PERENNIAL
GROUND
COVERS

PERENNIAL GROUND COVERS

David S. MacKenzie

Timber Press
Portland, Oregon

To all gardeners who value beauty,
the environment,
and the importance of their leisure time.

All photos by the author unless otherwise indicated.

Copyright © 1997 by Timber Press, Inc.
All rights reserved.

ISBN 0-88192-368-0

Printed in Hong Kong

Timber Press, Inc.
The Haseltine Building
133 S.W. Second Avenue, Suite 450
Portland, Oregon 97204, U.S.A.

Library of Congress Cataloging-in-Publication Data

MacKenzie, David S.
Perennial ground covers / David S. MacKenzie.
p.   cm.
Includes index.
ISBN 0-88192-368-0
1. Ground cover plants. I. Title.
SB432.M336   1997
635.9'32—dc20   96-23737
CIP

CONTENTS

Acknowledgments   7
Introduction   9
Useful Conversion Tables   11

PART 1
Chapter 1   Gardening with Ground Covers   15
Chapter 2   Finding the Right Ground Cover   19
Chapter 3   Planting and Maintaining Ground Covers   22
Chapter 4   Propagating Ground Covers   28
Chapter 5   The Fundamentals of Scientific Plant Names   31
Chapter 6   Native Ground Covers   34
Chapter 7   Variegated Ground Covers   41
Chapter 8   Ferns as Ground Covers   45
Chapter 9   Ornamental Grasses as Ground Covers   47

PART 2
Chapter 10 Ground Cover Descriptions   51

Ground Cover Selection Chart   323
Ground Covers under Walnut Trees   341
Glossary   343
Selected Sources for Additional Reading   346
Index of Plant Names   347

Color plates follow page 48.

ACKNOWLEDGMENTS

Marjory and Donald MacKenzie for helping with many non-book-related matters that helped free up my time for writing; Rita Hassert for reviewing the manuscript and researching and answering my many questions; Marnie Pavelich and Linda Willms for their diligence in editing; Mary Walters of Walters Gardens for loaning me her slides; Jeanette Kunnen for reviewing the manuscript; Steve Sloan for advising on the format of the manuscript; Gary Katerberg for reviewing the manuscript and answering plant related questions; Chuck Brower for reviewing the manuscript; Harlan and Shirley Hamernik of Bluebird Nursery for loaning me their slides; Monrovia Nursery Company for loaning me its slides; the Avdek family, Janet Coats, and Kathy Schmid for helping to review and select the illustrations; Jim Thompson for loaning me his slides; Steve VanderWoude for the use of his slide and for helping with the index; Dutchmill Herb Farm for furnishing descriptions of lavender cultivars.

For helping type and prepare the manuscript: Rachelle Staskiewicz, Stephanie Cole, Tammy Young, Marcia Wyant, Penny Polak, and Richard Sierra.

INTRODUCTION

Ground covers are materials used in landscaping expressly for the purpose of mulching or covering the soil. Such materials as wood chips, bark, the rinds or shells from fruits and nuts, stone, concrete, plastic, and turf grass are all ground covers. But this book is concerned with living, breathing ground covers, those vibrant plant species that oxygenate the air, control erosion, beautify our environment, and that when properly cultured and established, require little maintenance and densely cover the soil in a manner that discourages and prevents the growth of weeds.

For the most part, without pruning, ground covers range in height from less than an inch to about 4 feet tall. Ground covers may be woody, succulent, herbaceous, shrubby, or grasslike. They may be annual, biennial, or perennial. They can fall into the categories of clumping, vining, or sprawling. And they may be deciduous, evergreen, or semievergreen. Even primitive spore-bearing plants such as ferns and mosses can function as ground covers. Unlike turf grass and wood chips, which are plain green or boring brown, ground covers are available in an impressive array of colors and textures. In addition to green, there are red, blue, purple, silver, coppery, bronze, and gold types. Variegated (multicolored) forms provide exciting combinations of colors. And textures range from needle fine to coarse, and feather soft to stiff and prickly. In keeping with our objective to minimize the work and maximize the fun of creating a landscape, this book discusses only perennial ground covers, those which live indefinitely.

USEFUL CONVERSION TABLES

FAHRENHEIT/CELSIUS

45°	7°
40°	4°
35°	2°
32°	0°
30°	−1°
25°	−4°
20°	−7°
15°	−9°
10°	−12°
5°	−15°
0°	−18°
−5°	−21°
−10°	−23°
−15°	−26°
−20°	−29°
−25°	−32°
−30°	−34°
−35°	−37°
−40°	−40°
−45°	−43°

INCHES/CENTIMETERS

1	2.5 cm
1.5	4 cm
2	5 cm
2.5	6 cm
3	8 cm
3.5	9 cm
4	10 cm
4.5	11 cm
5	13 cm
5.5	14 cm
6	15 cm
6.5	16 cm
7	18 cm
7.5	19 cm
8	20 cm
8.5	21 cm
9	23 cm
9.5	24 cm
10	25 cm
11	28 cm
12	31 cm
13	33 cm
14	35 cm
15	38 cm
16	40 cm
17	43 cm
18	45 cm
19	48 cm
20	50 cm
25	63 cm
30	75 cm
35	88 cm

FEET/METERS

1	0.3 m
1.5	0.5 m
2	0.6 m
2.5	0.8 m
3	1.0 m
3.5	1.1 m
4	1.2 m
4.5	1.4 m
5	1.5 m
5.5	1.7 m
6	1.8 m
6.5	1.9 m
7	2.0 m
7.5	2.3 m
8	2.4 m
8.5	2.5 m
9	2.7 m
9.5	2.9 m
10	3.0 m
11	3.3 m
12	3.6 m
13	3.9 m
14	4.2 m
15	4.5 m
16	4.8 m
17	5.0 m
18	5.4 m
19	5.7 m
20	6.0 m
25	7.5 m
30	9.0 m
35	10.5 m

INCHES/MILLIMETERS

0.04	(1/24)	1 mm
0.06	(1/16)	1.5 mm
0.07	(1/15)	1.7 mm
0.08	(1/12)	2 mm
0.1	(1/8)	3 mm
0.2	(1/6)	4 mm
0.25	(1/4)	6 mm
0.3	(1/3)	8 mm
0.3	(5/16)	8 mm
0.4	(3/8)	10 mm
0.4	(7/16)	10 mm
0.5	(1/2)	13 mm
0.6	(9/16)	16 mm
0.6	(3/5)	16 mm
0.6	(5/8)	16 mm
0.7	(2/3)	17 mm
0.75	(3/4)	19 mm
0.8	(4/5)	20 mm
0.8	(13/16)	20 mm
0.9	(7/8)	22 mm
1		25 mm

FORMULAS

$$°C = °F − 32 \times 5 \div 9$$
$$cm = inches \times 2.5$$
$$mm = inches \times 25$$
$$cm = feet \times 30$$
$$m = feet \times 0.3$$

FEET/METERS

500	150 m
1,000	300 m
1,500	450 m
2,000	600 m
3,000	900 m
4,000	1,200 m
5,000	1,500 m
6,000	1,800 m
12,500	3,750 m

PART 1

Chapter 1

GARDENING WITH GROUND COVERS

GROUND COVERS AND THEIR BENEFITS

There are two classes of benefits to using ground covers, the material and the environmental. Each class is important to our enjoyment of the landscape.

Material Benefits

Much annual cleanup work and expense can be eliminated by using ground covers. In nature, a cycle exists in which microorganisms break down organic matter (i.e., dead animals, flowers, fruits, and leaves) to humus. The humus, in turn, releases the nutrients back to the earth, thus assuring the continuation of life. Unfortunately, instead of allowing this cycle to operate naturally, all too often we choose to pour concrete, spread stone, or plant manicured turf. Then we spend countless hours (usually on weekends) raking leaves or sweeping and vacuuming up fallen fruits, leaves, flowers, and twigs from their surfaces. If our trees and shrubs were instead underplanted with wisely selected ground covers, such debris (or gold, depending upon your perspective) would be concealed, and this work would be unnecessary. Indeed, most ground covers benefit from the nutrition released as the fallen fruits, leaves, and flowers decompose.

The trees and shrubs under which ground covers are planted benefit as well. Specifically, through the process of root growth (and death), the more shallowly rooted ground covers break up the soil and help increase its porosity and organic content. Because of this, the deeper roots of trees and shrubs benefit from better oxygen and water penetration and enhanced fertility. Also, the planting of a ground cover facing around shrubs and trees discourages foot and lawn mower traffic, which helps to reduce soil compaction and to protect the trunks of trees and shrubs from mechanical damage. The end result is better health and enhanced vigor for the shrubs and trees.

The reduced maintenance costs of ground covers in comparison to the upkeep of turf grass are their primary financial advantage. Generally speaking, turf grass is less expensive to plant, but considering its ongoing maintenance needs (e.g., frequent mowing, edging, fertilization, irrigation, disease and weed control, leaf removal), it proves to be more expensive in the long run.

Today, more and more gardeners are finding that ground covers are a practical alternative to turf grass for facing buildings, trees, and shrubs simply because they eliminate the tiresome and dangerous labor of mowing and trimming around and underneath them. Areas such as patios, courtyards, narrow strips paralleling walks and fences, underneath ornaments, and steep sloping hillsides can also be extremely difficult to navigate with a lawn mower. Planting ground covers eliminates the hazardous and intense work associated with turf care in such locations (see Plates 85, 286).

Environmental Benefits

The environmental benefits that ground covers exert upon their immediate surroundings, other than those related to the soil, should not be overlooked. Ground covers stabilize snow and reduce drifting during winter. Through transpiration (evaporative cooling) and photosynthesis, they cool and oxygenate the air during the warm season. Because they are typically green, they absorb light and reduce glare, an important factor making them useful in highway, roadside, and parking lot plantings. Furthermore, because ground covers are often deeply rooted and drought tolerant, they require less water than most turf grasses.

FUNCTIONS OF GROUND COVERS

Just as the benefits of using ground covers can be divided into two classes, the functions of using ground covers can also be divided into two classes, perceptual and practical.

Perceptual Functions

Psychologists define dissonance as the anxiety, confusion, or frustration that arises when there is a difference between our values or expectations and the reality that confronts us. People sometimes experience dissonance when confronted with a disharmonious landscape. For example, dissonance may be experienced when plants are not effectively linked to each other or when plants stand apart from the architectural elements of the landscape. Fortunately, in a number of ways, ground covers can help prevent such mental distress.

First, ground covers unify unrelated elements. For example, consider the substantial contrast between a house and a swimming pool. The house may be coarse-textured, vertically oriented, and dark colored. The swimming pool, on the other hand, is smooth-textured, horizontally oriented, and light (clear or blue) colored. In other words, the two structures have little in common. Yet, by effectively using ground covers, such as surrounding the pool with a broad bed of blue-green mounding junipers, this striking contrast can be lessened and the two structures can be joined in harmony.

Ground covers can also be used to soften the sharp edges and angles of natural and unnatural objects. Boulders (see Plates 7, 278), benches, walkways, fences, and stairs can all be brought into harmony with a house, each other, and trees, shrubs, and other plants when effectively linked with ground covers. Ground covers can be used for creating a rich, pleasant, inviting atmosphere or mood. Using broad lush beds of ground covers, walkways and entryways can be made to communicate a pleasant, welcoming feel to those who visit.

Additionally, ground covers can be used to alter our perception of space. To convey the impression of spaciousness, use small-leaved smooth-textured ground covers in wide, curving border plantings. On the other hand, use larger-leaved, coarse-textured ground covers to create a sense of intimacy. Shrubby ground covers, particularly those with horizontal branching, can be planted on steep slopes to make them seem more moderate. Brightly colored or fine-textured ground covers tend to light up areas and thereby elevate one's mood, while those in shades of blue, green, or gray tend to enhance feelings of tranquility and peacefulness.

For relieving monotony in the landscape, ground covers are paramount. Steps, entryways, decking, and shrubs are infinitely more interesting when accented with ground covers. With their intricate branch patterns, colorful foliage, and sometimes attractively flaking bark, ground covers are limitless in their variety. Evergreen ground covers exhibit year-round beauty, while others grace us with flowers of heavenly scent and bright, beautiful color. All kinds of wildlife, including numerous songbirds, are attracted to their flowers and fruits—an added bonus to the environment and to the people who benefit from the entertainment these creatures provide.

Practical Functions

GROUND COVERS FOR FACING BUILDINGS: In landscaping, any material applied as a screen or covering is referred to as a *facing*. Facings act as ornamental facades and are a simple, economical, and effective way to enhance the appearance of homes and commercial buildings. Ground covers employed as facings are most frequently used to conceal building foundations and as such are referred to as *foundation facers* or *foundation plants*. This practice is called *foundation planting* or *facing,* and the plants collectively are referred to as a *foundation planting*.

During the construction of a home or commercial building, the first few inches to a foot of the concrete foundation is often left exposed. In such circumstances, foundation plantings are extremely beneficial in concealing this unattractive feature (see Plate 120). Additionally, they aid in blending the building with other landscape elements. When planting close to buildings, standard shrubs and turf tend to look awkward or are functionally or physically inadequate (too short in the case of turf and too prone to damage or too cramped in the case of standard shrubs). However, many ground covers are ideally suited to such use.

The first 3 or 4 feet out from the base of a building is an extremely difficult area for plants to grow. Falling ice and heavy snow can be problems in the North, and reflected heat and torrents of rainwater can be troublesome in the South and along the coasts. Any of these circumstances will harm most plants, and clearly, foundation planting with standard shrubs is usually not the answer. On the other hand, horizontally spreading ground covers are bothered little from the harshness of winter, are far more visually interesting than turf grass, bind soil during the most torrential dousing, and in many cases can withstand reflected light and heat.

In addition to causing erosion, rainwater may also cause less obvious damage as it falls from the roof. If left unchecked, the rain can form a gutter that channels water down to the subterranean foundation where it may eventually saturate the surrounding soil, cause foundation damage, and eventually come into the basement. To help stabilize the soil and to prevent the formation of water channels, mat-forming, fibrous-rooted ground covers can be planted that will bind the soil, prevent erosion, and encourage the water to disperse away from the foundation. Because the soil around the foundation is often the poorest in the landscape (due to excavation and spilled mortar), be sure to have the soil tested and properly amended before installing a foundation planting.

Foundation planting with ground covers can prevent other more subtle complications as well. When erect or broad-spreading shrubs are planted too close to buildings, they often spread unnaturally and exhibit poor vigor due to reduced sunlight, particularly on the north side of buildings. Using ground covers (many of which are shade tolerant) as a facing near the foundation allows shrubs to be sited far enough away from the building to develop in a natural manner and to obtain sufficient sunlight for growth. Planting shrubs away from the foundation also permits easier access to utility meters, valves, and outlets and reduces the potential for damage to utility lines and pipes from the typically heavier-rooted shrubs.

When planted around foundations, certain ground covers may act as fire breaks, particularly those with succulent stems and leaves. In the event of fire, such ground covers can help decrease the spread of flames and therefore are especially useful in hot, dry areas.

Trees, shrubs, garden ornaments, statuary, and benches may also be faced with ground covers. In so doing, trunks, stems, and concrete bases may be partially concealed and in this way are more harmoniously linked with the turf, wood chips, water features, or concrete of the landscape.

COMBINING GROUND COVERS WITH BULBS, SPRING EPHEMERALS, AND ANNUALS: Ground covers combined with spring-flowering bulbs and ephemerals can be very attractive. Bulbs and spring ephemerals supply interest and beauty in early spring, a time when still-dormant deciduous ground covers are leafless. Later, when the bulbs and ephemerals die back, the fresh new season's foliage of the ground cover blankets the soil that would normally remain exposed if the bulbs or ephemerals had been planted alone. Some nice combinations are hosta and Virginia bluebell, dwarf plumbago and crocuses or trillium, and Ellacombe's stonecrop and daffodils. Annuals, on the other hand, can be used to provide color throughout the growing season. For this reason they combine nicely with low-growing evergreen ground covers, particularly those that are beautiful in foliage but lacking in bloom. A nice combination here is variegated lily-turf and yellow-flowered pansies. When interplanting with annuals, choose ground cover varieties with foliage no taller than one-third to one-half the height of the foliage of the annuals. Otherwise the annuals will become lost among the ground cover.

ACCENT PLANTING: To help emphasize or draw attention to particular features in the landscape, ground covers can be used as accent plants. Accent plants help draw one's eye to some significant feature of the landscape. In a complimentary fashion, they accentuate the features of other plants, benches, entryways, ornaments, statues, steps, or other garden structures. Aspects such as their bark, blossoms, foliage, and stems may provide accent. This may be conveyed subtly, moderately, or boldly, depending upon the degree of contrast between the ground cover and the element to which it is calling attention.

GROUND COVERS AS HEDGES: Ground covers may also be used for hedging, just as trees, shrubs, and tall ornamental grasses sometimes are. Obviously, they do not provide a screening effect because they are lower, nor do they defend against invasion from the neighbor's pets and children, except in the case of a few thorny plants such as barberry and firethorn. What they can help do, however, is to identify property; by delimiting garden and border periphery, they may contribute to a garden style that is both interesting, unusual, and aesthetically pleasing.

TRANSITION PLANTING: The use of plants for the purpose of unifying different elements or textures in the landscape is referred to as *transition planting*. The main purpose of transition planting is to ease one's perception of change from one landscape feature to another. Take, for instance, the contrast between the vertical orientation of a light pole, tree trunk, or the wall of a house and the horizontal orientation of the ground below. Ground covers help to unite these contrasting elements and to aid in the visual transition from one to the other. Similarly, a ground cover of intermediate texture or color can smooth the transition from two elements of sharp textural or functional contrast. For example, trees with very different characteristics, such as a smooth-barked beech tree and a coarse-barked black oak, can be harmonized by surrounding their trunks in a common bed of hosta, periwinkle, or pachysandra (see Plate 225). These ground covers, which are not as coarse-textured as the oak or as smooth-textured as the beech, provide an easy transition from one to the other. Similarly, a statue or bird bath and the surrounding turf, pavement, shrubs, and trees can be linked in harmony, even though they may differ in respect to color, shape, orientation, and size.

SPECIMEN GROUND COVERS: Unusual ground cover species or varieties can contribute unique character and style when planted alone as specimens, just as unusual shrubs and trees often do. Specimen planting of ground covers should be conducted in locations to which the eye naturally falls, such as on hillsides and berms, or along banks that parallel ascending walks or steps. Planting in these areas will expose exceptional ground covers to the attention that they deserve, and they will make your landscape unique and conversational (see Plate 60).

Chapter 2

FINDING THE RIGHT GROUND COVER

When you are landscaping with ground covers, it is important to choose the best one for the job. This process is very easy. After you determine the hardiness zone of your area, all you need to do is follow the three basic rules for ground cover use described later in this chapter. Then assess your landscape conditions and, using the Ground Cover Selection Chart in the back of this book, choose plants that will be hardy and that will perform the tasks assigned to them by you.

HARDINESS

When applied to plants, hardiness indicates how persistent and durable a plant will be under a particular set of circumstances. For example, a plant described as being very cold hardy could be expected to flourish in areas with a cold winter climate. Conversely, a plant described as not being cold hardy would at best struggle for survival under those conditions.

In this book I have used the United States Department of Agriculture (USDA) Plant Hardiness Zone Map (Plate 316). This map divides North America into 11 hardiness zones. Zone 1 represents the coldest areas, with a seasonal average low temperature below −50°F. As the zone numbers become larger, the average annual low temperature becomes higher. For each plant I have listed the coldest, lowest-numbered, northernmost hardiness zone in which it can be expected to flourish. Also, when the information is available, I have listed the warmest, highest-numbered, southernmost zone. Generally speaking, plants will grow well a few climatic zones warmer than their northernmost hardiness rating. Thus, if you have a plant that is rated hardy in Zone 5, and the southernmost hardiness zone is not listed in this book, the plant likely will do quite well in a Zone 7 garden. Usually it is worth a try.

Although hardiness zones are very helpful, one must remember that the USDA map (which takes only average annual low temperatures into consideration) has limitations. Wise gardeners know that factors other than minimum temperature affect the ability of a plant to remain healthy and flourish. Such factors as drought, sun and wind exposure, soil conditions, altitude, length of growing season, snow cover, humidity, water table, and pollution also influence the health, vigor, and survival of each plant. Because the USDA map is based only upon minimum temperature, it should only be used as a general guide in selecting your plant material. Do not be afraid to experiment a bit—many a gardener successfully grows plants one or two hardiness zones outside of their reported limits of hardiness. Knowledgeable gardeners make use of microclimates (small niches in the landscape that are climatically distinct). For example, in Zone 5, the shady north side of a home offers shelter from wintertime sun and wind and provides more consistent protective snow cover than an open southern exposure which is hit by drying wind and sun. Microclimates might exist, or can be created, that influence, one way or the other, most variables that affect hardiness—air temperature, sun and wind exposure, soil conditions, snow cover, humidity, and water table.

With this in mind, the USDA map should be used to make a reasonably accurate prediction of how well a particular plant will perform in a given part of North America. All you have to do is match up the plant's hardiness ratings with the geographic area in which you live. If they correspond, or if the plant is rated a few zones colder than where you live, chances are you will have success.

THREE RULES FOR USING GROUND COVERS

The uses of ground covers are limited only by your imagination. Even so, you should always attempt to follow three basic rules of ground cover use. Adhering to these rules will prevent you from using inappropriate or incompatible ground covers and will insure your success.

Rule 1.   Use only one or a few selected varieties. Combining too many different types in the same landscape results in a busy, cluttered appearance.

Rule 2.   Plant large-leaved ground covers when the scale is large and small-leaved ground covers when the scale is small. Ostrich fern, for example, is suitable as a foundation plant, whereas Corsican mint is not; the latter, however, is an excellent choice for filling in the cracks between paving stones or in a rock garden. Creeping mazus (Plate 200) is another example of a small-leaved plant that does best when the scale is small. By following this rule, you will create a harmonious setting and your plants will be in the proper proportion to the landscape. Ignoring this rule wastes the precious little space of the smaller landscape or leaves the large setting looking naked.

Rule 3.   Practice companion planting. In other words, combine only plants that will comfortably coexist. Choose plants with complementary cultural requirements, colors, textures, forms, and sizes. Companion planting is of utmost importance when you are combining ground covers with other plant types, such as trees, shrubs, perennials, and bulbs. If you put plants of different compatibility (companionship) together, not only will the landscape lack harmony, but extra maintenance will be required as well.

The third rule also applies to combinations of ground covers. Never combine ground covers that have incompatible growth habits. The worst offense is to combine a species of vigorous, horizontal-spreading habit (such as English ivy, goutweed, or fleece flower) with a species of diminutive or refined habit (such as Lydian stonecrop or dwarf astilbe). The vigorous plants will completely overrun (and kill) the smaller, slower-growing ones.

Nearly as bad would be the combination of two species of fast-growing, horizontal habit, such as English ivy and goutweed. In this case, the two would wage a constant struggle to take each other over, and the result would be a muddled, ugly appearance. Fast spreaders are almost always best used alone, but two or more slow spreaders can often be combined effectively.

ASSESSING THE SITE

To proceed with ground cover selection, first decide what you want to cover. Then assess the site to determine its soil condition (e.g., sand, clay), if it drains well or is saturated, and if it is acidic, alkaline, or neutral in pH. You can test the soil pH yourself with an inexpensive test kit or pH meter, available at most garden centers, or you can have the soil tested by your county horticultural extension agency.

Once you know the condition of the soil, check the light conditions. Light conditions are loosely described and inexact, as is almost everything in nature. Yet, for the sake of selecting ground covers, I classify and define light conditions as follows:

> FULL SUN: Locations receiving full sun are exposed to direct, unshaded sunlight for at least six hours per day.
>
> LIGHT SHADE: Light shade areas are exposed to partially filtered sun. Typically, the filter is an open-canopied tree, such as a locust, serviceberry, or birch. Often such sites receive a few hours of direct sun during some part of the day.
>
> MODERATE SHADE: Locations in moderate shade receive little direct sunlight. Reflected sunlight composes the bulk of the available light, such as at the floor of a typical hardwood forest.
>
> HEAVY SHADE: Sites in heavy shade receive almost no direct sunlight. Nearly all the light available is reflected light, such as at the base of a north-facing wall or below dense evergreens.

CHOOSING A GROUND COVER

When you know your hardiness zone, have had your soil tested, have evaluated the light conditions of your planting site, and have determined the function you want your ground cover to perform, you are ready to select the perfect plant. Use the Ground Cover Selection Chart at the back of this volume to match the conditions of your planting site with the characteristics you would like in the plant. Make a list of the suitable plants and look up their descriptions in Part 2 of this volume. With that information, you can make an informed purchasing decision.

If you have your heart set upon a particular type of ground cover that did not turn up on your list of possible choices, you need not despair. Just prepare yourself for some extra work and expense. Soil can be changed with amendments or even replaced. Moisture content can be modified with drainage or irrigation. Light conditions can be altered by planting trees or cutting them down (though this would be a shame), and even hardiness zones can be modified to some extent by planting a windbreak. No plant is out of the question, provided you have sufficient time and/or money.

Chapter 3

PLANTING AND MAINTAINING GROUND COVERS

Now that you know how to select ground covers, the next step is to properly plant them and maintain them. Proper planting and maintenance will allow your ground covers to fill in rapidly and will provide you maximum enjoyment with little work or expense.

WHEN TO PLANT

Exactly when to plant ground covers will vary with your climate. If you live in the North, you may plant successfully from spring through fall. Spring, because of predictable rains and the long growing season ahead, is the ideal time. Summer planting is fine also, provided water is available for irrigation. Planting in fall—most plants can be planted right up until the day before the ground freezes—is also fine, provided that the plant is good and hardy (i.e., capable of growing at least one zone colder than that of the planting site), and the site receives reliable snow cover and is sheltered from winter winds. If good root growth can be established prior to the ground's freezing, generally to the extent that a firm tug will not uproot the plants, mulching is not necessary. Otherwise, the soil between plants should be well mulched with wood chips or some other insulating material to prevent the soil's heaving from the cycle of freezing and thawing.

Unless water is readily available and relatively inexpensive, the hot climates of the Deep South and of the arid western regions necessitate planting in fall, winter, and spring.

PREPARING THE SITE FOR PLANTING

Before planting ground covers, remove all existing turf grass, weeds, and debris. Be sure to remove the roots of weeds and grass as well as the above-ground parts. This can be accomplished in a number of ways.

Black plastic mulching can be pinned on top of the site with rocks, bricks, or soil as a means of destroying weeds or turf. The black plastic makes it impossible for plants to manufacture food through photosynthesis, and the sun hitting the plastic causes the weeds and soil below to become very hot. The combination of sun and black plastic creates an opaque solar oven that destroys weeds. This method works best in locations exposed to direct sunlight, and works better in warm climates than cool ones. In general, the plastic should be left in place for two months. Then the site may be rototilled or spaded to loosen and aerate the soil before planting.

Herbicides may also be used to destroy existing turf or weeds. There are a number of different herbicides available, but those that work best are systemic herbicides that are absorbed into the plant and translocated throughout its sap stream. These types of herbicides kill the root system as well as the top growth, which is essential to effective eradication since most weeds and turf are capable of regenerating from the rootstock. Once the herbicide has killed the turf or weeds, rototill or spade up the area to loosen the soil. Your local garden center may be able to recommend the herbicide best suited to your area.

The final method of weed control is old-fashioned but provides marvelous exercise. It involves repeatedly rototilling or spading the planting site until all vegetation has essentially been converted into soil through decomposers such as fungi, bacteria, and earthworms. Typically three or four turns of the site over the course of five or six weeks will accomplish this objective.

After killing the weeds and loosening the soil, incorporate any amendments such as leaf mold, lime, organic compost, or topsoil with a spade or rototiller. Amendments enhance the soil's fertility, change its texture, or alter its chemical properties (such as pH), so that it will be suitable for a particular plant. For wide-spreading, woody, shrubby ground covers only the area in the vicinity of the root zone need be amended. This is usually the top 8 to 12 inches of soil in an area about 3 feet in diameter around the planting hole. The entire bed, however, must be amended for those plants that sprawl or spread by aboveground or belowground horizontal stems (stolons or rhizomes) or have trailing branches, or are planted very close together. After you remove the weeds and add the amendments, complete the final grading with a rake.

PLANTING GROUND COVERS

When planting, the soil line at the base of the ground cover should be the same depth as it was in the container prior to transplanting. Therefore if the container depth is 6 inches, the depth of your planting hole or trench should also be 6 inches. If planted too deep, the crown and stems will be covered with soil and will rot due to lack of oxygen. And, if planted too shallowly, the plants will not have enough soil contact for adequate anchoring or water absorption. Use a tool such as a spade, trowel, or hoe to dig the necessary holes or trenches for planting. Be sure to water the plants in thoroughly, then follow by top-dressing the exposed soil between them with a 1½- to 2-inch mulch of pine needles or wood chips. This not only helps to exclude weeds but also reduces the amount of watering that will be needed. Mulching, by the way, is best conducted before planting when using smaller plant material (for example, 2- to 3-inch-wide pots). In this case prepare the soil, conduct your final grading, add mulch, then plant right through the mulch.

SPACING THE PLANTS

Plants for ground cover need to be spaced evenly and at an appropriate distance apart so that plantings will be easy to maintain and will fill in at the same rate. Triangular spacing with plants staggered in parallel rows places all plants an equal distance apart. Square spacing places plants an equal distance from their neighbors above, below, or across, but not diagonally.

Both methods are fine and lead to an organized, professional-appearing planting. Random spacing takes less planting time and looks more natural, but to some people it looks less organized. However, for plants such as English ivy and purple winter creeper, which form a solid mat, the end appearance is the same. To calculate the number of plants needed, use the chart below. This chart is based upon the *on-square planting method,* with plants the same distance apart in rows as between rows. About the same number of plants will be needed for random or triangular spacing. This chart should be used with the recommendations expressed in the descriptions in Part 2 of this book. Spacing is based upon rate of growth and mature spread. In general these recommendations will allow your planting to fill in and become completely established in one and a half growing seasons. Planting at the closest recommended distance may speed this to one season, and the farthest recommendation may extend it to two seasons. Of course the rate will vary somewhat with soil fertility, maintenance practices, and climatic conditions.

GROUND COVER SPACING CHART

Inches between plants	Plants needed per			Square feet covered by each plant
	1 square foot	100 square feet	1000 square feet	
3	16.000	1,600.0	16,000	0.06
4	9.000	900.0	9,000	0.11
5	5.750	575.0	5,750	0.17
6	4.000	400.0	4,000	0.25
7	2.930	293.0	2,930	0.34
8	2.250	225.0	2,250	0.44
9	1.780	178.0	1,780	0.56
10	1.440	144.0	1,440	0.69
12	1.000	100.0	1,000	1.00
14	0.730	73.0	730	1.37
16	0.560	56.0	560	1.78
18	0.440	44.0	440	2.27
20	0.360	36.0	360	2.77
24	0.250	25.0	250	4.00
30	0.160	16.0	160	6.25
36	0.110	11.0	110	9.09
48	0.060	6.0	60	16.70
72	0.028	2.8	28	35.70
96	0.015	1.5	15	66.70
120	0.010	1.0	10	100.00

MAINTAINING GROUND COVERS

Probably the biggest advantage to using ground covers is that they require relatively little maintenance, especially in comparison to turf grass (see Plates 174, 225). Of course, the degree of maintenance will vary with the species (and the gardener) and can almost always be minimized by proper plant selection, site preparation, and installation. But, to believe that no maintenance will ever be needed is a misconception. Indeed, like other plants, ground covers may need occasional watering; weeding (until they become well established); pruning; fertilizing; disease, insect, and rodent control; thinning; grooming; misting; and in some cases, mowing.

Watering Ground Covers

The maintenance of ground covers begins immediately after planting. Be sure to water them in thoroughly. A good healthy soaking, to the point that the water penetrates a few inches deeper than the bottom of the roots, will eliminate large air pockets in the soil (created during planting) and will lessen the degree of transplant stress. Remember, the roots of newly installed ground covers are small, and until they expand and become well established, frequent watering may be needed to prevent wilting; three months is usually an adequate period for root establishment. From then on, water the plants only as needed.

Always water during the early morning so that the foliage can quickly dry, thus preventing fungal infection. Water to the extent that the soil becomes moistened through the entire root zone (6 to 12 inches deep), and only when necessary, evidenced by drying out of the soil or by a slight midday wilting of the leaves at the ends of the stems. Typically, little or no supplemental watering is necessary after the first year. If it is, it is usually only during extended hot, dry summer days. In areas of freezing winter temperatures, it is a good idea to water thoroughly in late fall before the ground freezes solid. This enables the plants to better cope with winter's harshness. When plants enter winter without drought stress, they come through in much better condition.

Controlling Weeds in Ground Cover Plantings

The most critical step in weed control occurs before the plants are ever placed in the ground. Completely eliminating all weeds (including their roots) before you plant is essential to the rapid establishment of ground covers. Mulching helps to keep weed seeds from germinating and becoming established. In time, as the ground covers fill in and outmuscle the weeds, the need for weeding will taper off, and eventually little or no weed control will be required.

After planting, ongoing weed control can be handled in three ways. The first method is manual hoeing or hand pulling. Consider it an opportunity to relax and be reflective. Weeding takes little mind power, produces little stress, and is safe for the environment. The second method is through the use of preemergent and postemergent herbicides. Preemergent herbicides prevent weeds from becoming established but do not kill existing weeds. Postemergent herbicides kill weeds after they have come up. They must be used carefully as they may also kill your ground cover, if you happen to spray it as well. The last and often the preferred method is to continue mulching around the ground covers with organic materials. Simply resupply 1½ to 2 inches of wood chips, bark, or pine needles as the initial mulch thins and decomposes. Mulching does not effectively eradicate emerged weeds but is useful in preventing weeds from becoming established, and works just as well as preemergent herbicides. The advantage, of course, is that it does not risk damaging the environment. Also, as they decompose, organic mulches add organic matter to the soil and help to supplement the soil's fertility. Nondegradable mulches, such as stone, can also be used but generally should be limited to rock gardens.

Pruning Ground Covers

Although seldom necessary, many gardeners give their ground covers an occasional pruning. The purpose of pruning ground covers is to make them look neater and to stimulate new growth and branching. The most useful tools for pruning are hand shears, hedge shears, a string trimmer, or scissors. In some cases, a modified lawn mower is even used. Converting a lawn mower for pruning ground covers involves adding extensions to the wheels to raise the elevation of the cutting deck—an easy task for any accomplished machinist or welder. Remember, safety shields on your lawn mower are there for a reason. They should also be extended so that you can safely operate your ground cover mower.

For pruning, follow these guidelines: prune spring-flowering plants immediately after they bloom, and prune summer-flowering and fall-flowering plants during spring. It is usually not wise to remove more than one-third of the length of the branches during a single pruning. Pruning more than one-third of the length of the branches removes excessive leaf tissue and risks stressing the plants and predisposing them to disease and insect attack.

Fertilizing Ground Covers

Many ground covers benefit from one or two annual applications of organic or slow-release fertilizer. Organic fertilizers are those that have come from the digestive tracts of animals (e.g., various manures, including horse, chicken, turkey, cow, and even human, as in the case of Milorganite, a product that comes from the Milwaukee sewage treatment facility). Slow-release fertilizers are chemical fertilizers that gradually release nutrients to the plant. Low-grade soluble fertilizers (non-slow-release types such as most 12–12–12 formulations) are less expensive but can wash through the soil before the plant can use them completely. Because of this they are more likely to contribute to contamination of the groundwater.

The ratio of nitrogen, phosphorus, and potassium in the fertilizer should be about 2–1–2, such as a 10–5–10 formulation. Such a fertilizer should be applied at the rate of 1 pound per 100 square feet (½ pound per 100 square feet for a 20–10–20 formulation), first in early spring and then again in early fall. A custom fertilizer program can be designed by your garden center or county extension agent. This involves sampling your soil during early spring and developing a fertilization program that more specifically meets the needs of your particular plant and soil.

Dry types of fertilizer should only be applied when the leaves of the plants are dry; otherwise, the granules of fertilizer will adhere to the leaves and spotting or rotting may occur. Following any application of fertilizer, immediately wash off (with a fast stream of water) any fertilizer that has adhered to or become trapped in the foliage.

Controlling Diseases and Pests

Like all plants, ground covers are susceptible to diseases and pests such as leaf spotting, aphids, and mites. This is why it is important to grow them under ideal conditions. Under ideal conditions plants are at their most vigorous state and thus most resistant to diseases and pests. If you ever find that frequent applications of chemicals become necessary to keep your ground covers healthy, chances are you have planted them in a location (e.g., soil, light, hardiness zone, or other climatic factor) to which they are ill-suited. Frequent chemical applications are harmful to the environment, tend to be very expensive, and do nothing to correct the underlying problem. The best thing to do is forget the chemicals and solve the problem by correcting any deficiencies in the planting site or by pulling up the plants and starting over with a different type of ground cover.

Thinning Overcrowded Ground Covers

Sometimes ground covers that spread by expanding from their bases can grow together so tightly that they become overcrowded, which may result in stunted growth, reduced floral display, and increased susceptibility to disease. To correct overcrowding, uproot, separate, and reinstall the plants, leaving more space around individual plants. This process, known as thinning or dividing, is best accomplished during early spring. Spring dividing allows time for the plants to rebuild their root systems before the onslaught of summer. In the North, it has the additional advantage of allowing the plant to become firmly anchored before the freezing and thawing of the soil that comes with fall and winter.

Controlling Animals

Occasionally, usually during late winter when food is scarce, mice, rabbits, and even deer may snack upon ground covers. Often they will feed without causing significant damage (i.e., affecting less than 5 percent of the planting) and therefore should be tolerated. At other times, generally following winters that were preceded by summer drought and thus diminished food reserves, they may feed heavily and cause significant damage. Extermination of mice is simple, mainly because they prefer the taste of poisoned grain to ground cover. Rabbits can often be trapped live and transported elsewhere. Deer can be repelled by hanging bars of soap from the branches of shrubs or by spreading human hair on the ground—available from your local barber. Wear rubber gloves when handling the hair.

Removing Leaves

Leaves should only be raked up or vacuumed when they smother and mat down the ground cover. If the ground cover is of such habit that the fallen leaves slip through its canopy, then allow the leaves to remain and decompose to supplement the soil. This is what nature intended, and it will save you time and money. Green Carpet Japanese spurge is an example of a ground cover that is coarse enough to absorb fallen oak leaves. The following spring the new growth obscures the oak leaves, which rot and furnish nutrients for the pachysandra.

Misting

When there is a long period between rains or in polluted urban landscapes where there is a lot of debris in the air, dust can accumulate on the foliage of ground covers. Although dust may not be directly harmful, in time it reduces the amount of sunlight penetration and gas exchange (oxygen and carbon dioxide) and will stress and weaken your plants. This condition can be alleviated simply by washing the leaves with a fast stream of water, a practice that may also remove any aphids or mites that might be present.

Chapter 4

PROPAGATING GROUND COVERS

Propagation, the practice of multiplying plants, is a rather involved (and interesting) science. On my shelf there are books dedicated solely to the propagation of herbs, trees, shrubs, wildflowers, and annuals. The largest one numbers over 600 pages, and there has been talk of expanding it. For our purposes, a brief description of the various techniques of ground cover propagation will suffice. Then, should you choose to explore propagation more thoroughly, you can purchase a book (or books) on the subject.

SEXUAL PROPAGATION

Typically, sexual propagation of plants involves the interaction of sperm (the male gamete, usually derived from pollen) and egg (the female gamete, usually found within the ovary). As with animals, the sperm and egg combine, but rather than form a fetus, they form a seed. If the seed germinates, the new plant will contain a mixture of genes from its parent, if both sperm and egg are from the same parent, or parents, if sperm and egg are from different parents. The traits that the new plant displays, however, often will be somewhat different from those of the parent or parents. The new plant may be taller, shorter, faster-growing, hardier, or differently colored. This phenomenon is known as variation or variability and is evidenced to different degrees according to the specific characteristics of the plants involved.

As with other plant types, the sexual propagation of ground covers is an important aspect of their perpetuation. As a practice, seed propagation can be quite challenging, since it may involve specific timing of seed collection, proper storage, and the administration of specific treatments, such as chilling, boiling, or scarring the seed coat to break seed dormancy. Some seeds may require several months or years to germinate, and even then, germination percentages may be quite low.

Ferns, which are started from spores not seeds, also undergo sexual reproduction. For the propagation of ferns, the term *challenging* may be an understatement. Two or more years are sometimes needed to produce a small garden-ready plant, and many types of ferns require very specialized conditions to successfully develop.

Throughout this book, various terms specific to the practice of propagation arise, and a knowledge of their meaning is helpful. Some of the more common ones are described as follows:

> DEPULP: The process of removing the fleshy part of the fruit from the seed. This can be accomplished by hand, or in the case of small, very hard seeds, by mixing them with water then blending the mixture in a kitchen blender.

Dormancy: The condition in which a seed is inactive and growth and development are suspended. Many seeds remain dormant for extended periods of time; to induce their germination, specific treatments such as refrigeration or abrading the seed coat may be necessary.

Germination: The physiological processes by which seed dormancy is overcome and the embryo begins to develop and display signs of growth.

Ripe: The condition of seed that is capable of germination. Usually ripeness has occurred when the fruit is no longer increasing in weight. Thereafter the fruit often opens up to disperse seed, becomes weakly attached to the plant (frequently falling to the ground), or begins to dry out and shrivel up. This is the time when fruit is usually harvested and seed collected.

Sowing: The process of scattering or planting seed. Unless otherwise stated, ground cover seed should be sown on a porous yet moisture-retentive medium or soil and covered with ¼ to ½ inch of the same. Until germination, the medium should be kept moist and warm, never allowed to dry out, and never overly saturated.

ASEXUAL PROPAGATION

Unlike sexual propagation, asexual propagation involves the production of new plants without the union of gametes. It does not involve the creation of a new genetic composition. A plant that is produced asexually, called a *clone,* is genetically identical to its parent. For this reason, asexual propagation is used when genetic uniformity is desired, such as to maintain a particular flower or leaf color. Indeed, unless some plants are propagated asexually, they are sure to display variable traits.

Asexual propagation is usually conducted by cuttings or division (less commonly by layering, and sometimes by tissue culture and grafting) and results in a complete plant that contains genes that are identical to those of its parent. For this reason, a plant that is asexually propagated will be identical to its parent in the traits that it displays when grown in a similar environment.

When discussing asexual propagation, you will need to understand the following terms:

Cutting: A cutting is a plant part that has been cut off from the parent plant for purposes of propagation. Usually a cutting is taken from the stem but sometimes from a leaf or root. It is then prepared in such a way (with trimming and sometimes the application of hormones) that when placed in a medium (usually coarse sand or a mixture of peat moss and perlite) and kept moist and warm or intermittently misted, the missing parts redevelop. For stem cuttings, one to three months is usually sufficient time for root formation. Root cuttings are typically made in late fall from 1- to 2-inch-long segments and are usually placed vertically in trays, covered with 1 inch of medium, and kept moist and warm. Normally two to four months are required for new shoots to form.

Mist, or intermittent mist: Intermittent mist refers to the practice of applying a light film of water at regular intervals. Generally, misting is carried out with a special sprinkler that produces a very fine spray and is controlled by a timer. Intermittent mist helps to keep unrooted cuttings cool and reduces wilting. When roots begin to form, the mist should be discontinued in favor of regular watering practices.

DIVISION, or crown division: Division is the easiest and most reliable means of propagating many ground covers. To perform division, simply dig up a plant and tug on its crown (the base of the plant) until it separates into individual plants. Each division is a smaller, completely functional version of the original clump.

LAYERING: Layering is an asexual propagation technique in which a stem is bowed over and pinned against or buried in the soil. In certain plants, roots form at the point of soil contact and the stem, with newly formed roots, can (with a sharp spade) be removed from the main plant and transplanted. In many plants, layering occurs naturally.

MEDIUM: The medium refers to the physical entity in which a plant is grown. It may be soil, sand, water, peat, perlite, vermiculite, or any other such material or combination thereof. Media is the plural of medium.

PLANTLETS: The practice of removing and transplanting the miniature plantlets that are formed on the stolons of stoloniferous plants such as strawberries and ajuga is another means of asexual propagation. When young, the plantlets may not have roots and may need to be placed under mist until roots can form.

ROOTING HORMONES: Invaluable to the propagator, rooting hormones are chemicals that stimulate root formation when applied to stem cuttings. Rooting hormones can be purchased in any garden shop and come in various strengths. Most ground covers root relatively easily and therefore require a hormone formulation of low strength. The most commonly used rooting hormone is a chemical called indole-3-butyric acid, or IBA. A concentration of 1000 parts per million (ppm) in a talc preparation is a low-strength formula; 3000 ppm is moderate; and 8000 to 16,000 ppm is a strong formula. You can also purchase liquid formulas but the powders are easier to work with as they require no soaking or mixing.

Chapter 5

THE FUNDAMENTALS OF
SCIENTIFIC PLANT NAMES

Probably the most intimidating aspect of the scientific names of plants is that they are derived from Latin and Greek. Since these languages are not used in everyday conversation, they are foreign to us. But Latin and Greek are an integral aspect of horticultural terminology, and scientific names are universal, indispensable, and even at times intriguing.

Granted, using common names is usually acceptable, but there can be disadvantages. Imagine, for example, if you called your local garden center and ordered 100 plants of the ground cover swamp loosestrife, for use along the edge of the creek that runs through your backyard. Instead of the native swamp loosestrife (*Decodon verticillatus*), you might receive the weedy European swamp loosestrife (*Lythrum salicaria*) that is the scourge of wetlands. If, however, you had originally specified *D. verticillatus,* you would have received exactly what you had wanted.

The origins of scientific names of plants can be very interesting. Many are derived from mythology. The genus *Baccharis,* for example, is named after Bacchus, the Greek god of wine, since a spicy extract of some species was added to wine, and the genus *Iris,* named after the Greek goddess of the rainbow and messenger of the gods, alludes to the rainbowlike array of flower colors of *Iris* species. Other names reveal aspects of the plants' uses. *Genista tinctoria* comes from *tinctus,* colored, and reveals that this plant is useful in dying fabric. Still other plant names tell about the characteristics of the plants. The common specific epithet *horizontalis* implies a horizontal habit of growth; and the genus *Xanthorhiza,* from Greek *xanthos,* yellow, and *rhiza,* root, was so named because it roots are yellow. Finally, many plants are named to commemorate someone, usually a prominent botanist or horticulturist, or the person who originally discovered the plant. *Heuchera* commemorates Johann Heinrich von Heucher, a German botanist and professor of medicine, and *Abelia* commemorates Dr. Clark Abel, who discovered *Abelia chinensis*.

The basic classification system used to identify and categorize plants was initially developed by Carolus Linnaeus (1707–1778), otherwise known as the father of modern botany. Linne, as he was called in his native Sweden, used flower structure traits as a means of classifying plants. In 1753 he published his original classification system in his book *Species Plantarum.* Even though the system has undergone numerous changes over the years, the fundamentals of Linnaeus's system are still the backbone of contemporary plant nomenclature.

Under this system, plant and animal species are named using a binomial (two-word) term consisting of a genus name and a species name. Sometimes a subspecies, variety, forma, or cultivar name is added behind the species name. The terms *genus, species, subspecies, variety, forma,* and *cultivar,* arranged in order of general to more specific, allow us to effectively and easily classify plants. *Genus* means general. Generic names are usually composed of a combination of Latin or Greek roots. In the binomial system, the genus name comes first and is always capitalized and italicized. All the plants in a genus share certain common characteristics. The plural of genus is genera.

Species means specific. The species name follows the genus name and is not capitalized but is italicized. The species name is more accurately called the specific epithet as it carries no meaning without being attached to a genus name. It is also commonly derived from Greek or Latin. The context determines whether species is singular or plural, although sometimes the abbreviations sp. and spp. are used after a genus name to indicate whether one or more species are being referred to.

Subspecies, infrequently mentioned, are naturally occurring biological strains of a species—in which 90 percent or more of the population (within the geographic region of the plant's discovery) is passed on from generation to generation, and is distinct from the typical species. Subspecies names follow the specific epithet, are preceded by the word subspecies (or the abbreviation subsp., sometimes ssp.), are not capitalized, but are italicized.

Occasionally, the term *variety* (or the abbreviation var.), followed by an italicized varietal name, appears after the specific epithet. This implies that the plant in question is a botanical variety that was discovered in the wild. Often these botanical varieties differ from the species in ways that only a botanist could appreciate (e.g., in the size of the fruit capsule; in the size, shape, density, orientation, and morphology of the hairs that cover the calyxes, leaves, and stems). Variety names usually come from Latin or Greek. The plural of variety is varieties.

A *forma* (abbreviated f.) is a taxonomic unit even smaller than a variety. Generally a forma is distinguished on the basis of an observable feature, such as flower color, that is important to gardeners but not so important to taxonomists.

Often following the genus name and specific epithet is a third word known as the *cultivar* name. A cultivar is a distinct strain that has arisen in cultivation or that has been vegetatively propagated from a variant occurring in wild populations. In effect, it is a cultivated variety, with the term *cultivar* being a compression of the words *cultivated* and *variety.* Cultivar names are taken from the most widely spoken language of the location where the plant was developed. Thus, a plant derived in the United States would have an English cultivar name, and a cultivar originating in Germany would have a German cultivar name. The nomenclatural rules, however, state that cultivar names may be transliterated to other languages, provided that the original meaning is held intact. Thus, the German-named cultivar *Deschampsia caespitosa* 'Goldschleier' may be represented as *D. caespitosa* 'Gold Veil' in English-speaking countries. Cultivar names are always capitalized, never italicized, and are enclosed in single quotation marks or preceded by the abbreviation cv., referring to cultivar. They are frequently descriptive in a manner that emphasizes uniqueness and consumer appeal. For example, the plant *Imperata cylindrica* 'Red Baron' has bright red leaves as opposed to the medium green leaves of the species, *I. cylindrica.*

Sometimes a genus name and a species name are separated by a multiplication sign, ×. This indicates that the plant in question is a *hybrid.* Hybrids are plants that have resulted from the interbreeding of different species, or, rarely, from the interbreeding of different genera. Interspecific hybrids, those resulting from crossbreeding two separate species within the same genus, are usually designated by a multiplication sign × between the genus name and the specific epithet. An example is *Lonicera* × *heckrottii,* which resulted from crossing *L. americana* with *L. sempervirens.* In intergeneric hybrids, the × precedes the genus name, as in × *Solidaster luteus,* in which the parents are *Aster* and *Solidago.* When a hybrid-indicating × appears in a name, it is written but not pronounced, and when alphabetizing plant names, the × is ignored (as are the abbreviations subsp., var., and f.).

One last word about scientific names must be made: sometimes they are changed. This can be very frustrating, especially after you have made the effort to memorize the proper name. Renaming becomes necessary, however, when research reveals an attribute that was previously overlooked during the original naming of the plant. When this happens, the scientist(s) will write a scientific paper chronicling the differences, then propose a new name and classification. Afterward, it is up to the readership, the botanical and horticultural communities, to decide whether to accept the proposed change. In this book, I have used the names that I believe to be the most up to date and accurate at the time of writing.

Chapter 6

NATIVE GROUND COVERS

Native plants are sometimes scorned as unattractive, untamed, too common, or too boring for landscape use. Many people fail to see the purpose of planting something in their yard that they could go out and dig up anywhere. People refer to building contractors—many of whom bulldoze every plant in their path—as being in the development business. Cleared land to many people is "improved land," and for them, native settings (see Plates 115, 161) are seen as unattractive representations of chaos.

Is it possible that these popularly held notions are wrong? I think so. Native plants do not grow chaotically. Instead, they grow in well-defined ecological niches. As to being unattractive, natives are often beautiful beyond description. Indeed, North American natives such as Point Reyes ceanothus and blue lyme grass are among the showiest of all ground covers. Once tried, they soon dispel the myth that a plant must be an unusual introduced species to be colorful, interesting, or worth growing. Another reason to recommend natives is because they look right. In other words, they appear to be at home in our landscapes.

Here are some examples of North American natives that may surprise you with their beauty, diversity, and adaptability. Virginia creeper, a robust native vine that often ascends to 40 feet, also makes a splendid, sturdy ground cover. It sprawls about the woodland floor, displaying glossy, deep green to blue-green, richly textured, massive, five-parted foliage. Although its flowers are tiny, they yield attractive blue grapelike fruit that helps to feed numerous woodland creatures and birds.

The lady fern was named for its grace and beauty. From central and northeastern North America, this plant has few equals when it comes to charm. No, it does not boast showy flowers— merely subtly beautiful horseshoe-shaped clusters of brown spores. Yet, after watching its fiddleheads unfurl to yield indescribably lush, cool green foliage, one might forget flowering plants altogether. In the landscape, it functions superbly as a general ground cover in shady sites.

Bearberry, occurring from Labrador to Alaska and as far south as Missouri, is among the most durable plants encountered anywhere. It can grow in full sun, face strong winds, and be anchored in pure sand—yet somehow thrive with no hint of unhappiness. Its foliage, flowers, and fruit are all attractive, and its landscape uses are many.

Rock garden enthusiasts will appreciate spatula-leaved stonecrop, a diminutive succulent that ranges from British Columbia to California. This drought-tolerant, low, matlike ground cover reaches only 2 to 4 inches tall and displays evergreen, bluish green, tightly set foliage. Vibrant yellow flowers in flat-topped clusters appear in mid- to late spring, enhancing its beauty. Various cultivars of this stonecrop have been selected, and at least two of them are exceptional. 'Cape Blanco', hailing from Cape Blanco, Oregon, displays sky blue foliage that during spring and fall becomes tipped with a white waxy coating that makes it appear to be frosted with snow. 'Atro-purpureum', another outstanding cultivar, has foliage deeply suffused with purple. It functions remarkably well either as a specimen or when mass planted as a small-scale general cover.

By planting native plants in our landscapes or preserving them during the construction process, we can help to maintain many species that might otherwise become extinct. This alone is reason to grow them. Coupled with their rich colors and interesting forms and textures, native plants give us no reason to not include them. Give them a chance in your garden and you will not be disappointed.

A complete list of North American native ground covers included in this book is as follows:

SCIENTIFIC NAME	COMMON NAME
Acacia angustissima var. *hirta*	Prairie acacia
Achillea ptarmica	Sneezewort
Acorus calamus	Sweet flag
Adiantum capillus-veneris	Southern maidenhair fern
Adiantum pedatum	Northern maidenhair fern
Ammophila breviligulata	Marram
Andromeda polifolia	Bog rosemary
Amdromeda glaucophylla	Marsh rosemary
Antennaria dioica	Common pussy-toes
Antennaria plantaginifolia	Plantainleaf pussy-toes
Arctanthemum arcticum	Arctic chrysanthemum
Arctostaphylos alpina	Alpine bearberry
Arctostaphylos edmundsii	Little Sur manzanita
Arctostaphylos hookeri	Hooker manzanita
Arctostaphylos nevadensis	Pinemat manzanita
Arctostaphylos nummularia	Coin-leaved bearberry
Arctostaphylos pumila	Dune manzanita
Arctostaphylos rubra	–
Arctostaphylos thymifolia	Thyme-leaved bearberry
Arctostaphylos uva-ursi	Common bearberry
Arenaria arctica	Arctic sandwort
Aronia melanocarpa	Black chokeberry
Artemisia frigida	Fringed sagebrush
Artemisia ludoviciana	–
Artemisia stelleriana	Beach wormwood
Asarum arifolium	Halberd ginger
Asarum canadense	Canadian wild ginger
Asarum caudatum	British Columbia wild ginger
Asarum hartwegii	Sierra wild ginger
Asarum memingeri	–
Asarum shuttleworthii	Mottled wild ginger
Asarum virginiana	Virginia wild ginger
Athyrium filix-femina	Lady fern
Athyrium pycnocarpon	Narrow-leaved spleenwort
Athyrium thelypteroides	Silvery glade fern
Baccharis pilularis	Baccharis
Calamovilfa longifolia	Sand reed-grass
Callirhoe involucrata	Poppy mallow
Carex atrata	Black sedge grass

Carex glauca	Blue sedge
Carex muskingumensis	Palm sedge
Carex nigra	Black sedge
Carex plantaginea	Plantain leaved sedge
Ceanothus gloriosus	Point Reyes ceanothus
Ceanothus griseus var. *horizontalis*	Yankee Point ceanothus
Ceanothus prostratus	Squaw carpet ceanothus
Ceanothus thyrsiflorus var. *repens*	Creeping blue blossom ceanothus
Chamaedaphne calyculata	Leatherleaf
Chelone glabra	–
Chelone lyonii	–
Chelone obliqua	–
Chimaphila maculata	Pipsissewa
Chimaphila umbellata	Spotted pipsissewa
Chrysogonum virginianum	Golden star
Clematis virginiana	Virgin's Bower
Clethra alnifolia 'Hummingbird'	–
Comptonia peregrina	Sweet fern
Conradina verticillata	Cumberland rosemary
Convallaria majalis	Lily-of-the-valley
Convallaria montana	Mountain lily-of-the-valley
Coptis groenlandica	Goldthread
Coptis laciniata	Western goldthread
Corema conradii	Broom crowberry
Coreopsis auriculata	Dwarf-eared coreopsis
Coreopsis rosea	Pink tickseed
Coreopsis verticillata	Threadleaf coreopsis
Cornus canadensis	Dwarf cornel
Cornus mas 'Nana'	Dwarf cornelian cherry dogwood
Cornus sericea 'Kelseyi'	Dwarf red osier dogwood
Dalea greggii	Trailing indigo bush
Decodon verticillatus	Willow herb
Deschampsia caespitosa	Tufted hair grass
Deschampsis flexuosa	Wavy hair grass
Dicentra eximia	Fringed bleeding heart
Dicentra formosa	Pacific bleeding heart
Dichondra micrantha	Dichondra
Diervilla lonicera	Bush honeysuckle
Diervilla sessilifolia	–
Dryas octopetala	Mountain avens
Dryopteris intermedia	Intermediate shield fern
Dryopteris filix-mas	Male fern
Dryopteris marginalis	Leatherleaf wood fern
Dryopteris wallichiana	Wallich's wood fern
Echeveria agavoides	Molded wax
Echevaria amoena	Baby echeveria
Echevaria derenbergii	Painted lady
Echevaria elegans	Mexican gem
Echevaria gibbiflora	Fringed echeveria
Echevaria × *gilva*	Green Mexican rose
Echevaria secunda	–

Empetrum nigrum	Black crowberry
Ephedra nevadensis	Nevada tea
Epigaea repens	Trailing arbutus
Equisetum hyemale	Common horsetail
Equisetum scirpoides	Dwarf scouring rush
Equisetum sylvaticum	Woodland horsetail
Equisetum variegatum	Variegated horsetail
Equisetum × trachyodon	–
Equisetum × nelsonii	–
Erigeron karvinskianus	Bonytip fleabane
Erigeron glaucus	Beach fleabane
Euonymus obovatus	Strawberry bush
Fragaria chiloensis	Chiloe strawberry
Fragaria virginica	Wild strawberry
Galax urceolata	Colt's foot
Gaultheria hispidula	Creeping pearl berry
Gaultheria ovatifolia	Oregon wintergreen
Gaultheria procumbens	Common wintergreen
Gaultheria shallon	Salal
Gaultheria hispidula	Creeping pearl berry
Gaultheria miqueliana	Miquel wintergreen
Gaylussacia brachycera	Box huckleberry
Gelsemium sempervirens	Carolina jessamine
Gelsemium rankinii	–
Geranium maculatum	Spotted cranesbill
Gymnocarpium dryopteris	Oak fern
Gymnocarpium robertianum	Northern oak fern
Hedyotis caerulea	Bluets
Heuchera americana	American alum root
Heuchera × brizoides	–
Heuchera micrantha	Small flowered alum root
Heuchera pilosissima	Hairy alum root
Heuchera sanguinea	Coral bells
Heuchera villosa	Hairy alum root
Hudsonia ericoides	Heathlike beach heather
Hudsonia montana	Mountain beach heather
Hudsonia tomentosa	Beach heather
Hypericum buckleyi	Blue Ridge St. John's-wort
Hypericum ellipticum	Pale St. John's-wort
Ilex vomitoria	Youpon holly
Iris cristata	Dwarf crested iris
Iris setosa	Alaskan iris
Iris versicolor	Larger blue flag
Itea virginica 'Henry's Garnet'	–
Jeffersonia diphylla	Twin leaf
Juniperus communis	Common juniper
Juniperus horizontalis	Creeping juniper
Juniperus scopulorum	Rocky Mountain juniper
Juniperus virginiana	Eastern red cedar
Ledum decumbens	Narrow-leaved Labrador tea
Ledum groenlandicum	Labrador tea

Leiophyllum buxifolium	Sand myrtle
Leucothoe axillaris	Fetterbush
Leucothoe fontanesiana	Dog hobble
Leymus arenarius 'Glaucus'	Blue lyme grass
Leymus mollis	Pacific lyme grass
Leymus racemosus 'Glaucus'	Giant blue lyme grass
Leymus tritichoides	Beardless wild rye
Linnaea borealis	Twin-flower
Lonicera flava	Yellow-flowered honeysuckle
Lonicera sempervirens	Evergreen honeysuckle
Lotus pinnatus	Deer vetch
Lycopodium clavatum	Staghorn club moss
Lycopodium complanatum	Christmas green
Lycopodium dendroideum	Treelike ground pine
Lycopodium lucidulum	Shining club moss
Lycopodium obscurum	Flat-branched ground pine
Lycopodium tristachyum	Ground pine
Mahonia nervosa	Cascades mahonia
Mahonia repens	Creeping mahonia
Matteuccia struthiopteris	Ostrich fern
Melampodium leucanthum	Black foot
Melampodium cinerium	—
Menispermum canadense	Moonseed
Mitchella repens	Partridge berry
Oenothera berlandieri	Mexican primrose
Oenothera drummondii	Baja primrose
Oenothera fruticosa	Common sundrops
Oenothera missouriensis	Missouri primrose
Oenothera tetragona	Sundrops
Onoclea sensibilis	Sensitive fern
Onoclea humifusa	Prickly pear
Opuntia erinacea var. *ursina*	Grizzly bear cactus
Opuntia juniperina	—
Opuntia macrorhiza	Big root opuntia
Opuntia phaeacantha	—
Osmunda cinnamomea	Cinnamon fern
Osmunda claytoniana	Interrupted fern
Osmunda regalis	Royal fern
Oxalis oregana	Oregon oxalis
Pachysandra procumbens	Allegheny pachysandra
Panicum virgatum	Switch grass
Parthenocissus quinquefolia	Virginia creeper
Paxistima canbyi	Ratstripper
Paxistima myrsinites	Oregon paxistima
Peltiphyllum peltatum	Umbrella plant
Penstemon pinifolius	Pineleaf penstemon
Persicaria filiformis	Virginia knotweed
Petasites palmata	Palmate sweet colt's foot
Petasites sagittata	Arrowleaf sweet colt's foot
Petasites trigonophylla	Arctic sweet colt's foot
Phalaris arundinacea	Ribbon grass

Phlox divaricata	Wild blue phlox
Phlox nivalis	Trailing phlox
Phlox stolonifera	Creeping phlox
Phlox subulata	Moss pink
Picea abies	Norway spruce
Picea pungens	Colorado spruce
Pinus banksiana	Jack pine
Pinus flexilis	Limber pine
Pinus strobus	Eastern white pine
Polemonium boreale	–
Polemonium caeruleum	Jacob's ladder
Polemonium reptans	Creeping Jacob's ladder
Polygonatum biflorum	Hairy Solomon's seal
Polygonatum commutatum	Smooth Solomon's seal
Polypodium virginianum	Rock polypody
Polypodium aureum	Golden polypody
Polystichum acrostichoides	Christmas fern
Polystichum braunii	Braun's holly fern
Polystichum lonchitis	Mountain holly fern
Polystichum munitum	Western sword fern
Potentilla anserina	Silver feather
Potentilla fruticosa	Bush cinquefoil
Potentilla tridentata	Wineleaf cinquefoil
Pyxidanthera barbulata	Pyxie moss
Pyxidanthera brevifolia	Short-leaved pyxie moss
Ranunculus repens	Creeping buttercup
Rhododendron lapponicum	Lapland rhododendron
Rhus aromatica	Fragrant sumac
Rosa blanda	Smooth rose
Salix tristis	Dwarf gray willow
Salix uva-ursi	Bearberry willow
Sanguinaria canadensis	Bloodroot
Satureja douglasii	Yerba buena
Satureja glabella	Smooth-leaved satureja
Sedum nevii	–
Sedum spathulifolium	Spatula-leaved stonecrop
Sedum ternatum	Wild stonecrop
Shortia galacifolia	Oconee bells
Stylophorum diphyllum	Celandine poppy
Symphoricarpos orbiculatus	Buck brush
Taxus canadensis	Canadian yew
Thelypteris connectilis	Long beech fern
Thelypteris hexagonoptera	Six cornered fern
Thelypteris noveboracensis	New York fern
Tiarella cordifolia	Allegheny foam flower
Tiarella wherryi	Wherry's foam flower
Tolmiea menziesii	Piggy-back plant
Tradescantia virginiana	Virginia spiderwort
Tsuga canadensis	Canadian hemlock
Vaccinium angustifolium	Low bush blueberry
Vaccinium crassifolium	Creeping blueberry

Vaccinium deliciosum	–
Vaccinium macrocarpon	American cranberry
Vaccinium vitis-idaea	Cowberry
Vancouveria chrysantha	Golden vancouveria
Vancouveria hexandra	American barrenwort
Vancouveria planipetala	Inside-out flower
Verbena bipinnatifida	Dakota verbena
Verbena canadensis	Rose verbena
Viola labradorica	Labrador violet
Viola sororia	Common violet
Vitis riparia	Riverside grape
Waldsteinia fragarioides	Barren strawberry
Woodwardia areolata	Netted chain fern
Woodwardia virginica	Virginia chain fern
Zauschneria californica	California fuchsia

Chapter 7

VARIEGATED GROUND COVERS

Literally meaning varied or diversified, the term *variegation,* when used to describe plants, refers to the quality of having multicolored leaves. Usually, leaf variegation involves green foliage in combination with gold, yellow, cream, or white. Colors such as pink, purple, red, or blue also sometimes arise. Patterns of variegation may include longitudinal striping, horizontal banding, spotting, splotching, or mottling.

Commonly occurring, variegated plants are usually mutants (variations) of the normal species. Rarely are they typical of a given species, yet so common is their incidence that one is hard pressed to name a species that does not contain at least one variegated selection. Japanese spurge is a shiny, dark green-leaved, evergreen ground cover, while a variegated cultivar has cream-colored leaf margins. Yellow archangel, a robust, green-leaved, herbaceous spreader, is far overshadowed in popularity by its cultivar 'Variegatum', of which the leaves show a brilliant silvery overlay inside medium green edges. The leaves of leopard plant are spotted like a leopard (albeit with a different color scheme: they flaunt brilliant golden spots upon a background of deep green). The Asian species from which it arose has plain green leaves. The popular and versatile genus of perennial herbs *Hosta* contains many interesting species with lush foliage and magnificent form. If it were not for its hundreds of variegated selections, however, enthusiasm for hostas would be greatly reduced.

LANDSCAPE USES OF VARIEGATED GROUND COVERS

In comparison with their single-colored parents, variegated ground covers are often as well or, some feel, better suited to enhance the landscape. For accent and specimen planting, variegated plants not only lend elements of form and texture, as do their corresponding nonvariegated parents, but they add an element of color variation. In a garden of subtly contrasting greens, a variegated selection jumps out and commands attention (see Plate 8), while its all-green parent might go unnoticed. In a woodland garden, an individual clump of Francis Williams hosta, with its magnificent gold-edged, bluish green leaves, draws the eye far more forcefully than its nonvariegated parent Siebold hosta. Similarly, variegated lily of the Nile, a vibrant lilylike cultivar for warm climates, boasts show-stopping leaves with white and green stripes and easily stands alone as a specimen or lends accent in a mixed border. In contrast, the all-green parent species functions best when mass planted or used as an edging.

Viewed from a distance, variegated ground covers convey an impression of color that is a blend of their component colors. Since variegation entails the addition or the loss of pigmentation, the resulting effect is that of an alteration in color or intensity compared with the original nonvariegated species. Blue hosta and blue lily-turf are valuable for their deep green color and extraordinary textures—both species imposing a cool tranquility when mass planted. Their gold-edged cultivars Aureo-marginata blue hosta and Gold Band blue lily-turf, however, appear sunny from a distance, and rather than lull the viewer, they stimulate feelings of excitement. White-and-green-variegated selections such as variegated bishop's weed and variegated pachysandra tend to appear ashen or silvery. Bronze-leaved two-row stonecrop, deeply suffused with red and purplish pigments, appears considerably more aristocratic when massed than its comparatively ordinary, all-green-leaved species of origin.

In using variegated ground covers a few rules of thumb should be applied. First, choose a color scheme and work with it. White-and-green-variegated ground covers generally should not be located next to variegated plants of another color, such as yellow and green. They do, however, combine wonderfully with all-green-foliaged plants—particularly those with pink, red, mauve, or purplish flowers. Also, striking color contrast can be brought to bear when purple-, bronze-, coppery-, red-, or blue-leaved plants are grown next to those of green-and-white variegation. By and large, green-and-white-patterned plants enhance our perception of spaciousness and seem to function best in mass plantings on a moderate to large scale. Exceptionally vibrant and attractive selections, of course, may be used as specimens or for accent, and they truly function quite well in those capacities.

Plants with yellow and green or gold and green variegation, as stated previously, appear bright and sunny in relation to their green counterparts. For this reason they lend themselves to specimen and accent planting—if used alone or in small groups. Border edging, which requires moderate to high contrast, primarily in relation to the dark green of turf grass, is another good use of gold-and-green selections. Compact gold-and-green-variegated selections of sedge, plantain lily, and lily-turf fill this role as well as any.

Selections displaying three or more colors, such as *Houttuynia cordata* 'Variegata' (Plate 160) with its combination of green, yellowish, cream, and purple hues, may behave similarly to those of yellow-and-green coloration. Appearing maroon from a distance, *H. cordata* 'Variegata' tends to look quite busy at close range, but it is this quality which enables this plant to command the attention of passersby. Other plants which capture the attention of passersby are three-colored stonecrop, with its cheerful Christmaslike leaves of frosted green that are first white-edged then surrounded by a thin margin of red, and spotted English ivy, with deep green, yellowish, cream, and white foliage.

HOW LEAF VARIEGATION OCCURS

Typically, plant tissue is colored according to its predominant pigmentation, which is usually green. Green-leaved species are green due to their abundance of chlorophyll, a green pigment present in such concentration that it masks the other pigments that may be present. Should a mutation occur in which chlorophyll production ceases or is reduced, the resulting tissue displays, to some degree, the coloration of the other pigments present in a leaf. If no other pigments are produced, the tissue will be white.

Plant growth occurs in *meristematic* tissues (literally tissues that divide into parts). These tissues are composed of embryonic cells that divide or develop into the various parts of the plant—such as the leaves, stems, flowers, roots, and so on. In *dicotyledonous* plants, or *dicots* (those which begin life with two seed leaves), meristematic tissue, or meristems, can be found in the leaf and stem buds, in the root tips, and in the living tissues of the stems. *Monocots* (those which begin life with a single seed leaf, encompassing such families as the grasses and lilies) harbor meristems at the base of each leaf and at the base of the stem segments between the leaves.

Variegation occurs for a variety of reasons, but it almost always involves a genetic change in the tissue of the meristems. When this occurs, the plant parts that are formed by the meristems display visible evidence of the mutation. For example, a normal leaf meristem is typically composed of cells which have a full compliment of chlorophyll, thus giving rise to normal green leaves. When a mutation occurs, the mutated meristematic tissue might become partially white, due to the absence of pigments. As the two tissue types (normal and mutated) divide and together form the leaves, the result may be a leaf that is partly white and partly green. Such plants are called *chimeras* (kie-*mee*-ras).

The term *chimera* comes from the Greek *chimaera,* a mythological monster composed of two or more parts of different animals, usually a fire-breathing monster with a serpent's tail, a goat's body, and a lion's head. Applied to plants, the word *chimera* identifies a plant which is composed of two or more genetically distinct types of tissue. Fortunately, rather than being scary, such plants are often attractive. The manner in which the different meristematic cells are arranged and develop accounts for the variety of colors and patterns in the leaves which they eventually form. The terms *sectorial, periclinal,* and *mericlinal* describe the chimeric type of most variegated plants.

TYPES OF VARIEGATION

In sectorial chimeras the different types of plant tissue occupy distinct sectors or regions within the plant. For example, the plant may be bilaterally colored with leaves half green and half white, or with one-half of the plant green and the other half white. Such variegation is usually short-lived with offspring propagated from cuttings (or another asexual method) soon producing new growth which possesses the normal all-green leaves. Even so, an occasional cultivar will prove to be stable. Variegated sweet iris is said to be a stable sectorial chimera (Plate 168).

Periclinal chimeras, in which one tissue type surrounds another, are far more stable than sectorial chimeras. In cross section, the meristem of a periclinal chimera appears to have one tissue forming an envelope around another. Such chimeras often result in plants with leaves that have edges which are a different color than their centers. For example, if a green layer of cells extends to the leaf margins above a thin layer of white, the plant will have green margins and a central splotch of whitish green. The reverse might result in a leaf with white margins and a whitish green center. The relative thickness of the layers and the intensity of their coloration determines the exact colors and patterns we see. Periclinal chimeras include variegated goutweed (Plate 8), gold-margined Fortune's hosta (Plate 159), and Shugert's periwinkle (Plate 308).

Mericlinal chimeras resemble periclinal chimeras except that the degree to which one tissue layer envelopes another is relatively incomplete. Like sectorial chimeras, the offspring of mericlinal chimeras usually prove unstable and quickly revert to normal or change to a more stable periclinal form. While periclinal chimera traits are demonstrated by all (or most of) the tissues of a given plant, the traits of a mericlinal chimera are unevenly distributed. Some leaves on the plant may appear variegated—yellow and green, for example—while others are all yellow, and still others completely green. In general, mericlinal chimeras tend to appear rather unattractive, and their use is limited to specimen or accent planting. Although I have observed mericlinal chimeras in many ground covers, I have not seen any that have struck me as being attractive enough to bother cultivating.

In addition to the three chimeras, variegation may develop due to a few other causes. Air pockets beneath the surface tissue are said to account for the spotting on the foliage of variegated lungwort. Periwinkle often exhibits iron deficiency chlorosis; in this condition, deprived of adequate iron, tissue between the leaf veins turns yellow, while the veins remain green. Nutrient deficiencies such as this result in rather unsightly variegation. Yellow-net honeysuckle, diseased with a viral infection, displays green leaves with yellow veins. In this instance, the foliage is quite striking, and in the years since its 1862 introduction by Robert Fortune, it has been the recipient of various awards of horticultural merit.

POSSIBLE PROBLEMS OF VARIEGATED GROUND COVERS

Knowledge that variegated plants are sometimes diseased, as is the case of yellow-net honeysuckle, has made some gardeners reluctant to incorporate them into the landscape. Some nursery professionals have been known to speak of variegated plants as sick (i.e., diseased). While such a statement is not true, variegated plants display certain characteristics of which you should be aware.

To begin, you should understand that white plant tissue, because it does not contain chlorophyll, does not manufacture its own food. It must then receive nourishment from surrounding tissue. Yellow or cream tissue may or may not be able to manufacture enough food to meet its own metabolic requirements. In general then, it may be said that chlorophyll deficient tissue imposes a nutritional burden upon a plant. For this reason, variegated selections usually display decreased vigor and slower growth than the typical green-colored species from which they are derived.

Slow growth is not necessarily a serious detriment to a plant's vitality, but other traits of variegated plants may be. Variegated ground covers frequently suffer from sun scorching and are more susceptible to diseases and insects than nonvariegated species. They also tend to be smaller, relatively shorter lived, and less cold and heat tolerant. Nevertheless, variegated plants are popular, and presumably forever will be. The consensus is that whatever drawbacks accompany variegated plants, their vivid, interesting, and often beautiful coloration makes them worthwhile components of the landscape.

Chapter 8

FERNS AS GROUND COVERS

Among the first plants to inhabit the earth, ferns evolved after algae and mosses, and they importantly marked the transition to plants with substantial water-conducting (vascular) tissue. Because of their ability to conduct water, ferns were able to grow larger than their more primitive predecessors, which simply absorbed water from their immediate surroundings, and were more able to aggressively exploit dry terrain. No less important was their development of *megaphylls* (literally, large leaves). Unlike the leaves of more primitive plants which contained only simple unbranched veins, fern leaves contained a network of veins—thus permitting them to grow larger, and thereby capture more of the sun's light. These two developments, in addition to the development of more extensive root systems, ultimately allowed the ferns to become as successful as they are today.

Ferns are diverse in size, habitat, and habit (see Plates 217, 222). They range from gigantic 75-foot-tall tree ferns of tropical rain forests to tiny aquatic organisms that drift on the surface of lakes and ponds. Some spread horizontally to form colonies, and others grow upright and form tight clumps or hummocks. Fern leaves, called *fronds,* are typically compound and finely divided, but vary to simple and unlobed forms. They may be evergreen or deciduous, and may reach several feet or less than an inch in length. Ferns that are suitable as ground covers are generally characterized by compact habit and mature heights of 4 feet or less.

When used as ground covers, ferns are about as versatile as any other type of ground cover. Clump-forming ferns with exceptional color or habit may be used as specimens, while those of greater simplicity or lesser brightness are best used for accent. In broad, sweeping beds, many spreading species make lushly beautiful, no-maintenance substitutes for turf. In woodland settings and naturalized landscapes, ferns are often the necessary cement for binding the other plants—trees, shrubs, and herbs—with the nonliving, physical elements of the landscape, such as the house, land, water, and rocks.

The propagation of ferns is most easily accomplished by division. Division can be attempted at any time of year but generally is most successful in early spring while plants are still dormant. Success is directly related to the size of the division, so use a spade and make divisions as large as possible. Seldom can one fail if half of the parent clump or crown, or a 6-inch or larger section of the creeping rhizome, is transplanted.

Division is not the only way in which to propagate ferns. In addition to spreading by underground stems or crowns, ferns also reproduce by dustlike structures called *spores,* rather than by seed, as do the flowering plants. Growing ferns by spores involves collecting the spores when ripe and then sowing them upon sterilized peat moss. With proper care, tiny green plantlets form, which eventually develop into mature ferns. The entire process takes about 1 to 2 years to produce a small garden-ready plant.

Like other plants, ferns are at times plagued by diseases and pests. If, however, they are properly cultured, they tend to be relatively trouble-free. Indeed, in most cases they remain very healthy and seldom if ever require the gardener's assistance.

The following ground-covering ferns are discussed in this book:

Scientific name	Common name
Adiantum capillus-veneris	Southern maidenhair
Adiantum pedatum	Northern maidenhair fern
Athyrium filix-femina	Lady fern
Athyrium nipponicum	Japanese lady fern
Athyrium thelypteroides	Silvery glade fern
Dryopteris atrata	–
Dryopteris cycadina	–
Dryopteris filix-mas	Male fern
Dryopteris intermedia	Intermediate wood fern
Dyopteris wallichiana	Wallich's wood fern
Gymnocarpium dryopteris	Oak fern
Gymnocarpium robertianum	Northern oak fern
Gymnocarpium × heterosporum	Hybrid oak fern
Matteuccia struthiopteris	Ostrich fern
Nephrolepis exaltata	Sword fern
Onoclea sensibilis	Sensitive fern
Osmunda cinnamomea	Cinnamon fern
Osmunda claytoniana	Interrupted fern
Osmunda regalis	Royal fern
Phegopteris connectilis	Long beech fern
Phegopteris hexagonoptera	Six cornered fern
Polypodium virginianum	Rock polypody
Polypodium aureum	Golden polypody
Polystichum acrostichoides	Christmas fern
Polystichum braunii	Braun's holly fern
Polystichum lonchitis	Mountain holly fern
Polystichum munitum	Western sword fern
Polystichum setiferum	Soft shield fern
Thelypteris noveboracensis	New York fern
Woodwardia areolata	Netted chain fern
Woodwardia virginica	Virginia chain fern

Chapter 9

ORNAMENTAL GRASSES AS GROUND COVERS

Some of the most exciting ground covers in use today are the ornamental grasses. Grasses, including the bamboos, are quite distinct among the flowering plants. Their stems are usually cylindrical, hollow, jointed, and as they contain chlorophyll, are active in food manufacture. In grasses two rows of leaves are arranged in alternating fashion and are usually very long in relation to their width. Veins run the length of the leaf, and the leaf itself is attached to the stem by means of a cylindrical sheath. The tiny flowers of grasses are known as florets and typically contain both male and female reproductive structures, not always the case with other types of flowering plants.

Ground-covering grasses of clump-forming habit (nonrunning, slow spreading) are typically used as accent plants or as specimens. Those that run have extensive root systems that make them most useful as general covers to bind the soil and control erosion.

For use as ground covers, the selection of grasses is quite diverse (see Plates 17, 125, 142, 166). They range in size from a few inches to about 3 feet tall. Foliar color variation is also broad. Selections are available with leaves of green, blue, brown, yellow, red, and gray. Some leaves even have combinations of these colors. In variegated selections, the patterns usually run in longitudinal stripes, or in rare cases, horizontal bands.

Flower clusters may be tiny or more than a foot long and also display diversity of color. Although most commonly straw-colored, some flowers are silvery, yellow, rosy, reddish, or purple. What is more, many grasses bloom in fall, when the flowers of many other plants have faded, and they persist through winter, protruding through the snow, a welcome sight when landscapes are at their least showy state.

Grasses grace the landscape with their vertical or arching orientation, adding interest and breaking up the dominant horizontal habits of other plants and landscape elements such as water, pavement, and garden structures. Consider using grasses as a background to horizontally spreading junipers and cotoneasters or at pondside where their beauty can be reflected off the mirrorlike surface of still water. In island beds of parking lots and as accent plants abreast of benches and statuary, ground-covering grasses are simply marvelous.

More so than most plants, the grasses respond to breezes with graceful, swaying motions. Many people do not find foliar and floral movement to be a momentous spectacle, but for the perceptive among us, it is subtly beautiful and extremely graceful—much appreciated for its calming effect on the tired mind. For these reasons, planting grasses in areas adjoining walkways, patios, decks, and landscape borders is highly recommended.

Grasses that are described in this book include the following:

SCIENTIFIC NAME	COMMON NAME
Ammophila arenaria	Sand reed
Ammophila breviligulata	Marram
Arundinaria pumila	Dwarf bamboo
Briza media	Quaking grass
Calamovilfa longifolia	Sand reed-grass
Deschampsia caespitosa	Tufted hair grass
Festuca ovina var. *glauca*	Blue fescue
Festuca amethystina	Large blue fescue
Festuca tenuifolia	Hair fescue
Glyceria maxima	Great water grass
Hakonechloa macra	Hakonechloa
Helictotrichon sempervirens	Blue oat grass
Holcus mollis 'Albo-variegatus'	Variegated velvet grass
Imperata cylindrica 'Red Baron'	Red cogon
Leymus arenarius 'Glaucus'	Blue lyme grass
Leymus mollis	Pacific lyme grass
Miscanthus sinensis	Japanese silver grass
Panicum virgatum	Switch grass
Pennisetum alopecuroides	Fountain grass
Pennisetum alopecuroides 'Japonicum'	Japanese fountain grass
Pennisetum caudatum	White-flowering fountain grass
Pennisetum incomptum	—
Pennisetum orientale	Oriental fountain grass
Pennisetum setaceum	Rose fountain grass
Phalaris arundinacea 'Picta'	Variegated ribbon grass
Pleioblastus auricoma	Dwarf yellow-stripe bamboo
Pleioblastus humilis	Dwarf bamboo
Pleioblastus pygmaeus	Pygmy bamboo
Pleioblastus variegatus	White-stripe bamboo
Sasa veitchii	Kumazasa
Zoysia tenuifolia	Mascarene grass

Plate 1. *Abelia* × *grandiflora*, glossy abelia

Plate 2. *Acacia redolens*, trailing acacia. Photo by Richard Shiell

Plate 3. *Acaena caesiiglauca*

Plate 4. *Acanthus mollis*, bear's breeches

Plate 5. *Achillea filipendula* 'Coronation Gold'

Plate 6. *Acorus gramineus* 'Ogon', Japanese sweet flag

Plate 7. *Adiantum capillus-veneris,* southern maidenhair fern

Plate 8. *Aegopodium podagraria* 'Variegatum', variegated bishop's weed

Plate 9. *Aeonium tabuliforme*

Plate 10. *Aethionema grandiflorum* 'Warley Rose', 'Warley Rose' Persian stonecress

Plate 11. *Agapanthus praecox* subsp. *orientalis* 'Variegatus', variegated Oriental agapanthus

Plate 12. *Aglaonema* cultivar, Chinese evergreen cultivar

Plate 13. *Ajuga reptans* 'Bronze Beauty', bronze-leaved creeping bugleweed

Plate 14. *Akebia quinata*, fiveleaf akebia

Plate 15. *Alchemilla mollis*, lady's mantle

Plate 16. *Aloe humilis*, spider aloe

Plate 17. *Ammophila breviligulata*, marram

Plate 18. *Ampelopsis brevipedunculata*, porcelain ampelopsis

Plate 19. *Anacyclus depressus*, Mount Atlas daisy

Plate 20. *Anagallis monellii*, Monell's pimpernel. Photo by Pamela Harper

Plate 21. *Andromeda polifolia* 'Nana', dwarf bog rosemary. Photo by Monrovia Nursery Company

Plate 22. *Anemone sylvestris*, snowdrop anemone. Photo by Walters Gardens

Plate 23. *Antennaria plantaginifolia*, plantainleaf pussytoes

Plate 24. *Aptenia cordifolia* 'Red Apple', 'Red Apple' baby sun rose

Plate 25. *Arabis caucasica* 'Snowcap', 'Snowcap' wall rock cress. Photo by Walters Gardens

Plate 26. *Arctanthemum arcticum*, arctic chrysanthemum. Photo by Pamela Harper

Plate 27. *Arctostaphylos uva-ursi*, bearberry

Plate 28. *Arctotheca calendula,* cape weed

Plate 29. *Ardisia japonica,* Japanese ardisia

Plate 30. *Arenaria montana,* mountain sandwort

Plate 31. *Armeria maritima* 'Bloodstone', 'Bloodstone' maritime thrift. Photo by Monrovia Nursery Company

Plate 32. *Aronia melanocarpa,* black chokeberry

Plate 33. *Artemisia stelleriana* 'Silver Brocade', 'Silver Brocade' beach wormwood. Photo by Monrovia Nursery Company

Plate 34. *Asarum shuttleworthii* 'Callaway', 'Callaway' mottled wild ginger

Plate 35. *Asparagus densiflorus* 'Sprengeri', Sprenger asparagus

Plate 37. *Athyrium nipponicum* 'Pictum', Japanese painted lady fern

Plate 36. *Astilbe × arendsii* 'Red Sentinel', 'Red Sentinel' hybrid astilbe. Photo by Walters Gardens

Plate 38. *Atriplex semibaccata*, creeping saltbush. Photo by Richard Shiell

Plate 39. *Aubrieta deltoidea*, purple rock-cress. Photo by Walters Gardens

Plate 40. *Aurinia saxatilis* 'Sulphurea', 'Sulphurea' golden tuft

Plate 41. *Azorella trifurcata*

Plate 42. *Baccharis pilularis* 'Pigeon Point', 'Pigeon Point' coyote bush

Plate 43. *Begonia grandis,* hardy begonia

Plate 44. *Bellis perennis,* English daisy

Plate 45. *Berberis thunbergii* 'Crimson Pygmy', 'Crimson Pygmy' barberry

Plate 46. *Bergenia cordifolia,* heartleaf bergenia

Plate 47. *Briza media,* quaking grass

Plate 48. *Brunnera macrophylla,* heartleaf brunnera

Plate 49. *Caladium* cultivar. Photo by Caladium Gardens

Plate 50. *Calamintha nepeta*, calamint savory

Plate 51. *Calamovilfa longifolia*, sand reed-grass

Plate 52. *Callirhoe involucrata*, poppy mallow

Plate 53. *Calluna vulgaris* cultivars, heather. Photo by Jim Thompson

Plate 54. *Campanula carpatica* 'Blue Clips', 'Blue Clips' Carpathian bellflower. Photo by Walters Gardens

Plate 55. *Carex hachioensis* 'Evergold', 'Evergold' Japanese sedge

Plate 56. *Carissa grandiflora,* Natal plum

Plate 57. *Carpobrotus edulis,* trailing Hottentot fig. Photo by Richard Shiell

Plate 58. *Caryopteris × clandonensis* 'Azure', 'Azure' bluebeard

Plate 59. *Ceanothus thyrsiflorus,* creeping blue blossom ceanothus

Plate 60. *Cedrus deodara* 'Golden Horizon', 'Golden Horizon' prostrate Deodar cedar. Photo by Steve Vanderwoude

Plate 61. *Centranthus ruber,* Jupiter's beard

Plate 62. *Cephalophyllum* cultivar, ice plant. Photo by Richard Shiell

Plate 63. *Cephalotaxus harringtonia* 'Prostrata', prostrate Japanese plum yew

Plate 64. *Cerastium tomentosum,* snow-in-summer

Plate 65. *Ceratostigma plumbaginoides,* dwarf plumbago

Plate 66. *Chamaedaphne calyculata,* bog leatherleaf

Plate 67. *Chamaemelum nobile,* Roman chamomile. Photo by Richard Shiell

Plate 68. *Chelone obliqua,* red turtle-head

Plate 69. *Chimaphila umbellata,* pipsissewa

Plate 70. *Chlorophytum comosum* 'Variegatum', variegated spider plant

Plate 71. *Chrysogonum virginianum,* golden star

Plate 72. *Cistus salviifolius,* sageleaf rock rose

Plate 73. *Clematis montana,* anemone clematis

Plate 74. *Clethra alnifolia* 'Hummingbird', 'Hummingbird' spiked alde

Plate 75. *Clivia miniata,* Kaffir lily

Plate 76. *Comptonia peregrina*, sweet fern

Plate 77. *Conradina verticillata*, Cumberland rosemary. Photo by Pamela Harper

Plate 78. *Convallaria majalis*, lily-of-the-valley

Plate 79. *Convolvulus cneorum*, bush morning glory

Plate 80. *Coprosma × kirkii* 'Variegata', Variegata creeping coprosma

Plate 81. *Coptis groenlandica*, goldthread

Plate 82. *Corema conradii,* broom crowberry

Plate 83. *Coreopsis verticillata* 'Moonbeam', 'Moonbeam' threadleaf coreopsis

Plate 84. *Cornus canadensis,* dwarf cornel

Plate 85. *Coronilla varia,* crown vetch

Plate 86. *Correa pulchella,* Australian fuchsia. Photo by Pamela Harper

Plate 87. *Cotoneaster horizontalis,* rock spray cotoneaster

Plate 88. *Cotula squalida,* New Zealand brass buttons

Plate 89. *Crassula multicava* (in foreground). Photo by John Trager

Plate 90. *Cuphea hyssopifola,* false heather

Plate 91. *Cymbalaria muralis* 'Alba', white-flowered Kenilworth ivy

Plate 92. *Cytisus decumbens,* prostrate broom. Photo by John Trager

Plate 93. *Dalea greggii,* trailing indigo bush

Plate 94. *Dampiera diversifolia*, dampiera. Photo by Pamela Harper

Plate 95. *Daphne × burkwoodii* 'Carol Mackie', 'Carol Mackie' Burk-wood daphne

Plate 96. *Decodon verticillatus*, willow herb

Plate 97. *Delosperma nubigena*, cloud loving hardy ice plant

Plate 98. *Dendranthema pacifica*, gold-and-silver chrysanthemum

Plate 99. *Deschampsia flexuosa* 'Aurea', golden wavy hair grass

Plate 100. *Deutzia gracilis* 'Nikko', 'Nikko' deutzia

Plate 101. *Dianthus* 'Zing Rose', 'Zing Rose' carnation. Photo by Walters Gardens

Plate 102. *Dicentra formosa* 'Alba', white-flowered Pacific bleeding heart

Plate 103. *Dichondra micrantha*, small lawn leaf. Photo by Pamela Harper

Plate 104. *Diervilla lonicera,* bush honeysuckle

Plate 105. *Disporum sessile* 'Variegatum', variegated Japanese fairy bells

Plate 106. *Drosanthemum floribundum,* rosy ice plant. Photo by Richard Shiell

Plate 107. *Dryas octopetala,* mountain avens. Photo by Steven Still

Plate 108. *Dryopteris filix-mas* 'Undulata Robusta', robust male fern

Plate 109. *Duchesnea indica,* mock strawberry. Photo by Walters Gardens

Plate 110. *Echeveria elegans*, Mexican gem. Photo by Pamela Harper

Plate 111. *Empetrum nigrum*, black crowberry. Photo by Donald Eastman

Plate 112. *Ephedra distachya*, joint fir

Plate 113. *Epigaea repens*, trailing arbutus

Plate 114. *Epimedium alpinum* 'Rubrum', red-flowered alpine epimedium

Plate 115. *Equisetum hyemale*, common horsetail

Plate 116. *Erica carnea* 'Springwood Pink', 'Springwood Pink' spring heath

Plate 117. *Erigeron karvinskianus*, bonytip fleabane

Plate 118. *Erodium reichardii*, alpine geranium

Plate 119. *Erysimum kotschyanum*, creeping gold wallflower. Photo by Pamela Harper

Plate 120. *Euonymus fortunei* 'Tricolor', 'Tricolor' Japanese euonymus

Plate 121. *Euphorbia polychroma,* cushion euphorbia

Plate 122. *Euryops acraeus,* Drakensberg daisy. Photo by Richard Shiell

Plate 123. *Fallopia japonica* 'Compacta', dwarf Japanese fleece flower

Plate 124. *Felicia amelloides,* blue marguerite. Photo by Pamela Harper

Plate 125. *Festuca ovina* var. *glauca,* blue fescue

Plate 126. *Ficus pumila* 'Variegata', variegated creeping fig

Plate 127. *Filipendula vulgaris,* dropwort. Photo by Steven Still

Plate 128. *Fittonia verschaffeltii* var. *verschaffeltii*, fittonia

Plate 129. *Forsythia viridissima* 'Bronxensis', dwarf Bronx forsythia. Photo by Pamela Harper

Plate 130. *Fragaria vesca,* European strawberry

Plate 131. *Francoa ramosa,* maiden's wreath

Plate 132. *Fuchsia procumbens,* trailing fuchsia

Plate 133. *Galax urceolata,* colt's foot

Plate 134. *Galium odoratum,* sweet woodruff

Plate 135. *Gardenia jasminoides* 'Radicans', creeping cape jasmine. Photo by Master Tag Corporation

Plate 136. *Gaultheria procumbens,* common wintergreen

Plate 137. *Gaylussacia brachycera,* box huckleberry

Plate 138. *Gazania rigens* cultivars, trailing gazania

Plate 139. *Gelsemium sempervirens,* Carolina jessamine. Photo by Steven Still

Plate 140. *Genista pilosa,* silky-leaf woadwaxen. Photo by Monrovia Nursery Company

Plate 141. *Geranium* 'Johnson's Blue'

Plate 142. *Glyceria maxima* 'Variegata', variegated great water grass

Plate 143. *Grevillea juniperina*

Plate 144. *Gunnera tinctoria*

Plate 145. *Gymnocarpium dryopteris,* oak fern

Plate 146. *Gypsophila repens* 'Rosea', pink creeping baby's breath

Plate 147. *Hakonechloa macra,* hakonechloa

Plate 148. *Haworthia radula*

Plate 149. *Hebe pinguifolia* 'Pagei'

Plate 150. *Hedera helix* 'Thorndale', 'Thorndale' English ivy

Plate 151. *Hedyotis caerulea,* bluets. Photo by Pamela Harper

Plate 152. *Helianthemum nummularium* 'Wisley Pink', 'Wisley Pink' sun rose

Plate 153. *Helictotrichon sempervirens,* blue oat grass

Plate 154. *Helleborus orientalis,* Lenten rose

Plate 155. *Hemerocallis* cultivar, daylily. Photo by Walters Gardens

Plate 156. *Herniaria glabra,* rupturewort

Plate 157. *Heuchera sanguinea,* coral bells

Plate 158. *Holcus mollis* 'Albo-variegatus', variegated velvet grass. Photo by Pamela Harper

Plate 159. *Hosta fortunei* 'Aureo-marginata', gold-margined Fortune's hosta

Plate 160. *Houttuynia cordata* 'Variegata', variegated houttuynia

Plate 161. *Hudsonia tomentosa,* beach heather

Plate 162. *Hydrangea anomala* subsp. *petiolaris,* climbing hydrangea. Photo by Bluebird Nursery

Plate 163. *Hypericum* 'Hidcote', 'Hidcote' goldencup St. John's-wort

Plate 164. *Iberis sempervirens* 'Snowflake', 'Snowflake' evergreen candytuft

Plate 165. *Ilex crenata* 'Helleri', 'Helleri' Chinese holly

Plate 166. *Imperata cylindrica* 'Red Baron', 'Red Baron' Japanese blood grass

Plate 167. *Indigofera incarnata,* white Chinese indigo. Photo by Pamela Harper

Plate 168. *Iris pallida* 'Aurea Variegata'

Plate 169. *Iris pseudacorus,* yellow water iris

Plate 170. *Itea virginica* 'Henry's Garnet', 'Henry's Garnet' Virginia sweetspire. Photo by Pamela Harper

Plate 171. *Jasminum nudiflorum,* winter jasmine

Plate 172. *Jeffersonia diphylla,* twinleaf

Plate 173. *Jovibarba heuffelii* 'Mystique'

Plate 174. *Juniperus horizontalis* 'Blue Chip' ('Blue Chip' creeping juniper) and *Pachysandra terminalis* (Japanese spurge)

Plate 175. *Juniperus davurica* 'Expansa Variegata', variegated Davurian juniper

Plate 176. *Kalanchoe blossfeldiana* cultivars, Christmas kalanchoe

Plate 177. *Lamiastrum galeobdolon* 'Variegatum', variegated yellow archangel

Plate 178. *Lamium maculatum* 'White Nancy', 'White Nancy' spotted dead nettle. Photo by Walters Gardens

Plate 179. *Lampranthus spectabilis,* showy ice plant. Photo by Richard Shiell

Plate 180. *Lantana hybrida* cultivar, hybrid lantana

Plate 181. *Lathyrus latifolius,* perennial pea vine

Plate 182. *Lavandula angustifolia* 'Lady Lavender' ('Lady Lavender' true lavender) and *Thymus* (golden thyme)

Plate 183. *Ledum groenlandicum,* Labrador tea

Plate 184. *Leiophyllum buxifolium,* sand myrtle

Plate 185. *Leucanthemum vulgare,* oxeye daisy. Photo by Steven Still

Plate 186. *Leucothoe fontanesiana* 'Girard's Rainbow', variegated drooping leucothoe

Plate 187. *Leymus arenarius* 'Glaucus', blue lyme grass

Plate 188. *Ligularia tussilaginea* 'Aurea-maculata', leopard plant

Plate 189. *Linnaea borealis,* twinflower

Plate 190. *Liriope muscari* 'Variegata', variegated blue lily turf

Plate 191. *Lithodora diffusa* 'Grace Ward', 'Grace Ward' spreading lithodora

Plate 192. *Lonicera pileata,* royal carpet honeysuckle

Plate 193. *Lotus corniculatus,* bird's-foot trefoil

Plate 194. *Luzula nivea,* snowy wood-rush

Plate 195. *Lycopodium complanatum,* Christmas green

Plate 196. *Lysimachia nummularia* 'Aurea', golden creeping Charley

Plate 197. *Mahonia nervosa*, Cascades mahonia

Plate 198. *Maranta leuconeura*, prayer plant

Plate 199. *Matteuccia struthiopteris*, ostrich fern

Plate 200. *Mazus reptans*, creeping mazus. Photo by Pamela Harper

Plate 201. *Melampodium cinerium*. Photo by Pamela Harper

Plate 202. *Melissa officinalis,* lemon balm

Plate 203. *Menispermum canadense,* Canadian moonseed

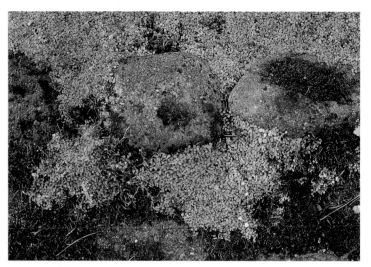

Plate 204. *Mentha requienii,* Corsican mint

Plate 205. *Microbiota decussata,* Siberian cypress

Plate 206. *Miscanthus sinensis* 'Adagio', 'Adagio' Japanese silver grass

Plate 207. *Mitchella repens,* partridge berry

Plate 208. *Muehlenbeckia axillaris,* creeping wire vine. Photo by Pamela Harper

Plate 209. *Myoporum parvifolium,* myoporum

Plate 210. *Myosotis scorpioides,* true forget-me-not

Plate 211. *Nandina domestica* 'Atropurpurea Nana', 'Atropurpurea Nana' heavenly bamboo

Plate 212. *Nepeta mussinii,* Persian catmint

Plate 213. *Nephrolepis exaltata*, sword fern

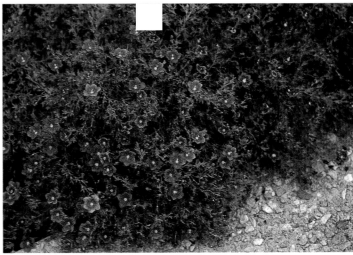

Plate 214. *Nierembergia hippomanica* var. *violacea*, dwarf cupflower

Plate 215. *Oenothera tetragona* 'Fireworks', 'Fireworks' four-angled sundrops. Photo by Walters Gardens

Plate 216. *Omphalodes verna*, blue-eyed Mary

Plate 217. *Onoclea sensibilis*, sensitive fern

Plate 218. *Ophiopogon japonica,* dwarf lily turf

Plate 219. *Opuntia humifusa,* prickly pear

Plate 220. *Origanum laevigatum* 'Herrenhausen', smooth-leaved oregano

Plate 221. *Orostachys iwarenge,* soft-leaved stonecrop

Plate 222. *Osmunda cinnamomea,* cinnamon fern

Plate 223. *Osteospermum fruticosum,* trailing African daisy

Plate 224. *Oxalis oregana,* Oregon oxalis

Plate 225. *Pachysandra terminalis,* Japanese spurge

Plate 226. *Panicum virgatum* 'Heavy Metal', 'Heavy Metal' switch grass

Plate 227. *Parthenocissus quinquefolia*, Virginia creeper

Plate 228. *Paxistima canbyi*, canby ratstripper

Plate 229. *Pelargonium fragans*, nutmeg geranium

Plate 230. *Peltiphyllum peltatum*, umbrella plant

Plate 231. *Pennisetum setaceum*, rose fountain grass

Plate 232. *Penstemon pinifolius,* pineleaf penstemon. Photo by Walters Gardens

Plate 233. *Peperomia obtusifolia,* oval leaf peperomia

Plate 234. *Pernettya mucronata,* Chilean pernettya. Photo by Monrovia Nursery Company

Plate 235. *Perovskia atriplicifolia* 'Longin', 'Longin' Russian sage

Plate 236. *Persicaria affinis,* Himalayan fleece flower. Photo by Walters Gardens

Plate 237. *Petasites japonicus* 'Giganteus', giant Japanese butterbur

Plate 238. *Phalaris arundinacea* 'Picta', variegated ribbon grass

Plate 239. *Phlox subulata* cultivar, moss pink. Photo by Walters Gardens

Plate 240. *Phyla nodiflora,* creeping lippia. Photo by Pamela Harper

Plate 241. *Picea abies* 'Pendula', weeping Norway spruce

Plate 242. *Pilea cadierei,* aluminum plant

Plate 243. *Pinus mugo,* mugo pine

Plate 244. *Pittosporum tobira* 'Wheeler's Dwarf', 'Wheeler's Dwarf' Japanese pittosporum

Plate 245. *Pleioblastus auricoma,* dwarf yellow-stripe bamboo

Plate 246. *Polemonium caeruleum*, Jacob's ladder

Plate 247. *Polygala chamaebuxus*, ground milkwort

Plate 248. *Polygonatum odoratum*, fragrant Solomon's seal

Plate 249. *Polypodium virginianum*, rock polypody

Plate 250. *Polystichum acrostichoides*, Christmas fern

Plate 251. *Potentilla anserina*, silver feather

Plate 252. *Pratia angulata*

Plate 253. *Primula japonica,* Japanese primrose

Plate 255. *Pulmonaria saccharata* 'Mrs. Moon', 'Mrs. Moon' Bethlehem sage

Plate 254. *Prunella grandiflora* cultivar, large-flowered self-heal

Plate 256. *Pulsatilla vulgaris* (European Pasque flower) with juniper

Plate 257. *Pyracantha* 'Ruby Mound', 'Ruby Mound' firethorn. Photo by Monrovia Nursery Company

Plate 258. *Pyxidanthera barbulata,* pyxie moss

Plate 259. *Ranunculus repens,* creeping buttercup

Plate 260. *Raoulia australis,* New Zealand scab plant

Plate 261. *Raphiolepis indica* dwarf cultivar, Indian hawthorn dwarf cultivar

Plate 262. *Rhododendron williamsianum*

Plate 263. *Rhus aromatica* 'Gro-low', 'Gro-low' fragrant sumac

Plate 264. *Rosa blanda,* smooth rose

Plate 265. *Rosmarinus officinalis* 'Huntington Carpet', 'Huntington Carpet' rosemary

Plate 266. *Rubus calycinoides* 'Emerald Carpet', Taiwanese creeping rubus

Plate 267. *Rudbeckia fulgida* 'Goldsturm', 'Goldsturm' orange coneflower

Plate 268. *Sagina subulata,* Corsican pearlwort

Plate 269. *Salix yezoalpina*

Plate 270. *Salvia argentea,* silver-leaved sage

Plate 271. *Sanguinaria canadensis,* bloodroot

Plate 272. *Santolina chamaecyparissus,* dwarf cypress. Photo by Jim Thompson

Plate 273. *Saponaria ocymoides,* rock soapwort

Plate 274. *Sarcococca hookeriana* var. *humilis,* dwarf Himalayan sarcococca

Plate 275. *Sasa veitchii* 'Nana', dwarf kuma bamboo grass

Plate 276. *Satureja douglasii,* yerba buena

Plate 277. *Saxifraga stolonifera,* strawberry saxifrage

Plate 278. *Sedum ellacombianum* (Ellacombe's stonecrop) and *Juniperus horizontalis* 'Blue Chip' ('Blue Chip' creeping juniper)

Plate 279. *Sedum spathulifolium* 'Cape Blanco'

Plate 280. *Sedum spectabile* 'Brilliant', 'Brilliant' purple stonecrop

Plate 281. *Sempervivum* species, houseleeks. Photo by Bluebird Nursery

Plate 282. *Shortia soldanelloides,* fringed galax

Plate 283. *Soleirolia soleirolii,* baby's tears

Plate 284. *Sorbus reducta,* dwarf Chinese mountain ash

Plate 285. *Spartina pectinata* 'Aureo-marginata'

Plate 286. *Spiraea* × *bumalda* 'Gold Mound', 'Gold Mound' spirea

Plate 287. *Stachys byzantina,* lamb's ear

Plate 288. *Stephanandra incisa* 'Crispa', dwarf cutleaf stephanandra

Plate 289. *Stylophorum diphyllum,* celandine poppy

Plate 290. *Symphoricarpos orbiculatus,* coralberry. Photo by Richard Shiell

Plate 291. *Symphytum grandiflorum,* large-flowered comfrey

Plate 292. *Tanacetum parthenium* 'Aureum', golden feverfew

Plate 293. *Taxus baccata* 'Repens Aurea', golden-leaved berried yew

Plate 294. *Teucrium chamaedrys* var. *prostratum*, prostrate ground germander. Photo by Walters Gardens

Plate 295. *Thelypteris noveboracensis*, New York fern

Plate 296. *Thymus × citriodorus,* lemon thyme

Plate 297. *Tiarella wherryi,* Wherry's tiarella

Plate 298. *Tolmiea menziesii,* piggyback plant

Plate 299. *Trachelospermum jasminoides,* star jasmine

Plate 300. *Tradescantia albiflora* 'Albovittata', white-striped white-flowered spiderwort

Plate 301. *Tsuga canadensis* 'Cole', 'Cole' Canadian hemlock

Plate 302. *Vaccinium macrocarpon,* American cranberry

Plate 303. *Vancouveria planipetala,* inside-out flower

Plate 304. *Verbena tenuisecta,* moss verbena

Plate 305. *Veronica incana,* woolly speedwell

Plate 306. *Viburnum davidii,* David viburnum

Plate 308. *Vinca minor* 'Ralph Shugert', 'Ralph Shugert' common periwinkle

Plate 307. *Vinca minor,* common periwinkle

Plate 309. *Viola labradorica,* Labrador violet

Plate 310. *Vitis riparia,* riverbank grape

Plate 311. *Waldsteinia fragarioides,* barren strawberry

Plate 312. *Woodwardia virginica,* Virginia chain fern

Plate 313. *Xanthorhiza simplicissima*, yellow-root

Plate 314. *Zauschneria californica*, California fuchsia

Plate 315. *Zoysia tenuifolia*, Mascarene grass

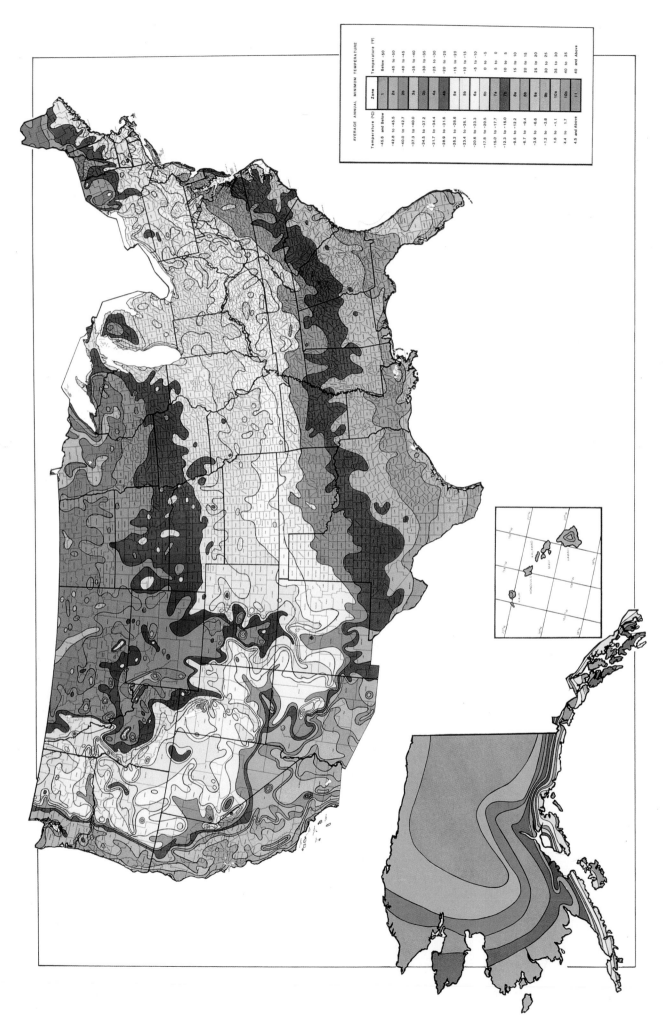

Plate 316. USDA Hardiness Map. Courtesy of the Agricultural Research Service, USDA.

PART 2

Chapter 10

GROUND COVER DESCRIPTIONS

This encyclopedic treatment of the most popular and useful ground covers for the North American landscape will help you discover many fascinating plants that, through their versatility and ease of maintenance, will make your gardening experiences all the more pleasant and rewarding. The plants are arranged alphabetically by scientific name; the most frequently used common name(s) is (are) listed below the scientific name. The topics that are included in the discussion under each genus heading, and for most species, are as follows:

INTRODUCTORY INFORMATION: Each description begins with an introduction to the particular genus or species of ground cover. In the case of genera with numerous ground-cover species, I give an overview of those species, and in the case of genera with only one or a few ground-cover species, I discuss the most common species first, then the less common species. Included in each introduction are common names most often applied to the particular genus or species. Common names are often very interesting and reveal secrets about the history and morphology of the plant. Next, I discuss size. In terms of height and width, I list the approximate dimensions of the plant at maturity. In the case of plants that send up shoots when in bloom, I indicate the height in bloom if it is significantly different from the height of the leaves. Landscape use is described, including the most common uses of the plant. Sometimes the discussion includes details about plants that make good companions to the ground cover in question. Finally, the ground cover's ability to withstand foot traffic is noted, and if it has any medicinal or economic uses or is shrouded in lore, these are discussed as well.

SCIENTIFIC NAME: Under this topic, I list the scientific name, its phonetic pronunciation, and many times, the source or derivation of the name. Many gardeners and even nursery professionals are intimidated by scientific names. They do not understand them and are even less secure about pronouncing them. This is unfortunate because scientific names are not difficult to understand. Remember, they are just two-word common names in Latin or Greek. Once you translate them to English you will be surprised at how much sense they make and how easy they are to remember. Pronunciation, too, should be easy; in fact, words in Latin and Greek are easier to pronounce than words in English because the vowel sounds are much more predictable. Unfortunately, however, those who grow and write about plants are not Latin and Greek scholars. They do, however, have opinions as to the correct pronunciation of plant names—usually the way they have been taught. I, like everyone else, have a particular way of pronouncing plant names. For example, I pronounce sempervirens as sem-per-*vie*-renz. On the other hand, many other authors and gardeners pronounce it sem-per-*veer*-enz. There are even inconsistencies within single books, and there are striking geographic differences in the English-speaking world. Because of the variation in pronunciation of scientific words, I often list two or three of the most common pronunciations and leave the final decision up to you. I am not ready to concede that there are numerous ways of correctly pronouncing each plant name, but you should know that other authors have said that very thing! The bottom line is, don't get distraught about pronunciation—you are probably as correct as the next person.

HARDINESS/ORIGIN: Under the topic of hardiness, I list the northern and southern (if known) limits of each species. The hardiness ratings I use come from the map of the United States Department of Agriculture Plant Hardiness Zone Map (Plate 316). Hardiness ratings are based upon the average seasonal low temperature of a given region and serve as a general guideline for determining whether a particular plant can be grown successfully. See Chapter 2 for further discussion of hardiness. Following the hardiness ratings, I usually list the origin or native habitat of the species. Normally I limit this to the country or region of origin, but when known, I often discuss the habitat in terms of its physical conditions: soil type, terrain, and light conditions.

LEAVES/FLOWERS/FRUIT: My discussion of these important morphological features is, for the most part, in easily understood nonscientific terms. Most people think that the leaves of ground covers are their only ornamental feature. In reality, the leaves are usually just the beginning. Often ground covers display exceptional floral and fruit characteristics. With the exception of the ferns, which do not flower but instead produce spores, I discuss floral characteristics—even if they are tiny and not very ornamental. Fruit is discussed only if it makes a contribution to the ornamental or aesthetic appeal of the plant.

RATE/SPACING: Here I indicate the relative rate of spread of each species and use terms such as slow, moderate, fast, and invasive. Following the rate of spread is a recommendation for spacing and a reference to the typical container sizes in which the plants are available. Loosely speaking, if you space your plants as recommended and their cultural and care requirements are met, they will fill in completely in one to two growing seasons. Some of the slow-to-mature types, particularly the broad-spreading woody shrubs, may take two, three, or even four years to fill in. Even so, they are easily weeded around and mulched between, and do not require much maintenance.

HORTICULTURAL SELECTIONS: This heading is a bit of a misnomer as I use it as a catch-all for any variation of a species that is likely to be found in cultivation. For this reason, it is used to encompass not only those forms that were selected in cultivation (cultivars), but for the botanical forms, varieties, and subspecies as well. All comparisons are to the title plant, unless otherwise stated. Where a cultivar has more than one name, synonyms are listed in parenthesis after the primary name). These additional names sometimes arise where sales-minded nursery professionals have inappropriately changed a preexisting name in an attempt to increase the marketability of a plant.

SPECIES, OTHER SPECIES or LESS COMMON SPECIES: Useful ground-covering species in the genus are discussed and described under these three headings, along with their subspecies, varieties, formas, cultivars, or related hybrids. Here I also explain any differences in cultural needs from the other species.

CULTURE/CARE: This is a discussion of the cultural needs; minimally the soil, moisture, and light requirements of each plant. At times I also discuss special needs as they relate to wind, humidity, pollution, or water table. Next is a discussion of the most common disease and insect problems, followed by the maintenance requirements.

PROPAGATION: Here I discuss the most common and useful methods of propagating a given species or genus. Most of the terminology here is pretty common, but at first you may find yourself referring to Chapter 4, Propagation, until you become comfortable with the different terms and methods of propagation.

Abelia × grandiflora   PLATE 1

Glossy Abelia

Thought to be a hybrid derived from a cross between *A. chinensis* and *A. uniflora,* this dense, rounded, semievergreen, many-stemmed shrub may reach 3 to 6 feet tall by 3 to 6 feet wide. It, and especially its cultivar 'Prostrata', are useful general covers for mass planting in large areas. Both bind the soil well and therefore are prized for use on steep slopes and freeway embankments. Because 'Prostrata' holds a nice, low, compact shape, it is sometimes used as a dwarf hedge. No foot traffic is tolerated.

SCIENTIFIC NAME: *Abelia × grandiflora* (a-*bee*-lee-a / a-*beel*-ya gran-di-*floe*-ra). *Abelia* is named for Dr. Clarke Abel (1780–1826), an English physician and author who reportedly discovered this naturally occurring hybrid species around 1816. *Grandiflora* refers to the large flowers.

HARDINESS / ORIGIN: Zones 6 to 9; both parent species are from China.

LEAVES / FLOWERS / FRUIT: The semievergreen, simple, oval, ⅗- to 1⅖-inch-long leaves are oppositely arranged upon fine-textured, reddish brown stems. Each leaf is toothed around the edges, lustrous dark green above and paler green below, and turns bronzy in fall and winter. Attractive to hummingbirds, the ¾-inch-long, ¾-inch-wide flowers of mid summer to early fall arise upon the new growth, are pale pink to white, funnel-shaped, and arranged in loose clusters upon the branch tips. As they age they turn purple, an interesting transition that makes for a very long and engaging floral show.

RATE / SPACING: Growth is slow. Plants from 1- to 2-gallon-sized containers are spaced 2½ to 4 feet apart.

HORTICULTURAL SELECTIONS: 'Francis Mason', leaves variegated yellow and green; 'Prostrata', 1½ to 2 feet tall by 4 feet wide, with compact, prostrate habit; 'Sherwoodii', 3 to 3½ feet tall by 4 to 4½ feet wide, with leaves reddish in youth and, like its flowers, a bit smaller than those of the species.

CULTURE / CARE: Glossy abelia grows best in well-drained, acidic, organically rich loam. It tolerates modest drought once established, but is most attractive and healthy if the soil is kept moist. It prefers light to moderate shade. Diseases are limited to leaf spots, powdery mildew, and root rots, and the only pest of consequence is the root-knot nematode. Other than an annual pruning to remove dead stems (primarily from winter damage in the North), it needs little maintenance.

PROPAGATION: Softwood cuttings root easily, especially when treated with 1000 to 2000 ppm IBA/talc. Seed is seldom used because of variability among the offspring. To develop new forms, collect ripe seed, store it in an airtight container at cool temperatures for one year, then sow.

Acacia redolens   PLATE 2

Trailing Acacia, Sweet Wattle

This is one of the best ground covers for use in the highly saline, arid soils of desert landscapes, where it performs well both for erosion control and as a replacement for turf in moderate-sized to large-sized level or sloping areas. It is low and shrubby, ranging from 1 to 4 feet tall by 10 to 15 feet wide. It graces the landscape with subtle grayish green foliage and in springtime adds a lively display of dainty ball-shaped yellow flowers.

SCIENTIFIC NAME: *Acacia redolens* (a-*kay*-sha *red*-a-lenz). *Acacia* comes from the Greek *akis,* a sharp point, in reference to the many acacias with thorns. *Redolens* means scented, the leaves emitting a sweet vanilla-like scent when rubbed in water.

HARDINESS / ORIGIN: Zones 9 to 10; Australia.

LEAVES / FLOWERS / FRUIT: Leaves are evergreen, narrow (3½ inches long by ½ inch wide), and an attractive subdued grayish green. Springtime flowers, which are arranged in round heads, are ⅛ inch long and yellow. The fruit that follows is a tiny pod.

RATE / SPACING: Growth is fast. Plants from 1- to 2-gallon-sized containers are spaced 4 to 6 feet apart.

OTHER SPECIES: *A. angustissima* var. *hirta* (an-gus-*tis*-i-ma *hir*-ta), named for its most narrow and hairy (hirsute) leaves, is commonly called fern or prairie acacia. It hails from the prairies, bluffs, and plains of the southern United States (from Florida to Arizona and as far north as Missouri), as well as Mexico and Costa Rica. It can be used in the same manner as *A. redolens,* displays a shrubby, semiwoody, sprawling character, and ranges from 1 to 3 feet tall. Its leaves are deciduous, compound, fernlike, 1 to 2 inches long, and composed of 8 to 14 pairs of narrowly oblong leaflets that in turn are divided into 10 to 50 pairs of ¼-inch-long, ⅟₁₂-inch-wide subleaflets. The flowers, which are tiny and white (often tinged pink to lavender), are borne during late spring and early summer. The fruit, an oblong legume to 4 inches, is interesting if not attractive. Hardy in Zones 6 or 7 to 10.

CULTURE / CARE: Well-drained, acidic, sandy, and rocky soils are best, yet soils of high salinity and alkalinity are also tolerated. Although plants require frequent watering during the first season, thereafter, tolerance to drought is excellent, and little or no irrigation is needed. Both species grow best in full sun, but a little shade does no harm. The diseases of greatest prevalence are twig canker, leaf spot, powdery mildew, and root rot, and pests include scale insects and caterpillars. Maintenance needs are few and normally consist only of periodic shearing to maintain a neat, compact appearance.

PROPAGATION: Stem cuttings from fresh new growth are the simplest and most common means of propagation, but root cuttings can also be used.

Acaena microphylla PLATE 3
Redspine Sheepburr

Although the genus *Acaena* contains numerous species that cover the ground, this species is the most prominent. Like the other species, it is a low-growing, horizontally spreading, herbaceous, mat-forming ground cover. It reaches 4 to 6 inches tall, spreads indefinitely, and like the others, is best used on a small scale as a general cover or as a filler between stepping stones—particularly along the Pacific Coast. Limited foot traffic is tolerated.

SCIENTIFIC NAME: *Acaena microphylla* (ak-*ee*-na / a-*seen*-a my-kroe-*fil*-a). *Acaena* comes from the Greek *akaina,* a thorn, in reference to the spiny fruits. *Microphylla* means small-leaved.

HARDINESS / ORIGIN: Zones 6 or 7 to 9; New Zealand.

LEAVES / FLOWERS / FRUIT: The leaves are compound, 1 inch long, divided into 7 to 15 leaflets $\frac{1}{8}$ inch wide and edged with rounded teeth. Colored purplish to olive or bronzy green, they display a soft fine texture. The rounded, grayish flower clusters are insignificant from an ornamental standpoint, but the bristly fruit, which ripens to an interesting shade of crimson, lends early-to-late summertime interest.

RATE / SPACING: Growth is fast. Plants from pint-sized to quart-sized containers are spaced 10 to 16 inches apart.

HORTICULTURAL SELECTIONS: 'Kupferteppich' ('Copper Carpet'), with attractive red-brown foliage.

OTHER SPECIES: **A. adscendens** (ad-*sen*-denz) is named for its branches that rise (ascend) from procumbent stems. Its leaves of bluish gray are held upon reddish stems.

A. buchananii (bu-kan-*an*-ee-eye) is named after John Buchanan (1819–1898), a botanist with the Geological Survey in New Zealand. It reaches 3 inches tall and displays tiny pale, jade green leaves.

A. caesiiglauca (see-zee *glaw*-ka), named for its bluish gray leaves, reaches only 2 inches tall.

A. inermis (in-*er*-mis), meaning unarmed or without thorns, reaches 3 inches tall and has leaves like those of *A. microphylla.*

A. novae-zelandiae (noe-vee-zee-*land*-ee-eye) comes from New Zealand, reaches 5 inches tall, and has leaves that are larger and darker green than those of *A. microphylla.*

A. sanguisorbae (san-gwi-*sor*-bee) is named for its supposed healing properties. It reaches 10 inches tall and displays hairy grayish leaves.

CULTURE / CARE: Sheepburrs do best in full sun in sandy, well-drained, alkaline, moist or dry soils. Accordingly, they tolerate considerable drought and seldom require watering. Disease and pest problems are minimal, and maintenance needs are few.

PROPAGATION: Division can be performed at any time as long as the soil is kept moist while the roots are becoming reestablished.

Acanthus mollis PLATE 4
Bear's Breech, Artist's Acanthus

Because the foliage of this species is often depicted in ancient art, it has the common name artist's acanthus. Stemless, with leaves arising from the crown, this 2- to 3-foot-tall, 6-foot-wide, herbaceous, clump-forming ground cover is exceptional for its huge leaves and tall flowers. For these reasons, it is often used as a specimen or background plant in perennial border plantings. On a larger scale it functions as a foundation facer or edging plant. No foot traffic is tolerated.

SCIENTIFIC NAME: *Acanthus mollis* (a-*kan*-thus *mol*-lis). *Acanthus* comes from the Greek *acanthos,* prickle or thorn, in reference to some species which are armed with spines. *Mollis,* soft, is probably a reference to the leaves not being spiny as they are in other species of *Acanthus.*

HARDINESS / ORIGIN: Zones 6 or 7 to 10; Mediterranean region.

LEAVES / FLOWERS / FRUIT: The dark glossy green, tooth-edged leaves are deeply cut, evergreen, oblong to oval, $1\frac{1}{2}$ to 2 feet long by 1 foot wide, and display conspicuous veins. The white to pinkish flowers of late spring and early summer are arranged in erect 1- to $1\frac{1}{2}$-foot-long spikes on $1\frac{1}{2}$- to 2-foot-long stems.

RATE / SPACING: Growth is moderate to fast. Plants from quart-sized to gallon-sized containers are spaced $2\frac{1}{2}$ to $3\frac{1}{2}$ feet apart.

HORTICULTURAL SELECTIONS: 'Latifolius', with broader leaves and greater cold tolerance; 'Oak Leaf', with oak-leaf-shaped leaves; 'Summer Dream', thought to be a hybrid from the cross between *A. mollis* and *A. spinosus,* 3 feet tall by 3 feet wide, with large, shiny, very deeply lobed leaves and numerous white tubular flowers with pinkish purple bracts.

OTHER SPECIES: **A. hungaricus** (hun-*gare*-i-kus), of the Balkan Peninsula, southwestern Romania, and northwestern Yugoslavia, is hardy in Zones 6 or 7 to 10. It is similar to *A. mollis* but with arching leaves that are edged with broad rounded teeth and with a smaller stalk at their bases. Reaching 2 to $3\frac{1}{2}$ feet and flowering like *A. mollis,* but during mid summer, this is a very impressive and commanding species.

A. spinosus (spy-*no*-sus), spiny bear's breeches, named for its spiny-edged leaves, is a fabulously impressive species with lustrous deep green, sharply and prominently toothed, deeply divided, oval to oblong leaves. Reaching 3 to 3½ feet tall by 3 feet wide with leaves reaching 10 inches wide by more than 3½ feet long, this robust Mediterranean/Italian native blooms during late spring to early summer with tall spikes of pinkish flowers and purple bracts. It is suitable for large scale, specimen and accent use, is hardy in Zones 6 or 7 to 10, and shows good tolerance to frost, heat, and humidity. Variety *spinosissimus* (sometimes classified as a variety of *A. mollis* or as a separate species *A. spinosissimus*) is exceedingly spiny with more and sharper teeth about the edges of its leaves.

CULTURE / CARE: Bear's breeches are adaptable to various soil types but perform best in slightly moist, richly organic, well-drained, acidic soil. They prefer light to moderate shade. No serious diseases seem to trouble them, and their primary pests are aphids, caterpillars, and slugs. Maintenance involves removing the flower stalks following bloom or trimming out tattered leaves.

PROPAGATION: Clumps are easily divided during fall or early spring. Root cuttings should be taken during early spring, sectioned to 2 to 3 inches, placed upright in a porous medium, and kept moist until new shoots form, usually four to six weeks. Early spring-sown seed germinates in three or four weeks at soil temperatures of 50 to 55°F.

Achillea   PLATE 5

Yarrow

Yarrows are the perfect example of entropy; that is, they are constantly moving in the direction of disorganization and chaos: they sprawl, reseed, collapse, and at times just plain annoy. Yet they remain popular, and the reason is simple: their flowers and fernlike foliage add color, texture, and fragrance to the landscape. Yarrows are said to be helpful to other landscape plants as they attract beneficial insects: they are an egg-laying site for ladybugs and are very attractive to butterflies.

The ground-covering yarrows are suitable for small-sized to moderate-sized, casual, wild, chaotic, or contained areas where they may spread freely. They are typically erect-stemmed, horizontally spreading herbaceous perennials. They range from 6 inches to 4½ feet tall, spread indefinitely, and are self-sowing, which often makes them invasive. Employ a single plant in the herbaceous border or rock garden as a specimen, or mass plant one of the lower-growing species as a lawn substitute. Infrequent foot traffic is tolerated.

Preparations of yarrow have been widely used in herbal medicines to help ease the pain of skin ulcerations, back problems, inflammations, fevers, toothaches, constipation, cramps, burns, earaches, and a host of other maladies. Although many of their alleged curative properties are questioned by authorities, several yarrow species contain salicylic acid derivatives that are closely related in structure and function to common aspirin.

SCIENTIFIC NAME: *Achillea* (a-*kil*-lee-a / a-kil-*lee*-a) is named after the Greek hero Achilles, who, on the advice of the goddess Aphrodite, used this plant to dress his wound during the siege of Troy.

HARDINESS / ORIGIN: Zones 2 or 3 to 9 or 10; Europe and Asia, naturalized in North America.

LEAVES / FLOWERS / FRUIT: Leaves vary from species to species, but are typically divided into many segments, giving a lacy, fernlike appearance. Flowers are easily dried and are very attractive alone or in arrangements with other dried flowers.

RATE / SPACING: Growth is fast. Plants from pint-sized to quart-sized containers are spaced 8 to 16 inches apart.

SPECIES: *A. ageratifolia* (a-jer-a-ti-*foe*-lee-a), named for its leaves, which resemble those of *Ageratum,* a genus of popular annuals, is commonly called Greek yarrow or white tansy. Native to the Balkan region and hardy in Zones 3 to 9, it ranges from 4 to 10 inches tall. Its hairy, silvery-gray, aromatic, evergreen leaves are arranged in rosettes, reach 1½ inches long by ⅛ to ¼ inch wide, are toothed along their edges, and are relatively fine-textured. The flowers, borne during summer and early fall, are solitary 1-inch-wide white heads atop 4- to 10-inch-tall stalks. Variety *aizoon,* one of the most popular varieties, has finely toothed, more straplike leaves.

A. filipendulina (fil-i-*pen*-du-lee-na), named for the leaves which resemble those of *Filipendula* (dropwort), is commonly called fernleaf yarrow. Native to Europe and Asia, this lacy-leaved perennial herb may reach 3 to 4½ feet tall. It displays linear to elliptical-shaped, 10-inch-long, fernlike, gray-green, hairy, strongly spice-scented leaves. Its yellow flowers, borne in early to late summer, are tiny yet so numerous that they form impressive dense heads to 5 inches wide. Horticultural selections include var. *alba,* with white flowers; 'Coronation Gold', claimed by some to be a hybrid between *A. filipendulina* and *A. clypeolata,* shorter than the species, vigorous, heat tolerant, with abundant mustard yellow 3-inch-wide flower clusters; 'Gold Plate', tall growing to 4 or 4½ feet with large mustard yellow flower clusters to 6 inches in diameter; 'Parker's Variety', 3½ feet tall, with clusters of 4-inch-wide yellow flowers. The species and its cultivars are hardy in Zones 3 to 10.

A. millefolium (mil-le-*foe*-lee-um), meaning thousand-leaved, is commonly called milfoil, common yarrow, sanguinary, thousand-seal, nose-bleed, bloodwort, stanchgrass, or thousand leaf. Hardy in Zones 3 to 10, it is native to Europe but widely naturalized in temperate regions. It reaches 3 feet tall and boasts fine-textured nearly evergreen 8-inch-long aromatic medium green leaves that are divided two or three times. Its tiny whitish flowers are arranged in flat-topped 2- to 3-inch-wide clusters and are effective from mid summer to early or mid autumn. Popular cultivars include 'Cerise Queen', with flat-topped clusters of bright cherry-red flowers atop 2-foot-tall stems; 'Crimson Beauty', with bright red flowers; 'Fire King', with rose-red flowers, stems to 18 inches, and silvery foliage; 'Heidi', with long-blooming clear pink flowers; 'Hope' ('Hoffnung'), with soft yellow flowers; 'Kelwayi', with magenta-red flowers; 'Lavender Beauty', with lavender flowers and deep green foliage; 'Paprika', with red flowers; 'Red Beauty', with red flowers; 'Roseum', with pink flowers and silvery-green foliage; 'Wesersandstone', with soft pastel reddish lavender flowers; and 'White Beauty', with large clusters of pure white flowers. Many different species of butterflies are attracted to the flowers of milfoil. There are also many myths about its miraculous healing properties, chief among them its ability to stop bleeding, as some of the common names suggest. Other claims range from its being able to heal toothaches to prolonging life. The Zuni Indians did not take long to employ introduced specimens of milfoil in treating burns. They ground up the entire plant and soaked it in cold water. The solution was then applied to the burned area, bringing about a cooling sensation, presumably due to the presence of the volatile oil cineol. Milfoil has also been used to ease the discomfort of earaches, head colds, fevers, and urinary tract infections. It is said to increase the inebriating quality of ale when used in place of hops.

A. 'Moonshine', a hybrid formed by crossing *A. taygetea* and *A. clypeolata*, was introduced into the United States by Adrian Bloom, son of Alan Bloom the famous English gardener and nurseryman. 'Moonshine' reaches 2 feet tall and spreads 1½ feet wide. Clothed in leaves of soft silvery-grayish green, it bears lemon yellow flowers in heads that reach 2½ inches wide from late spring to late summer. This cultivar is hardy in Zones 3 to 10.

A. ptarmica (*tar*-mi-ka), named from the Greek *ptarmos*, sneezing, for its ability to cause people to sneeze (and for its use as a snuff), is commonly called sneezewort, sneezeweed, or white tansy. It reaches up to 2 feet tall and bears 1- to 4-inch-long finely toothed, relatively fine-textured foliage. The ¾-inch-wide daisylike flowers are arranged in clusters that may reach 3 to 6 inches wide and are effective mid summer to early autumn. The central disk flowers typically are greenish white, while the ray flowers are white. Cultivars include 'Angel's Breath', with abundant snow-white flowers; 'Globe', with flowering stems 1½ feet tall topped with small rounded button-shaped white flowers; 'Perry's White', with double white flowers; 'Snowball', also with double white flowers and perhaps the same plant as the more commonly known 'The Pearl'; 'The Pearl' ('Boule de Neige'), a selection from 'Angel's Breath' that produces even more abundant snow-white flowers; 'Snow Sport', with narrow leaves, superb snowy-white flowers, 2 feet tall.

A. tomentosa (toe-men-*toe*-sa), named for its tomentose (woolly-haired) leaves, is commonly called woolly yarrow. Hardy in Zones 3 to 7 and native to Europe and western Asia, this species ranges from 6 to 12 inches tall and is characterized by evergreen 2-inch-long pungent grayish fernlike foliage. Each leaf is twice divided, linear, and hairy on both sides. The tiny yellow flowers form dense clusters 1 to 2 inches wide from late spring to early fall. Cultivars include 'Aurea', with darker, canary yellow flowers and gray downy foliage; 'King Edward', with primrose yellow flowers; 'Moonlight', with pale yellow flowers and a slower rate of spread; 'Nana', a dwarf selection with a compact habit and small white flowers.

CULTURE / CARE: A well-drained sandy loam of low fertility is best. Yarrows are very drought tolerant and actually are at their best in hot, dry, sunny locations. Their diseases include crown gall, powdery mildew, rust, and stem rot. Maintenance consists of dividing clumps every two to four years if symptoms of overcrowding, such as decreased floral display or mildewed leaves, become evident. Cutting flowers back in summer may produce extended bloom, and self-sowing may be prevented by removing the flowers as soon as they begin to fade.

PROPAGATION: Cuttings can be taken from the branches and rooted during the summer months. Division is most effective in spring and fall. Seed germinates readily.

Acorus   PLATE 6

Sweetflag

The two species of *Acorus*, *A. calamus* and *A. gramineus*, are rhizomatous, swordlike or grasslike, herbaceous perennials that inhabit bogs or swamps. Tolerant of wet soils, they are excellent for controlling erosion along stream and pond banks. Provided the soil is rich and retains moisture well, they may be mass planted or used on a smaller scale for accent or edging in more conventional landscape settings. As such, the colorful variegated selections excel.

SCIENTIFIC NAME: *Acorus* (a-*kore*-is / *ak*-oh-rus) is said to come from the Greek *a,* without, and *kore,* pupil of the eye, in reference to an ancient use of this plant to treat maladies of the eye.

HARDINESS / ORIGIN: See individual species for hardiness; Old World and North American wetlands.

LEAVES / FLOWERS / FRUIT: *Acorus* species have leaves that range from irislike to grasslike. They bloom with fleshy tiny-flowered spikes and later display gelatinous berries.

RATE / SPACING: Growth is moderate. Plants from pint-sized to quart-sized containers are spaced 8 to 12 inches apart.

SPECIES: *A. calamus* (*kal*-a-mus), named from the Latin *calamus,* reedlike, is commonly called sweetflag, flag-root, calamus, sweet-cane, sweet-grass, sweet-root, sweet-myrtle, myrtle-flag, sweet-rush, beewort, or sea-sedge. Hardy in Zones 5 to 10, it is native to North America and India, Sri Lanka, and the Celebes Islands. The leaves are keeled, 1 inch wide by 2 to 5 feet long, medium green, and lemonscented. Tiny greenish yellow flowers occur in 2- to 3½-inch-long, ½-inch-wide upright spadixes from spring through mid summer and give rise to fewseeded, green, gelatinous berries. Variety *angustifolius* has narrow leaves; 'Variegatus' has very attractive green and white leaves. Preparations of this species have been used since Hippocrates (460–377 B.C.) to treat intestinal gas and cramps, toothaches, menstrual disorders, and fevers, and have also been employed as an agent to facilitate quitting smoking. Now, however, such uses are considered unsafe as tests have linked them to cancer. A more sound application of this species might be its historical use as a fragrant floor covering. Spread upon the floor, the leaves of this species helped give buildings a fresh lemony scent.

A. gramineus (gra-*min*-ee-us), named for its graminoid or grasslike appearance, is commonly called Japanese sweetflag or grassy-leaved sweetflag. It hails from Japan, China, India, and Taiwan and is hardy in Zones 5 or 6 to 9. The shorter of the two species, it reaches 1 to 1½ feet tall, spreads indefinitely, and tolerates occasional foot traffic. The foliage is evergreen, handsome, shiny dark green, reaching ⅛ to ¼ inch wide by 12 to 18 inches long. Its numerous tiny yellow flowers of mid spring are arranged in erectly oriented, cylindrical, narrow, green 2- to 4-inch-long densely flowered spadixes and are surrounded by a leafy green hoodlike bract.

The fruit is a reddish fleshy berry. Cultivars include 'Argenteostriatus' ('Albo-variegatus'), nearly identical to 'Variegatus' (see below), with foliage striped white and green; 'Licorice', with licorice-scented leaves; 'Masamune', reaching 6 inches tall, with creamy white and green leaves; 'Minimus Aureus', reaching 4 inches tall, with yellow leaves; 'Oborozuki', with vibrant yellow leaves; 'Ogon' ('Wogon'), with foliage variegated with green and yellow; 'Pusillus', a dwarf selection reaching only 4 inches tall and sometimes grown as a house plant; 'Taninanoyuki', 12 inches tall, green foliage striped with patches of yellow; 'Yodonoyuki', 12 inches tall, variegated leaves of green and muted gold; 'Variegatus', with narrow leaves striped green and white, reaching only 6 inches tall.

CULTURE / CARE: The sweetflags grow best in moist or wet, organically rich, acidic to neutral soils in full sun to light shade. They are not prone to any serious diseases or pests and require no maintenance.

PROPAGATION: Division is easily accomplished in spring or fall. Seed should be collected fresh, depulped, and sown immediately, never allowed to dry out.

Adiantum pedatum   PLATE 7
Northern Maidenhair Fern, Five-finger Fern

This is an exceptional foreground plant for the shady perennial or wildflower border. It combines well with hostas, bergenias, foamflower, and countless other clump-forming, shade-loving herbs. It thrives underneath trees and shrubs and is marvelously effective as a moderate-scale to large-scale understory ground cover. Lovely when arranged in clumps for accent around trees with coarse-textured bark or among large rocks, it also creates a nice effect when allowed to overhang a wall or terrace embankment. If planted upon the side of a gently sloping, wooded hillside, the overall effect of the massed ferns is magnificent: one of lushness and tranquility as profound as that provided by any plant I have encountered. Mature plants are 18 to 24 inches tall by 3 to 5 feet wide. No foot traffic is tolerated.

SCIENTIFIC NAME: *Adiantum pedatum* (ad-ee-*an*-tum pe-*day*-tum). *Adiantum* is derived from the Greek *adiantos,* unwetted, referring to fronds supposedly remaining dry even after being plunged under water. *Pedatum,* foot, refers to the shape of the leaves, which resemble a bird's foot.

HARDINESS / ORIGIN: Zones 3 to 8; North American woodlands from Alaska and Canada, south to Georgia and Louisiana.

LEAVES / FLOWERS / FRUIT: The soft light green fronds are deciduous, compound, to 16 inches long by 10 inches wide, more or less broadly oval, and forked into two spreading branches on short, smooth, dark brown wiry stems that were used in basket weaving by American Indians.

RATE / SPACING: Growth is slow to moderate, by creeping rootstocks. Plants from quart-sized to gallon-sized containers are spaced 12 to 14 inches apart.

HORTICULTURAL SELECTIONS: Var. *subpumilum,* a dwarf only 4 to 8 inches tall.

OTHER SPECIES: ***A. capillus-veneris*** (ka-*pil*-us-*ven*-e-ris), named for its delicate foliage that resembles Venus' hair, is commonly called southern maidenhair, rock fern, black maidenhair, or Venus's-hair fern. A soft-textured, lush woodland fern, it is lacier in appearance than *A. pedatum* and has lighter green leaves. Its growth habit is similar, but it reaches only 18 inches tall. It frequently grows in limestone soil (unlike the more acid-loving *A. pedatum*). It has been used as an ingredient in hair tonic and cough syrup, as a diuretic and emmenagogue, and as a treatment for pleurisy and other respiratory conditions. Hardy in Zones 7 to 10.

CULTURE / CARE: Rich, acidic to neutral, consistently moist but well-drained soil that is high in organic matter is best. Dry conditions stunt growth. Light to relatively dense shade is preferred. Crown rot is sometimes a problem with very young plantlets; otherwise, diseases and pests are seldom serious.

PROPAGATION: Division is best performed during spring or fall.

Aegopodium podagraria   PLATE 8
Bishop's Weed, Goutweed, Ashweed, Ground Ash, Ground Elder, Herb Gerard

The common names of this species cause one to wonder if the plant is a weed or a tree. In fact, it is a very aggressive (potentially weedy) rhizomatous, herbaceous, 6- to 14-inch-tall, indefinite-spreading ground cover with foliage resembling that of an ash or elder tree. Well suited for covering moderate to large areas, provided that its stubbornly spreading rootstock can be kept in check, bishop's weed is both durable and attractive.

It is used effectively along woodland borders where it thrives in the shade of large deciduous trees and promotes a sense of continuity between the woodland and the artificial features of the landscape. It is excellent also for planting in less natural sites such as between a building foundation and sidewalk, where its spread can be held in check. The slightly less aggressive cultivar 'Variegatum' contrasts sharply when planted beneath dark-leaved shrubs such as purple-leaved barberry (*Berberis thunbergii* var. *atropurpurea*), Fraser's photinia (*Photinia fraseri*), or the purple-leaved plums (*Prunus cistena* or *P. cerasifera* 'Atropurpurea'). Foot traffic crushes the succulent leaf stalks, but walking across it infrequently causes no long-term harm.

Bishop's weed is said to be commonly named either for the resemblance of its leaves to the bishop's miter, or because bishops, who had the wealth to eat a rich diet, were more prone to gout than the average peasant. Historically, this species was used to treat gout, hence another of its common names. The plant was introduced in Great Britain in the Middle Ages as a pot herb, the leaves being boiled like spinach.

SCIENTIFIC NAME: *Aegopodium podagraria* (ee-go-*poe*-dee-um poe-da-*grar*-ee-a). *Aegopodium* comes from the Greek *aigo,* goat, and *podion,* foot, perhaps in reference to the shape of the leaves, which look somewhat like the foot of a goat. *Podagraria* comes from the Greek *podagra,* in the feet, and means gout. This species was once thought to be a remedy.

HARDINESS / ORIGIN: Zones 3 to 9; Europe.

LEAVES / FLOWERS / FRUIT: The deciduous medium green, carrot-scented leaves arise from the rootstock and are held on fleshy stalks. Each three-parted leaflet is further divided into three subleaflets, each 1½ to 3 inches long by 1½ inches wide. During early summer small whitish flowers are borne in large domed clusters on 1- or 2-foot-tall stems and look very much like those of its relative Queen Anne's lace. By most standards, they are considered relatively nonshowy. The fruit, a tiny brown capsule, is nonornamental.

RATE / SPACING: Growth is extremely rapid, even invasive, except under conditions of drought or infertile soil. Plants from 3- to 4-inch-diameter containers are spaced 10 to 14 inches apart.

HORTICULTURAL SELECTIONS: 'Variegatum' is far more popular than the plain green species, reaches 8 inches tall, and has foliage with silvery-white and green variegation. It is one of the best plants for brightening areas in deep shade. Like the species, it grows in full sun but often becomes unsightly as the leaf edges are prone to drying out and browning during the heat of summer. It is somewhat slower growing than the species, so plants should be spaced 6 to 10 inches apart.

CULTURE / CARE: Goutweed is very adaptable and grows in anything from sandy loam to heavy clay, from full sun to dense shade, and tolerates compacted soils and infertility. It is relatively drought tolerant yet often wilts during midday when soil moisture becomes depleted—thus it is one of the best indicators of water need. Pests and diseases are usually inconsequential, but mites, slugs, and leaf blight can be a problem from time to time. Although some gardeners mow goutweed after flowering to neaten and rejuvenate plantings, no maintenance is necessary. Goutweed is tenacious: once you plant it, resign yourself to the fact that you will probably have it for life.

PROPAGATION: Division can be performed any time.

Aeonium tabuliforme   PLATE 9

I have never come across any common names for this plant, but because of its saucerlike shape, which leads me to believe that it could fly if given a toss, I call it the Frisbee plant. In its native Tenerife it is called *pastel del risco,* which, the best I can figure, means pie of the rocks (or cliffs). Presumably, the implication is that the plant is pie-shaped and inhabits rocky terrain.

Frisbee plant is a low, dense, flat-topped, offset-spreading, mat-forming succulent ground cover that ranges from 4 to 8 inches tall and slowly spreads 8 to 14 inches wide. Often the topic of conversation because of its curious appearance, this plant is best used in small groupings for accent or facing to ornaments, statues, and small trees. It also works well on a moderate scale in public areas such as near walkways and building entrances where passersby might be charmed by its interesting features (cast light upon plantings at night for added effect).

The succulent foliage stores lots of water, reducing the need for supplemental watering. Walking on the foliage squashes it; therefore, plantings should be laid out to prevent foot traffic. Siting plants next to walks and footpaths facilitates this. Frisbee plant, in addition to being rather tolerant of drought, can also take a fair amount of heat and lives happily near the base of building foundations where light is often reflected.

SCIENTIFIC NAME: *Aeonium tabuliforme* (ee-*o*-nee-um tab-you-lee-*form*-ee). *Aeonium* reportedly was the name used by Dioscorides, the famous first-century Greek physician, for a close relative of this plant. *Tabuliforme,* tablelike, refers to the flat-topped shape formed by the leaves.

HARDINESS / ORIGIN: Zones 9 to 11 (best in southern coastal areas); Canary Islands.

LEAVES / FLOWERS / FRUIT: Leaves are evergreen, succulent, smooth, densely arranged in round, flat-topped, Frisbeelike, 100- to 200-leaved rosettes. Each light green leaf reaches 2½ to 5½ inches long by 1 to 1½ inches wide. Flowers are arranged in large clusters that arise above the foliage from the center of the rosette; they bloom in mid summer and are ½ to ¾ inch wide with yellow petals. The fruit is nonornamental.

RATE / SPACING: Growth is moderate. Plants from 4-

to 5-inch-diameter containers are spaced 10 to 14 inches apart.

CULTURE / CARE: *Aeonium tabuliforme* performs best in sandy loam or gravelly soils of excellent drainage and acidic pH. It is well adapted to withstand drought, and little supplemental watering is usually needed. Best light conditions are full sun or light shade, and no serious pests or diseases are typically encountered. Maintenance needs, which are minimal, include an occasional washing off with a hose to remove dust, and the removal of dried flower stalks with a pair of scissors. Aeoniums are, however, rather short-lived—just four to six years. Do not let this, however, discourage you from using them: just place them in easily serviced areas, and do not use them on too grand a scale.

PROPAGATION: Cuttings made by severing the stems of suckerlike offsets can be rooted in a moist, well-aerated medium throughout the year. Divisions, with a trowel, are best taken during late fall, winter, or early spring and transplanted to a container or planting bed.

Aethionema grandiflorum   PLATE 10
Persian Stonecress

This subshrubby species forms a low mound that has a tendency to spread horizontally. Reaching 6 to 8 inches tall and a foot or more wide, it functions well as a specimen, accent plant or as a small-scale general cover. Its cultural needs make it well suited for use in rock gardens. No foot traffic is tolerated.

SCIENTIFIC NAME: *Aethionema grandiflorum* (ee-thee-*oh*-nee-ma gran-di-*flore*-um). *Aethionema* comes from the Greek *aitho,* to burn, or *aethes,* unusual, and *nema,* a filament or thread, in reference to the charred or unusual appearance of the flower stamens. *Grandiflorum* means large-flowered.

HARDINESS / ORIGIN: Zones 5 to 8 or 9; Mediterranean region.

LEAVES / FLOWERS / FRUIT: The bluish green, 1½-inch-long, needlelike evergreen leaves are very narrowly oblong. Held upon thin wiry stems, they contrast nicely with the pink ½-inch-wide, slightly fragrant flowers of early to mid summer. The fruit is nonornamental.

RATE / SPACING: Growth is slow to moderate. Plants from ½-gallon-sized to gallon-sized containers are spaced 12 to 14 inches apart.

HORTICULTURAL SELECTIONS: 'Warley Rose', likely a hybrid of the cross between *A. grandiflorum* and *A. armenum,* forms a dense steel blue mound, is heat sensitive and hardy southward only to Zone 8; 'Warley Ruber', with darker flowers.

CULTURE / CARE: Persian stonecress grows best in

well-drained sandy loam. It tolerates acidic as well as alkaline conditions and is relatively drought resistant. It grows in full sun or in a lightly shaded, well-ventilated location. Other than aphids, it has few problems, and little or no maintenance is needed.

PROPAGATION: Softwood cuttings taken in early summer are effective, as is division in spring. Seed propagation also works but is seldom used because of the ease of the other methods.

Agapanthus
PLATE 11

Love Flowers

The agapanthuses are robust, lilylike, herbaceous, horizontally spreading ground covers. When mass planted and used as general covers, they are outstanding—both for magnificent flowers and for graceful, soft-textured, arching foliage. Additionally, they are excellent for edging borders and for use as accent plants when grouped together. Agapanthuses are tough, but they do not accept foot traffic. They grow from 20 inches to 3 feet tall.

SCIENTIFIC NAME: *Agapanthus* (ag-a-*pan*-thus) is derived from the Greek *agape,* love, and *anthos,* a flower, hence the common name love flower.

HARDINESS / ORIGIN: See individual species for hardiness; South Africa.

LEAVES / FLOWERS / FRUIT: The evergreen or deciduous leaves are elongated, broadly strap- or sword-shaped (like daylilies but wider), leathery, arching, and medium to dark green. The flowers are carried well above the leaves on stout, erect or arching floral stalks. Arranged in clusters of as many as 100, the flowers are trumpet-shaped and range from white to violet to dark blue. The fruit, a capsule, is non-ornamental.

RATE / SPACING: Growth is moderate. Plants from quart-sized to gallon-sized containers are spaced 18 to 24 inches apart.

SPECIES: *A. africanus* (af-ri-*kay*-nus), named for its African origin, is commonly called African agapanthus, blue African-lily, or lily-of-the-Nile. It is hardy in Zones 9 to 11. A stately plant, its foliage is evergreen, straplike (20 inches long by ½ inch wide), and arranged in clumps of 8 to 18. The deep violet-blue flowers are funnel-shaped, 1½ inches long, and arranged in clusters of 12 to 40 atop 1½-foot-tall stalks. They are effective from late spring through fall and are attractive to hummingbirds. Hardy in Zones 9 to 11. Some of the most popular horticultural selections include 'Albus', with white flowers; 'Albus Nanus', with white flowers and compact habit; 'Blue Giant', with large deep blue flowers; 'Blue Triumphator', with giant azure blue flowers, 2 to 3 feet tall; 'Queen Anne', with foliage 12 to 15 inches high, topped by bright blue flowers atop 2-foot-tall stalks; 'Variegatus', with leaves striped white and green.

A. inapertus (in-a-*per*-tis), literally means closed although normally open, but no one knows what it refers to. The plant itself is less of a mystery. Hailing from Africa, it is hardy in Zones 9 to 10. Its stiff, slightly arching, 2½-foot-long, 2-inch-wide deciduous leaves are bluish green and act as a subdued yet distant backdrop to the flower clusters that are borne atop 4- to 5-foot-tall stalks during late spring to fall. Each flower cluster is composed of about 100 tubular blue blossoms 1¼ inches long.

A. praecox subsp. *orientalis* (*pray*-koks or-ee-en-*tay*-lis), named *praecox,* early blooming, and *orientalis,* from the east (in this case, South Africa), is commonly called Oriental agapanthus. It is hardy in Zones 9 to 11. The evergreen leaves are considerably larger than those of the species, reaching up to 2 inches wide by 2 or more feet long. Colored dark glossy green and grouped 10 leaves per clump, the foliar mass gives rise to 4- to 5-foot-tall flower stalks in mid spring to early fall which support clusters of 40 to 110 blue funnel-shaped, hummingbird-attracting, 2-inch-long florets. Some of the most popular horticultural selections include 'Albidus', with white flowers; var. *aureovittatus,* with leaves striped yellow and green; 'Flore Pleno', with double blue flowers; var. *giganteus,* with sturdy spikes that carry clusters of about 200 dark blue flowers; var. *leichtlinii,* with deep blue flowers; 'Mooreanus', with dark blue flowers, somewhat hardier than the species (possibly to Zone 8); 'Peter Pan', a dwarf selection with leaves only 12 inches tall and deep blue flowers on 18-inch-tall stalks; 'Rancho White', similar to 'Peter Pan' but with white flowers; 'Variegatus', with broad streaks of white on the leaves.

HYBRID SELECTIONS: Perhaps the most popular, and clearly the most hardy of the agapanthuses are the hybrids, especially the series commonly known as the Headbourne Hybrids that was bred during the 1950s and 1960s by Lewis Palmer of Headbourne Worthy near Winchester, England. These hybrids, which are hardy in Zones 7 to 10 and often survive with mulching in Zone 6, are derived from crosses involving *A. campanulatus* and the more hardy, deciduous species *A. caulescens, A. coddii, A. inapertus,* and *A. nutans.* Cultivars that, arguably, should be classified among this group are 'Alice Gloucester', with purple flower buds and white flowers in mid to late summer; 'Bressingham Blue', 24 inches tall, with deep amethyst-blue flowers; 'Bressingham White', 24 inches tall, with large white flowers; 'Isis', with large clusters of lavender-blue flowers; 'Lilliput', 18 inches tall, with light blue flowers; 'Loch Hope', a late bloomer with deep violet flowers atop 4- to 5-foot-tall stems; 'Midknight Blue', with lush green 2-foot-long leaves and deep violet flowers carried upon 3- to 4-foot stalks; 'Snowy Owl', with creamy white flowers atop 3-foot-tall stems.

CULTURE / CARE: Sandy, well-aerated soil is ideal, but heavier types are tolerated, especially if drainage is good. The soil should receive enough water to maintain constant but relatively low soil moisture during the growing season. When plants are in bloom, they require more water, but the soil should not be saturated, especially in fall and winter, or crown rot will occur. Full sun to partial shade is preferred. Seldom are serious pests or diseases encountered. For maintenance, trim off flower stalks each year in the fall after blooming has finished. If plants become overcrowded (typically about every five to six years), dig them up, divide, and replant.

PROPAGATION: Division is best accomplished during the spring or fall.

Aglaonema commutatum   PLATE 12
Chinese Evergreen

Lush and basal-leaved (later becoming stemmed), this rhizomatous, herbaceous ground cover reaches 2½ feet tall and spreads 3 feet wide. It is very attractive in tropical settings for edging walkways and facing foundations and trees. Use it on a moderate to large scale and reap great ornamental benefits through its attractively variegated foliage. In front of dark green trees and shrubs, it provides contrast and imparts a subtle tranquilizing effect. No foot traffic is tolerated. Although the accepted common name of *Aglaonema commutatum* is Chinese evergreen, the name is more appropriately applied to *A. modestum,* which actually does hail from southern China.

SCIENTIFIC NAME: *Aglaonema commutatum* (ag-lay-oh-*nee*-ma kom-you-*tay*-tum). *Aglaonema* is derived from the Greek *aglaos,* bright, and *nema,* a thread, likely in reference to the stamens. *Commutatum,* changeable, refers to the multicolored leaves.

HARDINESS / ORIGIN: Zones 10 to 11; Philippines and the northeastern Celebes.

LEAVES / FLOWERS / FRUIT: Evergreen and exfoliating with age, the oblong-elliptic to lance-shaped 8- to 12-inch-long, 3- to 4-inch-wide leaves are leathery and glossy dark green with green-gray irregular streaking along their primary veins. The tiny summertime flowers are borne male above female in 1½- to 3½-inch-long spadixes, covered by a hood that is somewhat longer and pale green. The fruit is 1 inch long, single-seeded, elliptical-shaped, and yellow, maturing to bright red.

RATE / SPACING: Growth is moderate. Plants from 1-to 2-gallon-sized containers are spaced 2 to 2½ feet apart.

HORTICULTURAL SELECTIONS: 'Albovariegatum', with numerous gray-green irregular stripes on the leaves, and with white petioles, stems, and spathe; var. *elegans,* foliage somewhat smaller, with narrow veins limited to the upper surface of the foliage; var. *maculatum,* leaves with profuse gray-green markings; 'Pseudobracteatum' ('White Rajah'), reaching 1 to 2 feet tall, with white petioles and dark green foliage marked with pale green and creamy yellow; 'Treubii' ('Grafii'), smaller than the species with irregular pale green markings along primary veins on the upper leaf surface only.

OTHER SELECTIONS: *A.* 'Green Majesty', foliage broadly oval with large silver-green margins and dark green centers; *A.* 'Silver Frost', relatively narrow silvery-green foliage with dark green center; *A.* 'Silver Queen', leaves silvery-green with dark green mottling along the veins and leaf margin *A.* 'Stripes', introduced in 1988, derived by crossing *A.* 'Manila' and *A. nitidum* 'Curtisii', with 14-inch-long, 5- to 6-inch-wide, attractively variegated foliage with narrow silvery white bands overlaying medium green (variegation running parallel to the veins).

CULTURE / CARE: An organically rich, well-drained, slightly acidic loam is preferred. Although Chinese evergreen is moderately drought tolerant, it is at its best when the soil is maintained in a slightly moistened condition. It prefers light to dense shade. The most common diseases are leaf blight, leaf spot, soft rot, root and stem rot, and anthracnose, and pests such as lesion and root-knot nematodes are sometimes a problem. Little or no maintenance is needed, yet many gardeners prefer to remove the older leaves as they exfoliate.

PROPAGATION: Tip cuttings may be rooted in a porous mix. Division is easily accomplished by removing the new shoots from the rhizomes (with some roots attached), then transplanting. Air layering is said to be effective as well, as is simple layering when the stems are bent over and pinned to the soil surface. Seed is also sometimes used.

Ajuga reptans   PLATE 13
Creeping Bugleweed, Creeping Carpet Bugle, Comfrey, Sicklewort, Carpenter's Herb

Ajuga is one of the fastest spreading of the low-growing, herbaceous ground covers. This characteristic can be attributed to its stoloniferous mode of reproduction: in the spring it sends out multiple horizontal stems, or stolons, each of which bears several new plantlets along its length and one upon its end. As they come into contact with the soil, the plantlets set root and then go about their business of expanding from short underground stems called rhizomes. The following spring the process repeats itself, with all the new plantlets fulfilling the role of the mother. And, if this isn't enough, under the right conditions, ajuga supplements this system by self-seeding.

Ajuga reaches only 3 to 4 inches tall but seemingly spreads forever. This, in addition to its burst of springtime floral color, as well as the rich bronzy foliage of many of its cultivars, makes it nearly without parallel. Typically, it is used on a small to moderate scale as a substitute for turf grass or as a facing plant in narrow beds (2 to 3 feet wide) in front of taller ground covers such as purple-flowered stonecrop (*Sedum purpureum*), candytuft (*Iberis sempervirens*), hostas, and broad-spreading shrubs such as cultivars of Japanese spirea (*Spiraea japonica*) and bird's nest spruce (*Picea abies* 'Nidiformis'). Ajuga species are said to be able to grow underneath black walnut trees (*Juglans nigra*). Planted underneath and surrounding deep-rooted trees, ajuga blankets the ground, reduces the need for difficult and dangerous mowing, and softens the transition between the trunk of the tree and the surrounding turf or walkway. Occasional foot traffic is tolerated.

The foliage of *A. reptans* is said to produce a mild narcotic effect when ingested. The plant, which contains tannins and thus is astringent, has been applied to all sorts of ailments. The common name carpenter's herb comes from the plant's ability to stop bleeding, but it has also been used to treat coughs and other lung disorders, rheumatism, and ulcers. It is said to be an antihallucinogenic (following bouts of excessive drinking), and an extract of it has been used as a black dye for woolens.

SCIENTIFIC NAME: *Ajuga reptans* (a-*ju*-ga rep-*tanz*). *Ajuga* is derived from the Latin words *a,* no, and *zugon,* yoke, a reference to the calyx lobes (leaflike appendages surrounding the flower petals) which are not divided into two halves as is typical of many species of the mint family (to which *Ajuga* belongs). *Reptans* refers to the reptant, or creeping, habit of this species.

HARDINESS / ORIGIN: Zones 3 to 9; central Europe.

LEAVES / FLOWERS / FRUIT: The medium glossy green, 3- to 4-inch-long, oval-shaped, semievergreen to evergreen leaves are arranged in tight rosettes. During late spring 4- to 6-inch-long flower-laden spikes arise from the center of the rosettes, providing masses of long-lasting vibrant, highly visible, bluish violet, vaguely fragrant flowers. Bumblebees love these flowers. The fruit, unlike the leaves and flowers, is nonornamental.

RATE / SPACING: Growth is variable, depending on the particular variety, but in most cases relatively fast.

Plants from 2¼- to 5-inch-diameter containers are spaced 8 to 14 inches apart.

HORTICULTURAL SELECTIONS: The many selections are so mixed up and misnamed that trying to find a properly named cultivar can be very frustrating. Some of the more common selections include 'Alba', flowers creamy white; 'Alba Variegata' ('Variegata', 'Albo-variegata'), leaves mottled creamy white, often drying out along their edges when planted in full sun, best in light shade; 'Arboretum Giant', with enormous 8-inch-long, uprightly oriented, purple-margined leaves and light blue flowers on 12-inch-tall stalks; 'Arctic Fox', leaves green and grayish near their midribs, surrounded by broad margins of white; 'Atropurpurea', foliage bronzy purple, flowers dark purplish blue; 'Brightness', similar to 'Bronze Beauty', but somewhat more intensely purple-colored; 'Bronze Beauty', similar to 'Atropurpurea', but leaves more intensely purplish bronze; 'Brocade', with large silvery-purple leaves and blue flowers; 'Burgundy Glow', leaves burgundy, pink, creamy white, and green, less hardy than the species; 'Catlin's Giant', an exceptionally large cultivar with metallic bronzy foliage and large spikes of bluish flowers; 'Compacta', with habit denser than that of the species; 'Gaiety' ('Bronze Improved'), a robust, bronzy purple selection; 'Giant Green', larger, more robust, with bright green leaves; 'Jungle Bronze', to 10 inches tall, with bronze leaves that are crinkled along their edges; 'Jungle Green', with large green, relatively rounded, wavy-edged leaves; 'Mini Crispa Red', a miniature bronze-colored selection with wrinkled leaves; 'Multicolor', leaves mottled red, white, and yellow on the top of a green base, probably synonymous with 'Rainbow'; 'Pink Elf', with compact form, bronze leaves, and pink flowers; 'Pink Silver', a mutation of 'Burgundy Glow', more vigorous, with a metallic sheen to its purplish pink and silvery leaves; 'Pink Surprise', with bronze leaves and purplish pink flowers; 'Purple Brocade', with blue flowers in large 6-inch-tall spikes, foliage maroon and deeply furrowed; 'Purple Torch', with 12-inch-tall spikes of lavender flowers that emerge from whorls of bronze foliage; 'Rosea', flowers rose-pink; 'Royalty', somewhat larger than the species, with dark purple leaves; 'Rubra', flowers purplish red; 'Silver Beauty', leaves gray-green with silvery-white edges; 'Silver Carpet', with metallic silvery leaves; 'Thumbelina', with tiny shiny green leaves.

OTHER SPECIES: *A. genevensis* (jen-e-*ven*-sis), meaning of Geneva, is commonly called Geneva carpet bugle. It reaches 2 to 4 inches tall and is hardy in Zones 4 to 9. It displays rosettes of relatively coarse-textured, 3- to 4-inch-long, oblong leaves that are nearly evergreen. It differs from *A. reptans* in that it spreads only by rhizomes rather than by stolons and rhizomes. As a result, its rate of spread is slower, and for this reason it is preferred for use as an edging, specimen, or accent plant. Unfortunately, it lacks the diversity in leaf and flower color found in *A. reptans.* The blue-violet flowers arise upon upright stalks during late spring. Growth rate is relatively slow to moderate, and plants from 2¼- to 5-inch-diameter containers should be spaced on 6- to 12-inch centers. Horticultural selections include 'Alba', with white flowers; *A.* 'Brockbankii', a hybrid between *A. genevensis* and *A. pyramidalis,* resembling *A. genevensis* but dwarf in habit; 'Rosea', with rose-pink flowers; 'Variegata', foliage mottled with creamy white.

A. pyramidalis (pi-rim-i-*day*-lis), named because its flower spikes are pyramidal (or triangular), is commonly called pyramidal carpet bugle. Native to central Europe, it is somewhat less hardy than the others (Zones 5 to 9) and blooms in late spring with violet-blue flowers. It is most useful in smaller areas as a specimen, for accent, or for border edging. It reaches 3 to 4 inches tall and seldom spreads more than 12 inches wide. Its 4-inch-long, spatula-shaped, evergreen leaves are deep green and somewhat coarse in texture. Growth is slow, by short rhizomes, and plants from 2¼- to 5-inch-wide containers are spaced 6 to 12 inches apart. Like *A. reptans,* this species is valuable for the colorfully diverse cultivars that have arisen from it: 'Alexander', compact habit, with dark bronzy foliage; 'Metallica Crispa', very slow spreading with dark bronze, mounding, crinkled, spinachlike leaves; 'Nanus Compactus', similar to 'Metallica Crispa', from which it arose, very dwarf, slow growing (at a snail's pace), with deep green, wrinkled foliage; 'Pink Beauty', with pink flowers.

CULTURE / CARE: Although ajugas are difficult to match for the profusion and brightness of their flowers, they do have shortcomings. Several times I have witnessed apparently healthy plantings simply die out in just a few days, typically during early spring or mid fall. This is due to crown rot, a devastating condition caused by a fungus that becomes active during cool weather when soil moisture is high. In the North it often occurs in spring when the soil in the root zone is still frozen, but the sun has melted the surface soil and caused it to become slushy and oxygen depleted. To fight this condition, plant ajugas in shaded settings on the east or north side of taller shrubs or buildings to shelter them from bright afternoon sun. Dividing every few years prevents overcrowding, and may help fight this condition as well. Above all, learn to appreciate ajugas on a smaller scale to reduce the financial distress should your plants succumb to disease.

Although ajugas tolerate heavier soils to some extent (provided drainage is adequate), well-drained, sandy, acidic loam is their preference. Since the roots are relatively shallow, drought tolerance is not particularly good. Give them shelter from strong winds and plant in full sun only in the parts of their hardiness range that are moderated by the coast. Ajugas can also dry out in winter if snowcover is lacking, so attention to location is critical in this respect as well. Farther south and inland, light to moderate shade is necessary to cope with summer temperatures. Tobacco mosaic virus might be a problem, and pests such as aphids and root-knot nematodes may at times be encountered. These, by the way, are the vectors that spread the mosaic virus. The good news is that ajugas, if properly sited, will be relatively healthy and do not require much maintenance. Typically, all they need is to be trimmed back as they outgrow their bounds. In the case of the variegated selections, which rarely reseed true to type, the flowers can be mowed off before the seeds ripen.

PROPAGATION: Propagation is most easily accomplished by simple division; pull up or dig out the plants, then move them to their new home. This practice is most successful during early spring, but can be performed in summer and early fall when attention is paid to watering. Seed can also be used (primarily for the species); it germinates quickly if collected and sown shortly after the flowers fade.

Akebia quinata   PLATE 14

Fiveleaf Akebia, Chocolate Vine

This sturdy woody vine displays a twining, low-spreading (when unsupported) habit. As a ground cover it reaches 6 to 12 inches tall, spreads indefinitely, and is of greatest value as an erosion-controlling bank cover for moderate to large areas. It has few suitable companions other than large-trunked trees, which it cannot wrap itself around and overrun as it does other smaller trees and shrubs. No foot traffic is tolerated.

SCIENTIFIC NAME: *Akebia quinata* (a-*key*-bee-a kwi-*nay*-ta). *Akebia* is derived from the Japanese name for this genus. The Latin *quinata,* in fives, refers to the five leaflets of each leaf.

HARDINESS / ORIGIN: Zones 4 to 8 or 9; China, Korea, Japan.

LEAVES / FLOWERS / FRUIT: The compound, alternately arranged, semievergreen leaves are composed of five 1⅕- to 2⅖-inch-long, rounded to oblong, bluish green, fine-textured leaflets. Held upon wiry greenish to brownish stems, they combine nicely with the rather small, deep reddish purple, slightly fragrant springtime flowers. The edible purple-violet fleshy, sausage-shaped pod reaches 2¼ to 4 inches long and ripens in early to mid summer to expose black pealike seeds. More than one clone or cultivar seems to be needed for reliable fruit set.

RATE / SPACING: Growth is fast. Plants from quart-sized to gallon-sized containers are spaced 2½ to 3½ feet apart.

HORTICULTURAL SELECTIONS: 'Alba', flowers and fruit white; 'Rosea', flowers pinkish purple; 'Shirobana', flowers white, highly fragrant; 'Variegata', flowers pale pink, leaves with white variegation.

OTHER SPECIES: *A.* × *pentaphylla* (pen-ta-*fil*-a), the result of hybridizing *A. quinata* and *A. trifoliata,* is an interesting intermediate that has variable leaves—some with three and others with five leaflets.

A. trifoliata (try-*foe*-lee-aye-ta), named for the number of its leaflets (three), is commonly called threeleaf akebia. Each leaflet is larger and more rounded than those of *A. quinata,* which also is named for the number of its leaflets (five). Overall *A. trifoliata* has a coarser texture, its growth rate is a little slower, and its pale violet sausage-shaped fruit reaches 3 to 5 inches long by 1½ to 2½ inches wide.

CULTURE / CARE: Akebias grow best in moderately to highly fertile, well-drained neutral to acidic sandy loam. They withstand moderate drought as well as strong drying winds; yet, despite their ruggedness, are at their best when the soil is kept slightly moist. They prefer full sun or partial shade, and no serious disease or pest problems exist. Maintenance consists of trimming back the stems as they outgrow their bounds.

PROPAGATION: Cuttings root relatively well during early to mid summer and are aided by treatment with 3000 ppm IBA/talc. Naturally layered stems are easily dug up and transplanted. Seed that is sown immediately upon ripening quickly germinates.

Alchemilla vulgaris   PLATE 15
Lady's Mantle, Bear's Foot, Nine Hooks, Lion's Foot

This soft-textured, clump-forming, low-growing, herbaceous ground cover is a wonderful addition to almost any landscape. It ranges from 6 to 12 inches tall and gradually spreads to 2 feet wide. Often it is used as a small-scale to moderate-scale general cover along shady wooded borders or as a splendid edging alongside paths, where its pleated foliage and habit of forming dew about its edges (by a process called guttation) can be fully appreciated by early bird walkers. Medieval alchemists called the droplets of dew "water from heaven" and collected them for their experiments. Lady's mantle combines well with trees and shrubs such as pines, rhododendrons, and aza-

leas, and clump-forming herbaceous perennials such as ferns, hostas, lily turf, and a host of others. No foot traffic is tolerated.

This species was said to be used for adornment by the Virgin Mary, hence the common name lady's mantle. Another possibility is that the name reflects the pleated foliage, which is reminiscent of a woman's cloak. Lady's mantle is said to have astringent properties that make it effective in stopping bleeding. Historically, preparations of *A. vulgaris* have been used in the treatment of dysentery, diarrhea, vomiting, internal and menstrual bleeding, and sagging breasts. It has also been used to restore virginity, or at least a semblance thereof, through its powerful astringent powers.

SCIENTIFIC NAME: *Alchemilla vulgaris* (al-kem-*il*-a vul-*gay*-ris). *Alchemilla* is derived from the Arabic *alkemelych,* alluding to the use of lady's mantle in alchemy. *Vulgaris* means common.

HARDINESS / ORIGIN: Zones 3 to 7; Europe.

LEAVES / FLOWERS / FRUIT: The attractively pleated, evergreen leaves are rounded, 2 to 4 inches wide, hairy, and gray-green. Atop them in mid to late spring are borne numerous (more curious than lovely) yellowish green flowers, which are commonly dried and used in arrangements. The fruit is small, not ornamentally significant, and often occurs by apomixis, that is, fertile seed is produced without pollination. When this happens, such offspring are genetically identical to their parents.

RATE / SPACING: Growth is slow. Plants from 3- to 5-inch-diameter containers are spaced 6 to 10 inches apart.

HORTICULTURAL SELECTIONS: 'Auslese', with pale yellow, vertically oriented flowers.

OTHER SPECIES: *A. alpina* (al-*pine*-a), named for its mountainous habitat, is commonly called alpine lady's mantle. Hailing from high altitudes of Europe as well as from Greenland, it reaches 6 to 8 inches tall, spreads 12 inches wide, and is hardy in Zones 3 to 8. Its flowers are yellowish and not greatly ornamental, but its leaves are a pleasing silvery-green.

A. conjuncta (kon-*yunk*-ta), meaning joined (in reference to the leaflets being joined at the base), is similar to *A. vulgaris.* Hardy in Zones 3 to 7, it reaches 1 to 1½ feet tall and displays a more robust nature. It is not quite as heat tolerant as *A. vulgaris.*

A. mollis (*mol*-lis), named for its softly hairy leaves, is commonly called lady's mantle. It is very similar to *A. vulgaris,* thus often confused with it, and thought by some botanists to be a variety of it. It differs by being slightly taller, its leaves are deeper lobed and more hairy, and its flowers are slightly larger and a bit more yellowish.

CULTURE / CARE: Lady's mantle prefers moist, organically rich, well-drained, neutral to slightly acidic, loamy soil in full sun to moderate shade. Maintenance need not be performed at all, but some very fussy gardeners trim off the oldest leaves during late winter in an effort to neaten the plant's appearance. For large plantings, a lawn mower is the most practical means of performing this task. Plants sometimes reseed themselves and potentially can become weedy; if this seems to be a recurring problem, remove the flowers shortly after they fade.

PROPAGATION: Seed and division are both simple and effective means of propagation. Seed is best sown during spring, and division is best carried out during spring or fall.

Aloe   PLATE 16

The low-growing, succulent species of aloe (the genus contains shrubs and trees as well) make interesting and colorful ground covers for warm climates. Members of the lily family, the aloes which make the best ground covers are basal-leaved, rosettaceous, mat-forming succulents. On a small to moderate scale they function as general covers and accent plants and are particularly well suited to seaside gardens and rock gardens that feature cacti and other succulents. No foot traffic is tolerated.

Aloes are well known for the positive effects their juices have upon the skin, particularly the Mediterranean native *A. barbadensis* (syn. *A. vera*). Today, the juice of aloes is incorporated into many shampoos, cosmetics, and skin ointments. It has remarkable restorative properties when used on burned skin, but the juice of aloes can also function as a laxative. Reportedly aloe was used to embalm the body of Jesus Christ after the Crucifixion.

SCIENTIFIC NAME: *Aloe,* when used as the scientific name, has three syllables and is pronounced *al*-oh-ee. The common name is spelled the same way as the scientific name, but written in roman letters, not italic, and pronounced with two syllables as *al*-oh. *Aloe* is likely derived from the Arabic *alloch,* in reference to medicinal uses of some species. Other sources state that *Aloe* was simply the Greek word for this genus.

HARDINESS / ORIGIN: Zones 9 to 10 or 11; arid regions of the Old World and Africa.

LEAVES / FLOWERS / FRUIT: *Aloe* species are characterized by narrowly triangular, thick, fleshy, succulent leaves arranged in compact basal rosettes. Normally toothed about their edges, the leaves underlie typically red or yellow clusters of tubular flowers held aloft upon stout, round floral stems. The fruit, a capsule, is not ornamentally significant.

RATE / SPACING: Growth is moderate. Plants from 3-

to 5-inch-diameter containers are spaced 10 to 14 inches apart.

SPECIES: *A. aristata* (air-i-*stay*-ta), named for its long, bristle-tipped leaves, is commonly called torch plant or lace plant. It reaches 8 to 12 inches tall and spreads at a moderate pace to form mats several feet wide. A durable succulent from South Africa, it displays leaves that are arranged in rosettes of 100 to 150. Each narrow, fibrously bristled leaf reaches 4 inches long by ¾ inch wide, is covered with bands of white wartlike tubercles, and is edged with soft toothlike projections. The reddish yellow wintertime flowers reach 1¼ inches long and are arranged in simple or branched inflorescences that may ascend to 20 inches.

A. humilis (*hue*-mi-lis), meaning low growing or dwarf, is commonly called spider aloe, hedgehog aloe, or crocodile jaws. It reaches 4 to 6 inches tall, spreads 1 foot wide, and displays fleshy, basal, 4-inch-long, ¾-inch-wide, densely set, oval to lance-shaped, blue-green leaves that are wart-covered on their undersides and white-toothed along their margins. The flowers are red with green tips, reach 1½ inches long, and are borne during spring in long racemes on stalks that may reach 1½ feet tall. Variety *echinata* has smaller leaves with soft prickles and no tubercles on the upper surface; 'Globosa' has foliage tipped in purple when grown in sun.

A. variegata (vare-ee-i-*gay*-ta), named for its variegated foliage, is commonly called Kanniedood aloe, partridge breast aloe, tiger aloe, or pheasant's wings. It ranges from 9 to 12 inches tall, forms rosettes, and spreads to form mats up to several feet wide. Its fleshy leaves are covered with irregular transverse bands of white spots, are triangular to lance-shaped, range from 4 to 6 inches long, and are covered with white, horny, toothlike projections along their margins. The flowers are arranged in loose clusters 12 inches above the foliage. Pink to dull scarlet, they are borne intermittently throughout the year.

CULTURE / CARE: Aloes grow well in moderately acidic to neutral light-textured loamy or gravelly soils, but are adaptable to almost any well-drained soil. Their tolerance to drought is excellent due to water stored in their foliage, so little or no watering is required. They prefer full sun to light shade, and *A. humilis* is at its best in light shade. Root rots, mealybugs, and scale insects are sometimes a problem. Maintenance consists of removing the flower stalks following bloom to neaten the planting's appearance. Plants so cramped as to reduce the floral display may be dug up and divided.

PROPAGATION: Cuttings from young shoots can be rooted in gritty soil without mist. Division, the most common propagation method, is reliable from fall through early spring. Seed germinates in three to five weeks at 70 to 80°F.

Ammophila breviligulata   PLATE 17
Marram, Sand Reed, Beach Grass, American Beach Grass

This tough, drought-tolerant native grass is indispensable for binding soil. It reaches 1½ to 3 feet tall, spreads indefinitely by strongly rooted rhizomes, and offers season-long interest. In its native habitat, the shoreline of eastern North America, it plays a vital role in the ecology as it stabilizes blowing and drifting sand. Indiscriminate collecting from the wild is therefore discouraged. Although foot traffic is not recommended, it is usually a simple matter to step between the stems. Watch out, however, for emerging shoots. They are sharp and can puncture soft-soled shoes.

SCIENTIFIC NAME: *Ammophila breviligulata* (am-*mof*-i-la brev-i-lig-you-*lay*-ta). *Ammophila* is derived from the Greek *ammos,* sand, and *philos,* loving, in reference to the sites this genus naturally inhabits. *Breviligulata* refers to the short ligules (floral appendages) of the flowers.

HARDINESS / ORIGIN: Zones 4 to 8 or 9; coastal areas of Newfoundland and southern Labrador, south to North Carolina. It is also very common on the shores of Lake Ontario, Lake Superior, and Lake Michigan.

LEAVES / FLOWERS / FRUIT: The deciduous leaves reach 2 feet long and ½ inch wide. Best described as typically grasslike (long and narrow), they display a coarse texture and scaly roughness. In summer they are medium green, then become yellowish brown during autumn. Marram begins blooming in mid summer with foot-long cylindrical grayish green spikes composed of many ⅝-inch-long flowers held well above the arching foliage. By fall the spikes have turned a pleasing shade of light golden-brown and persist through winter. They dry well and are excellent in floral arrangements. The fruit, a small grain, is seldom produced and germinates very poorly.

RATE / SPACING: Growth is fast, once plants are established. Bare-root divisions or plants from pint-sized containers are spaced 14 to 18 inches apart.

OTHER SPECIES: *A. arenaria* (air-e-*nay*-ree-a), a European introduction, is much less common. The differences between the two species are subtle, but the primary one is that *A. arenaria* is somewhat smaller.

CULTURE / CARE: Marram is well adapted to growing in well-drained acidic to slightly alkaline sandy loam or beach sand. It is very capable of withstanding drought, shifting sand, salt, and high winds, and once its roots become established, no irrigation is ever needed. It prefers full sun. Seldom does anyone ever fertilize it, but one researcher reported increased vigor from an annual application of 12–12–12 fertilizer. Since sand has virtually no ability to hold fertilizer, a slow-release or controlled-release product should be used. When planting, be sure to set divisions deep enough so that the roots are in moist sand; do not worry about blowing sand piling up on the stem because these plants easily withstand such treatment. No serious diseases or pests have been reported, and although some gardeners mow their plantings once during springtime to neaten them up, little or no maintenance is required.

PROPAGATION: Division of the rhizomes should be taken from landscape plants or nursery stock beds and not from native stands; remember, marram is a critical element in the ecology of the dune landscape which is easily disturbed. Seed propagation is very difficult as seed production is scanty and germinability is poor.

Ampelopsis brevipedunculata   PLATE 18
Porcelain Ampelopsis

Most often appreciated for its tenacious climbing habit, porcelain ampelopsis, when unsupported, is also useful as a ground cover. As such this deciduous woody vine displays a horizontal, indefinite-spreading, low-sprawling habit with a height of 4 to 8 inches. It is durable, and for large sloping areas acts as an efficient soil-retaining general cover.

SCIENTIFIC NAME: *Ampelopsis brevipedunculata* (am-pel-*op*-sis brev-i-ped-unk-you-*lay*-ta). *Ampelopsis* comes from the Greek *ampelos,* a vine, and *opsis,* resemblance, referring to this genus's likeness to a grape vine. *Brevipedunculata* comes from the Latin *brevi,* short, and *pediculus,* a little foot, referring to the short peduncles or flower stalks of this species.

HARDINESS / ORIGIN: Zones 5 to 8 or 9; northeastern Asia.

LEAVES / FLOWERS / FRUIT: The simple, broadly oval, three-lobed, coarsely toothed medium green leaves reach 2½ to 5 inches long and are alternately arranged. The flowers, which are tiny, greenish, and held below the leaves, go all but unnoticed. The fruit, however, is anything but unnoticeable. First green, turquoise, or white, the ¼- to ⅓-inch in diameter round fruits eventually mature to lilac and porcelain blue. Often clusters contain fruit of different degrees of maturity and therefore multiple colors.

RATE / SPACING: Growth is fast. Plants from 1- to 2-gallon-sized containers are spaced 3 to 4 feet apart.

HORTICULTURAL SELECTIONS: 'Elegans', slower growing, smaller leaves variegated white and green, reported to come true from seed propagation; var. *maximowiczii,* leaves with three to five deep lobes, growth rate more vigorous than that of the species.

OTHER SPECIES: *A. aconitifolia* (ak-oh-nee-ti-*foe*-lee-a), named for the resemblance of its leaves to those of *Aconitum* (monkshood), is commonly called monkshood vine and hails from northern China. Its medium-textured leaves are compound, three-parted to five-parted (leaflets to 3 inches long), deep glossy green, and finely toothed along their edges. The flowers, which are tiny, green, and nondescript, bloom during late spring and give rise to ½-inch-wide berries that ripen to dull orange-yellow or, less commonly, blue.

A. humulifolia (hue-mue-lee-*foe*-lee-a), named for its leaves which resemble *Humulus* (hops), is a close relative of *A. brevipedunculata,* but differs in that its leaves are whitish on the underside and its fruits blue and yellow.

CULTURE / CARE: These species are durable and tolerate infertile, rocky, or sandy soils and lots of wind exposure. Even so, they welcome summertime watering and prefer to grow in loamy soil with good drainage and a pH of 4.5 to 7.0. They prefer light conditions ranging from full sun to moderate shade and have few serious diseases or pests. Maintenance typically consists of trimming back stems as they outgrow their bounds.

PROPAGATION: Stem cuttings taken during early to mid summer root well when treated with 3000 ppm IBA/talc. The trailing stems of *Ampelopsis* tend to root as they spread, thus creating the opportunity for transplanting them as they naturally become layered; this is best done during spring or early summer. If seed is used, it should not be allowed to dry out; instead, it should be harvested ripe then stratified at 40°F for three months prior to sowing.

Anacyclus depressus   PLATE 19
Mount Atlas Daisy

A sprawling, herbaceous ground cover that reaches 3 to 4 inches tall and spreads 14 or more inches wide, Mount Atlas daisy is impressive for its attractive fernlike foliage and beautiful daisylike flowers. It is interesting as a rock garden specimen, border or walkway edging, and mass planted as a general cover for small-sized to moderate-sized areas. No foot traffic is tolerated.

SCIENTIFIC NAME: *Anacyclus depressus* (an-a-*sy*-klus de-*pres*-sus / an-a-*sik*-lus day-*pres*-us). *Anacyclus* comes from the Greek *an,* without, *anthos,* flower, and *kuklos,* a ring, probably in reference to the circle of ovaries surrounding the disc. *Depressus* refers to the depressed (low) growth habit of this species.

HARDINESS / ORIGIN: Zones 6 to 10; alpine regions of Morocco.

LEAVES / FLOWERS / FRUIT: The leaves are evergreen, compound, fernlike, 3 to 5 inches long by ½ to ¾ inch wide, and gray-green with gray hairs. The flowers are solitary, daisylike, ¾ to 1½ inches wide, yellow in the center, and white around the outside. They open during the day, close at night, and are effective from early spring through summer. The tiny fruit is nonornamental.

RATE / SPACING: Growth is slow to moderate. Plants from 3- to 4-inch-diameter containers are spaced 8 to 12 inches apart.

CULTURE / CARE: Mount Atlas daisy requires well-drained (preferably gritty), rather infertile soil, but adapts to a pH ranging from alkaline to slightly acidic. Its tolerance to both heat and drought is good, and only occasionally is a summertime watering needed. It prefers a home in full sun. Although it is not greatly prone to pests and diseases, the taste of its flower petals seems to appeal to slugs. Maintenance needs are few to none.

PROPAGATION: Cuttings taken during the growing season root quite well. Division should be practiced during the spring or fall.

Anagallis monellii   PLATE 20
Monell's Pimpernel, Blue Pimpernel

This low-growing, sprawling, mounding, herbaceous ground cover reaches 12 to 18 inches tall, spreads over 3 feet wide, and is of great worth for its prolonged display of colorful flowers. A single plant is an excellent specimen for the rock garden or perennial border, or several plants can be combined on a small to moderate scale as a turf substitute. For level or sloping terrain, in an elevated planter, next to a retaining wall, or in a terrace, its cascading branches are very eye-catching. No foot traffic is tolerated.

SCIENTIFIC NAME: *Anagallis monellii* (an-a-*gale*-is moe-*nel*-ee-eye / an-a-*gah*-lis mon-*el*-ee-eye). *Anagallis* is said to be derived from a Greek word meaning delightful, presumably in reference to the fabled ability of this plant to alleviate melancholy. *Monellii* commemorates someone named Monelli.

HARDINESS / ORIGIN: Zones 7 to 10; Mediterranean region.

LEAVES / FLOWERS / FRUIT: The deciduous, oval to oblong, 1-inch-long leaves are dark green with reddish veins and are arranged loosely upon sprawling stems. Among them and at the tips of the stems, during summer, are borne solitary five-parted ¾- to 1-inch-diameter flowers. The petals are gentian blue above and reddish below. The fruit is nonornamental.

RATE / SPACING: Growth is moderate to fast. Plants

from pint-sized to gallon-sized containers are spaced 2 to 3 feet apart.

HORTICULTURAL SELECTIONS: Subsp. *linifolia,* commonly called flaxleaf pimpernel, with narrow foliage up to 1 inch long; 'Pacific Blue', more compact, 8 to 10 inches tall; 'Phillipii', 1 foot tall, deep gentian blue flowers.

CULTURE / CARE: Monell's pimpernel is adaptable to various soils provided drainage is good. Although it grows best when the soil is maintained in a slightly moistened condition, it tolerates short periods of drought. If not planted in full sun, the habit opens up and the flowers may fail. Aphids sometimes prey upon the stems and leaves, and if the soil becomes saturated, rotting may occur. Little or no maintenance is required, but the habit can be kept more compact and its appearance neatened by trimming plants back in late fall or early spring.

PROPAGATION: Stem cuttings root easily under mist and, while a mild root-inducing preparation may help, it is not essential. Division of the crowns also works and is best accomplished in early fall or spring.

Andromeda polifolia   PLATE 21
Bog Rosemary

Bog rosemary is a 1- to 2-foot-tall, 3- to 4-foot-wide, horizontally oriented shrublet that spreads by creeping rootstalk. It is not for every landscape but if you have moist acidic soil and a sunny location, it is well worth growing. It works well as an accent or specimen plant and can be massed as a small-scale to moderate-scale general cover. A member of the heath family, it combines with blueberries, cranberries, laurel, and numerous sedges (*Carex* species). No foot traffic is tolerated.

SCIENTIFIC NAME: *Andromeda polifolia* (an-*drom*-i-da pole-i-*foe*-lee-a). *Andromeda* is named after the Ethiopian princess of Greek mythology. *Polifolia* means the leaves are smooth or polished.

HARDINESS / ORIGIN: Zone 2; moist, boggy areas of northern Asia, northern Europe, and northeastern North America.

LEAVES / FLOWERS / FRUIT: The narrowly oblong leaves are dark green above and blue-green to light green below, evergreen, leathery, and 1½ inches long by ¼ inch wide, and tend to roll under around the edges. The lovely, five-lobed flowers, borne in clusters at the branch tips during early to mid spring, are urn-shaped, ¼ inch long, and pinkish fading to white. The fruit, a capsule, turns brown when ripe.

RATE / SPACING: Growth is slow to moderate. Plants from quart-sized to gallon-sized containers are spaced 1 to 1½ feet apart.

HORTICULTURAL SELECTIONS: 'Blue Ice', with ice blue foliage; 'Compacta', shorter, denser, and more compact than the species; 'Grandiflora Compacta', shorter, more compact habit, large coral pink flowers; 'Kiri-Kaming', a dwarf with narrower and shorter leaves, pinkish white flowers, and a mature size of 8 inches tall by 1 foot wide; 'Macrophylla', 8 inches tall by 1 foot wide, wider dark green leaves, deep pink flowers; 'Major', taller, with broader leaves than those of the species; 'Minima', with a nearly horizontal growth habit and threadlike leaves; 'Montana', lower and more compact than the species; 'Nana', only 12 inches tall; 'Nana Alba', white-flowered, 8 inches tall by 2 feet wide.

OTHER SPECIES: ***A. glaucophylla*** (glaw-koe-*fil*-a), named for its bluish leaves, is commonly called bog or marsh rosemary. Native from Greenland and Manitoba to Virginia, it is a variable species that is sometimes treated as a variety of *A. polifolia.* Compared with *A. polifolia,* its leaves are somewhat narrower with white felty undersides. Its habit is creeping, it is hardy to Zone 2, and it produces clusters of five to six white flowers in late spring.

CULTURE / CARE: Bog rosemary prefers to grow in boglike conditions, with organically rich, acidic, moist soil. It grows, however, in ordinary garden settings provided the soil is amended with liberal amounts of peat moss and watered during periods of drought. Full sun is best but light shade is tolerated. If grown in amended soil, it is a good idea to spade some peat into the ground every couple of years to keep the pH down and to hold moisture. Otherwise, very little maintenance is needed. Diseases seldom effect bog rosemary, and its pests—aphids, thrips, and mites—are seldom serious. Rabbits, however, find bog rosemary very tasty.

PROPAGATION: Division is effective during spring or fall. Stem cuttings may be taken during summer.

Anemone   PLATE 22
Windflower, Lily-of-the-field

This is an interesting genus of tuberous-rooted and fibrous-rooted, relatively low growing herbs that are remarkable for their flowers and soft fernlike foliage. Those that make the best ground covers are low-growing, compact species that have a tendency to spread by offsets or rhizomes. They are particularly useful in naturalized gardens, rock gardens, and Japanese gardens, and combine well with many afternoon-shade-loving shrubs such as rhododendrons and laurels.

SCIENTIFIC NAME: *Anemone* (a-*nem*-oh-nee) is derived from the Greek *anemos,* wind, and *mone,* a habitation, or possibly from Naamen, another name for Adonis, from whose spilled blood *A. coronaria* is said to have sprung. Some species enjoy windy places, hence the common name windflower.

HARDINESS / ORIGIN: See individual species.

LEAVES / FLOWERS / FRUIT: The deciduous leaves of most species of windflower originate from the base of the plant and are either simple and deeply divided, or palmately compound. The magnificent flowers get their color from petaloid sepals and are borne upon upright floral stems. Either borne singly or in loose clusters, they are numerous, cheery, and attention getting.

RATE / SPACING: Growth is moderate to fast. Plants from pint-sized to quart-sized containers are spaced 14 to 16 inches apart.

SPECIES: *A. hupehensis* (hue-pe-*en*-sis), named after Hupeh (now Hubei) Province, China, one of its native habitats, is commonly called Japanese anemone. It is hardy in Zones 6 to 10. Comparatively tall, it reaches 18 to 30 inches in height and spreads to 1½ feet wide. It displays deciduous, three-parted, light green leaves. Its 2- to 3-inch-diameter flowers are rose-colored and arise during late summer to early fall. The fruit is nonornamental. Variety *japonica,* noteworthy for its flowers which appear to be double due to the collection of small pink sepals underneath the petals, introduced into Europe during the seventeenth century by Robert Fortune; 'Praecox' has purple-pink flowers; 'Superba', more vigorous spreading, 2½ feet tall.

A. × *hybrida* (*hib*-ri-da), derived from the cross between *A. vitifolia* and *A. hupehensis* var. *japonica,* is more cold hardy (Zones 5 to 8) than *A. hupehensis.* It blooms from late summer to early fall and is the source of many cultivars, including 'Alba', with single white flowers from 2 to 3 inches wide; 'Alice', with rose-carmine flowers; 'Bressingham Glow'. with rose-red semidouble flowers on 2-foot-tall stems; 'Honorine Jobert', with numerous 2- to 3-inch-wide snowy-white flowers atop 3- to 4-foot-tall stalks; 'Krimhilde', with double light salmon-pink blossoms; 'Lady Gilmour', with semidouble 4-inch-wide pink flowers; 'Luise Uhink', with 4- to 5-inch-wide white flowers atop 4-foot-tall stalks; 'Margarete', with double pink flowers atop 3-foot-tall stalks; 'Max Vogel', with 4- to 5-inch-wide pink flowers atop 4-foot-tall stalks; 'Mont Rose', with double rose-pink flowers atop 3-foot-tall stalks; 'Pamina', with semidouble rose-pink flowers atop 3- to 4-foot-tall stalks; 'Prinz Heinrich' ('Prince Henry'), with semidouble deep rose flowers atop 3-foot-tall stalks; 'Queen Charlotte', with semidouble pink flowers; 'September Charm', with rose-pink flowers, darker on the outside than inside, and held atop 3-foot-tall stalks; 'Whirlwind', with white semidouble flowers atop 2- to 3-foot tall stalks.

A. sylvestris (sil-*ves*-tris), named for its sylvan habitat (limy, sunny woodland borders), is commonly called snowdrop anemone. Hailing from central and southern Europe, the Caucasus, and Siberia, it is hardy in Zones 3 to 9. This tenacious rhizomatous species reaches 12 to 18 inches tall and spreads indefinitely. It is stemless and gets its height from the long petioles of its five-parted, compound, unevenly tooth-edged, blue-green, soft-textured leaves. Above them, during late spring and early summer, are borne slightly fragrant, white, 1½- to 3-inch-wide flowers. 'Grandiflora' ('Macrantha'), with 3-inch-wide flowers; 'Plena' ('Elisa Fellmann', 'Flore Pleno') is a rare form with double flowers; 'Wienerwald' has flowers larger than those of the species.

CULTURE / CARE: Well-drained, mildly acidic loam or sandy loam with good drainage is best; *A. sylvestris,* however, tolerates limy soils. Tolerance to drought is only moderate, thus frequent watering may be required during hot, dry summers. The light preference of *A. hupehensis* and *A.* × *hybrida* is full sun to light shade, while *A. sylvestris* is best in light shade. Diseases such as leaf spot, rhizome rot, flower spotting, downy mildew, rust, smut, and viral mosaic are at times problematic. Although serious pest problems are rare, occasional aggravaters may include aphids, beetles, cutworms, and nematodes. Routine maintenance needs are few or nonexistent.

PROPAGATION: Root cuttings are best taken during fall; cover 2-inch-long cuttings with ½ inch of medium, and keep them moist and warm. Division should be practiced during spring and fall. Seed germinates in five or six weeks at 65 to 70°F.

Antennaria dioica   PLATE 23
Common Pussytoes

With prostrate stoloniferous habit, common pussytoes hugs the ground and spreads 8 to 12 inches wide. Best used on a small scale as a general cover, it looks nice below dwarf shrubs, clump-forming herbs, and as a rock garden specimen. No foot traffic is tolerated.

SCIENTIFIC NAME: *Antennaria dioica* (an-te-*nay*-ree-a die-*oy*-ka). *Antennaria* comes from the Latin *antenna,* a sail yard, in reference to the hairs attached to the seed which resemble the antennae of insects. *Dioica,* two houses, refers to the male and female reproductive parts being on separate plants.

HARDINESS / ORIGIN: Zones 3 to 9; north temperate grasslands and meadows, prairies, and dunes of Europe, Asia, and the Aleutian Islands.

LEAVES / FLOWERS / FRUIT: The semievergreen leaves with white-woolly bottom and green surface reach 1 inch long, are spatula-shaped, and are arranged in rosettes. Above them, during mid to late spring, are borne 3- to 12-flowered clusters of ¼-inch-wide fuzzy white or pale pink flower heads on stout, leafy, 6- to 12-inch-tall floral stalks. The fruit that follows is nonornamental.

RATE / SPACING: Growth is moderate. Plants from 4-inch-diameter containers are spaced 10 to 14 inches apart.

HORTICULTURAL SELECTIONS: 'Nyewood', with bright red flower heads; var. *rosea,* with rose-pink flower heads; 'Rubra', with dark red flower heads; 'Tomentosa', with leaves that appear silvery because of the silvery-white hairs on both sides.

OTHER SPECIES: ***A. plantaginifolia*** (plan-ta-jin-i-*foe*-lee-a), named for its plaintain-shaped leaves, is commonly called plantainleaf pussytoes. Hailing from Maine to Georgia west from Minnesota to Missouri, it is hardy to Zone 3, reaches 8 to 10 inches tall, and spreads indefinitely at a moderate rate. Plants from 4-inch-diameter containers are spaced 10 to 14 inches apart. The 3-inch-long conspicuously three-veined leaves are covered with hairs above and are white on their undersides. Arranged in a rosette, they are attractive and set a nice backdrop to the numerous heads of pale green to purplish flowers with white tips of mid to late spring.

CULTURE / CARE: Pussytoes thrive in rocky, sandy, infertile, neutral to slightly acidic soil. They tolerate drought quite well and actually prefer the soil a bit on the dry side. They prefer full sun to light shade. When grown in their preferred setting no serious disease or pests bother them. Little or no maintenance is needed.

PROPAGATION: Stem cuttings are easily rooted during early summer. Division is best performed in spring, before flowering, or during fall.

Aptenia cordifolia   PLATE 24
Baby Sun Rose

A glossy leaved, florific, succulent creeping ground cover, baby sun rose reaches only a few inches tall and spreads more than 4 feet wide. In the landscape it is effective at covering small-sized to moderate-sized expanses and is excellent in planters and rock gardens.

SCIENTIFIC NAME: *Aptenia cordifolia* (ap-*tin*-ee-a core-di-*foe*-lee-a). *Aptenia* comes from the Greek *apten,* wingless, in reference to the wingless seed capsules. *Cordifolia* means that the leaves are cordate (heart-shaped).

HARDINESS / ORIGIN: Zones 9 to 11; eastern South Africa.

LEAVES / FLOWERS / FRUIT: The shiny green succulent leaves are covered with shiny water-soaked pimple-like projections. Each leaf reaches 1 inch long by ¾ inch wide and is oval to heart-shaped. The purple to red flowers are borne on short stalks during spring and summer. The fruit is nonornamental.

RATE / SPACING: Growth is moderate to fast. Plants from 2½-inch-diameter to pint-sized containers are spaced 8 to 14 inches apart.

HORTICULTURAL SELECTIONS: 'Alba', flowers white; 'Red Apple', flowers cheery orangish apple-red; 'Variegata', leaves with white edges.

CULTURE / CARE: Baby sun rose is easy to grow and performs well in about any acidic or neutral well-drained soil. It tolerates a modest degree of salinity and performs best in full sun to light shade. After it becomes established, it requires water only during prolonged periods of heat and drought. It has few serious disease and insect problems and requires little or no maintenance.

PROPAGATION: Stem cuttings may be rooted any time. Division can be performed throughout the year.

Arabis caucasica   PLATE 25
Wall Rock Cress

Although few people have experience with wall rock cress, it is a very useful, small-scale soil stabilizer for rocky slopes. When planted between large stones in a rock garden or on top of a retaining wall, it performs admirably as a specimen or accent plant. It is useful in combination with such clump-forming ground covers as candytuft, showy sedum, pygmy barberry, blue fescue, and perhaps some of the nonrunning types of lily turf. Outstanding for its unusual leaf texture and pleasant flowers, wall rock cress is a somewhat tufted, somewhat trailing, herbaceous ground cover. It typically reaches 6 to 12 inches tall and spreads 18 inches wide. No foot traffic is tolerated.

SCIENTIFIC NAME: *Arabis caucasica* (*air*-a-bis kau-*kas*-i-ka). *Arabis* is derived from the word *Arabia,* which is the home of several rock cress species. *Caucasica* means of the Caucasus. Sometimes this species is listed as *A. albida.*

HARDINESS / ORIGIN: Zones 4 to 10; Caucasus Mountains.

LEAVES / FLOWERS / FRUIT: The semievergreen leaves are more or less oval-shaped with long, tapering bases. Colored grayish green, they reach 1 to 2 inches long, are covered with tiny hairs, and are slightly lobed or coarsely toothed on the edges toward the leaf tips. The fragrant flowers have white petals, are ⅜ to ⅝ inch wide, are held on 6- to 8-inch-long stems, and make a respectable show during early to mid spring.

RATE / SPACING: Growth is moderate. Plants from

pint-sized or quart-sized containers are spaced 8 to 12 inches apart.

HORTICULTURAL SELECTIONS: 'Floreplena', with striking, double white flowers; 'Rosabella', with pink flowers that fade to near white as they age; 'Snow Cap' ('Schneehaube'), with large, pure white flowers; 'Snow Peak', with single white flowers and compact habit to 4 inches tall; 'Spring Charm', with large clear pink flowers; 'Variegata', leaves with conspicuous creamy white, irregular patches that are, unfortunately, unstable in their variegation and often revert to all green.

OTHER SPECIES: *A. alpina* (al-*pie*-na), alpine rock cress, as its name indicates, comes from alpine regions, in this case, the mountains of Europe. Reaching up to 16 inches tall and spreading to 10 inches wide, it displays grayish green, oblong to oval, semievergreen, tooth-edged leaves. Its white, ⅜-inch-wide flowers appear in spring. Hardy in Zones 4 to 8. 'Compacta', with compact habit; 'Grandiflora', with larger flowers; 'Rosea', with pink flowers.

A. procurrens (pro-*cur*-enz), named for its procurrent habit of growth, is commonly called running rock cress. It is a herbaceous, evergreen, 12-inch-tall, indefinite-spreading European native. The foliage is lance-shaped to oval, rounded at the base, and colored glossy green. In bloom, which occurs during early to mid spring, it displays a good number of ¼-inch-wide flowers with white petals. Hardy in Zones 4 to 9.

CULTURE / CARE: Planting rock cresses in a poorly drained soil is to sentence them to pain and suffering (root and crown rot), humiliation (poor floral display), and eventual death (insufficient oxygen). To avoid this, plant them in sandy, well-drained, slightly acidic to alkaline soil. In accord with their rocky habitats, the rock cresses are relatively tolerant of drought. Once established, only an occasional summer watering will be necessary. They need full sun to light shade. At times they are subject to lily aphids, club root, downy mildew, white rust, and leaf spots. Although maintenance is not necessary, many gardeners shear or mow plantings after flowering to keep them looking neat and compact.

PROPAGATION: Cuttings taken after the flowering period root well in a porous, gritty medium. Division can be accomplished successfully during spring and fall. Seed is most successful when sown during spring; it germinates in three to four weeks.

Arctanthemum arcticum   PLATE 26
Arctic Chrysanthemum, Arctic Daisy

Formerly classified as *Chrysanthemum arcticum*, this species is a valuable florific herb that works nicely as a small-scale to moderate-scale edging plant or general cover. It forms a tight clump and reaches ½ to 1 foot tall by 1½ feet wide. Valued for its breathtaking, fragrant, sunflower-like blossoms, it blooms during fall and helps draw the growing season to a stunning close. No foot traffic is tolerated.

SCIENTIFIC NAME: *Arctanthemum arcticum* (ark-*tan*-the-mum *ark*-ti-kum). *Arctanthemum* refers to the flowers. *Arcticum* means from arctic regions.

HARDINESS / ORIGIN: Zones 2 to 9; coastal Alaska, Canada, and Kamchatka.

LEAVES / FLOWERS / FRUIT: Borne upon ascending stems, the deciduous, leathery, deep green, 1- to 3-inch-long spatula-shaped leaves are divided into three to five, tooth-edged, shallow lobes. Above them, during fall, are borne a multitude of 1- to 2-inch-wide, daisylike pink-tinged flowers with yellow centers and white petals. So late are the flowers borne that in the colder areas of the species' hardiness range, plants may be killed back by hard frost before flowering is completed. The fruit is nonornamental.

RATE / SPACING: Growth is slow, by short rhizomes. Plants from 1- to 2-gallon-sized containers are spaced 1 foot apart.

CULTURE / CARE: Arctic chrysanthemum prefers well-drained, moist, acidic to neutral soils in full sun to light shade. It feeds heavily, benefits from fertilization, is not tolerant of drought, and is susceptible to a number of diseases and pests, including leaf spot, wilt, rust, blight, powdery mildew, aster yellows, aphids, leaf miner, stalk borer, and mites.

PROPAGATION: Division is easily accomplished during spring. Stem cuttings root quickly in early summer, and root cuttings taken in fall also work. Seed germinates in seven to ten days at 70°F.

Arctostaphylos uva-ursi   PLATE 27
Bearberry, Kinnikinick, Bilberry, Bear's Grape, Barren Myrtle, Crowbars, Hog Cranberry, Creashak, Fox Plum, Meal Plum, Mountain Box, Mealberry, Rapper Dandies, Sandberry, Red Bearberry, Rockberry, Universe Plant, Uva-ursi, Manzanita

Common bearberry is an excellent ground cover for use on a moderate to large scale and is particularly effective around shrubs in informal and native-plant landscapes. Prostrate, low, woody and creeping, it is an excellent companion to magnolias, high and lowbush blueberries, witch hazels, dogwoods, pines, oaks, and the lovely white-flowered serviceberries. Ranging from 1 to 4 inches tall and spreading indefinitely, it thrives in rugged conditions such as the sand or gravel of lakeshores. Even in the face of prevailing winds, it blankets steep slopes and controls erosion as few others. Infrequent foot traffic is tolerated.

Herbalists have long appreciated this species for its medicinal properties as an astringent, diuretic, and blood purifier. It has also been used to stop bleeding and to promote the uterine contractions of childbirth. Native Americans, who called it kinnikinick (often spelled kinnikinic), steeped the foliage in water to make a tea that was used to treat kidney disorders. High in tannins, the foliage has been used in tanning hides in Iceland, Scandinavia, and Russia. The common name manzanita means little apple in Spanish.

SCIENTIFIC NAME: *Arctostaphylos uva-ursi* (ark-toe-*staf*-i-los oo-va-*er*-see). *Arctostaphylos* is derived from the Greek *arctos,* a bear, and *staphyle,* a bunch of grapes; the berries of some species are eaten by bears and may be borne in grapelike clusters. *Uva-ursi* literally means the bear's grape.

HARDINESS / ORIGIN: Zones 3 to 7; northern North America, Europe, and Asia.

LEAVES / FLOWERS / FRUIT: The attractive, dark green, leathery, 1-inch-long, evergreen leaves are teardrop-shaped and in fall and winter may turn bronzy or even reddish. Becoming green again in early to mid spring, they are a perfect backdrop for the multitude of miniature urnlike, white to pinkish, ¼-inch-long spring flowers that arise at the ends of the branches in spring. The fruit is very attractive, often copiously produced, berrylike, shiny, ¼ to ½ inch long, green in late summer, then red in autumn.

RATE / SPACING: Growth is slow to moderate. Plants from 3-inch-diameter to gallon-sized containers are spaced 12 to 24 inches apart.

HORTICULTURAL SELECTIONS: 'Alaska', very low growing with small dark green, rounded leaves; 'Big Bear', with larger leaves and more vigorous growth; 'Convict Lake', much shorter than the species; 'Emerald Carpet', more shade tolerant than the species, 10 to 18 inches tall by 6 feet wide, leaves densely set and dark green; 'Massachusetts', shorter and more compact than the species, with more flowers and fruit; var. *microphylla,* with leaves much smaller than those of the species; 'Pacific Mist', fast growing, 2 to 3 feet tall by 6 feet wide, grayish green leaves; 'Point Reyes', more heat and drought tolerant, with leaves darker green and more closely spaced; 'Radiant', leaves light green and widely spaced, fruiting heavily; 'Rax', from eastern Australia, a very low grower with smaller leaves than the species; 'Vancouver Jade', more vigorous, with flowers borne on semiupright branches and thus more visible; 'Vulcan's Peak', more prolific in flowers and fruit, leaves rounded and overlapping; 'Wood's

Compacta', low-growing and compact, 2 to 3 inches tall by 3 to 4 feet wide, leaves small and green, flowers white with pink tinge, leaf tips red in fall.

OTHER SPECIES: *A. alpina* (al-*pie*-na), alpine bearberry or black bearberry, hails from mountain peaks in northeastern North America and northern Europe. Compared to the other species, its stature (2 to 5 inches tall by 1 foot wide) is very small, but its features are no less attractive. Clothed in dark green (red in fall), evergreen, 1½-inch-long, ¼- to ½-inch-wide oval to narrowly oval leaves, it is hardy in Zones 1 to 4. In late spring to early summer the white, pink-tinged, urn-shaped flowers appear and are followed by edible ¼-inch-wide, ⅙-inch-long, purple to purplish black berries. It spreads at a slow to moderate rate, thus plants should be spaced 12 to 18 inches apart. Variety *japonica* displays larger, more spatula-shaped foliage.

A. edmundsii (ed-*mundz*-ee-eye), Little Sur manzanita, is native to California and hardy to Zone 7. It displays attractive elliptic to broadly oval ¼-inch-long grayish green evergreen leaves. Unlike the other species, its pinkish flowers of late winter to early spring are only sparsely borne. Its fruit is brown, berrylike, and effective in late autumn. In habit, it is a low, creeping, woody ground cover that reaches 12 inches tall by 6 feet wide. Growth is fast. Plants from gallon-sized containers are spaced 2 to 2½ feet apart.

A. '**Emerald Carpet**', emerald carpet manzanita, can spread to 6 feet wide and reach 9 to 15 inches tall. Its glossy emerald green leaves are oval and ½ inch long. Its flowers in early spring are white bells. Hardy in Zones 7 to 10.

A. hookeri (hook-*er*-eye), named after Sir Joseph Hooker, an English plant collector and nineteenth-century director of the Royal Botanic Gardens at Kew, is commonly called Hooker manzanita or Monterey manzanita (for Monterey, California, where it grows wild). Like *A. pumila* and *A. uva-ursi,* it is shrubby and horizontal growing. It reaches 18 to 25 inches tall and spreads to 6 feet wide or more. Hardy to Zone 7, it displays oval, 1-inch-long, bright green, evergreen foliage and numerous flowers of white to whitish pink in late winter and early spring. The fruit that follows is glossy and bright red. Growth is moderate. Plants from 1- to 2-gallon-sized containers are spaced 3 to 4 feet apart.

A. nevadensis (nev-a-*den*-sis), pinemat manzanita, is hardy northward to Zone 5. An interesting native shrublet from the Sierra Nevada, its bright shiny green, ¾- to 1-inch-long, ¼- to ¾-wide leaves are held neatly upon its 6- to 18-inch-tall, 4-foot-wide frame. They act as a splendid backdrop to the ⅓-inch-long, white (often pink-tinged) flowers of mid spring and the bright red fruit that follows. 'Chipeta' is uniformly prostrate, very drought tolerant, and exceptionally hardy. The as-yet-unnamed hybrid derived from crossing *A. nevadensis* and *A. canescens* (hoary manzanita, a 6-foot-tall shrubby species from the Pacific Northwest), makes a nice 2-foot-tall, 6-foot-wide silvery-green-leaved ground cover that is hardy to Zone 6.

A. nummularia (new-mew-*lay*-ree-a), coin-leaved bearberry, naturally displays either prostrate or upright habit. Clones of the prostrate forms, naturally, are those used as ground covers. They are hardy to Zone 7, hail from the coast of California, and display elliptic to oblong or oval, ¾-inch-long, dark shiny green hairless leaves. The flowers, borne during spring, are white and give rise to green fruit.

A. pumila (*pew*-mi-la), meaning dwarf, is commonly called dune manzanita. Ironically, this California species is actually tall compared with *A. uva-ursi* but dwarf compared with many of the other species. Typically, it spreads horizontally, displays a shrubby, ground-covering habit, and reaches 1 to 1½ feet tall. Growth is slow. Plants from gallon-sized containers are spaced 2 to 4 feet apart. The species is hardy to Zone 7 and displays narrow oval or spatula-shaped, 1-inch-long, dull green, evergreen leaves. In late winter and spring it produces lovely white to pink flowers that later give rise to brown, berrylike fruit.

A. rubra (*rew*-bra), named for the redness of its leaves during fall and winter, is commonly called red bearberry and is sometimes classified as a variety of *A. uva-ursi*. It is similar to *A. alpina* but has branchlets (1 to 6 inches tall) that are more ascending. Additionally, its foliage is brighter green, its corolla narrower, and its fruit larger. The species hails from western China and Korea and northwestern North America and is hardy to Zone 1.

A. thymifolia (tie-mee-*foe*-lee-a / thy-mee-*foe*-lee-a), thyme-leaved bearberry, apparently hails from an arctic locale. It is thought by some to be a variety or cultivar of *A. uva-ursi*. Its foliage is densely set and narrower than that of *A. uva-ursi,* and it is more prostrate, reaching only 3 inches tall by 3 feet wide. Presumably it is hardy in Zones 3 to 7.

A. 'Wood's Red' is a prostrate selection that reaches 6 inches tall by 3 feet wide. Hardy in Zones 5 to 9, it bears pink flowers in spring and reddish foliage in fall.

CULTURE / CARE: Well-drained, sandy or gritty, acidic soil is favored by all the species discussed here. They are highly drought resistant once established. Although they accept light conditions ranging from full sun to light shade, they are at their best when planted in exposed, open sites, particularly if air movement is good. Generally speaking, these species

are resistant to salinity, diseases, and pests. In almost all cases, if you try to grow them in poorly draining sites or climates hotter and drier than they prefer, you will be sentencing them to diseases and pests such as root rot, black mildew, leaf gall, leaf spots, rust, and mites. Maintenance demands are few, but for neatness buffs, shearing or mowing can be done following bloom.

PROPAGATION: Cuttings root best in spring or late fall when placed in a mixture of peat moss and perlite; some years they root in high percentages, and other years they do not. Divisions and rooted stem sections (layers) can also be taken from some species; the best time for this is during the spring. For the adventuresome who would like to try propagating from seed, the use of fire might be employed; sow seed in an outdoor bed (in fall), lightly cover the seed with soil, then cover the bed with 3 to 4 inches of excelsior or dry pine needles and set ablaze. Germination will occur the following spring.

Arctotheca calendula   PLATE 28
Cape Weed, Cape Dandelion

This tough, evergreen, coarse-textured, low-sprawling, herbaceous, leafy, carpeting ground cover is relatively aggressive, reaches 8 to 12 inches tall, and spreads indefinitely. Sometimes a bit ragged appearing, it is best used for erosion control on slopes and as a large-scale general cover where borders such as sidewalks or curbs check its spread. It is particularly attractive and useful when allowed to trail over the edge of a stone retaining wall and, when used in this way, its roots grow in between the stones and help prevent erosion. Occasional foot traffic is tolerated.

SCIENTIFIC NAME: *Arctotheca calendula* (ark-toe-*they*-ka ka-*len*-dew-la). *Arctotheca* is said to come from the Greek *arktos,* north, and *theke,* chest, but how this relates to the plant is unclear. *Calendula* refers to this species' resemblance to the marigold genus *Calendula.*

HARDINESS / ORIGIN: Zones 9 to 11; South Africa.

LEAVES / FLOWERS / FRUIT: The oblong to lyre-shaped, gray-green, rough, hairy, 6- to 8-inch-long evergreen leaves reach 2 inches wide and are deeply and irregularly furrowed about their edges. Atop them, borne profusely in spring and sporadically the rest of the year, are cheerful, solitary, daisylike, 1- to 2-inch-wide yellow flowers. Fruit is not always produced, as a sterile variety is most often used, but when it is produced, it is tiny and nonornamental.

RATE / SPACING: Growth is fast. Plants from 3- to 4-inch-diameter containers are spaced 14 to 20 inches apart.

CULTURE / CARE: Cape weed is adaptable to various

well-drained soils and, although it tolerates considerable heat and drought, it is best when the soil is kept slightly moist. It prefers full sun, has few problems (other than aphids and crown rot if the soil is inadequately drained), and is usually maintained with a single mowing after the main period of bloom to thicken plantings and neaten their appearance.

PROPAGATION: Division of the crown is an easy and effective means of propagation, as is transplantation of the naturally layered stem segments

---

Ardisia japonica   PLATE 29
Japanese Ardisia, Marlberry

This erect-branched, 8- to 12-inch-tall coarse-textured shrubby ground cover rapidly spreads by suckers to form broad leafy colonies. Nice looking throughout the year, it is usually planted in broad colonies at the edge of the woods. Here it not only acts as an effective backdrop to herbaceous perennials planted in its foreground but aids the transition between the trees and the lawn areas. No foot traffic is tolerated.

SCIENTIFIC NAME: *Ardisia japonica* (ar-*diz*-ee-a ja-*pon*-i-ka). *Ardisia* comes from the Greek *ardis,* a point, referring to the pointed anthers. *Japonica* means of Japan.

HARDINESS / ORIGIN: Zones 7 to 9; Japan and China.

LEAVES / FLOWERS / FRUIT: The superb coarse-textured, alternately arranged, leathery, shiny dark green, evergreen leaves are elliptic, crowded at the ends of the branches, and sharply serrated about their edges. Above them, during mid and late summer are borne the ½-inch-wide, star-shaped, five-petaled flowers carried in groups of two to six (rarely more). After flowering they yield ¼-inch-wide showy red fruit that matures during mid fall and persists well into winter.

RATE / SPACING: Growth is fast. Plants from 1- to 2-gallon-sized containers are spaced 2 to 3 feet apart.

HORTICULTURAL SELECTIONS: 'Beniyuki', leaves edged with a broad band of white; 'Chirimen', 2 to 6 six inches tall, deep green bronze-tinged leaves, pink and white flowers; 'Chiyoda', leaves edged with a narrow band of white; 'Hakuokan', larger, more robust, with leaves variegated green and white; 'Hinode', larger, more vigorous, and leaves with a broad splotch of yellow in their centers; 'Hinotsukasa', with irregularly shaped, sometimes white teeth about the leaf edges; 'Ito-Fukurin', with white-margined, light silvery-gray leaves; 'Variegata', reaching 12 to 15 inches tall, leaves variegated creamy white and green.

CULTURE / CARE: Japanese ardisia prefers fertile, cool, moist, acidic soil and light to moderate shade. It is

not greatly drought tolerant and should be given supplemental water during hot, dry weather. It has few disease and pest problems, and needs little maintenance.

PROPAGATION: Division of rooted suckers may be performed during spring and fall. Cuttings taken during the growing season root well if given bottom heat.

Arenaria verna   PLATE 30
Moss Sandwort

Low-growing (1½ to 2 inches tall), neat, and mosslike, this little herbaceous ground cover makes a good turf substitute when used on a small scale. It also is exceptional as a filler between patio cracks and stepping stones and makes a charming rock garden specimen. Infrequent foot traffic is tolerated.

SCIENTIFIC NAME: *Arenaria verna* (air-e-*nay*-ree-a *ver*-na). *Arenaria* is derived from the Latin *arena,* sand, referring to the plant's preferred habitat in sandy places. *Verna,* spring, refers to the time of flowering.

HARDINESS / ORIGIN: Zones 3 to 9; Spain to northern Russia.

LEAVES / FLOWERS / FRUIT: The evergreen, narrow, mosslike leaves to ¾ inch long are light green and reminiscent of artificial turf. During mid spring, tiny starlike flowers, arranged in groups of few or many, are borne upon the tops of erect, leafy stems.

RATE / SPACING: Growth is moderate to fast. Plants from 2¼- to 4-inch-diameter containers are spaced 8 to 12 inches apart.

HORTICULTURAL SELECTIONS: 'Aurea', with light yellow leaves prone to reverting back to green.

OTHER SPECIES: *A. arctica* (*ark*-ti-ka) arctic sandwort, is somewhat larger than *A. alpina,* reaches 6 to 8 inches high by 6 to 8 inches wide, and is hardy in Zones 1 to 4. Native to Asia as well as Greenland and Labrador to Quebec, in North America it naturally ranges westward to Alaska and southward to alpine areas of the Rockies. Its dark green leaves are evergreen and reach ⅓ inch long. The white flowers are borne in summer.

A. laricifolia (lar-is-i-*foe*-lee-a), named for its larchlike leaves, is commonly called larchleaf sandwort. Useful in the same ways as *A. verna,* this species ranges from 6 to 8 inches tall and spreads indefinitely. It is hardy to Zone 5 and native to the Swiss Alps. The dark green, thin, rather rigid, semievergreen leaves are neat and attractive. Showy white flowers are borne during early summer in groups of one to six held upon 12-inch-tall stems.

A. montana (mon-*tay*-na / mon-*tan*-a), meaning of the mountains, is commonly called mountain sandwort. It is best used between flagstones or as a lawn substitute for small yards. Hardy in Zones 5 to 7, it is native to Portugal and central and northwestern France and is characterized by evergreen leaves that are oval, tiny, grayish green, and pointed. Its flowers are white and borne in great profusion during mid spring. Ranging from 2 to 4 inches tall, it spreads 8 to 10 inches wide.

CULTURE / CARE: Sandy, well-drained, loamy soil with moderate acidity is best. Heavy clay or poorly drained soils should be avoided. The sandworts are not well adapted to withstand dry conditions as their root systems are shallow; therefore, they often require supplemental watering during the summertime. They should be grown in full sun or light shade. In the South they are best in light shade. No serious pests affect them. Crown rot, however, can be devastating when they are planted in poorly drained soil or in the North when the top part of the soil becomes covered with wet, slushy snow for extended periods of time. In these conditions, plant them on raised mounds and in northeastern exposures (to shade from afternoon sun). Other diseases such as leaf spot, powdery mildew, and rusts are sometimes encountered, yet are seldom serious. All species are notorious for self-seeding and can become weedy; because of this, many gardeners mow the flowers off before seed can ripen.

PROPAGATION: Division is best performed during spring or early fall. Seed is best sown in the spring.

Armeria maritima   PLATE 31
Maritime Thrift, Common Thrift

Common thrift is an easily appreciated plant. Not only is it magnificently showy during its extended flowering season, but its grassy, evergreen foliage is a lovely dark green year-round. It spreads slowly and requires little or no maintenance. Low, herbaceous, and tuft-forming, this tough little ground cover reaches only 4 to 6 inches tall and spreads 8 to 12 inches wide. Although its restricted spread makes it expensive for covering large areas, thrift is fine on a small to moderate scale and provides excellent contrast and color when interplanted with other tufted ground covers.

It performs well as a facing to open trees such as serviceberries, starry magnolias, dogwoods, crape myrtles, and erect or vase-shaped blue-leaved specimens of juniper. Single plants or small groups of thrift are splendid as specimens or accent plants in mixed herbaceous border or island groupings. For artistic gardeners, thrift holds its shape well and can be arranged in geometric patterns. Despite its grassy appearance, the tufted nature of thrift makes it rather intolerant of foot traffic. On the other hand, it is rel-

atively tolerant of salt, making it a good choice for coastal gardens.

SCIENTIFIC NAME: *Armeria maritima* (ar-*mee*-ree-a ma-*rit*-i-ma). *Armeria* is an old Latin name attributed to this genus. *Maritima* is a reference to the maritime or seaside environment these plants frequently inhabit.

HARDINESS / ORIGIN: Zones 4 to 8; southern Greenland, Iceland, and northwestern Europe.

LEAVES / FLOWERS / FRUIT: The thin, dark green to grayish, evergreen, grasslike leaves reach 4 inches long and arise from the base of the plant. During mid spring, thin green stalks arise from the foliar rosettes and are topped by bright pink to whitish, round, balloonlike flower heads. The initial springtime burst of color is nearly overwhelming. Later in the season (through the early part of summer), when flowering becomes sporadic, the effect is more charming than breathtaking.

RATE / SPACING: Growth is slow. Plants from 3- to 5-inch-diameter containers are spaced 6 to 10 inches apart.

HORTICULTURAL SELECTIONS: 'Alba', with white flowers; 'Brilliant', with bright pink flowers; 'California', with larger flowers on short stalks; 'Cotton Tail', 4 to 6 inches tall, with pure white flowers; 'Dusseldorf Pride', compact, with reddish to deep pinkish red flowers; 'Laucheana', deep crimson flowers, very compact habit; 'Purpurea', with purple flowers; 'Robusta', vigorous, with flower stalks to 15 inches tall; var. *rubra,* with light red flowers on 6- to 8-inch-tall stalks; 'Royal Rose', with abundant pink flowers; 'Ruby Glow', with ruby red flowers on 10-inch-tall stalks; 'Splendens', with bright red flowers; 'Vindictive', with deep rose-red flowers.

OTHER SPECIES: *A.* 'Bloodstone', probably the result of a cross between *A. plantaginea* and *A. maritima,* reaches 8 or 9 inches tall and produces bright red flowers.

A. juniperifolia (jew-ni-per-i-*foe*-lee-a), named for its leaves that resemble those of juniper, is commonly called juniper thrift. Hardy in Zones 4 to 8, it has a low, tufted habit, reaches only 2 inches tall, and spreads only 4 inches wide. It hails from Spain and displays awl-shaped, triangular, evergreen leaves that reach ¾ inch long and are arranged in tight rosettes. The lilac flowers compose ½-inch-diameter globe-shaped heads and are borne on short flowering stems during mid spring. Like *A. maritima,* it is slow spreading. Plants from 3- to 4-inch-diameter containers are spaced 4 inches apart. Because of its limited spread, it is best used as a specimen, for accent, or for edging. Variety *splendens* has bright pink, nodding flowers on 2- to 3-inch-tall stalks.

CULTURE / CARE: Light sandy loam is best, and good

drainage is essential. Avoid planting in heavy clay, and plan to water only during extended periods of drought. A location should be selected that is exposed to full sun or light shade. In the South, a location with increasing afternoon shade, such as along the northeastern side of a building, is preferred. No serious pests afflict the thrifts, and the most significant disease is stem rot, which invariably results from planting in poorly drained soils. Maintenance is nonexistent except for occasional division should plantings ever become brown in the center due to overcrowding.

PROPAGATION: Divisions from tuftlike offsets at the base of the parent clump are easily pulled off and rooted during mid to late summer. More disruptive but nearly foolproof is conventional division in which the entire clump is lifted and divided during spring or fall. Seed also works well; upon ripening it should be collected and stored in a cool, dry location until sown the following spring. Germination usually occurs in two to four weeks in a moist medium with temperatures of 70 to 75°F.

Aronia melanocarpa   PLATE 32
Black Chokeberry

A woody shrub that typically ranges from 1½ to 3 feet tall, and up to 5 feet in rich soil, black chokeberry spreads 6 to 10 feet wide. It is not real common but is a strong grower and a fine choice in very cold climates where an acid-loving plant is needed to retain soil in large-scale plantings, particularly around the edge of wooded borders in saturated soils. Because of considerable natural variation in height, it is a good idea to ask your local nursery about the mature size of any plants you purchase. No foot traffic is tolerated.

SCIENTIFIC NAME: *Aronia melanocarpa* (a-roe-*nee*-a me-lan-oh-*kar*-pa). *Aronia* comes from *aria,* the Greek name for *Sorbus aria,* a related species in the rose family. *Melanocarpa,* black fruited, is a Latin term.

HARDINESS / ORIGIN: Zones 3 to 7 or 8; eastern United States.

LEAVES / FLOWERS / FRUIT: The finely tooth-edged leaves are elliptic to oblong, 1½ to 3½ inches wide, and shiny dark green turning red in fall. The tiny flowers are bundled together in 1- to 1½-inch-wide hawthornlike clusters in late spring. They are attractive, pleasantly fragrant, and give rise to ⅓- to ½-inch-wide black to purplish black berrylike fruits.

RATE / SPACING: Growth is moderate to fast. Plants from 2- to 3-gallon-sized containers are spaced 3 to 4 feet apart.

CULTURE / CARE: Growing well in almost any acidic to neutral soil, black chokeberry tolerates short periods of saturation as well as drought and infertility. It prefers full sun to moderate shade and requires little or no maintenance. Diseases of greatest consequence are bacterial blight, leaf spots, twig and fruit blights, and rust. The only pest of significance is the round-headed apple tree borer.

PROPAGATION: Softwood cuttings that are taken during midsummer root relatively well if treated with 3000 ppm IBA/talc. Seed should be harvested and sown outdoors as soon as it ripens; germination will occur the following spring. Division, which consists of digging up and transplanting rooted suckers, is best accomplished during spring.

Artemisia   PLATE 33
Wormwood

The expansive genus *Artemisia* consists of various species (about 200) known as wormwood for their medicinal use in eradicating intestinal worms. Those that are best as ground covers are low-growing herbaceous or semiwoody perennials. Generally speaking, they work well for covering small plots, as specimens in rock gardens, or for accent or edging in border settings. Noteworthy primarily for their foliage, the flowers of artemisias are not very showy and are of limited ornamental value. No foot traffic is tolerated.

SCIENTIFIC NAME: *Artemisia* (ar-te-*meez*-ee-a / ar-te-*meesh*-ee-a) is named for Artemis (Diana), one of the divinities of ancient Greece.

HARDINESS / ORIGIN: Artemisias are quite cold tolerant, generally Zones 3 to 5, but are more sensitive to and limited by heat, particularly when accompanied by high humidity. Most species succeed in Zone 7 or 8 provided humidity is low, but the same plants barely survive during hot summers in Zone 6 if the humidity is high. Native to dry areas and sand dunes of the Northern Hemisphere, with a few species from South America and South Africa.

LEAVES / FLOWERS / FRUIT: The leaves vary from species to species, but those of most of the horticultural selections are finely divided, aromatic when crushed (the smell being used to help identify the different species), silvery to bluish green, and soft to the touch. The flowers are usually small, clustered, white, brownish, purplish, or yellowish and ornamentally less significant than the foliage. The fruit, a tiny seed, is nonornamental.

RATE / SPACING: Moderate to fast; see individual species for spacing recommendations.

SPECIES: *A. abrotanum* 'Nana' (ab-*rot*-a-num *nay*-na), commonly called dwarf southernwood, silver spreader, and dwarf lad's love or dwarf maid's ruin (in reference to its reputed aphrodisiac qualities), is native to Europe and hardy in Zones 5 to 8. It grows at a moderate pace, remains relatively low (reaching 20 inches tall), and spreads quite wide (reaching 7 feet wide). Its leaves are fine-textured, grayish, pungent when crushed, and sometimes used in toilet waters. Its yellowish white flowers of late summer are arranged in rounded heads to $\frac{3}{16}$ inch wide, and its fruit is of no ornamental significance. Plants from 1- to 2-gallon-sized containers should be spaced 2½ to 3 feet apart.

A. caucasica (kau-*kas*-i-ka), named for its native habitat, is commonly called Caucasian wormwood or silver spreader (the latter name also applied to *A. abrotanum*). It is a sturdy, mat-forming ground cover that ranges from 3 to 6 inches tall and spreads to 2 feet wide. It hails from the Caucasus region and is hardy to Zone 4. Growth is fast. Plants from 2¼- to 4-inch-diameter containers are spaced 10 to 12 inches apart. The species displays 1¼-inch-long evergreen leaves that are gray-green and silky haired. Its yellow flowers are arranged in heads to ¼ inch in diameter and are effective during late summer.

A. frigida (*frij*-i-da), named from the Latin *frigidus,* cold, for its frosty or frigid appearance, is commonly called fringed sagebrush. Hailing from the midwestern United States, it is hardy to Zone 2, grows in an upright manner, spreads by short underground stems, and displays a compact habit, 1½ feet high by 8 to 18 inches wide. Its leaves are clustered, to ½ inch long, silvery, silky, and pleasantly aromatic. The yellow flowers are arranged in tiny heads to ⅙ inch wide and are effective in late summer. Growth is moderate. Plants from pint-sized containers are spaced 8 to 12 inches apart.

A. ludoviciana (lew-doe-vik-ee-*aye*-na), meaning of Louisiana, is commonly called white sage, cudweed, or western mugwort. It hails from prairies and dry sandy sites of Michigan to British Columbia, south to Arkansas and Mexico and is hardy in Zones 4 to 9 or 10. A variable, durable, deciduous, gray-leaved species, it ranges from 1 to 4 feet tall and creeps by rhizomes to 2 or 3 feet wide. Its tiny gray flowers arise during late summer upon narrow upright inflorescences. Cultivars include 'Latiloba', with gray-green, 3-inch-wide, three-lobed to five-lobed leaves, 1 to 2 feet tall, hardy in Zones 4 to 7 as it is not as resistant to heat as is the species; 'Valerie Finnis', 1½ to 2 feet tall by more than 3 feet wide, hardy in Zones 4 to 9, with a pleasing medium-textured silvery-blue-green mat-forming habit, especially nice when trailing over the edge of a boulder or retaining wall, outstanding heat and humidity tolerance.

A. 'Powis Castle' a hybrid cultivar thought to be the result of crossing *A. abrotanum* with *A. ab-*

sinthium, is a non-flowering selection that forms neat compact mounds 1½ to 2½ feet tall by more than 3 feet wide. Its finely divided, ferny, silvery-white, aqua-tinted foliage is finer-textured than that of *A. ludoviciana* 'Valerie Finnis'. This cultivar is hardy in Zones 5 to 9.

A. schmidtiana (shmit-i-*aye*-na), commonly called satiny wormwood or angel's hair, is native to Japan. Hardy in Zones 3 to 7, it performs best in the northern part of its range. It spreads horizontally by creeping underground stems to 1 foot wide and reaches 18 to 24 inches tall. Its silvery, silky-haired, aromatic, bitter-tasting leaves reach 1¾ inches long and give it a very soft textured appearance. The flowers are arranged in heads that reach $\frac{3}{16}$ inch wide and bloom in late summer. As with other species of wormwood, the flowers are not considered of great ornamental value. Growth is moderate. Plants from 3- to 4-inch-diameter containers are spaced 8 to 14 inches apart. Horticultural selections include 'Nana', 4 inches tall; 'Silver Mound', seemingly not different from 'Nana' but considerably better known). Both cultivars are far more readily available than the species and are particularly good in small areas.

A. stelleriana (stel-lar-ee-*aye*-na), commonly called beach wormwood, dusty miller, or old woman, is hardy in Zones 3 or 4 to 9. A native of eastern North America, it is a herbaceous, shrubby ground cover that ranges from 2 to 2½ feet tall and spreads to 3 feet wide by underground stems. Its oblong to oval woolly white leaves reach 4 inches long, and its ¼-inch-diameter summertime flowers are yellow. The species possesses a relatively high tolerance to salt and therefore is popular in seaside plantings. Growth is moderate. Plants from quart-sized containers are spaced 1½ to 2 feet apart. 'Silver Brocade', which flowers little, reaches 6 to 12 inches tall and more than 12 inches wide, has a habit more horizontal than the typical species, and displays very attractive, lacy, silvery-white foliage on arching stems.

CULTURE / CARE: Tolerant of, and often best in, poor, infertile, relatively dry soils of acidic to neutral pH, wormwoods require supplemental water only during prolonged drought. They prefer full sun to light shade. No significant pests are usually encountered, but diseases include rusts and damping off, both most prevalent during hot, humid, and extended rainy weather. Maintenance consists of cutting back plantings when they become ragged or tattered; this not only neatens them but also stimulates fresh growth.

PROPAGATION: Cuttings placed in coarse sand root well. Division during spring or fall is almost foolproof.

Asarum   PLATE 34
Ginger

There is little doubt in my mind that if it were not for their slow growth (and concomitant high price), gingers would be commonplace in nearly every tree-shaded landscape of North America. Not only are these dense low-growing, horizontally spreading, leafy herbs excellent for covering the woodland floor, but they also display extremely handsome foliage and require absolutely no maintenance. They look beautiful in either small or large groups in woodland borders and underneath dense shade trees, where they carpet the soil and provide a lovely leafy element to the overall texture of the landscape. They combine well with forbs such as trillium, columbine, and bellflower, as well as other woodland ground covers such as bleeding heart and bunchberry. Interplanting with taller, clump-forming herbs such as hostas (particularly forms with white and green variegation) and some of the taller lungworts is an excellent practice when additional color is desired. No foot traffic is tolerated.

SCIENTIFIC NAME: *Asarum* (a-*sah*-rum / *as*-a-rum) is an ancient Greek name, the meaning of which is unclear.

HARDINESS / ORIGIN: Zones 4 to 6, and often Zones 8 to 9; most species are native to Japan but others can be found throughout the Northern Temperate Zone.

LEAVES / FLOWERS / FRUIT: The leaves may be either deciduous or evergreen. Normally they are kidney-shaped or heart-shaped, attached to the creeping rhizome by short petioles, and frequently are mottled with tones of gray or silver. The purplish or brownish bell-shaped flowers are interesting but not greatly ornamental, for they hang down and are usually covered by the leaves. The fruit is nonornamental.

RATE / SPACING: Growth is slow. Plants from pint-sized to quart-sized containers are spaced 8 to 12 inches apart.

SPECIES: *A. arifolium* (air-i-*foe*-lee-um), named for its arrow-shaped leaves, is commonly called halberd ginger. It hails from the woodlands of Tennessee to Virginia and Alabama to Florida. Hardy in Zones 6 to 9, it reaches 5 to 8 inches tall, spreads 18 inches wide, and displays evergreen, arrow-shaped, 2- to 6½-inch-long, 1¾- to 6½-inch-wide leaves. Colored glossy dark green with whitish gray mottling, they far overshadow the purplish flowers of early spring to early summer.

A. canadense (kan-a-*den*-see), named for its native habitat, Canada, is commonly called Canadian wild ginger, Indian snakeroot, or Indian ginger. Probably the most widely distributed species in the genus, its native range is eastern North America from New Brunswick to South Carolina, west to Missouri. It is hardy in Zones 3 to 8, reaches 4 to 6 inches tall, spreads indefinitely, and displays deciduous, paired, 6-inch-wide, kidney-shaped, leathery, dull gray-green leaves that originate from underground creeping stems. The solitary bell-shaped, purplish to reddish brown flowers, mostly obscured by the leaves, appear in mid spring. The fleshy fruit that follows wages the same struggle for recognition. Contact with the foliage causes dermatitis in sensitive persons, and the rhizomes, which smell much like *Zingiber officinale* (the popular seasoning of the East Indies), have been used as its substitute. Historically, Canadian herbalists used a preparation of *A. canadense* for treating heart palpitations. Native North Americans employed the species to normalize irregular menstrual cycles, as a flavoring, and as an agent to mask spoiled meat. Early settlers prepared a tonic for easing stomach gas, stimulating the appetite, reducing fever, and increasing perspiration.

A. caudatum (kaw-*day*-tum), named for the tail-like projections of the calyx lobes (the leafy component of the flowers), is commonly called British Columbia wild ginger. Native from British Columbia to California and hardy in Zones 5 or 6 to 9, this species reaches 7 inches tall and spreads 2 feet wide. The heart-shaped dark green evergreen leaves are arranged in pairs, reach up to 6 inches long by 6 inches wide, and arise from the base of the plant on 7-inch-long stems. The solitary, brownish purple flowers display the long taillike appendages (projecting backward up to 2 inches) for which the species is named. Borne during spring, the flowers are more interesting than ornamental. The fruit, a fleshy, globose capsule, also is of little ornamental significance.

A. europaeum (you-row-*pee*-um), meaning of Europe, is commonly called European wild ginger. Even though the species is not native to North America, it is the most frequently cultivated ginger in the New World. It is hardy in Zones 4 to 7 or 8, reaches 5 inches tall, and spreads to 14 inches wide. The evergreen, leathery, dark glossy green, paired, heart-shaped to kidney-shaped leaves, to 3 inches wide, are magnificently handsome (and account for its wide acceptance). The springtime, single, greenish to purple or brown, ½-inch-wide flowers are divided into three pointed lobes and often obscured by the foliage. The fruit, too, is usually hidden by the foliage and thus is of limited ornamental value.

A. hartwegii (hart-*wee*-gee-eye), commonly called Sierra wild ginger or cyclamen-leaved ginger, is hardy in Zones 5 to 9 and hails from Oregon and California. Its evergreen kidney-shaped leaves reach

5 inches wide and are dark green with silvery vena-tion and a grayish overlay. It reaches 4 to 6 inches tall, spreads 1 foot wide, and bears its dark brown to purplish flowers underneath the leaves during spring. 'Silver Heart' displays dark green leaves that are streaked through their centers with a broad splash of silvery-gray.

A. kumagianum (*kume*-age-ee-aye-num), Yaku-shima ginger, a rare Japanese species hardy in Zones 6 to 9, is exceptional for its shiny green, silvery-mar-bled foliage.

A. memmingeri (mem-*in*-jer-eye), named for Ed-ward Meminger, is related to *A. virginicum* but dif-fers in that its leaves are more rounded and the ca-lyxes of the flowers are shorter and broader.

A. shuttleworthii (shut-el-*worth*-ee-eye), com-monly called mottled wild ginger, is hardy in Zones 6 or 7 to 9 and is our showiest native ginger. Unfor-tunately, it is also one of the slowest growing and most difficult to obtain. Native from Virginia to Al-abama, it reaches 8 inches tall and spreads to 14 inches wide. Its leaves are semievergreen (in most areas, fully evergreen), thick, leathery, single or paired, to 3 inches wide, and attractively mottled with silvery-gray. Borne during mid summer, the urn-shaped, $\frac{3}{5}$- to $\frac{4}{5}$-inch-long flowers, like the leaves, are mottled. Inside they are solid purple. 'Callaway' displays smaller, silvery mottled and veined leaves.

A. splendens (*splen*-dens), hardy in Zones 5 to 9, reaches 6 inches tall, spreads vigorously by short rhi-zomes, and displays dark green, gray-mottled leaves.

A. virginicum (ver-*jin*-i-kum), commonly called Virginia wild ginger, southern wild ginger, heart leaf ginger, or black snakeweed, ranges from Virginia to North Carolina and is hardy to Zone 5. Typically, it reaches 6 to 8 inches tall and displays evergreen, heart-shaped leaves that are single, paired, or ar-ranged in groups of three. Each blade reaches 3 inches wide and frequently is mottled light and dark green.

CULTURE / CARE: The wild gingers are best in humus-rich, acidic soil. If the soil is light-textured, sandy, or gravelly, the best amendments are 6 inches of leaf mold or peat moss. Drought resistance is not very good, so plant gingers in locations that are sheltered from strong winds and that remain naturally moist throughout the season; otherwise, be prepared to water often. Light to dense shade is best in the North, and moderate to dense shade is needed in the South. The most serious pest is foliar nematode, which can mimic fungal decay. Serious diseases are seldom encountered, and no routine maintenance is required.

PROPAGATION: Division should be performed dur-ing spring or fall. Seed sown at the time of ripening germinates the following spring.

Asparagus densiflorus 'Sprengeri'   PLATE 35
Sprenger Asparagus

A tuberous (potato-like), shrubby, horizontally spreading, vinelike ground cover, Sprenger aspara-gus ranges from 2 to 3 feet tall (when unsupported) and spreads 2 to 3 feet wide. Often planted along the southern coasts and in the Deep South, it is known to many northern gardeners as a florist's plant, com-mon to cemetery urns and flower arrangements. As a ground cover, it excels in small-sized to moderate-sized areas and often is used to nice effect in raised beds and along the tops of retaining walls and sea walls, over which its vibrant green sprays of foliage can gracefully cascade. Because it tends to climb upon other plants, it should be used only by itself or underneath open-canopied trees and tall shrubs. It is not bothered by airborne salt, hence its usefulness along the coasts. Very little foot traffic is tolerated.

SCIENTIFIC NAME: *Asparagus densiflorus* 'Sprengeri' (a-*spare*-i-gus den-si-*floe*-rus *spreng*-er-eye). *Asparagus* is an ancient Greek name that is thought to come from *a*, intensive, and *sparasso*, to tear, referring to the prickles of some asparagus species. Another source claims that it comes from the Greek *spargan*, to swell, but does not say why. *Densiflorus* means densely flowered. The cultivar is named for Carl Sprenger (1846–1917), the German nursery owner who introduced it.

HARDINESS / ORIGIN: Zones 8 to 10 or 11; South Africa.

LEAVES / FLOWERS / FRUIT: The unusual, flattish, needlelike leaves are technically known as clado-phylls. Either borne alone or in groups of three or six, they range from $\frac{3}{8}$ to $1\frac{1}{4}$ inches long, curve slightly upward, and are colored light green. The flowers, borne from summer through fall, are $\frac{1}{4}$ inch wide, white to pale pink, mildly scented, but not of much ornamental value. The fruit, on the other hand, consists of numerous $\frac{1}{4}$- to $\frac{1}{2}$-inch-wide fleshy berries that change from green to red during the winter.

RATE / SPACING: Growth is slow to moderate. Plants from quart-sized to gallon-sized containers are spaced $2\frac{1}{2}$ to $3\frac{1}{2}$ feet apart.

HORTICULTURAL SELECTIONS: 'Sprengeri Deflexus', similar to 'Sprengeri' but with broader cladophylls and a metallic sheen; 'Sprengeri Nanus' and 'Spren-geri Compactus', both shorter and less open in habit; 'Sprengeri Robustus', more vigorous.

OTHER SPECIES: *A. officinalis* (oh-fis-i-*nay*-lis), com-mon asparagus, hails from southern Europe, reaches

3 feet tall, and spreads indefinitely. A superb backdrop plant, it is very finely textured with 1-inch-long, light green, wispy, slightly spurred cladophylls. Its flowers are small and ornamentally insignificant, but lead to bright red, ⅜-inch-wide, globose berries. Significantly more hardy than *A. densiflorus* 'Sprengeri', it is hardy to Zone 4. Variety *inermis* lacks spurs; var. *pseudoscaber*, native from Yugoslavia to the western Ukraine, reaches 4 feet tall, with longitudinally striped, warty branches; var. *pseudoscaber* 'Spitzenschleier' is said to be more graceful appearing than the species.

CULTURE / CARE: Loamy, well-drained, neutral to slightly acidic soil with good drainage is best. Drought detracts from the appearance of asparagus more than it threatens its survival, so if a neat, attractive, vibrant appearance is important to you, irrigate during extended dry periods. Asparagus prefers full sun to light shade. Particularly along its northern range, better color is obtained when grown in full sun. Pests include asparagus fern caterpillars, aphids, thrips, and scales. Diseases are blights, root rot, and crown gall. Yellowing often results from overwatering in poorly drained soils. Maintenance includes clipping plants back as they outgrow their bounds or become ragged looking.

PROPAGATION: Cuttings taken during spring root easily. Division is successful whenever the soil can be kept moist. Seed germinates in four to six weeks, but the seed coat must be cracked before sowing.

Astilbe   PLATE 36

Among the most easily cultured, most colorful, most durable, and most forgiving of ground covers, astilbes are great plants for all gardeners. They usually display a low, leafy, stemless habit, noninvasive horizontal spread, and upright floral stalks that ascend from a few inches to more than 4 feet. Alone or in combination with different species such as ferns, hostas, irises, bergenias, and many of the clump-forming ornamental grasses, they may be used on a small to large scale and are splendid as coarse-textured colorful turf substitutes. A small grouping of astilbes can be used as a facing to statuary, boulders, shrubs, and small trees. A broad facing of astilbes can literally transform an ordinary fence into a landscape spectacle and, when used in masses about the entrance of a home or building, their vibrant flowers and crisp foliage can help extend a cheerful greeting to visitors. Astilbes can also be used to line garden paths, soften pool edges, and enhance stream banks. Regardless of their use, they can be counted upon for nearly foolproof performance. With their vibrant upright clusters of tiny flowers, which in some spe-

cies are commercially valued as cut flowers, astilbes brighten the most dreary garden corner. They are said to grow underneath black walnut trees (*Juglans nigra*). No foot traffic is tolerated.

SCIENTIFIC NAME: *Astilbe* (a-*stil*-bee) comes from the Greek *a*, no, and *stilbe*, brightness, which, depending upon the reference, alludes to either the relatively colorless flowers or leaves. Considering the multitude of colorfully flowered/foliaged species and cultivars, it is a wonder that astilbe growers have not petitioned for a name change.

HARDINESS / ORIGIN: Zones 4 or 5 to 8 or 9. Two species come from North America but those that are useful as ground covers hail from eastern Asia.

LEAVES / FLOWERS / FRUIT: The leaves of most astilbes are two or three times compound, composed of several deeply toothed, more or less oval leaflets. They are course-textured, very attractive, and set the perfect stage for the profusion of bright, colorful (from white to purple to deep red), tiny flowers that are arranged in dense spike-shaped panicles and borne for an extended period during the summer season. The fruit is nonornamental.

RATE / SPACING: Growth is slow to moderate. Plants from quart-sized to gallon-sized containers are spaced 15 to 18 inches apart.

SPECIES: *A.* × *arendsii* (a-*renz*-ee-eye), named after George Arends (1862–1952) of Rosdorf, Germany, an avid hybridizer of astilbes, is commonly called hybrid astilbe, false spirea, meadowsweet, Arends' astilbe, or goat's beard. With masses of coarse-textured leaves and a height that ranges from 2 to 3½ feet, this is a rather imposing species. Typically, it spreads 2 to 3 feet wide and displays compound leaves that are doubly or triply divided. Each leaflet is oval to oblong with double-toothed edges and dark green to bronzy coloration. Its magnificent floral display occurs during summer and consists of 2½- to 3½-foot-tall stalks that are topped with 8- to 12-inch-long, erect clusters of thousands of tiny florets from white to salmon in color. Some of the most popular horticultural selections include 'Avalanche', with snowy-white flowers and slightly arching stems; 'Bremen', with deep carmine-rose flowers; 'Bridal Veil', with white flowers, 24 inches tall; 'Cattleya', with light pink flowers on stalks to 3 feet tall; 'Deutschland', with pure white flowers on 2-foot stems, compact habit, and vigorous growth; 'Diamond', with white flowers on stalks to 2½ feet tall; 'Emden', with soft pink flowers on 2- to 3-foot-tall stalks; 'Erica', 3 feet tall, with open clusters of clear pink flowers; 'Europa', with light pink flowers and deep green foliage; 'Fanal', with dark red flowers arranged in a narrow cluster; 'Federsee', with carmine-rose flowers; 'Garnet', with carmine-red flowers;

'Glow', with bright red flowers and compact form; 'Irrlicht', 2 to 2½ feet tall, with rosy white flowers and dark green leaves; 'Ostrich Plume', with showy salmon-pink flowers on nodding stalks to 30 inches tall; 'Purple Blaze', to 4 feet tall, with large purple flower clusters; 'Red Sentinel', with deep purplish red flowers in loose clusters, fine-textured reddish green leaves; 'Rheinland', with carmine-pink flowers on 2-foot-tall stalks; 'Snowdrift', with clear white flowers on 2½-foot-tall stalks; 'Spinell', with salmon-red flowers atop 3-foot-tall stalks; 'Vesuvius', with red flowers; 'White Gloria', early blooming, white flowers on 2-foot-tall stalks.

A. chinensis var. *pumila* (chi-*nen*-sis *pew*-mi-la), commonly called dwarf Chinese astilbe, is native to China. This tough little selection is far more robust than its 8- to 12-inch-tall, 8- to 12-inch-wide stature would imply. Often you can make five or more divisions of this plant at the end of the growing season, each as big as the original clump at the beginning of the season. The leaves are two or three times divided with 2- to 3½-inch-long, hairy, tooth-edged, oval leaflets. During mid to late summer, stout clusters of tiny rose-colored flowers appear on stout stalks above the mass of foliage. 'Finale', reaching 20 inches tall with bright pink flowers; 'Intermezzo', reaching nearly 30 inches tall, with salmon-pink flowers; 'Serenade', to 20 inches tall with pinkish red flowers; 'Vision', 12 to 14 inches tall, with light purple flowers.

A. × *crispa* (*kris*-pa), named for its crisped (i.e., crinkled) leaves, is commonly called crisped astilbe or hybrid astilbe. Very popular, it ranges from 4 to 6 inches tall and includes a number of small, low-growing, ground-covering selections that are noteworthy for their bronzy, deeply crinkled foliage and flowers that range from white to pink to red. Some authorities include this group among the hybrid group *A.* × *arendsii*. 'Liliput', with salmon-pink flowers; 'Perkeo', with dark pink flowers and shiny dark green crinkled leaves;

A. × *rosea* (*row*-zee-a), named for its pink flowers, is commonly called rose astilbe. It ranges from 2 to 3 feet tall (in flower) and spreads 2 feet wide. The flowers occur in summer. This hybrid species has given rise to two splendid selections: 'Peach Blossom', reaching 3 to 4 feet tall, introduced by George Arends in 1903, noteworthy for its large panicles of salmon-pink flowers; 'Queen Alexandra', similar to 'Peach Blossom' but with deep pink flowers.

A. simplicifolia (sim-pli-si-*foe*-lee-a), named for its leaves, which are simple instead of compound like those of most astilbes, is commonly called star astilbe. Native to Japan, it reaches 1 to 1½ feet tall and is graced with white flowers during summer. Al-though the species has long been cultivated, its hybrids are now more widely available than the species itself. Some of the more common varieties and hybrid selections are var. *alba,* with relatively pure white flowers; 'Aphrodite', with salmon-red flowers and a compact habit to 14 inches tall; 'Atrorosea', with rose-salmon flowers that ascend to a height of 20 inches; 'Bronce Elegans', with bronzy foliage and rose-pink flowers in late summer; 'Bronze Queen', with creamy flowers and bronze foliage; 'Hennie Graafland', reaching 16 inches tall, with upright trusses of delicate pink flowers; 'Inncerry', with vibrant pink flowers in mid spring and bronzy green foliage; 'Inshriach Pink', with bronze leaves and clear pink flowers; 'Purple Cats', with purple flowers; 'Snowdrift', with white flowers; and 'Sprite', a very popular cultivar displaying vibrant deep shiny bronzy green foliage and shell-pink flowers on stalks from 12 to 18 inches tall.

CULTURE / CARE: Astilbes grow best in cool, well-drained, humus-rich, acidic soil. The relatively shallow roots make these plants sensitive to drought, so make every effort to keep their soil moist. Astilbes need light to moderate shade, but tolerate full sun in alpine and coastal areas where the soil remains cool and moist. Pests include Japanese beetles and red spider mites, and the most common diseases are powdery mildew, wilt, and root rot. For the care-free gardener, maintenance will be minimal or nonexistent. The perfectionist, however, will trim off dried flower stalks as soon as the blooms fade and divide plants when they become crowded to improve flower production the following year.

PROPAGATION: Division in spring or fall is the standard method of propagation; the medium should be heated to 70 to 75°F and kept moist for two or three weeks, then the temperature reduced to 40°F.

Athyrium filix-femina   PLATE 37
Lady Fern

Lacy and delicate in appearance, the lovely lady fern displays lush, soft green foliage and slender, often burgundy-tinged leafstalks. To the surprise of even many avid gardeners, it is a splendid ground cover on a large or small scale, particularly in naturalistic landscapes. It arches gracefully, reaches 1½ to 3 feet tall by 1½ to 2 feet wide, and is excellent when planted randomly among lower-growing ground covers such as partridge berry, bearberry, or plumbago. Woodland borders take on an inviting lushness when lined with lady fern, and deciduous trees surrounded by a communal carpet of lady fern become harmoniously united. In the Pacific Northwest, where it propagates itself so freely from spores that it can become weedy, Indians reportedly made a tea from the stems that was said to ease the pain of labor. No foot traffic is tolerated.

SCIENTIFIC NAME: *Athyrium filix-femina* (a-*thee*-ree-um *fee*-liks-*fem*-i-na). *Athyrium* is probably from the Greek, *athyros,* doorless, referring to the late-opening spore covers. *Filix-femina,* lady fern, is a reference to the delicateness of this species in comparison to male fern, *Dryopteris filix-mas.*

HARDINESS / ORIGIN: Zones 3 to 8; widely distributed along both coasts, extending inward to the Plains States.

LEAVES / FLOWERS / FRUIT: The fronds are deciduous, large, to 30 inches long by 10 inches wide, broadly lance-shaped, compound, and twice divided with pinnae to 8 inches long by 1½ inches wide. Each pinna carries about 12 pairs of pinnules that are variable in shape, typically deeply cut, toothed along their margins, and colored bright green.

RATE / SPACING: Growth is moderate. Plants from pint-sized to ½-gallon-sized containers are spaced 10 to 14 inches apart.

HORTICULTURAL SELECTIONS: Many selections are available; the more popular include var. *angustum* (northern lady fern), native from Newfoundland south to Virginia and west to Iowa, with fronds that narrow toward their bases; 'Aristatum', with long pointed pinnae; var. *asplenioides* (southern lady fern), native from Rhode Island south to Florida and west to Texas, with fronds that are broad toward their bases; 'Crispum', with curly fronds; 'Minutissimum', reaching only 6 to 8 inches tall; 'Plumosum', with very finely divided foliage; 'Vernoniae Cristatum', with overlapping and curly pinnae, stems shiny crimson, reaching 2 to 3 feet tall.

OTHER SPECIES: *A. nipponicum* (ni-*pon*-i-kum), Japanese lady fern, is hardy in Zones 4 to 9. Sometimes listed as *A. goeringianum,* it displays dark green, tooth-edged, compound foliage. Its habit is drooping, and its mature height reaches 1½ feet. 'Pictum', Japanese painted lady fern, is noteworthy for its purple stems and leaves that are colorfully decorated with central gray and wine-colored markings. There are also rare crested and dwarf forms of 'Pictum' in circulation. 'Red Select', shows intensely reddish burgundy coloration in the center of the leaflets.

A. pycnocarpon (pik-no-*kar*-pon), narrow-leaved spleenwort, is an impressive, stately, robust species that reaches 3 feet tall and colonizes to several feet wide. Sometimes listed as *Diplazium pycnocarpon,* it has medium to deep green leaves that reach 3 feet long by 6 inches wide and are composed of numerous pairs of sharply pointed, narrowly triangular leaflets. Hardy to Zones 4 to 8.

A. thelypteroides (thee-lip-*tear*-oy-deez), named

for its resemblance to the genus *Thelypteris,* is commonly named silvery glade fern. Native to eastern North America, it is hardy in Zones 1 to 9, reaches 2 to 3 feet tall, spreads indefinitely (at a moderate pace), and should be spaced 12 to 16 inches apart. Its robust yellowish green leaves, which taper at both ends, reach 1 to 2½ feet long by 6 to 10 inches wide. Overall, this is one of the most lush and graceful of the hardy ferns.

CULTURE / CARE: For the most part, *Athyrium* species are best in moist, well-drained, highly organic, acidic loam, but tolerate a wide range of soil types. *Athyrium pycnocarpon* is best in neutral or slightly alkaline soil. In all cases, make every attempt to keep the soil moist during extended hot, dry weather, and plant these ferns out of windy locations. They prefer moderate to relatively heavy shade. The most common diseases and pests are leaf spot, slugs, and aphids. No maintenance is required.

PROPAGATION: Division of clumps is effective during spring or fall.

Atriplex semibaccata PLATE 38
Creeping Saltbush, Australian Saltbush

Creeping saltbush is a mounding, horizontally spreading, mat-forming, deep-rooted, woody ground cover—primarily planted in desert areas of the Southwest. It ranges from 1 to 1½ feet tall and spreads over 6 feet wide. Considered relatively fire resistant, it is recommended for use as a facing plant for commercial buildings, homes, and parks. It tolerates infertile, highly saline soil, a great deal of heat, but no foot traffic.

SCIENTIFIC NAME: *Atriplex semibaccata* (at-ri-pleks sem-eye-ba-*kay*-ta). *Atriplex* comes from the Greek *a,* no, and *traphein,* nourishment, possibly in reference to the plants' preference for infertile desert soils. *Semibaccata* means partially berried.

HARDINESS / ORIGIN: Zones 8 to 10; Australia.

LEAVES / FLOWERS / FRUIT: The gray, evergreen, fine-textured leaves are densely set and range from 1 to 1½ inches long. They are rather unevenly toothed about their edges and are the chief ornamental attribute of this durable plant. The flowers and fruit are very small and nonornamental.

RATE / SPACING: Growth is fast. Plants from 1- to 2-gallon-sized containers are spaced 3½ to 4½ feet apart.

HORTICULTURAL SELECTIONS: 'Corto', with uniform habit, 10 inches tall, gray-green foliage.

CULTURE / CARE: Creeping saltbush grows well in infertile, saline, sandy, well-drained soils. It tolerates drought and seldom requires watering once established. Even so, it achieves its best appearance and greatest vigor if given an occasional deep watering during the summer. It prefers full sun to light shade. No serious pests or diseases seem to affect it, and little routine maintenance is needed.

PROPAGATION: Stem cuttings may be rooted in a very porous medium during the growing season.

Aubrieta deltoidea   PLATE 39

Purple Rock Cress, False Rock Cress, Aubrietia, Aubretia

A matlike, herbaceous, horizontally spreading, slightly mound-forming, rhizomatous ground cover, purple rock cress reaches 3 to 6 inches tall and spreads 1 to 1½ feet wide. It is attractive for its handsome foliage as well as for its late-spring to early summer flowers. In the landscape it is at its best planted between large stones in rock gardens or allowed to trail over a retaining wall. As a small-scale general cover or a foreground plant for herbaceous perennial border plantings, it combines nicely with candytuft, phlox, alyssum, and other perennials of contrasting floral color. No foot traffic is tolerated.

SCIENTIFIC NAME: *Aubrieta deltoidea* (awe-*bree*-ta / awe-bree-*ay*-ta del-*toy*-dee-a). *Aubrieta* is named after French botanical artist Claude Aubriet (1668–1743). *Deltoidea*, three-angled, from the Greek letter *delta*, and *oidea*, likeness, refers to the triangular shape of the flower petals.

HARDINESS / ORIGIN: Zones 4 to 8, performing best in the northern part of its range; Greece.

LEAVES / FLOWERS / FRUIT: The evergreen, grayish green leaves are 1¼ inches long by ¼ inch wide, elongate, prominently toothed, and hairy. The ¾-inch-wide rose-lilac to rose-purple four-petaled flowers are borne from mid spring to early summer. The fruit that follows may reach ¾ inch long but is nonornamental.

RATE / SPACING: Growth is moderate. Plants from 3- to 4-inch-diameter containers are spaced 8 to 14 inches apart.

HORTICULTURAL SELECTIONS: There is some disagreement as to the exact classification of cultivars of *A. deltoidea*. Some horticulturists believe many to be hybrids with *A. deltoidea* as the dominant contributor to the gene pool. The most popular include 'Aurea', with golden-green leaves and blue to violet flowers; 'Aureo-variegata', leaves green with yellow variegation; 'Barker's Double', with purplish blue double flowers; 'Bengale', with lilac-blue, purple, and red semidouble flowers; 'Bob Sanders', with semidouble reddish purple flowers; 'Borsch's White', with white flowers; 'Bougainvillea', with violet flowers and dwarf, compact habit; 'Campbellii', somewhat taller with large purple flowers; 'Carnival', with

numerous purple-violet flowers; 'Dr. Mules', much like 'Carnival'; 'Gloriosa', with large, soft rose-colored flowers; 'Graeca', with large, light blue flowers; 'Greencourt Purple', with double bluish purple flowers; 'Henslow Purple', with bright purple flowers; 'J. S. Barker', with bluish flowers and white centers; 'Leichtlinii', with numerous bright reddish crimson flowers and dwarf habit; 'Moerheim', with large mauve flowers throughout the summer; 'Mrs. Rodewald', with large carmen flowers; 'Parkinsii', lavender flowers with white centers; 'Purple Cascade', with purple flowers and compact habit; 'Purple Gem', with blue flowers and silvery-white-margined red leaves; 'Red Cascade', with red flowers; 'Rosea Splendens', with bright rose-colored flowers; 'Royal Blue', with dark blue flowers; 'Royal Red', with flowers in various shades of magenta and red; 'Variegata', leaves with creamy white variegation; 'Vindictive', with rose-red, 1-inch-wide flowers; 'Whitewell Gem', with bright violet-purple blossoms.

CULTURE / CARE: Purple rock cress is at its very best in slightly acidic to slightly alkaline (pH 6.5 to 7.5), well-drained, sandy loam. It tolerates drought fairly well but appreciates having the soil kept slightly moist—especially during the summer. Full sun to light shade suits it well in the North, but light shade is required in the South. The primary problems are fungal damping off (usually only a threat in poorly drained soils), aphids, and mealybugs. Although fussy gardeners trim off the dried flower heads following bloom, maintenance needs are few if any.

PROPAGATION: Seed sown in spring germinates in two or three weeks at temperatures of 70 to 75°F; flowering will occur the following spring. Stem cuttings taken immediately after the plant blooms root well and, although it is not absolutely necessary, the application of 1000 ppm IBA/talc is helpful. Division should be performed during spring.

Aurinia saxatilis   PLATE 40

Golden Tuft, Basket-of-gold, Golden Alyssum, Rock Madwort, Gold Dust, Madwort

A very old-fashioned European herb, this tough, colorful ground cover is useful as a small-scale ground cover or accent plant. In herbaceous borders with such companions as sedums, candytuft, hen and chickens, and junipers, it adds textural contrast and seasonal color. In a rock garden it may be used as a specimen, and at the top of a retaining wall, its prolific, cascading flower-topped branches ensure that spring begins with grace and color. Indeed, the brightness of its yellow flowers takes a back seat to no others. Later, the grayish green foliage takes over and for the remainder of the season infuses a subtle yet pleasant element of subdued color. Horizontally growing, this low spreader reaches 6 to 10 inches tall and spreads 12 to 18 inches wide. Unfortunately for the southern gardener, it declines and dies if exposed to prolonged heat. No foot traffic is tolerated.

SCIENTIFIC NAME: *Aurinia saxatilis* (awe-*rin*-i-a saks-a-*til*-is). *Aurinia* comes from the Latin *aureus,* golden, a reference to the flowers. *Saxatilis* means inhabiting rocky places.

HARDINESS / ORIGIN: Zones 4 to 8; Europe.

LEAVES / FLOWERS / FRUIT: The spatula-shaped to linear evergreen leaves are grayish green due to the presence of white hairs on both sides and reach 2 to 5 inches long by ½ inch wide. The showy springtime flowers arise on 12-inch-tall stems, are bright golden-yellow, and reach ¼ inch wide. The fruit is non-ornamental.

RATE / SPACING: Growth is slow. Plants from 3- to 4-inch-diameter containers are spaced 10 to 14 inches apart.

HORTICULTURAL SELECTIONS: 'Citrinum', with many light yellow flowers; 'Compactum', most frequently cultivated, with light yellow flowers, more dense-growing than the species; 'Dudley Nevill Variegated', reaching 8 inches tall and noteworthy for its leaves with grayish white edges and for its creamy apricot flowers; 'Flore Pleno', with double flowers; 'Gold Ball' ('Goldkugel'), 8 inches tall, with globelike habit; 'Golden Globe', reaching only 6 inches tall, with bright yellow flowers; 'Nanum', more compact and lower growing than the species; 'Plenum', with double yellow flowers; 'Silver Queen', with lemon yellow flowers and compact habit; 'Sulphurea', with sulfur-yellow flowers; 'Sunny Border Apricot', with apricot-colored flowers; 'Tom Thumb', a vigorous selection reaching only 3 to 6 inches tall.

CULTURE / CARE: Nearly any acidic to neutral well-drained soil is acceptable. Drought tolerance is pretty good also, yet golden tuft appears best when the soil is kept slightly moist. It prefers full sun to light shade, with flowering being somewhat more profuse in full sun. Diseases such as leaf spot and crown rot are more common if the soil is poorly drained. Pests include aphids and soil mealybugs but are seldom serious. Maintenance includes mowing or shearing plantings after bloom to promote branching and to stimulate new growth.

PROPAGATION: Stem tip cuttings taken during late spring and early summer are easy to propagate; they should be treated with 1000 ppm IBA/talc, stuck in a very porous medium, and removed from mist as soon as they are rooted to prevent crown rot. Division, after flowering, can also be performed. Seed sown during late summer germinates in three to four weeks at soil temperatures of 70 to 85°F.

Azorella trifurcata   PLATE 41

A low, dense, creeping, herbaceous perennial often listed as *Bolax glebaria,* this species ranges from 1½ to 2½ inches tall and spreads to more than 12 inches wide. It is expensive due to its scarcity and slow growth; therefore, most gardeners use it as a rock garden specimen or accent plant. For those who can afford it (or are extremely patient), it may be employed as a small-scale to moderate-scale turf substitute. As such, its dense habit and deep green leaves give the appearance of artificial turf, and on level or sloping soil it controls erosion. It also conforms well to contours and thus is prized by creative gardeners who like to simulate waves by planting it on top of undulating soil. The leaves are very glossy and feel and look like plastic. To me, it gives the impression of dark green patio carpeting, especially in the case of the dwarf form. Limited foot traffic is tolerated.

SCIENTIFIC NAME: *Azorella trifurcata.* (az-oh-*rel*-a tri-fur-*kay*-ta). *Azorella* seems to refer to the Azores, but since the native range of this genus is South America, the meaning is questionable. *Trifurcata* refers to the three segmented tips of the leaves.

HARDINESS / ORIGIN: Zones 5 or 6 to 7; Peru, Chile, Ecuador, temperate South America, Falkland Islands, Antarctic islands.

LEAVES / FLOWERS / FRUIT: The evergreen, simple, opposite, crowded, 1-inch-long, ⅜-inch-wide leaves are tipped with three to five sharp points and each has a central dark green vein below. Colored vibrant, glossy, medium to dark green (lighter green below), they are thick and stiff to the touch. Not reliably produced from one year to the next, the tiny flowers with golden-yellow petals are arranged in groups of four and borne during summer.

RATE / SPACING: Growth is slow. Plants from 3- to 4-inch diameter containers are spaced 6 to 8 inches apart.

HORTICULTURAL SELECTIONS: 'Nana', a compact dwarf selection, seldom exceeding ¾ inch tall.

CULTURE / CARE: This species is best in gravelly, well-drained soil, and seems to be fairly adaptable to pH. It is very tolerant of heat and drought, and although an occasional deep watering may be to some benefit, it is rarely required. It prefers full sun, but tolerates light shade. Damping off may occur if the soil is too rich or does not drain adequately or if there is insufficient air movement. Little or no maintenance is usually required, but should its vigor become reduced or plantings thin out, mowing or division may prove helpful.

PROPAGATION: Cuttings root quite well in summer and fall when treated with 2000 to 3000 ppm IBA/talc. Division, the most common method of propagation, is successful during spring and fall.

Baccharis pilularis   PLATE 42
Coyote Bush

Reaching 1 to 2 feet tall and spreading to 10 feet wide, this low, prostrate, woody shrub is often recommended as much for its fire-retardant properties as for its ability to cover the ground. Along the West Coast and in desert areas, baccharis is often planted around building entrances and perimeters and along sidewalks where it can inhibit fires that might be started by careless people who toss their cigarettes into the bushes. Aside from resisting the efforts of would-be arsonists, baccharis is utilitarian in its ability to stabilize steep sloping banks. It may be used on a moderate to large scale as a general-purpose cover. It is highly resistant to salt spray and thus is useful in coastal regions. Its tolerance to heat and drought has led some authorities to claim that it is the most dependable ground cover for desert regions. No foot traffic is tolerated.

SCIENTIFIC NAME: *Baccharis pilularis* (*bak*-a-ris pil-you-*lay*-ris). *Baccharis* is named after Bacchus, the Greek god of wine; a spicy extract from some species was mixed with wine. *Pilularis* means with globular fruit.

HARDINESS / ORIGIN: Zones 7 to 10 or 11; dry regions of Oregon and California.

LEAVES / FLOWERS / FRUIT: The primary ornamental attribute of this ground cover is its dark green, evergreen, ¾-inch-long leaves that are coated with a sticky substance and are attractively toothed along their edges. The whitish yellow flowers of summer, on the other hand, are nonornamental. The dry, nutlike fruits that follow are also nonornamental. Since female plants produce a messy, cottony material, male clones are usually propagated.

RATE / SPACING: Growth is fast. Plants from 1- to 2-gallon-sized containers are spaced 3 to 6 feet apart.

HORTICULTURAL SELECTIONS: Var. *consanguinea,* more compact than the species; 'Pigeon Point', with larger, lighter green leaves and a more aggressive nature (reported to reach 9 feet wide in four years, with a mounding habit); 'Twin Peaks #2', with smaller dark green leaves and a moderate growth rate, eventually becoming 6 to 12 inches high by 6 or more feet wide.

CULTURE / CARE: This species is at its best when planted in full sun in dry, well-drained, sandy, acidic to neutral soil. It is extremely drought tolerant, so little or no supplemental water is needed once it becomes established. No serious pests have been reported, but diseases such as black mold and rust are sometimes troublesome. Maintenance involves watering regularly the first year until established, misting periodically to remove dust from the foliage, and shearing or mowing plantings in early spring to neaten their appearance.

PROPAGATION: Cuttings taken throughout the year root with relatively good results.

Begonia grandis   PLATE 43
Hardy Begonia

Either as a specimen in the perennial border or as a moderate-scale to large-scale general cover, this begonia is a lovely addition to the landscape. That it is considerably hardier than many other begonias makes it a bit of a curiosity. Selecting a site of high visibility, such as near an entrance or alongside a path, allows the greatest number of people to appreciate its interesting foliage and flowers. It is of intermediate height (8 to 24 inches tall), spreads several feet wide, has succulent foliage and stems, and is compatible with black walnut (*Juglans nigra*). No foot traffic is tolerated.

SCIENTIFIC NAME: *Begonia grandis* (be-*go*-nee-a *grandis*). *Begonia* commemorates Michael Begon (1638–1710), a governor of French Canada. Another source lists him as a botanist; possibly, he was both. *Grandis,* large or showy, probably refers to the flowers. This species was formerly called *B. evansiana* and may sometimes still be listed under this name.

HARDINESS / ORIGIN: Zones 7 or even 6 (when protected by mulch during winter) to 10; China, Japan, and the Malay Peninsula.

LEAVES / FLOWERS / FRUIT: The leaves are succulent, oval-shaped, to 6 inches wide by 8 inches long, with irregularly toothed edges. On top, the veins are suffused with red and are quite striking against the sparsely haired, dark green blades. Underneath, the veins are even more intensely red and are very eye catching when lifted by the wind. The showy, pinkish white, fragrant flowers of late summer and fall reach 1½ inches wide. The fruit, a three-winged capsule, is relatively ornamental as it develops attractive tones of pink during maturation.

RATE / SPACING: Growth is moderate. Plants from quart-sized to gallon-sized containers are spaced 1 to 2 feet apart.

HORTICULTURAL SELECTIONS: 'Alba', with white flowers.

CULTURE / CARE: Adaptable to most well-drained soils with acidic to neutral pH, hardy begonia displays only fair tolerance to drought and should be sheltered from drying winds. Its pests include mealybugs, aphids, mites, thrips, nematodes, and the greenhouse whitefly, while the diseases to which it is susceptible include leaf blight, powdery mildew, leaf spot, root rot, damping off, stem rot, crown gall, and viruses. Little or no maintenance is required.

PROPAGATION: Stem cuttings root easily and quickly during summer. Division is best accomplished during spring and early fall.

Bellis perennis   PLATE 44

English Daisy, True Daisy, Bachelor's Buttons, Marguerite

English daisy is an endearing, low-growing, horizontally spreading, somewhat tuft-forming, colorfully flowered ground cover. Serving well as a facer to shrubs, a small-scale turf substitute, or a walkway edging, it is a plant that is easy to appreciate. Not only are its leaves neat and handsome, its flowers are charming. Often it is used with spring-blooming bulbs, and occasionally it is included in the rock garden.

SCIENTIFIC NAME: *Bellis perennis* (*bell*-is per-*en*-is). *Bellis* is derived from the Latin *bellus,* pretty, in reference to the beautiful flowers. *Perennis,* perennial, also describes the flowers.

HARDINESS / ORIGIN: Zones 4 to 10; Europe.

LEAVES / FLOWERS / FRUIT: The deep green, wavy or somewhat tooth-edged leaves are spatula-shaped or oval-shaped, range from 1 to 2 inches long, and reach ½ to ¾ inch wide. Arranged in rosettes, they are neat and attractive and serve well as a backdrop to the daisylike 1- to 2-inch-wide flowers with yellow centers and white or pink petals that are borne mid to late spring. Held upon 3- to 6-inch-tall upright stems, the flowers give rise to tiny fruit that is nonornamental.

RATE / SPACING: Growth is slow. Plants from 2½- to 3-inch-diameter containers are spaced 8 to 10 inches apart.

HORTICULTURAL SELECTIONS: 'Brilliant', with deep red flowers; 'Carpet', with red, rose, or white, double 1-inch-wide flowers atop 4-inch-tall stems; 'China Pink', with pinkish red flowers; 'Dresden China', with light pink flowers; 'Monstrosa' (Monstrosa Hybrids), with double 3-inch-wide flowers in shades of white, pink, and red; 'Pomponette', with semidouble 1½-inch-wide flowers; 'Prolifera', with multiple flowers borne from upright flower stalks; 'Rob Roy', with double crimson flowers; 'Rosea', with rose-pink flowers; 'Tuberosa', with rose-colored flowers.

CULTURE / CARE: English daisy is not tolerant of drought and should to be sited in organically rich, fertile, moisture-retentive soil. It is adaptable to acid or alkaline conditions. In the North it performs best in full sun or light shade, but in the South it is best in light to moderate shade. Diseases of greatest significance are blight, leaf spot, root rots, aster yellows, and powdery mildew. Other than aphids, English daisy is relatively immune to insects and pests. When plants become crowded, their floral displays decline, but division of the clumps brings back the flowers and stimulates new growth.

PROPAGATION: Division of the clumps is very simple and most successful in spring or early summer. Seed is best sown during fall in a cold frame or garden and will germinate the following spring.

Berberis thunbergii 'Crimson Pygmy'   PLATE 45

Crimson Pygmy Barberry

Crimson pygmy barberry is a splendid, upright-branched, low-spreading, shrubby, dwarf, purple-leaved selection of Japanese barberry, the thorny upright shrub which has been popular for decades as a hedge plant and which, with its sharp thorns, works particularly well for deterring trespassers. Crimson pygmy barberry, like its taller parent, is also often used for hedging, but because of its small stature (1 ½ to 2 feet tall by 2½ to 4½ feet wide), it is more likely to be used as a specimen or for defining borders than for deterring trespassers. Its color is rich purple and therefore it is of great value for the contrast or accent which it brings when combined with selections having green, silvery, or golden leaves.

SCIENTIFIC NAME: *Berberis thunbergii* 'Crimson Pygmy' (*ber*-ber-is thun-*ber*-gee-eye). *Berberis* comes from the Arabic *berberys,* barberry. *Thunbergii* is named after Carl P. Thunberg (1743–1828), a Swedish physician, botanist, and explorer. The cultivar 'Crimson Pygmy' is also sometimes called 'Atropurpurea Nana' or variety *atropurpurea* 'Crimson Pygmy'.

HARDINESS / ORIGIN: Zones 5 to 8; *B. thunbergii* hails from Japan, while the cultivar 'Crimson Pygmy' arose in cultivation in the Netherlands in 1942.

LEAVES / FLOWERS / FRUIT: The deciduous, teardrop-shaped to oblong-shaped, ⅜- to 1-inch-long, ½-inch-wide leaves are alternately arranged and are colored a deep rich purple. The tiny yellow flowers are borne underneath the leaves in spring and are nonornamental. The fruit, an oval-shaped berry, matures to reddish purple during fall.

RATE / SPACING: Growth is slow. Plants from 1- to 2-gallon-sized containers are spaced 2 to 3 feet apart.

HORTICULTURAL SELECTIONS: Other useful dwarf selections of Japanese barberry include 'Bagatelle', only 12 to 16 inches tall, with deep reddish purple glossy foliage; 'Bonanza Gold', 1½ feet tall by 3 feet wide, low spreading, leaves yellowish golden; 'Concorde', with deep purple leaves, upright growth habit, 18 inches tall; 'Globe', with green leaves, a broad globe-shaped habit, 2 to 3 feet tall by 4 to 6 feet wide; 'Intermedia', similar to 'Crimson Pygmy' but faster growing and maturing to 3 feet tall; 'Kobold', to 2 ½ feet tall, with rich green leaves; 'Minor', compact, 3½ feet tall by 5 feet wide, with green leaves; 'Royal Burgundy', similar to 'Crimson Pygmy' but with richer burgundy foliage; 'William Penn', mound-shaped, 3 feet tall by 3 to 4 feet wide, with dark green leaves.

OTHER SPECIES: *B. stenophylla* 'Irwinii' (sten-oh-*fil*-a er-*win*-ee-eye), a selection from the cross between *B. darwinii* and *B. empetrifolia,* is commonly called Irwin's rosemary barberry. It displays a low, broad-spreading, shrubby habit and reaches 1½ feet tall by 1½ to 2½ feet wide. Its leaves are evergreen, 1 inch long by ¼ inch wide, alternately arranged or whorled, and are dark green above and grayish green below. Its flowers are yellow, up to ½ inch wide, and bloom in spring. The fruit, a black to purplish globe-shaped berry, reaches up to ½ inch in diameter. Hardy in Zones 6 to 9 or 10. 'Corallina Compact' forms dense 18-inch-high mounds of glassy dark green foliage.

CULTURE / CARE: Barberries are tolerant of a wide variety of well-drained, acidic soils. They are exceptionally tolerant of drought, and only during prolonged dry spells do they require watering. The green and purple forms are best in full sun to light shade, but light shade may prevent the golden-leaved cultivars from scorching during the heat of summer. Barberries are affected by few diseases and only occasionally have problems with aphids, scales, mealybugs, webworm, and nematodes. They need very little care, except for an occasional pruning.

PROPAGATION: Stem cuttings root relatively well during early summer; they should be placed in a well-drained medium, and treatment with 3000 ppm IBA/talc is helpful.

Bergenia cordifolia   PLATE 46
Heartleaf Bergenia, Pig Squeak

A low, laterally spreading, herbaceous ground cover that produces new plants from short underground stems, heartleaf bergenia reaches up to 12 inches in height and spreads 1 to 2 feet wide. It is one of the leafier-looking ground covers and one of the more durable and slow spreading. For these reasons, it is well suited for use as a general cover or facing plant for small-sized to moderate-sized areas, particularly in locations where its splendid foliage and interesting flowers will be visible to passersby. I like to see it used along entryways, corridors, and in front of statuary. It is often placed near the front of a border or along walks as an edging. Occasionally, it is attractively combined with hostas, ferns or daylilies. It is a very reliable, long-lived ground cover. No foot traffic is tolerated. The common name pig squeak is said to come from the squeaking noise that is made when the foliage is rubbed between one's fingers.

SCIENTIFIC NAME: *Bergenia cordifolia* (ber-*gen*-ee-a kor-di-*foe*-lee-a). *Bergenia* is named for Karl August von Bergen, an eighteenth-century botanist and physician of Frankfurt, Germany. *Cordifolia* means heart-shaped, referring to the leaves.

HARDINESS / ORIGIN: Zones 3 to 8 or 9; Siberia.

LEAVES / FLOWERS / FRUIT: The thick, leathery, shiny, evergreen leaves are not only large (to 12 inches long by 8 inches wide), they are colored a very deep shade of green and are often used in floral arrangements. In fall they become an intriguing shade of purplish bronze. During mid spring, long-lasting, ¼- to ½-inch-wide, nodding, clear rose flowers are borne atop stout flower stalks that ascend to 16 inches. The fruit, a small capsule, is nonornamental.

RATE / SPACING: Growth is moderate to slow. Plants from pint-sized to quart-sized containers are spaced 12 to 15 inches apart.

HORTICULTURAL SELECTIONS: 'Alba', white flowers; 'Perfecta', large purplish bronze leaves and purplish red flowers.

OTHER SPECIES: *B. ciliata* (sil-ee-*aye*-ta), named for its densely haired leaves, is commonly called winter begonia. It hails from western Pakistan, is hardy in Zones 6 to 10, reaches 12 inches tall, and spreads 1 to 2 feet wide. Its bronzy, leathery, evergreen, round to broadly oval leaves are 8 to 14 inches long by 3 to 4 inches wide and edged with teeth. The flowers, which range from white to rose-purple, are borne during late spring. Forma *ligulata* has flowers that are nearly white and leaves that are hairy only along the edges.

B. crassifolia (kras-i-*foe*-lee-a), leather bergenia, has thick leaves. Hardy in Zones 4 to 8, this native of Siberia and Mongolia reaches up to 12 inches tall, spreads 1 to 1½ feet wide, and displays evergreen leaves that are stemless, oblong or roundish, and to 8 inches long by 4½ inches wide. Each leaf is shallowly toothed on its edges and colored medium green. The ¾-inch-wide, pink to purplish, five-petaled flowers are borne during mid winter and spring and sit atop arching 10- to 18-inch-long stalks. The fruit is not ornamentally significant.

B. purpurascens var. *delavayi* (pur-pur-*as*-senz de-*lav*-aye-eye), purple bergenia, is sometimes listed as *B. purpurascens* or *B. beesiana.* It displays large magenta-colored springtime flowers and reaches 15 inches tall. It is hardy to Zones 4 to 9.

B.* × *smithii (*smith*-ee-eye), formed by the cross between *B. cordifolia* and *B. purpurascens,* is the name given to many hybrid cultivars whose origin is not always clear. All are hardy to Zone 4 and flower during later winter or spring. Some of the most popular cultivars include 'Abendglut' ('Evening Glow'), with dark green, large, rounded leaves, more prostrate habit, and rose-red flowers on 12-inch-tall stalks, somewhat less cold hardy than *B. cordifolia;* 'Ballawley', with very large leaves (8 to 12 inches wide) and sparsely borne magenta flowers; 'Bressingham Bountiful', with pink flowers arranged on many-branched stalks, more vigorous than the typical species; 'Bressingham Salmon', with salmon-red flowers; 'Bressingham White', with white flowers; 'Distinction', with pink flowers borne on brownish red stems; 'Morgenrote' ('Morning Red'), with bronzy green foliage and dark purplish red flowers often reblooming later in the season; 'Profusion', with rounded leaves and pink flowers; 'Pugsley's Purple', with purple flowers and foliage reaching 2 feet tall; 'Rotblum', with red flowers; 'Silberlicht' ('Silver Light'), pink-tinged flowers with red centers and white petals elevated above glossy deep green leaves, somewhat less cold hardy than *B. cordifolia;* 'Sunningdale', with reddish pink flowers and very durable foliage, height to 12 inches.

B. stracheyi (*stray*-kee-ee) is much like *B. ciliata* but is smaller in stature and blooms in late spring. Hardy in Zones 6 to 10.

CULTURE / CARE: Bergenias are about as accommodating as they are indestructible. They perform happily in any well-drained, slightly acidic to slightly alkaline soil. They tolerate short periods of drought yet perform best if their soil is kept moderately moist and if they are planted in a location sheltered from strong drying winds. They thrive in full sun to light shade in the North, and light to moderate shade in the South. Pests such as aphids, thrips, mealybugs, weevils, slugs, and snails are more annoying than serious, as is the most common disease, leaf spot. Careful gardeners in northern areas of unreliable snow cover lightly mulch plantings in early winter with pine or spruce branches to shade the leaves from the drying sun and wind. No other maintenance is required.

PROPAGATION: Division during spring or fall is simple and effective.

Briza media   PLATE 47

Quaking Grass, Cow Quakes, Didder, Dillies, Doddering Dickies, Intermediate Quaking Grass, Lady's Hair Grass, Maidenhair Grass, Pearl Grass, Perennial Quaking Grass, Quaker Grass, Quakers,

Rattle Grass, Shivering Grass, Totter Grass, Trembling Grass

The many common names all seem to refer to the flattened, heart-shaped, pendulous flower panicles that quiver, shiver, or quake at the lightest breath of wind. A loosely tufted, creeping, rhizomatous, erect-stemmed grass, quaking grass reaches 1 to 1½ feet tall and spreads 1½ feet wide. Of interest for its vibrant foliage and unusual flattened flower panicles, it is used for specimen and accent planting as well as for covering small to large areas as a general cover. It is easy to care for and attractive throughout the growing season.

SCIENTIFIC NAME: *Briza media* (*bri*-za *mee*-dee-a). Derived from the Greek *briza,* to nod, the name of this genus refers to the motion of the floral sprays. *Media,* midway, medium, or intermediate, refers presumably to the height of this species relative to *B. major* and *B. minor.*

HARDINESS / ORIGIN: Zones 4 to 8; originally from Eurasia, now naturalized from Ontario to Michigan and Connecticut.

LEAVES / FLOWERS / FRUIT: The flattened medium green, deciduous leaves reach 6 inches long and ¼ inch wide, taper to a blunt point, and have margins that are rough to the touch. The flattened broadly oval flower clusters, grouped in relatively open pyramidal-shaped panicles, are at first green then change to purplish then finally tan for a splendid effect that lasts from early summer to fall. The fruit, a grain, individually is not ornamental but collectively is rather showy.

RATE / SPACING: Growth is slow. Plants from pint-sized to gallon-sized containers are spaced 12 to 16 inches apart.

CULTURE / CARE: Quaking grass grows well in any infertile, well-drained soil. It is relatively tolerant of drought, needs little or no irrigation once established, and thrives in full sun. Pathology is uncommon and is usually limited to leaf spot. Maintenance typically consists of mowing plants back in late fall.

PROPAGATION: Clumps are easily divided during spring, summer, and fall. Seed, which is available commercially, germinates, although somewhat erratically, when lightly covered with soil and kept moist at a temperature of 70°F.

Brunnera macrophylla   PLATE 48

Heartleaf Brunnera, Siberian Forget-me-not, Siberian Bugloss, Dwarf Anchusa

Heartleaf brunnera is a sturdy, long-lived, large-leaved, herbaceous ground cover. Growing with a mounded, clump-forming habit, it reaches 18 to 24 inches tall by 1½ to 2 feet wide. Coarse-textured, it is a good choice for a general cover in shady or sunny locations, combining nicely with early flowering bulbs, hostas, astilbes, and trees with light-colored or coarse-textured bark.

SCIENTIFIC NAME: *Brunnera macrophylla* (brun-*nee*-ra mak-row-*fil*-a). *Brunnera* is named after Swiss botanist Samuel Brunner (1790–1844). *Macrophylla* means large-leaved.

HARDINESS / ORIGIN: Zones 3 to 8; Caucasus Mountains and Siberia.

LEAVES / FLOWERS / FRUIT: The coarse, deciduous, oval to kidney-shaped or heart-shaped leaves reach 8 inches wide, are sharply pointed at their ends, and are colored deep blackish green. Above them, during spring, ascend dainty, ⅛- to ¼-inch-wide, starlike blue flowers. The fruit that follows is tiny and nonornamental.

RATE / SPACING: Growth is slow. Plants from pint-sized to gallon-sized containers are spaced 16 to 24 inches apart.

HORTICULTURAL SELECTIONS: 'Hadspen Cream', leaves edged in creamy white, needs shade; 'Langtrees', leaves with silvery-gray speckles; 'Variegata', leaves irregularly edged with bands of creamy white, needs a cool, shaded location.

CULTURE / CARE: Heartleaf brunnera is best in well-drained, organically rich, acidic to neutral, loamy soil. It needs constant soil moisture and full sun to moderate shade. After two or three years plants may become so crowded that flowering is reduced. To correct this problem, divide the plants.

PROPAGATION: Division during spring or fall is quite easy and very effective. Root cuttings taken during spring or fall also work; they should be taken from relatively thick sections of root, cut into 3- to 4-inch-long segments, placed in a well-draining medium, and kept moist. Root cuttings taken during fall should be placed in an unheated greenhouse or cold frame. Seed, also commonly used, should be sown during fall in a cold frame or outdoor bed; it will germinate the following spring. Seed sown during late summer will germinate the same season if held at temperatures of 70 to 75°F.

Caladium   PLATE 49

Angel Wings, Elephant's Ear, Mother-in-law Plant

When considering caladium's common names, one is hard pressed to draw a mental image of these often strikingly colored, tuberous, stemless, tropical perennials. Even more difficult is finding the words to express how truly beautiful their pendant, triangular, oval, or heart-shaped foliage really is. The lush, rich, leafy appearance of caladiums imparts style and tranquility to the landscape like no other plants. Caladiums function remarkably well as facers to tall ferns, medium-sized shrubs, and small trees. Along a winding, junglelike path, they are exceptional for edging, specimen, or accent use. Companion plants are many and include shade-tolerant annuals of contrasting texture and color. In northern areas caladiums are often grown as annuals or house plants. No foot traffic is tolerated.

SCIENTIFIC NAME: *Caladium* (ka-*lay*-dee-um) is thought to be derived from the South American names for this plant, *kale* or *kaladi*.

HARDINESS / ORIGIN: Zones 10 to 11; tropical America.

LEAVES / FLOWERS / FRUIT: The leaves are large, colorful, and held upon sturdy leafstalks. The flowers, borne in a spadix, are unisexual, arise intermittently throughout the year, and although interesting, they are not significant ornamentally in comparison to the leaves. The fruit, a dull white berry, is nonornamental.

RATE / SPACING: Growth is slow to moderate. Plants from 1- to 2-gallon-sized containers are spaced 12 to 18 inches apart.

SPECIES: *C. bicolor* (*bye*-kul-er), named for its two-colored foliage, is commonly called common caladium or heart of Jesus. Hailing from Brazil, it reaches 2 feet tall and spreads about the same across. Its evergreen, peltate or oval leaves reach up to 14 inches long and 7 inches wide and are divided into two broad rounded lobes at the base. They are held upon 2-foot-long leaf stalks. The leaves are colored red with blue-green borders and blue-green on their undersides. The tiny flowers are arranged in a curious upright, cylindrical, 4-inch-long structure called a spathe.

C. × *hortulanum* (hort-you-*lay*-num), named for the garden origin of this hybrid group, is commonly called garden caladium, fancy-leaved caladium, or showy caladium. Indeed, caladiums have been hybridized to such an extent that not only have several splendid cultivars arisen, but confusion in nomenclature has been bred as well. As is often the case, hybrids of dubious origin are lumped together under the heading of a single hybrid species. Although *C. bicolor* is said to have been one of the parents involved in the original cross, the genealogy of most caladiums is uncertain and documentation has been poor. Most of the cultivars range from 1 to 2 feet tall and spread 2 feet wide. Typically their colorful leaves are much like those of *C. bicolor* but sometimes broader, narrower, or ruffled about the edges. Their colors include rose, red, green, white, pink, and various combinations of these. Of the dozens of cultivars described here, the amazing thing is that they are all uniquely different. Among the most popular are 'Ace of Hearts', with leaves colored green and red; 'Aaron', large leaves with white centers, white veins, and green edges; 'Blaze', leaves with crimson centers and narrowly edged in jade green; 'Brandy-wine', with large crimson leaves surrounded by a thin edge of green; 'Caloosahatchee', narrow leaves with whitish green centers and bordered by a broad margin of green; 'Candidum', with striking green veins against a background of almost pure white; 'Candidum Jr.', more compact, with leaf blades even whiter than those of 'Candidum'; 'Carolyn Whorton', leaves with large pink center, crimson veins, and green edges; 'Clarice', leaves with narrow scarlet veins, white speckles, and olive green edges; 'Fannie Munson', with deep pink leaves with crimson and green veins and green edges; 'Festiva', with purple leaves with green veins; 'Fire Chief', leaves with pink and white centers and irregular green margins; 'Florida Beauty', to 1½ feet tall, with light green leaves mottled red and yellow; 'Florida Elise', leaves with bronzy green edges and pinkish red dappling; 'Florida Fantasy', white leaves with brilliant pinkish red veins and a thin margin of green; 'Florida Sweetheart', leaves with bright maroon-red centers and wide wavy margins of olive green; 'Freida Hemple', wavy-edged leaves with crimson centers and veins and with uniform broad green margins; 'Gingerland', with narrow white-bladed, green-edged leaves dappled with splotches of crimson; 'Gypsy Rose', leaves with pink centers, green edges, and green flecks radiating inward from the margins; 'Irene Dank', with scarlet leaves edged in green with green penetrating inward from the margins; 'Ivory', with whitish leaves with a tinge of green most pronounced toward the margins and between the veins; 'Jackie Suthers', with white leaves with edges and overlays of near black; 'John Peed', leaves with crimson center radiating like a star toward iridescent green margins; 'June Bride', with white leaves, green veins, and thin green margins; 'Kathleen', with dull crimson leaves edged in coppery green; 'Lady of Fatima', narrow leaves with ivory centers and wavy green edges; 'Lance Whorton', with olive green wavy-edged leaves mottled with pink, green, and crimson; 'Lord Derby', leaves with narrow wavy edges, crimson centers, green veins, and green edges; 'Marie Moir', with bright white leaves, irregular crimson flecks, and green veins; 'Miss Chicago', habit erect, leaves attractive with crimson centers and veins, pink and white speckles, and green edges; 'Miss Muffet', with white leaves with pink veins, pink center splotch, and red speckles between the veins; 'Mrs. Arno Nehrling', with narrow green-edged white leaves with crimson centers and primary veins (the other veins are green); 'Mrs. F. M. Joyner', with green leaves flecked with white and crimson primary veins and midrib; 'Mumbo', with wavy olive-green-edged leaves with crimson centers; 'Pink Beauty', with red veins, pink center splotch, and green margins; 'Pink Cloud', leaves with purplish centers and speckled metallic green edges; 'Pink Gem', leaves with crimson centers surrounded by pinkish mottling and dark green margins; 'Pink Symphony', leaves pink with green veins; 'Poecile Anglais', leaves with crimson centers surrounded by purplish green and green edges; 'Postman Joyner', with attractively variegated leaves with a central deep red patch from which red veins extend outward toward bronzy green margins; 'Red Flash', 10 to 14 inches tall, with bright red midrib and primary veins, becoming burgundy as it merges with green margins and dappled with pink splotches between large veins; 'Red Frill', shiny leaves with crimson centers and wavy dark green margins; 'Rosalie', leaves with dark crimson centers tinged with overlays of near black that radiate inward from the thin greenish black margins; 'Rosebud', broad leaves with crimson centers that are green-edged and white between the margins and crimson center splotch; 'Torchy', flat leaves with crimson centers surrounded by a broad band of flat deep green; 'White Christmas', large leaves with green edges and white veins; 'White Queen', white leaves trimmed with green margins and with strikingly pinkish red primary veins and midrib; 'White Wing', flat leaves with white centers surrounded by dark green margins that radiate inward with greenish mottling.

C. humboldtii (hum-*bold*-ee-eye), named after German scientist Friedrich Wilhelm Heinrich Alexander von Humboldt (1769–1859), is a diminutive Venezuelan species that reaches only 6 to 8 inches tall. Its shield-shaped leaves are 4 to 5 inches long by 2½ inches wide, and painted green with white splotches and spots.

C. marmoratum (mar-moe-*ray*-tum), named from the Latin *marmoratum,* marbled, for its mottled leaves, is similar to *C. bicolor* except that its leaf stalks are a little longer (about twice the length of the leaves) in relation to foliage. Native to Ecuador, it has green leaves with gray, whitish, or yellowish green mottling.

C. picturatum (pik-too-*ray*-tum), named for its painted (variegated) leaves, is similar to *C. bicolor* but differs in that its leaves are narrower and reach 12 inches long by 4 inches wide.

CULTURE / CARE: Well-drained, highly organic soil of slight to moderately acidic pH is preferred. Tolerance to drought is poor, thus the soil should be kept moist with supplemental watering to prevent wilting. Ideally, the air also should be quite humid. Caladiums are good in light to relatively dense shade and display their best coloration in light to moderate shade. If the location also receives morning or evening sun it is even better. Bacterial and fungal tuber rots often occur if the soil is poorly drained or if the tubers become too moist in shipping or storage. Leaf spotting due to a fungus is sometimes encountered but seldom serious. Little or no maintenance is required. Tattered foliage can be removed with scissors and will soon regenerate.

PROPAGATION: Division, the primary method of propagation, involves digging up tubers in early spring, then dividing and replanting them to a depth of one or two inches; the soil should be kept slightly moist but not soggy. Adult leaf color does not fully develop until four to five leaves have been produced and fully expanded. Seed will germinate, but is useful primarily to hybridizers.

Calamintha nepeta   PLATE 50
Calamint Savory

Indefinitely spreading by rhizomes, this compact bushy herb reaches 2 feet tall and does a good job of covering up the soil as a general-purpose relatively low-care, small-scale to moderate-scale ground cover. No foot traffic is tolerated.

SCIENTIFIC NAME: *Calamintha nepeta* (kal-a-*min*-tha *nep*-e-ta / *ne*-pee-ta). *Calamintha* comes from the Greek *kalos,* beautiful, and *minthe,* mint. *Nepeta* refers to the related genus *Nepeta.*

HARDINESS / ORIGIN: Zones 6 to 10; southern Europe and the Mediterranean region.

LEAVES / FLOWERS / FRUIT: The soft green leaves covered with gray hairs are broadly oval, ¾ inch long by ⅜ inch wide, shallowly toothed around their edges, and pleasantly minty smelling when crushed. The mintlike, bee-attracting, ⅝-inch-long, white or lilac flowers are borne from spring to mid summer in such profusion as to nearly obscure the foliage. The fruit that follows is tiny and non-ornamental.

RATE / SPACING: Growth is moderate. Plants from pint-sized to quart-sized containers are spaced 1 to 1½ feet apart.

HORTICULTURAL SELECTIONS: Subsp. *glandulosa,* with smaller leaves; subsp. *nepeta,* more robust with larger leaves.

CULTURE / CARE: Calamint savory performs well in well-drained alkaline, neutral, or partially acidic soils. It requires full sun, is not greatly tolerant of drought, and should be given additional water during hot dry weather. Few pests and diseases affect it, and maintenance is normally limited to mowing once during late fall.

PROPAGATION: Propagation is easy by seed, division, or cuttings—the time of year not being important.

Calamovilfa longifolia   PLATE 51
Sand Reed-grass, Long Leaved Reed-grass

The primary landscape use of this coarse-textured rhizomatous grass is to reduce erosion in moderate to large sandy and hilly areas. Reaching 2 to 5 feet tall and spreading indefinitely, it does not tolerate being walked on, but stepping between the stems proves to be no problem. As a soil binder it works very well, and its foliage and flowers are attractive as they sway gracefully in the wind. Although less commonly cultivated than marram grass (*Ammophila breviligulata*), sand reed-grass ought to be considered for use more often. It is very cold hardy (like marram grass) and also has the advantage of being propagated economically from seed.

SCIENTIFIC NAME: *Calamovilfa longifolia* (kal-a-*moe*-vil-fa lon-ji-*foe*-lee-a). *Calamovilfa* comes from the Greek *calamos,* a reed. *Longifolia* is Latin for long-leaved.

HARDINESS / ORIGIN: Zone 3; sandy sites from western Ontario to the Mackenzie River northward, then south to northern Indiana, Kansas, and Colorado.

LEAVES / FLOWERS / FRUIT: Deciduous but persistent even after dying back in fall, the narrow leaves reach 8 to 12 inches long by ¼ to ½ inch wide. They taper to a narrow point, are coarse to the touch with prominent veins, and are colored medium to grayish green. In autumn they turn brown. The tiny florets are arranged in attractive narrow panicles to 12 inches long. Borne in fall upon thin stems that reach 6 feet tall, they are colored light brown and persist well into the winter. The fruit, a tiny grain, is nonornamental.

RATE / SPACING: Growth is moderate. Plants from pint-sized to quart-sized containers are spaced 2 to 3 feet apart.

HORTICULTURAL SELECTIONS: Var. *magna,* flower panicles broader, longer, and elevated much higher, leaves and flowering stems also taller, native to the dunes of Lakes Michigan, Superior, and Huron.

CULTURE / CARE: Sandy loam or 100-percent beach sand with good drainage is best. Sand reed-grass tolerates moderately alkaline to moderately acidic soil and, since its roots go very deep, no irrigation is needed once the plant is established. It prefers full sun to light shade. No serious diseases or pests have been reported. Although no maintenance is required, some gardeners mow back their plantings each spring.

PROPAGATION: Propagation is simple by seed, sown as soon as it ripens, or by division, which can be performed at any time.

Callirhoe involucrata   PLATE 52
Poppy Mallow, Wine Cups

An easy-to-grow native that is beginning to get some recognition, this low scrambling herb does a good job of blanketing the ground for general cover in moderate-sized areas. Semiwoody at its base, this plant typically ranges from 3 to 10 inches tall and sprawls 4 to 5 feet across. It is effective both for its flowers and foliage, and combines well with many other herbaceous perennials. Very little foot traffic is tolerated.

SCIENTIFIC NAME: *Callirhoe involucrata* (ka-*lir*-oh-ee in-voe-lew-kray-ta). *Callirhoe* commemorates the daughter of Achelous, a river god in Greek mythology. *Involucrata* refers to the involucre, circle of bracts, around the flowers.

HARDINESS / ORIGIN: Zone 4 or 5; sandy, often grassy areas of Missouri to Wyoming, south to Texas.

LEAVES / FLOWERS / FRUIT: With rough hairy stems, this sprawling perennial displays dark shiny green, round-outlined, coarse-textured deeply five-lobed to seven-lobed deciduous leaves that are first round-lobed before becoming angular in maturity. The 1- to 2½-inch-wide cerise flowers are composed of five rounded petals that arch upward to form distinctively cup-shaped blossoms. Under the blossoms are three leaflike bracts, collectively referred to as an involucre—hence the specific epithet. The fruit that follows is tiny and nonornamental.

RATE / SPACING: Growth is moderate. Plants from pint-sized to gallon-sized containers are spaced 2 to 3 feet apart.

CULTURE / CARE: Poppy mallow adapts to most soil types including dry clay and limy soils. It is most compact and flowers most impressively in warm sunny locations, but tolerates light shade. With its deep taproot it shows good tolerance to drought. It is seldom bothered by diseases or pests (except for crown rot in poorly drained soils) and requires little maintenance.

PROPAGATION: Seed is usually sown indoors under lights in late winter for production of transplantable plantlets that will flower the first season.

Calluna vulgaris   PLATE 53
Heather, Common Heather, Scotch Heather, Ling

A horizontally spreading alpine shrub that often reaches 3 to 4 feet across and mounds to heights of 18 to 36 inches, heather is a plant whose name is recognized by almost everyone; however, very few people have actually seen it or experienced the pleasure of growing it. This is for a number of reasons, not the least of which is heather's temperamental nature when it comes to propagation. Nursery owners find that the majority of gardeners are unwilling to pay the extra price due to the plant's slow growth and mediocre ability to root. Other reasons for the scarcity of heather in the landscape stem from its preference in soil type and limited range of hardiness. Heather shows a distinct preference for sandy or gravelly soils of relatively high acidity, yet a good deal of the soil in North America is on the heavy side (i.e., contains much clay). It is hardy only in Zones 4 to 6, sometimes with fair results in Zone 7.

Heather is exceptionally interesting on hillsides when mass planted as a general ground cover, especially when variously colored cultivars are combined. Often it is employed in shrub borders in conjunction with dwarf conifers, brooms, and heaths. In rock gardens it is one of the finest specimens available. No foot traffic is tolerated.

Herbalists have employed heather as a treatment for kidney stones, venomous bites, and insomnia (in a tea it has a mild sedative effect). The blossoms were previously processed to formulate a cough suppressant and to make a yellow dye for woolens. The dark honey derived from them is said to be an ingredient of Drambuie, the well-known Scottish liqueur. The white flowers of *C. vulgaris* 'Alba' are often incorporated in bridal bouquets in Scotland as they are believed to bring good luck. Dogs and cats for some unknown reason seem attracted to heathers and often relieve themselves on or around these plants.

SCIENTIFIC NAME: *Calluna vulgaris* (ka-*lew*-na vul-*gay*-ris). *Calluna* comes from the Greek *kalluno,* to cleanse, in reference to the use of branches in the heads of brooms. *Vulgaris* means common.

HARDINESS / ORIGIN: Zones 4 to 7; Asia Minor and Europe.

LEAVES / FLOWERS / FRUIT: The evergreen, tiny, scale-like, medium green leaves overlap and are oblong to oval-shaped. In winter they often take on bronzy hues. The flowers, borne from mid to late summer, are arranged in 1- to 10-inch-long, spikelike, rather upright clusters. Individually, they are urn-shaped, four-petaled, ⅛ inch wide, colored rose-pink or purplish pink, and attractive to bees. The fruit is nonornamental.

RATE / SPACING: Growth is slow to moderate. Plants from quart-sized to gallon-sized containers are spaced 16 to 22 inches apart.

HORTICULTURAL SELECTIONS: Authorities estimate that there are in excess of 600 cultivars. Some of the more popular selections include 'Alba', with white flowers; 'Aurea', with purple flowers August to October, height 18 inches, leaves yellow in summer and russet in winter; 'Corbett's Red', with compact mounding habit and late-opening red flowers; 'County Wicklow', with double pink flowers August to October on 3- to 6-inch-tall spikes; 'Cuprea', with purple flowers August to October, height 12 inches, leaves golden, turning bronzy in fall; 'Else Frye', selected in Seattle in 1940, only 8 inches tall, remarkable for its tiny dark green leaves and clear double white summertime flowers; 'Foxii Nana', with purple flowers August to October, mature height only 4 inches, leaves bright green; 'Golden Aurea', 18 to 24 inches tall by more than 2 feet across, blooming white above golden-yellow leaves; 'Golden Aureafolia', 18 to 24 inches tall by more than 2 feet wide, pink flowers, golden-yellow leaves; 'Hammondia Aurea', new growth bright gold, flowers white, ultimate size 18 inches tall by 14 inches wide; 'H. E. Beale', with pale pink flowers from late August to October, growth vigorous; 'J. H. Hamilton', with double pink flowers August to October, to 10 inches tall, leaves dark green; 'Kinlochruel', with superb double white flowers, dark green leaves, and compact habit; 'Long White', with white flowers, bright green leaves, and rather open upright habit; 'Mrs. Pat', only 6 inches tall by 10 inches wide, flowers lavender, bright green leaves with pink tips in spring; 'Mrs. R. H. Gray', low spreading, with bright green leaves, lavender-pink flowers; 'Nana Compacta', with pink flowers, bright green leaves, mature height only 6 inches; 'Peter Sparkes', showy, excellent for cutting with its deep pink flowers on 24-inch-tall branches; 'Plena Multiplex', with double pink flowers August to October, height to 18 inches; 'Robert Chapman', with rose-purple flowers August to September, foliage greenish yellow then reddish in winter, height 10 inches; 'Silver Queen', with woolly silvery leaves and lilac-pink flowers; 'Sister Anne', reaching 6 inches tall, with broad spread, silvery leaves, and a profusion of pink flowers; 'Spring Cream', with bright green leaves tipped cream in spring, height to 18 inches, and pink flowers in fall; 'Spring Torch', pink flowers, reaches 12 inches tall, leafs out vermilion in spring and then turns green; 'Tomentosa', with lavender flowers, height to 10 inches.

CULTURE / CARE: Heather prefers acidic, infertile, sandy, gritty, or sandy loam soils. The soil must be well drained yet moisture retentive. Drought tolerance is moderate, and excess humidity can be troublesome, so heathers should be planted in locations with good air circulation where plants are not exposed to strong, drying winds. They need thorough watering during hot, dry weather, and full sun to light shade (flowering is best in full sun). Pests include aphids, Japanese beetles, two-spotted mites,

oystershell scales, and chafer beetle larvae. Rabbits like to chew on the ends of the stems. Overfertilization results in leggy, open growth. Many gardeners mow or shear immediately after flowering to keep plants dense and compact.

PROPAGATION: Cuttings are used almost exclusively to propagate heather; they should be taken in late summer or fall from nonflowering shoots, placed in a mixture of two parts perlite and one part shredded peat, and heated from the bottom to keep the temperature of the rooting medium at 60°F.

Campanula PLATE 54
Bellflower

Low-growing, rhizomatous herbs, bellflowers make good general-use ground covers for smaller, contained, sunny areas of the landscape. They are superb for facing dark-leaved shrubs, such as English and Japanese yew, rhododendron, and holly; not only does their light green foliage lend a refreshing contrast, but in summertime their bright, crisp flowers bring yet another element of color variation. No foot traffic is tolerated.

SCIENTIFIC NAME: *Campanula* (kam-*pan*-you-la) in Latin means little bell and describes the flowers.

HARDINESS / ORIGIN: See individual species for hardiness; North America, but especially the Caucasus, Balkan, and Mediterranean regions.

LEAVES / FLOWERS / FRUIT: The ground-covering bellflowers are clothed in vibrant light to medium green deciduous to semievergreen leaves. The abundant flowers are bell-shaped and make a pleasing display of white, lilac, blue, or purple. The fruit is nonornamental.

RATE / SPACING: Growth is fast, with the potential to become weedy. Plants from pint-sized to quart-sized containers are spaced 8 to 12 inches apart and sited in a location where their spread is either contained or does not interfere with less aggressive plants.

SPECIES: *C. carpatica* (kar-*pat*-i-ka), named for its native habitat, the Carpathian Mountains of east central Europe, is commonly called Carpathian bellflower. A low, tufted, herbaceous ground cover 8 to 10 inches tall by 18 inches wide, this species is hardy in Zones 3 to 8. Its leaves are oval to triangular, 2 inches long by ½ inch wide, light green, and excellent for highlighting darker-foliaged plants. The bluish lilac flowers open in mid summer to relieve garden doldrums. Each flower is held upon a slender, elongated stem in nodding fashion slightly above the foliar mass. The fruit is inconsequential. Horticultural selections include 'Alba', with white flowers; 'Blue Carpet', with deep blue flowers, lower-growing and more compact than the species; 'Blue Clips'

('Blaue Clips'), with large violet-blue flowers from mid summer to early fall; 'China Cup', possibly the same as 'China Doll', with large mauve flowers and a lower-growing 8-inch-tall habit; 'Jingle Bells', reaching 8 to 12 inches tall, with both white and blue flowers; var. *turbinata,* with compact habit, reaching 6 to 9 inches tall, purplish blue flowers (also having given rise to numerous cultivars selected for flower colors ranging from white to violet); 'Wedge-wood Blue', with pale blue-violet flowers, reaching only 6 inches tall; 'White Carpet', with white flowers and compact habit; 'White Clips' ('Weisse Clips'), like 'Blue Clips' but with white flowers; 'White Star', with clear white flowers.

C. garganica (gar-*gan*-i-ka), named for Monte Gargano in Italy where it was discovered in 1827, is commonly called Adriatic bellflower or Dalmatian bellflower. Hardy in Zones 6 to 8, this lovely herbaceous ground cover of trailing habit ranges in height from 6 to 8 inches and spreads only 1 foot wide. Although slower growing than *C. carpatica,* it should be used in similar situations. It is noteworthy for its long-stemmed, oval to heart-shaped, 1-inch-long, 1-inch-wide, tooth-edged, grayish green foliage. Its violet-blue starlike flowers with white centers bloom from early summer through fall. Variety *hirsuta* is covered with grayish hairs and displays lighter blue flowers; var. *hirsuta* 'Alba' is covered with grayish hairs and displays white flowers.

C. portenschlagiana (por-ten-shlag-ee-*aye*-na), named after Austrian botanist and physician Franz von Portenschlag-Ledermeyer (1772–1827), is commonly called Dalmatian bellflower. It is a tenacious ground cover that spreads rapidly and indefinitely by underground stems. Ranging from 6 to 9 inches tall, this native of Dalmatia in the former Yugoslavia is hardy in Zones 4 to 8 and displays leaves that are semievergreen, 1 to 1½ inches long, round or heart-shaped, and medium to dark green with toothed margins. The continuously borne, ¾-inch-wide purple flowers are on display from mid spring to late summer and sometimes into the fall.

C. poscharskyana (po-shar-skee-*aye*-na), named for Gustav Adolph Poscharsky (1832–1914), a rock gardening specialist and head gardener of Dresden, Germany, who reportedly discovered this plant in 1895, is commonly called Serbian bellflower. Like the other species, this one is a herbaceous ground cover of sprawling habit. It typically reaches 4 to 6 inches tall but has been known to reach 12 inches and spreads with tenacity to more than 1 foot wide. Hardy in Zones 3 to 7, this native of the former Yugoslavia has oval, roundish, or heart-shaped, medium green, evergreen leaves that reach 1½ inches long by 1½ inches wide. Its 1- to 1¼-inch-wide flowers of lavender-blue are funnel-shaped and appear during the first few weeks of summer.

CULTURE / CARE: Well-drained, mildly acidic to mildly alkaline sandy loam soils are ideal for bellflowers. They are not particularly tolerant of drought and may require weekly watering during summer. Those planted in northern and coastal areas perform best in full sun; further south and inland, light shade is better. Pests include foxglove aphids, onion thrips, and slugs. Commonly encountered diseases include crown rot, leaf spot, rust, and powdery mildew. Bellflowers are maintenance-free except for an occasional trimming back as they sprawl outside of their bounds.

PROPAGATION: Simple division in spring or fall is the standard means of propagation, but seed (available from most seed companies) is also effective. Sown in spring, seed germinates in two or three weeks and yields mature plants by fall.

Carex   PLATE 55

Sedge

This enormous genus is composed of as many as 2000 species of perennial, grasslike, often rhizomatous herbs. Sedges are tough, colorful, and generally quite easily cultured. Those discussed here deserve more attention and no doubt will become more popular in the coming years. In general, *Carex* species that excel as ground covers are rather low to moderate in height (ranging from ¼ to 3 feet tall). They perform exceptionally well in linking and facing trees and shrubs and are best when mass planted for a bold effect in small-, moderate-, and large-scale plantings. Rather lax in habit, their arching foliage makes them perfect for planting in vast curvaceous beds, especially on gently undulating terrain where they impart a cool lushness. As with the lily turfs (*Liriope* and *Ophiopogon*), the sedges are excellent for walkway edging in both formal and informal landscapes, particularly in wooded settings. Occasional foot traffic is tolerated.

SCIENTIFIC NAME: *Carex* (*kay*-reks / *kare*-ex) is the Latin name for rush or sedge.

HARDINESS / ORIGIN: See individual species for hardiness; cosmopolitan, mostly from temperate and cold regions.

LEAVES / FLOWERS / FRUIT: Generally speaking *Carex* species have leaves which are narrow, pointed, parallel-veined and grasslike and which originate from a rhizomatous base. The flowers are borne in spikelike inflorescences that are typically composed of all-male or all-female flowers, usually with the male-flowered spikes above the female. The fruit is nutlike, usually brown but sometimes yellowish or purple, and usually nonornamental.

RATE / SPACING: Growth is slow to moderate. Plants from pint-sized to quart-sized containers are spaced 8 to 14 inches apart.

SPECIES: *C. atrata* (a-*tray*-ta), meaning clothed in black and named for its black seed heads, is commonly called black sedge, black sedge grass, or jet sedge. Hailing from northern Asia, North America (Rocky Mountains south to Utah), England, and Arctic Europe south to the Balkans and Pyrenees, this species is hardy in Zones 3 to 8 and displays a low-growing, rhizomatous, iris-like habit. It ranges from 6 to 9 inches tall, spreads indefinitely, and displays persistent, smooth or roughish, iris-like, keeled, 6-inch-long, blue-green leaves. Its flower spikes are arranged in groups of three to five. Each is oblong to oblong cylindric and ⅓ to 1 inch long by ⅙ to ¼ inch wide. Nodding in maturity, the deep brown flowers are displayed from early to mid summer. Variety *caucasia* displays smaller flower spikes than the species.

C. comans (*koe*-mans), named for reasons no longer known but likely named from the Latin *comans,* hairy, in reference to the leaves which resemble hair, is commonly called green wig or New Zealand hair sedge. Considered synonymous with *C. vilmorinii,* this species comes from New Zealand, is hardy in Zones 7 or 8 to 9, forms dense tufts, and although it normally reaches 14 inches tall, ranges from 12 to 24 inches. Its leaves give it a rather informal appearance. Each leaf is yellowish green to pale green, evergreen, narrow (almost hairlike), 18 inches long, erect in youth then later arching over to touch the ground. The flower spikes, arranged in groups of five to seven, are oblong or cylindrical, borne early to mid summer, and often are obscured by the foliage. Usually they are considered insignificant in relation to the ornamental qualities of the foliage. The horticultural selection 'Bronce' displays dull bronze-colored leaves.

C. digitata (di-ji-*tay*-ta), a green-leaved species of dryish hardwoods and glades from Maine to Wisconsin southward to Florida and Alabama, reaches 8 inches tall, is hardy in Zones 6 to 9, and lends itself well to mass planting.

C. elata (ee-*lay*-ta), hardy in Zones 5 to 9, has at least two outstanding golden selections to brighten the landscape when used for accent or massed on a moderate scale. These cultivars perform best in light shade to full sun and should have moist soil of relatively high fertility. 'Bowles Golden' reaches 2 feet tall and 1½ feet wide, is strikingly golden with a very thin green margin; 'Knightshayes', said to have arisen as a sport of 'Bowles Golden', is characterized by golden foliage like 'Bowles Golden' but without the thin green margin.

C. glauca (*glaw*-ka), named for its bluish foliage, is commonly named blue sedge, pink grass, carnation grass, gilliflower grass, or heath sedge. Considered by some to be *C. flacca,* this species reaches 6 inches tall, spreads slowly by creeping rhizomes, and displays narrow, rough-to-the-touch, medium to light blue leaves. Its tiny flowers are borne in 1- to 2-inch-long cylindric spikes (grouped two to three together) during early to mid summer. The species hails from meadows in eastern Canada and Europe and is hardy in Zones 5 to 9.

C. hachioensis 'Evergold' (hah-chee-oh-*en*-sis), Evergold Japanese sedge, is one of the most brightly colored plants in cultivation. Its creamy yellow center-striped leaves are visible from a long distance and impart a cheerful nature to lightly shaded landscape settings. Often listed as *C. morrowii* 'Old Gold', this slow-spreading clump-former originated in Japan and is hardy in Zones 5 or 6 to 9. It is quite adaptable to soil and in rich moist conditions may reach 12 inches tall, with gently arching 12- to 18-inch-long leaves.

C. morrowii (moe-*row*-ee-eye), named after someone called Morrow, is commonly called Japanese sedge or Morrow's sedge. Hardy in Zones 6 or 7 to 9, it is native to low, wooded, mountainous regions of Japan. Its stiff dark green leaves with narrow white edges are evergreen, 12 or more inches long by ¼ inch wide, and three angled to U-shaped in cross-section. A typical specimen is compact and nonrunning, reaching 12 inches tall (in very fertile soil it may reach 1½ to 2 feet), and forms a dense tuft 12 to 18 inches wide. The flower spikes are grouped four to six with the male-flowered spikes held above the female. The short-lived brown flowers are borne early to mid spring. The horticultural selections are more commonly cultivated than the species: var. *albomarginata,* with leaves longitudinally striped white, reaching 12 inches tall, sometimes listed as var. *expallida* or 'Variegata'; 'Aurea Variegata', with leaves decorated with a broad, golden central stripe, 12 inches tall; 'Aureo Variegata Nana', similar to 'Aurea Variegata' but more compact and reaching only 3 or 4 inches tall; 'Goldband', with gold-edged leaves; var. *temnolepis,* with narrow leaves.

C. muskingumensis (mus-kin-gum-*en*-sis), named after the Muskingum River, Ohio, is commonly called palm sedge (for its palmlike leaf arrangement). A slow-creeping rhizomatous spreader, this native of the Great Lakes, southward to Kentucky and Missouri, and west to Manitoba, is a strong-growing reliable species. It is best used for erosion control at the bank of a pond or stream and is interesting primarily for the tropical appearance of its droopy ¼-inch-wide, 4- to 8-inch-long deciduous leaves that are arranged in whorls on arching 2- to 3-foot-long stems. Although not highly ornamental, the flowers, formed at the ends of the stem during summer, lend interest and contrast. The species is hardy in Zones 4 to 9. 'Wachtposten' is like the species but displays greater resistance to drought and a more upright habit.

C. nigra (*nie*-gra), named in Latin for its black florets, is commonly called black sedge. Hailing from Greenland and northeastern North America, it displays grayish blue-green leaves to 6 or 8 inches. It spreads by creeping rhizomes, eventually forming a thick turf, and is hardy in Zones 4 to 8. Its black flowers are borne during summer. 'Variegata' is striped green and greenish yellow.

C. pendula (*pen*-dyu-la), named for its pendulous flower stalks, is commonly called drooping sedge or pendulous sedge. Found in moist woods and along streams in England, Europe, western Asia, and North Africa, it is hardy in Zones 5 or 6 to 9, reaches 1½ to 2 feet tall, and spreads about the same. It has a tufted habit. It is nonrunning and clothed in evergreen, lance-shaped, 18-inch-long (or longer), ½- to ¾-inch-wide, finely pointed, three-angled, yellowish green (above), bluish green (below) leaves. Its grayish flower spikes of mid to late spring are held upon tall arching stems with the male spikes located terminally and ranging from 2½ to 4 inches long. Below them are the pendulous female spikes that reach from 2¾ to 6 inches long.

C. plantaginea (plan-ta-jin-*ee*-a), commonly called plantain-leaved sedge for its broad plantain-shaped leaves, is a tufted species that reaches 1 to 2 feet tall. It has purple-sheathed, vibrant light green, evergreen foliage. It blooms from early spring to early summer, is native to eastern North America, and is hardy at least as far north as Zone 3 and as far south as Zone 8.

OTHER SELECTIONS: A couple of very good selections of *Carex* include *C*. 'Catlin', hardy in Zones 4 to 10, reaching 12 inches tall, unique for its narrow evergreen leaves which give it a weeping habit; *C. dolichostachya* var. *glaberrima* 'Gold Fountains', to 14 inches tall, with narrow leaves bordered in gold; 'Silver Curls', hardy in Zones 7 to 10, unique for its hair-thin silvery leaves.

CULTURE / CARE: Sedges grow best in organically rich, fertile, acidic loam. They are not greatly tolerant of drought, and their soil should be kept slightly moist with supplemental watering as needed. They prefer light to moderate shade. Few pests and diseases bother them. Although little or no maintenance is required, an annual spring mowing keeps them from becoming ragged looking.

PROPAGATION: The cultivars (and species) are usually increased by division in spring; however, division can be successful any time provided the soil is not allowed to dry out. Although difficult to obtain, commercial supplies of seed exist for some species; generally speaking, if sown during fall, seed germinates in high percentages the following spring.

Carissa grandiflora   PLATE 56
Natal Plum

A tough little shrubby ground cover, Natal plum spreads 3 to 5 feet across and ranges from 18 to 30 inches tall. Of greatest use in southern coastal and arid-climate landscapes, it displays some of the showiest fruit of any ground cover available today. Most often it is planted atop terraces or retaining walls or in elevated planters so that its branches can cascade attractively over the sides. It may also be put to use as an edging along walkways, patio borders, and building entrances. Natal plum is rather tolerant of salt spray, making it valuable in coastal landscapes. No foot traffic is tolerated.

SCIENTIFIC NAME: *Carissa grandiflora* (ka-*ris*-a grandi-*floe*-ra). The meaning of *Carissa* is unknown. *Grandiflora* means large-flowered.

HARDINESS / ORIGIN: Zones 7 to 10 or 11; South Africa.

LEAVES / FLOWERS / FRUIT: The evergreen leaves are leathery, dark green, oval-shaped, and typically reach 3 inches long. The funnel-shaped flowers are ½ inch long, waxy white, and effective during spring. The fruit, one of Natal plum's greatest ornamental features, is a scarlet berry to 2 inches long.

RATE / SPACING: Growth is slow until rooted, then moderate. Plants from 1- to 3-gallon-sized containers are spaced 3 to 3½ feet apart.

HORTICULTURAL SELECTIONS: 'Boxwood Beauty', with compact, mounding habit to 18 inches tall and dark green leaves; 'Green Carpet', 12 to 18 inches tall by 3 or 4 feet wide, dark green leaves; 'Horizontalis', with trailing stems, leaves arranged very densely, 18 to 24 inches tall by 4 feet wide; 'Minima', a dwarf form to 12 inches tall, with leaves and flowers reduced in size; 'Prostrata', low, spreading, to 2 feet tall by 5 feet wide; 'Tomlinson', 2 to 2½ feet tall by 3 feet wide with shiny mahogany tinged leaves; 'Tuttle' ('Nana Compacta Tuttlei'), 2 to 3 feet tall by 3 to 5 feet wide.

CULTURE / CARE: Although Natal plum prefers organically rich soils, it tolerates mineral soils of both light (sandy) and heavy (clayey) texture. It is not bothered by saline conditions—neither in the air nor in the soil—and it is fairly tolerant of drought. Although in most cases it can survive without supplemental irrigation, it almost always performs and looks better with occasional summer watering. It prefers full sun to moderate shade and has few or no serious pests or diseases. Maintenance typically consists of pruning out occasional upward-growing branches.

PROPAGATION: Cuttings in early summer are the ordinary means of propagation.

Carpobrotus edulis   PLATE 57

Trailing Hottentot Fig

A sturdy succulent from South Africa, trailing Hottentot fig reaches 12 to 18 inches tall and may spread more than 8 feet across. Not to be confused with the ordinary table fig (*Ficus carica*), the species described here is not known so much for its edible fruit as for its ability to effectively cover the ground in moderate to large plantings. In general, it (as well as its near relatives) may be characterized as low-growing, trailing, fleshy, and colorful. It is especially well suited for coastal landscaping and has few problems with shifting sand or airborne salt. On embankments of moderate repose it functions well as a soil binder, but on very steep slopes the weight of the stems and leaves may cause plants to pull away from their crowns. No foot traffic is tolerated.

SCIENTIFIC NAME: *Carpobrotus edulis* (kar-poe-*broe*-tus *ed*-you-lis / e-*dew*-lis). *Carpobrotus* comes from the Greek *karpos,* fruit, and *brotus,* edible, a reference to the edible fruit. *Edulis* also means edible. The common name is borrowed from the African tribe of the same name.

HARDINESS / ORIGIN: Zones 9 to 10 or 11; South Africa.

LEAVES / FLOWERS / FRUIT: The unusual leaves are evergreen, succulent, 3 to 5 inches long by ½ inch wide, curled upward somewhat, three-angled in cross section, and colored a fine shade of gray-green with a reddish keel below. Showy springtime flowers are solitary, to 4 inches across, many petaled, and light yellow, rose-pink, or purple. They open in the daytime sun, then close at night. The fruit is fleshy and edible but nonornamental.

RATE / SPACING: Growth is fast. Plants from pint-sized to quart-sized containers are spaced 16 to 24 inches apart.

OTHER SPECIES: *C. acinaciformis* (a-*sin*-a-si-form-is), ground Hottentot fig, displays rich magenta flowers.

C. chilensis (chil-*en*-sis), trailing sea fig or California beach plant, is hardy in Zones 9 to 10 or 11. Native from coastal Oregon to Baja California and Chile, it reaches 12 to 18 inches tall by more than 8 feet wide. Its fleshy leaves are 1¼ to 2 inches long, triangular, and green, sometimes with reddish tones. Sparsely borne summertime flowers reach 3½ inches

wide, open in the sun, and close at night. The fruit is fleshy, edible, and nonornamental.

C. deliciosus (dee-lis-ee-*oh*-sus), four fig or goukum, has magenta to purple flowers.

C. muirii (mew-*er*-ee-eye) bears smaller leaves and pink to purple flowers.

CULTURE / CARE: All species like full sun and adapt to soils of various textures provided that drainage is excellent. They easily withstand moderate periods of drought, benefit from occasional deep watering, and rarely suffer from serious diseases or pests. No special maintenance is required.

PROPAGATION: Cuttings and division are both practical and easy methods of propagation. The soil must be well drained.

Caryopteris × *clandonensis* 'Arthur Simmonds'   PLATE 58

Arthur Simmonds Bluebeard, Arthur Simmonds Blue-spirea, Arthur Simmonds Blue-mist

This woody-based, herbaceous-stemmed ground cover is superb for its magnificent late season floral display and attractive green-surfaced, silvery-undersided foliage. Reaching 2 feet tall and 4 feet wide, bluebeard makes an effective backdrop to other late bloomers like *Coreopsis rosea* and cultivars of *C. verticillata*. It is also superb as a foreground plant to tall fall-blooming grasses such as cultivars of *Miscanthus sinensis* and *Erianthus ravennae*. It is attractive to honeybees. No foot traffic is tolerated.

SCIENTIFIC NAME: *Caryopteris* × *clandonensis* 'Arthur Simmonds' (kar-i-*op*-ter-is klan-doe-*nen*-sis). Named for the Greek words *karyon,* a nut, and *pteron,* a wing, *Caryopteris* refers to the winged fruits. *Clandonensis* refers to Clandon, Surrey, England, where this hybrid originated. Arthur Simmonds was the hybridizer who named the original selection after himself.

HARDINESS / ORIGIN: Zones 4 to 9, usually dying back to the ground in the winter in Zones 4 to 6, then resprouting and blooming on the new growth the following season; Clandon Surrey, England, from crosses made by Arthur Simmonds (sometime before 1945) involving *C. incana* and *C. mongholica.*

LEAVES / FLOWERS / FRUIT: The oval, tooth-edged, eucalyptus-scented leaves reach 1 to 2 inches long by ½ to 1¼ inch wide and are oppositely arranged. Colored dull green above and silvery below, they nicely compliment the numerous whorls of vibrant purplish blue flowers borne in late summer to fall. The fruit is tiny and nonornamental.

RATE / SPACING: Growth is moderate. Plants from 1- to 3-gallon-sized containers are spaced 2½ to 3½ feet apart.

HORTICULTURAL SELECTIONS: 'Azure', with bright

blue flowers; 'Blue Mist', with powder blue flowers; 'Dark Knight', flowers colored deep bluish purple; 'Ferndown', with dark green leaves and dark blue flowers; 'Heavenly Blue', with compact habit, dark blue flowers, and earlier season of bloom; 'Kew Blue', with dark blue flowers; 'Longwood Blue', reaching 4 feet tall, with bluish violet flowers; 'Worcester Gold', with golden flowers and light blue flowers.

OTHER SPECIES: *C. incana* (*in*-kay-na), common bluebeard, ranges from 3 to 5 feet tall and is less commonly used as a ground cover. Hardy only to Zone 7, what this species lacks in hardiness it makes up for in bloom. Beginning in late summer and continuing through mid fall, it blooms with a profusion of bright violet-blue fragrant blossoms. Its dull green, 1- to 3-inch-long, ½- to 1½-inch-wide foliage is silvery below and edged with coarse, nearly round teeth. A native from Japan to northwestern China, it may, like *C.* × *clandonensis,* be grown as a herbaceous perennial in areas of cold winter—where it dies down in winter but quickly recovers the following spring and blooms well on the current season's growth. It has given rise to 'Blue Billows', a florific lavender-blue flowered selection that trails along the ground and displays compact habit, and 'Candida', with white flowers.

C. mongholica (mon-*go*-li-ka), Mongolian bluebeard, the other parent in the formation of *C.* × *clandonensis,* is similar to *C. incana.* Although less showy in flower, it is considerably more cold hardy (reported to be reliable in Zone 3).

CULTURE / CARE: Bluebeards prefer full sun and well-drained, light-textured, acidic to neutral soil. Like most plants they tolerate moderate periods of drought but benefit from occasional deep watering during such times. They are quite resistant to diseases and insects and seldom incur serious problems. Maintenance in the North consists of trimming back winter-killed stems in early spring; in warmer climates, one-third of the new growth should be trimmed back in late winter. Regardless of climate, a longer, more prolific blooming period may be induced by lightly pruning (to remove the first inch or so of the stem tips) in late summer.

PROPAGATION: Cuttings and division are both effective methods. Cuttings should be taken in early summer and rooted in a porous medium after being treated with 2000 to 4000 ppm IBA/talc. Division is successful any time the soil is kept moist.

Ceanothus gloriosus   PLATE 59
Point Reyes Ceanothus, Point Reyes Creeper

A prostrate, spreading shrub that reaches 24 inches tall and spreads to 5 feet across (rooting as it creeps), Point Reyes ceanothus is an excellent general cover for larger areas on flat or sloping surfaces. Often it is used as a specimen or in small groups as an accent plant. In such cases, it is best suited for more formal landscapes. Its ability to withstand high levels of salt makes it especially useful in coastal landscapes. None of the ceanothuses has showy fruit and none tolerates foot traffic.

SCIENTIFIC NAME: *Ceanothus gloriosus* (see-a-*no*-thus / kee-an-*oh*-thus glore-ee-*oh*-sus). *Ceanothus* is an ancient Greek name, supposedly applied to a now-unknown plant by Theophrastus, the Greek philosopher. *Gloriosus,* glorious or showy, refers to the colorful flowers and glossy leaves.

HARDINESS / ORIGIN: Zones 7 to 9; California.

LEAVES / FLOWERS / FRUIT: The radiant leaves are evergreen, elliptic to roundish, to 1½ inches long, dark glossy green, leathery-textured, and usually spiny-toothed about their edges. In bloom, which occurs during spring, this plant is magnificent. Against the glossy green foliage, the fluffy heads of lavender-blue flowers give more an impression of complement than contrast.

RATE / SPACING: Growth is moderate to fast. Plants of the species from 2- to 3-gallon-sized containers are spaced 3½ to 4½ feet apart, and cultivars are spaced a distance of two-thirds their mature spread.

HORTICULTURAL SELECTIONS: 'Anchor Bay', somewhat lower and more compact; var. *exaltatus* 'Emily Brown', 18 to 30 inches tall by 6 to 10 feet wide, with dark green leaves and blue-violet flowers; var. *porrectus,* low sprawling, 12 to 30 inches tall by 7 feet or more wide, fine-textured with deep blue flowers.

OTHER SPECIES: *C. griseus* var. *horizontalis* (gri-*see*-us / gris-*ee*-us hor-i-zon-*tay*-lis), Carmel creeper or Yankee Point ceanothus, is a California native hardy in Zones 8 to 10 or 11. Its leaves are evergreen, broadly oval-shaped, to 1¾ inches long, wavy edged, hairy below, and colored dark glossy green. The 2-inch-long blue flowers appear in spring and are very effective. Plants range from 18 to 30 inches tall by 8 to 15 feet wide. Growth is fast. Plants from 2- to 3-gallon-sized containers are spaced 6 to 11 feet apart. Horticultural selections include 'Compacta', with small, densely arranged foliage and a mature size of only 1 foot tall by 3 feet wide; 'Hurricane Point', more vigorous, 4 feet tall by as much as 30 feet wide, habit rather open; 'Yankee Point', to 3 feet high by 15 feet wide.

C. prostratus (pros-*tray*-tus), named for its prostrate (lying flat) growth habit, is commonly called squaw-carpet ceanothus or Mahala mat. This West Coast native is hardy in Zones 7 to 10 and reaches 3 to 6 inches tall by up to 10 feet wide. Growth is fast.

Plants from 2- to 3-gallon-sized containers are spaced 3½ to 5 feet apart. The leaves are evergreen, spine-edged, leathery, and dark glossy green. The flowers are small, blue, and effective during spring.

C. thyrsiflorus var. *repens* (thir-si-*floe*-rus *ree*-penz), creeping blue blossom ceanothus, is hardy in Zones 8 to 10 or 11 and native to the Pacific Coast from Oregon to California. It ranges from 18 to 24 inches tall by to 5 feet wide. Growth is moderate. Plants from 2- to 3-gallon-sized containers are spaced 3½ to 4½ feet apart. The name *thyrsiflorus* refers to the thyrsoid flower arrangement, that is, with flowers arranged in compact ball-like structures at the ends of the branches. The glossy green leaves are evergreen, oblong, to 2 inches long, and finely toothed. The flowers are small, blue, and effective in spring.

CULTURE / CARE: All species prefer light, sandy, well-drained, acidic to neutral soil. They are quite tolerant of short periods of drought: two deep waterings per month in summer are usually adequate. Overwatering results in root rot. Ceanothuses prefer full sun to light shade. Pests and diseases include scale insects, leaf spot, powdery mildew, rust, root rot, and crown gall. Maintenance needs are few; a light shearing each spring after blooming keeps plants looking neat and stimulates new growth.

PROPAGATION: Cuttings taken during early summer root quickly and in high percentages.

Cedrus deodara 'Prostrata'   PLATE 60
Prostrate Deodar Cedar, Prostrate Himalayan Cedar

Deodar cedar is not a ground cover but an evergreen tree that ascends to 70 feet. On the other hand, its prostrate-growing selection 'Prostrata' (syn. 'Pendula') is a ground cover of unparalleled grace and beauty. Indeed, as a specimen, particularly in terraced settings or elevated planter, its soft texture and droopy stems are awe inspiring.

SCIENTIFIC NAME: *Cedrus deodara* 'Prostrata' (*see*-drus dee-oh-*dar*-a pros-*tray*-ta). *Cedrus* is the ancient Greek name for this genus, some claiming that it is derived from the word *Kedron,* a river of Judea. *Deodara* is named after the northern Indian state Deodar. 'Prostrata' means low growing with a flat orientation.

HARDINESS / ORIGIN: Zones 7 to 8 or 9; Himalayas.

LEAVES / FLOWERS / FRUIT: The leaves are needlelike, 1 to 1½ inches long, and borne in whorls of 15 to 20. Held upon droopy branches, they tend to cascade down in a pendant fashion when overhanging a terrace wall and contribute a calming, subdued mood to the landscape. The fall flowers are either male or female and formed on the same plant. Each is a 2- to

3-inch-long, ½- to ⅝-inch-wide, erectly oriented cone. During the ripening process (which may take two years), the cones expand to 3 inches long by 2 inches wide. First green, they eventually mature to brown.

RATE / SPACING: Growth is moderate. Plants are spaced alone or in small groups with at least 4 feet on each side for natural development.

HORTICULTURAL SELECTIONS: 'Golden Horizon', with vibrant golden-yellow foliage; 'Prostrate Beauty', slow-growing, flat-topped, gray-blue leaves.

CULTURE / CARE: Deodar cultivars are best in a well-drained, somewhat dry acidic soil and a sunny to lightly shaded location. They are moderately tolerant to drought but prefer not to be located in a site exposed to strong winds. They sometimes die back a little from canker and occasionally are chewed on by weevils. They need no regular maintenance, but should plants develop an upright-growing leader, trim it to keep the plants growing horizontally.

PROPAGATION: Cuttings can be rooted during late fall; they should be treated with 8000 ppm IBA/talc, placed in a porous mix, and set in a poly tent with bottom heat of 70°F. Grafting is also successful in late winter using *C. deodara* as an understock.

Centranthus ruber   PLATE 61
Jupiter's Beard, Red Valerian, Fox's Beard

This compact 3-foot-tall, evergreen, herbaceous-stemmed, woody-based, sprawling ground cover gives a tremendous long lasting floral show. Yet, Jupiter's beard is also quite utilitarian. On steep banks it easily controls erosion, and on a moderate to large scale it makes a durable general purpose cover along streets, in rough fringe areas, and overhanging boulders and retaining walls. The use of a single specimen in the perennial border should not be overlooked either, especially since its rose-red flowers are complimentary to greens, blues, and yellows. No foot traffic is tolerated.

SCIENTIFIC NAME: *Centranthus ruber* (sen-*tran*-thoos *rew*-bur). *Centranthus* comes from the Greek *kentron,* a spur, and *anthos,* a flower, referring to the spurred flowers. *Ruber,* red or ruddy, also refers to the flowers.

HARDINESS / ORIGIN: Zones 5 to 8; Mediterranean region and Portugal, now naturalized in western and central Europe as well as in the western United States.

LEAVES / FLOWERS / FRUIT: The evergreen, broadly oval to lance-shaped, bluish green stemless leaves range from 2 to 4 inches long and often are toothed about their margins. The numerous fragrant flowers of late spring to late summer are dark crimson to rose-red, reach ½ inch long, and often repeat sporadically in fall. The fruit that follows is fuzzy like a dandelion and disperses in the wind—sometimes causing Jupiter's beard to show up in places where it is not wanted.

RATE / SPACING: Growth is fast. Plants from 1- to 2-gallon sized containers are spaced 2 to 2½ feet apart.

HORTICULTURAL SELECTIONS: 'Albus', with white flowers; 'Atrococcineus', with vibrant scarlet flowers; 'Red Valerian', with rose-red flowers; 'Roseus', with bright rose-red flowers.

CULTURE / CARE: Jupiter's beard grows best in sunny or lightly shaded, well drained, limy to slightly acidic soils. It is tolerant of drought and prefers the soil somewhat on the dry side. Occasionally, it is the host of aphids and mealybugs. In overly wet soil it develops crown rot, but otherwise is resistant to disease.

PROPAGATION: Division, stem cuttings, and seed are the customary means of propagation.

Cephalophyllum alstonii　　　　PLATE 62
Ice Plant, Vygie

Of the many ice plants discussed in this book, including species of *Delosperma, Drosanthemum,* and *Lampranthus,* this one, like the others, is a succulent and is called ice plant because its foliage glistens when wet and resembles ice. Another thing it has in common with the other ice plants is that it formerly belonged to the genus *Mesembryanthemum.* It forms low clumps ranging from 3 to 5 inches tall and 15 to 18 inches wide. Its best use is as a specimen in rock gardens or as a general cover on level or gently sloping terrain. It combines well with noninvasive succulents and herbaceous, arid-climate plants. Some good companions include haworthia, agave, aloe, and several species of cacti. No foot traffic is tolerated.

SCIENTIFIC NAME: *Cephalophyllum alstonii* (sef-a-loe-*fil*-um *all*-stun-ee-eye). *Cephalophyllum* in Latin implies that the leaves are arranged in heads; in other words, they are daisylike. *Alstonii* is a memorial.

HARDINESS / ORIGIN: Zones 9 to 10 or 11; South Africa.

LEAVES / FLOWERS / FRUIT: The leaves are evergreen, erect, upward curving, and 2¾ inches long by ⅜ inch across. They are nearly cylindrical in cross section and colored gray-green with dark dots. The magnificent daisylike flowers, although solitary, are numerous and create an outstanding show in late winter to mid spring. Each reaches 3¼ inches wide and opens to a rich wine red with the rising of the sun. The fruit is nonornamental.

RATE / SPACING: Growth is moderate. Plants from 3- to 4-inch-diameter containers are spaced 6 to 12 inches apart.

HORTICULTURAL SELECTIONS: 'Red Spike', with bronzy red, clawlike, erect leaves and bright cerise-red flowers.

OTHER SPECIES: *C. anemoniflorum* (a-nem-oh-ni-*floe*-rum), named for its salmon-pink flowers that resemble *Anemone,* is procumbent in habit.

C. aureorubrum (awe-ree-oh-*roob*-rum) trails along the ground with its branch tips ascending and displays bluish green leaves and yellow to rose-colored flowers.

C. cupreum (koop-*ree*-um) is low-growing with apricot-colored and coppery-colored flowers.

C. procumbens (pro-*kum*-benz) displays a low trailing habit, blue-green to rose-tinged leaves, and golden-yellow flowers.

C. subulatoides (sub-you-*lay*-toy-deez) has a trailing habit, light gray-green leaves, and purple-red flowers with yellow centers.

CULTURE / CARE: *Cephalophyllum* species are adaptable to a wide range of well-drained soils. Although quite tolerant of drought, occasional deep watering during the heat of summer is beneficial. They require full sun. Pests of greatest incidence are aphids and mealybugs.

PROPAGATION: Cuttings root well throughout the year. Division can be accomplished any time as long as the soil is kept moist until the roots become reestablished.

Cephalotaxus harringtonia 'Prostrata'　　PLATE 63
Prostrate Japanese Plum Yew

A fascinating conifer with extraordinary leaf characteristics, prostrate Japanese plum yew reaches 2 to 3 feet tall by 3 to 4 feet wide and displays large yew-like, nearly blackish green, stiff glossy green foliage upon slightly arching branches. It may be used both as a specimen or as a moderate-scale to large-scale general cover and is especially effective as a backdrop to lighter colored plants and landscape elements. No foot traffic is tolerated.

SCIENTIFIC NAME: *Cephalotaxus harringtonia* 'Prostrata' (sef-a-low-*tak*-sus hare-ing-*tone*-ee-a pros-*tray*-ta). *Cephalotaxus* comes from combining the Greek *kephale,* a head, with the genus *Taxus* (the yews), in reference to the resemblance of the species *C. harringtonia* to the treelike species of *Taxus. Harringtonia* commemorates the Earl of Harrington. 'Prostrata' means low growing with a flat orientation.

HARDINESS / ORIGIN: Zones 5 or 6 to 9; moist, semi-shaded mountains of Japan (from Kyushu to northern Honshu).

LEAVES / FLOWERS / FRUIT: The deep blackish green, sturdy, almost plasticlike, evergreen, ¾- to 1-inch-long, ⅛-inch-wide, sharply pointed, broad needlelike leaves are closely set in opposite fashion along medium green stems. Plants are either male or female; both are needed for fruit formation. Flowers are borne in spring. The female flowers are tiny, scalelike, and nonornamental, while the male flowers, composed of four to six stamens, are tiny and round. The olive to reddish brown fruit, formed only on the female plants, is an oval-shaped naked seed from 1 to 1¼ inches long and ¾ inch wide.

RATE / SPACING: Growth is slow to moderate. Plants from 2- to 3-gallon-sized containers are spaced 3½ to 4½ feet apart.

HORTICULTURAL SELECTIONS: 'Duke Gardens', much like 'Prostrata', 2 to 3 feet tall by 3 to 4 feet wide, branches carried in a more elevated horizontal fashion.

CULTURE / CARE: Prostrate Japanese plum yew requires well-drained sandy or loamy acidic soils. Although it is quite heat and drought tolerant, it is even more vibrant if given an occasional deep drink of water during the heat of summer. It prefers light shade but tolerates full sun, particularly in the northern part of its range. Its main pest problem is mites. Although it needs no maintenance, some gardeners prefer to shear it during the spring to promote branching and compactness.

PROPAGATION: Cuttings should be taken during late fall or early winter, treated with 3000 ppm IBA/talc, and stuck in a very porous medium with bottom heat of 75°F. Root formation may take up to three months.

Cerastium tomentosum   PLATE 64
Snow-in-summer

An old-fashioned herbaceous ground cover, snow-in-summer is low growing, creeping, matlike, and 6 to 12 inches tall by 12 inches wide. Although it tolerates no foot traffic, it performs well as a small-scale to moderate-scale general cover. It is particularly useful on sunny banks that are too steep to mow, between stepping stones, and in the cracks of stone walls and ledges as a filler.

SCIENTIFIC NAME: *Cerastium tomentosum* (sir-*as*-tee-um toe-men-*toe*-sum). *Cerastium* comes from the Greek *keras,* horn, in reference to the seed capsules, which look like horns. *Tomentosum,* woolly, refers to the grayish hairs that cover the leaves and stems.

HARDINESS / ORIGIN: Zones 3 to 10 (good drainage and air movement essential to prevent fungal diseases especially in warmer areas); Europe and Sicily.

LEAVES / FLOWERS / FRUIT: The evergreen leaves are grayish green and covered with soft-textured whitish hairs. Each reaches 1 inch long by ¼ inch wide and is oblong to lance-shaped. Atop the leaves and stems

during mid to late spring are borne a profusion of ½- to ¾-inch-wide, five-petaled white flowers. They are arranged in bundles of 3 to 15, and their effect reminds one of new-fallen snow. The fruit is tiny and nonornamental.

RATE / SPACING: Growth is moderate to fast. Plants from 3- to 4-inch-diameter containers are spaced 10 to 12 inches apart.

HORTICULTURAL SELECTIONS: Var. *columnae,* only 4 inches tall; 'Silver Carpet', frosty white leaves, 8 inches tall; 'Yo Yo', silvery leaves, many flowers, 10 inches tall.

OTHER SPECIES: *C. biebersteinii* (bee-bear-*stine*-ee-eye), taurus chickweed, is hardy in Zones 2 to 7. It is much like *C. tomentosum,* but its leaves are larger (to 1½ inches long by ⅕ inch wide), and its flower petals are notched on the ends.

CULTURE / CARE: Well-drained sandy or loamy soils with low fertility are best for these species. They are tolerant of drought and, although their performance may be enhanced with supplemental watering, rarely is it required. They prefer full sun, but plants in the South do better with light shade. If plants receive too much shade or humidity, they suffer from damping off, which causes them to rot off at the soil line. Aphids and mealybugs may also plague them at times but normally are not serious. Maintenance needs are nonexistent, but some gardeners prefer to mow plants in early spring before new growth begins, to keep plants neat and to remove any dried seed heads from the previous season.

PROPAGATION: Cuttings taken during summer will root but are prone to damping off unless the medium is very porous. Division during spring or fall is nearly foolproof. Seed, which is commercially available, germinates in two to four weeks.

Ceratostigma plumbaginoides   PLATE 65
Dwarf Plumbago, Blue Ceratostigma, Leadwort, Chinese Leadwort

If the top 100 gardeners of North America were asked to describe plumbago in three words or less, I think the resounding reply would be underrated, underappreciated, underutilized. In comparison to the big three, English ivy, pachysandra, and periwinkle, plumbago is every bit as durable and long lived and every bit as free of diseases and pests. In respect to its flowers and foliage, many feel that it is superior. One thing that it is not, though, is fully evergreen, and for this reason it will never gain the acceptance that the big three ground covers have enjoyed. Even so, plumbago clearly merits a bigger role in landscaping than it currently plays.

For rich, late-season color, plumbago deserves

rave reviews. Toward the middle part of summer its gentian blue flowers begin to unfold, and by the time the first few frosts have put a damper on its cheerful floral parade, the foliage has turned a rich coppery bronze. Low-growing, erectly branched, and horizontally spreading, the easy-to-care-for, stately plumbago is among the most aristocratic of the herbaceous ground covers. Attractive throughout the growing season, it is an unmistakable beacon signifying the end of summer and the onset of fall.

This durable, herbaceous ground cover reaches 6 to 10 inches tall and spreads indefinitely. It is excellent for providing contrast underneath light-green-leaved shrubs and small, open-canopied trees, particularly those with smooth or ashen-colored bark. Often it is used as an edging between paths and turf areas or as a turf substitute in tree-containing island beds of parking areas (to eliminate troublesome mowing). It should not be turned loose in a planting of refined perennials or interplanted with feeble annuals as its aggressive, spreading nature soon overruns less tenacious neighbors. When mass planted by itself, however, it is virtually foolproof. It combines well with bulbs such as crocus and daffodil, which lend early season interest while the plumbago is still dormant. Very infrequent foot traffic is tolerated.

SCIENTIFIC NAME: *Ceratostigma plumbaginoides* (ser-at-oh-*stig*-ma plum-ba-ji-*noy*-deez). *Ceratostigma* comes from the Greek *keras,* a horn, and *stigma,* the female floral apparatus that accepts the pollen, alluding to the hornlike branches of the stigmas. *Plumbaginoides,* plumbago-like, refers to the related genus *Plumbago.*

HARDINESS / ORIGIN: Zones 5 or 6 to 9; China.

LEAVES / FLOWERS / FRUIT: The semievergreen leaves usually are deciduous in the northern part of this species' range. They emerge in late spring (frequently a full month after expected), developing hues of burgundy, then later becoming a dull, almost platinum green. Finally, by the season's end, they have developed shades of bronze, copper, and even to some extent, maroon. Each elongated oval-shaped leaf reaches 1½ inches long by ¾ inch wide. The ½-inch-wide, star-shaped, five-petaled flowers are borne in dense clusters at the ends of the stems. Beginning in the latter part of summer, each day around mid morning they burst open and radiate their presence like brilliant gentian blue stars. Flowering generally lasts at least until the first frost, and the fruit which follows is interesting but not greatly ornamental.

RATE / SPACING: Growth is moderate to fast. Plants from 2- to 4-inch-diameter containers are spaced 8 to 10 inches apart, and those from pint-sized to ½-gallon-sized containers are spaced 10 to 16 inches apart.

CULTURE / CARE: Rich, well-drained, acidic loam is best, yet adaptability is plumbago's hallmark. As long as it is given good drainage, it performs more than adequately, even in sandy or clay-laden soils. Periodic watering during extended hot, dry weather is beneficial but usually not necessary, and full sun to moderate shade are the best conditions for light. Should any pests appear, they will likely be inconsequential aphids. Diseases should not present much of a problem, provided the soil is well drained.

PROPAGATION: Stem cuttings are best taken during late summer. Division, which is foolproof, can be performed any time the soil is not frozen. Rhizome cuttings may be taken during fall, sectioned into 3- to 4-inch-long segments, placed in a moist medium, and stored in a cold frame or unheated greenhouse; the next spring they will have formed new shoots and roots. Seed propagation is possible though seldom used; seed germinates best if stratified in moist sand for six weeks at 40°F prior to sowing.

Chamaedaphne calyculata   PLATE 66
Leatherleaf, Bog Leatherleaf, Ground Daphne, Cassandra

This little shrub is tough and virtually maintenance-free. With a sprawling, rhizomatous, woody, dense shrubby habit, it ranges from 2 to 4 feet tall and spreads over 4 feet across. Its foliage is attractive throughout the year, and its floral display during spring is lovely. It is best used in large masses surrounding rich acidic bogs, pond and lake shores, and along sandy stream beds. As a specimen in a moist corner of the rock garden it also functions well.

SCIENTIFIC NAME: *Chamaedaphne calyculata* (kam-e-*daf*-nee ka-lik-you-*lay*-ta). *Chamaedaphne* comes from the Greek *chamai,* on the ground, and *daphne,* literally meaning ground daphne. *Calyculata* refers to the prominent calyxes (leafy appendages) surrounding the flowers.

HARDINESS / ORIGIN: Zones 1 or 2 to 8 or 9; bog margins, and sandy, acidic, high-water-table meadows and ditches of northern Asia, North America, and northern Europe.

LEAVES / FLOWERS / FRUIT: The leathery leaves are flat green (bronzy in fall), evergreen, simple, alternate, elliptic to oblong, ½ to 2 inches long, short-stemmed, pointed at their ends, and minutely toothed about their edges. From the base of the stem to the ends, which terminate with flowers, the leaves become increasingly smaller. The creamy white flowers of spring are arranged in leafy racemes or solitarily in the axils of the branch tips. Nodding downward, they are urn-shaped, five-toothed, and ¼ inch long. The fruit, a brown capsule, is nonornamental.

RATE / SPACING: Growth is slow. Plants from 1- to 2-gallon-sized containers are spaced 2 to 3 feet apart.

HORTICULTURAL SELECTIONS: Var. *angustifolia,* native from Alaska to Newfoundland, then south to British Columbia, Iowa, and Georgia, is noteworthy for its narrow leaves; var. *latifolia,* broad-leaved, native from Labrador Peninsula west to MacKenzie River, then south to Newfoundland and New England; 'Nana', a dwarf only 1 foot tall.

CULTURE / CARE: Peaty or sandy acidic soil with a high water table is necessary. Drought tolerance, predictably, is poor. Full sun to light shade is preferred. Few serious diseases or pests affect it, and little maintenance is required.

PROPAGATION: Softwood cuttings during mid summer are easily rooted in a mixture of sand, perlite, and peat; treatment with 4000 ppm IBA/talc seems helpful. Individual stems that contain sections of roots or rhizomes are easily split off from the parent clump and then transplanted. Stems that are pinned to the ground will root, and later can be dug up and transplanted. Seed is said to germinate if placed uncovered on peat and kept constantly moist.

Chamaemelum nobile   PLATE 67
Roman Chamomile, Russian Chamomile, Garden Chamomile

This low, horizontally spreading, dense-growing, herbaceous ground cover ranges from 3 to 6 inches tall and spreads 1 foot across. It may be grown on a small or large scale and typically is used as a substitute for turf. Some gardeners even mow it regularly. Even so, since it tolerates only limited foot traffic, it should not be walked on too often.

This species is not to be confused with German chamomile, *Matricaria recutita,* a florific annual that grows considerably taller (2 to 3 feet). Both species are considered to be medicinally useful. Historically, they have been used in poultices to treat disorders of the liver, bladder, and kidneys and to relieve headaches. Their leaves have been used in potpourri, teas, air fresheners, hair tonics, and as a flavoring in liqueurs. Oil extracted from their flowers acts as an anti-inflammatory, antispasmodic, and skin tonic.

Note: it is also correct to spell chamomile as camomile.

SCIENTIFIC NAME: *Chamaemelum nobile* (kam-e-*mel*-um *noe*-bi-lee). *Chamaemelum* comes from the Greek *chamai,* on the ground, and *melon,* apple, here referring to the ground-hugging habit and apple-scented foliage of its species. *Nobile,* noble, refers to flowers that are very large for a plant so small.

HARDINESS / ORIGIN: Zones 5 to 8 or 9; Europe, Azores, and North Africa.

LEAVES / FLOWERS / FRUIT: The leaves are bright green, evergreen, finely divided, 2 inches long, fern-like, and strongly apple scented. The tiny, apple-scented flowers of summer are arranged in heads and look like daisies: yellow in the center and white petals around the outside. The fruit is a tiny brown seed.

RATE / SPACING: Growth is moderate to fast. Plants from pint-sized to quart-sized containers are spaced 10 to 14 inches apart.

HORTICULTURAL SELECTIONS: 'Flore Pleno', with double flowers; 'Treneague', nonflowering, only 2 to 3 inches tall, occasionally employed as a lawn substitute.

CULTURE / CARE: Chamomile grows best in sandy, well-drained acidic to slightly alkaline soils. It prefers full sun or light shade. Because its roots run deep, it is very tolerant of drought; if given only an occasional deep watering, it remains happy throughout summer. It is not greatly susceptible to diseases, and its primary pests are leaf and petal-eating slugs and snails. Maintenance normally consists of mowing plantings during spring to rejuvenate growth and in summer, after flowering, to remove dried flower heads. Some gardeners treat plantings like turf grass, mowing well-established plantings every couple of weeks with a rotary mower. Should you choose to do this, keep your mower on the highest setting to avoid injuring the crown of the plants.

PROPAGATION: Division of chamomile is simple and easily accomplished during spring or fall. Seed is commercially available or can be collected, and germination occurs readily. Many times plants will even reseed themselves naturally.

Chelone obliqua   PLATE 68
Red Turtle-head, Turtle-bloom, Shell-flower, Cod-head, Bitter-herb, Balmony, Salt-rheum Weed, Fish-mouth

Named for its flowers that look like the head of a turtle, this 2- to 3-foot-tall, 1½-foot-wide species and its two related species are upright-stemmed, rhizomatous spreaders that thrive in moist soils. Although used in perennial borders for many years, they have only recently become recognized as ground covers. As such they should be mass planted along the bank of streams and ponds in broad sweeps, or clumped here and there for accent. No foot traffic is tolerated.

SCIENTIFIC NAME: *Chelone obliqua* (kee-*loe*-nee / chel-*oh*-nee o-*blee*-kwa) *Chelone* takes its name from the Greek *chelone,* tortoise, in reference to the flowers. *Obliqua* means lopsided or oblique, but to what this refers is not clear.

HARDINESS / ORIGIN: Zones 5 or 6 to 9; wet thickets

and streamsides from Virginia to Illinois, south to Florida.

LEAVES / FLOWERS / FRUIT: The deciduous, oblong to broadly lance-shaped, tooth-edged, dark green leaves are oppositely arranged upon spreading or ascending stems. At the branch ends, the flowers are borne during mid summer to fall; they are 1 inch long, red to rose-purple, and turtle-shaped. The fruit, an ovoid capsule, is nonornamental.

RATE / SPACING: Growth is moderate. Plants from pint-sized to gallon-sized containers are spaced 1 to 1½ feet apart.

HORTICULTURAL SELECTIONS: 'Alba', with white flowers; 'Bethelii', with deep rose-colored flowers, more flowers per spike; 'Praecox Nana', with lilac-red flowers during mid to late summer, to 16 inches tall; var. *speciosa,* native from Indiana to Minnesota south to Missouri and Arkansas, with narrower leaves and larger bright rose-pink flowers.

OTHER SPECIES: *C. glabra* (*glay*-bra), named for its white flowers, is commonly called white turtle-head. Native from Newfoundland to northern Georgia and westward to Minnesota, this dark green lance-leaved species blooms with dense upright spikes of white, red-tinged to rose-tinged, late summertime flowers. It reaches 2 to 3 feet tall and spreads by rhizomes to 2½ feet across. It is hardy in Zones 3 to 8, but plants often languish in Zone 8 if not in constantly moist soil.

C. lyonii (lie-*on*-ee-eye), named after John Lyon (c. 1765–1814), Scottish gardener, botanist, and North American plant collector, is commonly called Lyon's turtle-head. This species is erect-stemmed and 1 to 3 feet tall by 1½ feet wide. Its oval leaves range from 3 to 7 inches long, are sharply pointed, rounded at their bases, and coarsely toothed along their margins. Hailing from mountainous swamps and wet thickets of Virginia to North Carolina, westward to Tennessee and Georgia, it blooms from mid summer to early fall with numerous spikes of 1-inch-long red or rose-purple turtle-shaped flowers. Hardy in Zones 3 to 8. 'Hot Lips' reaches 2 to 3 feet tall, displays rose-pink flowers, red stems, and leaves that are first bronzy green, then deep shiny green.

CULTURE / CARE: *Chelone* species prefer full sun to light shade and, if sited in full sun, tolerate dense shade late in the day. None are drought tolerant, and all prefer to be grown in organically rich, moist, acid soils. *Chelone lyonii* is most adaptable to soils of average moisture. Powdery mildew is the most common problem and can best be averted by growing in constantly moist soil in a site with good air circulation. Maintenance is simple and consists of shearing back the shoot tips in mid spring to promote vigor and density.

PROPAGATION: Cuttings taken during late spring and summer root easily. Division is effective any time the soil is kept adequately moist, and seed should be sown on moist peat at a temperature of 40°F. Then after six weeks the temperature should be raised to 60°F. Germination occurs 2 weeks later.

Chimaphila umbellata   PLATE 69

Pipsissewa, Prince's Pine, Noble Pine, Bitter Wintergreen, King's Cure, Ground Holly, Pine Tulip, Love-in-winter, Wax Flower, Pyrole, Fragrant Wintergreen, Rheumatism Weed, Butter Winter

Pipsissewa is a relatively rare, low-growing, rhizomatous, semiwoody ground cover that reaches 6 to 10 inches tall and spreads indefinitely. It is particularly well suited for use in naturalized gardens, especially underneath oak, beech, maple, and pine trees. There it functions as a sturdy, vibrant, shiny green general ground cover that combines well with pink lady slipper, *Trillium* species, checkerberry, low bush blueberry, and other woodland natives. Folk uses of pipsissewa are numerous. The foliage was used to treat kidney disorders, blisters, backache, rheumatism, typhus, gonorrhea, scrofula, and heart maladies. It was also used as an ingredient in root beer.

SCIENTIFIC NAME: *Chimaphila umbellata* (kye-*maf*-i-la um-bel-*lay*-ta). *Chimaphila* is derived from the Greek *cheima,* winter, and *phileo,* to love, in reference to the evergreen nature of these plants. *Umbellata* refers to the flowers which are arranged in umbels.

HARDINESS / ORIGIN: Zone 4; the species is native to Europe and Asia but two varieties are native to North America.

LEAVES / FLOWERS / FRUIT: The dark glossy green leaves are simple, evergreen, prominently veined, arranged in irregular whorls, oblong to oval or spatula-shaped, 1 to 2½ inches long by ¼ to 1 inch wide, and sharply toothed on the margins. At the apex the leaves are broadly or sharply rounded. The five-petaled flowers are borne early to mid summer, arranged in clusters of two to eight flowers (or sometimes solitary), are nearly round, cup-shaped, and slightly nodding, colored white to pinkish, and reach up to ½ inch across. The fruit, a five-celled globose capsule, is ⅓ inch in diameter, brown, and persists well into winter.

RATE / SPACING: Growth is slow. Plants from quart-sized to gallon-sized containers are spaced 6 to 14 inches apart.

HORTICULTURAL SELECTIONS: Var. *cisatlantica,* meaning on this side of the Atlantic, is comparatively larger (to 12 inches tall), more prominently veined, native from dry acidic woodlands of Quebec and Ontario, south to Michigan, Minnesota, Illinois, Georgia, New England, and Nova Scotia, and blooms from mid to late summer; var. *occidentalis,* native from British Columbia to southeastern Alaska, south to Colorado, Utah, and California, east to northern Michigan, with longer leaves (to 3½ inches), coarser-textured, very little venation.

OTHER SPECIES: *C. maculata* (mak-you-*lay*-ta), named for its spotted foliage, is commonly called spotted or striped pipsissewa or spotted or striped wintergreen. Native to North America but occurring further south than *C. umbellata,* this 4-inch-tall species differs from *C. umbellata* in that its foliage is lance-shaped to oval-lance-shaped and is variegated with white markings along the veins. Its flowers are white, fragrant, and borne during summer.

C. menziesii (men-*zeez*-ee-ee), named after Archibald Menzies (1754–1842), Scottish naval surgeon and botanist, displays oval to narrowly oblong, toothed, 1⅜-inch-long foliage that is sometimes variegated with white. Its height reaches 6 inches, and its white summertime flowers fade to pink as they age. It is native to coniferous forests from southern California to Idaho and Montana.

CULTURE / CARE: The pipsissewas perform best in acidic soils that range from well-drained sandy loam to organic peatlike soil. Their drought tolerance is pretty good, and they prefer light to moderate shade. Diseases of consequence are leaf spot, rust, and leaf blight—often occurring during propagation. No serious pest problems have been reported, and little or no maintenance is required.

PROPAGATION: Cuttings should be taken in midsummer from terminal shoots that contain a short segment of mature wood, treated with 3000 ppm IBA/talc, and stuck in a medium of sand or sand and peat. Patience is essential as cuttings may take until the following spring to root (although some will root within a couple of months). During rooting, the medium must be kept moist at all times but not saturated. A cold frame is a fine structure for propagating *Chimaphila* species, provided it is shaded and well vented during the summer months. Regardless of the method used, once plants are rooted, they should be transplanted immediately or they are likely to succumb to fungal infections. Division is probably the easiest means of propagation and should be conducted in spring. Natural populations of the pipsissewas, unfortunately, are ever decreasing; therefore, initial stock is best obtained by cutting propagation. To date, I have not heard of any surefire means of inducing seeds to germinate.

Chlorophytum comosum PLATE 70
Spider Plant, Ribbon Plant, Walking Anthericum, Spider Ivy

This tuberous-rooted, rhizomatous, stoloniferous, herbaceous, lilylike ground cover reaches 1 to 3 feet tall, spreads indefinitely, and in tropical areas is exceptional as a moderate-scale facing, general cover, or walkway edging. The variegated selections are most frequently cultivated and are popular house plants north of their hardiness limit.

SCIENTIFIC NAME: *Chlorophytum comosum* (klore-oh-*fie*-tum koe-*moe*-sum). *Chlorophytum* comes from the Greek *chloros,* green, and *phyton,* a plant, meaning green-colored plant. *Comosum,* tufted, refers to the arrangement of the foliage.

HARDINESS / ORIGIN: Zones 10 to 11; South Africa.

LEAVES / FLOWERS / FRUIT: The evergreen, tufted (basal-leaved), medium green, long, narrow, smooth-edged leaves (1½ feet long by ¾ inch wide) taper to a fine point and look like wide, drooping blades of grass with conspicuous veins. The ¾-inch-wide flowers, borne in fall and winter, are carried at the ends of curving cylindrical stalks and are six-petaled and white to greenish white.

RATE / SPACING: Growth is fast. Plants from quart-sized to gallon-sized containers are spaced 2½ to 3 feet apart.

HORTICULTURAL SELECTIONS: 'Variegatum', leaves with white and green longitudinal stripes.

CULTURE / CARE: Spider plant is at its best in slightly acidic or alkaline organically rich, well-drained loam. It is not tolerant of drought; often its leaf tips become brown or black due to desiccation if underwatered. For this reason, the soil should be kept slightly moist with supplemental irrigation as needed. Spider plant prefers light to moderate shade. Its most common diseases are crown rot (in poorly drained soils) and dieback of new growth (due to overly acidic soil). Slugs, snails, and caterpillars are common pests. Maintenance consists of removing the flower stalks following the fading of the flowers. Tattered plants can be mowed or clipped back to rejuvenate them.

PROPAGATION: Plantlets that are removed from stolons (particularly when they contain rootlets) will establish quickly when transplanted into moist soil. A short period of intermittent mist may be beneficial if temperatures are very hot.

Chrysogonum virginianum PLATE 71
Golden Star

Among the most endearing of our North American ground covers, this herbaceous, low-spreading,

2- to 4-inch-tall (4 to 8 inches when in bloom) florific charmer sprawls to 1½ feet across. A native to woodlands, it is excellent for use as an accent plant or facer in naturalized or native woodland gardens. It combines nicely with deciduous and evergreen shrubs, small trees of open habit, and numerous clump-forming ferns and herbaceous perennials. Limited foot traffic is tolerated.

SCIENTIFIC NAME: *Chrysogonum virginianum* (kris-*sog*-oh-num / kris-*oh*-go-num vir-jin-ee-*aye*-num). *Chrysogonum* comes from the Greek *chrysos,* gold, and *gonu,* a joint, in reference to the golden flowers that originate at the joints of the stems. *Virginianum* means of Virginia.

HARDINESS / ORIGIN: Zones 5 to 9; woodlands from Pennsylvania to Florida, west to Louisiana.

LEAVES / FLOWERS / FRUIT: The medium green, semi-evergreen, simple, oval to oblong, 1- to 3-inch-wide leaves are round-toothed about their edges and covered with sparse hairs. During spring, a profusion of vibrant, golden-yellow, star-shaped, five-petaled flowers rise above the foliage mass on stems that originate from the leaf axils. Through summer and into fall, the flowers continue to arise, but in much reduced numbers, particularly in cooler climates, and to a lesser degree in the South. The tiny fruit that follows is nonornamental.

RATE / SPACING: Growth is moderate. Plants from 2¼-inch-diameter to pint-sized containers are spaced 6 to 12 inches apart.

HORTICULTURAL SELECTIONS: Var. *australe,* with shorter stems, more rapid spread, and fewer flowers; 'Eco Lacquered Spider', with long purple strawberry-like runners and shiny green leaves; 'Springbrook', a dwarf strain of lower habit; var. *virginianum,* 4 to 6 inches tall when not in flower.

CULTURE / CARE: Golden star tolerates a wide range of well-drained soils, yet is particularly successful in richly organic soils of moderate acidity. Similarly, it tolerates a range of light conditions from full sun to moderate shade, but flourishes in light to moderate shade—essential in the South. Drought tolerance is marginal, so it may be necessary to water during the heat of summer.

PROPAGATION: Division is easily accomplished during spring. If seed is used it should be collected ripe, stored cool, and sown the following spring; germination takes about three weeks at 70°F.

Cistus

PLATE 72

Rock Rose

Those species of rock rose that are good for covering the ground are low-spreading shrubs. Because of their fire resistance they are well adapted for plant-ing in public areas, such as along pathways in parks and near building entrances (places where cigarettes are likely to be tossed). They also make nice foundation facers and soil retainers for terraced or sloping locations. Useful in desert or seaside locations, they show good resistance to soils that are highly saline. No foot traffic is tolerated.

SCIENTIFIC NAME: *Cistus* (*sis*-tus) was the ancient Greek name applied to the rock roses.

HARDINESS / ORIGIN: Zone 7 or 8; Mediterranean region.

LEAVES / FLOWERS / FRUIT: The leaves typically are evergreen, oppositely arranged, simple, and unlobed. The showy white, purple, or yellowish flowers are borne either alone or in branch-ending clusters. The fruit is nonornamental.

RATE / SPACING: Growth is fast. Plants from 1- to 2-gallon-sized containers are spaced 2½ to 3½ feet apart.

SPECIES: *C. crispus* (*kris*-pus), commonly called wrinkleleaf rock rose, is native to the western Mediterranean region and hardy to Zone 7. It reaches 1½ to 2 feet tall and spreads 4 to 5 feet wide. Its hairy, slightly aromatic, evergreen leaves are simple, oblong to elliptic, deep green, and reach 1½ inches long. The reddish pink five-petaled flowers with yellow centers are arranged in bundles of seven, reach 2 inches wide, and provide a superb show from late spring to mid summer.

C. hybridus (*hy*-brid-us), hybrid rock rose, comes from the cross between *C. populifolius* and *C. salviifolius.* It typically reaches 1½ to 2½ feet tall, is hardy in Zones 7 to 9, and displays evergreen, 2-inch-long, oval, green leaves. Its flowers with yellow centers and white petals arrive during late spring.

C. salviifolius (sal-vi-*foe*-lee-us), named for its leaves that resemble those of the genus *Salvia* (sage), is commonly called sageleaf rock rose. Like *C. crispus,* this species hails from the western Mediterranean. It reaches 2 feet tall, spreads to 6 feet wide, and is hardy in Zones 7 to 9. The leaves are evergreen, elliptic to oblong, hairy, wrinkled, and colored grayish green. The flowers reach 2 inches wide, have yellow centers and white petals (with yellow spots at their bases), and arise in profusion from late spring to mid summer.

CULTURE / CARE: *Cistus* species prefer coarse-textured, slightly alkaline, well-drained soils. They display considerable tolerance to drought, and in all but the driest and hottest climates need little supplemental watering. Full sun suits their light requirements, and seldom are they bothered by insects or diseases. Other than pruning out an occasional dead branch, they need little maintenance.

PROPAGATION: Stem cuttings taken during early

summer root well, and layered stems are easily dug and transplanted in early spring. If seed is used, it should be sown into containers to facilitate transplanting, as seedlings, dug from the ground, reportedly do not transplant well.

Clematis   PLATE 73

Vase Vine, Leather Flower, Virgin's Bower

Members of this genus of mostly woody vines tend to have compound leaves and showy solitary or paniculate flowers. Their fruit may be quite attractive with feathery persistent appendages. A few of these climbing species excel as vigorous attractively flowered ground covers. Such species exhibit a tendency to sprawl when unsupported. They are naturals for large-scale use as bank covers (with slight or moderate incline). They easily exclude weeds, and although their trailing stems are reluctant to root, they help control erosion by breaking the force of the rain. If placed in an elevated planter or alongside a retaining wall and allowed to cascade over, their brilliant fall floral display is brought to full attention, and their sweet fragrances easily picked up by air currents.

SCIENTIFIC NAME: *Clematis* (klem-a-tis / kle-*mat*-is) comes from the Greek *klema,* a vine branch, in reference to the climbing nature of many of the species in this genus.

HARDINESS / ORIGIN: See individual species for hardiness; North Temperate Zone.

LEAVES / FLOWERS / FRUIT: The leaves typically are opposite and compound or simple. The flowers are solitary or panicled, bell-shaped or flattish flaring, with the color show coming from the petallike sepals. The fruit, technically an achene, is exceptional on species where it develops a long feathery appendage (style).

RATE / SPACING: Growth is moderate to fast. Plants from quart-sized to gallon-sized containers are spaced 1½ to 2½ feet apart.

SPECIES: *C. alpina* (al-*pie*-na), commonly called alpine clematis, is named for its mountainous native habitat. This native of Europe and Asia is one of the toughest, most hardy, and carefree of the *Clematis* species. Easily cultured and growing well in Zones 5 to 8, it displays attractive coarsely toothed compound deciduous leaves with leaflets ranging from 1 to 2 inches long. During early spring it begins flowering, bearing masses of lovely 1½-inch-long, 1½-inch-wide lavender-blue to purplish blue nodding bell-shaped flowers—their color coming from four narrow pointed sepals and centers composed of often colorful stamens. Followed later by prominent seedheads, looking like fluffy gray balls, this plant is beautiful in all seasons. With luck, it may rebloom,

albeit to a lesser degree, during autumn. Several selections have been made including 'Alba', with pure white sepals contrasting subtly with creamy white stamens; 'Candy', flowers with pink sepals and centers that project outward as opposed to nodding; 'Columbine', with lovely nodding pale lavender sepals; 'Constance', with eight (double the normal four) bright, rich red sepals and creamy stamens; 'Francis Rivis', with 2¼-inch-long lantern-shaped rich medium blue sepals and white stamens in the center; 'Helsingborg', with deep purplish blue flowers and light green foliage; 'Jacqueline du Pre', of hybrid origin, with 2½-inch-long lantern-shaped deep rich pink sepals edged with a silvery margin, centered with pink-tinged, white stamens in the center; 'Pamela Jackman', with broad tapering medium blue sepals; 'Ruby', with rich reddish lilac flowers and mauve stamens; var. *siberica,* with sepals that range from creamy white to pure white, foliage light green; 'White Moth', with pure white flowers; 'Willy', with 1- to 2-inch-wide flowers of pale, pink-reddish-based sepals, center of white petallike stamens.

C. maximowicziana (maks-i-moe-witz-ee-*aye*-na), named to commemorate Carl Ivanovich Maximowicz (1827–1891), a Russian botanist and author of publications on plants of eastern Asia, is commonly called sweet autumn clematis. It was discovered in the late seventeenth century by the famous Swedish botanist Carl P. Thunberg (1743–1828) who named it *C. paniculata.* This name, however, had been used previously for a New Zealand native, and thus the species was renamed at a later date. Despite the name change, confusion still exists, and material offered as *C. paniculata* in the trade is usually *C. maximowicziana.* The species hails from Japan, China, and Korea and is hardy in Zones 4 to 9. Without support, this vine is a vigorous, dense, sprawling ground cover that reaches 8 to 14 inches tall and rapidly spreads more than 10 feet wide, forming a mulch impenetrable to weeds. The tendrilous petioles cling to any narrow support structures. For this reason, be sure to use this plant by itself or underneath large-trunked trees to which it cannot attach itself. A lattice support or wire frame along a deck or building foundation converts this clematis into an effective facer. The semievergreen, oppositely arranged, compound leaves are composed of five leaflets (occasionally three). Each long-stemmed leaflet is ¾ to 2½ inches long (those toward the bottom of the stem generally larger), ½ to 1½ inches wide, and oval to heart-shaped. Colored wine-red (suffused with green) in youth, they become flat medium green on both surfaces with age. The erectly oriented, 1-inch-wide flowers are borne in forked, 3- to 4-inch-long panicles and display four white, narrowly oval petals. Highly fragrant (some say reminiscent of hawthorn) and breathtakingly showy in late summer and early fall, the flowers are borne so profusely at times (particularly following very hot summers) that they nearly obscure the leaves. The fruit is attractive for its persistent feathery white seeds but, unfortunately, is not produced reliably.

C. montana (mon-*tay*-na / mon-*tan*-a), commonly called anemone clematis, is hardy in Zones 5 or 6 to 8. It is a vigorous Chinese species that displays rapid growth. Its handsome compound leaves are composed of three burgundy leaflets that mature to dark green. From the leaf axils are borne, in fall, the buds that will become the next season's flowers. Thus, in cold winters in the North when plants are killed back to the ground, they produce lush springtime growth but no flowers. When this species does flower, the result is a springtime spectacle of color as masses of attractive, 2- to 2½-inch-wide, white, sweetly scented flowers unfold in great number. 'Elizabeth', with pale pink, vanilla-scented flowers and purple-tinged new growth; 'Freda', with deep pink, dark pink-edged sepals and bronzy foliage; 'Grandiflora', with pure white 3- to 4-inch-wide flowers; 'Marjorie', with semidouble 2-inch-wide creamy salmon-pink flowers; 'Odorata', with pleasantly fragrant pale pink flowers; 'Pink Perfection', a floriferous selection with many fragrant soft pink flowers; var. *tetrarose,* with fragrant 3- to 4-inch wide lilac-rose flowers and attractive bronze-tinted new growth; 'Wilson', blooming somewhat later, fragrant, and with cream-colored somewhat twisted sepals.

C. paniculata (pan-ik-you-*lay*-ta), named for the panicles which hold the flowers, is native to both islands of New Zealand. It is a rapid-growing, compound-leaved vine species that is significantly less hardy than *C. maximowicziana,* reliable only in Zones 8 to 10. Most plants called *C. paniculata* in the North American horticultural trade are in reality *C. maximowicziana.* The evergreen, trifoliate leaves of *C. paniculata* are composed of 1½- to 3-inch-long, ¾- to 2-inch wide, oval, blunt-pointed, glossy, medium green leaflets. The leaflet margins are usually entire but occasionally lobed. This clematis is dioecious (that is, each plant bears only male or female flowers). The flowers are borne from spring to summer and arranged in loose axillary panicles to 1 foot long. On male plants each panicle displays six to eight white-sepaled flowers that reach 2 to 4 inches wide with rose-colored anthers and yellow filaments. The female flowers are somewhat smaller and produce attractive fruit with featherlike tails. Variety *lobata* displays leaves that are prominently lobed.

C. virginiana (ver-jin-ee-*aye*-na), meaning of Virginia, is commonly called Virgin's bower, woodbine, traveler's joy, old man's beard, love vine, devil's hair, darning needle, and wild hops. It is a scrambling native common along fence rows, roadsides, and moist low woodlands from Nova Scotia to Manitoba southward from Georgia to Tennessee. A deciduous species with five-parted compound rather dull medium green leaves (leaflets broadly oval to heart-shaped), it is popular among native plant gardeners. It blooms during mid summer to early fall with numerous 1-inch-wide white-sepaled airy flowers that are also attractive after flowering as they bear fluffy filamentous styles (appendages) on the seeds. Hardy in Zones 4 to 9. Extracts of this species were used by Native Americans to treat cuts and sores. Pioneers made a liniment to treat itches, and, in minute doses, took it internally as a treatment for rheumatism, palsy, venereal eruptions, and ulcers. Today it is considered too toxic for general use as it has been associated with causing blisters of the skin and mucous membranes, salivation, bloody vomiting, diarrhea, and even convulsions.

C. viticella (vie-ti-*kel*-a), meaning like a small *Vitis,* or grape species, is commonly called Virgin's bower, a name also applied to *C. virginiana.* It is a durable, dependable, relatively disease-free *Clematis* that, when unsupported, does a good job of covering the ground. From southern Europe and long cultivated there, this fast-growing species is likely to become popular in North America as well. It is hardy in Zones 5 to 9 and is clothed in medium green, often purple-mottled compound deciduous leaves of five to seven leaflets, which often reach 5 inches long, vary from narrowly oval to rounded, and may be further divided into three. It flowers during late summer and fall with masses of nodding 1½- to 2½-inch wide reddish purple to near blue flowers, each with four broadly oval sepals. Borne alone or in groups on slender stalks, the flowers appear in great profusion and make for a splendid late season burst of color. Woody at its base and more or less herbaceous above, the softer stem parts may get beat up a bit during winter and thus many gardeners cut plants back severely during spring to tidy them up. As flower buds are set during summer, this does not adversely affect flowering. 'Abundance', with creamy green stamens, pinkish red wavy edged sepals, 2- to 2½-inch-wide saucer-shaped flowers; 'Alba Luxurians', with vigorous growth and sometimes contorted sepals that often start out greenish then change to pure white; 'Betty Corning', a cross between *C. crispa* and *C. viticella,* with lightly fragrant pale lilac nodding, flaring bell-shaped flowers 2½ to 3 inches in diameter, difficult to propagate; 'Blue Belle', with deep violet sepals and golden stamens; 'Elvan', slightly twisted soft purple sepals with creamy white central stripe, nodding flowers 2 inches in diameter; 'Etoile Violette', early flowering with deep dark velvety purple-sepaled 3- to 4-inch-wide flowers; 'Kermesina' ('Rubra'), with small rich purplish crimson flowers; 'Little Nell', with pale lilac sepals and white stamens; 'Madame Julia Correvon', with twisted, backward curving bright wine red sepals and golden stamens, reaching 2 to 3 inches wide; 'Margot Koster', with large 4- to 6-inch-wide flowers, rich rosy red sepals, white stamens; 'Mary Rose', with a double set of bluish purple, early appearing, nonseeding extraordinarily beautiful flowers; 'Minuet', with green stamens and cream sepals bordered with mauve; 'Pagoda', with dainty nodding flowers, light lilac-pink sepals; 'Polish Spirit', of hybrid origin, rich deep purple sepals, numerous 3- to 4-inch-wide flowers; 'Purpurea Plena Elegans', with double, 2- to 2½-inch-diameter flowers, soft reddish purple sepals; 'Royal Velours', with deep velvety purple sepals, 1- to 2-inch-wide flowers; 'Tango', 2-inch-wide flowers, sepals with purplish red veins and edges, stamens greenish; 'Venosa Violacea', 3- to 4-inch-wide flowers, sepals white with red veins and purple edges.

CULTURE / CARE: These *Clematis* species adapt to well-drained soils ranging from sandy to clay loam with a pH of 4.5 to 7.0. Their drought tolerance is fair; however, their best appearance and growth is realized if periodic supplemental watering is provided during hot, dry weather. A fair amount of wind, too, can be tolerated. They prefer full sun to light shade. Diseases of greatest consequence are leaf spots, stem rot, crown gall, powdery mildew, rust, and smut. Their most pesky pests are the clematis borer, black blister beetle, Japanese weevil, mites, and whiteflies. Little maintenance is necessary beyond trimming back shoots as they outgrow their bounds.

PROPAGATION: Softwood cuttings taken during the summer months usually root quite well; treatment with 2000 to 3000 ppm IBA/talc may prove helpful. If seed is used, collect it during fall and sow immediately in a warm medium (70°F); germination takes about four months.

Clethra alnifolia 'Hummingbird'   PLATE 74
'Hummingbird' Summersweet, 'Hummingbird' Sweet Pepperbush, 'Hummingbird' White Alder, 'Hummingbird' Spiked Alder

Although the parent species of this cultivar is too large and open to be considered a ground cover, this compact, rounded, suckering, 2½-foot-tall, 3- to 4-foot-wide shrublet is a splendid ground cover. It is easy to grow, carefree, and attractive for its foliage as well as its superbly fragrant blossoms. It is functional in mass plantings as a general cover or foundation facer, as a dwarf hedge, and as a specimen. It is quite resistant to airborne salt and therefore of use in coastal gardens and near roads that are salted in winter. No foot traffic is tolerated.

SCIENTIFIC NAME: *Clethra alnifolia* 'Hummingbird' (*kleth*-ra or *klee*-thra al-ni-*foe*-lee-a). *Clethra* comes from the Greek *klethra,* alder. *Alnifolia* means with leaves like *Alnus,* the alders.

HARDINESS / ORIGIN: Zones 5 to 9; the species is native to swamps, moist woods, and occasionally dry soil, mostly along the coast from Maine to northern New Jersey, Florida, and Mississippi.

LEAVES / FLOWERS / FRUIT: The alternate, simple, oval to oblong, deciduous, sharply toothed, shiny dark green leaves range from 1½ to 3½ inches long by ¾ to 1¾ inches wide and often pick up hues of yellow and orange in autumn. The ⅓-inch-wide, white, fragrant flowers are borne in 2- to 5-inch-long, neat, ¾-inch-wide upright spikes. The flowering period lasts four to six weeks from mid to late summer. The fruit, a tiny dry capsule, is nonornamental.

RATE / SPACING: Growth is slow to moderate (faster with more moisture and fertility). Plants from 2- to 3-gallon-sized containers are spaced 2½ to 3½ feet apart as 'Hummingbird' suckers from the base.

CULTURE / CARE: 'Hummingbird' thrives in moist to wet organically rich soil of neutral to acidic pH. It grows well in full sun to moderate shade and tolerates only moderate drought. Although mites may show up during drought conditions, no serious diseases or pests plague this cultivar. Little maintenance is required.

PROPAGATION: Suckers can be divided from the parent clump with a sharp spade and transplanted from spring through fall into constantly moist soil. Cuttings taken during early and mid summer root well after dipping in 1000 ppm IBA/talc.

Clivia miniata   PLATE 75
Kaffir Lily, Scarlet Kaffir Lily

Kaffir lily is a very attractive, graceful, lilylike ground cover that functions beautifully along walkways as an edging or for accent, especially in high-traffic areas. Used in massed plantings, it makes a splendid general cover or facer for building foundations or taller shrubs, remaining attractive throughout the year. It is herbaceous and basal-leaved, reaches 1½ to 2 feet tall, and spreads 2½ feet across.

SCIENTIFIC NAME: *Clivia miniata* (*kly*-vee-a min-ee-*aye*-ta). *Clivia* is named for Lady Charlotte Florentina Clive, Duchess of Northumberland (d.

1868), granddaughter of General Robert Clive, founder of the empire of British India. *Miniata,* cinnabar red, refers to the flowers.

HARDINESS / ORIGIN: Zones 10 to 11; South Africa.

LEAVES / FLOWERS / FRUIT: The evergreen, basal, straplike, 2½-foot-long, 2-inch-wide leaves are dark glossy green. Above them, from early winter to early spring, are borne stout upright stems that give rise to terminal groups of 12 to 20 scarlet (yellow inside) funnel-shaped flowers 2 to 3 inches long. The bright red berries that follow are pulpy, globose, and 1 inch long.

RATE / SPACING: Growth is slow. Plants from quart-sized to gallon-sized containers are spaced 1 to 1½ feet apart.

HORTICULTURAL SELECTIONS: Var. *citrina,* with clear yellow flowers and yellow berries; 'Flame', with deep orange-red flowers and broader, richer green, more robust foliage; var. *flava,* with yellow flowers; 'Grandiflora', with larger-than-typical flowers; 'Striata', leaves with white and green variegation. A group of German and French hybrids are common in the trade and noteworthy for their showy yellow to deep orange flowers. Another group, the Zimmerman hybrids, is known for its white flowers, sometimes with hints of red, yellow, or orange.

OTHER SPECIES: *C.* × *cyrtanthiflora* (kur-tanth-i-*floe*-ra), another South African plant with lilylike flowers, is derived from the cross between *C. miniata* and *C. nobilis.* It has light red flowers, reaches 2 feet tall, and is intermediate between the parents in other respects.

C. gardenii (gaar-*deen*-ee-eye), a South African native, is not as showy as *C. miniata* but displays respectable groups of ten to fourteen 2- to 3-inch-long, yellow or orange flowers with green tips in late winter.

C. nobilis (*noe*-bi-lis) reaches 1½ feet tall. The red-and-yellow flowers have green tips and are borne in groups of 40 to 60.

CULTURE / CARE: *Clivia* species grow best in organically rich, well-drained, slightly acidic loam. They are not greatly tolerant of drought and should be kept moderately moist and located in a site that is sheltered from strong, drying winds. They prefer light to dense shade. Although they are not susceptible to any serious diseases, they sometimes are afflicted by nematodes, slugs, and snails. Maintenance typically consists of removing the leaves when they become tattered and cutting off the floral stalks after the fruit drops. Occasionally, plantings become overcrowded and the floral display declines; in this case, divide and replant.

PROPAGATION: Clumps are easily divided in fall, winter, or early spring; when replanting, be sure that the tops of the tubers are slightly above the soil surface. Ripe seed is reportedly viable and ready for sowing.

Comptonia peregrina PLATE 76
Sweet Fern, Meadow Fern, Shrubby Fern, Fern Bush, Spleenwort Bush, Canada Sweet Gale, Sweet Ferry

Although not a fern at all, sweet fern owes its common name to the spicy aroma of its foliage, especially during fall as it dries out, and to its resemblance to the leaves of *Asplenium,* a genus of ferns. A woody, rhizomatous, shrubby ground cover that reaches 2 to 4 feet tall and spreads 4 to 8 feet across, sweet fern is most useful for binding soil on sandy highway embankments and large hillsides. It shows exceptional tolerance to salt, drought, and infertility and combines well with acid-loving plants, including grasses such as little blue stem (*Schizacharium scoparium*) and eulalia (*Miscanthus sinensis*), shrubs such as low and high bush blueberries (*Vaccinium angustifolium* and *V. corymbosum*), and trees such as white pine (*Pinus strobus*), staghorn sumac (*Rhus typhina*), serviceberries (*Amelanchier* species), and witch hazels (*Hamamelis* species). No foot traffic is tolerated.

The folk uses of sweet fern are numerous. During the early 1900s the leaves and flowers were boiled to make a tea that was drunk to treat diarrhea or applied to the skin as a cooling wash with astringent properties. American Indians used an infusion of the leaves as a treatment for poison ivy.

Sweet fern plays an important role in the colonization of moist, acidic meadows, a property that is due in part to its symbiotic association with a bacterium of the genus *Frankia* that fixes nitrogen from the air surrounding the roots. The seed is said to be part of the diet of the flicker.

SCIENTIFIC NAME: *Comptonia peregrina* (komp-*toe*-nee-a pair-e-*grie*-na). *Comptonia* was named for Henry Compton (1632–1713), a bishop of London and connoisseur of North American plants. *Peregrina,* exotic or foreign, implies the species was presumably named by an overseas explorer, or it may mean wanderer, referring to the rhizomatous habit of spread.

HARDINESS / ORIGIN: Zones 2 to 8; acid-soil prairies of North America from Nova Scotia to North Carolina, west to Indiana and Michigan.

LEAVES / FLOWERS / FRUIT: The leaves are deciduous, fernlike, deeply notched, to 4½ inches long by ½ inch across, hairy, colored dark green, and slightly to highly aromatic depending on the season (most aromatic in fall). The yellowish male flowers, which bloom from late spring to mid summer, are arranged in elongated clusters up to ⅗ inch long. The reddish female flowers, which occur separately on the same plant, are arranged in rounded bundles and are effective in mid summer. The fruit, an olive-brown, 3/16-inch-long nutlet, is relatively nonornamental.

RATE / SPACING: Growth is slow. Plants from gallon-sized containers are spaced 2½ to 3½ feet apart.

HORTICULTURAL SELECTIONS: Var. *asplenifolia,* with smaller, less hairy leaves and smaller flower clusters; 'Variegata', with white and green leaves.

CULTURE / CARE: Sweet fern prefers acidic soils that range from moist and highly organic to dry, sandy, and infertile. Once established, it is extremely tolerant of drought; although it accepts deep watering during hot, dry weather, it is not likely to depend upon it. It prefers full sun. Pest and disease problems are likely to be minimal. No special maintenance is needed, except possibly an annual light shearing.

PROPAGATION: Stem cuttings root best in early summer, yet even at this time they may not root well and those cuttings that do root often die during transplanting. Root cuttings are best taken in late winter or early spring; simply dig up root segments, cut them into 4-inch-long pieces, place them ½ inch deep in a rich, acidic medium, and keep warm until new shoots begin to poke through in early summer. Alternatively, root cuttings can be taken during fall, bundled and refrigerated for three months prior to placing in flats. Divisions can be dug and transplanted in spring or fall. Seed is particularly stubborn due to the presence of chemical germination inhibitors that, rather uniquely, are not effectively neutralized by cold stratification. Researchers, however, have had success at inducing germination by soaking the seed in gibberellic acid (a potent plant hormone). Reports have been made of seed surviving for more than 70 years, then germinating when brought to the soil surface during logging operations. Generally, though, seedlings are very rare in the wild, presumably being more of an insurance policy for long-term survival. In the short run, the tenacious rhizomes seem aptly suited to take care of the natural propagation of this species.

Conradina verticillata   PLATE 77

Cumberland Rosemary, Rabbit Bane

Cumberland rosemary is a relatively rare native ground cover with attractive ornamental features. Sprawling and naturally layering, this shrubby species reaches 1 foot tall and spreads more than 3 feet across. On a moderate to large scale it works nicely as a general cover for streamsides. Its foliage remains attractive throughout the season and, because its stems root as they trail, they effectively stabilize the soil. For those not blessed with a stream in their back

yard, single plants (or small groups) make excellent specimens or accent plants in the rock garden, where they combine well with stonecrop (*Sedum*), heather (*Calluna*), broom (*Cytisus*), heath (*Erica*), and dwarf conifers such as *Chamaecyparis,* spruce, and juniper. Cumberland rosemary effectively combines with species of *Hosta, Iris,* and *Andromeda.* Apartment dwellers (or anyone with a patio) might appreciate this species as a container plant. The common name rabbit bane indicates the plant has rabbit-repelling properties.

SCIENTIFIC NAME: *Conradina verticillata* (kon-ra-*dee*-na ver-ti-si-*lay*-ta). *Conradina* commemorates Solomon White Conrad (1779–1831), a botanist from Philadelphia. *Verticillata* comes from the Latin *vertex,* whorl, and in this case refers to the whorled arrangement of the flowers, called *verticillasters.*

HARDINESS / ORIGIN: Zones 6 or 7 to 10; gravelly and sandy, moist, open woodlands, shores, and river banks of Kentucky and Tennessee.

LEAVES / FLOWERS / FRUIT: The evergreen, deeply scented leaves smell like the culinary rosemary, *Rosmarinus officinalis.* Similarly, they are needlelike, ¾ to 1 inch long, simple, and arranged in clusters. Typically they are colored dark green, then in fall pick up purplish bronzy tones. The flowers are arranged in whorls of two to seven and are borne toward the tips of the branches in late spring. Each flower is pealike, ¾ inch long by ½ inch wide, and colored lavender-pinkish to whitish. The fruit, each composed of four nutlets, is nonornamental.

RATE / SPACING: Growth is moderate. Plants from 1- to 2-gallon-sized containers are spaced 2 to 3 feet apart.

CULTURE / CARE: Cumberland rosemary prefers a sunny or lightly shaded location with moist, sandy, gravelly, or rocky soil. It is not greatly tolerant of drought yet shows fair tolerance to salt. No serious diseases or pests have been reported, and maintenance, at most, consists of a light shearing following bloom—to promote compactness.

PROPAGATION: Cuttings root well throughout the year; generally no hormones are needed, but treatment with 1000 to 3000 ppm IBA/talc will induce a heavier root system. Naturally layered stems can be dug up and transplanted throughout the growing season. Seed propagation is infrequently used due to the ease of the other methods.

Convallaria majalis   PLATE 78

Lily of the Valley, Conval Lily, Mayflower, Our Lady's Tears, Ladder to Heaven

If ever there were an old-fashioned ground cover, this is it. Leafy and herbaceous, this member of the lily family is a fixture in the landscape of countless homes and cottages that date back before the turn of the century. Lily of the valley is still commonly used as a general cover for small-, moderate-, or large-sized areas. It displays a low, horizontally spreading, lilylike, stemless nature and reaches a mature size of 6 to 8 inches tall with indefinite spread. Performing beautifully underneath trees (here supplement with a little more fertilizer than otherwise), it also combines well with low shrubs, ferns, and various cultivars of English ivy. Its quality of binding soil makes it particularly useful on shaded slopes. When freshly cut and placed in a small blue-, pink-, or mauve-colored vase, its fragrant, waxy white, springtime flowers smell wonderful and look lovely. The common name our lady's tears refers to the white flowers, a symbol of the Virgin Mary, and the name ladder to heaven was given by Medieval monks to describe the steplike arrangement of the flowers.

In the past, the rhizomes and roots of lily of the valley were used to treat heart maladies. In larger doses, these same plant structures are poisonous, as are the leaves, fruits, flowers, and the water in which flowers have been placed, causing irregular heartbeat and digestive and mental disorders. Small children should not be allowed to play near plants, particularly those with fruit.

SCIENTIFIC NAME: *Convallaria majalis* (kon-va-*lair*-ee-a ma-*jay*-lis). *Convallaria* comes from the Latin, *convallis,* a valley, the natural habitat of the species. *Majalis,* of May, refers to the time of flowering.

HARDINESS / ORIGIN: Zones 2 to 7; Europe, Asia, and eastern North America.

LEAVES / FLOWERS / FRUIT: The deciduous, lilylike, fleshy, medium green leaves are grouped in twos or threes, arise from the ground, and reach 4 to 8 inches long by 1 to 3 inches wide. During spring and into mid summer they appear vibrant and lush; by late summer they begin to deteriorate, and by early fall they are primarily yellow and brown and soon die back to the ground. During mid to late spring, many bell-shaped, ¼-inch-wide, waxy white, fragrant flowers are borne on erect green stalks. Fruiting does not always occur, but when it does, it takes the form of an orange-red, ¼-inch-diameter, many seeded, round berry.

RATE / SPACING: Growth is moderate to relatively fast. Bare-root divisions or rhizome segments are spaced 6 to 8 inches apart and plants from 4- to 5-inch-diameter containers 8 to 10 inches apart.

HORTICULTURAL SELECTIONS: 'Aurea Variegata', rare, rather unattractively variegated green and creamy yellow, far less interesting than the extravagant descriptions commonly read in mail order catalogs,

lackluster both in appearance and performance; 'Flore Pleno', with double flowers; 'Fortin's Giant', with leaves and flowers larger than typical; 'Fortunei', with larger leaves and flowers like 'Fortin's Giant'; 'Prolificans', with double flowers; 'Rosea', with light purplish pink flowers and less vigorous growth.

OTHER SPECIES: *C. montana* (mon-*tay*-na / mon-*tan*-a), meaning of the mountains, hails from rocky and sandy slopes of mountainous regions of Virginia and West Virginia to northern Georgia and eastern Tennessee. It flowers in late spring or early summer. Unlike the more popular *C. majalis,* it displays leaves that are narrower and a bit longer and, rather than running and colonizing, it tends to stay in a clump. Hardy in Zones 2 to 7.

CULTURE / CARE: Lily of the valley is tolerant of most soils, but does best in moderately acidic, organically rich, moist, well-drained loam. It survives extended periods of drought without supplemental water; however, its best appearance is attained when the soil is kept moist. It prefers light to dense shade, blooming most profusely in light to moderate shade. Although it accepts full sun, the foliage usually turns yellow or brown even earlier in the season than when planted in the shade. Pests include lily of the valley weevil, nematodes, Japanese weevil, and slugs. Diseases of greatest prevalence include stem rot (pansies are also a host, so do not plant the two near each other), anthracnose, leaf spot, leaf blotch, and crown rot. Blossom failure occurs occasionally when the soil does not drain well or when too much nitrogen is applied. Maintenance includes top-dressing lightly during fall with compost to supplement the soil. If flower production should decrease over time, dig up plants during the spring, divide, and replant them on 6- to 8-inch centers.

PROPAGATION: Division, the simplest method of propagation, can be effective any time but is best in spring and fall.

Convolvulus cneorum   PLATE 79
Bush Morning Glory

Bush morning glory is a good warm-climate, reputedly fire-resistant ground cover for soil retention on dry, sunny embankments. It reaches 2 to 4 feet tall by 3 to 4 feet wide and is best used on a moderate to large scale, or alone as a rock garden specimen. Limited foot traffic is tolerated.

SCIENTIFIC NAME: *Convolvulus cneorum* (kon-*vole*-view-lus nee-*oh*-rum). *Convolvulus* comes from the Latin *convolva,* to twine around, in reference to the stems of these plants. *Cneorum* comes from the Greek *kneorum,* resembling olive.

HARDINESS / ORIGIN: Zones 9 to 11; southern Europe.

LEAVES / FLOWERS / FRUIT: The evergreen, lance-shaped to spatula-shaped, white-hairy, conspicuously veined, ½- to 2½-inch-long, ¼- to ⅜-inch-wide leaves are borne in alternate fashion or in whorls upon brownish white-haired stems. The pink-tinged, white, morning-glory-like flowers are borne alone or in loose clusters of two to six from mid spring to early fall and reach 1½ to 2 inches wide. The fruit that follows, a round capsule, is non-ornamental.

RATE / SPACING: Growth is moderate to fast. Plants from quart-sized to 1-gallon-sized containers are spaced 2½ to 3 feet apart.

OTHER SPECIES: *C. sabatius* (sa-*bay*-tee-us), formerly classified as *C. mauritanicus,* and commonly called ground morning glory, reaches 1 to 2 feet tall and spreads 3 feet across. Native to South Africa, this woody-based herbaceous-stemmed vine displays ½- to 1½-inch-long, round to oval, conspicuously veined, grayish green, evergreen leaves. The flowers, borne from late spring to late fall, are 1 to 2 inches wide, solitary or clustered, and blue to violet purple with pale white throats. Hardy to Zone 8.

CULTURE / CARE: Both species are best in loose, well-drained, infertile, gravelly soil. They prefer full sun and show considerable tolerance to drought. Pests include black scale, mites, and nematodes. No maintenance is required except an occasional wintertime pruning to thin and shape.

PROPAGATION: Cuttings taken during the growing season root readily. Seed is said to germinate readily.

Coprosma × kirkii   PLATE 80
Creeping Coprosma, Kirk's Coprosma

Popular on the West Coast where it excels as a bank cover near the sea, creeping coprosma not only seems to enjoy being blasted by drying ocean breezes, but it also does not seem to mind the salt that they deposit. It is a woody ground cover that reaches 3 feet tall and spreads to more than 5 feet across. It is sometimes found in arid regions, provided water for irrigation is available, and is occasionally used along fences and buildings as a facing to reduce maintenance and to obscure meters and foundation blocks.

SCIENTIFIC NAME: *Coprosma × kirkii* (kop-*ros*-ma kirk-*ee*-eye). *Coprosma* comes from the Greek *kopros,* dung, and *osme,* a smell, in reference to the unpleasant odor of some of the species. *Kirkii* is named in honor of Sir John Kirk (1832–1922), an English botanist.

HARDINESS / ORIGIN: Zones 8 to 10; New Zealand as a natural hybrid between *C. acerosa* and *C. repens.*

LEAVES / FLOWERS / FRUIT: Although the evergreen

leaves are quite variable in shape, they typically range from oblong to narrowly oblong and reach 1½ inches long and ¼ inch wide. They are colored medium to yellowish green with reddish edges, and are neat and attractive. The flowers, on the other hand, borne in late spring, are nearly insignificant ornamentally. They are either male or female, funnel-shaped, and may reach ½ inch long. The fruit that follows is oblong, up to 1¼ inches long, and colored translucent bluish with red speckles.

RATE / SPACING: Growth is moderate. Plants from 2- to 3-gallon-sized containers are spaced 3 to 4 feet apart.

HORTICULTURAL SELECTIONS: 'Kirkii', with a horizontal to semierect habit, 4 feet tall by 6 feet wide, leaves narrower than the typical hybrid species; 'Variegata', with white-edged leaves.

OTHER SPECIES: *C. petriei* (pe-*tree*-eye), named after Donald Petrie (1846–1925), an amateur Scottish naturalist in New Zealand, is commonly called Petrie's coprosma. It is a fine New Zealand introduction that copes well in North America in Zones 7 to 9 and reaches 3 feet tall by 6 feet wide. Growth is moderate. Plants from 1- to 2-gallon-sized containers are spaced 2 to 3 feet apart. The evergreen, narrow to oblong, tiny, leathery, olive green foliage only reaches ¼ inch long. The flowers, like those of *C. × kirkii,* are not ornamental, but the round, ⅜ inch wide, purplish red to pale blue, translucent fruit is rather interesting.

CULTURE / CARE: Coprosmas are tolerant of most soil types, and once established, they become highly tolerant of drought. They prefer full sun to light shade. Seldom are they affected by pests or diseases. Maintenance consists of a light shearing in spring to promote neatness and density.

PROPAGATION: Cuttings are best taken during early summer.

Coptis groenlandica   PLATE 81
Goldthread, Golden Roots, Canker Root

Two of the common names refer to the bright gold roots and the third name to a use of the plant in treating canker sores. A low-growing (2- to 4-inch-tall), herbaceous, rhizomatous, creeping woodland ground cover that spreads indefinitely, goldthread is best used as a small-scale to moderate-scale general cover in naturalized gardens where it combines well with twin-flower, bunchberry, numerous ferns, and shade-loving, low-growing shrubs. Limited foot traffic is tolerated.

Goldthread contains the alkaloid berberine, which at one time was commonly used in the treatment of minor ailments. Many Native Americans used goldthread for the treatment of mouth sores. Typically they boiled the roots to create a mouthwash that was gargled (the Penobscots used such a gargle in the treatment of "smoker's mouth"). Others simply chewed the stems. Goldthread was also mixed with goldenseal (*Hydrastis canadensis*) in a formulation that was supposed to eliminate one's desire to consume alcohol.

SCIENTIFIC NAME: *Coptis groenlandica* (*kop*-tis *grone*-lan-di-ka). *Coptis* is derived from the Greek *coptein,* to cut, in reference to the divided leaves. *Groenlandica* means of Greenland.

HARDINESS / ORIGIN: Zones 2 to 7 or 8; northeastern North America and Greenland, extending south to Virginia and west to Iowa.

LEAVES / FLOWERS / FRUIT: The evergreen leaves emerge from the rootstalk and are composed of three short-stemmed leaflets. Each is more or less oval shaped, sharply toothed about the edges, and colored light to medium, shiny green. The solitary, dainty, white flowers are borne in late spring and are held atop thin, 3- to 5-inch-long stems. Each is composed of five to seven petals and reaches a width of ½ inch. The tiny fruit that follows is nonornamental.

RATE / SPACING: Growth is slow. Plants from 3- to 4-inch-diameter containers are spaced 4 to 8 inches apart.

OTHER SPECIES: *C. laciniata* (la-sin-ee-*aye*-ta), named for its deeply divided (laciniate) foliage, is commonly called western goldthread. It is native to Oregon, Washington, and northern California, and, like *C. groenlandica,* its evergreen foliage arises directly from the rootstalk. The leaves, composed of three leaflets, each held upon a long stalk, ascend 4 to 6 inches, and its small greenish white flowers are borne during spring. Much less common than *C. groenlandica,* this species is similar in hardiness but spreads at an even slower pace. Plants are spaced 3 to 5 inches apart.

CULTURE / CARE: Goldthread needs organically rich, very acidic soil (of pH 4.0 to 5.0). It is not tolerant of drought, so the site should be shady and cool and kept slightly moist at all times. Leaf spot is common but seldom serious. Maintenance needs are few if any.

PROPAGATION: Division any time during the growing season is successful, provided the soil is kept adequately moist.

shrubby. It reaches 6 to 24 inches tall (usually on the low end of this spectrum) and spreads more than 3 feet across. Unfortunately, however, it is not quite as easily cultivated as some of the more popular ground covers. Where the environment meets its rigorous standards, broom crowberry makes an excellent rock garden specimen, reminiscent of the heaths and heathers. When combined with these two or mass-planted alone, it makes a wonderful carpet—particularly on sloping terrain where it effectively controls erosion.

SCIENTIFIC NAME: *Corema conradii* (koe-*ree*-ma kon-*rad*-ee-eye). *Corema* comes from the Latin *corema,* a broom, in reference to the many-stemmed habit of these plants. *Conradii* commemorates Solomon White Conrad (1779–1831), the discoverer of this species.

HARDINESS / ORIGIN: Zone 3; sandy pine barrens and other gravelly and sandy areas (mostly coastal) of Newfoundland to Massachusetts, New Jersey, and New York (one county), usually growing in colonies.

LEAVES / FLOWERS / FRUIT: The evergreen, alternate, simple, linear leaves range from ⅙ to ¼ inch long by ¹⁄₂₄ inch wide and are medium green in maturity, with a central white line on their undersides. The numerous flowers of spring are male or female on each plant (dioecious), arranged in petal-less, stalk-less, branch-ending heads. The male flowers are highly visible with long purple stamens and purplish brown anthers, and the female flowers are less conspicuous, nearly concealed by the upper foliage. The fruit, a tiny dried drupe, is nonornamental.

RATE / SPACING: Growth is slow to moderate. Plants from 1- to 2-gallon-sized containers are spaced 1½ to 2½ feet apart.

CULTURE / CARE: Well-drained (preferably moisture-retentive), sandy or gravelly acidic soils are best. Drought and heat tolerance is considerable, although periodic deep watering during summer is beneficial. Plants prefer full sun to light shade. No serious disease or pest problems are likely to occur. A light shearing following bloom encourages development of a neat, compact habit.

PROPAGATION: Stem cuttings taken during early summer root fairly well if treated with 2000 ppm IBA/talc; the medium should consist of coarse sand.

Corema conradii   PLATE 82

Broom Crowberry, Poverty Grass, Brown Crowberry, Plymouth Crowberry, Conrad's Crowberry

This extremely neat and compact little shrublet is upright-stemmed, horizontally sprawling, and sub-

---

Coreopsis   PLATE 83

Tickseed

Coreopsis is a genus of about 100 species of annual and perennial herbs from North and South America. Of these, at least three species are very good ground covers. Two of them, *C. verticillata* and *C.*

rosea, are rhizomatous-spreading with upright habit. Rugged, attractive, and very florific, they are best applied in mass plantings along building foundations, walkways, and in public or commercial landscapes for such uses as surrounding the base of signs and statues, or adjoining entryways. In the smaller garden, or as an element in a herbaceous border or island planting, a single clump of *C. verticillata* is superb for accent use. During the 1980s *C. rosea* and *C. verticillata* have risen to a position of great prominence. The third species, *C. auriculata,* displays a low-spreading, stoloniferous, matlike habit, and is best used in small-sized to moderate-sized areas as a general cover.

SCIENTIFIC NAME: *Coreopsis* (kore-ee-*op*-sis) receives its name from the Greek *koris,* a bug or tick, and *opsis,* resemblance, in reference to the ticklike appearance of the seeds.

HARDINESS / ORIGIN: See individual species.

LEAVES / FLOWERS / FRUIT: The leaves are simple and range from opposite to alternate, and entire to pinnately lobed or cut. The yellow, brownish, purplish, or rose-colored flowers are borne in round sunflower-like heads and vary considerably in size. In some species they are borne singularly while in others they are grouped in panicles. The fruit is not showy but is attractive to birds of many species.

RATE / SPACING: See individual species.

SPECIES: *C. auriculata* (awe-rik-you-*lay*-ta), named in Latin for the auricles (earlike appendages) of its foliage, is commonly called dwarf-eared coreopsis or dwarf-eared tickseed. This native of the eastern United States, from Virginia to Florida, is a low-spreading, stoloniferous, herbaceous, mat-forming ground cover that reaches 6 to 12 inches tall by more than 1 foot wide. It is hardy in Zones 4 to 9. Growth is slow. Plants from pint-sized containers are spaced 10 to 14 inches apart. The medium green leaves range from semievergreen to evergreen, are oval to narrowly oval (with one or two lobes at their bases), and reach 2 to 5 inches long by 1 inch wide. Above them, upon leafy semiupright stalks, arise numerous 1½- to 2-inch-wide solitary heads of yellow daisy-like flowers from spring to fall. The fruit which follows is nonornamental. 'Nana' reaches only 8 inches tall; 'Superba' displays 2- to 3-inch-wide orange flowers with maroon centers.

C. pulchra (*pul*-kra), hardy in Zones 6 to 9 and reaching 15 inches tall, is similar to *C. verticillata* but is non-spreading and tends to stay in a clump.

C. rosea (*row*-zee-a), named for its rose-colored flowers, is commonly called pink tickseed or small rose. It is sometimes errantly represented as a variety or cultivar of *C. verticillata.* Hailing from swampy coastal terrain of eastern Massachusetts to Georgia, it tolerates saturated soils but does not display the same tolerance to drought as does *C. verticillata.* Even so, where the soil is rich and can be kept moist, it too is an exceptional contributor of summertime color. Beginning in July, the ½- to 1-inch-wide flowers with yellow centers and pink petals begin a long procession of petite floral splendor that lasts into the first weeks of September. The species is hardy in Zones 4 to 9. Growth is fast, by rhizomes. Plants from quart-sized to gallon-sized containers are spaced 1 to 1½ feet apart. 'Alba', with lovely snow-white flowers, is sometimes listed as *C. alpina* 'Alba'; forma *leucantha* is rare and has near-white petals.

C. verticillata (ver-tis-i-*lay*-ta), meaning with leaves arranged in whorls, is commonly called threadleaf coreopsis, whorled tickseed, or pot-of-gold. It is hardy in Zones 3 to 9, thrives in dry soil, and hails from the central and eastern part of the United States. Held upon erect, many-branched stems, the three-parted, very narrow, threadlike, medium green leaves act as a marvelous dark-hued backdrop to the numerous 1- to 1½-inch-wide heads of 6 to 10 ray flowers with yellow petals. The disk flowers, in the center of the flower heads, are dull yellow and very tiny. Their long-running bloom period lasts from early to late summer, but their tiny fruit is not ornamental. The species reaches 1½ feet tall by 3 feet wide. Growth is moderate, by rhizomes. Plants from pint-sized to gallon-sized containers are spaced 14 to 18 inches apart. Cultivars include 'Golden Showers', 1½ to 2 feet tall, a popular form, with larger, brighter yellow flowers; 'Grandiflora', more or less identical to 'Golden Showers'; 'Moonbeam', the most popular cultivar, 1½ to 2 feet tall, with numerous light sulfur-yellow flowers from early summer to mid fall, hardy southward to Zone 8; 'Zagreb', a compact, cushion-shaped, golden-flowered selection that reaches 1 foot tall.

CULTURE / CARE: All *Coreopsis* species discussed here perform best in acidic, fertile, loamy soil; *C. verticillata* tolerates drought and sandy soils, *C. rosea* tolerates excess moisture, and *C. auriculata* is somewhere in between. All species prefer full sun to light shade. Diseases of greatest consequence are leaf spot, rust, leaf blight, root and stem rots, powdery mildew, and beet curly top virus. Common pests, which seldom are injurious, are aphids, leafhoppers, four-lined plant bug, spotted cucumber beetle, soil mealybug, and mites. Little or no maintenance is required.

PROPAGATION: Cuttings taken in mid summer are easily propagated, as are divisions during mid spring. Seed is available commercially and typically takes two to three weeks to germinate.

Cornus canadensis   PLATE 84

Dwarf Cornel

Many Northerners refer to this dainty ground cover, one of our most lovely native ground covers, as bunchberry because its seeds are handsomely arranged in bunches. At 4 to 9 inches tall, it is leafy, dainty, and herbaceous, and spreads indefinitely by creeping rhizomes. It is the smallest species of dogwood and displays the same leaf shape and flowers (but smaller) as the popular spring-blooming tree species, *C. florida*. It is best suited for use in the shade of trees and shrubs in moist cool climates, and is most often used as an accent plant or as a lovely transition plant for use between the more formal aspects of the garden and surrounding woodland borders. Underneath specimen shrubs such as azalea, laurel, or blueberry it is superb, and its fruit is said to be a favorite food of ruffed grouse. No foot traffic is tolerated.

SCIENTIFIC NAME: *Cornus canadensis* (*kor*-nus kan-a-*den*-sis). *Cornus* is derived from the Latin *cornu*, horn, and refers to the hard nature of the seed. *Canadensis* indicates that the species is native to Canada.

HARDINESS / ORIGIN: Zones 2 to 7; mountainous woodlands of northern North America and eastern Asia.

LEAVES / FLOWERS / FRUIT: The deciduous, whorled in groups of four to six, conspicuously veined, medium green leaves are among the finest of all ground covers. In spring, they arise directly from the rootstalk upon thin wiry stems and soon unfold to reveal their 1- to 3-inch-long, oval to elliptic shape. Later, with the onset of fall, tones of yellow and red may become apparent. The tiny yellow and green flowers arise in the center of showy, white to greenish yellow, $\frac{1}{3}$- to 1-inch-long, oval-shaped bracts (modified leaves). It is these bracts that account for dwarf cornel's charming floral display. In time the flowers fade and give rise to green berrylike fruits, which ripen to shiny red during late summer and persist through much of autumn.

RATE / SPACING: Growth is slow. Plants from 3- to 4-inch-diameter containers are spaced 8 to 12 inches apart.

HORTICULTURAL SELECTIONS: A white-fruited form has been discovered but is rare in cultivation.

OTHER SPECIES: *C. mas* '**Nana**' (mahs *nay*-na), dwarf Cornelian cherry, is a dogwood that has yellow blossoms in early spring and bright cherry-red fruit in mid summer. It is similar to *C. sericea* 'Kelseyi', but more upright, slower growing, and hardy in Zones 5 to 8.

C. pumila (*pyu*-mi-la), dwarf dogwood, is a woody dwarf shrub hardy to Zone 4 or 5. It reaches 2 to 3 feet tall, forms neat compact mounds, and is exceptional for its terminal leaves that are crimson throughout the growing season. Against a background of the medium green mature leaves this gives a rather spectacular two-toned effect from summer to fall. The leaves surprisingly display no unique fall color, but simply dry up and fall off. The brown stems, however, have a unique irregular pattern that is interesting throughout the winter months. Quite resistant to mildew, this species produces clusters of tiny white florets, and makes a useful and attractive general cover when used in mass plantings.

C. sericea '**Kelseyi**' (sir-ee-*see*-a *kel*-see-eye), dwarf red osier dogwood, a compact, low-spreading, stoloniferous woody shrub, is a cultivar of the 7- to 10-foot-tall swamp and sand dune inhabiting species that reaches 18 to 30 inches tall by 2 feet wide. Its oval to narrowly oblong, deciduous leaves are bright green above and pale green below, then turn bronzy to purplish in fall. The off-white flowers are borne from mid spring to early summer and give rise to globe-shaped white fruit. The cultivar is hardy in Zones 3 to 8 and, in the landscape, is best used as a dwarf hedge or foundation planting. Growth is moderate. Plants from 2-gallon-sized containers are spaced $1\frac{1}{2}$ feet apart.

C. suecica (*swee*-si-ka), of Northern Europe south to Holland and West Germany, as well as northeastern Asia and northern North America from Greenland to Alaska, is a plant of lightly shaded bog margins where it grows in conjunction with thickets of moisture-tolerant and acid-tolerant shrubs. It reaches $\frac{3}{8}$ to 1 inch tall from horizontal rhizomes. The leaves are very much like those of *C. canadensis*, but are not clustered at the shoot tips. The flowers, borne in mid spring, are similar to those of *C. canadensis* as are the red fruits. Difficult to cultivate and hardy to Zone 3, this species is strict about its need for acidic saturated soils.

C. × *unalaschkensis* (un-a-lash-*ken*-sis), the result of crossing *C. canadensis* and *C. suecica*, reaches 3 inches tall by 12 inches wide. Rare, but naturally occurring in Greenland, this hybrid is said to be somewhat more sun tolerant than *C. canadensis* but otherwise seems nearly identical.

CULTURE / CARE: For *C. canadensis* and *C. suecica*, organically rich acidic soil is best. All species have poor tolerance to drought; for this reason, they require a site sheltered from strong drying winds where the soil remains naturally moist. They are fussy about their light preference, preferring light to moderate shade during spring and fall, but moderate to dense shade during summer. Fortunately, these demands can be met by planting underneath deciduous trees and shrubs. No serious pests seem to effect *C. cana-*

densis, but leaf spots and root rot are sometimes problematic. Maintenance is seldom if ever necessary. The shrubby *C. pumila, C. sericea* 'Kelseyi', and *C. mas* 'Nana' prefer moist, acidic, or neutral soil, but not saturated conditions, and *C. sericea* 'Kelseyi' does not tolerate drought. All three prefer full sun to light shade and tolerate exposure to wind.

PROPAGATION: Cuttings of *C. canadensis* taken during late spring or early summer should be started in a medium of one part peat moss and one part perlite. Division, which is more reliable but more time consuming, is best performed during spring and fall. For seed to be effective it must be collected fresh, stripped from the pulpy flesh that surrounds it, then sown immediately before drying out; germination occurs the following spring. The shrubby types, *C. sericea* and *C. mas,* are easily rooted from stem cuttings during early summer.

Coronilla varia   PLATE 85
Crown Vetch

Rather loose and informal in habit, crown vetch is a durable herbaceous ground cover that people seem to either love or hate. Those who hate it focus their attention on its aggressive spread and its tendency to naturalize, often at the expense of native plants. Those who love crown vetch admire it for its ability to bind steep slopes, its ease of maintenance, and its ability to manufacture its own nitrogen—actually a task performed by bacteria living upon its roots. They also like it for its lovely flowers of pink and white. Crown vetch is not neat or refined, but it binds and covers soil with a vengeance. Because the bacteria living in association with its roots extract nitrogen from the air (in the soil), crown vetch requires little fertilizer and is ideally suited for use in sandy soils, which are not capable of retaining nitrogen like organic soils. It is best grown on a steep hill that is dangerous to mow or in a sandy area requiring an inexpensive, informal, drought-tolerant covering. Crown vetch combines well with tall grasses such as marram grass (*Ammophila breviligulata*), sand reed grass (*Calamovilfa longifolia*), and lyme grass (*Leymus arenarius*), where its flowers add a nice splash of color during summer and its nitrogen-producing ability also benefits the grasses.

SCIENTIFIC NAME: *Coronilla varia* (kor-o-*nil*-la *vair*-ee-a). *Coronilla* in Latin means little crown; applied here it refers to the shape of the flower heads. *Varia,* also from Latin, indicates that the flowers vary in color, some being pink and others being white.

HARDINESS / ORIGIN: Zones 4 to 9; Europe.

LEAVES / FLOWERS / FRUIT: The leaves are deciduous, fine-textured, and arranged in pairs of oblong, ½-inch-long, emerald green leaflets. From early summer to early fall a multitude of dense, crownlike, pink and white flower heads arise—simply splendid for contrast against the emerald green foliage. The fruit consists of slender pods that are interesting but contribute little to the overall ornamental effect.

RATE / SPACING: Growth is very fast once plants are established, and plants may spread by self-sowing. Plants from 2- to 3½-inch-diameter containers are spaced 10 to 14 inches apart.

HORTICULTURAL SELECTIONS: 'Emerald', leaves a richer green than the species, flowers primarily pinkish white; 'Penngift', introduced by the Pennsylvania Highway Department, more vigorous (many times the plain species is sold under this cultivar name).

CULTURE / CARE: Although crown vetch tolerates nearly any type of well-drained soil, it prefers acidic to neutral soils. It also prefers sun over shade and, once established, tolerates considerable drought. No serious diseases or pests affect it, and if it is planted in a contained area or given sufficient room to spread, it requires only an annual late winter mowing to prevent the accumulation of dried stems which can become a fire hazard in periods of drought.

PROPAGATION: Division can be performed any time the soil can be kept moist. Seed also can be sown any time the soil is kept moist. Purchased seed usually comes with a packet of nitrogen-fixing bacterial spores for inoculation prior to sowing.

Correa pulchella   PLATE 86
Australian Fuchsia

With flowers similar to fuchsias, the common name of this plant is aptly descriptive. Its habit is woody, low spreading, 2 to 3 feet tall, and more than 8 feet across. It is quite durable and in the landscape is best used to cover large areas—usually as a general cover. It is particularly useful for binding soil on sloping terrain. No foot traffic is tolerated, and since it is sensitive to excess heat and light, it should not be planted in the foreground of south-facing or west-facing walls where intense sunlight is reflected.

SCIENTIFIC NAME: *Correa pulchella* (*kore*-ee-a *pul*-kel-a). *Correa* commemorates José Francesco Correa de Serra (1751–1823), a Portuguese botanist. *Pulchella,* beautiful, in Latin, refers to all aspects of this plant.

HARDINESS / ORIGIN: Zones 9 to 10; Australia.

LEAVES / FLOWERS / FRUIT: The evergreen leaves are 1½ inches long by ½ inch wide and oblong, elliptic, or oval. They are smooth and colored dark green on their upper surface, very attractive, and contrast with the ¼-inch-wide, four-petaled, pinkish red flowers of late fall to mid spring. The fruit is nonornamental.

RATE / SPACING: Growth is moderate. Plants from 1-

to 2-gallon-sized containers are spaced 3 to 4 feet apart.

CULTURE / CARE: Australian fuchsia is relatively tolerant of drought, but performs best when given an occasional deep drink during extended hot dry periods. It is adaptable to most loamy soils, requires good drainage, and tolerates infertile, sandy or rocky soils. It prefers full sun to light shade. Few serious disease or pest problems are encountered. Maintenance consists of shearing back plants as they outgrow their bounds or become taller than desired. Fertilizer should be applied sparingly.

PROPAGATION: Stem cuttings root throughout the year when stuck in a porous medium.

Cotoneaster   PLATE 87

To describe all the ground-covering cotoneasters would require more room than I am allotted, but the most common species are described here. Cotoneasters are woody shrubs of great utility. Generally they are durable, moderately aggressive, and resistant to drought and strong drying winds. Typical cotoneasters display leathery, shiny green, evergreen or deciduous leaves that turn bronzy in fall. In spring they bloom with a multitude of cheerful pink to white flowers that usually lead to showy fruit, scarlet to orangish red in color. Some ground-covering cotoneasters grow almost completely horizontally while others project upward with stiff woody branches. Their usefulness varies from covering banks and controlling erosion to standing alone as specimens. None of the cotoneasters tolerates foot traffic.

SCIENTIFIC NAME: *Cotoneaster* (koe-toe-nee-*as*-ter) is said to be derived from the Latin *cotoneum,* quince (a thicket-forming scraggly shrub that produces bitter fruit), and *aster,* a likeness, alluding to cotoneaster's resemblance to quince.

HARDINESS / ORIGIN: Mostly Zones 5 or 6 to 8 or 9, but see individual species; temperate regions of Europe and Asia.

LEAVES / FLOWERS / FRUIT: The leaves are alternate, simple, unlobed, usually under 1 inch long, and may be deciduous or evergreen. The flowers range from white to pink and may be solitary or clustered. The red, globose fruit is ornamentally valuable.

RATE / SPACING: See individual species.

SPECIES: *C. adpressus* (ad-*pres*-us), commonly called creeping cotoneaster, is a dense and horizontally creeping, coarse-textured shrub 4 to 10 inches tall by 4 to 6 feet wide. It is an exceptional rock garden specimen and performs all the same functions of the more common species *C. apiculatus*. Hailing from China, it is hardy in Zones 5 to 8 and is characterized by a stiff highly branched habit. Growth is slow.

Plants from 1- to 2-gallon-sized containers are spaced 2½ to 3 feet apart. The deciduous, 3/16- to 5/8-inch-long, broadly oval leaves are wavy-margined and colored dull dark green, sometimes turning reddish in fall. This species has many fine traits. During late spring and early summer, it produces pairs or single, ¼- to 3/8-inch-wide pinkish flowers. Later, ¼-inch-wide, berrylike, shiny green fruit emerges and reaches its peak of interest during late summer or fall when it turns a lustrous shade of red. Horticultural selections include 'Little Gem', a dwarf form that reaches 6 inches tall by 1½ feet wide but seldom flowers or fruits and is planted 12 to 16 inches apart; 'Praecox', early cotoneaster, a vigorous selection that reaches up to 3 feet tall and spreads to 6 feet wide, with leaves and fruit a bit larger than the species, flowers pink with a hint of purple.

C. apiculatus (a-pik-you-*lay*-tus), named for the little apices (projections) at the tips of its leaves, is commonly called cranberry cotoneaster. Native to China, it is hardy in Zones 5 to 8 and reaches 2 to 3 feet tall by 5 to 6 feet wide. The species works well on steep banks for erosion control and is outstanding atop retaining walls and within planters. Around building foundations, it performs well for facing, but never should it be used next to public walkways as its stiff branches tend to trap paper and debris. Growth is moderate. Plants from 2- to 3-gallon-sized containers are spaced 3 or 4 feet apart. The dark shiny green leaves are deciduous, roundish to oval, ¼ to ¾ inch long by ¼ to ¾ inch wide, and tipped with a tiny short point or apicule. In fall, they become bronzy red or purplish. This species does not put on a vibrant floral show. Rather, during late spring and early summer, tiny pinkish flowers arise, and although not magnificent, they are attractive. The fruit, which is the main ornamental feature, reaches ⅓ inch wide, is roundish, arises shortly after the flowers fade, and soon changes from pale green to deep cranberry red. Some of the most popular horticultural selections include 'Blackburn', a more compact form; 'Nana', a dwarf form that reaches 12 inches tall by 4 feet wide; 'Tom Thumb', a miniature selection that reaches 4 inches tall by 1 foot wide.

C. congestus (kon-*jes*-tus), commonly called Pyrenees cotoneaster or congested cotoneaster (for its crowded habit), is hardy in Zones 6 to 9. This tiny slow-growing species is best planted alone as a specimen or in small groups for accent. It excels in the rock garden and is of greatest merit in small-sized to moderate-sized areas. A Himalayan native, it displays bluish green, evergreen, oval-shaped foliage less than ½ inch long. Its pinkish springtime flowers reach ¼ inch long and give rise to roundish, bright red, fall-ripening fruit. Although plant height may reach 3 feet tall and spread may exceed 6 feet, growth is very slow. Plants from 1-gallon-sized containers are spaced 1½ to 2 feet apart. 'Likiang' displays a lower, more compact habit than the species.

C. conspicuus 'Decorus' (kon-*spik*-you-us day-*kore*-us), necklace cotoneaster, is hardy in Zones 6 to 9 and hails from western China. It is characterized by a prostrate to low-spreading habit and mature size of 1½ to 2 feet tall by 2 to 3 feet wide. An evergreen sometimes listed as var. *decorus,* this handsome plant displays simple, ⅜-inch-long, silvery leaves and white flowers in spring that give rise to round red fruit in fall. Growth is moderate. Plants from 1- to 2-gallon-sized containers are spaced 1½ feet apart.

C. dammeri (*dam*-er-eye), commonly called bearberry cotoneaster, is very popular in the northern United States, particularly the Midwest. Among the finest of evergreen ground covers, it is ideal for mass planting on a moderate to large scale where it blankets the soil and shuts out weed growth. It is excellent for controlling erosion, surrounding open-canopied trees, and facing building foundations. Hardy in Zones 6 to 9, this native of central China reaches 12 to 18 inches tall and spreads to more than 6 feet wide. The mostly evergreen, shiny, leathery, deep green leaves are oval to roundish and typically measure 1¼ inches long by ⅝ inch wide. In fall they turn bronzy to purplish and, by early spring the following year, they green up in time for a magnificent display of mid springtime, ½-inch-wide, fragrant, white flowers. The green fruit follows, turning bright red by late summer. Although not always produced in massive quantities, the fruit is very colorful and attractive. Growth is fast. Plants from 1- to 2-gallon-sized containers are spaced 2 to 3 feet apart. Many horticultural selections have been made, including 'Coral Beauty', sometimes also called 'Pink Beauty' or 'Royal Beauty', with moderate growth rate, seldom exceeding 16 inches tall, abundant white flowers in early spring, green fruit ripening to coral red in fall; 'Corbet', with large leaves and red fruit; 'Eichholz', with very low habit, foliage that turns gold to orange-red during fall; 'Juergl', with abundant flowers and orangish red fruit; 'Lowfast', small-leaved, with fast growth rate and habit lower than that of the species; 'Major', a more vigorous selection with leaves 1½ inches long; 'Mooncreeper', with white flowers and height of 2 inches; 'Oakwood', with low-growing habit, darker green leaves, and abundant red berries; 'Streibs Findling', reaching 3 inches tall and spreading more than 2 feet wide.

C. 'Hessei' (*hes*-see-eye), probably a hybrid of *C. adpressus* 'Praecox' and *C. horizontalis,* was bred by (and named for) H. A. Hesse. This low, compact, mounding selection reaches 1 to 1½ feet tall. Hardy in Zones 4 to 7, it spreads slowly and makes a good small-scale to moderate-scale general cover or rock garden specimen. Its shiny dark green foliage turns burgundy in fall. Its fruit is orangish red, but is only sparsely produced.

C. × *himalayense* (him-a-*lay*-en-see), a wide-spreading flat-topped, dense grower, is noteworthy for bright red fruit and tiny green leaves.

C. horizontalis (hor-i-zon-*tay*-lis), commonly called rock spray cotoneaster, is one of the finest species for specimen use. It has a stiffly symmetrical, herringbone branching pattern that can best be appreciated in elevated planters or retaining walls. Of course, it is also suitable for covering moderate-sized to large-sized areas as a general cover, and creative gardeners sometimes train it to grow against fences and walls. It is native to western China and is hardy in Zones 5 to 8. Low, dense, horizontally spreading, and coarse-textured, it reaches 2 to 3 feet tall and 6 to 8 feet wide. Growth is slow. Plants from 2-gallon-sized containers are spaced 4 to 5 feet apart. Its leaves are deciduous to semievergreen, roundish to broadly elliptic, with bristly tipped ends. Colored shiny dark green and showing reddish purple fall color, they seldom exceed ½ inch long. The tiny, pink, single or paired flowers which come in the latter weeks of spring are rather inconspicuous individually, but collectively they are quite showy. The fruit which follows is glossy, bright red, ⅕ to ¼ inch wide, globe-shaped, and effective from early fall to mid winter. Popular horticultural selections include 'Purpusilla', an exceptionally low-growing, compact selection that displays ¼-inch-long leaves and elliptical-shaped fruit; 'Robusta', a heavy-fruiting, more vigorous, more upright selection; 'Saxatilis', a slow-growing selection most noteworthy for its leaves that are edged in white, then pink during autumn.

C. microphyllus (mi-kro-*fil*-us), little-leaved cotoneaster, is a low-growing, horizontally branched ground cover that reaches to 3 feet high by 6 feet wide. Growth is moderate. Plants from 1- to 2-gallon-sized containers are spaced 4 to 5 feet apart. In the landscape it should be used on a medium to large scale on terraced hillsides or in rock gardens as a specimen. A native of the Himalayas, this species is hardy in Zones 6 to 9 and is characterized by 5/16-inch-long, ¼-inch-wide, oval, shiny, dark green, evergreen, thyme-like leaves. The white flowers of late spring and early summer may be solitary, in pairs, or in groups of three. The showy fruit that follows is ¼ inch wide and colored a bright shade of shiny red. Horticultural selections of merit include 'Cochleatus', a low-growing dwarf selection; 'Cooperi', a tiny dense mound-forming selection useful in the rock garden; 'Emerald Spray', with mounding habit and sprays of tiny shiny emerald green leaves on densely set branches; 'Thymifolia', with more compact habit and pink flowers.

C. salicifolius (sa-lis-i-*foe*-lee-us), named for its narrow willow-shaped leaves (*Salix* is the genus name for willow), is commonly called willow-leaved cotoneaster. This 15-inch-tall, 6-foot-wide, very attractive, horizontal spreader is an excellent choice for use alongside sidewalks, building foundations, and on a moderate to large scale as an alternative to turf grass. It is often used in slightly raised beds that are bounded by railroad ties, large timbers, or large rocks. No foot traffic is tolerated. Growth is fast. Plants from 1- to 2-gallon-sized containers are spaced 3 to 4 feet apart. The species comes to North America from western China and is hardy in Zones 6 to 9. Gracing the landscape with extremely attractive, shiny green, 1½- to 3-inch-long, evergreen, willow-shaped leaves, this species has other merits as well. During spring or early summer, it becomes literally loaded down with 2-inch-wide clusters of cheerful, small, white, fragrant flowers. By fall, bright red fruit takes the spotlight and often persists until mid winter. Horticultural selections include 'Autumn Fire', a fine 2- to 3-foot-tall, 8-foot-wide selection noteworthy for its larger, very shiny green foliage that becomes purplish red during fall; 'Gnom', low growing with mounding habit; 'Moner', sometimes offered under the trademarked name 'Emerald Carpet', said to be smaller leaved with tighter habit; 'Parkteppich', similar to 'Autumn Fire' but even taller growing; 'Repens', mostly horizontal in growth habit and somewhat smaller in fruit size; 'Saldam', much like 'Autumn Fire' but with leaves that stay green throughout the winter; 'Scarlet Leader', a low, trailing selection that reaches 6 to 12 inches tall, displays dark green, shiny leaves, and is said to have better resistance to disease and insects than most of the others.

CULTURE / CARE: Cotoneasters perform best when grown in a fertile, light-textured, loamy, neutral or acidic soil. Good drainage is a necessity, and acceptable light conditions range from full sun to light shade. Drought and wind tolerance are both good, thus supplemental watering is seldom needed. Pests include scale insects, webworm, pear tree borer, pear sawfly, blister mite, aphids, and root-knot nematode. The most frequently observed diseases include leaf spots, canker, and fire blight. To maintain cotoneaster, some effort is necessary. Typically, this consists of pruning during early spring to remove branches that were damaged during the previous winter. General shaping and pruning to control spread can be performed at the same time.

PROPAGATION: Cotoneasters are almost always propagated by cuttings taken in early summer.

Cotula squalida   PLATE 88
New Zealand Brass Buttons

Reaching only 2 to 4 inches tall and spreading 2 feet across, this diminutive, mat-forming, rhizomatous herb is sometimes employed as a small-scale substitute for turf or dichondra. A modest amount of foot traffic is tolerated. Like other low-growing ground covers, such as mother of thyme (*Thymus serpyllum*), moneywort (*Lysimachia nummularia*), and rupturewort (*Herniaria glabra*), it can be grown between stepping stones.

SCIENTIFIC NAME: *Cotula squalida* (*koe*-tew-la *skwol*-i-da). *Cotula* is said by some to come from the Greek *kotula,* a small cup, referring to the cuplike flower heads of some species. Others say that it is in reference to the base of the leaves which clasp the stems, making a small cup. *Squalida* refers to the squalid or dingy appearance of the nondescript flowers.

HARDINESS / ORIGIN: Zones 9 to 10; New Zealand.

LEAVES / FLOWERS / FRUIT: The evergreen leaves originate in clusters along the stem and are fernlike, soft-textured, hairy, narrowly oval, bronzy green, and 2 inches long. Above them, in solitary 5/16-inch-wide heads, arise the buttonlike, yellow, relatively nonshowy flowers of summer. The fruit is very tiny and even less ornamentally useful.

RATE / SPACING: Growth is fast. Plants from 3- to 4-inch-diameter containers are spaced 8 to 12 inches apart.

CULTURE / CARE: New Zealand brass buttons is best in rich loamy acidic soil. Because it is not greatly tolerant of drought, it grows best when the soil is watered enough to keep it slightly moistened. It prefers full sun to light shade. Few diseases or pests are serious. Maintenance normally consists of trimming back shoots as they outgrow their bounds. In the event that self-sowing becomes a problem or absolute neatness is desired, the flowers can be mowed off as they fade.

PROPAGATION: The easiest means of propagation is division of the naturally layered stems in spring and fall; simply dig them up and transplant them.

Crassula multicava   PLATE 89

This fleshy warm-climate succulent herb is colorful in leaf and flower. It ranges from 8 to 10 inches tall, spreads indefinitely, and makes a nice general cover for use in small-sized and medium-sized areas. No foot traffic is tolerated.

SCIENTIFIC NAME: *Crassula multicava* (*cras*-you-la /

cra-*sul*-a mul-tie-*kay*-va). *Crassula* is derived from the Latin *crassus,* thick, and refers to the thick fleshy leaves of many species. *Multicava* means much hollowed or with many cavities, but the application to this species is not clearly understood.

HARDINESS / ORIGIN: Zones 9 to 10; South Africa.

LEAVES / FLOWERS / FRUIT: The fleshy, evergreen, oval, shiny green leaves reach 1 to 3 inches long by ¾ inch wide and are held upon fleshy stems which root as they touch the ground. The flowers, which are small and four-petaled, are light pink, arranged in clusters at the ends of the branches, and make a nice show during late winter and spring. The fruit is nonornamental.

RATE / SPACING: Growth is fast. Plants from pint-sized to quart-sized containers are spaced 18 to 24 inches apart.

CULTURE / CARE: This species grows well in full sun to light shade, in about any well-drained soil. Like most succulents, it tolerates considerable drought. Diseases such as anthracnose, leaf spot and root rot are occasionally encountered. Mealybugs and cyclamen mite are its primary pests. It needs only to have its shoots trimmed back as it outgrows its bounds.

PROPAGATION: Stem cuttings root easily throughout the year. Division likewise is simple and works any time. Ripe seed is said to germinate in two to four weeks.

Cuphea hyssopifola   PLATE 90
False Heather, Elfin Herb

False heather is a ½- to 2-foot-tall dainty mound-forming shrublet. Nice as a dwarf hedge, massed as a general purpose ground cover, or used alone or in small groups in a rock garden, this plant requires little work and is very pleasing to the eye. No foot traffic is tolerated.

SCIENTIFIC NAME: *Cuphea hyssopifola* (*cup*-fee-a his-sop-i-*foe*-lee-a). *Cuphea* comes from the Greek *kyphos,* curved, in reference to the shape of the seed capsule. *Hyssopifola* refers to the leaves which are shaped like those of the herb *Hyssop.*

HARDINESS / ORIGIN: Zones 9 to 11; Mexico and Guatemala.

LEAVES / FLOWERS / FRUIT: The evergreen, medium green to coppery green, linear to lance-shaped, ¾-inch-long, neat leaves are crowded upon gently arching stems. The tiny, delightful, tubular flowers of summer range from pink to purple to white. The fruit that follows is nonornamental.

RATE / SPACING: Growth is slow. Plants from 1- to 2-gallon-sized containers are spaced 18 to 24 inches apart.

HORTICULTURAL SELECTIONS: 'Compacta', 1 to 2 feet

tall, with shiny bright green leaves and rose-purple flowers.

OTHER SPECIES: *C. procumbens* (pro-*kum*-benz), a herbaceous species, reaches 1½ feet tall. With lance-shaped, 3-inch-long green leaves and rose-purple flowers, it is an attractive ground cover. It has been crossed with the 3-foot-tall mound-forming woody species *C. llavea* in creating *C.* × *purpurea.*

C. × *purpurea* (pur-*pur*-ee-a), which reaches 1½ feet tall, displays oval to lance-shaped leaves and purple-tinged bright rose-colored flowers. It is hardy to Zone 9. 'Firefly' displays flowers that range from deep to bright red and purple.

CULTURE / CARE: *Cuphea* species prefer full sun to light shade, good air circulation, and well-drained neutral to acidic soils. They are quite drought tolerant, have few disease and insect problems, and require little maintenance.

PROPAGATION: Stem cuttings root easily throughout the year. Naturally layered branches may be divided and transplanted with good success any time the soil can be kept moist.

Cymbalaria muralis   PLATE 91
Kenilworth Ivy, Coliseum Ivy, Ivy-leaved Toadflax, Pennywort

Popular for planting in the cracks of walls, Kenilworth ivy functions well as a general cover for small locations, particularly if the terrain is steeply sloping. In such places its 1- to 2-inch-tall, indefinite-spreading habit lends a cool green, waterfall-like softness to the landscape. No foot traffic is tolerated.

SCIENTIFIC NAME: *Cymbalaria muralis* (cym-ba-*lay*-ree-a mew-*ray*-lis). *Cymbalaria* comes from the Latin *cymbalum* and refers to the cymbal-shaped foliage. *Muralis,* Latin for wall, is probably a reference to the use of this plant in conjunction with walls—often it is planted in the cracks of walls or on top and allowed to trail over.

HARDINESS / ORIGIN: Zones 5 to 9; Europe.

LEAVES / FLOWERS / FRUIT: The evergreen, succulent, light green, rounded to heart-shaped or kidney-shaped, ½- to 1-inch-long, ½- to 1-inch-wide leaves are three-lobed to seven-lobed and alternately arranged upon thin succulent stems. The flowers, which bloom from summer through fall, are shaped similar to snapdragon flowers and are colored lilac-blue with yellow throats. The tiny fruit is nonornamental.

RATE / SPACING: Growth is fast. Plants from 3- to 4-inch-diameter containers are spaced 10 to 16 inches apart.

HORTICULTURAL SELECTIONS: 'Alba', with white flowers; 'Alba Compacta', only 12 inches wide, tiny, mound-forming, creeping, leaves apple green, flow-

ers borne in summer, pure white with lemon throats.
OTHER SPECIES: *C. aequitriloba* (ee-kwee-try-*lo*-ba), named for its three equal lobes (the leaves), is commonly called toadflax basket ivy. It hails from southern Europe and is hardy in Zones 8 to 10. It reaches 4 inches tall, spreads indefinitely, and is clothed with evergreen, three-lobed to five-lobed, medium green foliage. Its ½-inch-long flowers, like those of *C. muralis,* are lilac-blue with a yellow throat, but borne only during the summer months.
CULTURE / CARE: These species need an acidic to slightly alkaline soil that is well drained yet moisture retentive. They are not greatly tolerant of drought or extreme heat and do their best in moderate to dense shade. Their primary disease problem is damping off, and their pest predators are slugs, snails, aphids, and mites. Little or no maintenance is needed.
PROPAGATION: Both species are easily increased by division. Seed germinates in one week.

Cytisus decumbens   PLATE 92
Prostrate Broom

If you have ever encountered any of the different species of broom, then no doubt you have noticed their many stiff, erectly oriented, green, relatively leafless branches. These, when tied tightly together and attached to a handle, are quite functional for sweeping, thus the common name broom. Prostrate broom, with its horizontal growth and mat-forming, semiwoody habit, reaches 8 inches tall (although often it stays much lower) and spreads more than 3 feet across. In comparison to the upright forms, it probably would not work well for sweeping, but as a ground cover, it more than passes the test. Prostrate broom makes an excellent rock garden specimen or small-scale general cover and is particularly effective when planted next to a wall or in an elevated planter that it can trail over. When combined with relatively drought-tolerant shrubs such as heather, juniper, and spring heath, very interesting and colorful hillside plantings can be created. No foot traffic is tolerated.
SCIENTIFIC NAME: *Cytisus decumbens* (*sit*-i-sus dee-*kum*-benz). *Cytisus* is derived from the Greek *kytisos,* trefoil, referring to the leaves of many species. *Decumbens* refers to the decumbent growth habit (horizontal with upturning branch tips).
HARDINESS / ORIGIN: Zones 6 to 8; southern Europe.
LEAVES / FLOWERS / FRUIT: The tiny, deciduous, dull medium green, oblong to oval leaves reach only ¼ to ¾ inch long by ¹⁄₁₆ to ⅛ inch wide. In bloom, which is outstanding, hundreds of ½- to ⅝-inch-long, yellow, pealike florets are borne in profusion in late spring and sporadically thereafter until fall. The fruit is podlike, nonornamental, and said to be poisonous.

RATE / SPACING: Growth is moderate. Plants from ½- to 1-gallon-sized containers are spaced 16 to 24 inches apart.
OTHER SPECIES: *C. albus* (*al*-bus), a slow spreader, hails from Europe, reaches 1 foot tall, and produces yellowish white to white flowers during summer.
C. × *beanii* (*bee*-nee-eye) reaches 14 inches tall by 16 inches wide. Its leaves are linear, to ½ inch long, and hairy in youth. The flowers, which arrive during summer, are golden yellow.
C. × *kewensis* (kew-*en*-sis) reaches 10 inches tall by 4 feet wide and is graced with creamy white to pale yellow flowers during late spring.
C. procumbens (pro-*kum*-benz) is similar to *C. decumbens* in habit, but taller—to 30 inches tall by 4 feet wide.
C. purpureus (pur-pur-*ee*-us) is a procumbent nearly hairless species that reaches 18 inches tall. Its oval-shaped leaves reach 1 inch long, and its purple, pink, or white flowers bloom during late spring.
CULTURE / CARE: Although prostrate brooms adapt to various well-drained soils, they perform best in sandy or gravelly, loamy soils. They prefer full sun, are highly resistant to drought, and are well suited for windswept locations. Their primary pests and diseases are nematodes, leaf spot, and blight. Maintenance needs are few to nonexistent, but some gardeners prefer to prune lightly immediately after flowering to encourage branching. It is important not to prune too heavily, as recovery may be slow.
PROPAGATION: Cuttings root quite well during the summer months. Division is best performed during spring or early fall.

Dalea greggii   PLATE 93
Trailing Indigo Bush, Trailing Smoke Bush

This species is best in desert areas of the Southwest as a general cover and soil retainer for moderate to large areas of level or sloping ground. It is a low, sprawling, woody shrub that reaches 12 inches tall (occasionally to 2 feet) and spreads from 4 to 8 feet across. No foot traffic is tolerated.
SCIENTIFIC NAME: *Dalea greggii* (*day*-lee-a *greg*-ee-eye). *Dalea* is named after Samuel Dale, an English botanist. *Greggii* likely honors another botanist.
HARDINESS / ORIGIN: Zones 9 to 10; Chihuahua desert of Mexico.
LEAVES / FLOWERS / FRUIT: The leaves are evergreen, compound, to ½ inch long by ¼ inch wide, and composed of about nine white-haired, narrowly oval, gray-green leaflets. The small, purple flowers are borne in dense round heads and are effective in spring and summer. The fruit, a small legume, is nonornamental.

RATE / SPACING: Growth is moderate to fast. Plants from gallon-sized containers are spaced 1½ to 2 feet apart.

CULTURE / CARE: Trailing indigo bush is tolerant of various soil types but always needs good drainage. It should be watered frequently until established, then little, if ever, thereafter. As with most arid-climate ground covers, it prefers full sun but tolerates light shade. No serious pests have been reported, yet sometimes fungi cause problems with young plants. Maintenance consists of trimming back the leading stems as they outgrow their bounds.

PROPAGATION: Cuttings root best during early summer when placed in a very well drained medium such as 50 percent perlite and 50 percent vermiculite.

Dampiera diversifolia   PLATE 94
Dampiera

Dampiera is exceptionally attractive, grows well in the cracks of a rock ledge, and looks beautiful when allowed to spill over the edge, especially when in bloom. Used en masse, it serves well as a general cover, and on sloping terrain it functions well as a soil binder. It is said to combine well with bulbs and with open-canopied Australian native trees and shrubs. It is low, trailing, subshrubby, and semi-woody, reaching 4 inches tall by 3 to 5 feet wide.

SCIENTIFIC NAME: *Dampiera diversifolia* (dam-*pe*-air-a di-ver-si-*foe*-lee-a). *Dampiera* commemorates William Dampier (1652–1715), an explorer, buccaneer, amateur botanist, and writer who first described many species of this genus. *Diversifolia* implies diversity and refers to the variable shape of the leaves.

HARDINESS / ORIGIN: Zones 9 to 10; southwestern Australia.

LEAVES / FLOWERS / FRUIT: The evergreen leaves at the base of the plant are simple, crowded, lance-shaped, somewhat concave, 1 to 2 inches long, quite narrow, and edged with small teeth. The leaves further up on the stems are somewhat more rounded. Both types are colored a vibrant shade of medium green. The flowers are borne profusely on short stems, reach ⅝ inch across, and contain five deep purplish blue (rarely pale blue) petals that radiate around a pollen-laden center of yellow. They are fragrant in hot weather and exceptionally attractive for many months during spring and summer. The tiny fruit is nonornamental.

RATE / SPACING: Growth is slow initially, but moderate when plants are established. Plants from ½- to 1-gallon-sized containers are spaced 1½ to 2½ feet apart.

CULTURE / CARE: A well-drained soil is required, but *Dampiera* species are not picky about texture and grow in a range of gravelly soils to clay loam. They have minimal drought and heat tolerance; for the best growth and appearance the soil should be slightly moistened. The site should be lightly shaded and somewhat sheltered from strong drying winds. No serious diseases or pests seem to exist. The only routine maintenance that is sometimes practiced is a light shearing after flowering to keep plants neat and compact.

PROPAGATION: Stem cuttings from late spring to late summer root quite easily. Rooted suckers can be cut off and transplanted during the cool seasons.

Daphne cneorum   PLATE 95
Rose Daphne, Garland Daphne

A low, mounding, rather loose, shrubby ground cover, rose daphne ranges from 6 to 12 inches tall and spreads 3 feet across. Although sometimes a little tricky to grow, this floriferous species can bring eye-catching rewards. Among its best uses is edging the sides of a garden path or walkway, but it is also effective as a rock garden specimen, accent plant, or, if mass planted, as a moderate-scale general cover or facing plant. No foot traffic is tolerated.

SCIENTIFIC NAME: *Daphne cneorum* (*daf*-nee nee-*oh*-rum). *Daphne* commemorates the nymph in Greek mythology who was turned into a laurel tree to escape from a pursuing Apollo. *Cneorum* is a Greek term for an olive-like shrub.

HARDINESS / ORIGIN: Zones 5 to 8; alpine regions of central and southern Europe.

LEAVES / FLOWERS / FRUIT: The evergreen, dark shiny green leaves appear neat and orderly. In maturity they reach ¾ to 1 inch long by ⅛ to ¼ inch across with an oblong outline. The flowers, which arise in clusters at the branch tips during mid spring (and often to a lesser extent in late summer), individually reach ⅖ inch across, are colored pink to rose-red, and are very pleasantly fragrant. To say the least, they are extremely attractive. The fleshy, leathery, yellowish brown fruit which follows is more of a curiosity than an ornamental feature.

RATE / SPACING: Growth is slow. Plants from 1- to 2-gallon-sized containers are spaced 1½ to 2 feet apart.

HORTICULTURAL SELECTIONS: 'Alba', somewhat smaller in size with white flowers; 'Albo-marginata' ('Variegata'), strikingly variegated green leaves with white margins; 'Eximia', with larger leaves and larger deep pink flowers; 'Major', with larger leaves; var. *pygmaea,* with rose-pink flowers and a rather horizontal habit; 'Ruby Glow', with darker green foliage and deep pink flowers; var. *verlotii,* with leaves and flowers somewhat longer than the species.

OTHER SPECIES: ***D. arbuscula*** (ar-*boos*-kew-la), literally meaning little tree in Latin, is commonly called shrubby daphne. It is hardy to Zone 4, hails from alpine regions of west central Europe, and displays a low, dwarf, mounded habit to 6 inches tall and more than 12 inches wide. Its growth occurs at a fairly slow rate, and plants from ½- to 1-gallon-sized containers should be spaced 10 to 14 inches apart. Upon its attractive reddish stems 1-inch-long, wavy-edged, dark green, lance-shaped, evergreen leaves are borne in a rather crowded arrangement. Its pink, pleasantly fragrant flowers are arranged in 1-inch-diameter clusters and appear in spring. Two subspecies of shrubby daphne are commonly grown. Subspecies *platycladus* is interesting in that its three-angled stems grow together in a parallel fashion (called fasciation). At their tips are borne 100-membered to 150-membered fanlike flower clusters. Plant size reaches 8 to 14 inches tall by 2 to 3 feet wide. Subspecies *septentianalis* reaches 6 to 12 inches tall and displays leaves that are narrower and longer than the species.

D. ashtonii (ash-*ton*-ee-eye), reaching 4 inches tall and spreading 12 inches wide, is hardy in Zones 6 to 9 and displays fleshy olive green leaves and numerous pink flowers with white centers.

D. × burkwoodii (burk-*wood*-ee-eye), Burkwood daphne, was formed by hybridizing *D. cneorum* with *D. caucasica.* The result was a lovely shrublet of broad, mound-forming habit. Typically, it reaches 3 feet tall and spreads to 5 or 6 feet across. Its flowers of late spring are pleasingly fragrant, colored white to pinkish, and arranged in magnificent 2-inch-wide clusters. Hardy in Zones 4 to 7, it is a parent of these significant cultivars: 'Carol Mackie', with leaf edges trimmed in creamy white, is one of the most beautifully variegated plants in existence; var. *laveniree,* reaching 3 feet tall by 3 feet wide, is vigorous and neat, and displays large clusters of purple and pink flowers; 'Somerset', with many pink flowers, is more robust than the typical species and reaches 4 feet tall by 6 feet wide.

CULTURE / CARE: Daphnes often do not transplant well bare root and thus are best purchased as container grown plants. Should transplanting be attempted, fall or spring are the preferred times. To have any success with daphnes, the soil must have excellent drainage. Rose and Burkwood daphnes require acidic to neutral soil; shrubby daphne prefers acidic soil but tolerates slight alkalinity. Daphnes are not markedly tolerant of drought and should be supplied with sufficient water to keep the soil slightly moist throughout the summer. They prefer full sun to light shade in coastal regions, otherwise light shade. Pests include aphids, scales, and mealybugs, while the most common diseases are leaf spots, canker, crown rot, twig blight, and viruses. Mainte-nance involves administering a light shearing following bloom to keep plants neat and compact.

PROPAGATION: Best success seems to be achieved with cuttings stuck in a mixture of perlite and peat moss during early summer.

Decodon verticillatus   PLATE 96
Willow-herb, Wild Oleander, Grass-poly, Milk Willow-herb, Swamp Loosestrife

A robust North American native somewhat woody-based, spongy or corky-stemmed rhizomatous ground cover, willow-herb is clearly not a ground cover for every landscape. It is, however, ideal for soil retention in swampy locations by lakes, ponds, or rivers. Its arching branches root as they touch the soil and form a dense thicket that effectively binds soil, while at the same time providing cover for aquatic and wetland inhabitants. Reaching 2 to 4 feet tall (rarely to 7 feet in the Deep South) and spreading indefinitely, it is both attractive and functional. It should not be confused with the noxious European import *Lythrum salicaria* that has been the scourge of our wetlands. Occasional foot traffic is easily tolerated.

SCIENTIFIC NAME: *Decodon verticillatus* (*dek*-oh-don ver-*tis*-i-lay-tus). *Decodon* takes its name from the Greek *deka,* ten, and *odous,* a tooth, in reference to the calyx which has ten teeth. *Verticillatus* refers to the flowers that are arranged in whorls, verticillasters, around the stems.

HARDINESS / ORIGIN: Zone 3; swamps and stream margins of central Maine to Florida, west to Minnesota, Missouri, and Louisiana.

LEAVES / FLOWERS / FRUIT: The deciduous, narrowly oval to lance-shaped (willowlike), 2- to 4-inch-long, ⅜- to 1-inch-wide, shiny green leaves are carried upon short leafstalks and turn reddish to orange in fall. The flowers, borne during mid summer, are pinkish, tubular, arranged in stem-surrounding whorls, and interesting although not greatly showy. The fruit that follows, a ¼-inch-diameter round capsule, is also interesting but not ornamentally spectacular.

RATE / SPACING: Growth is fast to invasive. Plants from 1- to 2-gallon-sized containers are spaced 2 to 3 feet apart.

CULTURE / CARE: Willow-herb is easy to grow, long-lived, and reliable in any acidic to neutral soil that remains constantly wet. It grows in water up to 15 inches deep and does well in full sun to moderate shade. It tolerates only short periods of drought. Although it is sometimes attacked by aphids, they are of minor consequence. Little or no maintenance is required.

PROPAGATION: There may be no easier plant to propagate than willow-herb. Because of preformed rootlets within the stems, cuttings stuck in moist soil root in less than one week. Seed and division are also effective but seldom practiced because division is so easy.

Delosperma

PLATE 97

Hardy Ice Plant

If you have ever visited the Los Angeles area, you have no doubt been impressed with the very showy roadside ground covers known as ice plants. Originating in western North America, Europe, South Africa, the Canary Islands, southwestern Asia, Chile, and Madeira, these plants are remarkable for their colorful, daisylike flowers and glistening foliage. Because they are so drought resistant, they are often planted along roadsides where they act as good soil binders. They are relatively disease-free, fire retardant, and, above all, very beautiful. In this book *Cephalophyllum, Drosanthemum,* and *Lampranthus* species are also discussed.

The only trouble with ice plants has been their lack of cold hardiness. Indeed, until relatively recently, only gardeners living in warm winter climates were able to fully appreciate their beauty. Now, however, a few outstanding introductions from the mountains of South Africa have changed that. Not only do these plants possess the ornamental characteristics of other ice plants, they are also relatively cold tolerant. For this reason they are called hardy ice plants.

Two of the most popular species, *D. nubigena* (cloud-loving ice plant) and *D. cooperi* (Cooper's ice plant), are colorful (both in flower and foliage), and relatively drought tolerant. They are attractive as single sprawling specimens, may be arranged in small groups for accent, or may be planted in large masses where they give the appearance of a vibrant green carpet (when not in flower) and display neonlike brilliance when in bloom.

Because the hardy ice plants are colorful and drought tolerant, they can be combined with drought-tolerant dwarf evergreens of uncomplicated green or blue foliage, such as spruces and junipers. Junipers are available in many sizes, shapes, and colors, and are among the best shrubs to plant with hardy ice plant. Suitable spruce companions are normally upright, pyramidal, and colored various shades of blue and green. When used for facing, ice plants also draw attention to garden statuary, public fountains and pools, and building entrances. For color fanatics with some open soil as their palette, a few flats of variously colored, upright-growing, clump-

forming stonecrops (*Sedum* species) interspersed among ice plants will create a beautiful montage of color. Tough in every other respect, the hardy ice plants do not tolerate foot traffic.

SCIENTIFIC NAME: *Delosperma* (del-*oh*-sper-ma) is derived from the Greek *delos,* manifest, and *perma,* seed, possibly in reference to the shininess of the seeds.

HARDINESS / ORIGIN: See individual species for hardiness; South Africa (often from alpine habitat).

LEAVES / FLOWERS / FRUIT: The dense branches are covered with numerous closely set, oppositely arranged, three-angled, cylindrical or nearly flat, often papillate (with raised dotlike projections) succulent leaves. The flowers are outstandingly colorful, solitary or in twos or threes (less commonly in clusters) and remind one of neon-colored daisies.

RATE / SPACING: Growth is moderate. Plants from 3- to 4-inch-diameter containers are spaced 12 to 16 inches apart.

SPECIES: *D. ashtonii* (ash-*tone*-ee-eye) reaches 4 inches tall, 12 inches wide, and is hardy in Zones 6 to 9. Its fleshy olive green leaves make a nice backdrop for its numerous pink summerborne flowers with white centers.

D. cooperi (*koo*-per-eye), named after Cooper, presumably the discoverer of this South African species, is commonly called Cooper's hardy ice plant and is very florific. Beginning in early summer, masses of neon pinkish purple, 2-inch-wide, daisy-like flowers begin to open and do not stop until after several heavy frosts in the fall. The plant reaches 6 to 7 inches tall by to 24 inches wide. Growth is fast. Plants from pint-sized to quart-sized containers are spaced 16 to 24 inches apart. The foliage is medium to dark, glistening green, $2^3/_{16}$ inches long by $^1/_4$ inch wide by $^3/_{16}$ inch thick, and nearly cylindrical in cross section. The only drawback of this plant is that it is less hardy (Zone 6 or 7 northward, Zone 10 to the south) than *D. nubigena.* The fruit is nonornamental. Several cultivars are said to exist, but their distribution thus far has been limited. Typically, they differ in having white, pink, rose, purple, or mauve flowers.

D. herbaeu (*herb*-ee-ew), an uncommon species, sometimes goes by the name *D.* 'Alba' or simply white-flowered ice plant. It is similar to *D. cooperi* but with somewhat smaller white flowers.

D. nubigena (nu-bi-*gee*-na), named from the Latin for born of a cloud, is commonly called cloud-loving hardy ice plant, trailing ice plant, or hardy ice. This species comes from the Drakensberg Mountains of South Africa, where at times it literally grows in the clouds. It reaches less than 2 inches tall by up to 3 feet wide. Growth is fast. Plants from 3- or 4-

inch pots are spaced 10 to 14 inches apart. Used on a small to moderate scale, they give a mossy, cheerfully colored, carpetlike effect. The species is hardy to Zone 5 or 6 northward and as far as Zone 9 or 10 to the south. Colored bright, light, shiny green, its 1¼-inch-long, ³⁄₁₆-inch-wide evergreen leaves are thick and fleshy. During fall they may take on reddish hues. The multitude of solitary, almost chartreuse-yellow, ¾-inch-wide, daisylike flowers that are borne during mid spring are exceptionally bright. The fruit, which sometimes follows, is nonornamental. 'Basutoland' displays smaller flowers.

D. obtusum (ob-*tew*-sum) is like *D. cooperi* but smaller in all respects, reaching only 4 inches tall.

CULTURE / CARE: Adaptable to almost any well-drained soil and tolerant of considerable drought, the hardy ice plants are quite accommodating. They do not object to an occasional deep watering during hot, dry weather. They prefer full sun. Their primary disease is crown rot (in poorly drained soils), and their predominant pests, mealybugs, are sometimes encountered. Maintenance needs are few, if any.

PROPAGATION: Cuttings root very easily and usually are ready for transplanting within three or four weeks. Division is nearly foolproof throughout the season. For *D. cooperi,* seed can be collected; germination occurs in 10 days.

Dendranthema   PLATE 98
Chrysanthemum

The large genus *Dendranthema* contains many fine ground covers that used to be classified as *Chrysanthemum* species. These valuable, florific herbs, particularly the more compact forms, work nicely as small-scale to moderate-scale edging plants and general covers. Those described here typically form tight clumps or cushions ½ to 3 feet in height and spread shyly by short rhizomes. Some species display highly ornamental foliage, yet, typically it is the breathtaking, fragrant, late season, sunflower-like blossoms that receive the most recognition. No foot traffic is tolerated.

SCIENTIFIC NAME: *Dendranthema* (den-dran-*the*-ma) comes from the Greek *dendron,* tree, and *anthemon,* flower, and refers to the woodiness of the flower stems of these species.

HARDINESS / ORIGIN: See individual species for hardiness; mainly China and Japan, with one species from eastern Europe.

LEAVES / FLOWERS / FRUIT: The leaves are deciduous with pinnately divided, lobed, tooth-edged, or rarely entire leaves. The flowers, like other plants that used to be classified as species of *Chrysanthemum,* are sunflower-like, composed of female ray florets in colors ranging from white, to pink, to yellowish. The central male disc florets are tiny and yellow. The fruit is nonornamental.

RATE / SPACING: See individual species.

SPECIES: *D. × morifolium* (mo-ri-*foe*-lee-um), named for its leaves, which are reminiscent of *Morus* (mulberry), is commonly called garden chrysanthemum or florist's chrysanthemum. Typically hardy in Zones 4 to 10, this very large and complex hybrid species contains thousands of cultivars. It has been in existence for hundreds of years, under one name or another, and is said to be derived from numerous deliberate and happenstance crosses. Most crosses took place in Asia, Europe, and North America, and probably involved *D. indicum, D. × grandiflorum, D. lavandulifolium, D. chanetti, D. japonense, D. makinoi,* and *D. odoratum.*

Selections of *D. × morifolium* range in height from 1 to 3 feet and are variable in hardiness (specific to each selection) in Zones 4 to 10. Plants from 1- to 2-gallon-sized containers are spaced 1½ feet apart. The flowers come in a wide range of colors, types, and bloom times and are classified as buttons, cushions, daisies, decoratives, and pompons. Buttons have small flowers less than 1 inch in diameter, and plant height typically does not exceed 1½ feet. Cushions have double flowers and a compact habit, normally less than 20 inches tall. Daisies are single flowers with yellow centers and variable height. Decoratives are taller cultivars with large double or semidouble flowers. Pompons have small ball-shaped flowers and a height that seldom exceeds 1½ feet.

Interestingly, it is the length of the night that triggers garden mums to flower. As summer passes and the nights grow longer, each plant encounters its critical night length, which triggers its flowering response. In the South this occurs while the weather is still warm, but in the North, with late-blooming varieties, it may not occur until too late in the season. For this reason, northern gardeners must select earlier blooming varieties since the late-blooming ones may be killed back by frost before their buds even open.

Garden mums need a lot of food and normally should be fertilized a couple of times each year. Use a fertilizer that is low in nitrogen, or you may spend all your time pruning. Fortunately, because most garden mums set their buds quickly late in the season, they can be maintained low and compact through summertime shearing without jeopardizing flowering. In the South, all pruning should occur before August 15, and in the North before August 1. Northern gardeners will experience good results with the University of Minnesota's 'Minn' series of mums, which have been bred to flower heavily before frost.

Related to *D.* × *morifolium* is *D.* 'Mei-kyo', which is hardy in Zones 6 to 9. Adorning this cultivar during fall are numerous 2-inch-wide, double flowers with yellow centers and rose-colored petals.

D. pacifica (pa-*sif*-i-ka), named for its Pacific, or Asian origin, is commonly called gold-and-silver chrysanthemum. It displays remarkable character. Spreading by rhizomes, it forms a tight, cushion-shaped mound from 10 to 16 inches tall by 3 feet wide. During late fall the foliage is topped with buttonlike yellow flowers, and although attractive in bloom and habit, it remains, uncharacteristically, a superb foliage plant. Trimmed with neat, ⅛-inch-wide laser sharp margins of white, the scallop-edged, oblong, grayish green leaves are remarkably attractive. Interestingly, the variegation comes from the overlap of the thick white hairs from the underside of the leaves rather than from two genetically different cells, as is most often the case (see Chapter 7 for a discussion on variegation). Hardy in Zones 6 to 9, it was brought into the United States from Japan in 1976 by Maryland nurseryman Kurt Bluemel.

D. × *rubellum* (rew-*bell*-um), presumably named after its pink flower petals, is commonly called hybrid chrysanthemum or red hybrid chrysanthemum. Selections range from 1 to 2½ feet tall and spread by rhizomes to form neat clumps. Its foliage is broadly oval to wedge-shaped, 1½ inches long, segmented and toothed about the edges, and colored medium to dark green. The daisylike flowers, which are borne in loose sprays during mid to late summer, are 2½ to 3½ inches wide and have yellow centers and pink petals. From Japan, Korea, northern China, and Manchuria, this hybrid is hardy in Zones 4 to 10 and often is listed as *D. zawadskii* var. *latilobum.* It, along with *D.* × *morifolium,* is said to be the parent of a very hardy group known as the Korean hybrids. A few common selections are 'Clara Curtis', with rose-pink flowers on 2- to 3-foot stems; 'Duchess of Edinburgh', to 2 feet tall, with muted red flowers; 'Mary Stoker', with brownish yellow flowers.

D. weyrichii (way-*rik*-ee-eye), named after Dr. Weyrich, a Russian naval surgeon, is a deep-green-leaved Japanese species hardy in Zones 3 to 8. It reaches 8 to 18 inches tall and spreads by creeping rootstock. Its 1- to 2-inch-wide daisylike flowers of late fall are white with yellow centers and mature to pink. Plants from pint-sized to gallon-sized containers are spaced 1 foot apart. 'Pink Bomb' has large pink flowers and compact habit of 8 to 10 inches tall; 'White Bomb' has white flowers and a height to 1 foot.

CULTURE / CARE: *Dendranthema* species prefer well-drained, moist, acidic to neutral soils in full sun to light shade. They feed heavily, benefit from fertiliza-

tion, and are not very tolerant of drought. They are susceptible to a number of diseases and pests, including leaf spot, wilt, rust, blight, powdery mildew, aster yellows, aphids, leaf miner, stalk borer, and mites. Many of the taller forms can become lanky and need pruning during mid summer.

PROPAGATION: Division is easily accomplished during spring. Stem cuttings root quickly in early summer. Root cuttings also work in fall. Seed germinates in seven to ten days at 70°F.

Deschampsia caespitosa PLATE 99
Tufted Hair Grass

Tufted hair grass is a densely tufted nonrunning grass that reaches 16 inches tall (2 to 3 feet when in flower) and spreads 10 to 18 inches across. As a ground cover, it is most effective when planted en masse in broad sweeping drifts as a background to lower ground covers or mixed perennials. It is also well suited for specimen planting in rock gardens or for accent or general cover in naturalized landscapes. Only infrequent foot traffic is tolerated.

SCIENTIFIC NAME: *Deschampsia caespitosa* (des-*kamp*-see-a seez-pi-*toe*-sa). *Deschampsia* commemorates Jean Louis Auguste Loiseleur-Deslongchamps (1774–1849). *Caespitosa* means tufted.

HARDINESS / ORIGIN: Zones 4 to 9; from Greenland to Alaska, south to California and North Carolina. Also Eurasia.

LEAVES / FLOWERS / FRUIT: The leaves are shiny, medium to dark green, evergreen, and arranged upon erect stems. They may reach 2 feet long by ⅕ inch wide and taper to a sharp or blunt point. The flowers, which are borne in feathery panicles during early to mid summer, reach up to 20 inches long by 8 inches across. Typically they are upright, but sometimes they nod. Each floret is tiny and varies in color—creating an overall color display that ranges from silver to gold, purple to green, or combinations thereof. The flowers are excellent in arrangements and can be cut off and preserved with hair spray prior to seed formation. The fruit, a grain, is nonornamental.

RATE / SPACING: Growth is slow. Plants from pint-sized to quart-sized containers are spaced 10 to 14 inches apart.

HORTICULTURAL SELECTIONS: Many selections have been made. A few of the more common are 'Bronze-schleier' ('Bronze Veil'), with bronze-colored inflorescences; 'Goldgehänge', with golden-yellow inflorescences; 'Goldschleier' ('Gold Veil'), with bright yellow inflorescences, hardy in Zones 6 to 9; 'Goldstaub', with yellow inflorescences, hardy in Zones 6 to 9; 'Schottland' ('Scotland'), with inflorescences ascending 4 to 6 feet; var. *tardiflora,* blooming later in the summer; 'Tautäger' ('Dew Bearer'), with narrow inflorescences; var. *vivipara,* excellent for viewing and conversation because, in place of seed, forms young plantlets on the flower panicle which, because of their weight, often cause the stems to bow, then upon touching the soil, develop as new plants, hardy in Zones 5 to 9; 'Waldschatt' ('Forest Shade'), 2 to 3 feet tall, with dark brown panicles.

OTHER SPECIES: **D. *flexuosa*** (fleks-you-*oh*-sa), meaning with wavy stems, is commonly called wavy hair grass. It hails from Europe, northern Asia, northeastern North America, and temperate South America and is very similar to *D. caespitosa* but is smaller and reaches only 2 feet tall when in flower. Its leaves reach 1 foot long, are stiff, and colored dark green. The flowers, which arise during summer, glisten with silvery, brownish, and purplish tones, and often give the overall appearance of a rich golden haze. Hardy in Zones 4 to 8. 'Aurea' has vibrant yellow leaves.

CULTURE / CARE: Although tufted hair grass is adaptable to most types of soil, it prefers a moist soil with a relatively high amount of organic matter. It is marginally tolerant of drought and prefers full sun to light shade. No serious diseases or pests seem to affect it. Little or no maintenance is required.

PROPAGATION: Division is required (to maintain uniformity) when propagating the cultivars. It is best performed in the spring; however, success is nearly as good in summer or fall. Seed, used only to propagate the species, germinates well and can be stored dry with good germination occurring after a year or more. Commercial supplies are available. In either case, sowing is usually performed in fall or late winter with plants ready for the landscape by late spring.

Deutzia gracilis 'Nikko'   PLATE 100
Nikko Deutzia

With tenacious spreading habit and compact form, this low-growing, broad-spreading, shrubby ground cover ranges from 2 to 2½ feet tall, spreads to 5 feet across, and roots in as it spreads. Planted en masse in moderate to large areas, it effectively conceals partially exposed foundations, and its habit of rooting allows it to excel as a soil binder on slopes of moderate incline. Single plants can be exceptional as specimens alongside stairs, in planters, or atop retaining walls, all locations where the eye more easily falls and where the graceful, trailing stems can be more fully appreciated. Nikko deutzia combines well with other dwarf shrubs in border plantings and looks especially attractive in front of taller, deep-green-leaved shrubs such as Japanese yew and holly. No foot traffic is tolerated.

SCIENTIFIC NAME: *Deutzia gracilis* 'Nikko' (*doot*-tsi-a *gra*-sil-is *nee*-koe). *Deutzia* commemorates Johann van der Deutz (1743–1788) of Amsterdam, who was a patron of the great Swedish plant collector and physician Carl Peter Thunberg. *Gracilis,* slender or graceful, refers to the narrow foliage.

HARDINESS / ORIGIN: Zones 5 to 8; Japan.

LEAVES / FLOWERS / FRUIT: The deciduous, narrow, oblong to lance-shaped leaves are quite durable, neat, and attractive. Colored medium green with toothed edges, they reach 1¾ to 2¼ inches long by ⅜ to ⅝ inch wide. Their fall color is often purplish. The numerous showy, tiny, white flowers of late spring are arranged in clusters 1 inch across. The fruit is nonornamental.

RATE / SPACING: Growth is moderate to fast. Plants from 1- to 2-gallon-sized containers are spaced 2½ to 3½ feet apart.

OTHER SPECIES: **D. × *lemoinei* 'Compacta'** (le-*moy*-nee-eye), commonly named Lemoine deutzia, after its hybridizer, who originally named it 'Boule de Neige', is an excellent cultivar with dwarf compact habit, height to 3 feet, and large clusters of pure white flowers in late spring. *Deutzia* × *lemoinei* is derived from a cross involving *D. gracilis* and *D. parviflora* in the late nineteenth century and itself is not a ground cover but a 5- to 7-foot-tall shrub.

CULTURE / CARE: Deutzias are easily satisfied and grow in well-drained, acidic soils that range from sandy to clay loam. They display moderate tolerance to drought and only require watering during extended periods of hot, dry weather. Full sun exposure in the North results in the best growth and flowering. In the South, full sun with afternoon shade is best. Pests and diseases are seldom serious, the most common being aphids, leaf miners, and leaf spot. Maintenance needs are few, normally a light shearing after flowering to promote compact growth.

PROPAGATION: Cuttings root easily during early summer. Division of rooted branch segments is best performed during spring or early fall.

Dianthus   PLATE 101
Carnation, Cloves, Pinks

Dianthus is a large (some 300 species), florific, herbaceous genus that offers some of the most beautifully flowered ground covers in cultivation. By the way, these are true carnations, the kind you buy from a florist, yet compact growing and cold hardy. Although carnations are adorable for their petite highly fragrant flowers and tufted grasslike habit, many tend to be disease prone and demanding in respect to maintenance. For this reason they are usually used on a small scale. A second note of caution concerns their names and nomenclature. Like all long-appreciated florific plants, carnations have been subject to selection and hybridization and therefore hundreds of cultivars exist. Thus, very often they are misnamed or classified as different species or hybrids by different horticulturists. If you don't find the plant you are looking for under one species heading (here or in your garden center), look under another. For all the confusion, generally speaking, there is agreement as to the cultivar names. No foot traffic is tolerated.

SCIENTIFIC NAME: *Dianthus* (die-*an*-thoos) is loftily named with the Greek roots *dios,* god or divine, and *anthos,* flower, and literally means divine flower.

HARDINESS / ORIGIN: Zones 3 to 9; Eurasia to South Africa.

LEAVES / FLOWERS / FRUIT: Normally narrow and near-grasslike, the leaves are oppositely arranged on prominently jointed stems. The typically five-petaled flowers are often strongly and pleasantly fragrant, and are borne in panicles or solitary fashion upon compact stems above the foliage. The fruit is nonornamental.

RATE / SPACING: Growth is slow to moderate. Plants from 3- to 5-inch-diameter containers are spaced 8 to 14 inches apart.

SPECIES: *D. × allwoodii* (awl-*wud*-ee-ii), named for the English nurseryman Mantague Allwood who created it during the 1920s, is commonly called Allwood pink. Hardy in Zones 4 to 8 and originating from crosses involving *D. plumarius* and *D. caryophyllus,* this hybrid species has given rise to a number of gray-green-leaved cultivars with two flowers per stem. Some of the most significant are 'Aqua', with pure white double flowers; 'Doris', with fragrant, pink-eyed, salmon-pink flowers that ascend to 15 inches; 'Essex Witch', with flowers ranging from pink to white and salmon; 'Ian', with double red flowers trimmed in crimson; 'Robin', with double flowers ranging from salmon to scarlet.

D. arenarius (air-e-*nay*-ree-us), named for the Latin *arena,* sand (the soil type which this species naturally inhabits), is commonly called sand pink. It is hardy throughout Zones 4 to 7, hails from Finland, and is good for edging and for small-scale, general applications. Tufted in habit, it ranges from 6 to 15 inches tall. Growth is moderate, and plants are spaced 8 to 12 inches apart. The evergreen leaves are very narrow, gray-green, and grasslike. During mid summer the plant is topped with fragrant white flowers.

D. deltoides (del-*toy*-deez), named for the deltoid (triangular) pattern on the flower petals, is commonly called maiden pink. Native from western Europe and eastern Asia, it too is a herbaceous, mat-forming ground cover, but unlike *D. arenarius* it only reaches 4 to 8 inches tall by 15 inches wide.

Hardy in Zones 3 to 9, it is good for edging and for small-scale, general applications. The leaves are evergreen, needlelike or grasslike, ½ inch long, and colored medium green to bluish green. The flowers, which appear solitarily during late spring or early summer, reach ¾ inch wide, are an attractive lavender, and have a lovely fragrance. Each petal has a dark V-shaped band at its base. Sometimes plants bloom again sparingly in the fall. Horticultural selections include 'Albus', with white flowers; 'Brilliant', with crimson flowers; 'Fanal', with dark green leaves and scarlet flowers; 'Flashing Red', with ruby red flowers; 'Microchip', with red and white flowers; 'Red Maiden', with reddish purple flowers and a height to 6 inches; 'Roseus', with flowers various shades of pink; 'Ruber', with red flowers; 'Samos', with dark green leaves and scarlet flowers; 'Serphyllifolius', lower growing than the species; 'Vampire', with carmine red flowers; 'Zing Rose', with magnificent deep red flowers.

D. gratianopolitanus (gra-tee-*aye*-no-poe-li-taynus), meaning of Grenoble, is commonly called cheddar pink (for Cheddar Gorge in southwestern England). Hardy in Zones 3 to 9 and native to Europe, it reaches 6 to 8 inches tall and displays ½- to ¾-inch-diameter, fragrant, rose-colored or pink flowers that contrast well against a background of fine-textured, gray-green foliage. Blooming begins in spring and lasts until late summer if fading flowers are continually removed before seed formation. The species is hardy in Zones 3 to 9 and performs well in the South. Cultivars include 'Bath's Pink', with soft pink, fringed flowers; 'Double Cheddar', with double pink flowers; var. *grandiflorus,* pink flowers to 1½ inch wide; 'Karlik', with deep pink, fringed, 1-inch-wide, fragrant flowers; 'Petite', with dwarf habit to 4 inches tall, gray-green leaves, and tiny pink flowers; 'Pink Feather', with feathery pink flowers; 'Splendens', with dark red flowers; 'Tiny Rubies', with double, deep pink flowers.

D. plumarius (plew-*may*-ree-us), named for its plumelike (feathered or frilled) petals, is commonly called cottage pink, grass pink, old-fashioned pink, or cottage carnation. This long cultivated species has a mat-forming habit and is hardy in Zones 3 to 9. It ranges from 12 to 18 inches tall and spreads more than 16 inches wide. Best used on a small scale for accent or general cover, it also functions well as an edging around herbaceous border plantings. The leaves are evergreen, grasslike, and gray-green, and range from 1 to 4 inches long. Their finely toothed edges give them a somewhat rough texture. The springtime flowers are solitary and fragrant, reach 1 inch long, and display deeply cut and fringed petals of rose, purple, or white.

HORTICULTURAL SELECTIONS: 'Spring Beauty', not really a cultivar (although usually represented as such), but rather a mixture of clove-scented semidouble and double flowered, usually seed-grown white, pink, and red flowered forms; 'Sonota', a mixture similar to 'Spring Beauty' but bred for earlier bloom and a larger percentage of fully double flowers.

HYBRID SELECTIONS: Because of their numerous fragrant and colorful flowers the pinks have been extensively hybridized and dozens of selections are available. There is considerable disagreement whether these are hybrid cultivars or cultivars of cottage pink. Since most of the species originated in Europe, I follow European authors in listing these as hybrid cultivars. In choosing them it is wise to pay attention to the foliar as well as floral characteristics. For use as ground covers, select plants with compact habit and resistance to fungal rot. Some of the best selections are 'Agatha', 8 inches tall, semidouble, purplish pink flowers with crimson centers; 'C. T. Musgrave', flower petals white with green bases; 'Dad's Favorite', with double, red-fringed, white petals; 'Excelsior', with dark-based, carmine petals; 'Inchmery', pink-flowered with compact habit to 10 inches tall; 'La Bourbille' ('La Bourboule'), foliage silvery-green, flowers clear pink; 'Little Bobby', one of my favorites, with pink and deep purplish red, spice-scented flowers atop 4-inch-tall mats of dusty blue evergreen leaves, often listed as a cultivar of *D. × allwoodii;* 'Painted Beauty', with fragrant deep crimson flowers; 'Mrs. Sinkins', with fragrant double white flowers; 'White Ladies', with strongly fragrant white flowers.

CULTURE / CARE: Carnations adjust to a range of soil types provided the drainage is good. Although some species tolerate acidic soils, they prefer a neutral to alkaline soil. Because they are shallowly rooted and not known for their tolerance to drought, they should be watered during the hot summer months. They prefer full sun to light shade, are susceptible to many insects and diseases, and are not always long lived. Close adherence to furnishing the proper cultural environment is the best means of maximizing their performance. Maintenance requirements are also a bit discouraging. After two or three years, in reaction to crowding, the center of the clump may thin out. At this time, plants must be dug up and divided. Flowers tend to persist after blooming, and many gardeners prefer to cut them back with scissors to neaten their appearance.

PROPAGATION: Division, the easiest method of propagation, is best done in spring. Cuttings taken during early summer root in about two weeks. Seed sown in spring often germinates in 10 days or less.

Dicentra PLATE 102
Bleeding Heart

Among the most popular and useful ground covers for shade gardens, bleeding hearts can be used alone as specimens or in small groups for accent, particularly in highly visible locations where their grace and charm can best be appreciated. Often they are combined with native ferns, such as Christmas fern (*Polystichum acrostichoides*) and lady fern (*Athyrium felix-femina*), and a host of native forbs including trillium, columbine, spring beauty, hepatica, and blood root. No foot traffic is tolerated.

SCIENTIFIC NAME: *Dicentra* (die-*sen*-tra) is derived from the Greek *di*, two, and *kentron*, spur, in reference to the dual spurlike appendages of the petals.

HARDINESS / ORIGIN: See individual species for hardiness; North America and eastern Asia.

LEAVES / FLOWERS / FRUIT: The leaves are typically compound with three leaflets, or deeply dissected and fernlike. They either arise from the base of the plant or, in species with ascending stems, are alternately arranged. The flowers, with flattened heart-shaped corollas, are arranged in racemose clusters and are usually nodding upon succulent flowerstalks. The fruit, a tiny capsule, is nonornamental.

RATE / SPACING: Growth is slow. Plants from pint-sized to quart-sized containers are spaced 12 to 16 inches apart.

SPECIES: *D. eximia* (eks-*im*-ee-a), named from the Latin *eximia*, distinguished, is commonly called fringed bleeding heart, turkey corn, staggerweed, or wild bleeding heart. It is a rhizomatous, medium-sized, herbaceous, 12- to 18-inch-tall ground cover. One of my favorites for woodland gardening, it is nearly unparalleled in grace and is one of the most lovely flowered, softly textured ground covers available in North America. It is hardy in Zones 3 to 9 and hails from the eastern United States from New York to Georgia. The leaves are deciduous, twice divided with the segments broadly oblong to oval, soft-textured, and colored a very soothing shade of medium gray-blue. The nodding flowers are elevated on floral stems that are frequently as tall as the foliage. Heart-shaped and pink to purplish, they bloom from mid spring to early fall but are most effective from early to mid summer. It is common to read about cultivars of *D. eximia,* but the same cultivars are often described elsewhere as selections of *D. formosa.* In reality, no one is certain as to which species they truly belong, and, of course, the situation is made more complicated by the hybridization of the two species. For the sake of simplicity, and because *Index Hortensis,* the nomenclatural guide that

I have relied upon extensively, lists them as *D. formosa* selections, I have done likewise.

D. formosa (fore-*moe*-sa), commonly called Pacific bleeding heart or western bleeding heart, is hardy in Zones 2 or 3 to 9. It is native to western North America from British Columbia to California and reaches 12 inches tall by 10 to 18 inches wide. Its leaves are deciduous, long-stemmed, oblong, and colored blue-green to greenish. Its flowers, which are borne from mid spring to early fall, are colored rose-purple to white and reach up to ⅝ inch long. Cultivars, which might as easily belong to *D. eximia,* are 'Adrian Bloom', with crimson-red flowers and blue-green foliage; 'Alba', with white flowers and light green foliage; 'Bacchanal', with carmine-pink flowers; 'Bountiful', with dark pink flowers heavily produced in mid spring and fall, blooming sparsely in between; 'Langtrees' ('Pearl Drops'), with blue-green leaves and numerous white flowers; 'Luxuriant', with red blossoms and blue-green foliage, said to be a hybrid between *D. formosa* and *D. eximia;* 'Margery Fish', with powder blue foliage, white flowers, and vigorous habit; 'Silver Smith', with white flowers that are suffused with pink; 'Snowdrift', with pure white flowers in spring, blooming again (but to a lesser extent) in fall, reaching 15 inches tall, grayish green foliage; 'Stuart Boothman', with dwarf habit, reaching only 10 inches tall by 24 inches wide, exceptional silvery-blue leaves, deep pink flowers; 'Sweetheart', with white flowers; 'Zestful', with pink flowers.

CULTURE / CARE: Bleeding hearts are adaptable to various soil textures, with their main requirement being good drainage. They are best in humus-rich moderately acidic soils. Since their drought tolerance is mediocre, the soil should be kept moist with supplemental water during the summer. Bleeding hearts prefer light to moderate shade. Although pest problems are unlikely, diseases such as stem rot, wilt, downy mildew, and rust may at times arise. No special maintenance is required.

PROPAGATION: Division during spring or fall is the main method of propagation. Cuttings can be rooted during early or mid summer. Seed sown in fall germinates the following spring.

Dichondra micrantha   PLATE 103
Small Lawn Leaf

An unusual leafy herb, dichondra is a dense, mat-forming creeper that epitomizes toughness and durability, accepting more foot traffic, probably, than any other nonturf ground cover. It ranges from 3 to 6 inches tall (shortest in the sun and tallest in the shade), spreads indefinitely, and is most apt to be en-countered in large, carpetlike plantings or as a substitute for turf grass. It is also useful as a filler between stepping stones and combines with almost any shrub or tree that would be found in a typical lawn setting. Considerable foot traffic is tolerated, but it should not be walked on it if becomes frozen. Dichondra utilizes a special type of carbon dioxide fixation known as the C4 carbon dioxide fixation cycle (Hatch-Slack cycle) of photosynthesis, which allows plants to grow in high temperatures with low carbon dioxide levels.

SCIENTIFIC NAME: *Dichondra micrantha* (die-*kon*-dra my-*kran*-tha). *Dichondra* comes from the Greek *di,* two, and *chondros,* grain, a reference to the two-lobed nature of its fruits, in this case, grains. *Micrantha* is Latin for small-flowered.

HARDINESS / ORIGIN: Zone 10 or 11; West Indies, China, Japan, Mexico, and Texas.

LEAVES / FLOWERS / FRUIT: The evergreen, kidney-shaped to almost round, dark green leaves are elevated upon rather weak stems. They normally reach ½ inch wide by ½ inch long. The very tiny, greenish yellow, ⅛-inch-wide flowers of spring are borne solitarily and are elevated upon long, upright, eventually arching stems. The fruit is nonornamental.

RATE / SPACING: Growth is moderate. Plants, typically available as small plugs, are spaced 8 to 12 inches apart.

CULTURE / CARE: Dichondra adapts to almost any soil condition, but if the soil is on the organically rich side, its performance will be even better. Because plants are relatively sensitive to drought, you might want to install an underground sprinkling system before planting large areas. Watering in the early morning permits the foliage to dry rapidly and reduces the risk of disease. Dichondra prefers full sun to moderate shade. Pests include dichondra flea beetle, cutworms, moths, weevils, mites, slugs, snails, and nematodes. Diseases of greatest incidence are root and crown rots, both caused by fungi when moisture is excessive. Maintenance varies with the location. If grown in the shade dichondra may reach 6 inches tall and need frequent mowing to obtain a low turf-like effect. In the sun it stays much lower and requires little or no mowing. Reel-type rather than rotary mowers give the best results. Dichondra requires considerable effort to keep it weed-free and needs to be fertilized more than most ground covers. Frequent light applications of fertilizer are better than infrequent heavy ones. Should dichondra ever dry up to the point that it turns brown, it normally recovers with regular watering.

PROPAGATION: Division and seeding are the standard methods of propagation. Division simply consists of digging up clumps and transplanting them. The best times are spring, late fall, and winter. To prepare the planting area, first roughly grade it, then remove weeds and install an irrigation system (if the area is too large to water by hand), then finish grading. Seed should be sown from late summer to early fall. Once germinated, the seedlings should be watered frequently during hot or dry weather. For the purposes of establishing a lawn or large ground-cover bed from seed, the normal sowing rate is 2 pounds of seed per 1000 square feet of soil area.

Diervilla lonicera   PLATE 104

Bush Honeysuckle, Blue Herb, Life of Man, Gravel Weed, Dwarf Bush Honeysuckle

The common name gravel weed speaks well of this plant's ability to withstand porous soils, such as found along the lakeshores of its native habitat. Sprawling, woody, and rhizomatous, this durable 2- to 4-foot-tall, indefinite-spreading ground cover is reliable and attractive on flat and sloping ground, and serves well to reduce soil erosion. It is used far too little. An attractive native, it resembles the prized Asian species *Leucothoe axillaris* to a certain extent. It is easy to cultivate, attractive, and quite functional. Its light to medium green, often burgundy tinged leaves contrast well against deep-green-leaved shrubs like yew (*Taxus*) and rhododendron, and the magnificent gray bark of magnolia and serviceberry (*Amelanchier*). For large-scale planting, its tenacious spreading habit binds gravelly and sandy slopes, but if planted in smaller areas, it should be surrounded with a deep edging to stave off the advance of its creeping rhizomes.

SCIENTIFIC NAME: *Diervilla lonicera* (die-er-*vil*-a lo-*nis*-er-a). *Diervilla* is named in honor of N. Dierville, a French physician and traveler who brought a plant of this genus back from Canada as a gift to the botanist Tournefort in 1699. *Lonicera,* commonly known as honeysuckle, is used as the specific epithet to show this species' resemblance to that genus.

HARDINESS / ORIGIN: Zones 3 to 7 or 8; midwestern and northeastern North America.

LEAVES / FLOWERS / FRUIT: The deciduous, opposite, simple, oval to elliptic, 2- to 4½-inch-long, short-stemmed, irregularly toothed leaves emerge light green then become medium green suffused with burgundy. The five-parted, ¾-inch-long flowers are borne in early summer, open pale yellow then darken to dark-yellow, scarlet, or maroon, and are effective during early to mid summer. The fruit, a slender, shiny, ½-inch-long capsule, is nonornamental.

RATE / SPACING: Growth is moderate to fast. Plants from 1- to 2-gallon-sized containers are spaced 2½ to 3 feet apart.

HORTICULTURAL SELECTIONS: 'Copper', with cop-

pery-colored new foliage arising on and off throughout the growing season; var. *hypomalaca,* leaves hairy on the bottom side.

OTHER SPECIES: **D. × *splendens*** (*splen*-denz), a cross between *D. lonicera* and the taller *D. sessilifolia,* is hardy in Zones 3 or 4 to 9. It displays burgundy new growth, bronzy green summer color, yellow summerborne flowers, spreading habit, height of 3 to 4 feet tall, and burgundy fall color.

CULTURE / CARE: Bush honeysuckle prefers sandy or gravelly well-drained neutral or acidic soil. It is very tolerant of drought; however, an occasional deep watering is beneficial during the heat of summer. It prefers full sun to moderate shade. No serious diseases have been reported, but aphids can be pesky at times. Bush honeysuckle can grow for many years without maintenance, but some people prefer to shear or mow it to promote compact growth.

PROPAGATION: Softwood cuttings root quickly and in high percentages; treatment with 3000 ppm IBA/talc is beneficial but not essential. Division is also easily accomplished and is best performed during early spring. Rhizomes can be sectioned during fall or winter, covered with ½ inch of soil, then kept moist; in time new shoots and roots will form.

Disporum sessile   PLATE 105

Japanese Fairy Bells

A herbaceous, rhizomatous, gracefully arching ground cover, Japanese fairy bells reaches 14 to 24 inches tall and spreads indefinitely by creeping rhizomes. Typically it is used for accent or general cover, and in the case of the variegated selection, which is more popular than the species, for contrast against dark-green-leaved species such as *Taxus* and *Rhododendron.* Walkway and border edging are also good uses, provided there is some type of barrier to contain its spread.

SCIENTIFIC NAME: *Disporum sessile* (die-*spore*-um / dis-*pore*-um *ses*-il / *ses*-i-lee). *Disporum* comes from the Greek *di,* two, and *spora,* a seed, referring to this characteristic of members of the genus, namely, that each chamber of the ovary houses two seeds. *Sessile,* without a stem, refers to the leaves, which originate from the rootstalk.

HARDINESS / ORIGIN: Zone 5; China and Japan.

LEAVES / FLOWERS / FRUIT: The deciduous, simple, oblong to oblong-lance-shaped, 4-inch-long, 1-inch-wide stemless leaves are held upon arching herbaceous stems and are colored deep green. The flowers are borne solitarily, paired, or sometimes grouped in threes. They are nodding, six-parted, bell-shaped, creamy white, and effective in spring. The fruit that follows, a berry, is nonornamental.

RATE / SPACING: Growth is slow to moderate. Plants from pint-sized to quart-sized containers are spaced 12 to 16 inches apart.

HORTICULTURAL SELECTIONS: 'Variegata', attractively edged and longitudinally striped with creamy white.

CULTURE / CARE: Best in organically rich, well-drained, moderately acidic loam, Japanese fairy bells tolerates a fair amount of drought, and interestingly, performs at its best when the soil is somewhat on the dry side. The site should be relatively cool and should offer light to moderate shade. No serious diseases or pests have been reported. No maintenance is needed.

PROPAGATION: Cuttings taken from the tips of the rhizomes form shoots and roots if covered by ½ inch of soil and kept moist and warm. Simple division of crowns is equally effective and is usually performed in spring or fall. Seed, the least common method of propagation, should be collected when ripe, stored cool and dry, then sown the following spring.

Drosanthemum floribundum   PLATE 106

Rosy Ice Plant, Rosea Ice Plant

This 6-inch-tall, succulent, matlike, trailing ground cover spreads indefinitely and functions as a general cover for use around shrubs and the foundations of homes and commercial buildings. It helps to control erosion on rocky slopes, and the floral show that it puts on during spring and summer is absolutely breath-taking. No foot traffic is tolerated. Other species of ice plant are discussed under *Cephalophyllum, Delosperma,* and *Lampranthus.*

SCIENTIFIC NAME: *Drosanthemum floribundum* (dro-*zan*-the-mum flor-i-*bun*-dum). *Drosanthemum* refers to the flowers being like those of *Drosera,* a genus of wetland herbs commonly called sundews. *Floribundum* means with abundant flowers.

HARDINESS / ORIGIN: Zones 9 to 10; South Africa.

LEAVES / FLOWERS / FRUIT: The three-angled, ½-inch-long, ⅛-inch-wide, succulent, evergreen leaves are covered with tiny, pimplelike protrusions, which reflect light and help the grayish, water-filled leaves earn for the plant the common name ice plant. The marvelous pale pink flowers of spring and summer are attractive to bees and reach ¾ inch across. The fruit which follows is nonornamental.

RATE / SPACING: Growth is fast. Plants from pint-sized to quart-sized containers are spaced 12 to 18 inches apart.

OTHER SPECIES: *D. hispidum* (*his*-pi-dum), hairy ice plant, another succulent, clump-forming ground cover, reaches 18 to 24 inches tall and spreads to 3 feet across. Hailing from South Africa, it is hardy only in Zones 9 to 10 and is characterized by evergreen, 1-inch-long, ⅛-inch-thick, nearly cylindrical, slightly flattened, light green or reddish, succulent foliage. Its deep purple flowers are borne alone, in pairs, or sometimes in threes. They reach 1¼ inches wide and make their colorful appearance during late spring.

LESS COMMON SPECIES: *D. bellum* (*bell*-um) is a South African species with white or pink flowers.

D. bicolor (*bye*-kul-er), a shrubby species that reaches 1 foot tall, is graced with bright yellow flowers that have orange tips.

D. speciosum (spee-see-*oh*-sum), a highly branched, South African shrubby succulent ground cover, has bright orange or cornelian-red flowers with green centers.

CULTURE / CARE: Rosy ice plant and its related species adapt to a wide range of well-drained soils. They withstand considerable drought once established, but occasional watering during the dry summer months keeps them at their best. Pests include scales, mealybugs, and aphids. Seldom are serious diseases encountered. Little or no maintenance is required.

PROPAGATION: Cuttings root easily throughout the year. Division can be performed anytime, although it is best during fall, winter, and early spring. Seed germinates quickly and in high percentages.

Dryas octopetala   PLATE 107

Mountain Avens, Mt. Washington Dryad, Wild Betony

Mountain avens is a semiwoody, prostrate-growing, mat-forming ground cover that ranges from 3 to 6 inches tall and spreads more than 2 feet across. In the landscape it functions well as a small-scale to moderate-scale general cover. In the rock garden it is fine for use as a specimen or accent plant and for occasional use as a border edging or living fountain when allowed to spill over the top of a retaining wall. Infrequent foot traffic is tolerated.

SCIENTIFIC NAME: *Dryas octopetala* (*dry*-as ok-toe-pe-*tay*-la). *Dryas* is probably from the Greek *drus,* oak, and implies that the leaves of this genus resemble those of an oak tree. Alternatively, it has been proposed that the genus name derives from *druas,* wood nymph, or from Dryades, daughters of Zeus, originally nymphs of the oak. *Octopetala,* with eight petals, refers to the flowers.

HARDINESS / ORIGIN: Zones 2 to 4; northern Asia, northern Europe, and northern North America.

LEAVES / FLOWERS / FRUIT: The leaves are evergreen, simple, alternate, oval, elliptic, or oblong, ½ to 1 inch long, and ¼ to ½ inch wide. They have a coarsely toothed margin, and the leathery blades are shiny, smooth, medium green above, and white and hairy (tomentose) below. The solitary flowers are borne upon 1- to 5-inch-long, erect, slender dark-hair-covered scapes. Each flower is 1 inch wide, effective late spring to mid summer, and has white petals. The fruit which follows is silvery and feathery.

RATE / SPACING: Growth is moderate to fast. Plants from 3- to 4-inch-diameter containers are spaced 8 to 12 inches apart.

HORTICULTURAL SELECTIONS: Var. *alaskensis,* with foliage widest toward the apex, margins deeply toothed, and lacking tomentum (downy hairs) below; var. *angustifolia,* with leaves that are narrower than the typical species; var. *argentea,* leaves shallowly toothed, broadest in the middle, nontomentose below; 'Minor', a dwarf reaching 2 inches tall by 9 inches wide; subsp. *octopetala,* foliage with thin scales, and white, tomentose, lower midvein.

CULTURE / CARE: For best results, mountain avens requires well-drained, sandy, slightly acidic soil. Although it is fairly drought tolerant, an occasional thorough watering keeps it at its best. It prefers full sun to light shade. The only disease of any significance is damping off, which sometimes is a problem with seedlings. Similarly, pest problems are minimal and typically limited to slugs. If any maintenance is practiced it usually consists of an occasional mowing to rejuvenate plantings.

PROPAGATION: Cuttings root rather easily when treated with 1000 ppm IBA/talc during the growing season. Division is also effective and can be performed anytime it is convenient. Commercial supplies of seed are readily available. Seed sown in a porous medium and kept at a temperature of 60 to 70°F germinates in 50 days.

Dryopteris
PLATE 108

Wood Fern

This group of sturdy, semievergreen to evergreen ferns ranges from 1 to 2½ feet tall and displays much greater durability than that expected of ferns. They work best on a moderate scale as general covers and accent plants, particularly in wooded settings that feature native plants. As would be expected, they combine well with native wildflowers such as trillium, columbine, dutchman's breeches, bellflower, and all species of Solomon's seal. No foot traffic is tolerated.

SCIENTIFIC NAME: *Dryopteris* (dry-*op*-ter-is) is probably derived from the Greek *drys,* tree, and *pteris,* fern.

HARDINESS / ORIGIN: Zones 3 to 9; see individual species for origin.

LEAVES / FLOWERS / FRUIT: The leaves are typically evergreen, stout-stalked, and leathery, and originate in vaselike fashion from a central crown. Each leaf is typically composed of oppositely arranged, deeply cut leaflets, giving a typically fernlike appearance. Of course, ferns have no flowers or fruit, but rather sori which contain spores. In the case of *Dryopteris,* the sori are horseshoe-shaped and often formed along the edges of the leaflets.

RATE / SPACING: Growth is slow. Plants from quart-sized to gallon-sized containers are spaced 1½ to 2 feet apart.

SPECIES: *D. cycadina* (sik-a-*deen*-a), also known as *D. atrata,* is commonly called shaggy wood fern or black wood fern (for the black scales that cover the leaf stalk). A rather extraordinary species, it ranges from 1½ to 3 feet tall, with stiff, leathery, erectly oriented, semievergreen leaves composed of narrowly lance-shaped shallowly lobed leaflets. It is hardy in Zones 5 to 8 and is native to Japan, Taiwan, China, and northern India.

D. erythrosora (e-rith-row-*so*-ra), named from the Greek *erythros,* red, and *sora,* sori, for its red sori, is commonly called autumn fern. This colorful Asian (Japan, China, and Taiwan) species is hardy in Zones 5 to 8. It reaches 1½ to 2 feet tall, with arching evergreen fronds that are tinged burgundy and bronze in youth and mature to deep glossy green by early summer. 'Prolifica' displays narrower leaflets and sometimes produces tiny plantlets along the upper surface of the rachis (leaf stalk).

D. filix-mas (*fee*-liks-mahs), literally meaning male fern, in reference to its robust nature, is commonly called sweet brake, shield fern, knotty brake, or bear's paw. A clump former, this native of England ranges from 2 to 4 feet tall and spreads to 2½ feet wide. It is composed of large, semievergreen, compound, toothed, leathery, yellow-green foliage. According to one myth, anyone who wore the ashes (derived from burning male fern) in a ringlike pattern around the finger would be able to understand the speech and songs of birds. The rhizome has been sometimes used to rid the body of tapeworms; reportedly it contains a chemical that paralyzes tapeworms, causing them to lose their grip on the intestinal wall so that they may be removed by purgatives such as salt water. The treatment, which was said to be most effective when preceded by a fat-free diet for three days, was also dangerous as it paralyzed the voluntary muscles of the patient. Cultivars include 'Barnesii', 3 to 4 feet tall, with unique ruffled leaves; 'Crispa Cristata', with dwarf habit, 12 to 15 inches tall, ruffled dark green leaflets; 'Cristata', with frilled leaflet tips; 'Grandiceps', a robust grower with narrow, finely crested leaflets; 'Linearis', with very thin leaflets, to 2½ feet tall; 'Linearis Cristata', with crested leaflets; 'Linearis Polydactyla', with thin leaflets that are frilled on their ends, 3 to 4 feet tall; 'Polydactyla Dadds', with finely crested and robust habit, maturing to 3 feet tall; 'Undulata Robusta', more robust habit, with wavy leaflet edges.

D. intermedia (in-ter-*mee*-dee-a), probably named for some characteristic of the plant, such as height, which is intermediate between two other species, is commonly called intermediate shield fern. It hails from eastern North America, reaches 1½ feet tall, and slowly spreads by creeping rootstock to form clumps 2 or more feet in diameter. Its large compound leaves are semievergreen, arise from a central crown, are rather coarsely toothed, and are colored medium to dark green. 'Prolifica' has narrower leaflets than the species and occasionally bears plantlets at the bases of the leaflets.

D. marginalis (mar-jin-*aye*-lis), named for the location of its spore-bearing sori which are located along the edges of the leaf margins, is commonly called leatherleaf wood fern or marginal shield fern. Native to the eastern United States, it reaches 15 to 18 inches tall and spreads 2½ feet across. Its compound leaves reach up to 2½ feet long and are composed of numerous pairs of staggered leaflets. Each leaflet is blunt-tipped, leathery, coarse-textured, and colored deep bluish green.

D. wallichiana (wal-*lik*-ee-*aye*-na), Wallich's wood fern, is a magnificent 2- to 4-foot-tall erectly oriented semievergreen species from Mexico, South America, the West Indies, Africa, Asia, and Hawaii. It is hardy in Zones 5 to 8. Its fiddleheads, which emerge during spring, are rather interesting for their dense covering of reddish black scales. As they mature, they become large, lustrous, deep green above, lighter below, and are composed of round lobed oblong to lance-shaped leaflets.

CULTURE / CARE: Like most ferns these species are at their best in rich, acidic, loamy, moisture-retentive soils; however, they grow nicely in sandy and infertile soils and survive considerable heat and drought. They prefer light to deep shade, have few disease or pest problems, and require little or no maintenance.

PROPAGATION: Division is best performed during fall or spring. Spores can also be used (see Chapter 8).

Duchesnea indica   PLATE 109
Mock Strawberry, Indian Strawberry

This low, herbaceous, mat-forming ground cover spreads in the typical strawberry fashion, that is, by stolons—above-ground horizontal stems that produce new plantlets at their tips. Mock strawberry typically reaches 2 inches tall and travels indefinitely. In the landscape it is of greatest value as a turf substitute for smaller areas, and it makes a good com-

panion to various small trees and shrubs. It is quite valuable as a soil stabilizer on steeply sloping banks. Limited foot traffic is tolerated.

SCIENTIFIC NAME: *Duchesnea indica* (due-*kes*-nee-a / due-*shez*-nee-a *in*-di-ka). *Duchesnea* is named after Antoine Nicolas Duchesne (1747–1827), a French horticulturist who was an authority on true strawberries (*Fragaria*). *Indica* means of India.

HARDINESS / ORIGIN: Zones 4 to 8; southern Asia.

LEAVES / FLOWERS / FRUIT: The leaves are evergreen, compound, and composed of three leaflets. The leaflets are oval, 1 inch long by ½ inch wide, coarsely toothed around their edges, somewhat hairy, and colored medium green with reddish bases. The flowers are solitary, ½ to 1 inch long, five-petaled, yellow, and borne intermittently throughout the growing season. Birds like the edible, bland-to-bitter-tasting fruit which follows. It is typically strawberry-like in shape, colored red, and ½ inch in diameter.

RATE / SPACING: Growth is fast. Plants from pint-sized to quart-sized containers are spaced 14 to 18 inches apart.

HORTICULTURAL SELECTIONS: 'Variegata', with white-edged leaves.

CULTURE / CARE: Mock strawberry is adaptable to various soil types and exhibits acceptable growth in nearly all well-drained soils. It is very tolerant of drought; however, during extended dry periods it is wise to water regularly and thoroughly to keep the soil moist and the plants from wilting. Mock strawberry prefers light shade but tolerates full sun provided the soil is kept adequately moist. Pests such as aphids and mites may at times be troublesome, and the most commonly encountered disease is rust. Maintenance includes mowing foliage in early spring to stimulate new growth and neaten appearance.

PROPAGATION: Division is best conducted during early spring or fall.

Echeveria   PLATE 110
Hen and Chickens

Echeveria is closely related to the genus *Sempervivum,* which also goes by the common name hen and chickens, a name that describes the habit of forming new rosettes (chicks) around a central rosette (hen). *Echeveria* is a genus of cold-tender, succulent-leaved, rosette-forming, colorful ground covers from Texas, Mexico, and Argentina. Typically these species are used in rock gardens as accent or specimen plants and in some cases perform remarkably well as small-scale to moderate-scale general covers.

SCIENTIFIC NAME: *Echeveria* (esh-e-*vee*-ree-a / ek-e-*vee*-ree-a) commemorates Athanasia Echeverriay

Godoy, an eighteenth-century botanical artist who illustrated plants during an expedition to Mexico from 1787 to 1797.

HARDINESS / ORIGIN: Zones 9 to 11; warm parts of the Americas, especially Mexico.

LEAVES / FLOWERS / FRUIT: See individual species.

RATE / SPACING: Growth is moderate. Plants from 3- to 4-inch-diameter containers are spaced 6 to 10 inches apart.

SPECIES: *E. agavoides* (ag-a-*voy*-deez), meaning like *Agave,* is commonly called molded wax and reaches 6 inches tall by 8 inches wide. Its green leaves, often red-tipped, are 1½ to 5 inches long, spiny pointed, and set a nice backdrop to the reddish, yellow-tipped flowers from spring to early summer.

E. amoena (am-*oh*-ee-na), baby echeveria, hails from Mexico. It reaches 3 to 6 inches tall, displays 1-inch-long, blue-green, oblong to spatula-shaped leaves and coral-red flowers during late spring.

E. derenbergii (dir-en-*ber*-gee-eye), named after J. Derenberg (1873–1928), is commonly called painted lady or baby echeveria. It is native to southern Mexico, reaches 3 inches tall, and displays blue-green, often red-tipped, 1- to 1¾-inch-long, 1¼-inch-wide leaves. Its yellow and cornelian-red flowers are borne during late winter and spring.

E. elegans (*el*-e-ganz), named for its elegant appearance, is commonly called Mexican gem, Mexican snowball, elegant stonecrop, or white Mexican rose. A native to Mexico, it reaches 3 inches tall and displays extraordinarily colorful, 1½- to 2½-inch-long, 1-inch-wide, bluish green, translucent-margined leaves. Its flowers, borne from late winter to early summer, are rose-red with yellow tips.

E. gibbiflora (gib-bi-*floe*-ra), named from the Latin *gibber,* hump-backed, in reference to its flowers that are swollen on one side, is commonly called fringed echeveria. It reaches 2 feet tall when in flower and is characterized by large rosettes of 12 to 25, oval to spatula-shaped, gray-green to purplish leaves that are 6 to 14 inches long by 4 to 10 inches wide. Its flowers are arranged in groups of 5 to 15 and are attractively colored red. Horticultural selections of note are 'Corniculata', with leaves that have warty outgrowths on upper surfaces; 'Crispa', with wavy leaf margins; 'Metallica', with purplish lilac leaves that may become brownish bronzy green with age; 'Pallida', with pale green leaves.

E. gilva (*gil*-va / *hil*-va), green Mexican rose, is the result of crossing *E. agavoides* and *E. elegans.* The species is characterized by oblong to oval, 3-inch-long, yellowish green to gray-green or blue-green leaves that are topped by 10-inch-tall stems of pink, yellow-tipped flowers during spring.

E. secunda (se-*kun*-da) reaches 6 inches tall and

displays 1- to 3-inch long, ½- to 1½-inch-wide, ³⁄₁₆-inch-thick, blue-green, often red-edged leaves. Its red, yellow-tipped flowers are borne atop 4- to 12-inch-tall stems during spring and early summer.

CULTURE / CARE: *Echeveria* species are best when grown in full sun to light shade in light-textured soils with excellent drainage. They require little water, and their maintenance requirements are few to none.

PROPAGATION: Division is best performed in fall and winter.

Empetrum nigrum   PLATE 111

Black Crowberry, Curlewberry, Heathberry, Crakeberry, Monox, Wire Ling, Crow Pea, Monox Heather, Blackberried Heath, Corbigeau

A many-branched, diffuse-spreading, subshrubby ground cover, black crowberry reaches 6 to 12 inches tall and spreads to form mats of several feet across. It has a heathlike appearance and tough, needlelike leaves. It is fussy about culture and clearly not for every landscape. When its conditions can be met, however, it forms a rather loose mat that combines well with species of cranberry, blueberry, and huckleberry (*Vaccinium* and *Gaylussacia*). It is not for the formal gardener either, but for those who appreciate the beauty and casualness of naturalized plantings. Infrequent foot traffic is tolerated.

The fruit is a source of food for many arctic birds. Eskimos also eat the fruit with that of *Vaccinium uliginosum* (bog bilberry). Others have found it acceptable for making pies and jams.

SCIENTIFIC NAME: *Empetrum nigrum* (em-*pe*-trum *nie*-grum). *Empetrum* is derived from the Greek *en,* upon, and *petros,* rock, and refers to the rocky habitat that species of this genus often exploit. *Nigrum,* black, refers to the color of the fruit.

HARDINESS / ORIGIN: Zone 3; rocky places from Greenland to Alaska, south to Maine, mountains of New England and northern New York, as well as Michigan and California. Also Asia and Europe.

LEAVES / FLOWERS / FRUIT: The evergreen, simple, whorled, crowded, oblong to oblong-linear, ⅜-inch-long, ⅛-inch-wide leaves are thick, leathery, rough to the touch, and colored dark green. The tiny, three-parted, purplish flowers of late spring are typically unisexual and solitary in the axils of the uppermost leaves. Later, they give rise to ¼-inch-wide, black, globose drupes, which are effective mid summer through fall.

RATE / SPACING: Growth is slow. Plants from quart-sized to gallon-sized containers are spaced 6 to 24 inches apart.

HORTICULTURAL SELECTIONS: Forma *leucocarpum,* with white fruit; var. *hermaphroditum,* meaning bisexual and descriptive of the flowers, sometimes called *E. eamesii* subsp. *hermaphroditum,* reaching 3 to 4 inches tall by 12 inches wide, with shorter and broader leaves and a denser habit, native from northern North America and northern Eurasia; var. *purpureum,* with purple fruit.

CULTURE / CARE: Black crowberry is best in sandy loam with a moderate amount of organic matter (for moisture and nutrient retention), and the pH should be from 7.0 to more acidic. Its drought tolerance is limited, and its best appearance comes when the soil is kept slightly moist at all times. It prefers light to moderate shade. The primary disease problem is rust, and pests seldom are a problem. Little or no maintenance is required.

PROPAGATION: Softwood and semihardened cuttings root under mist or in a plastic moisture-retentive tent. Double dormancy has been reported with the seed, thus it must first be treated with five months of stratification at warm temperatures, then three months at 40°F before germination can occur.

Ephedra distachya   PLATE 112
Joint Fir, Mexican Tea, Mormon Tea Bush

Unusual in most respects, *Ephedra* is composed of about 40 species of sprawling or upright green-stemmed semiwoody shrubs that resemble horsetails. *Ephedra distachya* is a sprawling, mounded to procumbent, rhizomatous, herbaceous-stemmed ground cover. It ranges from 1 to 2½ feet tall and spreads more than 8 feet across. In the landscape, with its sprawling, thin, jointed stems, it looks like a shaggy green head of hair. It is unique and lends itself well to specimen planting in rock gardens, elevated beds, and terrace-top locations. Presumably it would combine well with dwarf conifers and possibly brooms, heaths, and heathers of varying habit and color. On sandy sloping ground, its rhizomatous nature makes it a good choice for erosion control. No foot traffic is tolerated.

Asiatic species of *Ephedra* are a source of the drug ephedrine. Similar to adrenaline in its physiological effects, this potent alkaloid is used to treat asthma, sinusitis, colds, arthritis, gastritis, and hay fever. Commonly, it is an ingredient in nose sprays. A medicinal tea is made from the stems of various species by Mexicans and Native Americans. Russians and Chinese have been known to consume the fruit of *E. distachya* and to add the dried stems to tobacco.

SCIENTIFIC NAME: *Ephedra distachya* (e-*fee*-dra die-stay-*kee*-a). *Ephedra* literally means sitting on a chair or seat, yet the significance of this name in reference to this plant is unclear. Pliny the Elder, the famous Greek naturalist and writer (A.D. 23–79), applied this name to horsetails (*Equisetum*). *Distachya,* in two ranks or rows, possibly refers to the floral spikes at the stem joints.

HARDINESS / ORIGIN: Zones 5 to 9; southern Europe and northern Asia.

LEAVES / FLOWERS / FRUIT: The pithy, rushlike stems are gray-barked and woody at the base, yet their new growth is light green. These stems are the primary structures in which photosynthesis occurs. They are jointed every ½ to 2 inches, resemble horsetails, and support the sheathlike, ½-inch-long, paired leaves that reside at the stem joints. Each leaf ranges from ⅛ to ¼ inch long, is colored brownish yellow, and is divided into two triangular lobes. The tiny conelike yellow flowers are either male or female on any given plant. They are borne paired or solitarily, and although curious, contribute little ornamentally. They arise during early summer and are more numerous if the weather has been very hot. The fruit, borne only on the female plants, is a ¼-inch-long, red, berrylike, fleshy, globose structure that ripens in mid to late summer. Male plants are needed for pollination if fruit is to be formed.

RATE / SPACING: Growth is moderate. Plants from 1- to 2-gallon-sized containers are spaced 2½ to 3½ feet apart.

HORTICULTURAL SELECTIONS: Var. *helvetica,* with erect deep green stems; var. *monostachya,* low growing, with solitary female flowers.

OTHER SPECIES: *E. nevadensis* (ne-va-*den*-sis), commonly called Nevada tea, Mormon tea, Brigham tea, joint fir, Mexican tea, popotillo, and squaw tea, is a straggly rather loose branched shrub native to the southwestern United States and Mexico. Hardy in Zones 6 to 10 and ranging from 2 to 4 feet tall, it bears tiny yellow springborne flowers upon thin green twiggy branches, their joints covered only by tiny scalelike leaves borne in whorls of three. In time the flowers give rise to round, brown to black fruit. This plant is more interesting for the lore that surrounds it than for its landscape usefulness. Early Mormon settlers roasted and powdered the twigs and made a hot, coffeelike beverage of this plant. Native Americans used it in preparations to treat colds, headache, fever, syphilis, and various internal ailments. Dried and powdered twigs were also used to treat sores and burns, and a preparation of the scalelike leaves was applied to cuts to stop bleeding. Additionally, it was employed as a diuretic. Today, twigs of Mormon tea are often found in health food stores, but researchers have not been able to scientifically validate the effectiveness of any such uses.

E. minima (*min*-i-ma), dwarf joint fir, hails from China, reaches 2 inches tall, bears showy fruit, and is hardy in Zones 5 to 8.

E. minuta (mye-*new*-ta), also from China (mountainous regions), reaches 6 inches tall, is hardy in Zones 6 to 9, and displays the interesting habit of bearing purple flowers at the ends of its thin spaghetti-like branches.

E. monosperma (mon-oh-*sper*-ma) hails from very high elevations of Asia, reaches 2 inches tall, and bears bright red berries upon its tiny thin green stems.

E. regeliana (re-*gel*-ee-aye-na), also of Asian alpine origin, is a lovely 3- to 6-inch-tall, red-berried creeper hardy in Zones 6 to 9.

CULTURE / CARE: Joint fir is best in sandy or gravelly, well-drained, slightly acidic to neutral soil. It has excellent drought tolerance; however, an occasional deep watering in the heat of summer is beneficial if extended rain-free periods occur. It prefers full sun. No serious diseases or pests have been reported. Maintenance consists of trimming back shoots and digging up shoot-forming rhizomes that outgrow their bounds.

PROPAGATION: Divisions of the new shoots as they arise from rhizomes are best transplanted in spring or early summer. Layering is effective as well, but division is so easy, layering is seldom practiced. Seed propagation is said to be reliable.

Epigaea repens   PLATE 113

Trailing Arbutus, Mayflower, Trailing Mountain Laurel

Low, sprawling, and reaching 2 to 4 inches tall, trailing arbutus is an indefinite-spreading woodland ground cover. It is intriguingly beautiful, exquisitely fragrant in bloom, and would be out of place anywhere but in a naturalized garden or woodland border. In such places it should be planted about freely, and though it lacks the aggressiveness to blanket large patches of ground, it combines beautifully with woodland wildflowers and ferns, lending accent and setting a lovely backdrop to their varying colors and textures. Unfortunately, native populations of this once common plant have become depleted (due to over collection and destruction of habitat). Occasional foot traffic is tolerated.

Trailing arbutus was used as a diuretic by early settlers, and as an astringent by Native Americans. The common name trailing arbutus came as a result of its floral resemblance to the genus *Arbutus* (composed of evergreen trees and shrubs). The word *arbutus* is derived from the Celtic *arboise,* rough fruit.

Native to Japan and eastern North America, the two species that compose *Epigaea*, commonly referred to as ground laurel, are evergreen creeping woodland subshrubs.

SCIENTIFIC NAME: *Epigaea repens* (ep-e-*gee*-a *ree*-penz). *Epigaea* is derived from the Greek *epi,* upon, and *gaea,* earth, in reference to the prostrate habit (i.e., growing on the earth). *Repens,* creeping, also refers to the habit of growth.

HARDINESS / ORIGIN: Zones 2 to 8; woodlands and woodland edges of eastern North America from Newfoundland and Saskatchewan to Florida and west as far as Iowa.

LEAVES / FLOWERS / FRUIT: The evergreen, simple, alternate, oblong-oval leaves reach 3 inches long by 1½ inches wide. Each leaf is rounded at its end, attached to the horizontal stem by a slender stalk, and colored anywhere from bright green to grayish green to bronzy green, with soft hairs on both sides. The five-parted, white to pink flowers are borne in early spring, have a strong and pleasingly spicy fragrance, and are arranged in clusters at the tips of the stems. The fruit, a many-seeded ¼-inch-wide fleshy capsule, is nonornamental.

RATE / SPACING: Growth is slow. Plants from 3- to 4-inch-diameter containers or bare-root sods are spaced 6 to 10 inches apart.

HORTICULTURAL SELECTIONS: 'Rosea', very rare, with rose-colored flowers.

CULTURE / CARE: Trailing arbutus requires acidic soil of pH 4.0 to 5.0 and is adaptable to a range of organically rich to sandy soils. It also performs well in decaying wood and pine needles. Because it is not greatly tolerant of drought, its soil should be maintained slightly moist and its exposure to strong winds kept to a minimum. It prefers light to dense shade and thrives under both deciduous and evergreen canopies. Leaf spots and powdery mildew are occasionally encountered, but no serious pests seem to effect it. Little or no maintenance is required.

PROPAGATION: Division is best done in early spring, but can be difficult as the root system is small in proportion to the long trailing stems. Because the root system lives in association with an essential mycorrhizal fungus, the original soil attached to the roots should not be removed when transplanting divisions. Cuttings should be taken from new growth in late summer or early fall with a small heel of mature wood attached; inoculation with parent soil would be beneficial after root formation so as to introduce the proper mycorrhizal fungi. Rooting in a shady location with mild heat is preferable to rooting under a mist system. Seed ripens in early summer and should be depulped and sown immediately for germination in four to six weeks. Seed can be stored for up to one year, but germination percentages become reduced over time. Some claim that rotted wood is the best medium in which to germinate seeds.

Epimedium grandiflorum   PLATE 114

Long-spur Epimedium, Long-spur Bishop's Cap,
Long-spur Barrenwort

Reaching 9 to 12 inches tall and spreading more
than 1½ feet across, long-spur epimedium is one of
the best clump-forming ground covers for its floral
and foliar qualities. Clearly, with its refined habit,
unusually shaped leaves, and colorful springtime
flowers, it is a prize worthy of nearly every shady,
temperate-climate landscape. Its common name
bishop's cap supposedly arose from the resemblance
of the four-pointed flowers to the clergyman's
biretta, while the name barrenwort refers to a root
extract from the plant that was believed to prevent
conception when administered to women.

Although there are several excellent species and hybrids of epimedium, *E. grandiflorum,* arguably, is the
showiest. In the landscape it functions as a marvelous
edging plant for walkways, garden paths, alongside
steps, and around the periphery of herbaceous border
plantings. Single clumps or small groupings make excellent specimen or accent plants along woodland
borders, and mass plantings are superb for facing garden ornaments, trees, and building foundations.

SCIENTIFIC NAME: *Epimedium grandiflorum* (ep-i-
mee-dee-um gran-di-*floe*-rum). *Epimedium* is a
Greek name of obscure meaning. *Grandiflorum*
means large-flowered.

HARDINESS / ORIGIN: Zones 5 to 8; Japan, Korea, and
Manchuria.

LEAVES / FLOWERS / FRUIT: The compound leaves are
composed of rather heart-shaped, tooth-edged
leaflets that reach 2 to 3 inches long. In youth they
emerge beige, brownish, or coppery, and later turn
medium green. During bloom, which takes place in
spring, the lovely ¾- to 1½-inch-wide blossoms arise
with white and yellow sepals, rose or violet petals,
and white spurs. Selections are available with petals
that range from yellowish white to rose.

RATE / SPACING: Growth is slow to moderate. Plants
from pint-sized to quart-sized containers are spaced
10 to 12 inches apart.

HORTICULTURAL SELECTIONS: 'Album', with flowers
mostly white; 'Elf King' ('Elfkönig'), with creamy
white flowers and vigorous spread; 'Flavescens', with
yellowish white flowers; 'Lilac Fairy' ('Lilafee'), with
lavender-violet flowers and vigorous spread; 'Normale', with outer petals red, inner violet; 'Orion', to
18 inches tall, with shiny green leaves and large rose-
pink and white flowers; 'Rose Queen', with reddish
leaves and rose-pink and white flowers; 'Violaceum',
with light purple flowers; 'White Queen', with silvery white flowers.

OTHER SPECIES: *E. alpinum* (al-*pie*-num), alpine epimedium, named for its alpine habitat, is an exceptional, and some feel incomparable, ground cover
for facing low trees and shrubs. Others find it every
bit as useful as a specimen in perennial borders or as
edging along shady walkways, paths, and herbaceous
border plantings. In any case, like *E. grandiflorum,*
this species contributes a strong yet dainty beauty to
the landscape. Reaching 10 to 15 inches tall with a
dense, rather erect habit, it hails from southern and
central Europe, and displays deciduous to semievergreen leaves that are borne upon wiry, upright stems
and are leathery-textured, heart-shaped, tapering to
a fine point, 5 inches long, and colored pinkish in
youth then medium green before becoming bronzy
in fall. Texture is rather coarse, and the nodding
flowers with red sepals and yellow petals are arranged
in loose clusters that are elevated on slender stems in
mid spring. Typically, the flowers reach ½ inch wide,
but unfortunately are often partially obscured by foliage. Hardy in Zones 3 to 8. 'Rubrum', faster
spreading with brighter red sepals and brighter yellow petals than the species.

E. × *perralchicum* '**Fröhnleiten**' (pe-ral-*kee*-kum
froen-*leet*-en), a compact 4- to 6-inch tall cultivar
derived from crossing *E. perralderianum* with *E. pinnatum* subsp. *colchicum,* is considered to be even
more desirable than *E. perralderianum* as its slightly
brighter flowers are held higher above the foliage.

E. perralderianum (pe-ral-de-ree-*aye*-num),
named after the French naturalist Henri Rene le
Tourneux de la Perraudiere (1831–1861), is native
to Algeria. It is robust and remains fully evergreen
in the milder parts of Zones 5 to 8. In cooler areas it
is semievergreen but, regardless of locale, its young
leaves are bronzy and marbled with light green before maturing to medium glossy green with prickly
edges. Its bright yellow, ½-inch-wide flowers are
borne during spring in good number upon slender
stems slightly above the leaves. Height ranges from 1
to 1½ feet tall, and spread is indefinite.

E. pinnatum (pin-*nay*-tum), Persian epimedium,
is named for its pinnate, or featherlike, foliage. It is
hardy in Zones 5 to 8, comes from Iran (Persia) and
the Caucasus, and ranges from 9 to 12 inches tall.
The foliage is deciduous yet persistent and has spiny
leaf edges. In the landscape, this species is useful in
the same situations as the other species. Like them, it
flowers in spring, but its flowers are brownish red,
reach ⅝ inch wide, and are elevated to 1½ feet. Subspecies *colchicum* (sometimes listed as a variety),
golden bishop's hat, has fewer leaflets per leaf than
the species and more and larger flowers.

E. × *rubrum* (*roob*-rum), red epimedium, named
for the red sepals surrounding the petals, closely re-

sembles its parent *E. alpinum* (the other parent is *E. grandiflorum*). Possibly the most popular of all epimediums cultivated in North America today, it is outstanding for its bright crimson and creamy white flowers which are held well above the foliage during spring. It reaches 8 to 13 inches tall by 12 inches wide. Hardy in Zones 4 to 8.

E. versicolor (*ver*-si-cul-er), hybrid epimedium, is derived from a cross between *E. pinnatum* and *E. grandiflorum*. Its juvenile foliage is mottled green and red, later turning green, and then is tinged pinkish red in fall. This spring-bloomer displays rose-colored and yellow flowers that reach 1 inch wide. 'Cupreum' displays coppery red inner sepals while 'Sulphureum' is commonly cultivated and is noteworthy for pale yellow flowers but, unlike the species, its spring foliage is usually not mottled. Hardy to Zone 5.

CULTURE / CARE: Although epimediums prefer a nice organically rich loam, they are remarkably adaptable; however, they always insist upon good drainage and at least slightly acidic pH. In respect to drought tolerance, they can survive most summers without supplemental watering, but almost always grow better if watered periodically during the midsummer months. They prefer light to moderate shade. Pests include aphids, which may be the vector for transmitting mosaic virus, the main disease of epimediums. Maintenance needs are nonexistent, yet some gardeners remove the oldest leaves (or even cut them all back) in the fall or early spring as a means of neatening and rejuvenating plantings.

PROPAGATION: Division in early spring or fall is the standard means of propagation.

Equisetum   PLATE 115
Horsetail Snakegrass, Scouring Rush

Although most people consider horsetails to be weeds, the species described here are utilitarian, rhizomatous, upright to arching, herbaceous, perennial ground covers of relatively loose habit. They do not tolerate much foot traffic, but as moderate-scale to large-scale soil binders in moist places, such as ditches, pond perimeters, and low areas where water tends to pool during spring and fall, they have few equals. They are primitive spore-bearing, jointed, segmented, nearly leafless plants. They may be evergreen or deciduous and most frequently spread vigorously by rhizomes, which in time yield a single clone several feet across. They are known to occur naturally in all parts of the world with the exceptions of Australia and New Zealand, and are thought to have evolved about the same time as the mosses. Compared to mosses, they represent greater specialization with their increased ability to transport water,

encasement of spores in specialized structures called strobili, and evidence of hormonal control over the meristematic (growing) tissue within their stems. Their leaves are very minute, and their role in the manufacture of food is negligible. Nearly all photosynthetic function is assumed by chlorophyll contained in the stems.

Some *Equisetum* species have been given the common name scouring rushes. This is due to their use as a polish. The stems contain a siliceous material that is quite abrasive and works well for scouring. Native Americans made great use of the scouring rushes as medicine to treat diarrhea, as a hair tonic to repel lice, fleas, and mites, and, with the ashes of burned stems, as a treatment for burns. As abrasives, horsetails were used to sharpen arrows and to scour bowls and mussel shells. Certain species contain physiologically potent chemicals. Some have been employed as heart and nerve sedatives, wound dressings, and urinary tract cleansers. Unfortunately, when misused, they can be very dangerous. Some horsetails contain the alkaloid equestine, which is sometimes responsible for the poisoning of livestock; poisoning is said to be caused by the enzyme thiaminase, which destroys thiamine (vitamin B1), thus creating thiamine deficiency in the livestock.

SCIENTIFIC NAME: *Equisetum* (ek-we-*see*-tum) is derived from the Latin *eques,* horse, and *seta,* bristle. Commonly the genus is referred to as the horsetails for, as the Latin suggests, the plants resemble a horse's tail in appearance.

HARDINESS / ORIGIN: See individual species for hardiness; mostly from temperate regions, with the exception of Australia and New Zealand.

LEAVES / FLOWERS / FRUIT: The leaves are all but nonexistent. Typically they are tiny, colored white to black, borne in whorls about the joints of the green, photosynthetic, hollow stems. Like ferns, horsetails have no flowers or fruit, but bear spores in a conelike apparatus at the ends of the stems.

RATE / SPACING: Growth is moderate to relatively fast. Plants from sods or pint-sized to quart-sized containers are spaced 10 to 18 inches apart.

SPECIES: *E. hyemale* (hy-*mal*-lee), common horsetail, is native to nearly every locale in North, Central, and South America, as well as Europe and Asia, and is hardy in Zones 2 to 10. It is robust, evergreen, and stiffly jointed, and under ideal conditions reaches 5 feet tall (typically 2 to 3 feet tall). Its stems are dark green, ½ inch thick, unbranched (unless pruned), rough to the touch, and stiffly jointed. A vigorous spreader, it produces a strong system of rhizomes that branches out in all directions.

E. × *nelsonii* (nel-*sohn*-ee-eye), the result of naturally overlapping populations of *E. variegatum* and

E. laevigatum (which is taller and deciduous), most closely resembles *E. variegatum* but its stems are primarily deciduous.

E. scirpoides (skir-*poy*-deez), named for its resemblance to *Scirpus,* a genus of sedges, is commonly called dwarf scouring rush. It reaches 6 to 8 inches tall, spreads indefinitely, and is hardy in Zones 1 to 9. Native to North America from Greenland and Baffin Island to Alaska then south to Newfoundland, Maine, Michigan, and Oregon, it is adaptable to various moist sites ranging from sandy to organically rich woodlands, thickets, and semishady embankments. Its stems are densely matted together, in groups of 10 to 100, are very thin (1/30 inch wide), evergreen, prostrate to ascending, and display three deeply grooved ridges that appear as six to eight ridges due to the fissures that are cut into them. Their stem sheaths (leaflike appendages) are minute, display three to four short triangular teeth, and are white-margined. The strobili that they bear at their ends are nearly black, relatively small, and appear as swellings with pointed tips. Maturing in summer, they sometimes persist through winter.

E. sylvaticum (sil-*vat*-i-kum), meaning sylvan (i.e., of the woods), is commonly called woodland horsetail, although in addition to woodlands, it inhabits thickets and wet meadows. Native to Eurasia and North America, from Quebec to Alaska northward, and from New York to Washington southward, it is hardy in Zones 1 to 5. Ranging from 10 to 20 inches tall and with an indefinite spread, its non-spore-bearing stems are slender, deciduous, and rough to the touch. Overall, they create a lacy, open, airy appearance. In spring they are preceded by brownish stems that bear spores at their ends before dying back and being replaced by the sterile stems. Forma *multiramosum,* meaning many branched, is highly branched; var. *pauciramosum,* meaning few branched, has limited branching.

E. × *trachyodon* (tray-kee-*oh*-don), probably hardy in Zones 2 to 8, is considered a natural hybrid of *E. variegatum* and the taller more numerously ribbed *E. hyemale.* Presumably it is intermediate between the two species in its traits.

E. variegatum (var-i-e-*gay*-tum), named for the varied color of the tiny leaf scales that cover the sheaths of the stems, is commonly called variegated horsetail. It hails from moist sandy slopes and beach and bog margins from New Brunswick to Alaska northward and southward into Wyoming and the Midwestern states. It is hardy in Zones 1 to 8 or 9, reaches 14 to 20 inches tall, and spreads indefinitely. Its evergreen fertile and sterile stems are similar in appearance (in contrast to some of the other species that have greatly different fertile and sterile

stems). They are usually unbranched and 1/8 inch wide, and tend to arch over. Variety *alaskanum* is more robust and comes from the southern coast of Alaska.

CULTURE / CARE: Although minor individual differences exist between the species, generally speaking they are adaptable to a range of soils from gravelly or sandy to richly organic. They have been noted to grow in slightly alkaline to moderately acidic soils. *Equisetum scirpoides* has been witnessed growing in rotting logs, and *E. variegatum* on calcareous outcroppings. None of the species is greatly tolerant of drought (without severe disfigurement), thus they should be planted in a site that naturally maintains a constantly high moisture level. Ponds, streams, and bog periphery are ideal sites, as are low woodland areas. Sand dunes and waste places in which the substratum stays constantly moist also frequently support these species. *Epimedium* species prefer full sun to light shade, except for *E. sylvaticum,* which prefers light to moderate shade. No serious diseases or pests seem to effect them, and they need little or no maintenance.

PROPAGATION: Division of root masses, being sure to keep roots moist during the process, is the standard means of propagation. Spores contain chlorophyll and are usually very short-lived (about five days); ripe spores (ripeness evidenced by the splitting open of the strobili to expose them) can be germinated in a manner similar to fern spores.

Erica carnea   PLATE 116
Spring Heath

A close cousin to heather (*Calluna*), spring heath and its related species are small, woody, dense-growing, horizontally spreading, subshrubby ground covers. Spring heath typically reaches 1 foot tall and spreads 1 1/2 to 2 feet across. When mass planted, it is an excellent small-, moderate-, or large-scale general ground cover, particularly for sloping, sandy or gravelly terrain. In mixed plantings it is a perfect companion for heather, low forms of blueberry, bearberry, crowberry, and many other slow-growing, acid-loving shrublets and ground covers. Such combinations can cover large areas and slopes and serve as brilliantly colorful, multitextured lawn substitutes or foundation facers. In the rock garden or at the top of a rock retaining wall, heaths make exceptional specimens, and in combination with herbaceous perennials in a border setting, they are extraordinary. They are tolerant to salt, making them useful in coastal gardens. No foot traffic is tolerated.

SCIENTIFIC NAME: *Erica carnea* (*air*-i-ka *kar*-nee-a).

Erica is derived from the Greek *ereike,* heath or heather. *Carnea,* flesh-colored, refers to the pale, flesh pink flowers.

HARDINESS / ORIGIN: Zones 5 or 6 to 7 (reliable snow cover and shelter from winter wind is necessary in the extreme northern part of this range); central and southern Europe.

LEAVES / FLOWERS / FRUIT: The tiny, needlelike leaves are evergreen, whorled in fours, reach ¼ inch long, and are colored dark, shiny green. The flowers are ¼ inch long, urn-shaped, red to whitish, and effective from late winter to early spring. The fruit is non-ornamental.

RATE / SPACING: Growth is slow. Plants from quart-sized to gallon-sized containers are spaced 14 to 20 inches apart.

HORTICULTURAL SELECTIONS: 'Alan Coates', 6 inches tall by more than 15 inches wide, compact habit, pale rose-colored flowers which darken to purple as they age; 'Aurea', with light lime green leaves becoming golden yellow in winter and deep pink flowers from mid winter to spring; 'December Red', with red flowers December to February, vigorous, 6 to 9 inches tall; 'Eden Valley', reaching 10 inches tall by 15 inches wide, with light green leaves and lavender and white flowers; 'Eileen Porter', compact habit with dark green foliage and carmine-rose flowers; 'Foxhollow Fairy', relatively vigorous, light green foliage, white and pink flowers change to deep pink as they age, 6 inches tall by more than 18 inches wide; 'King George', leaves shiny dark green, flowers deep rose-pink, and height to 12 inches; 'Myretoun Ruby', with dark green needle-like leaves, mounding habit, and ruby red flowers; 'Pink Spangles', reaching 12 inches tall, mound-forming, with unique bicolor (lilac and deep pink) flowers; 'Prince of Wales', dark green leaves with rose-pink flowers and height to 12 inches; 'Spring-wood Pink', a vigorous spreader with medium green foliage and flowers from late winter to early spring that begin white then mature to clear pink, height to 8 inches; 'Springwood White', like 'Springwood Pink' but with white flowers; 'Vivelli', with dark green foliage that turns bronzy in winter, compact habit to 8 inches tall, and dark, almost blood-red flowers; 'Winter Beauty', slow-growing with dark green leaves and deep pink flowers from early winter to early spring.

OTHER SPECIES: *E. cinerea* (sin-er-*ee*-a), named for its gray or ashen-colored foliage, is commonly called twisted heath, Scotch heath, or bell heath. A woody, low-spreading, shrubby ground cover, it ranges from 12 to 24 inches tall, spreads to 2 feet across, is hardy in Zones 6 to 7, and hails from western Europe. It grows at a relatively slow to moderate rate, and plants

from quart-sized to gallon-sized containers are best set on 14- to 18-inch centers. Its leaves are evergreen, needlelike, arranged in threes, reach ¼ inch long, and are colored dark green. It displays purple to blue urn-shaped flowers from mid summer to early fall. Horticultural selections include 'Atropurpurea', with numerous dark violet flowers; 'Atrorubens', with ruby red flowers; 'C. D. Eason', with vivid deep pink flowers from mid to late summer; 'Coccinea', 4 inches tall by more than 12 inches wide, noteworthy for its profusion of deep red flowers, dark green foliage, and low habit; 'Golden Drop', with pink flowers and yellowish foliage that turn russet in winter; 'Golden Hue', with pale pink flowers and yellow leaves that turn golden during winter; 'Knap Hill Pink', with compact habit, rich pinkish purple flowers, and dark dull green leaves; 'Pink Ice', with pink flowers and bright green leaves that pick up hues of bronze in winter; 'P. S. Patrick', with purple flowers; 'Rosanne Waterer', 6 inches tall by more than 18 inches wide, with prostrate habit, deep green foliage, and maroon-purple flowers; 'Velvet Knight', with 10-inch-tall shrubby habit, dark shiny green leaves, and deep maroon purple flowers; 'Violacea', more upright in habit with purplish blue flowers.

E. × darleyensis (dar-lee-*en*-sis), Darley heath, winter heath, or hybrid heath, is a woody, relatively tall, spreading, shrubby hybrid ground cover that reaches 3 feet tall, spreads 1½ to 2 feet wide, and is hardy in Zones 6 to 7 or 8. Relatively fast growing, plants from quart-sized to gallon-sized containers should be spaced 1½ to 2 feet apart. Derived from a cross between *E. erigena* (an upright species) and *E. carnea* (a prostrate species), this hybrid is exceptional in that it inherited the long flowering period and bright colors of *E. carnea* along with the vigorous growth and abundant flower production of *E. erigena*. It shows very good drought tolerance and even during hot dry periods its dark, shiny evergreen, needlelike leaves remain attractive. Its flowers are pink, urn-shaped, and borne from late autumn to early spring. Popular horticultural selections include 'Arthur Johnson', with foliage light green, mauve-pink flowers, height to 2 feet; 'Ghost Hills', reaching 18 inches tall, with deep rose-colored flowers; 'Mediterranean Pink', with rose-lavender-colored flowers; 'Silberschmelze', with deep glossy green leaves, silvery-white flowers, and height reaching 1 foot.

E. tetralix (te-*tra*-liks), crossleaf heath, bog heath, moor heath, or bell heath, is a medium-sized, woody, upright-branched, subshrubby ground cover that reaches 12 inches tall, spreads 1 to 1½ feet wide, comes from western Europe, and is hardy in Zones 4 to 6 or 7. Its leaves are evergreen, needlelike, in fours (hence the scientific name), to ⅛ inch long, and covered with downy gray hairs. The flowers are urn-shaped, ¼ inch long, rose-colored, and effective from early summer to early or mid fall. The rate of growth is relatively slow to moderate, and plants from pint-sized to quart-sized containers should be spaced 12 to 16 inches apart. Popular horticultural selections include 'Alba', with white flowers and silvery-gray leaves that become greener with age; 'Con Underwood', with magenta flowers and gray-green leaves; 'George Fraser', with pale pink flowers and bluish foliage; 'Nana', reaching only 6 inches tall by 12 inches wide; 'Pink Star', with soft pink flowers and silvery-gray leaves.

E. vagans (*vay*-ganz), named from the Latin *vaga,* wandering (as in vagabond), is commonly called Cornish heath or wandering heath. Low-growing and horizontally spreading, this subshrubby species reaches 12 inches tall, spreads to 2 feet wide, is native to western Europe, and is hardy in Zones 6 to 7. It grows at a slow to moderate pace, and plants from quart-sized to gallon-sized containers should be spaced 16 to 20 inches apart. The leaves are evergreen, needlelike, in fours or fives, to ⅜ inch long, and are colored a bright shiny green. The tiny, ⅛-inch-long, purplish pink, urn-shaped flowers become effective during late summer. Some popular horticultural selections include 'Alba Minor', compact in habit with white flowers; 'Mrs. D. F. Maxwell', with dark shiny green leaves and deep red flowers on long spikes from early summer to fall; 'St. Keverne', with clear, bright pink flowers in late summer.

CULTURE / CARE: Well-drained, sandy, acidic, loamy soils are required. Although moderate periods of drought are not a problem, occasional deep watering enhances the floral display and the appearance of the foliage. The heaths typically perform at their best in areas of high humidity and moderate temperatures, and prefer full sun to light shade, with the best floral display in full sun. Rabbits and deer may at times nibble on them, but seldom cause much damage. Occasionally, diseases such as wilt, powdery mildew, and rust are a problem. Maintenance, if practiced at all, usually includes mowing or shearing plants following their bloom to keep them looking neat and to maintain a compact habit. A light mulch around the base is useful as it helps to moderate the temperature and moisture content of the soil.

PROPAGATION: Cuttings taken from mid summer through fall seem to root best. Division can be accomplished during spring and fall. Seed propagation is said to work well throughout the year but is seldom practiced with cultivars, which may not come true from seed.

Erigeron karvinskianus   PLATE 117
Bonytip Fleabane

The homely name bonytip fleabane fails to portray the beauty of this low-growing, trailing, herbaceous, 10- to 20-inch-tall ground cover. Of great utility in the Southwest, bonytip fleabane has the desirable attributes of being tolerant of high salinity and drought, and is of great use as a moderate-scale general cover around and underneath large shrubs and small trees. Because of its rambling nature, it should be used in areas that naturally check its spread. Never use it with smaller shrubs and herbs for it will quickly overrun them. No foot traffic is tolerated.

SCIENTIFIC NAME: *Erigeron karvinskianus* (e-*rij*-er-on kar-vin-skee-*aye*-nis). *Erigeron* comes from the Greek *eri,* early or springtime, and *geron,* old or old man, probably in reference to the fluffy white seed heads or the springtime hairiness of the leaves of some species. *Karvinskianus* commemorates botanist Wilhelm Friedrich Karwinski von Karwin (1780–1855).
HARDINESS / ORIGIN: Zones 9 to 11; Mexico south to Venezuela.
LEAVES / FLOWERS / FRUIT: The leaves are evergreen, elliptic to oval, often lobed and often with teeth about their edges. They are colored medium green and reach 1¼ inches long by ½ inch wide. The flowers, which appear throughout most of the growing season, are magnificent. Each is sunflower-like and ¾ inch wide, with a yellow center and white petals about the edges. As the white petals age they become pink then finally reddish purple—giving a multicolored effect as there are flowers in all colors (and in between) at all times. The fruit is nonornamental.
RATE / SPACING: Growth is fast. Plants from quart-sized to gallon-sized containers are spaced 14 to 20 inches apart.
HORTICULTURAL SELECTIONS: 'Profusion', with tiny pink and white flowers.
OTHER SPECIES: *E. glaucus* (*glaw*-kus), named for its grayish blue leaves, is commonly called seaside daisy or beach fleabane and hails from the Pacific Coast from southern California to northern Oregon. It is hardy in Zones 5 or 6 to 9, reaches 10 inches tall, spreads 18 inches wide, and is clothed in oval to spatula-shaped, fleshy, semievergreen leaves. Its daisylike flowers with violet petals are effective from mid to late spring. Horticultural selections include 'Albus', with white flowers; 'Olga', named after the late Olga Johnson who discovered it along the Oregon coast, 6 inches tall by 18 inches wide, noteworthy for its low-spreading habit and numerous large lilac flowers with yellow centers; 'Roseus', ray flowers with pink

petals; 'Wayne Rodrick', more compact and more floriferous than the species.

CULTURE / CARE: Fleabanes are at their best in well-drained sandy loam and adapt to varying degrees of acidity and alkalinity. They tolerate drought and infertility. Although they appreciate an occasional deep drink of water during summer, they open up and become leggy if given too much water or fertilizer. They prefer full sun, their primary disease problems are mildew, leaf spot, rust, and aster yellows, and aphids are sometimes pesky, especially during the summer months. Maintenance typically consists of shearing or mowing plantings in late fall to neaten them up.

PROPAGATION: Division in spring works well. Seed should be collected when ripe and stored cool until spring; germination occurs in one or two weeks. Stem cuttings can be rooted throughout the growing season.

Erodium reichardii   PLATE 118
Alpine Geranium

Unlike the florist's geranium (*Pelargonium* species), this dainty herbaceous ground cover (formerly *E. chamaedryoides*) reaches only 3 inches tall and spreads 4 to 6 inches across, but by no means is it insignificant. Its mat-forming dense habit is nearly impenetrable, and its long running floral show is most alluring. In other words, alpine geranium is charming and is an excellent choice for use as a small-scale general ground cover in place of turf or as a specimen in rock or alpine gardens. Periodic foot traffic causes no harm, but regular traffic should be avoided.

SCIENTIFIC NAME: *Erodium reichardii* (e-*row*-dee-um rye-*kard*-ee-eye). *Erodium* comes from the Greek *erodios,* a heron, in reference to the resemblance of the female floral apparatus to the head and beak of a heron. *Reichardii* commemorates Johann Jakob Reichard (1743–1782).

HARDINESS / ORIGIN: Zones 7 to 9; Mediterranean region.

LEAVES / FLOWERS / FRUIT: The leaves arise primarily from the rootstock. They are evergreen, held upon long thin leaf stalks, round to oval or heart-shaped, to ⅜ inch long by ⅜ inch wide, edged with rounded teeth, and colored medium to dark green. Profusely borne, beautiful, solitary, ½-inch-wide, pinkish white flowers with dark pink veins appear from mid spring to early fall. The fruit, a capsule, is nonornamental.

RATE / SPACING: Growth is slow. Plants from 3- to 4-inch-diameter containers are spaced 4 to 6 inches apart.

HORTICULTURAL SELECTIONS: 'Album', white flowers; 'Flore Pleno', single and double deep pink flowers; 'Roseum', rose-pink flowers with red veins.

CULTURE / CARE: Alpine geranium is adaptable to most soils but demands good drainage. Not notably tolerant to drought, it should be watered periodically to keep the soil slightly moist. Best growth is in full sun with afternoon shade or with constant light shade throughout the day. Pests include aphids and soil mealybug. The most common diseases are leaf spot, viral curly top, and stem and crown rots. Little or no maintenance is required.

PROPAGATION: Division of plants in spring or fall is the standard means of propagation.

Erysimum kotschyanum   PLATE 119
Creeping Gold Wallflower, Creeping Blister Cress, Kotschy Erysimum

Creeping gold wallflower is a low, mat-forming, herbaceous, stoloniferous ground cover. Quite useful in rock gardens as a specimen or for accent, at 3 to 6 inches tall by more than 2 feet wide, it can be used to fill the cracks of a rock wall, and in some cases, it has been used successfully as a small-scale general cover. No foot traffic is tolerated.

SCIENTIFIC NAME: *Erysimum kotschyanum* (e-*ris*-i-mum kotch-ee-*aye*-num). *Erysimum,* according to one source, comes from *erysimon,* the Greek name for this plant, while another source says the genus name comes from the Greek *eruo,* to draw up, referring to the use of some species in raising blisters. *Kotschyanum* commemorates Theodor Kotschy (1812–1890), an Austrian botanist and plant collector of western Asia and North Africa.

HARDINESS / ORIGIN: Zone 6; alpine regions of Asia Minor.

LEAVES / FLOWERS / FRUIT: The leaves are semievergreen, alternate, simple, and narrowly linear to spatula-shaped. They reach 1½ inches long by ¼ inch wide, are toothed about their margins, and display medium to deep green, hair-covered blades. The flowers, arranged in crowded, branch-ending racemes, are four-parted, showy, ½ inch in diameter, fragrant, bright yellow, and effective during spring and early summer. The fruit is nonornamental.

RATE / SPACING: Growth is moderate to fast. Plants from pint-sized to quart-sized containers are spaced 1½ to 2 feet apart.

CULTURE / CARE: Creeping gold wallflower is adaptable to a broad range of soil textures, provided the pH ranges from neutral to moderately alkaline. It needs good drainage, is quite tolerant of drought, and prefers full sun to light shade. Its primary disease problems are various mildews, leaf spot, root rot, club root, rusts, and wilt virus. Pests of greatest prevalence are aphids, mites, and soil mealybugs. Should creeping gold wallflower mound up off the ground and lose contact with the soil, the center should be cut out and the sides lightly tamped down. PROPAGATION: Mats with rooted stem sections are easily divided and transplanted. Seed is reported to be viable.

Euonymus fortunei   PLATE 120
Japanese Euonymus

Japanese euonymus is an evergreen of trailing or climbing habit. As a climber, it may reach 20 feet, but if not given support, it becomes a very thick, very useful ground cover. Even so, the ordinary species is seldom seen because its cultivars and varieties are better still. Indeed, cultivars of Japanese euonymus are so numerous and so useful that they have become a virtual ground-cover mainstay of modern North American horticulture. Like their parent species, these cultivars tend to climb if given support, although their tendency to do so is overshadowed by their propensity to blanket the ground. The dwarf, small-leaved varieties tend to be best for general use on a small scale where a dense carpet is needed. In planters, alongside steps, and trailing over walls, the colorful variegated selections are quite useful. Larger forms, with their greater vigor, make excellent general-purpose ground covers for moderate-sized to large-sized areas, especially on hillsides where their extensive root systems help to check erosion. Foot traffic is not encouraged, but to a certain extent is tolerated.

SCIENTIFIC NAME: *Euonymus fortunei* (you-*on*-i-mus / you-*oh*-nee-mus fore-*tew*-nee-eye). *Euonymus* is said to be named for Euonyme, mother of the Furies in Greek mythology, or it may be derived from the Greek *eu,* good, and *onoma,* a name, meaning with good reputation. *Fortunei* commemorates Robert Fortune (1812–1880), who collected in China.

HARDINESS / ORIGIN: Zones 4 or 5 to 9; China.

LEAVES / FLOWERS / FRUIT: The leaves, like those of English ivy (*Hedera helix*) and creeping fig (*Ficus pumila*), are dimorphic, meaning that the juvenile (nonflowering) form has a different leaf shape than the adult form. Seldom is the adult foliage observed unless the stems have ascended high above the ground, triggering the maturation process. Generally, the adult foliage is thicker, more leathery, and more rounded than the juvenile foliage. The juvenile leaves are evergreen, paired, elliptic to oval, to 2 inches long, edged with broad, shallow or rounded teeth, and colored dark green with prominent silvery-white veins. They are quite variable in size and color. Often branches displaying unique foliage appear and, when propagated, pass on these traits. Most of the cultivars have arisen in this manner. The

flowers, which are found only on branches that have matured from the juvenile state, are small, greenish, and not of great ornamental interest. The fruit that follows, however, is quite ornamental. It consists of pinkish, three-sectioned to five-sectioned capsules that become effective during fall and often persist well into winter.

RATE / SPACING: Moderate to relatively fast, but dwarf forms can be slow growing; space vigorous plants from 2- to 4-inch diameter containers 10 to 16 inches apart, or from gallon-sized containers 1½ to 3 feet apart; space slow-growing forms from 2- to 3-inch-diameter containers 8 to 10 inches apart, or from pint-sized to gallon-sized containers 1½ to 2 feet apart.

HORTICULTURAL SELECTIONS: 'Acutus', with narrow, dark green leaves and a vigorous, low-growing habit; 'Canadian Variegated', reaching 18 inches tall by 3 feet wide, leaves small, medium green with white edges and moderate rate of spread; 'Coloratus', purple wintercreeper, the most popular selection grown in North America, dark green foliage with purplish fall and winter color, rapid growth, and rooting stems that are exceptional for binding soil; 'Dart's Blanket', similar to 'Coloratus', but supposedly more salt tolerant and with deeper bronze fall color; 'Emerald 'n Gold', a low-growing branching shrub reaching 1½ to 2 feet tall, leaves relatively small, dark, glossy green with yellow margins, developing reddish tints in fall; 'Golden Princess', reaching 2 to 3 feet tall by 3 to 4 feet wide with medium green leaves and bright gold-tipped new growth; 'Kewensis', probably the smallest cultivar with leaves only ¼ inch long and a height of only 1 or 2 inches; 'Longwood', named after Longwood Gardens, the famous botanic garden in Pennsylvania, another small-leaved, dwarf form that reaches only 4 inches tall, with leaves ¼ to ½ inch long; 'Minimus', similar to 'Longwood' but often with upright-growing shoots; 'Moon Shadow', with yellow stems and yellow-centered, wavy green-margined foliage; var. *radicans,* moderate spreading with shiny medium to dark green, 1½- to 2-inch-long leaves; var. *radicans* 'Argenteo-variegata', similar to var. *radicans* in habit, but with dark green leaves edged in silvery white; var. *radicans* 'Harlequin', with extremely variable variegation (foliage ranging from all white to green with white margins, to green with speckles of white and yellowish green), rather sickly appearing; 'Sparkle 'n Gold', to 3 feet tall by 6 feet wide, foliage dark green with broad bright yellow edges; 'Sun Spot', slow-growing, with mounded habit, 3 feet tall by 6 feet wide, noteworthy for its dark green leaves with a vibrant yellow spot in the center (plant patent number 4340); 'Tricolor' ('Gaiety'), moderate spreading, 2 to 3 feet tall, with white, cream, and green leaves that take on hints of pink and red during fall; 'Vegetus', moderate spreading, with big, rounded, shiny green leaves and a tendency to be a bit shrubbier than the other cultivars.

OTHER SPECIES: *E. obovatus* (oh-bow-*vay*-tus), named for its inversely oval (obovate) leaves, is commonly called strawberry bush, running strawberry bush, or prostrate strawberry bush. It hails from northern North American rich, moist or dry woodlands and is often found growing in conjunction with beech, maple, oak, hickory, hemlock, and white cedar. It is hardy in Zones 3 or 4 to 8 or 9, displays a rather lax, sprawling (to 4 feet across), woody habit, and ranges from 8 to 24 inches tall. The leaves are medium green, deciduous, and 1 to 2 inches long by ½ to 1½ inches wide. The flowers are borne alone or in clusters of up to four from spring to early summer. Each is five-parted, ¼ inch wide, with green petals, and is relatively nonornamental. The fruit is quite showy and consists of three-celled capsules that ripen to crimson and scarlet in fall, thus adding a colorful touch to the late-season landscape. This species spreads at a moderate pace and is best used as a general cover or soil retainer on a moderate scale. It combines well with many native species and is at its best in native or naturalized settings. Plants from 1- to 2-gallon-sized containers should be spaced 2 to 3 feet apart.

CULTURE / CARE: All wintercreepers are amenable to acidic to slightly alkaline soils. Loamy soil is best, but high clay and sandy soils are nearly as good. *Euonymus fortunei* and its varieties tolerate moderate periods of drought, and they nearly always benefit from occasional deep summertime watering. *Euonymus obovatus* is more tolerant of moist conditions and less tolerant of drought. Wintercreepers prefer full sun to relatively dense shade. Pests include aphids, thrips, and scales. The most prevalent diseases are anthracnose, bacterial crown gall, dieback, powdery mildew, and leaf spot. Maintenance typically consists of trimming back the leading stems as they outgrow their designated bounds.

PROPAGATION: Cuttings are the standard means of propagation; they may be rooted throughout the year.

Euphorbia polychroma PLATE 121
Cushion Euphorbia, Cushion Spurge

Cushion euphorbia (formerly *E. epithymoides*) is a carefree, attractive, herbaceous, upright-stemmed, broad-cushion-shaped, 10- to 18-inch tall, 1½- to 3-foot wide, mound-forming ground cover. It performs beautifully as an edging along a formal walk or winding garden path, as a rock garden or border specimen, planted atop retaining walls, or massed in moderate expanses as a facing or general cover. It is best in areas of cool summers. No foot traffic is tolerated.

SCIENTIFIC NAME: *Euphorbia polychroma* (you-*fore*-bee-a poe-lee-*crow*-ma). *Euphorbia* is named after Euphorbus, physician to Juba, king of Mauritania. *Polychroma* refers to the two-colored (chartreuse and light green) flowers.

HARDINESS / ORIGIN: Zones 4 to 8; eastern Europe.

LEAVES / FLOWERS / FRUIT: The deciduous, simple, alternately arranged, oblong to oval-oblong, 2-inch-long, stemless leaves emerge light yellow. Later they become medium green and finally reddish in fall. The unusual poinsettia-like flowers are borne at the tips of the branches in clusters called *cyathia*. In this type of flower arrangement, which is characteristic of *Euphorbia,* the unisexual flowers sit above a cup-like whorl of bracts (leafy appendages). The individual flowers are greenish, single-sexed, and relatively inconspicuous. Instead, the showy, chartreuse, springtime display comes from the 1-inch-long, leafy bracts. The fruit is nonornamental.

RATE / SPACING: Growth is moderate. Plants from pint-sized to quart-sized containers are spaced 14 to 20 inches apart.

OTHER SPECIES: *E. amygdaloides* var. *robbiae* (a-*mig*-da-loy-deez rob-*ee*-aye), probably takes its specific epithet for the resemblance of its leaves to those of the genus *Amygdalus* (now known as *Prunus*). Spreading widely by rhizomes, var. *robbiae* is an attractive deep glossy green-leaved plant that is superb for its foliage, but even more interesting when its loose light green floral bracts emerge during spring. Often it is promoted for its greater tolerance to shade and drought. 'Rubra' displays reddish green leaves that turn rich purple in the fall.

E. cyparissias (sye-pa-*ris*-ee-is), cypress spurge, is aptly named for its needlelike blue-green leaves. Reaching 10 to 20 inches tall, this rhizomatous European native blooms with showy red-tinged yellow bracts from late spring to mid summer.

E. myrsinites (mur-sin-*eye*-teez), named for its resemblance to the genus *Myrsine,* is commonly called myrtle euphorbia. Hardy in Zone 5, it hails from the Mediterranean region, is evergreen, and reaches 4 to 8 inches tall. Although short-lived, it is worth growing for its unusual closely set, spiraling, fleshy, bright blue-green, oval to spatula-shaped foliage—topped during late spring to mid summer with vivid yellow bracts.

CULTURE / CARE: Euphorbias typically adapt to various soil types but are at their best in loose, light-textured, sandy or gravelly, well-drained neutral to limy soils. Although quite tolerant of drought, they appear best when the soil is kept just slightly moistened. They prefer full sun to moderate shade; in hot summer locations, they perform best with light to moderate shade (or at least afternoon shade). Wilt diseases of various types are common in areas of very hot summers, especially if grown in full sun with high humidity. No serious pests have been reported. A light shearing after flowering is sometimes given to keep clumps compact and neat in appearance.

PROPAGATION: Stem cuttings may be rooted soon after the bloom period has ended. Clumps may also be divided in spring and fall with good results. Seed is said to germinate irregularly when placed in a warm, moist medium.

Euryops acraeus   PLATE 122
Drakensberg Daisy

A low, sprawling, shrubby, stoloniferous ground cover, Drakensberg daisy reaches 1½ to 2 feet tall, and spreads more than 4 feet across. It has attractive foliage and flowers, and makes an excellent specimen in rock gardens or tucked into a crack between the boulders of a retaining wall. Occasionally used as a moderate-scale general cover or as a walkway border, it is useful in coastal landscapes as it withstands strong ocean breezes and airborne salt.

SCIENTIFIC NAME: *Euryops acraeus* (*yer*-ee-ops ak-*ree*-us). *Euryops* takes its name from the Greek *eu*, well, and *ops*, appearance, in reference to the good looks (i.e., large flowers) of some species. *Acraeus,* growing in high places, refers to the mountainous habitat of this species.

HARDINESS / ORIGIN: Zones 7 to 9; Drakensberg Mountains of South Africa.

LEAVES / FLOWERS / FRUIT: The grayish blue, oblong, ¾-inch-long leaves are evergreen, simple, leathery, and crowded toward the ends of the branches. The daisylike flowers with yellow centers and yellow petals are 1 inch wide and borne from late spring to early summer. Against the bluish foliage, the flower heads stand out like miniature suns.

RATE / SPACING: Growth is moderate to fast. Plants from gallon-sized containers are spaced 2½ to 3½ feet apart.

CULTURE / CARE: Drakensberg daisy is somewhat adaptable to soil, but performs best in well-drained, organically rich, slightly acidic loam. It is quite tolerant to heat, drought, and drying winds, but an occasional deep watering during summer keeps it looking its best. It prefers full sun. Maintenance is not required, although many gardeners prefer to shear plants lightly after blooming to keep them neat and compact.

PROPAGATION: Cuttings, the most common means of propagation, can be rooted during the summer. Seed is also said to be viable.

Fallopia japonica 'Compacta'   PLATE 123
Dwarf Japanese Fleeceflower, Dwarf Mexican Bamboo, Dwarf Japanese Knotweed

Dwarf Japanese fleeceflower (formerly classified as *Polygonum cuspidatum* 'Compactum', *P. reynoutria, Reynoutria japonica*) is a sprawling, rhizomatous, deciduous, herbaceous ground cover that reaches 18 to 35 inches tall and spreads indefinitely. Some consider it an overbearing thug, which it is not. It is a useful brute of a ground cover that should be employed as a low hedge or walkway border where it can be contained or as a large-scale blanket (particularly on slopes) where it can spread and bind soil, the two real joys of its long life.

Far underused for a plant so exceptional in its tolerance to climatic extremes, Japanese fleeceflower accepts cold and heat and seldom shows even the slightest sign of dissatisfaction. In the North, as a border around parking lots or alongside building entrances or walks, Japanese fleeceflower is an excellent choice as it withstands not only drought and heat but also reflected summer sun and radiant heat from the pavement. In winter it dies back, thus saving itself from the snowplow damage customarily associated with such plantings. Limited foot traffic is tolerated.

SCIENTIFIC NAME: *Fallopia japonica* (fa-*lope*-ee-a ja-*pon*-i-ka). *Fallopia* commemorates Gabriele Fallopi (1523–1562), an Italian anatomist and professor at Pisa and Padua, for whom the Fallopian tube was also named. *Japonica* means of Japan.

HARDINESS / ORIGIN: Zones 3 to 10; eastern Asia.

LEAVES / FLOWERS / FRUIT: The deciduous, simple, entire, variously shaped, alternate leaves are usually 3 to 4 inches long, oval, leathery, and colored medium green (reddish in youth and crimson in fall). They appear rugged and attractive. The flowers are borne in profusion in dense clusters and, remarkably, for all their radiance, have no petals. Instead, the showy reddish color comes when the flowers are still in bud. Later, when actually in bloom, the color show is tempered with the pink and white tones of the sepals, the tiny leaflike projections surrounding the base of the flowers. This continues for two weeks during late summer and early fall, then finally, the fruit appears with its showy pink-and-red winglike appendages. One can expect about six weeks of sensational color, a great way to finish out the growing season.

RATE SPACING: Growth is fast to invasive. Plants from quart-sized to gallon-sized containers are spaced 16 to 24 inches apart and should be given plenty of room to spread or be surrounded with concrete or a very deep plastic or metal edging.

HORTICULTURAL SELECTIONS: 'Variegata', flowers pink, leaves variegated green and white, height to 4 feet.

OTHER SPECIES: *F. aubertii* (awe-*bert*-ee-eye), silver lace vine or silvervine fleeceflower, is a vigorous twining vine with light to medium green, 1½- to 3½-inch-long oval to oblong-oval deciduous leaves. Hardy to Zone 5, this species climbs about anything, but if given no support can be used as a moderate-scale to large-scale general cover. It produces narrow panicles of tiny white flowers in mid to late summer.

F. baldschuanica (bald-*shwa*-ni-ka), Bokaravine fleeceflower, is like *F. aubertii* but reported to be evergreen. Other authors dispute this and say that it is deciduous and cannot be reliably distinguished from *F. aubertii*. Both species are functional but less common than *F. japonica*.

CULTURE / CARE: *Fallopia* species prefer full sun but tolerate light shade. They adapt to most types of well-drained soils and, as would be expected, spread more slowly in infertile soils, where they need more water. Dwarf Japanese fleeceflower is extraordinarily drought tolerant, while the other fleeceflowers tolerate short periods of drought. At times they may appeal to the ravenous appetites of pests such as deer, Japanese beetle, aphids, slugs, snails, and spittlebugs. A common disease is leaf spot. Annual maintenance is minimal, although some gardeners prefer to shear or mow dwarf Japanese fleeceflower following the blooming season to neaten plants.

PROPAGATION: Cuttings root readily and are best taken during spring or early summer while the new growth is still soft. Division is very successful as well with dwarf Japanese fleeceflower, and is best carried out during the spring and early fall.

Felicia amelloides   PLATE 124

Blue Marguerite, Blue Daisy, Cape Aster

Blue marguerite is a sprawling, semiwoody, sub-shrubby ground cover that reaches 1½ to 3 feet tall and spreads to more than 5 feet across. A single plant is rather showy as a rock garden or perennial border specimen. Mass plantings are striking. As an edging, atop of retaining walls, and in raised planters (and allowed to trail over), blue marguerite is excellent.

SCIENTIFIC NAME: *Felicia amelloides* (fe-*lis*-ee-a am-e-*loy*-deez). *Felicia* is named after a Mr. Felix, a German official. *Amelloides* refers to this species' resemblance to *Aster amellus*.

HARDINESS / ORIGIN: Zones 9 to 10; South Africa.

LEAVES / FLOWERS / FRUIT: The evergreen foliage is oblong to oval or elliptic, and 1 to 1¼ inches long by ½ inch wide. The daisylike flowers, 1⅜ inches wide, are sky blue with yellow centers and bloom from early summer through fall.

RATE / SPACING: Growth is moderate to relatively fast. Plants from 1- to 2-gallon-sized containers are spaced 3 to 3½ feet apart.

HORTICULTURAL SELECTIONS: 'Astrid Thomas', compact, with medium blue flowers; 'George Lewis', with dark blue flowers; 'Jolly', dwarf, 1 foot tall, medium blue flowers; 'Midnight', with deep blue flowers; 'Reed's Blue', with large blue flowers that have a golden center; 'Reed's White', flowers white with gold centers; 'Rhapsody in Blue', with dark blue flowers; 'San Gabriel', with large flowers; 'San Louis', also with larger than typical flowers; 'Santa Anita', with large blue flowers; 'Santa Anita Variegata', with stippled leaves and large blue flowers.

CULTURE / CARE: Although adaptable to most well drained soils, blue marguerite is best in moderately rich soils. Drought tolerance is good; however, for best appearance and floral display, the soil should be kept slightly moist with occasional deep watering. Blue marguerite prefers full sun to light shade. Its most common problems are powdery mildew and aphids. Although maintenance is not required, a hard shearing following bloom enhances its appearance and may induce further flowering.

PROPAGATION: Stem cuttings root quite well in early to mid summer and may be aided by application of 1000 ppm IBA/talc. Seed is usually sown outdoors in early spring when soil temperatures reach 55°F; germination takes four weeks. A pregermination treatment consisting of a few weeks of refrigeration (while seeds are placed atop of a moist paper towel) is said to improve the results.

Festuca ovina var. *glauca*   PLATE 125

Blue Fescue, Blue Sheep's Fescue

Although its proper classification is often debated (just as likely to be listed as *F. cinerea*, *F. glauca*, and *F. arvensis*), blue fescue is a tuft-forming, blue-leaved grass that serves as a colorful durable ground cover for areas of small, moderate, or large scale. Tufted in 8- to 10-inch-tall, 12- to 18-inch-wide hummocks, it is subtle in all respects, except for the blueness of its fine hairlike foliage. When it comes to blue-colored ground covers, this one has few parallels.

Blue fescue spreads slowly and, when grown in the proper climate, is reliable and has few maintenance needs. Although intense summer heat, especially with high humidity, is not to its liking, neither cold, wind, nor drought is a problem. A few plants grouped together do nicely for accent in front of large rocks and boulders, or even shrubby plants such as broad-spreading selections of spirea, abelia, nandina, and juniper. For an effect that is just as pleasing but much more exotic, try massing several hundred clumps together for a turf area that is as colorful and tranquilizing as a summertime sky. Occasionally and very interestingly, blue fescue is put to use as a border along the edges of a sunny walking path, and it is well suited for arrangement in geometric patterns or combination with taller clump-forming grasses and perennials such as fountain grass and *Sedum* 'Autumn Joy'. Occasional foot traffic is tolerated, but because of blue fescue's hummock-forming nature that could deal you a sprained ankle, it is not recommended.

SCIENTIFIC NAME: *Festuca ovina* var. *glauca* (fes-*tew*-ka oh-*vee*-na *glaw*-ka). *Festuca* comes from Latin and means a stem or blade; *ovina,* also from Latin, refers to sheep, the entire name meaning sheep's grass. Finally, *glauca* refers to a color that is formed by combining shades of blue and green.

HARDINESS / ORIGIN: Zones 4 to 9; central and southwestern Europe.

LEAVES / FLOWERS / FRUIT: The hairlike leaves are evergreen, sky blue, and sharply pointed but not prickly. Slender in cross section, they arch over gracefully and make an appropriate setting for the straw-colored, midsummer flower heads, which arise above the leaves on thin, light brown stems.

RATE / SPACING: Growth is slow. Plants from pint-sized to gallon-sized containers are spaced 10 to 16 inches apart.

HORTICULTURAL SELECTIONS: There are many cultivars that differ primarily in the intensity of their blueness and their height. 'Azurit', 12 inches tall; 'Blaufink' ('Blue Finch'), 6 inches tall; 'Blaufuchs' ('Blue Fox'), 12 inches tall, with light blue foliage; 'Blauglut' ('Blue Glow'), 6 inches tall; 'Blausilber' ('Blue Silver'), 6 inches tall, with bright blue leaves; 'Elijah's Blue', selected by The Plantage, NY, with deep silvery-blue foliage; 'Frühlingsblau' ('Spring Blue'), with good blue springtime color, 6 inches tall; 'Harz', with olive green leaves, 6 inches tall; 'Meer-blau' ('Sea Blue'), with bluish green leaves, 6 inches tall; 'Platinat', with silvery-platinum-blue leaves, 6 to 12 inches tall (sometimes listed as a cultivar of *F. amethystina*); 'Sea Urchin', with rigid spiny leaves and compact habit; 'Silberreiher' ('Silvery Egret'), 6 inches tall, with silvery-blue leaves; 'Soehrenwald', with olive green leaves, 8 inches tall; 'Solling', non-blooming, 8 inches tall, hardy in Zones 6 to 9; 'Tom Thumb' ('Daeumling'), 4 inches tall.

OTHER SPECIES: *F. amethystina* (a-me-*this*-tee-na), large blue fescue, is native to the Alps and outstanding for its vibrant blue, soft, filamentous foliage. Its purple inflorescences are a bit more showy than those of *F. ovina* var. *glauca.* Reaching 8 inches tall by 18 inches wide and hardy in Zones 4 to 8, it is quite compact and very attractive throughout the growing season. 'April Grün', with olive green leaves; 'Bronzeglanz', with bronzy leaves; 'Klose', with olive-colored leaves that turn bronze in winter.

F. tenuifolia (ten-you-i-*foe*-lee-a), from the Latin *tenui,* slender, and *folius,* leaved, is commonly called hair fescue. Indeed, the narrowness of its green foliage is a distinguishing feature of this grass. Tufted in habit, its height ranges from 4 to 6 inches tall. It is considered hardy in Zones 4 to 6 or 7.

CULTURE / CARE: Fescues need excellent drainage and prefer sandy or gravelly, light-textured soils. Their resistance to drought, wind, heat, and cold is far above average, and although they grow in a range of light conditions from light shade to full sun, their color is usually best in full sun. Most of their growth occurs during the spring and fall and, as is typical of other cool-season grasses, they may go through a period of summer dormancy. During this time, and especially in hot summer areas, they may look a bit unkempt. It is important, however, that they not be cut back or divided at this time, as they may not recover. No serious pests or diseases are usually of concern, but high humidity during the heat of summer may cause plants to thin in their centers; in such climates, springtime division every few years may be needed to maintain health and attractiveness. Mowing once during early spring is a good practice to neaten plantings.

PROPAGATION: Division works best during spring. Seed germinates readily but should only be used to propagate the species, not the cultivars (which will not come true). Seed of the species is readily available, takes about seven days to germinate, and fills out a 4-inch-pot (starting with 20 seeds/pot) in three months.

Ficus pumila   PLATE 126
Creeping Fig, Climbing Fig, Creeping Rubber Plant

A small, neatly leaved, woody vine, creeping fig is an easily grown, pleasant-appearing ground cover. One of my favorites for small areas in warm climates, this species, a true fig, clings by aerial rootlets. Without support, it makes a trailing ground cover of dense habit. As such, its height ranges from ½ to 1½ inches, and it spreads indefinitely. Unless one has unlimited space, creeping fig should be used in areas where its spread can be controlled. For this reason it is often planted within contained areas and is excellent in elevated planters. It forms splendid green carpets and makes a fine setting for shrubby and treelike species of figs, palms, and tall, clump-forming tropical herbs. Minimal foot traffic is tolerated.

SCIENTIFIC NAME: *Ficus pumila* (*fie*-kus *pew*-mi-la). *Ficus* comes from the Latin word for fig. *Pumila,* also Latin, means dwarf.

HARDINESS / ORIGIN: Zones 8 or 9 to 10; China, Japan, Australia, and northern Vietnam.

LEAVES / FLOWERS / FRUIT: The leaves, like those of English ivy (*Hedera helix*) and wintercreeper (*Euonymus fortunei*), are dimorphic, meaning that the juvenile (nonflowering) form has a different leaf shape than the adult form. The primary ornamental attribute of this species is the juvenile leaves, which are heart-shaped to oval-shaped, evergreen, 1 inch long, and colored a very attractive glossy green. As the plant climbs, certain branches become very stout and develop leaves that are thicker and more leathery than the typical juvenile growth. These are the branches that produce flowers and fruit. The mature leaves become oblong or elliptical and may reach 2 to 4 inches long. The minute flowers give rise to pear-shaped inedible fruit that may reach 2 inches long and is orange, then red-purple.

RATE / SPACING: Growth is tentative until plants are well rooted, then it is fast. Plants from pint-sized to gallon-sized containers are spaced 14 to 36 inches apart.

HORTICULTURAL SELECTIONS: 'Arina', a Danish selection, more vigorous spreading, more densely branched; 'Minima', with smaller leaves; 'Variegata', attractively variegated green with white margins.

OTHER SPECIES: *F. nipponicum* (ni-*pon*-i-kum), Japanese fig, is similar to *F. pumila* but with shiny, pointed evergreen leaves.

CULTURE / CARE: Creeping fig grows best in an organically rich, loamy soil. It tolerates short periods of drought, yet is best when the soil is kept moist. It prefers full sun to light shade, but the extreme heat and light that come from planting in front of a southern or western exposure should be avoided. No serious diseases plague it, and probably the most troublesome pests are mites. Maintenance consists only of cutting back branches as they outgrow their bounds.

PROPAGATION: Cuttings are easily rooted throughout the year. Divisions of rooted stem sections can be dug and transplanted during spring and fall.

Filipendula vulgaris   PLATE 127
Dropwort, Meadowsweet

Dropwort is a stemless, herbaceous, leafy ground cover with fernlike, soft-textured foliage. Although its leaves seldom ascend more than 1 foot, when in flower the plant reaches a height of 2 or 3 feet. Its

roots have been used for tanning, and its flowers contain an oil that smells like wintergreen. As a ground cover, however, it is used on a small to moderate scale to blanket the ground in place of turf. Or, it is used as a companion in herbaceous perennial borders. It spreads 1 foot across. No foot traffic is tolerated.

SCIENTIFIC NAME: *Filipendula vulgaris* (fil-i-*pen*-dyu-la vul-*gay*-ris). *Filipendula* takes its scientific name from the Latin *filum,* a thread, and *pendulus,* hanging, supposedly in reference to the root tubers of some species which are connected by threads. *Vulgaris* means common.

HARDINESS / ORIGIN: Zones 3 to 8; Europe.

LEAVES / FLOWERS / FRUIT: The deciduous, fernlike, 4- to 10-inch long, feathery leaves are composed of many pairs of 1-inch-long, equally fernlike, rich green leaflets. Soft and lacy in texture, they form a platterlike, leafy rosette that blends in well with most any plant and, with the creamy white, red-tinged, ¾-inch-wide flowers of early to mid summer, they lend an element of subtle contrast. Each flower cluster is held upon a tall upright or arching stalk, reaches ¾ inch wide, and is pleasantly fragrant. The fruit is nonornamental.

RATE / SPACING: Growth is moderate to fast. Plants from pint-sized to quart-sized containers are spaced 14 to 16 inches apart.

HORTICULTURAL SELECTIONS: 'Flore Pleno' (double dropwort), with double white flowers.

CULTURE / CARE: Dropwort grows well in most soils, but prefers slightly alkaline, well-drained loam. It shows moderate tolerance to drought and prefers full sun to moderate shade. It is prone to no serious diseases or pests. Its maintenance needs are limited to an occasional dividing—if overcrowding occurs—and clipping off the flower stalks following the blooming season.

PROPAGATION: Division of the tuberous rootstalk is most successful during spring or fall. Seed, which is available commercially, germinates readily.

Fittonia verschaffeltii var. *verschaffeltii*   PLATE 128
Fittonia, Mosaic Plant, Nerve Plant

Fittonia is exceptional for its attractively variegated foliage and makes a useful general cover or facer for tropical gardens. As such, it helps to brighten up shaded areas and provides color contrast with the green foliage of other ground covers and shrubs. Reaching 4 to 6 inches tall and spreading 1½ feet across, it is a splendid, easy-care, creeping, herbaceous ground cover.

SCIENTIFIC NAME: *Fittonia verschaffeltii* var. *verschaffeltii* (fi-*toe*-nee-a vare-sha-*felt*-ee-ee). *Fittonia* commemorates Elizabeth and Sarah Mary Fitton, botanical authors and sisters. *Verschaffeltii* commemorates M. Verschaffelt, a nineteenth-century Belgian nurseryman.

HARDINESS / ORIGIN: Zones 9 to 10 or 11, intolerant of extended temperatures below 50°F; Columbia to Peru.

LEAVES / FLOWERS / FRUIT: The evergreen, oppositely arranged, and ovate to elliptic leaves range from 3 to 4 inches long by ¾ to 1½ inches across. With broadly pointed ends, they display prominent rose-red veins against their dark green blades. The tiny flowers, which are borne in small spikes in the axils of bracts, have two-lipped, yellow, tubular corollas. Although interesting, in comparison to the foliage, the ornamental worth of the flowers is insignificant.

RATE / SPACING: Growth is moderate. Plants from pint-sized to quart-sized containers are spaced 10 to 14 inches apart.

HORTICULTURAL SELECTIONS: Var. *argyroneura* (silver nerve plant, silver threads, silver-net plant, silver plant, white leaf, nerve plant), is cultivated more often than the species and displays glossy green leaves with strikingly white midrib and veins.

CULTURE / CARE: Fittonia is best in organically rich loam with moderately acidic soil and excellent drainage. It is quick to wilt in dry weather and should be watered frequently enough to keep the soil slightly moist at all times. The humidity of the surrounding air should also be relatively high, and shelter from drying winds should be a priority when selecting a location. It prefers moderate to dense shade. Its primary disease problems are root rot, stem rot, and leaf blight. Aphids and slugs are sometimes problematic. Little or no maintenance is required, although shearing is sometimes practiced to thicken plantings.

PROPAGATION: Stem cuttings root very easily; treatment with 1000 ppm IBA/talc is beneficial but not necessary.

Forsythia × *intermedia* 'Arnold Dwarf'   PLATE 129
Dwarf Arnold Forsythia

This compact-growing, low-spreading, mound-forming, sprawling, woody shrub reaches only 2 to 4 feet high and spreads 6 to 7 feet across. It is truly a dwarf forsythia. Although it blooms very little in comparison to the tall forms, it has attractive foliage and is excellent for use as a dwarf hedge, or as an erosion-controlling bank cover or foundation facing. The foliage adds a nice, soft, cool green texture and communicates a warm, lush, inviting feeling. Suitable companions are nearly endless, but colorful foreground plantings of annuals, such as begonia or impatiens, and colorful ground covers, such as purple selections of coral bells (*Heuchera*) and bugle-

weed (*Ajuga*), the rich blue of blue fescue (*Festuca ovina* var. *glauca*), or the striking red of Japanese blood grass (*Imperata cylindrica* 'Red Baron'), work well. Behind or above dwarf Arnold forsythia one might consider nearly any type of deciduous tree or colorful or dark-green-leaved taller-growing shrubs, such as dwarf purple-leaved plum (*Prunus* × *cistena*), photinia (*Photinia fraseri*), holly (*Ilex* species), and boxwood (*Buxus* species). Forsythias are also said to be compatible with black walnut (*Juglans nigra*).

SCIENTIFIC NAME: *Forsythia* × *intermedia* 'Arnold Dwarf' (for-*sith*-ee-a in-ter-*mee*-dee-a). *Forsythia* is named after William Forsyth (1737–1805), superintendent of the Royal Gardens of Kensington Palace. *Intermedia* refers to the traits of this hybrid being between, or intermediate, to those of its parents. 'Arnold Dwarf' refers to this cultivar's origin at the Arnold Arboretum of Harvard University, and its size, small.

HARDINESS / ORIGIN: Zones 5 to 8; hybridized at the Arnold Arboretum in 1941 from *F.* × *intermedia* and *F. japonica* var. *saxatilis*.

LEAVES / FLOWERS / FRUIT: The lively light green, deciduous leaves are either entire or three-parted. Each leaf or leaflet is oval to oblong-oval and reaches 2½ inches long with teeth along its edges. Occasionally a few hints of purple creep in during the fall season. The flowers are not borne in great numbers. Alone or in groups of up to three, they are pale greenish yellow and open during early to mid spring. The fruit is nonornamental.

RATE / SPACING: Growth is moderate. Plants from 1- to 2-gallon-sized containers are spaced 2 to 3 feet apart.

OTHER SPECIES: ***F. viridissima* 'Bronxensis'** (vir-i-*dis*-i-ma bronks-*en*-sis), named after the Bronx, NY, as it originated at the New York Botanical Garden, is commonly called dwarf Bronx forsythia or dwarf green-stem forsythia. The only other significant ground-covering type of forsythia, it is also an excellent dwarf hedge or foundation-facing ground cover. It is somewhat more erect in habit than 'Arnold Dwarf' and, when planted en masse, makes a good bank stabilizer. It is a bit showier in flower than 'Arnold Dwarf', is hardy in Zones 5 to 8, and displays a low, broad, spreading habit and height of 1 to 3 feet tall, with spread of 2 to 4 feet wide. Entire or three-parted, like 'Arnold Dwarf', the bright green foliage of 'Bronxensis' reaches ¾ to 1¾ inches long by ½ inch wide and has toothed edges. Its flowers, more numerous than those of 'Arnold Dwarf', are bright yellow and effective from early to mid spring (prior to leaf emergence). Growth occurs at a moderate pace, and the same spacing should be used as for 'Arnold Dwarf'.

CULTURE / CARE: Forsythias are easy to grow, and although they perform best in medium-textured acidic loam, they adapt to almost any well-drained soil. Once they become established, they are moderately tolerant of drought and only require watering during the summer season. They prefer full to moderate shade. Their most common pests are four-lined plant bug, Japanese weevil, northern root knot nematode, aphids, and spider mites. Diseases of greatest significance are bacterial crown gall, leaf spots, and dieback. Maintenance needs are few if any, but some gardeners prefer to prune plants in the spring immediately after flowering.

PROPAGATION: Cuttings root quickly and reliably during early summer; treatment with 3000 ppm IBA/talc is helpful but not necessary.

Fragaria   PLATE 130
Strawberry

This genus, in addition to producing delicious fruits, also gives us some splendid herbaceous ground covers. Since they spread either by plantlet-producing stolons or creeping rhizomes, they are well suited for binding soil on gradually sloping banks. They are also good as turf substitutes in small-scale to moderate-scale plantings and are quite at home in naturalized, lightly shaded woodland settings. Attractive as facings to large shrubs and trees, they also produce fruit that, while not comparable to garden strawberries, can be flavorful. Very limited foot traffic is tolerated.

Interestingly, the common name strawberry came about as these plants were often mulched with straw, reputedly a means of reducing fungal problems during wet weather. Over the years, strawberries have been extensively employed in herbal remedies. They have been used as a treatment for constipation, indigestion, fever, and fainting. Blood, liver, and spleen disorders were also previously believed to be helped by the consumption of the fruit or teas made from the foliage.

SCIENTIFIC NAME: *Fragaria* (fra-*gay*-ree-a / fra-*gare*-ee-a) is derived from the Latin *fraga* or *fragans,* sweet smelling, here referring to the fruit.

HARDINESS / ORIGIN: Zones 4 or 5 to 9; Europe, North and South America.

LEAVES / FLOWERS / FRUIT: Typically the leaves are three-parted and evergreen. The flowers are dainty, five-petaled, white, and borne in spring. The red fruit is edible.

RATE / SPACING: Growth is moderate to relatively fast. Plants from pint-sized or quart-sized containers are spaced 8 to 14 inches apart.

SPECIES: *F. chiloensis* (chil-oh-*en*-sis), named for Chile, one of its native habitats, is commonly called chiloe strawberry or beach strawberry. Also native to North America from Alaska to California, it reaches up to 6 inches tall and spreads indefinitely. It is hardy in Zones 4 to 9 and exhibits evergreen leaves that are composed of three oval, 1- to 2-inch-long, toothed, shiny, dark green, silky-haired leaflets that turn reddish in fall. Its white five-petaled flowers reach ¾ inch wide and are effective during spring. The dark red fruit looks like a typical strawberry but is considerably smaller, firmer, and less palatable. 'Elsie Frye' has larger flowers; 'Green Pastures' is noteworthy for its giant 1½-inch-wide flowers and its habit of not forming fruit.

F. 'Pink Panda', strawberry potentilla, is hardy to Zone 6. It is an interesting hybrid formed by crossing unknown species of *Fragaria* and *Potentilla.* The result, a large pink-flowered strawberry-like herb, is beautiful in flower and even produces an occasional edible fruit. 'Lipstick', similar to 'Pink Panda' but with deep pink flowers; 'Shades of Pink', a mixed group of seedlings of 'Pink Panda', displays flowers that range from light to dark pink.

F. vesca (*ves*-ka), European strawberry, sow-teat strawberry, or woodland strawberry, is native to the European Alps, reaches up to 8 inches tall, and spreads indefinitely. Hardy in Zones 5 or 6 to 10, this species is similar in habit to *F. chiloensis,* but displays leaflets to 2½ inches long and flowers and fruit (⅜ to ¾ inch wide) throughout the season. Variety *albicarpa* ('Fructo-alba') has white fruit that although tasty is usually overlooked by birds; 'Alexandria', a dwarf form, does not produce runners; var. *monophylla,* with many simple leaves as well as compound leaves of three leaflets; 'Multiplex', with small double white flowers; var. *semperflorens,* nearly without runners and blooming spring through late summer; 'Variegata' has leaves with striking white and green variegation.

F. virginiana (ver-jin-ee-*aye*-na), wild strawberry, or Virginia strawberry, is native to the eastern part of North America and ranges from 4 to 12 inches tall. Hardy in Zones 5 or 6 to 9, it tends to spread indefinitely. Its leaflets range from 1 to 4 inches long and, during fall, often pick up hues of red. It flowers from spring to early summer and produces small, cone-shaped, tasty fruit well suited for making jam.

CULTURE / CARE: Strawberries are adaptable to a range of soils, but need good drainage for success. They are relatively tolerant of drought, but look best when the soil is kept slightly moist. They prefer full sun to light shade. Disease and pests include nematodes, anthracnose, leaf spot, blight, leaf rot, crown rot, wilt, and mosaic virus. Typical maintenance usually consists of mowing during late winter well before flowering as the growth of new foliage promotes density and renews vigor.

PROPAGATION: Rooted plantlets can be divided during fall or early spring.

Francoa ramosa   PLATE 131
Maiden's Wreath, Bridal Wreath

Maiden's wreath is a basal-leaved, clump-forming, rhizomatous, herbaceous ground cover. It reaches 1 to 2 feet tall (sometimes to 3 feet), spreads 2 to 3 feet across, and although not widely cultivated, is useful as a specimen or background plant in the perennial border. It prefers dry winter climates. As a general cover it is best in naturalistic settings.

SCIENTIFIC NAME: *Francoa ramosa* (frang-*koe*-a ra-*moe*-sa). *Francoa* is named in honor of Francisco Franco, a physician who encouraged the study of botany in sixteenth-century Spain. *Ramosa,* branching, is likely a reference to the inflorescence.

HARDINESS / ORIGIN: Zones 8 to 9 or 10; Chile.

LEAVES / FLOWERS / FRUIT: The leaves are mostly evergreen, leathery, lyre-shaped, 6 to 12 inches long by 2 to 3 inches wide and edged with irregular, wavy lobes. Their surfaces are smooth, medium green to gray-green above, with hairs on the veins on their undersides. The flowers, which are arranged in 6- to 12-inch-long terminal racemes, are elevated well above the foliage on 2- to 3-foot-tall stalks. Each flower is ¾ inch wide, four-petaled, white, and effective during mid summer. The cut flowers make an attractive ornament in a vase, either alone or in combination with other flowers.

RATE / SPACING: Growth is moderate. Plants from pint-sized to quart-sized containers are spaced 2 to 2½ feet apart.

CULTURE / CARE: Maiden's wreath prefers light to moderate shade and is adaptable to most well-drained soils. Although it displays good drought tolerance, it gives its best floral display when the soil is kept slightly moist and the location is relatively cool. No serious diseases seem to affect it, but slugs, snails, soil mealybugs, and aphids all are potential pests. To neaten its appearance, the flower stalks can be removed after the blossoms fade.

PROPAGATION: Clumps can be divided in spring or fall with good results. Seed is sometimes used.

Fuchsia procumbens   PLATE 132
Trailing Fuchsia

For warm-weather climates this horizontally growing, herbaceous, mat-forming ground cover provides season-long color and requires relatively little maintenance. It is known throughout North America as an exceptionally attractive hanging basket plant, but unfortunately only those living in the warmest zones (10 and 11) can appreciate it for the colorful ground cover that it is in its native New Zealand. Trailing fuchsia is best used on a moderate scale, and as one might expect from its use in hanging baskets, it is splendid when trailing over things. For this reason, plant it in elevated planters, on terraces, overhanging the edge of ponds and reflecting pools, and atop retaining walls. It combines well with tall ferns, rubber plants, tall caladium hybrids, and a host of tropical evergreen shrubs and small trees. No foot traffic is tolerated.

SCIENTIFIC NAME: *Fuchsia procumbens* (*few*-sha / *few*-shee-a / *fewks*-ee-a pro-*kum*-benz). *Fuchsia* commemorates Leonhart Fuchs, a sixteenth-century German physician and herbalist. *Procumbens* means procumbent or growing horizontally.

HARDINESS / ORIGIN: Zones 10 to 11; New Zealand.

LEAVES / FLOWERS / FRUIT: The leaves are evergreen, nearly round, ½ to ¾ inch long, and colored dark, shiny green. Attractive to hummingbirds and butterflies, the outstanding flowers of late summer and fall are solitary, ⁵⁄₁₆ inch long, and composed of dark green, leafy bracts that encase other intensely dark red bracts. For all their show, the flowers contain no true petals. The fruit, a bright red to purplish ¾-inch-wide persistent berry, is equally showy.

RATE / SPACING: Growth is moderate to fast. Plants from pint-sized to quart-sized containers are spaced 16 to 24 inches apart.

CULTURE / CARE: Trailing fuchsia is best in organically rich, well-drained soil. Since it is not markedly tolerant to drought, it requires a relatively cool location and moist soil. It prefers full sun and light shade. Pests include aphids, beetles, mealybugs, mites, scales, whitefly, and thrips. Diseases such as blight, root rot, rusts, wilt, dieback, leaf spot, and tomato spotted wilt virus are at times troublesome. Maintenance simply consists of trimming back the stems from time to time as they spread beyond their allotted space.

PROPAGATION: Cuttings and division are both simple and highly successful throughout the year.

Galax urceolata   PLATE 133
Colt's Foot, Beetleweed, Wand Plant, Wand Flower, Galaxy

Colt's foot stands 6 to 12 inches tall and spreads indefinitely by short rhizomes. A basal-leaved herbaceous ground cover, it is best used for general cover or accent planting in naturalized or woodland locations. It makes an excellent edging for woodland paths and functions as a specimen in shady rock gardens. Good companions are rhododendrons, azaleas, and pieris, and its attractive evergreen foliage is valued for flower arrangements. No foot traffic is tolerated.

SCIENTIFIC NAME: *Galax urceolata* (*gay*-laks ur-see-oh-*lay*-ta). *Galax* is derived from the Greek *gala*, milk, in reference to the milky white flowers. *Urceolata*, urn-shaped, also refers to the flowers.

HARDINESS / ORIGIN: Zone 4 or 5 to 9; moist woodlands of North America from Virginia to Georgia, west to Alabama.

LEAVES / FLOWERS / FRUIT: The shiny, evergreen, long-stemmed leaves are arranged in rosettes and arise from the crown. Each dark green leaf is heart-shaped to round, to 5 inches across, toothed on the edges, and often bronzy or reddish tinged in fall. The five-parted tiny white flowers are effective late spring to mid summer and are carried in spikes well above the foliage. The fruit is nonornamental.

RATE / SPACING: Growth is moderate. Plants from pint-sized to quart-sized containers are spaced 12 to 16 inches apart.

CULTURE / CARE: Colt's foot is best in well-drained, organically rich, slightly acidic loam. It is not greatly tolerant of drought, thus the soil should be kept moist with supplemental irrigation during extended periods of hot dry weather. Colt's foot prefers a cool, light to densely shaded, wind-sheltered site. Severe leaf spotting occasionally occurs and can be unsightly. Few serious pest problems have been reported. Little or no maintenance is required, although covering plants with evergreen boughs in winter (in the North where snowcover is unpredictable) is a good practice.

PROPAGATION: Division from early spring to summer is effective and probably better than waiting until fall, which may result in severe winter damage to the leaves as the roots will not have time to reestablish before the cold sets in. Seed can also be used; sow when ripe in a peaty medium and expect germination the following spring.

Galium odoratum　　　　PLATE 134
Sweet Woodruff, Bedstraw

Sweet woodruff is known by several other common names, but nearly all of them indicate its love of wooded habitat. The French refer to it as *musc de bois* (wood musk), while the Germans call it *waldmeister* (master of the woods). The name bedstraw alludes to its use as a pleasant-scented mattress and pillow stuffing.

A low, herbaceous, horizontally spreading, upright-stemmed ground cover, sweet woodruff ranges from 6 to 10 inches tall and spreads indefinitely. In the landscape it provides a soft texture and uniform growth underneath shallowly rooted trees and shrubs. Use sweet woodruff as a general cover for small, medium, and large areas and consider planting it under Sargent crab apples (*Malus sargentii*), which bloom at about the same time, or our lovely native dogwoods, pines, and serviceberries. Sweet woodruff thrives in very dense shade where few other plants can survive and combines well with spring-flowering bulbs, hostas, and ferns. It is even said to be compatible with black walnut (*Juglans nigra*). Occasionally, it is used as an edging for a perennial border or garden path, filling this role with style and grace. No foot traffic is tolerated.

Sweet woodruff contains coumarin (responsible for its vanilla-like scent, when dried) and has been used as an antispasmodic, wound dressing, laxative, antiarthritic, digestive aid, diuretic, calmative, and liver tonic. Due to some people's toxic reactions to coumarin, the medicinal use of sweet woodruff has fallen out of favor. Mixing the foliage into cattle fodder is said to give the milk a pleasant aroma; however this practice has its risks, since, if allowed to become wet, sweet woodruff becomes moldy and in the process produces an anticoagulant which can cause hemorrhaging in livestock. Although not fragrant while green, the dried stems and leaves become very aromatic and, in addition to having supposed insect-repelling properties, are useful in potpourri and perfumes. In the past they have been used as a stuffing for mattresses. Historically, a vanilla-like extract was taken from the stems and leaves. Today, the fresh leaves are still used as a garnish in wines, liquors, and other beverages. The leaves are an essential ingredient of *Maitrank*, the German wine traditionally consumed the first of May.

SCIENTIFIC NAME: *Galium odoratum* (*gay*-lee-um oh-der-*aye*-tum). *Galium* is derived from the Greek *gala*, milk, the leaves of one species having been used to curdle milk. *Odoratum*, fragrant, refers to the pleasant scent of the dried leaves and stems.

HARDINESS / ORIGIN: Zones 4 to 8; Europe and Asia (temperate regions and mountainous tropical areas).

LEAVES / FLOWERS / FRUIT: Depending upon the climate, the leaves are semievergreen or deciduous, in which case they persist late into fall. They are arranged in whorls of six to eight, are oval to narrowly oval, display minutely toothed edges, reach 1½ inches long, and are colored medium green. The tiny white, mildly fragrant flowers are borne atop the stems in 1-inch-diameter clusters during mid to late spring. The fruit, which sometimes follows, is nonornamental.

RATE / SPACING: Growth is moderate. Plants from 3- to 5-inch-diameter containers are spaced 8 to 12 inches apart.

CULTURE / CARE: Sweet woodruff performs best in acidic, rich, loamy, well-drained soil, yet tolerates sandy and heavy soils. It is relatively resistant to drought, but prefers a location where it is protected from strong winds in a cool setting with moderate to dense shade and moist soil. Usually no serious pests or diseases arise, although aphids can be a nuisance at times. Maintenance needs are few if any.

PROPAGATION: Cuttings should be taken in fall or from the first flush of new growth in spring. Division is simple and is best performed during the spring or fall.

Gardenia jasminoides 'Radicans'   PLATE 135
Creeping Cape-jasmine, Creeping Gardenia

Creeping cape-jasmine (sometimes listed under the cultivar name 'Prostrata') is a 1- to 2-foot-tall, 2- to 4-foot-wide, shrubby, spreading ground cover. It tends to be most functional in small-sized to medium-sized plantings as a general cover and is especially nice as a foundation facer or filler inside elevated planters or terrace embankments. No foot traffic is tolerated.

SCIENTIFIC NAME: *Gardenia jasminoides* (gar-*dee*-nee-a jas-min-*oy*-deez). *Gardenia* commemorates Dr. Alexander Garden (1730–1791), a South Carolina botanist. *Jasminoides* means resembling the genus *Jasminum*.

HARDINESS / ORIGIN: Zones 8 or 9 to 10; China.

LEAVES / FLOWERS / FRUIT: The attractive dark glossy green leaves are evergreen, oval, 1 to 2 inches long by ½ to 1 inch wide, and often streaked with white. Thick and leathery, they shine brightly and act as a splendid backdrop to the waxy white, exceptionally fragrant, 1-inch-wide flowers borne from mid summer to early fall. The fruit is an oval, orange, fleshy berry.

RATE / SPACING: Growth is slow. Plants from 1- to 2-gallon-sized containers are spaced 1½ to 2½ feet apart.

HORTICULTURAL SELECTIONS: 'Radicans Variegata', identical to 'Radicans' in habit, but leaves edged with creamy white; 'White Gem', only 1 to 2 feet tall and wide, good for dwarf hedging.

CULTURE / CARE: Creeping cape-jasmine grows best in rich, well-drained, loamy, acidic soil (pH 4.5 to 5.5 is optimal). In overly wet soil, the roots and crown develop fungal rot. On the other hand, it is quite tolerant of heat and drought, provided the soil is kept slightly moistened with an occasional deep watering. It prefers full sun to moderate shade. Northern and eastern exposures are best in desert regions, and moderate shade, especially during the afternoon hours, is best in inland locales. The primary disease problems are leaf spot, canker, powdery mildew, and bud rot. Aphids, mealybugs, thrips, scales, nematodes, and white fly are the most common pests. Maintenance normally consists of providing an annual mulching above the roots to help keep them cool and to conserve water.

PROPAGATION: Stem cuttings root easily during the growing season.

Gaultheria procumbens   PLATE 136
Common Wintergreen, Winterberry, Checkerberry, Teaberry

Common wintergreen is one of our most durable, aesthetically pleasing, and widely distributed natives; yet when it comes to intentionally planting it in our landscapes, most gardeners do not even consider it. Here is a classic example of America's fascination with the exotic to the exclusion of perfectly fine plants that grow right under our noses. It makes a fine, low (3 to 5 inches tall), indefinite-spreading, semi-herbaceous, subshrubby mat with a creeping habit. In the landscape it proves to be a wonderful companion to other taller-growing, acid-loving plants. In particular, it forms a magnificent setting for shrubs and trees such as rhododendrons, azaleas, Japanese pieris, witch hazel, dogwood, and high bush blueberry. Interplanting it with other ground covers such as trailing arbutus, partridge berry, or prince's pine adds naturalness to the landscape. Wintergreen is most at home in woodland gardens and makes a superb edging to woodland paths and borders. Occasional foot traffic is tolerated.

Wintergreen has a wide range of medicinal uses from treating stomachaches and fever to relieving sore muscles and arthritic joints and treating paralysis. The oil of wintergreen leaves and fruit contains methyl salicylate (a compound related to aspirin), which is quite effective when distilled and applied topically. Fall is said to be the best time to collect leaves for medicinal use because that is when the active compound is most concentrated. Thoreau reported drinking a tea of the leaves (a concoction said to posses diuretic and stimulant properties). While boycotting English tea, the American revolutionists employed wintergreen tea as one of their substitutes. Today, due to its ability to irritate the stomach, authorities recommend that wintergreen tea not be ingested. The fruit of wintergreen is edible and really quite tasty. Grouse, partridge, and deer feed on wintergreen fruit during late fall.

Many species of *Gaultheria* possess aromatic foliage and edible fruit. The leaves and fruit of *G. procumbens* were once used in the production of wintergreen flavoring. Today wintergreen flavoring is derived from the sweet birch (*Betula lenta*) or more commonly from the chemistry lab.

SCIENTIFIC NAME: *Gaultheria procumbens* (gaul-*thee*-ree-a pro-*kum*-benz). *Gaultheria* commemorates Jean-François Gaulthier, an eighteenth-century botanist and physician of Quebec. *Procumbens* refers to the procumbent, horizontal-spreading habit of growth.

HARDINESS / ORIGIN: Zones 3 to 7; eastern North America.

LEAVES / FLOWERS / FRUIT: The handsome evergreen leaves emerge either from the ground upon underground stems or immediately atop the foliage of the preceding year's growth. This occurs during the latter weeks of spring and is especially pleasing as the new leaves are light green and often have a wine tinge to them. Within a few short months, the new leaves become tough, leathery, and shiny dark green. They are elliptic to narrowly oval at maturity and reach 2 inches long by 1¼ inches across. They smell of wintergreen and take on lovely tones of purple during fall. The flowers look like little nodding, pinkish white urns. Borne during mid spring, they are reliably pollinated (possibly by ants). The fruit which follows is a fleshy, edible (pleasant-tasting), round, scarlet berry.

RATE / SPACING: Growth is slow. Plants from 3- to 6-inch-diameter containers or clumps are spaced 10 to 14 inches apart.

OTHER SPECIES: *G. adenothrix* (a-*den*-oh-thrix) is a relatively rare, spreading shrublet from Japan. Hardy in Zones 6 to 9, it reaches 9 inches tall, spreads 18 inches across, and is clothed in dark green, roughened, evergreen leaves. Its tiny white bell-shaped flowers are borne in summer and give rise to red fruit.

G. hispidula (*his*-pi-dyu-la), named for its hairy leaves, is commonly called creeping pearl berry, for its shiny white berries. It is a slow, indefinite-spreading, semiwoody, dense low-growing, mat-forming creeper. Plants from 2¼-inch-diameter containers are spaced 4 to 6 inches apart. The species hails from North America, is hardy to Zone 3, and displays shiny, leathery, oval, ⅜-inch-long, dark green leaves. Its white, urn-shaped flowers are borne in late spring.

G. miqueliana (mik-*el*-ee-aye-na), Miquel wintergreen, is a fine woody, low-spreading (to 12 inches tall), shrubby ground cover hardy to Zone 5 and originating in Japan. The leaves are evergreen, elliptic or oval, to 1⅜ inches long, with edges colored a splendid shiny dark green. The flowers of mid to late spring are borne in short, nodding clusters, each appearing as if it were a tiny, hair-covered, white to pinkish urn. The white or pink, small, berrylike fruit ripens in fall and is edible. Plants from 1-gallon-sized

containers are spaced 16 to 24 inches apart.

G. nummularioides (new-mew-*lay*-ree-oy-deez), a carpeting shrub that reaches 4 inches tall, hails from the Himalayas and is hardy to Zone 7. It displays small, attractive, oval, evergreen leaves that are borne upon long flattish stems. Flowering occurs during the summer with a display of white or pink-tinged tiny bells. The fruit that follows is bluish black.

G. ovatifolia (oh-vat-i-*foe*-lee-a), named for its oval-shaped leaves, is commonly called Oregon wintergreen. A sprawling, shrubby ground cover, it reaches 8 inches tall, is native from British Columbia to Idaho, is hardy to Zone 6, and is noteworthy for its tough, evergreen, 1½-inch-long leathery leaves. Its small white urn-shaped solitary flowers are covered with fine hairs and produced in spring. In time, they develop into berrylike scarlet beacons of summer. Plants from gallon-sized containers are spaced 12 to 16 inches apart.

G. shallon (*sha*-lon), named from the Native American name for this species, is commonly called salal or shallon. This superb western North American native is popular among florists who use its branches and leaves in flower arrangements. It is a shrubby, rhizomatous ground cover that is hardy to Zone 7 or 8 and is well suited to covering vast areas in large-scale shady settings. Typically it reaches 3 to 4 feet tall, spreads over 3 feet across, and is handsomely decorated with deep green, roughened, oval to nearly round, 4-inch-wide, rough-edged evergreen leaves. Its white or pinkish bell-shaped flowers are borne during late spring or early summer, and its purple fruit ripens to black by late summer. Plantings are best started from container-grown plants, as bare-root transplants may take up to two years to recover and show new growth. Plants from quart- to 2-gallon-sized containers are spaced 14 to 24 inches apart.

CULTURE / CARE: *Gaultheria* species are at their best in relatively organic, acidic soil of constant moisture. Even so, they often grow well in sandy soils, provided moisture levels are adequate. The best light conditions are light to moderate shade, yet at times these species can be coaxed into growing in full sun. Pests include aphids and thrips, and at times diseases such as leaf spots, black mildew, gall, and powdery mildew can be troublesome but rarely serious. Maintenance needs are few to nonexistent.

PROPAGATION: Cuttings taken in early summer will root, although they often take quite a while. For most purposes, division or seed is more efficient. Seed usually is sown in fall and germinates the following spring.

Gaylussacia brachycera PLATE 137
Box Huckleberry

Box huckleberry is an attractive, low, rhizomatous-spreading, shrubby ground cover. Ranging from 6 to 8 inches tall and spreading indefinitely, it is valued as a specimen in naturalized settings where it combines well with pines, rhododendrons, azaleas, heathers, and heaths. It is neat and tidy, needs little care, and can be used as a small-scale to moderate-scale general cover. It is interesting that box huckleberry was introduced into cultivation as far back as 1796. Later it was forgotten but now is receiving attention once again. In the Amity-Hall area of central Pennsylvania there exists a mile-long colony that covers 300 acres and is thought to have originated from a single plant over 12,000 years ago.

SCIENTIFIC NAME: *Gaylussacia brachycera* (gay-lou-*say*-shee-a bra-*kiss*-a-ra). *Gaylussacia* is named after J. L. Gay-Lussac. *Brachycera,* Latin for short-horned, likely refers to the appearance of the female floral apparatus.

HARDINESS / ORIGIN: Zones 5 or 6 to 9; Delaware to West Virginia and Tennessee.

LEAVES / FLOWERS / FRUIT: The evergreen, simple, elliptic to oval, dark shiny green leaves have a finely toothed edge, reach ¾ to 1 inch long, and often develop a reddish cast when grown in full sun. During winter they range from bronze to reddish purple. The flowers, which are effective from mid to late spring, are ¼ inch long, white to pinkish, and urn-shaped. Interestingly, in order for the summer-ripening bluish berrylike fruit to form, two different plants must be present since individuals are self-sterile. The fruit is edible, although full of seeds and relatively tasteless.

RATE / SPACING: Growth is slow. Plants from gallon-sized containers are spaced 2 to 3 feet apart.

CULTURE / CARE: Box huckleberry requires well-drained, porous, organically rich, acidic soils (pH 4.5 to 5.5). Because its drought tolerance is marginal, the soil must be kept moist at all times. Plants grow well in full sun to moderate shade. No serious pests or diseases seem to effect them. Maintenance needs are minimal.

PROPAGATION: Stem cuttings, which may be rooted during the growing season or during late fall with bottom heat, benefit from application of 8000 ppm IBA/talc. If seed is used it should be sown immediately upon ripening, with germination occurring the following spring.

Gazania rigens PLATE 138
Trailing Gazania

Marvelously utilitarian, this trailing, herbaceous, rugged ground cover ranges from 6 to 8 inches tall and spreads indefinitely. It is excellent for edging walkways, driveways, and for use as a turf substitute around driveways and parking areas. Needless to say, it is tough and withstands a fair amount of heat. It also is functional on a moderate to large scale around building foundations, in front of stone walls and fences as a facing plant, and on moderately sloping embankments for soil retention. Infrequent foot traffic is tolerated.

SCIENTIFIC NAME: *Gazania rigens* (ga-*zay*-nee-a *rye*-jenz). Some say that *Gazania* is named from the Latin *gaza,* treasure or riches, in reference to the large, showy flowers. Others claim that it commemorates Theodore of Gaza (1398–1478), a Greek scholar who translated the botanical works of Theophrastus into Latin. *Rigens,* rigid or stiff, refers possibly to the foliage.

HARDINESS / ORIGIN: Zones 8 to 10; South Africa.

LEAVES / FLOWERS / FRUIT: The evergreen, rather elongated leaves are formed in attractive rosettelike arrangements originating from the base of the plants. Each leaf reaches 4 to 5 inches long by ½ inch wide, is colored gray-green on top, and covered with white hairs below. In a word, the leaves are attractive, but the magnificent, daisylike flowers are responsible for trailing gazania's mass appeal. Due to extensive hybridization, there are numerous cultivars that come in various shades and combinations of yellow, orange, gold, and red. The typical species displays flowers that are 3 inches wide, held upon 4- to 6-inch-tall stalks, and colored orange with a dark brown, white-dotted splotch in the center. They open with the sun from spring through summer. The fruit is nonornamental.

RATE / SPACING: Growth is moderate to fast. Plants from 2½- to 4-inch-wide containers are spaced 10 to 14 inches apart.

HORTICULTURAL SELECTIONS: The horticultural selections are so many and so terribly mixed up that they are often categorized by hybrid group. Those described here represent a portion of what is offered. Most are probably hybrids (sometimes listed as cultivars of *G. splendens,* probably the same thing as *G. rigens*). 'Aztec Queen', a group of multicolored selections; 'Colorama', with flowers to 4 inches wide in mixed colors; 'Copper King', with orange flowers and markings in various colors; 'Fiesta Red', with dark reddish orange flowers; 'Fire Emerald', flowers 3 to 3½ inches wide in various colors but characteristically with emerald green petal bases; 'Gold Rush', with orange-yellow flowers and brown basal spots; var. *leucoleana,* with 1½-inch-wide yellow flowers; 'Moon Glow', with double yellow flowers; 'Sunburst', with 2-inch-wide orange flowers and black centers, leaves gray; 'Sun Glow', with yellow flowers.

OTHER SPECIES: **G. linearis** (li-nee-*air*-is), named for its linear (narrow) foliage, is commonly called treasure flower. It is a stemless, low-growing, herbaceous ground cover with hardiness about the same as that of *G. rigens.* Its gray-green, 4- to 8-inch-long, evergreen leaves are arranged in basal rosettes. The flowers are solitary, daisylike, to 2¾ inches across, and elevated on stalks to a height of 14 inches. Colored yellow or orange, sometimes with a dark brown spot at the base of their petals, they are effective spring to summer. The fruit is nonornamental.

CULTURE / CARE: Gazanias are tolerant of most soils (even those low in fertility) and thus are easily satisfied. They do, however, dislike saturated or poorly drained soils. Although tolerant of drought, they often require watering during extended dry periods. They prefer full sun. Their most common pests include soil mealybugs and thrips. Crown rot is the only disease of significance. Maintenance usually consists of mowing after flowering to neaten appearance and stimulate new growth.

PROPAGATION: Named cultivars should be propagated vegetatively. Division is easily accomplished during the cooler months. Cuttings may also be rooted at this time; they respond well to 1000 IBA/talc when stuck in a porous medium. If seed is used, it should be sown during spring, with germination occurring in about one or two weeks.

Gelsemium sempervirens   PLATE 139

Carolina Jessamine, Carolina Yellow Jessasmine, Yellow Jessamine, Evening Trumpet Flower, Carolina Wild Woodbine, Yellow False Jessamine

A shrubby, twining vine, Carolina jessamine, the state flower of South Carolina, climbs with support. When unsupported, it reaches 3 feet tall, spreads 20 to 30 feet across, and is useful for its sprawling, ground-covering habit. The tenacious nature of this native prize can be best appreciated as a large-scale covering for vast areas where it will not interfere with shrubs and trees. Sloping highway embankments and median sections are ideal, but on a smaller scale, it can be planted next to a retaining wall over which the stems can cascade gracefully and breezes can pick up the marvelous fragrance of the flowers. No foot traffic is tolerated.

The leaves, bark, stems, roots, and flowers are poisonous and when ingested will cause gastroin-

testinal and motor dysfunction and sometimes death through respiratory failure. Thus, Carolina jessamine should not be planted in a location where children play nor should it be planted within or around the perimeter of livestock corrals or pastures.

SCIENTIFIC NAME: *Gelsemium sempervirens* (jel-*sem*-ee-um sem-per-*vie*-renz). *Gelsemium* is the Latinized version of *gelsomino,* an Italian word for jasmine. *Sempervirens,* in Latin, means always green and refers to the evergreen leaves.

HARDINESS / ORIGIN: Zones 7 or 8 to 9; woodlands of eastern North America from Virginia south.

LEAVES / FLOWERS / FRUIT: The leaves, for the most part, are evergreen but tend to be only semievergreen in the northern part of the species' range. Colored dark shiny green, they are relatively long and narrow, to 4 inches long by 1¼ inches wide, and show lovely purplish tones during the winter. The bright yellow flowers borne from late winter to early spring (sometimes sporadically again in fall) are trumpet-shaped and very pleasantly fragrant. They reach 1½ inches wide and are unmistakable harbingers of spring. Oftentimes they alert us to fall as well, as they sometimes reappear, less numerously, for a late-season encore. The fruit is nonornamental.

RATE / SPACING: Growth is moderate. Plants from 1- to 2-gallon-sized containers are spaced 3 to 4 feet apart.

HORTICULTURAL SELECTIONS: 'Pride of Augusta' ('Plena'), double-flowering, with the normal spring bloom period extending into summer.

OTHER SPECIES: **G. rankinii** (rank-*in*-ee-eye) is far less common than *G. sempervirens,* which it resembles superficially but differs in its pleasing attribute of flowering profusely in late fall—in addition to sporadically during winter and heavily again in early spring—and in its somewhat slower growth rate. It is hardy in Zones 7 to 9 and hails from Alabama, Florida, and North Carolina. Its flowers are odorless, and its fruit reaches ½ inch long.

CULTURE / CARE: Although jessamines adapt well to most soils, they clearly prefer a rich, fertile, well-drained, acidic loam. They tolerate short periods of drought, yet appreciate an occasional deep watering during the summer months. They prefer full sun to light shade for maximum flower production.

PROPAGATION: Cuttings taken during early summer root fairly well. Seed should be collected as soon as it ripens, then stored in a cool, dry location prior to sowing the following spring.

Genista   PLATE 140

Broom

The common name broom comes from the long, narrow, nearly leafless, green, photosynthetic stems of the upright-growing species within this genus of some 75 to 90 species. In the past, and probably in some places still today, the stems were bound together and used for sweeping. The ground-covering forms are not so good for this as their stems have a greater tendency to branch. They are, however, very good for covering up the soil. Generally they range from ½ to 3 feet tall and spread 2 to 3 feet across. They are tough, dense, and showy in flower. As general covers, they can substitute for turf on a small to moderate scale, but more often they are employed as interesting rock garden and perennial border specimens. As such, they are superb in combination with heaths, heathers, carnations, and bell flowers, and are excellent upon slopes, terraces, and within planters. No foot traffic is tolerated.

SCIENTIFIC NAME: *Genista* (je-*nis*-ta) is the ancient Latin name for broom plant.

HARDINESS / ORIGIN: See individual species for hardiness; Europe to western Asia, with some species naturalized in North America.

LEAVES / FLOWERS / FRUIT: The leaves are usually quite small, either simple or trifoliate (with three leaflets), medium to dark or silvery-green, and deciduous. Their pealike flowers are usually arranged in clusters at the ends of the branches, and range from sulfur yellow to golden yellow. The fruit which follows is reminiscent of miniature pea pods.

RATE / SPACING: Growth is slow to moderate. Plants from quart-sized to gallon-sized containers are spaced 1½ to 2¼ feet apart unless noted otherwise.

SPECIES: *G. germanica* (ger-*man*-i-ka), named for its central and southern European origin, is commonly called German woadwaxen or German broom. Hardy in Zones 5 to 7, it reaches 12 inches tall by 12 inches wide and is simple-leaved and spiny-branched. The flowers, borne in early summer, produce a brilliant show of yellow blossoms. Plants from pint-sized to quart-sized containers are spaced 10 to 12 inches apart.

G. hispanica (his-*pan*-i-ka), meaning of Spain, is commonly called Spanish gorse or Spanish broom. It reaches 12 inches tall, spreads 2 feet wide, hails from Spain and northern Italy, and is hardy in Zones 7 to 9. Its stems are covered with simple, oblong leaves, and sharp spines and, during late spring and early summer, a multitude of bright yellow flowers.

G. horrida (hor-*i*-da), named from the Latin *horrida,* shaggy, rough, or bristly, for its spiny branches, is commonly called cushion woadwaxen. Native to Spain and southern France, it is hardy to Zone 7, reaches 1½ feet tall, and is very densely branched. Its silvery-gray leaflets are grouped in threes and lend subtle contrast to the yellow flowers of mid summer to early fall.

G. lydia (*lid*-ee-a), Lydian broom, named for the ancient maritime province of Lydia in western Turkey, this species reaches 1½ feet tall, hails from eastern Europe, and is hardy in Zones 7 to 9. It is an excellent dwarf shrublet with slender, pendulous branches and bright golden-yellow flowers from late spring to early summer.

G. pilosa (pie-*low*-sa), meaning downy in Latin, is commonly called silky-leaf woadwaxen. Native to Europe, this procumbent species is hardy in Zones 6 to 8, reaches 12 inches tall, and roots along its branches as it spreads. Its leaves are simple, silky-haired, and serve as a wonderful backdrop to the bright yellow flowers of early summer. Variety *procumbens* reaches only 2 inches tall by 3 feet wide; 'Vancouver Gold', a popular dark-green-leaved, 4- to 6-inch-tall, 3- to 4-foot-wide cultivar that is particularly easy to care for (and many feel more attractive) as it does not set seed, was selected by E. H. Lohbrunner of Victoria, British Columbia, and named in 1983 at the University of British Columbia Botanical Garden for its profusion of golden-yellow flowers from late spring to early summer.

G. sagittalis (saj-i-*tay*-lis), meaning like an arrow in Latin and named for its branches which are winged like the fletching of an arrow, is commonly called arrow broom. This intriguing species is hardy in Zones 3 or 4 to 8, hails from central Europe, reaches 4 to 18 inches tall, and spreads 2 or 3 feet wide. It displays a horizontal-spreading habit, simple ¾-inch-long, oval to oblong, hair-covered leaves, and numerous bright yellow, early summertime flowers. Plants from pint-sized to quart-sized containers are spaced 8 to 12 inches apart.

G. sylvestris (sil-*ves*-tris), meaning sylvan (wooded habitat), is commonly called forest broom or Dalmatian broom. Hailing from southeastern Europe, it reaches 6 inches tall and is hardy to Zone 6. It is clothed with sharp spines and narrow, simple leaves. Its flowers are bright yellow and borne during early to midsummer. Variety *pungens* is covered with even more spines than the species.

G. tinctoria (tink-*toe*-ree-a), named for its usefulness as a dye, is commonly called dyer's greenwood. It is characterized by furrowed branches (that appear striped), hails from Europe and western Asia, and reaches 2 to 3 feet tall. Hardy in Zones 4 to 7 or 8, it is clothed in bright green, deciduous, elliptic to oblong, 1-inch-long leaves. Its flowers, borne early summer to early fall, are bright yellow. Variety *humifusa* reaches only 2 inches tall by 1 foot wide; 'Plena' has brighter yellow flowers; 'Royal Gold', a low-growing selection, carries numerous golden-yellow flowers in mid summer.

CULTURE / CARE: Ground-covering brooms are able

to withstand considerable drought and are at their best in alkaline to partially acidic, infertile, well-drained, sandy or rocky soils. Even so, they prefer an occasional deep summer watering. Watering too frequently, however, makes them prone to rot and blight. They prefer full sun to light shade. If possible, they should be sighted in a location where there is air movement to help keep their leaves and stems dry and to prevent fungus infestations. The diseases of greatest consequence are fungal blight, dieback, powdery mildew, and rust. Bean aphid, scales, genista caterpillar, and rabbits are the most likely pests. Maintenance is usually limited to a light pruning after flowering, if a neat compact habit is desirable.

PROPAGATION: Division is simple and effective throughout spring and summer. Stem cuttings root well through the year and are said to be helped by treatment with 3000 to 8000 ppm IBA/talc. Seed propagation, although tricky, is also said to be successful if approached as follows: collect seed immediately upon ripening and, without allowing it to dry out, soak it in sulfuric acid for 30 minutes, then soak it in very hot water (190°F) for 180 hours before sowing.

Geranium
Cranesbill

PLATE 141

The "true" geraniums—not the geraniums you buy in hanging baskets each spring or grow in a planter on your patio (which are not geraniums at all but actually members of the genus *Pelargonium*)—are excellent ground covers for edging pathways and for facing shrubs, particularly in border settings. Also, they are fabulous as specimens in rock gardens, as small-scale lawn substitutes, foundation facers, and soil binders on moderate-sized slopes. They combine well with a host of trees, shrubs, and herbaceous perennials, and in some species, the fragrance exuded by the delightfully aromatic foliage perfumes the surrounding air. Geraniums are said to be capable of growing in conjunction with the roots of black walnut trees (*Juglans nigra*). No foot traffic is tolerated.

SCIENTIFIC NAME: *Geranium* (je-*ray*-nee-um) is derived from the Greek *geranos,* a crane, and refers to the fruit which resembles the head and beak of a crane.

HARDINESS / ORIGIN: Zones 3 to 10; Europe, Asia, and North America.

LEAVES / FLOWERS / FRUIT: The leaves typically are medium to dark green, tooth-edged, coarsely divided, hairy, long basal-stemmed, shield-shaped, and sometimes fragrant. Paired or in clusters, the flowers are five-petaled, showy, and colored from white to pink or blue. The ornamentally insignificant fruit is interesting in that at maturity it bursts to discharge its seed.

RATE / SPACING: Growth is moderate to fast. Plants are spaced a distance equal to two to three times their expected mature height.

SPECIES: *G.* '**Ann Folkard**' is a sterile hybrid from the garden of Rev. Oliver Folkard, Lincolnshire, United Kingdom. It is the result of a chance hybridization of *G. procurrens* and *G. psilostemon* in 1973. This superb selection is hardy in Zones 5 to 8. A robust spreader, it reaches 18 inches tall by 24 inches wide, and unlike *G. procurrens* does not root as it spreads. From mid summer to fall numerous 1½-inch-wide rich magenta-purple blossoms with black centers and veins are borne above yellowish green to medium green deciduous deeply five-lobed to seven-lobed leaves.

G. asphodeloides (as-pho-*del*-oy-deez), meaning like asphodel (*Asphodelus ramosus* and related species), is a stout-rooted, vibrant green, deeply lobed, semievergreen-leaved species that reaches 18 inches tall and is said to be hardy to Zone 6 northward. Its flaring, oblong-petaled, pink flowers are borne all summer long. Subspecies *asphodeloides,* native to southern Europe, displays 1-inch-wide star-shaped, pale to deep pink flowers with dark pink veins; subsp. *crenophilum,* native to Lebanon and Syria, has evergreen leaves and flowers with deep rose-pink petals and dark pink veins; 'Prince Regent' has many pale lilac ¾-inch-wide flowers; subsp. *sintenisii,* native to northern Turkey, has many pale pink to purple flowers and red-tipped glandular hairs covering the stems and leaves; 'Starlight' has clear white flowers and broader, less deeply divided leaves.

G. × *cantabrigiense* (kan-ti-brig-ee-*en*-see) is a sterile hybrid that originated in the Cambridge University Botanic Garden in 1974. It is a superb plant with aromatic, glossy light green, nearly evergreen, 2- to 3½-inch-wide, seven-lobed leaves. Carried upon trailing stems, the foliage is not the only merit, for during late spring and early summer are borne numerous 1-inch-wide bright pink or white flowers. Hardy in Zones 5 to 10, it reaches 12 inches tall by 18 inches wide. 'Biokovo', from the Biokovo Mountains of Yugoslavia, is more lax in habit and has white flowers with pale pinkish centers; 'Biokovo Karmina', 8 inches tall, with rose-pink flowers.

G. cinereum (sin-*air*-ee-um), named from the Latin for its grayish foliage, is commonly called grayleaf cranesbill. Hardy in Zones 5 to 7, it hails from the Pyrenees Mountains and forms attractive little mounds to 6 inches tall by 12 or more inches wide. The leaves are grayish green and five-lobed to seven-lobed, while the 1-inch-wide pink summertime flowers have petals with a dark stripe. Cultivars and varieties include 'Album', with white flowers; 'Ballerina', a hybrid, 6 inches tall, with 2-inch-wide long-blooming lilac-pink flowers with dark centers and purple veins; 'Laurence Flatman', similar to 'Ballerina' but with more vigorous growth; var. *obtusilobum,* native to Mount Lebanon, with rounded pale green leaves and 1⅜-inch-wide nearly white flowers with pink tinges and reddish veins; var. *subcaulescens,* with darker leaves and magenta flowers; var. *subcaulescens* 'Giuseppii', with magenta flowers and a dark spot in the center; var. *subcaulescens* 'Splendens', slow-growing, with flowers deep red with dark centers, height to 6 inches.

G. clarkei (*klark*-ee-eye), Clark's geranium, hails from Kashmir and reaches 1 to 1½ feet tall. Quickly spreading to 1½ feet wide, it blankets the ground with its deeply cut, 4- to 7-inch-wide, seven-segmented, sharp-pointed, fine-textured leaves. During spring and summer it bears abundant ½- to ¾-inch-wide upward-facing purplish violet or white flowers with dark veins. It is hardy in Zones 5 to 8. Noteworthy cultivars include 'Kashmir Purple', with deep blue flowers, and 'Kashmir White' (syn. *G. rectum* 'Album'), with pale clear-white flowers and lilac veins.

G. dalmaticum (dal-*ma*-ti-kum), Dalmatian cranesbill, is native to southwestern Yugoslavia and Albania and reaches only 4 to 6 inches tall. With cushionlike habit and dark shiny green, 2-inch-wide, aromatic, deeply five-lobed to seven-lobed leaves, it is a superb foliage plant. It is hardy in Zones 4 to 8. Even during fall the leaves are attractive and reliably pick up rich tones of red and orange—persisting this way well into winter. The mauve flowers of early to midsummer are not to be slighted. Reaching 1 inch wide, they are pink petaled and borne three to a flower stem. 'Album' is slower spreading and bears white flowers with pink tinges.

G. endressii (en-*dres*-ee-eye), named for P. A. C. Endress (1806–1831), a German plant collector, is commonly called Endress cranesbill. Hardy in Zones 5 or 6 to 8, it is a sizable species that reaches 15 inches tall by 18 inches wide. It is native to the Pyrenees Mountains and displays light green basal leaves and fragrant magenta-pink flowers in mid summer. 'Rose Claire', with bright rose flowers and white veins; 'Wargrave Pink', with salmon-pink flowers.

G. himalayense (him-a-*lay*-en-see), named for its home in the Himalayas, is commonly called Himalayan cranesbill. Hardy in Zones 4 to 8, it reaches 12 inches tall and sprawls to 2 feet wide. Its foliage is deeply cut, five-parted to seven-parted, 3 or 4 inches long, and turns reddish or orange in fall. Its lilac-colored flowers have purple veins and red-based petals.

Each flower reaches 1½ to 2 inches wide (possibly the largest of the geraniums). Collectively the flowers provide a very impressive show in mid summer. 'Baby Blue' has compact habit and very large blue-stained lavender flowers from mid spring to early summer; 'Gravetye', sometimes listed as *G. grandiflorum* var. *alpinum,* has 2-inch-wide deep blue flowers with reddish centers and dark veins and only reaches 12 inches tall; 'Irish Blue' is a vigorous selection with flowers that are like 'Gravetye' but paler blue and with a larger reddish center; 'Plenum' ('Birch Double') displays double purple-blue, sterile, persistent flowers.

G. incanum (in-*kay*-num), named in Latin for its grayish haired foliage, is commonly called carpet geranium. It reaches 6 to 10 inches tall and is hardy in Zones 9 to 10. Its leaves are mostly evergreen and dissected in the shape of a hand, each segment being linear and ¼ inch long by 3⁄16 inch wide. Overall, the leaves appear sparsely hairy, medium green above, and grayish and densely hairy below. The flowers, which are solitary, five-petaled, to 1 inch wide, are colored rose-purple, magenta, or pink and are effective during fall.

G. 'Johnson's Blue', a popular sterile hybrid, was named after its hybridizer, A. T. Johnson. With dense 12- to 18-inch-tall mounds of finely divided leaves, it is the result of crossing *G. himalayense* with *G. pratense.* It is noteworthy for its profusion of 1½- to 2-inch-wide clear blue red-centered flowers of summer and fall. Hardy in Zones 4 or 5 to 8.

G. macrorrhizum (mak-roe-*rye*-zum / mak-roe-*ree*-zum), named for its thick, fleshy roots, is commonly called bigroot geranium. Hardy in Zones 3 to 8, this native of southern Europe is a robust species and soon makes a dense weed-proof mat. Although the winter cold and snow tend to reduce it to a height of just a few inches, in spring it quickly rebounds and reaches 12 to 18 inches tall by mid season. Typical spread is 2 feet wide. The display of dark green, strongly scented, five-lobed to seven-lobed leaves forms a splendid backdrop to the magenta flowers that arise throughout summer. This species is relatively tolerant of drought, performs well in high temperatures, and is valued for blooming well in shady settings. Its cultivars include 'Album', with white flower petals and pink calyxes; 'Bevan's Variety', reaching only 10 inches tall and displaying magenta flower petals and dark red sepals; 'Czakor', with deep magenta-pink flowers; 'Ingwersen's Variety', with light pink flower petals and relatively shiny foliage; 'Lohfelden', with compact habit, pale pink flowers, dark pink veins; 'Pindus', similar to 'Czakor' but only about half the height; 'Ridsko', with smooth, shiny, deciduous leaves and magenta-pink flowers; 'Spessart', with light pink flowers; 'Variegatum', with grayish green leaves that are irregularly dappled with creamy white, flowers purplish pink; 'Velebit', similar to 'Pindus' but with green calyxes, which give its flowers more contrast; 'Walter Ingwersen', with rose-pink flowers.

G. maculatum (mak-you-*lay*-tum), named from the Latin *macula,* spot, referring to the mottled leaves, is commonly called spotted cranesbill. Native to eastern North America, it is hardy in Zones 3 to 8, reaches 1 to 2 feet tall, and spreads 2 to 3 feet wide. Rather loose in habit and oftentimes self-seeding, it is best suited to the wild or native plant garden, where it prefers a moist, partially shaded spot. It displays three-lobed to five-lobed, irregularly and coarsely toothed, medium green, grayish spotted foliage. During spring and early summer, five-petaled rose-purple flowers are borne in great profusion and help to brighten the surroundings.

G. × magnificum (mag-*nif*-i-kum), commonly called showy geranium, is a sterile hybrid resulting from the cross between *G. ibericum* and *G. platypetalum.* This fast-spreading hybrid has been around for more than a hundred years (often sold under the name of one of its parent species). Hardy in Zones 4 or 5 to 9 or 10, it reaches 1½ to 2 feet tall and spreads more than 2 feet wide. Its numerous 1½-inch-wide, saucer-shaped, deep violet-blue flowers with dark blue veins are borne during mid summer above rounded, hairy, five-lobed to seven-lobed deeply cut, broad segmented, 2- to 6-inch-wide leaves. Colored medium green to silvery-green during the growing season, the leaves become red and yellow during fall.

G. × oxonianum (ox-*on*-ee-aye-num) is a fertile hybrid from the cross between *G. endressii* and *G. versicolor.* Included among its numerous cultivars that make good moderate-scale to large-scale ground covers in Zones 5 to 8 are 'A. T. Johnson' ('Johnson's Variety'), bred by A. T. Johnson of North Wales in 1937, with more compact habit than that of *G. endressii* but similar in leaf, flowers light silvery-pink, borne in profusion during summer; 'Claridge Druce', selected by Dr. Claridge Druce around 1900, reaching 2 feet tall, flowers with rose-pink petals and dark pink veins, leaves dark grayish green, shiny, and evergreen; 'Hollywood', like 'Claridge Druce' but with smaller lighter green leaves and 1½-inch-wide pale pink flowers, magenta veins, and overlapping petals; 'Lady Moore', like 'Claridge Druce' but with deep pinkish purple flowers and purple veins; 'Rose Clair', long-blooming, with rose-pink flowers; 'Sherwood', with narrow pale pink flower petals; 'Southcombe Double', possibly short-lived, reaching only 15 inches tall, flowers many, ¾

inch wide, deep salmon-pink, and often with petal-like stamens which give a double-flowered effect; 'Southcombe Star', like 'Southcombe Double' but a bit taller and with starlike bluish pink flowers; 'Thurstonianum', to 2 feet tall, with dark green leaves that are often blotched purplish brown, flowers deeply notched, white-based, and colored bright reddish purple, stamens sometimes petallike creating a double-flowered appearance; 'Walter's Gift', to 2 feet tall, with shiny green leaves with deep reddish centers (the red spreads outward in irregular blotching pattern), small pale pink flowers with magenta-colored veins; 'Winscombe', discovered by the famous English garden designer and writer, Margery Fish, with pale, silvery-pink flowers that deepen as they mature.

G. procurrens (pro-*ker*-enz), which reaches 6 inches tall and more than 4 feet wide, is a tenacious spreader that roots as it goes. Hardy to Zone 6 or 7, it may not be the most showy species but it is surely one of the most useful for covering large areas fast. Its attractive five-lobed light green leaves with light mottling make a nice backdrop to the dainty dark-centered pinkish purple 1-inch-wide blossoms that are borne during summer and fall. Aside from *G.* 'Ann Folkard', mentioned previously, *G. procurrens* is a parent to these superb and less vigorous cultivars: 'Anne Thompson' (*G. procurrens × G. psilostemon*), with compact 22-inch-tall habit, 3-foot spread, young leaves that are slightly gold-tinged, and 1½-inch-wide magenta-purple flowers with black centers and veins; 'Dilys' (*G. procurrens × G. sanguineum*), to 9 inches tall by 3 feet wide, compact mounding habit, 1¼-inch-wide soft purple flowers with deep purple veins from late summer to fall.

G. pylzowianum (pil-zoe-ee-*aye*-num), Pylzow geranium, is hardy to Zone 7. Hailing from China, it reaches 12 inches tall. It has five-lobed, deeply cut leaves, and bears purple flowers in early summer.

G. sanguineum (san-*gwin*-ee-um), named for the blood-red color of its flowers, is commonly called bloody cranesbill. Hardy in Zones 3 to 8 and native to Europe and Asia, it reaches up to 12 inches tall and spreads 18 or more inches wide. The leaves are five-lobed to seven-lobed, deeply cut, and turn scarlet in autumn. The flowers of reddish purple to magenta are borne from mid spring to late summer. Horticultural selections include 'Alan Bloom', with numerous large bright pink flowers; 'Album', with white flowers; 'Cedric Morris', with large magenta-pink flowers and leaves that are larger than those of the species; 'Elspeth', with large bright purple flowers; 'Glenluce', with large rose-pink flowers; 'Holden', with vibrant pink flowers, 6 inches tall; 'Jubilee Pink', with deep green leaves, flowers 1½ inches wide, bright magenta-pink, with notched petals; 'Max Frei', 8 inches tall, with deep magenta flowers and bright autumnal foliar color; 'Minutum', with compact habit and small leaves; 'New Hampshire Purple', 8 inches tall by 24 inches wide, with vivid wine-red flowers; var. *prostratum,* with dwarf compact habit; 'Shepherd's Warning', with many 1-inch-wide deep magenta-pink flowers; var. *striatum* (var. *lancastriense*), with large pale pink flowers and dark pink veins.

G. wallichianum (wal-itch-ee-*aye*-num), named after Nathaniel Wallich (1786–1854), a Danish surgeon and botanist with the East India Company who introduced the plant in 1819, is hardy northward to Zone 6 and claims the Himalayas as its homeland. It reaches only 2 to 4 inches tall and spreads to more than 3 feet wide with trailing stems. Its leaves are three-lobed to five-lobed, soft green, and velvety to the touch. Its purple flowers of mid to late summer are attractive but not as showy as some of the other species. 'Buxton's Blue' has lavender-blue flowers with white centers and white-marbled leaves; 'Syabru', named for the Sherpa village near where it was collected in Nepal, is bright-green-leaved with bright magenta flowers.

CULTURE / CARE: Adaptable to most well-drained, acidic to slightly alkaline soils, geraniums (with the exception of bigroot geranium which is deep rooted and quite tolerant) display only average tolerance to drought. Often they need supplemental watering during the summer, as they are at their best when the soil is kept slightly moist at all times. They prefer full sun to light shade, with best flowering in full sun. Their primary pests are the four-lined plant bug and aphids. The most common diseases are bacterial and fungal leaf spots. Maintenance includes shearing growth back about halfway after bloom to promote compactness. Some gardeners perform this midway through the blooming season, thereby initiating another heavy flowering period. Seed is generally viable and self-sowing, but hybrid selections and cultivars may not come true from seed. In such cases, shear off fading flowers before their fruit has a chance to ripen and disperse seed. Over time, plants often show signs of deterioration; such plants can be divided to rejuvenate them.

PROPAGATION: Cuttings taken from the stems root very easily during most of the year. Root cuttings also work; cut 3-inch-long sections in fall, place them in flats, cover them with soil, and keep them lightly moist and warm until spring, when they will send up new shoots. Seed can often be purchased out of catalogs and typically germinates in two weeks or less. Alternatively, if you collect your own seed, it may need an after-ripening period; thus, storage for three to four weeks at room temperature is a good practice prior to sowing.

Glyceria maxima PLATE 142
Great Water Grass, Reed Manna Grass, Reed Meadow Grass, Reed Sweet Grass, Sweet Hay

Also known as *G. aquatica,* this water-tolerant species is not planted enough. The variegated selections are more common, but they, too, could be used more. The species and cultivars typically range from 2 to 2½ feet, spread vigorously by rhizomes, and are of great use for waterside planting as specimen or accent plants. Sometimes they are used to good effect in broad drifts along pond and stream banks; they are always better in such locations for they really do grow best at the water's edge.

SCIENTIFIC NAME: *Glyceria maxima* (gly-*seer*-ee-a / glik-*er*-ee-a *max*-i-ma). *Glyceria* comes from the Greek *glyks,* sweet, and refers to the sweet taste of the leaves—to the palette of horses and cattle. *Maxima* refers to the large stature of this species.

HARDINESS / ORIGIN: Zones 5 to 8; Europe and temperate Asia.

LEAVES / FLOWERS / FRUIT: The leaves are for the most part erectly oriented, smooth, and 1½ to 2 feet long by ½ to ¾ inch wide. The yellow or purple flowers of summer are tinged green and borne in panicles. In comparison to the foliage, the flowers and the tiny fruit, a grain, are of secondary interest.

RATE / SPACING: Growth is moderate. Plants from pint-sized to gallon-sized containers are spaced 10 to 16 inches apart.

HORTICULTURAL SELECTIONS: 'Pallida', leaves variegated green and pale, creamy white; 'Variegata', leaves variegated white, creamy yellow, and green.

CULTURE / CARE: This species and its cultivars need constantly moist to wet, acidic to neutral soil in full sun to light shade. They do not tolerate drought and only struggle in ordinary garden settings. They have few disease and insect problems, and require little or no maintenance.

PROPAGATION: Division during spring, summer, or fall is effective.

Grevillea PLATE 143
Spider Flower

Grevilleas compose a vast group of Australian trees and shrubs of which many are excellent ground covers, especially for use along the coast of California. The shrubby ground-cover types are either prostrate with long trailing stems or mound forming, often with cascading branches. Interesting both for unusual foliage and showy clusters of honeysuckle-like, hummingbird-attracting flowers, grevilleas function as specimens, accent plants, and en masse as general covers. Occasional foot traffic may be tolerated by the prostrate forms; no foot traffic is tolerated by the mound formers. There are many ground-covering species and cultivars, but because they have just recently begun to be used in the United States (primarily California and Arizona), little is known about their individual traits. Much of my information comes second hand from Australian publications, and here I discuss some of the more useful ground covers.

SCIENTIFIC NAME: *Grevillea* (gre-*vil*-ee-a) is named for Charles Francis Greville (1749–1809), a founder of the Horticultural Society of London and vice-president of the Royal Society.

HARDINESS / ORIGIN: Only limited hardiness testing has been conducted in North America, but Australian sources typically list *Grevillea* species as being frost tolerant, likely hardy in Zones 8 or 9 to 11, or frost intolerant, likely hardy in Zones 9 to 11. Whether the plants described below are listed as frost tolerant or intolerant, I encourage you to test them for yourself. Native habitat is Australia and Tasmania.

LEAVES / FLOWERS / FRUIT: The rich green to gray-green evergreen leaves vary greatly with individual species. Some are almost needlelike while others are broader and resemble a wide range of leaves from juniper and rosemary to ferns, holly, and oak. The flowers are typically honeysuckle-like and are attractive to hummingbirds. The tiny fruit is non-ornamental.

RATE / SPACING: Growth is moderate to fast. Plants from 2- to 3-gallon-sized containers are spaced a distance equal to ¾ to 1 times their expected mature spread.

SPECIES: *G. aquifolium* (ak-we-*foe*-lee-um), named for its rigid, prickly, gray-green, 3-inch-long holly-like leaves that resemble *Ilex aquifolium,* is commonly called holly leaf spider flower. It is a spreading shrub that reaches 4 feet tall by 6 to 7 feet wide. The profusion of red toothbrush-shaped flowers is borne from spring to summer. Frost tolerant.

G. 'Austraflora Canterbury Gold', a low-growing arching shrub, reaches 2 to 3 feet tall and spreads to 10 feet wide. Its glossy green, oval leaves set off the yellow flowers. Other related cultivars include 'Austraflora Copper Crest', a prostrate form with coppery new growth, prickly cascading leaves, and pink flowers, moisture-tolerant; 'Austraflora Fanfare', with prostrate habit, deeply lobed leaves and wine-red flowers; 'Austraflora Old Gold', reaching 2 feet tall by 5 feet wide, with bronzy gold new growth, a profusion of yellow and coral flowers, and mounding habit. Frost intolerant.

G. australis (as-*tray*-lis), Australian spider flower, is an alpine species that displays low prostrate habit and spread of 4 or more feet. It blooms with small creamy white, pleasantly scented summertime flowers. Frost tolerant.

G. banksii (*banks*-ee-eye) cultivars. Although the species may either be a tree or shrub, it is the prostrate cultivars that are useful as ground covers. These display low, broad-spreading habit, fernlike leaves, and spikes of red or cream flowers. Frost intolerant.

G. biternata (bi-ter-*nay*-ta), sometimes listed as *G. tridentifera,* hails from western Australia where it is a popular ground cover. Spreading 7 to 10 feet wide, it may reach 4 feet tall and is excellent for general cover as it forms thick light green fernlike-textured mats (leaves reach 4 inches long and are deeply dissected). Its creamy white flowers are carried upon upright spikes from winter to spring. Said to smell of honey, the flowers are attractive to bees. Frost tolerant.

G. brachystachya (bray-ki-stay-*key*-a), reaching 15 inches tall and more than 6 feet wide, displays fine-textured narrow gray foliage, loosely arranged pink flowers during winter and spring, and graceful cascading habit. Frost intolerant.

G. 'Bronze Rambler', a spreader of unknown origin, is noteworthy for its deeply divided sharply pointed oaklike foliage, which is carried upon weeping branches and is colored bronzy red in youth and bronze-tinged in cooler weather. Frost tolerant.

G. confertifolia (kon-*fer*-ti-foe-*lee*-a), dense-leaf grevillea, is a prostrate grower that reaches 3½ feet tall by 4 to 7 feet wide. Its needlelike leaves contrast nicely with its dusky mauve-pink flowers of spring. Frost intolerant.

G. × *gaudichaudii* (gaw-di-chau-*dee*-eye), a natural hybrid from the Blue Mountains, spreads 6½ to 10 feet wide. It hugs the ground and displays prickly lobed leaves that are coppery-red in youth. Its burgundy to red flowers are borne from spring to fall. Frost tolerant.

G. juniperina (jew-nip-er-*eye*-na), juniper-leaved spider flower, is a variable species with numerous selections. Typically the species displays prostrate habit with a spread of 6 or more feet. Its flowers may be either red or yellow, and its leaves are prickly and needlelike. 'Molonglo' has apricot-colored flowers in winter and spring; variety *trinervis* displays orange-red flowers in spring and summer. Frost intolerant.

G. lanigera (lan-i-*ger*-a), woolly spider flower, has softly hairy, densely set gray-green needlelike foliage. It displays a mounding habit with height from 3 to 4 feet tall and spread of 6 to 8 feet. Numerous clusters of deep pink and creamy yellow flowers appear from winter to summer. 'Mont Tamboritha' reaches 1 foot tall by 6 feet wide. Frost intolerant.

G. laurifolia (law-ri-*foe*-lee-a) is prostrate or trailing and spreads 10 feet wide. It has leaves that are bronze-tipped and flowers that are dark red during spring and summer. It is one of the parents of *G.* 'Poorinda Royal Mantle'. Frost intolerant.

G. 'Noell', a dense mounded cultivar that reaches 4 feet tall by 4 or 5 feet wide, is remarkable for its lovely rose-red and white springborne flowers and green needlelike foliage. Frost tolerant.

G. obtusifolia (ob-tew-si-*foe*-lee-a), with long narrow vibrant green leaves, has a low trailing habit and spread of 7 feet. It bears numerous scarlet flowers from winter to early summer. Frost tolerant.

G. paniculata (pan-ik-*you*-lay-ta) is similar to *G. biternata* in its scented, creamy white flowers. Its leaves, however, are fine-textured and prickly. Frost intolerant.

G. 'Poorinda Royal Mantle' displays deeply divided leaves that are red in youth and dark green in maturity. It is a strong bloomer, and its dark red flowers are borne above the foliage at the ends of short branchlets. Spreading more than 20 feet wide, this selection is one of the fastest growers and is superb for cascading over the edge of boulders and retaining walls. One of its parents is *G. laurifolia*. Frost intolerant.

G. pteridifolia (ter-id-i-*foe*-lee-a) has finely divided leaves that are silvery before maturing to green. It reaches 15 inches tall and spreads 6 to 10 feet wide. The golden-orange flowers are borne from fall to spring. Frost tolerant.

G. repens (*ree*-penz), creeping spider flower, carries its dark green hollylike leaves upon low trailing stems. Reaching 3 to 7 feet wide, it is not as dense growing as the other spider flowers, but makes a nice show of wine red flowers during summer. Frost tolerant.

G. rosmarinifolia (roze-ma-rine-i-*foe*-lee-a) cultivars. Although the species from New South Wales often reaches 6 feet tall, it has yielded some excellent mound-forming semiprostrate forms. The leaves, narrow and 1½ inches long (resembling rosemary), are covered with silky hairs below and are colored bluish green above. The reddish flowers, borne in short dense racemes, are splendid and make quite a show during winter and spring. Frost tolerant.

G. thelemanniana (*thel*-i-man-ee-aye-na), spider net spider plant, ranges from prostrate to upright. It is the two prostrate forms that make good ground covers. The gray form, with red, yellow-tipped flowers from fall to summer, reaches only a few inches tall. The green-leaved selection, with pinkish red flowers during winter and spring, reaches 2 feet tall with cascading stems. Frost intolerant.

G. 'White Wings', a fast-spreading selection of unknown origin, reaches 4 feet tall by 10 feet wide. It bears white flowers during winter and spring. Frost intolerant.

CULTURE / CARE: Spider flowers are best in sun or light shade. They tolerate only short periods of drought and typically prefer moist but well-drained soils of various textures. Little maintenance is required, but a light pruning after flowering can be used to promote compactness. An application (in spring) or two (spring and fall) of organic fertilizer such as blood and bone meal or cow manure, or a slow-release chemical fertilizer with low percentage of phosphorus, is said to keep them vibrant.

PROPAGATION: Cuttings are said to root easily after treatment with 1000 ppm IBA/talc. Seed is also said to be effective.

Gunnera   PLATE 144

Composed of both tiny-leaved, low mat-forming and huge-leaved, tall upright growers, the genus contains some magnificent ground covers. The low growers are quite cold tender and are often used in the foreground of other large-leaved species. The tall growers are magnificent, breathtaking specimens for use at water's edge in large garden settings. No foot traffic is tolerated.

SCIENTIFIC NAME: *Gunnera* (gun-*e*-ra) commemorates Johan Ernst Gunnerus (1718–1773), a Norwegian bishop and botanist who wrote *Flora Norvegica*.

HARDINESS / ORIGIN: Zone 7 or 8 depending upon the species; cool, moist, warm climates of Malaysia, Tasmania, Solomon Islands, New Zealand, Hawaii, Mexico to Chile, tropical and South Africa.

LEAVES / FLOWERS / FRUIT: Arising from stout rhizomes or woody crowns, the stout-stalked basal leaves may be small and nearly succulent or large, rough-textured, and ofttimes spiny. Not all species flower reliably, but some of the large species produce tiny flowers that are arranged in remarkably large inflorescences.

RATE / SPACING: Growth is moderate. Plants from 2- to 10-gallon-sized containers are spaced a distance equal to half their expected mature spread.

SPECIES: *G. dentata* (den-*tay*-ta), toothed gunnera, is native to New Zealand and naturally grows in subalpine lowlands in wet soil along stream banks and in swamps and wet meadows. It is hardy to Zone 8. Low growing, stoloniferous, and reaching only 18 inches tall, this vigorous spreader bears softly haired, leathery gray-green elliptic-oblong, coarse-textured, irregularly tooth-edged, ¼- to 1-inch-long leaves that are borne upon 2-inch-long petioles.

G. hamiltonii (ham-il-*tone*-ee-eye), also of New Zealand and hardy to Zone 8, is a dense cushion-forming species that hails from dunes and dune valleys. It carries its smooth, triangular to broadly oval, 1½-inch-wide, leathery to fleshy, brown-green, fine-toothed leaves upon 1¼- to 3-inch-long stout, flattish petioles.

G. magellanica (ma-jel-*lan*-i-ka) reaches 3 to 6 inches tall. A spreading ground cover, it hails from Patagonia, Tierra Del Fuego, and the Falkland Islands. It is hardy to Zone 7 and is characterized by stoloniferous spreading habit and 2- to 3-inch-wide smooth to softly haired, glossy green, round or kidney-shaped foliage. Tiny green flowers are borne on short red stalks as leaves develop during spring.

G. manicata (man-i-*kay*-ta) hails from moist rocky stream banks from Columbia to southern Brazil. It is a very large species that is hardy to Zone 7. It reaches over 6 feet tall and 8 feet wide and, perhaps unlike any other plant, commands attention. Indeed, with enormous 4- to 6-foot-wide, nearly round, coarse-textured leaf blades that are elevated upon petioles that arise from a stout furry brown rootstock (and may reach 8 feet long), any place this plant is grown people stop and look. By all accounts it is a huge plant (and I am sure to be criticized for calling it a ground cover, but cover the ground it does and to science-fiction proportions). Its summerborne flowers, too, are interesting. Although individually tiny, collectively they contribute to the composition of the 30- to 50-inch-long conical conelike flower clusters.

G. prorepens (pro-ree-*penz*), native to New Zealand, is a stoloniferous lowland species that hails from open swamps and moist woodlands. It is hardy to Zone 8. Its leaves are oval to heart-shaped, finely toothed to entire, brown to purplish green, smooth or hairy, and ⅜ to 2 inches long. Bearing insignificant flowers upon 3-inch clusters during summer, by fall it makes a nice show of bright red fruit.

G. tinctoria (tink-*toe*-ree-a), like *G. manicata,* is huge and displays monstrous 3- to 6-foot-wide, round to kidney-shaped, rough, deeply cut, prominently lobed, rusty green leaves that have veins covered with spiny prickles. Held upon leafstalks that reach 4 feet long with hard hooklike projections, the leaves are spectacular. The species is hardy to Zone 8, reaches more than 5 feet tall by 8 feet wide, and hails from moist Patagonian woodlands and stream sides. Unlike *G. manicata,* its reddish summertime flowers are borne in cylindrical panicles. It is sometimes listed as *G. chilensis.*

CULTURE / CARE: Organically rich, moist, acidic soil with lots of fertility suits gunneras. Time spent digging out their planting site and filling the site with equal parts of leaf mold or peat moss, cow manure, and top soil is well spent. Gunneras are fairly adaptable to light conditions and thrive in full sun or light to moderate shade. They are inflexible when it comes to drought and insist upon constantly moist to wet soils. They have few problems with diseases and insects and need little maintenance other than removal of leaves as they become tattered. If planted farther north than their hardiness limits (a temptation hard to resist), mulching is required. One authority states that leaves should be removed after the first killing frost, the crown covered with several inches of sphagnum peat, then covered with a wooden crate, and the crate in turn buried under leaf mold or dry leaves. The following March, the leaf mold and leaves can be removed, but not the crate, which should be left in place until the danger of frost has passed. Regardless of climate, gunneras are heavy feeders and should be given liberal amounts of organic fertilizer such as cow manure to help them reach their full potential.

PROPAGATION: Propagation is usually by division or cuttings. Division is effective in spring or fall. Cuttings from the leafy buds at the plant's base can be rooted like stem cuttings. Seed also works: sow it in the fall at the time of ripening, allow it to overwinter at cool temperatures, and it will germinate the following March.

Gymnocarpium dryopteris   PLATE 145

Oak Fern, Tender Three-branched Polypody, Pale Mountain Polypody

For moist wooded areas of the landscape, this diminutive, 8- to 11-inch tall, soft-textured, indefinite-spreading fern is supremely beautiful. Oak fern is at home and exceptionally lovely near the banks of a stream or along the sides of a moist woodland path, among conifers as well as deciduous trees. It can be used on a small to moderate scale where its soft-textured, mat-forming, rhizomatous habit can induce a hypnotic tranquility to the overall mood of the landscape.

SCIENTIFIC NAME: *Gymnocarpium dryopteris* (jim-noe-*kaar*-pee-um dry-*op*-ter-is). *Gymnocarpium,* with naked fruit, comes from the Greek *gymnos,* naked, and *karpos,* a fruit, in reference to the spore-bearing sori which lack covers (indusia). *Dryopteris,* oak fern, comes from the Greek, *drys,* oak, and *pteris,* a fern, and is so named because it often shares its home with oak trees.

HARDINESS / ORIGIN: Zones 2 to 7; Greenland, Europe, Asia, swamps and cool, moist thickets and woodlands of Newfoundland and Labrador to Alaska, extending south to Washington, Oregon, the tip of Nevada, North Dakota, Minnesota, Iowa, Illinois, and the New England States.

LEAVES / FLOWERS / FRUIT: The rich green, soft-textured leaves are deciduous and 4 to 10 inches long by 5 to 12 inches wide. Each is composed of three broadly triangular leaflets which themselves are divided one and one-half times. The sori, which house the spores, are rounded and located near the leaflet margins on the undersurface of the leaves.

RATE / SPACING: Growth is slow. Plants from quart-sized to gallon-sized containers are spaced 8 to 10 inches apart.

HORTICULTURAL SELECTIONS: 'Plumosum', with densely set leaflets.

OTHER SPECIES: *G.* × *heterosporum* (he-ter-oh-*spore*-um), a hybrid between *G. dryopteris* and *G. robertianum,* is intermediate in shape.

G. robertianum (roe-*bert*-tee-aye-num), commonly called northern oak fern, scented oak fern, limestone oak fern, limestone polypody, or Robert's oak fern, is native to northern North America, Europe, and Asia. It is hardy in Zones 2 to 6 and differs from *G. dryopteris* in its preference for limy soil and its more narrowly triangular fronds.

CULTURE / CARE: Organically rich, moist soils with a pH of 5.0 to 6.0 are ideal. *Gymnocarpium robertianum* tolerates slightly alkaline soil. None of the oak ferns tolerates drought; thus, they should be planted in locations that remain naturally moist. Oak ferns prefer light to dense shade. For a discussion of fern pathology and pests, see Chapter 8. Little or no maintenance is required.

PROPAGATION: The oak ferns are typically propagated by spores or division.

Gypsophila   PLATE 146
Baby's Breath

The ground-covering types of baby's breath are exceptional when their flower-laden branches are allowed to billow over the tops of rock ledges and retaining walls. As specimens in rock gardens, they lend a unique softening quality, just as they do when used for edging walks and accenting building entrances. The common name baby's breath comes from the soft effect of their cloudlike butterfly-attracting flowers. No foot traffic is tolerated.

SCIENTIFIC NAME: *Gypsophila* (jip-*sof*-i-la) comes from the Greek *gypsos,* gypsum, and *phileo,* to love, in reference to many of the species' love for chalky (alkaline) soil.

HARDINESS / ORIGIN: See individual species for hardiness; temperate Eurasia.

LEAVES / FLOWERS / FRUIT: The gray-green to blue-green fleshy leaves are elongate and round-pointed or spatula-shaped. They are oppositely arranged and fine-textured and make a suitable backdrop to the airy panicles of tiny white or pink flowers that are usually produced in spring or summer. The fruit is nonornamental.

RATE / SPACING: Growth is moderate. Plants from 3- to 5-inch-wide containers are spaced 14 to 24 inches apart.

SPECIES: *G. paniculata* (pan-ik-you-*lay*-ta), named for its flowers which are arranged in panicles, is commonly called common baby's breath. The loose, billowing, many-branched clusters of flowers make their striking appearance in mid summer with thousands of ¼-inch-wide white to pinkish balls. To say the least, the overall effect is astounding. The leaves are bluish green, 3 inches long, and more or less lance-shaped. The species originates in the Caucasus to central Asia and is hardy in Zones 3 to 9. Among the cultivars are 'Alba', with white flowers; 'Bristol Fairy', one of the most popular cultivars, 2 to 3 feet tall, with double white flowers; 'Compacta', with dense habit; 'Compacta Plena', with double pink flowers from late spring to mid summer, reaching only 15 inches tall; 'Dantzinger', promoted as tolerating more shade; 'Flamingo', with vigorous habit, reaching 3 or 4 feet tall, with double pink flowers; 'Flore Pleno', with double white flowers; 'Grandiflora', with flowers larger than those of the species; 'Perfecta', with large, double white flowers; 'Pink Fairy', with compact habit and pink flowers; 'Pink Star', with bright pink flowers and compact habit, only 18 inches tall; 'Red Sea', with double rose-pink flowers, 3 to 4 feet tall; 'Rosy Veil' ('Rosenschkier'), similar to 'Pink Star', but with paler pink flowers; 'Viette's Dwarf', 18 inches tall, with double white, pink-blushed flowers.

G. repens (*ree*-penz), named for its reptant (creeping) habit, is commonly called creeping baby's breath. An alpine from northwestern Spain, it is hardy in Zones 3 to 8 and is easily grown and long-lived. Unlike common baby's breath, it is much lower growing (only 6 inches tall by 18 to 24 inches wide), forms dense mats, and is tolerant of acidic soil. The gray-green foliage reaches 1 inch long and nearly disappears when the multitude of ⅓-inch-wide white to lilac-colored flowers arrive early to mid summer. Some of the most popular horticultural selections include 'Alba', with white flowers from early summer to frost, 4 inches tall; 'Bodgeri', with double light pink flowers; 'Fratensis', with rich pink flowers; 'Rosa Schönheit' ('Dorothy Teacher'), with compact habit and dark pink flowers; 'Rosea', with rose-pink flowers, 6 inches tall.

CULTURE / CARE: Baby's breath is best in light-textured or gravelly soil with excellent drainage. Neutral or alkaline pH is needed for common baby's breath, but creeping baby's breath tolerates acidic soils. Although these species are well suited to resisting drought, periodic deep watering during summer is beneficial. They prefer full sun. Pests include aphids, slugs, and snails. Diseases such as crown gall, blight, damping off, and aster yellows may sometimes be problematic. To encourage new growth and eliminate self-sowing, plants should be trimmed back shortly after their flowers begin to fade.

PROPAGATION: Cuttings are usually taken in mid-summer and are easily rooted in a porous medium. Seed is also available and usually takes only a week or two to germinate.

Hakonechloa macra PLATE 147

An unusual, attractive, ground-covering grass, this species is outstanding when used for accent, as a moderate-to large-scale general cover, or for a border or walkway edging. It is dense-growing and large-leaved, reaches 1 to 1½ feet tall, and spreads more than 2 feet across. Its drooping foliage appears graceful and soft-textured, and its brightly colored variegated selections can be used to add a vibrant highlight to dark corners. Both the species and the cultivars are naturals for use in Japanese theme gardens, but none of them tolerates foot traffic.

SCIENTIFIC NAME: *Hakonechloa macra* (ha-kone-ee-kloe-a *mak*-ra). *Hakonechloa* is named for Hakone, the region of Japan from which this genus comes, and the Greek *chloa,* grass. *Macra,* large, likely refers to the large leaves.

HARDINESS / ORIGIN: Zones 5 to 9; moist forests and mountainous regions of central Japan.

LEAVES / FLOWERS / FRUIT: The deciduous, arching, 8- to 10-inch-long, ⅜-inch-wide, smooth, tapering, bright green leaves are attractive and act as the foundation for the delicate, open, 6-inch-long, 2-inch-wide flower clusters. The tiny spikelets are yellowish to green and arise in late summer to early fall. The fruit, a grain, is nonornamental.

RATE / SPACING: Growth is slow to moderate. Plants from pint-sized to quart-sized containers are spaced 10 to 16 inches apart. The variegated selections tend to grow even more slowly and thus should be spaced closer together.

HORTICULTURAL SELECTIONS: 'Albo-aurea', with leaves brilliantly variegated white, golden yellow, and green; 'Albo-variegata' ('Albo Striata'), leaves variegated with narrow white and green streaks; 'Aureola', the most popular selection, with bright yellow leaves and with thin green lines running through them.

CULTURE / CARE: This species and its cultivars prefer an organically rich, well-drained, loamy soil with a pH from moderate acidity to slight alkalinity. Tolerance to drought is fair, although best growth occurs when the soil is kept slightly moist. Light to moderate shade is best, but more sun is tolerated in the northern limits of its range. Little or no maintenance is required.

PROPAGATION: Division in spring is the most successful method of propagation. Although seed may be difficult to locate, it is an effective means by which to propagate the species (but not the cultivars).

Haworthia PLATE 148

Species of this genus are useful general covers for small-scale applications, as specimen or accent plants in rock gardens, and as interesting facers to taller drought-tolerant shrubs and succulents. Members of the lily family, the species carry such interesting common names as wart plant, star cactus, and cushion aloe. For the most part, they are low-growing, mat-forming, basal-leaved, often sucker forming, aloelike, succulent, 3-inch-tall ground covers. No foot traffic is tolerated.

SCIENTIFIC NAME: *Haworthia* (hay-*wur*-thee-a) is named after Adrian Hardy Haworth (1768–1833), a botanist, writer, and entomologist who grew succulents at Chelsea, England.

HARDINESS / ORIGIN: Zones 10 to 11; South Africa.

LEAVES / FLOWERS / FRUIT: The flowers are usually tube-shaped with two liplike petals. Colored white with green or rose stripes, they are borne above the foliage in pyramidal clusters and may arise during any season. The fruit is nonornamental.

RATE / SPACING: Growth is slow to moderate. Plants from 3- to 4-inch-diameter containers are spaced 8 to 12 inches apart.

SPECIES: *H. cuspidata* (kus-pi-*day*-ta), named for its leaves that end in a sharp, short point, grows rather slowly and displays oval leaves that reach 1 inch long, ¾ inch wide, and ¼ inch thick. Concave and pale green with a translucent tip, each succulent leaf is edged with tiny teeth and helps form a fine green backdrop for the open clusters of ⅝-inch-long flowers, which are borne from spring through fall.

H. fasciata (fash-i-*aye*-ta), named for transverse bands on the leaves, is an attractive succulent with 1½-inch-long, ½-inch-wide, triangular dark green leaves. Each leaf is decorated with transverse bands of white tubercles on the lower surface. The flowers are whitish green and arranged in loose 6-inch-diameter clusters from spring through fall.

H. radula (rad-*dyew*-la) is another low-growing species that makes a splendid ground cover. Stemless and covered with minute hairs, it is characterized by narrowly triangular, 3-inch-long, medium green to grayish green leaves that are covered with white wartlike tubercles.

H. tessellata (tes-e-*lay*-ta), named for its checkered leaves, suckers freely, spreads quickly, and is characterized by thick, broadly triangular to oval, 2-inch-long, white-toothed, sharp-pointed, dark green leaves. Interestingly, the leaves are translucent and roughened on top with five to seven interconnected pale green lines. The flowers are arranged in 12-inch-long clusters. Variety *parva* is similar to the species but smaller in all respects.

CULTURE / CARE: A sandy or gritty soil with excellent drainage is required. Tolerance to drought is pretty good but an occasional deep watering during the summer months is appreciated. Light shade is best. Diseases such as crown and root rots may arise if the soil is poorly drained. Scale insects may be troublesome at times.

PROPAGATION: Rosettes can be divided from fall through early spring.

Hebe decumbens   PLATE 149
Ground Hebe

At 14 inches tall and 5 feet wide, this woody, low-spreading shrub makes a pleasing facer to taller shrubs and also performs well as a specimen for rock gardens. Ground hebe generally does not perform well away from the coasts, but near an ocean does fine and has proven tolerant to airborne salt. No foot traffic is tolerated.

SCIENTIFIC NAME: *Hebe decumbens* (*hee*-bee dee-*kum*-benz). *Hebe* is named for the Greek goddess of youth and spring, who was cupbearer to Zeus and the wife of Hercules. *Decumbens* describes the growth habit of the species—low spreading with upturned branch tips.

HARDINESS / ORIGIN: Zone 6 or 7; New Zealand.

LEAVES / FLOWERS / FRUIT: The evergreen leaves are relatively fleshy, arranged in four rows, and colored grayish with red margins. The white, ¾-inch-long flowers are borne in short, dense, vertical spikes in spring. The fruit is nonornamental.

RATE / SPACING: Growth is moderate. Plants from gallon-sized containers are spaced 2 to 3 feet apart.

OTHER SPECIES: *H. chathamica* (*chat*-am-i-ka), Chatham hebe, is native to the Chatham Islands of the South Pacific. Hardy only in Zones 8 to 10, it reaches 18 inches tall by 3 feet wide. The leaves are evergreen, elliptic to oblong, to 1 inch long, and colored dark green. During summer, 1-inch-long lavender flowers put on a pleasing show.

H. pinguifolia 'Pagei' (ping-gwi-*foe*-lee-a pag-*ee*-eye), a New Zealand native also hardy in Zones 8 to

10, is considerably shorter than the other hebes described here, reaching 9 inches tall by 5 feet across. The evergreen, bluish gray, leathery, fleshy foliage is elliptic to oval and reaches ¾ inch long by ³⁄₁₆ inch wide. The flowers, which are arranged in spikes, reach ⅜ inch wide, are colored white, and grace the landscape in splendid profusion during late summer.

HYBRID SELECTIONS: *H.* 'Autumn Glory', likely of hybrid origin, displays compact and cushionlike habit, reaches 2 feet tall by 2 feet wide, and is noteworthy for its sturdy leaves with purple undersides and numerous 2-inch-tall spikes of lavender-blue flowers borne late summer to fall. *H.* 'Carl Teschner', likely of hybrid origin, is a compact 9-inch-tall, 3-foot-wide dark-green-leaved ground cover that is decorated with violet and white flowers during summer.

CULTURE / CARE: Hebes tolerate various soils, but must have good drainage. Their drought tolerance is fair, but watering regularly throughout the summer encourages optimal growth. They prefer full sun in cool areas and light shade in warm climates. No serious pests or diseases have been reported. For maintenance, some gardeners give them only a light shearing following flowering.

PROPAGATION: Stem cuttings should be taken in mid to late summer.

Hedera   PLATE 150
Ivy

Ivies are among the most versatile, useful, and reliable woody ground covers. They flourish throughout most of North America and are magnificent for their shiny evergreen foliage, which comes in countless variations. Ivies are dimorphic, meaning that they have two forms, juvenile and adult. In the juvenile stage they are vinelike, climbing or trailing along the ground, nonflowering, with three-lobed or five-lobed leaves. In the adult form, flowers and fruit are produced, and the foliage is unlobed and darker green. Normally, branches of ivies only make the transition from juvenile to adult form when they have climbed upward as far as they can go, and there is no longer support for them. At this point their new growth displays the characteristics of the adult stage. Interestingly, if you root a cutting from one of these branches, it grows up to become a flowering shrub rather than a climbing vine.

Juvenile forms of ivy make good ground covers, reach 2 to 6 inches in height when unsupported, and spread indefinitely. They are best adapted for use in moderate or large areas and substitute well for turf grass. Their performance along building foundations (where the soil is often very poor) is admirable. Planted next to ledges and allowed to trail over, or near trees or walls that they can climb, they introduce an intriguing vertical dimension. On steep slopes and banks, they are among the most successful soil stabilizers. Regardless of their use, they project an image of aristocracy with their rich evergreen lushness. No regular foot traffic is tolerated.

The flowers of adult ivies contain great quantities of nectar and attract many bees. Birds frequently build nests in the security of ivy branches. Both the foliage and fruit contain a chemical called hederin, which, when ingested, causes a burning sensation in the throat and in severe cases, gastroenteritis, convulsions, and coma. The sap can cause dermatitis, sometimes with severe blistering and inflammation. The leaves are also harmful to livestock.

SCIENTIFIC NAME: *Hedera* (*hed*-er-a) is Latin for ivy.

HARDINESS / ORIGIN: Variable, depending on species and cultivar; Europe, North Africa, western Asia.

LEAVES / FLOWERS / FRUIT: The juvenile leaves are evergreen, leathery, usually dark green, and have three to five lobes, but there is much variation among the horticultural forms. The flowers are white to greenish in small clusters and are only borne on the mature forms of ivy. The fruit which follows is a ⅜-inch-long black capsule.

RATE / SPACING: Growth is slow at first, then faster as plants mature. Most plants from 2- to 3-inch-diameter containers are spaced 10 to 14 inches apart, but a few very slow-growing types should be planted 6 to 10 inches apart. There seems to be no advantage in using larger-sized material.

SPECIES: *H. canariensis* (ka-nare-ee-*en*-sis), named for its place of origin, is commonly called Canary Island ivy, Algerian ivy, or Madeira ivy. Native to the Canary Islands and North Africa, it is the staple ground cover of the California coast and hardy in Zones 8 or 9 to 10. The leaves are evergreen and very attractive. In their juvenile state, they display three to seven lobes, are heart-shaped, and reach 6 inches long by 6 inches wide. They range from light to medium green and are always shiny and smooth. The most popular selections are 'Azorica', with vigorous-spreading habit, leaves with five to seven lobes, 3 to 6 inches wide, vivid green; 'Souvenir de Marengo' ('Variegata, 'Gloire de Marengo'), with leaves edged in silvery white; 'Margino-maculata', leaf margins cream-colored and flecked or spotted with green; 'Ravensholst', with vigorous habit, leaves larger than those of the species; 'Striata', with leaf margins green and midsection streaked light green to ivory.

H. colchica (*col*-chi-ka), meaning of Colchis (the eastern coast of the Black Sea), is commonly called Persian ivy or fragrant ivy. It is a less common species hardy in Zones 5 to 9 or 10. Native to Asia and southeastern Europe, its evergreen leaves are heart-shaped, slightly lobed, thick and leathery, and may reach 10 inches long. They are colored dark dull green and smell very much like celery when crushed. Popular selections include 'Dentata', with shiny green, finely toothed leaves 10 inches long by 8 inches wide; 'Dentata Variegata', with leaves similar to 'Dentata' but edges irregularly variegated with creamy yellow; 'Sulfur Heart', sometimes listed as 'Gold Leaf' or 'Paddy's Pride', leaves light green with yellowish central variegation.

H. helix (*hee*-lix), named for the helical or spiraling pattern of the leaves about the stem, is commonly called English ivy. Beyond compare in popularity, this species comes from Europe and is the most widely cultivated species in North America. Like other *Hedera* species, its juvenile leaves are evergreen and somewhat variable in shape and size. Typically they are three-lobed to five-lobed, triangular to oval, 2 to 3 inches long, and smooth-textured. They are characteristically dark shiny green with whitish to cream-colored veins. The common species is hardy in Zones 5 or 6 to 9, but many cultivars are less cold hardy (see descriptions of individual cultivars).

According to an old folktale, if you place a stem of English ivy under your pillow, the face of your true love will appear in that night's dreams. The species contains fungicidal and insecticidal chemicals and extracts have been used to formulate commercial pesticides. The plant has been used in poultices for application to skin sores, eruptions, and cuts. A resin extracted from the bark has been processed into a tincture that has been used to treat menstrual irregularities and tooth decay. English ivy has long been implicated in the act of drinking, particularly wine. Bacchus (Dionysus), the mythological god of wine, is often pictured with a wreath of English ivy crowning his head and carrying a staff with English ivy wound around it. One source says ivy was thought to counteract the effects of alcohol and this is why Bacchus wore it. Mortal party-goers in ancient Athens are said to have similarly adorned themselves, probably with little sobering effect, and early European drinking establishments used poles adorned with garlands of ivy, called alestakes, to advertise their wares.

Well over 100 cultivars of English ivy are grown in the United States. Some are considered *ramulose* (branching freely), while others branch little or not at all and are referred to as *nonramulose.* The species and a few of the varieties are quite cold hardy (to Zone 5 or 6), yet others can cope only with the winters of Zone 7—these are designated as cold tender. The more popular selections are 'Argenteo-Variegata', with leaves variegated white, cold tender; 'Baltica', with leaves somewhat smaller, veins white, hardy to Zone 5, reportedly discovered in Latvia along the eastern side of the Baltic Sea in 1907 by Alfred Rehder, then herbarium curator of the Arnold Arboretum; 'Brocamp', freely branching, with leaves light green, willow-shaped, 2 inches long by 1 inch wide, hardy to Zone 6; 'Bulgaria', with broad, leathery, dark green leaves that turn purplish during winter, hardy to Zone 5; 'Buttercup', hardy only to about Zone 6, with leaves yellow in youth (if grown in the sun, otherwise green); 'Caecilia', hardy to Zone 6, with creamy white color on wavy leaf margins; 'California Fan', not cold-tolerant, interesting for its light green, fan-shaped, ¾- to 2-inch-wide leaves; 'California Gold', hardy to Zone 6, with leaves that are mottled green and butterscotch; 'Duckfoot', hardy to Zone 6, with small leaves that resemble a duck's foot; 'Flamenco', with twisted and curled leaves, hardy to Zone 6; 'Galaxy', free branching, hardy to Zone 6, with leaves star-shaped, colored medium green; 'Glacier', cold tender, with leaves small, five-lobed, colored green with pinkish and creamy white edges; 'Goldheart', cold tender, with leaves small, three-lobed to five-lobed, green with yellow and cream centers; 'Hahn's' ('Hahn's Self-Branching'), free branching, cold tender, with leaves small, light green; 'Harrison', similar to 'Baltica' but with leaves often reddish purple in winter; 'Hibernica', Irish ivy, hardy to Zone 5, with leaves bigger than those of the species (3 to 5 inches long) and colored shiny dark green, somewhat more vigorous than the species, thought to be the most commonly cultivated form in North America; 'Hummingbird', with green leaves that are sharply cut and resemble the feet of a hummingbird, hardy to Zone 6; 'Jubilee', hardy to Zone 6, with vigorous growth and miniature leaves; 'Little Diamond', hardy to Zone 6, with leaves variegated green and white; 'Maculata', cold tender, with leaves five-lobed, dark green, colored yellow-green with cream and white variegation; 'Midget', dwarf form, with densely set green leaves, compact habit, hardy to Zone 6; 'Miniature Green Ripples', with densely set green leaves, slow growth rate, hardy to Zone 6; 'Minima' (sometimes listed as 'Atropurpurea'), hardy to Zone 6, leaves small, three-lobed to five-lobed, heart-shaped, with wavy margins and dark, dull green coloration, often becoming purplish in fall; 'Needlepoint', freely branching, popular in the South, leaves smaller with a long, narrow center lobe, cold tender; 'Pedata', bird's foot ivy, small leaves with five sharp lobes, cold tender; 'Pixie', with small, crinkle-edged, deep green, deeply lobed leaves and prominent white veins, hardy to Zone 6; 'Savannah', with large glossy heart-shaped leaves, hardy to Zone 6; 'Schaffer Three', hardy to Zone 7, with leaves speckled white; 'Silverdust', with creamy-white-mar-

gined leaves, hardy in Zones 6 to 9; 'Thorndale', hardy to Zone 5, leaves slightly smaller than those of the species with pronounced central lobe and creamy white veins; 'Webfoot', with tiny (less than 1 inch wide) leaves shaped like a duck's foot, cold tender; 'Wilson', much like 'Thorndale', but considerably smaller, hardy to Zone 5; 'Walthamensis', hardy to Zone 5, with 1-inch-wide leaves; 'Woerner', vigorous habit, with dull green leaves that turn purple in winter, hardy to Zone 5.

CULTURE / CARE: As long as they are given good drainage, ivies are quite adaptive to soil type: they prefer rich, acidic, loamy soils, but heavier, lighter, and more alkaline conditions are also accepted. Drought tolerance is quite good, but watering thoroughly once or twice per week during the summer season creates optimum lushness. Ivies adapt to locations with full sun to dense shade. Pests include aphids, caterpillars, loopers, eight-spotted forester, mealybugs, blister beetle, and mites. Diseases of greatest significance are bacterial and fungal leaf spot, leaf blight, stem canker, powdery mildew, and sooty mold. Little or no maintenance is required, other than to clip back the stems as plants outgrow their bounds.

PROPAGATION: Cuttings are the most practical means of propagation and are best rooted during late summer and early fall. Division of rooted stems is an alternative, but because of typically very dense growth, division is difficult and time consuming. Should this be your means, however, divide plants during spring.

Hedyotis caerulea   PLATE 151

Bluets, Quaker Ladies, Innocence, Bright Eyes, Angels' Eyes, Venus's Pride, Star of Bethlehem, Wild Forget-me-not, Quaker Bonnets, Little Washerwoman

This herbaceous, broad-spreading, carpeting ground cover has been popular enough to warrant a whole host of common names. Bluets reach 4 to 6 inches tall, spread more than a foot across, and make good general covers or accent plants, particularly in saturated soils, such as those found in areas with a high water table and at the water line of a pond or stream. No foot traffic is tolerated.

SCIENTIFIC NAME: *Hedyotis caerulea* (hay-dee-*oh*-tis see-*roo*-lee-a). *Hedyotis* comes from the Greek *hedys*, sweet, and *otos*, ear, but exactly how this applies to bluets is unclear. *Caerulea*, dark blue, refers to the color of the flowers.

HARDINESS / ORIGIN: Zones 3 or 4; eastern North America.

LEAVES / FLOWERS / FRUIT: The leaves are semievergreen, light to medium green, simple, ⅜ inch long by

½ inch wide, and narrowly oval. The solitary, funnel-shaped flowers arise upon slender stalks at the tips of the stems. Each is four-petaled and violet, blue, or white with a yellow center. They reach ¼ inch wide and are borne from spring through summer. The fruit is nonornamental.

RATE / SPACING: Growth is moderate. Plants from pint-sized containers are spaced 12 to 14 inches apart.

CULTURE / CARE: Bluets prefer a moist, richly organic acidic soil and light to moderate shade. They tolerate saturated soils but not dry conditions and may need supplemental watering during hot summertime weather. Pests are insignificant, and the few diseases are leaf spots, downy mildew, and rust. Maintenance needs are few if any.

PROPAGATION: Division is easily accomplished during spring.

Helianthemum nummularium PLATE 152
Sun Rose

Low, trailing, somewhat open, this semiwoody, colorful, shrublike ground cover may be gaining popularity in North America. In Europe, it is greatly appreciated and has been incorporated into many gardens. Here, however, though long available, it has not yet caught on. Typically, sun rose reaches 6 to 12 inches tall and spreads to 3 feet across. It is best in rock gardens as a specimen or overhanging stone retaining walls. Additionally, it functions well as an edging for paths and walkways or as a colorful facing when massed on a small scale. The greatest attribute of sun rose is its outstanding floral display. No foot traffic is tolerated.

As with most plants that are of great floral value (such as rose, daylily, and crab apple), sun rose has been extensively hybridized. The result has been a horribly and irreversibly jumbled nomenclature and, fortunately, a multitude of variously flowered selections from which to choose. Sun roses can be purchased with flowers that are single as well as double and in a spectrum of colors that includes white, red, pink, cream, yellow, and all the above in various combinations.

SCIENTIFIC NAME: *Helianthemum nummularium* (hee-lee-*an*-the-mum new-mew-*lay*-ree-um). *Helianthemum* is derived from the Greek *helios,* sun, and *anthemon,* flower. The flowers are definitely colorful and bright and without a doubt justify this lofty analogy. *Nummularium* comes from the Latin *nummus,* a coin, and refers to the shape of the leaves.

HARDINESS / ORIGIN: Zones 5 to 7 in warm humid climates, but quite successful along the coastal regions of Zone 9; Mediterranean region.

LEAVES / FLOWERS / FRUIT: The leaves are oval to linear, evergreen, to 2 inches long by ¼ inch wide, graygreen, and rather unassuming. The large, brightly colored flowers, however, give this ground cover ornamental clout. Produced in quantity, they reach more than 1 inch wide, are five-petaled, colored pink or dusty rose fading to apricot, and last only one day. New flowers open daily from early to mid summer and are showy to say the least. The fruit is nonornamental.

RATE / SPACING: Growth is slow until the roots become well established, then moderate. Plants from gallon-sized containers are spaced 2 to 2½ feet apart.

HORTICULTURAL SELECTIONS: Depending upon what you read, the following cultivars are either classified as selections of the species or of hybrid origin (and thus named *H. × hybridus*). It is unlikely that they will ever be sorted out to everyone's satisfaction so I list the most noteworthy selections here and suggest that you simply appreciate them for their individual merits. 'Amy Baring', with buttercup-yellow flowers, and maybe the only selection that authorities agree is not of hybrid origin; 'Apricot', with apricot-colored flowers; 'Ben Afflick', with golden-yellow flowers and orange centers; 'Ben Nevis', with deep yellow flowers and bronzy red centers; 'Bright Spot', 6 inches tall by 24 inches wide, with hairy gray leaves and coppery-red flowers; 'Cerise Queen', with double red flowers; 'Dazzler', with numerous magenta flowers; 'Eloise', 6 inches tall by 24 inches wide, compact habit, with yellow flowers and an orange central ring; 'Fireball' ('Mrs. C. W. Earle'), with dark red single flowers; 'Flame', with 1-inch-wide flame-red flowers; 'Goldilocks', with bright golden-yellow flowers; 'Henfield Brilliant', 18 inches tall, bright coppery-yellow flowers; 'Jubilee', with double yellow flowers; var. *multiplex,* with small leaves and double, coppery-colored flowers; 'Mutabile', flowers pink in youth becoming light purple, and finally white; 'Pink', with long running pink floral display; 'Orange Surprise', 6 inches tall by 24 inches wide, noteworthy for its golden-orange flowers with dark orange centers and olive green leaves; 'Red', with red flowers; 'Rose Glory', with rose-pink flowers; 'Rose Queen' ('Rosa Konigin'), with rose-pink double flowers; 'Watergate Rose', with rose-crimson flowers and orangish centers; 'Wisley Pink', with pink flowers and grayish foliage; 'Wisley Primrose', much like 'Wisley Pink' but with light yellow flowers; 'Wisley White', with white flowers.

CULTURE / CARE: The best way to kill a sun rose is to place it in soil that does not drain well. Assuming this is not your intent, I suggest somewhat gravelly, slightly alkaline soil in full sun. In the South, light shade brings the best results. Sun roses are very tolerant of drought, but welcome an occasional watering during the summer months. They suffer from no serious pests, and their primary diseases are root rot and leaf spot. Of these, root rot is serious but rarely occurs if the soil is well drained. Maintenance consists of an occasional light shearing when plants become too lanky or when they begin to wander outside of their designated territories.

PROPAGATION: Stem cuttings can be taken during summer.

***

Helictotrichon sempervirens PLATE 153

Blue Oatgrass, Avena Grass

Blue oatgrass is a marvelously blue, tough, utilitarian grass that averages 2 feet tall and spreads 3 feet across. Appreciated both for its flowers and vibrant evergreen foliage, this grass is absolutely striking when used en masse as a general cover, walkway edging, or facing plant. Alone or in small groups, it is a valuable accent or specimen plant. It combines effectively with other clump-forming grasses and naturalizes with countless drought-tolerant, native and introduced herbaceous perennials. Avena is Latin for oatgrass.

SCIENTIFIC NAME: *Helictotrichon sempervirens* (he-lik-toe-*tri*-con sem-per-*vie*-renz). *Helictotrichon* is derived from the Greek *helix,* spiral, and *trichos,* a hair, presumably in reference to the shape of the awns (stiff bristlelike projections) of the florets. *Sempervirens,* forever green, refers to the evergreen foliage.

HARDINESS / ORIGIN: Zones 4 to 8; rocky, calcareous (chalky, alkaline) alpine and subalpine regions of central Europe.

LEAVES / FLOWERS / FRUIT: The evergreen leaves are borne on erect stems that tend to arch over. They reach 1 foot long by ¾ inch wide and taper to a fine point. Rather straight and stiff, they tend to roll inward, and are sparsely hairy. The one-sided, drooping clusters of pale blue flowers of summer reach 6 inches long, turn medium brown upon ripening, and are held upon arching stems to 4 feet tall. The fruit, a grain, is nonornamental.

RATE / SPACING: Growth is slow. Plants from pint-sized to gallon-sized containers are spaced 1 to 2 feet apart.

HORTICULTURAL SELECTIONS: 'Saphirsprudel', with brighter, more intensely blue foliage.

CULTURE / CARE: The soil must be well drained. Any texture, including gravel, will do, and high pH (alkaline) as well as acidic soils are tolerated. On the other hand, very acidic soils (below pH 5) should be avoided. Drought tolerance is pretty good, and only an occasional watering might be needed once plants become established. Blue oatgrass thrives in full sun

and tolerates light shade. Its primary disease problem, crown rot, seldom arises if the soil is well drained. Although no maintenance is required, sometimes people cut back the tattered flower clusters during late summer. The leaves can also be trimmed back to 2 or 3 inches in fall, winter, or early spring, for the same reason.

PROPAGATION: Division of clumps into smaller plantlets is most effective in early spring.

***

Helleborus niger PLATE 154

Christmas Rose

A stemless, herbaceous ground cover that reaches 12 to 18 inches tall and spreads about the same across, Christmas rose has, unfortunately, long been overlooked by North American gardeners. Appreciated in Europe for its early-season flowering (often blooming through the snow) and for its rugged, coarse-textured, leathery, shiny green foliage that remains attractive year-round, Christmas rose and its relatives seem about to come into their own in North America. Currently, there are a number of growers who stock good quantities of the hellebores, and they are constantly testing new hybrids and rare species. Hellebores are ideally suited for use on a small to moderate scale in naturalistic woodland landscapes and are best employed on sloping ground to increase the visibility of their subtle but charming flowers. Lining the edges of a sidewalk or garden path is a job that they perform remarkably well, especially since they must be observed up close to be fully appreciated. All species combine well with showily flowered bulbs, woodland lilies, and hostas. No foot traffic is tolerated.

All parts of the plant are poisonous, and in some individuals, skin contact with the sap can cause dermatitis. Historically, formulations of hellebores were believed to counteract witchcraft and to ward off evil: witches and sorcerers were said to use hellebores in their rituals, while ordinary folk spread hellebores on their floors to drive evil spirits from the home.

SCIENTIFIC NAME: *Helleborus niger* (he-*leb*-er-us / *hell*-e-bore-is *nie*-ger). *Helleborus* is derived from the Latin *elleboros,* a plant considered a remedy for madness. Indeed species of *Helleborus* contain the potent chemical helleborin, but rather than curing madness, helleborin is a potent cardiac glycocide that causes convulsions, delirium, and death from respiratory failure. *Niger,* black, refers to the roots.

HARDINESS / ORIGIN: Zones 3 to 8; Europe.

LEAVES / FLOWERS / FRUIT: The leaves are evergreen, erectly oriented, borne from the base of the plant, seven-segmented, edged with shallow teeth, and colored dark, shiny green. The flowers are borne in late winter and occasionally live up to their reputation of flowering on Christmas Day. They are solitary, held upon red-spotted stalks, 2½ inches wide, and saucer-shaped. Typically, they are colored whitish with tinges of pink. The fruit is nonornamental.

RATE / SPACING: Growth is slow. Plants from quart-sized to gallon-sized containers are spaced 14 to 18 inches apart.

HORTICULTURAL SELECTIONS: Var. *altifolius,* with larger, more prominently toothed foliage borne above the flowers (thus the scientific name which means high-leaved) and large (3- to 4-inch-wide) flowers lightly spotted with red; 'Angustifolius', with narrow leaves; 'Blackthorn Strain', with vigorous habit and flowers that are pink in bud, opening white, aging to pink, and carried upon tall dark stems; 'Eva', with large 4½-inch-wide flowers; 'Foliis Variegatus', leaves with cream and green variegation; 'Harvington Hybrids', flowering earlier than the species; 'Higham's Variety', selected for its reliableness in flowering at Christmas; 'Ladham's Variety', with robust habit and large flowers; 'Louis Cobbett', with flower buds pink, opening to expose pink flushed petals; subsp. *macranthus,* with smaller, relatively spiny leaves and white flowers suffused with rose; 'Madame Fourcade', with dwarf habit and large flowers; 'Major', with flowers like the species but larger; 'Marion', double flowers with white petals; 'Pixie', with semidouble short-petaled flowers; 'Potter's Wheel', distinctive flowers with green centers; 'Praecox', with flowers smaller than the species; 'St. Brigid', with tall dark green leaves; 'Sunset', with variably pink and red flowers; 'Trotter's Form', with large pure white long-blooming flowers; 'White Magic', with small bright green leaves carried upon sturdy dark green stems.

OTHER SPECIES: *H. atrorubens* (at-row-*rew*-benz), meaning very red, is named for its deep purplish flowers. Resembling *H. orientalis,* it is deciduous and displays large, richly purple flowers with green overtones in winter. Hardy to Zone 5 or 6.

H. foetidus (*fet*-i-dus / *fee*-tid-us), bear's foot hellebore, is named in reference to its foul-smelling flowers. Native to Europe and hardy in Zones 5 to 9, it is characterized by erect, stout-stemmed, herbaceous habit and a height of 8 to 14 inches. The leaves are evergreen, arise in a spiral manner around the stem, and are composed of three to nine, narrow, jagged-edged leaflets that are each 2½ to 4 inches long. Numerous pale green, red-edged, ½- to 1¼-inch-wide pendent flowers appear during late winter or early spring. 'Bowles Form', with finely divided leaves, vigorous habit, and numerous large flowers; 'Green Giant', a tall grower with pale green finely divided leaves and bright green bracts; 'Italian Form', similar to 'Bowles Form'; 'Miss Jekyll', with narrow leaflets and sweetly scented flowers; 'Sienna', with dark green leaves and pale green bracts; 'Sierra Nevada Form', with fewer but larger flowers than the species and dwarf habit to 12 inches tall; 'Sopron', with dark metallic foliage and large flowers; 'Tros-os-Montes', large dark green serrated leaves and open flowers with pale bracts; 'Wester Flisk', with red-tinted stems, sometimes extending up to the base of the flower petals, and grayish green leaves.

H. orientalis (or-ee-en-*tay*-lis), named for its native habitat of Asia Minor (also Macedonia and Thrace), is commonly called Lenten rose because it blooms during late winter and early spring during the period of Lent. Of all the hellebores discussed here, this one seems to be the easiest one to grow in North America. Hardy in Zones 5 to 9, this evergreen, stemless, herbaceous ground cover reaches 1½ feet tall by 1½ feet wide. Exceptional in flower, its 3-inch-wide, five-petaled, greenish, yellowish, pink, reddish, or purplish blossoms are usually grouped in fours atop reddish stalks. Often the colors appear in speckled patterns. 'Guttatus' flowers earlier than the species and lasts for more than two months, producing white flowers with tiny burgundy-red spots; 'Medallion', 18 inches tall by 24 inches wide, selected by Siskiyou Rare Plant Nursery, Oregon, displaying pure white, 2-inch-wide flowers that are purple spotted in their centers.

H. viridis (*vye*-ri-dis) is a clump-forming, herbaceous, 10-inch-tall, 18-inch-wide, deciduous, light-green-leaved species. Native to Europe, it produces drooping blossoms of rich green during late winter. It prefers rich soil with or without lime, and is hardy in Zones 4 to 9. Subspecies *occidentalis* 'Pailhès' displays leaves with creamy streaks.

CULTURE / CARE: Although many *Helleborus* species naturally grow in organically rich, well-drained, alkaline soil, they also show some adaptability to acidic soils. They are only moderately drought tolerant, with the lushest growth occurring when the soil is kept slightly moist at all times. They prefer light to moderate shade and seldom require any maintenance.

PROPAGATION: Seed and division are the normal means of propagation. Self-seeding often occurs in the landscape, and small plants are easily dug up and moved. Since seed does not typically store well, it should be sown in an outdoor bed immediately upon ripening for natural stratification and germination the following spring. Hellebores are not difficult to grow from seed but the seed must be fresh and must go through a wintertime cold treatment before spring germination. Division can also be performed and is most successful during spring or early fall.

Hemerocallis

PLATE 155

Daylily

Daylilies are among the most useful ground covers for small, moderate, or large areas. Nearly indestructible and even compatible with black walnut (*Juglans nigra*), they are often excellent choices for use as accent and specimen plants. Placed atop a retaining wall, on sloping terrain, or in beds paralleling steps brings them up to eye level where they can be appreciated to the fullest. Along walkways they are exceptional edgings and at building entrances they present a pleasing, colorful, welcoming appearance. Frequently they are employed as effective foundation plants or as erosion-controlling soil binders. Planted at the edge of a pond or stream, they stabilize the soil and promote a tranquil atmosphere. About the only thing that daylilies do not do is tolerate foot traffic.

Daylily flowers have been used as colorful garnishes. The flower buds and petals may be eaten fresh or dried or canned. The buds are said to be quite tasty when boiled and buttered or pickled, fried, or sauteed. Daylily roots are also edible and are reported to be quite nutritious. Generally, they are dug in the fall or winter and boiled or baked.

SCIENTIFIC NAME: *Hemerocallis* (hem-er-oh-*kal*-is) comes from the Greek *hemera,* a day, and *kallos,* beauty; meaning beautiful for a day, this name refers to the individual flowers that last only one day.

HARDINESS / ORIGIN: Daylilies are among the most adaptable plants in respect to hardiness and can generally be counted on to thrive in Zones 3 to 9, and in some cases as cold as Zone 2 and as warm as Zone 10. It is important to recognize, however, that because of the multitude of daylilies on the market, their rapid rate of introduction, and their varying genetic composition, these hardiness ratings are a mere generalization. There are some that have a much narrower range of hardiness, such as Zones 6 to 8. Thus, as with all plants, the most reliable information regarding hardiness comes from personal testing and experience and the sharing of such knowledge among gardeners, garden club members, and local horticultural professionals. Most daylilies in cultivation today are not species, but hybrids containing genes of several species, most of which hail from central Europe, China, Siberia, and Japan.

LEAVES / FLOWERS / FRUIT: The leaves usually look like giant, broad blades of grass. Either evergreen or deciduous, they originate from the base of the plant. Typically, they reach 6 to 14 inches long on varieties that are considered low, and up to 2 or even 4 feet long on some of the taller forms. Their colors range from light to medium green to grayish or even blue-green, and they are often arranged in such a way that they arch over and give the appearance of graceful, living fans. The flowers provide valuable nectar to hummingbirds and butterflies. Some are fragrant while others have no smell at all. They are arranged in clusters atop stout floral stems, typically above the mass of leaves. Normally they are six-parted, 2 to 6 inches wide, trumpet-shaped, short-lived, and replaced by new ones each day. The blooming period usually lasts about one month, but may run longer in some species and cultivars; some daylilies even flower for most of the growing season. Flower colors range from yellow, orange, reddish, or purplish, and all combinations of colors. A few species open at night, but most flower during the day, generally in late spring or summer. The fruit, an oblong, three-chambered capsule, is nonornamental.

RATE / SPACING: Growth is slow to fast, but generally moderate to fast. Plants from quart-sized to gallon-sized containers are spaced 14 to 30 inches apart.

SPECIES: ***H. aurantiaca*** (awe-ran-tee-*aye*-ka), named from the Latin *aurantiaca,* golden-orange, in reference to the flowers, is commonly called orange daylily. This species, one of the less hardy daylilies (to Zone 6), is a native of Japan. It reaches 3 feet tall and spreads to 5 feet wide. Characterized by 2- to 3-foot-long, 1-inch-wide, evergreen leaves, it appears rather coarse-textured when not in flower. The summertime flowers, which tend to soften the coarseness of the foliage, are orange, often flushed with purple. 'Major' has larger, reddish orange flowers.

H. fulva (*ful*-va), named for its fulvous, or tawny, flowers, is commonly called fulvous daylily, tawny daylily, or orange daylily. A rugged species, it is hardy to Zone 2 yet also thrives in the heat of the Midsouth, to Zone 9. It hails from Europe and Asia, reaches 2 feet tall, and rapidly spreads 3 to 5 feet wide. The leaves reach 1½ to 2 feet long by 1⅜ inch wide, and the unscented flowers reach 3½ inches wide by 5 inches long. Effective during mid summer, the flowers are colored rusty orange to orangish red and are quite visible, as the stalks that hold them may ascend to 6 feet. This very common species has naturalized throughout much of North America and can be seen growing in roadside ditches. It has often been used in daylily hybridizing and is the parent of many important hybrids. Some of its selections include 'Cypriana', with many brownish, 4½-inch flowers and glossy foliage; 'Europa', common along railroad tracks and ditches, very similar to the species but reported to contain three chromosomes where there would normally be only two (a condition known as triploidy) and thus (as is often the case with such plants) is stouter than the species; 'Kwanso', sometimes listed as 'Flore Pleno', noteworthy for its broad, coarse leaves that are sometimes striped white, double flowers borne slightly later in the season than those of the species; var. *littorea* with narrow, grayish yellow petals; 'Rosea', very attractive, with rose-red flowers.

H. hybridus (*hy*-brid-us), hybrid daylily. If in doubt about the classification of a particular daylily, especially one that displays multicolored flowers, guess that it is a hybrid. The species designated *H. hybridus* includes more than 40,000 hybrid selections. Those that receive the most attention are coveted for their floral displays, yet as ground covers, the color, density, texture, and durability of their leaves must also be taken into account. Vigor in respect to rate of spread is also important, and questions about each of these characteristics should be answered to your satisfaction before you make a purchase. Hybrids are hardy in Zones 3 to 8 or 9; deciduous selections (known by daylily aficionados as dormants) are typically regarded as more cold hardy than semievergreen and evergreen selections, but as mentioned previously, there is no substitute for testing or for another gardener's opinion. Should you have an interest in finding out about hybrid daylilies, there are a number of books on the topic, and there are several nurseries specializing in their propagation, hybridization, and sale.

With more than 40,000 registered daylily cultivars for sale, how would you ever know which ones to try? Your best bet, of course, is to visit your nearest daylily demonstration garden, where you can see hundreds of named varieties growing side by side. Not only can you view the plants when they are in flower (beginning about the first of June and extending through the summer months), thereby assessing the number and type of flowers that each produces, later in the fall you can assess the characteristics of the foliage and habit of the plant, after the flowers fade. Additionally, you can compare one variety to another, thereby comparing their flower colors and sizes, as well as the relative height of their foliage and flowers. Specialty daylily nurseries are fascinating as well and often offer more than a thousand cultivars. Of course you might just visit a garden center while its daylilies are in bloom or simply refer to color photos (usually only of the flowers) in catalogs of mail order nurseries. All these methods have their limitations, however, but with so many plants to choose from there is no perfect method. You can, nevertheless, hedge your bet somewhat by trusting in the evaluations of members of the American Daylily Society, who in their quest to develop, grow, and promote more colorful, longer blooming, and more florific cultivars, have developed elaborate methods of judging daylilies, and each year bestow awards upon the finest daylily cultivars.

AWARDS: The awards of distinction (awarded annually) are described below and the judges take into consideration when casting their votes such things as number of flowers, beauty of the flowers, substance of flowers, height of the bloom scape (flower stalk), growth performance, beauty of habit/form, and foliage quality.

AM   Award of Merit; given to ten outstanding daylilies.

ATG   Anne T. Giles Award; for outstanding small flowers.

DF   Donn Fischer Memorial Award; for the most outstanding miniature (flowers smaller than 3 inches).

DS   Don C. Stevens Award; for best eyed or banded daylily.

EF   Eugene S. Foster Award; for outstanding late blooming variety.

HM   Honorable Mention; one step below the Award of Merit, given for excellent quality and performance. Plants must have been introduced two or more years and have demonstrated excellent performance beyond a single region.

HO   Harris Olson Spider Award; for outstanding spider-shaped flowers.

IM   Ida Munson Award; for best double-flowered selection (double or more the usual number of petals).

JC   Junior Citation; for promising seedlings or unintroduced cultivars. These plants that have not been around long enough to impress the judges as to their long-term merits.

JEM   James E. Marsh; for best lavender or purple flower. Discontinued in 1991.

LEN   Lenington All-American Award; for the variety that performs outstandingly in all parts of the country. Plants must have been in cultivation and for sale at least 10 years. Participating judges cast their votes from all parts of the country.

LEP   L. Ernest Plouf Consistently Very Fragrant Award; for highly fragrant deciduous-leaved cultivars. Must have previously won an HM.

RCP   Richard C. Peck Memorial Award; for the best tetraploid daylily.

RPM   Robert P. Miller Memorial Award; for the best near-white-colored flower.

ST   Stout Silver Medal; the most prestigious and considered to be the top daylily award, for the single cultivar that is considered to be the very best. Only previous AM winners are eligible three to six years after winning an AM.

The top daylily selections are described below. Most of them have won awards and thus are in high demand and tend to be more expensive than those that have not been awarded such honors. For each known award, I have included the year the award was given.

BLOOM SEASONS: The bloom season designates the onset of flowering. Most cultivars display a main bloom period of about one month (although the range may be two to six weeks). Those that are considered rebloomers may rest for a short while (which may be virtually imperceptible as is the case with 'Stella de Oro' or maybe three or four weeks with other cultivars) after the primary bloom season, then continue to produce flowers. Although the second period of flowering is not as prolific as the first, it may last for much of the remainder of the growing season. These are the cultivars that I recommend most strongly, as they give you more color and interest for your money, and why not get the most out of your limited garden space?

In the middle of the United States (around Tennessee and Kentucky), the onset of flowering occurs approximately as follows: early begins around late May/early June, mid begins about mid-June, and late begins around late June/early July. For regions farther north, the seasons begin a week or two later and for areas to the south a week or two sooner.

DIPLOIDS/TETRAPLOIDS: Included in the description of each cultivar, I have indicated whether the plant is a diploid, having the normal compliment of chromosomes (11 pairs), or tetraploid having twice the normal number of chromosomes (22 pairs). Naturally occurring species are diploids but sometimes mutations occur spontaneously in nature which causes the chromosome number to double. Even more often, such mutations are induced by experimenters who use a chemical called *colchicine* to cause a doubling of the chromosome numbers. The significance of this is that tetraploid daylilies typically have stouter stems, larger leaves and flowers of greater substance (that is, with thicker and more durable flower petals).

HEIGHT: The height listed in the following cultivar descriptions is the height of the flowers. The leaves will be somewhat shorter than the flowers.

'Alec Allen', early to midseason diploid, repeat blooming, flowers 26 inches tall, 5½ inches wide, creamy yellow, foliage evergreen, awarded AM.

'Always Afternoon', early season tetraploid, repeat blooming, flowers 22 inches tall, 5½ inches wide, with medium mauve-purple centers and green throats, foliage semievergreen, awarded HM92, DS93, AM95.

'Amadeus', early to midseason diploid, repeat blooming, flowers 26 inches tall, 6 inches wide, scarlet-red with green throats, foliage evergreen.

'Antique Carrousel', early to midseason diploid, repeat blooming, flowers 25 inches tall, 7 inches wide, lemon-yellow with green throats, foliage evergreen.

'Apple Tart', early to midseason tetraploid, repeat blooming, flowers 28 inches tall, 6 inches wide, dark red with green throats, foliage deciduous, awarded HM77, AM80, RCP80.

'Barbara Mitchell', midseason diploid, repeat blooming, flowers 20 inches tall, 6 inches wide, with pink petals and green throats, foliage semievergreen, awarded HM87, AM90, ST92.

'Baroody', early to midseason diploid, flowers 29 inches tall, 9½ inches wide, greenish yellow, spider-shaped, foliage deciduous.

'Becky Lynn', early season diploid, repeat blooming, flowers 20 inches tall, 6¾ inches wide, fragrant, with rosy petals and green-throats, foliage semievergreen, awards HM80, AM83, ST87.

'Bertie Ferris', early season diploid, flowers 20 inches tall, 2½ inches wide, with persimmon-orange petals, foliage deciduous, awarded DF73, AM75, ST80, HM87.

'Bette Davis Eyes', early season diploid, repeat blooming, flowers 23 inches tall, 5¼ inches wide, lavender with purple centers and green throats, foliage evergreen, awarded AM, DS.

'Betty Woods', early season diploid, repeat blooming, flowers 26 inches tall, 5½ inches wide, yellow, double, foliage evergreen, awarded IM83, AM87, ST91.

'Black Eyed Stella', early season diploid, repeat blooming, flowers 14 inches tall, 3¼ inches wide, golden yellow with reddish orange centers, foliage deciduous.

'Black Eyed Susan', midseason diploid, flowers 26 inches tall, 5½ inches wide, bright yellow with deep red centers, foliage deciduous.

'Blake Allen', early to midseason diploid, repeat blooming, flowers 28 inches tall, 7 inches wide, deep yellow with green throats, foliage evergreen, awarded AM.

'Brocaded Gown', early to midseason diploid, repeat blooming, flowers 26 inches tall, 6 inches wide, lemon-yellow with chartreuse throats, foliage semievergreen, awarded HM83, AM86, ST89.

'Chester Cyclone', midseason diploid, repeat blooming, flowers 30 inches tall, 8½ inches wide, fragrant, lemon-yellow with green throats, foliage deciduous.

'Chicago Knobby', early to midseason tetraploid, flowers 22 inches tall, 6 inches wide, purple with deep purple centers, foliage semievergreen, awarded HM77, RCP79, AM80.

'Chorus Line', early season diploid, repeat blooming, flowers 20 inches tall, 3½ inches wide, medium pink with rose bands and yellow rims, foliage evergreen, awarded ATG86, LEP88, AM88.

'Christmas Is', early to midseason diploid, repeat blooming, flowers 26 inches tall, 4½ inches wide, deep Christmas red with green throats, foliage deciduous, awarded AM.

'Condilla', early to midseason diploid, flowers 22 inches tall, 4½ inches wide, deep gold, foliage deciduous, awarded IM84, AM85, LEN91.

'Dan Tau', early season diploid, repeat blooming, flowers 24 inches tall, 6 inches wide, creamy green with pink tones and green throats, foliage evergreen, awarded AM.

'Dancing Shiva', early season tetraploid, repeat blooming, flowers 22 inches tall, 5 inches wide, medium pink blend with greenish yellow throats, foliage deciduous, awarded HM76, AM79, RCP80.

'Ed Murray', midseason diploid, flowers 30 inches tall, 4 inches wide, blackish red with green throats, foliage deciduous, awarded HM75, ATG76, AM78, ST81, LEN83.

'Eenie Weenie', midseason diploid, repeat blooming, flowers 10 inches tall, 1¾ inches wide, yellow, foliage deciduous, awarded JC76, HM80.

'Ellen Christine', midseason diploid, repeat blooming, flowers 23 inches tall, 7 inches wide, pink-gold blend with dark green throats, foliage semievergreen, awarded HM90, AM93, IM94.

'Fairy Tale Pink', midseason diploid, repeat blooming, flowers 24 inches tall, 5½ inches wide, pink with green throats, foliage semievergreen, awarded HM84, AM87, ST90.

'Fama', early season diploid, repeat blooming, flowers 26 inches tall, 5½ inches wide, creamy yellow with lavender edges and green throats, foliage evergreen, awarded HM.

'Flutterbye', early season diploid, repeat blooming, flowers 26 inches tall, 6 inches wide, fragrant, lavender with green throats, spider-shaped, foliage deciduous, awarded HM87.

'Forsyth Lemon Drop', early season diploid, repeat blooming, flowers 24 inches tall, 3½ inches wide, very fragrant, lemon-yellow with green throats, foliage evergreen, awarded HM93.

'Frances Joiner', midseason diploid, repeat blooming, flowers 24 inches tall, 5½ inches wide, fragrant, double, rose blend with green-yellow throats, foliage deciduous, awarded HM92, IM93, AM95.

'Fred Ham', midseason tetraploid, repeat blooming, flowers 24 inches tall, 7 inches wide, fragrant, yellow, foliage evergreen, awarded HM88, AM91.

'Golden Prize', late season tetraploid, flowers 7 inches tall, 7 inches wide, golden, foliage deciduous, awarded HM72, AM75, LEN87.

'Golden Scroll', early season diploid, repeat blooming, flowers 19 inches tall, 5½ inches wide, tangerine-orange, foliage deciduous, awarded HM85, AM88, LEP89.

'Hamlet', early to midseason diploid, flowers 18 inches tall, 4 inches wide, purple with dark blue centers and green throats, foliage deciduous, awarded HM, JEM.

'Happy Returns', early season diploid, repeat blooming, flowers 18 inches tall, 3¼ inches wide, fragrant, bright yellow, foliage deciduous.

'Janet Gayle', early season diploid, repeat blooming, flowers 26 inches tall, 6½ inches wide, fragrant, pink-cream blend with green throats, foliage evergreen, awarded AM82, ST86.

'Janice Brown', early to midseason diploid, flowers 21 inches tall, 4¼ inches wide, bright pink with rose-pink centers and green throats, foliage semievergreen, awarded ATG90, DS90, AM92, ST94.

'Jason Salter', early to midseason diploid, flowers 18 inches tall, 2¾ inches wide, yellow with lavender-purple eyes and green throats, foliage evergreen, awarded DF93, DS94, AM95.

'Joan Senior', early to midseason diploid, repeat blooming, flowers 25 inches tall, 6 inches wide, near white with lime-green throats, foliage evergreen, awarded HM81, AM84, LEN90.

'Kate Carpenter', early to midseason tetraploid, repeat blooming, flowers 28 inches tall, 6 inches wide, pale pink with cream throats, foliage evergreen, awarded HM86, AM89.

'Kindly Light', midseason diploid, flowers 28 inches tall, yellow, spider-shaped, foliage deciduous, awarded HO89.

'Lemon Lollypop', early season diploid, repeat blooming, flowers 24 inches tall, fragrant, light lemon-yellow, foliage deciduous, awarded HM90, LEP94.

'Little Business', early to midseason diploid, repeat blooming, flowers 15 inches tall, 3 inches wide, red with green throats, foliage semievergreen, awarded HM74, ATG75, AM77.

'Little Deeke', early season diploid, repeat blooming, flowers 20 inches tall, 4½ inches wide, fragrant, orange-gold blend with green throats, foliage evergreen, awarded HM83, AM86, ATG93.

'Little Grapette', early season diploid, repeat blooming, flowers 12 inches tall, 2 inches wide, grape-purple, foliage semievergreen, awarded HM74, DF75, AM77.

'Lots of Pizazz', early season diploid, repeat blooming, flowers 26 inches tall, 5½ inches wide, golden with ivory edges, foliage evergreen.

'Lullaby Baby', early to midseason diploid, flowers 19 inches tall, 3½ inches wide, fragrant, light pink with green throats, foliage semievergreen, awarded HM80, ATG82, AM83, LEN88.

'Magic Obsession', midseason diploid, repeat blooming, flowers 26 inches tall, 5 inches wide, bright magenta-rose with ruffled gold edges and green throats, foliage semievergreen.

'Malaysian Monarch', early to midseason tetraploid, repeat blooming, flowers 24 inches tall, 6 inches wide, burgundy-purple with creamy white throats, foliage semievergreen, awarded HM90, AM93.

'Mandala', early to midseason diploid, flowers 27 inches tall, 5 inches wide, creamy lavender with ruffled gold edges and yellow centers, foliage evergreen.

'Martha Adams', early to midseason diploid, repeat blooming, flowers 19 inches tall, 6¾ inches wide, rich pink, foliage evergreen, awarded AM.

'Mary Todd', early season tetraploid, flowers 22 inches tall, 6 inches wide, buff-yellow, foliage semievergreen, awarded HM70, AM73, RCP74, ST78.

'Merry Witch', midseason tetraploid, repeat blooming, flowers 30 inches tall, 6 inches wide, rose with lavender overlays, foliage evergreen.

'Ming Snow', early to midseason tetraploid, repeat blooming, flowers 26 inches tall, 5 inches wide, fragrant, creamy pink, foliage deciduous, awarded RPM79.

'Mini Pearl', early to midseason diploid, repeat blooming, flowers 16 inches tall, 3 inches wide, bluish pink with green-lemon throats, foliage deciduous.

'Mini Stella', similar to 'Stella de Oro' but flowers reaching only about 10 inches tall.

'Moroccan Summer', early to midseason diploid, flowers 22 inches tall, 4¾ inches wide, fragrant, double, intense gold with green throats, foliage evergreen.

'My Belle', early season diploid, flowers 26 inches tall, 6½ inches wide, flesh pink with green throats, foliage evergreen, awarded HM77, AM80, ST84.

'My Friend Nell', early season diploid, repeat blooming, flowers 20 inches tall, 4 inches wide, creamy pink with plum-colored edges and green throats, foliage evergreen, awarded HM.

'My Pet', early season diploid, repeat blooming, flowers 20 inches tall, 3½ inches wide, beige with red centers, foliage deciduous.

'Nagasaki', early to midseason diploid, repeat blooming, flowers 19 inches tall, 4½ inches wide, fragrant, double, ivory, cream, pink, and lavender, foliage evergreen, awarded HM82.

'Neal Berry', midseason diploid, flowers 18 inches tall, 5 inches wide, rose-pink with deep pink edges, foliage semievergreen, awarded HM, AM, ST95.

'Olive Bailey Langdon', early to midseason tetraploid, flowers 28 inches tall, 5 inches wide, purple with yellowish green throats, foliage semievergreen, awarded HM77, AM80, LEN85.

'Open Hearth', midseason diploid, flowers 26 inches tall, 9 inches wide, spider-shaped, red and copper with ruby rims, foliage deciduous, awarded HM83.

'Ornate Ruffles', midseason diploid, repeat blooming, flowers 24 inches tall, 5½ inches wide, near white with ruffled edges, foliage deciduous.

'Paper Butterfly', early season tetraploid, repeat blooming, flowers 24 inches tall, 6 inches wide, creamy peach with violet eyes, foliage semievergreen, awarded HM87, DS87, AM90.

'Pardon Me', midseason diploid, flowers 18 inches tall, 2¾ inches wide, bright red with yellow-green throats, foliage deciduous, awarded HM84, DF84, AM87.

'Picotee Princess', midseason diploid, flowers 30 inches tall, 3½ inches wide, soft pink with deep pink frilly edges, foliage deciduous.

'Pink Corduroy', midseason diploid, 28 inches tall, 5½ inches wide, fragrant, rich pink with dark green throats, night-opening, foliage semievergreen, awarded HM88.

'Praire Blue Eyes', midseason diploid, flowers 28 inches tall, 5¼ inches wide, lavender with bluish centers and green throats, foliage semievergreen, awarded HM73, AM76.

'Prester John', early to midseason, flowers 26 inches tall, 5 inches wide, orange-gold, double, foliage deciduous, awarded IM76, AM77, LEN81.

'Princess Ellen', early to midseason diploid, repeat blooming, flowers 18 inches tall, 5½ inches wide, cream with rose edges, foliage evergreen, awarded HM.

'Rachael My Love', early to midseason diploid, repeat blooming, flowers 18 inches tall, 5 inches wide, fragrant, golden-yellow, double, foliage evergreen, awarded HM88, IM89, AM91.

'Raindrop', diploid, repeat blooming, flowers 14 inches tall, 2½ inches wide, medium yellow, ruffled, foliage deciduous.

'Red Rum', midseason diploid, flowers 15 inches tall, 4 inches wide, rusty red with yellow throats, foliage semievergreen, awarded HM79, ATG79, AM82, LEN84.

'Ruffled Apricot', early to midseason tetraploid, flowers 28 inches tall, 7 inches wide, apricot with golden-apricot throats, foliage deciduous, awarded HM76, RCP77, AM79, ST82.

'Russian Rhapsody', midseason tetraploid, repeat blooming, flowers 30 inches tall, 6 inches wide, violet-purple with yellow throats, foliage evergreen, awarded HM76, AM79, LEN89.

'Sebastian', early to midseason diploid, repeat blooming, flowers 20 inches tall, 5½ inches wide, vivid purple with lime-green throats, foliage evergreen, awarded HM83, JEM83, AM87.

'Seductor', early season tetraploid, repeat blooming, flowers 28 inches tall, 6 inches wide, fragrant, apple-red with green throats, foliage evergreen, awarded HM86, AM90.

'Seductress', early to midseason tetraploid, repeat blooming, flowers 18 inches tall, 5½ inches wide, fragrant, beige-lavender with purple edges, foliage evergreen, awarded HM83, AM86.

'Siloam Bertie Ferris', early to midseason diploid, flowers 16 inches tall, 2¾ inches wide, deep rose-shrimp with deep rose centers and green throats, foliage deciduous, awarded HM, DF, DS.

'Siloam Bo Peep', early to midseason diploid, flowers 18 inches tall, 4½ inches wide, orchid-pink blend with deep purple centers, foliage deciduous, awarded HM81, ATG83, AM84.

'Siloam Byelo', midseason diploid, flowers 16 inches tall, 3¼ inches wide, fragrant, rose with red centers and green throats, foliage deciduous, awarded HM83, AM88.

'Siloam Double Classic', early to midseason diploid, flowers 16 inches tall, 5 inches wide, fragrant, pink, double, foliage deciduous, awarded LEP85, IM88, AM91, ST93.

'Siloam Jim Cooper', early to midseason diploid, repeat blooming, flowers 16 inches tall, 3½ inches wide, red with deep red centers, foliage deciduous.

'Siloam June Bug', early to midseason diploid, repeat blooming, flowers 23 inches tall, 2¾ inches wide, gold with maroon centers, foliage deciduous.

'Siloam Merrill Kent', midseason diploid, flowers 18 inches tall, 3½ inches wide, orchid-pink with purple centers and green throats, foliage deciduous, awarded HM87, AM90, ATG92.

'Siloam Virginia Henson', early to midseason diploid, flowers 20 inches tall, 4½ inches wide, pink with ruby centers and green throats, foliage deciduous, awarded HM83, ATG85, AM86, DS89.

'Smoky Mountain Autumn', early season diploid, repeat blooming, flowers 18 inches tall, 5¾ inches wide, fragrant, rose-pink with rose-lavender rims and green throats, foliage evergreen, awarded HM89, LEP90, AM92.

'Sombrero Way', mid to late season tetraploid, repeat blooming, flowers 24 inches tall, 5½ inches wide, orange-apricot with deeper orange throats, foliage deciduous, awarded HM80, RCP78, AM83.

'Snowy Apparition', early to midseason tetraploid, repeat blooming, flowers 30 inches tall, 6½ inches wide, fragrant, near white with green throats, foliage deciduous, awarded RPM80, HM85.

'Stella de Oro', the most popular, longest-blooming daylily in the United States, early to late season diploid, repeat blooming, flowers 14 inches tall, 2¾ inches wide, golden, foliage deciduous, awarded DF79, HM79, AM82, ST85.

'Strawberry Candy', tetraploid, repeat blooming, flowers 26 inches tall, 4¼ inches wide, bright strawberry-pink with rose centers and red spots about their edges, foliage semievergreen, awarded ATG, DS, HM.

'Sugar Cookie', early to midseason diploid, flowers 21 inches tall, 3¼ inches wide, fragrant, creamy with green throats, foliage evergreen, awarded HM86, AM89, ATG89.

'Super Purple', early season diploid, repeat blooming, flowers 26 inches tall, 5⅝ inches wide, fragrant, deep purple with lime-green throats, foliage semievergreen, awarded HM84, JEM86, AM89.

'Sweet Shalimar', midseason diploid, repeat blooming, flowers 24 inches tall, 5½ inches wide, fragrant, with deep persimmon-colored veins, orange petals, and olive throats, foliage evergreen, awarded AM91, EF94.

'Tuscawilla Dave Talbott', early to midseason diploid, repeat blooming, flowers 26 inches tall, 4 inches wide, almond with bold raisin centers and emerald-green throats, night-opening, foliage evergreen, awarded HM94.

'Venetian Lace', midseason diploid, repeat blooming, flowers 30 inches tall, 6 inches wide, light lavender, foliage semievergreen.

'Vintage Bordeaux', early season diploid, repeat blooming, flowers 27 inches tall, 5¾ inches wide, black cherry with yellow edges and chartreuse throats, foliage evergreen, awarded HM91, AM94.

'Vision of Beauty', midseason diploid, repeat blooming, flowers 21 inches tall, 6 inches wide, light pink with pink rims, foliage deciduous.

'Whooperee', early season diploid, repeat blooming, flowers 24 inches tall, 6½ inches wide, fragrant, rose-red with dark red centers and chalky-green throats, foliage evergreen, awarded HM92.

'Wilson Spider', midseason diploid, flowers 28 inches tall, 7½ inches wide, two-tone purple with white centers and chartreuse throats, spider-shaped, foliage deciduous, awarded HO94.

'Winsome Lady', early season diploid, repeat blooming, flowers 24 inches tall, 5½ inches wide, blush pink with deep pink throats, foliage deciduous, awarded HM86, AM71, LEN74.

'Wynnson', early to midseason diploid, flowers 24 inches tall, 4½ inches wide, yellow, foliage deciduous.

'Zinfandel', early to midseason tetraploid, repeat blooming, flowers 26 inches tall, 6½ inches wide, fragrant, burgundy-wine with chartreuse throats, foliage evergreen, awarded HM84, JEM90.

H. lilioasphodelus (lil-ee-oh-*as*-foe-dell-us), named for *Lillium* and *Asphodelus,* two genera with which it shares attributes, is commonly called lemon daylily or yellow daylily. It displays cold tolerance northward to Zone 3, reaches 3 feet tall, and spreads to 3 feet across. A native of eastern Asia, its fragrant, lemon-yellow flowers are borne atop tall arching stalks in spring.

H. middendorffii (mid-den-*dorf*-ee-eye), named after Alexander Theodor von Middendorff (1815–1894), a Russian plant collector, is commonly called Middendorff daylily. Native to Siberia and hardy in Zones 3 to 9, this species reaches only 1 foot tall and displays pale orange flowers during late spring and early summer.

CULTURE / CARE: Daylilies adapt to almost any soil, preferring moist, rich, acidic, well-drained loam. Because of their fleshy, water-storing roots and rhizomes, they are particularly well suited to withstand drought; for mere survival, they seldom require watering other than that provided by nature, but to maximize flower production an occasional deep watering, sufficient to keep the soil slightly moist at all times, is beneficial throughout the flowering season. Daylilies like to grow in full sun to moderate shade and, in general, those with dark flowers are at their best with afternoon shade. Pests include flower thrips, long-horned weevil, Japanese beetle, grasshoppers, mites, slugs, and root-knot nematode. Disease problems such as leaf spot, russet spot, root rot, and crown rot may at times arise. Low or high maintenance is possible, depending upon how fastidious one is. Some gardeners deadhead (pick off faded flowers) at 6:00 A.M. throughout the blooming season; others have learned to appreciate the beauty of faded flowers. Over time daylilies may become crowded and suffer from diminished flower production; this condition can be alleviated by division.

PROPAGATION: Division is the most sensible means of propagation, unless one is a seed-propagating hybridizer of daylilies. Clumps can be divided any time of year, provided the soil can be kept moist for a few weeks until the roots become reestablished.

Herniaria glabra   PLATE 156
Rupturewort, Burstwort, Herniary

This species is one of the most boring ground covers in cultivation today. With nearly unnoticeable flowers and fruit, and a height of only 2 or 3 inches, one might wonder why rupturewort is used at all. But rupturewort is functional. This trailing plant dutifully smothers the ground, excludes weeds, and accepts limited foot traffic. It is useful between stepping stones and, as a turf substitute in smaller areas, it provides a nice uniform green cover. Colorful bulbs and herbaceous perennials can be interplanted with it to add interest.

SCIENTIFIC NAME: *Herniaria glabra* (her-nee-*air*-ee-a *glay*-bra). *Herniaria* comes from the Latin *hernia,* a rupture, in reference to the use of this species at one time in treating hernias. *Glabra,* hairless, refers to the leaves.

HARDINESS / ORIGIN: Zones 5 to 10; Europe, northern and western Asia, Africa, and Turkey.

LEAVES / FLOWERS / FRUIT: The evergreen, simple leaves are oppositely arranged, are oval to elliptic, and reach only ⅛ to ⅜ inch long by ⅛ inch wide. They are colored bright shiny green, turning bronzy in winter, and are the main feature of this plant. The tiny greenish white flowers are formed during mid summer and go all but unnoticed. The fruit which follows is nonornamental.

RATE / SPACING: Growth is slow to moderate. Plants from 2- to 4-inch-diameter containers are spaced 6 to 12 inches apart.

CULTURE / CARE: Rupturewort grows in about any well-drained neutral to acidic soil. It is shallowly rooted and therefore often needs to be watered during the summer. It prefers full sun to light shade. Other than aphids, it has few problems with pests or disease. Trimming back stems as they outgrow their bounds is all the maintenance it ever requires.

PROPAGATION: Propagate by seed, division, and cuttings.

Heuchera sanguinea   PLATE 157
Coral Bells

One of our most prized herbaceous native ground covers, coral bells is sturdy and very easily grown. The typical species reaches 12 to 18 inches tall and forms broad clumps 2 or 3 feet across. It is most frequently used in small-sized to moderate-sized plantings as a general cover or as a facing to buildings, trees, and woodland borders. Not too rambunctious, it is also excellent as an edging to garden paths and sidewalks and border plantings of perennials. It combines well with many deciduous shrubs and trees, as well as lower-growing herbaceous perennials. No foot traffic is tolerated.

SCIENTIFIC NAME: *Heuchera sanguinea* (*hew*-ker-a san-*gwin*-ee-a). *Heuchera* is named after Johann Heinrich von Heucher (1677–1747), a German botanist. *Sanguinea,* blood red, refers to the color of the flowers.

HARDINESS / ORIGIN: Zones 3 to 9; Mexico and Arizona.

LEAVES / FLOWERS / FRUIT: The attractive evergreen leaves arise from the short, stout stems and are held upon 5-inch-long, hair-covered stalks. Roundish to heart-shaped, they are colored dark to rather grayish green (with reddish winter pigmentation) and may reach 1 to 2 inches long by 1 to 2 inches wide. The ¼-inch-wide, red to pink, five-petaled, bell-shaped flowers are borne atop 20-inch-long slender flower stalks that project upward though the center of the foliar mass. They are effective from mid spring through early fall. The fruit is nonornamental.

RATE / SPACING: Growth is slow. Plants from pint-sized to quart-sized containers are spaced 12 to 14 inches apart.

HORTICULTURAL SELECTIONS: Horticulturists have had a field day selecting varieties that differ in their floral characteristics. Most of the time, however, they have been more interested in plants than paperwork and have poorly documented the parentage of many cultivars. Some of the most common, typically sold as selections of *H. sanguinea* are listed below. Other texts may list some of these as selections of *H. × brizoides,* but it is unlikely they will ever be unequivocally classified. 'Alba', with white flowers; 'Apple Blossom', with white flowers that are delicately trimmed in red; 'Bressingham Blaze', with intense salmon-scarlet flowers; 'Bressingham Hybrids', a hybrid group with flowers ranging from white to pink to coral red; 'Chartreuse', with chartreuse-colored flowers and compact growth habit; 'Chatterbox', with deep rose-pink flowers; 'Cherry Splash', leaves with gold and white splashes, flowers cherry-red; 'Coral Splash', vigorous growing, with white overlays to the foliage, flowers coral-red; 'Fairy Cups', with cupped leaves and red flowers; 'Firebird', with deep rose-red flowers on stems to 2 feet tall; 'Fire Sprite', with rose-red flowers borne in compact panicles on stiff stems to 1½ feet tall; 'Freedom', freely blooming with rose-pink flowers and marbled leaves; 'Garnet', with deep rose-pink flowers; 'Green Ivory', vigorous growing, with many white flowers; 'Jack

Frost', with rose flowers and silvery leaves; 'June Bride', with white flowers on 15-inch-tall stems; 'Matin Bells', with coral-red flowers from early summer to early fall; 'Mt. St. Helens', with deep red flowers from late spring to late summer; 'Patricia Louise', with bright pink flowers; 'Pink Splash, slow-growing, leaves with white variegation, flowers pink; 'Queen of Hearts', with larger, redder flowers than the species; 'Rhapsody', with clear rose-pink flowers; 'Rosamund', with many dark pink flowers; 'Salt and Pepper', with white and dark green spots on the leaves; 'Scarlet Sentinel', with scarlet foliage, very vigorous growth; 'Shere Variety', with large deep pinkish red flowers and semievergreen leaves with reddish overlay; 'Silver Veil', large variegated leaves overlaid with silver; 'Snowflakes', outstanding white flowers; 'Snowstorm', flowers cerise, leaves with white and green variegation; 'Splendens', with dark crimson flowers; 'Splish Splash', vigorous growing, with pink flowers and intense winter color; 'Virginalis', with white flowers.

OTHER SPECIES: *H. americana* (a-mer-i-*kay*-na / a-mare-i-*kay*-na), American alum root or rock geranium, bears the name of its homeland, North America. Rugged and coarse appearing, this low-growing woodland species is hardy to Zone 4 and is excellent for planting in dry, rocky, wooded landscapes. Its flowering stems ascend 2 or even 3 feet high, but the leaf mass typically peaks at 3 to 7 inches. The leaves are mostly evergreen, heart-shaped to rounded or oval, and more or less toothed about their edges. They reach 3 to 4 inches wide and measure slightly more in length. Occurring throughout the season, the leaves unfold with purple mottling then become uniformly medium green and sparsely covered with stiff short hairs across their surface. Tiny, greenish, and interesting at best, the late spring flowers unfortunately do not compare favorably with those of coral bells.

Several botanical varieties are discussed in Chapter 6, "Native Ground Covers." They differ from the species chiefly in physical characteristics that are primarily of botanical interest. Cultivars are also available, many the result of hybridization among other cultivars of *H. americana.* Thus there is no guarantee as to exact classification. 'Chocolate Veil', with leaves 6 inches wide and purple highlights; 'Dale's Strain', selected by Dale Hendricks for silvery veins and variably colored leaves, flowers white but relatively insignificant in relation to the leaves; 'Emerald Veil', with 6-inch-wide emerald to metallic green leaves and silver veins; 'Garnet', with garnet-red flowers throughout summer; 'Ring of Fire', with silver leaves and dark purple veins during the growing season, becoming edged bright coral red in fall; 'Sunset', with purple veins that radiate from the midvein to the edges of the leaves.

H. × *brizoides* (bri-*zoy*-deez) refers to several hybrids of uncertain origin, with genes from *H. micrantha, H. sanguinea, H. americana,* and others. They are excellent for one reason or another, and all are hardy in Zones 4 to 9. Many of them are classified differently by different horticulturists. For example, I have seen 'Palace Purple' listed as a cultivar of no fewer than four species. The bottom line then is this: use them—they are good plants, with or without exact nomenclature. 'Amethyst Myst', foliage plum-purple with a metallic gray overlay; 'Bloom's Variety', with dark coral-red flowers; 'Can-Can', leaves deeply divided with silvery-gray overlays and purple veins; 'Canyon Pink', with compact habit to 3 inches tall, 12 inches wide, pink flowers, medium green leaves; 'Cappuccino', with deep brownish purple leaves; 'Carousel', with nearly round leaves that are splashed with silver and with large, bright, vermillion-red flowers; 'Cascade Dawn', with deep purple veins and metallic lavender blades; 'Cathedral Windows', with dark gray veins and purple tones on top of dark green leaves; 'Chiqui', reaching 18 inches tall by 12 inches wide, selected from a cross involving *H. cylindrica* and *H. sanguinea,* characterized by large, long blooming, shrimp-pink flowers above compact rosette-forming leaves; 'Chocolate Ruffles', ruffled leaves with chocolate surface and burgundy undersides; 'Chocolate Veil', with 9-inch-wide purple-highlighted chocolate-black leaves; 'Coral Cloud', with coral-salmon-colored flowers; 'Frosty', leaves with bright silver variegation, flowers deep red; 'Lace Ruffles', with shiny, dark-green-margined leaves that are overlaid with hues of metallic gray; 'Martha's Compact', with compact habit, green leaves, and sprays of tiny white and pink flowers; 'Mayfair', reaching 12 inches tall by 8 inches wide, with a dwarf habit and bright rose-colored foliage, hardy in Zones 4 to 9; 'Mint Julip', with broad silver-frosted mint green leaves; 'Montrose Ruby', the result of crossing *H. americana* and *H.* 'Palace Purple', with dark purple, silver-mottled leaves and tiny wispy white flowers in summer; 'Oakington Jewel', lovely shell-pink, medium green silver-frosted leaves with purple veins; 'Palace Passion', with purple leaves and rose-pink flowers; 'Palace Purple', perhaps the most popular cultivar, with 8- to 12-inch-long leaves a royal shade of burgundy-purple, plant height to 20 inches tall in flower, excellent for color contrast with light green or golden-foliaged companions; 'Persian Carpet', 8-inch-wide metallic blue leaves with purple veins; 'Pewter Moon', with purplish leaves and light silvery-pink overlays, flowers whitish pink; 'Pewter Veil', with new growth coppery pink maturing to pewter-silver; 'Pluie de Feu' ('Rain of Fire'), with cherry-red flowers; 'Plum Puddin', with shiny purple foliage and compact habit; 'Purple Petticoats', with deep purple ruffled foliage; 'Purple Sails', with deep purple maple-shaped, wavy-edged, metallic silver overlaid foliage; 'Raspberry Regal', with many large muted-red flowers and medium green rough-surfaced leaves that are scalloped along their edges; 'Regal Robe', with silver and lavender 10-inch-wide leaves; 'Ruby Ruffles', heavy blooming with leaves that display ruffled edges and a shiny metallic overlay; 'Ruby Veil', with 8-inch-wide leaves and dark purple veins that separate pewter-colored blades which are suffused with ruby-purple; 'Ruffles', with woolly, ruffled, apple green leaves; 'Scintillation', with red-tipped, pink flowers; 'Silver Shadows', with deep silver 7-inch-wide leaves; 'Splendour', with orangish scarlet flowers; 'Stormy Seas', large undulating leaves colored silver, lavender, pewter, and charcoal-gray; 'Tattletale', with clear pink flowers; 'Velvet Night', 7-inch-wide purplish black leaves with dark purple veins; 'Whirlwind', with bronzy green fluted foliage; 'White Cloud', with many tiny white flowers; 'White Marble', with silvery foliage and large white flowers; 'White Spires', with white wispy flowers and ruffled, apple green leaves.

H. pilosissima (pye-low-*sis*-i-ma), hairy alum root, is native to California, 9 inches tall by 18 inches wide, and clump-forming. The hair-covered evergreen leaves are colored flat green with grayish marbling and are transcended by sprays of tiny white flowers in early summer. Hardy in Zones 7 or 8 to 9.

H. villosa var. *macrorhiza* (vil-*oh*-sa mak-roe-*rye*-za) has large fuzzy leaves and stout roots. The parent species hails from Virginia to Georgia and Tennessee and has also given rise to the cultivar 'Purpurea', which is similar to *H.* × *brizoides* 'Palace Purple', but displays a habit that is smaller and more compact, with foliage that is even more intensely purple. Hardy in Zones 5 to 9.

CULTURE / CARE: *Heuchera americana, H. pilosissima, H. micrantha,* and many related hybrids have a definite preference for light to moderate shade. On the other hand, *H. sanguinea* and *H. villosa* prefer full sun to light shade. In other respects, both groups are similar: each prefers well-drained, loamy, slightly acidic soil and tolerates gravelly or stony soils. *Heuchera sanguinea* tolerates neutral and slightly alkaline soil. Fairly drought tolerant, heucheras do better with occasional watering during the heat of summer. Pests include strawberry root weevil, foliar nematode, mealy bugs, and four-lined plant bug. Diseases such as leaf spot, powdery mildew, stem rot, and leaf and stem smut are occasionally encountered. No maintenance is necessary, but some gardeners prefer to trim off the flower stalks at the end of the blooming season.

PROPAGATION: Cuttings are easily rooted during early summer. Division of clumps works best during spring and fall.

Holcus mollis 'Albo-variegatus'   PLATE 158

Variegated Velvet Grass, Calf Kill, Feather Grass, Creeping Soft Grass, Wood Soft Grass, Yorkshire Fog, White Timothy, Dart Grass, Salem Grass

'Albo-variegatus' is a deciduous, rhizomatous, erect-stemmed, soft-textured grass and an eye-catching ground cover. It may be used on a small to large scale as a border edging or as a rock garden specimen. It ranges from 6 to 8 inches tall and spreads indefinitely. The ordinary green species is generally considered too invasive for cultivation as a ground cover. Because of its slower growth rate and showy variegated leaves, 'Albo-Variegatus' is preferentially used. Infrequent foot traffic is tolerated.

SCIENTIFIC NAME: *Holcus mollis* 'Albo-variegatus' (*hole*-kus *mol*-lis *al*-bo-vare-ee-i-*gay*-tus). *Holcus* is derived from the Greek *holkus,* sorghum, in reference to this genus' resemblance to sorghum. *Mollis* means soft in Latin and refers to the soft hairs that often cover the foliage and branches of the inflorescences. 'Albo-Variegatus' means white-variegated.

HARDINESS / ORIGIN: Zones 5 to 9; *H. mollis* is originally native to Europe and Asia but now is naturalized in many parts of North America. The date and place of origin of the variegated selection are a mystery.

LEAVES / FLOWERS / FRUIT: With broad, white, marginal streaks and a narrow central green stripe, the leaves reach 6 to 8 inches long but are less than ½ inch wide. Only a few wispy flowers are borne on narrow oblong panicles in early to late summer. The fruit, a grain, is nonornamental.

RATE / SPACING: Growth is moderate to fast. Plants from pint-sized to quart-sized containers are spaced 8 to 14 inches apart.

CULTURE / CARE: Variegated velvet grass adapts to most well-drained, acidic to neutral soils. It tolerates a fair amount of drought, but is best when periodically watered during hot, dry weather. It prefers full sun to light shade. Other than leaf spot, it has few problems. An occasional mowing neatens its appearance, but even this is not absolutely necessary.

PROPAGATION: Division is best performed during spring.

Hosta   PLATE 159

Plaintain Lily, Funkia

The endlessly useful, clump-forming hostas rank among the most popular herbaceous ground covers. Their popularity is due in part to their ease of culture, the public's greater awareness of the value of landscaping upon property values, and the positive effect hostas have on our ecology. Hostas require no maintenance, become larger and more valuable each year, offer food to bees and hummingbirds, and enrich the soil as they die back to the earth each fall. More than this, I suspect it is the sheer beauty and lushness of hostas that account for their popularity. In my mind, hostas are beyond compare for returning so much beauty and usefulness for so little work.

Hostas range from a couple of inches tall to more than 3 feet, and their spread may range from one to five times their height. They are widely employed for edging walks and perennial borders and are useful as accent plants among ornamental beds containing shrubs and low-growing trees. A dramatic lush appearance is obtained when masses of hostas are planted as bank coverings or facings to trees and foundations, and a single specimen is always very attention getting. Hostas combine well with astilbes, ferns, lilies, spring-flowering bulbs, and countless varieties of deciduous and evergreen trees and shrubs. Reports indicate that *H. fortunei, H. lancifolia, H. undulata* 'Variegata', and likely many other species are compatible with black walnut (*Juglans nigra*). No foot traffic is tolerated.

Hybrid cultivans of hosta number over 4000. Unfortunately, their names are often erroneous, and identical plants are sometimes listed by more than one name. Because of this situation, be sure to exercise caution when ordering hostas, and be sure to read catalog descriptions thoroughly. Reportedly, the Japanese sometimes eat hosta leaves as a vegetable. I haven't found them to be very palatable, but raw fish does not appeal to me either. The common name funkia, originally the genus name, commemorates German botanist Heinrich Funk (1771–1839), a collector of alpine ferns.

SCIENTIFIC NAME: *Hosta* (*hos*-ta) is named after Austrian botanists Nicolas Tomas Host (1761–1834) and Joseph Host.

HARDINESS / ORIGIN: Zones 3 to 8 or 9; China, Korea, and Japan.

LEAVES / FLOWERS / FRUIT: The leaves are deciduous and originate from the base of the plant. They range from long and narrow to short and broad and may be oval or heart-shaped and are often quite conspicuously veined. The trumpet-shaped flowers normally range from white to purple, may or may not be fragrant, and are usually elevated well above the foliage on stout flowering stalks. Both hummingbirds and bees are attracted to their nectar. The fruit is nonornamental.

RATE / SPACING: Growth is moderate, except for some dwarf forms, which spread slowly. Plants, normally available in pint-sized to gallon-sized containers, are spaced a distance equal to their expected mature spread, usually 12 to 36 inches depending upon the variety.

SPECIES: *H. decorata* (dek-oh-*ray*-ta), named for its decorative leaves, is commonly called blunt-leaved hosta. Sometimes listed as *H.* 'Thomas Hogg', it ranges from 12 to 24 inches tall and spreads to 2 feet wide. Its leaves are oval to elliptic, to 6 inches long, blunt or abruptly pointed, and colored green with prominent white edges. The flowers are dark violet in late summer.

H. fluctuans (fluk-*too*-anz), hardy to Zone 4 and hailing from Japan, reaches 36 inches tall by 80 inches wide. The oval to elliptic leaves are colored bright shiny green and make a nice backdrop to the clusters of purple flowers borne in summer. The species is somewhat uncommon, but its extraordinary cultivar, 'Variegata', is readily available. 'Variegata' reaches 30 inches tall by 70 inches wide. The somewhat wavy leaves with blue-green centers and iridescent yellow edges reach 13 inches long by 11 inches wide. By mid summer the leaf edges change to creamy white and above the foliage, on 4-foot-tall stalks, are borne lavender flowers.

H. fortunei (for-*tewn*-ee-ee), named after Robert Fortune (1812–1880), a plant collector, is commonly called Fortune's hosta. It reaches 2 feet tall and spreads to 2 feet wide. Its leaves are heart-shaped to oval, to 5 inches long by 3 inches wide, and colored pale green. The flowers of mid summer are pale lilac to violet and borne upon stalks to 3 feet tall. Some of the most popular selections include 'Aoki', with gray-green leaves, lavender-purple flowers, and a height to 2 feet; 'Aureo-marginata', with dark green leaves and gold margins; 'Gloriosa', with deeply grooved lanceolate leaves edged with a thin border of white; 'Hyacinthina', with green to blue-gray leaves; 'Gold Standard', reaching 2 feet tall, with pale lavender flowers in summer, golden leaves edged with green; 'Marginato-Alba', with large leaves (to 11 inches long), broadly edged in white.

H. lancifolia (lan-si-*foe*-lee-a), narrow-leaved hosta, reaches 1½ to 2 feet tall and spreads to 18 inches wide. Its dark glossy green leaves are oval to lance-shaped and 5 to 7 inches long by ½ to 3½ inches wide. The flowers are pale lavender, borne in late summer to early fall, and are held upon 2-foot-tall stems.

H. montana (mon-*tay*-na / mon-*tan*-a), named for its mountainous habitat, is hardy to Zone 4. Native to Japan, it has dark green elongate to heart-shaped leaves that reach 20 inches long by 11 inches wide. The surfaces of the leaves are roughened by the impressed veins, and the leaves tend to droop at their tips. The whole foliar mass reaches 30 inches tall by 4 feet wide and is transcended during early summer with pale purple flowers. 'Aureo-marginata' is slightly smaller and has leaves edged with bright yellow; 'Mountain Snow', with large medium green, white-edged, heart-shaped leaves; 'On Stage', leaves with green margins and yellow centers; var. *praeflorens* is slower growing and shorter than the species.

H. plantaginea (plan-ta-*jin*-ee-a), fragrant hosta, reaches 10 inches tall, and spreads to 3 feet wide. Its leaves are glossy yellowish green, to 10 inches long by 7 inches wide, and oval to heart-shaped. The horizontally held white flowers bloom from late summer to early fall and are more valuable than those of many other hostas. Cut and placed in a vase, they fill entire rooms with their lovely fragrance. 'Aphrodite', with superbly fragrant, pure white double flowers; 'Grandiflora', with foliage and flowers longer and narrower than those of the species, the magnificent flowers resemble Easter lilies.

H. sieboldiana (see-bold-ee-*aye*-na), Siebold hosta, reaches 18 inches tall and spreads to 3 feet wide. Its leaves are oval with heart-shaped bases, reach 10 to 15 inches long by 6 to 10 inches wide, and sometimes partially obscure the pale lilac, mid to late summertime flowers. Popular horticultural selections include 'Alba', with green leaves and pure white flowers; 'Aurora Borealis', similar to 'Frances Williams' (see below) but with colors more intense and growth more vigorous, reaching 4 feet tall by 5 feet wide; 'Elegans', with broad, rounded, bluish green leaves; 'Frances Williams', with blue-green leaves and gold margins; 'Golden Sunburst', with golden leaves; 'Great Expectations', 30 inches tall, leaves blue-green with cream centers, flowers near white; 'Helen Doriot', with white flowers and puckered blue leaves; 'Louisa', slow-growing, diminutive, with white flowers and wide, white-margined leaves; 'May T. Watts', leaves puckered with gold centers and white margins; 'Northern Halo', from Walter's Gardens in Holland, Michigan, with bluish green foliage edged in creamy white; 'Robusta', with very large, blue-green foliage.

H. undulata (un-dew-*lay*-ta), named for its undulating leaf margins, is commonly called wavy-leaved hosta. This magnificent species reaches 2 to 3 feet tall and spreads to 2 feet wide. Its leaves are elliptic to oval, to 8 inches long by 3 inches wide, pointed, wavy edged, and variegated green with cream or white in the middle. The pale lavender flowers are 2 inches long and are elevated atop 3-foot-tall stalks during summer. Horticultural selections include 'Albo-marginata', with leaves edged in white; 'Erromena', slightly larger and more robust; 'Univittata', less vigorous with less wavy-edged leaves showing a narrow central white stripe; 'Univittata Middle Ridge', with large dark green leaves and prominent creamy white streaks; 'Variegata', reaching only 10 inches tall, leaves with white centers and green margins.

H. ventricosa (ven-tri-*koe*-sa), blue hosta, is native to Japan and Siberia and reaches 3 feet tall by 3 feet wide. Its leaves are dark shiny green, oval to heart-shaped, large (to 9 inches long by 8 inches wide), with slightly twisted, short pointed tips. The abundant flowers of late summer are dark violet to near blue and reach 2 inches long on 3-foot-tall stalks. Two of the more popular selections are 'Aureo-maculata', with leaves mottled green and yellow in spring, and 'Aureo-marginata', with yellow-margined foliage.

H. yingeri (ying-*er*-eye) reaching 18 inches in bloom, was collected and named by Barry Yinger. Hardy in Zones 3 to 8 or 9, it displays narrow, medium green, heavy-textured foliage. Its flowers of pale lavender are held horizontally on the flower stalk and are among the most lovely of the hostas.

OTHER SELECTIONS: Many hostas are useful as ground covers. Often they are derived from hybridization, and their parentage is not well documented. Some of the finest ones include 'Abiqua Drinking Gourd', 16 inches tall, with round deeply cupped blue-green leaves, clumps 16 inches wide with white flowers; 'Antioch', 24 inches tall, oval leaves with wide white margins and two-tone green center, clumps to 5 feet wide, flowers pale lavender in mid summer; 'August Moon', with large round yellow-puckered leaves and pale lavender flowers; 'Big Daddy', 24 inches tall, 3 feet wide, with deep blue, round, puckered leaves and white flowers; 'Blue Angel', with huge blue heavy-textured leaves, 30 inches tall by 6 feet wide, white summerborne flowers; 'Blue Cadet', less than 10 inches tall, with dark lavender flowers and heart-shaped blue-green leaves; 'Blue Diamond', 19 inches tall by 34 inches wide with 7-inch-long, 4½-inch-wide frosty blue-green oval leaves, flowers pale lavender on 30-inch-tall scapes during mid to late summer; 'Blue Wedgewood', 13 inches tall by 2 feet wide, with lavender early summerborne flowers above blue wedge-shaped relatively slug resistant leaves; 'Bright Glow', 13 inches tall by 36 inches wide, with leaves 7 inches

long by 6 inches wide, chartreuse early in the season, then bright golden yellow by mid summer, near white flowers borne mid summer atop 20-inch-tall stalks; 'Brim Cup', less than 10 inches tall, with seersuckered rich green, white-margined leaves and light blue flowers; 'Camelot', 14 inches tall by 26 inches wide, with prominently veined frosty blue leaves 7 inches long by 6½ inches wide, near white flowers on 2-foot-tall stalks during mid to late summer; 'Daybreak', 22 inches tall by 3 feet wide with exceptionally bright deep golden-yellow heavy-textured, prominently veined leaves and lavender-blue flowers in late summer; 'Diamond Tiara', 15 inches tall by 2 feet wide, with small rounded medium green, white-edged leaves and dark purple flowers in early summer; 'Don Stevens', 18 inches tall by 2 feet wide, with glossy green, wide creamy yellow bordered, red-stalked leaves and dark purple flowers in late summer; 'Ellerbroek', 18 inches tall, with deep green, gold-edged leaves and lavender flowers; 'Fragrant Blue', 8 inches tall by 12 inches wide, with near white fragrant flowers above chalky deep blue foliage; 'Fragrant Bouquet', 16 inches tall by 2 feet wide, with apple green leaves and wide creamy margins, fragrant white flowers in early summer; 'Francee', leaves light green with white-edges, one of the most attractive selections, reaches 2 feet tall, lavender flowers in late summer; 'Frosted Jade', 32 inches tall by 5 feet wide, attractive soft green, white-edged narrowly shield-shaped slightly wavy leaves 14 inches long by 10 inches wide, flowers pale lavender borne upon 3-foot-tall stalks during mid summer; 'Ginko Craig', 8 inches tall by 20 inches wide, with vigorous spread and attractive lance-shaped green, white-edged leaves, flowers medium lavender in late summer; 'Gold Edger', 8 inches tall, with neatly arranged gold leaves and lavender flowers in mid summer; 'Golden Scepter', 12 inches tall by 18 inches wide, with rounded bright golden leaves, flowers light lavender, vigorous growth; 'Golden Tiara', 15 inches tall by 20 inches wide, round green leaves with chartreuse edges and medium lavender flowers; 'Gold Standard', 15 inches tall, leaves with bright yellow centers and deeply green border, flowers lavender; 'Green Fountain', sometimes listed as a cultivar of *H. kikutii,* has a lush green, leafy effect in the landscape, shiny green leaves 3 inches wide by 10 inches long and arranged in tiers to create neat, 3-foot-tall fountainlike mounds, numerous lavender flowers in late summer; 'Green Gold', 18 inches tall, with oval, deep green, creamy-yellow-edged leaves, lavender flowers during mid summer; 'Ground Master', a wonderful ground cover that covers and binds the soil completely, slow growing at first, 12 inches tall, leaves 10 inches long by 4 inches wide, green with wavy white margins, abundant lavender flowers in late summer; 'Hadspen Blue', one of the finest blue forms, mound-forming, 1 foot tall, leaves 4 inches wide by 5 inches long and rich blue-lavender flowers in late summer; 'Halcyon', 16 inches tall by 32 inches wide, with deep bluish green leaves 8 inches long by 5⅓ inches wide, lavender summerborne flowers; 'Honeybells', 20 inches tall, with large elongated light green leaves topped by violet-white flowers in late summer; 'Inniswood', 24 inches tall by 30 inches wide, leaves wide with deep green edges and golden centers, clumps to 4 feet wide with lavender flowers atop 30-inch-tall stems; 'Janet', with bright yellow, golden, or whitish leaves (varying throughout the growing season) edged in green, lavender flowers in summer, 16 inches tall at maturity; 'June', a sport of 'Halcyon' with blue and green edged, golden leaves often bleaching to creamy white in sun; 'Krossa Regal', to 3 feet tall, with frosty blue upright oriented leaves and lavender flowers on tall stalks in mid summer; 'Leona Fraim', 11 inches tall by 24 inches wide, leaves rounded with wide white margins and deep green centers, flowers light lavender in mid summer; 'Love Pat', 14 inches tall by 2 feet wide, round wavy leaves colored intense blue, with flowers borne during early summer; 'Midas Touch', golden leaves deeply wrinkled and with margins that roll up in a cusplike manner, 14 inches tall, lavender flowers in summer; 'Night Before Christmas', 18 inches tall by 30 inches wide, attractive leaves 8 inches long by 3 inches wide with white central stripe, broad medium green edges, and prominent veins, flowers lavender on 30-inch-tall stalks in early summer; 'North Hills', 18 inches tall, with medium green, white-edged leaves, stoloniferous habit, lavender flowers in mid summer; 'Patriot', with compact habit, 12 inches tall by 30 inches wide, leaves dark green with bright broad edges of white; 'Paul's Glory', 15 inches tall, leaves with gold centers and wide blue edges, flowers near white; 'Royal Standard', 24 inches tall, with glossy green leaves forming 4-foot-wide clumps, fragrant white flowers in mid summer; 'Sea Thunder', 12 inches tall by 12 inches wide, vigorous habit, leaves glossy green with bright creamy white centers, lavender flowers during mid summer; 'Shade Fanfare', light green leaves with creamy white margins, mound-forming, 1½ feet tall, lavender flowers in mid summer; 'Shade Master', with reliably golden foliage, vigorous growth, and lavender flowers in summer, 2 feet tall; 'Snow Crust', 24 inches tall by 4 feet wide, with lovely narrowly oval, soft medium green, white-edged leaves 12 inches long by 8 inches wide, and pale lavender flowers upon 30-inch-tall stalks during mid summer; 'So Sweet', 15 inches tall, leaves with medium green centers and creamy yellow edges, flowers very fragrant, near white, in late summer; 'Spritzer', 14 inches tall by 2 feet wide, leaves with chartreuse centers and two-tone green edges, flowers bluish purple in mid summer; 'Striptease', 20 inches tall, leaves dark green with a narrow central cream-colored stripe; 'Sugar and Cream', 18 inches tall, green leaves wavy and puckered, edged in creamy white, flowers near white in late summer; 'Sum and Substance', 20 inches tall by 6 feet wide, extraordinary selection with giant rounded chartreuse foliage, pale lavender flowers atop 30-inch-tall spikes; 'Sun Power', 22 inches tall by 3 feet wide, with superb twisted golden-yellow leaves arranged in vase-shaped habit, light lavender flowers; 'Tiny Tears', 5 inches tall by 18 inches wide, with medium green oval-shaped leaves 3½ inches long by 2½ inches wide, purple flowers borne upon 18-inch-tall scapes in mid summer; 'White Christmas', 12 inches tall by 2 feet wide, with white centers and wavy green margins, flowers lavender; 'Wide Brim', 18 inches tall, round leaves colored bluish green with wide creamy margins, flowers lavender on 20-inch-tall stalks in mid summer; 'Yellow River', 28 inches tall by 5 feet wide, with deeply veined medium green, gold-edged leaves 12 inches long by 8 inches wide, lavender flowers borne upon 3-foot-tall stalks mid to late summer; 'Yellow Splash Rim', 16 inches tall, oval leaves with dark green centers and creamy edges, flowers purple in mid summer.

CULTURE / CARE: Hostas prefer acidic sandy or light loamy soil with good drainage, but well-drained clayey soils are fine as well. They do not tolerate drought well and, unless irrigation is readily available, should be kept out of windy locations. They prefer light to dense shade, although in cool climates with high humidity, they often thrive in full sun. Their main pests are snails and slugs, blister beetle, earwigs, cutworms, inchworms, weevils, leaf-cutter bees, and deer. Rodents may also eat hostas, particularly immature plants in woodland settings. The most common diseases are leaf spots and crown rot. Maintenance needs are few if any.

PROPAGATION: Division, the standard method of propagating hostas, is best performed during spring or fall.

Houttuynia cordata   PLATE 160

A rather unusual herbaceous ground cover, houttuynia functions well in small to large areas. It reaches 12 to 15 inches tall, spreads indefinitely, and because of its tenacious rhizomatous habit, must be either given room to spread or surrounded by a deep edging or sidewalk. Once used in Japan to treat respiratory diseases, here it is used to cover the ground, and the variegated and bronzy colored selections provide contrast and heighten interest. Houttuynia is remarkably capable of withstanding high moisture, and thus is well suited to stabilize the soil around ponds and streams. So tolerant of water is it that it is sometimes grown in containers placed directly in the water. Only limited foot traffic is tolerated.

SCIENTIFIC NAME: *Houttuynia cordata* (howt-toe-*in*-ee-a kore-*day*-ta). *Houttuynia* commemorates the Dutch botanist Dr. Martin Houttuyn (1720–1794). *Cordata,* heart-shaped, refers to the shape of the leaves.

HARDINESS / ORIGIN: Zones 4 or 5 to 8; Japan, south to the mountains of Java and Nepal. Houttuynia may be killed back by late spring frost, but will quickly recover.

LEAVES / FLOWERS / FRUIT: The deciduous, deep green, simple, alternate, oval to heart-shaped leaves reach 2 to 3 inches long by 1½ inches wide and smell of citrus. The tiny yellowish flowers are arranged in ½-inch-long spikes subtended by four white petal-like bracts, reminiscent of dogwood. They appear in June.

RATE / SPACING: Growth is moderate to fast. Plants from 3- to 4-inch-diameter containers are spaced 8 to 10 inches apart.

HORTICULTURAL SELECTIONS: 'Plena', with bronzy green foliage and extra bracts, giving the appearance of semidouble flowers; 'Variegata' (sometimes listed as 'Chameleon'), with foliage interestingly colored yellow, green, pale green, gray, cream, and scarlet (yellow and red becoming predominant in fall).

CULTURE / CARE: This species and its cultivars are adaptable to various types of soil provided the soil remains constantly moist or wet. They are not tolerant of drought. They prefer full sun to moderate shade, with the variegated selection coloring best in full sun. The primary pests are leaf spot, aphids, and slugs. Although no maintenance is needed, some gardeners mow plantings once or twice each season to rejuvenate and thicken them.

PROPAGATION: Stem cuttings root well throughout the growing season. Division can be performed with good success during spring and fall.

Hudsonia tomentosa   PLATE 161

Beach Heather, Woolly Beach Heather, Poverty Grass, False Heather, Woolly Hudsonia, Bear Grass, Poverty Plant, Dog's Dinner, Ground Moss, Ground Heather

A low-growing, decumbent, subshrubby ground cover, beach heather reaches 6 to 10 inches tall and spreads 3 to 4 feet across. The landscape use of hud-sonias is uncommon; however, in naturalized landscapes by lakes, rivers, or oceans, these plants add an element of uniqueness. Here they may be used alone or in small groups for specimen or accent planting. In sand dunes, when planted in colonies, they make very unusual general covers that help reduce the blowing and drifting of sand. They combine well with grasses such as little blue stem (*Schizachyrium scoparium*) and beach grasses (*Ammophila breviligulata, Calamovilfa longifolia*), and shrubby ground covers such as bearberry (*Arctostaphylos uva-ursi*) and sweet fern (*Comptonia peregrina*). No foot traffic is tolerated. The genus *Hudsonia* contains only three species; the most likely to be encountered is *H. tomentosa.*

SCIENTIFIC NAME: *Hudsonia tomentosa* (hud-soe-*nee*-a toe-men-*toe*-sa). *Hudsonia* is named in honor of William Hudson (1730-1793), an English botanist. *Tomentosa,* hairy, refers to the foliage.

HARDINESS / ORIGIN: Zone 3; sand dunes and pine barrens from New Brunswick to Virginia along with isolated colonies westward to the Mackenzie River in northwestern Canada, North Dakota, Minnesota, and the Great Lakes region.

LEAVES / FLOWERS / FRUIT: The simple, evergreen, scalelike, stemless, overlapping, ⅛-inch-long leaves are pale green and covered with hoary grayish hairs. In winter they turn bronzy to grayish bronze. The numerous solitary, five-parted flowers are carried on short, stout stalks toward the ends of the branches. They are borne in early summer. Each petal is oblong-oval and colored a vibrant shade of sulfur-yellow. The fruit that follows is ornamental.

RATE / SPACING: Growth is slow. Plants from pint-sized to gallon-sized containers are spaced 2½ feet apart.

HORTICULTURAL SELECTIONS: Var. *intermedia,* sometimes represented as a hybrid of *H. tomentosa* and *H. ericoides,* with leaf tips projecting outward and flowers on longer stalks than those of *H. tomentosa.*

OTHER SPECIES: *H. ericoides* (er-i-*koy*-deez), meaning similar to *Erica* (heath), is commonly called heathlike hudsonia, beach heather, and golden heather. It is hardy to Zone 3, reaches 7 inches tall, and resembles *H. tomentosa* with the exception that the flowers are carried on longer stalks and the foliage is more greenish and more closely pressed toward the stems. It is native from Nova Scotia to North Carolina. Forma *leucantha* is a white-flowered variant.

H. montana (mon-*tay*-na / mon-*tan*-a), mountain beach heather, is found in the mountains of North Carolina. It is closely related to *H. ericoides* but much less common.

CULTURE / CARE: Beach heather requires beach sand

with excellent drainage and neutral or acidic pH. Because the root system goes down very deep into the sand, tolerance of drought is excellent; even so, an occasional deep watering may be helpful during the summer, though it is seldom essential. Beach heather prefers full sun. Few diseases have been reported, but fungal blight can sometimes be a problem, and rabbits, which chew the branch tips, are an occasional pest. Maintenance seldom goes beyond a light shearing after flowering to rejuvenate growth and promote compactness.

PROPAGATION: Typically, only small (8 inches or less in diameter) plants are successfully transplanted. Be sure to dig deep and wide when taking up the rootball, otherwise the plants will likely live for a short while then die. Natural populations of these species are not what they once were; therefore, transplanting should only be conducted from one garden to another, or from native populations that are scheduled to be destroyed by building or road construction. Fresh seed should be sown in trays or deep plugs. The medium should be moist acidic or neutral sand, and the container should be covered with clear plastic until germination occurs. When well rooted, seedlings should be transplanted to a deep container (6 to 10 inches deep by 3 inches wide) still using sand as the medium. When they fill these pots, upgrade them to pint-sized or quart-sized containers, then finally, transplant them into the landscape.

Hydrangea anomala subsp. *petiolaris*   PLATE 162
Climbing Hydrangea

Climbing hydrangea is a clinging vine which harmlessly attaches itself to trees by means of rootlike holdfasts. Although it is most often encountered as a climber, if unsupported, it holds its own as a moderate-scale to large-scale general cover.

SCIENTIFIC NAME: *Hydrangea anomala* subsp. *petiolaris* (hy-*dran*-gee-a / hy-*drain*-jee-a a-*nom*-a-la pet-ee-oh-*lay*-ris). *Hydrangea* is derived from the Greek *hydor,* water, and *angeion,* a vase or vessel, in reference to the shape of the seed capsule, presumably resembling a vessel used for carrying water. *Anomala,* from the Greek *anomalas,* deviating from what is usual, may be in reference to the vinelike nature of this plant—most other species being shrubby. *Petiolaris* refers to the long leafstalks, or petioles.

HARDINESS / ORIGIN: Zones 5 to 7 or 8; China, Korea, and Japan.

LEAVES / FLOWERS / FRUIT: The deciduous dark green, broadly oval leaves are oppositely arranged and reach 2 to 4 inches long by 1½ to 3 inches wide. Along their edges are rather coarse teeth. The fragrant flowers of late spring to early summer, which are borne in broad 6- to 10-inch-wide flat-topped clusters, are of two types: sterile and fertile. The fertile flowers are dull white, not very showy, and located in the middle of the clusters. The sterile flowers are found around the edges of the clusters, reach 1 to 1¾ inches wide and display showy white petals. Although the fruit is nonornamental, the flower clusters are persistent and are of interest even after they fade away and dry out.

RATE / SPACING: Growth is slow until plants are established, then moderate. Plants from 1- to 2-gallon-sized containers are spaced 2½ to 3½ feet apart.

HORTICULTURAL SELECTIONS: 'Skyland's', with larger flower clusters.

CULTURE / CARE: Climbing hydrangea is a bit temperamental, especially during its first few years. Until it becomes well rooted, its stems grow very little. Once established, it spreads much faster, often covering 12 or more inches during a season. To help it become established quickly, water it amply during the first season and fertilize it each spring. It prefers fertile, well-drained, acidic to neutral, loamy soils. Drought tolerance is fair, but unless the ground is kept moist, the floral display will be unimpressive. Climbing hydrangea prefers light to moderate shade, but full sun is tolerated if the ground is kept moist. Stem rot, bud blight, leaf spots, rust, and powdery mildew are the main disease problems. Aphids, two-spotted mite, rose chafer, scales, leaf tier, rabbits, and nematodes are the main pests.

PROPAGATION: Stem cuttings root relatively well during early summer if treated with 3000 ppm IBA/talc and stuck in a very well-drained medium. Seed is sometimes available commercially and is said to germinate well after two to three months of cold stratification.

Hypericum   PLATE 163
St. John's Wort

The St. John's worts may be better known for the tall representatives of the genus, but some of the slower-growing, more refined, low-shrubby forms can be used as ground covers for walk and driveway edging. In addition, there are a number of outstanding low, trailing, subshrubby forms that excel as ground covers. Of great usefulness on medium to large slopes, they are exceptional for their dense network of erosion-controlling roots and rhizomes, dark green semisucculent foliage, assertive spreading qualities, and extraordinary bright yellow flowers. The flowers are important to bees, not because they produce nectar, but because they provide copious amounts of pollen, the source of protein for bees. No foot traffic is tolerated.

SCIENTIFIC NAME: *Hypericum* (hi-*per*-i-kum) is a Greek name of obscure meaning, possibly from *hyper,* over, and *ereike,* a heath, in reference to the natural habitat of some species being at higher elevations than that of *Erica* (heath) species. Or, possibly it comes from the Greek *hyper,* above, and *eikon,* a picture, alluding to it having been hung above pictures to ward off evil spirits.

HARDINESS / ORIGIN: See individual species for hardiness; temperate and subtropical regions of the Northern Hemisphere.

LEAVES / FLOWERS / FRUIT: The green to blue-green leaves vary with the species and may be deciduous, semievergreen, or evergreen, and range from narrow to broad. The flowers, the outstanding feature of most species, are bright sunny yellow and give rise to nonornamental fruit.

RATE / SPACING: Moderate, varies somewhat with the species; see individual species for spacing recommendations.

SPECIES: *H. buckleyi* (buk-*lee*-eye), Blue Ridge St. John's-wort, is native to North Carolina and Georgia. Hardy in Zones 6 to 8, this semiwoody, low, matlike, rather small, shrubby ground cover reaches only 12 inches tall. Its leaves are deciduous, oval, ½ to ¾ inch long, and colored medium to dark green. The yellow flowers may be solitary or arranged in bundles of three and reach 1 inch wide. They are borne on last season's growth and are effective in early summer. While growth is moderate to fast, rate of spread is easily controlled. Plants from quart-sized or gallon-sized containers are spaced 1½ to 2¼ feet apart.

H. calycinum (kal-*is*-e-num / kal-i-*sye*-num / kal-i-*kee*-num), named for its large cup-shaped calyxes (rings of leaflike scales found below the petals of the flowers), is commonly called Aaron's beard, rose-of-Sharon, gold flower, or creeping St. John's-wort. It is most commonly used for ground cover and displays a dense, trailing, semiwoody habit. It spreads tenaciously by underground stems. Plants from pint-sized to gallon-sized containers are spaced 2½ to 3 feet apart. Hardy in Zones 6 to 10, occasionally with top growth being killed to the ground in winter in Zone 6, this species hails from southeastern Europe and Turkey, reaches 12 to 18 inches tall, and spreads indefinitely. Its leaves are semievergreen, oval to oblong, to 4 inches long by 1 inch wide, medium to dark green above and bluish green below, becoming purplish in fall. During early summer to early fall, they serve as a splendid backdrop to the many enormous solitary 3-inch-wide, stupendously showy, brilliantly yellow, pollen-laden flowers.

H. coris (*kore*-ris), meaning bedbug in Greek, is possibly named for its resemblance to *Coris,* a genus of woody-based perennial or biennial herbs. Native to southern Europe and hardy to Zone 7, it is a low-spreading, sprawling, mat-forming, herbaceous ground cover with a height of 6 to 12 inches and a spread of more than 3 feet wide. Growth is fast. Plants from pint-sized to quart-sized containers are spaced 1½ to 2½ feet apart. The grayish green foliage is evergreen, simple, and linear, and reaches ½ to 1 inch long. In bloom, which occurs during mid summer, it bears bright yellow, five-petaled, ¾- to 1-inch-wide blossoms.

H. ellipticum (e-*lip*-te-kum), named for its elliptical leaves, is commonly called pale St. John's-wort. Hailing from southeastern Canada and the eastern seaboard of the United States as far south as Virginia, it is hardy to Zone 4. It is a herbaceous, 12-inch-tall, dense ground cover that spreads by underground horizontal stems at a moderate rate. Plants from pint-sized to quart-sized containers are spaced 1 to 1½ feet apart. The leaves are semievergreen, elliptic, and 1¼ inches long. The numerous yellow flowers are borne in clusters on the ends of the branches from mid to late summer.

H. olympicum (o-*lim*-pi-kum), meaning of Mt. Olympus, is commonly called Olympic St. John's-wort. It is native to southern Europe, western Asia, and Turkey. Hardy in Zones 6 to 8, this woody, low-spreading, shrubby ground cover reaches 12 inches tall. Its leaves are oblong to lance-shaped or elliptic, to 1½ inches long, and colored gray-green. The showy golden-yellow flowers are 2½ inches wide and produced in clusters from spring to mid summer. Growth is moderate. Plants from quart-sized to gallon-sized containers are spaced 2½ to 3 feet apart. Variety *citrinum* displays pale yellow flowers; forma *minus* (formerly *H. polyphyllum*) differs in having flowers that are 1½ to 2 inches wide in clusters of four to ten, and leaves more grayish colored; forma *minus* 'Sulphureum' has sulfur-colored flowers.

H. patulum (pat-*tyew*-lum), named from the Latin *patulus,* to spread out, is commonly called goldencup St. John's-wort. Hardy in Zones 6 or 7 to 8 or 9, this broad-spreading Chinese species is more or less upright in its branch orientation. It reaches 3 feet tall by 4 to 5 feet wide. Growth is moderate. Plants from gallon-sized containers are spaced 2½ to 3 feet apart. The leaves are semievergreen, oval to narrowly oblong, and medium green. During mid summer the stunning yellow, clustered or solitary, five-petaled, 2-inch-wide flowers make their colorful presence on the stems of last year's growth.

Many cultivars were attributed to this genus in the past, but at present there is considerable confusion and cultivars are likely to be listed by one of any number of names. Even though most nurseries continue to offer selections of *H. patulum,* authorities have been reclassifying these plants and have either given them species status or determined them to be of hybrid origin. As far as I know, the species has been left with only one cultivar, 'Sunshine, with mounding habit, from 1½ to 2 feet tall, with green leaves and vibrant yellow summertime flowers.

The plants that have been reclassified are *H. beanii* (formerly *H. patulum* var. *henryi, H. acmosepalum, H. pseudohenryi*), which is comparatively more vigorous with larger flowers to 2½ inches across; *H.* 'Hidcote' (formerly *H. patulum* 'Hidcote'), thought by some to be a cross of *H.* × *cyanthiflorum* 'Gold Cup' × *H. calycinum* but thought by others to be a cross of *H. forrestii* × H. *calycinum,* with shorter habit, 18 to 24 inches tall in cold climates and to 3 feet tall in warm climates, as wide as it is tall, yellow flowers 2 inches in diameter from early summer to mid fall; *H. kouytchense* 'Sungold' (formerly *H. patulum* 'Sungold'), with somewhat greater cold tolerance and larger flowers than the species; *H. olympicum* f. *uniflorum* 'Sunburst' (formerly *H. patulum* 'Sunburst'), reaching 2 feet tall, with blue-green leaves and bright golden-yellow flowers in summer and fall.

H. reptans (*rep*-tanz), creeping St. John's-wort, is hardy to Zone 7 or 8 and hails from western China and the Himalayas. It displays a woody, horizontally sprawling, shrubby habit of growth. Normally it ranges from 4 to 6 inches tall and spreads indefinitely, rooting along the branches. The leaves are elliptic to oblong, ½ inch long, and colored medium green. The flowers of summer and fall are solitary, to 1¾ inches wide, and colored bright yellow. Growth is moderate. Plants from quart-sized containers are spaced 1 to 2 feet apart.

LESS COMMON SPECIES: *H. androsaemum* (an-droes-ee-mum), named from the Greek *andros,* man, and *haima,* blood, is much like *H. calycinum,* but differs in that it is hardy in Zones 5 to 7 and has a more woody habit. It reaches 3 feet tall and hails from Europe and western Asia. The bright yellow, 1-inch-wide flowers are followed by fruit that is first yellow, then red, and finally maturing to black. 'Albury Purple', with dark purplish green leaves; 'Glacier', with leaves that are mottled green and white and fruit that begins orange but ripens to black.

H. cerastoides (sir-as-*toy*-deez), hardy to Zone 6 northward, is characterized by hairy, grayish green foliage, buttercup-yellow flowers, and growth to 6 inches tall by more than 18 inches wide.

H. moseranum (moe-ser-*aye*-num), derived from a cross between *H. calycinum* and *H. patulum,* reaches 3 feet tall and displays an extended bloom of 3-inch-diameter yellow flowers. It is said to perform

well in Zones 6, 7, and possibly 8. 'Tricolor' is hardy in Zones 7 to 9, reaches 20 inches tall, and is uniquely variegated with white and green, with edges trimmed in pink if grown in the sun.

H. tomentosum (toe-men-*toe*-sum), hardy in Zones 5 to 9, displays horizontal habit and a height to 6 inches with blue-green leaves and vibrant yellow flowers.

CULTURE / CARE: Although the various St. John's worts show some degree of flexibility with respect to soil type, they are at their best in fertile, loamy, acidic, well-drained soils. Their tolerance to drought is sufficient to allow them to survive short hot, dry periods, but if the conditions are prolonged, they need supplemental watering. They prefer full sun to partial shade. Their pests include nematodes (microscopic roundworms which cause the roots to rot), mites, and aphids. Diseases of greatest significance are leaf spots, powdery mildew, rust, and root rot. Maintenance, if you feel inspired, consists of a light shearing or mowing during late winter. In most cases it is optional.

PROPAGATION: Cuttings can be easily rooted during the early part of summer. Division is accomplished with great success during spring and fall.

Iberis sempervirens   PLATE 164
Evergreen Candytuft, Edging Candytuft

"Tidy" is the single most descriptive adjective that can be applied to evergreen candytuft. It is a low, semiwoody, densely growing, upright-stemmed, shyly spreading subshrub (woody-based herb) that reaches 12 inches tall and 3 to 4 feet across. Because of these features, evergreen candytuft makes a very effective edging along walkways and terrace margins. It also performs exceptionally well as a specimen in rock gardens or as a small-scale general cover, particularly in beds that are slightly elevated and surrounded by a rocky border. As a facing, candytuft is effective before building foundations, ornaments, and dwarf shrubs such as *Spiraea* × *bumalda* 'Gold Mound', *S. japonica* 'Little Princess', and the compact forms of glossy abelia. Should your goal be to use evergreen candytuft in the background of another lower growing-ground cover, try facing it with a bronze form of *Ajuga,* golden creeping Charley (*Lysimachia nummularia* 'Aurea'), hardy ice plant, or a colorful sedum such as *Sedum spurium* 'Bronze Carpet' or 'Dragon's Blood', or *S. kamtschaticum.*

SCIENTIFIC NAME: *Iberis sempervirens* (eye-*beer*-ris sem-per-*vie*-renz). *Iberis* is derived from the Greek *Iberia,* the ancient name of Spain. *Sempervirens,* in Latin, means always green, referring to the evergreen foliage.

HARDINESS / ORIGIN: Zones 5 to 7; Europe and Asia.

LEAVES / FLOWERS / FRUIT: The evergreen, deep shiny green, linear leaves reach 1 to 1½ inches long by ⅛ to ¼ inch wide. The flowers, which are produced in late spring or early summer, are four-petaled, white, ⅜ inch wide, and arranged in many-flowered clusters that reach 2 inches across. They provide an excellent floral show and later give rise to flattened almost podlike seeds. The seeds are interesting but add little ornamental effect.

RATE / SPACING: Growth is slow. Plants from pint-sized to gallon-sized containers are spaced 1½ to 2 feet apart.

HORTICULTURAL SELECTIONS: 'Alexander's White', compact habit, early bloom; 'Autumn Beauty' ('Autumn Snow'), with vibrant white flowers, compact habit, blooming early in spring and then again in fall, more prone to damping off and root rot than the species and some of the other cultivars; 'Autumn Snow', likely the same as 'Christmas Snow', blooming in spring and again in early fall; 'Kingwood Compact', compact habit, heavy blooming, 8 inches tall; 'Little Gem' ('Weisserzwerg'), compact habit, 5 inches tall by 8 or 10 inches wide; 'October Glory' (often listed as 'Autumn Beauty'), blooming in spring and fall, more prone to crown rot; 'Purity', with flowers more numerous and longer lasting; 'Pygmaea', low-growing, horizontally spreading; 'Snowflake', larger waxy white flowers formed in broad clusters, leaves broader and darker green than the species; 'Snowmantle', similar to 'Snowflake' but more compact in habit.

OTHER SPECIES: *I. gibraltarica* (ji-brawl-*tare*-i-ka), Gibraltar candytuft, reaches 12 inches tall and spreads 3 to 4 feet wide. Hailing from Spain and Morocco, it is similar in many respects to *I. sempervirens,* but is hardy only in Zones 6 to 9. Its dark green leaves are evergreen, shaped like oblong spatulas, reach 1 inch long, and sport small teeth along their edges. The flowers, which arise during late spring, are colored light lilac and are arranged in flat-topped clusters to 2 inches across.

I. pruitii (prew-*it*-ee-eye), formerly *I. candolleana,* is an uncommon miniature spring-flowering alpine that reaches only 2 inches tall and spreads to 8 inches across. Typically, it is used as a specimen in the rock garden. Hardy to Zone 4.

I. saxatilis (saks-*at*-i-lis), named for its ability to inhabit rocky places, is commonly called rock candytuft. Hardy in Zones 3 to 7 and native to southern Europe, this low, sprawling species reaches only 6 inches tall and spreads to 4 feet wide. The leaves are evergreen, very narrow, and colored medium to deep green. The white flowers begin to awaken about mid spring and may continue until summer. They are four-parted and arranged in clusters at the branch tips. The growth rate is slow to moderate, so plants from pint-sized to gallon-sized containers should be spaced 2 to 2½ feet apart.

I. sayana (say-*an*-a) reaches only 2 inches tall but spreads to 12 inches across and flowers in fall as well as spring. Hardy to Zone 4.

CULTURE / CARE: Candytufts adapt to various soils and require only one absolute—excellent drainage. Without this, they succumb to crown rot and are short lived. Their tolerance to drought is fair, but occasional deep watering is required during extended periods of hot, dry weather. They prefer full sun to light shade, with the best floral display in full sun. Pests and diseases are seldom serious, but any of the following are potentially troublesome: oystershell scale, diamond back moth, southern root-knot nematode, club root, damping off, downy mildew, powdery mildew, and white root. Maintenance needs are few or none. Some gardeners prefer to lightly shear their plants after flowering to induce branching and to rejuvenate growth. No more than 3 inches should be sheared off.

PROPAGATION: Cuttings root with fairly good percentages from early spring to late fall. Division can also be effective provided adequate water is supplied.

Ilex

PLATE 165

Holly

The genus contains several species of shrubs that are not themselves ground covers. Some of their cultivars, on the other hand, fill the role admirably. Typically, they are mounding selections that reach a few feet tall and spread about twice their height. Their best uses are for edging walkways and driveways, as dwarf hedges, and as foundation facers. Not all of these plants are typically hollylike with scallop-edged evergreen leaves, thorns, and red wintertime fruit, what most people think of as hollies. Some have deciduous leaves with rounded edges, no thorns, and black fruit. Most are separate sexed, with male and female plants needed for fruit production, but others are polygamodioecious, that is, having mostly male or female flowers but with some flowers that are both-sexed.

Some people believe that the common name holly is a corruption of the Anglo-Saxon word *holegn* (holy). This may stem from the symbolism of the white flowers for the virgin birth of Christ, and of the thorns and fruit for His suffering and the redness of His blood. Some English people considered the presence of holly in the home shortly before Christmas to be an omen of bad luck. Those from the county of Derbyshire believed that smooth-leaved hollies in the home indicated year-long rule by the wife; prickly leaved species, on the other hand, gave the reins to the husband for a year. Native Americans considered sprigs of holly to be symbols of courage. Followers of the Zoroastrian religion of Persia sprinkled their newborns with an infusion of the holly bark.

SCIENTIFIC NAME: *Ilex* (*eye*-leks) is the Latin name for *Quercus ilex* (holm oak), which holly is said to resemble.

HARDINESS / ORIGIN: See individual species for hardiness; from temperate and tropical regions worldwide.

LEAVES / FLOWERS / FRUIT: See individual species.

RATE / SPACING: Relatively slow; space cultivars on centers at a distance of 75 percent of their expected mature width.

SPECIES: *I. cornuta* (korn-*new*-ta), meaning horned in Latin, in reference to the spiny projections along the margins of the leaves, is commonly called Chinese holly or horned holly. Hardy in Zones 7 to 9, this species hails from China and is clothed in evergreen, heart-shaped to oblong or quadrangular leaves. Leathery, thick, and dark glossy green, they are the primary ornamental feature. The springtime flowers, although fragrant, are tiny and dull white, and appear on both male and female plants. The fruit, which is formed only on female plants, is a bright red berry that persists through winter. 'Berries Jubilee' is a slow-growing, compact, mounding selection that produces quantities of large red berries; 'Burfordii Nana' has a compact habit to 3 feet tall (sometimes to 5 or 6 feet if not pruned), a spread of 5 to 6 feet, lustrous dark green leaves, and sparse fruit production; 'Carissa', a dense, nonfruiting, dwarf selection, ranges from 3 to 4 feet tall by 4 to 6 feet wide; 'Rotunda', dwarf Chinese holly, is a compact, dark green, mounding selection that reaches 3 to 4 feet tall, spreads more than 6 feet wide, and only rarely sets fruit.

I. crenata (kree-*nay*-ta), named for its leaves that are edged with rounded teeth (crenate), is commonly called Japanese holly or box-leaved holly (for its resemblance to *Buxus,* the boxwood genus). Hailing from Japan, it is hardy in Zones 6 to 9 and displays evergreen, crowded, elliptic, oblong, or narrowly oval, 1¼-inch-long, ⅝-inch-wide leaves that are edged with rounded or pointed teeth. The shiny and smooth leaves are colored dark green above and pale green below. The flowers are dull white, small, and borne during late spring and early summer. The fruit, which matures in fall, is a ¼-inch-wide, rounded, black berry. 'Compacta', a low-growing, compact, globe-shaped selection reaches 3 feet tall (with minimal pruning) and spreads to 6 feet wide;

'Convexa' is much like 'Compacta' but has convex (cup-shaped) leaf surfaces; 'Green Island' has a loose, broad, spreading habit, to 3 feet tall by 6 feet across; 'Helleri', reaching little more than 3 feet tall, is dwarf, mounded, and compact; 'Hetzii' is much like 'Compacta' but with larger leaves and a faster rate of growth; 'Kingsville' has a loose habit and is 3 feet tall by 6 feet wide; 'Kingsville Green Cushion' has a dense habit and reaches 10 inches tall by 3 feet wide.

I. vomitoria (vom-i-*tore*-ee-a), named for its emetic and purgative qualities, is commonly called yaupon, cassina, cassena, or cassine. Hailing from the southeastern United States, it is hardy in Zones 7 to 10 and displays evergreen, oval to oblong or elliptic, 1½-inch-long, ½- to ¾-inch-wide leaves that are shallowly toothed about their edges, dark green, and glossy on their upper surface. The flowers of mid spring are tiny, and greenish white, with male and female on separate plants. The fruit which follows is a ¼-inch-diameter scarlet berry. A mild tea can be made from this plant and was used as a substitute for coffee and tea during the Civil War (a concentrated brew, however, can cause hallucinations and vomiting). 'Nana', typically reaching 3 or 4 feet tall by up to 8 feet wide, is a compact dwarf selection with smaller leaves; 'Shelling's Dwarf' ('Stoke's Dwarf') is much like 'Nana' but with darker green leaves, a more compact habit, and no berries; 'Straughans' has a vigorous growth habit from 1½ to 2 feet tall.

CULTURE / CARE: Ground-covering hollies are relatively drought tolerant and prefer to grow in full sun or light shade. They grow best in well-drained, loamy, slightly acidic soil with a pH of 5.0 to 6.5 and, like most plants, benefit from supplemental watering during the summer. Their primary disease problems are various blights—bacterial, leaf, twig, and flower—leaf spots, mildew, root rot, rust, and sooty mold. Pests of greatest consequences are nematodes and mites. Maintenance consists of a light shearing in spring.

PROPAGATION: Stem cuttings taken in fall root well when treated with bottom heat of 70°F; treatment with 3000 ppm IBA/talc is beneficial and will yield a much larger root system than otherwise.

Imperata cylindrica 'Red Baron'   PLATE 166
Japanese Blood Grass, Red Cogon

With foliage that is so unusual as to make it a conversation piece, this erect-stemmed, 1½- to 2-foot-tall grass is one of the most exciting ground covers in cultivation today. Although a slow grower, for the patient gardener or for one who has the money to space them closely, Japanese blood grass is a plant well worth growing. It is best known for its erectly oriented red-tipped leaves that look like the flickering tips of red flames. It is one of the most unusually colored moderate-scale to large-scale ground-covering grasses available and although effective as an accent plant, is also impressive when laid out in broad, sweeping border plantings or used as a foundation facer. By placing a border of red cogon around stone or metal statuary or in front of light colored stonework, the vibrant interplay of colors will appear very modern and, depending on who you talk to, either gaudy or sophisticated. No one, however, contests that red cogon is attention-getting. Due to its dense network of horizontal stems (rhizomes) and fibrous root system, Japanese blood grass also serves to control erosion on sloping terrain, and if its spread is not desired, it can be surrounded by a deep edging. Although this is not a turf grass, walking through it on occasion will do no harm.

In its native range—tropical regions of the Old World to the Mediterranean—*I. cylindrica* has been used for thatching and forage (although some say not palatable to most livestock). Today, it (but not the cultivar *I. cylindrica* 'Red Baron') has begun to naturalize in Florida, where it is feared for its aggressive spread, propensity to seed, and ability to overpower native vegetation. 'Red Baron', however, spreads very slowly and does not produce seed. One note of caution: should all-green-leaved mutations ever occur, dig them up and destroy them immediately. Not only will they be more aggressive and eventually overrun the red-leaved form, but they might also become a hazard by producing seed.

SCIENTIFIC NAME: *Imperata cylindrica* 'Red Baron' (im-per-*aye*-ta si-*lin*-dri-ka). *Imperata* commemorates Ferrante Imperato (1550–1625), an apothecary in Naples, Italy. *Cylindrica* likely refers to the cylindrical shape of the flower clusters.

HARDINESS / ORIGIN: Zones 5 to 10; Japan, Manchuria, China, and Korea.

LEAVES / FLOWERS / FRUIT: The tall, narrow, and sharply pointed, grassy leaves are green at the base and red from the midsection to their tips. The erectly oriented, spikelike flower clusters may reach 4½ to 9 inches long, are produced in late summer, and are an attractive silvery white. No fruit is produced.

RATE / SPACING: Growth is slow. Plants from quart-sized to gallon-sized containers are spaced 8 to 12 inches apart.

CULTURE / CARE: Even though red cogon can succeed in any type of soil, its spread is best in an acidic, organically rich, well-drained loam; in sandy or heavy clay soils, its slow spread is even slower. Red cogon happily accepts occasional deep watering during the summer. Its best color is obtained in full sun, but light shade is tolerated. Diseases are nearly nonexis-

tent. Slugs, however, at times consume the leaves. Maintenance consists of rejuvenating tattered and tired-looking plantings by mowing.

PROPAGATION: Sections of the plant mass can be divided and repotted or transplanted any time throughout the growing season.

Indigofera kirilowii
PLATE 167
Kirilow Indigo

With low dense suckering habit, this 3-foot-tall shrubby ground cover gives a nice display of soft-textured pealike foliage for general cover or soil stabilization in moderate to large areas. No foot traffic is tolerated.

SCIENTIFIC NAME: *Indigofera kirilowii* (in-di-*gof*-er-a / in-di-*go*-fer-a kir-i-*low*-ee-eye). *Indigofera* is from the Latin *indigo,* a dye, and *fera,* to produce, the popular dye being derived from members of this genus. *Kirilowii* commemorates Ivan Petrovich Kililov (Kirilow) (1821–1842).

HARDINESS / ORIGIN: Zones 5 to 7; northern China and Korea.

LEAVES / FLOWERS / FRUIT: The compound leaves are composed of three to five pairs of ¾-inch-long, elliptic to oval semievergreen leaflets and range from 1¼ to 1¾ inches long. The bright rose, ¾-inch-long pealike flowers, borne in mid summer, are arranged in 5-inch-long rather elongate upright inflorescences. The fruit, a legume, is interesting but nonornamental.

RATE / SPACING: Growth is fast. Plants from 1- to 2-gallon-sized containers are spaced 3 to 4 feet apart.

OTHER SPECIES: *I. incarnata* (in-car-*nay*-ta), meaning flesh-colored, is named for its flowers and is commonly called white Chinese indigo. Hailing from China and Japan, it is hardy to Zone 5, reaches 18 inches tall by 6 to 8 feet wide, and sports semievergreen pinnately compound leaves. Each 2½-inch-long leaf is composed of three to six pairs of elliptic soft medium green leaflets. Its pealike, ¾-inch-long, pinkish white flowers are borne during mid summer and give rise to podlike fruit. Variety *alba* has white flowers.

CULTURE / CARE: Indigoferas need full sun and exhibit their best growth in well-drained, loamy, acidic to slightly alkaline soils. They are not greatly tolerant of drought and should be watered often enough to keep the ground slightly moist. They experience no serious diseases or pests. Shoots often die back during winter; thus it is a good idea to cut plants back to the living wood in spring, or to mow them to the ground shortly after winter. They grow back quickly and flower on the current year's growth.

PROPAGATION: Softwood stem cuttings respond well

to 4000 ppm IBA/talc. Root cuttings should be made in late fall. Division of rooted suckers is effective as well and is best accomplished in spring or fall. Seed should be harvested when ripe, soaked in hot water (190°F) for 12 hours, then sown.

Iris   PLATES 168, 169

Heralded for their marvelous flowers and attractive sword-shaped foliage, irises are normally planted in small clumps and clearly are not what most people think of as ground covers. However, in mass plantings their foliar and floral features are still special—there are just more of them. Besides, in nature, many irises do tend to form colonies.

Irises are leafy herbaceous ground covers that spread either by creeping rhizomes or offsets of bulbous crowns. The former produce sodlike mats, while the latter tend to form broad clumps. Regardless, both are fine for use in mass plantings. The flowers, which typically are formed on stout ascending floral stems, are outstanding, and the combination of foliar and flower color is often just plain lovely. Although irises bear rather conspicuous fruit capsules, most gardeners believe they do not contribute to the overall ornamental worth of the plant.

Planting irises along walks and drives as edging is often very attractive, as is planting them about the edge of a mixed herbaceous border. Many irises tolerate wet soil and therefore are useful near streams, ponds, and reflecting pools. On the sloping sides of a drainage ditch, irises bind soil beautifully and eliminate the treachery of mowing. Planting a compact clump in the rock garden or one of the larger cultivars next to the base of a boulder can infuse a much needed vertical dimension. No foot traffic is tolerated.

Native Americans used a preparation of the roots to treat leg sores and as a cathartic. Like most medicines, the usefulness of this preparation depends upon the dosage and, when administered improperly, can be dangerous. All parts of wild and cultivated iris are poisonous and can cause intestinal distress if ingested. The sap can irritate the skin.

Irises have been hybridized beyond reason, and I suspect that with only a little effort, one could lay one's hands upon a few thousand different varieties. The trick is to know what to call them, for as is true of every large genus that has been put through the hybridizing mill, the end result is a lot of beautiful plants and nearly as many erroneous names.

Although there are countless irises that make effective ground covers, there is only enough space here to discuss the more common. I encourage you to try other species, cultivars, and hybrids which you may come across, for there are hundreds which make good ground covers. Additionally, for those who wish to learn more, there are entire books that have been written about irises.

SCIENTIFIC NAME: *Iris* (*eye*-ris) is named for Iris, the Greek goddess of the rainbow and a messenger of the gods. It is likely to have been applied to this genus because of its many flower colors, which nearly span the rainbow and include shades of red, pink, blue, violet, and purple, as well as white, brown, yellow, orange, and black. Furthermore, there are multicolored forms that may have combinations of any of the above colors. The Greek word *iris* also means eye of heaven; since one of the responsibilities of goddess Iris was to lead the souls of women to the Elysian fields, the classical world's equivalent of heaven, it is unsurprising that the Greeks developed a habit of adorning the graves of women with iris. Louis VII used the iris as a victory symbol in the twelfth century, thus the name fleur-de-lis (flower of Louis); today it is the provincial symbol of Quebec.

HARDINESS / ORIGIN: See individual species for hardiness; Northern Temperate Zone.

LEAVES / FLOWERS / FRUIT: Basal swordlike leaves and distinctive flowers with three upright petals (*standards*) and three drooping sepals (*falls*) characterize most *Iris* species. The seed pods that follow are large and noticeable, but nonornamental.

RATE / SPACING: Slow to moderate; see individual species for spacing recommendation.

SPECIES: *I. cristata* (kris-*tay*-ta), dwarf crested iris, shows good hardiness in Zones 3 to 9. A North American native, it ranges from Maryland to Michigan, and south to Georgia and Missouri. Although its height seldom exceeds 7 inches, it spreads indefinitely, and in time forms lush dense mats. Its deciduous, 4- to 9-inch-long foliage is medium green, and, like that of all irises, sword-shaped. Despite their small size, the 1- to 2½-inch-long pale lilac (with white or yellow crests on the falls) springtime flowers are splendid. Plants from pint-sized or quart-sized containers are spaced 10 to 14 inches apart. Horticultural selections include 'Abbey's Violet', with deep violet-blue flowers; 'Alba', with white flowers; 'Baby Blue', with 4-inch-long leaves and pale purplish blue flowers; 'Eco Little Bluebird', with numerous bright blue flowers; 'Shenandoah Sky Light', with light blue flowers; 'Summer Storm', with deep blue flowers; 'Vein Mountain', with orange-crested purple flowers.

I. ensata (en-*say*-ta), named for its sword-shaped leaves, is commonly called Japanese iris. Hardy in Zones 5 to 10, this lovely acid-loving species with attractive long narrow tapering foliage prefers full sun and moist soil during spring and summer and drier conditions during fall and winter. Formerly named *I. kaempferi* (and still often labeled as such), this species hails from Manchuria and Korea as well as Japan. It reaches about 3 feet tall and displays lovely bright green foliage. During mid summer groups of three or four graceful 5-inch-wide, three-parted flowers, composed of reddish purple falls with yellow centers, dark veins, and white upright standards, are borne upon leafy round floral stalks. The hundreds of cultivars of this species differ primarily in their floral characteristics. Double flowering forms with six-parted flowers are common, and twelve-parted flowers exist (and may look more like peonies than like irises). Because of space considerations I am limited to describing a few fine selections, but of course there are several others worth growing. 'Beni-Tsubaki', with dark rose-violet, white-rayed falls; 'Confettii Shower', flowers light blue with violet veins; 'Crystal Halo', flowers with reddish purple centers and white edges; 'Ebb and Flow', flowers medium blue with violet edges and dark blue centers; 'Freckled Geisha', falls with white centers, purple ruffles and edges; 'Frilled Enchantment', flowers with white ruffles and rose-red edges; 'Frosted Pyramid', with pure white, ruffled flowers resembling peonies; 'Henry's White', with attractive white flowers; 'Joyous Troubadour', white, blue-edged flowers; 'Joy Peters', with soft orchid-pink falls softening to white toward their edges; 'Light At Dawn', with white, narrowly blue-violet bordered falls; 'Lilac Peaks', white flowers with lilac-lavender veins; 'Little Snow Man', only 15 inches tall, with large bright white flowers; 'Over The Waves', magnificent double, reddish purple flowers with white veins; 'Oriental Eyes', falls purple with violet centers and light violet edges; 'Pink Pearl', with soft lavender-pink flowers; 'Prairie Noble', double flowers with white and blue-violet ruffles and red veins; 'Reign of Glory', flowers with white veins and soft purple falls; 'Rose Adagio', ruffled flowers with white centers and rose-violet stippled margins; 'Sparkling Sapphire', with dark regal blue flowers; 'Storm At Sea', with large blue and violet bicolored falls; 'Summer Moon', with soft white, ruffled flowers; 'Summer Storm', with dark purple, ruffled flowers; 'Tideline', with purple-edged white flowers; 'Variegata', foliage with lovely white and green variegation; 'Winged Sprite', with bluish violet flowers darkest at their edges.

I. pallida (*pa*-li-da), named for the paleness of its soft violet summerborne flowers, is commonly called sweet iris for its pleasantly fragrant scent. This floriferous, attractive iris is easily cultured. Hailing from northern Italy and hardy in Zones 4 to 8, it displays lovely gray-green broad sword-shaped leaves, reaches

24 to 36 inches tall by 24 inches wide, and is one of the parents in the creation of the popular hybrid bearded irises. Popular selections include 'Argentea', leaves with gray and white streaks; 'Albo-variegata' ('Zebra'), blue-green leaves with white and cream streaks; var. *dalmatica,* lovely blue-green leaves; 'Variegata' ('Aurea-variegata'), leaves with yellow and green stripes.

I. pseudacorus (sood-*a*-kore-is), named for its appearance which closely resembles that of *Acorus* species, is commonly called yellow water iris. It inhabits moist marshy areas, is hardy in Zones 5 to 9, and originally came from Europe, Siberia, Caucasus, Western Asia, and North Africa but is now naturalized in North America. It displays massive grasslike, medium green foliage up to 4 feet tall. Its yellow flowers grace the plant from mid spring to mid summer. Excellent for planting at stream and pondside, this species happily tolerates saturated soils. It has been employed in wound dressings, as a treatment for inflammations and various gynecological irregularities, and as a purgative, emetic, and diuretic. The roots have been used to produce black and brown dyes and ink, and the yellow flowers, possibly the original fleur-de-lis, have been used to produce yellow dyes. Seeds of this species have been used as a substitute for coffee during times of scarcity. Horticultural selections include 'Alba', with pale, creamy yellow flowers; 'Bastardii', with light yellow flowers; 'Flore-Plena', with double flowers; 'Golden Queen', with larger flowers; 'Nana', about half the size of the species; 'Variegata', leaves with yellow and cream stripes that turn green during summer.

I. pumila (*pyu*-mi-la), named from the Latin *pumila,* dwarf or diminutive, is commonly called dwarf bearded iris. Interestingly, older references to this species are straight forward in describing and classifying it, while modern botanists are not so sure. It has been listed as synonymous with *I. attica* and reported to be of possible hybrid origin, which might explain the significant variation among the cultivars. Another source says that plants offered as *I. pumila* are almost always hybrids of *I. chamaeiris*. Regardless, it is hardy in Zones 4 to 10, hails from Europe and Asia Minor, ranges from 4 to 5 inches tall and spreads indefinitely. Its deciduous green leaves are sword-shaped and 4 to 8 inches long. The flowers, which occur during springtime, are 2 to 3 inches long and range from yellow to deep lilac with a beard of bluish, white, or yellow. Plants from pint-sized or quart-sized containers are spaced 14 to 16 inches apart. Some of the more popular horticultural selections that are represented as cultivars of dwarf bearded iris (just as likely of hybrid origin) include 'Alba', with cream-colored flowers; 'Atropurpurea', with purple flowers; 'Aurea', with clear bright yellow flowers; 'Cherry Garden', with violet flowers; 'Cyanea', with deep blue flowers; 'Lena', with red flowers, 'Lutea', with golden-yellow flowers; 'Navy Doll', with white flowers and purple markings; 'Ritz', with yellow flowers and blue markings; 'Sunrise Pink', with apricot-pink flowers; 'Truely', with purple and white flowers.

I. setosa (say-*toe*-sa), named from the Latin word meaning bristled, in reference to the apex of the floral standards, is commonly called Alaskan iris. This attractive, relatively small, easy-to-grow native of Siberia, Japan, and North America displays hardiness in Zones 4 to 9, reaches 20 to 26 inches tall by 16 inches wide, and makes a lovely early summertime display of petite flowers bearing rich purple falls with white centers. Preferring to grow in sunny or lightly shaded sites of rich well-drained moderately and constantly moist acidic soil, it is a pleasant, well-behaved, clump-forming species that is excellent for edging pathways, accent use, and as a rock garden specimen. Selections include variety *canadensis,* native to coastal Labrador and Maine, smaller than the species, white spotted at the base of its falls; 'Kosho En', with pure white flowers; 'Nana', reaching only 8 inches tall, with rich blue flowers.

I. tectorum (tek-*toe*-rum), named from the Latin *tectum,* roof, was once grown atop thatched roofs in Japan and is commonly called roof iris or wall iris. It is hardy in Zones 5 to 9, hails from China and Japan, reaches more than 10 inches in height, and spreads indefinitely. The leaves are sword-shaped, to 12 inches long, exceptionally attractive and durable. In flower it is lovely, producing late springtime blossoms of deep lilac to bluish purple with brownish violet and lilac streaking. Plants from pint-sized to quart-sized containers are spaced 10 to 16 inches apart. 'Alba' has white and yellow flowers.

I. versicolor (ver-si-*cul*-er or ver-*sik*-o-lor), named for its multicolored flowers, is commonly known as larger blue flag, wild iris, poison iris, water flag, liver lily, snake lily, and flag lily. Arising from shyly creeping rhizomes, the lovely blue-green swordlike gently arching ½- to 1-inch-wide leaves reach 2 to 3 feet tall and combine beautifully with the flowers that are carried slightly above them (on slender stalks) during late spring to mid summer. At this time, the plant makes a colorful display of 2½- to 3-inch-wide widely spreading violet-blue falls that are decorated with yellow and white. Naturally inhabiting marshes, thickets, ditches, and wet meadows, the species is a superb choice for soil stabilization along stream and pond banks, as well as a moderate-scale to large-scale general cover or accent plant in garden settings of more moderate soil moisture. Rated hardy

in Zones 3 to 9, it is pleasing to the eye and easy to grow. It is, however, mired in a haze of confusion that relates to its native distribution: no one seems to agree on exactly what its native range is. Involved in this discussion is the closely related species *I. virginica* (similarly known as blue flag), which is also an effective ground cover.

In researching blue flags, I read one article that claims *I. versicolor* hails from Labrador to Manitoba southward to Ohio, Wisconsin, and Minnesota. In another article, the species is listed as spanning the areas from Newfoundland to Manitoba and south to Florida and Arkansas. In a third, it is listed as ranging only as far south as the middle portion of the lower peninsula of Michigan. The related species, *I. virginica* (vir-*jin*-i-ka), meaning of Virginia, is said to range from the Virginia coastal plain southward to Florida and Texas. Sometimes listed as *I. hexagona, I. virginica* is reported by some sources as being hardy northward only to Zone 7. By others, it is reported hardy to Zone 4.

Finally, there are those who claim that *I. versicolor* and *I. virginica* have hybridized freely in the wild and that over time they have become essentially the same plant, differing as follows: the stems of the flower stalks of *I. versicolor* are shorter than the foliage, and the bases of its leaves are often flushed with purple. *Iris virginica* displays leaves that frequently overtop the flowers, and the bases of its leaves are only sometimes flushed with purple. None of this is of horticultural significance. The important thing, of course, is that whether you are planting *I. versicolor* or *I. virginica,* they are very similar and equally fine plants. Cultivars, which not surprisingly are ascribed to both species, include 'Alba', with white flowers; 'Kermesina', with reddish purple flowers; and several clones which vary in the intensity of the blueness of the flowers.

CULTURE / CARE: For the most part, irises are at their best when growing in moist to slightly wet, fertile, loamy soils. Even so, they can tolerate many other soil types and even withstand a fair bit of drought. They prefer full sun to moderate shade. They are host to a number of pests and diseases. These include aphids, lesser bulb fly, iris borer, Florida red scale, iris thrips, verbena bud moth, iris weevil, zebra caterpillar, bulb mite, and various nematodes. Diseases of greatest prevalence are bacterial soft rot, leaf spots, blossom blight, rust, rhizome rot, crown rot, black rot, ink spot, fusarium basal rot, blue mold, and iris mosaic virus. For the most part, maintenance consists of shearing back the foliage to ground level each fall to encourage compact growth and good health. If you are successful in this pursuit, you will eventually end up with overcrowded plantings (as evidenced by reduced flowering), in which case you will need to divide and replant them. Keep repeating this cycle and you will never have to worry about how you are going to spend your time!

PROPAGATION: Rhizomes can be divided during late summer. New offsets that arise from the base of the plants can be separated and transplanted in spring or early fall.

Itea virginica 'Henry's Garnet'   PLATE 170

Henry's Garnet Virginia Sweetspire, Henry's Garnet Virginia Willow, Henry's Garnet Tassel-white

A marvelous dwarf selection of its taller, more open native parent species, 'Henry's Garnet' reaches only 3 to 4 feet tall by 5 or 6 feet wide. Valuable for its compact habit, attractive foliage, and pleasantly scented summertime flowers, it makes a nice foundation plant, can be massed for bold effect, and even stands alone as a specimen. It works well for controlling erosion. No foot traffic is tolerated.

SCIENTIFIC NAME: *Itea virginica* (it-ee-a / eye-*tee*-a / ee-tee-a vir-*jin*-i-ka). *Itea* is simply the Greek name for willow. *Virginica* means of Virginia.

HARDINESS / ORIGIN: Zones 5 to 9; the species hails from the pine barrens of New Jersey, south to Florida, extending west to Missouri and Louisiana.

LEAVES / FLOWERS / FRUIT: The simple, dark green, elliptic to oblong or oval, deciduous to semievergreen leaves are alternately arranged. Ranging from 1½ to 3 inches long by ¾ to 1¼ inches wide, they give an exceptional color show during fall as they change to bright reddish purple. The ⅓- to ½-inch-wide, sweet-scented flowers are carried upon upright 3- to 6-inch-long bottlebrush-shaped branch-ending spikes during late spring and early summer. The tiny brown fruit which follows is nonornamental.

RATE / SPACING: Growth is moderate. Plants from 2- to 3-gallon-sized containers are spaced 4 to 5 feet apart.

OTHER SELECTIONS of *I. virginica*: 'Beppu', 2½ to 3 feet tall by 3 to 5 feet wide, vigorous rhizomatous spreading habit; 'Sarah Eve', 3 to 4 feet tall by 4 to 6 feet wide, with remarkable reddish new growth, pink flowers, and brilliant red fall leaf color.

CULTURE / CARE: Sweetspires are very adaptable and grow well in full sun to moderate shade, in well-drained, moist, or relatively wet, neutral or acidic soils. They are moderately tolerant of drought but more lush if given supplemental water during dry weather and an annual application of fertilizer or organic compost. No serious diseases or pests occur, and little or no maintenance is required.

PROPAGATION: Division of sucker growth during spring or fall is effective. Softwood cuttings, treated with 3000 ppm IBA/talc, root well during mid summer.

Jasminum   PLATE 171

Jasmine

For covering the ground, this large genus offers at least three species that can do the job. Although they vary considerably in hardiness, each species is relatively woody and vinelike, and displays a distinctive scrambling habit. Jasmine species produce numerous showy, pleasantly scented flowers, tend to be somewhat lax or casual in appearance, and are normally best when their trailing branches can cascade over the edge of something. Hillsides, planters, terraces, and atop retaining walls are all good sites for jasmines. No foot traffic is tolerated.

SCIENTIFIC NAME: *Jasminum* (jas-*mine*-um / *jas*-min-um) is said to be derived from *yasmin*, the Persian name for jasmine.

HARDINESS / ORIGIN: See individual species for hardiness; mostly from tropical and some temperate regions of the Old World.

LEAVES / FLOWERS / FRUIT: The leaves typically are opposite or alternate, and composed of three to seven leaflets. The white, yellow, or pink flowers are arranged in branch-ending clusters. The fruit is usually a black berry.

RATE / SPACING: Relatively fast. Plants from 1- to 2-gallon-sized containers are spaced 3 to 4 feet apart.

SPECIES: *J. floridum* (*flor*-i-dum), possibly named for its many flowers, is commonly called showy jasmine. It shows good hardiness in Zones 7 to 9, hails from China, and reaches 3 to 4 feet tall by 5 to 7 feet wide. Its leaves are semievergreen and compound with three, or rarely five leaflets; leaflets elliptical to oblong, to 1½ inches long, and dark green. The yellow flowers that arise during early summer are trumpet-shaped and ¾ inch long. The fruit is a black berry.

J. mesnyi (*mez*-nee-eye), named after William Mesny (1842–1919), an officer in the Chinese national army who collected in China, is commonly called primrose jasmine. Hardy in Zones 8 to 10 or 11, it hails from western China, may reach 5 to 6 feet tall, and spreads 6 to 8 feet wide. Its shiny dark green leaves are evergreen and compound with leaflets in threes, each oblong to lance-shaped, to 3 inches long by ⅓ to ¾ inch wide. Its springtime flowers are solitary, often double-petaled, trumpet-shaped, and are yellow with darker centers. Seldom produced, the fruit is a black berry.

J. nudiflorum (new-di-*flore*-um), named for its stems which are nude (devoid) of leaves when the plant flowers during early spring, is commonly called winter jasmine. Hardy in Zones 6 to 9, this native of China reaches 2 or 3 feet tall and spreads 4 to 7 feet wide. The deciduous compound leaves are composed of three leaflets, each being shiny green, oval to oblong-oval, and 1¼ inches long by ½ inch wide. The bright yellow flowers are solitary, trumpet-shaped, 2 inches long by 1 inch wide, and open in early spring before the leaves appear. The sparse fruit, a black berry, is savored by hummingbirds.

CULTURE / CARE: Jasmines are adaptable to most well-drained, acidic soils. They are moderately tolerant of drought, yet benefit from occasional deep watering during the heat of summer. They prefer full sun to moderate shade and are susceptible to nematodes, scales, and citrus whitefly. Diseases such as bacterial crown gall, blossom blight, leaf spot, and root rot are also at times problematic. Maintenance includes cutting plants to within 6 inches of the ground every few years to neaten appearance and rejuvenate growth.

PROPAGATION: Cuttings root relatively well during early summer. Also, stems that root as they contact the ground can be dug and transplanted during spring and early fall.

Jeffersonia diphylla   PLATE 172
Twinleaf, Ground Squirrel Pea, Helmet Pod, Rheumatism Root

A very handsome woodland native of eastern North America, twinleaf is a useful clump-forming, basal-leaved, herbaceous ground cover. It typically reaches 10 to 12 inches tall and spreads more than 16 inches across. It is best in deciduous woodlands where it receives dappled springtime sun and summertime shade. It may be mass planted as a general cover, used in clumps for accent, or planted along the sides of a path as a dwarf hedge. Regardless of its specific application, this attractive, lush, leafy ground cover is remarkable for contributing a mood of tranquility to the understory of any woodland setting. No foot traffic is tolerated.

SCIENTIFIC NAME: *Jeffersonia diphylla* (jef-er-*so*-nee-a dye-*fil*-a). *Jeffersonia* is named in honor of the third president of the United States, Thomas Jefferson (1743–1826). *Diphylla,* two-leaved, refers to the double lobes of each leaf.

HARDINESS / ORIGIN: Zone 5; from Ontario, Canada, west to Iowa (including New York and eastern Pennsylvania), south to Alabama.

LEAVES / FLOWERS / FRUIT: The deciduous, unusual leaves are composed of two kidney-shaped lobes that are joined in the center by a wiry green stem. These smooth, blue-green leaves range from 3 to 6 inches long and 2 to 4 inches wide. The saucerlike flowers of spring are solitary, 1 inch wide, with eight oblong white petals. The fruit, a l-inch-long, leathery, pear-shaped capsule, is interesting but not greatly ornamental.

RATE / SPACING: Growth is slow. Plants from quart-sized containers are spaced 10 to 14 inches apart.

OTHER SPECIES: *J. dubia* (*dub*-ee-a), from the Manchurian woodlands, is an exquisite species with single, kidney-shaped bluish green leaves. Its height may reach 10 inches, and its flowers are a fine blue and said to look like large *Hepatica* blossoms. Hardy in Zones 5 to 8.

CULTURE / CARE: Twinleaf is adaptable to most well-drained, acidic to neutral soils. It tolerates drought once established; although an occasional deep watering during hot dry weather enhances its appearance, watering usually is not essential. It prefers light to moderate shade. No serious diseases or pests seem to affect it. Little if any maintenance is required.

PROPAGATION: Division during spring or fall is the standard means of propagating twinleaf.

Jovibarba   PLATE 173
Houseleek

This genus consists of five species that were formerly included in the genus *Sempervivum* (hen and chicks). Most nurseries still refer to them as such, but experts differentiate between the two genera based on the flowers and growth habit. *Jovibarba* species have bell-shaped flowers, and they self-propagate by developing offsets that arise from the base and develop into twin rosettes. *Sempervivum* species have flowers that flare outward, and they produce single new rosettes at the ends of leafy stolons. In other respects the two genera are much alike. Species of both genera reach only a few inches tall, spread a foot or so across, and are suitable for covering small areas as general covers, accent plants, or rock garden specimens.

SCIENTIFIC NAME: *Jovibarba* (jove-i-*bar*-ba), comes from the Latin name *Jovis barba,* beard of Jupiter, said to have been used by Charlemagne (c. 742–814) for *Sempervivum tectorum,* which Charlemagne is said to have ordered planted on top of the house of an imperial gardener, likely in adherence to the popular belief of the day that it protected against lightning.

HARDINESS / ORIGIN: Zones 5 or 6 to 8; Alps, northern Italy, Tatra Mountains of central Europe, and the Balkans.

LEAVES / FLOWERS / FRUIT: Like the leaves of *Sempervivum*, those of *Jovibarba* species are evergreen and arranged in dense rosettes. Usually they are oblong to oval, broad-based, with hairy edges and a sharply pointed tip. They are usually light or medium green, sometimes with edges colored shades of purplish or brown. Usually during summer, the mother rosette bears numerous bell-shaped flowers (⅜ inch wide) on an erect, leafy, flowering stem. The petals are usually yellow and their edges fringed with hairs. The fruit is nonornamental.

RATE / SPACING: Growth is slow. Plants from 3- to 5-inch-diameter containers are spaced 3 to 5 inches apart.

SPECIES: *J. arenaria* (air-e-*nay*-ree-a) is named from the Latin *arena,* sand, for its liking of sandy places. Native to the eastern Alps, it reaches 9 inches tall in flower and forms dense mats of tiny rosettes ⅛ to ¾ inch in width. Each rosette is composed of 60 to 80 very narrow, smooth, often red-brown-tipped, hairy-edged leaves. The summertime flowers are pale yellow with tinges of red.

J. heuffelii (hyu-*fel*-ee-eye), a very slow spreader, produces no runners but instead forms new rosettes by buds that originate at the base of the leaves from the parent rosette. Hailing from southeastern Europe, it is characterized by flat rosettes of dark or gray-green, often red-tipped leaves. Its flowers are pale yellow. Cultivars include 'Apache', with sea green and violet leaves trimmed with frosty white hairs; 'Beacon Hill', with rose-purple and gray-green leaves; 'Bermuda', with leaves flushed purple and light green at their bases; 'Bloodstone', with dark purple leaves colored green at their bases; 'Cameo', with soft bluish gray leaves, those on the outside of the rosette suffused with reddish coral; 'Giuseppi Spiny', with lime green and bronze sharply pointed leaves; 'Gold Bug', with russet-tipped yellowish green leaves; 'Inferno', with green rosettes in the center surrounded by large maroon-red leaves; 'Miller's Violet'; with purple-violet leaves colored gray at their bases; 'Mystique', with tightly compressed rich plum-purple leaves; 'Tan', with broad bronzy red leaves colored blue-green at their bases; 'Xantho-heuff', with leaves that overwinter as apple green then change to yellow during the growing season.

J. hirta (*hir*-ta), of the eastern Alps, Carpathians, Hungary, Yugoslavia, and Albania, displays 3-inch-wide, green-leaved (often with a reddish upper surface) rosettes that produce offsets upon short thin stolons. The funnel-shaped flowers are pale yellow to greenish white. Horticultural selections include 'Borealis', with orange-backed green leaves; 'Bulgaria', with red and green leaves that turn purple in winter; 'Emerald Spring', with red and green rosettes and with round red balls like chicks that rest above the foliage mass; 'Sierra Nevada', with red-tipped green leaves; 'Smeryouka', with deep red sharply pointed leaves.

J. sobolifera (sob-ol-*if*-er-a), named from the Latin *soboles,* to sprout or bear offspring, is commonly called hen and chickens. Native to Austria, it reaches 9 inches tall in flower and displays rosettes of only ½ to 1¼ inches wide. The leaves number 60 to 80 per rosette and are smooth, ¾ inch long, and light green, often with red tips and tones of brown. The flowers are greenish yellow, ⅝ inch long, and effective in summer.

CULTURE / CARE: Houseleeks are adaptable to most soils, excellent drainage being their biggest concern. They tolerate infertility and drought and seldom need watering except during long stretches of hot, dry weather. They prefer full sun to light shade or a combination of full sun with light or moderate afternoon shade. They experience few pest problems, and their most common diseases are rust, leaf rot, stem rot, and root rot. Mother plants die soon after flowering, and the dead rosettes are best removed so that the progeny can more readily fill in the gaps.

PROPAGATION: Division proves to be most practical and consists merely of pulling up the small offsets and replanting them.

Juniperus   PLATES 174, 175
Juniper

Ground-covering species of juniper are some of the finest, most durable, drought-resistant, low-maintenance plants available. They are excellent when mass planted on a moderate to large scale as turf substitutes and foundation facers, and they are superior for erosion control on slopes of light to moderate incline. Many forms are excellent for facing open shrubs and trees (such as honey locust and mature white pine). Next to a rock ledge over which their branches can hang, they appear graceful and eye-catching. Junipers are said to be tolerant of growing near black walnut (*Juglans nigra*). Little or no foot traffic is tolerated.

Only a few juniper species fit the description of ground cover: *Juniperus conferta, J. horizontalis,* and *J. procumbens.* These are horizontal growing evergreens covered with needlelike leaves of green, blue, or gray. Where it becomes complicated, though, is with the hundreds of ground-covering cultivars from these and several other species that are normally treelike or shrubby. In the following pages I present the basics of ground-covering junipers. There are many, many more, and others popping up all the time.

Juniper berries have been widely used as a flavoring and herbal medicine. They are also attractive to several types of birds and other wildlife. Even though many of the ground-covering selections fruit less heavily than the species, they too are attractive to wildlife. The pfitzer juniper is said to attract cedar waxwings, robins, and mockingbirds. In addition, many selections serve well as nesting sites for a variety of birds.

SCIENTIFIC NAME: *Juniperus* (jew-*nip*-er-us / yoo-*ni*-pe-rus) is the Latin name for the juniper tree.

HARDINESS / ORIGIN: See individual species for hardiness; Northern Hemisphere, anywhere from polar regions to tropical mountains.

LEAVES / FLOWERS / FRUIT: The leaves are either needlelike or scalelike. The male and female flowers are ornamentally insignificant. The fruit is a dark blue berrylike cone.

RATE / SPACING: Slow to moderate; see individual species for spacing recommendations. The ground-covering junipers are characterized by broad-spreading or horizontal habits of growth and must be compact enough to discourage weed growth.

SPECIES: *J. chinensis* (chi-*nen*-sis) cultivars. The species, commonly called Chinese juniper, is native to China, Mongolia, and Japan. Hardy in Zones 4 to 9, it generally is shrubby or treelike and may reach 60 feet tall. Its green to blue-green or grayish green evergreen leaves are of two forms: juvenile leaves are awl-shaped, 1/3 inch long, ending in a spiny point; adult leaves are scalelike, overlapping, 1/16 inch long, and blunt-tipped. The flowers are small, yellowish, and ornamentally inconsequential. Although the species is not a ground cover, it has produced selections which make good ground covers. Growth of these cultivars is slow to moderate. Plants from 2- to 5-gallon-sized containers are spaced 3 to 4 feet apart. Among the popular selections are 'Emerald Sea', with emerald green leaves, low habit, spreading to more than 8 feet wide; 'Fruitlandii', compact, with low-growing habit, 1½ to 2 feet tall by 6 feet wide, foliage dull green and rather coarse-textured; 'Gold Coast', a graceful, compact, low-spreading clone with golden-yellow new foliage that intensifies with cold weather in fall; 'Gold Lace', 4 feet tall by 6 feet wide, compact habit, with bright golden-yellow foliage; 'Holbert', with blue leaves, 3 feet tall by more than 8 feet wide; 'Old Gold', similar to 'Pfitzeriana Compacta' (see below) but with golden or bronzy golden new foliage and a somewhat more delicate and refined habit; 'Pfitzeriana', pfitzer juniper, broad spreading, usually 4 to 5 feet tall by 10 feet wide, with light green foliage, new branches somewhat pendulous; 'Pfitzeriana Aurea', with foliage light golden yellow in youth, otherwise similar to 'Pfitzeriana' but a bit smaller and flatter growing; 'Pfitzeriana Compacta', with broad-spreading habit, 12 to 18 inches tall by 6 feet wide, foliage gray-green; 'Pfitzeriana Sarcoxie', Ozark compact pfitzer juniper, 3 to 4 feet tall, with dense habit; 'San Jose', 12 to 18 inches tall by 8 feet wide, foliage dull green and

coarse-textured, but soft, not prickly; var. *sargentii,* with leaves blue-green and scaly, low and broad-spreading habit, generally 12 to 24 inches tall by 9 feet wide; var. *sargentii* 'Glauca', shorter than var. *sargentii,* only 18 inches tall, with bluish and soft-textured foliage; 'Saybrook Gold', with very compact habit, 30 inches tall by 6 feet wide, new foliage bright golden; 'Sea Spray', with blue-green leaves, 15 inches tall by more than 6 feet wide.

J. communis (koe-*myu*-nis), named from the Latin *communis,* common, is commonly called common juniper. Hardy in Zones 2 to 6 (unique for its intolerance of heat), it hails from Europe, Asia, and North America, and is highly variable in shape and size. Its height may be anywhere from a few inches to 35 feet, and its habit ranges from a straggly spreading shrub to a medium-sized tree. The needlelike foliage is evergreen, prickly, and narrowly triangular; it persists for about three years, reaches 3/8 inch long, and is concave above with broad white longitudinal striping. The flowers are small, yellow, and ornamentally insignificant, but they yield numerous blue or blackish, ½-inch-long berrylike fruits. Growth of ground-covering selections is slow. Plants from 2- to 5-gallon-sized containers are spaced 2½ to 3½ feet apart. The species is seldom cultivated; however, many useful selections are available. Some of the more popular include var. *depressa,* Canadian juniper, a low, spreading or prostrate shrub rarely reaching 4 feet tall by 8 feet wide, with foliage light yellowish or brownish green, becoming bronzy in winter; 'Depressa Aurea', similar to var. *depressa* in habit but with yellow foliage in youth; 'Depressed Star', a uniformly shaped selection that ranges from 1 to 1½ feet tall and spreads to more than 8 feet wide; 'Effusa', a low, spreading, horizontal selection with foliage dull green above and silvery-white below, 9 to 12 inches tall by 4 or more feet wide; 'Nana', sometimes listed as 'Saxatilis' or 'Siberica', a slow, horizontally growing selection with dark green leaves that reaches 2 or 3 feet tall.

J. conferta (kon-fer-ta), named from the Latin *confertus,* crowded, in reference to its leaves, is commonly called shore juniper. Hardy in Zones 6 to 8, it comes from the seacoast of Japan and is characterized by a dense, horizontal, wide-spreading habit. In time it reaches 1 to 1½ feet tall and spreads to more than 6 feet wide. Its needlelike leaves are evergreen, ¼ to 5/8 inch long by 1/16 inch wide, and prickly. Like the other junipers, its flowers are of no ornamental significance. Growth is slow. Plants from 1- to 3-gallon-sized containers are spaced 3 to 4 feet apart. Some popular horticultural selections include 'Blue Pacific', 6 to 12 inches high, with blue-green needles; 'Boulevard', with blue-green needles; 'Compacta', more compact and horizontal than the species; 'Emerald Sea', 6 to 12 inches tall, with a gray-green band on emerald green needles that become yellow-green in winter.

J. davurica (day-*vure*-i-ka), Davurian juniper, hails from southeastern Siberia. It is closely related to *J. sabina* and is hardy in Zones 5 to 9. Growth is slow to moderate. Plants from 2- to 3-gallon-sized containers are spaced 3 to 4½ feet apart. While the species is seldom cultivated, some of its cultivars make excellent ground covers: 'Expansa' ('Parsonii'), 3 feet high by 7 to 9 feet wide, with dark foliage arranged in dense clusters on rigid horizontal branches; 'Expansa Aureospicata', a less vigorous selection with occasional yellow-leaved branches; 'Expansa Variegata', similar to 'Expansa' but taller and denser with white-leaved branches scattered among the green-leaved branches.

J. horizontalis (hor-i-zon-*tay*-lis), creeping juniper, creeping cedar, creeping savin, or horizontal juniper, is a horizontal, mat-forming ground cover. Hardy in Zones 2 to 9, it is native to North America, occurring from Nova Scotia to British Columbia, in the mountains and along the shores of the Great Lakes. It reaches 1 to 2 feet tall by 4 to 6 feet wide. The evergreen leaves are blue-green to steel green and often turn purple during fall. The adult leaves are scalelike, ¹⁄₁₆ inch long, and sharply pointed, while the juvenile leaves are awl-shaped. Although the flowers are small and not very ornamental, they often yield roundish blue fruit. Growth of ground-covering selections is slow to moderate. Space plants from 1-to 3-gallon-sized containers 3 to 4 feet apart. Some popular selections include 'Adpressa', green with blue-green new growth, a dense, mat-forming habit, and a mature height of 4 to 6 inches; 'Aurea', with golden-yellow new foliage; 'Bar Harbor', low spreading, with excellent landscape qualities, to 10 inches tall by 6 or more feet wide, steel blue, mostly awl-shaped foliage, turning purplish blue in fall; 'Blue Chip', with silvery-blue foliage, mounding habit, to 8 or 10 inches tall; 'Blue Horizon', similar to 'Wiltonii' (see below) but lower growing and never mounding in the center; 'Emerald Spreader', with feathery-textured, emerald green foliage, very low growing; 'Hughes', with silvery-blue foliage becoming slightly purplish in winter, low-growing, 12 inches tall; 'Huntington Blue', densely branched, wide spreading, with blue-gray foliage becoming purplish in winter; 'Icee Blue', with compact habit and silvery-blue foliage; 'Jade Spreader', compact, very low growing, with jade green foliage; 'Mother Lode', with bright yellow foliage becoming yellow-orange and plum-tinged during winter; 'Pancake', said to be the most horizontal cultivar of the species,

reaching only 2 inches tall and spreading more than 30 inches wide; 'Plumosa', a dense, wide-spreading selection with coarse scalelike grayish green foliage that becomes purplish in winter; 'Turquoise Spreader', with a low, spreading habit and dense, turquoise-green feathery foliage; 'Variegata', blue-green with creamy-white-tipped branchlets, vigorous and low growing; 'Wiltonii' ('Blue Rug'), probably the most popular cultivar, with low, trailing habit, silvery-blue foliage sometimes with a hint of purple in winter, 3 to 6 inches tall.

J. procumbens (pro-*kum*-benz), named for its procumbent (i.e., horizontal trailing but not rooting) habit, is commonly called Japanese garden juniper. Native to Japan, it is hardy in Zones 5 to 9, reaches 10 to 12 inches tall, and may spread 10 or more feet across. Its ⅓-inch-long leaves are needle-like and sharply pointed. The flowers are small, yellow, and relatively insignificant. Its fruit reaches ⅓ inch wide but is seldom seen in cultivation. Growth is slow. Plants from 2- to 3-gallon-sized containers are spaced 3 to 4 feet apart. The most popular horticultural selections include 'Green Mound', 8 inches tall by 6 feet wide with vibrant light green foliage; 'Nana', lower and denser than the species, seldom more than 4 inches tall, eventually reaching 6 to 8 feet wide, with blue-green foliage becoming slightly purplish in winter; 'Nana Californica', similar to 'Nana' but with leaves deeper blue-green and finer-textured, to 8 inches tall and spreading to 4 feet wide; 'Nana Greenmound', much like 'Nana Californica' but more bluish in color; 'Variegata', with leaves variegated creamy white and green.

J. sabina (sa-*been*-a / sa-*bine*-a) cultivars. The specific epithet is taken from the Latin name for this plant, which is commonly called savin. Characterized by dark, dull green, pungent-smelling (when crushed), evergreen, ¹⁄₂₀- to ⅕-inch-long adult scale-like leaves and ⅙-inch-long awl-shaped juvenile needles, the species hails from Europe and is hardy in Zones 3 to 8. It has a broad-spreading habit from 4 to 6 feet tall by 5 to 10 feet wide and is not often classed as a ground cover. Many of its selections, however, are excellent for this purpose. Growth is slow to moderate. Plants from 2- to 3-gallon-sized containers are spaced 3½ to 4½ feet apart. Among the more common ground-covering cultivars are 'Arcadia', similar to 'Tamariscifolia' (see below), with a dense, horizontally growing habit, arching branch tips, in time reaching 20 inches tall by 4 to 7 feet wide; 'Arcadia Compacta', like 'Arcadia', but compact in habit, with lacy green foliage; 'Blue Danube', semiupright in habit, with feathery bluish green foliage; 'Blue Forest', 18 inches tall, giving the unique appearance of a miniature blue-green forest;

'Broadmoor', low-spreading, mound-forming habit with grayish green foliage, 2 to 3 feet tall by 8 to 10 feet wide; 'Buffalo', similar to 'Tamariscifolia' but foliage colored bright green, mature height only 12 inches, and spread sometimes exceeding 8 feet; 'Calgary Carpet', similar to 'Arcadia' but lower growing, foliage soft green; 'Moor-Dense', similar to 'Broadmoor' but more compact in habit; 'Skandia', with broad-spreading habit, 12 to 18 inches tall by 10 feet wide, foliage grayish blue-green; 'Sierra Spreader', 1 foot tall by 6 to 8 feet wide, noteworthy for its year-round intense green foliage; 'Tamariscifolia', tam juniper, an excellent, attractive, low-spreading (1½ feet tall by 15 feet wide), mounding selection with feathery bluish green foliage held on branches arranged in horizontal tiers; 'Tamariscifolia New Blue', similar to 'Tamariscifolia' but with a vibrant blue cast to the foliage; 'Variegata', 2 to 3 feet tall by 3 to 4½ feet wide, foliage white-streaked.

J. scopulorum (skop-you-*lore*-um) 'Blue Creeper' ('Monam'), an outstanding selection with a low (to 2 feet tall), broad-spreading (from 6 to 8 feet wide), many-branched habit has bright blue foliage that becomes more intense in cold weather. The species, named for its habit of growing on cliffs, is commonly called Rocky Mountain juniper or Colorado red cedar. Native to dry rock outcroppings from British Columbia to Texas, *J. scopulorum* is hardy in Zones 3 to 6 or 7. It generally is a rather small tree (sometimes reaching 35 feet tall) with a narrow pyramidal form.

J. squamata (skwa-*may*-ta) cultivars. The species, named from the Latin *squama,* scale, for its scaly bark, is commonly called singleseed juniper. Its gray-green needlelike leaves are sharp pointed, stiff, ⅛ to 5⁄16 inch long, and curved slightly outward. Native to China, the species is hardy in Zones 4 to 8. Because it is greatly variable in habit and size, it is seldom used. A number of interesting selections, however, are useful for ground covers: 'Blue Carpet', a vigorous, flat, broad selection with blue-gray foliage; 'Blue Star', a dwarf form with beautiful, deep silvery-blue foliage, usually not exceeding 12 inches in height, 4 to 5 feet wide; 'Holger', a broad-spreading, blue-green, yellow-tipped selection reaching less than 1 foot tall and more than 4 feet wide; 'Prostrata', a horizontal slow-spreading selection with leaves bluish white above and green below; 'Variegata', a low-growing horizontal selection reaching 10 inches tall and spreading 4 or 5 feet wide, with new growth cream-colored.

J. virginiana (ver-jin-ee-*aye*-na) 'Silver Spreader' is a silvery-gray-leaved cultivar with a low, wide-spreading habit. Plants from 2- to 3-gallon-sized containers are spaced 4 to 5 feet apart. The species,

named for its Virginia origin, is commonly called eastern red cedar. Native to eastern North America from Canada to Florida, it is hardy in Zones 3 to 9 but cannot be used as a ground cover because it is an upright-growing, pyramidal tree. 'Gary Owl' reaches 3 feet tall by 6 feet wide, has fine-textured silvery-gray foliage, and is a good ground cover for large-scale use.

CULTURE / CARE: All the junipers are best in well-drained, loamy, neutral to acidic soil, but they tolerate sandy or gravelly, often infertile soils. They are well adapted to withstand drought and seldom need supplemental watering. Excessive humidity often does more harm than drought, so do not hesitate to plant them in windy sites, as this will help to keep their foliage dry and reduce the incidence of fungus diseases. They prefer full sun. Their pests and diseases are juniper twig blight, cedar apple rust, mites, and root-knot nematode. Maintenance is easy; seldom is anything needed beyond cutting off the branch tips as plants outgrow their designated bounds.

PROPAGATION: Cuttings taken in mid to late fall are the normal means of propagating junipers. Rooting is greatly aided by the use of a hormone containing 3000 to 8000 ppm IBA and bottom heat.

Kalanchoe   PLATE 176

The genus *Kalanchoe* contains more than 125 species of tropical, erectly oriented, succulent, subshrubby ground covers. When mass planted they do a good job of blanketing small-sized or moderate-sized areas. They are attractive edging plants for flower beds, walkways, and building entrances. Small groups may be used for accent. Due to their fleshy and shrubby nature, they tolerate no foot traffic.

SCIENTIFIC NAME: *Kalanchoe* (ka-*lan*-koe-ee / ka-*lan*-choe) is the Chinese name for one species in the genus.

HARDINESS / ORIGIN: Zones 10 to 11; Old World tropics, especially Africa and Madagascar.

LEAVES / FLOWERS / FRUIT: Most species have oppositely arranged, entire or lobed (rarely pinnate) succulent leaves. The tubular flowers, borne from summer to winter (with some species flowering in spring), are arranged in clusters at the ends of the stems. The fruit is nonornamental.

RATE / SPACING: Growth of most species is moderate. Plants from pint-sized to gallon-sized containers are spaced 8 to 14 inches apart.

SPECIES: *K. blossfeldiana* (blos-feld-ee-*aye*-na), named after Robert Blossfeld, a German nurseryman, is commonly called Christmas kalanchoe. Native to Madagascar, it reaches 12 to 15 inches tall by 12 to 15 inches wide. Its fleshy, opposite, evergreen leaves are narrowly oblong, 1 to 3 inches long by 1 inch wide, and colored glossy green with a reddish outline. The numerous tiny scarlet trumpet-shaped flowers are borne on long stalks and provide an excellent winter and early springtime floral display.

K. fedtschenkoi (fet-*shenk*-oh-ee), named after Boris Fedtschenko (1872–1933), a Russian traveler, is commonly called Fedtschenkoi kalanchoe. It reaches 12 inches tall, has ½- to 2-inch-long metallic gray-green, fleshy, scallop-edged leaves and late winterborne flowers of brownish rose. Also native to Madagascar, it is cultivated mainly for its foliage.

K. laciniata (la-sin-ee-*aye*-ta) is erect-stemmed to 4 feet. It bears fragrant yellowish orange or pink ¼-inch flowers in clusters in late winter and spring. The leaves are fleshy, to 5 inches long, and colored greenish bronze to red.

K. marmorata (mar-moe-*ray*-ta), named from the Latin *marmor,* marbled, for its leaves, is commonly called pen-wiper. Hailing from eastern Africa, it is stout and erectly oriented. The marbled leaves are rounded, grayish, and waxy with brown markings. The white flowers are often tinged pink or yellow.

K. tomentosa (toe-men-*toe*-sa), named for its foliage that is densely covered with fuzzy white down, is commonly called panda plant or pussy ears. It is native to Madagascar and reaches 12 to 36 inches tall. The 2-inch-long leaves have strong brown markings at their tips and in their notches around the edges. The flowers are yellow-green with purple-tinged petals. Variegated selections are also available.

K. tubiflora (tube-i-*floe*-ra), named for its tubular flowers, is commonly called chandelier plant. It is interesting for its narrow pinkish leaves which are borne in whorls of three and which bear young plantlets at their tips. The tubular flowers are salmon-red or scarlet and ascend 12 to 18 inches.

CULTURE / CARE: Kalanchoes grow best in well-drained, sandy, somewhat acidic loam and are relatively tolerant of drought. An occasional deep watering during periods of hot, dry weather is beneficial but seldom absolutely necessary. They prefer full sun. Crown rot—especially in poorly drained soils—is the most common disease; wilt, leaf spot, powdery mildew, and viral mosaic are less common problems. The primary pests are aphids and mealybugs. The only maintenance required is division of overcrowded plants (as evidenced by the floral display becoming reduced over time).

PROPAGATION: Division is best accomplished during spring and fall, and leafy stem sections are rooted easily throughout the year. Additionally, the small plantlets that form along the leaf margins of some species can be detached and transplanted. Plantlets that have not yet developed roots can be detached and rooted as if they were cuttings. Seed germinates in a temperature range of 85 to 95°F but may be very slow.

Lamiastrum galeobdolon   PLATE 177
Yellow Archangel, Golden Dead Nettle, Lamiastrum

Almost vinelike, yellow archangel trails along the ground with long herbaceous stems which root as they come in contact with the soil. As such, it is best suited for use in large open areas and especially on sloping ground, terraced hillsides, and within elevated planters. The variegated selections are excellent in the shade surrounding tree trunks or in mass plantings in shady woodland borders where their silvery coloration adds a pleasant brightening effect. The clump-forming selections spread very slowly and are best as specimens or accent plants. No foot traffic is tolerated.

SCIENTIFIC NAME: *Lamiastrum galeobdolon* (lay-mee-as-trum gal-lee-*ob*-da-lon). *Lamiastrum,* meaning resembling *Lamium,* dead nettle, refers to a closely related genus. *Galeobdolon,* according to some authorities, is an old name meaning weasel and/or a bad smell. Others say that the name is commemorative. Still others say that it is a Latin name for a nettlelike plant, from *galeo,* to cover with a helmet, and *dolon,* a fly's sting. Some authorities believe the species should be called *Galeobdolon luteum* in reference to its yellow (*luteum*) flowers.

HARDINESS / ORIGIN: Zones 4 to 9; woodlands from western Europe to Iran.

LEAVES / FLOWERS / FRUIT: The leaves are evergreen, oval to nearly round, to 3 inches long, covered with sparse hairs, toothed along the edges, aromatic when crushed, and colored medium green. The colorful yellow, ½- to ¾-inch-long flowers are arranged in upright spikes and are effective during late spring. The fruit is nonornamental.

RATE / SPACING: Growth is fast. Plants from 2½- to 3-inch-diameter containers are spaced 12 to 18 inches apart.

HORTICULTURAL SELECTIONS: 'Compacta', similar to 'Variegatum', but slower growing and with smaller leaves; 'Herman's Pride', clump-forming, nontrailing, leaves oval and sharply tapering with intensely silver and green variegation (at least during spring), sometimes fading to a rather unattractive mottled pattern during the heat of summer, best in a cool shady location; 'Variegatum', with silvery and green foliage that develops a blood-red to purplish center splotch in autumn, more common than the species and all other cultivars combined.

CULTURE / CARE: This species and its cultivars are at their absolute best in rich, fertile, loamy, acidic soil, yet they also tolerate every other type of soil. Many gardeners prefer to grow them in infertile sandy soils to slow their growth; this works in the shade, but not in sunny locations as the ability of these plants to cope with drought is poor, and even in rich shady sites, occasional summer watering may be necessary. The species and its cultivars prefer light to moderate shade, yet fine results can be achieved in full sun as long as the soil is rich and ample water is provided. Leaf blight is the primary disease problem, and the only real pest problems are mites (spider and bud scale types). Maintenance is easy: a single mowing in early summer (after flowering) to neaten appearance and rejuvenate growth is optional but certainly not necessary.

PROPAGATION: Cuttings root quickly and easily throughout the growing season. Division is best accomplished during spring and fall.

Lamium maculatum   PLATE 178
Spotted Dead Nettle

Clump-forming and horizontally spreading, this charming, colorful little herbaceous ground cover reaches 6 to 8 inches tall and spreads 12 to 16 inches across. Most often used on a small scale, its variegated foliage contrasts nicely with the darker leaves of other plants, making it an excellent facing for hedges of Japanese yew or for grouped plantings of shrubs such as boxwood, purple-leaved plum, rhododendron, and others. No foot traffic is tolerated.

SCIENTIFIC NAME: *Lamium maculatum* (*lay*-me-um mak-you-*lay*-tum). *Lamium* is from the Greek *laimos,* throat, alluding to the throatlike appearance of the basal portion of the blossoms. *Maculatum,* spotted, refers to the silvery splotch in the center of each leaf.

HARDINESS / ORIGIN: Zones 3 to 8; Europe.

LEAVES / FLOWERS / FRUIT: The evergreen, crinkled leaves with rounded teeth about their margins are oval to heart-shaped, 1 inch long by ½ inch wide, and green with a silvery-gray splash in their centers. They are unpleasantly scented when rubbed, bruised, or crushed. The flowers reach ⅝ inch long, consist of an upper and lower petallike lip, are colored lavender, and are effective during spring and early summer. The fruit, a tiny nutlet, is nonornamental.

RATE / SPACING: Growth is moderate. Plants from 2 ¼- to 4-inch-diameter containers are spaced 6 to 10 inches apart.

HORTICULTURAL SELECTIONS: 'Album', with flowers creamy white; 'Aureum', leaves yellowish with a whitish blotch along the midrib, less aggressive, per-forming better in shade than sun, susceptible to diseases; 'Beacon Silver', an exceptionally attractive selection (when not infected with leaf spot or blight), with radiant silver leaves surrounded with a light border of green, needs excellent drainage, relatively low humidity, light to moderate shade, and cool temperatures; 'Beedham's White', with bright yellow leaves and white flowers; 'Chequers', somewhat more vigorous, flowers pinkish, and foliage a bit larger; 'Elizabeth de Maas', with chartreuse, green, silver, and yellow variegation; 'Pink Pewter', with pink flowers atop coarsely toothed dark silver, green-edged foliage; 'Shell Pink', leaves with irregular white variegation in their centers, flowers soft pastel pink; 'White Nancy', similar to 'Beacon Silver' in respect to its foliage, but with white flowers.

CULTURE / CARE: Spotted dead nettle and its cultivars require well-drained soils, preferably a rich acidic loam; elsewhere, they suffer an agonizing death. They are not well adapted to heat, drought, or high humidity, so be sure to plant them in a cool site, with full sun to moderate shade (more shade with the cultivars, particularly further south). Should they need additional watering, do so in the morning so that the leaves dry quickly. Pests include slugs and aphids, and the most common diseases are leaf scorch, crown rot, leaf blight, and leaf spots. While the species is quite disease resistant, the same cannot, unfortunately, be said of all the cultivars. Especially where summers are hot and humid, or during greenhouse propagation, certain cultivars ('Aureum' and 'Beacon Silver' among them) are likely to be in some state of decay (that eventually will lead to their demise) at any time. Maintenance is minimal, but some gardeners prefer to shear or mow in summer (after flowering) to help keep plantings rejuvenated and vibrant.

PROPAGATION: Cuttings can be rooted easily during early summer. Division is best performed during spring and early fall.

Lampranthus   PLATE 179
Ice Plant

There are several ground covers that can be tagged ice plant, including species of *Cephalophyllum, Delosperma,* and *Drosanthemum.* Of those grown in North America, however, *Lampranthus* has been the most common. Subshrubby or sprawling, it, like the other ice plants, provides many succulent, drought-tolerant, durable cultivars, which are outstanding for their bright colorful daisylike flowers and glistening water-soaked leaves and stems. Ice plants are resistant to fire and are therefore a good choice for rest areas and along sidewalks and foundations of public buildings. Also, because of their sprawling nature, they work well as soil stabilizers, often being used on highway embankments and gently sloping berms. In a rock garden they make splendid specimens, and in elevated planters, terrace plantings, along the side of stairways, and atop retaining walls—places that lift them closer to the eye—they are particularly valuable. No foot traffic is tolerated.

SCIENTIFIC NAME: *Lampranthus* (lam-*pran*-thus / lam-*pranth*-us) receives its name from the Greek *lampros*, brilliant, and *anthos*, flower, in reference to the very showy flowers.

HARDINESS / ORIGIN: Zones 9 to 11; South Africa.

LEAVES / FLOWERS / FRUIT: The leaves are evergreen, succulent, round or three-angled, and colored glistening shades of gray to green. The daisylike flowers are borne alone or in clusters and come in near-neon shades of red, pink, white, purple, yellow, or orange. They are attractive to bees. The fruit is nonornamental.

RATE / SPACING: Growth is moderate. Plants from pint-sized to quart-sized containers are spaced 10 to 18 inches apart.

SPECIES: *L. aurantiacus* (awe-ran-tee-*aye*-kus), named for its orange flowers, is commonly called bush ice plant. It ranges from 10 to 15 inches tall and spreads more than 2 feet wide. An outstanding species, it has subdued gray-green, 1-inch-long, three-sided leaves that tend to lull the observer into a sense of tranquility. Then, all at once, it bursts forth with magnificent orange, 1- to 1½-inch-wide springtime flowers. Cultivars include 'Glaucus', with bright yellow flowers; 'Gold Nugget', with bright orange flowers; 'Sunman', with golden-yellow flowers.

L. filicaulis (fil-i-*kau*-lis), named from the Latin *filum*, thread, and *caulis,* stem, for its threadlike stems, is commonly called Redondo creeper. It reaches only 3 inches tall and spreads indefinitely to form a mat of handsome, fine-textured, glistening green foliage—an appropriate backdrop for the small pink flowers of early spring. Growth is slow. Plants from 3- to 4-inch-diameter containers are spaced 8 to 12 inches apart.

L. productus (pro-*duk*-tus), named for its floral productivity, is commonly called purple ice plant. It is smothered with showy purple flowers from late winter to spring—to the point that one must strain the eyes to glimpse the gray-green, bronzy-tipped leaves that lie below. At maturity plants reach 15 inches tall by 2 feet wide.

L. spectabilis (spek-*tab*-i-lis), meaning spectacular in Latin, in reference to its floral display, is commonly called showy ice plant or trailing ice plant. It reaches 15 inches tall by 1½ to 2 feet wide. The leaves are 2 to 3 inches long by ¼ inch wide, three-angled to cylindrical, and colored an attractive gray

with reddish tips. In bloom, hundreds of striking, 2- to 3-inch-wide, bright purple solitary flowers put on a lively springtime display.

CULTURE / CARE: Despite their flamboyance, ice plants are pretty simple when it comes to cultural needs. Adaptable to a wide range of soils, they insist only upon excellent drainage. Discouraged but undaunted, they persevere in the most infertile soils and face drought with the confidence of camels. They prefer to bask in full sun and find aphids and mealybugs sometimes annoying. Little or no maintenance is needed.

PROPAGATION: Cuttings root easily throughout the year. Division is possible any time.

Lantana

PLATE 180

Lantanas are sturdy, woody covers for use in warm climates in moderate-sized to larger-sized areas, both on flat or sloping terrain, and particularly in elevated beds or planters. They bear bright, cheerful, fragrant flowers (primarily in spring, sparsely in other seasons), and are useful in controlling erosion, as accent plants in borders, or when planted as an edging along paths and walkways. The green, unripe fruits can be fatally poisonous. Some species are considered serious weeds in parts of the United States.

SCIENTIFIC NAME: *Lantana* (lan-*tay*-na / lan-*tan*-a) is an ancient name for *Viburnum,* the inflorescences of the two genera sometimes being similar.

HARDINESS / ORIGIN: Zones 9 to 11; tropical America.

LEAVES / FLOWERS / FRUITS: The coarse-textured, evergreen or deciduous leaves are toothed about their edges and smell somewhat like citrus when touched. On the other hand, the brightly colored flowers, which occur in hemispherical heads and change color as they mature, are often quite pleasant smelling. The fruit, a berrylike drupe, turns blackish in maturity.

RATE / SPACING: Growth is fast. Plants from gallon-sized containers are spaced 3 to 4 feet apart.

SPECIES: *L.* × *hybrida* (*hye*-bri-da), named for its hybrid origin, is commonly called hybrid lantana. Most of the cultivated lantanas that are suitable for use as ground covers are hybrids between *L. camara, L. montevidensis,* and their cultivars. As with most large hybrid groups, the accuracy of its names and classification are often doubtful. Regardless, these plants are very worthwhile ground covers. They can be categorized as displaying low-spreading or trailing habits, mature heights of 2 to 3 feet, and spreads of 4 to 8 feet. Popular horticultural selections include 'American Red', with bright red and yellow florets; 'Carnival', to 2 feet tall by 4 to 5 feet wide, flowers mixed pink, yellow, lavender, and crimson; 'Christine', with bright cerise-pink flowers; 'Confetti', to 3 feet tall by 8 feet wide, flowers yellow, pink, or purple; 'Cream Carpet', to 3 feet tall by 8 feet wide, flowers creamy white with bright yellow throats; 'Dwarf Pink', compact habit, flowers pink; 'Dwarf White', compact habit, white flowers; 'Dwarf Yellow', compact habit, corn yellow flowers; 'Golden Glow', less than 3 feet tall, flowers golden yellow; 'Gold Mound', 2 feet tall by 6 feet wide, flowers orange-yellow; 'Gold Rush', with masses of golden-yellow flowers; 'Irene', with compact habit, flowers lemon-yellow and magenta; 'Kathleen', to 2 feet tall by 6 feet wide, flowers rose-pink with golden centers; 'Miss Huff', to 36 inches tall, may be somewhat more hardy, noteworthy for its orange and pink flowers throughout summer; ' New Gold', sometimes represented as a selection of *L. camara,* flowers vibrant yellow; 'Radiation', flowers orange-red; 'Spreading Sunset', to 3 feet tall by 8 feet wide, flowers orange-red; 'Spreading Sunshine', flowers bright sunny yellow; 'Sunburst', to 3 feet tall by 8 feet wide, flowers bright yellow; 'Tangerine', 2 to 3 feet tall by 6 to 8 feet wide, flowers orange-red; 'Variegata', leaves green with chartreuse edges and mottling, flowers lemon-yellow; 'Yellow Spreader', with bright yellow flowers and mound-forming habit to 3 feet tall.

L. montevidensis (mon-te-vid-*en*-sis), named for Montevideo, the capital of Uruguay, is commonly called polecat geranium, trailing lantana, or weeping lantana. Its leaves are evergreen, usually deeply furrowed, oval, ½ to 1 inch long by ½ inch wide, coarsely toothed and haired about the edges, dark green becoming darker with cold weather. The profusely borne springtime flowers (sparse in other seasons) are arranged in compact heads to 1 inch or more in diameter. Individually they reach ¼ inch wide and are attractively colored rose-pink to lilac. The fruit is nonornamental. Horticultural selections include 'Lavender Swirl', with clusters of all-white, all-purple, and combined white-and-purple-flowers on individual plants; 'Veluntina White', with white flowers; 'White Lightnin', with low habit and masses of snowy white flowers.

CULTURE / CARE: Lantanas are adaptable to almost any soil with good drainage. They tolerate drought very well, but an occasional deep watering in summer is recommended. They prefer full sun to light shade, but flower best in full sun. Pests include caterpillars, greenhouse whitefly, mites, lantana aphid, southern root-knot nematode, and mealybugs. Diseases such as black mildew, leaf spot, rust, and wilt are occasionally problematic and are almost always less prevalent in full sun. In time, lantanas may de-velop open dead centers; this can be prevented, and new growth stimulated, by annual shearing (on the moderate to heavy side), following flowering.

PROPAGATION: Cuttings taken during late spring, summer, and fall root relatively well.

Lathyrus latifolius   PLATE 181
Perennial Pea Vine, Wild Sweet Pea, Vetchling

Often thought of as an old-fashioned cottage garden plant, perennial pea still makes its way into the modern landscape. Normally it is put to use as a moderate-scale to large-scale general cover for sloping sandy or gravelly sunny embankments, where it helps to prevent erosion and adds seasonal interest with its long-lasting floral display. Reaching 4 to 8 inches tall, it climbs as well as sprawls, and thus is often used against the base of a fence so that it can perform the dual roles of a ground cover and screening plant. No foot traffic is tolerated.

SCIENTIFIC NAME: *Lathyrus latifolius* (*lath*-i-rus / *la*-thi-rus lat-i-*foe*-lee-us). *Lathyrus* is the Greek name for the pea. *Latifolius* means broad-leaved.

HARDINESS / ORIGIN: Zones 4 to 9; southern Europe, naturalized in North America.

LEAVES / FLOWERS / FRUIT: The compound leaflets are alternately arranged, narrowly oblong, colored medium green, reach 4 inches long, and are held upon curious winged stems which grasp for support by means of threadlike tendrils. The many pealike, 1-inch-wide rosy, pinkish purple, or white flowers are borne from early summer through early fall. The pealike seedpods which follow are poisonous if eaten in quantity, as are the seeds.

RATE / SPACING: Growth is fast. Plants from pint-sized containers are spaced 1 foot apart.

HORTICULTURAL SELECTIONS: 'Albus', with white flowers; 'Pink Pearl', with pink flowers; 'Red Pearl', with red flowers; 'Splendens', with dark purple and red flowers; 'White Pearl', with clear white flowers.

CULTURE / CARE: Perennial pea grows well in about any well-drained, mildly acidic to mildly alkaline soil. It is tolerant of drought and infertility and grows well in full sun to light shade. Anthracnose, viral mosaic, black root rot, and downy mildew are its primary disease problems. Its most common pests are aphids, pea moth, mites, corn earworm, and southern root-knot nematode. Maintenance usually is limited to trimming back shoots as they outgrow their bounds.

PROPAGATION: Clumps may be divided during spring or fall. Seed germinates in only two or three weeks.

Lavandula angustifolia   PLATE 182
True Lavender

Among the most popular garden plants, true lavender is a semiwoody subshrub that ranges from 1½ to 2½ feet tall and spreads 1 to 2 feet across. It is frequently used as a specimen in herb gardens but is often overlooked as a ground cover. Used as a ground cover, it is valuable for edging walkways and garden borders as a dwarf hedge and can also be used as a foundation plant or rock garden specimen. No foot traffic is tolerated.

Pleasantly scented, the foliage and flowers of true lavender are frequently dried and used in sachets. Extracts from the flowers are used in the manufacture of perfume. Since lavender oil is said to repel insects, such perfume might be very practical for hunters and fishermen. Incorporated with other compounds, oil of lavender has been used to make smelling salts and spirits that aid in the prevention of fainting. Topically, the oil functions as an antiseptic, a treatment for skin disorders, and a cosmetic. The culinary uses of lavender are extensive and include using the flowers for flavoring jellies and vinegars and incorporating the leaves in salads. Honey from the flowers is supposed to be very good. Medicinally, lavender has been used to relieve toothaches and soreness of the joints and feet. It has been used as a stimulant, antispasmodic, and carminative to relieve gas and colic.

SCIENTIFIC NAME: *Lavandula angustifolia* (la-*van*-dyu-la an-gus-ti-*foe*-lee-a). *Lavandula* is thought to come from the Latin word *lavo,* to wash, as the Greeks and Romans used lavender in their bath water. *Angustifolia* means narrow-leaved.

HARDINESS / ORIGIN: Zones 5 to 9; southern Europe and North Africa.

LEAVES / FLOWERS / FRUIT: The evergreen, narrowly oblong, pleasantly aromatic leaves reach 2 inches long by ¼ inch wide. Colored a soft blue-green, they provide a subtle contrast to the spikes of purple ¼-inch-long flowers of mid to late summer. The fruit is nonornamental.

RATE / SPACING: Growth is moderate. Plants from pint-sized to quart-sized containers are spaced 14 to 18 inches apart.

HORTICULTURAL SELECTIONS: 'Alba', with white flowers; 'Baby White', 12 inches tall, with pure white flowers; 'Bowles', the earliest blooming cultivar, reaches 18 to 20 inches tall, with very fragrant lavender flowers; 'Carrol Gardens', with pale purple flowers; 'Compacta', only 10 inches tall; 'Dutch', with deep blue flowers; 'Dwarf Blue', with compact habit and deep blue flowers; 'Fragrance', flowers more heavily scented than the species; 'Gigantea', 2½ to 3 feet tall, with wispy spikes of lavender-blue flowers; 'Graves', with attractive and fragrant lavender-blue flowers atop 10-inch-tall stems; 'Grey Lady', with very fragrant bright lavender flowers; 'Hidcote Blue', with silvery-gray leaves, rich purple flowers, and vigorous habit, 15 to 20 inches tall; 'Hidcote Giant', 2½ to 3 feet tall, with lavender flowers; 'Hidcote Pink', 16 inches tall, with soft pastel pink flowers; 'Jean Davis', with pinkish white flowers, 18 inches tall; 'Lady Lavender', with frosty green leaves, rather open habit, and lovely intensely purple flowers; 'Mitchem', with fragrant deep purple flowers; 'Mitchem Grey', 18 to 20 inches tall by 20 to 24 inches wide, with soft lavender-gray flowers; 'Munstead Dwarf', with dark lavender-blue flowers, 12 to 18 inches tall; 'Nana', with purple flowers, only 12 inches tall; 'Nana Baby White', similar to 'Nana' but with pure white flowers; 'Rosea', with rose-pink flowers; 'Royal Velvet', with fragrant dark purple flowers; 'Sachet', with superior fragrance, 15 to 18 inches tall by 20 inches wide, flowers violet atop 12-inch-tall stems; 'Silver Frost', with powdery white frosted foliage, 15 inches tall, bluish lavender flowers; 'Twickle Purple', with dark blue flowers on short spikes, 18 inches tall; 'Waltham', with deep purple flowers.

OTHER SPECIES: *L.* × *intermedia* (in-ter-*mee*-dee-a), a gray-green-leaved cross between *L. latifolia* and *L. angustifolia*, is said to be extremely fragrant and tolerant of hot, humid summertime weather. 'Dutchmill', named after Dutchmill Herb Farm, a strong grower, 2 feet tall by 3 feet wide, with very fragrant lavender-blue flowers; 'Fred Boutin', with compact habit, silvery-gray leaves and fragrant violet flowers in late summer; 'Grosso', 20 to 24 inches tall, violet very fragrant flowers, raised commercially in France for lavender oil; 'Provence', 24 inches tall by 24 inches wide, very fragrant, long-blooming lavender flowers from late spring to fall; 'Seal', 36 inches tall, with mauve-purple fragrant flowers.

L. latifolia (lat-i-*foe*-lee-a), meaning broad-leaved, is commonly called spike lavender. It is hardy to Zone 6, reaches 1 to 1½ feet tall, displays denser growth than true lavender, and has silvery-green foliage.

L. stoechas (*stoy*-kis), meaning from the Stoechades islands off the coast of southern France near Toulon (now known as the Isles d'Hyeres), is commonly called French lavender. It is hardy to Zone 6, may reach 3 feet tall, and attracts butterflies with its purple blooms during summer. More showy than its flowers, however, are the petallike, veined, purple bracts that surmount the flowers. 'Alba', with pure white bracts; 'Atlas', with large flower heads on long floral stems; 'Otto Quest', with larger than typical flowers; 'Papillon', only 2 feet tall, with floral bracts larger than those of the species; subsp. *pedunculata,* with flowers that look like purple pineapples.

CULTURE / CARE: Lavenders grow best in well-drained, light-textured, loamy, slightly acidic to slightly alkaline soils. They are quite tolerant of drought, but benefit from an occasional deep watering during the heat of summer. They prefer full sun. Diseases of greatest incidence are leaf spot and root rot, and the most common pests are caterpillars, four-lined plant bug, and northern root-knot nematode. No maintenance is required beyond an annual trimming, after flowering, to keep plantings looking neat and to insure abundant flowers the next year.

PROPAGATION: Cuttings that are taken from side shoots during the summer months root very well. Division of clumps in spring must be performed carefully to prevent damaging the stems. Seed germinates in two or three weeks at 70 to 80°F.

Ledum groenlandicum　　PLATE 183
Labrador Tea

Labrador tea, a member of the heath family, is an attractive, fine-textured, erect-stemmed shrub that ranges from 1 to 4 feet tall and 3 to 4 feet across. Relatively uncommon, it is useful to gardeners in the North as a specimen, accent, or facing plant, and can even be put to use as a dwarf hedge. It grows well in moderate to large settings in moist, peaty or sandy acidic soils and combines with other ground covers such as bunchberry (*Cornus canadensis*), dwarf crested iris (*Iris cristata*), and bog rosemary (*Andromeda* species).

SCIENTIFIC NAME: *Ledum groenlandicum* (*lee*-dum grun-*land*-i-kum). *Ledum* is derived from *Ledon,* the Greek name for *Cistus* (the rock roses), which yield aromatic resin from their leaves—the young leaves of *L. groenlandicum* also being aromatic. *Groenlandicum* means from Greenland.

HARDINESS / ORIGIN: Zones 3 to 6 or 7; Greenland, west to Alberta, Canada, and Washington, south to Wisconsin and Pennsylvania.

LEAVES / FLOWERS / FRUIT: The simple, alternate, evergreen, oval to oblong leaves range from ¾ to 2 inches long by ¼ to ½ inch wide. They are shiny green above and rusty brown below and fragrant when crushed. The pleasantly fragrant white flowers, borne in 2-inch-wide branch-ending clusters during late spring, range from ½ to ¾ inch wide. The fruit, a brown capsule, is nonornamental.

RATE / SPACING: Growth is slow. Plants from 2- to 5-gallon-sized containers are spaced 2½ to 3 feet apart.

HORTICULTURAL SELECTIONS: 'Compactum', with woolly stems, short broad leaves, small flower clusters, to 1 foot tall; forma *denudatum,* with thin flat-tened leaves that lack the rusty brown tomentum on their undersides.

OTHER SPECIES: *L. decumbens* (dee-*kum*-benz) is commonly called narrow-leaved Labrador tea, crystal tea, or wild rosemary. It also is hardy in Zones 3 to 6 or 7, but reaches only 1 foot tall and displays leaves that are shorter and narrower (⅓ to ¾ inch long by 1/12 to ⅙ inch wide), and white, ¼- to ⅜-inch-wide flowers in summer. It hails from North America and Asia.

CULTURE / CARE: *Ledum* species need cool, moist, boggy or sandy, moderately to highly acidic soils (pH from 3.5 to 5.5). They prefer full sun or light shade and, if correctly sited in a location where the soil remains constantly moist, are not hampered by wind. Diseases such as anthracnose, leaf galls, rusts, and leaf spots are all caused by fungi and, provided the cultural requirements are adequately met, are seldom serious. Maintenance needs are nonexistent other than trimming out branches that break during winter.

PROPAGATION: Root-containing suckers can be split off from the base of the plant and transplanted during spring. Cuttings taken during fall can be rooted with bottom heat and seem to respond best to treatment with 8000 ppm IBA/talc.

Leiophyllum buxifolium　　PLATE 184
Sand Myrtle

An attractive general cover when mass planted in moderate-sized areas, sand myrtle is a compact, upright-stemmed, horizontally spreading, subshrubby ground cover. It reaches 14 to 18 inches tall (sometimes to 2½ feet) and spreads more than 1½ feet across. In small groups, it also functions nicely for accent and is particularly well adapted for use in seashore gardens along the Atlantic Coast. No foot traffic is tolerated.

SCIENTIFIC NAME: *Leiophyllum buxifolium* (lee-oh-*fil*-um / lay-oh-*fil*-um buks-i-*foe*-lee-um). *Leiophyllum* is derived from the Greek *leios,* smooth, and *phyllon,* leaf, in reference to the smooth and glossy foliage of the single species of this genus. *Buxifolium* refers to the resemblance of the leaves to boxwood (*Buxus*).

HARDINESS / ORIGIN: Zones 5 to 8; sandy pine barrens of New Jersey, south to Florida.

LEAVES / FLOWERS / FRUIT: The evergreen, simple, crowded, oval to oblong, leathery leaves reach 5/16 inch long, are sharply pointed at their ends, and colored shiny dark green with bronzy tones in fall. The flowers, borne from spring to early summer and arranged in branch-ending clusters, are five-parted, pink in bud opening to white, waxy, rather small, and resemble those of blueberries. Although quite attractive against the dark leaves, the fruit they yield is nonornamental.

RATE / SPACING: Growth is slow. Plants from quart-sized to gallon-sized containers are spaced 12 to 16 inches apart.

HORTICULTURAL SELECTIONS: Var. *hugeri,* with glandular flower stalks (covered with oil secreting organs), more of a cushionlike habit, longer leaves, and pink flowers; 'Nanum', a dwarf with highly branched stems; 'Procumbens' (sometimes referred to as var. *prostratum*), Allegheny sand myrtle, low-growing, prostrate, native to the mountains of Tennessee, North Carolina, and northern Georgia, 6 to 10 inches tall.

CULTURE / CARE: Sand myrtle is best in full sun in well-drained, acidic loam. It shows good tolerance to drought, yet displays its best growth if given an occasional, thorough watering in summer. Leaf gall is the only known pathology. Although sand myrtle needs no maintenance, a light shearing after the blooming season helps to promote branching and keeps plants looking neat and compact.

PROPAGATION: Leafy 1- to 1½-inch-long stem cuttings can be rooted from early summer through fall; sometimes they root better if covered with a plastic tent to maintain a high level of humidity. Naturally layered branches can also be used; simply dig them up and transplant them. Ripe seed is ready to germinate; it should be surface sown, not covered, and given high humidity. Alternatively, seed may be stored in a cool, dry place for up to one year prior to sowing.

Leucanthemum vulgare   PLATE 185
Oxeye Daisy, Field Daisy, White Daisy

This attractively flowered species was previously classified as *Chrysanthemum leucanthemum* and, like most of the other former chrysanthemums, is valuable for its late season flowers. It works well as a small-scale to moderate-scale edging plant or general cover, forms clumps reaching 1 to 2 feet tall, and spreads indefinitely by short rhizomes. No foot traffic is tolerated.

SCIENTIFIC NAME: *Leucanthemum vulgare* (lew-*can*-the-mum vul-*gay*-re). *Leucanthemum* means white-flowered. *Vulgare* means common.

HARDINESS / ORIGIN: Zones 3 to 10; Europe and Asia, now naturalized in North America.

LEAVES / FLOWERS / FRUIT: Borne upon ascending stems, the deciduous, leathery, spoon-shaped dark green basal leaves reach up to 6 inches long and are edged with lobes and rounded teeth. Toward the tip of the stem the leaves become blunt-toothed or may

be divided so as to appear featherlike. The 1- to 2-inch-wide daisylike flowers with yellow centers and white petals are formed at the ends of the stems during late summer and fall. The fruit is nonornamental.

RATE / SPACING: Growth is moderate. Plants from gallon-sized containers are spaced 1 foot apart.

HORTICULTURAL SELECTIONS: 'May Queen', with more flowers.

CULTURE / CARE: Oxeye daisy prefers well-drained, moist, acidic to neutral soils in full sun to light shade. It feeds heavily, benefits from fertilization, and is not very tolerant of drought. It is susceptible to a number of diseases and pests, including leaf spot, wilt, rust, blight, powdery mildew, aster yellows, aphids, leaf miner, stalk borer, and mites. Some gardeners prefer to prune it during midsummer to prevent lankiness.

PROPAGATION: Division is easily accomplished during spring. Stem cuttings root quickly in early summer. Fall propagation with root cuttings also works. Seed germinates in seven to ten days at 70°F.

Leucothoe axillaris   PLATE 186
Fetterbush, Coast Leucothoe

This superb species is a subshrubby, rhizomatous ground cover with a gracefully arching, fountainlike branch pattern. It typically reaches 2 to 4 feet tall and spreads somewhat less than twice that in width. In the landscape it makes an excellent general cover and facing plant for moderate-sized to large-sized areas. Due to its spreading nature, it is useful for binding soil on sloping terrain. No foot traffic is tolerated.

SCIENTIFIC NAME: *Leucothoe axillaris* (lew-*koth*-oh-ee / lew-*koo*-thoe-ee aks-i-*lay*-ris). *Leucothoe* is named for Leucothoe, daughter of Orchamus (king of Babylon) and Eurynome; according to Greek mythology, she was turned into a shrub by Apollo, her lover, after being buried alive by Clytia, her rival for Apollo's affection. *Axillaris* refers to the flower clusters, which originate from the leaf axils.

HARDINESS / ORIGIN: Zones 5 or 6 to 9; coastal southeastern North America from Virginia to Florida.

LEAVES / FLOWERS / FRUIT: Evergreen, simple, and alternate, the leathery, dark shiny green leaves are elliptic to narrowly oblong, 2 to 5¼ inches long by 1 to 1½ inches wide, and taper to an abrupt point. The springtime flowers are arranged in pendulous fashion, in solitary or grouped clusters, from the leaf axils. Each cluster is 1 to 3 inches long and contains a number of urn-shaped, ¼-inch-long, white (sometimes with hints of pink), fragrant flowers. When in flower, the shiny, dark green, zigzag branches can be cut and placed in vases for a lovely tabletop display. The fruit is nonornamental.

RATE / SPACING: Growth is slow to moderate. Plants

from 1- to 2-gallon-sized containers are spaced 2½ to 3½ feet apart.

OTHER SPECIES: ***L. fontanesiana*** (fon-ta-neez-ee-*aye*-na), named for René Louiche Desfontaines (1750–1833), a French botanist and professor, is commonly called dog hobble, switch ivy, and drooping leucothoe. Hailing from Virginia to Georgia and Tennessee, it is hardy in Zones 4 to 6 and is similar to *L. axillaris* but has slightly larger flowers, longer leafstalks, and supposedly greater susceptibility to leaf spot. Horticultural selections include 'Girard's Rainbow' ('Rainbow'), with new growth green and later developing yellowish, pinkish, and whitish splotches; 'Nana', compact habit reaching 2 feet tall by 6 feet wide.

L. 'Scarletta' is a compact cultivar, the new leaves of which emerge bright red (throughout the year) before turning dark green in maturity. During fall they become burgundy or purplish and remain so until spring. Of hybrid origin, this cultivar is said to come from crossbreeding *L. axillaris* and *L. fontanesiana* and is presumed hardy in Zones 4 to 7 or 8. Seldom does its height exceed 20 inches.

CULTURE / CARE: Leucothoes are at their best in organically rich, acidic, well-drained loam. Once established they tolerate drought quite well, yet always look their best when the soil is kept slightly moist. They need shelter from strong drying winds and prefer a location with light to dense shade. Leaf spot is their most common disease; black mildew, canker, leaf gall, and anthracnose occur but are less common. Pests such as whitefly and southern root-knot nematode are occasionally troublesome. No maintenance is required.

PROPAGATION: Stem cuttings from early to mid summer root quite well, and a treatment of 1000 to 2000 ppm IBA/talc is helpful. Hardwood cuttings taken during winter will also root; they tend to root best if treated with 3000 to 5000 ppm IBA/talc and given bottom heat. Rooted stems can also be divided throughout the growing season. Seed is ready to germinate upon ripening; sow it immediately and never allow the seed to dry out once it is in the ground.

Leymus arenarius 'Glaucus'   PLATE 187

Blue Lyme Grass, Blue-downy Lyme Grass, Sea Lyme Grass, Narrow Bent, Rancheria Grass, Marram Sea Grass

Formerly named *Elymus arenarius* 'Glaucus' and often errantly represented as *E. glaucus* (see below), this outstanding blue-colored grass has a penchant for covering the ground and is every bit as eye-catching as blue fescue (see *Festuca*) but much more aggressive. Where blue fescue is shy about spreading, blue lyme grass travels as if it were scared. Three years ago I obtained four divisions of this grass, and today I have more than 500 divisions.

Blue lyme grass is a broad-bladed evergreen grass that spreads by underground stems. It is relatively erect in habit, but as its foliage elongates, it tends to arch over. In general, it ranges from 3 to 4 feet tall and spreads indefinitely. In the landscape it is best used on a moderate to large scale as a tall soil-binding substitute for conventional turf. It effectively controls erosion in dune landscapes. In all cases it should have plenty of spreading room, or its spread should be contained by a deep edging, sidewalk, driveway, or building foundation. Because of its height and evergreen foliage, blue lyme grass is well suited for facing foundations. It also functions well as a general cover for open expanses or on a slope for soil retention. Suitable companions are limited to open-canopied trees such as locust, mature pines, poplars, and erect junipers and cedars. Like blue fescue, blue lyme grass tolerates occasional foot traffic.

The true *Elymus glaucus* bears mention here. Unfortunately, because of the confusion in nomenclature and popular interest in *Leymus arenarius* 'Glaucus', the real *E. glaucus,* well known to botanists, ecologists, and foresters (who often use it for revegetation after fires) has not been given much horticultural attention, but it too is a good ground cover. Commonly called blue wild rye, it is actually a semi-evergreen native from moist soils of western and the midwestern United States and Canada. Its foliage color varies from bright green to nearly blue—the blue strain being the source of its name and all the confusion with *Leymus arenarius* 'Glaucus'. Like the latter, it is aggressive, useful for erosion control, and blooms during early to mid summer (first green then maturing to straw-colored). It differs in that it is more tolerant of light shade or half-day sun and it tends to be more apt to produce seed and reseed itself—a good thing as plants tend to last only for a few years, and population renewal comes from self-seeding.

SCIENTIFIC NAME: *Leymus arenarius* 'Glaucus' (*lay*-mus air-i-*nay*-ree-us *glaw*-kus). The origin of *Leymus* is uncertain. *Arenarius,* from the Latin *arena,* sand, refers to the species' penchant for growing in sand. 'Glaucus' refers to the color of the foliage—bluish green.

HARDINESS / ORIGIN: Zones 3 or 4 to 9; Europe, Asia, shores of Greenland and Labrador to Alaska, south to Maine, Lake Superior, and Washington.

LEAVES / FLOWERS / FRUIT: The leaves are evergreen, flattish, often arching, to 12 inches long by ⅝ inch wide, rough to the touch, and prominently colored deep bluish green to bluish gray. The summertime flowers are arranged in 5- to 7-inch-long, dense, slender unbranched spikes. Compared to the foliage, the flowers contribute little to the overall ornamental quality of this species. The fruit also is nonornamental.

RATE / SPACING: Growth is fast. Plants from 1- to 2-gallon-sized containers are spaced 16 to 28 inches apart.

OTHER SPECIES: *L. mollis* (*mol*-lis), meaning soft, in reference to the soft texture of its foliage, was formerly named *Elymus mollis* and has the common names pacific dune grass or pacific lyme grass. Native to sand dunes of coastal central California to Alaska, it is hardy in Zones 7 to 10 and is noteworthy for its 2- to 3-foot-tall display of soft blue-gray foliage that arches over as it matures. Its flowers, noticeable but not greatly showy, are borne early to mid summer and mature to a soft wheat color.

L. racemosus 'Glaucus' (ray-si-*moe*-sus *glaw*-kus), named for its racemelike flowers, was also previously classified in the genus *Elymus* and is commonly called volga wild rye, Siberian wild rye, or giant dune grass. It comes from Siberia and is hardy in Zones 4 to 10. Other than being a bit more robust and about one-third larger in every respect, it very closely resembles *L. arenarius* 'Glaucus' and is every bit as durable and useful.

L. tritichoides (trit-i-*koy*-deez), beardless wild rye, hails from heavy soils in valleys, foothills, and mountain flats of the western United States. A dense colonizing, rhizomatous spreader that makes a good turf substitute and soil stabilizer, particularly along shorelines of ponds, lakes, and streams, it is at once relatively moisture-tolerant and drought-tolerant. With green to blue-green (attractively brown then gray from late fall through winter), ½- to 2-inch-wide leaves, this is a variable species that ranges from 2 to 4 feet tall and blooms (first green then straw-colored) with narrow ¼- to ½-inch-wide, 4- to 6-inch-long spikes during early to mid summer. The subject of intense hybridization and selection, numerous cultivars will soon be available. At present 'Gray Dawn' displays bluish gray leaves in mid summer and 'Shoshone' is a prolific grower for saline-alkaline soils.

CULTURE / CARE: *Leymus* species are adaptable to most well-drained soils and hold up well in extremes of heat and cold. They prefer full sun. Because they are capable of withstanding drought, little or no water is needed once they root in. Being cool season grasses, however, they tend to slow their growth during summer, and in extreme heat may even go dormant. Should this be undesirable in your garden, you can keep plantings looking spry by mowing them back and supplying fertilizer and regular irrigation. They are not susceptible to serious pests or diseases. The only regular maintenance that you might anticipate is an annual mowing, usually during early spring, to neaten them up.

PROPAGATION: Division is easy and effective in all seasons. Seed is not always produced and is variably effective, depending upon the species.

Ligularia tussilaginea   PLATE 188
Daempfer Golden-ray

Coarse-textured with large colorful leaves, this sizable herb makes a bold statement. In maturity, it reaches 1½ to 2 feet tall and spreads indefinitely by creeping rootstock. Quite often it is used as a walkway or border edging and is most impressive as a facing to trees along a wooded periphery setting. For the most part, this plant is best used on a moderate to large scale, but a single clump (especially of the colorful cultivars) stands out as a unique specimen. In any event, it flaunts some of the most magnificent foliage of any ground cover and, considering its preference for shady terrain, is no less impressive for its midsummer show of golden-yellow flowers. No foot traffic is tolerated.

SCIENTIFIC NAME: *Ligularia tussilaginea* (lig-you-*lay*-ree-a tus-e-lah-*gin*-ee-a). *Ligularia* comes from the Latin *ligula,* a strap, in reference to the straplike appearance of the ray florets surrounding the centers of its daisylike flowers. *Tussilaginea* simply means like *Tussilago,* a related genus.

HARDINESS / ORIGIN: Zones 6 to 9 or 10; Japan, China, Korea, and Taiwan.

LEAVES / FLOWERS / FRUIT: The evergreen, gigantic kidney-shaped leaves are colored medium to dark green and commonly reach 6 inches long by 12 inches wide. Their edges are shallowly toothed, and although in youth they are covered with fine hairs, as they mature they become shiny and hairless. Mid summer initiates their commanding floral exposition. Each yellow daisylike head ranges from 1½ to 2½ inches in diameter and is carried atop a 2-foot-long floral stalk. The fruit that follows is nonornamental.

RATE / SPACING: Growth is moderate. Plants from quart-sized to gallon-sized containers are spaced 1½ to 2 feet apart.

HORTICULTURAL SELECTIONS: 'Argentea', with leaves irregularly mottled dark green, gray-green, and ivory; 'Aurea-maculata' (leopard plant), with dark green foliage randomly dappled with bright round yellow spots; 'Crispata' (parsley ligularia), with leaf edges ruffled and crinkled.

OTHER SPECIES: *L. dentata* (den-*tay*-ta), named for its dentate or toothed-edged leaves, is commonly called toothed ligularia. This rugged, coarse-textured, marvelous herb ascends to 4 feet and displays very attractive shiny green foliage more than 12 inches wide. The flowers, which appear during mid to late summer, look like large orange daisies. It and its cultivars are hardy in Zones 5 to 8. 'Dark Beauty', with fabulous coarsely textured leaves that are purplish green above and intensely maroon-purple below; 'Desdemona', 3 to 4 feet tall, with colorful bronzy green and mahogany heart-shaped, tooth-edged, 12-inch-wide foliage; 'Orange Queen', more luxuriant with deep green leaves and larger, deeper orange flowers; 'Othello', similar to 'Desdemona' but with leaves that are less deeply purple-pigmented.

L. stenocephala (sten-oh-*sef*-e-la), from the Greek *stenos,* narrow, and *kephalo,* head, is named for its narrow-headed flowers and is commonly called narrow spiked ligularia. This species is not as impressive as the others in respect to its foliage; however, its bright show of yellow flowers in summer is far superior. It is hardy in Zones 5 to 8, reaches 3 to 4 feet tall, and displays light green, heart-shaped or triangular tooth-edged, 8- to 12-inch-long, 8- to 12-inch-wide leaves. The flowers individually are 1 to 1½ inches wide and are arranged in narrow spikes 12 to 18 inches tall. 'The Rocket', a cultivar of high acclaim, is more compact in habit, with a great number of lemon-yellow somewhat smaller flowers that are arranged in 18- to 24-inch-long upright spikes.

CULTURE / CARE: Ligularias are at their best when grown in organically rich, slightly acidic loam. They are not greatly tolerant of drought and may be very quick to wilt. They prefer moderate to dense shade (in the North and coastal areas tolerating more sun or morning sun with afternoon shade), where the soil remains slightly moist even during summer. No serious pests or diseases affect them, and little or no maintenance is required for their success.

PROPAGATION: Divisions may be split off the main clumps during spring and fall.

Linnaea borealis   PLATE 189
Twinflower, Deer Vine

This low growing, trailing (and naturally layering), semiwoody, native ground cover reaches 1 to 3 inches tall and spreads indefinitely. It is appropriate in a wooded setting, where it functions superbly as a small-scale to moderate-scale general cover. Particularly in spring when it has just put on new growth, it radiates a superb greenness—the essence of which is so fresh as to appear iridescent. Twinflower is excellent on steep hillsides and combines beautifully with trillium, goldthread (*Coptis* species), hostas, rhododendrons, azaleas, oaks, spruces, and white cedar. Limited foot traffic is tolerated.

SCIENTIFIC NAME: *Linnaea borealis* (lin-*nee*-a bor-ree-*aye*-lis). *Linnaea* is named for Carolus Linnaeus (1707–1778), who, by popularizing the binomial system of plant names, is considered the father of modern botany; this is said to have been a favorite plant of his. *Borealis,* northern, refers to this plant's prevalence in northern latitudes.

HARDINESS / ORIGIN: Zones 3 to 6 or 7 and portions of Zone 8 moderated by the coast; Northern Hemisphere.

LEAVES / FLOWERS / FRUIT: The evergreen, neat, oppositely arranged, simple, rounded to oval, ⅝-inch-long, ½-inch-wide, shiny, medium green leaves are edged with rounded teeth and attached to the slender, reddish, trailing, somewhat hairy stems by short medium green stalks. In pairs, the nodding, five-lobed, funnel-shaped, ½-inch-long, whitish pink, fragrant, summertime flowers are borne atop 4- to 6-inch-long wiry, erect stems. Occasionally, although sparingly, they rebloom in autumn. The tiny fruit is nonornamental.

RATE / SPACING: Growth is moderate. Plants from 2- to 3-inch-diameter containers are spaced 6 to 8 inches apart.

HORTICULTURAL SELECTIONS: Var. *americana,* with flowers longer and more tubular than the species; var. *longiflora,* with flowers and leaves somewhat larger than the species.

CULTURE / CARE: Twinflower is at its best in well-drained, organically rich loam of pH 4.0 to 5.0. Although it is fairly tolerant of drought, it displays its best appearance and optimal vigor when the soil is kept slightly moist and the location is relatively cool. It prefers light or moderate shade. Although leaf spot or mildew are potential diseases, neither is likely to present a great risk. Similarly, there are no pests of consequence, and no maintenance is required.

PROPAGATION: Stem cuttings should be taken in early summer; root formation is aided by treatment with 1000 ppm IBA/talc. Sods or small divisions should be dug in spring, as time is needed for the roots to become well established before winter. Seed is reported to germinate adequately, but since division and cutting propagation are so easy, seed propagation is seldom practiced.

Liriope   PLATE 190
Lily-turf

Exceptional for edging borders or lining walks and driveways, lily-turf is often used underneath trees for facing, as a foundation facer, and as a moderate-scale to large-scale substitute for turf grass. Small groups of plants can be used for accent, and in shaded corners of rock gardens, single specimens of the nonrunning forms can add a striking vertical dimension. They are widely used in Oriental garden settings and are especially nice for edging paths and walkways. Little or no foot traffic is tolerated. See also *Ophiopogon*.

SCIENTIFIC NAME: The name *Liriope* (la-*rye*-a-pee) is of uncertain origin. Some say that it comes from the Greek *leiron,* a lily; others claim it was named after Liriope, a fountain nymph and mother of Narcissus in Greek mythology.

HARDINESS / ORIGIN: See individual species for hardiness; Japan, China, and Vietnam.

LEAVES / FLOWERS / FRUIT: The basal leaves are grassy. The flowers are held near the top or above the foliage in dense spikes. The beadlike fruit is colored shiny black.

RATE / SPACING: Slow to moderate; see individual species for spacing recommendations.

SPECIES: *L. exiliflora* (ex-il-i-*flore*-a), meaning meager flowered, is a rather uncommon species with thin-leaved grasslike sod-forming habit and height of 8 to 12 inches. Native to Japan and China, it is hardy to Zone 5, spreads at a modest pace by long underground runners, and blankets the ground with deep green evergreen foliage. Its pale violet-blue flowers are borne during spring and give rise to black fruit that ripens in fall.

L. muscari (mus-*kay*-ree), named for its resemblance to *Muscari,* grape hyacinth, is commonly called blue lily-turf. It is a clumplike, tuberous (bearing small potato-like swellings), grassy, lilylike cover that is hardy in Zones 6 or 7 to 10 and hails from Japan and China. (A few cultivars are said to be hardy in Zone 5.) It reaches 18 to 24 inches high and spreads 8 to 12 inches wide. The evergreen leaves originate from the base of the plant, are long and narrow (to 2 feet long by $\frac{3}{8}$ inch wide), and colored dark green. The flowers are formed atop upright stems in dense, spikelike clusters that reach 6 to 8 inches long. They often extend above the foliage on young plants and are partially hidden in mature plants. Each is dark purple, six-petaled, $\frac{1}{2}$ inch wide, and effective in mid to late summer. The showy $\frac{1}{3}$-inch-wide round fruit that follows is at first green, ripening to shiny black. Growth is slow. Plants from pint-sized to quart-sized containers are spaced 12 to 16 inches apart. Some popular horticultural selections include 'Big Blue', with deep blue flowers and dark green, larger, erectly oriented foliage, 2 feet tall, hardy to Zone 5(?); 'Christmas Tree', with light purple flowers in clusters that taper to a point like a Christmas tree; 'Densiflora', with densely set, slender, slightly longer leaves of dark green; 'Evergreen Giant', a stiffly upright, taller selection; 'Gold Band', with leaves shorter, broader, and edged in gold; 'Green Midget', less than 8 inches tall in the sun, a compact, tuft-forming, dwarf, with dark green leaves, at its best in small areas, becoming somewhat taller in the shade; 'John Burch', very large leaved with cockscomb-shaped flower clusters; 'Lilac Beauty', shorter, with deep violet flowers; 'Majestic', to 2 feet tall, with many deep violet flowers, hardy to Zone 5(?); 'Monroe's #2', with dark green leaves and white flowers; 'Monroe's White', with pure white flowers, hardy to Zone 8; 'Peedee Ingot', with golden-yellow leaves when grown in full sun (chartreuse in the shade), lavender-blue flowers, good for lending color contrast in the landscape; 'Purple Bouquet', very similar to 'Lilac Beauty'; 'Royal Purple', with dark purple flowers, hardy to Zone 5(?); 'Samantha', robust, with pink flowers, somewhat less hardy; 'Silver Midget', low growing to 8 inches, foliage narrowly banded with white; 'Silvery Sunproof', leaves pale green with white to yellow stripes, tolerates more sun, blooms profusely; 'Variegata', new leaves with yellow edges that become green their second year, 1 to 1½ feet tall, with violet flowers, hardy to Zone 8; 'Webster's Wideleaf', hardy to Zone 7, medium height, with very broad leaves and tufted habit.

L. spicata (spie-*kay*-ta), named for its spikelike clusters of flowers, is commonly called creeping lily-turf. It is the most cold-adapted species of the genus, displaying hardiness in Zones 4 to 9 or 10. A rhizomatous lilylike ground cover native to Japan and China, it reaches 8 to 12 inches tall and spreads 6 to 12 inches wide. Its leaves are evergreen, straplike, to 18 inches long by ¼ inch wide, colored dark green until fall, then bronzy green until spring. The flowers are formed in spikelike clusters atop sturdy purplish stems. Each floret is ¼ inch wide, colored pale violet to white, and effective mid to late summer. The fruit is a blue-black, berrylike, round capsule. Growth is moderate. Plants from pint- to ½-gallon-sized containers are spaced 8 to 16 inches apart. There seem to be two forms of the species that are sold interchangeably: the form described above, which is rather fine-textured and narrow-leaved, and a second form that is somewhat shorter and broader leaved. 'Franklin Mint', claimed by some to be a cross between *L. muscari* and *L. spicata,* reaches 12 to 15 inches tall, with dark green foliage; 'Silver Dragon' displays dark green leaves with silvery-white longitudinal variegation, is a bit less hardy, and has the unfortunate habit of sending up shoots of all-green-colored leaves.

CULTURE / CARE: Lily-turfs are adaptable to almost any well-drained nonalkaline soil. With massive root systems that contain water storage nodules, lily-turfs are well able to withstand drought and, in the worst case, only infrequent summer watering is needed. A broad range of light conditions from full sun to moderately dense shade suits them, and they are relatively free from pests and diseases. Snails and slugs are partial to the foliage, and at times scale insects and mealybugs may pose a problem. Maintenance includes mowing back foliage in spring, before new growth begins, to promote a healthy, youthful appearance and to stimulate vigor.

PROPAGATION: Division of plants is effective most any time. Ripe seed may be sown after removing the pulpy covering; germination occurs late the following spring.

Lithodora diffusa   PLATE 191
Spreading Lithodora, Acid-soil Lithodora

This lovely horizontally growing evergreen shrublet ranges from 6 to 12 inches tall, spreads 2 to 2½ feet across, and performs well as a small-scale general cover. In rock gardens and border settings as a specimen or accent plant, it combines particularly well with azaleas, rhododendrons, and pieris. No foot traffic is tolerated.

SCIENTIFIC NAME: *Lithodora diffusa* (lith-oh-*door*-a di-*few*-sa). *Lithodora* comes from the Greek *lithos,* a stone, and *dorea,* a gift, but how these terms apply to this species is not exactly clear. Possibly it means this plant is a gift from rocky terrain. *Diffusa* refers to the diffuse or spreading habit of this plant.

HARDINESS / ORIGIN: Zones 6 to 8; southern and western Europe and Morocco.

LEAVES / FLOWERS / FRUIT: The hairy leaves are evergreen, dark green above, grayish below, and ½ inch long by ⅛ to ¼ inch wide. The funnel-shaped flowers, borne during spring and early summer, are five-petaled, ½ inch wide, and colored a stunning iridescent blue.

RATE / SPACING: Growth rate is moderate. Plants from quart-sized to gallon-sized containers are spaced 1½ to 2½ feet apart.

HORTICULTURAL SELECTIONS: 'Alba', with white flowers; 'Grace Ward', with dark blue flowers somewhat larger than the species; 'Heavenly Blue', with sky blue flowers; 'Lohbrunner White', with white flowers, 6 inches tall by 18 inches wide at maturity.

CULTURE / CARE: Spreading lithodora needs moist, fertile, well-drained acidic soil. It is not greatly tolerant of drought and grows best in light to moderate shade. Its primary disease problem is damping off, a fungus disease that affects small plants. Its most common insect predators are aphids. Maintenance needs are few if any.

PROPAGATION: Stem cuttings can be rooted during the summer months; treatment with 3000 ppm IBA/talc is helpful and mist, if it is used, should be discontinued immediately upon root formation to prevent damping off. Seed propagation can be successful but is less frequently practiced; ripe seed should be soaked in water for 48 hours prior to sowing.

Lonicera   PLATE 192
Honeysuckle

Ground-covering honeysuckles share many of the same traits (beautiful fragrant flowers and shiny deciduous or evergreen foliage) as the more common shrubby and climbing forms that have so popularized the genus. Many of the climbing vines, when unsupported, double as ground covers. They excel in moderate to large, open areas, particularly in elevated planters around the foundations of public and commercial buildings or as soil stabilizers on large open slopes. They love to grab hold of and strangle other plants and, therefore, are only compatible with themselves and with trees whose trunks are too broad for them to grip. Normally, the vine types reach 8 to 16 inches tall without support (or on occasion mound to a couple of feet) and spread indefinitely. Shrubby ground-covering types, on the other hand, typically are most useful as specimens, facing plants, and low hedges. No foot traffic is tolerated by either type.

SCIENTIFIC NAME: *Lonicera* (lo-*nis*-er-a) is named after Adam Lonitzer, Latinized Lonicerus (1528–1586), a German naturalist and author.

HARDINESS / ORIGIN: See individual species for hardiness; Northern Hemisphere to Mexico and the Philippines.

LEAVES / FLOWERS / FRUIT: The leaves are usually more or less deciduous, and the very fragrant flowers are followed by a sometimes edible but not very tasty berry.

RATE / SPACING: Growth of vinelike species is moderate to fast and, especially in the South, can become invasive. Plants from 2¼-inch-diameter to 1- to 2-gallon-sized containers are spaced 12 to 30 inches apart. Growth of shrubby species is slower than that of the vinelike species. Plants from 1- to 2-gallon-sized containers are spaced 2½ to 3½ feet apart.

SPECIES: *L. × brownii* (*brown*-ee-eye), named for Brown (probably the hybridizer), is commonly called Brown's hybrid honeysuckle and is derived from crossing *L. sempervirens* and *L. hirsuta.* Vinelike in habit, it is hardy in Zones 3 to 9 and is characterized by semievergreen oval to oblong leaves that reach 3 inches long and are colored blue-green below and green above. Its flowers, which are borne in spikes during late spring (then again in late summer), arise at the ends of the stems. Each is trumpet-shaped, 1 to 1¾ inches long, and colored orange-scarlet. 'Dropmore Scarlet', one of the most popular selections, flowers profusely from early summer to early fall and boasts reddish orange flowers and exceptional cold hardiness.

L. caprifolium (kap-ri-*foe*-lee-um), named from the Latin *capra,* goat, and *folium,* leaf, supposedly not so much in reference to the foliage but to the ability of this plant to climb like a goat, is commonly called sweet honeysuckle, or Italian woodbine. It is clearly sweet smelling when its 2-inch-long flowers of white to purplish open during early summer and fall. Its blue-green leaves are large and often reach 4 inches long. The fruit is an orange-red berry. This European native is hardy to Zone 5.

L. flava (*flay*-va), named for its yellow flowers, is commonly called yellow-flowered honeysuckle. This vinelike species is hardy in Zones 5 to 9 and hails from the southeastern United States. It displays leaves that are elliptic, 3 inches long, green above and bluish green below. Its flowers are borne in whorls, reach 1¼ inches long, are trumpet-shaped, fragrant, and effective from late spring to early summer. The fruit is red, ¼ inch in diameter, and berrylike.

L. × *heckrottii* (hek-*rot*-ee-eye), named after its hybridizer, Heckrott, is commonly called everblooming honeysuckle or goldflame honeysuckle and is derived from crossing *L. americana* and *L. sempervirens.* Of the more popular honeysuckles, this one is exceptional for its extremely long-running floral display. It is hardy in Zones 5 to 9, displays 2-inch-long, dark—almost jade green—evergreen leaves that turn purplish during winter. Its magnificent trumpet-shaped flowers are carmine-colored in bud, reach 2 inches long, and open from late spring through much of fall, exposing their soft yellow interiors. Their fragrance is superior to the finest perfume and on a still morning can be smelled from more than 50 feet away.

L. henryi (*hen*-ree-eye), named after Augustine Henry (1857–1930), an Irish doctor who collected it in China, is commonly called Henry's honeysuckle. Hardy to Zone 4, it is a semievergreen twining vine that resembles *L. japonica* in many respects, but spreads with considerably less abandon. Its leaves are dark shiny green, evergreen, oval (ending in a fine point), 2 to 3 inches long, and virtually disease-free. It blooms from early to late summer with pleasantly fragrant trumpets of yellowish to reddish purple. When fruit is produced, it is a persistent black berry.

L. japonica (ja-*pon*-i-ka), meaning of Japan, is commonly called Japanese honeysuckle or gold and silver flower. It is a fast-spreading vine that has created environmental problems by overrunning shrubs and small trees, particularly in the southern United States. Farther north, however, it is reduced in vigor and is relatively easily cultured and confined. In the South, it sets seed (which it seldom does in the North) and of course, grows faster and enjoys the longer growing season. Its strong twining branches can strangle small trees or, simply by running over the tops of plants, it smothers them. Some states have outlawed the planting of this species. It is hardy in Zones 5 to 9, and if you live in a state where its use is not outlawed, in Zone 5 or 6, it should be safe to use. It displays semievergreen to evergreen, oval to oval-oblong, 1¼- to 3-inch-long, shiny green leaves that often become yellowish during autumn. Its flowers are paired, white with tinges of pink or purplish, then mature to yellow. They reach 1½ inches long, are fragrant, and become effective in early summer. The fruit is black, berrylike, ¼ inch wide, and ripens in early to mid autumn. Some of the popular horticultural selections include 'Aureo-reticulata', yellow-net honeysuckle, much like the species but with smaller leaves, to 2 inches long, colored bright green with striking yellow or golden veins (due to the presence of a virus, which consequently makes this cultivar weaker, slower growing, and less cold hardy—Zones 6 to 9), best in shade and rich moist soil; 'Halliana', named after Dr. George Hall, who introduced it to the United States in 1862, by far the most popular selection, more common as a ground cover than all the other species combined, with pure white flowers turning yellow as they age; 'Purpurea', a bit less vigorous, with leaves attractive bluish purple below and greenish purple above, flowers purplish red with white interiors; var. *repens,* with young shoots and leaf veins colored purplish, white flowers, sometimes with a hint of purple, aging to light yellow, not as strong growing as 'Halliana'.

L. pileata (pie-lee-*aye*-ta), named for its cap (like the pileated woodpecker) which resides atop the fruit, is commonly called royal carpet honeysuckle or privet honeysuckle. It is characterized by a neat, low-spreading, shrubby habit. Chinese in origin, it is hardy in Zones 7 to 9 and typically reaches 12 to 18 inches tall by 3 to 4 feet wide. The leaves are semievergreen, oval to narrowly oblong, ½ to 1¼ inches long by ⅕ to ½ inch wide, and colored lustrous medium green. Although fragrant, the yellowish white, ⁵⁄₁₆-inch-long flowers are not very showy and in many cases pass almost unnoticed during mid spring. The fruit is small, violet-purple, translucent, berrylike, and more interesting than showy.

L. sempervirens (sem-per-*vie*-renz), named from the Latin *semper,* always, and *virens,* green, for its evergreen foliage, is commonly called evergreen honeysuckle. Hardy in Zones 4 to 9, this North American twining vine displays 1- to 1¾-inch-long, purplish to bluish green, oval leaves. Its flowers of orange to red (yellow or orange inside) are displayed during early to late summer. 'Cedar Lane', with narrow blue leaves; 'Sulphurea', with yellow flowers and much broader, medium green foliage; 'Superba', sometimes listed as 'Dreer's Everblooming', 'Magnifica', 'Red Coral', 'Red Trumpet', or 'Rubra', with scarlet flowers throughout the summer.

L. xylosteum 'Nana' (zie-*loe*-stee-um), probably named from the Greek *xylon,* wood, in reference to the woody nature of the stems, is commonly called dwarf emerald mound honeysuckle. Native to Europe and Asia, it is an excellent low-mounding dwarf shrubby species with bluish green attractive leaves and neat compact, hemispherical growth to 3 feet tall by 6 feet wide. Its springborne flowers are rather inconspicuous, and it is hardy in Zones 3 to 8. 'Emerald Mound' is said to be the same as 'Nana'; 'Miniglobe' resembles 'Nana' but is said to be more cold tolerant and more compact.

CULTURE / CARE: Honeysuckles are adaptable to most acidic to alkaline soils with good drainage. Typically, they are quite tolerant, or moderately tolerant, to drought and require only an infrequent deep watering in hot, dry weather. For the vigorous vine-type species, allowing the soil to become somewhat dry slows growth. Honeysuckles grow best in full sun to light shade. Pests include the woolly honeysuckle aphid, leaf rollers, honeysuckle sawfly, four-lined plant bug, plant hopper, leaf miners, and greenhouse whitefly. Diseases that affect the honeysuckles are leaf blight, leaf spots, powdery mildew, bacterial crown gall, twig blight, thread blight, and hairy root. Maintenance consists of pruning heavily each year during late winter. An elevated lawn mower can be used on vines and helps remove dead undergrowth. Later in the season the leading stems can be cut back as they outgrow their bounds or begin to climb trees or shrubs.

PROPAGATION: Cuttings root with relative ease during the early part of summer. Stem segments, which naturally root as they contact the soil, can also be dug and replanted during spring and fall.

Lotus corniculatus   PLATE 193

Bird's-foot Trefoil, Cat's Clover, Crow Toes, Sheep Foot, Bird's-eye, Ladies Finger, Devils Fingers, Eggs-and-bacon, Shoes-and-stockings

The common name bird's-foot trefoil comes from the shape of the seedpods, which spread out in the shape of a bird's foot; the word *trefoil* means three-leaved. Matlike, trailing, and semiwoody, this ground cover reaches 1½ to 2 feet tall and spreads 2 feet across. It is usually used to prevent erosion on a

moderate to large scale, particularly in infertile sandy soil. Like other members of the pea family, it has the ability to fix nitrogen (convert soilborne atmospheric nitrogen) into a form it can use. It was originally introduced into North America for fodder and for a pigment derived from the flowers and used for dying cotton and wool. Herbal applications were and, to some extent, still are common. Lotus has been used for treating heart palpitations, depression, insomnia, nervousness, and conjunctivitis. Scientifically, its effectiveness has not been validated. Some southern populations contain cyanide, however, and animals have died from eating it.

SCIENTIFIC NAME: *Lotus corniculatus* (*lo*-tus kor-nik-you-*lay*-tus). *Lotus* is a name that Greek naturalists applied to many plants. *Corniculatus,* with small horns, refers to the shape of the flowers.

HARDINESS / ORIGIN: Zones 5 to 10; Europe and Asia.

LEAVES / FLOWERS / FRUIT: The leaves are compound and composed of three leaflets which are narrowly oval, colored medium to dark green, and of greatest ornamental value for the color contrast they provide with the clusters of strikingly yellow, red-tinged, pealike, ½- to ¾-inch-long, summertime flowers. The fruit is a slender 1-inch-long green pod.

RATE / SPACING: Growth is moderate to fast. Plants from pint-sized to quart-sized containers are spaced 14 to 24 inches apart.

HORTICULTURAL SELECTIONS: 'Pleniflorus', with double flowers, not as likely to become weedy as it does not set seed; var. *tenuifolium,* with prostrate stems and linear to oblong leaves.

OTHER SPECIES: *L. berthelotii* (birth-e-*lot*-ee-eye), possibly named for Sabin Berthelot (1794–1880), is known by such common names as coral gem, parrot's beak, pelican's beak, and winged pea. Native to Tenerife, largest of the Canary Islands, it is hardy in Zones 10 to 11, reaches 1½ to 2 feet tall, and spreads to 6 feet wide. It displays evergreen, compound, grayish green leaves. Each leaf is made up of three to seven narrow (almost needlelike), ½-inch-long, 1/16-inch-wide leaflets. The flowers are pealike, up to 1 inch long, scarlet, and bloom profusely from early to mid summer. The fruit is narrow and podlike.

L. pinnatus (pi-*nay*-tus), named for the pinnate or featherlike arrangement of its compound leaves, is commonly called deer vetch. Native from Washington state to central California, it reaches 2 to 4 inches tall, is hardy to Zone 8, and displays yellow flowers throughout the summer.

CULTURE / CARE: *Lotus* species have a preference for somewhat infertile, gritty or sandy, well-drained alkaline soils but tolerate mild acidity. They are only marginally tolerant to drought; therefore, during extended periods of heat and drought, they should be given supplemental water when they begin to wilt. They prefer to grow in full sun. Other than mealybugs and black scale, they are plagued by few pests or diseases. If desired, plantings can be kept neat by mowing or shearing.

PROPAGATION: Cuttings can be rooted during early summer. Divisions can be taken any time they can be kept moist. Seed is commercially available for some species.

Luzula   PLATE 194
Wood Rush

Wood rushes are loosely tufted, rhizomatous, herbaceous, broad clump-forming, grasslike ground covers. They are most useful for naturalizing as large-scale general covers among shrubs and trees in woodland settings. They are attractive both for their flowers and foliage. Infrequent foot traffic is tolerated.

SCIENTIFIC NAME: *Luzula* (*lewz*-ew-la) is derived from the Italian *lucciola,* a firefly, or originally from the Latin *lux,* light, and refers to at least one species that has the habit of reflecting light from dew trapped on its leaves.

HARDINESS / ORIGIN: See individual species for hardiness; Eurasia.

LEAVES / FLOWERS / FRUIT: The leaves are grasslike and edged or covered with soft hairs that catch dew. The flowers, typically borne above the foliage during late winter or early spring on erect or aching stems, are tiny, but clustered together and therefore quite showy. The fruit, a nutlet, is nonornamental.

RATE / SPACING: Growth is slow to moderate. Plants from pint-sized to quart-sized containers are spaced 12 to 18 inches apart.

SPECIES: *L. luzuloides* (lewz-ew-*loy*-deez) is very similar to the more popular *L. nivea* (see below), but differs in having light green foliage and grayish white flowers. It is generally considered less ornamental and is less frequently cultivated.

L. nivea (nie-*vee*-a), named from the Latin *nivea,* snowy white, in reference to the flowers, is commonly called snowy wood rush. It reaches 1½ to 2 feet tall, spreads to form a broad mat, is reliably hardy in Zones 5 to 9, and hails from mountainous forested areas of west and central Europe. Its semievergreen, grasslike, 1-foot-long leaves are first erectly oriented then arch over as they age. Colored medium to dark green, they are covered with white hairs on their blades and margins. The snowy white flowers, which are quite striking during late spring, are borne in loosely arranged clusters elevated well above the foliage on slender stalks.

L. sylvatica (sil-*vat*-i-ka), meaning of woods, is commonly called greater wood rush. It hails from

the Caucasus region, Europe, and Asia Minor and is hardy in Zones 4 to 9. It forms densely tufted, stoloniferous mats, appears grasslike, reaches 12 inches tall (to 3 feet when in flower), and spreads indefinitely. Its leaves are evergreen, linear (grasslike), to 12 inches long by ⅜ to ⅝ inch wide. They are bright shiny green and taper to a fine point, their margins are somewhat filamentous, and their surfaces sparsely hairy. The brown flowers, effective during mid to late spring, are borne in loose groups upon erect to oblique, short-leaved, 2½- or 3-foot-long stems. Variety *marginata* has leaves that are strikingly edged in white.

CULTURE / CARE: Adaptable to about any soil, the wood rushes are best in organically rich soils. They tolerate short periods of drought and waterlogging, but are best when the soil is maintained in a slightly moistened condition. Light to moderate shade is their preference for light. Rust and smut are occasional problems, and seldom are pests encountered. Maintenance consists of mowing back the foliage in late fall.

PROPAGATION: Division of crowns is effective; they must be kept moist until reestablished. Seeds are sometimes offered commercially and germinate in a few weeks if kept warm and moist.

Lycopodium   PLATE 195
Club Moss

Probably because many species are difficult to propagate, club mosses are only rarely offered for sale. Many times, however, they are found growing wild. Thus, if your property contains club mosses, or if you know of some whose habitat is going to be destroyed by commercial development, it is my hope that you will recognize, appreciate, and preserve them. They are perennial, low-growing, relatively primitive (about 300 million years old), evergreen, coarse-textured, spore-producing herbaceous plants. The common name refers to their club-shaped spore-bearing appendages or strobili. The genus is thought to contain between 100 and 450 species from woodlands and jungles throughout the world.

Cultivated too infrequently, club mosses are unique, rugged, attractive ground covers. They seldom exceed 12 inches tall, and although most species grow very slowly, in time they may spread more than 20 feet across. They are typically green throughout the year and interesting in all seasons. In most cases they spread out in a circular fashion from the center and form a thick mat that excludes other plants. For this reason, their companions are limited to robust clump-forming perennials and woodland trees and shrubs—natives being the most appropriate. Occasional foot traffic is tolerated.

The historical uses of club mosses are many and very interesting. Various species were and, unfortunately to some extent, still are used as greens in Christmas decorations. Coupled with their slow growth, increasing numbers of collectors, and habitat destruction, it has become necessary to protect many species. Interestingly, the spores of some species are explosively flammable and historically were used in fireworks, photographic flashes, and as flash powder by Native American medicine men and women. Spores of club mosses are very uniform in size and therefore have been used as standards for comparison in microscopic measurement, to perform sound experiments in physics, as miniature ball bearings in pill coatings (to keep pills from sticking together), and as lubricating dusts for surgical gloves, condoms, and rectal suppositories. Some species have been used for stuffing upholstery and for making baskets, bags, and fish nets. Medicinally, the spores of club mosses have been applied to wounds to absorb fluids and speed coagulation and have been used to treat urinary tract ailments, including kidney stones. Some Native American tribes inhaled the spores to stop nose bleeds. Concoctions prepared from the foliage and stems were used as emetics and poisons and as dye fixatives in woolen manufacture. Today, research using extracts of stems and leaves is being conducted to determine their effectiveness in treating viral diseases, and spores are sometimes administered in homeopathic remedies.

SCIENTIFIC NAME: *Lycopodium* (lie-koe-*poe*-dee-um) comes from the Greek *lycos,* a wolf, and *pous,* foot, in reference to the pawlike or clawlike appearance of the trailing end of the stems of some species.

HARDINESS / ORIGIN: See individual species for hardiness; tropical and temperate regions of the world.

LEAVES / FLOWERS / FRUIT: The leaves typically are small, dark green, evergreen, and scalelike or needlelike. Like ferns, these species reproduce by spores and thus do not produce flowers or fruit.

RATE / SPACING: Growth is slow. Plants from deeply rooted divisions or 4- to 5-inch-diameter containers are spaced 10 to 14 inches apart.

SPECIES: **L. clavatum** (kla-*vay*-tum), named from the Latin *clava,* a staff or cudgel, in reference to the club-shaped spore cases (or possibly the trailing stems), is commonly called staghorn club moss, wolf's claw club moss, vegetable sulfur (for the yellow spores), foxtail, ground pine, or clubfoot moss. From dry shady woodlands of northern North America, Europe, and Asia, this species is hardy in Zones 1 to 8. It displays a trailing, low, herbaceous, mosslike habit and reaches 1 to 3 inches tall, with erect spore-bear-

ing stems that ascend higher than 10 inches. Spread is indefinite and oftentimes exceeds 20 feet. The evergreen leaves, densely set in many ascending staggered rows, are lance-shaped, reach ⅛ to ¼ inch long by ¹⁄₃₂ inch wide, are soft to the touch, and colored vibrant green. The spore-bearing structures, or strobili, are borne at the tips of 10-inch-long erect shoots. Alone or grouped in twos or threes, the strobili are round in cross section, 2 to 3½ inches long, scalelike, and colored yellowish green.

L. dendroideum (den-*droy*-dee-um), sometimes still considered a variety of *L. obscurum,* is commonly called tree club moss or princess pine. It is similar in appearance to *L. obscurum* but differs in that its stem leaves flare out from the branches and its leaves are more yellowish and more arching. It is hardy in Zones 2 to 6 or 7.

L. obscurum (*ob*-skyur-um), meaning obscure, was so named by Carl Linnaeus because of his unfamiliarity with the structure of the strobili, and is commonly called flat-branch ground pine, bunch evergreen, or tree club moss. It is a rhizomatous, erectly oriented, broad-spreading, herbaceous, miniature umbrella-topped, treelike dweller of damp, rich, shady woodland edges. Its natural range is from Newfoundland to Alaska to the north, south to Oregon, and east to northwestern Illinois. Additionally, it is found in northeastern Asia. It is hardy in Zones 1 to 7 or 8, and its height ranges from 6 to 12 inches. Growth is slow. Plants from pint-sized to quart-sized containers are spaced 10 to 16 inches apart. The leaves are evergreen, arranged in six to eight linear rows, needlelike, ⅛ to ¼ inch long, smooth-edged, and tapered to a fine point. Densely set, they are numerous, colored deep green, and borne upon upright, mostly unbranched stems. Upon the tips of the branches, the cylindrical 1- to 2-inch-long, yellow, pussy-willow-like strobili are arranged in groups of up to 12 (or sometimes more).

L. tristachyum (try-*stay*-key-um), meaning three-spike in Latin and named for the three spikelike shoots that ascend to hold the strobili, is commonly called ground pine or ground cedar. It inhabits dry, cool, sandy, lightly shaded woodlands and pastures of northern North America and Europe and is hardy in Zones 1 to 8 or 9. It is erect-stemmed, reaches 5 to 12 inches tall, spreads indefinitely by rhizomes, and looks like a grove of miniature pine trees. Growth is slow. Plants from pint-sized to quart-sized containers are spaced 10 to 16 inches apart. The evergreen, tiny, scalelike leaves are arranged in four rows, pressed toward the stems, lance-shaped, and tapered to sharp points. Colored deep green, they are held upon branches that flare out to form fanlike patterns. The upper stems are often flat-topped and hold leaves that are bluish green. The strobili are cylindrical, 2 to 3 inches long, and held at the ends of thin 3- to 4-inch-long stalks that fork twice to give the appearance of a candelabra.

LESS COMMON SPECIES: The above-mentioned club mosses are relatively common and are the most likely to be available for purchase. Many others, however, may be encountered in the wild. *Lycopodium complanatum,* commonly called Christmas green or running pine, and superficially resembling *L. tristachyum,* has many forms and varieties, reaches 6 to 10 inches tall, and thrives in shady, moist, woodland locations. *Lycopodium lucidulum* (*Huperzia lucidula*), shining club moss, has stiff, bright green, lance-shaped foliage, is slow to spread, in time forms dense mats, reaches 6 to 8 inches tall, and is at its best in shady, moist, woodland settings.

CULTURE / CARE: Club mosses vary in their preference for soil. Some species grow in sandy or richly organic, slightly alkaline to acidic soils. *Lycopodium clavatum* performs well under pines and in open thickets with loose, relatively sandy soils, while *L. obscurum* prefers the damp soils of moist forest and bog margins, and *L. tristachyum* grows in sandy, somewhat drier soils. Although the club mosses can tolerate a good deal of drought during summer, they are most vibrant if a slightly moist soil condition is maintained; *L. obscurum* tolerates relatively wet soils. None do as well in extreme heat, and all prefer light to moderate shade. No serious diseases have been reported, but slugs and rodents often feed upon new transplants. No maintenance is required.

PROPAGATION: Although division is the only practical means of propagation, it is difficult because the root systems are very sparse. Should you try it, do so in early spring during cool weather. Taking a good deal of soil is helpful, and close attention to soil moisture during the first season is essential.

Lysimachia nummularia   PLATE 196
Creeping Charley, Creeping Jenny, Moneywort, Loosestrife

I don't know who Charley is or was, but the adjective "creeping" is well deserved, as this species displays more than a mere penchant to spread and spread and spread. The common name moneywort comes from the round coin-shaped leaves. This plant remains a low-growing (only 1 or 2 inches tall), indefinite-spreading (sometimes into places where it is unwanted), tenacious, herbaceous ground cover. As a rule, it should not be combined with other low-growing plants because it has a habit of smothering them. It makes a mossy blanket in contained areas underneath low-growing trees such as Japanese

maple, crape myrtle, purple-leaved plum, or even shrubs such as red twig dogwood, hydrangea, or burning bush.

Used in smaller confined locations, such as elevated planters where its stems can trail over (like a green waterfall), creeping Charley is at its best. It performs admirably as a turf substitute in smaller contained areas or along the edge of a stream or pond where its spread is naturally controlled by the water. Because it is not averse to occasionally being trod upon, it is ideal for planting between stepping stones and alongside wooded garden paths. The contrast that exists between its flowers and foliage is outstanding, but when not in flower, it would take a generous individual to consider it handsome.

Historically, extracts of creeping Charley were used in hair dyes and reportedly, when the plant was burned, the smoke was effective in driving away serpents. Serpent problems are rare today, but one might try burning a little creeping Charley in an effort to repel the neighbor's dog.

SCIENTIFIC NAME: *Lysimachia nummularia* (lis-i-ma-kee-a new-mew-*lay*-ree-a). *Lysimachia* is said to commemorate King Lysimachus (306–281 B.C.) of Thrace; according to legend, the king was being chased by a raging bull when he grabbed a bundle of loosestrife, waved it in front of the bull's face, and, to his relief, quieted the bull and was able to escape unharmed. In Greek, the word *lysimachia* means ending strife. *Nummularia* comes from the Latin *nummus,* a coin, and refers to the shape of the leaves.

HARDINESS / ORIGIN: Zones 4 to 9; Europe and central Russia, now naturalized in North America.

LEAVES / FLOWERS / FRUIT: The leaves are evergreen, nearly round, to 1 inch wide, and colored medium to dark green. Borne at their bases are ¾-inch-wide buttercup yellow flowers that nicely lend contrast during early summer (and sometimes sparingly thereafter until fall).

RATE / SPACING: Growth is moderate to fast. Plants from 3- to 4-inch-diameter containers are spaced 10 to 16 inches apart.

HORTICULTURAL SELECTIONS: 'Aurea' (golden creeping Charley), with exceptionally bright golden leaves, grows slower than the species but can still be invasive.

OTHER SPECIES: *L. clethroides* (cleth-*roy*-deez), gooseneck loosestrife or shepherd's crook, takes its common name from its 12- to 18-inch-long, arching, gooseneck-shaped floral racemes, which later straighten out as the flowers fade and the fruit matures. Native to China and Japan, it is hardy in Zones 3 to 9, and produces masses of ½-inch-wide white flowers in summer. The deciduous leaves are slightly pubescent, oval to lance-shaped, medium green, tapered at both ends, and from 3 to 6 inches long by ¾ to 1¼ inches wide; they are oppositely arranged upon upright 2- to 3-foot-tall stems. A tenacious, fast to invasive rhizomatous spreader (reaching 3 feet across), this species is also known to spread by seed. It should be planted 1½ to 2 feet apart from 4-inch to gallon-sized containers and preferably used on a large scale as a general cover, or contained so as to keep it from spreading.

L. congestiflora (kon-jes-ti-*floe*-ra), commonly called dense-flowered loosestrife, is native to China and hardy only to Zone 6. It is characterized by a growth habit similar to that of *L. nummularia*. Its ½- to ¾-inch-wide yellow flowers are borne terminally. 'Eco Dark Satin', named for Eco Gardens, Georgia, displays yellow flowers with red throats.

L. japonica (ja-*pon*-i-ka), meaning of Japan, is commonly called Japanese loosestrife or Japanese moneywort. It grows in thickets and open areas in both low and high elevations of China, Taiwan, Japan (including the Ryukyu Islands), and Malaysia. It has been reported hardy to Zone 5, and with its creeping, herbaceous, mat-forming habit, it reaches 1 inch tall and spreads indefinitely. On a small to moderate scale, it makes a pleasant, low-maintenance turf substitute. It has a rather neat green appearance and is quite tough. The dark green leaves are evergreen, simple, opposite, oval to broadly oval, and from ⅓ to 1 inch long by ⅓ to ¾ inch wide. The barely visible, solitary flowers range from ⅕ to ⅓ inch wide. The tiny variety *minuta* is useful for filling in between the paving stones of a shaded path, and both the species and the variety are pleasantly mosslike when grown on rocks or on banks alongside of streams or fountains.

CULTURE / CARE: The loosestrifes are adaptable to most soil conditions, possibly with the exception of gravelly soils. They show modest tolerance to drought, prefer constant soil moisture, and even tolerate relatively wet soils—hence their usefulness at the margins of ponds and streams. They prefer light to moderate shade. Pests and diseases that might be encountered include bud scale mites, woolly aphids (above and below the ground), and fungal leaf blight. Maintenance consists of trimming back or digging up the trailing stems as they outgrow their bounds.

PROPAGATION: Cuttings may be rooted throughout the year. Division can be practiced any time during the growing season.

Mahonia   PLATE 197

Mahonias are low, rhizomatous, woody shrubs that make excellent ground covers for use as specimens in rock gardens, as edging alongside walkways, and as shrubby border plantings. Between their flowers, fruit, and foliage, they are interesting year-round, so plant them where they will be fully appreciated. No foot traffic is tolerated.

SCIENTIFIC NAME: *Mahonia* (ma-*hoe*-nee-a) is named after American horticulturist Bernard McMahon (d. 1816).

HARDINESS / ORIGIN: Zones 5 or 6 to 8 or 9; North and Central America, the Himalayas to Japan and Sumatra.

LEAVES / FLOWERS / FRUIT: The leaves typically are spiny-edged and evergreen. The clusters of bright yellow flowers are followed by prominent bluish black fruit.

RATE / SPACING: Growth is slow. Plants from quart-sized to gallon-sized containers are spaced 12 to 16 inches apart.

SPECIES: *M. aquifolium* (a-kwi-*foe*-lee-um) cultivars. The species, commonly called Oregon grape holly, hails from British Columbia to Oregon and is too tall to be considered a ground cover. It has, however, given rise to some splendid cultivars that are useful ground covers in Zones 4 or 5 to 8: 'Apollo', similar to 'Compactum' but lower growing and with orangish yellow flowers; 'Compactum', the most popular cultivar, 2 to 3 feet tall by 3 to 4 feet wide, with evergreen, 6- to 12-inch-long compound leaves containing 5 to 9 oval to oblong-oval, 1½- to 3½-inch long, spine-tipped, stiff, leathery, shiny dark green leaflets that provide a fine backdrop to the abundant bright yellow springtime flowers and the blue-black ⅓-inch-wide fruit, foliage turns bronzy during the winter; 'Mayhan Strain', 30 to 40 inches tall, fewer and more closely spaced leaflets per leaf.

M. nervosa (ner-*voe*-sa), Cascades mahonia, longleaf mahonia, or Oregon grape (*M. aquifolium* is also called Oregon grape), reaches 12 to 18 inches tall and spreads 4 to 5 feet wide. From the mountains of British Columbia south to California, it is hardy in Zones 6 to 9 and bears evergreen, pinnately compound leaves that reach 7 to 16 inches long and are made up of 11 to 19 dark green (reddish during winter) 2- to 3-inch-long, spiny-toothed leaflets. Its yellow flowers are arranged in clusters to 8 inches long and add a splendid element of color contrast against the foliage during late spring. The fruit that follows is a round blue-black berry.

M. repens (*ree*-penz), named for its reptant (creeping) growth habit, is commonly called creeping mahonia. It reaches 1 to 2 feet tall and spreads 4 to 5 feet across. Hardy in Zones 5 to 9, it hails from the western coast of North America from British Columbia to California. It bears semievergreen compound leaves with three, five, or seven oval, spiny-toothed leaflets 1 to 3 inches long. Colored dull green above and gray-green below, they form a fine background for the small, fragrant, attractive deep yellow flowers of late spring and early summer. The early summer fruit is a globe-shaped, blackish berry that is covered with a rich blue waxy material.

CULTURE / CARE: Ground-covering mahonias are adaptable to various soils but prefer those that are relatively high in organic matter. They need good drainage and mild acidity (*M. nervosa* is quite strict about its need for acidic soil). They tolerate moderate drought, but their best growth and appearance are realized if the soil is kept slightly moist. They prefer full sun to light shade. In areas of hot, dry summers, they must be placed where they will be shaded in the afternoon. In the North, they may need to be covered with pine branches to protect plants from winter wind and sun if snow cover is inadequate to cover them. Pests include the barberry aphid, greedy scale, and various caterpillars. The most common diseases are rusts (several types occur) and leaf spots. Maintenance normally consists of a single light pruning in late summer to promote compactness.

PROPAGATION: Cuttings taken during mid summer can be rooted. Seed sown at the time of ripening will germinate the following spring. Division is most effective during early spring.

Maranta leuconeura   PLATE 198
Prayer Plant, Ten Commandments, Rabbit
Tracks, Banded Arrowroot

In the North this plant is used indoors in hanging baskets and planters, but in tropical gardens, it can be appreciated as a colorful ground cover. Low spreading, leafy, and herbaceous, it reaches 8 to 12 inches tall, spreads to more than 3 feet across, and is an excellent choice for facing shrubs and trees in moderate to large areas. It works well as an edging along footpaths, but no foot traffic is tolerated.

SCIENTIFIC NAME: *Maranta leuconeura* (ma-*ran*-ta lew-koe-*ner*-a). *Maranta* is named for Bartolommeo Maranta, a sixteenth-century Venetian botanist. *Leuconeura* comes from the Latin *leuco*, white, and *neura*, vein, referring to the white veins of the leaves.

HARDINESS / ORIGIN: Zones 10 to 11; moist soils and clearings of evergreen and deciduous forests of Brazil.

LEAVES / FLOWERS / FRUIT: The unique leaves are evergreen, simple, elliptic, and reach 5 inches long by 3 to 3½ inches wide. They are open and flat during the daytime and fold up at night, hence the common name prayer plant. The upper surface of the leaves is attractively variegated light and dark green. Sometimes the leaves show additional hues of purplish brown and occasionally the venation is red or grayish. The lower surface is bluish green. The three-

parted seldom-borne flowers are white with purple spots. The small fruit is nonornamental.

RATE / SPACING: Growth is moderate. Plants from quart-sized to gallon-sized containers are spaced 14 to 20 inches apart.

HORTICULTURAL SELECTIONS: Var. *erythroneura*, lateral veins rose-red, leaves variegated light green with dark green splotches along either side of the midvein; var. *kerchoveana*, with leaves spotted red underneath; var. *massangeana* (cathedral windows), with leaves smaller than the species, tinted blue with dull rusty-brown markings in their centers, colored deep purple below, and, when held up to the light, looking like stained glass (hence the common name).

CULTURE / CARE: Prayer plant requires organically rich, slightly acidic, well-drained loam. It is not greatly tolerant of drought; therefore, it should be given some shelter from strong, dry winds and should be watered as frequently as needed to keep the soil slightly moistened. It prefers light to moderate shade. Few pests present problems, although leaf spot and rust diseases sometimes arise. Maintenance consists primarily of trimming back the shoots as they outgrow their bounds.

PROPAGATION: Stem cuttings are easily rooted throughout the year. Division of the crowns works well from late fall through early spring.

Matteuccia struthiopteris   PLATE 199
Ostrich Fern

Gracefully vase-shaped, this robust, lush, rhizomatous fern reaches 3 to 5 feet tall and spreads indefinitely. It tends to colonize and thus is exceptional when it has room to roam without adversely affecting smaller, less vigorous plants. The vibrant sterile fronds are exceedingly attractive, as are the shorter brown fertile fronds—particularly when they poke up through the snow in the winter. Ostrich fern works well in a number of situations. Broad sweeping woodland borders are transformed into lush, junglelike entrances with ostrich fern edging. Large oaks can be effectively linked when underplanted with an island of this leafy companion. I've even seen ostrich fern excel as a foundation facing. In all cases, use it on a moderate to large scale and expect your friends to constantly ask for divisions. No foot traffic is tolerated.

The springtime fiddleheads of ostrich fern are sometimes eaten. They can be made into soup or sauteed in butter.

SCIENTIFIC NAME: *Matteuccia struthiopteris* (ma-*too*-ke-a / ma-*too*-see-a stroo-thee-*op*-ter-is). *Matteuccia* commemorates the nineteenth-century Italian physics professor Carlo Matteucci. *Struthiopteris* is said to be derived from the Greek *struthokamelos,* an ostrich, and *pteris,* a fern, referring to the fronds which resemble the graceful plumes of the ostrich.

HARDINESS / ORIGIN: Zones 2 to 8; from Newfoundland west and south to Virginia, Michigan, Iowa, and Missouri; Europe and Asia are also places of natural distribution.

LEAVES / FLOWERS / FRUIT: The magnificent sterile leaves are deciduous, vibrant green, graceful, with a habit of arching over in a feathery vaselike manner. They appear cool, lush, and stately. Widest above their midpoint, they range from 2½ to 5 feet long by 8 to 16 inches wide. The semiwoody lyre-shaped fertile fronds are much shorter (generally 1 to 2 feet). First green then ripening to dark brown, they are composed of tightly rolled, beadlike leaflets, which enclose the sporangia. The sporangia persist through winter then release their spores in the spring.

RATE / SPACING: Growth rate is moderate. Plants from 1- to 2-gallon-sized containers are spaced 2 to 3 feet apart.

CULTURE / CARE: Ostrich fern prefers organically rich loam with a pH from moderately acidic to slightly alkaline. It grows best in light to moderate shade, and although it tolerates short periods of drought, it is at its very best when the soil remains moist at all times. Ostrich fern has few problems with diseases or pests and, if given plenty of room, needs no maintenance. If planted in a smaller area, however, gardeners might need to dig up and remove the shoots and rhizomes that creep into areas where they are not desired.

PROPAGATION: Division is easily performed during spring and fall. Spore culture also works (see Chapter 8).

Mazus reptans   PLATE 200
Creeping Mazus

Herbaceous and rooting as it spreads, a single plant of this lowly, indefinite-spreading ground cover holds the potential for a quick, efficient cover or for weediness, depending upon your interpretation. Creeping mazus will never be as popular as Japanese spurge or periwinkle, but with its curious purple flowers, cheerful green foliage, and assertive spreading nature, it does have its place. It is best used in small areas and is particularly useful underneath small trees and tall single-stemmed shrubs. It is also an effective filler between stepping stones, or edging around the perimeter of a shaded patio. Finally, it is rather interesting lining the banks of a shaded reflecting pool or koi pond and performs admirably as a carpet underneath large bonsai, dwarf conifers, and Japanese maple. It is pretty tough and tolerates limited foot traffic.

SCIENTIFIC NAME: *Mazus reptans* (*may*-zoos *rep*-tanz).

Mazus comes from the Greek *mazos,* a teat, in reference to the projections at the mouth of the flowers. *Reptans,* a term very often applied to ground covers, describes the creeping habit of growth.

HARDINESS / ORIGIN: Zones 4 to 9; Himalayas.

LEAVES / FLOWERS / FRUIT: The semievergreen, light green leaves are rather fleshy and almost succulent. They may reach 2 inches long, are somewhat oval, and are more or less toothed about the edges. The flowers borne in late spring reach ¾ inch long, are very interesting, and although typically borne alone, they may also be grouped in twos or threes. Each is formed in two halves, or lips, and is colored a lovely violet-blue. The uppermost lip is composed of two lobes, and the lower, which is white with yellow and purple spots, is composed of three. The fruit is non-ornamental.

RATE / SPACING: Growth is slow initially, then moderate to fast. Plants from 2- to 3-inch-diameter containers are spaced 8 to 12 inches apart.

OTHER SPECIES: *M. japonicus* '**Albiflorus**' (ja-*pon*-i-kus al-bi-*floe*-rus), white-flowered Japanese mazus, is hardy northward to Zone 7 and is nearly identical to *M. reptans* except that it may be a little bit taller and its flowers are white.

M. pumilio (pew-*mil*-ee-oh), dwarf mazus, is another mat-forming, creeping, herbaceous ground cover that reaches only 1 or 2 inches tall. Hardy to Zone 7, this native of Australia and New Zealand spreads indefinitely and is characterized by oval-shaped, smooth or tooth-edged leaves that may reach 3 inches long. The 5⁄16-inch-long flowers of early to mid summer are white or bluish with yellow centers.

CULTURE / CARE: Although the mazuses prefer rich, well-drained, loamy soil, they show a certain degree of tolerance to other types, provided that drainage is excellent. They are not markedly resistance to drought and may require frequent watering during the summer, particularly if grown in sandy soils. They prefer full sun to moderate shade. Few if any disease or insect problems ever arise, and maintenance needs are also few.

PROPAGATION: Simple division in spring remains the standard means to propagate mazus; simply dig, divide, and replant.

Melampodium leucanthum   PLATE 201
Blackfoot Daisy, Black Foot, Melampodium, White-flowered Black Foot, White-flowered Melampodium

Blackfoot daisy is a clump-forming, herbaceous to semiwoody, taprooted ground cover. Reaching 6 to 14 inches tall by 36 inches across, it is best used in rock gardens as a specimen, as a small-scale general cover, or as an accent plant to compliment other plants and landscape features. Several plants can be arranged in a row and used as a dwarf hedge or for edging walkways or defining boundaries.

SCIENTIFIC NAME: *Melampodium leucanthum* (mel-am-*poe*-dee-um lew-*kan*-thum). *Melampodium,* black-footed, comes from the Greek *melas,* black, and *pous* foot, and refers to the darkened stems. *Leucanthum,* white-flowered, comes from the Greek *leucos,* white, and *anthos,* a flower.

HARDINESS / ORIGIN: Zones 4 to 9; Colorado, Arizona, New Mexico, Texas, and northern Mexico.

LEAVES / FLOWERS / FRUIT: The leaves are simple, linear, and oppositely arranged. They have a grayish color due to an overlay of ashen hairs and have purple veins on their bottom sides. The daisylike composite flowers have yellow central disc florets surrounded by seven to thirteen broad, creamy white ray florets. Borne profusely from spring through summer, then sporadically through winter in mild areas, the flowers range from ¾ to 1 inch wide. In cold climates they sometimes flower again in fall. The fruit is nonornamental.

RATE / SPACING: Growth is moderate. Plants from pint-sized to quart-sized containers are spaced 8 to 12 inches apart.

OTHER SPECIES: *M. cinerium* (sin-*er*-ee-um) is named for its ashen foliage. Native to Texas, Kansas, Colorado, and New Mexico, it is like *M. leucanthum* but shorter and bears wavy-margined leaves that are often divided so as to appear featherlike.

CULTURE / CARE: *Melampodium* species grow well in full sun to light shade in coarse-textured, calcareous (chalky), well-drained soils. With long taproots, they are well equipped to tolerate drought, and although a deep watering during the heat of summer may be appreciated, it typically is not essential. Plants tend to be short lived but often reseed themselves. Sometimes they are damaged by late-season frosts, in which case shearing or mowing, a good annual practice anyway, can be performed during late winter to neaten and rejuvenate them.

PROPAGATION: Propagate by seed or cuttings. Because of its taproot, blackfoot daisy is difficult to transplant after it becomes established; for this reason one must usually start with container plants and should place them in their permanent location when first planted out.

Melissa officinalis PLATE 202
Lemon Balm, Bee Balm, Sweet Balm, Balm Leaf, Honey Plant, Sweet Mary

The word balm comes from the Greek *balsamon* (an oily resin of sweet aroma) and, as its common names indicate, this species gives off a very sweet lemony aroma. Lemon balm reaches 14 to 24 inches tall, forms clumps that may exceed 2 feet across, and displays a dense, erect or sprawling, herbaceous habit. Frequently included in herb or scent gardens, it should not be overlooked as a ground cover. It works well as a splendid backdrop to lower-growing herbs and ground covers, particularly those whose leaf color contrasts with its own crisp medium green. It is also an ideal edging to walkway and garden paths because its leaves give off their pleasant fragrance each time they are brushed against. No foot traffic is tolerated.

Lemon balm has a number of uses that go beyond landscaping. It has been used in natural medicine for several hundred years to treat colds and influenza, fever, depression, anxiety, nervousness, stomach upsets, insomnia, and cramps. Dioscorides, the famous Greek physician, used it as a component of medicinal wine and as a wound dressing. Arabs used it as a treatment for heart disorders, and others made a pleasant-tasting tea from its foliage. Containing an oil that has been proven to be a central nervous system depressant, lemon balm tea is often substituted for alcohol as a mild nightcap. Pleasantly aromatic, its fragrance is predominately lemony, but some say with a hint of mint. The pleasant fragrance alone relaxes one's mind. Lemon balm is also used as a flavoring in salads, cool drinks, and poultry and vegetable recipes. The dried leaves give a lemon scent to sachets and potpourri. Oil of lemon balm makes a good polish for furniture, repels certain insects, attracts bees, and is an important component of various cosmetics and perfumes. Bathing in water containing lemon balm refreshes the skin, and companion-plant enthusiasts say that when planted near tomato plants, lemon balm enhances their productivity.

SCIENTIFIC NAME: *Melissa officinalis* (me-*lis*-a oh-fis-i-*nay*-lis). *Melissa* is derived from the Greek word for honeybee, likely in reference to the attraction bees have to the flowers; beekeepers were said to have rubbed the foliage and stems of *M. officinalis* on hives to entice the bees to return. *Officinalis* means common.

HARDINESS / ORIGIN: Zone 5; southern Europe, western and central Asia.

LEAVES / FLOWERS / FRUIT: The vibrant medium green, intensely lemon-scented deciduous leaves are simple, arranged oppositely, range from oval to heart-shaped, and reach 1 to 3 inches long by 2 inches wide. Their edges are lined with rounded teeth, and their surface is covered with furrows and sparse hairs. During summer the white, somewhat-trumpet-shaped, ¼-inch-long, two-lipped flowers appear in whorls about leafy, squarish, erect stems that arise above the leaf mass. The fruit is nonornamental.

RATE / SPACING: Growth is moderate. Plants from 3- to 4-inch-diameter containers are spaced 8 to 12 inches apart.

HORTICULTURAL SELECTIONS: 'Aurea', with yellow foliage in springtime that later turns green; 'Variegata', with leaves variegated yellow and green before turning all green.

CULTURE / CARE: Lemon balm adapts to a wide range of soils, but is at its best in richly organic, well-drained, slightly acidic loam. It is not greatly tolerant of drought and therefore should be watered as needed to keep the soil slightly moistened. It prefers full sun. Diseases of greatest prevalence are gray mold, leaf spot, and leaf blight. Aphids are at times pesky but cause little real damage. Maintenance is not needed, but some gardeners trim off the dried flower stalks after they bloom to neaten plantings.

PROPAGATION: Cuttings root easily in summer and need no root-inducing hormones. Clumps can be divided during spring or fall with good results. Commercial seed is available. If you collect your seed, do so when it becomes ripe, then store it in a cool, dry location for sowing the following spring; germination takes two weeks at 70°F.

Menispermum canadense   PLATE 203

Moonseed, Canadian Moonseed, Yellow Parilla, Yellow Sarsaparilla, Texas Sarsaparilla, Vine Maple

Moonseed is not commonly used as a ground cover, but it has enough recognition to have been given a diverse assignment of common names. It is a strong twining and rhizomatous vine, which, if supported, ascends in excess of 15 feet. As a ground cover, however, it reaches only 8 to 12 inches tall and sprawls about to form dense, indefinite-spreading mats. Its chief ornamental attribute is its lush foliage, and its best use is as a very large scale cover in native landscapes, particularly underneath a canopy of mature hardwoods. If planted among shrubs and small trees, it can quickly overrun them. It is also useful for retaining soil on sloping terrain, especially on steep riverbanks. Occasional foot traffic is tolerated.

The fruit, which looks like wild grapes, is poisonous. Its ingestion has the effect of quickening the pulse and inducing convulsions and vomiting. There have been reports of fatalities—the causative agents being alkaloids that display strychninelike properties. Native Americans employed the roots, stems, and leaves in the preparation of medicines that were used to treat arthritic, lymphatic, and respiratory disorders. Others have used its roots as a diuretic, laxative, appetite stimulator, and tonic. Root extracts

were also employed as a substitute for sarsaparilla in the flavoring of soft drinks.

SCIENTIFIC NAME: *Menispermum canadense* (men-i-*sper*-mum kan-a-*den*-see). *Menispermum*, moonseed, is derived from the Greek *mene*, moon, and *sperma* seed, and refers to the crescent shape of the seeds. *Canadense* means of Canada.

HARDINESS / ORIGIN: Zones 5 to 8; moist woods and streambanks from Quebec and Manitoba to Nebraska, Arkansas, and Georgia.

LEAVES / FLOWERS / FRUIT: The deciduous, simple, alternate, thin-stemmed, shield-shaped to broadly oval leaves are 4 to 10 inches long by 4 to 7 inches wide, unlobed to seven-lobed, medium green above, and lighter green below. The unisexual flowers, male and female occurring on separate plants, are unspectacular, reach $\frac{1}{6}$ inch across, and, because of their greenish color, barely show up during their early summer bloom season. The poisonous fruit, which ripens in early fall, is formed only on female plants, is globose to oblong, $\frac{1}{4}$ to $\frac{1}{3}$ inch wide, and colored black.

RATE / SPACING: Growth is fast. Plants from 1- to 2-gallon-sized containers are spaced 2 to 3 feet apart.

OTHER SPECIES: **M. dauricum** (*daw*-ri-kum), of Asian origin, is similar to *M. canadense* but has two clusters of flowers originating at each leaf axil instead of one.

CULTURE / CARE: Moonseeds prefer organically rich, acidic soil. They are modestly tolerant of drought and strong winds. They prefer full sun to moderate shade. No serious diseases or pests have been reported. Maintenance consists of trimming back the leading stems as they outgrow their bounds.

PROPAGATION: Division of shoots that arise from the rhizomes is simple any time during the growing season and consists of digging up and transplanting them. Seed should be collected during fall, depulped, and sown immediately. If the seed has been stored for any period of time, cold stratification at 40°F for two months prior to sowing is recommended.

Mentha   PLATE 204

Mint

Several species of mint make wonderful ground covers. Common spearmint and peppermint fall into this category, but there are others as well. Some mints are low and trailing and spread by rooting as their stems contact the ground. Others are more erect and spread by underground stems. Still others spread by little shoots sent up from their bases. All the ground-covering mints are herbaceous perennials that contain high quantities of pleasantly scented volatile oils. Their flowers may or may not be significant, and their uses range from filling cracks between stepping stones to stabilizing steep moist embankments.

The tales about and uses for the mints are endless and no doubt were inspired by their strong and pleasant fragrances. For hundreds of years mints have been considered a symbol of hospitality, and the leaves of various species were strewn around the home to freshen it. Today the scent of mint is frequently incorporated into room fresheners. The oil of mints is often employed as a flavoring for chewing gum, cigarettes, candies, ice cream, toothpaste, chocolate, tea, creme-de-menthe, and mint jelly. Native Americans utilized mints in the preparation of mouth rinses. Today, the chief medicinal uses of mints are relieving intestinal gas and as an ingredient in ointments for sore muscles. Oil of the peppermint plant is a rich source of menthol, an agent that increases the secretion of bile to the stomach and acts to reduce spasms in muscles of the digestive system. Thus peppermint tea and after dinner mints are not only tastefully satisfying but beneficial to one's digestion and overall comfort. The leaves and stems of mints are often used in sachets, and fresh leaves in bath water soften the skin and increase its tone.

Planting mints in proximity to cabbage and tomatoes is reported to enhance the yields of these crops. Among the pests that mints repel are aphids, flea beetle, whitefly, and ants. Mint species contain various naturally occurring fungicides and insect repellents that no doubt account for some of their tenacity. Salicylic acid (of which aspirin is a chemical analog) has fungicidal properties, and the camphor, menthol, and citronella which mints contain, account for their insect-repelling abilities.

SCIENTIFIC NAME: *Mentha* (*men*-tha) is named for the nymph Minthe in Greek mythology, who was turned into this plant by Persephone (daughter of Zeus and Demeter) upon finding out that her husband Pluto, god of the underworld, was in love with Minthe. Although Pluto could not reverse the spell, he avenged Minthe somewhat by giving the plant a pleasant fragrance.

HARDINESS / ORIGIN: See individual species for hardiness; North Temperate Zone, South Africa, and Australia.

LEAVES / FLOWERS / FRUIT: All the mint species have very aromatic leaves, four-angled stems, and lavender, pink, or white flowers clustered in whorls, usually in terminal spikes. The seed is nonornamental.

RATE / SPACING: See individual species.

SPECIES: *M. gentilis* 'Emerald-N-Gold' (jen-*tee*-lis), also sometimes called variegated red mint, scotch mint, downy mint, or ginger mint, is a colorful cultivar characterized by gold-and-green-mottled fo-

liage. Hardy in Zones 4 or 5 to 10, it is 8 to 14 inches tall by more than 4 feet wide. Growth is fast. Plants from 2½- to 3½-inch-diameter containers are spaced 10 to 14 inches apart. Its pinkish purple flowers bloom from mid to late summer.

M. × *piperita* (pie-per-*eye*-ta), named from the Latin *piper,* pepperlike, is commonly called peppermint or black peppermint. It is useful as a soil binder along streams, pools, ditches, and ponds, but tolerates no foot traffic. Hardy to Zone 4, it hails from Europe, displays a herbaceous, strong spreading habit, and reaches 12 to 24 inches tall with an indefinite spread. Its leaves are 2½ inches long, edged with teeth, colored medium green, and strongly scented with a pungent peppermint fragrance. The flowers are formed in oblong, 1- to 3-foot-long spikes, colored lilac-pink to purple, and are effective in late summer. Growth is fast. Plants from 2½- to 3½-inch-diameter containers are spaced 10 to 14 inches apart. Variety *citrata,* lemon mint, sometimes classified as a separate species, has lemon-scented leaves; var. *vulgaris* has dark red stems and long-stemmed dark green leaves. The medical uses of peppermint are many and range from relieving menstrual cramps, headaches, colds and influenza, and insomnia. Reportedly, the Menominee Indians of Wisconsin and the Upper Peninsula of Michigan used the leaves with catnip leaves to treat pneumonia. Peppermint oil is effective in alleviating stomach and intestinal gas and may act as a mild stimulant.

M. pulegium (pew-*lee*-jee-um), named from the Latin *pulex,* a flea, in reference to its ability (when rubbed on the skin) to repel fleas, gnats, and mosquitos, is commonly called pennyroyal. A herbaceous mat-forming ground cover that reaches 1 to 3 inches tall and spreads indefinitely, it, like *M. requienii,* is useful as a filler between stepping stones or as a general cover in small areas where it can be contained. Limited foot traffic is tolerated. The leaves are oval to round, 1 inch long, medium to dark green, and pungent smelling when crushed. The flowers are small, lilac-blue, and effective in summer. Hardy to Zone 7, the species hails from Europe and Asia. Growth is fast. Plants from 2½- to 3½-inch-diameter containers are spaced 12 to 16 inches apart. 'Nana', dwarf pennyroyal, ranges from ½ to 1¼ inches tall and is clothed in ½-inch-long, ½-inch-wide leaves. Pennyroyal has been used to relieve spasms, but its use today is uncommon because, when taken internally, pennyroyal is very potent and potentially dangerous. It has also been used to induce abortion and menstruation. Its effectiveness comes from the high concentration of pulegone in the oil, a toxic chemical that can cause coma, convulsions, and even death. For this reason, the ingestion of pennyroyal and the preparation of teas from its foliage are vehemently discouraged.

M. requienii (rek-wee-*en*-ee-eye), named for Esprit Requien (1788–1851), a student of the flora of southern France and Corsica, is commonly called Corsican mint or creeping mint. This matlike species, the original flavoring for the drink crème de menthe, is excellent for filling the cracks between stepping stones and patio blocks. As a small-scale lawn substitute, it is as charming as it is functional. Growth is slow. Plants from 2½- to 3½-inch-diameter containers are spaced 6 to 10 inches apart. Native to Corsica, in North America this species is hardy in Zones 6 to 10. It reaches only ½ to 1½ inches tall and displays tidy, oval to round or heart-shaped, ⅛- to 3/16-inch-long, dark green, strongly aromatic foliage. Its flowers are small, lavender, and effective during summer. Limited foot traffic is tolerated.

M. spicata (spie-*kay*-ta), named for its flowers that are borne in spikes, is commonly called spearmint or garden mint. It is useful as a soil binder along streams, pools, ditches, and ponds. No foot traffic is tolerated. Hailing from Europe and hardy to Zone 4, it is a strong-growing, tenaciously spreading, herbaceous ground cover that reaches 12 to 24 inches tall and spreads indefinitely. Its medium green leaves are narrow in proportion to their 2-inch length and are pleasantly scented. The small lilac, pink, or white flowers are arranged in terminal spikes and are effective during summer. Growth is fast. Plants from 2½- to 3½-inch-diameter containers are spaced 12 to 16 inches apart. A mouthwash made from spearmint leaves is said to be quite effective in soothing sore or scratchy throats and sore gums. The relatively mild taste of spearmint is excellent in jellies, salads, beverages, candies, and as a seasoning in dishes.

CULTURE / CARE: Mints are adaptable to almost any soil type and are highly tolerant of saturated conditions. Under drought conditions, however, they do not fair quite so well. During summer, watering should be frequent enough to keep the soil slightly moistened at all times. Mints prefer full sun to light shade; they are shorter in the sun and taller in the shade. They have very few disease or pest problems. Maintenance needs of the low mat-forming species are few to none; taller forms are often mowed after flowering to neaten appearance and rejuvenate growth.

PROPAGATION: Cuttings root quickly and easily during the growing season. Divisions can be taken any time the soil can be kept adequately moist. Seed usually germinates in a few days.

Microbiota decussata   PLATE 205
Siberian Cypress

From southeastern Siberia, this wonderfully soft-textured evergreen conifer reminds one of a feathery-leaved, horizontal juniper, yet botanically speaking it is in a category all by itself. It is a low-spreading, dwarf, woody, 8-inch-tall shrub. It spreads 9 to 12 feet across, attractively displays its soft foliage upon gracefully drooping branches, and imparts a lush tranquilizing effect to the landscape. Masses of Siberian cypress may be planted to face foundations, yet single plants used as specimens can be just as eye-catching, particularly on sloping terrain where one can more fully appreciate its feathery foliage and graceful branch pattern. Siberian cypress combines well with upright and widespreading junipers, dwarf upright and horizontally growing spruce, arborvitae (*Thuja* or white cedar), *Chamaecyparis* species, and various forms of rhododendron and Japanese maple. No foot traffic is tolerated.

SCIENTIFIC NAME: *Microbiota decussata* (mie-kroe-bie-oh-ta day-koo-*say*-ta). *Microbiota* comes from the Greek, *micros,* small, and *biota,* the Greek name for the genus *Thuja. Decussata* refers to the leaves formed in pairs.

HARDINESS / ORIGIN: Zones 2 to 8; discovered in 1921 in Siberia.

LEAVES / FLOWERS / FRUIT: The wonderfully soft-textured evergreen leaves are a pleasure in any season. Scalelike or awl-shaped, each leaflet is small and feathery, and throughout summer appears dull green. By autumn the leaves have turned a bronzy almost burgundy color, and poking through the wintertime snow, lend excellent contrast. The very tiny flowers are not an important ornamental feature. The fruit, which is berrylike, reaches ¼ inch across on female plants, yet it too is ornamentally unimportant. Most plants in cultivation are male clones that produce tiny inconspicuous cones.

RATE / SPACING: Growth is moderate. Plants from 2- to 3-gallon-sized containers are spaced 3½ to 5 feet apart.

CULTURE / CARE: Siberian cypress is at home in a wide range of soils provided drainage is good. It shows pretty good resistance to moderate drought, but an occasional deep watering is welcomed during the summer. It grows in full sun to light shade and encounters no serious pests or diseases. Although it requires little or no maintenance, it is sometimes given an annual light shearing.

PROPAGATION: Cuttings taken during late fall root relatively well, particularly if given bottom heat.

Miscanthus sinensis   PLATE 206
Japanese Silver Grass, Eulalia

A robust 6- to 10-foot-tall clump former, Japanese silver grass is unlikely to be considered a ground cover. Yet, some of its dwarf offspring are nothing short of extraordinary for covering the ground. Not only are they neat, compact, and cheerful during spring and summer, they add the element of motion as they move about in the wind, and during fall they put on an impressive floral display that persists throughout the winter months. These dwarf cultivars are impressive when planted on a moderate to large scale in broad sweeping drifts and when combined with such popular perennials as sedums, black-eyed Susan (*Rudbeckia*), and Russian sage (*Perovskia*).

SCIENTIFIC NAME: *Miscanthus sinensis* (mis-*kan*-thus sye-*nen*-sis). *Miscanthus* comes from the Greek words *miskos,* a stem, and *anthos,* a flower, likely in reference to the flowers being borne atop prominent stalks.

HARDINESS / ORIGIN: Zones 5 to 9; the parent species hailing from China and Japan.

LEAVES / FLOWERS / FRUIT: Narrow and pointed, the rough-edged leaves are green with a silvery midrib. By mid to late summer flowers begin to grace the landscape with magnificent silvery plumes that rise above the foliage, dry to a soft shade of brown, then persist and decorate the landscape throughout the summer months. The fruit, a tiny grain, is nonornamental but is appreciated by winter songbirds.

HORTICULTURAL SELECTIONS: 'Adagio', 2 feet tall, with neat compact habit, silvery-gray leaves and flowers that are first pink before maturing to white then finally drying to coppery tan; 'Gracillimus Nana', 3 to 4 feet tall, leaves green with narrow silvery veins, flowers purple before maturing to silver; 'Kleine Fontaene', 3 to 4 feet tall, with lovely fountainlike habit and silvery flowers developing continually from late summer through fall; 'Kleine Silberspinne', with narrow silvery leaves, upright habit, 3 to 4 feet tall; 'Morning Light', narrow leaves variegated silvery-white, giving a soft silvery, billowy appearance; 'Nippon', 4 feet tall, with compact, upright habit, excellent reddish bronze fall foliage color, and attractive flowers that are carried well above the foliage; 'Yaku Jima', 3 to 4 feet tall, narrow soft green foliage with silvery center.

RATE / SPACING: Growth rate is moderate. Plants from 1- to 2-gallon-sized containers are spaced 2 to 3 feet apart.

CULTURE / CARE: Dwarf cultivars of this species grow well in about any well-drained acidic to neutral soil. They display good tolerance of wind and drought, moderate tolerance of saturated soils, and are at their best in full sun. Occasionally they are afflicted by leaf spot and their only serious pest is Miscanthus mealybug, which can live inside the stems and stunt their growth.

PROPAGATION: Cultivars are best propagated by division during early spring.

Mitchella repens   PLATE 207
Partridge Berry, Twinberry, Squaw Berry, Squaw Vine, Two-eyed Mary, Running Box

Partridge berry is a lovely trailing vinelike species that is attractive not only for its evergreen foliage but also for its dainty early summertime flowers and bright red fruits that follow. In the landscape the 1- to 2-inch-tall indefinite-spreading, semiwoody species may be used on a small to large scale. It is particularly well adapted for shady naturalized settings, and it is good company for mosses, lady slipper orchids, wintergreen, hostas, rhododendrons, kalmias, azaleas, and pieris. Limited foot traffic is tolerated.

United at their base and self-sterile, the paired flowers of partridge berry are interesting for two curious traits. The first is that a pair of flowers together (not an individual flower) produces a double berrylike fruit. Reportedly, the fertilization of both flowers is a requirement for fruit formation. Second, the flowers in each pair display different characteristics. One flower usually has long stamens (male flower structures) and a short pistil (the female flower structure), and the other has short stamens and a long pistil.

The common name partridge berry comes from its fruit being part of the diet of partridge. The berries are also consumed by deer, wild turkey, and quail. Since the fruit is low in fat, it is particularly resistant to rotting, and uneaten fruit remains well preserved through the winter. After the snow melts in early spring, when food is especially scarce, wildlife can resume feeding. Humans can also eat the berries, but they are virtually tasteless. Teas of partridge berry were used for their diuretic and astringent properties. Native American women drank a tea made from the leaves to stimulate uterine contractions and assist and induce labor. Following childbirth, the new mother sometimes formulated a lotion from the foliage and applied it to her breasts to alleviate the soreness associated with nursing. The Menominee Indians of Michigan's Upper Peninsula are said to have used it as a treatment for insomnia, and others employed its astringent properties to shrink swollen tissue. Early colonists from England used it as a treatment for menstrual cramps.

SCIENTIFIC NAME: *Mitchella repens* (mi-*chel*-a *ree-*

penz). *Mitchella* is named after Dr. John Mitchell (1711–1768), a botanist and physician who is credited with the development of a treatment for yellow fever during the Philadelphia epidemic. *Repens* means creeping.

HARDINESS / ORIGIN: Zones 5 to 8 or 9; woodlands of eastern North America.

LEAVES / FLOWERS / FRUIT: The leaves are evergreen, round to oval, to ¾ inch long, and glossy dark green with whitish veins. The flowers are funnel-shaped, to ½ inch long, pinkish, and effective during early summer. The fruit, an eight-seeded, brilliant scarlet berry, reaches ¼ inch in diameter, ripens during fall, and persists through winter.

RATE / SPACING: Growth is slow. Plants from 3- to 4-inch-diameter containers are spaced 6 to 8 inches apart.

HORTICULTURAL SELECTIONS: Var. *leucocarpa,* with pale yellowish white fruit.

CULTURE / CARE: Partridge berry prefers organically rich, moist, acidic loam. It also grows in sandy loam, but with less vigor. It is not greatly tolerant of drought; an effort should be made to keep the soil moist during periods of little rainfall. Other than rabbits, which like to eat the stems, it has few pests, and its most common diseases are leaf spot and stem rot. No maintenance is needed.

PROPAGATION: Cuttings root easily from early summer through fall. Division can be most effectively accomplished during spring and fall. Seed germinates during spring if sown the preceding fall.

Muehlenbeckia   PLATE 208
Wire Vine, Wire Plant

There are two valuable species of wire vine that function well in covering the ground. Both are relatively small, sprawling, mounding, semiwoody, mat-like vines. In the landscape, they are used as general covers for moderate-sized to large-sized contained areas. Often they are combined with small spring-flowering bulbs for color. In the rock garden they are planted by themselves as specimens. On sloping terrain, their sprawling habits and dense network of roots effectively control erosion, and their high tolerance to salt makes them useful in seaside landscapes. Little or no foot traffic is tolerated.

SCIENTIFIC NAME: *Muehlenbeckia* (myu-len-*bek*-ee-a) commemorates Henri Gustave Muehlenbeck (1789–1845), a French physician and botanist.

HARDINESS / ORIGIN: Zones 7 to 10; Australia, New Zealand, South America.

LEAVES / FLOWERS / FRUIT: The leaves typically are alternate, rounded, and evergreen. The small single-sexed greenish or yellowish flowers, borne alone, in pairs, or clusters, originate from the leaf axils or stem tips. The fruit, a nutlike seed surrounded by a white berrylike structure, is interesting but nonornamental.

RATE / SPACING: See individual species.

SPECIES: *M. axillaris* (aks-i-*lay*-ris), named for its flowers that are born in the leaf axils, is commonly called creeping wire vine. It reaches 2 to 12 inches tall and spreads 4 to 5 feet wide. It is hardy in Zones 7 to 10, hails from Australia, New Zealand, and Tasmania, and displays neat ⅜-inch-long, oblong to round, dark green to bronzy green, reddish edged evergreen foliage. Of little ornamental merit, the flowers are solitary or paired, five-petaled, yellowish green, and reach ³⁄₁₆ inch across. The fruit, similar to that of *M. complexa,* is a black shiny three-angled nutlike seed surrounded by a shiny white, berrylike covering. Growth is slow to moderate. Plants from gallon-sized containers are spaced 2 to 2½ feet apart.

M. complexa (com-*pleks*-a), named from the Latin *complexus,* to embrace, because the perianth swells, enclosing the fruit, is commonly called complex wire vine. Native to New Zealand, it reaches 2 to 18 inches tall and spreads several feet wide. It is hardy in Zones 7 to 10 and sports variable oval to rounded, often lobed, evergreen, ½- to ¾-inch-long dark green leaves. In flower it is not impressive. In fall it displays relatively unnoticeable auxiliary and terminal clusters of minute greenish yellow florets in 1- to 1½-inch-long spikes. The fruit is similar to that of *M. axillaris.* Growth is moderate to fast. Plants from gallon-sized containers are spaced 3 to 4 feet apart.

CULTURE / CARE: Wire vines are at their best in light-textured, well-drained, slightly acidic to slightly alkaline soils. They tolerate infertile soils as well as short periods of drought, but prefer moderately moist soil at all times. If these conditions are met, wire vines can be used in exposed windswept sites. They prefer full sun to light shade and have no serious pests or diseases. Maintenance consists of trimming back the trailing stems as they outgrow their bounds.

PROPAGATION: Cuttings root quite well during the summer. Divisions can be dug and successfully transplanted during spring, fall, and winter,

---

Myoporum parvifolium   PLATE 209

Woody, low growing (3 to 6 inches tall), horizontally spreading (to 9 feet across), myoporum is a staple ground cover for many warm coastal and arid climates, where its lush green appearance, few maintenance needs, and drought tolerance make it one of the best. For these reasons it is usually planted on a moderate to large scale as a general cover and foundation facer. Its fleshy leaves and stems store moisture, making it fire resistant, and therefore a good choice for public locations such as parks, rest areas, and near entrances of buildings, where people are apt to discard cigarettes or matches. Because myoporum roots well and forms dense mats, it is excellent for use on slopes and along highway embankments for erosion control. No foot traffic is tolerated.

SCIENTIFIC NAME: *Myoporum parvifolium* (my-*op*-orum / my-oh-*pore*-um par-wa-*foe*-lee-um / par-vi-*foe*-lee-um). The meaning of *Myoporum* is unknown. *Parvifolium,* small-leaved, comes from the Latin *parva,* small, and *folium,* leaf.

HARDINESS / ORIGIN: Zones 9 to 10 or 11; New Zealand.

LEAVES / FLOWERS / FRUIT: The leaves are evergreen, more or less lance-shaped, to ½ inch long by ¼ inch wide, and irregularly toothed around their edges at their ends. Typically colored bright green, in winter they often take on purplish tints. Waxy white starlike flowers, ⅜ inch across, cover the plants in spring and summer. The fruit is a tiny purplish berry that reaches ⅛ inch in diameter.

RATE / SPACING: Growth is moderate to fast. Plants from gallon-sized containers are spaced 3 to 5 feet apart.

HORTICULTURAL SELECTIONS: 'Burgundy Carpet', 6 inches tall by 6 to 8 feet wide, tips of new stems and leaves deep reddish purple when grown in sun; 'Pink', with clear pink flowers; 'Putah Creek', reportedly more symmetrical in habit, 12 inches tall by more than 4 feet wide.

OTHER SPECIES: *M. debile* (day-*bee*-lay), a little less cold hardy, is similar in habit to *M. parvifolium,* but differs in being taller (to 12 inches), and displays foliage that is narrower, almost needlelike.

M. 'Pacifica', reputed to be of hybrid origin, reaches 3 feet tall by 10 feet wide.

CULTURE / CARE: *Myoporum* species prefer well-drained sandy loam that is slightly acidic. They are relatively tolerant of drought. They prefer full sun and have few serious pests or disease problems. Maintenance includes periodic edging or trimming back of growth when stems outgrow their bounds. Occasional mowing rejuvenates growth and helps to keep plantings neat.

PROPAGATION: Cuttings root easily throughout the growing season.

Myosotis scorpioides   PLATE 210
True Forget-me-not

Used as a long-blooming general cover for small-sized to moderate-sized areas, the soft, lacy, delicate-textured look of true forget-me-not (a.k.a. swamp forget-me-not) is effective in softening up hard lines of brick or wood structures, and coarse-textured trees and shrubs. As a rhizomatous herb, it works well near streams, ponds, and lakes, and is useful in bogs and at poolside. No foot traffic is tolerated.

The name forget-me-not is said to come from the tale of a young man who was collecting the flowers for his lady near the bank of a river. In the process he slipped and fell into the fast-moving water. Clenching the flowers in his hand, as he was quickly swept downstream, he cried out to his lover on the shore, "Forget me not."

SCIENTIFIC NAME: *Myosotis scorpioides* (my-oh-*soe*-tis skore-pee-*oy*-deez). *Myosotis* comes from the Greek *mus,* a mouse, and *otes,* an ear, in reference to the leaves which look like the ears of a mouse. *Scorpioides,* like a scorpion's tail, refers to the shape of the flower clusters.

HARDINESS / ORIGIN: Zones 5 to 9; moist meadows of Europe to Siberia.

LEAVES / FLOWERS / FRUIT: The simple, oblong to lance-shaped, 2-inch-long, bright shiny green, deciduous leaves are an attractive backdrop to the small five-parted flowers of spring through summer, which are bright blue to pink (sometimes with yellow, pink, or white eye). The tiny shiny nutlets that follow are nonornamental.

RATE / SPACING: Growth is moderate. Plants from 3- to 4-inch-diameter containers are spaced 8 to 12 inches apart.

HORTICULTURAL SELECTIONS: 'Alba', with white flowers; 'Graf Waldersee' ('Count Waldersee), with deep blue early flowers; 'Meernixe' ('Sea Nymph'), with light blue flowers; 'Perle von Ronneberg', with dark blue flowers; 'Pinkie', with bright pink flowers; 'Rosea', with pink summertime flowers; 'Sapphire', with brilliant sapphire blue flowers; 'Semperflorens', with dwarf habit and many flowers; 'Thuringen', with large dark blue flowers.

CULTURE / CARE: Forget-me-not prefers cool, sunny to moderately shady conditions, and adapts to most soils, including wet conditions, that are neutral to acidic. It is not tolerant of drought and should be kept out of windy conditions. Its most common diseases are blight, mildew, wilt, rust, and aster yellows. It seems to have no serious pest problems. Little maintenance is required; however, division every fourth or fifth year improves bloom.

PROPAGATION: Cuttings taken during summer and treated with 1000 ppm IBA/talc root well in a porous medium. Division is effective during spring and fall. Ripe seed germinates shortly after sowing.

Nandina domestica PLATE 211

Heavenly Bamboo, Sacred Bamboo, Nandina

A woody-based, semievergreen, multistemmed suckering shrub, heavenly bamboo reaches heights of 6 to 8 feet and spreads 6 to 8 feet across. It is the lower-growing dwarf selections, however, that are useful as ground covers. They can be planted as a low hedging along walkways, arranged in small groups near the trunk of a tree or next to a garden ornament or large boulder to create accent, or massed in moderate to large groups and used for facing foundations. They are particularly effective if the background is light-colored. The dwarf cultivars combine well with a host of ornamental grasses as well as several sprawling ground covers such as ice plant, trailing African daisy, and gazanias. The fruit provides wintertime food for songbirds.

SCIENTIFIC NAME: *Nandina domestica* (nan-*die*-na do-*mes*-ti-ka). *Nandina* comes from *nanten,* the Japanese name for this shrub. *Domestica* means cultivated.

HARDINESS / ORIGIN: Zones 7 to 9; central China and Japan.

LEAVES / FLOWERS / FRUIT: The leaves are evergreen, divided into two or three leaflets, each leaflet being 1 to 3½ inches long by 1 to 1½ inches wide, rather elliptic, and leathery-textured. The young leaves are often tinged pink or bronzy as they open; in summer they become light green, and in fall, they often pick up bronzy or purplish hues. Pinkish in bud, the small ¼- to ⅜-inch-wide flowers are assembled in erect panicles that range from 8 to 15 inches long and are attractively displayed during early summer. The showy fall-ripening fruits that follow are ⅓-inch-wide, round, bright red berries. Typically they are borne in such profusion so as to cause the branches to bow under their weight.

RATE / SPACING: Growth is slow to moderate. Plants from gallon-sized containers are spaced 2 to 3 feet apart.

HORTICULTURAL SELECTIONS: 'Atropurpurea Nana' ('Purpurea Dwarf'), with a stiff upright habit, to 2 feet tall, leaves reddish purple in fall; 'Harbor Dwarf', an excellent selection that develops into a 2- to 3-foot-tall graceful mound, foliage orange to bronzy red or purple-tinged in winter, flowers smaller than the species; 'Moon Bay', to 2 feet tall, with bright lime green foliage that turns red in fall; 'Nana' ('Compacta'), 2 to 4 feet tall, dense mounds, fruiting less than the species; 'Pygmaea' ('Minima'), with compact habit, 3 feet tall, fall color bright red; 'Wood's Dwarf', with compact habit and densely set light green leaves that become crimson-orange in cold weather.

CULTURE / CARE: Heavenly bamboo is adaptable to various soil types, but clearly prefers a fertile, acidic loam. In alkaline soils it soon develops iron-deficiency chlorosis. It is relatively tolerant to drought and only requires an occasional deep watering during summer. It prefers full sun to moderate shade, with the best foliage color in full sun. Pests include northern root-knot nematode. Diseases include red leaf spot, anthracnose, and root rot. Maintenance consists of an annual pruning at which time the oldest stems are removed just above the crown, and the remainder headed back to promote a neat, compact growth habit.

PROPAGATION: Cultivars do not come reliably true from seed and must be propagated vegetatively. Cuttings are best rooted during spring and early summer. Rooted suckers (shoots that arise from the base of the plant) also work and can be divided and transplanted during fall, winter, and spring.

Nepeta × faassenii PLATE 212

Faassen's Catmint, Mauve Catmint, Blue Catmint

This hybrid is an attractive, long-blooming, herbaceous, mound-forming ground cover. It reaches 1½ to 2 feet tall, spreads 2 to 3 feet across, and is of great value as a small-scale to moderate-scale general cover, accent plant, pathway edger, or rock garden specimen. Like catnip (*N. cataria*), it attracts cats, and its flowers furnish nectar for hummingbirds.

SCIENTIFIC NAME: *Nepeta × faassenii* (*nep*-i-ta / ne-*pee*-ta fah-*sen*-ee-eye). *Nepeta* is probably named for Nepete, a city in Etruria, the ancient country that was the center of Etruscan civilization and was located in the area of Tuscany, a region of western Italy. Another source says that it is simply the Latin name for the plant. *Faassenii* is named after J. H. Faassen, a Dutch nurseryman.

HARDINESS / ORIGIN: Zones 4 or 5 to 8 or 9; Faassen's catmint was developed by crossing *N. mussinii* with *N. nepetella* at the Copenhagen Botanic Gardens in 1939.

LEAVES / FLOWERS / FRUIT: The leaves are deciduous to semievergreen (basal leaves often staying green), oblong to oval, 1¼ inches long, with rounded teeth about their margins. They are colored gray-green and, when crushed, are aromatic. Above the leaves are borne spikes of ½-inch-long, showy violet-blue flowers in summer. No fruit is produced as this is a sterile hybrid.

RATE / SPACING: Growth is moderate. Plants from 3- to 4-inch-diameter and gallon-sized containers are spaced 1 to 1½ feet apart.

HORTICULTURAL SELECTIONS: 'Six Hills Giant' (sometimes classified as *N. gigantea*), very impressive, with a foliar mass that reaches 3 feet tall by 4 feet wide, flower stalks 9 to 12 inches tall, flowers numerous and dark violet.

OTHER SPECIES: *N. mussinii* (moo-*sin*-ee-eye). One of the parents of *N. faassenii,* this species, commonly called Persian catmint, reaches 1 to 1½ feet tall, is hardy in Zones 3 to 8, and is the forerunner of many attractive cultivars. Hailing from the Caucasus, it is clothed in gray, heart-shaped, 1-inch-long leaves. Above the strongly aromatic foliage are borne spikes of pale blue ½-inch-long flowers in spring. The flowers often bear a great deal of seed, but the seed are not of any ornamental value. 'Blue Dwarf' is a compact form that flowers profusely. 'Blue Wonder', reaching 12 to 15 inches tall, has dark blue flowers. 'Snowflake' has white flowers. 'White Wonder' is similar to 'Blue Wonder' but white flowered.

CULTURE / CARE: Catmints are not particular about soil, tolerating any texture and pH. They do, however, need good drainage, and, without it, soon develop crown rot. Relatively durable, they show good drought tolerance; even when planted in full sun, which they prefer, they need little watering in summer. Maintenance needs are few if any. For an autumnal repeat of the summertime flowers, plantings can be sheared back toward the end of the summertime blooming period. This also keeps plants compact, rejuvenated, and neat looking.

PROPAGATION: Stem cuttings root easily during the summer months. Division is almost foolproof during spring. Catmints are seldom propagated from seed as the hybrid does not produce seed and the cultivars of *N. mussinii,* which are typically what are being grown, often do not come true from seed.

Nephrolepis exaltata   PLATE 213
Sword Fern, Ladder Fern

Quite common as a house plant, especially the cultivar 'Bostoniensis' (Boston fern), which ranks among the most popular of all time, sword fern is also a good ground cover in the warmer parts of North America. It is an evergreen, stoloniferous and rhizomatous, graceful, lush fern. It ranges from 2 to 6 feet tall—depending upon soil fertility and moisture—and spreads somewhat broader than its height. In coastal areas of southern Florida and California it grows beautifully as a moderate-scale to large-scale ground cover for walkway edging, general covering, turf substitution, facing, and as an accent or specimen plant. Regardless of how it is employed, sword fern imparts a lush, tranquil element to the landscape.

SCIENTIFIC NAME: *Nephrolepis exaltata* (nef-roe-*lep*-is eks-al-*tay*-ta). *Nephrolepis* is derived from the Greek *nephros,* kidney, and *lepis,* scale, referring to the kid-

ney-shaped scales, or indusia, that cover the spore-bearing sori. *Exaltata* means extremely tall.

HARDINESS / ORIGIN: Zones 10 to 11; tropics of the Old World, now naturalized in southern Florida.

LEAVES / FLOWERS / FRUIT: The evergreen, medium green, tufted, divided, compound leaves are erect, then arching over, and reach 1 to 5 feet long by up to 6 inches wide. Each leaflet is 3 inches long, eared at the base, narrowly triangular with a blunt point, and smooth or slightly toothed about its edges. The round or kidney-shaped sori (spore cases) are located near the edges on the underside of the leaves.

RATE / SPACING: Growth is moderate. Plants from 1- to 3-gallon-sized containers are spaced 3 to 4 feet apart, depending on the mature size of the particular variety.

HORTICULTURAL SELECTIONS: There are more than 50 selections of this species. 'Bostoniensis' (Boston fern), a common house plant in the North, the most popular selection, discovered in Philadelphia in 1894 among a shipment of plants from Boston; 'Compacta' (Dallas fern, sometimes listed as 'Dallasii'), very attractive, compact, vigorous, with emerald green leaves, able to withstand more shade and lower humidity than the species; 'Compacta Cristata', similar to 'Dwarf Boston' but with crested foliage; 'Dwarf Boston', considerably smaller and more compact than the species; 'Fluffy Ruffles', with ruffled leaf edges; 'New York', vigorous growing, with somewhat shorter fronds and wavy leaflets; var. *rooseveltii,* with wavy leaflets; 'Teddy Junior', compact, derived from var. *rooseveltii*; 'Whitmanii', with long, arching, sometimes three-parted, light green fronds.

CULTURE / CARE: Sword fern and its cultivars require good drainage and perform best in fertile, rich, acidic loam. They are not greatly tolerant of drought or extremely high temperatures. They achieve their most robust appearance when the soil is kept slightly moist, the climate is moderated by coastal conditions, and the light conditions range from light to moderate shade. Their most common diseases are anthracnose, gray mold, damping off, leaf spot, and rust. Their primary pests are aphids and mites. Maintenance needs include dividing plants when they become crowded and removing dead fronds from their bases.

PROPAGATION: Division is easily accomplished in winter and early spring. Spores may also be used (see Chapter 8).

Nierembergia repens   PLATE 214
White Cupflower

White cupflower is not very common, but for those privileged to be growing it, it brings the rewards of attractive flowers and leaves and minimal maintenance. Reaching 4 to 6 inches tall and spreading 12 inches across, this herbaceous, trailing, mat-forming species performs well as a small-scale general cover. It combines beautifully with thymes, candytuft (*Iberis*), and *Cymbalaria* species, especially in rock gardens. No foot traffic is tolerated.

SCIENTIFIC NAME: *Nierembergia repens* (nee-rem-*ber*-gee-a *ree*-penz). *Nierembergia* is named after Juan Eusebio Nieremberg (1595–1658), a Spanish Jesuit. *Repens,* creeping, refers to the trailing habit.

HARDINESS / ORIGIN: Zones 7 or 8 to 10; South America.

LEAVES / FLOWERS / FRUIT: The leaves are bright green, oblong to spatula-shaped, and 1¼ inch long. The morning-glory-like flowers of summer are five-petaled, 1½ inches wide, and creamy white or rose-streaked with purple. The tiny fruit is non-ornamental.

RATE / SPACING: Growth is moderate. Plants from pint-sized containers are spaced 12 inches apart.

OTHER SPECIES: *N. hippomanica* var. *violacea* (hip-oh-*man*-i-ka vee-oh-*lay*-see-a) is named from the Greek *hippomanes,* in reference to this plant's impact on horses, apparently driving them mad or perhaps meaning that horses are mad about eating it. Commonly known as dwarf cupflower, it is a 6- to 12-inch tall, sprawling, evergreen, herbaceous ground cover that displays blue to violet, bell-shaped, 1-inch-wide flowers in summer. It is hardy in Zones 7 or 8 to 10. 'Purple Robe' has flowers that are darker violet.

CULTURE / CARE: Cupflowers prefer fertile, well-drained soils. They are not tolerant of drought and should be watered often enough to keep the soil slightly moist. They prefer full sun when grown at their northernmost limits, and light shade in the mid to southern portions of their hardiness range. Pests and diseases are normally not a problem. Maintenance typically consists of mowing or trimming plants back during early spring before new growth occurs.

PROPAGATION: Stem cuttings may be rooted during early summer. Division during spring is nearly foolproof. Seed, which is sometimes sold commercially, germinates in only two or three weeks.

Oenothera   PLATE 215
Evening Primrose, Sundrops

Evening primroses and sundrops are attractive both for their foliage and for their exceptional floral displays. They work well as general covers for facing taller shrubs (especially dark green evergreens), garden ornaments, and building foundations. Plant them on slopes, in parking strips, as walkway or border edging, or for accent. Planting in locations of high visibility where passersby can appreciate their beauty is highly recommended. No foot traffic is tolerated.

The classic evening primrose is *O. biennis,* a native biennial forb of wide distribution. Although this species is seldom grown as a garden plant, it is said to be a favorite food for Japanese beetles. Thus, interplanting a perennial border with evening primrose may reduce damage as the beetles consume it preferentially to the other plants.

SCIENTIFIC NAME: *Oenothera* (ee-noe-*thee*-ra / e-*noth*-er-a) is said to be an English version of *oinotheras,* the Greek name for this genus. It is also said to be the name that Theophrastus used for a species of *Epilobium.*

HARDINESS / ORIGIN: See individual species.

LEAVES / FLOWERS / FRUIT: The leaves vary from evergreen to deciduous, depending on the species. In most species they are alternately arranged, simple, anywhere from completely unlobed to very prominently lobed, and act as a backdrop to numerous four-parted prominent flowers that either bloom during the day (sundrops or suncups) or evening (evening primroses). The fruit, a capsule, is interesting and ornamental on only a few cultivars.

RATE / SPACING: See individual species.

SPECIES: *O. berlandieri* (ber-lan-dee-*a*-ree), named after J. L. Berlandier (d. 1851), a German botanist who explored Texas and Mexico, is commonly called Mexican primrose. Hailing from Texas and Mexico, it is hardy in Zones 8 to 9, exhibits a low, herbaceous, spreading habit, and ranges from 6 to 12 inches tall. Growth is moderate to fast. Plants from pint-sized to quart-sized containers are spaced 14 to 18 inches apart. The leaves are alternately arranged. Each is narrowly oblong to oval, 1 to 3 inches long, gray-green, and evergreen. The springtime flowers, borne in the upper portions of the stems, are solitary, rose-pink, and effective during the day. 'Siskiyou', 10 inches tall, with large 2-inch-wide silvery-pink flowers and robust spread.

O. drummondii (drum-*mond*-ee-eye), named after James (c. 1784–1863) or Thomas Drummond (c. 1790–1831), two brothers who collected for Messrs Veitch, is commonly called Baja primrose. Native to Texas and Mexico, it is hardy in Zones 8 to 9. It reaches only 4 inches tall, spreads by stolons, and displays a low, spreading habit. Its leaves are narrowly oblong to oval and ¼ to 3 inches long at the base of the plant. The stem leaves, on the other hand, are oblong and ½ to 1½ inches long. Both types of leaves are evergreen, medium green, and turn reddish during periods of cold or drought. The solitary flowers are elevated above the leaves on 6- to 8-inch-long stems. Each is soft yellow, 2½ inches wide, and effective during the evening, night, and early morning in spring, then intermittently throughout summer. Growth is moderate to fast. Plants from pint-sized to quart-sized containers are spaced 14 to 18 inches apart.

O. fruticosa (frew-ti-*koe*-sa), meaning shrubby (somewhat of a misnomer as it is actually only semi-shrubby), is commonly called common sundrops, suncups, wild beet, and scabish. Often confused with *O. tetragona* in the trade, this is one of the most impressive natives. It displays erect-stemmed, rhizomatous habit and ranges from 1½ to 3 feet tall by more than 2 feet wide. It is hardy in Zones 4 to 7 or 8 and hails from woodland borders, meadows, and swales of Nova Scotia to Minnesota, then south to Louisiana to Florida. It is said to be compatible with black walnut (*Juglans nigra*). Growth is moderate to relatively fast. Plants from quart-sized to gallon-sized containers are spaced 12 to 16 inches apart. The stem leaves are deciduous, and the basal leaves (formed in ground-hugging rosettes) are evergreen in the warmer parts of its range. The stem leaves tend to be narrowly oval while the basal leaves are broader and more rounded. In either case they are dark green and may range from 1 to 4 inches long by ¾ to 1½ inches wide. The flowers, which live up to the name sundrops, are borne at the ends of the stems in clusters from late spring to mid summer. Open during the day and night, each magnificent flower is four-petaled and ranges from 1 to 2 inches wide. 'Erica Robin', leaves unfurling bright yellow with red and pink tones, flowers bright yellow; subsp. *glauca,* with bright yellow flowers; var. *linearis,* narrower leaves and slightly smaller flowers than the species; 'Summer Solstice', 15 inches tall, dark leaves.

O. missouriensis (mi-sur-ree-*en*-sis), of Missouri, is commonly called Missouri primrose, flutter-mills primrose, or Ozark sundrops. Native from Missouri to Nebraska, as well as Texas and Colorado, it is hardy in Zones 4 to 8 and is characterized by a sprawling, rhizomatous habit. It ranges from 10 to 15 inches tall, spreads more than 3 feet wide, and displays silvery-green deciduous or evergreen leaves. The stem leaves, which are deciduous, are narrowly oval and range from 3 to 5 inches long by ⅜ to 1¼ inches wide. The basal leaves are broader and evergreen. The afternoon-opening, solitary flowers are borne from spring through fall. In bud they are held erect and often droop once they open. Magnificently showy, their 1- to 2-inch-long yellow petals form a corolla that may reach more than 5 inches wide. Persistent, decorative seedpods follow and the petals, which are effective mid spring to late summer, often become red-tinged as they fade. Growth is moderate.

Plants from quart-sized to gallon-sized containers are spaced 14 to 18 inches apart.

O. tetragona (te-tra-*goe*-na), meaning four-angled, likely referring to the four-lobed stigma of the flowers, is commonly called four-angled sundrops (as is *O. fruticosa*). This day bloomer hails from meadows and thickets of the eastern United States and is hardy to Zone 4. Herbaceous, spreading, and floriferous, it reaches 1 to 2 feet tall and spreads indefinitely. Its simple leaves are alternately arranged upon reddish pubescent stems. Each leaf is narrowly oblong, 1 to 3 inches long, and vibrant green. The flowers, which are borne in leafy branching spikes, are 2 inches wide, four-petaled, bright vibrant yellow, and effective during the summer. Growth is moderate to fast. Plants from pint-sized to quart-sized containers are spaced 14 to 18 inches apart. Cultivars include 'Fireworks' ('Fyrverkeri'), to 18 inches tall, with red flower buds and stems, and bright yellow, 2- to 3-inch-wide flowers from mid to late spring; 'Highlight' ('Hoheslicht'), with compact habit, only 12 inches tall; 'Yellow River', with deep yellow 2- to 2½-inch-wide flowers, 18 inches tall.

CULTURE / CARE: *Oenothera* species prefer full sun to light shade and are adaptable to most well-drained, sandy to loamy, organically rich, acidic to slightly alkaline soils. All are modestly tolerant of heat and drought, and only occasionally do they need supplemental summertime watering. Their primary diseases are leaf spots, rust, downy mildew, powdery mildew, blight, gray mold, gall, and root rot, and their most common pests are aphids and slugs. Maintenance normally consists of removing straggly or broken stems, with a lawn mower or shears, during early spring.

PROPAGATION: Stem cuttings are easily rooted during early summer and may be aided with the use of 1000 ppm IBA/talc. Division is simple and best performed during early spring by separating the rosettes that arise from the rhizomes. *Oenothera* species can easily be divided and transplanted during any season. Fresh seed can be sown in the greenhouse during late summer or outdoors in fall or mid spring; germination is said to take two to three weeks at 68 to 85°F.

Omphalodes verna   PLATE 216
Blue-eyed Mary, Creeping Navel-seed, Creeping Forget-me-not, Navelwort

Truly a charmer, this leafy little herb reaches 8 inches tall and 12 or more inches wide. It is often difficult to purchase because many growers overlook it in favor of more conventional ground covers, but certainly it is a plant worth having in your landscape so, should you happen upon a few pots of it, buy them. The plant is easy to propagate and, within a short time, you will have enough to cover a modest-sized area. Then you can go into business selling divisions to your admiring neighbors.

Creeping navel-seed is best used as a general cover in small-sized or moderate-sized areas where its spreading short rhizomes can easily be contained. It forms a nice living mulch underneath most deciduous trees and is particularly attractive and effective between sidewalks and building foundations. No foot traffic is tolerated.

This plant was a favorite of Queen Marie Antoinette. The common name creeping navel-seed comes from the deep grooves in the nutlets, which presumably look like tiny navels.

SCIENTIFIC NAME: *Omphalodes verna* (om-fa-*loe*-deez *ver*-na). *Omphalodes* is derived from the Greek, *omphalos,* navel, and *eidos,* like, referring to a navellike depression in the seed. *Verna,* spring, refers to the time of flowering.

HARDINESS / ORIGIN: Zones 6 to 9; Europe.

LEAVES / FLOWERS / FRUIT: The semievergreen leaves are both rugged and attractive, oval to narrowly oval-shaped, 1 to 3 inches long, prominently veined, and medium to dark green. The flowers that arise during mid to late spring are five-parted, ½ inch wide, and blue with white centers. The fruit consists of four tiny nutlets and is nonornamental. Considering that the plant is named for its fruit, the fruit is rather disappointing.

RATE / SPACING: Growth is slow in the northern portion of its hardiness limits and relatively fast in the southern portion. Plants from 3- to 4-inch-diameter containers are spaced 10 to 14 inches apart.

HORTICULTURAL SELECTIONS: 'Alba', with white flowers; 'Grandiflora', with larger flowers.

CULTURE / CARE: This species adapts to a wide range of soil types. Its only strict requirements are that drainage be good and that moisture be maintained during the heat of summer. It prefers moderate shade and has few pests, diseases, or maintenance problems.

PROPAGATION: Division of plants is simple with a spade; it can be done any time, although early spring is best so that plants will be well rooted before summer arrives.

Onoclea sensibilis   PLATE 217
Sensitive Fern, Bead Fern

If ever there were a ground cover for moist soil, this is it. It is a plant of great tenacity. Reaching 12 to 24 inches tall, sensitive fern spreads indefinitely and forms a dense network of roots. These properties make it particularly well suited to binding soil along the banks of streams and ponds. Here, the reflection of its neat light green foliage in the water enhances its appeal. In other areas where the soil remains constantly moist, sensitive fern fulfills the role of foundation facer or general cover. It also looks quite nice when naturalized along the edges of a soggy wooded setting, and it combines well with red maple, red-stem dogwood, spice bush (*Lindera benzoin*), and taller clump-forming ferns such as royal fern (*Osmunda regalis*) and cinnamon fern (*O. cinnamomea*). It said to be compatible with black walnut (*Juglans nigra*). No foot traffic is tolerated.

The young fiddleheads can be steamed and eaten. During times of scarcity, Native Americans consumed the rhizomes. The mature leaves contain thiaminase, an enzyme that breaks down thiamine (vitamin B1) and thus creates thiamine deficiency in livestock.

SCIENTIFIC NAME: *Onoclea sensibilis* (on-oh-*klee*-a / a-nok-*lee*-a sen-*si*-bil-is). *Onoclea* is derived from the Greek *onokleia,* a plant with leaves rolled up into the semblance of berries; in this case, the reference is to the beadlike spore capsules of the fertile leaves. *Sensibilis,* sensitive, refers to the plant's sensitivity to early frost in fall.

HARDINESS / ORIGIN: Zone 3; marshy soils of the North Temperate Zone.

LEAVES / FLOWERS / FRUIT: Spores are borne on special, modified leaves, fertile fronds, that are considerably different from the sterile fronds. Each erectly oriented fertile frond reaches 12 inches long and is composed of many medium green beadlike spore cases. In maturity the spore cases and stalk turn brown and persist through the winter to release their spores during spring. In the minds of most people, they do not resemble leaves at all, yet they are very interesting to look at and are often used in dried flower arrangements. In contrast, the sterile fronds are deciduous, light green, flattened and typically leaflike. They may reach 4 feet long, yet usually range from 1½ to 2½ feet long by 1 foot wide. Along their edges are about 12 pairs of rounded lobes, each covered with tiny teeth.

RATE / SPACING: Growth is moderate to fast. Plants from pint-sized or gallon-sized containers are spaced 14 to 20 inches apart.

HORTICULTURAL SELECTION: Var. *interrupta* (Asian sensitive fern), from Japan, Korea, Manchuria, and eastern Russia, with the beads of fertile fronds widely separated (i.e., interrupted).

CULTURE / CARE: Sensitive fern prefers rich, acidic, highly organic loam, yet sandy soils present few problems. For a swamp-inhabiting fern, this species shows remarkable tolerance to drought, yet unquestionably it is best when grown in constantly moist soils. It prefers full sun to moderate shade. Seldom are serious diseases or pests encountered. Maintenance is a word that should not be associated with this plant; however, some very meticulous gardeners mow off the foliage during fall in the name of neatness. This is a costly shame as, by doing so, one is foregoing the intriguing wintertime display of the snow-capped fertile fronds.

PROPAGATION: Division is the most practical means of propagation; simply dig up sections and transplant them in spring or fall.

Ophiopogon   PLATE 218
Dwarf Lily-turf, Mondo Grass

This genus is similar to *Liriope* in that it displays grassy foliage, dainty yet showy flowers, and shiny black fruit. Like *Liriope,* its grassy leaves arch over to form a graceful fountain shape; yet in *Ophiopogon* they tend to be smaller, slower growing, and more refined. Use *Ophiopogon* in the same manner as *Liriope,* but on a somewhat smaller scale.

SCIENTIFIC NAME: *Ophiopogon* (oh-fee-oh-*poe*-gon) is from the Greek *ophis,* a serpent, and *pogon,* a beard.

HARDINESS / ORIGIN: See individual species for hardiness; Southeast Asia from India to Japan.

LEAVES / FLOWERS / FRUIT: The evergreen leaves are grasslike. The white or lilac flowers are borne in spikelike clusters. The fruit is shiny blue in color.

RATE / SPACING: Relatively slow to moderate; see individual species for spacing recommendations.

SPECIES: *O. clarkei* (*klark*-ee-eye) reaches 8 inches tall and grows in sun or light shade. Hailing from the Himalayas, the species is narrow-leaved, colored grayish green, and seems to be hardy at least to Zone 6. Plants from pint-sized to gallon-sized containers are spaced 10 to 14 inches apart.

O. jaburan (jab-*you*-ran), commonly called white lily-turf, Jaburan lily-turf, or snakebeard, is hardy to Zone 7 or 8 and native to Japan. This species reaches 24 to 36 inches tall and spreads 6 to 8 inches wide. Its evergreen leaves are grasslike, to 2 feet long by $\frac{1}{2}$ inch wide, and colored dark green. The $\frac{1}{2}$-inch-wide flowers are six-parted, white, and effective during summer. The fruit is berrylike, oblong, and colored violet-blue. Growth is moderate. Plants from pint-sized to quart-sized containers are spaced 6 inches apart. Some popular horticultural selections include 'Aureus', hardy only to Zone 9, with leaves longitudinally striped with yellow; 'Evergreen Giant', 18 to 30 inches tall, with thick, straplike olive green leaves; 'Variegatus' ('Vittatus'), leaves with attractive white and green stripes.

O. japonicus (ja-*pon*-i-kus), dwarf lily-turf or mondo grass, is hardy in Zones 7 to 9 and reaches 6 to 15 inches tall. It tends to form dense sods and spread indefinitely, and its dwarf cultivars can be used to form a foot-tolerant no-mow turf substitute. Growth is slow to moderate. Plants from pint-sized to gallon-sized containers are spaced 10 to 14 inches apart. A native of Japan and Korea, this species exhibits evergreen, grasslike, 10- to 15-inch-long dark green leaves. Its flowers are colored light lilac to white, reach $\frac{1}{4}$ inch wide, and are effective during early summer. The fruit is a blue globe-shaped capsule to $\frac{1}{4}$ inch wide. Some popular horticultural selections include 'Comet', 6 inches tall, leaves with narrow vertical white stripes; var. *compacta,* only 2 inches tall and 6 inches wide; 'Gyoku Ryu', 3 inches tall, with dark green leaves; 'Kigimafukiduma' ('Silver Mist'), with foliage longitudinally variegated white and green, relatively slow growing; 'Kioto', with dwarf habit, reaching 3 inches tall; 'Nanus Variegatus', with white-streaked leaves and dwarf habit; 'Nippon', with dark green foliage, only 2 inches tall by 3 to 4 inches wide; 'Shiroshima Ryu', said to be hardy to Zone 5 or 6, slow spreading, only 3 or 4 inches tall, with dark green leaves and white stripes; 'Super Dwarf', reaching only 1 inch tall, good potential for a lovely no-mow lawn; 'Variegatus' ('Silver Showers'), clump-forming, leaves with green and white stripes, flowers white, 1 to 2 feet tall.

O. planiscapus '**Nigrescens**' (plahn-i-*skah*-pus nie-*gres*-ens) is commonly called black lily-turf. The species name refers to the flat floral stems (scapes), and the cultivar name indicates the color of the leaves—black. Hardy in Zones 5 or 6 to 10 and native to Japan, this unique selection reaches only 6 inches tall and spreads indefinitely (but at a snail's pace). The leaves, which make it outstanding, are evergreen, grasslike, 12 inches long by $\frac{1}{4}$ inch wide, and are colored such a dark shade of purple as to appear black. The flowers are bell-shaped, colored pinkish to purplish, $\frac{1}{4}$ inch long, and borne in summer. They are attractive, but compared to the unusual foliage, their ornamental value is of little importance. The fruit is a blackish berry.

This cultivar is exceptional and unique for its unusual foliage coloration. Outstanding contrast is attained when it is combined with lighter-foliaged plants such as some of the smaller variegated (white and green) hostas, clump-forming variegated lily-turfs (*Liriope muscari* cultivars), golden creeping Charley, burgundy glow bugleweed, and blue fescue. Two notes of caution before you start designing acres of black lily-turf into your landscape plan: first, it is slow to spread and must be spaced on 4-inch centers, and second, because of its slow-spreading nature, it is rather expensive. The species, by the way, is somewhat taller and more robust with jade green leaves.

CULTURE / CARE: The *Ophiopogon* species described here are adaptable to most well-drained soils, but in comparison to *Liriope,* they are not very tolerant to drought. The soil should be kept slightly moist with regular watering, and the location should be such that plants receive full sun to moderate shade, full sun being best in coastal areas and light to moderate shade best further inland. No serious pests or diseases have been reported, and little or no maintenance is required.

PROPAGATION: Division should be performed during spring or early fall. Seed should be stored in moist sand at 75°F for six weeds prior to sowing. Alternatively, ripe seed can be sown outdoors in the fall to germinate late the following spring.

Opuntia humifusa   PLATE 219
Prickly Pear, Indian Fig

Although not everyone wants a hardy ground-covering cactus in their garden, this is a plant for those intrigued by the unusual. Prickly pear is relatively low growing (4 to 8 inches tall), sprawls to more than 3 feet across, and is interesting both for its succulent pads and brilliant flowers. The best uses of this species are as a small-scale general cover, a facing to shrubs and tall succulents, and as a rock garden specimen. Prickly pear also grows well on sandy slopes where it does a wonderful job of erosion control. It combines well with various species of *Sedum, Yucca, Haworthia,* and other drought-tolerant plants.

The fruits (tunas) of prickly pear cactus were an important food of Native Americans and were either eaten fresh, mashed and cooked as an applesauce-like dish, or dried in the sun and saved for the wintertime. In a pinch, Native Americans and early settlers ate the pads as well, usually roasted over hot coals. Today, candy, jams, and other condiments made from the fruit are staple items of Western tourist traps.

Native Americans applied the sap of prickly pear to their wounds. Poultices were applied to insect bites, warts, and moles. Today, medical researchers have discovered that the leaves of many *Opuntia* species, including *O. humifusa,* are effective in treating diabetes mellitus and obesity. It is believed that preceding a meal with an appetizer of a few pads of prickly pear significantly reduces blood sugar and cholesterol levels following the meal.

SCIENTIFIC NAME: *Opuntia humifusa* (oh-*pun*-shee-a hume-i-*few*-sa). *Opuntia* is named after Opuntis (Opus), a town in Greece; although it is a New World genus, it apparently resembled a different plant that grew near Opus. *Humifusa* comes from the Latin *humilis,* on or near the ground, and refers to the plant's growth habit.

HARDINESS / ORIGIN: Zones 5 to 9 or 10; from Montana to Massachusetts in the North and from eastern Texas to Florida in the South.

LEAVES / FLOWERS / FRUIT: The evergreen, fleshy, wrinkled, round to oval, medium to dark green pads (flattened, highly modified stems) reach 2 to 10 inches long and are covered with tiny spines. The minute leaves that are located between the pads are deciduous and colored brown. Blooming in early summer, the flowers are solitary, 2½ to 4 inches wide, and composed of 8 to 12 bright yellow petals. The berry, or tuna as it is usually called, is edible and contains white, compressed seeds. First green, then ripening to dark purple, its pulpy flesh is edible and very tasty.

RATE / SPACING: Growth is slow to moderate. Plants from quart-sized to gallon-sized containers are spaced 1½ to 2 feet apart.

HORTICULTURAL SELECTIONS: Var. *greenii,* very coarsely spined, somewhat more erect growing.

OTHER SPECIES: *O. erinacea* var. *ursina* (air-i-*nay*-see-a ur-*see*-na), grizzly bear cactus, is native from southeastern California to Arizona and is an attractive, broad-spreading species that reaches 1½ feet tall. Its flattened 4-inch-long segments tend to ascend in upright fashion and are covered by numerous 2-inch-long white bristles. The red, yellow, or sometimes pink summerborne flowers reach 2½ inches wide and lead to spiny 1¼-inch-long fruit. Variety *hystricina,* porcupine cactus, displays erectly oriented 4- to 8-inch-wide spine-covered joints. Also a spreader, it blooms with orange or pink flowers, and its 1½-inch-long dry fruit is oval to oblong and prickly tipped.

O. juniperina (jew-ni-per-*eye*-na), a procumbent somewhat ascending wide-spreader, is hardy to Zone 5. Native to New Mexico, it is composed of 6½-inch-long oval joints that tend to be more broadly rounded and spiny away from the crown of the plant. Its light yellow flowers bear reddish non-prickly fruits.

O. macrorhiza (mak-roe-*rye*-za), big root opuntia, is native to California, Idaho, Louisiana, and Kansas to Texas, and is hardy to Zone 5. It is a low-growing species that forms 4-foot-wide colonies. Its 4-inch-long, 1½-inch-wide rounded joints are bluish green, and its yellow flowers turn orange-centered or red-centered as they age. The oval fruit that follows is reddish purple and reaches 1½ inches long. Variety *pottsii* has joints 2½ inches long and reddish flowers.

O. phaeacantha (fee-a-*kan*-tha), from New Mex- ico, Arizona, and Texas, is hardy to Zone 6. With variable low sprawling habit, it displays round to oval, 4- to 8-inch long, 6-inch-wide, ¾-inch-thick segments. Covered with 1- to 2½-inch-long brown spines, it is well armed. Yet, when covered with its yellow, ofttimes red-based, flowers, or with its su- perb barrel-shaped 1¼-inch-long spineless fruit, it is as attractive as any. Variety *camanchica,* native from Oklahoma to New Mexico, is a low grower with round or oval pads 5 to 7 inches long by 4 inches wide and yellow to orange flowers. It is more tolerant of wetness.

CULTURE / CARE: As one might expect, cacti perform best in full sun, in sandy or gravelly, well-drained soil. They are not particular about pH and seem con- tent in a range of 5.5 to 8.0. Drought tolerance is good, and little or no irrigation is needed once plants are established. Anthracnose rot, charcoal spot, dry rot, fusarium rot, soft rot, stem rot, bacterial rot, and mosaic virus are the common diseases, and cactus fruit gall midge and aphids are the most troublesome pests. Little or no maintenance is required.

PROPAGATION: Segments of the pads that are broken off and laid upon or stuck in moist sand will root in a short period of time. Rooted segments or crown divisions can be dug and transplanted throughout the year. In nature, seed germinates after passing through the digestive tract of animals. Horticultur- ists imitate this by treating seed with concentrated sulfuric acid. Plants are so easily propagated vegeta- tively, however, that seed propagation is seldom practiced.

Origanum dictamnus PLATE 220
Dittany of Crete, Crete Dittany, Hop Marjoram

Dittany of Crete is an interesting subshrubby ground cover that may reach 12 inches tall by 12 inches across. Typically used in smaller areas, espe- cially in rock gardens, it provides both foliar and flo- ral interest and is complimentary to a host of other noninvasive species. No foot traffic is tolerated.

The essential oils of oregano species have antisep- tic properties and thus infusions of their foliage have been used in cleansing wounds. And, because of its fragrant foliage, the foliage and stems of various spe- cies were strewn about the home and used in per- fumes, soaps, and sachets.

SCIENTIFIC NAME: *Origanum dictamnus* (oh-*rig*-a- num / ore-i-*gay*-num dik-*tam*-nus). *Origanum* comes from the Greek *oros,* mountain, and *ganos,* beauty, in reference to the typical origin and appearance of these species and literally means joy (or beauty) of the mountains. *Dictamnus* is simply the Greek name

for this plant and refers to its native habitat, Mount Dikte.

HARDINESS / ORIGIN: Zones 8 to 10; Greece and Crete.

LEAVES / FLOWERS / FRUIT: The simple, oppositely ar- ranged, oval to round, 1-inch-long, 1-inch-wide, woolly, whitish gray-green leaves are attractive as well as aromatic. At the tips of the squarish stems, in late summer and fall, are borne many loose clusters of showy ½-inch-long flowers with purple bracts and pink petals. The fruit that follows is nonornamental.

RATE / SPACING: Growth is moderate. Plants from pint-sized to quart-sized containers are spaced 10 to 12 inches apart.

OTHER SPECIES: *O. laevigatum* (lee-vi-*gay*-tum), meaning smooth leaved, is named for its ⅜-to ½- inch-long, triangular-oval, dark gray-green leaves that are, unusually for this genus, nearly hairless. Hailing from rocky mountainous sites of Asia Minor and Syria, this species is excellent in rock gardens or as a small-scale general cover. It blooms from mid summer until early fall and produces an astounding burst of color with its numerous butterfly-attracting purple flowers. 'Herrenhausen' reaches 15 inches tall and displays young leaves that are suffused with bur- gundy and lavender flowers with deep red-violet bracts.

O. vulgare (vul-*gay*-ree), named from the Latin *vulgaris,* common, is commonly called creeping oregano, dwarf marjoram, or dwarf oregano. Hardy to Zone 4 or 5, it displays a 4-inch-tall, rhizomatous spreading, mat-forming, herbaceous habit. Its leaves are oval to narrowly oval, reach ¾ inch long, are often wavy and somewhat toothed about their edges, and are colored dark green. The dried leaves are commonly used as a culinary seasoning. When flow- ering in late summer, the plant is covered by numer- ous spikelets of flowers with purple bracts and white or purple petals. 'Aureum' is golden-leaved and reaches only 8 inches tall; 'Compacta Nana' has dark green leaves that turn purple in winter.

In ancient Rome, newlyweds wore wreaths of *O. vulgare* as a symbol of their happiness. Greeks, on the other hand, laid oregano leaves beside grave sites to delight the departed. Tea prepared from this spe- cies is said to be a calmative and useful for treating insomnia.

CULTURE / CARE: *Origanum* species perform best in full sun in gritty or gravelly soil that contains suffi- cient leaf mold or peat to maintain moisture but not enough to inhibit drainage. They can take periods of dry weather and are no worse when the soil be- comes a bit dry. On the other hand, they quickly rot in overly saturated soils. Few pest or disease prob- lems seem to effect them. Little maintenance is required, but most gardeners prefer to give plants a hard pruning in early spring to rejuvenate and promote compactness.

PROPAGATION: Cuttings taken from nonflowering stems root well in mid to late summer when treated with 1000 ppm IBA/talc. Division is effective as well and seems most successful in spring.

Orostachys iwarenge   PLATE 221
Soft-leaved Stonecrop

Soft-leaved stonecrop is an unusual 2- to 4-inch-tall succulent for use as a rock garden specimen, accent plant, or small-scale general ground cover. It resembles *Sempervivum* species (hen and chicks) in three ways: its leaves are borne in a rosette; it spreads by plantlets at the tips of its stolonlike branchlets, which arise from the leaf axils; and its flowers are borne on special erect stalks that die back after flowering.

SCIENTIFIC NAME: *Orostachys iwarenge* (ore-oh-*stak*-is eye-wa-*ren*-gee). *Orostachys* comes from the Greek *oros,* mountain, and *stachys,* spike, presumably in reference to the habitat and floral spikes. *Iwarenge* is likely a commemorative.

HARDINESS / ORIGIN: Reliably hardy at least to Zone 6; Japan.

LEAVES / FLOWERS / FRUIT: The leaves, which are arranged in a basal rosette, are evergreen, thick and fleshy, oblong to oval, ½ to 1 inch long by ¼ to ½ inch wide, and colored first grayish green then purplish in fall. The flowers are arranged in spikelike fashion upon erect leafy stems and are borne in mid fall. Each curious flower is five-parted with pale white and light yellowish petals. The fruit is nonornamental.

RATE / SPACING: Growth is moderate to fast. Plants from 2¼- to 3½-inch-diameter containers are spaced 10 to 16 inches apart.

OTHER SPECIES: *O. aggregatum* (ag-ra-*gay*-tum) is similar to *O. iwarenge* but with somewhat larger, pale green foliage.

CULTURE / CARE: *Orostachys* species prefer to be grown in full sun in well-drained, slightly acidic to neutral sandy or loamy soils. Because of their fleshy roots and succulent leaves, they are highly resistant to drought. Crown rot is sometimes encountered, especially in areas of cool, wet springtime weather, or during other seasons if soil drainage is inadequate. Other than aphids, no serious pests have been reported, and little or no maintenance is usually required.

PROPAGATION: The plantlets that form at the tips of the stolons may be removed, placed in a moist medium, and rooted like cuttings; in a couple of weeks roots begin to form, and shortly afterward the plantlets can be transplanted. Simple crown division is also effective throughout the year.

Osmunda   PLATE 222

This genus of durable, tall, strong-growing ferns contains at least three species from North America that may be classified as ground covers. Because they tend to be tall (generally 2½ to 5 feet), they are best suited for use as specimen or accent plants in combination with trees and tall shrubs in naturalized woodland settings. Since they tolerate moisture, they are also of value for lining the banks of streams and ponds. They can also be used in large groups as a general cover to link together trees or as a nice divider between woodlot and perennial border, where they act as a backdrop for lower-growing perennials. No foot traffic is tolerated.

There are a number of myths associated with this genus. Biting the fiddlehead of an *Osmunda* fern was once believed to bring a full year without toothaches, and preparations of royal fern, *O. regalis,* were thought to be very useful in healing injuries, particularly those involving the bones.

SCIENTIFIC NAME: *Osmunda* (os-*mun*-da). There are two possible explanations for the genus name. One theory states that it comes from the Saxon language and means strength, presumably because species of *Osmunda* tend to be tall and robust. A second theory states that it commemorates the Scandinavian god Thor, who was also known as Osmunder.

HARDINESS / ORIGIN: See individual species for hardiness; temperate and tropical regions of eastern Asia and North and South America.

LEAVES / FLOWERS / FRUIT: Osmundas do not produce flowers or fruit but reproduce by spores that are borne in spore cases (sporangia). Among ferns, the osmundas display unusually large deciduous fronds (leaves). With some species, the fronds have special fertile leaflets that bear the spore cases. In others the fertile and sterile fronds are completely separate. So prominent and so unique are the fertile fronds on some species that their shape, color, or arrangement are the source of the common or scientific names.

RATE / SPACING: Growth is slow to moderate. Plants from quart-sized to gallon-sized containers are spaced 2 to 2½ feet apart.

SPECIES: *O. cinnamomea* (sin-a-*moe*-mee-a), meaning cinnamon-like, in reference to the cinnamon-colored fertile fronds that ripen during late spring and look like tall cinnamon sticks, is commonly called cinnamon fern, swamp brake, fiddleheads, or bread root. This 2½- to 5-foot-tall species is erectly oriented and fans out in a vaselike manner. It hails from moist woodlands and swamps from New-foundland to Minnesota south to the Gulf states and New Mexico, and is also found in Mexico, Brazil, the West Indies, and eastern Asia. It is a magnificent, stately fern that is a fine addition to any shady garden from Zones 3 to 9 or 10. Interestingly, it is said to be compatible with black walnut (*Juglans nigra*). The nonspore-forming sterile foliage looks like magnificent light green feathers—up to 5 feet long by 5 to 10 inches wide. The shorter, narrower fertile fronds are markedly different. Each is composed of leaflets that are made up of numerous beadlike sacs, the sporangia, which house the green spores. In time the spores ripen to a cinnamon brown and later, during late spring, are liberated.

O. claytoniana (klay-tone-ee-*aye*-na), named after John Clayton (1686–1773), an American botanist, is commonly called interrupted fern for its fronds which, after the fertile spore-bearing leaflets fall off, are left with a leafless gap or "interruption" in their middle section. From North America and Asia, this species is hardy to Zone 3, reaches 2 to 4 feet tall, spreads 2 feet wide, and displays a nearly erect habit. It is deciduous with light to medium green fronds to 4 feet tall. Composed of numerous narrowly triangular leaflets, the fronds look like giant feathers with a gap in the center. In fall they turn yellow.

O. regalis (ree-*gay*-lis), meaning royal, is commonly called royal fern, buckhorn brake, king's flowering fern, water fern, snake fern, tree fern, ditch fern, bog onion, herb Christopher, Hartshorn bush, or royal osmund. This stately fern is hardy in Zones 2 or 3 to 9. It hails from Europe, while its varieties are found from Canada south to Florida and Missouri as well as tropical America and Africa. It is tall (2 to 6 feet), with fronds emerging in a circular, crownlike manner (hence the name royal fern) from hilly hummocks that often extend more than 2 feet wide. The fronds are locustlike, wine-colored in youth, maturing to a flat deep green to bronzy green. Borne upon forked stalks, they reach 6 to 12 inches long by 2 to 4 inches wide. Each is composed of numerous oblong-oval leaflets. The fertile fronds are a bit shorter and are composed of rounded pinnae that enclose the green spores in beadlike sacs. Upon maturity the spores turn brown, are liberated to the wind, and leave behind shriveled brown sacs. Variety *cristata* reaches 3 to 4 feet tall, with leaflets curled and frilly; var. *gracilis* has bronze-colored leaves; var. *palustris* is only 3½ feet tall, with reddish fronds; 'Purpurascens' is 3 to 6 feet tall, with purple stems; var. *spectabilis* has a more open habit than that of the species.

CULTURE / CARE: Although tolerant of saturated soils, *Osmunda* species are best in acidic, moist, rich soils, and do not cope well with drought. They prefer light to moderate shade, have few problems with disease and insects, and require no maintenance.

PROPAGATION: Division is easily accomplished during spring or fall. Spores can also be used (see Chapter 8).

Osteospermum fruticosum   PLATE 223
Trailing African Daisy, Freeway Daisy

A thick, mat-forming, horizontally spreading, herbaceous ground cover, trailing African daisy reaches 6 to 14 inches tall and spreads 4 or more feet across. Known to many Californians as freeway daisy, this low-growing member of the sunflower family is an excellent general cover or soil stabilizer. Superb for difficult-to-maintain slopes, berms, terraces, and highway embankments, it is almost always used in moderate-sized to large-sized plantings. High salt tolerance allows it to be used near the shore as well as inland. It is also considered to be relatively fire retardant. No foot traffic is tolerated.

SCIENTIFIC NAME: *Osteospermum fruticosum* (ost-ee-oh-*sper*-mum frew-ti-*koe*-sum). *Osteospermum* is derived from the Greek *osteon,* a bone, and *sperma,* seed, likely in reference to the hardness of the seed. *Fruticosum* means shrubby.

HARDINESS / ORIGIN: Zones 9 to 10 or 11; South Africa.

LEAVES / FLOWERS / FRUIT: The gray-green leaves are evergreen, oval to spatula-shaped, 2 inches long by ¾ inch wide, thick, and almost succulent appearing. Abundant 2-inch-wide lilac-purple daisylike flowers carried upon 4-inch-tall upright stems grace the landscape during late fall to early spring. The relatively tiny fruit is nonornamental.

RATE / SPACING: Growth is moderate to fast. Plants from 2¼- to 4-inch-diameter containers are spaced 12 to 20 inches apart.

HORTICULTURAL SELECTIONS: 'African Queen', with leaves deeper green, flowers deep purple, habit similar but somewhat taller than the species; 'Burgundy Mound', with deep purple flowers; 'Snow White' ('White Cloud'), thought to be a hybrid, noteworthy for its showy white flowers in late winter and early spring, somewhat taller and more upright than the species.

CULTURE / CARE: Although trailing African daisy prefers moderately fertile loam, it is adaptable to a wide range of soil types, provided drainage is good. Once established, it becomes very tolerant of drought, yet occasional thorough watering is needed to maintain best summertime appearance. Full sun, or full sun with a little afternoon shade are the best light conditions, and only rarely do serious pest infestations occur. Fungal diseases such as damping off can be prevalent if the soil is poorly drained or if plants are overwatered or exposed to atypically rainy weather. Maintenance consists of trimming back stems as they outgrow their bounds and mowing off dried flowers at the end of the blooming season.

PROPAGATION: Cuttings and division are both simple and effective, and meet with best success during spring, fall, and winter.

Oxalis oregana   PLATE 224

Oregon Oxalis, Redwood Sorrel

Low, herbaceous, and as lush appearing as any moss or fern, Oregon oxalis reaches 10 inches tall and shyly spreads to several feet across. This rhizomatous ground cover, which resembles giant shamrocks, should be considered for use as edging along shaded walkways and as a moderate-scale to large-scale ground cover underneath trees in wooded border settings. It is especially useful in northwestern naturalized gardens and makes a splendid companion to ferns and rhododendrons. No foot traffic is tolerated.

SCIENTIFIC NAME: *Oxalis oregana* (ok-*say*-lis / *oks*-a-lis or-e-*gay*-na). *Oxalis* is derived from the Greek *oxus*, acid, and alludes to the sharp, acid taste of the leaves of many species. *Oregana* means from Oregon.

HARDINESS / ORIGIN: Moist coastal areas of Zones 7 to 10; Pacific Northwest coastal areas.

LEAVES / FLOWERS / FRUIT: The giant cloverlike leaves reach 4 inches across and are held horizontally atop thin 6- to 8-inch-long stems. Each is composed of three broadly heart-shaped, 1½-inch-long medium green leaflets. The solitary pink, rose, or white, five-petaled, springtime flowers are also borne atop wiry 6-inch stems. With luck, they bloom again (although less profusely) during autumn. The fruit that follows is nonornamental.

RATE / SPACING: Growth is slow. Plants from 2- to 4-inch-diameter containers are spaced 10 to 14 inches apart.

OTHER SPECIES: *O.* 'Iron Cross', iron cross false shamrock, is hardy in Zones 7 to 10 and reaches 12 inches tall. Thought to be of hybrid origin, it blooms with light pink flowers and forms clumps of green leaves which are purple-colored in the inner corner of the four leaflets—thus forming the four corners of the cross.

O. regnelii (reg-*nell*-ee-eye), false shamrock, is hardy in Zones 7 to 10. It is 8 inches tall and bears white flowers in spring and summer atop vibrant green leaves of four leaflets, each with three lobes. 'Purpurea' has deep purple leaves with lighter purple centers and pink flowers; 'Triangularis', purple leaf

false shamrock, reaches 8 inches tall and is noteworthy for its deep velvety purple leaves that are topped by light pink flowers in summer.

CULTURE / CARE: Oregon oxalis and its relatives require organically rich, moderately acidic soil. They should be kept moist at all times and should be planted in a moderate to densely shaded location that is sheltered from strong drying winds. If grown in too much sun the leaflets droop and stay folded up much of the time as a means of conserving water. Serious pests are seldom encountered, but diseases such as beet curly top virus, seed smut, root rot, and leaf spot may appear. Little or no maintenance is required.

PROPAGATION: Division of clumps is effective in spring or fall, if watered until the roots become well established.

Pachysandra terminalis   PLATE 225

Japanese Spurge, Japanese Pachysandra

Pachysandra is among the most popular ground covers in use today, and for good reasons. It thrives in a broad geographic range, seldom encounters serious pest or disease problems, and once it fills in, it can be relied upon for many years of maintenance-free service. It is an evergreen semiwoody subshrub that spreads indefinitely by underground stems and reaches 6 to 12 inches tall. In the landscape it should be employed on a moderate to large scale. It thrives underneath trees, around shrubs, near walkways, and around building foundations. Excellent shrub companions are rhododendrons, pieris, azaleas, photinias, and dwarf conifers, and tree companions include serviceberry, dogwood, redbud, Japanese maple, purple-leaved plum, oaks, maples, and witch hazel. For a lovely infusion of tranquilizing lushness, try interplanting pachysandra with hostas, or cinnamon, lady, and royal ferns.

SCIENTIFIC NAME: *Pachysandra terminalis* (pak-i-*san*-dra ter-mi-*nay*-lis). *Pachysandra* comes from the Greek *pachys*, thick, and *andros*, masculine, and refers to the thick stamens (male flower parts). *Terminalis* implies that the flowers are borne terminally (at the ends of the stems).

HARDINESS / ORIGIN: Zones 4 to 7 or 8; Japan.

LEAVES / FLOWERS / FRUIT: The leaves are more or less oval-shaped, 2 to 4 inches long by ½ to 1½ inches wide, and shiny medium green year-round. The pleasantly fragrant, short-lived, spikelike, white flowers are borne in profusion during spring. Occasionally they give rise to white berries in fall, but this is not the norm since cross-pollination is required, and usually the plants are all genetically identical and are not capable of cross-pollination.

RATE / SPACING: Growth is slow. Plants from 2- to 3-

inch-diameter containers are spaced 6 to 10 inches apart.

HORTICULTURAL SELECTIONS: 'Cabbage Leaf', with larger, medium green, scallop-edged leaves; 'Cutleaf', with deeply toothed medium green leaves; 'Green Carpet', more compact and slower spreading with somewhat broader leaves that are a darker and shinier green; 'Green Sheen', more tolerant of heat, slow spreading with smaller, very glossy (like plastic), dark green leaves; 'Kingwood', with prominent teeth about the leaf margins; 'Variegata', with creamy white and green leaves.

OTHER SPECIES: *P. axillaris* (ak-si-*lay*-ris), named for its flowers that are borne in the axils of the leaves, is hardy in Zones 5 to 7. A relatively rare species, it is an evergreen, rhizomatous, herbaceous, 8- to 12-inch-tall Asian native. Its foliage is colored a medium shiny green, and its slightly sweet-smelling tiny white flowers are formed during mid spring. By summer, round green fruit forms, and by fall it ripens to bright crimson. Plants spread at a slow pace and should be spaced 4 to 8 inches apart from 3- to 4-inch-diameter pots. This species is much like *P. stylosa,* also of Asian origin, which displays slightly broader leaves and slightly lower habit.

P. procumbens (pro-*kum*-benz), Allegheny pachysandra, is hardy in Zones 5 to 7 or 8 and is an American native with semievergreen foliage and a clump-forming habit. Its foliage is deciduous, roughened, and bronzy in fall. In bloom, it is similar to *P. terminalis* but malodorous. The fruit, a purplish capsule, is formed low on the stem and often is obscured by the foliage. 'Forest Green' displays smaller leaves with consistent mottling. Although *P. procumbens* is a splendid plant, its use is minimal in comparison to its Japanese cousin. I have successfully cross bred *P. terminalis* and *P. procumbens* and, although the resultant plant is still unnamed, it is evergreen (like *P. terminalis*) and has leaves like those of *P. procumbens.*

CULTURE / CARE: Pachysandras grow in well-drained acidic loamy soil and require additional water only during periods of extreme heat and drought. They are best in light to dense shade. Pests include slugs, mites, scales, nematodes, and aphids. Occasionally the leaves become infected with leaf blight, which in the South can at times be serious. No maintenance is required.

PROPAGATION: Cuttings root year-round. Division is best performed during the spring or fall.

Panicum virgatum PLATE 226
Switch Grass, Wild Red Top, Thatch Grass, Wobsqua Grass, Black Bent Grass

Increasingly popular, this versatile and widely distributed North American native is a superb choice for moderate-scale to large-scale massing, where its attractive foliage and wispy flowers lend interest throughout the year. Durable, moisture-tolerant and drought-tolerant, this shy-creeping broad clump former reaches 3 to 6 feet tall with flowers ascending to 4 or 7 feet. Ranging from upright to vase-shaped and from 3 to 4 feet wide, switch grass is excellent for erosion control in moist or dry sites and combines nicely with other ornamental grasses—especially natives, such as little blue stem (*Schizachyrium scoparium*), big blue stem (*Andropogon gerardii*), Indian grass (*Sorghastrum nutans*), and floriferous fall bloomers, such as showy sedum (*Sedum spectabile*), Russian sage (*Perovskia atriplicifolia*), bluebeard (*Caryopteris* × *clandonensis*), and goldenrod species (*Solidago*).

SCIENTIFIC NAME: *Panicum virgatum* (*pan*-i-kum vir-*gay*-tum). *Panicum* is the Latin name for millet, and *virgatum,* wandlike, refers to the flowers.

HARDINESS / ORIGIN: Zone 5 to 11; moist and dry soils of tall grass prairies and dunes of central and eastern North America from Maine to Saskatchewan southward to Florida and Arizona; also native to Costa Rica and the West Indies.

LEAVES / FLOWERS / FRUIT: Smooth, flat, 1/3 to 1/2 inch wide by 18 to 24 inches long, the deep green to gray-green or blue-green leaves often pick up tones of purple to wine-red during fall. Above them, beginning during mid summer, are borne airy open panicles of florets that are first pinkish, purplish, or silvery, maturing to grayish white or brown. Persisting well into winter, they produce a small grain that is eaten by birds during the winter months.

HORTICULTURAL SELECTIONS: 'Cloud Nine', very large, for use on a large scale or as a specimen, 7 to 8 feet tall, with light blue foliage topped with wispy golden fallborne flowers; 'Haense Herms', red switch grass, with compact upright habit, 3 to 3½ feet tall, bright red-orange fall color; 'Heavy Metal', popular, upright growing, 3 to 3½ feet tall, with steel blue leaves and bright yellow fall color; 'Pathfinder', 4 to 5 feet tall, with feathery open panicles and orange-yellow fall color; ''Rehbraun', meaning deer red, 3 to 4 feet tall, with soft reddish brown fall color; 'Rotstrahlbusch', meaning red rays, has the brightest red fall color of all the switch grasses; 'Squaw', 3 to 4 feet tall, with red fall color; 'Strictum', an early bloomer with tall upright habit and blue-green leaves; 'Warrior', a tall selection with reddish brown fall color.

RATE / SPACING: Growth rate is moderate to relatively fast. Plants from 1- to 2-gallon-sized containers are spaced 3 to 4 feet apart.

CULTURE / CARE: Switch grass grows well in a broad range of soil types, from moist to very dry, sand to clay, and acidic to slightly alkaline. It tolerates light shade, where it may flower somewhat less, but is at its best in full sun. Drought and salt tolerance are excellent. Aside from leaf spot and grasshoppers, it has few disease and pest problems.

PROPAGATION: Seed germinates rapidly and in high percentages. Cultivars are best propagated by division during spring.

Parthenocissus quinquefolia   PLATE 227
Virginia Creeper, Woodbine, American Ivy, Five-leaved Ivy

This woody, creeping native vine, when unsupported, makes a handsome, rather coarse-textured ground cover. It reaches 3 to 8 inches tall without support and spreads indefinitely. Regardless of season, it is primarily attractive for its foliage, which is lustrous blue-green during summer and scarlet during early fall. Indeed, its fall color is so early and so bright, that Virginia creeper is considered the standard harbinger of autumn. It is best suited for use on a moderate to large scale. It spreads quickly, shows little respect for artificial boundaries, and is especially good on shady slopes for erosion control. It also exhibits a fair degree of tolerance to salt spray and is said to be tolerant of growing under black walnut (*Juglans nigra*). Should your Virginia creeper begin to climb, do not panic! In most cases it does not harm trees but instead enhances their appearance, especially in autumn when it turns red. Eastern kingbird, pileated woodpecker, the great crested flycatcher, brown thrasher, American robin, chickadees, and scarlet tanagers are attracted to the fruit. No foot traffic is tolerated.

SCIENTIFIC NAME: *Parthenocissus quinquefolia* (par-thin-oh-*sis*-us kwin-kwe-*foe*-lee-a). *Parthenocissus* likely comes from the Greek *parthenos,* a virgin, and *kissas,* ivy, referring to the common name Virginia creeper. *Quinquefolia,* five-leaved, refers to the five leaflets that compose each leaf.

HARDINESS / ORIGIN: Zones 3 to 9; woodlands of eastern United States.

LEAVES / FLOWERS / FRUIT: Waxy bronze to reddish in youth, the large five-parted deciduous leaves mature to bluish green then become intensely reddish purple to crimson in early fall. Each is elliptic to oval, measures up to 6 inches long by 2½ inches wide, and is edged with prominent coarse teeth. The tiny five-parted, relatively nonornamental flowers of early to mid summer are colored greenish white and, for the most part, are obscured by the foliage. The ¼-inch-wide, berrylike, clustered fruit that follows is first green then bluish black and is most effective in fall, as it persists after the foliage has dropped.

RATE / SPACING: Growth is fast. Plants from gallon-sized containers are spaced 2½ to 3½ feet apart.

HORTICULTURAL SELECTIONS: 'Engelmannii' (often listed as var. *engelmannii*), with leaflets smaller than the species; 'Saint Paulii' (often listed as var. *saint paulii*), with smaller leaflets that are hairy below, said to display a greater ability to cling than the species.

OTHER SPECIES: *P. henryana* (hen-ree-*ah*-na), silvervein creeper, a Chinese species discovered by the Irish plant collector, dendrologist, and medical man Augustine Henry (1857–1930) in 1885, is hardy to Zone 8. Noteworthy for its smaller 4-inch-wide leaves that are bright red in youth, strikingly dark green with silvery white venation (if grown in shade) at maturity, then bright red in fall, it differs from *P. quinquefolia* in that it is slower growing and not a very strong climber.

P. inserta (in-*ser*-ta), hardy to Zone 2, is another North American native and looks like *P. quinquefolia* but lacks adhesive discs at the end of its tendrils.

P. thomsonii (tom-*son*-ee-eye), of China to the Himalayas, is much like *P. henryana* but hardy to Zone 7 with smaller leaflets that lack the silvery venation.

CULTURE / CARE: *Parthenocissus* species grow successfully in both heavy (high clay content) and light soils (those which are predominantly composed of sand or gravel). Good drainage, however, is essential, and soil pH should range from acidic to neutral. These species display moderate tolerance to drought, and mid summer is about the only time they are likely to need supplemental watering. Acceptable light conditions vary from full sun to moderate shade, but light to moderate shade is best. Pests include beetles, leaf hoppers, several types of scales, aphids, and mites. Diseases such as canker of the stems, downy mildew, leaf spots, powdery mildew, wilt, anthracnose, blight, and root rot may at times prove problematic yet are seldom serious. The only maintenance need that might arise is an occasional trimming back of the leading stems as they outgrow their bounds.

PROPAGATION: Cuttings root quickly and easily during early summer. Divisions are best made during spring or summer. Seed should be sown in fall for germination the next spring.

Paxistima canbyi   PLATE 228
Canby Ratstripper, Cliff Green, Mountain Lover, Canby Paxistima

Often sought after but unfortunately seldom offered for sale (because it is very difficult to grow in a container), Canby ratstripper is a dense growing, 8- to 12-inch-tall, spreading (sometimes to more than 10 feet across), woody ground cover. It combines well with rhododendrons, pieris, and azaleas, and works best as a moderate-scale general cover or specimen plant. No foot traffic is tolerated.

SCIENTIFIC NAME: *Paxistima canbyi* (paks-*i*-sti-ma *kan*-bee-eye). *Paxistima* comes from the Greek *pachys,* thick, and *stigma,* the female reproductive apparatus, in reference to the thick stigmas of plants within this genus. *Canbyi,* commemorates William Marriot Canby (1831–1904), who discovered this species.

HARDINESS / ORIGIN: Zones 4 or 5 to 6 or 7; eastern North America in the central Appalachian Mountains.

LEAVES / FLOWERS / FRUIT: The narrow, evergreen, coarse-textured, leathery, dark green, 1-inch-long leaves reach up to ³⁄₁₆ inch wide and turn coppery green during fall. The flowers, which are tiny and greenish to reddish, are borne during late spring but are hardly noticeable. The fruit, a white leathery capsule, is also very small and nonornamental.

RATE / SPACING: Growth is slow to moderate. Plants from quart-sized to gallon-sized containers are spaced 12 to 24 inches apart.

OTHER SPECIES: **P. myrsinites** (mur-sin-*eye*-teez) is named for its foliage which resembles that of *Myrtus,* or myrtle, a genus of evergreen trees and shrubs, and is commonly called myrtle paxistima, Oregon paxistima, or Oregon boxwood. It hails from the western coast of North America from British Columbia to California. Hardy in Zones 5 to 7, it reaches 1½ feet tall, spreads to 3 feet across, and bears evergreen, oval to oblong, 1¼-inch-long, dark shiny green, leathery, tooth-edged leaves. Its flowers and fruit, like those of *P. canbyi,* are nonornamental.

CULTURE / CARE: *Paxistima* species need well-drained acidic soils and tolerate infertility and moderate periods of drought. They prefer full sun to light shade. Their most common problems are fungal leaf spot and root rot. Scale insects and mites also, at times, are problematic. Little or no maintenance is required.

PROPAGATION: Cuttings taken during summer or fall are best rooted in a mixture of one part peat and one part perlite or sand; they are aided by treatment with 3000 ppm IBA/talc, and care must be taken to insure that the medium does not become overly saturated.

Pelargonium peltatum　　　　PLATE 229
Ivy Geranium, Trailing Geranium, Hanging Geranium

Known to northern gardeners as a colorfully florific annual for hanging baskets, ivy geranium is, in warm climates, an effective herbaceous perennial ground cover for use as a general cover on sloping banks or atop retaining walls. In such locations it is brought up close to eye level so that its graceful trailing stems and beautiful flowers can easily be appreciated. It reaches 16 to 26 inches tall and spreads more than 3 feet across. It is normally used on a small to moderate scale. Because of its succulent nature, it does not tolerate foot traffic.

One common gardening myth is that planting *Pelargonium* species helps to repel Japanese beetles and other garden insects. Even if it is ineffective at repelling beetles, planting pelargoniums brings the enjoyment of this lovely species to the garden. The genus is very large with about 280 species, undoubtedly some with as-yet-unsung merit as ground covers. One such group are the scented geraniums. These are the species sold in garden centers as potted herbs. They are amazing in that their rubbed foliage gives off scents that range from chocolate-mint to rose to lemon to pineapple. As with trailing geranium, the scented geraniums are native to South Africa. When dried, they are excellent in sachets and potpourris. They have also been utilized in toilet waters, ointments, teas, and recipes. A few are described below.

SCIENTIFIC NAME: *Pelargonium peltatum* (pel-are-*goe*-nee-um pel-*tay*-tum). *Pelargonium* comes from the Greek *pelargos,* a stork, and refers to the resemblance of the seed heads to the head and beak of a stork. *Peltatum,* shieldlike, refers to the shape of the leaves.

HARDINESS / ORIGIN: Zones 9 to 11; South Africa.

LEAVES / FLOWERS / FRUIT: The leaves are evergreen and shield-shaped with a broadly oval to round outline and five shallowly cut, pointed lobes. The leaves reach 2 to 3 inches long and wide, are leathery, succulent, and colored light to medium shiny green. The flowers, which are striking, are arranged in clusters of five to seven, have five petals, and are rose-carmine to white with dark veins. Flowering occurs continually from late winter to early fall (provided the soil is kept moist). The fruit that follows is nonornamental.

RATE / SPACING: Growth is fast. Plants from pint-sized to gallon-sized containers are spaced 1½ to 2½ feet apart.

HORTICULTURAL SELECTIONS: There are numerous horticultural selections. Among the most common are 'Charles Monselet', with red flowers; 'Charles Turner', with rose-pink flowers; 'Comtesse Degrey', with salmon-pink flowers; 'Giant Lavender', with lavender flowers and red marks; 'Jeanne d'Arc', with lavender flowers and dark striping; 'L'Elegante', flowers pink, leaves variegated green and white; 'Riga', with numerous rose-pink flowers; 'Sugar Baby', with compact habit and rose-pink flowers; 'Tavira', with numerous bright red flowers.

OTHER SPECIES: **P. crispum** (*kris*-pum) has small crinkled foliage with a pleasant lemon fragrance. It reaches 3 feet tall and has lavender flowers. Several cultivars have been selected.

P. denticulatum (den-tik-you-*lay*-tum) is pine-scented, reaches 12 inches tall, and has a compact habit with deeply incised foliage and pink or lilac flowers.

P. × *fragans* (*fray*-ganz) is nutmeg-scented, 1 foot tall, gray-foliaged, and white-flowered. It is the result of a cross involving *P. exstipulatum* and *P. odoratissimum.*

P. grossularioides (gross-*you*-lair-ee-oy-deez) is coconut-scented and has dark green foliage and magenta flowers.

P. mellissinum (mee-*lis*-i-num) is lemon-scented. Its upper petals are white suffused with red, while the lower petals are white only.

P. nervosum (ner-*voe*-sum) is lime-scented and has lavender flowers.

P. odoratissimum (oh-der-a-*tis*-i-mum) is apple-scented, has velvety foliage and white flowers, and is 1½ feet tall.

P. tomentosum (toe-men-*toe*-sum) is intensely mint-scented, has velvety foliage and white flowers, and is 3 feet tall.

CULTURE / CARE: Geraniums need well-drained soils yet are not picky about texture or pH. Every effort should be made to keep the soil constantly moist; failure to do so impairs the floral display and may even stop it. Geraniums prefer full sun with partial afternoon shade. Pest problems include aphids, caterpillars, moths, mealybugs, weevils, whitefly, termites, nematodes, slugs, scales, and mites. Diseases of greatest prevalence are bacterial and fungal leaf spots, crown gall, stem rot, flower blight, root rot, and viral infections that cause leaf curl, wilt, and mosaic. Maintenance consists of trimming back branches as they outgrow their bounds.

PROPAGATION: Stem cuttings root easily any time of year. Seed, which may be obtained commercially, germinates well at 70°F.

Peltiphyllum peltatum   PLATE 230
Umbrella Plant

One of the most unusual ground covers, umbrella plant displays the curious trait of flowering, rather showily, before the leaves emerge. Its extraordinary foliage is nothing to slight either. Umbrella plant spreads 6 feet or more, and thus is clearly not a plant for the small garden. Rather, it is a plant for use at waterside along the bank of a stream, pond, lake, or reflecting pool. It combines well with large clump-forming, moisture-tolerant grasses like Japanese silver grass (*Miscanthus sinensis* and its larger cultivars), the magnificent moisture-loving 5-foot-tall rush

Scirpus cyperinus (commonly called wool grass), as well as the yellow flag iris (*Iris pseudacorus*). No foot traffic is tolerated.

SCIENTIFIC NAME: *Peltiphyllum peltatum* (pel-ti-*fill*-um pel-*tay*-tum). *Peltiphyllum* comes from the Greek *pelte*, a shield, and *phyllon*, a leaf, in reference to the shape of the leaves. *Peltatum*, peltate (shield-shaped), simply reiterates this.

HARDINESS / ORIGIN: Zones 5 to 7; mountains of northern California, north to southwestern Oregon.

LEAVES / FLOWERS / FRUIT: The magnificent, long, round, deep green, hairy-stalked leaves are tooth-edged and range from 6 to 18 inches wide. They are coarse-textured, deeply lobed, and during fall turn beautiful shades of bronze. The flowers are carried atop rough-haired, round, succulent, 3- to 6-foot tall stems in spring. Each flower is ½ inch wide, pink to white, and arranged in many-flowered, stalk-ending, round-topped clusters. Attractive before and after the leaves unfurl, they are enchanting as they wave above the soil or water atop their leafless stems. The fruit that follows is nonornamental.

RATE / SPACING: Growth is moderate to fast. Plants from 2- to 3-gallon-sized containers are spaced 3 to 4 feet apart.

HORTICULTURAL SELECTIONS: Var. *nana,* only 12 to 18 inches tall.

CULTURE / CARE: Umbrella plant needs a cool, moist to wet location and is not tolerant of drought. Plants will be larger in rich soil, but are adaptable to soil texture and pH. They prefer light to moderate shade, but can be grown in the sun where they remain shorter and more compact. Pests and diseases are insignificant. Little maintenance is required.

PROPAGATION: Plants are easily divided from late spring to fall. Seed, available commercially, is also said to be effective.

Pennisetum alopecuroides   PLATE 231
Fountain Grass, Chinese Fountain Grass

Reaching 2½ to 3½ feet tall and spreading about the same across, fountain grass is a graceful, loosely tufted, erect-stemmed ornamental grass. Even though it has been widely accepted as a specimen ornamental grass, it is not often considered for use as a ground cover. Nonetheless, mass plantings are exceptionally attractive for use in foundation facings, bordering walkways, and for accent. They are also superb companions to such popular fall bloomers as *Sedum* 'Autumn Joy', *S.* 'Brilliant', *Caryopteris* species and cultivars, Russian sage (*Perovskia*) cultivars, and cultivars of the lovely Japanese silver grass (*Miscanthus*).

SCIENTIFIC NAME: *Pennisetum alopecuroides* (pen-i-

see-tum al-low-pek-you-*roy*-deez). *Pennisetum* is derived from the Latin *penna,* a feather, and *seta,* a bristle, in reference to the feathery bristles that are attached to the floral spikelets. *Alopecuroides* means resembling *Alopecurus* (the foxtails), a genus of grasses from the North Temperate Zone.

HARDINESS / ORIGIN: Zones 5 to 9; Asia.

LEAVES / FLOWERS / FRUIT: The deciduous, lance-shaped, medium green leaves reach 6 inches long by ¼ inch wide, are tapered to a fine point, and arise from erect stems. In time they arch over giving a fountainlike appearance, and in fall they turn brown. The purplish flowers, which poke through the center of the foliage mass during late summer and fall, are arranged in bristly spikes. As they fade they become brown, then tan, and persist well into the winter.

RATE / SPACING: Growth is moderate. Plants from quart-sized to gallon-sized containers are spaced 1½ to 2 feet apart.

HORTICULTURAL SELECTIONS: 'Cassian', leaves only 10 inches tall; var. *compressum,* 2 to 3 feet tall, with arching habit and white flowers; 'Hameln', 1½ to 2½ feet tall, with coppery-tan flowers; 'Herbstzauber' (autumn sorcery fountain grass), somewhat smaller than the species at 15 to 30 inches tall; 'Japonicum', sometimes listed as species *P. japonicum,* the largest fountain grass, 4 to 5 feet tall; 'Little Bunny', a perfectly named "cute" selection, only 12 inches tall when in flower; 'Moudry', late-blooming with dark purplish black flowers and very broad dark green leaves; 'National Arboretum', reaching 2 feet tall, with dark flowers and sharply pointed slender leaves; 'Purpurea', with purple-black inflorescences on 2-foot-tall stems in early fall; var. *viridescens,* 2 feet tall, with vibrant green foliage; 'Weserbergland', a dwarf similar to 'Hameln' but a bit lighter green and broader spreading.

OTHER SPECIES: *P. caudatum* (caw-*day*-tum), white-flowering fountain grass, is sometimes considered a variety of *P. alopecuroides.* Hardy in Zones 6 to 9, it is native to eastern Asian open meadows and streamsides. It blooms earlier than *P. alopecuroides,* with white flowers that fade to tan. It reaches 3 to 3½ feet tall with flower spikes held 1 to 1½ feet above its deciduous foliage that turns brown and persists through winter.

P. incomptum (in-*comp*-tum), meadow fountain grass, is hardy in Zones 6 to 9 and hails from open woodlands and moist slopes of northeastern China to the Himalayas. Unlike the other species, it spreads aggressively to colonize large areas. It reaches 2 to 3 feet tall and is clothed with bluish green (brownish yellow to tan in fall) leaves that are 12 to 18 inches long by ¼ to ⅜ inch wide. During late spring the flowers, first purplish pink then creamy white, arise in cylindrical spikes and are held well above the foliage to give a pleasing show right through fall and into winter. This species is especially good for large-scale use as a general cover or erosion controller in utility areas such as along roadways, in parks, and around golf course ponds.

P. orientale (or-ee-en-*tale*-ee), Oriental fountain grass, is hardy in Zones 7 to 9 and originated in meadows and woodland clearings of central Asia to the Caucasus region and northern and western India. Like *P. alopecuroides* it is a clump former. Its leaves are shiny bluish green (yellow-brown in fall), are from 4 to 8 inches long, and are held on arching stems to a height of 12 to 18 inches. The flowers, borne during late spring or early summer, are open and airy with a silky soft texture. First they are violet-pink, then mature to creamy light brown, remaining this way through winter.

P. setaceum (se-*tay*-see-um), named for its flower spikes (the specific epithet means bristlelike), is commonly called rose fountain grass. It hails from Ethiopia, is hardy in Zones 7 to 10, reaches 2 to 3½ feet tall, and spreads about the same across. Its medium green leaves, like those of *P. alopecuroides,* are deciduous, lance-shaped, narrow (only ⅛ inch wide), and originate from erect stems. With age, they, too, gracefully arch over in a fountainlike array. The flowers are showy, arranged in spikelike fashion in inflorescences that nod downward and reach 14 inches long. Prominently bristled, they are colored pink to purplish, and give their outstanding show during fall. Cultivars include 'Atrosanguineum', with purple flower spikes and foliage, robust form, wide dark purple leaves, broad inflorescences that may reach as high as 5 feet; 'Cupreum', with coppery-colored spikes and reddish foliage; 'Rubrum', with rosy spikes and purplish foliage, 2 to 3 feet tall; 'Rubrum Compactum', about 1½ to 2 feet tall, with rosy spikes and light purple foliage.

CULTURE / CARE: The fountain grasses grow best in rich, well-drained, acidic loam. Although they can tolerate moderate periods of drought, ideally the soil should be maintained in a slightly moistened condition. A little shelter from strong drying winds is recommended, and full sun to light shade is preferred. Few disease problems occur, and the only maintenance that is needed is an annual trimming back during late winter or early spring.

PROPAGATION: Division of clumps in spring, summer, or fall is effective. This is the only manner in which cultivars should be propagated as they may not come true from seed. For the species, seed germinates readily and matures very rapidly. I haven't found a time of year in which it isn't successful. Commercial supplies are available.

Penstemon pinifolius
PLATE 232

Pineleaf Penstemon, Creeping Red Penstemon, Pineleaf Beard Tongue

A sprawling, low, subshrubby ground cover, pineleaf penstemon ranges from 4 to 12 inches tall, spreads more than 1½ feet across, and attracts hummingbirds with its bright red tubular flowers. This interesting species is excellent in hot, low-rainfall areas. It is resilient, colorful, and functions well as a general cover and soil stabilizer on flat and sloping terrain. Consider using pineleaf penstemon also as a border edging, accent plant, or rock garden specimen. No foot traffic is tolerated.

SCIENTIFIC NAME: *Penstemon pinifolius* (pen-*stee*-min / *pen*-ste-min / pen-*stay*-mon pie-ni-*foe*-lee-us). *Penstemon* comes from the Greek *pente,* five, and *stemon,* stamen, a reference to the flowers which have five stamens (male flower parts). *Pinifolius* implies that the leaves are like those of a pine.

HARDINESS / ORIGIN: Zones 2 or 3 to 9 or 10; mountainous regions of southwestern New Mexico, southeastern Arizona, and adjoining Mexico.

LEAVES / FLOWERS / FRUIT: Mostly evergreen, the simple ¾-inch-long, needlelike leaves are crowded, oppositely arranged, and colored medium green. The numerous reddish flowers are five-parted, trumpet-shaped, 1½ inches long, yellow-bearded (due to stamens), and effective throughout summer. The tiny fruit is many seeded and nonornamental.

RATE / SPACING: Growth is slow to moderate. Plants from pint-sized to quart-sized containers are spaced 10 to 14 inches apart.

HORTICULTURAL SELECTIONS: 'Mersea Yellow', 6 inches tall by 18 inches wide with yellow flowers.

OTHER SPECIES: **P. fructicosus** var. **scouleri** (frew-ti-*koe*-sus *skow*-ler-eye), shrubby penstemon, of British Columbia to Idaho, is hardy to Zone 6. It is a woody-based, herbaceous-stemmed spreader that ranges from 12 to 14 inches tall and makes an attractive mat of leathery deep green foliage. It has toothed-edged or smooth-edged, 2-inch-long semievergreen leaves that vary from lance-shaped to elliptic and bears lavender-blue (rarely purple) flowers during early summer. 'Albus', with white flowers during summer; 'Purple Gem', only 3 to 6 inches tall, with violet-purple flowers in late spring or early summer; 'Red Cultivar', with rose-purple flowers in late spring or early summer; 'Six Hills', with fuchsia-pink flowers in spring.

CULTURE / CARE: Best in full sun, these species of *Penstemon* prefer moisture-retentive (due to some organic matter), gritty soils with excellent drainage. *Penstemon pinifolius* prefers a neutral pH, while *P. fructicosus* needs acidic soil. Both species tolerate heat and drought fairly well. Leaf spot, rusts, mildew, and crown rot, especially if soil drainage is inadequate, are sometimes problematic. The most common pests are root and stem nematodes. Some gardeners shear their plants lightly in spring to promote compactness and neatness.

PROPAGATION: Stem tip cuttings are best taken in spring, treated with 1000 to 3000 ppm IBA/talc, and given a modest amount of bottom heat; as soon as the cuttings become rooted, reduce the amount of moisture or they will rot. Commercial supplies of seed are also available and germinability is said to be good.

Peperomia
PLATE 233

Trailing, fleshy, herbaceous perennials, peperomias are right at home as ground covers in tropical landscapes. Usually they are employed on a moderate to large scale as general covers or pathway edgers, but they are also excellent in elevated planters and around the trunks of trees as facing.

SCIENTIFIC NAME: *Peperomia* (pep-er-*oh*-mee-a) is derived from the Greek *piperi,* pepper, and *homoios,* similar, referring to the foliage which is similar to that of the pepper plant.

HARDINESS / ORIGIN: Zones 10 to 11; tropical and subtropical areas throughout the world.

LEAVES / FLOWERS / FRUIT: The leaves are arranged in alternate, opposite, or whorled fashion. Normally they are simple, unlobed, prominently veined, and fleshy. The flowers are small, stemless, and arranged in narrow upright spikes.

RATE / SPACING: Growth is moderate to fast. Plants from quart-sized to gallon-sized containers are spaced 12 to 16 inches apart.

SPECIES: **P. argyreia** (ar-ji-*ree*-a), named from the Latin *argyreia,* silvery, in reference to the foliage, is commonly called Sander's peperomia, watermelon peperomia, or watermelon begonia. It is a leafy, succulent, colorful herb that reaches 6 to 12 inches tall and spreads more than 1½ feet wide. Hailing from the tropics of South America, it is often used as a house plant in the North. The evergreen leaves, held upon short red stems, are arranged in near-rosette-like fashion. Individually, they are simple, round to oval, and 3 to 5½ inches long by 2½ to 4 inches wide. Their edges are smooth, the ends pointed, the surface somewhat roughened, and they are dark green in color with gray striping between their 9 to 11 prominent veins. The flowers that arise above the mass of foliage are tiny and individually almost imperceptible. Together, however, they are arranged in clusters of elongate spikes. The fruit is nonornamental.

P. arifolia (air-i-*foe*-lee-a) is similar to *P. argyreia* except that it has all-green leaves and its flower spikes are borne on longer stems.

P. obtusifolia (ob-toos-e-*foe*-lee-a), meaning blunt-leaved, in reference to the rounded ends of the leaves, is commonly called oval-leaf peperomia, baby rubber plant, American rubber plant, or pepper face. Native to southern Florida and tropical America, it is 6 to 12 inches tall by more than 3 feet wide. The evergreen, alternately arranged leaves, borne on reddish fleshy stems, are spatula-shaped, oval, 5 to 8 inches long by 2 to 3 inches wide, smooth-edged, round-ended, and dark green. They serve as a lush backdrop to the tiny flowers that are borne upon solitary or paired 6-inch-long upright spikes. The fruit is nonornamental. Horticultural selections include 'Alba', new leaves whitish yellow with bright red markings; 'Albo-marginata' ('Silver Edge'), with gray-green leaves and white edges; 'Albo-marginata Minima', similar to 'Albo-marginata' but smaller in all respects; 'Minima', with leaves that reach only 1½ to 2 inches long; 'Variegata', leaves with a central gray-green blotch and creamy white edges.

CULTURE / CARE: Peperomias are best in light-textured, moderately fertile, slightly acidic, well-drained loamy soil. They are not greatly tolerant of drought, thus they should be placed where they are sheltered from drying winds, and the soil should be kept slightly moist with supplemental watering during periods of little rainfall. They prefer light to moderate shade. The most common diseases are anthracnose, root rot, crown rot, ring spot virus, and corky scab. Their main predators are nematodes. Little maintenance is required, but occasionally stems might have to be clipped back as plants outgrow their bounds.

PROPAGATION: Stem cuttings are easily rooted and may be aided with treatment of 500 to 1000 ppm IBA/talc. Division of crowns and rooted stem sections is equally effective and is best carried out during fall, winter, or early spring.

Pernettya mucronata   PLATE 234
Chilean Pernettya

Good for edging paths or for moderate-scale facing near building entrances, this low-growing, horizontally spreading (by underground stems) shrublet is one of the more colorful ground covers. Typically, it ranges in height from 18 to 36 inches and spreads to more than 3 feet across. In addition to being used for edging and foundation planting, it works well as a border around swimming pools and ponds and along the banks of streams. Its primary merit is its exquisite display of colorful but poisonous fruit. Its

foliage and flowers, also poisonous, are quite pleasant as well. No foot traffic is tolerated.

Ingestion of the fruit has been associated with such symptoms as burning in the mouth, diarrhea, headache, weakness, and cardiac distress. Severe cases have resulted in coma or even death.

SCIENTIFIC NAME: *Pernettya mucronata* (per-*net*-ee-a mew-kro-*nay*-ta). *Pernettya* is named for Antoine Joseph Pernetty (1716–1801), an author of a book about the Falkland Islands. *Mucronata* comes from mucronate and refers to the leaves which end in a point.

HARDINESS / ORIGIN: Zones 6 or 7; Chile and Argentina.

LEAVES / FLOWERS / FRUIT: The shiny, prominently veined, deep green leaves are evergreen, oval to elongate, ¾ inch long by ⅜ inch wide, with somewhat toothed edges and pointed tips. Fall color is bronzy green. The flowers are solitary, ¼ inch long, white to pink, and effective during spring and summer. The outstanding fruits are ½-inch-wide, shiny, almost metallic-appearing, variously colored white to red or lilac globes. Long-lasting, they radiate their vibrant colors from fall until the following spring. Different cultivars must be present to ensure fruit production as cross-pollination is required.

RATE / SPACING: Growth is moderate. Plants from 1- to 2-gallon-sized containers are spaced 2 to 2½ feet apart.

HORTICULTURAL SELECTIONS: The selections differ in the color and size of their fruit. Some of the most popular are 'Alba', white fruit slightly pink-tinged; 'Cherry Ripe', big, bright, cherry red fruit; 'Coccinea', scarlet fruit; 'Davis's Hybrids,' a group of hybrids characterized by large and variously colored fruit; 'Dwarf Form', a dwarf only 1 foot high by 3 feet wide; 'Lilacina', lilac-purple fruit; 'Pink Pearl', lilac-pink fruit; 'Purpurea', violet-purple fruit; 'Rosie', red young stems, dark green leaves, pinkish rose fruit larger than the species; 'Sea Shell', pinkish fruit ripening to rose; 'White Pearl', medium to large shiny white fruit.

OTHER SPECIES: *P. tasmanica* (tas-*man*-i-ka), Tasmanian pernettya, is low and creeping, ranges from 2 to 6 inches tall, and is hardy to Zone 7. The leathery leaves are evergreen, ⁵⁄₁₆ inch long, oblong, somewhat toothed around the edges, and colored bright green. The white flowers appear during early summer and yield ⅜-inch-wide bright red fruit.

CULTURE / CARE: Pernettyas are best in acidic, loamy, well-drained soil. They are able to tolerate short periods of drought, but achieve their best appearance when the soil is kept moist. In very hot climates plants should be placed in a location that is shaded in the afternoon. In climates that are more temperate, full sun to light shade is best. There are no serious pests or diseases. Maintenance consists of an occasional light shearing if plants become too lanky.

PROPAGATION: Cuttings and division both work quite well and, for best results, should be practiced during the cooler months of the year.

Perovskia atriplicifolia   PLATE 235
Russian Sage

Reaching as high as 4 or 5 feet tall and spreading to 4 feet across, Russian sage is a large-scale ground cover that fills a valuable niche as a backdrop or accent plant for use on a moderate to large scale. It is particularly stunning when planted in broad drifts and performs best in areas of hot summer weather. Thus, in July and August, when many plants fade and languish, Russian sage starts to look good, and it stays looking good until fall's first hard frost. It is excellent in the background of *Coreopsis rosea* and *C. verticillata* cultivars as well as shasta daisy (*Chrysanthemum × maximum*), white and pink forms of purple coneflower (*Echinacea purpurea*), and dwarf forms of fountain grass (*Pennisetum alopecuroides*). It makes a wonderful companion next to orange coneflower (*Rudbeckia fulgida*) or white boltonia (*Boltonia asteroides*), and is superb in front of Japanese silver grass (*Miscanthus sinensis* and cultivars) as well as numerous other tall grasses. It is tough, reliable, and long-lived, and offers unparalleled mid to late season color. About the only thing it does not do is tolerate foot traffic.

SCIENTIFIC NAME: *Perovskia atriplicifolia* (pe-*rof*-skee-a a-tri-plis-i-*foe*-lee-a). *Perovskia* commemorates the Russian General V. A. Perovski (1794–c. 1857). *Atriplicifolia* means that the leaves are like those of *Atriplex*, salt-bush.

HARDINESS / ORIGIN: Zones 5 to 9; Afghanistan to Tibet.

LEAVES / FLOWERS / FRUIT: The silky-hair-covered bluish gray-green leaves range from 1 to 2½ inches long by ½ to 1 inch wide. Borne upon stiff square silvery-gray stems, the pleasantly aromatic (like menthol) leaves are elongate, lanceolate to narrowly oval, sparsely toothed, and prominently wavy along their edges. As the stems ascend they give rise to oppositely paired side shoots that in turn bear numerous whorls of tiny, two-lipped, purplish blue, mintlike flowers from mid summer to fall. The tiny fruit is nonornamental.

RATE / SPACING: Growth is slow, by short rhizomes. Plants from 1- to 2-gallon-sized containers are spaced 2 to 2½ feet apart.

HORTICULTURAL SELECTIONS: 'Blue Haze', with paler blue flowers and leaves nearly without teeth; 'Blue Mist', a bit earlier blooming with lighter blue flowers; 'Blue Spire', with deep violet-blue flowers and deeply cut foliage; 'Filigran', with finely divided lacy textured leaves and lavender-blue flowers; 'Longin', said to be of hybrid origin, more upright than the species, resists flopping or blowing over, which can sometimes occur late in the season.

OTHER SPECIES: *P. abrotanoides* (a-broe-ta-*noy*-deez), Caspian perovskia, is hardy to Zone 5 and native from Turkestan to northeastern Iran. It is more branched than *P. atriplicifolia*, reaches 3 to 4 feet tall, and displays deeply once-dissected or twice-dissected (nearly to the midrib) leaves and deeper blue flowers. Sometimes the cultivars I have listed under *P. atriplicifolia* are considered the result of hybridization with *P. abrotanoides*.

P. artemesioides (ar-tay-*mis*-ee-oy-deez), from southeastern Iran to northern Pakistan, reaches 3 feet tall with oval 1¼-inch-long deeply cut leaves. Its flowers are purplish blue in summer.

CULTURE / CARE: Russian sage is best in acidic to neutral, well-drained soils. It is more compact and less prone to flopping over in heavy winds when grown in light-textured soils of lower fertility. It prefers full sun, is quite tolerant of drought, and needs little maintenance. Most gardeners find that it looks best if pruned back to a height of 12 inches after the first hard frost in fall or to the live growth the following spring.

PROPAGATION: Cuttings should be treated with 3000 ppm IBA/talc and stuck in a porous medium during early summer. Division is best performed during spring. Seed is also available and is said to germinate readily.

Persicaria filiformis   PLATE 236
Virginia Knotweed

Formerly known as *Tovara virginica* or *Polygonum filiforme*, this native herb from eastern North America is uncommon in cultivation. Even so, it has spawned two extraordinary ground covering cultivars: 'Painter's Palette' and 'Variegata'. Both are colorful and interesting in woodland gardens, and both are rhizomatous spreading ground covers suitable for general use on a moderate to large scale. No foot traffic is tolerated.

SCIENTIFIC NAME: *Persicaria filiformis* (*per*-si-kare-ee-a fil-i-*form*-is). *Persicaria*, the Medieval name for knotweed, comes from *Persica*, peach, and refers to the shape of the leaves. *Filiformis*, threadlike, likely describes the thin floral spikes.

HARDINESS / ORIGIN: Zones 4 to 7/8; eastern and central United States, eastern Canada, and Japan.

LEAVES / FLOWERS / FRUIT: The deciduous oval to elliptic leaves range from 4 to 8 inches long. The tiny red flowers, borne from summer to early fall, are held on thin, upright to arching, slender spikes.

RATE / SPACING: Growth is moderate. Plants from pint-sized to gallon-sized containers are spaced 12 to 18 inches apart.

HORTICULTURAL SELECTIONS: 'Painter's Palette', with leaves mottled creamy white and green and brightly marked with a deep maroon V-shaped overlay; 'Variegata', with leaves marbled creamy white and green.

OTHER SPECIES: *P. affinis* (a-*fin*-is), meaning kindred or allied (that is, related to some other species), is commonly called Himalayan fleece flower (formerly listed as *Polygonum affine*). It is a remarkable general cover for small-sized to moderate-sized areas and is attractive both in bloom (which may be for six full months) and when out of bloom. It is more than effective for use as a facing to south or west sides of open deciduous or evergreen shrubs and small trees, and it receives high marks when planted alone in raised beds surrounded by turf. It tolerates very infrequent foot traffic, but is happier when not trod upon. It is a pretty but not always tough ground cover (needs moderate temperatures, good fertility, and plenty of water), but what it lacks in endurance, it more than makes up in charm. Characteristically, it is a mat-forming, erect-leaved, horizontally stemmed, herbaceous, trailing ground cover that reaches 4 to 6 inches tall and spreads to more than 4 feet wide. Its leaves, which may reach 4 inches long by 1 inch wide, are deciduous, narrowly oblong with finely toothed edges, and colored dark to medium green during the growing season. With the onset of fall they become rusty red, and with the first few hard frosts change to brown. The thousands of tiny, faintly fragrant flowers are arranged in dense, erect, 3-inch-long, narrow, pokerlike spikes on sparsely leafy, 1- to 1½-foot-tall upright stems. To state it mildly, the flowers are attractive, and their varied patterns of pinkish, white, and rose from early summer to mid autumn are simply charming. The fruit, on the other hand, is not ornamental. Growth is moderate. Plants from 2½- to 4-inch-diameter containers are spaced 10 to 16 inches apart. Although this species is considered to be hardy to Zone 3, occasionally in Zone 5 or 6 it has difficulties with growing prematurely in early spring and then being killed back by late frost. Usually recovery is complete, but it may take more than one season to repair all the damage. Some popular horticultural selections include 'Border Jewel', similar to the species, but with larger foliage and blooming spring to fall; 'Darjeeling Red', with flowers predominately dark pink, from early summer through fall; 'Donald Lowndes', with flowers bright pink and quite showy.

P. bistortum (bis-*tore*-tum), a medieval Latin name meaning twice twisted, from *bis,* twice, and *tortus,* twisted, refers to the contorted appearance of the rhizomes. Formerly listed as *Polygonum bistorta* and commonly called snakeweed or simply bistort, this attractively foliaged, clump-forming, showily flowered herbaceous ground cover reaches 1½ to 2 feet tall and displays oblong to oval, large, shiny green leaves that for the most part arise from the base of the plant. During late spring and extending through late summer, erect flower stalks emerge from the mass of foliage to give rise to sizable spikes of tiny pink and white florets. Bistort is hardy in Zones 4 to 8, hails from Europe and Asia, and is useful in many of the same situations as *P. affinis.* The magnificent flowers of 'Superbum' reach 2 to 3 feet tall and bloom even more profusely than those of the species. Historically, the medicinal applications of bistort were numerous. It is high in tannins, is an astringent and anticoagulant, and has been a component of skin cleansers and mouth washes as well as a treatment for diarrhea. In Shakespearean times, the juice of bistort was applied as a treatment for nasal polyps. Today, tender leaves are occasionally used in green salads and are sometimes used in soups. Roasted or dried and ground into flour, the starchy rhizomes have provided sustenance during times of famine. In parts of England the dried rhizome was consumed in a pudding as it was thought to aid in conception and prevent miscarriages.

P. capitatum (ka-pi-*tay*-tum), pinkhead knotweed, is a mat-forming herbaceous Himalayan native hardy in Zones 7 to 10. Like other *Persicaria* species, it was formerly classified as a species of *Polygonum.* It reaches 3 to 6 inches tall, spreads indefinitely, grows at a fast pace, and should be spaced 8 to 12 inches apart from 2- to 3-inch-diameter containers. Its semievergreen foliage, which reaches 1½ inches long by ¾ inch wide, is colored bronzy purplish red and acts as a colorful backdrop to the springtime pink, ball-shaped clusters of tiny flowers.

P. vacciniifolia (vak-*sin*-i-foe-lee-a), blueberry-leaved fleece flower, is splendid. A low trailing herbaceous species from the Himalayas, it is hardy to Zone 6 or 7, blooms during late summer and fall with bright pink flowers, and is clothed in attractive glossy green elliptic deciduous leaves.

CULTURE / CARE: *Persicaria* species prefer rich, moisture-retentive soil, shelter from strong winds, and regular watering. They grow well in light to moderate shade and have few disease problems, but are occasionally hampered by aphids. Maintenance needs are few if any.

PROPAGATION: Cultivars of *P. filiformis* tend to come true from seed and thus are often propagated sexually. Stem cuttings of all species and cultivars also work during early summer. Division is easily accomplished any time the soil can be kept moist.

Petasites   PLATE 237
Butterbur, Lagwort

These stemless, robust, perniciously rhizomatous, rhubarblike herbaceous perennials from Asia, Europe, and North America command a great deal of attention for their unusual flowers and foliage. Clearly they are not suitable for every garden, particularly in consideration of their robustness and the ever-shrinking dimensions of the average residential lot. But for the privileged few who are fortunate enough to be surrounded by vast expanses of land, with moist wooded terrain, butterburs might be considered as large-scale backdrops for woodland border plantings. Alternatively, of course, they may be surrounded with a deep edging and used on a smaller scale. This is certainly worth the effort with *P. japonicas* 'Gigantus'.

When planted along streams and ponds, the fleshy pink or black, aggressively spreading root systems of *Petasites* species help stabilize banks and impart a bold, near-tropical richness to the landscape. Once established, however, plants are difficult to eradicate. Their tenacity and dense canopy excludes all smaller plants and, therefore, just the right site must be selected. Choose a place where they will not interfere with herbs or small shrubs and combine them only with trees and large shrubs. No foot traffic is tolerated.

The name butterbur comes from the historic use of the leaves as a protective wrap for butter. Lagwort refers to the late emergence of the leaves, which lag behind the flowers in the spring. Colt's foot and a variety of other names such as butterdock, bladderdock, umbrella plant, bog rhubarb, langwort, capdockin, flapperdock, and bogshorns are also at times applied to *Petasites* species.

Petasites species have important medical applications. *Petasites hybridus* is reported to contain such compounds as inulin, helianthenine, tannic acid, petasitine, petasine, and petasin. Its dried rhizomes, flowers, and leaves have been used for diuretic, expectorant, antispasmodic, menstrual, cardiological, and dermatological applications. Since the Middle Ages this species has been used as an anticonvulsive and a febrifuge. Some people have claimed that preparations of *Petasites* eradicate intestinal worms, alleviate asthma, and cure back pains. Because of these many uses, the common name plague flower has sometimes been applied. Young leaves, stalks, and flowers of the Eurasian species are used as veg-

etables by the Japanese and reportedly are quite tasty. Because of their characteristics of early and prominent flowering, butterburs are sometimes planted near beehives to lure bees in as soon as possible in springtime.

SCIENTIFIC NAME: *Petasites* (pe-ta-*sy*-teez) comes from the Greek *petasos,* hat, referring to the large leaves.

HARDINESS / ORIGIN: See individual species for hardiness; North Temperate Zone.

LEAVES / FLOWERS / FRUIT: The flowers are arranged in predominantly single-sexed heads that in turn are held singularly or numerously in clusters upon stout stalks that stick up through the bare earth (or emerge concurrently with the leaves) during early spring. The flower heads are usually white or purple and, when fertile, contain mostly female flowers. The sterile flower heads, on the other hand, are composed of bisexual disc and female ray flowers, both of which are sterile. The tiny cylindrical fruit is nonornamental.

RATE / SPACING: Growth is very fast. Plants from 1- to 5-gallon-sized containers are spaced 2 to 4 feet apart.

SPECIES: *P. albus* (*al*-bus), meaning white, either in reference to the flowers or the white woolly tomentum on the underside of the foliage, is commonly called white butterbur. Native to European and western Asia, it is hardy to Zone 5 and reaches 12 inches tall with the flower stem elongating to 30 inches after blooming. It spreads indefinitely. The flowers appear in late winter to early spring and are followed by round to broadly heart-shaped leaves that are white-woolly at first, later woolly only on the undersides, simple, arising from the rootstock, and edged with conspicuous teeth. The whitish flower clusters occur on 6- to 12-inch-tall stalks with many lance-shaped bracts.

P. fragans (*fray*-grans), winter heliotrope or sweet-scented colt's foot, hails from the Mediterranean region. It is hardy to Zone 7, reaches 6 to 10 inches tall, and spreads indefinitely. The matte green leaves are deciduous to semievergreen, simple, kidney-shaped to heart-shaped, and 5 inches wide. Arising from the rootstalk with or shortly after the flowers, they are edged with small teeth, are hairless above, and begin to unfurl during (or slightly after) full bloom. The lilac, pinkish, or whitish flowers, which are arranged in dense clusters atop ½- to 1½-foot-stalks, are vanilla-scented and effective from late winter to early spring.

P. hybridus (*hy*-brid-us), named to imply hybrid origin but arguably a misnomer (as botanists argue that this plant does not appear to be a hybrid), is commonly called bog rhubarb, butterfly dock, hybrid butterbur, or common butterbur. Some authorities list it as *P. vulgaris* or *P. officinalis*. It is a robust, rhizomatous, 2- to 4-foot-tall, large-leaved, Eurasian, indefinite-spreading ground cover hardy in Zones 4 to 8. Its deciduous, simple, medium green, stout-stalked, heart-shaped to kidney-shaped leaves are enormous and may reach 3 feet wide. Toothed along their edges, they are hairless and come up from the rootstalk shortly after the unusual springtime flowers. The purple flowers, which are carried atop stout clublike spikes, upon thick hollow stalks, arise from the ground during late winter—often through the snow.

P. japonicus (ja-*pon*-i-kus), meaning of Japan, in reference to its native habitat, is commonly called Japanese butterbur. It is hardy in Zones 4 to 9, reaches 3 to 4 feet tall, spreads indefinitely (is less invasive than *P. hybridus*), and displays deciduous, simple, thick-stalked, kidney-shaped to heart-shaped, 3½- to 4-foot-wide, irregularly toothed, green leaves. Its fragrant white to purplish disk-shaped flowers, held upon stalks to 18 inches tall, are effective from late winter to early spring. 'Giganteus', 5 to 6 feet tall with leaves to 4 or 5 feet wide, is a bit faster spreading than the species.

LESS COMMON SPECIES: As is often the case, the exotic species of a genus are more commonly cultivated than the natives. In the case of *Petasites,* there are a number of native species that can be grown for the same purposes as the exotics. *Petasites palmata,* named for its leaves that are shaped like a hand, is commonly called palmate sweet colt's foot, and hails from northeastern and midwestern North America. *Petasites sagittata,* arrowleaf sweet colt's foot, comes from northwestern North America. *Petasites trigonophylla,* Arctic sweet colt's foot, hails from Quebec, Saskatchewan, and Minnesota.

CULTURE / CARE: *Petasites* species prefer moist, organically rich, boggy soil, but seem to adapt easily to typically drier ordinary garden soils with an acidic to alkaline pH. Most wilt rather easily, but when watered, recover almost as fast. Light to moderate shade is best and little or no maintenance is required.

PROPAGATION: Simple division is successful from spring through fall.

Phalaris arundinacea 'Picta'   PLATE 238
Variegated Ribbon Grass, Gardener's Garters, Variegated Reed Canary Grass

This colorful, ground-covering, horizontally spreading, upright-stemmed grass spreads with a vengeance. Knowing this, keep in mind that to safely use ribbon grass, it must be given lots of space or surrounded by a deep edging, house foundation, sidewalk, or driveway. In such places it can be effectively used as a cheery, light-colored edging, facing, or general cover. Use it on a moderate to large scale as it reaches 2 to 3 feet tall and spreads wherever there is open ground. It can be used safely and effectively for erosion control along stream banks, on open slopes, and in ditches. Infrequent foot traffic is tolerated.

SCIENTIFIC NAME: *Phalaris arundinacea* 'Picta' (*fal*-a-ris / fa-*lare*-is a-run-di-*nay*-see-a *pik*-ta). *Phalaris* is an ancient Greek name, possibly from *phalaros,* shining, referring to the polished seeds. Another source says that it is simply a Greek name for this grass. *Arundinacea* comes from Latin *arundo,* reedlike. 'Picta' means painted, referring to the leaves.

HARDINESS / ORIGIN: Zone 3; the all-green-leaved species hails from the North Temperate Zone. Plain green and weedy looking, it is not cultivated.

LEAVES / FLOWERS / FRUIT: The long, narrow, typically grasslike, deciduous leaves reach 6 to 12 inches long by ½ to ¾ inch across. They are rough to the touch, striped lengthwise with white and green, and often contain hints of purplish red or yellow. When grown in dry conditions, the bottom leaves often turn brown. The flowers are borne in narrow clusters during summer, but are of limited ornamental significance. The fruit also is nonornamental.

RATE / SPACING: Growth is fast. Plants from pint-sized to 1-gallon-sized containers are spaced 14 to 24 inches apart.

HORTICULTURAL SELECTIONS: 'Dwarf Garters', reaching only 12 to 15 inches tall, slow spreading, leaves with green and white stripes tinged pink in spring; 'Feesey's Form', leaves with green and white stripes that emerge with strong tints of pink during spring, reaching 1½ to 2½ feet tall; 'Luteo-Picta', golden ribbon grass, leaves with yellow and green stripes as they emerge in spring, later becoming white and green, 1½ to 2½ feet tall; 'Tricolor', with pink, white, and green striping during spring, later becoming white and green, 1½ to 2 feet tall.

CULTURE / CARE: Ribbon grass adapts to most soil types, but growth is slower and more dense (both often desirable) if grown in heavy clay or sandy soils. If grown in moist, rich loam, the plantings often open up and become extremely vigorous, and the leaves may lose much of their variegation. Soil fertility, regardless of soil type, is best kept low. Ribbon grass prefers full sun to moderate shade. It has no serious pests or diseases. Plantings that become top heavy and topple over should be mowed with a rotary mower to cause them to resprout vibrant and new.

PROPAGATION: Division is simple and effective throughout the growing season, provided the soil is kept moist until the root system becomes reestablished.

Phlox   PLATE 239

Although most people immediately think of moss pink (*P. subulata*) whenever anyone mentions phlox, there are other species that work well as ground covers. Generally speaking, they are useful in rock gardens as specimens, as edging along the foreground of perennial borders, paths, or walkways, or as general covers for small areas. Often they work well as a facing to the sunny side of a low hedge or as accent plants when tucked into the cracks of a retaining wall. Wildlife gardeners value phlox for its ability to attract hummingbirds and butterflies.

SCIENTIFIC NAME: *Phlox* (*floks*) gets its name from the Greek *phlox*, a flame, in reference to the brightly colored flowers.

HARDINESS / ORIGIN: See individual species for hardiness; North America, with one species from Siberia.

LEAVES / FLOWERS / FRUIT: The leaves vary considerably depending on the species. They range from deciduous to evergreen and narrow, almost grasslike, to broad and rounded. What they all have in common, however, is that their basal leaves are oppositely arranged and their upper leaves may be either opposite or alternate. The vibrant five-lobed flowers, borne alone or in groups, originate from the ends of the branches. Depending upon the species and variety, they may be white, pink, red, rose, violet, or blue. The tiny fruit is nonornamental.

RATE / SPACING: Growth is moderate. Plants from pint-sized to quart-sized containers are spaced 10 to 12 inches apart.

SPECIES: *P. divaricata* (die-vare-i-*kay*-ta), named from the Latin *divaricatus,* to spread apart or branch off, in reference to its sprawling habit, is commonly called wild blue phlox or wild sweet William. It is native to the eastern United States (as well as the Midwest), is hardy to Zone 3, and is characterized by a semiwoody, low-spreading, mat-forming habit from 8 to 12 inches tall by 18 to 36 inches wide. Its leaves are oval to oblong, to 2 inches long, and colored dark green. The showy, trumpet-shaped pale violet-blue to lavender flowers are slightly fragrant, reach 1 inch across, and are borne from mid spring to early summer. Watering should be frequent enough to maintain soil in a slightly moistened condition, and plants should receive full sun to moderate shade. The species makes a nice accent plant when mixed with lower covers such as periwinkle (*Vinca minor*). There are many attractive cultivars: 'Dirigo Ice', with pale blue flowers, height to 10 inches; 'Fullers White', with white flowers, reportedly more tolerant of shade than the species; subsp.

lamphamii, with fragrant lavender-blue flowers that have more-rounded petals and oval leaves, more vigorous, with a longer flowering period than the species; subsp. *lamphamii* f. *candida,* similar to subsp. *lamphamii* but with white flowers; 'Louisiana', with early purple-blue flowers and magenta centers.

P. 'Frondosa', from the cross between *P. stolonifera* and *P. subulata,* is hardy to Zone 3, reaches 6 inches tall, and displays rose-red flowers.

P. nivalis (nie-*vay*-lis), trailing phlox, is hardy in Zones 6 to 9 and is a horizontally spreading, semiwoody, 12-inch-tall, 18-inch-wide ground cover. It is clothed in narrow, green, ½-inch-long leaves and is graced during early summer with purple to pink or white flowers. It is native to the eastern United States from Virginia to Florida. Growth is moderate, and plants are spaced 10 to 12 inches apart. Best growth occurs when the soil is kept moist and the light conditions range from full sun to light shade. 'Eco Brilliant', flowers with mauve centers; 'Eco Flirtie Eyes', flowers with white centers.

P. 'Perfection', from the cross between *P. stolonifera* and *P. subulata,* has pink flowers.

P. × *procumbens* (pro-*kum*-benz), named for its procumbent (trailing horizontally without rooting) habit of growth, is commonly called hybrid phlox or trailing phlox. A semiwoody, mat-forming ground cover that is hardy to Zone 5, this species is the result of a cross between *P. stolonifera* and *P. subulata.* Reaching 10 to 12 inches tall and spreading 12 to 18 inches across, it displays elliptic to lance-shaped, 1-inch-long, evergreen leaves. Its flowers are bright purple, ¾ inch wide, and effective in mid to late spring. It is best when its soil is only slightly moist and allowed to dry somewhat between infrequent deep watering. It prefers full sun to light shade. 'Millstream Variety' has rose-pink flowers with blue streaks, and 'Variegata' has leaves edged in creamy yellow and grows to 6 inches tall.

P. stolonifera (sto-lon-*if*-er-a), named for its stoloniferous habit (i.e., it spreads by above-ground, plantlet-bearing, leafy horizontal stems), is commonly called creeping phlox. A low, mat-forming, trailing, semiwoody ground cover, it reaches 6 to 12 inches tall and spreads indefinitely. It is native to the eastern part of the United States from Pennsylvania to Georgia and hardy northward to Zone 3. Its evergreen attractive spatula-shaped to oval leaves are colored dark green and reach only 1 inch long. The trumpet-shaped, purple or violet, 1-inch-wide flowers are effective mid to late spring. The species is best in organically rich acidic to neutral loam. It is not notably tolerant to drought, so the soil should be kept moist with regular watering. It prefers light to moderate shade. Var. *alba*, white flowers with golden centers; 'Blue Ridge', bluish lilac flowers; 'Bruce's White', white flowers with yellow centers; 'Iridescens', blue and mauve flowers; 'Light Pink', large pale pink flowers; 'Pink Ridge', mauve-pink flowers on 6-inch-tall stems; 'Porter's Purple', dark purple flowers; 'Sherwood Purple', fragrant purplish blue flowers on 6-inch-tall stems; 'Violet Queen', dark reddish violet flowers.

P. subulata (sub-you-*lay*-ta), named in Latin for its awl-shaped leaves, is commonly called moss pink, ground pink, mountain phlox, and moss phlox. The most common of the cultivated phloxes, it is a low, mosslike, mat-forming, semiwoody ground cover that reaches 4 to 6 inches tall and spreads to 2 feet across. Hardy in Zones 3 to 9, it hails from sandy woodlands of New York to North Carolina and is most greatly appreciated for its astounding floral show during mid to late spring. Thousands of five-parted, trumpet-shaped, red-purple to violet-purple, pink, or white, ¾-inch-wide flowers burst forth in such masses so as to completely obscure the foliage. Shy by comparison, its narrow, sharply pointed, evergreen, light green to gray-green leaves reach only 1 inch long. This species is adaptable to most well-drained soils, whether acidic or alkaline. It tolerates gravelly soils, is not bothered by moderate drought, and grows in full sun. There are many cultivars, some of the favorites being 'Alba', with white flowers; 'Alexander's Surprise', with pink flowers; 'Alexander's Wild Rose', with deep rose-pink flowers; 'Atropurpurea', with rose-purple flowers and a crimson ring; 'Blue Emerald', with blue flowers, compact habit; 'Blue Hills', with sky blue flowers; 'Brilliant', with magenta flowers; 'Chuckles', with pink flowers; 'Crimson Beauty', with bright red flowers; 'Daniel's Cushion', with magenta-pink flowers and leaves that remain vibrant green throughout the season; 'Emerald Cushion', with pink flowers, smaller in habit; 'Emerald Pink', with pink flowers, compact habit; 'Exquisite', with orchid-pink flowers; 'Laura', with shell-pink flowers; 'Millstream Daphne', with pink flowers and yellow centers, vigorous growth, compact habit; 'Millstream Jupiter', with blue flowers and yellow centers, compact habit; 'Profusion', with white flowers and red centers; 'Red Wings', with red flowers; 'Rosea', with rose-pink flowers; 'Scarlet Flame', with scarlet flowers, vigorous growth; 'Sneewittchen', with pure white flowers, dwarf habit, 3 inches tall by 9 inches wide; 'White Delight', with pure white, large, profuse flowers.

P. '**Vivid**', from the cross between *P. stolonifera* and *P. subulata*, has deep reddish pink flowers.

CULTURE / CARE: Phloxes tend to prefer sandy, well-drained, acidic to neutral loamy soils, although *P. subulata* is said to tolerate alkaline soils. Their pests include beetles, scales, wireworms, two-spotted mite, bulb and stem nematode, stalk borer, and aster leafhopper. Diseases such as leaf spots, powdery mildew, rusts, crown rot, stem blight, and bacterial crown gall are of greatest significance. To maintain phlox, some gardeners prefer to shear or mow it following bloom to promote a neat, compact habit. Division every three years is often performed to rejuvenate and increase flowering, and only slow-release fertilizers are recommended as the roots are shallow and tend to be damaged by rapid changes in fertility levels.
PROPAGATION: Cuttings are typically rooted during the summer. Division is best performed during spring or early fall. Seed germinates in three or four weeks at 70°F.

Phyla nodiflora   PLATE 240
Creeping Lippia, Frog Fruit, Garden Lippia, Mat Grass, Cape Weed, Turkey Tangle

This creeping herbaceous ground cover and former member of the genus *Lippia* is a strong stoloniferous spreader that tolerates considerable foot traffic and quickly covers the ground. In the landscape it is commonly utilized as a lawn substitute on a moderate to large scale. It reaches 1 to 2 inches tall in full sun and 3 to 6 inches in the shade and seems to do very well around ponds, pools, and even in rock gardens. It tolerates salt spray and airborne salt and therefore is valuable to coastal gardeners.
SCIENTIFIC NAME: *Phyla nodiflora* (*fie*-la noe-di-*floe*-ra). *Phyla* is Greek for tribe; here it likely refers to the flowers, which are borne in groups. *Nodiflora* refers to the nodes (joints) of the stems as the point of origin of the flowers.
HARDINESS / ORIGIN: Zones 9 to 10; South America.
LEAVES / FLOWERS / FRUIT: The evergreen, oppositely arranged, simple, grayish to medium green, spatula-shaped leaves are toothed, 1¾ inches long by ¼ inch wide, and covered with coarse hairs. The small flowers, which arise from spring to fall in dense ½-inch-wide heads, are colored white or lilac. The fruit is nonornamental.
RATE / SPACING: Growth is fast. Rooted stolon segments, small pieces of sod, or plants from small containers are spaced 8 to 12 inches apart.
HORTICULTURAL SELECTIONS: Var. *canescens,* flowers lilac-colored with yellow throats; var. *rosea* ('Rosea'), flowers rose-colored.
CULTURE / CARE: Creeping lippia grows well in almost any well-drained soil. It is tolerant of drought but gladly accepts an occasional deep drink of water during the summer. It prefers full sun to moderate shade. Its main pest problem is nematodes. Maintenance can be as little or as much as one cares to pro-

vide. Should a low height and compact habit be your objective, then mow it just as you would a turf lawn. Otherwise, let it creep about naturally.

PROPAGATION: Division may be practiced with great success from late fall to early spring.

Picea abies   PLATE 241
Norway Spruce

Although Norway spruce is a tall (100- to 150-foot) evergreen, needle-leaved tree, over the years numerous mutations have led to varieties that reach only 1 to 2 feet tall and spread 3 to 5 feet across. These variations make splendid specimen and accent ground covers, contributing an extravagant flair to rock gardens and terraced slopes as mounded specimens or as cascading living waterfalls over the side of retaining walls. Along walkways they can be used as low-maintenance dwarf hedges, and if combined with dwarf forms of pine, juniper, cedar, and false cypress (*Chamaecyparis*), they act as vital components in the formation of an interesting theme garden of dwarf conifers.

SCIENTIFIC NAME: *Picea abies* (*pie*-see-a *aye*-beez). *Picea* is the Latin name for a pitch-producing pine; it comes from *pix*, pitch, and refers to the viscous sap of spruce trees. *Abies* is Latin for the silver fir.

HARDINESS / ORIGIN: Zones 2 to 7; northern and central Europe.

LEAVES / FLOWERS / FRUIT: The needlelike evergreen leaves are ½ to 1 inch long, medium green, and sharply pointed. The flowers, like those of many conifers, are barely noticeable, but the fruit that follows is a 4- to 6-inch-long, 1½- to 2-inch-wide, light brown cone. Much of the time, however, the cultivars, are sterile and do not form cones.

RATE / SPACING: Growth is slow. Plants from 1- to 2-gallon-sized containers are spaced 3 to 4 feet apart.

HORTICULTURAL SELECTIONS: 'Nidiformis' (bird's nest spruce), dense, low-growing, medium green leaves, 2 to 4 feet tall by 5 feet wide, with center sometimes opening up to form a nest (hence the common name); 'Pendula', with gracefully pendulous branches and sprawling habit; 'Procumbens', flat-topped, with compact growth, medium green leaves, 2 to 3 feet tall, horizontally spreading and mounded habit; 'Pseudoprostrata', medium green leaves, somewhat rare, a nice specimen, 8 to 12 inches tall by 6 to 8 feet wide; 'Repens', compact and wide spreading, slightly mounded, 2 feet tall by more than 5 feet across, with medium green needles.

OTHER SPECIES: *P. pungens* (*pun*-jenz) is named from the Latin *pungens*, pointed, which either refers to the sharp points or the sharp taste of its rigid bluish or silvery-white needles, and is commonly called Col-orado spruce. It hails from the southwestern United States, is hardy in Zones 2 to 7, and like *P. abies*, is a tall (100 to 130 feet) evergreen, needle-leaved tree. Its cultivar 'Glauca Pendula' is a strikingly silvery-blue-green, 1- to 2-foot-tall, broad-spreading (to more than 10 feet), weeping form useful as a ground cover. Similar and maybe the same plant are 'Glauca Procumbens' and 'Glauca Prostrata'.

CULTURE / CARE: Ground-covering spruces grow best in well-drained, acidic, loamy soils. Like most plants they are at their finest if their soil is kept moderately moist. Even so, they tolerate considerable drought and prefer full sun. Diseases of greatest prevalence are canker, needle casts, rusts, and wood decay. Pests include aphids, budworms, scales, needle miners, weevils, mites, and bagworms. Little or no care is required.

PROPAGATION: Cuttings are best taken in November or December and treated with 8000 ppm IBA/talc and bottom heat of 65 to 70°F. Late wintertime grafting is sometimes practiced as well; use a 2- or 3-year-old seedling of the parent species as the root stock and graft a branch of the desired cultivar on top.

Pilea   PLATE 242

This genus of 250 species of tropical and warm-temperate herbaceous annuals and perennials in the nettle family contains at least three distinctive perennial ground covers. Described below, they are foliaceous, fleshy, and robust.

SCIENTIFIC NAME: *Pilea* (*pie*-lee-a) comes from the Latin *pileus*, a felt cap, in reference to the sepals (leaflike appendages) which cover the fruit like a cap.

HARDINESS / ORIGIN: Zones 10 to 11; tropics and warm temperate areas.

LEAVES / FLOWERS / FRUIT: The leaves typically are attached by short stalks and oppositely arranged—those of each pair often of different size. They may be toothed about their edges or entire. The flowers are tiny, single-sexed, and borne in clusters that may contain one or both sexes of flowers. The tiny fruit which follows is nonornamental.

RATE / SPACING: See individual species.

SPECIES: *P. cadierei* (ka-dee-*aye*-ree-eye), named to commemorate R. P. Cadiere, who collected the species in its native habitat, Vietnam, in 1938, is commonly called aluminum plant or watermelon pilea. Hardy in Zones 10 to 11, it reaches 12 to 18 inches tall, spreads 2 or more feet wide, is fleshy, herbaceous, and laxly upright. Growth is fast. Plants from quart-sized to gallon-sized containers are spaced 1 to 2 feet apart. In the landscape, this species is prized for its colorful foliage, which allows it to excel as a facing to taller, dark-green-foliaged herbs, shrubs, and trees.

No foot traffic is tolerated. The evergreen, succulent, oppositely arranged, and oval leaves reach 3 inches long, are pointed at their tips, colored green with interrupted bands of silvery-gray along their margins and middles, and are edged with rounded teeth. The tiny greenish summertime flowers are arranged in stalked heads. 'Minima' is a lower growing, more compact selection with pink stems.

P. depressa (dee-*pres*-sa) is commonly called creeping pilea, in reference to its low habit of growth. Hailing from the West Indies, it is hardy in Zones 10 to 11, reaches 1 to 3 inches tall, and spreads indefinitely. It is a low, dense, mat-forming, creeping, succulent ground cover. Growth is moderate to fast. Plants from 2¼- to 3-inch-diameter containers are spaced 6 to 12 inches apart. As is true of many tropical species, this one is commonly grown as a house plant in the North. As an outdoor ground cover, it functions well as a general cover for small areas and is especially nice in elevated planters or terraced settings, where it does not hesitate to climb out and display itself in a graceful pendent manner. No foot traffic is tolerated. The leaves are evergreen, glossy green, succulent, and oppositely arranged on short stems. They are oval to spatula-shaped, reach ⅜ inch long by ⅜ inch wide, are edged with rounded teeth near their ends, and are closely set upon the trailing succulent stems. Like other *Pilea* species, this one bears tiny green nonornamental flowers during summer.

P. nummularifolia (new-mew-lay-ree-*foe*-lee-a), named from the Latin *nummus,* a coin, in reference to its coin-shaped leaves, is commonly called creeping Charlie or round-leaved pilea. Hailing from the West Indies, Panama, and northern South America, it is hardy in Zones 10 to 11, reaches 1 to 3 inches tall, and spreads indefinitely. Growth is moderate to fast. Plants from 2¼- to 3-inch-diameter containers are spaced 6 to 10 inches apart. Like *P. depressa*, it is a trailing, low, dense, mat-forming, succulent ground cover. The evergreen, round, ¼- to ¾-inch-wide leaves are shiny medium to dark green and edged with smooth teeth. The summertime flowers are also tiny, green, and nonornamental.

CULTURE / CARE: *Pilea* species perform well in most well-drained loamy soils. Although their tolerance to drought is fairly good, they grow best when the soil is kept moistened and the relative humidity is high. They prefer light to moderate shade. Their primary problems are blights (leaf, stem, and bud), leaf spot, crown rot, and root-knot nematode. Little if any maintenance is required.

PROPAGATION: Cuttings are easily rooted throughout the year without the aid of rooting hormones. Division is easily accomplished in fall, winter, and spring.

Pinus
PLATE 243
Pine

Pines are not normally considered ground covers; indeed, the genus is composed of about 90 species of tall, evergreen, needle-leaved, coniferous trees. But, like every plant group, they are subject to mutations that lead to botanical and horticultural varieties, and some of these variations are ground covers. Among the pines, there are two types of ground covers: those derived from witches'-brooms and those derived from mutations. Witches'-brooms on pines are branches that display exceptionally dense bushy growth, apparently caused by a fungus that creates a permanent change in the growth and development of the affected branch. When a branch of a witches'-broom is removed and grafted onto the stem of a normal pine seedling, the plant develops into a broad, compact, pincushion-shaped ground cover. In the landscape, such plants are excellent for specimen or accent use and are sometimes grouped together as general covers and foundation facers. When a seed from a normal pine germinates and grows horizontally, the resultant plant, a true genetic mutation, will also retain its habit when vegetatively reproduced. But in this case, rather than displaying a tight pincushion-like habit, the plant will creep horizontally with trailing stems. For landscape use, such pines are at their best as specimens, particularly when grown in planters or at the top of retaining walls and allowed to creep over like a living waterfall.

SCIENTIFIC NAME: *Pinus* (*pie*-nus) is the classical name for pine trees.

HARDINESS / ORIGIN: See individual species for hardiness; North Temperate Zone, south to Central America, Java, and Sumatra.

LEAVES / FLOWERS / FRUIT: The leaves are slender, pointed, and referred to as needles. They vary in their degree of stiffness, coloration, pointedness, and in the number grouped in each bundle, or fascicle. The flowers are tiny, without petals, and arranged in separate male or female, globose or elongate cones. Should pollination occur, the seed develops within the larger female cone.

RATE / SPACING: Growth of the witches's-broom type of ground-covering pines is slow. Plants from 3- to 5-gallon-sized containers are spaced 3 to 4 feet apart. The ground-covering pines arising from genetic mutations are normally planted alone as specimens.

SPECIES: *P. banksiana* '**Uncle Foggy**' (banks-ee-*aye*-na) is a horizontal creeping form that reaches 2 feet tall and up to 15 feet wide. The species, named to commemorate Sir Joseph Banks (1743–1820), an influential English scientist and plant collector, is commonly called Jack pine, scrub pine, or gray pine. A typically scrubby, ¾- to 2-inch-long, olive-green-needled pine, *P. banksiana* is native to North America and hardy in Zones 2 to 6 or 7.

P. densiflora 'Prostrata' (den-si-*floe*-ra) has a horizontal ground-hugging habit, reaches 1 to 2 feet tall, and spreads more than 8 feet across. The species, named for its dense-flowering habit, is commonly called Japanese red pine. Native to Japan, Korea, and China, *P. densiflora* is hardy in Zones 3 or 4 to 7, sometimes exceeds 100 feet, and is clothed in 3- to 5-inch-long, lustrous, bright green needles.

P. flexilis 'Glauca Pendula' (*fleks*-i-lis) displays needles that are more horizontal in habit. The species, named for its flexible trunk, is commonly called limber pine. Hardy in Zones 4 to 7 and native to western North America, *P. flexilis* has 2½- to 3½-inch-long, dark green to bluish green needles and may reach more than 50 feet tall.

P. mugo (*myu*-go), from the old Tyrolean name for this species, is commonly called dwarf mountain pine, mugo pine, or Swiss mountain pine. It is a European native that grows well in Zones 2 to 7. The typical species is covered with 1- to 2-inch-long rigid, medium to dark green needles that turn yellowish in winter. Plants range from 1 to 6 feet tall and display no predictable shape. Ground-covering forms include 'Gnom', with low, compact, cushionlike habit, 15 inches tall by 3 feet wide and with deep green needles. Variety *mugus* (var. *mugho*), Tyrolean mugo pine, has a variable habit and probably includes several clones, the smaller of which (those less than 4 feet tall and spreading 6 or more feet wide) might be considered for use as very large scale ground covers. Variety *pumilio*, dwarf mugo pine, is shorter than 5 feet, spreads more than 10 feet wide, and is also appropriate for large-scale use.

P. nigra 'Hornibrookiana' (*nye*-gra) is a dwarf form much smaller than the species. Originating from a witches'-broom found in Rochester, New York, this compact, cushionlike selection ranges from 1½ to 2 feet tall and spreads to 6 feet wide. The species, named from the Latin word meaning black, is likely named in reference to the dark fissures in the bark but may be named for the darkness of its needles. Commonly called Austrian pine, this native to Europe displays deep green, stiff, 4- to 6-inch-long, sharply pointed needles. It is hardy to Zone 4 and may ascend to 90 feet tall.

P. parviflora 'Bergman' (par-wa-*floe*-ra) is a low-growing selection that reaches 16 inches tall and spreads only 3 feet wide. The species, named from the Latin for small-flowered, is commonly called Japanese white pine. Native to Japan and hardy to Zone 5, *P. parviflora* typically ranges from 25 to 50 feet

tall and is a slow-growing tree decorated with bluish to medium green, stiff, 1¼- to 2½-inch-long, blunt-tipped needles.

P. strobus (*stroe*-bus) ground-covering cultivars include 'Haird's Broom', a compact, cushionlike dwarf that reaches 12 inches tall by 3 feet wide; 'Merrimack', much like 'Haird's Broom' but with bluish green needles and 2 to 3 feet tall; 'Ottawa', a selection I discovered in Muskegon, Michigan, in 1984 that trails along the ground, seldom exceeds 12 inches tall, is named for the Ottawa Indians of the area, and will likely exceed 25 feet wide. The species, named for its prominent strobili, or floral clusters, is commonly called eastern white pine or white pine. Native to eastern North America, it is the state tree of Michigan. It is hardy to Zone 3 and known to reach 80 to 150 feet tall. It displays 3- to 5-inch-long, soft green, flexible, stiffly pointed needles. Northeastern Native Americans made a scurvy-preventing tea from the young green needles (they contain up to five times as much vitamin C as lemons and are also rich in vitamin A). Others utilized the inner bark of various pines as a food source (or treatment for gonorrhea): it was often eaten raw or boiled and could be dried and stored for later use. The seeds of many pines are edible, and today they are available in health food and grocery stores. Ojibwa Indians used the seeds as a flavoring for meat, and today the seeds are still sometimes used for this purpose. Early settlers to the New World valued the white pine so much that they celebrated its image on the face of seventeenth-century silver shillings.

P. sylvestris (syl-*ves*-tris) ground-covering cultivars include 'Albyn's Prostrate', a loosely sprawling, somewhat mounded clone that reaches 1 foot tall, spreads more than 5 feet wide, and holds its medium green color throughout winter, and 'Hillside Creeper', much like 'Albyn's Prostrate' but a bit coarser-textured and yellow during winter. The species, named from the Latin *sylvestris,* of woods, is commonly called Scotch pine, Scot's pine, or Scotch fir. It hails from Norway and Scotland south to Spain, through Europe, Siberia, and western Asia. It may grow to 90 feet tall. Its needles, arranged in bundles of two, reach 1 to 4 inches long, are stiff and blue-green, and sometimes take on a yellowish color in fall and winter. The species is hardy in Zones 2 to 8.

CULTURE / CARE: The ground-covering pines are not identical in their likes and dislikes, but by and large they all grow in well-drained, sandy to sandy-loamy, acidic soils. They are relatively tolerant of drought, seldom need summertime watering and, with the exception of *P. strobus,* do not tolerate high soil moisture. They prefer full sun, but in most cases do equally well in light shade. They are usually quite healthy, but may be subject to a number of diseases and pests. Damping off, root rot, dieback, tip blight, stem blister, rust, twig blight, and wood decay are the most prevalent diseases, and the most common insect pests are aphids, webworms, sawflies, scales, needle miners, spittlebugs, weevils, borers, and moths. Maintenance needs are few if any.

PROPAGATION: Because pines resist layering and cutting propagation, and because the ground-covering forms do not reproduce true from seed, they are usually propagated by grafting: graft a dormant shoot (usually in December or January) of a ground-covering form on top of an actively growing understock (greenhouse forced) of a 2-year-old or 3-year-old seedling of the typical treelike species. Care must be taken during the first two or three years to trim off any branches that develop below the graft union, as such branches will bear the characteristics of the normal treelike form and will quickly overrun the less aggressive branches of the ground-covering variety. In time, the bark will become so thick on the understock that no new buds and stems (of the understock) will be able to push through it.

Pittosporum tobira 'Wheeler's Dwarf'   PLATE 244
Wheeler's Dwarf Japanese Pittosporum, Dwarf Australian Laurel, Dwarf Mock Orange

This little mound-shaped shrub displays a low, compact, horizontally spreading, upright-branched, woody habit. It reaches 2 to 3 feet tall, spreads 3 to 4 feet across, and is useful in a number of different ways. As a low hedge along sidewalks its attractive foliage and fragrant white flowers can be easily appreciated. As a low foundation facer its thick branches and closely set foliage completely obscure the bricks or blocks in the background. Several dozen plants can be grouped together to cover moderate to large areas, creating an interesting sea-of-green effect. Used on a slope, this shrub is excellent for controlling erosion. No foot traffic is tolerated.

SCIENTIFIC NAME: *Pittosporum tobira* (pi-tos-*poe*-rum / pit-oh-*spoe*-rum toe-*bye*-ra). *Pittosporum* comes from the Greek *pitte,* pitch tar, and *sporum,* seed, in reference to the sticky seeds. *Tobira* is the native name for this species.

HARDINESS / ORIGIN: Zones 8 to 9; China and Japan.

LEAVES / FLOWERS / FRUIT: The evergreen, densely set, leathery, oval, 2- to 3-inch-long, ½- to ¾-inch-wide leaves are attractively colored dark shiny green. They lend nice contrast to the pleasantly fragrant, creamy white, ⅜-inch-wide, five-petaled flowers of mid to late spring. The fruit, a small pear-shaped capsule, is nonornamental.

RATE / SPACING: Growth is slow. Plants from 1- to 2-gallon-sized containers are spaced 2½ to 3 feet apart.

HORTICULTURAL SELECTIONS: 'Cream de Mint', 2 to 2½ feet tall, compact habit, mint green and creamy white leaves.

CULTURE / CARE: This cultivar grows best in full sun to light shade in acidic to slightly alkaline, well-drained soils. It tolerates drought fairly well, but prefers the soil to be slightly moist. It is occasionally affected by leaf spot, stem rot, blight, root rot, and mosaic. Its most frequent pests include aphids, mealybugs, and southern root-knot nematode. Seldom does it need any maintenance.

PROPAGATION: Stem cuttings root easily in early summer; treatment with 1000 to 3000 ppm IBA/talc may be helpful but is not necessary.

Pleioblastus   PLATE 245
Reed Bamboo

This genus contains a number of low-growing, moderate-spreading to relatively fast-spreading rhizomatous grasses formerly classified as *Arundinaria.* These small-scale to large-scale, soil-retentive general covers are useful along streams, ponds, and pools, for accent or specimen use, and for edging paths and walkways in both formal and informal landscapes. Because of their ability to spread rapidly, they should be sited in locations that naturally check their spread or provide a lot of space to travel. Limited foot traffic is tolerated.

Bamboos are unusual in that they flower very infrequently, a feature that distinguishes them from the other grasses, which flower annually. Flowering is unpredictable and, amazingly, when one species flowers, it often flowers throughout the world. This may result in the starvation of animal species that depend upon bamboos for food, as the plants sometimes die after they flower and produce seed.

SCIENTIFIC NAME: *Pleioblastus* (plee-oh-*blas*-tus) comes from the Greek *pleios,* many, and *blastos,* buds, in reference to the branches which arise several per node.

HARDINESS / ORIGIN: While most people think of bamboos as tropical plants, several species are quite cold tolerant and will survive in Zone 5 or 6; see individual species for specific hardiness ranges. Native habitat is southern North America and eastern and southern Asia.

LEAVES / FLOWERS / FRUIT: The leaves, like those of other grasses, are flattened, narrow, and elongate, but in most cases are arranged in clusters of four to ten. The flowers and fruit are not ornamental and seldom if ever are formed.

RATE / SPACING: Growth is fast. Plants from 1-gallon-sized containers are spaced 1½ to 2 feet apart.

SPECIES: *P. auricoma* (awe-ri-*koe*-ma), formerly classified as *P. viridi-striata* and *Arundinaria viridi-striata,* is commonly called dwarf yellow-stripe bamboo. With 8-inch-long, 1¼-inch-wide leaves that have longitudinal green and yellow stripes, this is a welcome addition to many landscapes in Zones 6 to 10. It ranges from 1½ to 2½ feet tall. Two dwarf forms, both called 'Nana', are said to exist. One reaches 1 foot tall and the other 1½ to 2 feet tall.

P. humilis (*hyu*-mi-lis), meaning low growing or dwarf, is commonly called dwarf bamboo. Native to Japan, it reaches 2½ feet tall, spreads indefinitely, and is hardy to Zone 8. Its slightly hairy leaves reach 6 inches long by ¾ inch wide, are grasslike, sharply pointed, deciduous, colored medium green, and are held upon thin, light green stems. Variety *pumilus* is more robust, reaches 2 feet tall, and is colored a lighter but more vibrant green.

P. pygmaeus (pig-*may*-us), named for its dwarf stature, is commonly called pygmy bamboo. Native to Japan, it reaches only 6 to 10 inches tall (in sun) and 1½ feet tall in the shade. It spreads indefinitely and is hardy at least to Zone 5. Its leaves, which reach 5 inches long by ½ inch wide, are sharp pointed, deciduous, fringed with bristles, and colored bright green above and silvery-green below. 'Akebeno' has leaves crowded upon longer, narrower branches; 'Tanake' has leaves longer than those of the species.

P. variegatus (vare-ee-e-*gay*-tus), meaning varied in leaf color, is commonly called white-stripe bamboo. It hails from Japan, is hardy northward to Zone 6, reaches 3 feet tall, and spreads indefinitely. Its deciduous leaves are decorated with a striking pattern of dark green and silvery white and reach 8 inches long by 1 inch wide.

CULTURE / CARE: Bamboos are best in organically rich, loamy, fertile soil. Although they are often associated with wet soil, these species rot if planted in standing water. Remarkably, they tolerate a fair amount of drought and thrive in full sun to moderate shade. Other than smut and scale insects, they have few problems. Maintenance usually consists of mowing plantings in fall to clean up dead stems and leaves.

PROPAGATION: Divisions, normally taken during spring, will reestablish quite well if kept constantly moist. Rhizome cuttings, on the other hand, should be taken during fall; section them into 12-inch-lengths, place them in flats, cover with 3 inches of soil, and keep them moist and warm. In about six months they will have developed into small transplantable plantlets.

Polemonium reptans   PLATE 246
Creeping Jacob's Ladder, Greek Valerian,
Creeping Polemonium

Creeping Jacob's ladder is a sprawling, weak-stemmed, 8- to 12-inch-tall herbaceous ground cover. Contrary to its name it is more of a crown spreader than creeper. It is very easy to grow, is right at home in wild gardens, and not only does it have pleasing foliage but a robust flower show as well. Grown in masses it makes a nice general-purpose ground cover in shady areas. It combines well with bloodroot (*Sanguinaria canadensis*) and trilliums, and looks splendid in the foreground of hostas with green and white, green, or blue leaves. No foot traffic is tolerated.

SCIENTIFIC NAME: *Polemonium reptans* (po-lee-*moe*-nee-um *rep*-tanz). *Polemonium* is simply the Greek name for this plant, which presumably was used for medicinal purposes by Polemon of Cappadocia. *Reptans,* creeping, refers to the habit.

HARDINESS / ORIGIN: Zone 3 to 8 or 9; moist woodlands and meadows of eastern North America.

LEAVES / FLOWERS / FRUIT: The superb light to medium green compound evergreen leaves are composed of 7 to 15 paired lance-shaped leaflets arranged in ladderlike fashion along the stems, hence the common name creeping Jacob's ladder. During late spring and early summer arise numerous loose, nodding clusters of light blue, ½-inch-wide flowers. The fruit, tiny and hardly noticeable, is nonornamental.

RATE / SPACING: Growth is slow to moderate, although sometimes a bit invasive by self-sowing. Plants from pint-sized to gallon-sized containers are spaced 1 to 1½ feet apart.

HORTICULTURAL SELECTIONS: 'Alba', with white flowers; 'Blue Pearl', 8 to 10 inches tall, with bright blue flowers; 'Konigsee', rare, with deep blue flowers.

OTHER SPECIES: *P. boreale* (bore-ee-*al*-ee), from *borealis,* northern, hails from northern latitudes throughout the world and is hardy to Zone 4. It reaches only 9 inches tall (previously called *P. humile,* meaning dwarf), displays 13 to 23 pairs of leaflets per leaf, and produces ½-inch-wide bluish purple flowers during summer.

P. caeruleum (se-*rew*-lee-um), named for its intensely blue flowers, is commonly called Jacob's ladder. An upright grower, it hails from Europe, Asia, and North American mountains, is hardy in Zones 3 to 7, reaches 2 feet tall by 2 feet wide, and displays 3- to 5-inch-long, long-stalked compound leaves that are composed of up to 20 paired tapering leaflets—said to represent the ladder in Jacob's dream. The flowers, borne during late spring or early summer, reach 1 inch wide, are colored deep blue, and are arranged in drooping clusters. Var. *album* (var. *lacteum*), with white flowers; 'Brise d'Anjou' ('Breeze of Anjou'), lovely foliage with yellowish white edges and dark green centers, flowers violet-blue in summer; 'Sapphire', with light blue flowers. Variety *himalayanum,* hardy to Zone 5, displays deeper blue 1½-inch-wide flowers, is considered by some authorities to be a separate species, and has given rise to the following useful cultivars: 'Album', with white flowers; 'Gracile', more compact growing with blue flowers; 'Variegatum', with leaves variegated white and green.

P. carneum (*kar*-nee-um), salmon polemonium, requires sandy peat-enriched soil, is hardy in Zones 6 to 8 and, although somewhat temperamental, is worth trying. Native to the Cascades, it reaches 1 to 1½ feet tall by 1 foot wide and looks like *P. caeruleum* but is smaller and less upright growing, and has flowers with pinkish white to pink blossoms that fade to purplish white as they age.

CULTURE / CARE: Jacob's ladders prefer to be grown in light to moderate shade in richly organic, moist, well-drained acidic soils. They also tolerate full sun, but the soil should never be allowed to dry out. Even in the shade, they are not tolerant of drought, and during extended hot dry weather, if the soil is not kept moist, their leaf tips dry out. Their primary pest is slugs, and disease problems are seldom seen. Little to no maintenance is required. In time they may become crowded, decreasing their floral display, and thus require division.

PROPAGATION: Division during spring is foolproof. Ripe seed readily germinates.

Polygala chamaebuxus   PLATE 247
Ground Milkwort

Ground milkwort, an attractive florific, 6-inch-tall, 1-foot-wide suckering alpine, is a ground cover for those who have just the right location—well-drained, gritty, yet moisture-retentive soil in alpine regions or along the Pacific Coast. In any other location, it is likely to be short-lived. It is a natural for combining with dwarf conifers and dwarf rhododendrons and makes a dense weed-impenetrable mat for use on a small to moderate scale. No foot traffic is tolerated.

SCIENTIFIC NAME: *Polygala chamaebuxus* (poe-*lee*-ga-la ka-*mee*-*buks*-us). *Polygala* comes from the Greek *polys,* much, and *gala,* milk, referring to the belief that ingestion of the leaves will enhance lactation. *Chamaebuxus* comes from the Greek *chamai,* on the ground, and *Buxus,* the boxwood genus, and refers to the resemblance of this plant to a dwarf boxwood.

HARDINESS / ORIGIN: Zones 6 to 8; well-drained limy or acidic mineral or humus-rich sunny alpine regions of western central Europe, south to southern Italy and western Yugoslavia.

LEAVES / FLOWERS / FRUIT: Reaching ¾ to 1½ inches long by ¼ to ½ inch wide, the oval to linear-shaped, boxwoodlike leaves are dark shiny green and give strong contrast to the solitary or paired yellow or whitish, often red-spotted, fragrant flowers that are borne in their axils during late winter to late spring. The tiny fruit is nonornamental.

RATE / SPACING: Growth is slow to moderate. Plants from pint-sized to ½-gallon-sized containers are spaced 10 to 12 inches apart.

HORTICULTURAL SELECTIONS: 'Grandiflora', with larger pinkish red flowers; var. *rhodoptera,* a dwarf, 5 inches tall by 10 inches wide, with vivid wine-red and yellow flowers.

OTHER SPECIES: *P. vayredae* (*vay*-re-dee), of the eastern Pyrenees, is hardy in Zones 7 to 8. A short spreader that reaches a mature size of 4 inches tall by 1½ feet wide, this species differs from *P. chamaebuxus* in its lower habit and in its pinkish purple and yellow springtime flowers. Plants from pint-sized to ½-gallon-sized containers are spaced 12 to 14 inches apart.

CULTURE / CARE: Ground-covering milkworts can be successfully grown in alkaline or acidic soils, but they absolutely demand excellent drainage in conjunction with moderate moisture holding capacity—from a combination of coarse gravelly soils and rotted leaf mold. They prefer full sun, but often tolerate light shade, and should receive supplemental watering during extended hot, dry weather. Rabbits and aphids can sometimes be pesky. Little maintenance is required.

PROPAGATION: Division during early summer or fall is effective. Ripe seed should be sown immediately. Cuttings can be taken during mid summer.

Polygonatum   PLATE 248
Solomon's Seal

Solomon's seal is a genus comprised of about 30 species of rhizomatous, herbaceous, erect-stemmed, arching perennials. Primarily from temperate areas of Asia, Europe, and North America, they serve as useful accent and specimen plants for woodland gardens. Often overlooked is their ability to function as mass-planted general ground covers. Indeed, when several plants are grouped together in sweeping drifts at the back of a wooded border, they contribute a magnificent soft, motion-filled gracefulness. The springtime flowers are attractive as are the fruits that follow. At all times they appear graceful and at the slightest breeze sway hypnotically in the wind. Solomon's seal species combine well with hostas, primroses, rhododendrons, and various ferns. Indeed, alone or in combination, for woodland and semishady border plantings, they are among the loveliest of ground covers. No foot traffic is tolerated.

In accord with the "Doctrine of Signatures" (see *Pulmonaria*), the jointed rhizomes of Solomon's seal suggested to early herbalists that the plant would be useful in treating disorders of the joints. Although their effectiveness in such cases is questionable, researchers have been able to substantiate that rhizome extracts are effective treatments for cuts, bruises, skin ulcerations, and as an agent to stop vomiting. Presumably their effectiveness is due to the presence of allantoin, a substance that promotes healing of local wounds and infections. The common name Solomon's seal comes from the round leaf scars that are left on the rhizome from one year to the next. Similar to the annual rings of a tree, each scar indicates one year's growth.

SCIENTIFIC NAME: *Polygonatum* (poe-lig-oh-*nay*-tum / pol-ee-*goe*-nay-tum) is derived from the Greek *polys,* many, and *gony,* knee, in reference to the jointed rhizome.

HARDINESS / ORIGIN: See individual species for hardiness; North Temperate Zone, especially southwestern China.

LEAVES / FLOWERS / FRUIT: Long, graceful, nodding, unbranched stems, alternate leaves, and small white, cream-colored or greenish pendulous flowers hanging from the leaf axils characterize Solomon's seal. Typically the fruit is ⅓ inch in diameter and blueblack.

RATE / SPACING: Growth is slow. Plants from ½- to 1-gallon-sized containers are spaced 8 to 12 inches apart.

SPECIES: *P. biflorum* (bie-*floe*-rum), named from the Latin *biflorum,* two-flowered, in reference to flowers which occur in pairs, is commonly called hairy Solomon's seal, true King Solomon's seal, or small Solomon's Seal. Native to the northeastern United States (extending from Connecticut south to Florida and west to the Mississippi River), it reaches 1 to 3 feet tall by 2 feet wide and is hardy in Zones 3 to 9. Its smooth-textured, soft bluish green leaves lend a mild coolness to the shady woodland sites in which the species thrives. The deciduous, simple, elliptic, narrow or broadly oval leaves are either joined directly to the arching stems or attached by way of short stalks. They reach 2 to 4½ inches long by ½ to 2 inches wide, are pointed at their ends, rounded at their bases, and colored a cool bluish green above and paler green below. The flowers reach ½ to ¾ inch long, are colored greenish white, and dangle

solitarily or in groups of up to four from the arching stems (most often, however, in pairs, as the specific epithet suggests). Each flower is cylindrical to bell-shaped, six-parted, and ⅓ to ½ inch long, arises mid to late spring, and gives rise to ¼- to ⅓-inch-diameter dark blue berries. Historically the rhizome had been employed medicinally in the treatment of vomiting, cuts, bruises, and skin ulcerations. John Gerard, a sixteenth-century herbalist (and presumably the world's top-ranking male chauvinist), made the claim that the rhizome was a wonderful cure for the physical pains "gotten by falls, or women's willfulness in stumbling on their hasty husbands' fists." Unlike false Solomon's seal (*Smilacina racemosa*), which looks like *P. biflorum* and shares its habitat, *P. biflorum* has pendent paired flowers along and below the stem (keel) instead of flowers borne in clusters at the end of the stems. One way to remember the distinction is with the mnemonic rhyme: "You can tell that I'm real by the flowers under my keel."

P. commutatum (kom-you-*tay*-tum), meaning changeable, is commonly called smooth, giant, or great Solomon's seal, and sealwort. It reaches 3 to 5 feet tall (large by ground-cover standards but excellent under medium-sized to large-sized trees), spreads more than 4 feet wide, and is native from Manitoba east to New Hampshire and south to New Mexico and Georgia. It is hardy in Zones 3 to 7. The deciduous, simple, narrowly oval leaves are 4½ to 6 inches long by 3 to 4 inches wide, smooth-margined with sharply pointed ends, dark green (lighter below), somewhat coarse-textured, and alternately arranged upon stout arching stems. The pendent, ½- to ¾-inch-long, ⅙-inch-wide, cylindrical to bell-shaped flowers are whitish green and borne alone or in groups of up to eight from mid spring to early summer. The large and prominent, ⅓- to ½-inch-wide globose berries are first green, then blackish blue.

P. × *hybridum* (*hy*-brid-um), a sterile hybrid from crossing *P. odoratum* with *P. multiflorum,* is hardy in Zone 6 and has given rise to a double-flowered cultivar, 'Flore Pleno'.

P. odoratum (oh-der-*aye*-tum), named for its fragrant flowers, is commonly called fragrant Solomon's seal. Hailing from Europe and Asia, it is hardy in Zones 3 to 9, reaches 1½ to 2 feet tall, and spreads by creeping rootstock to 2 feet wide. It is adorned with elliptic to oval, 4-inch-long, 1½-inch-wide, medium green leaves that are held upon arching stems. The white cylindrical to bell-shaped flowers are ½ to ⅞ inch long with yellowish green bases. Solitary or in pairs, they are borne during mid to late spring and are very pleasantly lilylike in fragrance. Later they give rise to blackish blue berries. Variety *thunbergii* is more robust than the species, with height to 3 feet, flowers to 1½ inches long, and leaves to 6 inches long; 'Variegatum', with foliage strikingly decorated with creamy white margins, is hardy only to Zone 4 and a bit less heat tolerant than the species.

CULTURE / CARE: Solomon's seals are adaptable to a range of sandy, gravelly, loamy, or acidic soils. They prefer moderate to dense shade and drought tolerance is fairly good. They are susceptible to no serious diseases and play host only to slugs. No maintenance is needed.

PROPAGATION: Division of rhizomes and stem segments is effective during late spring. Seed should be sown in a cold frame or seed bed during fall for germination the following spring.

Polypodium virginianum
PLATE 249

Rock Polypody, American Wall Fern

This neat little fern is just as comfortable residing in the side of a rock ledge, retaining wall, or shady corner of a rock garden, as it is growing in moderate-sized hillside plantings as a soil stabilizer. Typically it reaches 10 inches tall and spreads to 5 feet across. A sturdy, rhizomatous spreader, it is not rampant and will not overpower its native companions, which often include trailing arbutus (*Epigaea repens*), partridge berry (*Mitchella repens*), false Solomon's seal (*Smilacina racemosa*), blue stem golden rod (*Solidago caesia*), leatherleaf wood fern (*Dryopteris marginalis*), and Christmas fern (*Polystichum acrostichoides*), nor is it incompatible with such imported ground covers as *Hosta, Helleborus* (Lenten and Christmas rose), and cultivars of Solomon's seal (*Polygonatum*). No foot traffic is tolerated.

SCIENTIFIC NAME: *Polypodium virginianum* (poe-lee-*poe*-dee-um ver-jin-ee-*aye*-num). *Polypodium* comes from the Greek *polys,* many, and *pous,* foot, referring to the furry, footlike divisions of the creeping stems. *Virginianum* means of Virginia.

HARDINESS / ORIGIN: Zone 3; eastern North America.

LEAVES / FLOWERS / FRUIT: The fronds are evergreen, oblong to lance-shaped or triangular, deeply lobed along their edges, to 1 foot long by 3 inches wide, and colored dark medium green on both sides. There are no flowers but rather prominent, rounded spore-producing sori that are visible from both sides of the fronds.

RATE / SPACING: Growth is slow to moderate. Plants from pint-sized to ½-gallon-sized containers are spaced 1 to 1½ feet apart.

OTHER SPECIES: *P. aureum* (*awe*-ree-um), golden polypody or hare's foot fern (named for its hairy creeping rhizomes that look like the foot of a rab-

bit), is a robust fern hardy in Zones 10 to 11. Native to Florida, the West Indies, and Argentina, it reaches 3 feet tall and displays attractive blue-green 10-inch-wide fronds.

CULTURE / CARE: *Polypodium virginianum* may be difficult to culture and often fails in too rich or too moist soils. For best results, it should be located on sloping ground or in cracks in a wall or boulder. Here it does quite well if the substrate is a soil of relatively organic, rocky or sandy, infertile, acidic composition. *Polypodium aureum* is a bit less fussy, but in either case the soil should be kept moist and plants located out of drying winds in light to dense shade where the temperatures stay relatively cool. Diseases and pests are seldom serious.

PROPAGATION: Division is best performed during fall or spring.

Polystichum acrostichoides
PLATE 250

Christmas Fern, Dagger Fern, Canker Brake

Christmas fern is so named because its evergreen fronds were used by early New England settlers for decoration at Christmas time. It ranges from 1½ to 2½ feet tall and does not spread extensively. Instead it stays in solitary crowns that reach 2½ or 3½ feet wide. It performs well on a moderate to large scale on woody slopes as a general cover. Along the shady banks of streams, ponds, and pools, where its lush foliage and stiff habit can be reflected, it functions well as a specimen, accent plant, or general cover. No foot traffic is tolerated.

SCIENTIFIC NAME: *Polystichum acrostichoides* (poe-lees-ti-kum a-kros-ti-*koy*-deez). *Polystichum* comes from the Greek *polys,* many, and *stichos,* a row, referring to the multiple rows of sori (spore cases) found upon the undersides of the leaves. *Acrostichoides* means like *Acrostichum,* another genus of ferns.

HARDINESS / ORIGIN: Zones 4 to 7; eastern North America.

LEAVES / FLOWERS / FRUIT: The fronds are evergreen, from 1½ to 2½ feet long by 4 to 5 inches wide at the base, lance-shaped, compound, and composed of 20 to 40 pairs of leathery, medium green, triangular-oval pinnae. Upon their bottom sides, during summer, are borne numerous, round, spore-laden sori.

RATE / SPACING: Growth is slow. Plants from pint-sized to gallon-sized containers are spaced 1½ to 2 feet apart.

HORTICULTURAL SELECTIONS: 'Crispum', with ruffled leaflet margins; 'Cristatum', with the tip of the leaf blade being crested; 'Incisum', with leaflets deeply and coarsely toothed; 'Multifidum', leaflets with deeply cut lobes.

OTHER SPECIES: *P. braunii* (*brawn*-ee-eye), Braun's holly fern or shield fern, is native to northeastern North America, Europe, the Caucasus, and Japan. It is hardy to Zone 4 and reaches 1½ to 2 feet tall by 2 feet wide. Its semievergreen, featherlike, compound leaves reach up to 2 feet long by 6 to 8 inches wide and are attractively arranged in an upright, outward arching, vase-shaped cluster. Narrowly elliptical, they are composed of 6 to 18 pairs of oblong to oval, leathery, deep shiny green leaflets.

P. lonchitis (lon-*kye*-tis), named for its spearlike leaves, is commonly called mountain holly fern or holly fern. Native to Europe, north and central Asia, the Himalayas, and North America, it is hardy to Zone 4 and reaches 9 to 20 inches tall by 3 feet wide. The leaves are narrow, featherlike, and evergreen, and reach up to 2 feet long. Edged with small spiny teeth, they display a rich, vibrant green color.

P. munitum (mew-*nee*-tum) is named from the Latin *munitus,* armed (that is, with teeth), in reference to the edges of the pinnae, and is commonly called western sword fern. This very large plant is hardy in Zones 6 to 9, hails from the Pacific Northwest, and ranges from 3 to 5 feet tall. Displaying long (to 5 feet) and narrow, deep green singly divided fronds, it is rather spectacular, especially in the Northwest where it reaches its maximum size. Out East, however, it is said to languish in the summer heat and barely survives. 'Crested' has crested frond tips, and 'Crisped Form' displays twisted pinnae.

P. setiferum (say-*ti*-fe-rum / se-*tif*-er-um), soft shield fern, is native to Tsu-shimaj, Japan, and displays lovely featherlike, doubly divided, 1½- to 4-feet-long, erect to arching, glossy, medium to dark green semievergreen fronds. Hardy in Zones 5 to 8, it has given rise to several interesting cultivars: 'Capitatum', with crested apical pinna; 'Congestum', with leaves originating from the crown in a swirling pattern; 'Congestum Cristatum', with dense overlapping pinnae and a tip that is crested; 'Cristatum', with crested apical and terminal pinnae; 'Cristulatum', with small crests on the frond apex and pinnae; 'Divisilobum Plumosum', with 2- to 3-foot-long fronds that are four times divided and appear plumelike; 'Imbricatum', similar to 'Congestum' but slightly taller; 'Percristatum', with prominently crested apical pinnae; 'Polydactylum', with a narrow forklike or fingerlike pattern to the pinnae; 'Plumosum Bevis', with dark green, tall, gracefully arching fronds; 'Plumosum Gracillimum', with feathery narrow pinnules that are finely crested at their tips; 'Plumosum Grande', with large fronds that may reach 4 feet tall; 'Pulcherrimum', with narrow, widely spaced pinnules'; 'Rotundatum', with nearly round pinnules.

CULTURE / CARE: These species adapt well to most soil types. They usually attain their best growth in acidic to neutral, organically rich loam. They tolerate moderate periods of drought, even in sandy soils, but prefer to be planted in cool locations with moist soil. Light to dense shade is best, and few diseases or pests threaten them.

PROPAGATION: Division during spring is easy and effective. Spores can also be used (see Chapter 8).

Potentilla   PLATE 251
Cinquefoil

The potentillas are excellent general covers for moderate-sized areas. Neither their foliage nor their flowers are to be slighted, and their endurance is exceptional. In cultivation for centuries, this group of plants offers a fair amount of diversity. Ground-covering types range from herbs with slow, clump-forming habits to low, sprawling woody shrubs. All have their particular niche in the landscape, which, interestingly, may range from a relatively dry rock garden to a nearly aquatic environment. The herbaceous potentillas do not seem to suffer greatly from infrequent foot traffic, but those of woody composition prefer not to be trod upon. Unless otherwise mentioned, the potentillas discussed here perform well as general covers or lawn substitutes.

SCIENTIFIC NAME: *Potentilla* (poe-ten-*til*-a) comes from the Latin *potens,* powerful and refers to the medicinal properties of some species.

HARDINESS / ORIGIN: See individual species for hardiness; North Temperate Zone, boreal regions, and a few in the South Temperate Zone.

LEAVES / FLOWERS / FRUIT: True to their common name five-finger, most *Potentilla* species display compound hand-shaped (palmate) five-parted leaves. Other species, like *P. anserina,* are feather-shaped with many leaflets. The flowers, normally yellow, are white or red in some species. The tiny fruit is nonornamental.

RATE / SPACING: See individual species.

SPECIES: *P. anserina* (an-sir-*eye*-na), from the Latin *anserina,* goose, is commonly called goose grass (interestingly, the foliage of this plant is one of the favorite foods of geese), silver feather, wild tansy, goose tansy, argentine, dog's tansy, silverweed, goosewort, moon grass, or crampweed. Native to the sandy and rocky shores and salt meadows of Greenland, much of North America, Asia, and Europe, this species is hardy in Zones 3 to 7, reaches 3 to 14 inches tall, spreads indefinitely, and is best used in sandy or rocky shoreside locations as a general cover. Growth is moderate to fast. Plants from quart-sized to gallon-sized containers are spaced 10 to 14 inches apart.

The leaves are compound and featherlike, oblong to oval, many segmented, and arranged in tufts that originate from sprawling stolons. From 3 to 16 inches long and 2 to 4 inches wide, the leaves are silky, silvery, and hairy in youth, then smooth and medium green in maturity. Each tooth-edged leaflet, of which there are 7 to 25 per leaf, is oblong to oval, ½ to 2 inches long by ½ to ¾ inch wide. The yellow flowers are borne individually upon thin stems that arise from the base of the leaves. They are ¾ to 1¼ inches across, five-petaled, and effective from early to mid summer. Forma *sericea* has leaves covered on both sides with silky silvery hairs. Herbalists often recommend a preparation of *P. anserina* as a soothing mouthwash and gargle. Its effectiveness in this capacity is likely due to its high tannin content and astringent properties. Tea made from steeping the foliage has been employed in the treatment of toothaches, stomachaches, and menstrual cramps. Combined with honey, such a tea is reported to be very soothing to sore throats. Although the foliage is quite appealing to geese, it is the edible rootstock that has more appeal to the human species. Eskimos, northern Europeans, and Native North Americans have eaten the roots, which are said to taste something like sweet potatoes, chestnuts, or parsnips, and which are typically boiled or roasted.

P. atrosanguinea (a-*tro*-san-gwin-ee-a), commonly called ruby cinquefoil, is native to the Himalayas. A sturdy, herbaceous spreader that reaches 1½ feet tall by 2 feet wide, it is hardy in Zones 5 to 8, displays silky haired green leaves, and is noteworthy for its 1-inch-wide blood-red summertime flowers. Growth is moderate. Plants from pint-sized to gallon-sized containers are spaced 12 to 16 inches apart. Horticultural selections include 'Firedance', heavy flowering, with small salmon-orange flowers and red centers; 'Gibson's Scarlet', with dark green leaves and extended bloom season; var. *leucochroa,* with cheery yellow flowers; 'Red', with rich red flowers; 'William Rollison', with flame-orange semidouble flowers and yellow centers; and 'Yellow Queen', with bright yellow flowers, red centers, and silvery leaves.

P. cinerea (ki-*ne*-ree-a / si-*nee*-re-a), named for its gray hairy leaves, is commonly called rusty cinquefoil. Hailing from the Alps and hardy in Zones 3 to 9, it reaches 2 inches tall and spreads indefinitely. Plants are spaced 10 to 16 inches apart. The palmate gray-green leaves are composed of five oval leaflets, and the yellow flowers are borne on 4-inch-stems in spring.

P. fruticosa (frew-ti-*koe*-sa) cultivars. The species, named for its fructose (shrubby) habit, is commonly called bush cinquefoil. It is woody and grows upright, thus cannot function as a ground cover. A few

of its cultivars, however. are outstanding for their wide, flat or mounding growth. These, as with the parent species, are magnificent in flower and provide a seemingly endless display of color throughout most of the growing season. They are best when functioning as foundation facers, as specimens in rock gardens and shrub borders, and as walkway edgings. Most important, they demand little care and give much beauty. Widely distributed throughout the Northern Hemisphere and hardy in Zones 2 to 8, the species typically reaches 4 feet tall and spreads about 4 feet wide. The ground-covering cultivars, however, tend to reach 1 to 2 feet tall and spread 3 to 5 feet wide. Growth is moderate. Plants from 1- to 3-gallon-sized containers are spaced 2 to 3 feet apart. They prefer full sun in a location that provides good air circulation. Once these criteria are met, difficulties with powdery mildew, enemy number one, should nearly be eliminated. The deciduous leaves consist of three to seven (typically five) fingerlike leaflets, each elliptical to oblong and ⅜ to 1 inch long. The leaves are medium green and covered with silky hairs. The flowers are borne solitarily or in dense clusters and range from ⅘ to 1½ inches wide. They are composed of bright yellow roundish petals, and they bloom continually from early summer through fall.

Among the ground-covering cultivars are 'Abbotswood', 2 feet tall by 3 feet wide, with fine-textured blue-green leaves and white flowers; 'Donard Gold', to 20 inches high, creeping habit, golden-yellow to orangish flowers; 'Elizabeth' ('Sutter's Gold'), with broadly rounded habit, 3 feet tall by 3 feet wide, golden-yellow 1½-inch-wide flowers, blue-green leaves; 'Farreri Prostrata', 1½ feet tall by 3 feet wide, buttercup-yellow flowers; 'Gold Carpet', like 'Elizabeth', but with greater resistance to mildew; 'Gold Finger', 3 feet tall by 4 feet wide, golden-yellow flowers; 'Gold Star', 2 feet tall by 3 feet wide, with large 2-inch-wide golden-yellow flowers and rich green leaves; 'Goldteppich', flatter and lower growing than 'Elizabeth', green leaves, golden-yellow flowers; 'Hollandia Gold', with low mounded habit and dark yellow flowers; 'Klondike', 2 feet tall, with bright green foliage, bright yellow flowers, and mound-forming habit; 'Kobold', compact habit, 18 inches tall, bright green leaves, small yellow flowers; 'Longacre', broad-spreading, cushion-forming, seldom exceeding 2½ feet tall, with medium-sized sulfur-yellow flowers; 'McKay's White', 3 feet tall, with single and semidouble creamy white flowers; 'Manchu' (var. *mandshurica*), reaching 12 to 16 inches tall, white flowers, grayish foliage; 'Mount Everest', with snow white flowers and broad mounding habit, 3 feet tall by 4 feet wide; 'Pink Pearl', with pink flowers, mounding habit, and mature height of 16 to 20 inches; 'Pretty Polly', with small salmon-pink flowers, 14 to 20 inches tall; 'Red Ace', reaching 2½ feet tall by 4 feet wide, densely branched, mounding habit, exceptional for its flowers that are vermillion-red above and pale yellow below; 'Royal Flush', with rose-pink flowers and yellow centers, compact habit, 12 to 18 inches tall by 3 feet wide, dark green leaves; 'Sunset', with brick-orange flowers, 2 feet tall by 3 feet wide; 'Tangerine', mounding habit, medium yellow flowers flushed orange-red (yellow in full sun), gray-green leaves, mature height of 2 to 3 feet; 'Tilford Cream', with white flowers, bright green leaves, mature height of 12 to 18 inches; 'Woodbridge Gold', with buttercup-yellow flowers, rich green leaves, mature height of 2 to 3 feet; 'Yellow Gem', mounding habit, to 18 inches tall, bright yellow 1¼-inch-wide flowers; 'Yellow Queen', broad spreading habit, less than 12 inches tall, yellow semidouble flowers borne in profusion from mid summer through fall.

P. nepalensis (nep-el-*en*-sis), Nepal cinquefoil, is a 12-inch-tall indefinite-spreading herb. Hardy in Zones 5 to 8, it hails from the Himalayas, spreads at a moderate pace, and is clothed in semievergreen, dark green leaves composed of five leaflets that range from 1 to 2½ inches long. Its rose-red flowers are borne during summer.

P. tabernaemontani (ta-ber-nee-mon-*tan*-ee), named for Jakob Theodor von Bergzabern (Tabernaemontanus), a sixteenth-century physician and herbalist, is commonly called spring cinquefoil. This low, mat-forming, herbaceous, horizontally trailing species is a relatively pleasing and uncomplicated plant. Formerly known as *P. verna,* it is frequently confused with *P. crantzii,* which grows more upright and is taller. Spring cinquefoil reaches 3 to 6 inches tall and spreads indefinitely. It is hardy in Zones 4 to 9, displays semievergreen, palmate, five-parted, 1½-inch-long, medium green, coarsely toothed leaves. During spring and early summer (often again, but more sparsely in the fall), it produces golden-yellow, 1-inch-diameter flowers. Growth is moderate to fast. Plants from pint-sized to gallon-sized containers are spaced 10 to 16 inches apart. Some popular horticultural selections include 'Nana', with very compact, nontrailing habit, 2 inches tall, deep green leaves, abundant bright yellow flowers, slow growth, plants from 4-inch-diameter containers are spaced 4 inches apart; 'Orange Flame', similar to 'Nana' but with orange flowers and slightly taller habit.

P. tonguei (*ton*-gee-eye), probably resulting from the cross between *P.* × *anglica* and *P. nepalensis,* is a low, herbaceous, trailing hybrid that ranges from 3 to 8 inches tall and spreads more than 18 inches

wide. It is hardy in Zones 4 to 9. Its palmate leaves are semievergreen and composed of three to five, 1½-inch-long, oval, coarsely toothed leaflets. The unusual flowers, borne in mid summer, are yellow to orangish with red centers. Growth is moderate, by strawberry-like stolons. Plants from pint-sized to gallon-sized containers are spaced 10 to 14 inches apart.

P. tridentata (tri-den-*tay*-ta), named for its three-parted leaves that have three teeth at the apex, is commonly called wineleaf cinquefoil or three-toothed cinquefoil. Hailing from Greenland and Canada south to northern Georgia and west to Michigan, Wisconsin, Minnesota, and North Dakota, this is one of our more refined native ground covers. It is variable in height from 2 to 12 inches tall and eventually forms dense, neat, shiny green mats. Growth is slow. Plants from pint-sized to quart-sized containers are spaced 10 to 16 inches apart. Seldom does the leathery ½- to 2-inch-long dark green foliage show a blemish, yet in fall, the leaves turn scarlet and the older ones turn yellow and fall off. The flowers are five-petaled, ¼-inch-wide, white, and effective throughout the summer. Extraordinarily cold hardy (to Zone 2), this species is not for warm climates (Zone 8 and northward). 'Minima' is a dwarf cultivar.

CULTURE / CARE: As a rule, the cinquefoils prefer sandy or loamy well-drained, acidic soils and are relatively tolerant of drought. Even so, they appreciate a little water during the heat of summer. They prefer full sun or light shade (shade is best for *P. tridentata*) and require a location with good air movement. Pests include rose aphid, strawberry weevil, rabbits, and slugs. Diseases such as mildew, leaf spots, and leaf rust are sometimes encountered but are rarely serious. Maintenance includes mowing or shearing after flowering to promote compactness and to rejuvenate growth.

PROPAGATION: Cuttings should be taken during early summer. Divisions can be performed at any time. Self-seeding occurs in some climates, and small plantlets are easily uprooted and transplanted.

Pratia pedunculata   PLATE 252
Blue-star Creeper

Blue-star creeper, sometimes listed as *Laurentia fluviatilis* or *Isotoma fluviatilis,* is a low-growing, mat-forming, herbaceous, stoloniferous and rhizomatous ground cover that ranges from 2 to 5 inches tall and spreads indefinitely. Hardy only in warmer climates, it is typically used as a general cover for small-sized to moderate-sized areas and, since it tolerates light foot traffic, as a filler between stepping stones.

SCIENTIFIC NAME: *Pratia pedunculata* (pray-*tee*-a pe-dunk-you-*lay*-ta). *Pratia* commemorates Ch. L. Prat-Bernon, a French naval officer. *Pedunculata* means with flowers borne on stalks.

HARDINESS / ORIGIN: Zones 7 or 8 to 10; southern Australia, Tasmania, and New Zealand.

LEAVES / FLOWERS / FRUIT: The ½-inch-long oval leaves are evergreen, medium dull green above, and purplish below. About their edges are small lobes and tiny hairs. The attractive ⅜-inch-wide, irregularly star-shaped light blue or whitish flowers arise during late spring and intermittently throughout summer. The fruit that follows is nonornamental.

RATE / SPACING: Growth is moderate to fast. Plants from 2- to 3-inch-diameter containers are spaced 8 to 12 inches apart.

OTHER SPECIES: *P. angulata* (an-gyu-*lay*-ta), meaning angled, displays rounded or broadly oval ½-inch-long evergreen, medium green leaves that are furrowed by a prominent central vein and edged with four or six teeth. The ⅜- to ¾-inch-wide white flowers have purple venation, are borne upon thin elongate stalks (peduncles) during summer, and later give rise to ¼-inch-wide reddish to purplish round berry-like fruits. Hardy in Zones 7 to 10, this species resembles *P. pedunculata* in habit and size. Variety *treadwellii,* sometimes listed as the cultivar 'Tread-wellii', has flowers that are larger than those of the species.

CULTURE / CARE: *Pratia* species prefer full sun in the northern part of their range to light shade in hotter climates, and grow well in most acidic, neutral, or alkaline, sandy, peaty, or organically rich soils—provided they receive regular watering during the summer. No serious diseases affect them, and aphids, their most common pest, are rarely serious. Maintenance typically consists of trimming back plants as they outgrow their bounds, and mowing during spring to promote vigor and to stimulate new growth.

PROPAGATION: Stem cuttings will root throughout the growing season. Division is easily conducted during fall, winter, and spring. Seed is effective also but may be difficult to obtain; sow it during early fall in a cold frame for germination the following spring.

Primula × polyantha   PLATE 253
Polyanthus Primrose, English Primrose,
Polyanthus

This hybrid species is represented by a collection of leafy, herbaceous, low-growing, stemless ground covers. They are often grown as annuals in hot, dry climates, but where the conditions are cool and moist they may be very long lived. The cultivars are noteworthy for their attractive foliage as well as masses of brightly colored flowers, which, in the landscape, have the effect of brightening the overall mood. Oftentimes they are employed on a small to moderate scale for edging walkways, paths, and perennial borders. They are best suited for growing on moist hillsides and stream or pond banks, and when planted in large masses, they eliminate the work and hazards of mowing. Sometimes they are very effectively interplanted with large hostas and deciduous ferns, each of which allow light to penetrate during spring, then later mature by summer and provide the primroses with increasing shade that helps them withstand the rigors of mid season. Polyanthus primrose is said to be compatible with black walnut (*Juglans nigra*). No foot traffic is tolerated.

SCIENTIFIC NAME: *Primula polyantha* (*prim*-you-la / *prie*-myu-la poe-lee-*anth*-a / pol-ee-*anth*-a). *Primula* is derived from the Latin *primus,* first, and refers to the early flowers of many species. *Polyantha* means many-flowered.

HARDINESS / ORIGIN: Zones 3 to 8; resulting from crosses involving *P. veris, P. elatior, P. vulgaris,* and *P. juliae.*

LEAVES / FLOWERS / FRUIT: The oval leaves are arranged in rosettes and, with good snow cover, often remain evergreen through the winter. Reaching 10 inches long by 3 to 4 inches wide and colored light green, they are typically wrinkled and puckered with wavy margins and are an ideal backdrop for the numerous flowers borne above them on 8- to 15-inch-long stems. Each early springtime, fragrant flower reaches 1 inch long, is funnel-shaped, has five petals, and might be colored white, gray, yellow, blue, brown, coppery, orange, or various combinations, but always with a yellow center. The fruit, if produced at all, is tiny and nonornamental.

RATE / SPACING: Growth is moderate. Plants from pint-sized to quart-sized containers are spaced 10 to 14 inches apart.

HORTICULTURAL SELECTIONS: There are dozens of named and unnamed cultivars. New ones are introduced each year, and old ones are discontinued with about the same frequency. For this reason it is best to just go to your garden center and see what it has in stock. Read the descriptions carefully, then make the choice that best suits your needs. Some strains that you are likely to encounter are described here: Barnhaven Hybrids, with relatively small leaves and large flowers; 'Giant Bouquet', with large 2- to 2½-inch-diameter flowers; 'Monarch', with large 2-inch-diameter flowers in mixed colors, similar to 'Giant Bouquet'; 'Pacific Giant Hybrids', with white, red, and pink flowers.

OTHER SPECIES: *P. auricula* (awe-*rik*-you-la), from

the Latin *auricula,* an ear, is named for its leaves. Native to the Alps, the species is hardy in Zones 2 or 3 to 8 and reaches 8 inches tall by 9 inches wide. The evergreen foliage is thick and fleshy to leathery, ranges from oval to narrowly oval, and from 2 to 4 inches long. Like the leaves of *P. × polyantha,* the wavy-edged leaves form a rosette from whose center rises a 2- to 6-inch-tall flower stalk. At the top of the flower stalk are borne clusters of from 3 to 20, fragrant, ½- to 1-inch-wide flowers. Borne in spring, the flowers are funnel-shaped, composed of five overlapping petals, and colored bright yellow. Having been cultivated for hundreds of years, *P. auricula* has been cross bred with other species, primarily *P. rubra* and *P. viscosa.* The result, along with confused nomenclature, is a large group of hundreds of floriferous cultivars—usually in shades and combinations of yellow, red, and purple, often with a large, paler eye in combination with a darker contrasting rim. Collectors divide the cultivars into four major groups, which are sometimes further subdivided: (1) common garden auriculas, with single-colored flowers and often a mat-white eye; (2) Belgian auriculas, with flowers of one or two main colors that tend to be darker toward the center, lighter toward the rim, and normally with a yellow or olive-colored eye; (3) English auriculas, with a white center that radiates outward to the margin of the petals giving a striped appearance, often with a third color at the edges of the petals, and the leaves covered with farina, a mealy material; and (4) double-flowered auriculas. Some of the most popular selections include 'Alba', with white flowers and compact habit; 'Blue Wave', with violet-blue flowers and yellow centers and wavy edges; 'Copper King', flowers with yellow centers, ruffled, coppery-colored petals; 'Dale's Red', with brick-red flowers and yellow centers; 'Gold of Ophir', with vibrant yellow flowers; 'Old Red Dusty Miller', with rose-red flowers and farina-covered stems; 'Old Yellow Dusty Miller', similar to 'Old Red Dusty Miller' but with yellow flowers; 'The Mikado', with deep red flowers, a vigorous grower; 'Winifred', reaching 6 inches tall, noteworthy for its vigorous growth and red flowers with gold centers.

P. denticulata (den-tik-you-*lay*-ta), named for its irregularly fine-tooth-edged leaves, is commonly called toothed primrose and Himalayan primrose (for its native habitat). This 10-inch-tall, 12-inch-wide species is hardy in Zones 4 to 8. Its leaves are oblong, soft green, to 6 inches long. It blooms in spring with a dense, ball-shaped cluster of ½-inch-wide flowers in shades of purple to pinkish purple with white or yellow centers held atop 12-inch-tall stems.

P. japonica (ja-*pon*-i-ka), Japanese primrose, is a candelabra-type, meaning that its flowers occur in whorls one above the other on a stalk. Hardy in Zones 5 to 7, it reaches 18 to 24 inches tall (in flower) by 2 feet across. Its oblong to spatula-shaped leaves reach 10 inches long and are colored medium green. The rose-purple or white flowers, which reach 1 inch across, are carried on stout stalks in one-tiered to six-tiered whorls. Selections of this easy-to-grow primrose include 'Miller's Crimson', with vibrant red flowers; 'Postford White', with large yellow-eyed, white flowers; var. *rosea,* with variably rose to pink flowers.

P. × variabilis (vare-ee-a-*bi*-lis), formerly *P. tommasinii,* is the result from crossing *P. vulgaris* and *P. veris.* It has many vibrant yellow flowers, yet is rather rare in cultivation.

P. veris (*vee*-ris / *ver*-is), meaning first flower of spring, is commonly called cowslip. This variable European species, which by some standards is split into several subspecies, is hardy in Zones 5 to 9. Typically it is oval-leaved, reaches 4 inches tall (to 12 inches when in flower), and bears a one-sided cluster of fragrant ½- to ¾-inch-long bell-shaped, bright yellow flowers atop a 4- to 8-inch-long flower stalk. Horticultural selections include 'Coccinea', with crimson flowers; 'Kleynii', with yellow flowers fading to apricot; 'Lutea', with pale yellow flowers; subsp. *macrocalyx,* with orange-yellow flowers, native to Asia.

P. vulgaris (vul-*gay*-ris), meaning common, is commonly called English primrose. Native to Europe, it is hardy in Zones 5 to 8, reaches 6 to 9 inches tall, and spreads more than 1 foot wide. Its leaves are broadly lance-shaped to oval, reach 10 inches long, and display a prominent central rib, irregularly toothed margin, and wrinkled, medium to deep green blade. The numerous slightly fragrant flowers, which are effective in spring, are borne on 6-inch-long, slender, slightly hairy stalks. Each blossom reaches up to 1½ inches across, has five petals, and is colored sulfur-yellow. It has been used extensively to create new plants through hybridization. Nosegay and Biedermeier strains are noteworthy for the profusion of flowers that they bear, while Barnhaven hybrids, reputed to be hardier, bear pastel-colored flowers. Horticultural selections include 'Alba', with white flowers; 'Atropurpurea', with purple flowers; 'Lilacina', with light purplish blue flowers; 'Lutea', with yellow flowers; 'Rosea', with pinkish red flowers; 'Rubra', with red flowers.

CULTURE / CARE: All primulas prefer rich soils and perform best when the soil is somewhat acidic. *Primula polyantha, P. auricula,* and *P. vulgaris* need excellent drainage, while *P. japonica,* and *P. veris* prefer soil with a high moisture content. Primulas also need to be sheltered from strong drying winds. They tolerate full sun in cool summer climates. In warmer climates light to moderate shade is best. None is very tolerant of drought. Pests of greatest consequence are aphids, weevils, nematodes, mites, and mealybugs. Diseases such as bacterial leaf spot, root rot, anthracnose, crown rot, leaf blight, viral mosaic, and aster yellows are sometimes problematic. Maintenance consists of applying an annual top-dressing of an inch or so of organic compost. When plants become crowded, they should be lifted, divided, and replanted.

PROPAGATION: Division is simple and best performed during the spring. Seed is sometimes used as well and is often available commercially; it should be stratified under moist conditions for one month at 35°F, then sown in early spring for germination three to five weeks later.

Prunella grandiflora   PLATE 254

Large-flowered Self-heal, Carpenter Weed, Allheal

Large-flowered self-heal is a low-growing, herbaceous, basal-leaved, rhizomatous, mat-forming ground cover. Reaching 6 to 12 inches tall and spreading to 1½ feet across, it does an excellent job of covering the soil (similar to *Ajuga*) and can be used as a small-scale to moderate-scale general cover as well as a specimen or accent plant in the rock garden or perennial border. During the seventeenth century, herbalists used the closely related species *P. vulgaris* as a treatment for various infections and maladies. Over time, the name self-heal, became applied to *P. grandiflora* as well.

SCIENTIFIC NAME: *Prunella grandiflora* (prew-*nel*-a gran-di-*flore*-ra). Reportedly the name *Prunella* came from the German *Braune,* quinsy (tonsillitis), a disease these plants supposedly cured. Other sources suggest the name came from the Latin *prunum,* purple, in reference to the color of the flowers. *Grandiflora* means large-flowered.

HARDINESS / ORIGIN: Zones 5 to 9; Europe, naturalized in temperate regions worldwide.

LEAVES / FLOWERS / FRUIT: The semievergreen, simple, oval, and deeply veined leaves range from 1½ to 2 inches long by ½ to ¾ inch wide. Colored medium to dark green, they lend strong contrast to the whitish, purple-lipped, 1-inch-long flowers which are held in 2- to 3-inch-tall cylindrical spikes in summer.

RATE / SPACING: Growth is moderate. Plants from 3- to 4-inch-diameter containers are spaced 8 to 12 inches apart.

HORTICULTURAL SELECTIONS: 'Alba', with white flowers; 'Loveliness', a hybrid group with pink, white, and pale violet-blue flowers; 'Rosea', with

pink flowers; 'Rotkappchen', with red flowers; 'Rubra', with red flowers.

CULTURE / CARE: This species is best in organically rich, moderately acidic, well-drained loam. It is not greatly tolerant of drought, and its soil should be kept slightly moist with summertime watering as needed. It prefers full sun to moderate shade. Diseases such as blight, leaf spot, powdery mildew, and root rot are common, and aphids are the most prevalent pest. Maintenance consists of mowing plantings as soon as the flowers begin to fade to prevent self-sowing (cultivars seldom come true to type) and to promote a neat appearance.

PROPAGATION: Cultivars must be propagated asexually. Division of clumps is effective almost any time. Ripe seed germinates in a couple of weeks without pretreatment.

Pulmonaria saccharata   PLATE 255

Bethlehem Sage, Spotted Mary, Virgin Mary's Milkdrops, Soldiers and Sailors, Hundreds and Thousands, Lungwort

Bethlehem sage is a herbaceous, low-growing, usually clump-forming ground cover that reaches 9 to 12 inches tall and spreads to 2 feet across. Three of its common names suggest that this plant might have played a role in the birth of Christ. The common name soldiers and sailors refers to the flower colors, which change from red to blue as they mature, and hundreds and thousands, to this plant's ability to proliferate by crown expansion. The name lungwort is applied because the speckled leaves supposedly resemble a lung, and pulmonarias were once used as a treatment for pulmonary maladies. The Swiss physician and alchemist Theophrastus Bombast von Hohenheim (otherwise known as Paracelsus, 1493–1541) advanced the Doctrine of Signatures, according to which plants were believed to possess medical value for ailments of the organs that they most closely resembled. For example, *Hepatica,* with its liver-shaped leaves, was thought to cure ailments of the liver, and walnuts, with their deeply convoluted brainlike nutmeats, to cure ailments of the brain. The principle was applied to countless other plants, including pulmonarias.

Bethlehem sage is a unique ground cover well suited for edging shady paths and herbaceous perennial borders. Its slow rate of spread and eye-catching foliage are a splendid combination that allows it to perform its job in both a carefree and aesthetically pleasing manner. The plant holds a nice shape and seldom presents encroachment problems. It is very effective when planted underneath and around deciduous shrubs and trees and is said to be compatible with black walnut (*Juglans nigra*). It may be employed on a small, moderate, or large scale. No foot traffic is tolerated.

SCIENTIFIC NAME: *Pulmonaria saccharata* (pul-moe-*nay*-ree-a sak-a-*ray*-ta). *Pulmonaria* comes from the Latin *pulmo,* lung, and *saccharata,* sugared, referring to the white-spotted leaves that appear to be powdered by sugar.

HARDINESS / ORIGIN: Zones 3 to 8; Europe.

LEAVES / FLOWERS / FRUIT: The more than 6-inch-long, elliptic, evergreen leaves arise directly from the rootstock or are held upon stems that ascend and give rise to flowers. The leaves are rough to the touch and profusely spotted white upon dark green. The floral-stem leaves are more oval-shaped and somewhat smaller than the basal leaves. During early spring, the five-parted, pink to rose-red flower buds open to expose ¾- to 1-inch-long, ½ inch wide, strikingly bright blue to violet flowers. The tiny nut-like fruit that follows is nonornamental.

RATE / SPACING: Growth is moderate. Plants from pint-sized to quart-sized containers are spaced 12 to 18 inches apart.

HORTICULTURAL SELECTIONS: 'Alba', with white flowers; 'Argentea', with narrow almost solid silver leaves; 'Baby Blue', with compact habit, silvery splotched foliage, and sky blue flowers that fade to pink as they age; 'Boughton Blue', with clear blue flowers, long, narrow, and randomly blotched foliage; 'British Sterling', reaching 15 inches tall, with numerous silvery spots that overlap to make the leaves almost completely silver, flowers blue and pink; 'Coral', with pale orange flowers; 'Highdown', with early blooming rich blue flowers, somewhat taller than the species; 'Leopard', with reddish purple flowers and green leaves with silvery blotches; 'Mrs. Moon', with large pink flower buds that open to showy gentian blue; 'Pierre's Pure Pink', with shell-pink flowers that remain pink as they age; 'Pink Dawn', with uniform pink flowers; 'Regal Ruffles', a hybrid with compact habit, silver-spotted leaves, and large unique ruffled flowers; 'Roy Davidson', sometimes billed as a hybrid, with lance-shaped leaves, prominent silver spotting, mounding habit, and showy sky blue flowers; 'Sissinghurst White', with silvery-whitish-spotted foliage and white flowers.

OTHER SPECIES: *P. angustifolia* (an-gus-ti-*foe*-lee-a), which means narrow-leaved, is commonly called cowslip lungwort. Typically it reaches 8 to 12 inches tall by 12 to 18 inches wide. It has evergreen foliage that may exceed 6 to 12 inches in length and is colored a good dark green year-round. The five-parted, pink-budded flowers mature to blue or violet in early to mid summer. The fruit that follows is nonornamental. The species is hardy in Zones 2 to 8. Horti-

cultural selections include 'Alba', with white flowers; 'April Opal', with intense blue flowers; 'Azurea', with sky blue flowers; 'Benediction', with compact habit, white-spotted leaves, and large cobalt blue flowers; 'Mawson's Variety', with leaves not as evergreen; 'Munstead Blue', with deep blue flowers and deciduous leaves; 'Rubra', with red to deep reddish violet flowers.

P. longifolia (long-gi-*foe*-lee-a), long-leaved lungwort, is native to western Europe and is hardy in Zones 3 to 8. It is characterized by narrow, 12- to 18-inch-long dark green, gray-spotted foliage in spring, and it displays purplish blue flowers arranged in terminal racemes. 'Bertram Anderson', with blue flowers and star-shaped rosettes of fuzzy, gray-blotched, narrow green leaves; subsp. *cevennensis,* hardy in Zones 5 to 9, 6 inches tall by 4 feet wide, with narrow, nearly 2-foot-long silver-spotted leaves, dark violet-blue flowers; 'Little Blue', with numerous flowers and tall, narrow, lance-shaped leaves.

P. mollis (*mol*-lis), soft lungwort, is hardy in Zones 4 to 8 and hails from southeastern and central Europe. With upright, tapered, softly haired, dark green evergreen leaves, this clump former strongly resembles primrose. It reaches up to 18 inches tall by 2 feet wide, and its flowers, borne in tight clusters at the tips of 10-inch-tall flower stalks, are intense blue fading to purple or salmon-red. 'Royal Blue' was selected for especially deep blue flowers.

P. officinalis (oh-fis-i-*nay*-lis), Jerusalem cowslip or common lungwort, is hardy in Zones 3 to 10 and reaches 1 foot tall by 1½ feet wide. Native to Europe, it displays bristle-covered, oval, 2- to 4-inch-long leaves and violet-blue ½- to ¾-inch wide bell-shaped flowers. 'Alba' is white flowered; 'Cambridge Blue', has powder blue flowers; 'White Wings' is white flowered.

P. rubra (*rew*-bra), red lungwort, is hardy in Zones 4 to 7 and has coral-red flowers and pale green leaves. It is noteworthy for its unique bloom time of early to mid winter. 'Albocorollata' has white flowers; 'Bowles' Variety' has mottled foliage and salmon-red flowers; 'Redstart' has deep red flowers and compact habit; 'Salmon Glow' has attractive salmon-colored flowers.

P. villarsae (vil-*lar*-see) is hardy in Zones 4 to 8 and hails from Italy. It resembles *P. mollis* but is less upright in habit and displays broader more heavily mottled evergreen leaves. The well-known selection 'Margery Fish' is more common than the species, displays evergreen dark green silvery-white-marbled foliage, and strong vigor.

Numerous species and cultivars of lungwort have been crossbred to produce a number of interesting cultivars that are hardy to Zone 4: 'Apple Frost', with compact habit, rose-colored flowers, and apple-green leaves that are overlaid with silver; 'Berries and Cream', leaves with silver centers, dark green ruffled edges, flowers pink; 'David Ward', leaves with pale green centers and white edges, flowers salmon-pink; 'Excalibur', with mounding and spreading habit, good vigor and unique narrow, silver, dark-green-margined leaves; 'Little Star', with azure blue flowers for 2½ months, narrow silvery spotted leaves, good vigor; 'Milky Way', with very large, heavily spotted foliage, wine-red flowers; 'Purple Haze', with compact habit, silvered and spotted leaves which are suffused with purple at their bases, flowers first blue then rose; 'Regal Ruffles', with compact habit and unique ruffled broadly oval, milky-spotted foliage, deep lavender-purple flowers; 'Silver Dollar', with broad, nearly round, silver foliage; 'Silver Streamers', an extraordinary, iridescent silvery-white-leaved selection with interesting wavy leaf margins; 'Spilled Milk', with compact habit, broad silvery leaves, pink flowers.

CULTURE / CARE: Lungworts are at their best when grown in moderate to dense shade in organically rich, constantly moist, loamy soils. They adapt to almost any soil provided drainage is good; however, they are sure to suffer in very hot, dry weather. Make every effort to place them in locations where the temperature stays relatively cool, and few serious diseases will occur. Slugs are the most problematic pest. Little or no maintenance is required, although vigor might be increased with occasional thinning should plantings become overcrowded. Also, an annual top-dressing with a light application of rotted leaf mold is good for the soil.

PROPAGATION: Division is effective in late summer or fall. Seed can be sown in late summer.

Pulsatilla vulgaris   PLATE 256
European Pasque Flower

An extract of the bracts is said to have been used in dyeing Easter eggs, hence the common name European pasque flower (*pasque* meaning Easter in French). Until recently this species was considered to be a member of the genus *Anemone* and named *A. pulsatilla*. It differs from *Anemone* species in that its seeds contain feathery appendages called styles that, in addition to being botanical curiosities, add summertime ornamental appeal after the flowers have faded. Perennial enthusiasts and florists have long appreciated European Pasque flower (and the closely related cultivars of *Anemone* × *hybridus*), but to a great extent, gardeners have overlooked its usefulness as a ground cover. This is unfortunate, for in foliage as well as flower, it is simply beautiful. Herba-

ceous, relatively dense-growing, and reaching 12 inches tall by 18 inches wide, it is a ground cover well suited for background planting behind low-growing ground covers such as ajuga and thrift. Next to low, sprawling junipers it not only infuses floral color but also provides an effective element of textural contrast with its soft, fernlike foliage. Clumps of European Pasque flower are marvelous for accent beside reflecting pools, next to boulders, in planters, and next to building entrances. They are effective in edging sidewalks and garden paths, and, of course, they make fine specimens in herbaceous border plantings. No foot traffic is tolerated.

SCIENTIFIC NAME: *Pulsatilla vulgaris* (pul-sa-*til*-la vul-*gay*-ris). *Pulsatilla* comes from the Latin *pulso,* to strike, but the application to this plant is unclear. *Vulgaris* means common.

HARDINESS / ORIGIN: Zones 5 to 8; Europe and Asia.

LEAVES / FLOWERS / FRUIT: The deciduous leaves arise from the base of the plant and have a very lacy, almost fernlike texture. Upon maturation, which occurs after flowering, the three-parted leaves reach 4 to 6 inches long and are colored bluish green. The outstanding apetalous flowers get their appeal from the brightly colored bracts that surround them. Appearing during early spring, they reach 2 inches wide, are bell-shaped, and display reddish purple sepals (leaflets that compose each bract). The fruit consists of fuzzy seed heads, which are persistent and attractive.

RATE / SPACING: Growth is slow to moderate. Plants from pint-sized to gallon-sized containers are spaced 10 to 14 inches apart.

HORTICULTURAL SELECTIONS: Var. *alba,* with creamy white flowers; var. *grandis,* more vigorous and a bit taller than the species; var. *rubra,* with intensely purplish bracts.

CULTURE / CARE: This species prefers well-drained, slightly acidic soils with enough organic matter to maintain moisture. Even so, it is does not tolerate saturated or poorly draining soils and will soon die if planted in such. It requires watering during periods of drought and prefers full sun in the North and full sun to light shade in the South. Maintenance needs are few if any, but some gardeners prefer to trim off the dried flower heads after the seeds fall off.

PROPAGATION: Seed should be sown immediately upon ripening, never allowing it to dry out or dormancy may be prolonged; germination will occur in five or six weeks at 68°F. Division of mature plants can also be performed but often with some loss. Root cuttings should be made during fall; cut 2-inch-long sections, lay them on the surface of 2-inch-deep soil in nursery flats, and cover with ½ inch of soil.

Pyracantha koidzumii Cultivars   PLATE 257
Formosa Firethorn Cultivars

While Formosa firethorn, at 8 to 12 feet tall, is not a ground cover, it is the parent of many fine ground-covering cultivars. They generally range from 1½ to 3 feet tall, mound up in the center, and spread 3 to 6 feet across. In the landscape they are often used on a moderate to large scale as low, informal hedges, particularly on uneven or rocky terrain. They are colorful in flower and fruit and lend themselves well to planting as specimens. No foot traffic is tolerated.

SCIENTIFIC NAME: *Pyracantha koidzumii* (pie-ra-*kan*-tha koyd-*zoom*-ee-eye). *Pyracantha* comes from the Greek *pyr,* fire, and *akantha,* a thorn, referring to the red berries and thorns. *Koidzumii* is a commemorative of unknown origin.

HARDINESS / ORIGIN: Zones 7 or 8 to 10; Taiwan.

LEAVES / FLOWERS / FRUIT: The typically evergreen leaves may be semievergreen in the northern part of the species' range. They are dark shiny green and from 1 to 3 inches long by and ½ to ¾ inch wide. Along their edges may be small teeth. At the ends of the branches are borne clusters of numerous ¼-inch-wide, five-petaled, white, not-so-pleasantly-fragrant flowers in mid summer. The ¼-inch-wide round fruit that follows is outstanding. Maturing in early fall, it becomes bright red and persists throughout the winter months.

RATE / SPACING: Growth is moderate. Dwarf plants are spaced 3 to 4 feet apart.

HORTICULTURAL SELECTIONS: 'Santa Cruz', 2 to 3 feet tall by 5 to 6 feet wide, good disease resistance; 'Walderi Prostrata', 3 to 4 feet tall by 5 to 6 feet wide, large red fruit.

HYBRID SELECTIONS: *P.* 'Red Elf', a dwarf, 2 feet tall by 3 or 4 feet wide, mounded habit, dark green leaves, bright red fruit, less susceptible to fireblight, hardy in Zones 7 to 9; *P.* 'Ruby Mound', 1½ feet tall by 3 feet wide, mounded habit, drooping branches, hardy in Zones 7 to 9.

OTHER SPECIES: *P. coccinea* 'Lowboy' (kok-*kin*-ee-a), 'Lowboy' scarlet firethorn, is a vigorous grower that reaches 2 to 3 feet tall by 6 to 8 feet wide. It displays rich green leaves, bright orange fruit, and is hardy to Zone 5.

CULTURE / CARE: Ground-covering pyracanthas grow best in full sun in soils that are neutral or acidic. They need good drainage, are relatively drought tolerant, and, if located in areas where there is good air movement, remain relatively disease-free. Should they encounter problems, the cause is likely to be a blight infection, scab, canker, or root rot. Pests of greatest consequence are aphids, lace bugs, scales, mites, and leaf rollers. Maintenance is generally limited to pruning out any upright-growing shoots as they appear.

PROPAGATION: Stem cuttings can be rooted during early to mid summer; the application of 3000 ppm IBA/talc aides rooting but is not necessary.

Pyxidanthera barbulata   PLATE 258
Pyxie Moss, Pyxie, Flowering Moss, Moose Flower, Pine Barren Beauty

Pyxie moss is a low, mat-forming, evergreen, mosslike, semiwoody ground cover. It reaches 2 inches or less in height, spreads 3 feet across, and gives the appearance of green carpeting. Attractively flowered with many tiny pink or white blooms and bright green foliage, it unfortunately is rather temperamental and thus uncommon in cultivation. Should one be fortunate enough to successfully cultivate it, the rewards are worth the effort. It is best used as a specimen or general cover and turf substitute on a small to moderate scale. Occasional foot traffic is tolerated.

SCIENTIFIC NAME: *Pyxidanthera barbulata* (piks-i-*dan*-the-ra bar-byu-*lay*-ta). *Pyxidanthera* comes from the Greek *pyxis,* a small box, and *anthera,* in reference to the anthers which open like the lid of a box). *Barbulata,* Latin for little beard, likely refers to some aspect of the flowers.

HARDINESS / ORIGIN: Zone 6; sandy pine barrens of New Jersey, Virginia, and southward to South Carolina.

LEAVES / FLOWERS / FRUIT: The evergreen, linear, lance-shaped, or linear oblong, ⅙- to ⅓-inch-long, 1/12-inch-wide leaves are colored bright shiny green. The springtime solitary flowers are tiny but very numerous, attractive, and noticeable when in bloom. Five-parted and ranging from ⅙ to ¼ inch across, they look like little white to pinkish bells.

RATE / SPACING: Growth is slow. Plants from 3- to 4-inch-diameter containers are spaced 6 to 8 inches apart.

OTHER SPECIES: *P. brevifolia* (brev-i-*foe*-lee-a), short-leaved pyxie moss, is very similar to *P. barbulata* but has smaller, hairy, narrower leaves. It is hardy to Zone 6.

CULTURE / CARE: Pyxie moss needs acidic sandy soil and full sun to light shade. Its drought tolerance is fair but an effort should be made to keep the soil slightly moist during dry weather. No serious diseases or insects have been reported. The only maintenance this plant needs is a good raking should it become matted with fallen leaves.

PROPAGATION: Cuttings may be rooted in a porous,

acidic medium during fall and winter; they reportedly respond well to bottom heat. Divisions can be made throughout the growing season.

Ranunculus repens PLATE 259

Creeping Buttercup, Creeping Crowfoot, Sitfast, Yellow Gowan, Butter Daisy, Spotted-leaf Buttercup, Ram's-claws, Gold-knops, Creeping Yellow Gowan

Normally used on a moderate to large scale, particularly in naturalized landscapes, creeping buttercup spreads fast and forms an effective 8- to 24-inch-tall ground cover in moist areas where few other broad-leaved ground covers will survive. It is attractive both in foliage and flower and combines well with moisture-tolerant native shrubs and trees.

SCIENTIFIC NAME: *Ranunculus repens* (ra-*nun*-kue-les *ree*-penz). *Ranunculus* comes from the Latin, *rana,* a frog, in reference to the marshy habitat of many species. *Repens,* also from Latin, means creeping and refers to the habit.

HARDINESS / ORIGIN: Zones 4 to 9; Europe, Asia, and western Canada, naturalized throughout much of northeastern United States and Canada.

LEAVES / FLOWERS / FRUIT: Deciduous, shiny dark green, and often grayish-mottled, the compound leaves are divided into three coarsely toothed leaflets. Each leaflet is 2 inches long by 2 inches wide and is sparsely covered with stiff bristles on either side. From mid spring through late summer are borne ½- to 1-inch-wide, bright yellow, five-parted flowers. Although they are not large, against the dark green background of the leaves, they show up remarkably well. The small fruit is nonornamental.

RATE / SPACING: Growth is fast. Plants from 3- to 4-inch-diameter containers are spaced 1 to 1½ feet apart.

HORTICULTURAL SELECTIONS: 'Pleniflorus' ('Flore-Pleno'), showy double flowers.

CULTURE / CARE: Creeping buttercup performs well in both acidic and alkaline soils in full sun to moderate shade. The soil should be moist at all times and should have a moderate to high organic content. Diseases of greatest incidence are leaf spots, mildew, root rot, rust, viral curly-top, and aster yellows. Aphids sometimes feed on the tender new growth but do little real harm. Maintenance consists of little more than cutting back the runners as they outgrow their bounds.

PROPAGATION: Propagation is easy by division any time during the growing season. Seed can also be used and should be collected when ripe, stored dry and cool, then sown the following spring.

Raoulia australis PLATE 260

New Zealand Scab Plant, Raoulia

Forming a dense, flat, silvery-white mosslike carpet, this slow-growing temperamental creeper makes a charming cover in rocky alpine gardens in areas of mild climate—generally the west coast from San Francisco to Vancouver. Needing little care, raoulia reaches no more than ¼ inch tall and slowly spreads to more than 1 foot across. It grows across small rocks and is used as a carpeter. It combines well with other rock garden plants such as *Hebe* species, *Carex buchananii,* and *Jovibarba* species and cultivars. Limited foot traffic is tolerated.

SCIENTIFIC NAME: *Raoulia australis* (ray-*ew*-lee-a aus-*tray*-lis). *Raoulia* commemorates Edward Raoul (1815–1852), a French surgeon and student of New Zealand plants. *Australis* means southern.

HARDINESS / ORIGIN: Zone 7; barren ground and dry streambeds of New Zealand, from the plains to an altitude of 5500 feet.

LEAVES / FLOWERS / FRUIT: The evergreen, crowded, oblong, silvery white-haired, alternately arranged leaves reach only 1/10 inch long. Perched atop the foliage during mid to late summer arise the tiny, sunflower-like flowers with yellow bracts. The tiny fruit is nonornamental.

RATE / SPACING: Growth is very slow. Plants from 3- to 4-inch-wide containers are spaced 2 to 4 inches apart.

OTHER SPECIES: ***R. glabra*** (*glay*-bra), meaning leaves without hairs, hails from grassy open areas of lowlands up to 4000 feet. More loosely branched with ascending stems than *R. australis,* it sprawls 12 inches across, displays yellowish green ⅕-inch-long leaves, and produces flowers with yellow or white bracts during mid summer.

R. subsericea (sub-*sir*-ee-see-a), meaning with silky hairs below (i.e., undersurface of the leaves), is another flat spreader. It naturally inhabits grassy open mountainous terrain from 1000 to 4500 feet. Clothed in light green ⅙- to ⅓-inch-long leaves, it covers the ground in mosslike fashion and during mid to late spring produces ⅕-inch-wide flowers with white bracts.

R. tenuicaulis (ten-yew-i-*kaw*-lis), meaning slender-stemmed, is also slender leaved. Indeed, its foliage, which reaches ¼ inch long by ⅑ inch wide, is more lance-shaped than oblong, as is the case for most other species. Another creeper, this one naturally inhabits sandy or gravelly dry stream beds from sea level to 5000 feet. Its branchlets, like those of *R. glabra,* tend to ascend. Its ⅓-inch-wide flower heads display dark-tipped bracts during mid to late summer.

LESS COMMON SPECIES: *R. eximia* (eks-*im*-ee-a) reaches 16 inches tall by 3 feet wide and has oblong to spatula-shaped ⅛-inch-long leaves and tiny ⅛-inch-wide flowers with white bracts.

R. grandiflora (gran-di-*floe*-ra) forms mats or cushions to 6 inches wide and is clothed in densely set ⅜-inch-long silvery haired foliage. Its flowers reach ⅝ inch wide with white-tipped bracts.

R. haastii (*hahst*-ee-eye) forms cushions 12 inches tall by 3 feet wide, roots as it creeps, and is clothed in densely set ¹⁄₁₆-inch-long foliage. Its flowers reach ³⁄₁₆ inch wide and are decorated by creamy-white-tipped bracts.

R. mammilaris (mam-i-*lay*-ris), named for its white-tipped floral bracts, forms dense woody cushions to 2 feet wide.

CULTURE / CARE: *Raoulia* species like sunny sites in well-drained gravelly, sandy, or gritty moisture-retentive (from incorporated humus), acidic to neutral soils. Their drought tolerance is only fair but neither do they like excess moisture or humidity, especially during the winter. Plants should be protected from winter cold by covering them with open evergreen boughs, but seldom is any other maintenance needed.

PROPAGATION: Although these species can be propagated by seed, most gardeners find division to be the easier method.

Raphiolepis umbellata Cultivars   PLATE 261
Yeddo, Indian Hawthorn, Raphiolepis

This species is a florific evergreen that needs little care and brings great pleasure. The species itself, ranging from 4 to 6 feet tall by 4 to 6 feet across, is probably a little large to be considered a ground cover. The dwarf, compact forms, however, which typically range from 2 to 4 feet tall by 3 to 4 feet across, are exceptional. Common in southern and coastal landscapes, these cultivars are normally used in mass plantings as facers and hedge plants. Even so, a single specimen placed in a rock garden, an elevated planter, or atop a terrace embankment is quite effective. Similarly, groups of three to five plants can be used to lend accent to specimen trees, walls, or sculpture. In Japan a brown dye is made from the bark of yeddo.

SCIENTIFIC NAME: *Raphiolepis umbellata* (raf-ee-oh-*le*-pis um-bel-*lay*-ta). *Raphiolepis* comes from the Greek *raphis,* a needle, and *lepis,* a scale, likely in reference to the floral bracts. *Umbellata* refers to the arrangement of the flowers in umbel-like clusters, but this seems to be a bit of a misnomer, as the flowers are actually arranged in wide panicles or racemes.

HARDINESS / ORIGIN: Zones 8 or 9 to 10; Japan and Korea.

LEAVES / FLOWERS / FRUIT: The evergreen leaves are simple, alternately arranged, range from 1 to 1½ inches long by ¾ to 1¼ inches wide, and are oval to broadly oval. The leaves that are carried near the ends of the stems are smooth-edged while those closer to the base are toothed about their margins. Each is leathery, shiny dark green above and dull green below and during winter takes on a slight purplish tinge. The flowers, borne from reddish purple buds during mid spring, are fragrant, white, ¾ inch wide, and borne in good numbers. The attractive fruit which follows is a ⅜- to ½-inch-diameter purplish black to bluish black berry that ripens during early fall and persists well through the winter.

RATE / SPACING: Growth is moderate. Plants from 1- to 5-gallon-sized containers are spaced 3 to 3½ feet apart.

HORTICULTURAL SELECTIONS: *R. × delacourii* (dee-la-*kore*-ee-eye), the result of crossing *R. indica* (Indian hawthorn, hardy in Zones 9 to 10) and *R. umbellata,* reaches 6 feet tall and has 2- to 3-inch-long leaves that are narrower and more sharply tooth-edged than *R. umbellata.* This hybrid species has led to ground-covering cultivars.

Very often the following cultivars are represented as members of *R. × delacourii* or *R. umbellata.* In reality, the origin of the cultivars is not well documented and, therefore, their assignment to a particular species is often no better than a guess. 'Ballerina', 3 to 4 feet tall, with reddish wintertime foliage and rose-pink flowers that are borne intermittently during summer; 'Charisma', with double softly pink flowers, vibrant green leaves, and tight compact habit; 'Clara', to 4 feet tall by 4 feet wide, with white flowers and red juvenile leaves that mature to dark green; 'Coates Crimson', 2 to 4 feet tall by 2 to 4 feet wide, with crimson-pink flowers; 'Indian Princess', broadly mounded, compact habit, with bright pink flowers that fade to white as they age; 'Minor', 2 to 3 feet tall and wide, dark green leaves and small fragrant flowers in early spring; 'Pink Cloud', with pink flowers and compact habit, 3 feet tall by 3 to 4 feet wide; 'Pink Dancer', with compact mounding habit, 16 inches tall by 3 feet wide, pink flowers, and shiny leaves with wavy margins that turn bronzy or maroon during winter; 'Snow White', a compact dwarf with spreading habit and pure white flowers from early spring to early summer; 'Spring Rapture', with rose-red flowers and compact mounding habit; 'White Enchantress', with low compact habit and white flowers.

CULTURE / CARE: The compact yeddos prefer well-drained acidic or slightly alkaline soil and full sun to light shade. Their tolerance to drought is fair, and they do best if given frequent deep drinks of water during extended periods of intense heat and drought. Nematodes are sometimes problematic, as are scale insects. Twig blight and leaf spots can be serious in locations that are too shady or where the soil is inadequately drained. They require little or no maintenance and should not be pruned, except to remove dead stems, as it interferes with the development of their natural character.

PROPAGATION: While the species is propagated by seed, the cultivars need to be propagated vegetatively. Cuttings taken during midsummer should be treated with 10,000 to 20,000 ppm IBA/talc and rooted under mist.

Rhododendron   PLATE 262

Encompassing what we usually refer to as rhododendrons and azaleas, this genus of, by some accounts, about 900 species is comprised of small to large evergreen, semievergreen, and deciduous, usually spring-blooming shrubs (and a few small trees). Those plants that are commonly referred to as rhododendrons are evergreen and have 10 or more stamens per flower. Azaleas are usually deciduous and have 5 stamens per flower. For the most part *Rhododendron* species are native to temperate regions of the Northern Hemisphere. Due to their ability to hybridize, the number of cultivars is astounding. Species and cultivars (many of hybrid origin) for ground-cover use are relatively low growing, mounding, and compact in habit with horizontal or erect branches. Generally speaking, these types range from 6 inches to 4 feet tall and spread 2 to 5 feet across. The ground-covering cultivars are usually used as specimens for shrub borders and rock gardens. Additionally, they are excellent for edging and accent, and, like heather (*Calluna*), make very interesting general covers and lawn substitutes when mass planted in various color combinations. They are especially effective on slopes or terraced hillsides where they eliminate the need to mow and where their visibility is enhanced. It has been said that the low-growing rhododendrons combine beautifully with wildflowers, but using them in combination with heavy feeding ground covers such as *Epimedium* or *Vinca* may stunt their growth and decrease their floral display.

SCIENTIFIC NAME: *Rhododendron* (roe-doe-*den*-dron) comes from the Greek *rhodo*, a rose, and *dendron*, a tree, thus literally rose tree. The name was probably first applied to *R. ferrugineum*, alpine rose. Others, however, claim that *Rhododendron* was the Greek name for oleander (*Nerium oleander*), the popular florific evergreen shrub so commonly planted in Zones 8 to 10.

HARDINESS / ORIGIN: See individual species or groups.

LEAVES / FLOWERS / FRUIT: For the most part the leaves are evergreen or deciduous, opposite, simple, oval, smooth along the edges, from ¾ to 2½ inches long by ½ to ¾ inch across, and colored dark shiny green. Usually the tube-shaped to trumpet-shaped flowers are clustered at the ends of the stems in spring. Each is five-parted and very showy. Typical colors are white, pink, red, yellow, orange, and shades in between. The fruit is nonornamental.

RATE / SPACING: Growth is slow. Plants from 2- to 3-gallon-sized containers are spaced 2 to 3 feet apart.

HYBRID GROUPS AND SPECIES: **Girard Hybrids.** This group of hybrids originated from breeding efforts at Girard Nurseries in Geneva, Ohio. Well adapted to withstand cold (hardy in Zone 5 or 6), these evergreen azaleas are large-flowered. A couple of the compact forms make good ground covers. 'Girard National Beauty' reaches 2 feet tall by 3 feet wide and displays ruffled rose-pink flowers above large dark green leaves. 'Girard's Scarlet' reaches 1½ to 2 feet tall by 3 feet wide and displays deep glossy green leaves and red flowers with orange-red blush.

Glenn Dale Hybrids. A group of cold-tolerant (to Zone 5 or 6) cultivars, the Glenn Dale Hybrids display much diversity in respect to habit and flowers. A few that make nice ground covers are 'Guerdon', with light lavender flowers and lavender-rose blotches, low spreading habit, and height to 2 feet; 'Polar Sea', with height to 3 feet tall, broad spreading habit, frilly white flowers and chartreuse blotches; 'Sagittarius', with low spreading habit to 2 feet, pink flowers suffused with salmon; 'Seafoam', with height to 3 feet tall, broad spreading habit, frilly white flowers with chartreuse throats; 'Snowclad', with low spreading habit to 3 feet tall, ruffled white flowers and chartreuse blotches; 'Vestal', with wide spreading habit, height to 4 feet tall, white flowers and chartreuse blotches.

Indicum Hybrids. Although the name of this hybrid group comes from the species *R. indicum,* the role of this parent in their development may actually be overshadowed by that of *R. simsii, R. pulchrum, R. mucronatum,* and others. Nevertheless, this group of low-growing azaleas, which was originally developed for the indoor plant market, is composed of a number of showy single-flowered and double-flowered forms that have become popular outdoor plants. The first varieties are reported to have appeared in England around 1830. They are hardy in Zones 6 or 7 to 9. Some of the more common ground-covering selections include 'Balsaminiflorum', disputably claimed to be a cultivar of the species *R. indicum* (rather than the hybrid *R. × in-*

dicum), with double salmon-red flowers in early summer and a height of only 4 inches; 'Flame Creeper', with orangish red flowers and a height to 10 inches; 'Kozan', with pink flowers; 'Macrantha', with compact habit, height of 3 feet, and double red flowers; 'Macrantha Double', with double orange-pink flowers.

R. kiusianum (kye-*ew*-see-aye-num), one of the parents of the Kurume Azaleas (see below), this dense-spreading dwarf displays 1-inch-long evergreen or semievergreen leaves. It hails from Japan, is hardy to Zone 7, and in late spring produces attractive funnel-shaped purple, white, or crimson florets that are grouped in clusters of two to five. Cultivars include 'Album', with white flowers; 'Benichidori', with small, bright reddish orange flowers; 'Benisuzume', with low spreading habit, reddish orange flowers; 'Hanekomachi', with bright pinkish red flowers; 'Harunoumi', with soft pink flowers; 'Komo Kulshan', with small rose-margined pale pink flowers; 'Rose', with rose-colored flowers, low habit, small leaves; 'Ukon', with petite pink flowers.

Kurume Azaleas. With more than 50 selections, this large hybrid group originated in Kurume, Japan, in the late 1800s from crosses involving *R. kaempferi, R. obtusum,* and *R. kiusianum.* The cultivars were not introduced into the United States until 1918. For the most part, they are characterized by a densely branched habit and small leaves. Their height may reach 3 feet tall and their profusion of 1-inch-wide flowers comes in various shades of red. Hardiness northward is usually limited to Zone 6. Noteworthy selections include 'Album', with white flowers; 'Bridesmaid', with bright red flowers; 'Coral Bells', with double pink flowers; 'Hexe', with crimson flowers; 'Hino-crimson', with bright red flowers; 'Hinodegiri', with cerise-red flowers; 'Sherwood Orchid', with reddish violet flowers; 'Sherwood Red', with orange-red flowers; 'Snow', with vivid white flowers; 'Wards', with ruby red flowers.

R. lapponicum (la-*pon*-i-kum), meaning of Lapland, is commonly called Lapland rhododendron or Lapland rosebay. Native to arctic and subarctic regions of North America, Europe, Greenland, and Asia, often it is found growing in barrens, on bluffs, and in high alpine regions. Occasionally disjunct populations are found farther south, and the species is of interest for its adaptability to calcareous and magnesian soils. Hardy to Zone 2 or 3, this relatively low-growing, dense, compact, shrubby ground cover reaches 1½ feet tall and spreads more than 2½ feet wide. Growth is slow. Plants from 1- to 2-gallon-sized containers are spaced 2 to 3 feet apart. Usually this species is used as a rock garden specimen, but when massed on a moderate to large scale, it might

make a functional and rather attractive general cover or foundation plant. It also could perform nicely as a border edging, especially in combination with taller rhododendrons, blueberries, and other members of the heath family. Unfortunately, *R. lapponicum* is rare, for it is quite difficult to propagate and culture. Often it fails shortly after propagation or dies after a lengthy decline. Its leaves are evergreen, simple, alternate, narrowly oval, ¼ to 1 inch long by ⅛ to ⅖ inch wide, thick, and leathery, and turn dark bronzy green in fall. Arranged in few-flowered clusters, the flowers are five-parted on short, scaly stalks. Each is ½ to 1 inch wide, oblong-petaled, purple, and effective in early summer. No foot traffic is tolerated.

Pennington Hybrids. This group of hybrids was bred by Ralph Pennington of Covington, Georgia. 'Beth Bullard', which reaches 2½ feet tall by 5 feet wide, has dark green leaves that contrast nicely with its 4-inch-wide reddish pink flowers.

P.J.M. cultivars. The result of crossing *R. carolinianum* and *R. dauricum* var. *sempervirens,* the P.J.M. cultivars are hardy to Zone 4, typically range from 3 to 6 feet tall, have evergreen leaves, are rounded in habit, and produce abundant lavender-pink flowers in early spring. They were developed at Weston Nurseries in Hopkinton, Massachusetts, and named after Peter J. Mezitt, founder of Weston Nurseries. Most of the work was done by Edmund V. Mezitt. A couple of selections are lower growing and work well as ground covers. These include 'Low Red Frilled', with low growing, broad spreading compact habit, dark green leaves, and red flowers with frilled edges; 'Molly Fordham', with small shiny green leaves, compact habit, and white flowers.

Polly Hill's North Tisbury Hybrids. Polly Hill of Martha's Vineyard has been selecting Japanese azaleas since 1957 with the objective of producing prostrate, evergreen, hardy ground covers. Reportedly, these hybrids arose from crosses involving *R. nahakarai* (a prostrate evergreen species that reaches only 5 inches tall in 10 years). Hardy to Zone 5 or 6, this group of evergreen azaleas is characterized by a height of 10 to 15 inches and a spread to 4 feet, with mounding or prostrate habit. The leaves are rather small, and the flowers, borne in spring, tend toward shades of red. Mrs. Hill has had considerable success, and today her exceptional plants grace landscapes throughout North America. Among the useful cultivars are 'Alex', with low spreading habit and red flowers; 'Alexander', reaching 1½ feet tall and blooming during mid to late spring with salmon-red flowers; 'Gabrielle Hill', reaching 15 inches tall, spreading 5 feet, relatively open-growing habit, light pink flowers with crimson blotches; 'Hill's Single Red', with salmon-red flowers, compact spreading habit; 'Hotline', with large, ruffled, bright purplish red flowers, mounded habit, 16 inches tall by 4 feet wide; 'Jeff Hill', with deep pink flowers, 1½ feet tall by 2½ feet wide; 'Joseph Hill', with bright red flowers, 1 foot tall by 3½ feet wide; 'Marilee', with purplish green leaves, rose-red flowers, 15 inches tall by 4 feet wide; 'Michael Hill', 17 inches tall by 45 inches wide, with soft pink, frilled flowers and dark throats; 'Pink Pancake', with robust habit, large wavy-edged, bright pink flowers; 'Susannah Hill', with vigorous low mounding habit, 15 inches tall by 5 feet wide, deep red flowers; 'Trill', reaching 14 inches tall by 2½ feet wide, with large ruffled red flowers; 'Wintergreen', mounded habit, pink to light red flowers, 15 inches tall by 3½ feet wide; 'Yaku', with low habit, large white flowers with soft pink stripes.

R. '**Purple Gem**', a compact selection from a cross involving *R. fastigiatum* and *R. carolinianum,* produces attractive and profuse violet flowers in early spring. It reaches only 8 inches tall, has blue-green evergreen leaves, and performs well in Zones 6 to 8. 'Purple Imp' is similar to 'Purple Gem' but smaller, denser growing, and bluer in flower.

R. racemosum '**Compactum**' (ray-se-*moh*-sum) reaches only 1 to 2 feet tall and produces light pink flowers.

R. '**Ramapo**', another compact selection, is hardy to Zone 4 or 5. It displays blue-green leaves and vibrant violet-pink flowers in spring.

Robin Hill Hybrids. Bred by Robert Gartrell using the Japanese Satsuki azaleas, this group is composed of innumerable low prostrate evergreen selections that are hardy to Zone 7 and display large open-faced flowers in soft muted pastels. Cultivars include 'Barbara M. Humphreys', pure white single flowers above bright green glossy foliage; 'Betty Ann Voss', double light pink flowers, weeping habit, and dark green leaves; 'Blue Tip', with lavender flowers and white centers; 'Chanson', semidouble to double pink flowers; 'Christie', with low mounding habit and pink flowers; 'Congo', with reddish purple flowers; 'Conversation Piece', with rich pink 4-inch-wide flowers that are dotted and blotched with pink, red, and white; 'Dorothy Hayden', with broad white flowers and green throats; 'Dorothy Rees', with large pure white, wavy edged flowers and green throats; 'Early Bent', with semidouble coral-red flowers, 28 inches tall by 3 feet wide; 'Eunice Updike', with pale scarlet flowers and mound-forming habit; 'Flame Dance', with weeping habit and large tubular red flowers; 'Frosty', with dark blotched, frosty overlaid, pink flowers; 'George Harding', with vivid red flowers and white throats; 'Gillie', with rose-salmon flowers; 'Givenda', with light pink flowers; 'Glamora',

with large semidouble lavender-tinted white flowers, 1½ feet tall by 3 feet wide; 'Glencora', with dwarf habit and medium red, double, 2½-inch-wide flowers; 'Gresham', with compact habit and large pink, variably striped flowers; 'Greta', with low mounding habit and dark pink, wavy-margined flowers; 'Gwenda', with 3-inch-wide pale pink ruffled flowers, 1½ feet tall by 3 feet wide; 'Hilda Niblett', with vigorous, low, cushionlike habit, 1 foot tall by 3 to 4 feet wide, lovely soft pink, reddish marked, 4-inch-wide flowers in late spring; 'Jeanne Weeks', with double lavender-pink flowers and compact mounded habit; 'Le Belle Helene', with pink, white-throated flowers; 'Lady Louise' with single or semidouble pink flowers and dark pink splotches; 'Lady Robin', with white flowers that are variably striped or flushed with pink and dark pink, 21 inches tall by 3 feet wide; 'Laura Morland', with semidouble soft pink flowers and dark pink stripes, 16 inches tall by 2 feet wide; 'Maria Derby', with bright red double flowers and compact growth habit; 'Mrs. Emil Hager', only 12 inches tall by 2 feet wide, with semidouble to double, vibrant pink flowers; 'Mrs. Villars', with frilly pink-splashed white flowers; 'Octavian', with light creamy pink flowers; 'Olga Niblett', with 2- to 2½-inch-wide clear white flowers that are frosted with hues of yellow, relatively upright branched habit, 4 feet tall by 3 feet wide; 'Peg Hugger', with compact habit and soft pink flowers; 'Redmond', with large red flowers; 'Red Tip', with white flowers and rose-red edges; 'Robin Dale', with pink-splashed, wavy flowers, white petals, and green throats; 'Robin Hill Gillie', 30 inches tall by 40 inches wide, mounded habit, superb foliage, 4- to 5-inch-wide flowers with red throats and rose-salmon petals; 'Roseanne', with large white flowers and pink margins, broad spreading habit; 'Sir Robert', compact mounding habit, 2 to 3 feet tall by 3 feet wide, white to soft pink 4-inch-wide flowers; 'Watchet', with mounding habit and large, flat-faced, frilly margined, rich pink flowers; 'White Moon', with large wavy-edged, sometimes red-flecked, white flowers.

R. williamsianum (wil-yum-*see*-aye-num), reaching 3 to 5 feet tall and spreading somewhat broader, this florific species has been used extensively as a parent in breeding projects. From scrubby cliffs of Sichuan, China, and hardy to Zone 7, its pale rose tubular 2¼-inch-wide flowers make a magnificent display in early spring. Its elliptical to oval or rounded, 2¼-inch-long evergreen leaves are attractive as well.

R. yakusimanum (ya-koo-si-*may*-num), from granite outcroppings and sphagnum bogs of Yakushima Island, Japan, reaches 3 feet tall by 5 feet wide, makes a neat dense mound, and is covered with dark green evergreen leaves. Its flowers are rose-pink in bud before opening to white. Hardy to Zone 5 or 6, it has given rise to such noteworthy cultivars as 'Mist Maiden', with rose-colored buds that open to pinkish white then fade to white; 'Yaku Duchess', with low habit and light red flowers; 'Yaku Princess', with low habit and flowers that open light pink before turning to sparkling white; 'Yaku Queen', with low habit and bright pink flower buds that open to pale pink before changing to white.

CULTURE / CARE: Most species and cultivars of *Rhododendron* grow best in organically rich, well-drained soil with a pH of 6.0 or lower. Most do not tolerate extended drought and for this reason, should be watered enough to keep the soil constantly moist during dry spells. *Rhododendron lapponicum,* on the other hand, is unique in that it has been successfully grown in peat, loam, gravel, and limestone with a pH ranging from acidic to alkaline. Most rhododendrons prefer light to moderate shade. Their primary diseases are canker, crown rot, dieback, petal blight, gall, leaf spot, scorch, mildew, shoot blight, rust, root rot, and wilt. Rhododendron aphid, Japanese beetle, nematodes, lace bugs, leaf miner, midge, weevils, white fly, scales, leafhopper, leaf tier, and mealybugs are their primary pests. Yellowing, due to iron deficiency from a too high soil pH, is common. Salt injury and winter desiccation of the leaves are also common if snow cover is inadequate in cold winter areas. Maintenance needs are few if any.

PROPAGATION: Cuttings taken throughout summer root marginally well if placed in a porous medium in the shade and misted frequently enough to keep them from drying out; treatment with 8000 to 10,000 ppm IBA/talc has proven helpful in some cases but is not always essential. Mound layering is occasionally practiced on a small scale; this involves mounding soil up around the bottom stems which, in time, form roots; later the rooted stems may be cut off with a spade and transplanted.

Rhus aromatica   PLATE 263
Fragrant Sumac, Sweet-scented Sumac, Lemon Sumac, Polecat Bush

A low, variable-sized, dense, suckering, woody shrub that reaches 1½ to 6 feet tall and spreads 6 to 10 feet across, fragrant sumac is not showy; however, it does have significant ornamental attributes and, in certain demanding situations, performs like few others. It is valuable as a salt-tolerant erosion-controlling cover for banks and slopes. It is a tough ground cover for northern climates, and for general use in large-sized or moderate-sized areas, particularly along highways, in median strips, and close to

parking areas. It seldom fails. Since it is aggressive and woody, it does not combine well with many other plants, but in front of tall, coarse-barked trees, it makes an acceptable facing plant. No foot traffic is tolerated.

The fruit of this species, like other species of *Rhus,* particularly *R. trilobata,* is lemon-flavored and edible. Typically, the pulp is removed from the fruit and used as an ingredient in jellies. The fruit is also used to make a very tasty lemonade-like beverage.

SCIENTIFIC NAME: *Rhus aromatica* (*roos* air-oh-*mat*-i-ka). *Rhus* is an ancient Greek name for this genus. *Aromatica,* aromatic, refers to the scented foliage.

HARDINESS / ORIGIN: Zones 3 to 9; eastern North America from Vermont and Ontario to Minnesota, south to Florida and Louisiana.

LEAVES / FLOWERS / FRUIT: If not showy, at least the deciduous leaves are interesting, resembling miniature oak leaves, and like some of the oaks, their glossy greenness turns to vibrant yellow or scarlet during autumn. Each is rather oval with significant lobes along the edges. They range from 1½ to 3 inches long, are grouped in threes (the central one being larger than the two that are paired at its base). Best fall color occurs when grown in full sun with well-drained soil. The leaves typically are fragrant when crushed. The flowers, which may be male, female, or both, are borne in elongate clusters called catkins or in a more rounded arrangement known as a panicle. In either case, they are more curious than showy and appear very early in the spring, before the leaves even begin to unfold. The fruit that follows is red, ¼ inch across, effective from late summer to early fall, and often persists, becoming brownish, into winter. Sometimes it is eaten by wildlife.

RATE / SPACING: Growth is slow at first then moderate. Plants from 1- to 2-gallon-sized containers are spaced 3½ to 4½ feet apart.

HORTICULTURAL SELECTIONS: 'Gro-low', more readily available than the species, with a low, wide-spreading habit, 2 feet tall by up to 8 feet wide.

CULTURE / CARE: Although fragrant sumac is adaptable to most well-drained soils, its best growth is displayed in infertile, dry, well-drained soils of moderate acidity. Established plants are well equipped to withstand drought, yet they welcome an occasional deep watering during the hottest days of summer. Plants prefer full sun to moderate shade. Pests include aphids, mites, and scales. Diseases such as fusarium wilt, cankers, leaf spots, powdery mildew, rusts, and root rot are also at times problematic. Maintenance typically consists of pruning out branches in spring that may have broken during winter.

PROPAGATION: Cuttings are probably the easiest way in which to propagate fragrant sumac. About 70 percent of cuttings taken during the first few weeks of summer will root.

Rosa

PLATE 264

Rose

I suspect that because of the multitude of upright, shrubby, and vinelike roses, most often the ground-covering types go overlooked. This is unfortunate as there are a number of good roses that cover the ground with style and beauty. Popular for centuries and surrounded by folklore, the rose is the national flower of the United States. Red-colored roses, according to the Turks, received their pigment from the blood of Mohammed. Greeks claimed the color was due to the shed blood of Aphrodite, who pricked her foot on a thorn. Some Christians claim that the original rose had no thorns, but that thorns arose after the fall of Adam and Eve in the Garden of Eden.

Unquestionably beautiful, roses are also highly useful. Perfumes, room fresheners, and soaps often employ their rich fragrances. Rosewater, derived from the petals, is a mild astringent excellent for the skin as it eases the discomfort of minor irritations and inflammations. The petals can be dried for pot-pourris and sachets, made into preserves, and used to flavor honey and vinegar. The fruits of roses, called hips or rosehips, are rich in vitamin C and contain substantial quantities of vitamins A, B, E, and K, as well as pectin and some organic acids. Often consumed as a dietary supplement, they are mealy and vaguely taste like cranberries. Occasionally they are used in teas, soups, and wines, as well as in pies, breads, and muffins.

SCIENTIFIC NAME: *Rosa* (*row*-za) is the ancient Latin name for the rose. Some authorities believe the name comes from the Greek, *rhod,* rose or red.

HARDINESS / ORIGIN: See individual species for hardiness; temperate and subtropical regions of the Northern Hemisphere.

LEAVES / FLOWERS / FRUIT: The deciduous or sometimes evergreen leaves are typically compound, alternately arranged, and have broadly oval leaflets. The flowers, with five petals, are borne alone or in groups. They are typically very showy and come in shades of pink, red, yellow, white, and cream. Their fleshy fruit is often large, red, and quite effective for late-season interest.

RATE / SPACING: See individual species.

SPECIES AND GROUPS: *R. blanda* (*bland*-a), named for its nearly thornless stems (*blanda* means pleasant), is commonly called smooth rose (for the same reason) or meadow rose. Native to eastern North America, this species is best characterized as a variable, sprawling, suckering shrubby ground cover that reaches 2 to 5 feet tall by more than 5 feet wide. It can be mass planted to give a quick cover in medium to large areas. It is also very attractive on a gently sloping bank or when its graceful, vibrant green branches are allowed to cascade over the side of a stone wall or terrace embankment. Growth is moderate. Plants from 1- to 2-gallon-sized containers are spaced 2 to 3 feet apart. Hardy to Zone 3, it thrives in sandy or rocky, moist to dry, windswept areas along lake shores, in meadows, and on the banks of streams, and is not hampered by infertile gravelly soils. Good companions are mature, open-canopied pines, serviceberry, dogwoods, honey locust, and poplar. Lower-growing herbaceous species such as fountain grass (*Pennisetum alopecuroides*), beach grass (*Ammophila* and *Calamovilfa* species), and golden rod (*Solidago* species) also combine well. No foot traffic is tolerated. The rather pale medium green, tooth-edged leaves are deciduous and compound, composed of five to seven short-petioled, oval, 1- to 1½-inch-long leaflets. The five-petaled flowers are solitary or arranged in clusters, to 3 inches wide, colored pink (or rarely white), and appear during early summer. The fruit is round to pear-shaped, ½ to ¾ inch wide, first green then ripening to red in mid to late summer. Forma *alba* has white flowers; forma *augustier* has narrower, wavy-edged, smooth (rather than toothed) foliage.

R. 'Flower Carpet', promoted as more disease resistant than other roses, bears masses of vibrant rosy-pink 1½-inch-wide double, subtly fragrant flowers from spring through fall. Hardiness is reported to range from Zones 2 to 8. Mature plants reach 2 to 2½ feet tall by 3 feet wide and are clothed in deep shiny green foliage. This floriferous hybrid was originally registered as *R.* 'Noatraum', named after its breeder, Werner Noack. The recipient of numerous awards in Europe where it has exhibited good disease resistance in North America, it has not been thoroughly tested. I have seen disease-ridden plants in North Carolina, but this hybrid may prove to be fine in cooler climates.

Meidiland Roses. The results of breeding efforts of the House of Meilland, a group of French rose breeders, the Meidiland roses, typically hardy in Zones 4 to 9, are a group of cultivars introduced into the United States in the late 1980s. Growth is moderate. Plants from 1- to 2-gallon-sized containers are spaced a distance equal to about three fourths their expected mature spread. 'Alba Meidiland', a care-free, hardy, erosion-controlling ground cover, is characterized by hundreds of small white, ever-blooming flowers; it reaches 2½ feet tall by 6 feet wide, displays moderate vigor, and is ideal for sloping terrain. 'Fuchsia Meidiland', a superb low growing long-blooming (early summer until frost) selection, reaches 2 feet tall by 3 to 4 feet wide and displays numerous 2-inch-wide superb fuchsia-rose flowers with white centers. 'Pearl Meidiland', with a horizontal, mounded habit, deep green leaves, and masses of dainty ivory-pink flowers in summer, reaches 2½ feet tall by 6 feet wide. 'Pink Meidiland', 4 feet tall by 3 feet wide, has long-lived 2- to 2½-inch-wide, single, pink flowers followed by bright orange-red hips that last well into winter. 'Red Meidiland', only 1½ feet tall by 2 feet wide, with a mounded habit, has double red flowers with yellow centers in summer and fall. 'Scarlet Meidiland', with bright scarlet, 1- to 1½-inch-wide, continuously blooming flowers in spring and fall, has rich green leaves and ranges from 3 to 4 feet tall by 5 to 6 feet wide. 'White Meidiland', 2 feet tall by 5 feet wide, is a horizontal, mound-forming selection with large, leathery, dark green leaves that make a splendid backdrop for the 4-inch-wide double flowers from late spring until frost.

R. polyantha 'Nearly Wild', of dubious origin and hardy to Zone 2, is a shiny green-leaved shrubby rebloomer with lovely fragrant five-petaled rose-pink single flowers throughout summer. Reaching 3 feet tall by 4 feet wide, it is one of the finest ground-covering roses.

R. spinosissima 'Petite Pink Scotch' (spy-no-*sis*-i-ma) is derived from an Eurasian species named for its thorniness. Hardy in Zones 4 to 8, this particular selection reaches 2 to 3 feet tall by 3 to 4 feet wide. It displays a horizontal mounded habit, dark green leaves, and double pink flowers for two to three weeks during early summer. Growth is moderate. Plants from 1- to 2-gallon-sized containers are spaced 3 feet apart.

R. wichuraiana (wi-shure-aye-*an*-a), named to commemorate Max E. Wichura, a Prussian diplomat who collected this East Asian species, is commonly called memorial rose in reference either to this commemoration or to the use of this species in decorating grave sites. It displays a trailing habit but, with support, shows some inclination to climb. As a ground cover, it reaches 12 to 18 inches tall and spreads 6 to 15 feet wide. It is useful in medium-sized to large-sized areas as a general cover. With its dense network of stems and roots, it is well suited to control erosion on sloping terrain. Its floral display is excellent, and the effect of the flowering branches as they cascade over the sides of a stone wall, terrace embankment, or elevated planter is superb. It is hardy in Zones 5 or 6 to 9. The leaves are semievergreen and composed of seven to nine leaflets, each of which is ⅖ to 1 inch long, rounded to broadly oval, edged with coarse teeth, and colored shiny dark

green. From late spring to mid summer, 2-inch-wide, fragrant, five-petaled, white flowers make their appearance and eventually give way to ½-inch-wide, egg-shaped, red rosehips. Growth is moderate to fast. Plants from gallon-sized containers are spaced 2½ to 4 feet apart. Horticultural selections include 'Curiosity', variegated memorial rose, unique for its shiny green leaves that are splashed with creamy white; 'Hiawatha', red-flowered memorial rose, with bright red flowers, white centers, perhaps of hybrid origin; 'Poterifolia', a lower-growing, less dense growing selection 3 to 5 inches tall.

OTHER HYBRIDS: Among numerous hybrids, most of uncertain origin, there are several other low-growing ground-covering roses that are available readily: *R.* 'Hindawn', with deep pink semidouble flowers, deep green leaves, trailing habit, and hardiness to Zone 5; *R.* 'Hinvory', with ivory-white semidouble flowers throughout summer, hardy to Zone 5; *R.* 'Scarlet Spreader', with semidouble scarlet summerborne flowers, dark green leaves, hardy to Zone 5; *R.* 'Snow Carpet', with double white summerborne flowers, hardy to Zone 5.

CULTURE / CARE: Roses usually perform best in full sun in organically rich, well-drained, acidic to neutral soils. *Rosa blanda* grows in almost any type of well-drained, acidic to neutral soil, even beach sand. Drought tolerance is fair, although watering may sometimes be needed during the summer. Watering should be deep and only as often as needed; frequent light watering should be avoided as it may encourage fungus or bacterial diseases of the leaves, including black spot, canker, mildew, rust, viral mosaic, and viral streak. Insects and pests that favor roses are sawflies, aphids, leaf hoppers, thrips, Japanese beetles, rose bugs, chaffers, mites, and slugs. Maintenance ordinarily consists of selectively pruning out dead or diseased stems and any upright growing shoots. The best time for pruning is immediately after flowering. Some gardeners treat their roses to a light mulching of organic matter each year to increase fertility and enhance the soil texture.

PROPAGATION: Cuttings root quickly during early summer. Division of rooted stem sections also works well and is best practiced during the spring or early fall. Seed should be sown during the fall as it ripens, for germination the following spring. Naturally layered stem sections may be dug and transplanted during the spring or fall.

Rosmarinus officinalis   PLATE 265
Rosemary

The culinary herb rosemary with its shrubby habit ranging from 2 to 4 feet tall is only a fair ground cover. Its cultivars, on the other hand, which are typically more uniform in habit and lower growing, are really quite good for this purpose. When single specimens or small groups are placed in a location where their neat foliage, attractive branch patterns, and graceful trailing stems are easily viewed, they are spectacular. Such places as gentle slopes and atop retaining walls bring rosemary closer to eye level, where it may be best enjoyed. Other uses include turf substitution in moderate to large areas, walkway edging, dwarf hedging, and as a rock garden specimen. No foot traffic is tolerated.

Throughout history, rosemary has been considered to have potent curative properties ranging from returning speech to the dumb to reversing baldness and aging to preventing drowsiness to tightening loose teeth. The validity of such claims has never been substantiated, but rinsing one's skin in rosemary water is said to be invigorating, and the leaves of the cultivars, as well as the species, can be used for seasoning.

SCIENTIFIC NAME: *Rosmarinus officinalis* (rose-ma-*rye*-nus oh-fis-i-*nay*-lis). *Rosmarinus* comes from the Latin *ros,* dew (spray), and *marinus,* sea, a reference to the native habitat on sea cliffs, where, presumably, the plant becomes misted with sea spray during heavy storms. *Officinalis* indicates that this is the common species.

HARDINESS / ORIGIN: Zones 7 to 9; Mediterranean region.

LEAVES / FLOWERS / FRUIT: The leathery, hairy, grayish green, narrow, evergreen leaves reach ½ to 1½ inches long and are very pleasantly aromatic. The spring flowers, which are arranged in short clusters on the previous year's growth, are pale blue, rarely pink or white, two-lobed, and reach 5/16 inch long. The fruit is nonornamental.

RATE / SPACING: Growth is moderate. Plants from quart-sized to gallon-sized containers are spaced 2½ to 4 feet apart.

HORTICULTURAL SELECTIONS: 'Collingwood Ingram', graceful, 2 feet tall by 4 feet wide; 'Huntington Carpet', very compact, dwarf, mounded habit, 1 foot high by 4 feet wide, with light green leaves and flowers darker blue than the species; 'Lockwood de Forest', semiprostrate, mounded habit, 2 feet tall by 4 to 5 feet across, with dark blue flowers; 'Prostratus' (trailing rosemary), prostrate habit, with foliage and flowers like the species, probably hardy only to Zone 8.

CULTURE / CARE: Rosemary and its cultivars, although best in acidic to neutral soils, tolerate slight alkalinity and always need good drainage. They are also tolerant of infertile soils and of modest drought. They prefer full sun, have few disease problems, and should be watched for aphids and mites. Mainte-

nance normally consists of a light shearing immediately following bloom to promote branching and to keep plants dense and neat looking.

PROPAGATION: Cuttings may be taken during the early part of the growing season. Seed is available for the species and germinates in two or three weeks.

Rubus calycinoides 'Emerald Carpet' PLATE 266
Taiwanese Creeping Rubus, Creeping Bramble

A low, trailing, relatively woody, densely branched ground cover, this species ranges from 2 to 4 inches tall, spreads over 3 feet across, and is best used as a soil binder on moderate to large sloping areas. Its few maintenance requirements make it well suited to roadside plantings, and it functions well as a large-scale facing for mixed tree and shrub borders. No foot traffic is tolerated.

SCIENTIFIC NAME: *Rubus calycinoides* (*roo*-bus kay-li-ki-*noy*-deez / kal-i-sin-*oy*-deez). *Rubus* is said by some to come from the Latin *ruber,* red, and refer to the red fruit of many of the species. Others say that it was simply the Latin word for the blackberry. *Calycinoides* means resembling (*R.*) *calycinus.*

HARDINESS / ORIGIN: Zone 7; the species hails from high elevations in Taiwan, and the cultivar 'Emerald Carpet' was selected from a seedling at the University of British Columbia in 1978.

LEAVES / FLOWERS / FRUIT: The semievergreen to evergreen, simple, alternate, somewhat ivy-shaped leaves with three to five lobes are deeply furrowed, shiny dark green above, lighter green below, and hairy. They are ¾ to 1½ inches long, just as wide, and densely cover the prickly stems. During fall and winter they become copper-colored. The summerborne white flowers, ½ inch wide, are paired or solitary and not very conspicuous. The fruit is composed of an orange base (receptacle) and a bright red black-berry-like aggregate of drupelets ½ inch long.

RATE / SPACING: Growth is moderate. Plants from pint-sized to gallon-sized containers are spaced 16 to 30 inches apart.

CULTURE / CARE: Adaptable to most well-drained soils, once established, Taiwanese creeping rubus displays modest drought tolerance and requires only an occasional thorough watering in hot, dry weather. It is at its best in full sun but tolerates light to moderate shade. No serious diseases or pests have been reported. The only maintenance needed is to trim back trailing shoots as they outgrow their bounds.

PROPAGATION: Cuttings root readily during the growing season; the application of 1000 ppm IBA/talc is not essential but may speed the rooting process and result in a greater root mass.

Rudbeckia fulgida   PLATE 267
Orange Coneflower

Although uninspiring when not in bloom, the extended flower season of orange coneflower easily offsets the coarse, rather dull foliage of late spring and early summer. With rhizomatous rootstock, it spreads at a moderate pace to 2 or 3 feet across. It reaches 6 inches or so when not in bloom and flowers to a height of 2 to 2½ feet. Often confused with black-eyed Susan (*R. hirta*), orange coneflower (somewhat misnamed as the flowers are really orangish yellow) is utterly reliable and a superb companion to Japanese silver grass (*Miscanthus sinensis*) and its cultivars, feather reed grass (*Calamogrostis* species and cultivars), and Russian sage (*Perovskia atriplicifolia*). No foot traffic is tolerated.

SCIENTIFIC NAME: *Rudbeckia fulgida* (rud-*bek*-ee-a *ful*-gi-da). *Rudbeckia* commemorates a prominent father-son pair of botanists: Olof Rudbeck (1630–1702), professor of botany, antiquarian, and anatomist, founded the Uppsala Botanic Garden; his son Olof (1660–1740), also a professor in Uppsala, is said to have befriended Linnaeus when he was a poverty-stricken student. *Fulgida,* shining, likely refers to the seeds.

HARDINESS / ORIGIN: Zones 3 to 9; eastern United States from Connecticut to West Virginia, west to Michigan and Missouri.

LEAVES / FLOWERS / FRUIT: The deciduous, deep green, tooth-edged leaves are of two types, basal and stem. The oval to lance-shaped basal leaves are long-stemmed and range from 3 to 6 inches long, are rather coarse-haired, and arise from the creeping rhizomes. Those borne on the upright flower-laden stems are smaller and stemless. Flowering begins during mid summer and continues until the first hard frost. Each magnificent 1½- to 3-inch-wide daisylike head is composed of a prominent dark brown center or cone surrounded by narrowly oval petals of vibrant buttery orange. The tiny brown fruit persists well into winter and furnishes nutrition to numerous birds.

RATE / SPACING: Growth is moderate to fast (faster in loose, fertile, moist soils). Plants from 1- to 2-gallon-sized containers are spaced 1½ to 2 feet apart.

HORTICULTURAL SELECTIONS: Var. *deamii* (syn. *R. deamii*), with more leaves, which are broader and coarser toothed; var. *fulgida,* native from New Jersey to Illinois south to northern Alabama, with nearly lance-shaped basal leaves; 'Oraile', with larger deeper golden-yellow flowers; var. *sullivantii* (syn. *R. speciosa* var. *sullivantii*), similar to var. *deamii* but with stem leaves becoming successively smaller up the stem until they are reduced to large bracts at the stem ends; var. *sullivantii* 'Goldsturm', a popular selection with compact habit and profuse display of large vibrant flowers.

CULTURE / CARE: Orange coneflower thrives in about any soil, but is at its best in a loose, organically rich, acidic loam. It is tolerant of moderate drought, but is larger and more showy if the soil is kept slightly moist. Maintenance consists of pruning off dead growth during late winter. A lawn mower does this nicely.

PROPAGATION: Stem cuttings root easily during early summer. Division during early spring is foolproof. Seed is also available and germinates readily.

Sagina subulata   PLATE 268
Corsican Pearlwort

A low, mat-forming, mosslike, herbaceous ground cover that reaches 2 to 4 inches tall and spreads indefinitely, Corsican pearlwort is one of those little plants that is often overlooked in favor of something taller or showier. It is, however, a wonderful choice to perform the tough job of filling in between stepping stones or the pavers of a patio or walkway, where it holds the soil solidly in place and endures the occasional misplaced footstep. When used as a small-scale general cover or turf substitute, it appears vibrant and lush but occasionally has to be tamped down as it has a tendency to mound upward.

SCIENTIFIC NAME: *Sagina subulata* (sa-*jie*-na sub-you-*lay*-ta). *Sagina* is possibly an ancient name for spurrey (*Spergularia*), among which this plant was formerly classified. Others claim that the name comes from the Latin *sagina,* fodder, as sheep were fed on a related plant. *Subulata,* awl-shaped, refers to the leaves.

HARDINESS / ORIGIN: Zones 5 to 9 or 10; Europe.

LEAVES / FLOWERS / FRUIT: The evergreen, thin, lance-shaped or awl-shaped leaves are united at their bases in whorls about thin upright stems. Each is ¼ inch long and colored a light vibrant shade of green. Tiny (³⁄₁₆ inch wide), white, star-shaped, solitary flowers are borne in mid summer upon even thinner stems. The fruit is so tiny as to be virtually unnoticeable.

RATE / SPACING: Growth is moderate. Plants from 3- or 4-inch-diameter containers are spaced 6 to 10 inches apart.

HORTICULTURAL SELECTIONS: 'Aurea', with light yellowish colored leaves, often partially reverts to green and thus looks blotchy and unhealthy.

CULTURE / CARE: Organically rich, loamy acidic to neutral soil is necessary for best growth, but light-textured (sandy), well-drained soils are tolerated. In heavy clay, crown rot is a certainty. Drought tolerance is poor, so plants must be watered frequently during hot, dry weather. They prefer full sun to light shade. Although no serious pests or diseases affect *Sagina*, crown rot can be devastating if humidity is excessive or drainage inadequate. If plantings mound up when overcrowded, the mounded portion should be cut out and the surrounding mat gently pressed down to cover up the open area. 'Aurea' should be used on a small scale and its flowers must be mowed off before they fade, set seed, and (often) bear green-colored offspring.

PROPAGATION: Division is probably the easiest method; all one has to do is dig up plugs and transplant them. Since they are shallowly rooted, the best time is when the weather is relatively cool and moist (typically, spring or fall). Seed can be found with a little shopping around and normally it germinates in two weeks.

Salix   PLATE 269
Willow

Most people think of willows as moisture-tolerant, upright or drooping shrubs and trees valued for their velvety springtime flowers and graceful forms. Yet, there are other species, particularly the small alpine species, which are low growing, sometimes nearly herbaceous, and which perform well as ground covers. Like the shrubs and trees, they often display showy, spring-borne catkins. Normally their growth habits are upright or broad and spreading, with heights ranging from 1 to 4 feet tall. They generally make good specimens and accent plants, especially in gritty, moisture-retentive soils, oftentimes along streambanks and sometimes in rock gardens. No foot traffic is tolerated.

Native Americans found willows to be of great value. The bark was often used in treating colds and fevers, and extracts prepared from the roots were used in the treatment of itchy scalp, dysentery, and nosebleeds. Pharmacologists later found the active ingredient to be salicin, a chemical closely related to aspirin.

SCIENTIFIC NAME: *Salix* (*say*-liks) is the Latin name for willow.

HARDINESS / ORIGIN: See individual species for hardiness; cold and temperate regions of the Northern Hemisphere, with some in the Southern Hemisphere (except Australia).

LEAVES / FLOWERS / FRUIT: The leaves are typically deciduous and lanced-shaped. The flowers are tiny and borne in catkins. The fruit is nonornamental.

RATE / SPACING: See individual species.

SPECIES: *S. purpurea* 'Nana' (pur-*pur*-ee-a *nay*-na), named from *purpurea,* purple, for its stem color and

nana, dwarf, in reference to its height, this cultivar is commonly called dwarf purple osier, dwarf arctic willow, or dwarf basket willow and is also listed as *S. purpurea* 'Gracilis'. It was selected from the 8- to 15-foot-tall species that hails from Europe, the Mediterranean region, and Japan. Hardy in Zones 3 to 7, the cultivar reaches 3 to 4 feet high by 3 to 5 feet wide. It makes an attractive small hedge and its branches are useful for weaving baskets. It is woody and upright branched. Growth is fast, by suckering stems. Plants from 1- to 2-gallon-sized containers are spaced 2½ to 3 feet apart. The leaves, borne upon slender, purplish to light grayish brown stems, are soft-textured, attractive, blue-green, deciduous, and narrowly oblong, and reach 1 to 1½ inches long. The flowers, which arise upon the naked stems in early spring, are yellow and gray, and arranged in woolly catkins. The fruit consists of a small hair-covered capsule that is not particularly ornamental.

S. repens (*ree*-penz), named for its reptant (creeping) habit, is commonly called creeping willow. It has a low-growing, wide-spreading, rhizome-forming habit, and reaches 2 to 3 feet tall by up to 8 feet wide. Hardy in Zones 4 to 9, it is native to Europe, Asia Minor, and Siberia. Growth is moderate. Plants from 1- to 3-gallon-sized containers are spaced 2½ to 3 feet apart. This species is deciduous, displays oval, ¾- to 2-inch-long, gray-green leaves with grayish white undersides. Its flowers, borne during early spring, are held upon brown (oftentimes with hints of purple and red) stems and are arranged in attractive white cylindrical catkins that reach ½ to 1½ inches long. The fruit is relatively nonornamental. 'Argentea' (syn. *S. repens* var. *arenaria, S. repens* var. *nitida, S. arenaria*) displays silvery-colored leaves; 'Boyd's Pendulous' reaches 6 inches tall by more than 2 feet wide.

S. rosmarinifolia (roze-ma-rine-i-*foe*-lee-a), named for its rosemary-like leaves, is native to eastern Europe. It is much like *S. repens,* differing in having narrower leaves and catkins that are rounded. It is reported to be hardy in Zones 4 to 9 and requires low humidity.

S. tristis (*tris*-tis), named from the Latin *tristis,* sad, in reference to its weeping habit, is commonly called dwarf gray willow. It ranges from 1½ to 4 feet tall by more than 3 feet wide. Woody, shrubby, and hardy in Zones 2 to 9, it hails from eastern North America (Maine to Minnesota and Montana, south to Oklahoma and northern Florida). It is slow growing and prefers soil conditions on the dry side. Plants from 1- to 2-gallon-sized containers are spaced 2 to 3 feet apart. The leathery leaves are deciduous, crowded, oval, bluntly pointed at their ends, and edged with small teeth. Colored gray-green above, underneath they are gray and hairy. The catkins, which arise during spring before the foliage, are oval to rounded and very small, thus of little ornamental consequence.

S. uva-ursi (oo-va-*er*-see), literally meaning bear's grape, is named for its resemblance to bearberry (*Arctostaphylos uva-ursi*) and is commonly called bearberry willow. It is a mat-forming species that reaches 2 inches tall by 3 feet wide. Its oval to elliptic, ½- to 1-inch-long, ¼- to ½-inch-wide, prominently veined, shiny green leaves are held upon thick brown stems. About the same time the leaves emerge, the reddish, oblong, ½-inch-long catkins are borne. Native from Greenland and Labrador to Alaska, south to the mountain summits of the northeastern United States, this slow-growing alpine species is hardy in Zones 1 to 5.

S. yezoalpina (yay-zoe-al-*pine*-a), a very interesting Japanese species, has large oval leaves reminiscent of trailing arbutus (*Epigaea repens*). Its new stems are covered with a thick coat of silvery hairs, and the pure white, 2-inch-long, erect catkins are magnificent in late winter. It reaches 6 inches tall, spreads to 3 or more feet, and is reportedly hardy in Zones 4 to 8.

CULTURE / CARE: Willows prefer sandy, moisture-retentive, somewhat infertile soil; if grown in rich soils, their growth often becomes leggy and open. They prefer neutral soil, but grow in mildly acid or alkaline conditions. They are somewhat tolerant of drought. but are at their best if the soil is kept slightly moist. They prefer full sun, but tolerate light shade. They are rather susceptible to diseases and pests. Among the diseases are bacterial twig blight, crown gall, leaf blight, cankers, leaf spots, gray scab, mildew, and rust. Pests such as leaf beetle, pine cone gall, aphids, gall midge, lace bug, flea beetle, willow borer, poplar borer, satin moth, sawfly, and scale are sometimes a problem. With the exception of a light annual shearing after flowering, these plants seldom require maintenance.

PROPAGATION: Stem cuttings during early summer are effective; IBA can be applied but is usually not needed.

Salvia officinalis   PLATE 270
Sage, Common Sage, Garden Sage, True Sage, Meadow Sage

With more than 800 species, the genus *Salvia* is composed of a cosmopolitan collection of herbs, subshrubs, and shrubs. *Salvia officinalis* is an excellent ground cover for edging sidewalks or garden pathways where its attractive foliage and flowers can be appreciated. An erect-stemmed, dense, semiwoody

ground cover, it reaches 1½ to 2½ feet tall by 2 to 2½ feet wide, and is useful as a specimen in the rock garden or herb border. No foot traffic is tolerated.

With its strong aromatic fragrance and pungent taste, sage is a versatile culinary herb used in many recipes. Native Americans once used the leaves of some species and bear grease to treat skin sores. Others have touted it as a mind stimulator, prolonger of life, cure for insomnia, and treatment for epilepsy, excessive sweating, measles, excessive menstrual bleeding, dysentery, fevers, worms, intestinal gas, and lack of sexual interest. Modern science has proven that sage does reduce intestinal gas and aid digestion. It is also known to display astringent, antiseptic, calmative, and insect-repellent properties. Its flowers are attractive to bees and hummingbirds.

SCIENTIFIC NAME: *Salvia officinalis* (*sal*-vee-a oh-fis-i-*nay*-lis). *Salvia* is the name reported to have been used by Pliny, the first-century Roman naturalist and writer. Derived from *salvus,* safe or healthy, the name refers to the healing properties of many species. *Officinalis* means common.

HARDINESS / ORIGIN: Zones 6 to 9; northern and central Spain to the western Balkan Peninsula and Asia Minor.

LEAVES / FLOWERS / FRUIT: The grayish green (lighter below), somewhat hairy leaves are roughened, evergreen, opposite, oblong, 1 to 3¼ inches long by ½ to 1 inch wide, with smooth or slightly toothed margins. Among the leaves, arising from their axils and at the ends of the stems, originate the five-flowered to ten-flowered clusters of trumpet-shaped, two-lipped, 1¼- to 1⅜-inch-long, blue or purple (rarely white), fragrant flowers of spring. The tiny fruit that follows is nonornamental.

RATE / SPACING: Growth is moderate. Plants from pint-sized to quart-sized containers are spaced 1½ to 2½ feet apart.

HORTICULTURAL SELECTIONS: 'Albiflora', with white flowers; 'Aurea', compact habit (to 18 inches tall), with foliage variegated gold and green; 'Dwarf', to 18 inches tall, with smaller foliage; 'Purpurascens' ('Purpurea'), with reddish purple foliage; 'Tricolor', with foliage edged in white and purplish red.

OTHER SPECIES: *S. argentea* (ar-jen-*tee*-a) silver-leaved sage, is very interesting and attractive for its densely woolly, roughened leaves that look like silver velvet. Hardy in Zones 5 to 9, it ranges in height from 8 inches to 3 feet (in flower) and during summer produces white flowers that are often tinged pink or yellow. Native to Europe, it is somewhat rare in North America, where it is often short-lived.

S. × *superba* (soo-*per*-ba), hardy in Zones 4 to 7, is a showy sterile hybrid. It ranges from 1½ to 3 feet tall and is notable for its tremendous display of beautiful purple flowers on long spikes in early to mid summer. Its cultivars include 'East Friesland' ('Ostfriesland'), which reaches 1½ feet tall, with purple flowers; 'Lubeca', 2½ feet tall; 'May Delight', which is similar to 'East Friesland' but begins blooming in spring; 'May Night', with blue-violet flowers from spring to fall.

CULTURE / CARE: Although the sages are quite adaptable to soil type, they are at their best in well-drained, gravelly or sandy, slightly alkaline to slightly acidic soils. Heat and drought do not seem to bother them much, so one should not hesitate to use them in exposed locations. They prefer full sun to light shade. Their diseases, which are many, include leaf blight, damping off, downy mildew, leaf spot, root rot, rust, California aster yellows virus, and viral induced wilt. Pests of greatest consequence include aphids, stalk borers, grape leafhopper, leaf tier, greenhouse whitefly, tarnished plant bug, yellow woollybear, and leaf and root nematodes. To keep plants looking neat, they should be sheared after flowering; division every three to four years keeps them growing vigorously.

PROPAGATION: While some propagators swear by making stem cuttings with a heel of mature basal wood attached, this does not seem to be essential as long as a node is present below the surface of the rooting medium. Normally stem cuttings are rooted in a very porous medium and, although treatment with 500 to 1000 ppm IBA/talc will induce a heavier root system, it is not necessary. Clump division is also effective, and is usually performed in early spring or fall. Seed, which is available commercially, germinates in two to three weeks at 60 to 70°F.

Sanguinaria canadensis   PLATE 271
Bloodroot, Puccoon-root, Tetterroot, Red Puccoon, Indian-paint, Red Root, Turmeric, Pauson, Sweet Slumber, Snake Bite, White Puccoon

Bloodroot is among the most precious wildflowers for ground-cover use. It is not common in the nursery trade for it takes a patient grower to coax it to a saleable size, nor is it easily transplanted—and for this reason is protected in many states. Nonetheless, it can be cultivated and is well worth the effort. It reaches 4 to 6 inches tall, slowly spreads by stout, red, surface-oriented rhizomes (for which it takes its common name bloodroot), and makes lush coarse-textured mats. It grows well in small-sized to moderate-sized areas. Because it tolerates being submersed in water for several weeks, it is excellent for use next to streams and creeks where spring flooding often occurs. It is at its best in native-plant or natural woodland gardens and combines superbly

with trilliums, Jack-in-the-pulpit, dicentra, hepatica, sedges, ferns, and a host of other woodland natives. No foot traffic is tolerated.

SCIENTIFIC NAME: *Sanguinaria canadensis* (san-gwi-nay-ree-a kan-a-*den*-sis). *Sanguinaria* comes from the Latin *sanguis,* blood, referring to the redness of the roots. *Canadensis* means from Canada and refers to the northern habitat of this species.

HARDINESS / ORIGIN: Zones 4 to 9; eastern North America.

LEAVES / FLOWERS / FRUIT: The deciduous leaves start out rather inauspiciously as they poke through the cool ground of early spring. Still juvenile as the lovely 3-inch-wide anemone-like flowers with white petals begin to bloom, the blue-green prominently veined leaves with whitish gray undersides often encircle the succulent flower stems until the end of the short two-week-long blooming season. Once flowering ceases the leaves mature quickly and, as they unfold, change their orientation to horizontal. They may reach 6 inches wide and are typically deeply lobed and heart-shaped or kidney-shaped. By late summer the leaves may begin to die back and go dormant, especially during dry seasons. The prominent erectly oriented pod-shaped fruit is interesting and yields numerous round beadlike seeds.

RATE / SPACING: Growth is slow. Plants from pint-sized to gallon-sized containers are spaced 8 to 12 inches apart.

HORTICULTURAL SELECTIONS: 'Major', with larger flowers; 'Multiplex', with exceptionally attractive, longer-lasting, sterile, double flowers.

CULTURE / CARE: Bloodroot requires a cool, moist, humus-rich, acidic soil. It is not tolerant of drought, needs light to moderate shade, has few disease or insect problems, and needs no maintenance.

PROPAGATION: Seed should be sown immediately upon ripening for germination the following spring. Plants take two or three years before they will bloom. Division can also be performed successfully but should not be attempted during the summer; do it during early spring or late fall and do not plant the rhizomes deeper than their original depth.

Santolina   PLATE 272
Lavender Cotton

The two lavender cotton species that are used as ground covers are both interesting, aromatic, semi-woody/semiherbaceous, mound-forming, spreading ground covers. Typically they reach 1½ to 2 feet tall and spread 2 to 4 feet across. They are superb rock garden specimens and make excellent dwarf hedges for along walkways. Also, because they are relatively resistant to fire, they are often favored in public areas such as parks or around the entrance of public buildings as foundation facers, areas where smoldering cigarette butts are likely to land.

SCIENTIFIC NAME: *Santolina* (san-toe-*line*-a) is said to be derived from *sanctum linum,* holy flax, the Latin name for *S. rosmarinifolia.* Another possibility is that it comes from the Latin *santonica,* a herb of the Santoni, a people of Roman Aquitaine.

HARDINESS / ORIGIN: Zones 7 to 9; Mediterranean region.

LEAVES / FLOWERS / FRUIT: The leaves are grayish, evergreen, compound, and alternately arranged. The segments are tiny and beadlike. The flowers, borne in heads, are sunflower-like and produce tiny, nonornamental seed.

RATE / SPACING: Growth is moderate to fast. Plants from quart-sized to gallon-sized containers are spaced 2½ to 3½ feet apart.

SPECIES: **S. chamaecyparissus** (kam-i-sip-*air*-i-sus), named for its low-growing or dwarf cypress-like habit, is commonly called ground cypress. It is a spicy-smelling shrub native to southern Europe and North Africa that is hardy in Zones 7 to 9. Its silvery-gray foliage is compound, evergreen, 1⅜ inches long, and composed of several ⅛-inch-long, beadlike, hair-covered segments. For about one month in summer, numerous solitary ¾-inch-wide, buttonlike heads of tiny yellow flowers are carried on stalks above the foliage.

   S. virens (*vie*-rens), green lavender cotton, is a Mediterranean native that is hardy in Zones 7 to 9. It is like *S. chamaecyparissus* except that its leaflets are larger, hairless, and dark green, giving it a ferny appearance, and its buttonlike heads of tiny yellow flowers occur from mid to late spring.

CULTURE / CARE: Lavender cottons require excellent drainage. They tolerate gritty soils and, if given an occasional deep watering, are not hampered by drought. They prefer full sun. No serious diseases or pests effect them. As for maintenance, many gardeners prefer to shear plantings lightly after they flower to remove the flower heads, which would normally dry up and persist, and to promote a neat, compact habit.

PROPAGATION: When stuck in a very porous medium, stem cuttings root relatively well during the growing season. Seed, which should be collected as soon as it ripens, should be stored dry and cool, then sown in spring.

Saponaria ocymoides   PLATE 273
Rock Soapwort
   Low-growing and mat-forming, this trailing-but-usually-not-strongly-rooting herbaceous ground

cover reaches 4 to 8 inches tall and spreads to more than 3 feet across. Most of the year it looks like a green mop, but when in full bloom, what a show! The colorful pink flowers rival neon and are enough to awaken the spirit of even the most preoccupied passerby. For this reason, rock soapwort is ideal for visible locations and particularly well suited for edging walkways, filling elevated planters, or planting atop a retaining or terrace wall. Single specimens can be used to good effect in rock gardens and in smaller areas. If the ground is sloping, masses of rock soapwort make splendid low-maintenance turf substitutes. No foot traffic is tolerated.

SCIENTIFIC NAME: *Saponaria ocymoides* (sap-oh-*nay*-ree-a o-sim-*oi*-deez). *Saponaria* comes from the Latin *sapo,* soap, in reference to the lather-producing qualities of the leaves of *S. officinalis,* which have at times been used as a substitute for soap. *Ocymoides* means like *Ocimum,* a related genus.

HARDINESS / ORIGIN: Zones 2 to 7; southern and central Europe.

LEAVES / FLOWERS / FRUIT: The dark green, evergreen leaves are small, to 1 inch long by ⅜ inch wide, and teardrop-shaped. The flowers are five-petaled, bright purplish pink, and totally obscure the leaves for about four weeks in late spring and early summer, thereafter sporadically until fall. The fruit is nonornamental.

RATE / SPACING: Growth is moderate to fast. Plants from 3- to 4-inch-diameter containers are spaced 10 to 16 inches apart.

HORTICULTURAL SELECTIONS: 'Alba', with pure white flowers; 'Carnea', with flesh pink flowers; var. *floribunda,* with soft pink flowers borne in profusion; 'Gillian Shermon', with white-edged leaves but no flowers; 'Rosea', with bright rose flowers; 'Rubra', with bright rose-pinkish-red flowers; 'Rubra Compacta', with crimson flowers, and a compact habit with little propensity to spread; 'Splendens', with large, deep rose-colored flowers; 'Splendissima', presumably identical to 'Splendens' but sometimes represented as having larger flowers; 'Versicolor', reported to be a hybrid of 'Splendens' and 'Alba', with flowers that are first white then rose in maturity.

OTHER SPECIES: **S. × lempergii** (lem-per-*gee*-eye), named after Dr. Fritz Lemperg, Styria, Austria, reaches 16 to 22 inches tall, sprawls with horizontal to semiupright habit, and is covered with dark green leaves and, during mid to late summer, with large carmine-pink flowers. 'Max Frei', an earlier flowering cultivar, is especially popular.

CULTURE / CARE: Rock soapwort prefers a well-drained loamy soil, but tolerates light-textured infertile soils. It is not hampered greatly by drought, although it may appear a bit more vibrant if given occasional deep watering throughout the summer. Aphids and leaf spot are about its only pest and disease problems. Maintenance consists of shearing or mowing plantings immediately after flowering to thicken and neaten them.

PROPAGATION: Cuttings during summer and division in spring or early fall are the only ways to reliably propagate the cultivars. Division can be tricky because the stems root very little as they spread. Seed works well for the species and is available from most seed houses; germination occurs in 10 days at 70°F.

Sarcococca hookeriana var. *humilis*   PLATE 274
Dwarf Himalayan Sarcococca, Dwarf Himalayan Sweet Box

Dwarf Himalayan sarcococca, sometimes listed as the species *S. humilis,* is a plant that is very easy to appreciate once you see it. The problem, however, is in becoming exposed to it, for unfortunately, its shy-spreading nature, one of its greatest assets once established, is one of its greatest drawbacks initially. Fast growers such as English ivy and myrtle take less time and less money to produce; therefore, they sell for less, and because they are less expensive, such plants meet with greater acceptance from the consumer. Also, because they fill in quickly, they require less initial maintenance during the establishment period. Nevertheless, dwarf Himalayan sarcococca is a superb plant and, slow-spreading nature aside, should be used to a greater extent.

This rather unobtrusive, low-spreading, woody shrublet reaches anywhere from 1 to 2 feet tall and, by underground stems, spreads (taking an eternity to do so) more than 6 feet across. For the patient gardener, the use of dwarf Himalayan sarcococca pays great dividends. Not only are its late wintertime/ early springtime flowers pleasantly fragrant, but its dark green lustrous foliage is simply superb and its round black ¼-inch-wide berries are very attractive as well. Its best applications are as a general cover or facing to trees in wooded settings on a moderate to large scale. On shady slopes, because of its considerable network of roots and stolons, it helps to bind soil and prevent erosion. Good shrubby companions include acid-loving plants such as rhododendrons, azaleas, laurel, witch hazel, blueberry, juniper, and dogwood. It looks lovely with some of the more robust hostas such as *H. sieboldiana* 'Elegans' and *H.* 'Krossa Regal', and seems to enjoy the companionship and protection offered by trees such as pine, oak, and fir. An interesting merit of dwarf Himalayan sarcococca is that it is relatively tolerant of air pollution. No foot traffic is tolerated.

SCIENTIFIC NAME: *Sarcococca hookeriana* var. *humilis* (sar-koe-*koke*-a hook-er-ee-*aye*-na hue-*myu*-lis). *Sarcococca* comes from the Greek *sarx,* flesh, and *kokkos,* a berry, the fruit being fleshy. *Hookeriana* commemorates Sir Joseph Hooker (1817–1911), the English botanist. *Humilis* means low-growing or dwarf.

HARDINESS / ORIGIN: Zones 7 to 9; western China.

LEAVES / FLOWERS / FRUIT: The evergreen elliptic or lance-shaped, 1- to 3-inch-long, ½- to ¾-inch-wide, leathery, deep green leaves radiate a truly striking glossiness. Indeed, the leaves are among the most attractive of any shade-loving ground cover. The small white fragrant flowers are grouped in fours and arranged in clusters, with the male flowers carried above the female. Partially obscured by the foliage, the flowers are of little consequence except for their sweet fragrance. The female flowers give rise to ⅓-inch-wide, round, black berries.

RATE / SPACING: Growth is slow. Plants from ½- to 1-gallon-sized containers are spaced 12 to 16 inches apart.

HORTICULTURAL SELECTIONS: Var. *digyna,* with uniform height of 2 feet.

OTHER SPECIES: *S. ruscifolia* (rus-ki-*foe*-lee-a), fragrant sarcococca, is named for its leaves that resemble butcher's broom (*Ruscus*). It hails from central and western China, is hardy only in Zones 7 to 9, reaches 2½ feet tall by 4 to 6 feet wide, and blooms with tiny white fragrant flowers during fall. Its leaves are evergreen, shiny, leathery, sharply pointed and 1¼ to 2 inches long. Its deep red fruit is rounded, ¼ inch across, and matures during late fall. Variety *chinensis* displays longer and narrower leaves.

CULTURE / CARE: Sarcococcas grow best in organically rich, well-drained, acidic loam. Their drought tolerance is fair, but supplemental watering may be needed during extended periods of heat and drought. They prefer moderate to dense shade. Pest and disease problems are rare. No maintenance is necessary, but a light shearing every other spring encourages branching and may help to speed the filling-in process.

PROPAGATION: Cuttings may be rooted in late fall and normally are given heat from the bottom to encourage rooting. Division works quite well during spring and early fall. In this case, sections are simply dug up and replanted.

Sasa veitchii   PLATE 275
Kumazasa, Kuma Bamboo Grass

Kumazasa is a rapid-growing, indefinite-spreading, running bamboo that reaches 2 to 3 feet tall in sun and 4 to 5 feet tall in the shade. It is best used as a general cover for moderate to large areas where there is ample room for it to spread without interfering with other plants. In small sites, or next to a property line it should be used only if it can be surrounded by a deep edging to control its spreading rhizomes. It is excellent for use at the side of an ornamental pool, pond, or stream and, of course, is right at home in Oriental-style gardens. Foot traffic is not well tolerated.

SCIENTIFIC NAME: *Sasa veitchii* (*sah*-sa *veech*-ee-eye). *Sasa* is the Japanese name for this genus. *Veitchii* commemorates J. Veitch and Sons Nursery, London.

HARDINESS / ORIGIN: Zones 8 to 10; temperate eastern Asia.

LEAVES / FLOWERS / FRUIT: The oval leaves are 8 inches long by ¼ to 1½ inches wide, with 12 to 18 veins, a prominent midrib, wedge-shaped base, and abruptly pointed tip. Colored deep green above and bluish green with minute hairs below, they are deciduous, turn straw-colored about their edges in fall, and persist to provide interest in the winter landscape. Attached to dull purple stems (green in youth), the leaves are fringed about their edges. Flowering and fruiting are seldom observed.

RATE / SPACING: Growth is fast to invasive. Plants from quart-sized to gallon-sized containers are spaced 2 to 3 feet apart.

HORTICULTURAL SELECTIONS: 'Nana', lower-growing, less invasive than the species.

CULTURE / CARE: Adaptive to almost any soil, kuma bamboo tolerates moderate periods of drought as well as temporarily saturated soils. It grows well in full sun to moderate shade. The most frequently observed disease and pest problems are bamboo smut and scale insects. Maintenance typically consists of shearing or mowing plantings to the ground during early spring.

PROPAGATION: Division works well and should be performed during early spring. Rhizome cuttings may also be used and should be taken during late winter; make them 12 inches long from new rhizomes and keep them moist during the entire propagation procedure; plant the sections 5 to 6 inches deep. Keep the soil well moistened during shoot formation.

Satureja douglasii   PLATE 276
Yerba Buena, Savory

Yerba buena, meaning good herb in Spanish, was the original name for San Francisco, in commemoration of this mat-forming, herbaceous, 2-inch-tall, 3-foot-wide ground cover. Truly it is a good herb, for in addition to being a flavorful seasoning and useful medicinal, it works well to cover the soil. As such, it is most often applied as a small-scale to moderate-scale general cover. Limited foot traffic is tolerated.

SCIENTIFIC NAME: *Satureja douglasii* (sat-you-*ree*-a dug-*las*-ee-eye). *Satureja* may come from the Arabic *sattar,* which was applied to this and other members of the mint family. Pliny, the first-century Roman writer, contended that the name came from *satyr,* the half-man, half-goat creature of ancient mythological forests. *Douglasii* is a commemorative and likely honors David Douglas (1799–1834), a famous Scottish plant collector who spent much time in the Pacific Northwest.

HARDINESS / ORIGIN: Zone 5; western United States from Los Angeles County to British Columbia.

LEAVES / FLOWERS / FRUIT: The aromatic, evergreen, oval leaves reach 1¼ inches long by 1 inch wide. Along their edges are rounded teeth, and at their bases originate the singular, ¾-inch-long, white to purple flowers of early spring to late summer. The fruit is nonornamental.

RATE / SPACING: Growth is moderate to fast. Plants from pint-sized to quart-sized containers are spaced 10 to 16 inches apart.

OTHER SPECIES: *S. glabella* (gla-*bell*-a), smooth-leaved satureja, is sometimes listed as *S. glabra,* but both names indicate that this plant has smooth, hairless foliage. Like *S. douglasii,* this species is a mat-forming herb. It ranges from 1 to 2 feet tall, spreads relatively fast to 4 feet wide, hails from Kentucky to Arkansas, and should be planted on 1½-foot centers. It is hardy to Zone 6. The leaves are narrowly oblong, ¾ to 1½ inch long by ¾ inch wide, dark green, and aromatic. During summer the purple flowers are borne upon thin 3-inch-long stems.

CULTURE / CARE: These savories are not greatly tolerant of drought and should be grown in a moist, organically rich, well-drained acidic loam. In humid or cooler climates, such as along the coast, they do well in full sun, but in warmer inland climates they prefer partial shade. They have no serious diseases and pests. Other than an early springtime mowing to keep them neat and compact, they need little maintenance.

PROPAGATION: Stem cuttings root easily during the summer.

Saxifraga stolonifera   PLATE 277
Strawberry Saxifrage, Mother-of-thousands, Strawberry Geranium, Strawberry Begonia, Creeping Sailor, Beefsteak Geranium

Strawberry saxifrage by all accounts is a well-liked, low-spreading, wonderfully carefree, herbaceous ground cover that reaches 6 to 8 inches tall and spreads indefinitely. Colorful year-round, it is easily cultured and is so pleasing that the biggest problem you might have with it is deciding which common name to use! Not only is this species a good general cover for small-sized to moderate-sized areas, it makes a splendid facing for azaleas, pieris, rhododendrons, lilies, and other shade-loving and acid-loving plants. Sometimes it is even used as a rock garden specimen. No foot traffic is tolerated.

SCIENTIFIC NAME: *Saxifraga stolonifera* (saks-*if*-ray-ga sto-lon-*if*-er-a). *Saxifraga,* breaking rocks, comes from the Latin *saxum,* a rock, and *frangere,* to break, a likely reference to the ability of these plants to exploit rocky terrain; by growing in rock crevices they appear to break rocks. *Stolonifera* means with stolons.

HARDINESS / ORIGIN: Zones 7 to 10; China and Japan.

LEAVES / FLOWERS / FRUIT: The attractive, colorful leaves are evergreen, roundish to heart-shaped, 2 to 4 inches long and wide, with edges often toothed and fringed with hairs. They are gray-green with conspicuous silvery-gray veins and sparse hairs all over. The bottom side is purplish maroon, warty, and covered with long pink hairs. During spring and summer, dainty 1-inch-wide, five-petaled, wispy flowers arise on slender 1- to 2-foot-long stems and make for a lovely display. The tiny fruit that follows is non-ornamental.

RATE / SPACING: Growth is fast. Plants from pint-sized to quart-sized containers are spaced 10 to 16 inches apart.

HORTICULTURAL SELECTIONS: 'Tricolor', rose-flushed leaves variegated dark green, gray-green, and ivory-white.

OTHER SPECIES: *S. umbrosa* (um-*broe*-sa), a parent of the hybrid *S. × urbium,* this species has somewhat shorter leaf blades, few rounded crenations on the margins, and more densely haired leaf stalks. It reaches a height of 1½ feet tall and is hardy in Zones 6 to 7.

S. × urbium (*er*-bee-um), meaning of towns, is commonly called London pride. Derived from the cross between *S. umbrosa* and *S. spathularis,* this hybrid is hardy to Zone 6 or 7. With leaves arranged in rosettes, it forms dense, herbaceous mats through its stoloniferous spreading habit. It ranges from 6 to 12 inches tall (to 20 inches while in flower). Like *S. stolonifera,* it is evergreen with oval to oblong, 2½-inch-long, thickened, medium to dark green leaves that are often red-tinged below. The tiny spring flowers are borne in many-flowered billowy clusters, 8 to 10 inches above the foliage, on thin, red stems. Colored white to pinkish, they seem to billow due to the stamens that are longer than the petals. The species spreads at a moderate rate, and plants from pint-sized to quart-sized containers should be spaced 10 to 14 inches apart. Its cultivars include 'Aureopunc-

tata', foliage variegated gold; 'Chamber's Pink Pride', with light pink flowers on scapes to 10 inches tall; 'Covillei', only 6 inches tall, with neat serrated leaves and white flowers; var. *primuloides* ('Minor'), of the Pyrenees, 6 inches tall, rose-pink flowers; var. *primuloides* 'Elliott's Variety', compact habit with rose-pink flowers on 6-inch-tall reddish scapes; var. *primuloides* 'Ingwersen's Variety', unique for its bronzy-colored foliage and deep red flowers; 'Variegata', with leaves variegated white and green.

CULTURE / CARE: These species are best in organically rich loam with good drainage and a pH from neutral to moderately acidic. They are not greatly tolerant of drought, thus their soil should be kept moist with regular watering, and a site should be selected with moderate to dense shade (particularly during the afternoon). Temperatures during the summer should range from cool to moderate, and shelter should be given from strong drying winds. Pests include slugs, snails, and grape rootworm. Diseases that might occur are leaf spots, powdery mildew, and rusts.

PROPAGATION: Newly rooted plantlets are easily dug up and transplanted during spring and fall.

Sedum   PLATES 278, 279, 280

Stonecrop, Sedum, Orpine

Sedums by some accounts are the most underrated and underused ground covers in North America today. They require nearly no maintenance, are easy to grow, have superb drought tolerance, display beautiful flowers (and sometimes beautiful fruit), and come in a variety of foliage and flower colors. Although they have long been overlooked, I am convinced—particularly in light of the increasing need for water conservation—they will become increasingly popular in our landscapes. *Sedum* is one of the most expansive genera of ground covers in cultivation with more than 600 species and many times more horticultural selections. Many insightful nursery owners now specialize in stonecrops, and there is even an American society for sedum enthusiasts. So why, then, don't more people use sedums in their landscape? Primarily because nursery owners have not done their part in promoting the merits of this exceptional plant group, and uncreative gardeners have been content to reside in the ground-cover triangle of myrtle, pachysandra, and ivy.

Stonecrop species are wonderfully diverse. Most are succulent herbs, but some are shrublike. They may be aggressive or slow spreading, tall and twiggy or low and mosslike. Leaves range from roundish and ball-shaped to needlelike to broad and flat. They may be colored anywhere from blue to green to red or even variegated. Flowers, too, are available in an array of colors, and happily, species can be found that bloom during spring, summer, fall, or winter.

Stonecrops are tough and long-lived. The Greeks called them *aeozoon* (live forever) and considerable mythology has been associated with the tenacity of stonecrops. As a rule, stonecrops are well adapted to withstand drought because of their crassulacean acid metabolism. With this special type of metabolism, gas exchange occurs at night; thus the stomata (leaf pores) remain closed during the day and open up at night (just opposite the norm). This way, less moisture is lost due to transpiration, since nights are typically cooler than days. This is a distinct advantage for survival in their rocky native haunts.

In the landscape, stonecrops thrive in sandy and rocky soils and seldom need watering. Generally, they are exceptionally cold hardy and, impressively, are often just as tolerant of heat. Plant them in sunny borders, at poolside or patioside, along walkways, against foundations, and here and there about rock gardens and herbaceous border plantings. Fast-spreading types should be bounded by natural barriers or edging or used as turf substitutes. The smaller species are best planted between cracks in stone retaining walls. Unless otherwise noted, the selections described below form tight mats or crowns.

SCIENTIFIC NAME: *Sedum* (*see*-dum), from the Latin *sedare,* to calm, presumably refers to the historical use of stonecrop in healing the sick. Others believe that it comes from the Latin *sedere,* to sit, in reference to the species that seem to sit (or grow) upon rocks.

HARDINESS / ORIGIN: See individual species for hardiness; North Temperate Zone and tropical mountain areas.

LEAVES / FLOWERS / FRUIT: The leaves vary considerably, depending on the species. They range from minute beadlike segments to broad flat oval forms and may be either alternate, opposite, or whorled in their arrangement. On some species they overlap, most are without stalks and attach directly to the stem, and all are succulent. The white, yellow, pink, red, or purple flowers, typically five-parted, are tiny but usually borne in clusters in such profusion as to make quite a show. The fruit that follows, technically called a follicle, in some species becomes swollen and colorful. With others it turns brown. In either event, the mature (and later dried) flowers and fruit are an added ornamental feature that often contrasts well with the foliage and frequently persists and adds interest to the winter landscape.

RATE / SPACING: Growth is fast. Plants from 2- to 4-inch-diameter containers are spaced 6 to 10 inches apart.

SPECIES: *S. acre* (*ack*-ree), named for its acrid taste, is commonly called goldmoss stonecrop (for its golden-yellow flowers of spring and its mosslike habit). This diminutive, 1- to 2-inch-tall carpeting species displays light green evergreen leaves, spreads at a moderate pace, and tolerates occasional foot traffic. It is hardy in Zones 3 to 8. Horticultural selections include 'Aureum' (syn. *S. acre* var. *aureum*), with bright yellow shoot tips that turn green during mid season; 'Elegans' (syn. *S. acre* var. *elegans*), with silvery shoot tips; 'Majus' (syn. *S. acre* var. *majus*), with larger leaves and flowers; 'Minus' (syn. *S. acre* var. *minus*), with smaller leaves and flowers.

S. alboroseum (al-bo-row-*ze-um*), named for the white and pink carpels of its floral apparatus, is a 16- to 20-inch-tall species with unbranched erect stems and oppositely arranged fleshy, somewhat toothedged, oval, gray-green 2- to 3-inch long leaves. At the ends of the stems, during early fall are borne tight clusters of whitish green flower buds which open to reveal whitish green petals and pinkish carpels (fruit bodies). From Asia and hardy in Zones 4 to 8, this is not the most showy or attractive sedum, but its cultivar 'Mediovariegatum', more often planted, is quite interesting. Displaying broad green leaves with yellow centers and wavy margins, it is often included in rock garden plantings. *Sedum* 'Frosty Morn', likely of different parentage, reminds me of *S. alboroseum* 'Mediovariegatum' in that it displays the same growth habit and flower cluster shape. Its leaves, however, are bluish green with white edges, and its flowers, white in bud, open to light pink.

S. ellacombianum (el-la-koe-mee-*aye*-num), named after Canon Henry Nicholson Ellacombe (1822–1916), an English horticulturist and clergyman, is commonly called Ellacombe's stonecrop. This deciduous, light green, clump-forming species is one of the most popular of the cultivated stonecrops. It reaches 6 to 10 inches tall and blooms bright yellow during early summer. Native to Japan, it is hardy in Zones 3 to 9.

S. 'Harvest Moon' is derived from the cross between *S. spathulifolium* var. *carneum* and *S.* 'Silver Moon'. Hardy to Zone 6 northward, it has large rosettes of grayish blue leaves that often turn reddish during the cold season. It is vigorous and may reach 4 inches tall by 12 inches wide with yellow flowers.

S. kamtschaticum (kam-*chat*-i-kum), named for its place of origin, Kamchatka, Siberia, is commonly called Kamchatka stonecrop and, not surprisingly, is very cold tolerant (Zones 3 to 9). Virtually trouble-free and maintenance-free, it is beautiful throughout the year. The semievergreen, narrow, succulent, dark green foliage is tightly set on compact stems. Reaching 3 to 4 inches tall and spreading indefinitely, its sprawling stems never need pruning, and the flowers that arise during early summer are both long-lived and superb in their ornamental qualities. In Michigan, they open about the second week of June and dazzle us with the intensity of their orangish yellow coloration. Weeks later, after the petals have faded, the fruit swells and turns russet-red. This has the effect of prolonging the blooming period and the display is just as effective as it was when the petals were present and fully expanded. Variety *floriferum*, with more flowers; 'Takahira Dake', taller and more upright in habit; 'Variegatum', green-leaved with irregular off-white margins.

S. lydium (*lid*-ee-um), meaning of Lydia, is commonly called Lydian stonecrop. Although only 2 inches tall, it more than makes up for its small stature with its attractive evergreen foliage and habit reminiscent of light green moss. Native to Asia Minor, it serves as a living reminder of ancient Lydia. The tiny white flowers, borne in summer on tall erect stems, are both numerous and endearing. The species performs best in colder climates, Zones 3 to 6, and spreads indefinitely at a rather slow pace.

S. middendorfianum (mid-den-door-fee-*aye*-num), named after the distinguished Russian plant collector Alexander Theodor von Middendorff (1815–1894), is commonly called Middendorff stonecrop. It is much like *S. kamtschaticum,* but more vigorous and more sprawling in habit. A native of eastern Siberia, Mongolia, Manchuria, and North Korea, it is hardy in Zones 3 to 9. Its evergreen foliage is medium green, and its yellow flowers make a pleasant show during mid to late summer. Variety *diffusum* has somewhat wider leaves and is laxer in habit.

S. 'Moonglow', to 2 inches tall and more than 12 inches wide, is noteworthy for its silvery-green rosettes that during summer often take on hues of gold, orange, and green. Hardy to Zone 6, it arose as a seedling of *S.* 'Silver Moon', which itself is a hybrid selection of *S. laxum* subsp. *heckneri* and *S. spathulifolium*. 'Moonglow' is a tightly rosetted selection noteworthy for its gray-green foliage that often displays hues of pink, red, and orange. It is hardy to Zone 6 northward.

S. nevii (*nev*-ee-eye), named after Dr. R. D. Nevius, is an interesting rosettaceous evergreen native with low compact habit. It hails from limestone, sandstone, and shale cliff crevices, and mossy places of the southern Appalachian highlands, Alabama, Tennessee, and Georgia. Its neat broadly pointed ⅜-inch-long succulent leaves are colored medium green above and reddish brown below. It blooms in late spring with a multitude of tiny white petals and prominent rose-colored anthers. Unlike most sedums, this one likes a bit of shade and soil that is relatively moist, but not wet. It is hardy to Zone 4.

S. populifolium (pop-you-li-*foe*-lee-um), now by some reclassified as *Hylotelephium populifolium,* is commonly called poplar-leaved stonecrop (for its light green deciduous foliage shaped like that of a poplar tree). It is native to western Siberia, has stems that are nearly woody, and resembles a small shrub in habit. It may reach 14 inches tall and may spread to 18 inches wide. It is hardy in Zones 3 to 7 and its rate of growth is moderate. The pink and white flowers, to ⅜ inch wide, appear during summer. Plants from quart-sized to ½-gallon-sized containers are spaced 14 inches apart.

S. purpureum (pur-pur-*ee*-um), named for its purple flowers, is commonly called purple stonecrop, evergreen stonecrop, frog plant, life-of-man, live long, live forever, orpine, garden orpine, and witch's moneybags. Native to North Korea and Japan, this species, a taxonomist's nightmare, is now classified by some as *Hylotelephium telephium,* or sometimes referred to as a subspecies of *S. telephium* (others say *S. telephium* is not an acceptable name and has been replaced by *S. purpureum*). Hardy in Zones 3 to 9 or 10, it is rather laxly clump forming in habit and tends to grow upright. It ranges from 12 to 18 inches tall and spreads generally from 18 to 24 inches wide. Plants from pint-sized to gallon-sized containers are spaced 16 to 24 inches apart. Exceptionally showy when mass planted as a general cover or foundation plant, it also excels as an edging to pathways and sidewalks. Often single or small groups of plants are featured in rock gardens and herbaceous perennial borders as specimens or for accent. It withstands considerable drought, tolerates being planted near black walnut (*Juglans nigra*), and its late-season floral display is among the best. The stalkless, flattened, medium green, succulent deciduous leaves are alternately arranged along stout stems. Generally they are 2 to 3 inches long, oval, irregularly toothed, and attached by tapering bases. Toward the terminal portion of the stems, they tend to be more elliptic, and their bases are more rounded. The flowers are five-parted, star-shaped, ⅜ inch wide, and colored pink to light purple. Arranged in many-flowered, convex, branch-ending clusters, the flowers are very effective from late summer to early fall. Historically, the astringent sap of this species was used as an ointment for the treatment of skin diseases, fistulas, and wounds. Taken internally, the juice has been used to treat ulcers, dysentery, and lung disorders. The lore associated with *S. purpureum* generally revolves around its tenacity (one common name comes from its Greek name *aizoon*, which means live forever). Scandinavians grew it on their roofs to ward off lightning, and if a plant were to suddenly wilt, they expected a death in the household. In some countries, plants were kept inside the home to insure the health of the inhabitants. Unfortunately, there is a great deal of confusion as to the classification of cultivars within this species. Poor documentation of interspecific hybrids is the main cause and thus it is common to see varying representations of the cultivars. Some of the more common cultivars, typically represented as members of the species *S. purpureum,* include 'Autumn Joy' ('Herbstfreude'), 12 to 18 inches tall (24 in rich soil), with large rounded clusters of pinkish mauve to bronzy red flowers, probably a hybrid between *S. purpureum* and *S. spectabile* that originated at Arends Nursery (circa 1955) but also claimed to be a cultivar of *S. spectabile* or *S. purpureum* (syn. *S. telephium*); 'Indian Chief', similar to 'Autumn Joy' but with even larger flower clusters; 'Munstead Dark Red', with reddish bronze leaves and flowers; 'Rosea-variegatum' ('Bittoniense'), with foliage that is pink in youth, later maturing to green.

S. reflexum (ree-*fleks*-um), named for its leaves which are bent backwards (reflexed), is commonly called spruce-leaved stonecrop for its blue leaves that look like succulent spruce needles. Originally from Europe, where its evergreen leaves are eaten in salads, it is hardy to Zone 3, reaches 8 to 10 inches tall, and spreads indefinitely. Growth is moderate. Plants from quart-sized to gallon-sized containers are spaced 8 to 12 inches apart. In early summer, tall, narrow, upright stems rise like pillars above the leaf mass. Atop them are borne thousands of tiny yellow flowers that collectively compose the 1- to 1½-inch-wide flat-topped clusters.

S. rubrotinctum (roob-row-*tink*-tum), named for its red-tinged leaves, is commonly called Christmas cheer stonecrop or pork and beans (for its color and the shape of its leaves). For diversity of color and durability, this 6- to 8-inch-tall, broad spreading, Guatemalan native is one of the finest warm-climate ground covers. It is hardy in Zones 9 to 10 and seldom needs watering. Throughout the year its evergreen, clublike, ½- to ⅔-inch-long, shiny green foliage is suffused with varying amounts of coppery-red pigment. During spring and early summer, yellow flowers further enhance the color show.

S. **'Ruby Glow'**, likely a hybrid of *S. cauticola* × *S. purpureum* 'Autumn Joy', displays a low sprawling habit and height to 9 inches. Its foliage is suffused with purple, and its flowers are ruby red.

S. spathulifolium (spath-e-le-*foe*-lee-um), named for its evergreen spatula-shaped leaves, is commonly called spatula-leaved stonecrop. An attractive plant native to the Pacific Northwest, it is slow to spread, easy to manage, and charming in appearance. It prefers cool weather, and although hardy northward to Zone 5, it fails in many inland areas, particularly in the South, as it does not tolerate the combination of high humidity and summertime heat. The bluish green foliage reaches ½ to 1¼ inches long and is densely arranged in rosettes upon short erect stems. The yellow flowers in spring add a dash of early season interest. Horticultural selections include 'Cape Blanco', with frosty blue-colored foliage, and 'Purpureum', with deeply purple-tinged foliage.

S. spectabile (spek-*tab*-i-lee), named for its spectacular flowers, is commonly called showy stonecrop. It produces a most breathtaking floral display and, for this reason, is near the top of the list in popularity. Blooming during fall, it punctuates the season—not as a period but as an exclamation point! The cultivars of *S. spectabile* are often the subject of controversy as to exact classification (likewise the species is under the scrutiny of botanists that have proposed a name change to *Hylotelephium spectabile*). Because of the extent of hybridization of this species, many popular garden forms exist. Typically they are hardy in Zones 3 to 9, range in height from 12 to 18 inches, spread 12 to 18 inches wide, are upright clump-forming in habit, and display opposite, 1½- to 2-inch-long, oval, tooth-edged (near their ends), blue-green deciduous leaves. Growth is slow to moderate. Plants from quart-sized to gallon-sized containers are spaced 16 to 24 inches apart. Some of the most popular horticultural selections include 'Album', with white flowers; var. *atropurpurea,* with rose to purplish pink flowers; 'Brilliant', with deep pink flowers; 'Carmen', with dark carmine-pink flowers; 'Chubby Fingers', like the species but with plumper leaves; 'Coral Carpet', with striking salmon-orange highlights to the new leaves before they mature to bright green; 'Humile', reaching only 8 inches tall; 'Meteor', with huge clusters of rose-pink flowers; 'Nigra', with chocolaty-maroon-tinged leaves; 'Pink Chablis', discovered as a sport of 'Brilliant', with blue-green leaves edged in creamy white, topped in late summer with flat clusters of frosty white flower buds that open to clear pink flowers; 'Purpureum', with purple-tinged leaves; 'Star Dust', with white flowers; 'Variegatum', with leaves variegated cream and blue-green.

S. spurium (*spew*-ree-um), meaning false or doubtful (for the frequent misapplication of names to this species), is commonly called two-row stonecrop (for its leaves that are more or less arranged in two columns along the length of the stems). Native to Asia Minor, it is one of the most popular stonecrops. It makes a tight cover 2 to 6 inches in height, spreads slowly to more than 8 inches wide, and is hardy in Zones 3 to 8. Its green foliage is interesting in that it is deciduous toward the base of the stems and evergreen toward the tips. In fall the leaves often take on burgundy hues, and in summer, they contrast marvelously with the pink to purplish star-shaped flowers that appear on 6-inch-tall erect stems. Plants from 2- to 4-inch-diameter containers are spaced 4 to 6 inches apart. Horticultural selections of note are 'Bronze Carpet', an excellent robust selection with bronzy, broad leaves that turn a deep burgundy during fall and winter; 'Dragon's Blood' ('Scharbuser Blut'), with variably greenish and burgundy, narrower leaves that turn bronzy reddish during fall and winter; 'Elizabeth' ('Glowing Fire', 'Purple Carpet', 'Purpurteppich', 'Red Carpet'), with bronzy purplish, broad, fan-shaped leaves that are scalloped along the margins, relatively slow growth; 'Splendens', somewhat larger than the species, with deep carmine flowers; 'Tricolor', unique for variegated foliage that is green in the center surrounded by a white border, which in turn has a pinkish purple margin, leaves narrower than the species and somewhat toothed, moderate growth rate, reversion to all-green-leaved stems is common (in which case such shoots should be removed as they are more vigorous and will eventually smother the variegated stems).

S. 'Sunset Cloud', with wine-red flowers, is related to *S.* 'Vera Jameson' (which see below).

S. ternatum (ter-*nay*-tum), named for its habit of bearing its leaves in threes (ternate), is commonly called wild stonecrop, Iceland moss, three-leaved stonecrop, or mountain stonecrop. This species hails from rocky areas of the eastern and midwestern United States. It is hardy in Zones 3 to 8 and is characterized by a low, mat-forming habit of 2 to 3 inches tall, with indefinite spread. Unusual in its preference for light to moderate shade and cool moist soil, this species is best used as a specimen in rock gardens or wooded settings as a small-scale general cover. Growth is moderate. Plants from 2- to 4-inch-diameter containers are spaced 6 to 12 inches apart. On its arching, nonflowering stems it bears semievergreen, flat, oval, medium green leaves that are arranged in whorls of three. These leaves reach ½ to 1 inch long by ⅓ to ¾ inch wide. The flowering stems, on the other hand, are erect with much narrower foliage. They ascend to 8 inches and are adorned with two to four terminally borne, dense, flat-topped, forked clusters. Each flower is four-parted, white, and borne rather sparsely during late spring and early summer. 'White Waters' is said to be more florific than the species.

S. 'Vera Jameson', derived from crosses involving *S. maximum* 'Atropurpureum' and *S.* 'Ruby Glow' (and some say *S. cauticola* as well), is 9 to 12 inches tall, has blue-green to purplish leaves, and bears showy pinkish mauve flowers in late summer.

CULTURE / CARE: Stonecrops grow in well-drained, acidic, sandy, or gravelly soil. Normally, they need watering only during extended periods of drought and heat. They prefer full sun with either afternoon or morning shade. Pests include slugs, nematodes, aphids, and weevils. Occasionally leaves become blighted during excessive hot rainy weather, but in most cases the severity of infection is insignificant. The only maintenance that might be required is to mow off the dried flower stalks after flowering.

PROPAGATION: Cuttings root well throughout the spring and summer for the deciduous types, and for the evergreen ones, cuttings can be taken any time. Seed, if obtainable, germinates well. Division, the simplest method, can be carried out at any time.

Sempervivum   PLATE 281

Houseleeks, Hen and Chicks

Although houseleeks are excellent, interesting rock garden specimens, they are seldom treated justly when it comes to covering small-sized to moderate-sized areas. Yet, until they are used in patches of 3 or more feet across, their seasonal variations in leaf color, low maintenance requirements, and drought tolerance often go unappreciated. These low-growing, rosette-forming, succulent ground covers spread by producing horizontal stems that bear new plantlets (chicks) at their tips. Each year, only the mother rosette of each plant flowers. This is the large rosette that is surrounded by several smaller plantlets. Upon the fading of the flowers, the mother rosette dies and is replaced by the "chicks" that it has produced.

A typical houseleek displays a mass of foliage ranging from 1 to 4 inches tall, and a flower stalk that may ascend to 1½ feet. The individual heights listed below reflect the height of the flowering stems, not the foliar mass. The next time that you are planting a walkway or border edging in a sunny location, or you need to control erosion on a sunny, sandy, gentle slope or terrace, perhaps you would do well to use houseleeks. They are good in coarse-textured, infertile soil and are excellent as foreground plants to the taller, nontrailing stonecrops, such as *Sedum purpureum* and its varieties. No foot traffic is tolerated.

In Europe, houseleeks were planted on roofs to hold the slates in place and were thought to protect the house from lightening and fire.

Among the houseleeks there are hundreds of species and even more cultivars. There is also an astounding (and countless) array of hybrids. Specialty nurseries often stock more than 1000 selections, all different in color combinations, leaf and rosette size, and floral characteristics. Be sure to ask for varieties that hold their color and perform well in your climate.

SCIENTIFIC NAME: *Sempervivum* (sem-per-*vie*-vum) comes from the Latin *semper,* always, and *vivus,* alive, alluding to the tenacity of these plants.

HARDINESS / ORIGIN: Zones 4 or 5 to 8; Europe, Morocco, and western Asia.

LEAVES / FLOWERS / FRUIT: The leaves are evergreen and arranged in dense rosettes. Usually they are oblong to oval, broad-based, with hairy edges and a sharply pointed tip, and their edges are colored shades of pink to purple or brown, while their thick, fleshy blades are colored varying shades of green, blue, bronze, or gray. During summer the mother rosette bears numerous flowers (⅜ inch wide) on an erect, leafy, flowering stem. The petals are red, purple, yellow, or white, and the edges are frequently fringed with hairs. The fruit is nonornamental.

RATE / SPACING: Growth is slow. Plants from 3- to 5-inch-diameter containers are spaced 3 to 5 inches apart.

SPECIES: *S. arachnoideum* (a-rak-*noy*-dee-um), named from the Greek *arachnoeides,* like a cobweb, is commonly called Spiderweb houseleek or cobweb houseleek for the curious thin, white cobweblike hairs that extend from leaf tip to leaf tip. Native to the mountains of southern Europe, this little species seldom exceeds 3 or 4 inches tall in flower. Its leaves, which reach ¾ inch long by ¼ inch wide, are colored pale green, sometimes tipped brown or red, and covered with cobwebby white hairs. About mid summer, a little flower stalk ascends from the mother rosette bearing 5 to 15 bright rose-red flowers arranged in compact, flattish clusters. Variety *tomentosum* has flattish rosettes that are nearly concealed by their masses of cobweblike hairs.

S. calcareum (kal-*care*-ee-um), named for its habitat in calcareous rocks in the French Alps, was, and by some still is, considered a subspecies of *S. tectorum.* It is characterized by relatively large rosettes, usually more than 2½ inches wide, that are composed of blue-green leaves with reddish brown tips. The pale red flowers are smaller than those of *S. tectorum* with narrower petals. Common cultivars include 'Greenii', with smaller more compact habit; 'Mrs. Giuseppi', more compact habit and deep-red-tipped foliage; 'Sir William Lawrence', with red-tipped leaves and larger more globose habit.

S. montanum (mon-*tay*-num /mon-*tan*-um), named for its mountain origins, in this case the Alps, the Pyrenees, and the Carpathian Mountains, is commonly called mountain houseleek. It reaches 6 inches tall in flower and is a fine-textured species with 1- to 1½-inch-diameter rosettes of 40 to 50 hairy, dark green leaves ½ to 1 inch long. Its bluish

purple flowers reach 1½ inches wide and are effective in early to late summer. Variety *braunii* has yellowish flowers and rosettes that reach 2 inches wide.

S. ruthenicum (rew-*then*-i-kum), named for Ruthenia, a region of European Russia, is commonly called Russian houseleek. Native to southeastern Europe, it reaches 12 inches tall in flower and displays rosettes that range from 1½ to 2½ inches wide. Its 1¼-inch-long green leaves are covered with dense hairs and are sometimes tipped with purple (older ones are typically flushed with hues of rose). The flowers are pale yellow with purple centers, reach ¾ to 1 inch wide, and bloom during mid to late summer.

S. tectorum (tek-*tore*-um), from the Latin *tectum,* roof, is so named because it used to be grown on roofs and is commonly called common houseleek, hen-and-chickens, old man and old woman, St. Patrick's cabbage, or roof houseleek. Native to Europe, it reaches 12 inches tall in flower and is probably the most frequently cultivated species of *Sempervivum.* It is characterized by flattish, 3- to 4-inch-diameter (sometimes larger) rosettes of 50 to 60 smooth, 1½- to 3-inch-long, green, often purple-tipped leaves. The purplish red flowers are ¾ to 1 inch wide and effective in summer. Many cultivars and varieties exist. A few of the most common are subsp. *alpinum,* with smaller rosettes (1 to 2½ inches in diameter) and red leaf bases; 'Robustum', with purple-tipped leaves in rosettes to 6 inches wide.

HYBRID SELECTIONS: To mention a single hybrid is to neglect hundreds of worthy selections. Here are a few with nice sunfast color patterns, but hundreds of other worthy selections are available. 'Collector Anchisi', with small mahogany-red-tipped emerald green leaves; 'Emerald Giant', with large rosettes of broad light green leaves that often turn bright orange-red in late season; 'Godaert', with lightly fringed red leaves; 'Lilac Time', with gray-green leaves that are attractively overlaid with rose; 'Maria Laach', with deep mahogany-tipped dark green medium-sized leaves; 'Maroon Queen', with red-backed olive green leaves; 'Pistachio', with brown-tipped bright yellowish green leaves; 'Red Devil', with deep purplish red leaves; 'Royanum', with bright green dark red-tipped leaves; 'Wendy', with flat rosettes of rose-tipped green leaves.

CULTURE / CARE: Houseleeks are adaptable to most soils, excellent drainage being their biggest concern. They tolerate infertility and drought, and seldom need watering except during long stretches of hot dry weather. They prefer full sun to light shade or a combination of full sun with light or moderate afternoon shade. They experience few pest problems, and the most common diseases that occur are rust, leaf rot, stem rot, and root rot. Maintenance consists of removing the dead rosettes from mother plants (which die soon after flowering) so that their progeny can more readily fill in the gaps.

PROPAGATION: Division proves to be most practical and consists merely of pulling up the small offsets and replanting them.

Shortia galacifolia   PLATE 282
Oconee Bells

Oconee bells, a 6- to 8-inch-tall herbaceous ground cover native to eastern North America, spreads more than 16 inches wide with a rhizomatous, basal-leaved habit. It and two related species from Japan, *S. soldanelloides* and *S. uniflora,* are excellent ground covers for use in an acid soil in deciduous woodland settings, where they work well for general cover, pathway edging, or as accent plants. They are not, however, easy to grow. They require exact adherence to their cultural needs and are certainly not a good choice for impatient gardeners. Typically, they are used on a relatively small to moderate scale and may take several years to become well established.

SCIENTIFIC NAME: *Shortia galacifolia* (*shore*-tee-a ga-las-i-*foe*-lee-a). *Shortia* is named for Charles W. Short (1794–1863), a botanist from Kentucky. *Galacifolia* means that the leaves are like those of *Galax.*

HARDINESS / ORIGIN: Zones 4 to 8; wooded mountains of Virginia to Georgia.

LEAVES / FLOWERS / FRUIT: The evergreen, simple leaves arise in rosettes from rhizomes and are round to oval, 1 to 3 inches wide, wavy-edged to toothed-edged, and glossy green, often turning bronze in winter. The nodding flowers arise upon slender upright stalks during early spring. Each flower is five-petaled, 1 inch wide, and resembles a little bell, first white then pink or rose.

RATE / SPACING: Growth is slow. Plants from pint-sized to quart-sized containers are spaced 8 to 10 inches apart.

SPECIES: *S. soldanelloides* (sol-da-nel-*oye*-deez), named for its resemblance to the genus *Soldanella,* is commonly called fringed galax or fringe bell. From Japan, it is hardy to Zone 6, reaches 4 to 9 inches tall, and spreads over 12 inches across. Fringed galax, like Oconee bells, is basal leaved, herbaceous, and evergreen. Its leaves, which range from round to kidney-shaped, are 1½ to 2½ inches long and wide. Their edges are typically coarsely toothed, their blades leathery gray-green and bronzy edged, and their winter color is bronzy maroon. The flowers of mid spring are carried in groups of four to six, elevated well above the foliage on slender scapes, and display themselves in nodding fashion. Each is five-

parted, bell-shaped, with fringed, deep rose to pinkish petals. Forma *alpina* is more compact and somewhat smaller than the species; variety *ilicifolia,* has leaves with fewer and coarser teeth; variety *magna,* has larger leaves with margins ringed with several tiny teeth.

S. uniflora (yew-ni-*flore*-a), commonly called nippon-bells, is native to Japan, hardy in Zones 4 to 8, and closely resembles *S. galacifolia.* Its foliage, however, is more heart-shaped and more deeply wavy margined. The cultivar 'Grandiflora' has larger flowers than the typical species.

CULTURE / CARE: *Shortia* species need well-drained, highly organic, acidic loam. They are not notably tolerant of drought, their soil should be kept moist, and preferably the site should be cool and somewhat sheltered from strong winds. Because they need sun in early spring during bloom, then moderate to dense shade later on, they are best used in conjunction with deciduous trees and shrubs. Crown rot is sometimes a problem if plants are subjected to excess moisture. Aphids are encountered occasionally but are rarely serious. No maintenance is needed except in northern climates with unreliable snowfall, where plants should be covered with evergreen boughs in winter to keep the foliage from drying out.

PROPAGATION: Division is best accomplished during spring immediately following bloom. Seed, which is said to germinate very poorly, is seldom used.

Soleirolia soleirolii   PLATE 283
Baby's Tears, Angel's Tears, Irish Moss, Peace in the Home, Corsican Curse, Japanese Moss, Pollyana Vine, Corsican Carpet Plant, Helxine, Mind-your-own-business, Mother-of-Thousands

This low, herbaceous, creeping, mosslike ground cover, which reaches 3 inches tall and spreads indefinitely, is an excellent carpeting plant to put between patio blocks and stepping stones, particularly in naturalized settings. On a small scale it is fine as a turf substitute, and it makes an outstanding setting for statuary and bird baths. In Mexico City I have seen it used as a mannequin facing! It was planted wall to wall, carpeting the inside of an east-facing store front. Baby's tears is an excellent companion to clump-forming ferns and hostas in woodland settings and to astilbes, daylilies, and lily turf (particularly black lily turf) in more sunny exposures. It is a tough little plant, despite its delicate appearance. Infrequent foot traffic is tolerated.

SCIENTIFIC NAME: *Soleirolia soleirolii* (soe-lay-*role*-ee-a soe-lay-*role*-ee-eye). Both names are for Joseph Francois Soleirol (1796–1863), who originally collected this species in Corsica.

HARDINESS / ORIGIN: Zones 9 to 11; Corsica, Sardinia, and other islands in the western Mediterranean Sea.

LEAVES / FLOWERS / FRUIT: Held on threadlike stems, the shiny light green leaves are evergreen, nearly round, relatively succulent, to ¼ inch long and just as wide, with both sides sparsely hairy. The flowers are solitary, very small, without petals, and of little or no ornamental significance.

RATE / SPACING: Growth is fast. Plants from 4-inch-diameter containers are spaced 10 to 14 inches apart.

HORTICULTURAL SELECTIONS: 'Aurea', with golden leaves.

CULTURE / CARE: Baby's tears is best in organically rich, loamy soil. Because it is intolerant of drought, the soil should be kept moist with regular watering. Exceedingly high temperatures should also be avoided, and light conditions should range from light to dense shade. No serious pests or disease problems are likely to occur, and little or no maintenance is required.

PROPAGATION: Cuttings are not difficult to root. Division, however, is so simple and effective that it is the standard method of propagation; simply dig up small plugs and transplant to their new location in fall, winter, or early spring.

Sorbus reducta   PLATE 284
Dwarf Chinese Mountain Ash

Dwarf Chinese mountain ash is a rhizomatous, shrubby ground cover that reaches 2½ feet tall and spreads more than 4 feet across. Rather coarse in texture, and relatively large, this ground cover clearly is not suitable for use in every landscape. It needs a good deal of room and probably is at its best when mass planted on large slopes as a means of retaining soil. It might also be employed as a specimen in a border planting or alpine garden featuring dwarf shrubs.

SCIENTIFIC NAME: *Sorbus reducta* (*sore*-bus ree-*duck*-ta). *Sorbus* is simply the Latin name for this genus, commonly called mountain ash. *Reducta,* reduced, refers to the dwarf size of the species.

HARDINESS / ORIGIN: Zone 5 with snow cover, otherwise Zones 6 to 8; northern Burma and western China.

LEAVES / FLOWERS / FRUIT: The deciduous, alternate, compound leaves with 13 to 15 paired, dark glossy green, sharply toothed leaflets turn spectacular tones of bronze and bright red during autumn. The flowers, effective during late spring and arranged in branch-ending clusters, are tiny, five-parted, white, and fragrant. They are interesting in that they yield fruit without fertilization. The berrylike fruit is round, ¼ inch wide, pink, persistent, and very attractive.

RATE / SPACING: Growth is moderate. Plants from 2- to 3-gallon-sized containers are spaced 2½ to 3 feet apart.

CULTURE / CARE: Adaptable to a range of well-drained, acidic soils, this species tolerates a modest amount of drought, yet is best when the soil is kept slightly moist. It prefers full sun to light shade. Diseases such as powdery mildew and blight are often encountered. The primary pest problem is mites. Little or no maintenance is required.

PROPAGATION: During spring, simply divide out new shoots that arise from the rhizomes. Seed, also commonly used, should be harvested in fall at the time of fruit ripening; depulp it, then stratify it moist for 3 or 4 months at 35 to 40°F prior to sowing.

Spartina pectinata   PLATE 285
Prairie Cord Grass

As durable as it is attractive, this species is a rhizomatous spreading 3- to 5-foot-tall colonizer, ideal for soil retention on a moderate to large scale. Tolerant of moisture, it displays lovely vertically oriented foliage that moves in the wind and gives off a soothing rustling sound. The variegated cultivar 'Aureo-marginata' is exceptional for its lovely gold and green stripes.

SCIENTIFIC NAME: *Spartina pectinata* (spar-*teen*-a pek-ti-*nay*-ta). Spartina comes from the Greek word *spartion,* esparto grass, which was used for making cord or rope, and *pectinata,* comblike, in reference to the one-sided flower spikes.

HARDINESS / ORIGIN: Zones 4 to 9; from marshes and high water table areas of Maine to eastern Oregon, southward to North Carolina and Texas.

LEAVES / FLOWERS / FRUIT: Sharp-edged, the shiny green leaves range from ¼ to ¾ inch wide by 1½ to 2½ feet long. During mid summer it bears one-sided soft brown spikes that arch and wave about in the wind 2 to 3 feet above the foliage. Producing a small brown grain, their fruit is not showy; however, during fall the leaves turn a lovely shade of golden-yellow.

RATE / SPACING: Growth is relatively fast. Plants from 1- to 2-gallon-sized containers are spaced 2 to 3 feet apart.

HORTICULTURAL SELECTIONS: 'Aureo-marginata' ('Variegata'), leaves magnificent with green and golden-yellow stripes.

CULTURE / CARE: This grass tolerates drought, wetness, and salt. It prefers acidic soils of light sandy or loamy texture and is tolerant of infertility. Too much fertilizer may cause it to flop over midseason. Problems with insects or diseases are unlikely.

PROPAGATION: Seed may be used to propagate the species, but most often propagation is conducted by division during spring or early summer.

Spiraea

PLATE 286

Spirea

Almost every gardener is familiar with spireas and almost always thinks of them as broad, upright-growing, medium-sized shrubs. Certain varieties and hybrids, however, are useful as ground covers because they exhibit low, mounding, dense, shrubby habits. Such varieties typically reach 12 to 36 inches tall, spread 3 to 4 feet across, and are useful as specimens in rock gardens and border plantings, or in mass plantings along foundations. They can be used also as edgings along walkways or steps or for accent when placed alongside boulders and statuary. No foot traffic is tolerated.

SCIENTIFIC NAME: *Spiraea* (spie-*ree*-a) is likely derived from the Greek *speira,* a wreath, or *speiraira,* a plant used in garlands.

HARDINESS / ORIGIN: See individual species for hardiness; North Temperate Zone to Mexico and the Himalayas.

LEAVES / FLOWERS / FRUIT: Generally speaking the leaves are deciduous, 1 to 3 inches long, lance-shaped to oval with sharply pointed tips and double-toothed edges. Usually green, the leaves form the perfect backdrop for the pink, deep pink, or whitish flowers borne in large flat-topped clusters during early to mid summer. The tiny fruit is nonornamental.

RATE / SPACING: Growth is slow to moderate. Plants from 1- or 2-gallon-sized containers are spaced 2 to 3½ feet apart.

SPECIES: *S.* × *bumalda* (bew-*mal*-da), named for Ovidio Montalbani (1601–1671), of Bologna, whose Latinized name was Bumaldes, was derived by crossing *S. albiflora* and *S. japonica* and is the parent of many fine ground-covering cultivars—mostly hybrids from crosses with *S. japonica,* 'Alpina'. They seem to have picked up some of the greater hardiness of *S.* × *bumalda* (Zones 3 or 4 to 9) and typically can survive in Zones 4 to 9. Those that function well as ground covers include 'Anthony Waterer', 3 feet tall and wide, with rose-pink flowers; 'Crispa', with twisted coarse-textured prominently toothed leaves and pink flowers, 3 feet tall by 3 feet wide; 'Dakota Goldcharm', 12 to 15 inches tall, with gold leaves and pink flowers; 'Dart's Red', 2 to 3 feet tall, with carmine-red flowers; 'Flaming Mound', 2 feet tall, with reddish foliage and deep carmine-red flowers; 'Flowering Mound', with leaves reddish in youth maturing to yellow, flowers dark pink throughout summer, mature size 28 inches tall by 36 inches

wide; 'Glowing Mound', with diminutive habit, maturing to form broad mounds 2 feet tall by 2½ feet wide with small pink flowers and golden-yellow foliage that turns coppery pink in the fall; 'Golden Carpet', interesting for its unusual habit of rooting as it trails, a very low growing (to only 12 inches tall) selection reminiscent of gold carpeting; 'Gold Flame', 2 to 3 feet tall by 3 to 4 feet wide, with bright gold leaves and pink flowers; 'Gold Mound', 2 feet tall, with golden leaves, mounded habit, pink flowers; 'Gumball', 2 feet tall, compact habit and pink flowers; 'Lightening Mound', with creamy lemon leaves that mature to lime in late summer, seldom flowers, does best in light shade, and reaches 1½ feet tall by 2 feet wide; 'Neon Flash', 3 feet tall, purple new growth changing to green, red flowers borne from late spring through fall; 'Norman', 15 to 18 inches tall, with pink flowers and red fall color; 'Sparkling Carpet', like 'Golden Carpet', with prostrate habit, densely branched, graced with reddish pink juvenile leaves that become yellow in maturity, does not exceed 12 inches tall, seldom flowers.

S. japonica (ja-*pon*-i-ka), meaning of Japan, is commonly called Japanese spirea. It is a variable species that may reach 4 or 5 feet tall, with stiff, erectly oriented branches. Its pink-red flowers, ¼ inch wide, occur in flat-topped clusters 6 to 8 inches wide in June and July. Hardy in Zones 5 to 9, it is an attractive plant, but too unpredictably shaped to be much of a ground cover. It has, however, contributed a couple of superb cultivars that are wonderful ground covers: 'Alpina' ('Nana', var. *alpina*), commonly called daphne spirea, with dwarf mounding habit, 1 to 2½ feet tall, leaves medium green, densely set, ½ inch long, and fine-textured, pink flowers in summer; 'Little Princess', also a dwarf selection with mounding habit, more robust than 'Alpina', reaching 30 inches tall, blooming deep pink in early spring; 'Magic Carpet', 18 to 24 inches tall by 2½ feet wide, new growth red all summer changing to rich bronzy yellow-tipped, flowers deep pink; 'Nyewoods' (sometimes listed as a cultivar of *S.* × *bumalda*), said by some to be identical to 'Little Princess' (which it closely resembles), 2 feet tall, with cheery pink flowers in spring; 'Shirobana', 2 to 3 feet tall, with red flower buds opening to pink and white florets carried in the same clusters.

OTHER SELECTIONS: *S.* 'Dolchica', with attractive leaves that are reddish in youth and dark green in maturity, reaches 2 feet tall by 3 feet wide, flowers purplish pink from early to late summer.

CULTURE / CARE: Spireas are not picky about soil type, other than to insist upon good drainage and acidic pH (to avoid chlorosis from iron deficiency). Once established, they withstand considerable drought, only requiring supplemental watering during prolonged hot, dry weather. All selections prefer to be grown in the sun, although they tolerate dappled shade. Diseases include fire blight, hairy root, leaf spots, powdery mildew, and root rot. The most prevalent pests are aphids, leaf rollers, scales, nematodes, and caterpillars. Maintenance at most consists of a light shearing after flowering.

PROPAGATION: Stem cuttings root easily in early to mid summer.

Stachys byzantina   PLATE 287

Lamb's Ears, Woolly Betony

Lamb's ears is the perfect name for this plant with velvety soft, lamb's-ear-shaped leaves. It is a herbaceous, laxly spreading, 12- to 18-inch-tall (when in flower, otherwise 4 to 6 inches), 3-foot-wide ground cover. It is useful to gardeners who are looking for contrast because its light gray leaves show up well in the foreground or background of green-, purple-, and yellow-leaved perennials. No foot traffic is tolerated.

SCIENTIFIC NAME: *Stachys byzantina* (*stay*-kis bye-zan-*teen*-a). *Stachys* comes from the Greek *stachys,* a spike, in reference to the pointed flower clusters. *Byzantina* means of Byzantium, now Istanbul.

HARDINESS / ORIGIN: Zones 4 to 8; southwestern Asia.

LEAVES / FLOWERS / FRUIT: The deciduous leaves are pleasantly scented when crushed and densely covered with velvety white hairs. Reaching 4 inches long, they are this species' chief ornamental attribute. The flowers, although considered of secondary importance, are attractive as well. Colored pink to purple, they reach ½ inch long and are borne in upright leafy spikes from mid summer until frost. The fruit is nonornamental.

RATE / SPACING: Growth is moderate. Plants from 3- to 4-inch-diameter containers are spaced 12 to 16 inches apart.

HORTICULTURAL SELECTIONS: 'Cotton Ball' ('Sheila McQueen'), a compact, slightly larger leaved cultivar, reaches only 1 foot tall, with leaves less hairy than the species; 'Helen von Stein' ('Big Ears'), sparsely flowering, reaches up to 3 feet tall, holds up well in heat and humidity; 'Primrose Heron', primrose-yellow leaves in spring that mature to grayish green in summer; 'Silver Carpet', a nonflowering form, with thicker, woollier leaves.

OTHER SPECIES: *S. macrantha* (ma-*kran*-tha), large-flowered or big betony, reaches 12 to 24 inches tall by 1 foot wide, and is of interest for its 1-inch-wide, violet-purple flowers that bloom from late spring to early summer. Adding to its appeal are its broadly oval leaves that are dark green, wrinkled, roughly

haired, and scalloped about their edges. Its growth rate is relatively fast, and in rich soils it quickly fills in and forms thick mats. It is hardy in Zones 3 to 8 and hails from the Caucasus Mountains. It has given rise to the following selections: 'Alba', with white flowers; 'Robusta', reaching 24 inches tall, with rose-pink, somewhat earlier flowers than the species; 'Rosea', with rose-red flowers; 'Superba', with deep purplish violet flowers; 'Violacea', with deep violet flowers, much like 'Superba'.

CULTURE / CARE: These two species of *Stachys* grow well in almost any type of well-drained soil, yet are at their best in a constantly moist, rich loam. They tolerate a moderate amount of drought and should be sited in full sun or light shade. The primary disease problems, leaf spot, powdery mildew, and leaf gall, can be reduced or prevented by watering during the morning (or drip irrigating) so that the leaves dry out quickly. Slugs are the primary pest problem, and nematodes are occasionally destructive. Maintenance needs are minimal.

PROPAGATION: Division is the standard means of propagating the selections, and the species are usually propagated by seed. Seed propagation is simple, and germination occurs in one or two weeks.

Stephanandra incisa 'Crispa'   PLATE 288

Dwarf Cutleaf Stephanandra, Crisped Stephanandra, Lace Shrub

Similar to dwarf Arnold forsythia in that it is a rather low-growing woody shrub that sprawls about and displays greater foliar merits than floral, dwarf cutleaf stephanandra functions best as a dwarf hedge, foundation facer, or soil stabilizer for moderate-sized slopes. Typically it reaches 1½ to 3 feet tall and spreads 4 feet across. No foot traffic is tolerated.

SCIENTIFIC NAME: *Stephanandra incisa* 'Crispa' (stef-a-*nan*-dra in-*sie*-sa *kris*-pa). *Stephanandra* comes from the Greek *stephanos,* a crown, and *andros,* a man, in reference to the stamens (the male floral apparatus) being arranged like a crown. *Incisa* comes from the Latin *incis,* to carve into, and indicates that the leaves have deep cuts carved into their edges. 'Crispa' means wrinkled.

HARDINESS / ORIGIN: Zones 5 to 8 or 9; the species is native to Japan and Korea, and the cultivar 'Crispa' originated in Denmark in 1930.

LEAVES / FLOWERS / FRUIT: The deciduous leaves are carried on weeping, downward bowed branches, range from 1½ to 2½ inches long, are colored a light bright green, and are remarkable for the many deep irregular cuts in their margins. Fall color is often reddish purple or reddish orange. The flowers, which arise during early summer, contribute little to the ornamental effect of this plant. They are tiny, yellowish white, and arranged in loose, 1- to 1½-inch-wide clusters. The fruit is nonornamental.

RATE / SPACING: Growth is moderate. Plants from 1- to 2-gallon-sized containers are spaced 2½ to 3 feet apart.

CULTURE / CARE: Best growth is usually realized in organically rich, well-drained, loamy, acidic soil. Tolerance to drought is only fair, and often a few deep waterings are needed during the summer. A site in full sun to light shade is preferred. No serious pests or diseases seem to effect this plant. Maintenance needs are minimal; an annual shearing during late spring is practiced by some gardeners but is not necessary.

PROPAGATION: Cuttings during early summer root easily. Naturally layered stem sections can be dug up and replanted during spring and fall.

Stylophorum diphyllum   PLATE 289
Celandine Poppy, Yellow Poppy

Celandine poppy is an aggressive, 1- to 1½-foot-tall, indefinite-spreading (mostly by seed), long-blooming native herbaceous woodland ground cover. Most at home in moist shady areas where it has room to roam, it is quite effective as a general cover when mass planted. No foot traffic is tolerated. The yellow sap in the stems was once used as a dye by Native Americans.

SCIENTIFIC NAME: *Stylophorum diphyllum* (sty-*lof*-oh-rum dye-*fil*-um). *Stylophorum* comes from the Greek *stylos*, a style, and *phoros*, bearing, in reference to the long styles (female floral apparatus between the carpel and stigma). *Diphyllum*, two-leaved, refers to the foliage which is often paired toward the end of the stems.

HARDINESS / ORIGIN: Zones 4 to 9; moist woodlands of western Pennsylvania and Ohio to Tennessee, west to Wisconsin and Missouri.

LEAVES / FLOWERS / FRUIT: Upon succulent yellow-sap-filled stems, the bluish green, almost succulent, semievergreen, 10- to 15-inch-long, deeply divided, five-lobed to seven-lobed compound leaves appear very lush and robust. The bright yellow flowers are eye-catching, too. They are borne from spring to mid summer, reach 1½ to 2 inches in diameter, and light up shaded woodlands like few other flowers. The fruit that follows, an oblong fuzzy pod, is also quite interesting.

RATE / SPACING: Growth is moderate. Plants from quart-sized to gallon-sized containers are spaced 1½ to 2 feet apart.

CULTURE / CARE: Celandine poppy grows in about any moist soil and thrives in light to moderate shade.

It does not tolerate drought and should be given supplemental watering during extended hot, dry weather. Few pests or diseases affect it, and it requires no maintenance if given sufficient room to spread.

PROPAGATION: Division during spring and fall is simple and effective. Seed is also effective; sown in fall, it germinates the following spring.

Symphoricarpos × chenaultii 'Hancock'   PLATE 290
Hancock Chenault Coralberry

Hancock Chenault coralberry is a low woody spreading shrub that reaches 2 feet tall by 12 feet across. Definitely not a ground cover for small gardens, this one is best used on a large scale in informal settings and because of its suckering nature is excellent for erosion control on steep embankments. No foot traffic is tolerated.

SCIENTIFIC NAME: *Symphoricarpos × chenaultii* 'Hancock' (sim-foe-ri-*kar*-pos sha-*nolt*-ee-eye). *Symphoricarpos* comes from the Greek *symphoreo*, to accumulate, and *karpos*, a fruit, in reference to the clustered fruits. *Chenaultii*, a hybrid, is presumably named for its hybridizer.

HARDINESS / ORIGIN: Zones 4 to 8; *S. × chenaultii* is a hybrid of the cross between *S. orbiculatus × S. microphyllus* around 1910, and the cultivar 'Hancock' was selected at Hancock Nurseries, Ontario, Canada, around 1940.

LEAVES / FLOWERS / FRUIT: The deciduous, oppositely arranged, elliptic, ¾-inch-long simple leaves are colored soft medium blue-green. Pink bell-shaped flowers are borne in mid summer and give rise to ¼-inch-wide berries that are white on the side away from the sun and reddish pink toward the sun.

RATE / SPACING: Growth is fast. Plants from 1- to 3-gallon-sized containers are spaced 4 to 5 feet apart.

OTHER SPECIES: *S. orbiculatus* (ore-bik-you-*lay*-tus) is named for its orbicular (round) fruit and is commonly called buck brush, coralberry, Indian current, or turkeyberry. Native to the south central United States, it is hardy in Zones 2 to 7 and reaches 2 to 5 feet tall by 4 to 8 feet wide. It has a low, dense, suckering habit, spreads relatively fast, and should be spaced 3 to 4 feet apart from 1- to 2-gallon-sized containers. Its leaves, like those of *S. × chenaultii* 'Hancock', are simple and oppositely arranged. They vary in shape from elliptic to oval, reach ⅗ to 1⅖ inches along, and are colored dull gray-green during the growing season and bluish gray in fall. The tiny yellowish white, ofttimes pinkish-tinged or purple-tinged flowers are borne from mid to late summer, reach ⅛ to ⅙ inch long, and give rise to clusters of ¼-inch-long coral red to purplish berries. 'Leucocarpus' has white fruits, while 'Variegatus' ('Foliis

Variegatus') has leaves that are irregularly trimmed in yellow.

CULTURE / CARE: Adaptable to pH and tolerant of nearly any soil, the coralberries also handle drought quite well once established. Like most plants, however, they benefit from supplemental watering during the heat of summer. They prefer full sun to moderate shade. Their most common disease problems include anthracnose, berry rot, leaf spot, powdery mildew ('Hancock' seems to be quite resistant), rusts, and stem gall. Pests such as aphids, whitefly, scale insects, and snowberry clearwing are problematic at times. Maintenance typically involves pruning during early spring.

PROPAGATION: Stem cuttings root well during the growing season; treatment with 7000 to 8000 ppm IBA/talc is necessary for 'Hancock' Chenault coralberry, and 1000 to 2000 ppm IBA/talc for *S. orbiculatus.* Rooted suckers can also be dug and transplanted throughout the season.

Symphytum grandiflorum   PLATE 291
Large-flowered Comfrey

Leafy and herbaceous, large-flowered comfrey ranges from 8 to 12 inches tall and spreads more than 1½ feet across. With a coarse texture and rather plain appearance, it is not one of the world's most exciting ground covers, nor is it likely ever to become very popular; however, it puts on a respectable floral show and serves quite well in a woodland border as a general cover, specimen, or edging plant. The composted leaves, rich in potassium and nitrogen, are said to make an excellent mulch, especially for tomatoes.

SCIENTIFIC NAME: *Symphytum grandiflorum* (*sim*-fie-tum gran-di-*flore*-um). *Symphytum* is derived from the Greek *symphysis,* to grow together or fuse, and *phyton,* a plant, in reference to the plant's folk use in healing broken bones. *Grandiflorum* means large-flowered.

HARDINESS / ORIGIN: Zones 4 to 8; Caucasus.

LEAVES / FLOWERS / FRUIT: The simple, semievergreen, coarse, rough-to-the-touch leaves are oval, oblong oval, or heart-shaped. Formed upon stems as well as arising from the rootstalk, they are deeply veined, hairy on both sides, and colored medium to dark green. The flowers, effective during spring and summer, are borne in nodding clusters. Each is five-parted, ¾ inch long by ¾ inch wide, tube-shaped, and colored white.

RATE / SPACING: Growth is moderate. Plants from pint-sized to quart-sized containers are spaced 10 to 14 inches apart.

OTHER SPECIES: *S. × rubrum* (*rew*-brum), red-flowered comfrey, differs from *S. grandiflorum,* one of its parents (the other being *S. officinale* 'Coccineum'), in that its flowers are red, its leaves are less hairy, and it is somewhat slower spreading.

S. × uplandicum (up-*land*-i-kum), Russian comfrey, the result of the cross between *S. asperum* and *S. officinale,* is a robust, bristly, coarse-textured, deep green leafy ground cover that is hardy to Zone 6. Reaching over 12 inches tall and bearing its lilac-pink to purple, 1-inch-long flowers upon upright 3-foot-tall stalks from spring to mid summer, it spreads at least 3 feet wide. 'Variegatum' is lilac-blue flowered and prominently cream-edged when grown on fertile soil, otherwise plain green.

CULTURE / CARE: Adaptable to most well-drained soils, large-flowered comfrey withstands considerable drought but is best when the soil is kept slightly moist. It prefers full sun to light shade and is affected by few diseases or pests. Maintenance, at most, consists of shearing or mowing plants in late fall.

PROPAGATION: Division of crowns, the standard means of propagation, is easily accomplished spring through fall, provided attention is given to moisture needs.

Tanacetum parthenium   PLATE 292
Feverfew

The name feverfew is derived from *febrifuge* (a fever-reducing agent), as parts of the entire plant are said to reduce fever. Feverfew is said to also be effective in alleviating nervous disorders and repelling insects, and is, of course, a good ground cover. It is best as a small-scale general cover, for contrast, or as a lacy-leaved herbaceous accent plant. It reaches 1 to 2½ feet tall and spreads 1½ to 2 feet across. No foot traffic is tolerated.

SCIENTIFIC NAME: *Tanacetum parthenium* (tan-a-*see*-tum par-*thee*-nee-um). *Tanacetum* is thought to be derived from the Greek *athanatos,* immortal, in reference to the longevity of the flowers. *Parthenium* is named after the Parthenon, as the species reputedly was used to save the life of a man who fell during its construction.

HARDINESS / ORIGIN: Zones 6 to 8; Caucasus.

LEAVES / FLOWERS / FRUIT: The leaves are aromatic, dark green, and oblong to broadly oval. They reach 3 inches long and are so deeply divided as to appear feathery. In mid to late summer are borne numerous ¾-inch-wide flowers with yellow centers and white petals. The fruit that follows is nonornamental.

RATE / SPACING: Growth is moderate. Plants from pint-sized to quart-sized containers are spaced 14 to 20 inches apart.

HORTICULTURAL SELECTIONS: 'Alba', with white flowers; 'Aureum', with young foliage yellowish green, later turning light to medium green; 'Crispum', with crinkled foliage; 'Golden Ball', compact habit, 1 foot tall, with small double yellow flowers; 'Golden Feather', to 10 inches tall, with chartreuse foliage; 'Golden Moss', compact habit, to 18 inches tall, with golden flowers; 'Silver Bell' ('Snowball'), with double white flowers; 'Tom Thumb White Stars', with a compact habit and white flowers; 'Ultra Double White', with double white flowers and a height of 15 to 18 inches.

CULTURE / CARE: Feverfew prefers well-drained, acidic to neutral, relatively organic soils. It needs full sun and should receive sufficient water during the summer to keep the soil constantly moist.

PROPAGATION: Division is easily accomplished during spring. Stem cuttings root quickly in early summer. Root cuttings can be taken in fall. Seed germinates in 7 to 10 days at 70°F.

Taxus canadensis PLATE 293

Canadian Yew, American Yew, Ground Hemlock, Dwarf Yew, Shinwood, Creeping Hemlock

The many common names might lead one to conclude that Canadian yew is a plant of considerable horticultural merit. In reality, it is seldom planted in our landscapes, and its many common names come from having been frequently encountered by pioneers and botanists. In the future, it may become better known to gardeners as a plant of horticultural merit, for it is useful on a moderate to large scale in northern climates, particularly in landscapes that feature native species. It ranges from 3 to 5 feet tall, spreads more than 8 feet wide, displays a sprawling, rather open, woody habit, and thrives in the shade of deciduous trees such as oak, maple, beech, and ash as well as under conifers such as hemlock, pine, fir, and cedar. It has very dark green foliage and works well with light-colored ground covers and perennials in its foreground. It functions remarkably well for binding dry sandy slopes, as in the dunes of the Great Lakes, and its branches grow up to the water's edge, in contrast to some of the other *Taxus* species that are very intolerant of excess soil moisture. It is extraordinarily winter hardy.

Every part of the yew is poisonous except for the fleshy red aril surrounding the seeds, which is edible and considered tasty by some people. The seeds, like the rest of the plant, contain toxic substances and are considered very poisonous. In severe cases, poisoning from yew leads to death through respiratory and heart failure. Birds seem able to pass the seed through their systems, and as long as the seed coat is not chewed or otherwise cracked, it does them no harm. Yews have been used since prehistoric times in both Europe and North America for medicinal purposes. Indians of Canada and Michigan used the plant in the preparation of beverages. Scientists have isolated a useful compound called taxol from Pacific yew (*T. brevifolia*), which has proven effective in the treatment of ovarian cancer. Since it takes about 10,000 pounds of *T. brevifolia* bark to produce one pound of taxol, it is fortunate that scientists have discovered taxol in cultivated species of yew, and recently have devised a way to manufacture semisynthetic taxol (starting with a naturally occurring precursor), making it no longer necessary to harvest the slow-growing tree.

SCIENTIFIC NAME: *Taxus canadensis* (*tak*-sus kan-a-*den*-sis). *Taxus,* the Latin name for this genus, probably comes from the Greek *taxon,* a bow, in reference to the resilient wood that has long been prized for making archery bows. *Canadensis* means of Canada.

HARDINESS / ORIGIN: Zones 3 to 6; woodlands from Newfoundland to Manitoba, south to Minnesota and Iowa, east to Virginia and New Jersey.

LEAVES / FLOWERS / FRUIT: The evergreen, narrow, ½- to 1-inch-long, $\frac{1}{12}$- to $\frac{1}{10}$-inch-wide, needlelike leaves are smooth-edged, relatively flat, leathery, waxy, dark green above, and light green below. Borne in spring, the flowers are individually sexed. The male flowers are scaly, numerous, globe-shaped, and $\frac{1}{12}$ inch long. The female flowers are fewer, erectly oriented, and fleshy with bracts at their bases. Neither flower is ornamental, but the females give rise to red, fleshy fruits that surround the bony, olive-colored seeds. Individually they are rather attractive, but because they are not borne in great numbers, they usually go unnoticed.

RATE / SPACING: Growth is slow. Plants from 3- to 5-gallon-sized containers are spaced 3 to 4 feet apart.

OTHER SPECIES: *T. baccata* (ba-*kay*-ta), meaning berried, or bearing berries, is also known as English yew. From Europe, western Asia, North Africa, and the Caucasus, it is hardy in Zones 6 to 7 and reaches 40 to 80 feet tall. Its flowers, like those of *T. canadensis,* are nondescript, but its ¼-inch-wide, fleshy, coral-red to purplish, clustered fruit is quite effective during fall and persists well into winter. In cultivation for centuries, this species has given rise to many cultivars, a few of which are suitable ground covers. With low spreading habit, they are impressive shrubby ground covers for use in large landscapes. Most common are 'Cavendishii', 3 feet tall by 12 feet wide, with wide spreading habit; 'Repandens', 2 to 4 feet tall by 12 to 15 feet wide; 'Repens Aurea', an attractive, low-growing broad-spreading form with vibrant golden foliage.

T. cuspidata (kus-pi-*day*-ta), Japanese yew, is named for its cuspidate leaves (constricted into a concave sharply pointed tip). A native of Japan, Korea, and China, it is a tree that reaches 10 to 40 feet high by 10 to 40 feet wide. It, like other species in the genus, displays dark green, ½- to 1-inch long, ¹⁄₁₂- to ⅛-inch wide evergreen foliage. Its fruit is also a hard, ovoid, olive-colored seed covered by a fleshy red aril. Hardy in Zones 4 to 7, the species has given rise to the following low spreading cultivars: 'Aurescens', a nonfruiting (male) cultivar that reaches 1 foot tall by 3 feet wide with new leaves deep yellow gradually changing to green; 'Cross Spreading', selected by Cross Nurseries of Minnesota, 3 to 4 feet tall by 8 to 10 feet wide, said to be very resistant to winter desiccation; 'Densa', a fruiting (female) cultivar that reaches 4 feet tall by 8 feet wide.

T. × *media* (mee-*dee*-a), Anglo-Japanese or intermediate yew, is hardy in Zones 5 to 7 or 8. Derived from crossing *T. baccata* and *T. cuspidata*, it is popular for its countless varieties of broad-spreading and upright-growing, medium-sized to large-sized shrubs. The following selections are the most useful as ground covers: 'Chadwickii', reaching 3 to 4 feet tall by 5 feet wide; 'Densiformis', with spreading habit, 3 to 4 feet tall by 5 to 6 feet wide; 'Everlow', reaching 1½ feet tall by 4 to 5 feet wide; 'Sebian', 3 to 4 feet tall by 4 to 5 feet wide; 'Ward' ('Wardii'), reaching 6 feet tall and up to 20 feet wide (in 20 years).

CULTURE / CARE: All the yews listed here grow in various soil types and all are relatively tolerant of drought. Only *T. canadensis,* however, tolerates soil that sometimes becomes saturated—the others are quick to develop root rot in such conditions. None are fussy about light conditions, growing in full sun to moderate shade. Their most common diseases are twig and needle blights, root rot, leaf drop, and dieback. Pests of greatest consequence are black vine weevil, strawberry root weevil, taxus and grape mealybugs, bud mites, termites, and nematodes. Other than an occasional (optional) light springtime shearing, plants need little attention.

PROPAGATION: Stem cuttings are usually taken in late fall after a few hard frosts and typically root well if treated with 8000 ppm IBA/talc. *Taxus canadensis* seems to root easily during summer, and *T. baccata,* the most difficult to root, is sometimes grafted upon easier-to-root species and hybrids.

Teucrium chamaedrys　　　　PLATE 294
Germander, Ground Germander, Common Germander, Wall Germander

Low-growing and dense in habit, this semiwoody, shrubby ground cover reaches only 8 to 18 inches tall and spreads 1½ to 2 feet across. It is a tidy, easy-to-care-for, effective ground cover which is used as a

dwarf edging along walkways or as a facing to garden statuary or building foundations. It can also be used as a specimen or massed in small groups or for accent. It works well in rock gardens, and because of its slow growth and compact habit, it is exceptionally well suited for use in formal landscape settings. Germander is tough and relatively tolerant of drought, but does not take to being walked upon.

SCIENTIFIC NAME: *Teucrium chamaedrys* (tew-kree-um *kam-e*-dris). *Teucrium* is named for Teucer, a Trojan prince who used one of the species in medicine. *Chamaedrys,* dwarf oak, comes from *chamai,* on the ground, and *drys,* oak, in reference to its height and the shape of its leaves.

HARDINESS / ORIGIN: Zones 4 to 9; central and southern Europe.

LEAVES / FLOWERS / FRUIT: Thick and tough but very attractive, the shiny green, semievergreen, oblong to oval, ½- to ¾-inch long, tooth-edged leaves account for 90 percent of this species' ornamental appeal. Even so, the rose to purplish, occasionally white flowers appearing in early summer to fall are not to be slighted. They are borne in compact upright spikelets, and although they are not blatantly showy, they compliment the fine foliage and add another dimension of appeal. The fruit is nonornamental.

RATE / SPACING: Growth is slow to moderate and does not spread out of control. Plants from quart-sized to gallon-sized containers are spaced 12 to 16 inches apart.

HORTICULTURAL SELECTIONS: Var. *prostratum,* low-growing, only 8 inches tall, more tenacious in its habit of spreading and flowering.

CULTURE / CARE: These germanders happily reside in just about any well-drained soil. They are moderately tolerant of drought, but are clearly better if soil moisture is maintained with watering during periods of drought. Similarly, they tolerate light shade, but prefer to bask in full sun. Pests and diseases that sometimes give them trouble include mites, mildew, leaf spots, and rust. Maintenance consists of an annual shearing in early spring to promote compactness and to remove any tattered foliage that might have resulted from winter's harshness.

PROPAGATION: Cuttings are easily rooted year-round. Division can be accomplished any time the soil is not frozen.

Thelypteris　　　　PLATE 295
Maiden Ferns

Thelypteris, a large genus with several species, both spreaders and clump formers, is attractive as well as useful. Of the species listed here two had formerly been classified as members of the genus *Phegopteris.*

The differentiating character is that members of *The-lypteris* have distinct, minute, needlelike hairs on their stipes (leaf stalks), two water-conducting bundles (within the middle of the stipe), and different numbers of spores and chromosomes. In the landscape they infuse a cool soft texture and function well on a small-scale to moderate-scale for accent at the base of trees or as an underplanting to link together trees and shrubs.

SCIENTIFIC NAME: *Thelypteris* (thee-*lip*-ter-is / the-*lip*-ter-is / *theel*-teer-is) comes from the Greek *thelys,* female, and *pteris,* fern, and refers to the more delicate appearance of these ferns in comparison to the male fern, *Dryopteris felix-mas.*

HARDINESS / ORIGIN: See individual species for hardiness; tropical wet forests and temperate woodlands.

LEAVES / FLOWERS / FRUIT: The leaves range from relatively small to more than 2 feet long, with thin blades and kidney-shaped sori on their lower surfaces. Like other ferns, *Thelypteris* species reproduce by spores and have no flowers.

RATE / SPACING: See individual species.

SPECIES: *T. connectilis* (ka-*nekt*-e-lis), probably named for its lowest set of leaflets, which are disconnected from the other pairs, is commonly called long beech fern, beech fern, common beech fern, northern beech fern, or sun fern. Formerly called *Phegopteris connectilis,* it hails from thickets and moist to relatively dry woodlands (although typically near running water) of the North Temperate Zone. It is hardy to Zone 5, medium-textured, and slow spreading. In time it reaches 8 to 18 inches tall and spreads more than 3 feet wide. Growth is slow to moderate. Plants from pint-sized to gallon-sized containers are spaced 10 to 14 inches apart. The light green, deciduous, feathery, compound leaves are triangular, 6 to 14 inches long by 5 to 9 inches wide, and are composed of numerous leaflets that are oppositely arranged along a fine-hair-covered cylindrical stalk. Each leaflet is narrowly triangular with a long tapering tip and has lobes that are deeply cut and veins and margins that are hairy. The bottom pair of leaflets is disjunct from the pair above it and gradually flares forward.

T. hexagonoptera (heks-i-goe-*nop*-ter-a), six-cornered fern, broad beech fern, or southern beech fern, was also formerly considered a species of the genus *Phegopteris.* It is sometimes confused with *T. connectilis,* but is distinguished by its more erect and taller (2 feet tall) habit, broader lowest leaflets, and veins that usually lack hairs. From eastern North America, it is hardy in Zones 3 to 7.

T. noveboracensis (noe-vee-bore-e-*sen*-sis), New York fern, is a graceful, rhizomatous, medium-sized fern that reaches 1 to 2 feet tall and spreads indefi-

nitely. It is best suited for use as a woodland ground cover on a moderate to large scale and is of great value for its graceful arching fronds that, with their vibrant yellowish green coloration, brighten woodland landscapes. It is an excellent choice for low-lying areas, as it withstands considerable moisture. No foot traffic is tolerated. Hardy to Zone 2, it hails from moist woodlands and thickets from Ontario eastward to Newfoundland, bordered on the west by Michigan, Illinois, Tennessee, and Mississippi, then east to South Carolina. It displays featherlike, deciduous, elliptical leaves that taper gradually at their ends and bases—hence easily recognized by anyone who realizes that New Yorkers "burn the candle at both ends." The leaves reach 10 to 24 inches long by 3½ to 7 inches wide, are divided into smaller leaflets, and are colored a cheerful vibrant yellowish green. On the undersides, during summer, are formed small, kidney-shaped sori that house brown, summer-ripening spores. Growth is moderate to fast. Plants from quart-sized to gallon-sized containers are spaced 1 to 1½ feet apart.

CULTURE / CARE: *Thelypteris* species are best grown in organically rich, moderately acidic soil. They (especially *T. noveboracensis*) tolerate considerable moisture, but only short periods of drought. Light to dense shade suits them best. Seldom are they bothered by pests or disease. No maintenance is required.

PROPAGATION: Division is easily accomplished during spring or fall. Spores also may be germinated (see Chapter 8).

Thymus   PLATE 296
Thyme

In addition to their culinary uses, thymes are valuable for such ornamental characteristics as colorful, pleasantly scented foliage, lovely flowers, endurance, low maintenance, and drought resistance. Low, sprawling or mat-forming, herbaceous or woody-based, the ground-covering thymes function well as aromatic fillers for between patio blocks and stepping stones, releasing their comforting fragrances in response to the slightest step. Sometimes, and I think too infrequently, they are used as small-scale lawn substitutes or simply as maintenance-saving general covers in small-sized or moderate-sized areas. Then, and perhaps at their best, they can be used for edging sidewalks and patios. Occasional foot traffic is tolerated.

Historically, the foliage was used as a stuffing for pillows because it was believed to alleviate depression and epilepsy. The foliage was also eaten, rubbed over the body, and drunk in teas for protection from the plague and leprosy. Thymes have been utilized in the treatment of dysmenorrhea, skin sores, worms, hysteria, colic, flatulence, and headaches. Thymol, the essential oil in thyme, is a potent antiseptic used as a fungicide and a preservative. Diarrhea, cardiac depression, respiratory disruption, vomiting, headaches, nausea, and dizziness have been experienced when too much thyme is consumed. Today the most common household use of thyme is as a seasoning with a host of meats, poultry, and vegetables. Specialty soups, liqueurs, and beer also occasionally derive their flavor from the leaves and stems of thyme.

Of interest to gardeners is that planting thyme in proximity to tomatoes, eggplant, and potatoes is said to enhance their performance. Pests that thyme is said to discourage are whitefly, cabbage worm, and cabbage looper. Not surprisingly, insecticidal sprays and dusts of dried ground thyme leaves occasionally appear in the retail market.

SCIENTIFIC NAME: *Thymus* (*tie*-mus / *thy*-mus) may be the Greek name for this plant; it was used by Theophrastus for either this plant or savory. It has also been said that it comes from the Greek *thymos,* mind or spirit, probably in reference to the trait of courage. Others claim that it means to fumigate, likely from *thyein,* to make a burnt offering or sacrifice, since smoke from burning thyme was once thought to repel insects from the home.

HARDINESS / ORIGIN: Zones 4 to 10 (see individual species); temperate Eurasia.

LEAVES / FLOWERS / FRUIT: The leaves are for the most part evergreen, oval-shaped, and small (⅛ inch wide by ⅜ inch long), but in respect to color vary greatly with the particular species and variety. Leaves may be dark glossy green, fuzzy blue, yellow, reddish, grayish, or have variegated patterns of yellow and green or green and cream. Attractive to bees, the flowers are either solitary or combined in spikelets; they are two-lipped, ¼ inch long, colored a shade of pink or purple, and borne during late spring or early summer. The fruit is nonornamental.

RATE / SPACING: Growth is moderate, spreading more than 12 inches wide. Plants from 3- to 4-inch-diameter containers are spaced 8 to 12 inches apart.

SPECIES: *T. caespitosa* (seez-pi-*toe*-sa), named for its leaves that are arranged in tufted fashion, is commonly called Azorican thyme. Native to the Azores, Canary Islands, and northwest Iberian Peninsula, it reaches ¾ to 2½ inches tall and rapidly spreads in prostrate mat-forming fashion so as to densely blanket the ground. Its green linear leaves are densely set and make a nice backdrop to the purplish pink to whitish flowers of summer. It is hardy to Zone 5.

T. × citriodorus (sit-ree-oh-*dore*-is), named for its lemon-scented leaves, is commonly called lemon thyme. This naturally occurring hybrid between *T.*

pulegioides and *T. vulgaris* comes from southern France and is hardy in Zones 4 to 10. It displays a densely upright, branched habit that takes it to heights of 4 to 8 inches. Its dark glossy green foliage is narrowly oval to lance-shaped, ⅜ inch long, smooth, and scented like lemon. The pale lilac flowers are effective in early summer. One note of caution: slugs and snails love to nibble upon the foliage of this species and, if unchecked, can progress to ravenous grazing, which soon results in dead, leafless stems. Some popular horticultural selections include 'Aureus', with leaves variegated gold and green and a mature height somewhat lower than the type; 'Argenteus', with leaves variegated silver and green; 'Bertram Anderson' ('Anderson's Gold', 'E. B. Anderson'), with congested gold-splashed leaves, a height to 2 inches, and pink flowers; 'Minus', low-growing to 3 inches tall; 'Silver Queen', more open in habit, with leaves edged in white.

T. herba-barona (*her*-ba-ba-*rone*-a), meaning herb of nobility, is commonly called caraway thyme. Hailing from Corsica, it is hardy to Zone 5, reaches 2 inches tall, and displays oval to lance-shaped, ⁵⁄₁₆-inch-long, hairy-edged, dark green leaves. The clear pink flowers appear in mid summer.

T. praecox (*pray*-cox), meaning early flowering, reaches 3 to 6 inches tall and displays purple flowers in summer and shiny dark green leaves. It hails from Europe, is hardy to Zone 5, and tolerates alkaline soils. Seldom cultivated, it is not as popular as its two subspecies *arcticus* and *skorpilii*. Subspecies *arcticus* displays hairy stems, rose-purple flowers, and height to 4 inches. Its cultivar 'Alba' is white-flowered, and 'Minus' seldom exceeds 1 inch tall. Subspecies *skorpilii* displays only minor foliar differences, but has given rise to white-flowered and red-flowered cultivars.

T. pseudolanuginosus (soo-doe-lan-you-jin-*oh*-sis), woolly thyme, is thought by some to be a hairy variety of *T. praecox.* It is remarkable for its dense carpeting habit and densely gray-haired ⅕-inch-long leaves. This evergreen species is hardy to Zone 6 and decorated with pale pink flowers (unreliably) during summer. A fair amount of foot traffic is tolerated.

T. serpyllum (sir-*pil*-um), named for the Greek word for this species, is commonly known as wild thyme, creeping thyme, creeping red thyme, or mother of thyme. It is hardy to Zone 4 and native to Europe, western Asia, and northern Africa. It sprawls about haphazardly, reaching heights of only 1 to 3 inches. Cloaked with elliptic to oblong ¼- to ⅓-inch-long, dark green, slightly hairy, mint-scented leaves, in bloom this species is nothing short of remarkable. Its multitudes of lilac to royal purple flowers seemingly jump into view during late spring and early summer. Horticultural selections include 'Albus', with white flowers; 'Argenteus', with leaves variegated silvery-white; 'Aureus', with leaves variegated golden yellow; var. *coccineus,* with scarlet flowers; 'Minus', less than ½ inch tall, with gray-green leaves and white flowers; 'Roseus', with pink flowers.

T. vulgaris (vul-*gay*-ris), common thyme or garden thyme, reaches 6 to 10 inches tall and is hardy as far north as Zone 5. Native to southern Europe, it displays aromatic linear to elliptic, ³⁄₁₆- to ⅝-inch-long, hairy, medium to dark green leaves. Its subtly beautiful flowers of late spring are colored pale whitish and lilac.

CULTURE / CARE: Most thymes prefer acidic to neutral soil. Although they tolerate organic and clay soils (only with excellent drainage), they are at their best in well-drained light-textured soils (sandy or gritty) of low fertility. Well adapted to withstand drought, their growth is best when the weather is warm and the soil somewhat dry. They prefer full sun, but light shade is tolerated. Other than snails and slugs, they are not subject to serious pest problems. The only disease of significance is a leaf blight that sometimes occurs during cold, rainy weather. Maintenance consists of shearing or mowing plantings after blooming to keep plants looking neat and tidy. If they become densely woody at their bases, they can be rejuvenated by division and a hard shearing.

PROPAGATION: Cuttings seem to root well any time the plants are not in flower. Division works well throughout the year. Seed, which is available commercially, takes two weeks to germinate.

Tiarella cordifolia   PLATE 297

Allegheny Foamflower, False Mitrewort

Known as foamflower because of its white, loosely arranged, and airy or foamlike flowers, this attractive, coarse-textured, shy spreading (by short rhizomes), eastern North American native is a good choice for use in small clumps or on a moderate scale as a general cover underneath deciduous trees in naturalized woodland landscapes. Some gardeners have reported good success using foamflower as a specimen in shady rock gardens or in herbaceous perennial borders. No foot traffic is tolerated.

SCIENTIFIC NAME: *Tiarella cordifolia* (tie-a-*rel*-a kore-di-*foe*-lee-a). *Tiarella,* literally little turban, is a diminutive of the Greek *tiara,* a turban, and refers to the shape of the seed pods. *Cordifolia,* heart-shaped, refers to the shape of the leaves.

HARDINESS / ORIGIN: Zones 3 to 8; moist woodlands throughout eastern Canada and the United States, south to the Carolinas and Tennessee, west to Michigan.

LEAVES / FLOWERS / FRUIT: The evergreen basal leaves arise from the rootstock on downy 4-inch-long stalks. Each leaf is oval to heart-shaped, five-lobed to seven-lobed, reaches 4 inches long, displays unevenly toothed edges, and is colored rich green becoming bronzy in fall. The flowers are tiny, five-petaled, colored white, and held atop thin, erect stems during mid spring. The fruit, a capsule, is nonornamental.

RATE / SPACING: Growth is moderate. Plants from pint-sized to quart-sized containers are spaced 10 to 16 inches apart.

HORTICULTURAL SELECTIONS: Var. *collina,* with pink-blushed white flowers and softly mottled, matte-textured, slightly lobed, light green leaves, often confused with *T. wherryi,* which has more deeply cut foliage. This variety is said to have many interesting cultivars, most of them probably of hybrid origin: 'Major', with rose or reddish flowers; 'Marmorata', with bronze to black-green foliage, marbled with purple; 'Montrose Selection', selected from a seedlot at Montrose Nursery, dark green leaves, light pink flowers, clumping habit, extended spring bloomer; 'Purpurea', purple flowers.

Other cultivars said to be derived from the species are 'Dunvegan', with pinkish flowers 4 to 6 inches above the leaves, heavy blooming, clumping habit, deeply dissected, medium green, softly haired palmlike leaves; 'Erika Leigh', with flowers that open white then become pink-tinged and stand 4 to 6 inches above dark green slightly hairy, 4½-inch-wide, palmlike, deeply divided leaves; 'Filigree Lace', with lacy leaves and white flowers; 'Oakleaf', with dark green oak-shaped leaves borne in profusion, clumping habit.

OTHER SPECIES: × *Heucherella tiarelloides* (hew-ke-*rel*-la tee-a-rel-*loy*-deez), a sterile hybrid, the result of crossing *Heuchera brizoides* with *T. cordifolia,* is a stoloniferous, low-growing, basal-leaved ground cover with attractive, nearly round, 3½-inch-long foliage that is mottled with brown in youth prior to becoming dull green in maturity. Pinkish summer-borne flowers are attractive but not greatly showy. This hybrid, which is hardy in Zones 3 to 8, is a nice choice for the woodland garden. Cultivars include 'Bridget Bloom', leaves decorated with a central red splotch, flowers deeper pink with white centers; 'Crimson Clouds', with pink flowers above densely set crimson dotted leaves; 'Pink Frost', with silver leaves and flowers that are colored blush pink; 'Rosalie', with deep green foliage and numerous ice pink flowers, 8 inches tall; 'Snow White', with white flowers; 'White Blush', with white flowers that are suffused with pink above silver mottled leaves.

T. trifoliata (try-*foe*-lee-aye-ta), native to the

West Coast, this species is hardy to at least Zone 6, displays evergreen, light green, densely hairy leaves and a habit that resembles piggyback plant, *Tolmiea menziesii*. Its flowers are white and ascend 12 inches above the foliar mass.

T. wherryi (*ware*-ee-eye). Named for its discoverer, Edgar Theodore Wherry, an American botanist who was born in 1885, this species, commonly known as Wherry's tiarella or mapleleaf tiarella, is sometimes listed as *T. cordifolia* var. *collina*. Hardy in Zones 3 to 8, it hails from eastern North America from Virginia and Tennessee south to Georgia, Alabama, and Mississippi. It is similar to *T. cordifolia* but lacks stolons and displays leaves that are maple-shaped with rich burgundy tones in fall. Flowering occurs during early summer with wispy sprays of tiny white pink-tinged stars.

OTHER SELECTIONS: There are a number of other selections of *Tiarella* that are derived from hybridization: 'Brandywine', vigorous running, with pink flowers, light green heart-shaped leaves with red centers; 'Eco Eyed Glossy', 12 inches tall, glossy leaves, white flowers; 'Eco Rambling Silhouette', 12 inches tall, indefinite spreading, shiny green leaves with dark reddish purple centers below white springtime flowers; 'Eco Red Heart', clump forming, with light green leaves that radiate from the center with a splash of deep red, flowers pink-tinged and 10 to 12 inches above the leaves; 'Eco Running Tapestry', running form, leaves deeply cut and fuzzy green with reddish black pigment extending out from their midribs; 'Eco Splotched Velvet', with fragrant pale pink flowers borne in spring, leaves velvet-textured with dark reddish purple pattern at their bases; 'Filigree Lace', with lacy deeply cut leaves and white flowers; 'Laird of Skye', stoloniferous, with large white flowers above large dark green deeply lobed, rough surfaced, ruffle-edged leaves; 'Slick Rock', low growing, vigorous spreading, stoloniferous, with small dark green deeply dissected leaves and pink-tinted, fragrant flowers.

CULTURE / CARE: Tiarellas are best in organically rich, acidic, loamy soils. They are not notably tolerant of drought; therefore, the soil should be kept moist with regular watering and they should be placed in cool locations with light to dense shade. No serious pests or diseases have been reported. Maintenance needs are few if any. Supplying a light mulch of leaf mold each fall is a good means of building the organic content of the soil and providing natural fertilizer.

PROPAGATION: During spring or fall (summer also, provided that adequate water is available) plants can easily be lifted and divided. Seed also germinates readily; it should be collected during summer and sown immediately for germination the following spring.

Tolmiea menziesii   PLATE 298
Piggyback Plant, Youth-on-age, Pickaback Plant, Thousand Mothers

A low-spreading, herbaceous ground cover that reaches 12 to 24 inches high and spreads indefinitely, piggyback plant is a ground cover that will never be very popular. Yet, for those who appreciate novelty, namely, its trait of producing new plantlets atop mature leaves, it will always have a small place in the landscape or in the home as a handsome hanging basket plant. It combines with most deciduous shrubs and trees and various herbaceous perennials such as hosta, bleeding heart, heartleaf bergenia, purple-leaved heuchera, and clump-forming lily turfs. No foot traffic is tolerated.

SCIENTIFIC NAME: *Tolmiea menziesii* (toll-*mee*-a men-*zeez*-ee-eye). *Tolmiea* is named after Dr. William Fraser Tolmie (1830–1886), a Scottish surgeon and botanist of the Hudson Bay Company. *Menziesii* is named after Archibald Menzies (1754–1842), a naval surgeon and botanist who collected the species in western North America.

HARDINESS / ORIGIN: Zones 7 to 10; western coast of North America from Alaska to California.

LEAVES / FLOWERS / FRUIT: The hairy, light to medium dull green leaves are heart-shaped, reach 4 inches across, are covered with bristly hairs, and arise from a creeping rootstock. Interestingly, new plantlets arise at the junction of the leaf blade and the leaf stalk; as they grow, their increased weight causes the parent leaf to bend down, and when it comes in contact with the ground, it forms roots. The late spring-borne flowers are greenish purple, $\frac{3}{8}$ inch wide, and although interesting, overall they are rather inconspicuous and not of great ornamental significance. The fruit also is nonornamental.

RATE / SPACING: Growth is moderate. Plants from 3- to 4-inch-diameter containers are spaced 8 to 14 inches apart.

CULTURE / CARE: Piggyback plant easily adapts to most soils and even tolerates wet soils. Drought, on the other hand, is a bit of a problem; thus, the soil should be kept constantly moist with regular watering, and plants should be located only in light to dense shade. The main disease and pest problems are powdery mildew, mites, and mealy bugs. The only maintenance that might be required consists of trimming back shoots as they outgrow their bounds.

PROPAGATION: New plantlets can be separated from the bases of the mature leaves any time; they should be kept moist until their roots become well developed. If the new plantlets have not yet sprouted roots at the time they are separated from the parent plant, they can be treated as cuttings and kept extra moist for a few days until roots begin to form.

Trachelospermum jasminoides   PLATE 299
Star Jasmine, Chinese Star Jasmine, Confederate Jasmine

Star jasmine is a low-growing, creeping, woody, vinelike plant that when unsupported forms a ground cover 10 to 16 inches tall and more than 10 feet across. Useful only in the South and warm coastal and desert areas, it is a tenacious, rather rugged plant that is best suited to cover moderate or large areas, particularly on sloping ground as a soil stabilizer. It grows over shallow tree roots and thus may be used as a turf substitute or facing around tree trunks. No foot traffic is tolerated.

SCIENTIFIC NAME: *Trachelospermum jasminoides* (tray-ka-low-*sper*-mum jas-min-*oy*-deez). *Trachelospermum* comes from the Greek *trachelos,* neck, and *sperma,* seed, referring to the narrow seeds. *Jasminoides* means resembling jasmine.

HARDINESS / ORIGIN: Zones 9 to 10 or 11; China.

LEAVES / FLOWERS / FRUIT: The elliptic to oblong evergreen leaves with dark veins are colored shiny green and reach 1½ to 4 inches long by ½ to 1 inch wide. The 1-inch-wide flowers are five-petaled, white, and pleasantly fragrant during mid spring and early summer. The fruit is nonornamental.

RATE / SPACING: Growth is moderate to fast once plants are established. Plants from gallon-sized containers are spaced 1½ to 3 feet apart.

HORTICULTURAL SELECTIONS: 'Madison', more cold hardy (Zones 7 to 10), originated in Madison, Georgia; 'Variegatum', with leaves variegated green and white, sometimes with a reddish tinge.

OTHER SPECIES: *T. asiaticum* (aye-shee-*at*-i-kum), yellow star jasmine, from Asia, is hardy to Zone 8 or 9 and similar to *T. jasminoides* in habit. It reaches 10 to 14 inches tall when unsupported and spreads 8 to 10 feet across. Its evergreen leathery-textured leaves are elliptic to oblong, colored dark green with whitish veins, reach 1 to 2 inches long, and in northern climates, become an attractive purplish red during the winter months. Its flowers are similar to those of *T. jasminoides,* but are colored yellowish white, and its fruit, like that of *T. jasminoides,* provides no ornamental display. 'Elegant', is said to display mounding habit from 8 to 12 inches tall; 'Nana' ('Nortex') is characterized by leaves that are more lance-shaped than those of the species.

CULTURE / CARE: Both species are at their best when grown in fertile, loamy, acidic soil. They are not greatly tolerant of drought and should receive supplemental watering during hot, dry weather. They prefer full sun or light shade in the northern part of their hardiness range, while light to moderate shade is better farther south. Pests that may at times cause problems include mites, scales, and the greenhouse whitefly. Seldom are serious diseases encountered. Maintenance normally consists of shearing plantings during early spring to promote compactness.

PROPAGATION: Cuttings root quite well during early summer. Division of rooted stem sections is easily accomplished during spring, fall, and winter.

Tradescantia   PLATE 300
Spiderwort

As far as the ground-covering spiderworts go, there are three species of note. The first, Virginia spiderwort (*T. virginiana*), is a cold hardy, lily-leaved, laxly upright, herbaceous ground cover. Its companions, both called wandering Jew (*T. albiflora* and *T. fluminensis*) are cold tender and tend to sprawl about with horizontal habits of growth. All are herbaceous, nearly succulent, and best suited for informal landscape situations.

SCIENTIFIC NAME: *Tradescantia* (trad-es-*kan*-shee-a) is named after John Tradescant (1608–1662), gardener to King Charles I.

HARDINESS / ORIGIN: See individual species for hardiness; the Americas.

LEAVES / FLOWERS / FRUIT: The leaves are rather fleshy, almost succulent, and vary considerably in size and shape (see individual species for further details). The flowers, normally borne in branch-ending or axillary clusters or pairs, bloom from late spring through summer and are typically open only during the morning.

RATE / SPACING: Growth is moderate to fast. Plants from pint-sized to ½-gallon-sized containers are spaced 1 to 1½ feet apart.

SPECIES: *T. albiflora* (al-bi-*flore*-a), meaning white-flowered, is commonly called wandering Jew or giant inch plant. It is quite similar to *T. fluminensis* (below); however, the leaves are oblong to elliptic, 2 to 3 inches long by 1 inch wide, and colored green above and below. Native to South America, this species is a common house plant in the North. Cultivars include 'Albovittata', with leaves that are evenly streaked with white; 'Aurea', with yellow leaves; 'Laekenensis', pale green leaves with white stripes and purple bands; 'Variegata', leaves with white and yellow stripes. Hardy in Zones 8 to 10.

T. fluminensis (flew-*min*-en-sis), meaning of Rio de Janeiro (Flumen Januarii) or possibly named from the Latin *flumen,* a river, is commonly called wandering Jew or spiderwort. Known to many northern gardeners only as a hanging basket plant, this South

American native functions as an excellent general cover for small-sized or medium-sized bounded areas in Zones 8 to 10. It is a low, trailing, succulent ground cover that reaches 2 to 4 inches tall and spreads indefinitely. Its leaves are semievergreen, oval, to 1⅝ inch long by ¾ inch wide, colored green above and deep violet below, and are smooth with thinly haired margins. The flowers are paired, reach ¼ inch long by ½ inch wide, are colored white to pinkish, and are effective summer through fall. 'Variegata' displays green and white leaves.

T. virginiana (ver-jin-ee-*aye*-na), Virginia spiderwort, common spiderwort, or widow's-tears, is native to northeastern North America and at its best in border plantings either on a moderate or large scale. As such, it fits well into naturalized landscapes, particularly in shaded ditches where it functions well for erosion control. It is hardy in Zones 4 to 9 and ranges from 1 to 3 feet tall with an indefinite spread. It is characterized by a grassy appearance and medium green leaves to 1 foot long by ½ to 1 inch wide. Its 1- to 1½-inch-wide flowers of violet-purple to deep blue, or rarely white, are three-parted and, although short-lived (only one day), bloom continually and provide a succession of color from late spring through late summer. Unlike the flowers of most plants, when the flowers of this species die, the petals turn into a slimy liquidlike substance, reportedly caused by an enzyme in the petals. This species seems to be particularly sensitive to pollution. It takes relatively little radiation or chemical pollution to alter its genes (manifested as various morphological or physiological mutations, including changes in floral color), and the plant has been employed by researchers to test relative levels of pollution. There are numerous theories as to the derivation of some of the common names. The name spiderwort may have been derived from its use as a cure for the bite of the phlangium spider, which is not even poisonous. Another possibility (and generally considered to be closer to the truth) is that the name describes the leaves which look like the legs of a spider. The common name widow's-tears supposedly comes from the unusual habit of the flowers of this plant turning to liquid as they fade. Several cultivars have been named and ascribed to *T. virginiana,* yet it is more likely that they belong to the hybrid *T. × andersoniana* (from crosses involving *T. virginiana* with *T. ohiensis* or *T. subaspera*). Some of these include 'Bilberry Ice', with narrow leaves and soft lavender-colored flowers overlaid with brush strokes of darker lavender; 'Blue Stone', with dark blue flowers; 'Blushing Bride', with light pink flowers, petals rounded; 'Carmine Glow', with deep carmine flowers; 'China Blue', with soft blue flowers and tight

clump-forming habit; 'Concord Grape', with rich purple 1½-inch-wide flowers and frosty blue foliage; 'Hawaiian Punch', with large pinkish red flowers; 'Innocence', with white flowers, clump-forming habit, to 24 inches tall; 'Iris Prichard', with white flowers, tinged with blue; 'Isis', with Oxford blue flowers 3 inches wide; 'James C. Weguelin', with larger pale blue flowers; 'Leonora', with violet-blue flowers and height of 18 inches; 'Little Doll', with light blue 1½-inch-wide flowers and compact foliage; 'Navajo Princess', with lavender tinged white flowers; 'Osprey', with large white, blue feathery flowers; 'Pauline', with lilac-colored flowers 2 to 2½ inches wide; 'Purple Passion', with rich velvety purple semidouble flowers and low vigorous habit; 'Purple Dome', with bright rose-purple flowers; 'Purewell Giant', with deep rose and purple flowers; 'Purple Profusion', leaves emerging with purple stripes, flowers royal purple and long lasting; 'Red Cloud', with rose-red flowers; 'Snowcap', with snowy white flowers; 'Valor', with crimson-purple flowers and height of 1½ to 2 feet; 'True Blue', with light clear blue flowers and vigorous habit; 'Zwanenburg', with violet-purple flowers.

CULTURE / CARE: The spiderworts are best in organically rich, loamy soil and are exceptional in their tolerance to poorly drained soils. They are not notably tolerant to drought and should be maintained in a nonwilted condition with supplemental irrigation as needed during the summer. *Tradescantia albiflora* grows best in light to moderate shade, and *T. virginiana* is best in full sun. Their pests include greenhouse leaf tier, morning-glory leaf cutter, orange tortix caterpillar, citrus mealybug, chaff scale, southern root-knot nematode, and aphids. Diseases of greatest prevalence are leaf spots, rust, and blight. Other than trimming back the stems and leaves as they become tattered or outgrow their bounds, little or no maintenance is needed.

PROPAGATION: Division of all species is very simple and is easily accomplished during spring and early fall. With *T. albiflora* and *T. fluminensis,* cuttings root very quickly and in high percentages throughout the year.

Tsuga canadensis   PLATE 301
Canadian Hemlock

This species is a very attractive evergreen tree that ascends to heights of 80 feet or more. It does not fit the description of a ground cover, of course; but a number of low-growing, prostrate selections are useful for this purpose. Typically these cultivars are gracefully arching, shrubby, 1½ to 2½ feet tall, and spread several feet across. The high cost, scarcity, and uniqueness of these selections predisposes them to use as specimens. They should be positioned at eye level whenever possible to fully display their unique arching branches and vibrant foliage. They are said to be tolerant of planting in near proximity to black walnut (*Juglans nigra*) and if there is a reflecting pool in their foreground, the effect is even more dramatic. The bark is rich in tannins and was at one time used in the tanning of hides. Native Indians used the young leaves in a tea.

SCIENTIFIC NAME: *Tsuga canadensis* (*tsu*-ga kan-a-*den*-sis). *Tsuga* is the Japanese name for the species *T. sieboldii. Canadensis* means of Canada.

HARDINESS / ORIGIN: Zones 3 to 7 or 8; the species comes from hilly and rocky as well as moist, rich woodlands from New Brunswick and Nova Scotia, south to Minnesota and Maryland, and to mountainous regions of Georgia and Alabama.

LEAVES / FLOWERS / FRUIT: The evergreen, simple, flattened, linear, ¼- to ⅔-inch long, ¹⁄₁₂- to ⅛-inch wide leaves are edged with fine teeth and colored shiny dark green above with two whitish bands below. The conelike flowers are small and ovoid, with woody scales, and turn brown in maturity.

RATE / SPACING: Growth is relatively slow. Use specimen-grade material from 2-gallon-sized (or larger) containers. Normally, single plants are used for specimen planting.

HORTICULTURAL SELECTIONS: 'Bennett', slow-growing, weeping form, with compact low-growing habit; 'Cole' ('Cole's Prostrate'), faster-spreading, prostrate habit that follows the contour of the ground, often less than 12 inches tall by more than 3 feet wide; 'Pendula', usually a weeping, broad-spreading form that may reach 2 or 3 feet tall by more than 8 feet wide, but there is a lot of variation in plant material offered as 'Pendula'; 'Pendula Sargentii', 2 feet tall by 4 to 6 feet wide, mounded habit; 'Prostrata', presumably the same as 'Cole'; 'Sherwood Compact', attractive mounds with twisted, contorted branches.

CULTURE / CARE: Canadian hemlock is adaptable to various well-drained, acidic soils with texture ranging from sandy or rocky to relatively rich and loamy. It is not very tolerant of drought when compared with many other conifers. For this reason, its soil should be kept slightly moist and exposure to strong drying winds should be kept to a minimum. Excess heat can also be devastating, so plants should be sited away from walls that reflect the sun's heat. Canadian hemlock prefers full sun to dense shade, but it is only successful in full sun if given ample water and shelter from strong drying winds. Diseases such as blister rust, leaf and twig blights, needle rust, sapwood rot, damping off (if soil is poorly drained), and root rot

are occasionally encountered. Pests such as fir flat-headed borer, bagworm, mites, scales, spruce leaf miner, hemlock looper, gypsy moth, hemlock woolly aphid, spruce budworm, hemlock sawfly, and Japanese weevil are the most common. Maintenance, if practiced, typically consists of a light shearing in spring to promote branching, compactness, and neat appearance.

PROPAGATION: Cuttings are typically taken in winter, lightly wounded, treated with 5000 to 8000 ppm IBA/talc, then given bottom heat of 60 to 70°F. Softwood cuttings in early to mid summer have also been rooted but require frequent misting. Cultivars that are difficult to root can be grafting upon seedlings of the species.

Vaccinium angustifolium   PLATE 302
Low Bush Blueberry, Low Sweet Blueberry, Sweet-hurts, Late Sweet Blueberry

Who would ever guess that the same genus that gives us one of the finest table fruits could also produce a species that covers the ground, produces delicious fruit, provides lovely springtime flowers, and dazzles with brilliant autumnal color? Low bush blueberry is such a creation, and for some unexplained reason (probably because it is a native and thought too common or because it is not the easiest to propagate), it is seldom used in our landscapes. But this splendid plant is surely worthy of much greater use. Low growing, as its common name indicates, low bush blueberry is low in relation to high bush blueberry (*V. corymbosum*), which is the source of the fruit we all love to consume. Low bush blueberry is a stiffly woody, often somewhat open, shrubby plant that reaches 6 to 24 inches tall and spreads to more than 4 feet across. In the landscape, it is a natural for acid-soil native-plant gardens, gardens that feature edible fruit, or gardens that are designed to attract wildlife—particularly birds. Use low bush blueberry in moderate to large areas and combine it with open-canopied trees such as dogwood, pines, serviceberry, oak, and witch hazel. Shrubs that it befriends are too numerous to count, but some of the best include rhododendron, azalea, serviceberry, magnolia, huckleberry, and high bush blueberry. No foot traffic is tolerated.

SCIENTIFIC NAME: *Vaccinium angustifolium* (vak-*sin*-ee-um an-gus-ti-*foe*-lee-um). *Vaccinium* is the Latin name for blueberry. *Angustifolium* means narrow-leaved.

HARDINESS / ORIGIN: Zones 2 to 6; northeastern North America from Newfoundland to Saskatchewan, south to Illinois and Virginia.

LEAVES / FLOWERS / FRUIT: The leathery, narrow, deciduous leaves reach 1 inch long by ½ inch wide. In summer they are shiny medium green to blue-green, and in fall they turn bronzy scarlet and crimson. The dainty ¼-inch-long urnlike greenish white flowers are borne in spring and soon give rise to small but sweet blueberries.

RATE / SPACING: Growth is slow. Plants from 1- to 2-gallon-sized containers are spaced 12 to 18 inches apart.

OTHER SPECIES: *V. crassifolium* (crass-i-foe-*lee*-um), creeping blueberry, is named from the Latin *crassus,* thick, and *folium,* leaf, in reference to its thick leaves. A rather low-growing, horizontal-branching species native to the southeastern United States, it forms an attractive evergreen mat with its shiny, deep green to bronzy, uniformly fine-textured foliage. Blooming during mid to late spring, it bears small clusters of rosy-red ¼-inch-diameter flowers. Selections such as 'Well's Delight, and 'Bloodstone' are noteworthy for larger foliage and greater cold tolerance (to Zone 6), while the species is only reliably hardy to Zone 7.

V. deliciosum (day-li-see-*oh*-sum), aptly named for its tasty fruit, is a deciduous slow growing Pacific Northwestern native (Washington to northern Oregon) that is hardy to Zone 4. It branches densely and reaches only 12 to 18 inches tall.

V. macrocarpon (mack-row-*kar*-pon), commonly known as American cranberry, is named from the Greek *macro,* large, and *carpus,* fruit. This traditional Thanksgiving Day fruit hails from acidic swamps, bogs, moist shores, and occasionally moist meadows from Minnesota to Newfoundland and from Arkansas to North Carolina. It displays extreme cold hardiness and is reliable in Zones 1 to 6 or 7. As a landscape plant, it has a low-growing (1- to 4-inch-tall), sprawling (to 1½-feet-wide), trailing, wiry-stemmed, subshrubby habit and makes a good ground cover in places where the soil is sandy or organic (peaty), acidic, and constantly moist. As such, it is not only functional, forming a very dense, small-scale to moderate-scale, long-lived cover, but supplies an abundance of attractive red edible fruit. It spreads at a moderate rate and should be spaced 10 to 14 inches apart from pint-sized to quart-sized containers. The leaves are evergreen, simple, alternate, oblong to oval, ¼ to ¾ inch long by ⅒ to ⅓ inch wide, thick, leathery, light green and maroon in youth, maturing to shiny dark green with a prominent central midrib. Its branched clusters of four-parted to five-parted, ⅓- to ½-inch-wide, light pink flowers are borne during early to mid summer. The tart fall-ripening fruit is an oblong to globose, four-celled, red berry of ⅓ to ⅔ inch width and length. Infrequent foot traffic is tolerated. Horticultural selections include 'Beckwith', with late-ripening me-

dium to large, red fruit; 'Ben Lear', with early ripening medium to large, deep red fruit; 'Bennett', with egg-shaped fruit; 'Cropper', with fruit ripening in mid season, noteworthy for the durability of its fruit after harvest; 'Hamilton', with dwarf mounding habit, forming tussocks 4 inches tall by 6 inches wide, hardy in Zones 2 to 7; 'Langlois', with pendent flowers and large fruit, a hybrid formed by crossing *V. macrocarpon* with *V. ovatum,* said to reach 8 inches tall by 24 inches wide with leaves that are larger and more round than those of *V. macrocarpon;* 'LeMunyon Honkers', very fruitful, said to perform well as a commercial variety in New Jersey and Wisconsin; 'Olsons', with very large fruit; 'McFarlin', with abundant late-ripening medium-sized, firm, deep red fruit.

V. vitis-idaea (*vie*-tis-eye-*dee*-a), which means grape of Mount Ida, is commonly called cowberry, foxberry, or lingonberry. It is a low, woody shrub that, like low bush blueberry, also spreads by underground stems. It may reach 6 to 12 inches tall and more than 2 feet wide. It is hardy in Zones 4 to 7 and hails from arctic North America, Japan, Siberia, and northern Europe. The leaves are evergreen, to 1¼ inch long, leathery, glossy dark green with metallic reddish brown winter color. The drooping flowers of spring are about the same size and shape as those of low bush blueberry but are colored white or pinkish white rather than greenish white. They give rise to bright red, bitter, peg-sized, edible fruits somewhat like cranberries. Popular horticultural selections include 'Erntesegen', of Germany, a vigorous grower that reaches 12 to 18 inches tall and just as wide, with medium-sized to large-sized fruit, noteworthy for its disease resistance; 'Korealle, 12 inches tall by 12 inches wide, reported to be hardy to Zone 5, noteworthy for its prolific production of large red fruit and neat clump-forming habit; var. *majus,* from Eurasia, with leaves and fruit somewhat larger than the species, prefers a warmer climate than var. *minus*; var. *minus,* with leaves and fruit somewhat smaller than the species, 8 inches tall by 8 inches wide, seems be more useful in the North (to Zone 2) than var. *majus;* 'Red Pearl', of Germany, a vigorous grower, reaches 12 to 18 inches tall and just as wide, noteworthy for its disease resistance and heavy production of early ripening fruit.

CULTURE / CARE: Sunny or lightly shaded sites in which the soil is acidic and organically rich with good drainage are best, although sandy, constantly moist soils are often just as good. Tolerance to drought is fair. Pests that might be encountered include stem gall wasp, scales, azalea stem borer, and forest tent caterpillar. Diseases that might become a problem include dieback, leaf spots, viral ring spot, and stunt. Although no maintenance is required, gardeners who prefer a more manicured effect shear their plantings during late winter.

PROPAGATION: Division is often hard work with these species, but remains a reliable means of propagation. Cuttings taken during early summer will root, but sometimes the percentages are disappointing.

Vancouveria PLATE 303
Barrenwort

Rather fancy looking with their thin upright stems and dainty leaves, vancouverias are dense, spreading, herbaceous ground covers that perform well in cool, moist, shady conditions. They slowly decline and often perish in areas of hot dry summers, but in the proper climate and site, they will increase steadily and are excellent in small-sized or moderate-sized sites, particularly in native or naturalized settings. They are good companions to taller clump-forming species of ferns, hosta, rhododendron, azalea, pieris, kalmia, blueberry, and a host of herbaceous and woody noninvasive species that grow in wooded sites. No foot traffic is tolerated.

SCIENTIFIC NAME: *Vancouveria* (van-koo-*veer*-ee-a) is named after Captain George Vancouver (1758–1798), an English explorer.

HARDINESS / ORIGIN: See individual species for hardiness; western North America.

LEAVES / FLOWERS / FRUIT: The leaves are basal and usually heart-shaped. The yellow or white flowers are borne in nodding panicles. The fruit is nonornamental.

RATE / SPACING: Growth is relatively slow. Plants from pint-sized to quart-sized containers are spaced 10 to 14 inches apart.

SPECIES: *V. chrysantha* (kris-*san*-tha), meaning yellow-flowered, is commonly called golden vancouveria. Native to Oregon and northern California, it is noteworthy for its ½-inch-long, yellow flowers. Its leathery leaves are mostly evergreen, divided two or three times with five leaflets per segment, and rise upon wiry leafstalks to a mature height of 1 foot. Hardy in Zones 6 to 8.

V. hexandra (heks-*an*-dra), named for its six stamens, is commonly called American barrenwort. Hardy in Zones 5 to 8, it reaches 12 to 18 inches tall and spreads to more than 1 foot wide. It is native to coastal forests from northern Washington to northern California and is characterized by attractive deciduous leaves atop slender stalks arising from its creeping rootstalk. Each leaf is rather heart-shaped, somewhat three-lobed, to 1½ inches long, very thin, and colored blue-green. The white ½-inch-long flowers that arise during mid to late spring droop

downward in a pendent fashion. The fruit that follows is nonornamental.

V. planipetala (plan-i-*pe*-tay-la), named for its flat flower petals, is commonly called inside-out plant and hails from Oregon and California. Unlike *V. hexandra,* this species is evergreen and less cold hardy (Zones 6 to 8). Typically, it reaches 7 to 12 inches high and spreads to 1 foot wide. Its leaves are compound with five leaflets and are carried atop thin stems that arise from the rootstalk. The attractive glossy green leaflets reach 1½ inches long by 1½ inches wide and, although dainty, are more rugged looking than those of *V. hexandra.* Atop upright flower stalks, the six-petaled white-tinged or lavender-tinged flowers are borne in clusters of 25 to 30 and are effective during mid to late spring. They are attractive yet lead to no significant fruit.

CULTURE / CARE: These species are at their best in organically rich, well-drained, loamy, acidic soils. None is very tolerant of drought. All inevitably perish if not planted in soil that stays constantly moist and cool, and should therefore be placed in wind-sheltered sites of moderate to dense shade. No serious pests or diseases seem to effect them. Although no maintenance is required, an annual light top-dressing with compost (in the fall) does no harm.

PROPAGATION: Division of plants in spring or fall is best.

Verbena PLATE 304
Vervains

Low, mat-forming, trailing herbaceous ground covers, verbenas enjoy a modest popularity. As general purpose covers, their chief values are their good, persistent butterfly-attracting floral displays and pleasing trailing habit of growth. They are best suited for use in small-sized to medium-sized bounded areas and are most striking when trailing over the edge of an elevated planter or down the sides of a raised bed. No foot traffic is tolerated.

SCIENTIFIC NAME: *Verbena* (ver-*bee*-na) is the ancient Latin name of the common European vervain, *V. officinalis.* Some authorities say that it is derived from the Latin *verbenae,* the sacred branches of olive, laurel, and myrtle that were used for ceremonial and medicinal purposes. Perhaps it resembles them in some respect.

HARDINESS / ORIGIN: See individual species for hardiness; temperate and tropical North and South America, with some species from the Old World.

LEAVES / FLOWERS / FRUIT: The leaves are typically opposite, sometimes whorled or alternate, toothed, often deeply dissected, and colored medium green. The flowers, of various colors, usually originate from the ends of the branches and may be spikelike, solitary, or arranged in broad panicles. The fruit is nonornamental.

RATE / SPACING: Growth is moderate. Plants from 3- to 4-inch-diameter containers are spaced 12 to 18 inches apart.

SPECIES: *V. bipinnatifida* (bie-pin-*aye*-tif-i-da), named for the shape of its leaves which are twice pinnate (twice divided), is commonly called Dakota verbena or Dakota vervain. Native to the United States from South Dakota to Alabama westward to Arizona, it is hardy to Zone 4, reaches 3 inches tall, and spreads 1½ to 2½ feet across. Its leaves are triangular, to 2 inches long, three-parted, with each leaflet being oblong or linear. The ½-inch-long, trumpet-shaped, lilac-purple flowers are arranged in dense spikes and bloom from late spring throughout the growing season until frost. The fruit is very tiny and is nonornamental.

V. canadensis (kan-a-*den*-sis), rose verbena, clump verbena, creeping vervain, or rose vervain, would presumably be a Canadian native. In fact, it hails from sandy and rocky barrens from Virginia to Florida, westward to Iowa, Colorado, and Mexico. It normally reaches 4 to 6 inches tall and spreads 2 or more feet across. It is hardy in Zones 6 to 10 and sports oval to oval-oblong, 3- to 4-inch-long, shiny dark green leaves. The flowers, which bloom heavily during late spring (then sporadically until fall), are borne in dense spikes. Each is five-parted, trumpet-shaped, to ⅝ inch across, and colored reddish purple, lilac, rose, or white. The fruit is nonornamental. Popular horticultural selections include 'Candidissima', with white flowers; 'Compacta', with a dense, compact, lower growing habit; 'Gene Cline', with compact habit (6 to 9 inches tall), attractive deep rose flowers, named for Gene Cline, a plantsman from Canton, Georgia; 'Homestead Purple', with deep violet-purple flowers; 'Lavender', with predominantly lavender flowers, height of 8 to 12 inches; 'Rosea', more compact, with season-long, rose-purple flowers; 'St. Paul', with pink flowers.

V. peruviana (pe-roov-ee-*aye*-na), Peruvian verbena, an evergreen species native to Argentina and Brazil, reaches 4 to 6 inches tall and displays attractive dark green, oblong to narrowly oblong toothed leaves and flowers of scarlet or crimson. It blooms throughout the summer and is hardy only to Zone 8. 'Bubble Gum', with light pink flowers; 'Lipstick', with purple flowers; 'Mini Red', with compact habit and bright red flowers; 'Red', with red flowers; 'Saint Paul', with hot pink flowers.

V. tenuisecta (ten-you-i-*sec*-ta), moss verbena, a stunningly florific species displays spikelike inflorescences of 5 to 15 flowers that range from blue to purple, violet, to lilac. A tenacious trailer, it hails from South America, is naturalized from Georgia to Louisiana, reaches 12 inches tall, and displays triangular dark green leaves 1 to 1½ inches long. 'Alba' is white-flowered. Hardy in Zones 8 or 9 to 10.

CULTURE / CARE: Verbenas are adaptable to a wide range of slightly acidic to neutral well-drained soils and tolerate sandy soils and infertility. They are relatively tolerant of drought once established, although they may require occasional deep watering during the summer. They prefer full sun. Pests include aphids, beetles, mites, nematodes, verbena leaf miner, verbena bud moth, greenhouse whitefly, and caterpillars. Diseases of greatest significance are bacterial wilt, flower blight, powdery mildew, stem rot, and root rot. Maintenance consists of a light shearing after the main blooming period is finished.

PROPAGATION: Cuttings are easily rooted throughout the growing season. Division is most effective during spring and fall.

Veronica   PLATE 305
Speedwell

The common name speedwell comes from the word *speed,* which once meant to thrive, and indicates that members of this genus thrive well, growing rapidly and showing good hardiness. Indeed, with only a few exceptions, this is true. Another derivation is that speedwell means goodbye and refers to the corolla falling as soon as the flowers are picked.

There are many veronicas that fulfill the role of covering the ground. For the most part, these species grow rather low to the ground and spread horizontally with aggressive tenacity. They make good specimens in rock gardens, and if contained, are interesting planted along garden paths and sidewalks as edging. The lower forms can be used as fillers for cracks in stepping stone paths and patio slabs, and on a small to moderate scale, where their spread can be contained, they are an interesting alternative to grass. No foot traffic is tolerated.

SCIENTIFIC NAME: *Veronica* (ve-*ron*-i-ka) is believed by some to be a Latin form of the Greek *betonika,* previously a small genus of herbs. Possibly it comes from *hiera eicon,* sacred image, or from the Arabic term *viroo nikoo,* beautiful remembrance. It may simply commemorate St. Veronica, who wiped the face of Christ during his march to Calvary. The flowers of the plant reputedly resemble the markings left upon the cloth when she performed her kind act.

HARDINESS / ORIGIN: See individual species for hardiness; North Temperate Zone with a few species found in tropical mountain areas and the South Temperate Zone.

LEAVES / FLOWERS / FRUIT: The deciduous to semi-evergreen leaves typically vary from broadly oval to lance-shaped, depending on the species, and are colored medium to deep green and are either smooth or tooth-edged. The flowers are borne in the leaf axils or are arranged in little spikelets or clusters at the branch tips; normally composed of four petals (usually three that are broadly rounded, and one that is much narrower), they are colored blue, purplish, pink, or white, and bloom during spring and summer. The fruit that follows is nonornamental.

RATE / SPACING: Growth is moderate to fast, often invasive. Plants from 3- to 4-inch-diameter containers are spaced 8 to 12 inches apart.

SPECIES: *V. chamaedrys* (*kam*-e-dris), named from the Latin *chamae,* on the ground, and *drys,* oak, is perfectly fitting for a plant that grows along the ground and displays leaves that are shaped like those of an oak tree. Otherwise known as germander speedwell, angel's eyes, and bird's-eye (for its bicolored flowers with a center spot), this interesting Eurasian species spreads by stolons. Now naturalized in North America, it reaches 12 to 18 inches tall, displays a compact habit, is hardy to Zone 4, and has semievergreen leaves that typically range from ½ to 1½ inches long. Its flowers, which appear during late spring to early summer, are colored vibrant blue with light violet centers and are arranged in elongate 3- to 6-inch-long clusters. 'Alba' is white-flowered.

V. incana (in-*kay*-na), named for its hairy leaves, is commonly called woolly speedwell. A herbaceous species from the steppes of Russia, it reaches 12 to 18 inches tall and forms dense mats. It is hardy to Zone 4 and has silvery-gray-haired, oblong to lance-shaped, 3-inch-long, semievergreen, smoothly tooth-edged, soft-textured foliage. The flowers are bright blue and contrast sharply with the leaves during early to mid summer. 'Rosea' has rose-pink flowers.

V. latifolia '**Prostrata**' (lat-i-*foe*-lee-a pros-*tray*-ta), as the cultivar name indicates, is named for its horizontal habit of growth. The species name, on the other hand, indicates that the leaves are flattened (from the Latin *folia,* leaves, and *lat,* broad or flat). Commonly called Hungarian speedwell, this herbaceous, dense-growing, hairy, matlike European selection reaches 8 inches tall and thrives northward to Zone 4. Its leaves are lance-shaped to oval, toothed about their edges, and colored dark green. The flowers are colored blue to reddish and become effective during late spring and early summer.

V. officinalis (oh-fis-i-*nay*-lis), from the Latin word for common, is commonly called drug speedwell (for its reputed medicinal qualities, such as treating coughs and curing skin ailments), common veronica, gypsy weed, or fluellen. It is a low, herbaceous, horizontal, hairy, spreading ground cover that reaches 12 inches tall and is hardy to Zone 4. Native to Europe, Asia, and North America, it displays leaves that are evergreen, oval to elliptic or oblong, to 2 inches long, with teeth about their edges. Its ½-inch-wide, pale blue flowers are arranged in many-flowered branch-ending clusters from mid spring to mid summer.

V. prostrata (pros-*tray*-ta), like hundreds of other ground covers, is named for its prostrate (horizontal) habit of growth and is commonly called harebell speedwell. It is a herbaceous, dense, mat-forming ground cover that reaches a mature height of 6 to 10 inches tall and spreads indefinitely. Hardy in Zones 5 to 8, it is native to Europe and displays dark green, semievergreen, linear to oval, 1- to 1½-inch-long leaves. Its dark blue flowers, which are found at the ends of the branches, are arranged in clusters and are borne from late spring to early summer. Horticultural selections include 'Alba', with white flowers; 'Heavenly Blue', with sapphire blue flowers; 'Lodden Blue', with deep blue flowers, height to 4 inches; 'Mrs. Holt', with bright pink flowers, height to 6 inches, slow growing; 'Nana', dwarf with lighter blue flowers; 'Rosea', with reddish pink flowers; 'Spode Blue', with light blue flowers; 'Trehane', with bright chartreuse leaves and bright blue flowers.

V. repens (*ree*-penz), named for its reptant (creeping), low mat-forming habit, is commonly called creeping speedwell. It reaches 4 inches tall, spreads indefinitely, hails from the mountains of Corsica and southern Spain, and is hardy to Zone 5. Its narrowly oval leaves are semievergreen, to ½ inch long, toothed about their edges, and colored shiny dark green. During late spring to early summer and to the nearly complete obscurement of the foliage, a multitude of remarkable ¼-inch-wide, light blue flowers are borne. 'Alba' has white flowers; 'Rosea' has reddish pink flowers.

OTHER CULTIVARS: Of uncertain parentage are 'Goodness Grows', named for a Lexington, Georgia, nursery, 12-inch-tall bushy habit, blue flowers from spring to fall; 'Sunny Border Blue', named for Sunny Border Nurseries, with violet-blue flowers atop sturdy spikes throughout summer, 18 to 20 inches tall.

CULTURE / CARE: Speedwells are fairly accommodating in respect to soil types, but they prefer to have their feet anchored in slightly to moderately acidic soils, and they absolutely abhor saturated soils. Their tolerance to infertility is not bad, yet because they are shallowly rooted, they can withstand only short periods of drought without supplemental irrigation. They prefer full sun to light shade. Their primary pests are checkerspot butterfly, Japanese weevil, and southern root-knot nematode. Diseases such as downy mildew, leaf spot, leaf galls, root rot, and leaf smut are those most often encountered. When fertilizing, be particularly careful to wash granules from the foliage immediately, as leaves are exceedingly prone to fertilizer damage. Shearing or mowing plantings after they bloom neatens their appearance and rejuvenates growth.

PROPAGATION: Cuttings root well during summer. Division is best accomplished during spring and early fall. Seed should be collected as soon as it ripens and stored in a cool dry location prior to sowing the following spring.

Viburnum davidii PLATE 306
David Viburnum

A member of the honeysuckle family, this 3-foot-tall, 4-foot-wide, woody, mounding, shrubby ground cover is excellent for use along walkways for edging and as a general cover in moderate-sized to large-sized areas. It works well as an accent plant, particularly with rhododendrons, azaleas, pieris, and kalmia. Because it does not tolerate extremes of temperature, it is most common in the Pacific Northwest from northern California to British Columbia.

SCIENTIFIC NAME: *Viburnum davidii* (vie-*ber*-num da-*vid*-ee-eye). *Viburnum* is the Latin name for the wayfaring tree (*V. lantana*). *Davidii* is named for Abbé Armand David (1826–1900), a French missionary and plant collector who spent his working life in China.

HARDINESS / ORIGIN: Zones 7 to 9; western China.

LEAVES / FLOWERS / FRUIT: From 2 to 5½ inches long by 1 to 2½ inches wide, the elongate-oval, sometimes slightly tooth-edged leaves are prominently veined, evergreen, and colored a very distinct shade of dark green. The small, white, five-parted flowers that arise during early summer are arranged in broad 3-inch-wide clusters. Although the flowers themselves are not greatly impressive, by late summer to mid autumn they produce superb ¼-inch-long bright blue fruit.

RATE / SPACING: Growth is slow. Plants from 1- to 2-gallon-sized containers are spaced 2½ to 3 feet apart.

HORTICULTURAL SELECTIONS: 'Jermyn's Globe', rounded, more compact than the species.

CULTURE / CARE: David viburnum grows best in moist, acidic, well-drained soils. It is not greatly tolerant of heat or drought and prefers constant soil moisture and full sun to moderate shade. It is prone to diseases such as leaf spot, crown gall, shoot blight, mildew, and rusts, and at times is afflicted by aphids, beetles, and thrips. Maintenance typically consists of giving plants a light shearing during spring to promote branching.

PROPAGATION: Softwood cuttings taken during mid summer and treated with 8000 ppm IBA/talc are effective. Division also works and can be performed at any time.

Vinca PLATES 307, 308
Periwinkle

Excellent for moderate-sized or large-sized areas, periwinkles are low-growing, horizontally creeping, nonclimbing, herbaceous, vinelike ground covers that make interesting and effective edgings along walkways, shrubby border plantings, and fillers in elevated planters. Their main attribute is their ability to blanket the ground in such a manner as to totally exclude weeds, bind the soil, and completely eliminate erosion. They are entirely at home underneath shallowly rooted trees, and currently are so widely distributed that most people believe them to be American natives instead of the European imports they are. Infrequent foot traffic is tolerated.

SCIENTIFIC NAME: *Vinca* (*ving*-ka) is the Latin name for this genus, probably from *vincio,* to bind, alluding to the tough runners, which when bound together could be used to form rope.

HARDINESS / ORIGIN: See individual species for hardiness; Europe to North Africa and central Asia.

LEAVES / FLOWERS / FRUIT: The leaves are evergreen, broadly oval, and oppositely arranged. The flowers, borne during spring and often to a lesser degree in summer and fall, are five-parted, funnel-shaped, relatively showy, and colored violet. The fruit that follows is nonornamental.

RATE / SPACING: See individual species.

SPECIES: *V. major* (*may*-jor), named for its leaves that are large in comparison to those of *V. minor* (common or lesser periwinkle), is commonly called big-leaved periwinkle or greater periwinkle. Hardy in Zones 6 to 9 (and protected sites in Zone 5), it reaches 8 to 18 inches tall and spreads indefinitely. It is native to southern Europe and western Asia and is characterized by robust growth and oval evergreen leaves, 1½ to 3 inches long by 1 inch wide. From their axils, the dark green leaves give rise to short, thin stalks that bear solitary, five-parted, funnel-shaped, bright blue, 1- to 2-inch-wide flowers at their tips. Flowering, for the most part, occurs during early spring, but often repeats, albeit less profusely, during fall. The fruit, which reminds me of a pair of miniature beans, is nonornamental. Plants from 3- to 4-inch-diameter containers are spaced 10 to 16 inches apart. Horticultural selections include 'Alba', with white flowers; 'Gold Vein', with leaves colored yellow in the middle, surrounded by green; 'Morning Glory', with bluish purple flowers;

var. *pubescens* (syn. *V. major* var. *hirsuta*), with reddish purple flowers, narrower petals, and leaves that are more pubescent than those of the species; 'Reticulata', leaves with yellow veins (appearing to be yellow-netted); 'Variegata' ('Elegantissima'), with large leaves blotched and edged in creamy white. There is also an English selection that goes by the same name. Its leaves are smaller, thicker, and more strikingly variegated.

V. minor (*my*-ner), named for its leaves and stature, which are small in comparison to those of *V. major,* is commonly called common periwinkle, dwarf periwinkle, running myrtle, myrtle, or lesser periwinkle. During the Middle Ages, the heads of criminals who were to be executed were adorned with stems of *V. minor,* hence the Italian name *Fiore di morte* (flower of death). In France the species had been called *violette des sorciers* (violet of the sorcers)—by one account because it was thought to repel witches and evil spirits, and by another because it was used during witches' sabbaths. This species is among the most popular ground covers for use in temperate climates. It is hardy in Zones 4 to 7 or 8 and hails from Europe and western Asia. It reaches 4 to 6 inches tall, spreads indefinitely, and displays evergreen, oblong to oval, shiny dark green evergreen leaves. The flowers, which are borne in great numbers during early spring, lack only fragrance, but with their lovely lilac-blue, ½-inch-wide, funnel-shaped collection of petals, this is a minor flaw. They often continue to flower sparsely throughout the remainder of the season and usually produce one more strong show during fall (but less significant than that in spring). The nonornamental fruit is similar to that of *V. major* but smaller.

Herbal uses of both *V. minor* and *V. major* included employing them as agents to reduce blood pressure and to stop bleeding. Their astringent properties were well reputed, and they were employed in cleansing the skin and treating nervous disorders.

Horticultural selections include 'Alboplena', with double white flowers; 'Argenteo-variegata', with light blue flowers and large irregularly variegated leaves of creamy white and pale green; 'Atropurpurea', with deep purple flowers; 'Aureo-variegata', with variegated leaves and irregular dull golden-yellow margins; 'Blue & Gold', with blue flowers and bright yellow edged foliage; 'Bowlesii' ('La Grave', 'Bowles' Variety'), an exceptional selection, with flowers more intense blue and larger than the species, a more reliable bloomer, continuing to bloom in summer and fall (after its primary springtime flowering period), leaves more rounded and broader than the species and curling under somewhat at their edges, more expensive than the species, slower grow-

ing, more apt to stay in a clump than the species, named for the great English plantsman Edward Augustus Bowles (1865–1954) who introduced it after bringing home a few plants from an alpine churchyard; 'Dart's Blue', similar to 'Bowlesii' but flowers a bit paler and though to have greater disease resistance; 'Emily', with large white flowers; 'Flore Pleno' ('Alpina', 'Multiplex'), with double purplish blue flowers; 'Gertrude Jekyll', with dainty white flowers, small leaves, trailing lower to the ground than the species; 'Golden', with yellow edged leaves and white flowers; 'Gold Heart', with irregular splashes of golden yellow in the center of the leaves; 'Ralph Shugert', with the same floral characteristics as 'Bowlesii', from which it arose, and deep glossy green leaves trimmed neatly with a thin edge of white, a 1987 selection named for a dear friend from Michigan whom I consider to be the nursery industry's most enthusiastic, kind, and sharing horticulturist; 'Sterling Silver', with leaves similar to 'Ralph Shugert' but flowers paler violet and smaller; 'Valley Glow', with golden new growth and white flowers.

OTHER SPECIES: *V. difformis* (die-*form*-is), a cold-tender species (Zone 7 or 8) that resembles *V. major* but with somewhat smaller leaves and flowers. Variety *dubia* displays darker violet flowers.

V. herbacea (her-*bay*-see-a), suitable for sun or shade, is a rare herbaceous species from Eastern Europe and Asia Minor that is characterized by arching to horizontal spreading stems that root at their nodes to form loose mats. The green leaves are narrow and the pale violet flowers with narrow petals are formed during late spring.

CULTURE / CARE: Periwinkles produce their best growth in fertile, organically rich, well-drained, loamy soils. A pH ranging from acidic to neutral is acceptable, and although summer drought rarely hurts them, they are much more florific and attractive if given an occasional deep drink of water. In the North, periwinkles need a sunny or densely shaded location that receives protection from dry winter winds and sun. In the South, their best growth is attained in moderate to dense shade. Pests include aphids and nematodes, and diseases such as blight, canker, dieback, leaf spots, and root rot are the most serious. Maintenance needs are few or nonexistent, although some gardeners prefer to mow plantings with a rotary mower in the fall to rejuvenate and to thicken them the following season.

PROPAGATION: Division, the standard means of propagation, can be conducted any time the soil can be kept adequately moist. Cuttings also root, yet typically a high percentage rot in the process; early fall seems to be the best time for rooting cuttings. Some stems of *V. minor* are strictly vegetative, producing no flowers but rooting at all their nodes. It is wise to select these stems when rooting cuttings as they root in higher percentage.

Viola
Violet

Although nearly all gardeners have experienced violets at one time or another in their gardening past, very few people consider them when they need a sturdy edging or general purpose, small-scale to moderate-scale ground cover. This is unfortunate, as violets perform these tasks admirably. Ground-covering violets tend to be low-growing, tufted, rhizomatous, rather assertive leafy herbs. Usually they are best contained with an edging to control their spread or given room in a naturalized setting to travel without harming less aggressive species. Violets combine marvelously with many nonspreading, clump-forming ferns. Such native species as the cinnamon fern (*Osmunda cinnamomea*), royal fern (*O. regalis* var. *spectabilis*), and Christmas fern (*Polystichum acrostichoides*) are just a beginning. Shrubs, as well as trees, are excellent in combination with violets. Try underplanting your favorite species with a living mulch of violets, and see how violets infuse both color and texture. Violets are tough, but do not tolerate foot traffic.

Reportedly, the flowers of all violet species are edible. They are not tasty, but when incorporated into salads or desserts, the flowers add a splash of color. They can also be crystallized as a food decoration, or pureed and used as a food coloring. The foliage is also edible and can be used as salad greens, pickled, canned, or added to soups for flavoring. As a herbal remedy, violets have a long history. Hippocrates recommended them for headaches, hangovers, and bad eyesight. In the Middle Ages they were believed to cure cancer. In general they are said to have a soothing and tonic effect, especially for the respiratory and digestive systems.

SCIENTIFIC NAME: *Viola* (*vie*-oh-la) is the ancient Latin name for this plant.

HARDINESS / ORIGIN: See individual species for hardiness; temperate regions, especially in the Northern Hemisphere and Andes.

LEAVES / FLOWERS / FRUIT: The leaves are either directly attached to the rhizome or crown of the plant, or attach to the stem. Generally they have stalks that are long in proportion to their blades which range from broad and nearly round to narrow, almost grasslike. The flowers, borne in early spring, are of two types in some species: one type is sterile, showy, and five-petaled (one spurred and the other four in unlike pairs). The other type is fertile, cleistogamous

(without petals), nonopening, and self-pollinated. In species that bear only one type of flower, the flowers are showy and petaled but with a full compliment of reproductive parts. Often the flowers are pleasantly fragrant. The fruit, usually a small capsule, is nonornamental.

RATE / SPACING: Growth is moderate to fast and can become invasive. Plants from 3- to 4-inch-diameter containers are spaced 8 to 12 inches apart.

SPECIES: *V. hederacea* (hed-er-*aye*-see-a), named for its ivy-shaped leaves (*Hedera* being the genus name of English ivy), is commonly called ivy-leaved violet or Australian violet. It is hardy in Zones 9 to 10 and, as you might have guessed, comes from Australia. It reaches 1 to 4 inches tall, spreads indefinitely by stolons, and displays evergreen round or kidney-shaped, ½- to 1½-inch-wide, medium green leaves. The solitary flowers are five-petaled, to ½ inch long by ¾ inch wide, colored purple with white tips, and bloom from spring through summer.

V. labradorica (lab-ra-*dore*-i-ka), meaning of Labrador, is commonly called Labrador violet. From Greenland and Labrador to Alaska, and from Newfoundland south to New Hampshire and west to Minnesota, this species is hardy northward to Zone 3. It reaches 4 inches tall, spreads indefinitely by stolons, and displays very attractive, deep purplish heart-shaped leaves that reach 1 inch wide. The solitary flowers, borne in mid summer, reach 1 inch wide and are deep violet but have no fragrance. Variety *purpurea* has leaves that display hues of purple, particularly the new growth, during spring and fall.

V. odorata (oh-do-*ray*-ta), named for its sweet-scented flowers, is commonly called sweet violet or florist's violet. This aggressive stoloniferous spreader reaches 6 to 8 inches tall in maturity and is lovely in flower but should not be trusted to stay within its bounds. It comes from Europe, Asia, and Africa and is hardy in Zones 6 to 7 (not as successful in areas of extreme summer heat). Its leaves are evergreen, oval or heart-shaped, 1 to 2 inches long by 1 to 2 inches wide, and colored medium green. The flowers are of two types: (1) fertile cleistogamous flowers are borne in summer, are not showy, and look like greenish capsules; (2) sterile flowers, on the other hand, are borne in mid to late spring, are quite showy, reach ¾ inch wide, are pleasantly fragrant, five-petaled, and colored violet or, rarely, pink or white.

Very common and endearing, this species has been coveted through the ages and has even served as the symbol of Athens, where it was sold in the flower markets as early as 400 B.C. It is mentioned in various Greek myths and was awarded as a prize for poetic achievement in France during troubadour times from the eleventh to the thirteenth centuries. It has been utilized in the treatment of insomnia, pleurisy, jaundice, skin cancers, epilepsy, constipation, coughs, and respiratory, urinary, and digestive disorders. Sufferers of dizziness and headaches were believed to gain relief when a garland of violets was worn about the head. When mixed with vinegar, the steeped roots were regarded as a cure for gout. Scientific evidence for all but its effect as a diuretic is lacking. In times past, the flowers were used as an ingredient in cosmetics. Today, the petals are sometimes used as a coloring and ingredient in salads, liqueurs, jams, jellies, desserts, cough medications, and perfumes. In potpourris, the fragrance of sweet violet flowers is pleasant though short-lived. Like most plants that are prized for their flowers, *V. odorata* has many horticultural selections and, of course, there is the usual controversy as to exact classification. Some authors claim them to belong to *V. odorata,* others to *V. alba* (mistakenly ascribed to *V. odorata*), and still others claim them to be hybrids. Generally they vary in the color of their flowers or the number of sets of petals (single vs. double), and, because they have been around for many decades, it is unlikely that their classification will ever be completely resolved. Those that are most common include 'Charm', with white flowers; 'Czar', with deep violet, single flowers; 'Double Russian', small, with double purple flowers; 'Duchesse de Parme', likely the same as 'Parma' (which see below); 'Lady Hume Campbell', with lavender-colored, double flowers; 'Marie Louise', with double, white to bluish lavender flowers; 'Parma', with double flowers; 'Queen Charlotte', with deep blue flowers on stems to 8 inches tall; 'Red Giant', with large, reddish violet flowers; 'Rosina', with fragrant, rose-pink flowers; 'Royal Elk', with violet flowers; 'Royal Robe', with large, dark purple, highly fragrant flowers; 'White Czar', with white flowers and purple markings on yellow centers; 'White Queen', with small white flowers and height to 6 inches.

V. sororia (sa-*rore*-ee-a), meaning sisterly, is named for its sisterly resemblance to *V. odorata* and is commonly called common violet, woolly blue violet, butterfly violet, sister violet, or dooryard violet. Preferring full sun to light shade, it is an inhabitant of moist meadows and open woodlands of North America from southwestern Quebec to Minnesota, South Dakota, and Montana extending to Oklahoma, Missouri, Kentucky, and North Carolina. Hardy in Zones 4 to 8, it spreads indefinitely and reaches 6 to 8 inches tall. Its leaves are deciduous, simple, and borne from the rootstalk on 6- to 8-inch-long hairy leafstalks. They are dark green, oval to round or kidney-shaped, 2 to 4 inches wide

(somewhat less in length), with round-toothed margins. Their showy sterile flowers are held upon long stems that elevate them to or above the height of the foliage. Typically, they reach about ¾ inch wide and are composed of five petals of deep blue, violet, red, or white (often on the same plant) effective mid to late spring. The three lower petals are white-based with purple veins, and the two lateral petals are densely white-bearded. The nonshowy, oval-shaped cleistogamous fertile flowers, are colored brown and purple. Forma *albiflora* has pure white flowers, and 'Freckles' has flowers with purple centers.

V. tricolor (*try*-cul-er), named for its three-colored (purple, yellow, and white) flowers, is commonly called European wild pansy, miniature pansy, field pansy, Johnny-jump-up, heart's-ease, ladies-delight, Johnny-jumper, none-so-pretty, stepmother, kisses, kiss-me, monkey's-face, fancy-biddy's-eyes, herb-trinity, cats'-faces, love-in-idleness, gardengate, cupid's-delight, garden-violet, trinity, and tricolor violet (my favorite name). As you may have guessed from the flamboyance of some of these names, this plant is very colorful. Indeed, its masses of tricolored flowers are difficult not to notice. Unfortunately, although a perennial, it is rather short-lived. For this reason, it should be used in moderation as a walkway edging or as a facing for low trees or specimen shrubs where a splash of color is desired. It grows in full sun to light shade. No foot traffic is tolerated. Hardy northward to Zone 5, this species is native to the mountains of southern and central Europe and is naturalized in North America. It reaches 4 to 12 inches with an indefinite spread. Its medium green leaves range from oval to oblong or even lance-shaped and have toothed edges. The five-petaled flowers reach ¾ to 1 inch wide, are variously colored yellow, white, or purple, and bloom during spring. The fruit is nonornamental. Because its growth rate is fast and it is prone to self-sowing, be sure to select an appropriate location. Plants from 3- to 4-inch-diameter containers are spaced 6 to 12 inches apart. There are a number of horticultural selections that are annual or biennial. These are excellent as short-term colorful ground covers, but should not, of course, be relied upon for long-term effect. It is interesting to note that European wild pansy has, at times, been used as an ingredient in love potions. Its three colors are said to represent souvenirs, memories, and loving thoughts; hence, the common name heart's-ease, as these three forms of endearment help assuage the emotions of separated lovers. The flowers have been extensively used in folk medicine in the treatment of respiratory maladies, skin irritations, and fevers. They have also been employed as an agent for purifying the blood, as a diuretic, as a treatment for relieving constipation, as a gargle, and as a sedative.

CULTURE / CARE: Violets grow best in organically rich, loamy, well-drained, acidic soils. They do not tolerate drought well; thus watering may be needed periodically throughout the drier months of the year. They prefer light to dense shade, except in hot summer areas, where moderate to dense shade is preferred. Pests include aphids, cutworms, violet gall midge, greenhouse leaf tier, violet sawflies, slugs, mites, and nematodes. Diseases such as anthracnose, crown rot, downy mildew, gray mold, leaf spots, powdery mildew, root rots, rusts, scab, and smut may at times plague violets. Maintenance needs are few, but an annual light top-dressing of leaf mold is a good practice for enhancing the composition of the soil.

PROPAGATION: Division during spring or fall is nearly foolproof and is probably the easiest means of propagation. Seed propagation also is effective if seed can be found or collected; normally, seed germinates within four weeks when sown during spring.

Vitis riparia   PLATE 310

Riverbank Grape, Riverside Grape, Sweet-scented Grape, Bull Grape, Winter Grape, Arroyo Grape, River Grape, Frost Grape

This very robust ground cover is tough, attractive, and fast spreading. It is a coarse-textured, high climbing, tendrilous woody vine that, when unsupported, makes an effective sprawling ground cover that ranges from 6 to 12 inches tall and spreads more than 12 feet across. Normally it is used in naturalized landscapes along moist riverbanks or sandy duneland locations where, as a ground cover, it may grow several feet each year. It should be used on a large scale, away from trees and shrubs as it will climb rather than sprawl if given the option. It combines well with beach grasses such as *Calamovilfa longifolia, Ammophila breviligulata,* and *Leymus arenarius* 'Glaucus', and seems to grow well underneath black walnut trees (*Juglans nigra*).

A number of different bird species nest in the stems of riverbank grape, and humans have found a host of culinary uses for this species. Typically the fruit is used in making wine, grape juice, and jelly, but less common is the preparation of *dolma,* a dish from the Middle East in which minced beef or lamb is combined with rice and seasonings, then rolled in young, fully expanded riverbank grape leaves (they are said to become too tough when mature) and placed in a pot, covered with water to two-thirds their height, and boiled gently for an hour.

SCIENTIFIC NAME: *Vitis riparia* (*vie*-tis ri-*pair*-ee-a). *Vitis* is the Latin name for the grape vine. *Ripa,* river,

indicates this plant's preference for growing in the moist soil along the banks of rivers.

HARDINESS / ORIGIN: Zones 3 to 7; thickets, dunes, and riverbanks from Quebec to Manitoba and Montana, south to New Brunswick, New England, West Virginia, Missouri, Tennessee, and Texas.

LEAVES / FLOWERS / FRUIT: The leaves are deciduous, simple, 3 to 7 inches long by 3 to 6¾ inches wide, more or less heart-shaped (typically with three lobes, of which the center is usually the longest), and coarsely toothed along the margins; they are colored green to dull red in youth, green in summer, and bright yellow in fall, and are held upon green stems that become stout and covered with dark brown bark that flakes off as it ages. When allowed to climb, the stems may become very large, and in mature forests, it is not uncommon to find specimens that have stem diameters of more than 5 inches. Borne in 3- to 5-inch-long narrow clusters and positioned opposite the leaves, the tiny, five-parted, greenish white to cream, relatively nonornamental but strongly and pleasantly fragrant (some say similar to the annual herb, mignonette, *Reseda odorata*) flowers bloom during late spring and early summer. The fruit that follows is a ⅓- to ½-inch-wide dark purple berry; sweet tasting and edible, it matures during summer and early fall.

RATE / SPACING: Growth is moderate to fast. Plants from 1- to 2-gallon-sized containers are spaced 3 to 5 feet apart.

HORTICULTURAL SELECTIONS: Var. *praecox* (meaning early ripening), commonly called June grape, native from sand dunes and dune borders of Michigan, Indiana, and New York, flowers in 1¾- to 2½-inch-long clusters, fruit ripens in early summer, is ¼ to ⅓ inch across, very sweet tasting, and more blackish than blue; var. *syrticola,* native from southwestern Illinois to central Missouri, is named for its sand dune habitat (from Latin *syrtis,* a sandbank) and is distinguished by leaf stalks and lower leaf blades that are more hairy than those of the species.

CULTURE / CARE: Sandy loam, beach sand, and gravelly soils with a neutral to acidic pH are best for this plant. Remarkably, despite its vigorous growth, it thrives in very infertile conditions and withstands strong winds if the soil consistently maintains a moderate degree of moisture. It prefers full sun to light shade. Diseases such as crown gall, leaf and shoot blights, leaf spot, downy and powdery mildews, nematodes, root rot, and viruses are the most common. Pests such as Japanese beetles, cutworm, grape berry moth, leafhopper, sawfly, nematodes, and rose chafer beetle are occasionally troublesome. Maintenance consists simply of trimming back the leading shoots as they outgrow their bounds.

PROPAGATION: Softwood cuttings root quite well under mist in late spring or early summer; they are helped with the use of a low-strength root-inducing preparation and should not be transplanted until the following spring after they have resumed growth. Layered stems can be dug up and transplanted during early spring. If seed is used it should be harvested as soon as the fruit ripens and immediately depulped and stratified under cool, moist conditions for three months prior to sowing. Alternatively, it can be sown outdoors upon ripening for germination next spring.

Waldsteinia
PLATE 311

Mock Strawberry

Mock strawberry is a herbaceous mat-forming ground cover with a strawberry-like appearance, low growth, and great reliableness. Two fairly common species are barren strawberry (*W. fragarioides*), a North American native, and dry strawberry (*W. ternata*), from Europe, Siberia, and Japan. Other species are worth trying. Waldsteinias are at their best as turf substitutes for small-sized or medium-sized areas, or as edgings for shrub-filled or herbaceous border plantings. They also make good transition plants around the base of deciduous lawn trees as they help to ease the change from coarse bark to fine-textured turf. Among their many suitable companions are trees such as serviceberry, redbud, oak, maple, dogwood, cherry, plum, and elm, as well as shrubs such as viburnum, privet, and forsythia. Limited foot traffic is tolerated.

SCIENTIFIC NAME: *Waldsteinia* (wald-*stine*-ee-a / vald-*stine*-ee-a) is named after Count Franz Adam von Waldstein-Wartenberg (1759–1823), an Austrian officer and botanist.

HARDINESS / ORIGIN: See individual species for hardiness; North Temperate Zone.

LEAVES / FLOWERS / FRUIT: The evergreen leaves are borne basally or from a horizontal stem. Usually they are three-lobed or five-lobed, somewhat strawberry-like, and act as a fine backdrop to the 3/8- to 3/4-inch-wide yellow, five-parted flowers which are borne in spring. The tiny, green fruit, reminiscent of strawberry, is nonornamental.

RATE / SPACING: Growth is slow to moderate. Plants from pint-sized to quart-sized containers are spaced 10 to 16 inches apart.

SPECIES: *W. fragarioides* (fra-gay-ree-*oy*-deez), named for its leaves which are like those of *Fragaria*, the strawberry genus, is commonly called barren strawberry. Hardy in Zones 4 to 7, it comes from southern Canada and northern and eastern parts of the United States. It reaches 4 to 8 inches high and

spreads indefinitely. The leaves are evergreen, arise from the base, and are composed of three wedge-shaped, 3-inch-long, coarsely toothed, deep shiny green leaflets that turn bronzy in winter. The cheery 3/4-inch-wide yellow flowers are borne in clusters of four to seven, are held slightly above the foliage on floral stems, and appear in late spring.

W. geoides (gee-*oye*-deez), meaning earthlike, was likely named for the rounded shape of its leaves. In reality, only some of the leaves appear rounded, most are fine-lobed in the shape of a palm. This species is not as common as *W. fragarioides* or *W. ternata*, but is attractive and useful in its own right. Hardy to Zone 5, it hails from Europe and slowly spreads by expanding crowns. It ranges from 3 to 10 inches tall and has coarsely textured, medium green evergreen three-lobed to five-lobed leaves that are 2 to 3 inches wide. Its flowers, borne during mid to late spring, are 3/4 to 1 inch wide, yellow, and carried slightly above the foliage.

W. lobata (low-*bay*-ta), an uncommon species, blooms during spring with tiny yellow flowers, reaches 4 to 6 inches tall, and displays evergreen leaves that turn bronzy during winter.

W. ternata (ter-*nay*-ta), named for its ternate (in threes) leaves composed of three leaflets, is commonly called dry strawberry or yellow strawberry. It resembles *W. fragarioides* but differs in being somewhat more coarse-textured and its leaves are not quite so dark or shiny green. Hardy to Zone 4 and native from Central Europe to Siberia and Japan, it reaches 4 to 6 inches high and spreads indefinitely. Its three-parted evergreen leaves are composed of wedge-shaped, 1- to 2-inch-long irregularly toothed leaflets that are colored glossy green. The yellow, five-petaled flowers, which are arranged in three-flowered to eight-flowered clusters atop flowering stems that are 8 inches tall by 1/2 to 3/4 inch in diameter, bloom from late spring to early summer.

CULTURE / CARE: Although best in rich soils, waldsteinias are adaptable to most well-drained, acidic to neutral soils. They are moderately tolerant of drought, yet best when their soil is kept moist with regular watering. They prefer full sun to light shade. Other than slugs, which can do serious damage to their foliage, waldsteinias are relatively free of problems. Maintenance, although not mandatory, includes an annual light dressing of leaf compost, which helps to boost organic content and enhance moisture retention. When fertilizing these species, always wash the granules from the foliage immediately afterward; otherwise, spotting is sure to occur.

PROPAGATION: Stem cuttings root well throughout the growing season. Rooted plantlets that have formed on stolons or divisions of the parent crowns can be taken with a spade during spring and fall.

Woodwardia   PLATE 312
Chain Fern

For moist woodland settings, chain ferns are beautiful and functional ground covers. The light to medium shiny green color of netted chain fern (*W. areolata*) lightens a dark area and lends an element of cool lushness. The taller Virginia chain fern (*W. virginica*) can be grown in several inches of water, is darker green, and is interesting as its fronds often align themselves in one direction. The common name came about because of the chainlike patterns formed by the sori (spore cases). No foot traffic is tolerated.

SCIENTIFIC NAME: *Woodwardia* (wood-*war*-dee-a) commemorates T. J. Woodward (1745–1820), an English botanist.

HARDINESS / ORIGIN: See individual species for hardiness; warm temperate and subtropical zones.

LEAVES / FLOWERS / FRUIT: See individual species.

RATE / SPACING: See individual species.

SPECIES: **W. areolata** (air-ee-oh-*lay*-ta), from the Latin *areolata,* divided into small open spaces, is named for the spaces between the veins of its fronds and is commonly called netted chain fern, net-veined chain fern, or small chain fern. Hardy in Zones 4 to 9, it hails from acidic swamps and bogs from Nova Scotia to Michigan, south to Florida, with isolated locales in the Southwest. It prefers rich acidic soils, reaches 1 to 1½ feet tall, and spreads indefinitely by rhizomes. Growth is moderate to fast. Plants from quart-sized to gallon-sized containers are spaced 1 to 1½ feet apart. The deciduous, light green, fleshy fronds are of two types: fertile or sterile. The spore-bearing fertile fronds are from 10 to 26 inches long with purplish to blackish stalks 6 to 12 inches long. Each frond ranges from 3 to 8 inches wide, is colored shiny medium green, is oval to oblong, and is composed of numerous narrow divisions. Along their midveins, in pairs, run the sausage-shaped spore-bearing sori. The sterile fronds are broadly triangular to oval and reach 6 to 15 inches long on green or tan stalks 6 to 14 inches long. They are smooth-surfaced, finely toothed along their edges, light yellowish to coppery green, and interlaced with a prominent network of veins.

W. virginica (ver-*jin*-i-ka), meaning of Virginia, is commonly called Virginia chain fern. It is an erectly oriented, densely spreading, rhizomatous, 1½- to 2-foot-tall species. It is hardy in Zones 3 to 10 and hails from marshes and bogs of eastern North America from Nova Scotia south to Florida and Texas and also in Bermuda. It spreads at a relatively fast pace. Space bare-root divisions or plants from gallon-sized containers 1½ to 2 feet apart. The deciduous, lush, and leathery, 1½- to 2-foot-long, 12-inch-wide leaves are attached to the creeping rootstalk by stout, 1- to 3-foot-long, shiny purplish brown stalks. Each blade is narrowly oblong, compound, and composed of numerous medium to dark green, wavy edged leaflets. Unlike *W. areolata,* this species does not have separate sterile and fertile fronds. All fronds bear sausage-shaped sori that are strung together like links in a chain. In maturity, during late summer, they turn brown and look like links of sausage. A form that grows wild in Michigan has very fragrant resin-dotted (glandular) foliage.

CULTURE / CARE: Acidic or neutral, very moist to saturated, highly organic (mud or muck) soil is preferred. Each species requires a considerable amount of moisture for best growth; therefore, plantings are ideally made in locations that naturally remain moist or saturated year-round. These ferns prefer light to moderate shade and require no maintenance.

PROPAGATION: Division during spring or fall or spore culture works well.

Xanthorhiza simplicissima   PLATE 313
Yellow-root, Shrub Yellow-root

The common names of this rugged native ground cover describe it well, namely, it is shrublike and displays distinctly yellow roots. It reaches 2 to 3 feet tall, spreads indefinitely by suckers and rhizomes, and is excellent for planting in moist shady sites. At home along pond and stream banks, it can be used as an edging or dwarf hedge, where a deep border or other feature such as a sidewalk or building foundation can keep it contained. It also functions well as a foundation facer and thrives beneath open-canopied trees as a moderate-scale to large-scale general cover. No foot traffic is tolerated.

Like many other yellow-sapped species such as Japanese barberry (*Berberis thunbergii*), *X. simplicissima* contains the bright yellow chemical berberine. Berberine is distributed throughout the plant but tends to concentrate in the grayish brown outside layer of the larger roots. This crystalline alkaloid has been used as a mouthwash and medicine for the treatment of stomach and throat disorders. The bitter taste of extracts of yellow-root are still sometimes consumed prior to meals to stimulate the taste buds.

SCIENTIFIC NAME: *Xanthorhiza simplicissima* (zan-thoe-*rye*-za sim-pli-*kis*-i-ma). *Xanthorhiza,* yellow root, comes from *xanthos,* yellow, and *rhiza,* root.

Simplicissima, most simple or, in this case, un-branched, refers to the habit of the stems of this species.

HARDINESS / ORIGIN: Zones 4 to 9; eastern United States from New York to Florida.

LEAVES / FLOWERS / FRUIT: The alternate leaves on short, unbranched, upright stems are compound, deciduous, and composed of three to five, oval to oblong-oval, 1½- to 2¾-inch-long, tooth-edged, medium shiny green leaflets. During fall, the leaves take on hues of yellow, reddish orange, and purple for several weeks. The tiny flowers are arranged along 2- to 4-inch-long stems; each is ⅛ inch wide, not very showy, brownish purple, star-shaped, and borne early to mid spring. The tiny fruit is nonornamental.

RATE / SPACING: Growth is moderate. Plants from 1- to 2-gallon-sized containers are spaced 1½ to 2½ feet apart.

CULTURE / CARE: Yellow-root grows well in full sun to dense shade in a range of sandy to clayey, acidic soils. Its best growth, however, occurs in moderate shade in organically rich, moist, well-drained loam. Drought and moisture tolerance are both above average, and although beneficial, summertime watering is seldom necessary. Diseases and pests are rarely a problem, and maintenance, if practiced at all, consists merely of lightly shearing plantings during early spring.

PROPAGATION: Cuttings can be made from the stem tips during early summer and rooted in a peat-based compost after treating with 3000 ppm IBA/talc. Root cuttings may be made from rhizome segments during fall. Division, the easiest means of propagation, consists simply of dividing and transplanting rooted suckers during early to mid spring.

Zauschneria californica   PLATE 314
California Fuchsia

California fuchsia, a colorfully florific southwestern native, is splendid as a bank cover or rock garden specimen and combines well with lavender, rock rose (*Cistus* species), basket-of-gold (*Aurinia saxatilis*), and wormwood (*Artemisia* species). It thrives in drought conditions, normally reaches 3 feet wide by 1 foot tall, and is valued not only for its bright scarlet flowers but also for the hummingbirds they attract.

SCIENTIFIC NAME: *Zauschneria californica* (zawsch-*neer*-ee-a kal-i-*for*-ni-ka). *Zauschneria* is named after Johann Baptist Zauschner (1737–1799), a professor of natural history from Prague. *Californica* means of California.

HARDINESS / ORIGIN: Zones 7 or 8 to 9; Sierra Nevada of California.

LEAVES / FLOWERS / FRUIT: The gray-green, glandu-

lar, white-woolly leaves are oval to narrowly oval and range from ½ to 1½ inches long. The trumpet-shaped flowers, borne in late summer to fall, are brilliantly scarlet and reach 1½ to 2 inches long.

RATE / SPACING: Growth is moderate. Plants from 1- to 2-gallon-sized containers are spaced 2 to 3 feet apart.

HORTICULTURAL SELECTIONS: Subsp. *alba,* pure white flowers; subsp. *arizonica,* large flaring blossoms; subsp. *cana,* narrower silky silvery leaves; 'Catalina Form', with grayer leaves; 'Compact Form', 6 inches tall by 18 inches wide, covered with light green, gray-hair-covered leaves; 'Dublin', more florific than the species; 'Etteri', low-growing, with gray leaves; subsp. *latifolia,* 2 feet tall, more vigorous growth, more profuse bloom; 'Solidarity Pink', 12 inches tall by 24 inches wide, with soft peach-colored flowers; subsp. *splendens,* low growing, with dark green leaves; 'U.C. Hybrid', incandescent flowers.

CULTURE / CARE: The best location for California fuchsia is one exposed to full sun with light-textured sandy or gravelly acidic to neutral soil. It is remarkably tolerant of drought and seldom needs any summertime watering. Disease problems are seldom encountered, provided the soil is well drained, and pests are inconsequential. Typical maintenance consists of removing dead stems during late winter.

PROPAGATION: Underground rhizomes that are dug up and transplanted will soon develop new shoots and root systems. Stem cuttings from nonblooming shoots can be rooted during summer. Ripe seed, which is ready to be germinated, will produce flowering plants within two years.

Zoysia tenuifolia   PLATE 315
Mascarene Grass, Korean Grass

A low, stoloniferous, mounding, herbaceous, grass, this species ranges from 2 to 8 inches tall and spreads indefinitely, making a bumpy, fine-textured surface that creates a mossy, Oriental effect. Its greatest usefulness is as a small-scale to large-scale turf substitute or as a filler between stepping stones. Typically, it is used in informal landscapes in areas that are difficult to reach with a lawn mower. Limited foot traffic is tolerated.

SCIENTIFIC NAME: *Zoysia tenuifolia* (*zoy*-see-a / zoe-*is*-ee-a ten-you-i-*foe*-lee-a). *Zoysia* is named after Karl von Zoys, an Austrian botanist. *Tenuifolia* comes from the Latin *tenuis,* slender, and *folia,* leaf, in reference to the narrow leaves.

HARDINESS / ORIGIN: Zones 9 to 10; Mascarene Islands (east of Madagascar).

LEAVES / FLOWERS / FRUIT: The evergreen, sharply pointed, 1½- to 3-inch-long, bright green leaves are the primary ornamental attribute. The flowers and fruit are insignificant.

RATE / SPACING: Growth is slow. Plants from 2- to 4-inch-wide divisions are spaced 6 to 8 inches apart.

CULTURE / CARE: Adaptable to most well-drained soils, Mascarene grass withstands drought and only requires occasional watering during the summer. It grows best in full sun to light shade and has few disease or pest problems. Little or no maintenance is required. Unlike other zoysias, Mascarene grass does not take well to mowing.

PROPAGATION: Division may be accomplished during spring or fall.

GROUND COVER SELECTION CHART

The Ground Cover Selection Chart is designed to help you determine which plants will work in a particular landscape setting. All you have to do is match the categories with the conditions of your particular planting site. This will enable you to make a list of plants that you might consider, then you can refer to a detailed description of each plant in Part 2 of this book.

Italicized abbreviations indicate that a characteristic is partially applicable.
? = information currently unknown.

PLANT TYPE
Bamboo = a member of the grass family with woody stems and infrequent flowering.
Cactus = a member of the cactus family.
Fern = a member of the fern family.
Grass = a member of the grass family.
Grasslike = a herbaceous plant that is not a member of the grass family, but displays long narrow leaves that are reminiscent of those of grasses.
Herbaceous = a plant with a herbaceous, nonwoody stem.
Herblike = a plant that is predominately herbaceous but tends to be woody at its base.
M. tree = mutated tree
Sedge = a member of the sedge family.
Shrub = a woody plant that typically has a single or multiple stems.
Shrublike = a semiwoody plant that has a single or multiple stems.
Succulent = a herbaceous plant with fleshy water filled stems and leaves.
Vine = a plant with a woody based, flexible stem that will climb when supported.
Vinelike = a plant that is like a vine but tends to trail along the ground and can not climb well even when supported.

HARDINESS
Numbers correspond to zones of USDA hardiness map.

HEIGHT
S = Small, less than 6 inches tall
I = Intermediate, 6 inches to 2 feet tall
T = Tall, more than 2 feet tall

BLOOM SEASON
Sp = Spring
Su = Summer
F = Fall
W = Winter

FOLIAGE
E = Evergreen
S = Semievergreen
D = Deciduous

SCALE OF PLANTING
S = Small areas
M = Medium areas
L = Large areas

LIGHT
FS = Full sun
LS = Light shade
MS = Moderate shade
DS = Dense shade

SOIL TYPE
Ac = Acidic
N = Neutral
Al = Alkaline

SOIL MOISTURE
DT = Drought tolerant
MT = Moisture tolerant (tolerates saturated soils)

OTHER
FT = Tolerates foot traffic
CE = Controls erosion
FR = Fire retardant
ST = Salt tolerant

Name of ground cover	Plant type	Hardi-ness	Height	Bloom season	Foliage	Scale of planting	Light	Soil type	Soil moisture	Other
Abelia × grandiflora	Shrub	6-9	I-T	Su, F	S	M-L	LS, MS	Ac	DT	CE
Acacia angustissima var. *hirta*	Shrub	6/7-10	I-T	Sp, Su	D	M-L	FS, LS	Ac	DT	CE, ST
Acacia redolens	Shrub	9-10	I-T	Sp	E	M-L	FS, LS	*Ac,* N, Al	DT	CE, ST
Acaena adscendens	Herbaceous	6/7-9	S	Su	E	S	FS	N, Al	–	*FT*
Acaena buchananii	Herbaceous	6/7-9	S	Su	E	S	FS	N, Al	–	*FT*
Acaena caesiiglauca	Herbaceous	6/7-9	S	Su	E	S	FS	N, Al	–	*FT*
Acaena inermis	Herbaceous	6/7-9	S	Su	E	S	FS	N, Al	–	*FT*
Acaena microphylla	Herbaceous	6/7-9	S	Su	E	S	FS	N, Al	–	*FT*
Acaena novae-zelandiae	Herbaceous	6/7-9	S	Su	E	S	FS	N, Al	–	*FT*
Acaena sanguisorbae	Herbaceous	6/7-9	I	Su	E	S	FS	N, Al	–	*FT*
Acanthus hungaricus	Herbaceous	6/7-9	T	Su	E	M-L	LS, MS	Ac	–	–
Acanthus mollis	Herbaceous	6/7-10	T	Sp, Su	E	M-L	LS, MS	Ac	–	–
Acanthus spinosus	Herbaceous	6/7-9	T	Sp, Su	E	M-L	LS, MS	Ac	–	–
Achillea ageratifolia	Herbaceous	3-9	S-I	Su, F	D	S-M	FS	Ac, N, Al	DT	*FT,* FR
Achillea filipendula	Herbaceous	3-10	T	Su	D	M-L	FS	Ac, N, Al	DT	FR
Achillea millefolium	Herbaceous	3-10	T	Su, F	D	M-L	FS	Ac, N, Al	DT	FR
Achillea ptarmica	Herbaceous	3-9	I	Su, F	D	M	FS	Ac, N, Al	DT	–
Achillea tomentosa	Herbaceous	3-7	I	Sp, Su, F	E	S-M	FS	Ac, N, Al	DT	*FT,* FR
Acorus calamus	Grasslike	5-10	T	Sp, Su	D	M-L	FS, LS	Ac, N	MT	CE
Acorus gramineus	Grasslike	5/6-9	I	Sp	E	S-M	FS, LS	Ac, N	MT	CE
Adiantum capillus-veneris	Fern	7-10	I	–	D	M	LS, MS, DS	AC, N	–	–
Adiantum pedatum	Fern	3-8	I-T	–	D	M	LS, MS, DS	Ac, N	–	–
Aegopodium podagraria	Herbaceous	3-9	I	Su	D	M-L	FS, LS, MS, DS	Ac, N, Al	–	CE
Aeonium tabuliforme	Succulent	9-11	S-I	Su	E	S-M	FS, LS	Ac	DT	FR
Aethionema grandiflorum	Shrublike	5-8/9	I	Su	E	S	FS, LS	Ac, N, Al	DT	–
Agapanthus africanus	Lilylike	9-11	I	Sp, Su, F	E	M-L	FS, LS	Ac, N, *Al*	–	–
Agapanthus inapertus	Lilylike	9-10	I	Sp, Su, F	D	M-L	FS, LS	Ac, N, *Al*	–	–
Agapanthus orientalis	Lilylike	9-11	T	Sp, Su, F	E	M-L	FS, LS	Ac, N, *Al*	–	–
Aglaonema commutatum	Herbaceous	10-11	T	Su	E	M-L	LS, MS, DS	Ac	–	–
Aglaonema 'Stripes'	Herbaceous	10-11	I	Su	E	M-L	LS, MS, DS	Ac	–	–
Ajuga genevensis	Herbaceous	4-9	S	Sp	E	S	FS, LS, MS	Ac, N	–	–
Ajuga pyramidalis	Herbaceous	5-9	S	Sp	E	S-M	FS, LS, MS	Ac, N	–	–
Ajuga reptans	Herbaceous	3-9	S	Sp	E	S-M	FS, LS, MS	Ac, N	–	–
Akebia quinata	Vine	4-8/9	I	Sp	S	L	FS, LS, MS	Ac, N	–	CE
Akebia trifoliata	Vine	4-8/9	I	Sp	S	L	FS, LS, MS	Ac, N	–	CE
Akebia × pentaphylla	Vine	11-8/9	I	Sp	S	L	FS, LS, MS	Ac, N	–	CE
Alchemilla alpina	Herbaceous	3-8	I	Sp	E	S-L	FS, LS, MS	Ac, N, *Al*	–	–
Alchemilla conjuncta	Herbaceous	3-7	I	Sp	E	S-L	FS, LS, MS	Ac, N, *Al*	–	–
Alchemilla mollis	Herbaceous	3-7	I	Sp	E	S-M	FS, LS, MS	Ac, N, *Al*	–	–
Alchemilla vulgaris	Herbaceous	3-7	I	Sp	E	S-M	FS, LS, MS	Ac, N, *Al*	–	–
Aloe aristata	Succulent	9-10/11	S	W	E	S	FS, LS	Ac, N	DT	FR
Aloe humilis	Succulent	9-10/11	S	?	E	S	LS	Ac, N	DT	FR
Aloe variegata	Succulent	9-10/11	I	*Sp, Su, F, W*	E	S	FS, LS	Ac, N	DT	FR
Ammophila arenaria	Grass	4-8/9	I-T	F	D	L	FS	Ac, N, *Al*	DT	*FT,* CE, ST
Ammophila breviligulata	Grass	4-8/9	I-T	F	D	L	FS	Ac, N, *Al*	DT	*FT,* CE, ST
Ampelopsis aconitifolia	Vine	5-8/9	S-I	Sp	D	L	FS, LS, MS	Ac, N	–	CE
Ampelopsis brevipedunculata	Vine	5-8/9	S-I	Su	D	L	FS, LS, MS	Ac, N	–	CE
Anacyclus depressus	Herbaceous	6-10	S	Sp, Su	D	S-M	FS	*Ac,* N, Al	DT	–
Anagallis monellii	Herbaceous	7-10	I	Sp, Su	D	M-L	FS	Ac, N, *Al*	*DT*	–
Andromeda glaucophylla	Shrublike	2-?	I	Sp	E	S	FS, *LS*	Ac	MT	–
Andromeda polifolia	Shrublike	2-?	I	Sp	E	S	FS, *LS*	Ac	MT	–
Anemone hupehensis	Herbaceous	6-10	I-T	Su, F	E	S-M	FS, LS	Ac	–	–
Anemone × hybrida	Herbaceous	5-8	I-T	Su, F	D	S-M	FS, LS	Ac	–	–
Anemone sylvestris	Herbaceous	3-9	I	Sp, Su	D	M	FS, LS	Ac	–	–

Name of ground cover	Plant type	Hardi-ness	Height	Bloom season	Foliage	Scale of planting	Light	Soil type	Soil moisture	Other
Antennaria dioica	Herbaceous	3-9	S	Sp	S	S	FS, LS	Ac, N	DT	–
Antennaria plantaginifolia	Herbaceous	3-10	I	Sp	D	S-M	FS, LS	Ac, N	DT	–
Aptenia cordifolia	Succulent	9-11	S	Sp, Su	E	S-M	FS, LS	Ac, N, *Al*	DT	FR, *ST*
Arabis alpina	Herbaceous	4-8	I	Sp	D	M	FS, LS	*Ac*, N, Al	DT	–
Arabis caucasica	Herbaceous	4-10	I	Sp	D	M	FS, LS	*Ac*, N, Al	DT	–
Arabis procurrens	Herbaceous	4-9	I	Sp	D	M	FS, LS	*Ac*, N, Al	DT	–
Arctanthemum arcticum	Herbaceous	2-9	I	F	D	M	FS, LS	Ac, N	–	–
Arctostaphylos alpina	Shrub	1-4	S	Sp, Su	E	S-M	FS, *LS*	Ac	DT	CE, ST
Arctostaphylos edmundsii	Shrub	7-?	I	W, Sp	E	M	FS, *LS*	Ac	DT	CE, ST
Arctostaphylos 'Emerald Carpet'	Shrub	7-10	I	Sp	E	M-L	FS, *LS*	Ac	DT	CE, ST
Arctostaphylos hookeri	Shrub	7-?	I	W, Sp	E	M-L	FS, *LS*	Ac	DT	CE, ST
Arctostaphylos nevadensis	Shrub	5-?	I	Sp	E	M-L	FS, *LS*	Ac	DT	CE, ST
Arctostaphylos nummularia	Shrub	7-?	S	Sp	E	M-L	FS	Ac	DT	CE, ST
Arctostaphylos pumila	Shrub	7-?	T	W, Sp	E	M-L	FS, *LS*	Ac	DT	CE, ST
Arctostaphylos rubra	Shrub	1-?	S	Sp	E	S-M	FS, *LS*	Ac	DT	CE, ST
Arctostaphylos thymifolia	Shrub	3-7	S-I	Sp	E	S-L	FS, *LS*	Ac	DT	CE, ST
Arctostaphylos uva-ursi	Shrub	3-7	S-I	Sp	E	S-L	FS, *LS*	Ac	DT	CE, ST
Arctostaphylos 'Wood's Red'	Shrub	5-9	S	Sp	E	S-L	FS, *LS*	Ac	DT	CE, ST
Arctotheca calendula	Herbaceous	9-11	I	Sp, *Su, F, W*	E	M-L	FS	Ac, N, Al	DT	*FT*, CE
Ardisia japonica	Shrub	7-9	I	Su	E	L	LS, MS	Ac	–	CE
Arenaria arctica	Herbaceous	1-4	I	Su	E	S-M	FS, *LS*	Ac	DT	CE, ST
Arenaria montana	Herbaceous	5-7	S	Sp	E	S	FS, LS, MS	Ac, N, *Al*	–	–
Arenaria verna	Herbaceous	3-9	S	Sp	E	S	FS, LS, MS	Ac, N, *Al*	–	–
Armeria 'Bloodstone'	Herbaceous	4-8	I	Sp, Su	E	S-M	FS	Ac, N, *Al*	DT	ST
Armeria juniperifolia	Herbaceous	4-8	S	Sp	E	S	FS	Ac, N, *Al*	DT	ST
Armeria maritima	Herbaceous	4-8	I	Sp, Su	E	S-M	FS	Ac, N, *Al*	DT	ST
Aronia melanocarpa	Shrub	3-7/8	I-T	Sp	D	L	FS, LS, MS	Ac, N	–	–
Artemisia abrotanum 'Nana'	Herbaceous	5-8	I	Su	E	M	FS, *LS*	Ac, N, *Al*	DT	ST
Artemisia caucasica	Herbaceous	4-?	S	Su	D	S	FS, *LS*	Ac, N, *Al*	DT	ST
Artemisia frigida	Herbaceous	2-?	I	Su	E	M	FS, *LS*	Ac, N, *Al*	DT	ST
Artemisia ludoviciana	Herbaceous	4-9/10	I-T	Su	D	M	FS	Ac, N, *Al*	–	ST
Artemisia schmidtiana	Herbaceous	3-7	I	Su	D	S-M	FS, *LS*	Ac, N, *Al*	DT	ST
Artemisia stelleriana	Herbaceous	3/4-9	I-T	Su	D	M	FS, *LS*	Ac, N, *Al*	DT	ST
Asarum arifolium	Herbaceous	6-9	I	Sp, Su	E	S-M	LS, MS, DS	Ac	–	–
Asarum canadense	Herbaceous	3-8	S	Sp	D	S-M	LS, MS, DS	Ac	*MT*	–
Asarum caudatum	Herbaceous	5/6-9	I	Sp	D	S-M	LS, MS, DS	Ac	–	–
Asarum europaeum	Herbaceous	4-7/8	S	Sp	E	S-M	LS, MS, DS	Ac	–	–
Asarum hartwegii	Herbaceous	5-9	S	Sp	E	S-M	LS, MS, DS	Ac	–	–
Asarum shuttleworthii	Herbaceous	6/7-9	I	Sp	E	S	LS, MS, DS	Ac	–	–
Asarum virginicum	Herbaceous	5-?	S	Sp	E	S-M	LS, MS, DS	Ac	–	–
Asparagus densiflorus 'Sprengeri'	Herbaceous	8-10/11	T	Su, F	S	S-l	FS, LS	Ac, N	*DT*	–
Asparagus officinalis	Herbaceous	4-?	T	Sp	D	M	FS, LS	Ac, N	*DT*	–
Astilbe × arendsii	Herbaceous	4/5-8/9	T	Su	E	M	FS, LS, MS	Ac	–	–
Astilbe chinensis 'Pumila'	Herbaceous	4/5-8/9	I	Su	D	S-M	FS, LS, MS	Ac	–	–
Astilbe crispa	Herbaceous	4/5-8/9	S	Su	D	S	FS, LS, MS	Ac	–	–
Astilbe × rosea	Herbaceous	4/5-8/9	T	Su	D	M	FS, LS, MS	Ac	–	–
Astilbe simplicifolia	Herbaceous	4/5-8/9	I	Su	D	M	FS, LS, MS	Ac	–	–
Athyrium felix-femina	Fern	3-8	I-T	–	D	S-L	LS, MS, DS	Ac	–	–
Athyrium nipponicum	Fern	4-9	I	–	D	S-L	LS, MS, DS	Ac	–	–
Athyrium pycnocarpon	Fern	4-8	T	–	D	M-L	LS, MS, DS	N, *Al*	–	–
Athyrium thelypteroides	Fern	1-9	T	–	D	M-L	LS, MS, DS	Ac	–	–
Atriplex semibaccata	Shrub	8-10	I	–	E	M-L	FS, LS	*Ac*, N, Al	DT	ST
Aubrieta deltoides	Herbaceous	4-8	S	Sp, Su	E	S	FS, LS	*Ac*, N, Al	–	ST
Aurinia saxatilis	Herbaceous	4-8	I	Sp	D	S-M	FS, LS	Ac, N	*DT*	–
Azorella trifurcata	Herbaceous	5/6-7	S	Su	E	S-M	FS, *LS*	*Ac*, N, Al	DT	*FT, CE*

Name of ground cover	Plant type	Hardi-ness	Height	Bloom season	Foliage	Scale of planting	Light	Soil type	Soil moisture	Other
Baccharis pilularis	Shrub	7-10/11	I	Su	E	L	FS	Ac, N, *Al*	DT	CE, FR
Begonia grandis	Herbaceous	7-10	I-T	Su, F	D	M-L	LS, MS	Ac, N	–	FR
Bellis perennis	Herbaceous	5-10	S	Sp	D	S	FS, LS	AC, N, Al	–	*FT*
Berberis thunbergii 'Crimson Pygmy'	Shrub	5-8	I-T	Sp	D	M-L	FS, LS	Ac	DT	–
Berberis stenophylla 'Irwinii'	Shrub	6-9/10	I	Sp	E	M-L	FS, LS	Ac	DT	
Bergenia ciliata	Herbaceous	6-10	I	Sp	E	S-M	FS, LS	*Ac*, N, *Al*	–	
Bergenia cordifolia	Herbaceous	3/4-8/9	I	Sp	E	S-M	FS, LS	*Ac*, N, *Al*	–	
Bergenia crassifolia	Herbaceous	3/4-8	I	W, Sp	E	S-M	FS, LS	*Ac*, N, *Al*	–	
Bergenia purpurascens	Herbaceous	4-9	I	Sp	E	S-M	FS, LS	*Ac*, N, *Al*	DT	
Bergenia smithii	Herbaceous	4-8	M	W, Sp	E	S-M	FS, LS	*Ac*, N, *Al*	–	
Bergenia stracheyi	Herbaceous	6-10	I	Sp	E	S-M	FS, LS	*Ac*, N, *Al*	DT	
Briza media	Grass	4-8	I	Su, *F*	D	M-L	FS	Ac, N, Al	DT	CE
Brunnera macrophylla	Herbaceous	3-8	I	Sp	D	M	FS, LS, MS	Ac, N	–	
Caladium bicolor	Herbaceous	10-11	I	*Sp, Su, F, W*	E	M	LS, MS, DS	Ac, *N*	–	
Caladium × *hortulanum*	Herbaceous	10-11	I	*Sp, Su, F, W*	E	M	LS, MS, DS	Ac, *N*	–	
Caladium humboldtii	Herbaceous	10-11	I	*Sp, Su, F, W*	E	S	LS, MS, DS	Ac, *N*	–	
Caladium marmoratum	Herbaceous	10-11	I	*Sp, Su, F, W*	E	M	LS, MS, DS	Ac, N	–	
Caladium picturatum	Herbaceous	10-11	I	*Sp, Su, F, W*	E	M	LS, MS, DS	Ac, *N*	–	
Calamintha nepeta	Herbaceous	6-10	I	Su	D	M	FS	*Ac*, N, Al	–	
Calamovilfa longifolia	Grass	3-?	T	Su	D	L	FS, LS	*Ac*, N, *Al*	DT	CE, ST
Callirhoe involucrata	Herbaceous	4/5-?	S-I	Sp, Su	D	M	FS, LS	Ac, N, Al	DT	
Calluna vulgaris	Shrub	4-7	I-T	Su, F	E	M-L	FS, LS	Ac	–	
Campanula carpatica	Herbaceous	3-8	I	Su	E	S-M	FS, LS	*Ac*, N, *Al*	–	
Campanula garganica	Herbaceous	6-8	S	Su, F	D	S-M	FS, LS	*Ac*, N, *Al*	–	
Campanula portenschlagiana	Herbaceous	4-8	I	Sp, Su, *F*	D	S-M	FS, LS	*Ac*, N, *Al*	–	
Campanula poscharskyana	Herbaceous	3-7	S	Su	S	S-M	FS, LS	*Ac*, N, *Al*	–	–
Carex atrata	Sedge	5-8	I	Su	S	S-L	LS, MS	Ac	–	*FT*, CE
Carex comans	Sedge	7/8-9	T	Su	E	M-L	LS, MS	Ac		CE
Carex digitata	Sedge	6-9	M	Sp, Su	D	S-M	LS, MS	–	–	–
Carex elata	Sedge	4-?	I	Sp	D	S-L	LS, MS	Ac	MT	*FT*
Carex glauca	Sedge	5-9	I	Su	E	S-L	LS, MS	Ac	–	FT, CE
Carex hachioensis	Sedge	5/6-9	S-I	Sp	E	S-M	LS, MS	Ac	–	FT
Carex morrowii	Sedge	6/7-9	I	Sp	E	S-L	LS, MS	Ac	–	*FT*, CE
Carex muskingumensis	Sedge	4-9	T	Su	D	M-L	FS, LS, MS	Ac	MT	CE
Carex nigra	Sedge	4-8	I	Su	E	S-L	LS, MS	Ac	–	FT, CE
Carex pendula	Sedge	5/6-9	I	Sp	E	M-L	LS, MS	Ac	MT	–
Carex plantaginea	Sedge	3-8	I	Sp	E	S-M	LS, MS	Ac	–	*FT*
Carissa grandiflora	Shrub	7-10/11	I-T	Sp	E	M	FS, LS, MS	Ac, N, Al	–	ST
Carpobrotus chilensis	Succulent	9-10/11	I	Su	E	L	FS	Ac, N, Al	DT	CE
Carpobrotus edulis	Succulent	9-10/11	I	Su	E	L	FS	Ac, N, Al	DT	CE
Caryopteris × *clandonensis*	Semiwoody	4-9	T	Su, F	D	M-L	FS	Ac, N	DT	CE
Ceanothus gloriosus	Shrub	7-9	T	Sp	E	M-L	FS, LS	Ac, N	DT	CE
Ceanothus griseus var. *horizontalis*	Shrub	8-10/11	T	Sp	E	L	FS, LS	Ac, N	DT	CE
Ceanothus prostratus	Shrub	7-10	S	Sp	E	L	FS, LS	Ac, N	DT	CE
Ceanothus thyrsiflorus var. *repens*	Shrub	8-10/11	I-T	Sp	E	L	FS, LS	Ac, N	DT	CE
Cedrus deodara	M. tree	7-8/9	I-T	F	D	M-L	FS, LS	Ac	*DT*	CE
Centranthus ruber	Herbaceous	5-8	T	Sp, Su	E	M-L	FS, LS	*Ac*, N, Al	DT	CE
Cephalophyllum alstonii	Succulent	9-10/11	S	W, Sp	E	M-L	FS	Ac, N, Al	DT	CE, FR
Cephalophyllum anemoniflorum	Succulent	9-10/11	S	W, Sp	E	M-L	FS	Ac, N, Al	DT	CE, FR
Cephalophyllum aureorubrum	Succulent	9-10/11	S	W, Sp	E	M-L	FS	Ac, N, Al	DT	CE, FR
Cephalophyllum procumbens	Succulent	9-10/11	S	W, Sp	E	M-L	FS	Ac, N, Al	DT	CE, FR

Name of ground cover	Plant type	Hardi-ness	Height	Bloom season	Foliage	Scale of planting	Light	Soil type	Soil moisture	Other
Cephalophyllum subulatoides	Succulent	9-10/11	S	W, Sp	E	M-L	FS	Ac, N, Al	DT	CE, FR
Cephalotaxus harringtonia	Shrub	5/6-9	T	Sp	E	M-L	*FS*, LS	Ac	DT	CE
Cerastium biebersteinii	Herbaceous	2-7	I	Sp	E	S-M	FS	*Ac*, N, *Al*	DT	*CE*
Cerastium tomentosum	Herbaceous	3-7	I	Sp	E	S-M	FS	*Ac*, N, *Al*	DT	*CE*
Ceratostigma plumbaginoides	Herbaceous	5/6-9	I	*Su*, F	E	S-L	FS, LS, MS	Ac, N, Al	–	CE
Chamaedaphne calyculata	Shrub	1/2-8/9	T	Sp	E	L	FS, LS	Ac	MT	CE
Chamaemelum nobile	Herbaceous	5-8/9	S	Su	E	S-L	FS, LS	Ac, N, *Al*	DT	*FT*
Chelone glabra	Herbaceous	3-8	T	Su	D	M	FS, LS	Ac	MT	–
Chelone lyonii	Herbaceous	3-8	I-T	Su, F	D	M	FS, LS	Ac	MT	–
Chelone obliqua	Herbaceous	5/6-9	T	Su, F	D	M	FS, LS	Ac	MT	–
Chimaphila umbellata	Herblike	4-?	I	Su	E	S-M	LS, MS	Ac	*DT*	–
Chimaphila maculata	Herblike	4-?	S	Su	E	S	LS, MS	Ac	*DT*	–
Chimaphila menziesii	Herblike	4-?	S-I	Su	E	S-M	LS, MS	Ac	*DT*	–
Chlorophytum comosum	Herbaceous	10-11	I-T	F, W	E	M	LS, MS	*Ac*, N, *Al*	–	–
Chrysanthemum leucanthemum	Herbaceous	3-10	I	Su, F	D	M	FS, LS	Ac, N	–	–
Chrysogonum virginianum	Herbaceous	5-9	S	Sp	S	S	LS, MS	Ac, *N*	–	*FT*
Cistus crispus	Shrub	7-?	I	Sp, Su	E	M-L	FS	Al	DT	CE, ST
Cistus salviifolius	Shrub	7-9	I	Sp, Su	E	M-L	FS	Al	DT	CE, ST
Cistus × *hybridus*	Shrub	7-9	I-T	Sp	E	M-L	FS	Al	DT	CE, ST
Clematis alpina	Vine	5-8	M	Sp	D	L	FS, LS	Ac, N	–	*CE*
Clematis maximowicziana	Vine	4-9	I	F	S	L	FS, LS	Ac, N	*DT*	*CE*
Clematis montana	Vine	5/6-8	I	Sp	E	L	FS, LS	Ac, N	*DT*	*CE*
Clematis paniculata	Vine	8-?	I	?	E	L	FS, LS	Ac, N	*DT*	*CE*
Clematis virginiana	Vine	4-9	M	Su, F	D	M-L	FS, LS	Ac, N	–	*CE*
Clematis viticella	Vine	5-9	M	Su, F	D	M-L	FS, LS	Ac, N	–	*CE*
Clethra alnifolia 'Hummingbird'	Shrub	5-9	T	Su	D	M-L	FS, LS, MS	Ac, N	MT	CE, ST
Clivia miniata	Lilylike	10-11	I	W, Sp	S	M-L	LS, MS, DS	*Ac*, N	–	CE
Comptonia peregrina	Shrub	2-8	T	Su	S	L	FS	Ac	DT, *MT*	CE, ST
Conradina verticillata	Shrub	6/7-10	I	Sp	E	M-L	FS, LS	Ac, N, ?Al	*MT*	CE, *ST*
Convallaria majalis	Herbaceous	2-7	I	Sp	D	S-L	LS, MS, DS	Ac, N, *Al*	–	CE
Convallaria montana	Herbaceous	2-7	I	Sp	D	S-M	LS, MS, DS	Ac, N, *Al*	*DT*	CE
Convolvulus cneorum	Shrub	9-11	T	Sp, Su, F	E	M-L	FS	Ac, N, *Al*	DT	FR
Convolvulus sabatius	Shrub	8-?	I	Sp, Su, F	E	M-L	FS	Ac, N, *Al*	DT	FR
Coprosma petriei	Shrub	7-9	T	Sp	E	L	FS, LS	Ac, N, Al	DT, MT	CE, ST
Coprosma × *kirkii*	Shrub	8-10	T	Sp	D	L	FS, LS	Ac, N, Al	DT, MT	CE, ST
Coptis groenlandica	Herbaceous	2-7/8	S	Su	E	S-M	LS	Ac	*MT*	*FT*
Coptis laciniata	Herbaceous	2-7/8	S	Su	E	S-M	LS	Ac	–	*FT*
Corema conradii	Shrublike	3-?	I	Sp	E	M	FS, LS	Ac	DT	–
Coreopsis auriculata	Herbaceous	4-9	I	Sp, Su, F	D	S-M	FS, LS	Ac	–	–
Coreopsis rosea	Herbaceous	4-9	I	Su	D	M-L	FS, LS	Ac	MT	–
Coreopsis verticillata	Herbaceous	3-9	I	Su	D	M-L	FS, LS	Ac	DT	–
Cornus canadensis	Herbaceous	2-7	S	Sp, Su	E	S-M	LS, MS	Ac	*MT*	–
Cornus mas 'Nana'	Shrub	5-8	T	Sp	D	S-M	LS, MS	Ac, N	–	–
Cornus pumila	Shrub	4-/5-?	T	–	D	M	FS, LS	Ac, N	–	–
Cornus sericea 'Kelseyi'	Shrub	3-8	I-T	Sp, Su	D	S-M	LS, MS	Ac, N	*MT*	CE
Coronilla varia	Herbaceous	4-9	I	Su, F	D	L	FS, LS	Ac, N	DT	*FT*, CE
Correa pulchella	Shrub	9-10	T	Sp, Su, F	E	L	FS, LS	Ac, N, *Al*	*DT*	–
Cotoneaster adpressus	Shrub	5-8	I	Sp, Su	D	M-L	FS, LS	Ac, N, *Al*	DT	–
Cotoneaster apiculatus	Shrub	5-8	T	Sp, Su	D	M-L	FS, LS	Ac, N, *Al*	DT	–
Cotoneaster congestus	Shrub	6-9	T	Sp	E	S-M	FS, LS	Ac, N, *Al*	DT	–
Cotoneaster conspicuus 'Decorus'	Shrub	6-9	I	Sp	E	M	FS, LS	Ac, N, *Al*	DT	–
Cotoneaster dammeri	Shrub	6-9	I	Sp	S	M-L	FS, LS	Ac, N, *Al*	DT	–

Name of ground cover	Plant type	Hardi-ness	Height	Bloom season	Foliage	Scale of planting	Light	Soil type	Soil moisture	Other
Cotoneaster 'Hessei'	Shrub	4-7	I	Sp	D	M-L	FS, LS	Ac, N, *Al*	DT	–
Cotoneaster horizontalis	Shrub	5-8	I	Sp, Su	S	M-L	FS, LS	Ac, N, *Al*	DT	–
Cotoneaster microphyllus	Shrub	6-9	T	Sp, Su	E	M-T	FS, LS	Ac, N, *Al*	DT	–
Cotoneaster salicifolius	Shrub	6-9	I	Sp, Su	E	M-L	FS, LS	Ac, N, *Al*	DT	–
Cotula squalida	Herbaceous	9-10	S	Su	E	S-M	FS, LS	Ac	–	*FT*
Crassula multicava	Succulent	9-10	I	W, Sp	E	S-M	FS, LS	Ac, N, *Al*	DT	FR
Cuphea hyssopifola	Shrub	9-11	I	Su	E	S-M	FS, LS	Ac, N	–	–
Cuphea procumbens	Semiwoody	9-11	I	Su	E	M	FS, LS	Ac, N	–	–
Cuphea × purpurea	Semiwoody	9-11	I	Su	E	M	FS, LS	Ac, N	–	–
Cymbalaria aequitriloba	Herbaceous	8-10	S	Su, F	E	S	MS, DS	Ac, N, *Al*	–	–
Cymbalaria muralis	Herbaceous	5-9	S	Su, F	E	S	MS, DS	Ac, N, *Al*	–	–
Cytisus decumbens	Shrub	6-9	I	Sp, *Su*	D	M	FS	Ac, N, Al	DT	–
Dalea greggii	Shrub	9-10	I	Sp, Su	E	M-L	FS, LS	Ac, N, Al	DT	ST
Dampiera diversifolia	Herbaceous	9-10	S	Sp, Su	E	M	LS	*Ac*, N, *Al*	–	CE
Daphne arbuscula	Shrub	4-?	I	Sp	E	S-M	FS, LS	Ac, N, *Al*	–	–
Daphne cneorum	Shrub	5-8	I	Sp, *Su*	E	M-L	FS, LS	Ac, N	–	–
Daphne × burkwoodii	Shrub	5-?	T	Sp	E	M-L	FS, LS	Ac, N	–	–
Delosperma ashtonii	Succulent	6-9	S	Su	E	S	FS	Ac, N, Al	–	FR
Delosperma cooperi	Succulent	6/7-10	S-I	Su, F, W	E	M-L	FS	Ac, N, Al	–	CE, FR
Delosperma herbaeu	Succulent	6/7-10	S-M	Su, F	E	S-M	FS	Ac, N, Al	×	FR
Delosperma nubigena	Succulent	5/6-9/10	S	Sp	E	S-M	FS	Ac, N, Al	–	CE, FR
Dendranthema × morifolium	Herbaceous	4-10	I-T	Su, F	D	M	FS, LS	Ac, N	–	–
Dendranthema pacifica	Herbaceous	6-9	I	F	D	M	FS, LS	Ac, N	–	–
Dendranthema × rubellum	Herbaceous	4-10	I-T	Su	D	M	FS, LS	Ac, N	–	–
Dendranthema weyrichii	Herbaceous	3-8	I	F	D	M	FS, LS	Ac, N	–	–
Deschampsia caespitosa	Grass	4-9	I	Su	E	M-L	FS, LS	Ac, N, Al	*DT*	CE
Deschampsia flexuosa	Grass	4-8	I	Su	E	M-L	FS, LS	Ac, N, Al	*DT*	CE
Deutzia gracilis	Shrub	5-8	T	Sp	D	M-L	FS, LS	Ac	*DT*	–
Dianthus × allwoodii	Herbaceous	4-8	I	Sp	E	S	FS, LS	*Ac*, N, Al	–	–
Dianthus arenarius	Herbaceous	4-7	I	Su	E	L	FS, LS	*Ac*, N, Al	–	–
Dianthus deltoides	Herbaceous	3-9	S-I	Sp, Su, *F*	E	S	FS, LS	*Ac*, N, Al	–	–
Dianthus gratianopolitanus	Herbaceous	3-9	I	Sp, Su	E	S	FS, LS	*Ac*, N, Al	–	–
Dianthus plumarius	Herbaceous	3-9	I	Sp	E	S	FS, LS	*Ac*, N, Al	–	–
Dicentra eximia	Herbaceous	3-9	I	*Sp*, Su, *F*	D	S-M	LS, MS	Ac, N, *Al*	–	–
Dicentra formosa	Herbaceous	2/3-9	I	*Sp*, Su, *F*	D	S-M	LS, MS	Ac, N, *Al*	–	–
Dichondra micrantha	Herbaceous	10-11	S	Sp	E	S-L	FS, LS, MS	Ac, N, Al	–	FT, CE
Diervilla × splendens	Shrub	3/4-9	T	Su	D	L	FS, LS, MS	Ac, N	DT	CE
Diervilla lonicera	Shrub	3-7/8	T	Sp, Su	D	M-L	FS, LS, MS	Ac, N	DT	CE
Disporum sessile	Herbaceous	5-?	I	Sp	D	S-M	LS, MS	Ac	*DT*	–
Drosanthemum floribundum	Succulent	9-10	S	Sp, Su, F	E	M-L	FS	Ac, N, Al	DT	CE, FR
Drosanthemum hispidum	Succulent	9-10	I	Sp	E	M-L	FS	Ac, N, Al	DT	FR
Dryas octopetala	Herbaceous	2-4	S	Sp, Su	E	S	FS, LS	*Ac*, N	*DT*	*FT*
Dryopteris cycadina	Fern	5-8	M	–	E	M	LS, MS, DS	Al	*DT*	–
Dryopteris erythrosora	Fern	5-8	I	–	E	M	LS, MS, DS	Ac	*DT*	CE
Dryopteris filix-mas	Fern	3-9	T	–	S	M	LS, MS, DS	Ac	*DT*	–
Dryopteris intermedia	Fern	3-9	I	–	E	M	LS, MS, DS	Ac	MT	CE
Dryopteris marginalis	Fern	3-9	I	–	E	M	LS, MS, DS	Ac	*DT*	CE
Dryopteris wallichiana	Fern	5-8	T	–	E	L	LS, MS, DS	Ac	–	CE
Duchesnea indica	Herbaceous	4-8	S	*Sp, Su, F*	E	S-M	*FS*, LS	Ac, N, Al	DT	*FT*, CE
Echeveria agavoides	Succulent	9-11	S	W, Sp	E	S-M	FS, LS	Ac, N, *Al*	DT	–
Echeveria amoena	Succulent	9-11	S	Sp	E	S-M	FS, LS	Ac, N, *Al*	DT	–
Echeveria derenbergii	Succulent	9-11	S	W, Sp	E	S-M	FS, LS	Ac, N, *Al*	DT	–
Echeveria elegans	Succulent	9-11	S	W, Sp	E	S-M	FS, LS	Ac, N, *Al*	DT	–
Echeveria gibbiflora	Succulent	9-11	S	?	E	S-M	FS, LS	Ac, N, *Al*	DT	–
Echeveria × gilva	Succulent	9-11	S	Sp	E	S-M	FS, LS	Ac, N, *Al*	DT	–
Echeveria secunda	Succulent	9-11	S	Sp, Su	E	S-M	FS, LS	Ac, N, *Al*	DT	–

Name of ground cover	Plant type	Hardiness	Height	Bloom season	Foliage	Scale of planting	Light	Soil type	Soil moisture	Other
Empetrum nigrum	Shrublike	3	I	Sp	E	M	LS, MS	Ac, N	–	*FT*
Ephedra distachya	Shrublike	5-9	I-T	Su	E	M	FS	*Ac*, N	–	CE
Ephedra nevadensis	Shrublike	6-10	M-T	Sp	E	M-L	FS	*Ac*, N	–	CE
Epigaea repens	Shrublike	2-8	S	Sp	E	S-M	LS, MS, DS	Ac	–	*FT*
Epimedium alpinum	Herbaceous	3-8	I	Sp	D	S-L	LS, MS	Ac	–	–
Epimedium grandiflorum	Herbaceous	5-8	I	Sp	D	S-L	LS, MS	Ac	–	–
Epimedium perralderianum	Herbaceous	5-8	I	Sp	D	S-L	LS, MS	Ac	–	–
Epimedium pinnatum	Herbaceous	5-8	I	Sp	D	S-L	LS, MS	Ac	–	–
Epimedium × rubrum	Herbaceous	4-8	I	Sp	D	S-L	LS, MS	Ac	–	–
Epimedium × versicolor	Herbaceous	5-?	I	Sp	D	S-L	LS, MS	Ac	–	–
Equisetum hyemale	Grasslike	2-10	T	–	E	M-L	FS, LS	*Ac*, N, *Al*	MT	–
Equisetum scirpoides	Grasslike	1-9	I	–	S	S-M	FS, LS	*Ac*, N, *Al*	MT	–
Equisetum sylvaticum	Grasslike	1-5	I	–	E	S-M	MS	*Ac*, N, *Al*	MT	–
Equisetum variegatum	Grasslike	1-8	I	–	E	S-M	FS, LS	*Ac*, N, *Al*	MT	–
Erica carnea	Shrublike	5/6-7	S-I	W, Sp	E	S-M	FS, LS	Ac	*DT*	CE, ST
Erica cinerea	Shrublike	6-7	I	Sp, Su, F	E	S-L	FS, LS	Ac	*DT*	CE, ST
Erica × darleyensis	Shrublike	6-7/8	T	Sp, F, W	E	M-L	FS, LS	Ac	*DT*	CE, ST
Erica tetralix	Shrublike	4-6	I	Su, F	E	S-L	FS, LS	Ac	*DT*	CE, ST
Erica vagans	Shrublike	6-7	I	Su	E	M-L	FS, LS	Ac	*DT*	CE, ST
Erigeron karvinskianus	Herbaceous	9-11	I	Sp, Su, F, W	E	M	FS	Ac, N, Al	DT	ST
Erigeron glaucus	Herbaceous	5/6-9	I	Sp, Su, F, W	E	M	FS	Ac, N, Al	DT	ST
Erodium reichardii	Herbaceous	7-9	S	Sp, Su, F	E	S	FS, LS	Ac, N, Al	–	*FT*
Erysimum kotschyanum	Herbaceous	6-?	S	Sp, Su	S	S	FS, LS	*Ac*, N, *Al*	DT	–
Euonymus fortunei	Vine	4/5-9	S-T	–	E	S-L	FS, LS, MS, DS	Ac	*DT*	*FT*, CE
Euonymus obovatus	Shrublike	3/4-8/9	I	Sp, Su	E	S-L	FS, LS, MS, DS	Ac	*MT*	*FT*, CE
Euphorbia amygdaloides var. *robbiae*	Herbaceous	7-?	I	Sp	E	M	FS, LS	Ac, N, Al	DT	–
Euphorbia cyparissias	Herbaceous	4-?	I	Sp, Su	D	M	FS	Ac, N, Al	–	–
Euphorbia myrsinites	Herbaceous	5-?	I	Sp, Su	E	S	FS	Ac, N, Al	DT	–
Euphorbia polychroma	Herbaceous	4-8	I	Sp	D	S-M	FS, LS, MS	Ac, N, Al	DT	–
Euryops acraeus	Shrub	7-9	I	Sp, Su	E	S-M	FS	*Ac*, N	DT	ST
Fallopia japonica 'Compacta'	Herbaceous	3-10	I-T	F	D	M-L	FS, LS	Ac, N, *Al*	DT	–
Felicia amelloides	Shrub	9-10	I-T	Su, F	E	S-M	FS, LS	Ac, N, Al	*DT*	–
Festuca amethystina	Grass	4-8	I	Su	E	S-L	FS	Ac, N	DT	*FT*
Festuca ovina var. *glauca*	Grass	4-9	I	Su	E	S-L	FS	Ac, N	DT	*FT*
Festuca tenuifolia	Grass	4-6/7	S	Su	E	S-M	FS	Ac, N	DT	–
Ficus pumila	Vine	8/9-10	S	–	E	S	FS, LS	Ac	*DT*	*FT*
Filipendula vulgaris	Herbaceous	3-8	I-T	Su	D	S-M	FS, LS, MS	*Ac*, N, Al	*DT*	–
Fittonia versicolor var. *versicolor*	Herbaceous	9/10-11	S	?	E	S-M	MS, DS	*Ac*, N	–	–
Forsythia viridissima 'Bronxensis'	Shrub	5-8	T	Sp	D	M-L	FS, LS, MS	Ac	–	CE, *ST*
Forsythia 'Arnold Dwarf'	Shrub	5-8	T	Sp	D	M-L	FS, LS, MS	Ac	–	CE, *ST*
Fragaria chiloensis	Herbaceous	4-9	S	Sp	E	S-M	FS	Ac	–	*FT*, CE
Fragaria 'Pink Panda'	Herbaceous	5/6-?	S	Su	E	S-M	FS	Ac	–	*FT*, CE
Fragaria vesca	Herbaceous	5/6-10	I-T	Sp, Su, F	E	S-M	FS	Ac	–	CE
Fragaria virginiana	Herbaceous	5/6-9	S-I	Sp, Su	E	S-M	FS	Ac	–	CE
Francoa ramosa	Shrub	8/9-10	I	Su	E	S-M	LS, MS	Ac, N, Al	*DT*	–
Fuchsia procumbens	Herbaceous	10-11	S-I	Su, F	E	S	FS, LS	Ac, N, Al	–	–
Galax urceolata	Herbaceous	4/5-9	I	Sp, Su	E	S	LS, MS, DS	Ac, N	–	–
Galium odoratum	Herbaceous	4-8	I	Sp	S	S-M	MS, DS	Ax	–	–
Gardenia jasminoides 'Radicans'	Shrub	8/9-10	I	Su, F	E	S-M	FS, LS, MS	Ac	DT	–
Gaultheria adenothrix	Shrublike	6-9	I	Su	E	S-L	FS, LS, MS	Ac	–	–
Gaultheria hispidula	Shrublike	3-?	S	Sp	E	?	LS, MS	Ac	–	–
Gaultheria humifusa	Shrublike	5-?	S	Su	E	S-L	LS, MS	Ac	*MT*	*FT*
Gaultheria miqueliana	Shrublike	5-?	I	Sp	E	M-L	LS, MS	Ac	*MT*	–

Name of ground cover	Plant type	Hardi-ness	Height	Bloom season	Foliage	Scale of planting	Light	Soil type	Soil moisture	Other
Gaultheria nummularioides	Shrublike	7-?	S	Su	E	M-L	LS, MS	Ac	–	–
Gaultheria ovatifolia	Shrublike	6-?	I	Sp	E	M-L	LS, MS	Ac	*MT*	–
Gaultheria procumbens	Shrublike	3-7	S	Sp, Su, F	E	S-L	LS, MS	Ac	*MT*	*FT*
Gaultheria shallon	Shrublike	7/8-?	T	Sp, Su	E	M-L	LS, MS	Ac	–	–
Gaylussacia brachycera	Shrublike	5/6-9	I	Sp	E	S-M	FS, LS, MS	Ac	–	–
Gazania linearis	Herbaceous	8-10	I	Sp, Su	E	S-M	FS	Ac, N, Al	*DT*	–
Gazania rigens	Herbaceous	8-10	I	Sp, Su	E	S-M	FS	Ac, N, Al	*DT*	–
Gelsemium rankinii	Vine	7-9	T	Sp, *F*	S	L	FS, LS	Ac	–	CE
Gelsemium sempervirens	Vine	7/8-9	T	Sp, *F*	S	L	FS, LS	Ac	–	CE
Genista germanica	Shrub	5-7	I	Su	D	S-M	FS, LS	*Ac*, N, Al	DT	–
Genista hispanica	Shrub	7-9	I	Sp, Su	D	S-M	FS, LS	*Ac*, N, Al	DT	–
Genista horrida	Shrub	7-?	I	Su, F	D	S-M	FS, LS	*Ac*, N, Al	DT	–
Genista lydia	Shrub	7-9	I	Sp, Su	D	S-M	FS, LS	*Ac*, N, Al	DT	–
Genista pilosa	Shrub	6-8	I	Su	D	S-M	FS, LS	*Ac*, N, Al	DT	–
Genista sagittalis	Shrub	3/4-8	I	Su	D	S-M	FS, LS	*Ac*, N, Al	DT	–
Genista sylvestris	Shrub	6-?	S	Su	D	S-M	FS, LS	*Ac*, N, Al	DT	–
Genista tinctoria	Shrub	4-7/8	I-T	Su, F	D	S-M	FS, LS	*Ac*, N, Al	DT	–
Geranium alpinum	Herbaceous	7-10	S	Sp, Su, F	E	S	FS, LS	Ac, N, Al	–	–
Geranium 'Ann Folkard'	Herbaceous	5-8	I	Su, F	D	S-M	FS, LS	Ac, N, *Al*	–	–
Geranium asphodeloides	Herbaceous	6-?	I	Su	S	S-M	FS, LS	Ac, N, *Al*	–	–
Geranium × *cantabrigiense*	Herbaceous	5-10	I	Sp, Su	S	S-M	FS, LS	Ac, N, *Al*	–	–
Geranium cinereum	Herbaceous	5-7	S	Su	D	S	FS, LS	Ac, N, *Al*	–	CE
Geranium clarkei	Herbaceous	5-8	I	Sp, Su	D	S-M	FS, LS	Ac, N, *Al*	–	–
Geranium dalmaticum	Herbaceous	4-8	S	Su	E	S	FS, LS	Ac, N, *Al*	–	–
Geranium endressii	Herbaceous	4/6-8	I	Su	D	S	FS, LS	Ac, N, *Al*	–	CE
Geranium himalayense	Herbaceous	4-8	I	Su	D	S	FS, LS	Ac, N, *Al*	–	CE
Geranium incanum	Herbaceous	9-10	I	Sp, Su, F	S	S	FS, LS	Ac, N, *Al*	–	CE
Geranium 'Johnson's Blue'	Herbaceous	4/5-8	I	Su, F	D	S-M	FS, LS	Ac, N, *Al*	–	–
Geranium macrorrhizum	Herbaceous	3-8	I	Su	D	S-L	FS, LS	Ac, N, *Al*	–	CE
Geranium maculatum	Herbaceous	3-8	I	Sp, Su	D	S	FS, LS	Ac, N, *Al*	–	CE
Geranium × *oxonianum*	Herbaceous	5-8	I	Su	E	M-L	FS, LS	Ac, N, *Al*	–	–
Geranium procurrens	Herbaceous	6/7	I	Su, F	D	M-L	FS, LS	Ac, N, *Al*	–	–
Geranium pylzowianum	Herbaceous	7-?	I	Su	D	S	FS, LS	Ac, N, *Al*	–	CE
Geranium sanguineum	Herbaceous	4-8	I	Sp, Su	D	S-M	FS, LS	Ac, N, *Al*	–	CE
Geranium wallichianum	Herbaceous	6-?	S	Su	D	S	FS, LS	Ac, N, *Al*	–	CE
Glyceria maxima	Grass	5-8	T	Su	D	S-L	FS, LS	Ac, N	MT	–
Grevillea aquifolium	Shrub	8/9-10/11	T	Sp, Su	E	M-L	FS, LS	Ac, N	*DT*	CE
Grevillea 'Australflora Canterbury Gold'	Shrub	9-10/11	T	Su	E	L	FS, LS	Ac, N	*DT*	CE
Grevillea australis	Shrub	8/9-10/11	T	Su	E	M	FS, LS	Ac, N	*DT*	CE
Grevillea banksii	Shrub	9-10/11	S	Su	E	M-L	FS, LS	Ac, N	*DT*	CE
Grevillea biternata	Shrub	8/9-10/11	T	W, Sp	E	M-L	FS, LS	Ac, N	*DT*	CE
Grevillea brachystachya	Shrub	9-10/11	T	W, Sp	E	M-L	FS, LS	Ac, N	*DT*	CE
Grevillea confertifolia	Shrub	9-10/11	T	Sp	E	M-L	FS, LS	Ac, N	*DT*	CE
Grevillea × *gaudichaudii*	Shrub	8/9-10/11	S	Sp, Su, F	E	L	FS, LS	Ac, N	*DT*	CE
Grevillea juniperina	Shrub	9-10/11	S	W, Sp	E	M-L	FS, LS	Ac, N	*DT*	CE
Grevillea lanigera	Shrub	9-10/11	T	W, Sp, Su	E	L	FS, LS	Ac, N	*DT*	CE
Grevillea obtusifolia	Shrub	8/9-10/11	S	W, Sp, Su	E	L	FS, LS	Ac, N	*DT*	CE
Grevillea paniculata	Shrub	8/9-10/11	T	W, Sp	E	L	FS, LS	Ac, N	*DT*	CE
Grevillea 'Poorinda Royal Mantle'	Shrub	9-10/11	S	W, Sp, Su	E	L	FS, LS	Ac, N,	*DT*	CE
Grevillea pteridifolia	Shrub	8/9-10/11	I	F, W, Sp	E	M-L	FS, LS	Ac, N	*DT*	CE
Grevillea repens	Shrub	8/9-10/11	S	Su	E	M-L	FS, LS	Ac, N	*DT*	CE
Grevillea rosmarinifolia	Shrub	9-10/11	I-T	W, Sp	E	M	FS, LS	Ac, N	*DT*	CE
Grevillea thelemanniana	Shrub	9-10/11	S-I	F, W	E	M-L	FS, LS	Ac, N	*DT*	CE
Grevillea 'White Wings'	Shrub	9-10/11	T	W, Sp	E	L	FS, LS	Ac, N	*DT*	CE
Gunnera dentata	Herbaceous	8-10/11	I	–	D	M-L	FS, LS, MS	Ac	MT	–
Gunnera hamiltonii	Herbaceous	8-10/11	I	–	D	M	FS, LS, MS	Ac	MT	–

Name of ground cover	Plant type	Hardi-ness	Height	Bloom season	Foliage	Scale of planting	Light	Soil type	Soil moisture	Other
Gunnera magellanica	Herbaceous	7-10/11	S	Sp	D	M	FS, LS, MS	Ac	MT	–
Gunnera prorepens	Herbaceous	8-10/11	S	Su	D	M	FS, LS, MS	Ac	MT	–
Gunnera manicata	Herbaceous	7-10/11	T	Su	D	L	FS, LS, MS	Ac	MT	–
Gunnera tinctoria	Herbaceous	8-10/11	T	Su	D	L	FS, LS, MS	Ac	MT	–
Gymnocarpium dryopteris	Fern	2-7	I	–	D	S-M	LS, MS, DS	Ac, N, *Al*	MT	–
Gymnocarpium robertianum	Fern	2-6	I	–	D	S-M	LS, MS, DS	*Ac,* N, Al	MT	–
Gypsophila paniculata	Herbaceous	3-9	T	Su, F	D	M	FS	N, Al	*DT*	–
Gypsophila repens	Herbaceous	3-8	S	Su	E	S-M	FS	Ac, N, Al	*DT*	–
Hakonechloa macra	Grass	5-9	I	Su, F	D	S-M	LS, MS	*Ac,* N, *Al*	*DT*	–
Haworthia cuspidata	Succulent	10-11	S	Sp, Su, F	E	S	LS	Ac, N, *Al*	DT	–
Haworthia fasciata	Succulent	10-11	S	Sp, Su, F	E	S	LS	Ac, N, *Al*	DT	–
Haworthia radula	Succulent	10-11	S	?	E	S	LS	Ac, N, *Al*	DT	–
Haworthia tessellata	Succulent	10-11	S	?	E	S	LS	Ac, N, *Al*	DT	–
Hebe chathamica	Shrub	8/9-10	I	Su	E	M	FS, LS	Ac, N, Al	–	–
Hebe decumbens	Shrub	6/7-?	I	Sp	E	M	FS, LS	Ac, N, Al	–	–
Hebe pinguifolia 'Pagei'	Shrub	8/9-10	I	Su	E	M	FS, LS	Ac, N, Al	–	–
Hedera canariensis	Vine	8-9/10	S-I	–	E	M-L	FS, LS, MS, DS	Ac, N, *Al*	–	*FT*, CE
Hedera colchica	Vine	6-9/10	S	–	E	M-L	FS, LS, MS, DS	Ac, N, *Al*	–	*FT*, CE
Hedera helix	Vine	5/6-9	S	–	E	M-L	FS, LS, MS, DS	Ac, N, *Al*	–	*FT*, CE
Hedyotis caerulea	Herbaceous	3/4-?	S	Sp, Su	S	S-M	LS, MS	Ac	MT	–
Hedyotis nummularium	Shrub	5-7	I	Su	E	M	FS	N, Al	DT	–
Helictotrichon sempervirens	Grass	4-8	I	Su	E	S-M	FS, *LS*	*N,* Al	DT	–
Helleborus atrorubens	Herbaceous	5/6-?	I	W	E	S-M	LS, MS	Ac, N, Al	–	–
Helleborus foetidus	Herbaceous	5-9	I	W, Sp	E	S-M	LS, MS	Ac, N, Al	–	–
Helleborus niger	Herbaceous	3-8	I	W	E	S-M	LS, MS	Ac, N, Al	–	–
Helleborus orientalis	Herbaceous	5-9	I	W, Sp	E	S-M	LS, MS	Ac, N, Al	–	–
Helleborus viridis	Herbaceous	4-9	I	W	E	S-M	LS, MS	Ac, N, Al	–	–
Hemerocallis aurantiaca	Lilylike	6-8	T	Su	E	M-L	FS, LS, MS	Ac, N, Al	*DT, MT*	CE
Hemerocallis fulva	Lilylike	2-9	I	Su	D	M	FS, LS, MS	Ac, N, Al	*DT, MT*	CE
Hemerocallis × hybrida	Lilylike	3-8/9	I-T	*Sp, Su, F*	S	M-L	FS, LS, MS	Ac, N, Al	*DT, MT*	CE
Hemerocallis lilioasphodelus	Lilylike	3-?	T	Sp	D	M-L	FS, LS, MS	Ac, N, Al	*DT, MT*	CE
Hemerocallis middendorffii	Lilylike	3-9	I	Sp, Su	D	S-M	FS, LS, MS	Ac, N, Al	*DT, MT*	CE
Herniaria glabra	Herbaceous	5-10	S	Su	E	S-M	FS, LS	Ac, N, Al	–	*FT*
Heuchera americana	Herbaceous	4-?	S	Sp	E	S	LS, MS	Ac	*DT*	–
Heuchera brizoides 'Palace Purple'	Herbaceous	4-9	I	Sp	E	S-M	LS, MS	Ac	*DT*	–
Heuchera pilosissima	Herbaceous	7/8-9	I	Sp	E	S	LS, MS	Ac	*DT*	–
Heuchera sanguinea	Herbaceous	3-9	I	*Sp,* Su, *F*	E	S	FS, LS	Ac, N, *Al*	*DT*	–
Heuchera villosa var. *macrorhiza*	Herbaceous	5-9	I	Sp	E	S-M	FS, LS	Ac	*DT*	–
Heucherella tiarelloides	Herbaceous	5-9	I	Sp, Su	E	S-M	LS, MS	Ac, N	–	–
Holcus mollis 'Albo-variegatus'	Grass	5-9	I	Su	D	S-L	FS, LS	Ac, N	–	*FT*
Hosta decorata	Herbaceous	3-8/9	I	Su	D	M	*FS,* LS, MS, DS	Ac	*MT*	–
Hosta fortunei	Herbaceous	3-8/9	I	Su, F	D	M	*FS,* LS, MS, DS	Ac	*MT*	–
Hosta lancifolia	Herbaceous	3-8/9	I	Su, F	D	M	*FS,* LS, MS, DS	Ac	*MT*	–
Hosta montana	Herbaceous	4-8/9	I	Su	D	M-L	*FS,* LS, MS, DS	Ac	–	CE
Hosta plantaginea	Herbaceous	3-8/9	I	Su	D	S-M	*FS,* LS, MS, DS	Ac	*MT*	–
Hosta sieboldiana	Herbaceous	3-8/9	I	Su	D	M-L	*FS,* LS, MS, DS	Ac	*MT*	–
Hosta undulata	Herbaceous	3-8/9	T	Su	D	M-L	*FS,* LS, MS, DS	Ac	*MT*	–
Hosta ventricosa	Herbaceous	3-8/9	T	Su	D	M-L	*FS,* LS, MS, DS	Ac	*MT*	–
Hosta yingeri	Herbaceous	3-8/9	I	Su	D	M-L	*FS,* LS, MS, DS	Ac	*MT*	–
Houttuynia cordata	Herbaceous	4/5-8	I	Su	S	S-L	FS, LS, MS	Ac, N, Al	–	*FT*
Hudsonia tomentosa	Shrublike	3-?	I	Su	E	S	FS	Ac, N	–	CE
Hudsonia ericoides	Shrublike	3-?	I	Su	E	S	FS	Ac, N	–	CE

Name of ground cover	Plant type	Hardiness	Height	Bloom season	Foliage	Scale of planting	Light	Soil type	Soil moisture	Other
Hydrangea anomala subsp. *petiolaris*	Vine	5-7/8	T	Sp, Su	D	M-L	LS, MS	Ac, N	*DT*	–
Hypericum androsaemum	Shrublike	5-7	T	Su, F	E	M-L	FS, LS	Ac	–	CE
Hypericum buckleyi	Shrublike	6-8	I	Su	D	M-L	FS, LS	Ac	–	–
Hypericum calycinum	Shrublike	6-10	I	Su, F	S	M-L	FS, LS	Ac	–	CE
Hypericum coris	Shrublike	7-?	I	Sp, Su	E	M-L	FS, LS	Ac	–	CE
Hypericum ellipticum	Shrublike	4-?	I	Su	S	M-L	FS, LS	Ac	–	CE
Hypericum olympicum	Shrublike	6-8	I	Su	D	M-L	FS, LS	Ac	–	–
Hypericum patulum	Shrub	6/7-8/9	T	Su	S	L	FS, LS	Ac	–	–
Hypericum reptans	Shrublike	7/8-?	S	Su, F	D	M-L	FS, LS	Ac	–	CE
Iberis gibraltarica	Shrublike	6-9	I	Sp	E	S	FS, LS	Ac, N, *Al*	DT	–
Iberis pruitii	Shrublike	4-?	S	Sp	E	S	FS	Ac, N, *Al*	–	–
Iberis sayana	Shrublike	4-?	S	Sp, F	E	S	FS	Ac, N, *Al*	–	–
Iberis saxatilis	Shrublike	3-7	S	Sp	E	S-M	FS, LS	Ac, N, *Al*	DT	–
Iberis sempervirens	Shrublike	5-7	I	Sp	E	S-M	FS, LS	Ac, N, *Al*	DT	–
Ilex cornuta	Shrub	7-9	T	Sp	E	M	FS, LS	Ac	*DT*	–
Ilex crenata	Shrub	6-9	T	Sp, Su	E	M	FS, LS	Ac	*DT*	–
Ilex × vomitoria	Shrub	7-10	T	Sp	E	M	FS, LS	Ac	*DT*	–
Imperata cylindrica 'Red Baron'	Grass	5-10	I	Su	D	S-L	FS, LS	Ac, *N, Al*	*DT*	CE
Indigofera incarnata	Shrub	5-?	I	Su	S	L	FS	Ac, N, *Al*	–	CE
Indigofera kirilowii	Shrub	5-7	T	Su	S	L	FS	Ac, N, *Al*	–	CE
Iris cristata	Herbaceous	3-9	S	Sp	D	S-M	FS, LS, MS	Ac, N, *Al*	*MT*	CE
Iris ensata	Herbaceous	5-10	T	Su	D	S-L	FS, LS	Ac	*MT*	CE
Iris pseudacorus	Herbaceous	5-9	T	Sp, Su	D	M-L	FS, LS, MS	Ac, N, *Al*	*MT*	CE
Iris pumila	Herbaceous	4-10	S	Sp	D	S-M	FS, LS, MS	Ac, N, *Al*	*MT*	CE
Iris setosa	Herbaceous	4-9	I	Su	D	S-M	FS, LS	Ac	–	–
Iris tectorum	Herbaceous	5-9	I	–	D	S-M	FS, LS, MS	Ac, N, *Al*	*MT*	CE
Iris versicolor	Herbaceous	3-9	T	Su	D	M-L	FS, LS, MS	Ac, N, Al	*MT*	CE
Itea virginica 'Henry's Garnet'	Shrub	5-9	T	Sp, Su	S	M-L	FS, LS, MS	Ac, N	*MT*	CE
Jasminum floridum	Shrub	7-9	T	Su	S	L	FS, LS, MS	Ac	*DT*	CE
Jasminum mesnyi	Vinelike	8-10/11	T	Sp	E	L	FS, LS, MS	Ac	*DT*	–
Jasminum nudiflorum	Vinelike	6-9	T	Sp	D	L	FS, LS, MS	Ac	*DT*	CE
Jeffersonia diphylla	Herbaceous	5-?	I	Sp	D	S	LS, MS	Ac, N	–	–
Jovibarba arenaria	Succulent	5/6-8	S	Su	E	S	FS, LS	Ac, N, *Al*	DT	FR
Jovibarba heuffelii	Succulent	5/6-8	S	Su	E	S	FS, LS	Ac, N, *Al*	DT	FR
Jovibarba hirta	Succulent	5/6-8	S	Su	E	S	FS, LS	Ac, N, *Al*	DT	FR
Jovibarba sobolifera	Succulent	5/6-8	S	Su	E	S	FS, LS	Ac, N, *Al*	DT	FR
Juniperus chinensis cultivars	Shrub	4-9	I-T	W, Sp	E	M-L	FS	Ac, N	DT	CE
Juniperus communis cultivars	Shrub	2-6	S-I	–	E	M-L	FS	Ac, N	DT	CE, ST
Juniperus conferta	Shrub	6-8	I	–	E	M-L	FS	Ac, N, *Al*	DT	CE, ST
Juniperus × davurica	Shrub	5-9	T	–	E	L	FS	Ac, N	DT	CE
Juniperus horizontalis	Shrub	2-9	S-I	–	E	M-L	FS	Ac	DT	CE, ST
Juniperus procumbens	Shrub	5-9	S-I	–	E	S-M	FS	Ac	DT	CE
Juniperus sabina	Shrub	3-8	I-T	–	E	M-L	FS	Ac, N, *Al*	DT	CE
Juniperus scopulorum cultivars	Shrub	3-6/7	I	–	E	M	FS	Ac, N	DT	CE
Juniperus squamata cultivars	Shrub	4-8	I	–	E	M	FS	Ac, N	DT	CE
Juniperus virginiana cultivars	Shrub	3-9	I	Sp	E	M	FS	Ac, N, *Al*	DT	CE, ST
Kalanchoe blossfeldiana	Succulent	10-11	I	W, Sp	E	S-M	FS	Ac	*DT*	–
Kalanchoe fedtschenkoi	Succulent	10-11	I	W	E	S-M	FS	Ac	*DT*	–
Kalanchoe laciniata	Succulent	10-11	I	?	E	S-M	FS	Ac	*DT*	–
Kalanchoe marmorata	Succulent	10-11	?	?	E	S-M	FS	Ac	*DT*	–
Kalanchoe tomentosa	Succulent	10-11	I-T	?	E	S-M	FS	Ac	*DT*	–
Kalanchoe tubiflora	Succulent	10-11	I	?	E	S-M	FS	Ac	*DT*	–

Name of ground cover	Plant type	Hardi-ness	Height	Bloom season	Foliage	Scale of planting	Light	Soil type	Soil moisture	Other
Lamiastrum galeobdolon	Herbaceous	4-9	I	Sp	E	M-L	FS, LS, MS	Ac, N, ?Al	*MT*	CE
Lamium maculatum	Herbaceous	3-8	S-I	Sp	E	S	FS, LS, MS	Ac, N, ?Al	–	–
Lampranthus aurantiacus	Succulent	9-11	I	Sp	E	M-L	FS	Ac, N, Al	DT	CE, FR
Lampranthus filicaulis	Succulent	9-11	S	Sp	E	S	FS	Ac, Al	DT	CE, FR
Lampranthus productus	Succulent	9-11	I	W, Sp	E	M-L	FS	Ac, N, Al	DT	CE, FR
Lampranthus spectabilis	Succulent	9-11	I	Sp	E	M-L	FS	Ac, N, Al	DT	CE, FR
Lantana × hybrida	Shrub	9-11	I-T	Sp, *Su, F, W*	E	M-L	FS, LS	Ac, N, Al	DT	CE
Lantana montevidensis	Shrub	9-11	T	Sp, *Su, F, W*	E	M-L	FS, LS	Ac, N, Al	DT	CE
Lathyrus latifolius	Herbaceous	4-9	I	Su, F	D	M-L	FS, LS	Ac, N, *Al*	DT	CE
Lavandula angustifolia subsp. angustifolia	Herbaceous	5-9	I-T	Su	S	S-M	FS	Ac	*DT*	–
Lavandula latifolia	Herbaceous	6-?	I	Su	S	S-M	FS	Ac	*DT*	–
Lavandula stoechas	Herbaceous	6-?	T	Su	S	S-M	FS	Ac	*DT*	–
Ledum decumbens	Shrub	3-6/7	I	Su	E	M	FS, LS	Ac	MT	–
Ledum groenlandicum	Shrub	3-6/7	I-T	Sp	E	M-L	FS, LS	Ac	MT	–
Leiophyllum buxifolium	Shrublike	5-8	I	Sp, *Su*	E	M	FS	Ac	*DT*	–
Leucanthemum vulgare	Herbaceous	3-10	I	Su, F	D	S-M	FS, LS	Ac, N	–	–
Leucothoe axillaris	Shrublike	5/6-9	T	Sp	E	M-L	LS, MS, DS	Ac	*DT*	CE
Leucothoe fontanesiana	Shrublike	4-6	T	Sp	E	M-L	LS, MS, DS	Ac	*DT*	CE
Leucothoe 'Scarletta'	Shrublike	4-7/8	I	Sp	E	M-L	LS, MS, DS	Ac	*DT*	CE
Leymus arenarius	Grass	3/4-9	T	Su	E	M-L	FS	Ac, N, Al	DT	CE
Leymus mollis	Grass	7-10	T	Su	D	L	FS	–	DT	CE
Leymus racemosus 'Glaucus'	Grass	4-10	T	Su	D	L	FS	–	DT	CE
Leymus tritichoides	Grass	4-10	T	Su	D	L	FS	–	DT	CE
Ligularia dentata	Herbaceous	5-8	T	Su	D	M-L	MS, DS	Ac	–	–
Ligularia stenocephala	Herbaceous	5-8	T	Su	D	M-L	MS, DS	Ac	–	–
Ligularia tussilaginea	Herbaceous	6-9/10	I	Su	D	M-L	MS, DS	Ac	–	–
Linnaea borealis	Shrublike	3-6/7	S	Su	E	S-M	LS, MS	Ac	–	*FT*
Liriope exiliflora	Lilylike	5-?	I	Sp	E	M	FS, LS, MS	Ac	DT	–
Liriope muscari	Lilylike	6/7-9	I	Su	E	S-L	FS, LS, MS	Ac	DT	–
Liriope spicata	Lilylike	4-9/10	I	Su	E	S-L	FS, LS, MS	Ac	DT	–
Lithodora diffusa	Shrub	6-8	I	Sp, Su	E	S	LS, MS	Ac	–	–
Lonicera × brownii	Vine	3-9	I	Sp, Su	D	M-L	FS, LS	Ac, N, *Al*	*DT*	CE
Lonicera caprifolium	Vine	5-?	I	Su, F	D	M-L	FS, LS	Ac, N, *Al*	*DT*	CE
Lonicera flava	Vine	5-9	I	Sp, Su	D	M-L	FS, LS	Ac, N, *Al*	*DT*	–
Lonicera × heckrottii	Vine	5-9	I	Sp, Su, F	S	M-L	FS, LS	Ac, N, *Al*	*DT*	–
Lonicera henryi	Vine	4-?	I	Su	E	M-L	FS, LS	Ac, N, *Al*	–	CE
Lonicera japonica	Vine	5-9	I	Su	S	M-L	FS, LS	Ac, N, *Al*	DT	ST
Lonicera pileata	Shrub	7-9	I	Sp	S	S-L	FS, LS	Ac, N, *Al*	DT	–
Lonicera sempervirens	Vine	4-9	I	Su	E	M-L	FS, LS	Ac, N, *Al*	–	CE
Lonicera xylosteum 'Nana'	Shrub	3-8	T	Sp	D	M-L	FS, LS	Ac, N, *Al*	DT	–
Lotus berthelotii	Herbaceous	10-11	I	Su	E	L	FS	Ac, N, Al	*DT*	CE
Lotus corniculatus	Herbaceous	5-10	I	Su	D	M-L	FS	Ac, N, Al	*DT*	CE
Lotus pinnatus	Herbaceous	8-?	S	Su	D	M	FS	Ac, N, Al	*DT*	CE
Luzula luzuloides	Sedge	5-9	I	Sp	S	M-L	LS, MS	Ac, N, Al	–	*FT*
Luzula nivea	Sedge	5-9	I	Sp	S	M-L	LS, MS	Ac, N, Al	–	*FT*
Luzula sylvatica	Sedge	4-9	I	Sp	S	M-L	LS, MS	Ac, N, Al	–	*FT*
Lycopodium clavatum	Fernlike	1-8	S	–	E	M-L	LS, MS	Ac, N, *Al*	–	–
Lycopodium complanatum	Fernlike	1-8/9	I	–	E	M-L	LS, MS	Ac, N, *Al*	–	–
Lycopodium obscurum	Fernlike	1-7/8	I	–	E	M-L	LS, MS	Ac, N, *Al*	–	–
Lycopodium tristachyum	Fernlike	1-8/9	I	–	E	M-L	LS, MS	Ac, N, *Al*	–	–
Lysimachia clethroides	Herbaceous	3-9	I	Su	D	M-L	FS, LS	Ac, N, Al	MT	CE
Lysimachia congestiflora	Herbaceous	6-?	S	Su, *F*	E	S-M	FS, LS, MS	Ac, N, Al	–	*FT*
Lysimachia japonica	Herbaceous	5-?	S	Su, *F*	E	S-M	FS, LS, MS	Ac, N, Al	–	*FT*
Lysimachia nummularia	Herbaceous	4-9	S	Su, *F*	E	S	FS, LS, MS	Ac, N, Al	*MT*	*FT*
Mahonia aquifolium	Shrublike	4/5-8	T	Sp	E	M-L	FS, LS	Ac	–	–
Mahonia nervosa	Shrublike	6-9	I	Sp	E	S-M	FS, LS	Ac	–	–

Name of ground cover	Plant type	Hardi-ness	Height	Bloom season	Foliage	Scale of planting	Light	Soil type	Soil moisture	Other
Mahonia repens	Shrublike	5-9	S-I	Sp, Su	S	S-M	FS, LS	Ac, N, *Al*	–	–
Maranta leuconeura	Herbaceous	10-11	I	?	E	M-L	LS, MS	Ac	–	–
Matteuccia struthiopteris	Fern	2-8	T	–	D	L	LS, MS	*Ac,* N, *Al*	–	–
Mazus japonica 'Alba'	Herbaceous	7-?	S	Su	S	S	FS, LS, MS, DS	Ac, N, *Al*	–	*FT*
Mazus pumilio	Herbaceous	7-?	S	Su	D	S	FS, LS, MS	Ac, N, *Al*	–	FT
Mazus reptans	Herbaceous	4-9	S	Sp	S	S	FS, LS, MS	Ac, N, *Al*	–	*FT*
Melampodium cinerium	Herbaceous	?	I	Sp, Su, *F, W*	D	S	FS, LS	?	DT	–
Melampodium leucanthum	Herbaceous	4-9	I	Sp, Su, *F, W*	D	S	FS, LS	?	–	–
Melissa officinalis	Herbaceous	5-?	I	Su	D	S	FS	Ac, N, Al	–	–
Menispermum canadense	Vine	5-8	I	Su	D	M-L	FS, LS, MS	Ac	*DT*	*FT,* CE
Menispermum dauricum	Vine	5-8	I	Su	D	M-L	FS, LS, MS	Ac	*DT*	*FT,* CE
Mentha × gentilis 'Emerald-N-Gold'	Herbaceous	4/5-10	I	Su	D	S	FS, LS	Ac, N, Al	MT	CE
Mentha × piperita	Herbaceous	4-?	I	Su	D	M	FS, LS	Ac, N, Al	MT	CE
Mentha pulegium	Herbaceous	7-?	S	Su	D	S	FS, LS	Ac, N, Al	MT	*FT*
Mentha requienii	Herbaceous	6-10	S	Su	D	S	FS, LS	Ac, N, Al	MT	*FT*
Mentha spicata	Herbaceous	4-?	I	Su	D	M	FS, LS	Ac, N, Al	MT	–
Microbiota decussata	Shrub	2-8	I	?	E	M-L	FS, LS	Ac, N, ?Al	*DT*	–
Miscanthus sinensis dwarf cultivars	Grass	5-9	T	F	D	M-L	FS	Ac, N	DT, *MT*	CE
Mitchella repens	Herblike	4-8/9	S	Su	E	S-M	LS, MS	Ac	–	*FT*
Muehlenbeckia axillaris	Vine	7-10	S-I	F	E	M-L	FS, LS	Ac, N, *Al*	DT	ST
Muehlenbeckia complexa	Vine	7-10	S-I	F	E	L	FS, LS	Ac, N, *Al*	DT	–
Myoporum debile	Shrub	9-10/11	I	Su	E	M-L	FS	Ac, N	DT	CE, FR
Myoporum parvifolium	Shrub	9-10/11	S	Su	E	M-L	FS	Ac, N	DT	CE, FR
Myosotis scorpioides	Herbaceous	5-9	S	Sp, Su	D	M	FS, LS, MS	Ac, N	MT	–
Nandina domestica	Shrub	7-9	T	Su	E	M-L	FS, LS, MS	Ac	*DT*	–
Nepeta × faassenii	Herbaceous	3-8	I	Su	E	S-M	FS	Ac, N, Al	DT	–
Nepeta mussinii	Herbaceous	3-8	I	Sp	E	S-M	FS	Ac, N, Al	DT	–
Nephrolepis exaltata	Fern	10-11	T	–	E	M-L	LS, MS	Ac	–	–
Nierembergia hippo-manica var. *violacea*	Herbaceous	7/8-10	I	Su	E	S	FS	Ac, N, Al	–	–
Nierembergia repens	Herbaceous	7/8-10	S	Su	E	S	FS	Ac, N, Al	–	–
Oenothera berlandieri	Herbaceous	8-9	I	Sp	E	S	FS, LS	Ac, N, *Al*	DT	–
Oenothera drummondii	Herbaceous	8-9	S	Sp, *Su*	E	S	FS, LS	Ac, N, *Al*	DT	–
Oenothera fruticosa	Herbaceous	4-7/8	I-T	Sp, Su	E	M-L	FS, LS	Ac, N, *Al*	DT	–
Oenothera missouriensis	Herbaceous	4-8	I	Sp, Su	E	S-M	FS, LS	Ac, N, *Al*	DT	–
Oenothera tetragona	Herbaceous	4-?	I	Su	E	S-M	FS, LS	Ac, N, *Al*	DT	–
Omphalodes verna	Herbaceous	6-9	I	Sp	S	S-M	MS	Ac, N, Al	–	–
Onoclea sensibilis	Fern	3-?	I	–	D	M-L	FS, LS, MS	Ac	DT, MT	CE
Ophiopogon clarkei	Lilylike	6-?	I	Su	E	S	LS, MS	Ac, N, Al	–	FT
Ophiopogon jaburan	Lilylike	7-8	T	Su	E	M-L	LS, MS	Ac, N, Al	–	–
Ophiopogon japonica	Lilylike	7-9	I	Su	E	S-L	FS, LS, MS	Ac, N, Al	–	FT
Ophiopogon planiscapus 'Nigrescens'	Lilylike	5/6-10	I	Su	E	S-L	FS, LS, MS	Ac, N, Al	–	*FT*
Opuntia erinacea var. *ursina*	Cactus	5-9/10	I	Su	D	M-L	FS	Ac, N, Al	DT	CE, FR
Opuntia humifusa	Cactus	5-9/10	S	Su	D	S-L	FS	N, Al	DT	*CE,* FR
Opuntia juniperina	Cactus	5-9/10	S	?	D	M	FS	Ac, N, Al	DT	CE, FR
Opuntia macrorhiza	Cactus	5-9/10	S	?	D	M	FS	Ac, N, Al	DT	CE, FR
Opuntia phaeacantha	Cactus	5-9/10	S	?	D	M	FS	Ac, N, Al	DT	CE, FR
Origanum dictamnus	Herbaceous	8-10	I	Su, F	D	S-M	FS	Ac, N, Al	*DT*	–
Origanum vulgare 'Compacta Nana'	Herbaceous	4/5-?	S	Su	D	S	FS	Ac, N, Al	*DT*	–
Origanum laevigatum	Herbaceous	6-?	I	Su, F	D	S-M	FS	Ac, N, Al	*DT*	–
Orostachys aggregatum	Succulent	6-?	S	F	E	S	FS	*Ac,* N	DT	–
Orostachys iwarenge	Succulent	6-?	S	F	E	S	FS	*Ac,* N	DT	–
Osmunda cinnamomea	Fern	3-9/10	T	–	D	S-M	LS, MS	Ac	MT	–
Osmunda claytoniana	Fern	3-?	T	–	D	S-M	LS, MS	Ac	MT	–
Osmunda regalis	Fern	2/3-9	T	–	D	S-M	LS, MS	Ac	MT	–

Name of ground cover	Plant type	Hardiness	Height	Bloom season	Foliage	Scale of planting	Light	Soil type	Soil moisture	Other
Osteospermum fruticosum	Succulent	9-10/11	I	Sp, *Su*, F, *W*	E	M-L	FS	Ac, Al	DT	FR
Oxalis oregana	Herbaceous	7-10	I	Sp, *F*	D	S-L	MS, DS	Ac	–	–
Oxalis regnelii	Herbaceous	7-10	M	Sp, Su	D	S-M	MS	Ac	–	–
Pachysandra axillaris	Shrublike	5-7	I	Sp	E	M-L	LS, MS, DS	Ac, N	–	–
Pachysandra procumbens	Shrublike	5-7/8	I	Sp	S	M-L	LS, MS, DS	Ac, N	–	–
Pachysandra terminalis	Shrublike	5-7/8	I	Sp	E	M-L	LS, MS, DS	Ac, N	–	CE
Panicum virgatum	Grass	5-11	T	Su, F	D	M-L	FS, LS	Ac, N, *Al*	DT	CE, ST
Parthenocissus henryana	Vine	8-?	I	Su	D	L	FS, LS	Ac, N	–	*FT,* CE, ST
Parthenocissus quinquefolia	Vine	3-9	S-I	Su	D	L	FS, LS, MS	Ac, N	–	*FT,* CE, ST
Paxistima canbyi	Shrub	4/5-6/7	I	Sp	E	M	FS, LS	Ac	*DT*	–
Paxistima myrsinites	Shrub	5-7	I	Sp	E	M	FS, LS	Ac	*DT*	–
Pelargonium crispum	Herbaceous	9-11	T	Sp, Su, *F, W*	E	S-M	FS, LS	Ac, N, Al	–	–
Pelargonium denticulatum	Herbaceous	9-11	I	Sp, Su, *F, W*	E	S-M	FS, LS	Ac, N, Al	–	–
Pelargonium × fragans	Herbaceous	9-11	I	Sp, Su, *F, W*	E	S-M	FS, LS	Ac, N, Al	–	–
Pelargonium grossularioides	Herbaceous	9-11	I	Sp, Su, *F, W*	E	S-M	FS, LS	Ac, N, Al	–	–
Pelargonium mellissinum	Herbaceous	9-11	I	Sp, Su, *F, W*	E	S-M	FS, LS	Ac, N, Al	–	–
Pelargonium nervosum	Herbaceous	9-11	I	Sp, Su, *F, W*	E	S-M	FS, LS	Ac, N, Al	–	–
Pelargonium odoratissimum	Herbaceous	9-11	I	Sp, Su, *F, W*	E	S-M	FS, LS	Ac, N, Al	–	–
Pelargonium peltatum	Herbaceous	9-11	I	Sp, Su, *F, W*	E	S-M	FS, LS	Ac, N, Al	–	–
Pelargonium tomentosum	Herbaceous	9-11	T	Sp, Su, *F, W*	E	S-M	FS, LS	Ac, N, Al	–	–
Peltiphyllum peltatum	Herbaceous	5-7	T	Sp	D	M-L	FS, LS, MS	Ac, N, Al	MT	–
Pennisetum alopecuroides	Grass	5-9	T	Su, F	D	M-L	FS, LS	Ac	DT	–
Pennisetum caudatum	Grass	6-9	T	Su	D	M-L	FS	Ac	DT	–
Pennisetum incomptum	Grass	6-9	T	Sp	D	M-L	FS	Ac	DT	–
Pennisetum orientale	Grass	7-9	T	F	D	M-L	FS, LS	Ac	DT	–
Pennisetum setaceum	Grass	7-10	T	F	D	S-M	FS, LS	Ac	DT	–
Penstemon pinifolius	Shrublike	2/3-9/10	I	Su	S	M	FS	Ac, *N*	DT	–
Peperomia argyreia	Herbaceous	10-11	I	?	E	M-L	LS, MS	*Ac,* N	–	–
Peperomia obtusifolia	Herbaceous	10-11	I	?	E	M-L	LS, MS	*Ac,* N	–	–
Pernettya mucronata	Shrub	6/7-?	T	Sp, Su	E	M	FS, *LS*	Ac	–	–
Pernettya tasmanica	Shrub	7-?	S-I	Su	E	S-M	FS, *LS*	Ac	–	–
Perovskia abrotanoides	Semiwoody	5-?	T	Su	D	M-L	FS	Ac, N	DT	–
Perovskia atriplicifolia	Semiwoody	5-9	T	Su, F	D	M-L	FS	Ac, N	DT	–
Persicaria affine	Herbaceous	3-7	S	F	S	S-M	FS, LS	Ac, N, *Al*	–	*FT*
Persicaria bistortum	Herbaceous	4-8	M	Sp, Su	S	M-L	FS, LS	Ac, N, *Al*	–	–
Persicaria capitatum	Herbaceous	7-10	S	Sp	S	S-M	FS, LS	Ac, N, *Al*	–	*FT*
Persicaria filiformis	Herbaceous	4-7/8	M	Su, F	D	M-L	LS, MS	Ac, N, Al	MT	–
Petasites albus	Herbaceous	5-?	I	W, Sp	D	L	LS, MS	Ac, N, Al	MT	*FT*
Petasites fragans	Herbaceous	7-?	I	W, Sp	S	L	LS, MS	Ac, N, Al	MT	*FT*
Petasites × hybridus	Herbaceous	4-8	T	Su	D	L	LS, MS	Ac, N, Al	MT	*FT*
Petasites japonicus	Herbaceous	4-9	T	*F,* W, Sp	D	L	LS, MS	Ac, N, Al	MT	*FT*
Phalaris arundinacea var. *picta*	Grass	3-?	T	Su	D	M-L	FS, LS, MS	Ac, N, Al	DT, MT	*FT,* CE
Phlox divaricata	Herbaceous	3-?	I	Sp, Su	D	S-M	FS, LS, MS	Ac, N	–	–
Phlox × frondosa	Herbaceous	3-?	S	?	D	S	FS, LS	Ac, N	–	–
Phlox nivalis	Herbaceous	6-9	I	Su	D	S	FS, LS	Ac, N	–	–
Phlox procumbens	Herbaceous	5-?	S	Sp	D	M	FS, LS	Ac, N	–	–
Phlox stolonifera	Herbaceous	3-?	S	Sp	E	M	LS, MS	Ac, N	–	–
Phlox subulata	Herbaceous	3-9	S-I	Sp	E	S-M	FS	Ac, N, Al	–	*FT*
Phyla nodiflora	Herbaceous	9-10	S	Sp, Su, F	E	M-L	FS, LS, MS	Ac	DT	FT
Picea abies cultivars	M. tree	2-7	I	Sp	E	S-L	FS	Ac	DT	–
Picea pungens cultivars	M. tree	2-7	I	–	E	S-L	FS	Ac	DT	–
Pilea cadierei	Herbaceous	10-11	I	Su	E	S-M	LS, MS	Ac, N, Al	*DT*	–

Name of ground cover	Plant type	Hardi-ness	Height	Bloom season	Foliage	Scale of planting	Light	Soil type	Soil moisture	Other
Pilea depressa	Herbaceous	10-11	I	Su	E	S	LS, MS	Ac, N, Al	*DT*	–
Pilea nummularifolia	Herbaceous	10-11	I	Su	E	S	LS, MS	AC, N, Al	*DT*	–
Pinus banksiana cultivars	M. tree	2-6/7	I	Sp, Su	E	S-L	FS, LS	Ac	*DT*	–
Pinus densiflora cultivars	M. tree	3/4-7	I	?	E	S-L	FS, LS	Ac	*DT*	–
Pinus flexilis cultivars	M. tree	4-7	I	?	E	S-L	FS, LS	Ac	*DT*	–
Pinus mugo cultivars	M. tree	2-7	I-T	?	E	S-L	FS, LS	Ac	*DT*	–
Pinus nigra cultivars	M. tree	4-?	T	Sp, Su	E	S-L	FS, LS	Ac	*DT*	–
Pinus parviflora cultivars	M. tree	5-?	T	?	E	S-L	FS, LS	Ac	*DT*	–
Pinus strobus cultivars	M. tree	3-?	T	Sp, Su	E	S-L	FS, LS	Ac	*DT*	–
Pinus sylvestris cultivars	M. tree	2-8	T	Sp, Su	E	S-L	FS, LS	Ac	*DT*	–
Pittosporum 'Wheeler's Dwarf'	Shrub	8-9	T	Sp	E	S-L	FS, LS	Ac, N, *Al*	*DT*	CE
Pleioblastus auricoma	Bamboo	6-10	I-T	?	D	M-L	FS, LS, MS	Ac, N	*DT*	CE
Pleioblastus humilis	Bamboo	8-?	I	?	D	M-L	FS, LS, MS	Ac, N	*DT*	CE
Pleioblastus pygmaea	Bamboo	5-?	I	?	D	M-L	FS, LS, MS	Ac, N	*DT*	CE
Pleioblastus variegatus	Bamboo	6-?	I-T	?	D	M-L	FS, LS, MS	Ac, N	*DT*	CE
Polemonium boreale	Herbaceous	4-?	I	Su	D	S-M	FS, LS, MS	Ac	–	–
Polemonium caeruleum	Herbaceous	3-7	I	Sp, Su	D	M	FS, LS, MS	Ac	–	–
Polemonium reptans	Herbaceous	3-8/9	I	Sp, Su	E	S-L	FS, LS, MS	Ac	–	–
Polygala chamaebuxus	Herbaceous	6-8	S	W, Sp	D	S	FS, *LS*	Ac, N, Al	–	–
Polygala vayredae	Herbaceous	7-8	S	Sp	D	S	FS, *LS*	Ac, N, Al	–	–
Polygonatum biflorum	Herbaceous	3-9	I-T	Sp	D	M	MS, DS	Ac	DT	–
Polygonatum commutatum	Herbaceous	3-7	T	Su	D	M-L	MS, DS	Ac	DT	–
Polygonatum odoratum	Herbaceous	3-9	I	Sp	D	M	MS, DS	Ac	DT	–
Polypodium aureum	Fern	10-11	T	–	E	M	LS, MS, DS	Ac	*MT*	–
Polypodium virginianum	Fern	3-?	I	–	E	M	LS, MS, DS	Ac	*MT*	–
Polystichum acrostichoides	Fern	4-7	T	–	E	S-L	LS, MS, DS	Ac, N, *Al*	–	–
Polystichum braunii	Fern	4-7	I	–	S	M	LS, MS, DS	Ac, N	*DT*	–
Polystichum lonchitis	Fern	4-?	I	–	E	S-M	LS, MS, DS	Ac, N, *Al*	–	–
Polystichum munitum	Fern	6-9	T	–	E	L	LS, MS, DS	Ac, N	*DT*	–
Polystichum setiferum	Fern	5-8	I-T	–	S	M-L	LS, MS, DS	Ac, N	*DT*	–
Potentilla anserina	Herbaceous	3-7	I	Su	D	M-L	FS	Ac	MT	*FT*, CE
Potentilla atrosanguinea 'Gibson's Scarlet'	Herbaceous	5-8	I	Su	D	M	FS	Ac	MT	*FT*, CE
Potentilla cinerea	Herbaceous	3-9	S	Sp	E	M	FS	Ac	–	CE
Potentilla fruticosa	Shrub	2-8	I-T	Su, F	D	M-L	FS	Ac	DT	–
Potentilla nepalensis	Herbaceous	5-8	I	Su	S	M	FS	Ac	–	–
Potentilla tabernaemontani	Herbaceous	4-9	S	Sp, Su, *F*	S	M	FS, LS	Ac, N, *Al*	–	–
Potentilla × tonguei	Herbaceous	4-9	S-I	Su, F	S	M	FS, LS	Ac, N, *Al*	–	*FT*
Potentilla tridentata	Herbaceous	2-8	S-I	Su	S	S-L	FS, LS	Ac	–	*FT*
Pratia angulata	Herbaceous	7-10	S	Sp, Su	E	S	FS, LS	Ac, N, Al	–	–
Pratia pedunculata	Herbaceous	7/8-10	S	Sp, *Su*	E	S	FS, LS	Ac, N, Al	–	–
Primula auricula	Herbaceous	2/3-8	I	Sp	E	S-M	*FS*, LS, MS	*Ac*, N	–	–
Primula denticulata	Herbaceous	4-8	I	Sp	E	S-M	*FS*, LS, MS	*Ac*, N	–	–
Primula japonica	Herbaceous	5-7	I	Su	E	S-M	*FS*, LS, MS	*Ac*, N	–	–
Primula × polyantha	Herbaceous	3-8	I	Sp	E	S-M	*FS*, LS, MS	*Ac*, N	–	–
Primula veris	Herbaceous	5-9	S	Sp	E	S-M	*FS*, LS, MS	*Ac*, N	–	–
Primula vulgaris	Herbaceous	5-8	I	Sp	E	S-M	*FS*, LS, MS	*Ac*, N	–	–
Prunella grandiflora	Herbaceous	5-9	I	Su	S	S-M	FS, LS, MS	Ac	–	–
Pulmonaria angustifolia	Herbaceous	2-8	I	Su	E	M	MS, DS	Ac, N, Al	–	–
Pulmonaria longifolia	Herbaceous	3-8	I	Sp	E	M	MS, DS	Ac, N, Al	–	–
Pulmonaria mollis	Herbaceous	4-8	I	Sp	E	M	MS, DS	Ac, N, Al	–	–
Pulmonaria officinalis	Herbaceous	4-9	I	Sp	E	M	MS, DS	Ac, N, Al	–	–
Pulmonaria rubra	Herbaceous	4-7	I	W	E	M	MS, DS	Ac, N, Al	–	–
Pulmonaria saccharata	Herbaceous	3-8	I	Sp	E	M	MS, DS	Ac, N, Al	–	–
Pulmonaria villarsae	Herbaceous	4-8	I	Sp	E	M	MS, DS	Ac, N, Al	–	–
Pulsatilla vulgaris	Herbaceous	5-8	I	Sp	D	S-M	FS, LS	Ac	–	–

Name of ground cover	Plant type	Hardiness	Height	Bloom season	Foliage	Scale of planting	Light	Soil type	Soil moisture	Other
Pyracantha coccinea 'Lowboy'	Shrub	5-?	T	Su	S	M	FS	Ac, N	DT	–
Pyracantha koidzumii	Shrub	7/8-10	I-T	Su	S	M-L	FS	Ac, N	DT	–
Pyracantha 'Red Elf	Shrub	7-9	I	Su	S	M-L	FS	Ac, N	DT	–
Pyracantha 'Ruby Mound'	Shrub	7-9	I	Su	S	M-L	FS	Ac, N	DT	–
Pyxidanthera barbulata	Shrublike	6-?	S	Sp	E	S-M	FS, LS	Ac	*DT*	*FT*
Pyxidanthera brevifolia	Shrublike	6-?	S	Sp	E	S-M	FS, LS	Ac	*DT*	*FT*
Ranunculus repens	Herbaceous	4-9	S-I	Sp, Su	D	M-L	FS, LS, MS	Ac, N, Al	MT	–
Raoulia australis	Herbaceous	7-?	S	Su	E	S	FS	Ac, N	–	*FT*
Raoulia glabra	Herbaceous	7-?	S	Su	E	S	FS	Ac, N	–	–
Raoulia subsericea	Herbaceous	7-?	S	Sp	E	S	FS	Ac, N	–	*FT*
Raoulia tenuicaulis	Herbaceous	7-?	S	Su	E	S	FS	Al, N	–	*FT*
Raphiolepis umbellata cultivars	Shrub	8/9-10	T	Sp	E	M-L	FS	Ac, N, *Al*	*DT*	–
Rhododendron hybrids	Shrub	5/6-9	I	Sp	D, S, E	S-M	LS, MS	Ac	–	–
Rhododendron kiusianum	Shrub	7-?	I	Sp	S	S-M	LS, MS	Ac	–	–
Rhododendron l apponicum	Shrub	2/3-?	I	Su	E	S-L	LS, MS	Ac, N, Al	–	–
Rhododendron 'Purple Gem'	Shrub	5-?	I	Sp	E	S-M	LS, MS	Ac	–	–
Rhododendron williamsianum	Shrub	7-?	T	Sp	E	L	LS, MS	Ac	–	–
Rhododendron yakusimanum	Shrub	5/6-?	T	Sp	E	L	LS, MS	Ac	–	–
Rhus aromatica 'Grow Low'	Shrub	3-9	I-T	Sp	D	L	FS, LS	Ac	DT	CE
Rosa blanda	Shrub	3-?	I-T	Su	E	M-L	FS	Ac	DT	CE
Rosa Meidiland cultivars	Shrub	4-9	I-T	Su, F	D	M-L	FS	Ac, N	–	CE
Rosa spinosissima 'Petite Pink Scotch'	Shrub	4-8	T	Su	D	M-L	FS	Ac, N	–	–
Rosa wichuraiana	Shrub	5/6-9	I	Su	S	M-L	FS, LS	Ac, N	–	ST
Rosmarinus officinalis	Shrublike	7-9	I-T	Sp	E	M-L	FS	Ac, N, *Al*	DT	–
Rubus calycinoides 'Emerald Carpet'	Shrub	7-?	S	Su	S	M-L	FS, LS	Ac, N, Al	–	CE
Rudbeckia fulgida	Herbaceous	3-9	T	Su, F	D	M-L	FS	Ac	–	–
Sagina subulata	Herbaceous	5-9/10	S	Su	E	S	FS, LS	Ac, N	–	*FT*
Salix purpurea 'Gracilis'	Shrub	3-7	T	Sp	D	M	FS, LS	*Ac*, N, Al	*DT*	–
Salix repens	Shrub	4-9	T	Sp	D	M-L	FS, LS	*Ac*, N, Al	*DT*	–
Salix rosmarinifolia	Shrub	4-9	T	Sp	D	M-L	FS, LS	*Ac*, N, Al	*DT*	–
Salix tristis	Shrub	2-9	I-T	Sp	D	S	FS, LS	*Ac*, N, Al	*DT*	–
Salix uva-ursi	Shrub	1-5	S	W	D	S	FS, LS	*Ac*, N, Al	*DT*	–
Salix yezoalpina	Shrub	4-8	S	W	D	S-M	FS, LS	*Ac*, N, Al	*DT*	–
Salvia argentea	Herbaceous	5-9	I-T	Su	D	S-M	FS, LS	*Ac*, N, Al	*DT*	–
Salvia officinalis	Herbaceous	6-9	I-T	Sp	E	S-M	FS, LS	*Ac*, N, Al	*DT*	–
Salvia × superba	Herbaceous	4-7	I-T	Su	E	S-M	FS, LS	*Ac*, N, Al	*DT*	–
Sanguinaria canadensis	Herbaceous	3-9	S-I	Sp	D	S-M	LS, MS	Ac	*MT*	–
Santolina chamaecyparissus	Shrublike	7-9	I	Su	E	S-M	FS	?	DT	*FR*
Santolina virens	Shrublike	7-9	I	Sp	E	S-M	FS	?	DT	*FR*
Saponaria ocymoides	Herbaceous	2-7	S-I	Sp, Su, *F*	E	S-M	FS	Ac, N, Al	–	–
Sarcococca hookeriana var. *humilis*	Shrub	7-9	I	F, W	E	M-L	*LS,* MS, DS	Ac	*DT*	–
Sarcococca ruscifolia	Shrub	7-9	T	F	E	L	*LS,* MS, DS	Ac	*DT*	–
Sasa veitchii	Bamboo	8-10	T	?	D	L	FS, LS, MS	Ac, N, *Al*	DT, MT	CE
Satureja douglasii	Herbaceous	5-?	S	Sp, Su	E	S-M	FS, LS	Ac	–	*FT*, CE
Satureja glabella	Herbaceous	6-?	I	Su	E	S-M	FS, LS	Ac	–	*FT*, CE
Saxifraga stolonifera	Herbaceous	7-10	S-I	W, Sp, Su	E	S-M	MS, DS	Ac, N, *Al*	–	–
Saxifraga umbrosa	Herbaceous	6-7	I	W, Sp, Su	E	S-M	MS, DS	Ac, N, *Al*	–	–
Saxifraga × urbium	Herbaceous	6-7	I	W, Sp, Su	E	S-M	MS, DS	Ac, N, *Al*	–	–

Name of ground cover	Plant type	Hardi-ness	Height	Bloom season	Foliage	Scale of planting	Light	Soil type	Soil moisture	Other
Sedum acre	Succulent	3-8	S	Sp	E	S-M	FS	Ac, N, *Al*	DT	FR
Sedum alboroseum	Succulent	4-8	M	F	D	M-L	FS	Ac, *N*, *Al*	DT	FR
Sedum ellacombianum	Succulent	3-9	I	Su	D	M-L	FS	Ac, N, *Al*	DT	CE, FR
Sedum kamtschaticum	Succulent	3-9	S	Su	E	S-M	FS	Ac, N, *Al*	DT	*FT*, CE, FR
Sedum lydium	Succulent	3-6	S	Su	E	S	FS	Ac, N, *Al*	DT	FR
Sedum midden-dorffianum	Succulent	3-9	S	Su	S	S-L	FS	Ac, N, *Al*	DT	CE, FR
Sedum nevii	Succulent	4-?	S	Sp	E	S	LS, MS	Ac, N, *Al*	–	FR
Sedum populifolium	Succulent	3-7	I	Su	D	M	FS	Ac, N, *Al*	DT	FR
Sedum purpureum	Succulent	3-9/10	M	F	D	M-L	FS	Ac, N, *Al*	DT	FR
Sedum reflexum	Succulent	3-?	S-I	Su	E	S-M	FS	Ac, N, *Al*	DT	CE, FR
Sedum rubrotinctum	Succulent	9-10	I	Sp, Su	E	S	FS	Ac, N, *Al*	DT	FR
Sedum spathulifolium	Succulent	5-?	S	Sp	E	S	FS	Ac, N, *Al*	DT	FR
Sedum spectabile	Succulent	3-9	I	F	D	M-L	FS	Ac, N, *Al*	DT	FR
Sedum spurium	Succulent	3-8	S	Su	S	S-M	FS, LS	Ac, N, *Al*	DT	FR
Sedum ternatum	Succulent	3-8	S	Sp, Su	S	S	LS, MS	Ac	DT	FR
Sempervivum arachnoideum	Succulent	4/5-8	S	Su	E	S	FS	Ac, N, Al	DT	FR
Sempervivum calcareum	Succulent	4/5-8	S	Su	E	S	FS	Ac, N, Al	DT	FR
Sempervivum montanum	Succulent	4/5-8	S	Su	E	S	FS	Ac, N, Al	DT	FR
Sempervivum ruthenicum	Succulent	4/5-8	S	Su	E	S	FS	Ac, N, Al	DT	FR
Sempervivum tectorum	Succulent	4/5-8	S	Su	E	S	FS	Ac, N, Al	DT	FR
Shortia galacifolia	Herbaceous	4-8	S	Sp	E	S-M	*FS*, MS, DS	Ac	–	–
Shortia soldanelloides	Herbaceous	6-?	S-I	Sp	E	S-M	*FS*, MS, DS	Ac	–	–
Shortia uniflora	Herbaceous	4-8	S	Sp	E	S-M	*FS*, MS, DS	Ac	–	–
Soleirolia soleirolii	Herbaceous	9-11	S	?	E	S	LS, MS, DS	Ac, N, ?Al	*MT*	*FT*
Sorbus reducta	Shrub	5-?	T	Sp	D	S-L	FS, LS	Ac	–	CE
Spartina pectinata	Grass	4-9	T	Su	D	M-L	FS	Ac, N	*DT*, MT	CE, *ST*
Spiraea × bumalda cultivars	Shrub	3/4-9	M-T	Sp	D	M-L	FS	Ac	*DT*	–
Spiraea japonica	Shrub	5-9	I-T	Su	D	M-L	FS	Ac	–	–
Stachys byzantina	Herbaceous	4-8	S	Su, F	E	S	FS, LS	Ac, N, Al	*DT*	–
Stachys macrantha	Herbaceous	3-8	I	Sp, Su	E	S	FS, LS	Ac, N, Al	*DT*	–
Stephanandra incisa 'Crispa'	Shrub	5-8/9	I-T	Sp, Su	D	M	FS, LS	Ac	–	CE
Stylophorum diphyllum	Herbaceous	4-9	I	Sp, Su	S	M-L	LS, MS	Ac, N, Al	–	–
Symphoricarpos × chenault 'Hancock'	Shrub	4-8	I	Su	D	M-L	FS, LS, MS	Ac, N, Al	–	CE
Symphoricarpos orbiculatus	Shrub	2-7	T	Su	D	L	FS, LS, MS	Ac, N, Al	–	CE
Symphytum grandiflorum	Herbaceous	4-8	I	Sp, Su	S	M-L	FS, LS	Ac, N, Al	DT	–
Tanacetum parthenium	Herbaceous	6-8	I-T	Su	D	M	FS, LS	Ac, N	–	–
Taxus baccata	Shrub	6-7	T	Sp	E	L	FS, LS, MS	Ac, N, Al	DT	–
Taxus canadensis	Shrub	3-6	T	Sp	E	M-L	FS, LS, MS	Ac, N, Al	DT, *MT*	–
Taxus cuspidata cultivars	Shrub	4-7	T	Sp	E	M-L	FS, LS, MS	Ac, N, Al	DT	–
Taxus × media cultivars	Shrub	5-7/8	I	Sp	E	M-L	FS, LS, MS	Ac, N, Al	DT	–
Teucrium chamaedrys	Herbaceous	4-9	I	Su, F	S	M-L	FS, LS	Ac, N, Al	*DT*	–
Thelypteris connectilis	Fern	5-?	I	–	D	S-M	LS, MS	Ac	*MT*	–
Thelypteris hexagonoptera	Fern	5-?	T	–	D	S-M	LS, MS	Ac	*MT*	–
Thelypteris noveboracensis	Fern	2-?	I	–	D	M-L	LS, MS, DS	Ac	*MT*	–
Thymus caespitosa	Herbaceous	5-?	S	Su	E	S-M	FS, LS	Ac, N, *Al*	DT	*FT*
Thymus × citriodorus	Herbaceous	4-10	S-I	Su	E	S-M	FS, LS	Ac, N, *Al*	DT	–
Thymus herba-barona	Herbaceous	5-?	S	Su	E	S	FS, LS	Ac, N, *Al*	DT	–
Thymus praecox	Herbaceous	5-?	S	Su	E	S-M	FS, LS	Ac, N, *Al*	DT	–
Thymus pseudolanuginosus	Herbaceous	4-?	S	Su	E	S	FS, LS	Ac, N, *Al*	DT	*FT*
Thymus serpyllum	Herbaceous	4-?	S	Su	E	S	FS, LS	Ac, N, *Al*	DT	*FT*

Name of ground cover	Plant type	Hardi-ness	Height	Bloom season	Foliage	Scale of planting	Light	Soil type	Soil moisture	Other
Thymus vulgaris	Herbaceous	5-?	I	Su	E	S-M	FS, LS	Ac, N, *Al*	DT	–
Tiarella cordifolia	Herbaceous	3-8	I	Sp	D	S-M	LS, MS, DS	Ac	–	–
Tiarella wherryi	Herbaceous	3-8	I	Su	D	S-M	LS, MS, DS	Ac	–	–
Tolmiea menziesii	Herbaceous	7-10	I	Sp	D	M	MS, DS	Ac, N, *Al*	MT	–
Trachelospermum asiaticum	Vine	8-9	I	Sp, Su	E	M-L	FS, LS, MS	Ac	–	CE
Trachelospermum jasminoides	Vine	9-10/11	I	Sp, Su	E	M-L	FS, LS, MS	Ac	–	CE
Tradescantia albiflora	Herbaceous	8-10	S	Su, F	S	S-M	LS, MS	Ac, N	MT	–
Tradescantia × andersoniana	Herbaceous	4-9	I-T	Sp, Su	D	M-L	FS	*Ac, N, Al*	MT	CE
Tradescantia fluminensis	Herbaceous	8-10	S	Su, F	S	S-M	LS, MS	Ac, N	MT	–
Tradescantia virginiana	Herbaceous	4-9	I-T	Sp, Su	D	M-L	FS	Ac, N, *Al*	MT	CE
Tsuga canadensis cultivars	M. tree	3-7/8	T	Sp	E	S-L	FS, LS, MS	Ac	–	–
Vaccinium angustifolium	Shrub	2-6	I	Sp	D	M	FS, LS	Ac	MT	–
Vaccinium crassifolium	Shrub	7-?	I	Sp	E	M	FS, LS	Ac	–	–
Vaccinium deliciosum	Shrub	4-?	I	Sp	D	M-L	FS, LS	Ac	*DT*	CE
Vaccinium macrocarpon	Shrublike	1-6/7	S	Su	E	S-M	FS, LS	Ac	MT	*FT*
Vaccinium vitis-idea	Shrublike	4-7	I	Sp	E	M	FS, LS	Ac	MT	–
Vancouveria chrysantha	Herbaceous	6-8	I	Sp	S	S-L	MS, DS	Ac	–	–
Vancouveria hexandra	Herbaceous	5-8	I	Sp	D	S-L	MS, DS	Ac	–	–
Vancouveria planipetala	Herbaceous	6-8	I	Sp	E	S-L	MS, DS	Ac	–	–
Verbena bipinnatifida	Herbaceous	4-?	S	Sp, Su, F	D	S-M	FS	*Ac*, N	DT	–
Verbena canadensis	Herbaceous	6-10	S	Sp, Su, *F*	D	S-M	FS	*Ac*, N	DT	–
Verbena peruviana	Herbaceous	8-?	S	Su	E	S-M	FS	Ac, N	DT	–
Verbena tenuisecta	Herbaceous	8/9-10	I	Su, F	E	M-L	FS	Ac, N	DT	–
Veronica chamaedrys	Herbaceous	4-?	I	Sp, Su	S	M-L	FS, LS	Ac	–	–
Veronica incana	Herbaceous	4-?	I	Su	S	M-L	FS, LS	Ac	–	–
Veronica latifolia 'Prostrata'	Herbaceous	4-?	I	Sp, Su	S	M-L	FS, LS	Ac	–	–
Veronica officinalis	Herbaceous	4-?	I	Su	E	M-L	FS, LS	Ac	–	–
Veronica prostrata	Herbaceous	5-8	I	Sp, Su	S	M-L	FS, LS	Ac	–	–
Veronica repens	Herbaceous	5-?	S	Sp, Su	S	S-M	FS, LS	Ac	–	–
Viburnum davidii	Shrub	7-9	T	Su	E	M-L	FS, LS, MS	Ac	–	–
Vinca difformis	Vinelike	7/8-10	I	Sp	E	M-L	FS, LS, MS, DS	Ac, N, *Al*	–	CE
Vinca major	Vinelike	6-9	I	Sp, *F*	E	M-L	FS, LS, MS, DS	Ac, N, *Al*	–	*FT,* CE
Vinca minor	Vinelike	4-7/8	S	Sp, *F*	E	S-L	FS, LS, MS, DS	Ac, N, *Al*	–	*FT,* CE
Viola hederacea	Herbaceous	9-10	S	Sp, Su	E	S-L	LS, MS, DS	Ac, N, ?Al	–	–
Viola labradorica	Herbaceous	5-?	S	Su	E	S-L	LS, MS, DS	Ac, N, ?Al	–	–
Viola odorata	Herbaceous	6/7-10	S	Sp, Su	E	S-L	LS, MS, DS	Ac, N, ?Al	–	–
Viola sororia	Herbaceous	4-8	I	Sp	E	S-L	FS, LS	Ac, N, ?Al	–	–
Viola tricolor	Herbaceous	5-?	S-I	Sp	D	S-M	FS, LS	Ac, N, ?Al	–	–
Vitis riparia	Vine	3-7	I	Sp, Su	D	L	FS, LS	Ac, N	*MT*	–
Waldsteinia fragarioides	Herbaceous	4-7	S-I	Sp	E	S-M	FS, MS	Ac, N	*DT*	*FT*
Waldsteinia geoides	Herbaceous	5-?	S	Sp	E	S-M	LS, MS	Ac, N	*DT*	*FT*
Waldsteinia ternata	Herbaceous	4-?	S	Sp, Su	E	S-M	FS, MS	Ac, N	*DT*	*FT*
Woodwardia areolata	Fern	4-9	I-T	–	D	M-L	LS, MS	Ac, N	MT	–
Woodwardia virginica	Fern	3-10	I-T	–	D	M-L	LS, MS	Ac, N	MT	–
Xanthorhiza simplicissima	Shrublike	4-9	I-T	Sp	D	M-L	FS, LS, MS, DS	Ac	DT	–
Zauschneria californica	Herblike	7/8-9	I	Su, F	D	M-L	FS	Ac, N	DT	–
Zoysia tenuifolia	Grass	9-10	S-I	?	E	S-M	FS, LS	Ac, N, Al	DT	FT

GROUND COVERS
UNDER WALNUT TREES

Many ground cover species cannot tolerate planting under or near black walnut (*Juglans nigra*), and to some extent English walnut (*J. regia*), butternut (*J. cinerea*), shagbark hickory (*Carya ovata*), and pecan (*Carya illinoinensis*). This is due to the toxin juglone that is found in the roots, leaves, and bark of such plants. Symptoms of juglone toxicity range from stunting to partial or total wilting or even death.

A handful of species, however, have shown reasonable resistance. Those that are described in this book include the following:

Ajuga reptans
Astilbe species
Begonia species
Forsythia species
Galium odoratum
Geranium sanguineum
Hemerocallis fulva
Hosta fortunei
H. lancifolia
H. undulata 'Variegata'
Juniperus virginiana
Oenothera fruticosa
Onoclea sensibilis
Osmunda cinnamomea
Parthenocissus quinquefolia
Primula × *polyantha*
Pulmonaria species
Sedum spectabile
Tsuga canadensis

GLOSSARY

Alternate. An arrangement, usually in reference to leaves, where they are attached to the stem in staggered fashion, one per node, as opposed to opposite or whorled.

Annual. A plant that completes its life cycle in a single season (i.e., germination, flowering, seed formation, and death).

Anther. The part of the male floral reproductive apparatus that bears the pollen.

Apetalous. Without petals.

Apex. The tip or terminal end of a branch or leaf.

Apomixis. Yielding fruit without fertilization.

Aromatic. With a detectable fragrance.

Axil. The upper angle formed by the junction of a leaf and stem.

Basal. The base (crown) of a plant; often used in reference to plants, such as *Ajuga,* whereby the leaves arise from the crown instead of upon stems.

Bisexual. A plant with both male and female reproductive structures (stamens and pistil) present in a single flower.

Bract. Leafy appendage.

Ciliate. A leaf margin fringed with hairs.

Cladophyll. A leaflike flattened branch.

Cleistogamous. A flower that pollinates itself without opening.

Clone. A plant that is derived (vegetatively) from a single parent plant.

Compact. Having dense arrangement, normally in reference to the branch and leaf arrangement.

Compound leaf. A leaf that is composed of two or more leaflets.

Corolla. The inner whorl (usually of petals) that surrounds a flower.

Crown. The part of the plant near ground level from which new shoots arise.

Cultivar. A plant variety which originated in cultivation.

Cultivated. A plant that is maintained and cared for.

Deltoid. Shaped like a triangle.

Dentate. A leaf margin surrounded by teethlike projections.

Dioecious. A plant that has only male or female flowers.

Disk flowers. The tiny flowers in the center of sunflower-like and daisylike inflorescences.

Double flower. A flower that has double the normal complement of petals.

Downy. Covered with fine hairs.

Dwarf. An atypically small plant when compared to the normal species.

Elliptical. Shaped like an ellipse.

Erect. With upright growth habit.

Evergreen. Having leaves that remain attached throughout the year.

Fertile. Being able to produce seed.

Fleshy. Pulpy or juicy at maturity, usually in reference to leaves or fruit.

Floret. A tiny flower, usually in reference to flowers of plants in the sunflower and grass families.

Foliage. Leaves collectively.

Frond. The leaf of a fern.

Fruit. The structure that comes from the ovary of a flower and encloses the seeds.

Globose. Globe-shaped in outline.

Glossy. Reflecting light, shiny.

Habit. The typical form, shape, and mode of growth that a plant exhibits.

Habitat. The conditions, (climate, soil, light, etc.) under which a plant grows.

Herbaceous. Herblike, not woody.

Hybrid. A plant that arose from cross-pollination of two or more types of plants.

IBA. Indole-3-butyric acid, the most commonly used root-inducing hormone.

Inflorescence. The arrangement of flowers about an axis.

Internode. The section of stem that is between two nodes.

Introduced. A plant that has been moved (imported) from one region or country and planted in a location where it is not indigenous.

Juvenile. The early stage of plant growth, as exemplified by the following traits: nonflowering, hairiness, and fast growth.

Loose. With an open habit of branch arrangement, as opposed to being compact.

Margin. The leaf edge.

Mature. A stage of plant growth characterized by the following traits: flowering, fruit formation, and a slowing of growth rate.

Mossy. Displaying a matted, low habit of growth—resembling that of a moss.

Mutation. Any change in genetic composition.

Needle. A slender, often pointed leaf, like that of a conifer.

Nodding. Drooping or bending over, usually in reference to flowers.

Node. The joint of a stem.

Oblong. Being longer than wide, when one end is wider than the other, usually in reference to leaves or fruits.

Opposite. Leaves that are grouped two per node.

Papillate. With raised dotlike projections.

Peltate. Shield-shaped.

Perennial. Any plant that lives for three or more years.

Persistent. Adhering for an extended period of time, usually in reference to flowers or fruit.

Petal. The single unit of a floral corolla.

Pinnae. Leaflets.

Pinnatifid. Leaves that are deeply cut.

Pod. A fruit that is beanlike in shape.

Procumbent. Trailing along the ground without forming roots as it spreads.

Procurrent. Running forward with extending stems.

Prostrate. Lying flat on the ground, usually in reference to the stems or overall habit of a plant.

Pungent. Sharp smelling or tasting.

Ray. The tiny flowers of a sunflower-like inflorescence that are arranged around the outside of the central disc. Normally they contain petals.

Rhizome. A horizontally spreading underground stem that contains nodes, buds, or scalelike leaves and often sprouts up through the ground and forms a new plant at its tip.

Rhizomatous. A plant that bears rhizomes.

Rosette. A group of leaves that encircles the stem.

Runner. A horizontal growing shoot (stolon) that typically gives rise to a plantlet or plantlets at its tip.

Seed. The structure that arises from a fertilized ovule and contains an embryo and a food supply.

Semievergreen. Having only a portion of the leaves fully held throughout the year—often affected dramatically by winter temperatures.

Sepal. A leaflike part of the whorl of leaves that protect a flower.

Shrub. A woody plant that is generally lower growing than 14 feet and has a tendency to produce many branches.

Silky. Covered with soft fine hairs.

Smooth. Smooth to the touch.

Solitary. Occurring alone.

Sorus. A group of spore-bearing structures (sporangia).

Sori. The plural of the word *sorus*.

Spadix. A fleshy spike of tiny flowers.

Spathe. A hoodlike leaf or bract that encloses the spadix.

Spike. An unbranched, elongate type of inflorescence.

Spore. A simple, asexual, reproductive body (as opposed to an egg), characteristic of primitive plants such as mosses and ferns.

Stamen. The collective male reproductive apparatus that is composed of an anther and filament.

Stolon. A horizontally oriented, above-ground stem (runner) that roots from, or produces plants at, its tip—as in strawberries. See also runner.

Stoloniferous. Bearing stolons.

Subshrub. A woody-based herb.

Suffrutescent. Herbaceous-stemmed.

Texture. The overall effect or impression displayed by a plant, often listed in terms of soft, rough, coarse, or smooth.

Tomentose. Densely hairy.

Toothed. A leaf margin that is surrounded by teethlike projections.

Trailing. Horizontal growing but not rooting as it spreads. See also procumbent.

Tuber. A short, thick, potato-like, underground storage stem.

Tufted. A type of habit whereby the leaves are held tightly together, originate from a single point at the plant's base, then flare outward. Common particularly in grasses and grasslike perennials.

Unisexual flowers. Flowers that are of only one sex.

Variegated. Composed of more than one color.

Venation. The pattern formed by the veins of the leaf or flower.

Vine. A trailing or climbing plant with limp stems that depends on other plants or structures for support.

Weeping. Hanging down in a pendant manner.

Whorl. The floral or leaf arrangement whereby three or more structures originate from a single node.

SELECTED SOURCES
FOR ADDITIONAL READING

The information garnered in writing *Perennial Ground Covers* came not only from my own experience and the experiences recounted to me by countless gardeners and nursery professionals, but also from a careful review of hundreds of books, magazine articles, nursery catalogs, and reference guides. A few of the books that I found most helpful are listed below. I recommend them for further reading as I have found them to be full of useful and fascinating information.

Aden, Paul. 1988. *The Hosta Book.* Timber Press.
Armitage, Allan. 1989. *Herbaceous Perennial Plants.* Varsity Press.
Bath, Trevor, and Joy Jones. 1994. *Hardy Geraniums.* Timber Press.
Clausen, Ruth Rogers, and Nicholas H. Ekstrom. 1989. *Perennial for American Gardens.* Random House.
Dirr, Michael. 1990. *Manual of Woody Landscape Plants.* Stipes Publishing Company.
Greenlee, John. 1992. *The Encyclopedia of Ornamental Grasses.* Rodale Press.
Jelitto, Leo, and Wilhelm Schacht. 1990. *Hardy Herbaceous Perennials.* Timber Press.
Mickel, John. 1994. *Ferns for American Gardens.* Macmillan Publishing Company.
Munson, R. W., Jr. 1989. *Hemerocallis, The Daylily.* Timber Press.
The American Horticultural Society. 1992. *Encyclopedia of Garden Plants.* Macmillan.

INDEX OF PLANT NAMES

Aaron's beard, 190
Abelia, glossy, 53, Plate 1
Abelia × *grandiflora,* 53, Plate 1
    'Francis Mason', 53
    'Prostrata', 53
    'Sherwoodii', 53
Acacia
    fern, 53
    prairie, 35, 53
    trailing, 53, Plate 2
Acacia angustissima var. *hirta,* 35, 53
Acacia redolens, 53, Plate 2
Acaena adscendens, 54
Acaena buchananii, 54
Acaena caesiiglauca, 54, Plate 3
Acaena inermis, 54
Acaena microphylla, 54
    'Copper Carpet', see
        'Kupferteppich'
    'Kupferteppich', 54
Acaena novae-zelandiae, 54
Acaena sanguisorbae, 54
Acanthus, artist's, 54
Acanthus hungaricus, 54
Acanthus mollis, 54, Plate 4
    'Latifolius', 54
    'Oak Leaf', 54
    var. *spinosissimus,* see *A. spinosus*
        var. *spinosissimus*
    'Summer Dream', 54
Acanthus spinosus, 55
    var. *spinosissimus,* 55
Acanthus spinosissimus, see *A. spinosus*
        var. *spinosissimus*
Achillea, 55
Achillea ageratifolia, 55
    var. *aizoon,* 55
Achillea clypeolata 'Gold Plate', 55, 56
    'Moonshine', 56

'Parker's Variety', 56
Achillea filipendulina, 55
    var. *alba,* 55
    'Coronation Gold', 55, Plate 5
Achillea millefolium, 56
    'Cerise Queen', 56
    'Crimson Beauty', 56
    'Fire King', 56
    'Heidi', 56
    'Hoffnung', see 'Hope'
    'Hope', 56
    'Kelwayi', 56
    'Lavender Beauty', 56
    'Paprika', 56
    'Red Beauty', 56
    'Roseum', 56
    'Wesersandstone', 56
    'White Beauty', 56
Achillea 'Moonshine', 56
Achillea ptarmica, 35, 56
    'Angel's Breath', 56
    'Boule de Neige', see 'The Pearl'
    'Globe', 56
    'Perry's White', 56
    'Snowball', 56
    'Snow Sport', 56
    'The Pearl', 56
Achillea taygetea, 56
Achillea tomentosa, 56
    'Aurea', 56
    'King Edward', 56
    'Moonlight', 56
    'Nana', 56
Acorus calamus, 35, 56
    var. *angustifolius,* 57
    'Variegatus', 57
Acorus gramineus, 57
    'Albo-variegatus', 57
    'Argenteostriatus', 57
    'Licorice', 57

    'Masamune', 57
    'Minimus Aureus', 57
    'Oborozuki', 57
    'Ogon', 57, Plate 6
    'Pusillus', 57
    'Taninanoyuki', 57
    'Variegatus', 57
    'Wogon', see 'Ogon'
    'Yodonoyuki', 57
Adiantum capillus-veneris, 46, 35, 58, Plate 7
Adiantum pedatum, 46, 35, 57
    var. *subpumilum,* 58
Aegopodium podagraria, 58
    'Variegatum', 58, Plate 8
Aeonium tabuliforme, 59, Plate 9
Aethionema grandiflorum, 59
    'Warley Rose', 59, Plate 10
    'Warley Ruber', 59
Agapanthus
    African, 60
    Oriental, 60, Plate 11
Agapanthus, Headbourne Hybrids, 60
Agapanthus africanus, 60
    'Albus', 60
    'Albus Nanus', 60
    'Blue Giant', 60
    'Blue Triumphator', 60
    'Queen Anne', 60
Agapanthus 'Alice Gloucester', 60
Agapanthus 'Bressingham Blue', 60
Agapanthus 'Bressingham White', 60
Agapanthus campanulatus, 60
Agapanthus coddii, 60
Agapanthus inapertus, 60
Agapanthus 'Isis', 60
Agapanthus 'Lilliput', 60
Agapanthus 'Loch Hope', 60
Agapanthus 'Midknight Blue', 61

Agapanthus nutans, 60
Agapanthus praecox subsp. *orientalis,*
    60
    'Albidus', 60
    var. *aureovittatus,* 60
    'Flore Pleno', 60
    var. *giganteus,* 60
    var. *leichtlinii,* 60
    'Mooreanus', 60
    'Peter Pan', 60
    'Rancho White', 60
    'Variegatus', 60, Plate 11
Agapanthus 'Snowy Owl', 61
Aglaonema, Plate 12
Aglaonema commutatum, 61
    'Albovariegatum', 61
    var. *elegans,* 61
    'Grafii', 61
    var. *maculatum,* 61
    'Pseudobracteatum', 61
    'Treubii', 61
    'White Rajah', see
        'Pseudobracteatum'
Aglaonema 'Green Majesty', 61
Aglaonema 'Manila', 61
Aglaonema modestum, 61
Aglaonema nitidum 'Curtisii', 61
Aglaonema 'Silver Frost', 61
Aglaonema 'Silver Queen', 61
Aglaonema 'Stripes', 61
Ajuga 'Brockbankii', 63
Ajuga genevensis, 62
    'Alba', 63
    'Rosea', 63
    'Variegata', 63
Ajuga pyramidalis, 63
    'Alexander', 63
    'Metallica Crispa', 63
    'Nanus Compactus', 63
    'Pink Beauty, 63
Ajuga reptans, 61
    'Alba', 62
    'Alba Variegata', 62
    'Albo-variegata', see 'Alba
        Variegata'
    'Arboretum Giant', 62
    'Arctic Fox', 62
    'Atropurpurea', 62
    'Brightness', 62
    'Brocade', 62
    'Bronze Beauty', 62, Plate 13
    'Bronze Improved', see 'Gaiety'
    'Burgundy Glow', 62
    'Catlin's Giant', 62
    'Compacta', 62
    'Gaiety', 62
    'Giant Green', 62
    'Jungle Bronze', 62
    'Jungle Green', 62
    'Mini Crispa Red', 62

    'Multicolor', 62
    'Pink Elf', 62
    'Pink Silver', 62
    'Pink Surprise', 62
    'Purple Brocade', 62
    'Purple Torch', 62
    'Rainbow', 62
    'Rosea', 62
    'Royalty', 62
    'Rubra', 62
    'Silver Beauty', 62
    'Silver Carpet', 62
    'Thumbelina', 62
    'Variegata', see 'Alba Variegata',
Akebia
    fiveleaf, 63, Plate 14
    threeleaf, 64
Akebia × pentaphylla, 64
Akebia quinata, 63, Plate 14
    'Alba', 64
    'Rosea, 64
    'Shirobana', 64
    'Variegata', 64
Akebia trifoliata, 64
Alchemilla alpina, 64
Alchemilla conjuncta, 64
Alchemilla mollis, 64, Plate 15
Alchemilla vulgaris, 64
    'Auslese', 64
Alder
    'Hummingbird' white, 109
    'Hummingbird' spiked, 109,
        Plate 74
Allheal, 268
Aloe
    cushion, 168
    hedgehog, 65
    Kanniedood, 65
    partridge breast, 65
    spider, 65, Plate 16
    tiger, 65
Aloe aristata, 65
Aloe barbadensis, 65
Aloe humilis, 65, Plate 16
    var. *echinata,* 65
    'Globosa', 65
Aloe variegata, 65
Aloe vera, see *A. barbadensis*
Aluminum plant, 255, Plate 242
Alum root
    American, 37, 182
    hairy, 37
    small flowered, 37, 183
Alyssum, golden, 83
Ammophila arenaria, 48, 66
Ammophila breviligulata, 35, 48, 66,
        Plate 17
Ampelopsis aconitifolia, 67
Ampelopsis brevipedunculata, 66,
        Plate 18

    'Elegans', 66
    var. *maximowiczii,* 67
Ampelopsis humulifolia, 67
Ampelopsis, porcelain, 66, Plate 18
Amygdalus, 146
Anacyclus depressus, 67, Plate 19
Anagallis monellii, 67, Plate 20
    subsp. *linifolia,* 68
    'Pacific Blue', 68
    'Phillipii', 68
Anchusa, dwarf, 88
Andromeda glaucophylla, 35, 68
Andromeda polifolia, 35, 68
    'Blue Ice', 68
    'Compacta', 68
    'Grandiflora compacta', 68
    'Kiri-Kaming', 68
    'Macrophylla', 68
    'Major', 68
    'Minima', 68
    'Montana', 68
    'Nana', Plate 21
    'Nana Alba', 68
Anemone
    dwarf Japanese, 69
    Japanese, 69
    snowdrop, 69, Plate 22
Anemone hupehensis, 69
    var. *japonica,* 69
    'Praecox', 69
    'Superba', 69
Anemone × hybrida, 69
    'Alba', 69
    'Alice', 69
    'Bressingham Glow', 69
    'Honorine Jobert', 69
    'Krimhilde', 69
    'Lady Gilmour', 69
    'Luise Uhink', 69
    'Margarete', 69
    'Max Vogel', 69
    'Mont Rose', 69
    'Pamina', 69
    'Prince Henry', see 'Prinz
        Heinrich'
    'Prinz Heinrich', 69
    'Queen Charlotte', 69
    'September Charm', 69
    'Whirlwind', 69
Anemone sylvestris, 69, Plate 22
    'Elisa Fellmann', see 'Plena'
    'Flore Pleno', see 'Plena'
    'Grandiflora', 69
    'Macrantha', see 'Grandiflora'
    'Plena', 69
    'Wienerwald', 69
Anemone vitifolia, 69
Angels' eyes, 171
Angel's eyes, 312
Angel's hair, 77

Angel wings, 89
Antennaria dioica, 35, 69
  'Nyewood', 70
  var. *rosea,* 70
  'Rubra', 70
  'Tomentosa', 70
Antennaria plantaginifolia, 35, 70,
  Plate 23
Aptenia cordifolia, 70
  'Alba', 70
  'Red Apple', 70, Plate 24
  'Variegata', 70
Arabis albida, 71
Arabis alpina, 71
  'Compacta', 71
  'Grandiflora', 71
  'Rosea', 71
Arabis caucasica, 70
  'Floreplena', 71
  'Rosabella', 71
  'Schneehaube', see 'Snow Cap'
  'Snow Cap', 71, Plate 25
  'Snow Peak', 71
  'Spring Charm', 71
  'Variegata', 71
Arabis procurrens, 71
Arbutus, trailing, 37, 138, Plate 113
Archangel, yellow, 204, Plate 177
Arctanthemum arcticum, 35, 71,
  Plate 26
Arctostaphylos alpina, 35, 72
  var. *japonica,* 72
Arctostaphylos canescens, 73
Arctostaphylos edmundsii, 35, 72
Arctostaphylos 'Emerald Carpet', 72
Arctostaphylos hookeri, 35, 72
Arctostaphylos nevadensis, 35, 72, 73
  'Chipeta', 72
Arctostaphylos nummularia, 35, 73
Arctostaphylos pumila, 35, 72, 73
Arctostaphylos rubra, 35, 73
Arctostaphylos thymifolia, 35, 73
Arctostaphylos uva-ursi, 35, 71, Plate
  27
  'Alaska', 72
  'Big Bear', 72
  'Convict Lake', 72
  'Emerald Carpet', 72
  'Massachusetts', 72
  var. *microphylla,* 72
  'Pacific Mist', 72
  'Point Reyes', 72
  'Radiant', 72
  'Rax', 72
  'Vancouver Jade', 72
  'Vulcan's Peak', 72
  'Wood's Compacta', 72
Arctostaphylos 'Wood's Red', 73
Arctotheca calendula, 73, Plate 28
Ardisia, Japanese, 74, Plate 29

Ardisia japonica, 74, Plate 29
  'Beniyuki', 74
  'Chirimen', 74
  'Chiyoda', 74
  'Hakuokan'
  'Hinode', 74
  'Hinotsukasa', 74
  'Ito-Fukurin', 74
  'Variegata', 74
Arenaria arctica, 35, 74
Arenaria laricifolia, 74
Arenaria montana, 74, Plate 30
Arenaria verna, 74
  'Aurea', 74
Argentine, 263
Armeria 'Bloodstone', 75, Plate 31
Armeria juniperifolia, 75
  var. *splendens,* 75
Armeria maritima, 75
  'Alba', 75
  'Brilliant', 75
  'Californica', 75
  'Cotton Tail', 75
  'Dusseldorf Pride', 75
  'Laucheana', 75
  'Purpurea', 75
  'Robusta', 75
  'Royal Rose', 75
  'Rubra', 75
  'Ruby Glow', 75
  'Splendens', 75
  'Vindictive', 75
Aronia melanocarpa, 35, 76, Plate 32
Arrowroot, banded, 222
Artemisia, 76
Artemisia abrotanum, 77
  'Nana', 76
Artemisia caucasica, 77
Artemisia frigida, 35, 77
Artemisia ludoviciana, 35, 77
  'Latiloba', 77
  'Valerie Finnis', 77
Artemisia 'Powis Castle', 77
Artemisia schmidtiana, 77
  'Nana', 77
  'Silver Mound', 77
Artemisia stelleriana, 35, 77
  'Silver Brocade', 77, Plate 33
Arundinaria viridi-striata, see
  Pleioblastus auricoma
Asarum arifolium, 35, 78
Asarum canadense, 35, 78
Asarum caudatum, 35, 78
Asarum europaeum, 78
Asarum hartwegii, 35, 78
  'Silver Heart', 79
Asarum kumagianum, 79
Asarum memingeri, 35, 79
Asarum shuttleworthii, 35, 79
  'Callaway', Plate 34

Asarum splendens, 79
Asarum virginicum, 35, 79
Ash, ground, 58
Ashweed, 58
Asparagus
  common, 79
  Sprenger, 79, Plate 35
Asparagus densiflorus
  'Sprengeri', 79, Plate 35
  'Sprengeri Compactus', 79
  'Sprengeri Deflexus', 79
  'Sprengeri Nanus', 79
  'Sprengeri Robustus', 79
Asparagus officinalis, 79
  var. *inermis,* 80
  var. *pseudoscaber,* 80
  var. *pseudoscaber* 'Spitzenschleier',
    80
Aster, Cape, 148
Astilbe
  Arends', 80
  crisped, 81
  dwarf Chinese, 81
  rose, 81
  star, 81
Astilbe × arendsii, 80
  'Avalanche', 80
  'Bremen', 80
  'Bridal Veil', 80
  'Cattleya', 80
  'Deutschland', 80
  'Diamond', 80
  'Emden', 80
  'Erica', 80
  'Europa', 80
  'Fanal' 80
  'Federsee'
  'Garnet', 80
  'Glow', 81
  'Irrlicht', 81
  'Liliput', 81
  'Ostrich Plume', 81
  'Purple Blaze', 81
  'Red Sentinel', 81, Plate 36
  'Rheinland', 81
  'Snowdrift', 81
  'Spinell', 81
  'Vesuvius', 81
  'White Gloria', 81
Astilbe chinensis var. *pumila,* 81
  'Finale', 81
  'Intermezzo', 81
  'Serenade', 81
  'Vision', 81
Astilbe × crispa, 81
  'Perkeo', 81
Astilbe × rosea, 81
  'Peach Blossom', 81
  'Queen Alexandra', 81
Astilbe simplicifolia, 81

[*Astilbe simplicifolia*]
  var. *alba,* 81
    'Aphrodite', 81
    'Atrorosea', 81
    'Bronce Elegans', 81
    'Bronze Queen', 81
    'Hennie Graafland', 81
    'Inncerry', 81
    'Inshriach Pink', 81
    'Purple Cats'
    'Snowdrift', 81
    'Sprite', 81
Athyrium filix-femina, 46, 35, 81
  var. *angustum,* 82
    'Aristatum', 82
  var. *asplenioides,* 82
    'Crispum', 82
    'Minutissimum', 82
    'Plumosum', 82
    'Vernoniae Cristatum', 82
Athyrium goeringianum, 82
Athyrium nipponicum, 46, 82
    'Pictum', 82, Plate 37
    'Red Select', 82
Athyrium pycnocarpon, 35, 82
Athyrium thelypteroides, 46, 35, 82
Atriplex semibaccata, 82, Plate 38
    'Corto', 82
Aubretia, 83
Aubrieta deltoidea, 83, Plate 39
    'Aurea', 83
    'Aureo-variegata', 83
    'Barker's Double', 83
    'Bengale', 83
    'Bob Sanders', 83
    'Borsch's White', 83
    'Bougainvillea'
    'Campbellii', 83
    'Carnival', 83
    'Dr. Mules', 83
    'Gloriosa', 83
    'Graeca', 83
    'Greencourt Purple', 83
    'Henslow Purple', 83
    'J. S. Barker', 83
    'Leichtlinii', 83
    'Moerheim', 83
    'Mrs. Rodewald', 83
    'Parkinsii', 83
    'Purple Cascade', 83
    'Purple Gem', 83
    'Red Cascade', 83
    'Rosea Splendens', 83
    'Royal Blue', 83
    'Royal Red', 83
    'Variegata', 83
    'Vindictive', 83
    'Whitewell Gem', 83
Aubrietia, 83
Auriculata, 267

Auriculas
  Belgian, 267
  common garden, 267
  double-flowered, 267
  English, 267
Aurinia saxatilis, 83
    'Citrinum', 84
    'Compactum', 84
    'Dudley Nevill Variegated', 84
    'Flore Pleno', 84
    'Gold Ball', 84
    'Golden Globe', 84
    'Goldkugel', see 'Gold Ball'
    'Nanum', 84
    'Plenum', 84
    'Silver Queen', 84
    'Sulphurea', 84, Plate 40
    'Sunny Border Apricot', 84
    'Tom Thumb', 84
Avens, mountain, 133, Plate 107
Azaleas, Kurume, 275
Azorella trifurcata, 84, Plate 41
    'Nana', 84

Baby's breath
  common, 167
  creeping, 167, Plate 146
Baccharis, 35
Baccharis pilularis, 35, 85
  var. *consanguinea,* 85
    'Pigeon Point', 85, Plate 42
    'Twin Peaks #2', 85
Bachelor's Buttons, 86
Balm
  bee, 224
  lemon, 224, Plate 202
  sweet, 224
Balm leaf, 224
Balmony, 103
Bamboo
  dwarf, 48, 259
  dwarf Mexican, 147
  dwarf yellow-stripe, 48, 259,
    Plate 245
  heavenly, 231, Plate 211
  pygmy, 48, 259, Plate 45
  reed, 258
  sacred, 231
  white-stripe, 48, 259
Bane, rabbit, 111
Barberry
  crimson pygmy, 86
  Irwin's rosemary, 87
Barrenwort
  American, 40, 310
  golden, 310
  long-spur, 139
Basket-of-Gold, 83
Beach grass, 66
Beach heather, 37

heathlike, 37
Mountain, 37
Bearberry, 34, 71, Plate 27
  alpine, 35, 72
  black, 72
  coin-leaved, 35, 73
  common, 35, 71
  red, 71, 73
  thyme-leaved, 35, 73
Beard, goat's, 80
Beard, old man's, 108
Beard tongue, pineleaf, 247
Bear's foot, 64
Bear's paw, 134
Bedstraw, 154
Beetle weed, 153
Beewort, 57
Begonia
  hardy, 85, Plate 43
  strawberry, 287
  watermelon, 247
  winter, 87
Begonia grandis, 85, Plate 43
    'Alba', 85
Bell, fringed, 294
Bellflower
  Adriatic, 94
  Carpathian, 93, Plate 54
  Dalmatian, 94
  Serbian, 94
Bellis perennis, 86, Plate 44
    'Brilliant', 86
    'Carpet', 86
    'China Pink', 86
    'Dresden China', 86
    'Monstrosa', 86
    Monstrosa Hybrids, 86
    'Pomponette', 86
    'Prolifera', 86
    'Rob Roy', 86
    'Rosea', 86
    'Tuberosa', 86
Bent, narrow, 211
Berberis darwinii, 87
Berberis empetrifolia, 87
Berberis stenophylla 'Irwinii', 87
    'Corallina Compact', 87
Berberis thunbergii, 86
  var. *atropurpurea* 'Crimson
    Pygmy', see 'Crimson Pygmy'
    'Atropurpurea Nana', see
      'Crimson Pygmy'
    'Bagatelle', 86
    'Bonanza Gold', 86
    'Concord', 86
    'Crimson Pygmy', 86, 87, Plate 45
    'Globe', 87
    'Kobold', 87
    'Minor', 87
    'Royal Burgundy', 87

'William Penn', 87
Bergenia
  heartleaf, 87, Plate 46
  leather, 87
  purple, 87
Bergenia beesiana, 87
Bergenia ciliata, 87, 88
  forma *ligulata,* 87
Bergenia cordifolia, 87, 88, Plate 46
  'Alba', 87
  'Perfecta', 87
Bergenia crassifolia, 87
Bergenia purpurascens, 88
  var. *delavayi,* 87
Bergenia × smithii, 88
  'Abendglut', 88
  'Ballawley', 88
  'Bressingham Bountiful', 88
  'Bressingham Salmon', 88
  'Bressingham White', 88
  'Distinction', 88
  'Evening Glow', see 'Abendglut'
  'Morgenrote', 88
  'Morning Red', see 'Morgenrote'
  'Profusion', 88
  'Pugsley's Purple', 88
  'Rotblum', 88
  'Silberlicht', 88
  'Silver Light', see 'Silberlicht'
  'Sunningdale', 88
Bergenia stracheyi, 88
Berry
  partridge, 228
  squaw, 228
  tea, 155
Betony
  big, 297
  large flowered, 297
  woolly, 297
Bilberry, 71
Bird's-eye, 217, 312
Bird's-foot trefoil, 217, Plate 193
Bishop's cap, long-spur, 139
Bishop's weed, 58, Plate 8
Bistort, 250
Bitter-herb, 103
Black foot, 38
  white-flowered, 223
Bleeding heart
  fringed, 36, 130
  Pacific, 36, 131, Plate 102
  western, 131
  wild, 130
Bloodroot, 39, 284, Plate 271
Bloodwort, 56
Bluebeard, Plate 58
  common, 97, 98
  Mongolian, 97, 98
Blueberry
  creeping, 39, 309

late sweet, 308
low bush, 39
low sweet, 308
Blue-eyed Mary, 234, Plate 216
Bluets, 37, 171, Plate 151
Bolax glebaria, see *Azorella trifurcata*
Box
  mountain, 71
  running, 228
Boxwood, Oregon, 244
Brake
  buckhorn, 240
  canker, 262
  knotty, 134
  swamp, 239
  sweet, 134
Bramble, creeping, 280
Bread root, 239
Breeches
  bear's, 54, Plate 4
  spiny bear's, 55
Bright eyes, 171
Briza media, 48, 88, Plate 47
Broom
  arrow, 159
  German, 159
  prostrate, 122, Plate 92
  Spanish, 159
Brunnera, heartleaf, 88, Plate 48
Brunnera macrophylla, 88, Plate 48
  'Hadspen Cream', 89
  'Langtrees', 89
  'Variegata', 89
Buck brush, 39, 298
Bugle, creeping carpet, 61
Bugleweed, creeping, 61, Plate 13
Bugloss, Siberian, 88
Bunchberry, 116
  white fruited form, 116
Burstwort, 181
Bush
  Hartshorn, 240
  Mormon tea, 137
  polecat, 277
  prostrate strawberry, 146
  running strawberry, 146
  spleenwort, 110
  strawberry, 37, 146
  trailing indigo, 36, 122, Plate 93
  trailing smoke, 122
Butter winter, 104
Butterbur
  common, 251
  fragrant, 251
  Japanese, 252, Plate 237
  spotted-leaf, 272
  white, 251
Buttercup
  creeping, 39, 272, Plate 259

Cactus
  grizzly bear, 38, 237
Caladium
  common, 89
  fancy-leaved, 89
  garden, 89
  showy, 89
  star, 168
Caladium, 89, Plate 49
Caladium bicolor, 89
Caladium × hortulanum, 89
  'Aaron', 90
  'Ace of Hearts', 89
  'Blaze', 90
  'Brandywine', 90
  'Caloosahatchee', 90
  'Candidum', 90
  'Candidum Jr.', 90
  'Carolyn Whorton', 90
  'Clarice', 90
  'Fannie Munson', 90
  'Festiva', 90
  'Fire Chief', 90
  'Florida Beauty', 90
  'Florida Elise', 90
  'Florida Fantasy', 90
  'Florida Sweetheart', 90
  'Freida Hemple', 90
  'Gingerland', 90
  'Gypsy Rose', 90
  'Irene Dank', 90
  'Ivory', 90
  'Jackie Suthers', 90
  'John Peed', 90
  'June Bride', 90
  'Kathleen', 90
  'Lady of Fatima', 90
  'Lance Whorton', 90
  'Lord Derby', 90
  'Marine Moir', 90
  'Miss Chicago', 90
  'Miss Muffet', 90
  'Mrs. Arno Nehrling', 90
  'Mrs. F. M. Joyner', 90
  'Mumbo', 90
  'Pink Beauty', 90
  'Pink Cloud', 90
  'Pink Gem', 90
  'Pink Symphony', 90
  'Poecile Anglais', 90
  'Postman Joyner', 90
  'Red Flash', 90
  'Red Frill', 90
  'Rosalie', 90
  'Rosebud', 90
  'Torchy', 90
  'White Christmas', 90
  'White Queen', 90
  'White Wing', 90
Caladium humboldtii, 90

Caladium marmoratum, 90
Caladium picturatum, 90
Calamintha nepeta, 91, Plate 50
    subsp. *glandulosa*, 91
    subsp. *nepeta*, 91
Calamovilfa longifolia, 35, 48, 91,
    Plate 51
    var. *magna*, 91
Calamus, 57
Calf kill, 184
California beach plant, 97
Callirhoe involucrata, 35, 92, Plate
    52
Calluna vulgaris, 92, Plate 53
    'Alba', 92
    'Aurea', 92
    'Corbett's Red', 93
    'County Wicklow', 93
    'Cuprea', 93
    'Else Frye', 93
    'Foxii Nana', 93
    'Golden Aurea', 93
    'Golden Aureafolia', 93
    'Hammondia Aurea', 93
    'H. E. Beale', 93
    'J. H. Hamilton', 93
    'Kinlochruel', 93
    'Long White', 93
    'Mrs. Pat', 93
    'Mrs. R. H. Gray', 93
    'Nana Compacta', 93
    'Peter Sparkes', 93
    'Plena Multiplex', 93
    'Robert Chapman', 93
    'Silver Queen', 93
    'Sister Anne', 93
    'Spring Cream', 93
    'Spring Torch', 93
    'Tomentosa', 93
Campanula carpatica, 93
    'Alba', 93
    'Blaue Clips', see 'Blue Clips'
    'Blue Carpet', 93
    'Blue Clips', 93, Plate 54
    'China Cup', 94
    'China Doll', 94
    'Jingle Bells', 94
    var. *turbinata*, 94
    'Wedgewood Blue', 94
    'Weisse Clips', see 'White Clips'
    'White Carpet', 94
    'White Clips', 94
    'White Star', 94
Campanula garganica, 94
    var. *hirsuta*, 94
    var. *hirsuta* 'Alba', 94
Campanula portenschlagiana, 94
Campanula poscharskyana, 94
Candytuft
    edging, 191

evergreen, 191, Plate 164
    Gibraltar, 192
    rock, 192
Canker root, 113
Cape-jasmine, creeping, 155, Plate
    135
Cape weed, 73, 254, Plate 28
Carex atrata, 35, 95
    var. *caucasica*, 95
Carex 'Catlin', 96
Carex comans, 95
    'Bronce', 95
Carex digitata, 95
Carex dolichostachya var. *glaberrima*
    'Gold Fountains', 96
Carex elata, 95
    'Bowles Golden', 95
    'Knightshayes', 95
Carex flacca, 95
Carex glauca, 36, 95
Carex hachioensis 'Evergold', 95,
    Plate 55
Carex morrowii, 95
    var. *albomarginata*, 95
    'Aurea Variegata', 95
    'Aurea Variegata Nana', 95
    var. *expallida*, 95
    'Goldband', 95
    'Old Gold', 95
    var. *temnolepis*, 95
    'Variegata', 95
Carex muskingumensis, 36, 95
    'Wachtposten', 96
Carex nigra, 36, 96
    'Variegata', 96
Carex pendula, 96
Carex plantaginea, 36, 96
Carex 'Silver Curls', 96
Carex vilmorinii, 95
Carissa grandiflora, 96, Plate 56
    'Boxwood Beauty', 96
    'Green Carpet', 96
    'Horizontalis', 96
    'Minima', 96
    'Nana Compacta Tuttlei', see
        'Tuttle'
    'Prostrata', 96
    'Tomlinson', 96
    'Tuttle', 96
Carnation, Plate 101
    cottage, 129
Carpenter weed, 268
Carpet Bugle
    Geneva, 62
    pyramidal, 63
Carpobrotus acinaciformis, 97
Carpobrotus chilensis, 97
Carpobrotus deliciosus, 97
Carpobrotus edulis, 97, Plate 57
Carpobrotus muirii, 97

Caryopteris × *clandonensis*
    'Arthur Simmonds', 97
    'Azure', 97, Plate 58
    'Blue Mist', 98
    'Dark Knight', 98
    'Ferndown', 98
    'Heavenly Blue', 98
    'Kew Blue', 98
    'Longwood Blue', 98
    'Worcester Gold'
Caryopteris incana, 97, 98
    'Blue Billows', 98
    'Candida', 98
Caryopteris mongholica, 97, 98
Cassandra, 102
Cassena, 193
Cassina, 193
Cassine, 193
Cathedral windows, 222
Catmint
    blue, 231
    Faassen's, 231
    mauve, 231
    Persian, 232, Plate 212
Cats' faces, 316
Cat's clover, 217
Ceanothus
    creeping blue blossom, 36, 99,
        Plate 59
    Point Reyes, 36, 98
    squaw-carpet, 36, 98
    Yankee Point, 36
Ceanothus gloriosus, 36, 98
    'Anchor Bay', 98
    var. *exaltatus* 'Emily Brown',
        98
    var. *porrectus*, 98
Ceanothus griseus var. *horizontalis*,
    36, 98
    'Compacta', 98
    'Hurricane Point', 98
    'Yankee Point', 98
Ceanothus prostratus, 36, 98
Ceanothus thyrsiflorus, Plate 59
    var. *repens*, 36, 99
Cedar
    creeping, 202
    eastern red, 37
    ground, 219
    prostrate deodar, 99, Plate 60
    prostrate Himalayan, 99
Cedrus deodara
    'Golden Horizon', 99, Plate 60
    'Prostrata', 99
    'Prostrate Beauty', 99
Centranthus ruber, 99, Plate 61
    'Albus', 100
    'Atrococcineus', 100
    'Red Valerian', 100
    'Roseus', 100

Cephalophyllum, 125, 133, 205, Plate 62
Cephalophyllum alstonii, 100
  'Red Spike', 100
Cephalophyllum anemoniflorum, 100
Cephalophyllum aureorubrum, 100
Cephalophyllum cupreum, 100
Cephalophyllum procumbens, 100
Cephalophyllum subulatoides, 100
Cephalotaxus harringtonia
  'Duke Gardens', 101
  'Prostrata', 100, 101, Plate 63
Cerastium biebersteinii, 101
Cerastium tomentosum, 101, Plate 64
  var. *columnae,* 101
  'Silver Carpet', 101
  'Yo Yo', 101
Ceratostigma, blue, 101
Ceratostigma plumbaginoides, 101, Plate 65
Chamaedaphne calyculata, 36, 102, Plate 66
  var. *angustifolia,* 103
  var. *latifolia,* 103
  'Nana', 103
Chamaemelum nobile, 103, Plate 67
  'Flore Pleno', 103
  'Treneague', 103
Chamomile
  garden, 103
  Roman, 103, Plate 67
  Russian, 103
Chandelier plant, 204
Charley
  creeping, 220, 256, Plate 196
  golden creeping, 220
Checkerberry, 155
Chelone glabra, 36, 104
Chelone lyonii, 36, 104
  'Hot Lips', 104
Chelone obliqua, 36, 103, Plate 68
  'Alba', 104
  'Bethelii', 104
  'Praecox Nana', 104
  var. *speciosa,* 104
Chickweed, taurus, 101
Chimaphila maculata, 36, 105
Chimaphila menziesii, 105
Chimaphila umbellata, 36, 104, Plate 69
  var. *cisatlantica,* 104
  var. *occidentalis,* 105
Chlorophytum comosum, 105
  'Variegatum', 105, Plate 70
Chokeberry, black, 35, 76, Plate 32
Christmas green, 38, 220, Plate 195
Chrysanthemum
  arctic, 35, 71, Plate 26
  florist's, 126
  garden, 126

gold-and-silver, 127, Plate 98
  Korean hybrids, 127
  Minn series, 126
  red hybrid, 127
Chrysogonum virginianum, 36, 105, Plate 71
  var. *australe,* 106
  'Eco Lacquered Spider', 106
  'Springbrook', 106
  var. *virginiana,* 106
Cinquefoil, 263
  bush, 39, 264
  Nepal, 265
  ruby, 264
  rusty, 264
  spring, 265
  three-toothed, 265
  wineleaf, 39, 265
Cistus crispus, 106
Cistus × hybridus, 106
Cistus populifolius, 106
Cistus salviifolius, 106, Plate 72
Clematis
  alpine, 107
  anemone, 108, Plate 73
  sweet autumn, 107
Clematis alpina, 107
  'Alba', 107
  'Candy', 107
  'Columbine', 107
  'Constance', 107
  'Francis Rivis', 107
  'Helsingborg', 107
  'Jacqueline du Pre', 107
  'Pamela Jackman', 107
  'Ruby', 107
  var. *siberica,* 107
  'White Moth', 107
  'Willy', 107
Clematis crispa, 108
Clematis maximowicziana, 107, 108
Clematis montana, 108, Plate 73
  'Elizabeth', 108
  'Freda', 108
  'Grandiflora', 108
  'Marjorie', 108
  'Odorata', 108
  'Pink Perfection', 108
  var. *tetrarose,* 108
  'Wilson', 108
Clematis paniculata, 107, 108
  var. *lobata,* 108
Clematis virginiana, 36, 108
Clematis viticella, 108
  'Abundance', 108
  'Alba Luxurians', 108
  'Betty Corning', 108
  'Blue Belle', 108
  'Elvan', 109
  'Etoile Violette', 109

'Kermesina', 109
  'Little Nell', 109
  'Madame Julia Correvon', 109
  'Margot Koster', 109
  'Mary Rose', 109
  'Minuet', 109
  'Pagoda', 109
  'Polish Spirit', 109
  'Purpurea Plena Elegans', 109
  'Royal Velours', 109
  'Rubra', see 'Kermesina'
  'Tango', 109
  'Venosa Violacea', 109
Clethra alnifolia 'Hummingbird', 36, 109, Plate 74
Cliff green, 243
Clivia
  French hybrids, 110
  German hybrids, 110
  Zimmerman hybrids, 110
Clivia × cyrtanthiflora, 110
Clivia gardenii, 110
Clivia miniata, 109, 110, Plate 75
  var. *citrina,* 110
  'Flame', 110
  var. *flava,* 110
  'Grandiflora', 110
  'Striata', 110
Clivia nobilis, 110
Cloves, 128
Club moss, 218
  shining, 37, 220
  staghorn, 38, 219
  tree, 219
  wolf's claw, 219
Cod-head, 103
Cogon, red, 193
Colt's foot, 37, 153, Plate 133
  Arctic sweet, 38
  arrowleaf sweet, 38
  palmate sweet, 38
  sweet-scented, 251
Comfrey
  large-flowered, 299, Plate 291
  middle, 61
  red-flowered, 299
  Russian, 299
Comptonia peregrina, 36, 110, Plate 76
  var. *asplenifolia,* 111
  'Variegata', 111
Coneflower, orange, 281, Plate 267
Conradina verticillata, 36, 111, Plate 77
Convallaria majalis, 36, 111, Plate 78
  'Aurea Variegata', 112
  'Flore Pleno', 112
  'Fortin's Giant', 112
  'Fortunei', 112

[*Convallaria majalis*]
  'Prolificans', 112
  'Rosea', 112
Convallaria montana, 36, 112
Convolvulus cneorum, 112, Plate 79
Convolvulus mauritanicus, 112
Convolvulus sabatius, 113
Coprosma
  creeping, 113, Plate 80
  Kirk's, 113
  Petrie's, 113
Coprosma × kirkii, 113
  'Kirkii', 113
  'Variegata', 113, Plate 80
Coprosma petriei, 113
Coptis groenlandica, 36, 113, Plate 81
Coptis laciniata, 36, 114
Coral bells, 37, 181, Plate 157
Coralberry, 298, Plate 290
  Hancock Chenault, 298
Coral gem, 217
Corbigeau, 136
Corema conradii, 36, 114, Plate 82
Coreopsis
  dwarf-eared, 36, 115
  threadleaf, 36, 115, Plate 83
Coreopsis, 114
Coreopsis alpina 'Alba', 115
Coreopsis auriculata, 36, 115
  'Nana', 115
  'Superba', 115
Coreopsis pulchra, 115
Coreopsis rosea, 36, 115
  'Alba', 115
  forma *leucantha,* 115
Coreopsis verticillata, 36, 115
  'Golden Showers', 115
  'Grandiflora', 115
  'Moonbeam', 115, Plate 83
  'Zagreb', 115
Cornel, dwarf, 36, 116, Plate 84
Cornus canadensis, 36, 116, Plate 84
Cornus mas 'Nana', 36, 116
Cornus pumila, 116
Cornus sericea 'Kelseyi', 36, 116
Cornus suecica, 116
Cornus × unalaschkensis, 116
Coronilla varia, 117, Plate 85
  'Emerald', 117
  'Penngift', 117
Correa pulchella, 117, Plate 86
Corsican carpet plant, 294
Corsican curse, 294
Cotoneaster
  bearberry, 119
  congested, 118
  cranberry, 118
  creeping, 118
  little-leaved, 119

necklace, 119
Pyrenees, 118
rock spray, 119, Plate 87
willow-leaved, 120
Cotoneaster adpressus, 118
  'Little Gem', 118
  'Praecox', 118
Cotoneaster apiculatus, 118
  'Blackburn', 118
  'Nana', 118
  'Tom Thumb', 118
Cotoneaster congestus, 118
  'Likiang', 119
Cotoneaster conspicuous
  'Decorus', 119
  var. *decorus,* see 'Decorus'
Cotoneaster dammeri, 119
  'Coral Beauty', 119
  'Corbet', 119
  'Eichholz', 119
  'Juergl', 119
  'Lowfast', 119
  'Major', 119
  'Mooncreeper', 119
  'Oakwood', 119
  'Pink Beauty', see 'Coral Beauty'
  'Royal Beauty', see 'Coral Beauty'
  'Streibs Findling', 119
Cotoneaster 'Hessei', 119
Cotoneaster × himalayense, 119
Cotoneaster horizontalis, 119, Plate 87
  'Purpusilla', 119
  'Robusta', 119
  'Saxatilis', 119
Cotoneaster microphyllus, 119
  'Cochleatus', 119
  'Cooperi', 119
Cotoneaster salicifolius, 120
  'Autumn Fire', 120
  'Emerald Carpet', 120
  'Gnom', 120
  'Moner', 120
  'Parkteppich', 120
  'Repens', 120
  'Saldam', 120
  'Scarlet Leader', 120
Cotula squalida, 120, Plate 88
Cowberry, 40, 309
Cow quakes, 88
Cowslip, 267
  Jerusalem, 269
Coyote bush, 85, Plate 42
Crakeberry, 136
Crampweed, 263
Cranberry
  American, 40, 309, Plate 302
  hog, 71
Cranesbill
  bloody, 162
  Endress, 161

Himalayan, 161
  spotted, 37, 161
Crassula multicava, 120, Plate 89
Creashak, 71
Creeper
  blue-star, 265
  Carmel, 98
  Point Reyes, 98
  Redondo, 206
  silvervein, 243
  Virginia, 243, Plate 227
Creeping forget-me-not, 234
Creeping Jenny, 220
Creeping navel-seed, 234
Creeping sailor, 287
Cress
  alpine rock, 71
  creeping blister, 144
  false rock, 83
  Persian stone, 59, Plate 10
  purple rock, 83, Plate 39
  running rock, 71
  wall rock, 70, Plate 25
Crete dittany, 238
Crocodile jaws, 65
Crowbars, 71
Crowberry
  black, 37, 136, Plate 111
  broom, 36, 114, Plate 82
  brown, 114
  Conrad's, 114
  Plymouth, 114
Crowfoot, creeping, 272
Crow toes, 217
Cudweed, 77
Cupflower
  dwarf, 233, Plate 214
  white, 232
Cuphea hyssopifola, 121, Plate 90
  'Compacta', 121
Cuphea llavea, 121
Cuphea procumbens, 121
Cuphea × purpurea, 121
  'Firefly' 121
Cupid's delight, 316
Curlewberry, 136
Current, Indian, 298
Cymbalaria aequitriloba, 122
Cymbalaria muralis, 121
  'Alba', 121, Plate 91
  'Alba Compacta', 121
Cypress
  ground, 285, Plate 272
  Siberian, 227, Plate 205
Cytisus albus, 122
Cytisus × beanii, 122
Cytisus decumbens, 122, Plate 92
Cytisus × kewensis, 122
Cytisus procumbens, 122
Cytisus purpureus, 122

Daisy
    Arctic, 71
    blackfoot, 223
    blue, 148
    butter, 272
    Drakensberg, 147, Plate 122
    English, 86, Plate 44
    field, 210
    freeway, 240
    Mount Atlas, 67, Plate 19
    oxeye, 210, Plate 185
    seaside, 143
    trailing African, 240, Plate 223
    true, 86
    white, 210
Dalea greggii, 36, 122, Plate 93
Dampiera diversifolia, 123, Plate 94
Dandelion, Cape, 73
Daphne
    Burkwood, 124, Plate 95
    garland, 123
    ground, 102
    rose, 123
    shrubby, 124
Daphne arbuscula, 123
    subsp. *platycladus,* 124
    subsp. *septentianalis,* 124
Daphne ashtonii, 124
Daphne × burkwoodii, 124
    'Carol Mackie', 124, Plate 95
    var. *laveniree,* 124
    'Somerset', 124
Daphne caucasica, 124
Daphne cneorum, 123, 124
    'Alba', 123
    'Albo-marginata', 123
    'Eximia', 123
    'Major', 123
    var. *pygmaea,* 123
    'Ruby Glow', 123
    'Variegata', see 'Albo-marginata'
    var. *verlotii,* 123
Darning needle, 108
Daylily, 175, Plate 155
    fulvous, 175
    lemon, 181
    Middendorff, 181
    orange, 175
    tawny, 175
    yellow, 181
Decodon verticillatus, 36, 124, Plate 96
Delosperma, 100, 133, 205
Delosperma 'Alba', 125
Delosperma ashtonii, 125
Delosperma cooperi, 125
Delosperma herbaeu, 125
Delosperma nubigena, 125, Plate 97
    'Basutoland', 126
Delosperma obtusum, 126

Dendranthema, 126
Dendranthema chanetti, 126
Dendranthema × grandiflorum, 126
Dendranthema indicum, 126
Dendranthema japonense, 126
Dendranthema lavandulifolium, 126
Dendranthema makinoi, 126
Dendranthema 'Mei-kyo', 127
Dendranthema × morifolium, 126, 127
Dendranthema odoratum, 126
Dendranthema pacifica, 127, Plate 98
Dendranthema × rubellum, 127
    'Clara Curtis', 127
    'Duchess of Edinburgh', 127
    'Mary Stoker', 127
Dendranthema weyrichii, 127
    'Pink Bomb', 127
    'White Bomb', 127
Dendranthema zawadskii var. *latilobum,* 127
Deschampsia caespitosa, 36, 48, 127, 128
    'Bronzeschleier', 127
    'Bronze Veil', see 'Bronzeschleier'
    'Dew Bearer', see 'Tauträger'
    'Forest Shade', see 'Waldschatt'
    'Goldgehänge', 127
    'Goldschleier', 127
    'Goldstaub', 127
    'Gold Veil', see 'Goldschleier'
    'Schottland', 127
    'Scotland', see 'Schottland'
    var. *tardiflora,* 127
    'Tauträger', 128
    var. *vivipara,* 128
    'Waldschatt', 128
Deschampsia flexuosa, 36, 128
    'Aurea', 128, Plate 99
Deutzia
    Lemoine, 128
    Nikko, 128, Plate 100
Deutzia gracilis 'Nikko', 128, Plate 100
Deutzia × lemoinei
    'Boule de Neige', 128
    'Compacta', 128
Deutzia parviflora, 128
Devils fingers, 217
Devil's hair, 108
Dianthus, 128
Dianthus × allwoodii, 129, 130
    'Aqua', 129
    'Doris', 129
    'Essex Witch', 129
    'Ian', 129
    'Robin', 129
Dianthus arenarius, 129
Dianthus caryophyllus, 129

Dianthus deltoides, 129
    'Albus', 129
    'Brilliant', 129
    'Fanal', 129
    'Flashing Red', 129
    'Microchip', 129
    'Red Maiden', 129
    'Roseus', 129
    'Ruber', 129
    'Samos', 129
    'Serphyllifolius', 129
    'Vampire', 129
    'Zing Rose', 129, Plate 101
Dianthus gratianopolitanus, 129
    'Bath's Pink', 129
    'Double Cheddar', 129
    var. *grandiflorus,* 129
    'Karlik', 129
    'Petite'
    'Pink Feather', 129
    'Splendens', 129
    'Tiny Rubies', 129
Dianthus plumarius, 129
    'Agatha', 130
    'C. T. Musgrave', 130
    'Dad's Favorite', 130
    'Excelsior', 130
    'Inchmery', 130
    'La Bourbille', 130
    'La Bourboule', see 'La Bourbille'
    'Little Bobby', 130
    'Mrs. Sinkins', 130
    'Painted Beauty', 130
    'Sonota', 130
    'Spring Beauty', 130
    'White Ladies', 130
Dicentra eximia, 36, 130
Dicentra formosa, 36, 130, 131
    'Adrian Bloom', 131
    'Alba', 131, Plate 102
    'Bacchanal', 131
    'Bountiful', 131
    'Langtrees', 131
    'Luxuriant', 131
    'Margery Fish', 131
    'Pearl Drops', see 'Langtrees'
    'Silver Smith', 131
    'Snowdrift', 131
    'Stuart Boothman', 131
    'Sweetheart', 131
    'Zestful', 131
Dichondra, 36, 131, Plate 103
Dichondra micrantha, 36, 131, Plate 103
Dickies, doddering, 88
Didder, 88
Diervilla lonicera, 36, 132, Plate 104
    'Copper', 132
    var. *hypomalaca,* 132
Diervilla sessilifolia, 36, 132

Diervilla 'Splendens', 132
Dillies, 88
Diplazium pycnocarpon, see *Athyrium pycnocarpon*
Disporum sessile, 132
   'Variegata', 133, Plate 105
Dittany of Crete, 238
Dock, butterfly, 251
Dog hobble, 38
Dog's dinner, 188
Dogwood
   dwarf, 116
   dwarf cornelian cherry, 36, 116
   dwarf red osier, 36, 116
Dropwort, 150, Plate 127
   double, 150
Dryad, Mt. Washington, 133
Dryas octopetala, 36, 133, Plate 107
   var. *alaskensis*, 134
   var. *angustifolia*, 134
   var. *argentea*, 134
   'Minor', 134
   subsp. *octopetala*, 134
Dryopteris filix-mas, 82
Drosanthemum, 100, 125, 205
Drosanthemum bellum, 133
Drosanthemum bicolor, 133
Drosanthemum floribundum, 133, Plate 106
Drosanthemum hispidum, 133
Drosanthemum speciosum, 133
Dryopteris, 134
Dryopteris atrata, 46, 134
Dryopteris cycadina, 46, 134
Dryopteris erythrosora, 134
   'Prolifica', 134
Dryopteris filix-mas, 46, 36, 134
   'Barnesii', 134
   'Crispa Cristata', 134
   'Cristata', 134
   'Grandiceps', 134
   'Linearis', 134
   'Linearis Cristata', 134
   'Linearis Polydactyla', 134
   'Polydactyla Dadds', 135
   'Undulata Robusta', 135, Plate 108
Dryopteris intermedia, 46, 36, 135
   'Prolifica', 135
Dryopteris marginalis, 36, 135
Dryopteris wallichiana, 36, 135
Duchesnea indica, 135, Plate 109
   'Variegata', 135
Dusty miller, 77

Echeveria
   baby, 36, 136
   fringed, 36, 136
Echeveria, 136
Echeveria agavoides, 36, 136

Echeveria amoena, 36, 136
Echeveria derenbergii, 36, 136
Echeveria elegans, 36, 136, Plate 110
Echeveria gibbiflora, 36, 136
   'Corniculata', 136
   'Crispa', 136
   'Metallica', 136
Echeveria × *gilva*, 36, 136
Echeveria secunda, 36, 136
Eggs-and-bacon, 217
Elder, ground, 58
Elephant's ear, 89
Elymus glaucus, 211
Empetrum eamesii subsp. *hermaphroditum*, 137
Empetrum nigrum, 37, 136, Plate 111
   var. *hermaphroditum*, 136
   forma *leucocarpum*, 136
   var. *purpureum*, 137
Ephedra distachya, 137, Plate 112
   var. *helvetica*, 137
   var. *monostachya*, 137
Ephedra minima, 137
Ephedra minuta, 138
Ephedra monosperma, 138
Ephedra nevadensis, 37, 137
Ephedra regeliana, 37, 138
Epigaea repens, 138, Plate 113
   'Rosea', 138
Epimedium
   alpine, 139, Plate 114
   long-spur, 139
   Persian, 139
   red, 139
Epimedium alpinum, 139
   'Rubrum', 139, Plate 114
Epimedium grandiflorum, 139
   'Album', 139
   'Elf King', 139
   'Elfkönig', see 'Elf King'
   'Flavescens', 139
   'Lilac Fairy', 139
   'Lilafee', see 'Lilac Fairy'
   'Normale', 139
   'Orion', 139
   'Rose Queen', 139
   'Violaceum', 139
   'White Queen', 139
Epimedium × *perralchicum*
   'Fröhnleiten', 139
Epimedium perralderianum, 139
Epimedium pinnatum, 139
   subsp. *colchicum*, 139
Epimedium × *rubrum*, 139
Epimedium × *versicolor*, 140
   'Cupreum', 140
   'Sulphureum', 140
Equisetum, 140

Equisetum hyemale, 37, 140, Plate 115
Equisetum laevigatum, 141
Equisetum × *nelsonii*, 37, 140
Equisetum scirpoides, 37, 141
Equisetum sylvaticum, 37, 141
   forma *multiramosum*, 141
   var. *pauciramosum*, 141
Equisetum × *trachyodon*, 37, 141
Equisetum variegatum, 37, 141
   var. *alaskanum*, 141
Erica carnea, 141, 142
   'Alan Coates', 142
   'Aurea', 142
   'December Red', 142
   'Eden Valley', 142
   'Eileen Porter', 142
   'Foxhollow Fairy', 142
   'King George', 142
   'Myretoun Ruby', 142
   'Pink Spangles', 142
   'Prince of Wales', 142
   'Springwood Pink', 142, Plate 116
   'Springwood White', 142
   'Vivelli', 142
   'Winter Beauty', 142
Erica cinerea, 142
   'Atropurpurea', 142
   'Atrorubens', 142
   'C. D. Eason, 142'
   'Coccinea', 142
   'Golden Drop', 142
   'Golden Hue', 142
   'Knap Hall Pink', 142
   'Pink Ice', 142
   'P. S. Patrick', 142
   'Rosanne Waterer', 142
   'Velvet Knight', 142
   'Violacea', 142
Erica × *darleyensis*, 142
   'Arthur Johnson', 142
   'Ghost Hills', 142
   'Mediterranean Pink', 142
   'Silberschmelze', 142
Erica erigena, 142
Erica tetralix, 142
   'Alba', 143
   'Con Underwood', 143
   'George Fraser', 143
   'Nana', 143
   'Pink Star', 143
Erica vagans, 143
   'Alba Minor', 143
   'Mrs. D. F. Maxwell', 143
   'St. Keverne', 143
Erigeron glaucus, 37, 143
   'Albus', 143
   'Olga', 143
   'Roseus', 143

'Wayne Rodrick', 144
Erigeron karvinskianus, 37, 143,
    Plate 117
    'Profusion', 143
Erodium chamaedryoides, see *E.
    reichardii*
Erodium reichardii, 144, Plate 118
    'Album', 144
    'Flore Pleno', 144
    'Roseum', 144
Erysimum, Kotschy, 144
Erysimum kotschyanum, 144, Plate
    119
Eulalia, 228
Euonymus, Japanese, 145, Plate 120
Euonymus fortunei, 145, 150
    'Acutus', 145
    'Canadian Variegated', 145
    'Coloratus', 145
    'Dart's Blanket', 145
    'Emerald 'n Gold', 145
    'Gaiety', see 'Tricolor'
    'Golden Princess', 145
    'Kewensis', 145
    'Longwood', 145
    'Minimus', 145
    'Moon Shadow', 145
    var. *radicans,* 145
    var. *radicans* 'Argenteo-variegata',
        145
    var. *radicans* 'Harlequin', 145
    'Sparkle 'n Gold', 145
    'Sun Spot', 145
    'Tricolor', 145, Plate 120
    'Vegetus', 146
Euonymus obovatus, 37, 146
Euphorbia
    cushion, 146, Plate 121
    myrtle, 146
Euphorbia amygdaloides
    var. *robbiae,* 146
    'Rubra', 146
Euphorbia cyparissias, 146
Euphorbia myrsinites, 146
Euphorbia polychroma, 146, Plate
    121
Euryops acraeus, 147, Plate 122
Evergreen
    bunch, 219
    Chinese, 61, Plate 12

Fairy bells, Japanese, 132, Plate 105
Fallopia aubertii, 148
Fallopia baldschuanica, 148
Fallopia japonica
    'Compacta', 147, Plate 123
    'Variegata', 148
Fancy biddy's eyes, 316
Felicia amelloides, 148, Plate 124
    'Astrid Thomas', 148

'George Lewis', 148
'Jolly', 148
'Midnight', 148
'Reed's Blue', 148
'Reed's White', 148
'Rhapsody in Blue', 148
'San Gabriel', 148
'San Louis', 148
'Santa Anita Variegata', 148
Fern
    American wall, 262
    bead, 235
    beech, 301
    black maidenhair, 58
    black wood, 134
    Boston, 232
    Braun's holly, 39, 46, 263
    broad beech, 302
    Christmas, 39, 46, 262, Plate 250
    cinnamon, 38, 46, 239, Plate 222
    common beech, 301
    dagger, 262
    Dallas, 232
    ditch, 240
    five-finger, 57
    hare's foot, 262
    holly, 263
    hybrid oak, 46
    intermediate shield, 36, 135
    intermediate wood, 46
    interrupted, 38, 46, 240
    Japanese lady, 46, 82, Plate 37
    Japanese sword, 134
    King's flowering, 240
    ladder, 232
    lady, 34, 35, 46, 81
    leatherleaf wood, 36, 135
    limestone oak, 167
    long beech, 39, 46, 301
    maiden, 301
    male, 36, 46, 82, 134, Plate 108
    marginal shield, 135
    meadow, 110
    mountain holly, 39, 46, 263
    netted chain, 40, 46, 319
    net-veined chain, 319
    New York, 39, 302, Plate 295
    northern beech, 301
    northern maidenhair, 35, 46, 57
    northern oak, 37, 46, 167
    oak, 37, 46, 166, Plate 145
    ostrich, 38, 46, 222, Plate 199
    Robert's oak, 167
    rock, 58
    royal, 38, 46, 240
    scented oak, 167
    sensitive, 38, 46, 235, Plate 217
    shaggy wood, 134
    shield, 134, 263
    shrubby, 110

    silvery glade, 35, 46, 82
    six cornered, 39, 46, 302
    small chain, 319
    snake, 240
    soft shield, 46, 263
    southern beech, 302
    southern lady, 82
    southern maidenhair, 35, 46, 58,
        Plate 7
    sun, 301
    sword, 46, 232, Plate 213
    tree, 240
    Venus's-hair, 58
    Virginia chain, 40, 46, 319, Plate
        312
    Wallich's wood, 36, 135
    water, 240
    western sword, 39, 46, 263
    wood, 134
Fescue
    blue, 48, Plate 125
    hair, 48, 149
    large blue, 48, 149
Festuca amethystina, 48, 149
    'April Grün', 149
    'Bronzeglanz', 149
    'Klose', 149
Festuca ovina
    'Azurit', 149
    'Blaufink', 149
    'Blaufuchs', 149
    'Blauglut', 149
    'Blausilber', 149
    'Blue Finch', see 'Blaufink'
    'Blue Fox', see 'Blaufuchs'
    'Blue Glow', see 'Blauglut'
    'Blue Silver', see 'Blausilber'
    'Daeumling', see 'Tom Thumb'
    'Elijah's Blue', 149
    'Frühlingsblau', 149
    var. *glauca,* 48, 148, Plate 125
    'Harz', 149
    'Meerblau', 149
    'Platinat', 149
    'Sea Blue', see 'Meerblau'
    'Sea Urchin', 149
    'Silberreiher', 149
    'Silvery Egret', see 'Silberreiher'
    'Soehrenwald', 149
    'Solling', 149
    'Spring Blue', see 'Frühlingsblau'
    'Tom Thumb', 149
Festuca tenuifolia, 48, 149
Fetterbush, 38, 210
Feverfew, 299, Plate 292
Ficus nipponicum, 150
Ficus pumila, 149
    'Arina', 150
    'Minima', 150
    'Variegata', 150, Plate 126

Fiddleheads, 239
Fig
    climbing, 149
    creeping, 149, Plate 126
    four, 97
    ground Hottentot, 97
    Indian, 237
    Japanese, 150
    trailing Hottentot, 97, Plate 57
    trailing sea, 97
Filipendula vulgaris, 150, Plate 127
    'Flore Pleno', 150
Fir
    dwarf joint, 137
    joint, 137, Plate 112
Firethorn, Plate 257
    Formosa, 271
    'Lowboy' scarlet, 271
Fish-mouth, 103
Fittonia, 150, Plate 128
Fittonia verschaffeltii
    var. *argyroneura,* 151
    var. *verschaffeltii,* 150, Plate 128
Flag
    grassy leaved sweet, 57
    Japanese sweet, 57, Plate 6
    larger blue, 197
    sweet, 35, 56, 57
    water, 197
    yellow, 196
Flag-root, 56, 57
Fleabane
    beach, 37, 143
    bonytip, 37, 143, Plate 117
Fleeceflower
    blueberry leaved, 250
    Bokaravine, 148
    dwarf Japanese, 147, Plate 123
    Himalayan, 250, Plate 236
    silvervine, 148
Fluellen, 312
Foamflower
    Allegheny, 39, 304
    Wherry's, 39
Fog, Yorkshire, 184
Forget-me-not
    Siberian, 88
    swamp, 230
    true, 230, Plate 210
Forget-me-nots, wild, 171
Forsythia
    dwarf Arnold, 151
    dwarf Bronx, 151, Plate 129
    dwarf green-stem, 151
Forsythia × intermedia 'Arnold
        Dwarf', 151
Forsythia viridissima 'Bronxensis',
        151, Plate 129
Foxberry, 309
Fox's beard, 99

Foxtail, 219
Fragaria chiloensis, 37, 152
Fragaria 'Lipstick', 152
Fragaria 'Pink Panda', 152
Fragaria 'Shades of Pink', 152
Fragaria vesca, 152, Plate 130
    var. *albicarpa,* 152
    'Alexandria', 152
    'Fructo-alba', see var. *albicarpa*
    var. *monophylla,* 152
    'Multiplex', 152
    var. *semperflorens,* 152
    'Variegata', 152
Fragaria virginiana, 37, 152
Francoa ramosa, 153, Plate 131
Frisbee plant, 59
Frog fruit, 254
Frog plant, 290
Fuchsia
    Australian, 117, Plate 86
    California, 40, 320, Plate 314
    trailing, 153, Plate 132
Fuchsia procumbens, 153, Plate 132
Funkia, 184

Galax, fringed, 294, Plate 282
Galax urceolata, 37, 153, Plate 133
Galaxy, 153
Gale, Canada sweet, 110
Galeobdolon luteum, see *Lamiastrum
        galeobdolon*
Galium odoratum, 154, Plate 134
Garden gate, 316
Gardener's garters, 252
Gardenia, creeping, 155
Gardenia jasminoides
    'Radicans', 155, Plate 135
    'Radicans Variegata', 155
    'White Gem', 155
Gaultheria adenothrix, 156
Gaultheria hispidula, 37, 156
Gaultheria miqueliana, 37, 156
Gaultheria nummularioides, 156
Gaultheria ovatifolia, 37, 156
Gaultheria procumbens, 37, 155,
        Plate 136
Gaultheria shallon, 37, 156
Gaylussacia brachycera, 37, 157, Plate
        137
Gazania, trailing, 157, Plate 138
Gazania linearis, 158
Gazania rigens, 157, 158, Plate 138
    'Aztec Queen', 157
    'Colorama', 157
    'Copper King', 157
    'Fiesta Red', 157
    'Fire Emerald', 157
    'Gold Rush', 158
    var. *leucoleana,* 158
    'Moon Glow', 158

    'Sunburst', 158
    'Sun Glow', 158
Gazania splendens, 157
Gelsemium rankinii, 37, 158
Gelsemium sempervirens, 37, 158,
        Plate 139
    'Plena', 158
    'Pride of Augusta', 158
Genista germanica, 159
Genista hispanica, 159
Genista horrida, 159
Genista lydia, 159
Genista pilosa, 159, Plate 140
    'Vancouver Gold', 159
Genista sagittalis, 159
Genista sylvestris, 159
Genista tinctoria, 159
    'Royal Gold', 159
Geranium
    alpine, 144, Plate 118
    apple-scented, 245
    beefsteak, 287
    bigroot, 161
    carpet, 161
    Clark's
    coconut-scented, 245
    hanging, 244
    ivy, 244
    lemon-scented, 245
    lime-scented, 245
    mint-scented, 245
    nutmeg, 245, Plate 229
    pine-scented, 245
    polecat, 207
    Pylzow, 162
    rock, 182
    strawberry, 287
    trailing, 244
    Wallich, 163
Geranium 'Ann Folkard', 160
Geranium asphodeloides, 160
    subsp. *asphodeloides,* 160
    subsp. *crenophilum,* 160
    'Prince Regent', 160
    subsp. *sintenisii,* 160
    'Starlight', 160
Geranium × cantabrigiense, 160
    'Biokovo', 160
    'Biokovo Karmina', 160
Geranium cinereum, 160
    'Album', 161
    'Ballerina', 161
    'Laurence Flatman', 161
    var. *obtusilobum,* 161
    var. *subcaulescens,* 161
    var. *subcaulescens* 'Giuseppii', 161
    var. *subcaulescens* 'Splendens', 161
Geranium clarkei, 161
    'Kashmir Purple', 161
    'Kashmir White', 161

Geranium dalmaticum, 161
    'Album', 161
Geranium endressii, 161, 162
    'Rose Claire', 161
    'Wargrave Pink', 161
Geranium grandiflorum var. *alpinum,*
        see *G. himalayense* 'Gravetye'
Geranium himalayense, 161
    'Baby Blue', 161
    'Birch Double', see 'Plenum'
    'Gravetye', 161
    'Irish Blue', 161
    'Plenum', 161
Geranium ibericum, 162
Geranium incanum, 161
Geranium 'Johnson's Blue', 161,
        Plate 141
Geranium macrorrhizum, 161
    'Album', 161
    'Bevan's Variety', 161
    'Czakor', 161
    'Ingwersen's Variety', 161
    'Lohfelden', 161
    'Pindus', 161
    'Ridsko', 161
    'Spessart', 162
    'Variegatum', 162
    'Velebit', 162
    'Walter Ingwersen', 162
Geranium maculatum, 37, 161
Geranium × magnificum, 162
Geranium × oxonianum, 162
    'A. T. Johnson', 162
    'Claridge Druce', 162
    'Hollywood', 162
    'Johnson's Variety', 162
    'Lady Moore', 162
    'Rose Clair', 162
    'Sherwood', 162
    'Southcombe Double', 162
    'Southcombe Star', 162
    'Thurstonianum', 162
    'Walter's Gift', 162
    'Winscombe', 162
Geranium platypetalum, 162
Geranium pratense, 161
Geranium procurrens, 162
    'Anne Thompson', 162
    'Dilys', 162
Geranium psilostemon, 162
Geranium pylzowianum, 162
Geranium rectum 'Album', see *G.
        clarkei* 'Kashmir White'
Geranium sanguineum, 162
    'Alan Bloom', 162
    'Album', 162
    'Cedric Morris', 162
    'Elspeth', 162
    'Glenluce', 162
    'Holden', 162

'Jubilee Pink', 162
    var. *lancastriense,* see var. *striatum*
    'Max Frei', 163
    'Minutum', 163
    'New Hampshire Purple', 163
    var. *prostratum,* 163
    'Shepherd's Warning', 163
    var. *striatum,* 163
Geranium versicolor, 162
Geranium wallichianum, 163
    'Buxton's Blue', 163
    'Syabru', 163
Germander, 301
    common, 301
    ground, 301, Plate 294
    wall, 301
Ginger
    British Columbia wild, 35, 78
    Canadian wild, 35, 78
    European wild, 78
    Halberd, 35, 78
    heart leaf wild, 79
    Indian, 78
    mottled wild, 35, 79, Plate 34
    Sierra wild, 35, 78
    southern wild, 79
    Virginia wild, 35, 79
    Yakushima, 79
Glyceria maxima, 48, 163
    'Pallida', 163
    'Variegata', 163, Plate 142
Gold and silver flower, 216
Gold dust, 83
Golden-ray, Daempfer, 212
Golden roots, 113
Golden star, 36, 105, Plate 71
Gold flower, 190
Gold-knops, 272
Goldthread, 113, Plate 81
    western, 36, 114
Goosewort, 263
Gorse, Spanish, 159
Goukum, 97
Goutweed, 58
Gowan, creeping yellow, 272
Grape
    arroyo, 317
    bear's, 72, 282
    bull, 317
    frost, 317
    June, 317
    riverbank, 317, Plate 310
    riverside, 40, 317
    sweet scented, 317
    winter, 317
Grass
    American beach, 66
    autumn sorcery fountain, 246
    avena, 173
    bear, 188

black bent, 242
black sedge, 35, 95
blue-downy lyme, 211
blue lyme, 38, 48, 211, Plate 187
blue oat, 48, 173, Plate 153
carnation, 95
Chinese fountain, 245
creeping soft, 184
dart, 184
feather, 184
giant blue lyme, 38
giant dune, 212
gilliflower, 95
goose, 263
great water, 48, 163, Plate 142
intermediate quaking, 88
Japanese blood, 193, Plate 166
Japanese fountain, 48, 245
Japanese silver, 48, 228, Plate 206
Korean, 320
kuma bamboo, 286, Plate 275
lady's hair, 88
maidenhair, 88
marram sea, 211
Mascarene, 48, 320, Plate 315
mat, 254
meadow fountain, 246
mondo, 236
moon, 263
oriental fountain, 48, 246
Pacific dune, 38, 212
Pacific lyme, 212
pearl, 88
perennial quaking, 88
pink, 95
poverty, 114
prairie cord, 295
Quaker, 88
quaking, 48, 88, Plate 47
rancheria, 211
rattle, 88
reed manna, 163
reed meadow, 163
reed sweet, 163
ribbon, 38
rose fountain, 48, 246, Plate 231
Salem, 184
sand reed, 35
sea lyme, 211
shivering, 88
snake, 140
switch, 38, 48, 242, Plate 226
thatch, 242
totter, 88
trembling, 88
tufted hair, 36, 48, 127
variegated reed canary, 252
variegated ribbon, 48, Plate 238
variegated velvet, 48, 184, Plate
    158

[Grass]
    wavy hair, 36, 128, Plate 99
    white flowering fountain, 48, 246
    Wobsqua, 242
    wood soft, 184
Grass-poly, 124
Gravel weed, 132
Greenwood, dyer's, 159
Grevillea, 163
Grevillea aquifolium, 164
Grevillea 'Austraflora Canterbury Gold', 164
Grevillea 'Austraflora Copper Crest', 164
Grevillea 'Austraflora Fanfare', 164
Grevillea 'Austraflora Old Gold', 164
Grevillea australis, 164
Grevillea banksii, 164
Grevillea biternata, 164
Grevillea brachystachya, 164
Grevillea 'Bronze Rambler', 164
Grevillea confertifolia, 164
Grevillea × *gaudichaudii,* 164
Grevillea juniperina, 164, Plate 143
    'Molonglo', 164
    var. *trinervis,* 164
Grevillea lanigera, 164
    'Mont Tamboritha', 165
Grevillea laurifolia, 165
Grevillea 'Noell', 165
Grevillea obtusifolia, 165
Grevillea paniculata, 165
Grevillea 'Poorinda Royal Mantle', 165
Grevillea pteridifolia, 165
Grevillea repens, 165
Grevillea rosmarinifolia, 165
Grevillea thelemanniana, 165
Grevillea tridentifera, 164
Grevillea 'White Wings', 165
Ground moss, 188
Ground pine, 38
    flat-branched, 38
    treelike, 38
Gunnera, toothed, 165
Gunnera chilensis, 166
Gunnera dentata, 165
Gunnera hamiltonii, 166
Gunnera magellanica, 166
Gunnera manicata, 166
Gunnera prorepens, 166
Gunnera tinctoria, 166, Plate 144
Gymnocarpium dryopteris, 37, 46, 166, 167, Plate 145
    'Plumosum', 167
Gymnocarpium heterosporum, 46, 167
Gymnocarpium robertianum, 37, 46, 167
Gypsophila paniculata, 167
    'Alba', 167

'Bristol Fairy', 167
'Compacta', 167
'Compacta Plena', 167
'Dantzinger', 167
'Flamingo', 167
'Flore Pleno', 167
'Grandiflora', 167
'Perfecta', 167
'Pink Fairy', 167
'Pink Star', 167
'Red Sea', 167
'Rosenschkier', see 'Rosy Veil'
'Rosy Veil', 167
'Viette's Dwarf', 167
Gypsophila repens, 167
    'Alba', 167
    'Bodgeri', 167
    'Dorothy Teacher', see 'Rosa Schönheit'
    'Fratensis', 167
    'Rosa Schönheit', 167
    'Rosea', 167, Plate 146
Gypsy weed, 312

Hakonechloa, 48, 168, Plate 147
Hakonechloa macra, 48, 168, Plate 147
    'Albo-aurea', 168
    'Albo Striata', see 'Albo-variegata'
    'Albo-variegata', 168
    'Aureola', 168
Hardy ice, 125
Haworthia, 168
Haworthia cuspidata, 168
Haworthia fasciata, 168
Haworthia radula, 168, Plate 148
Haworthia tessellata, 169
    var. *parva,* 169
Hawthorn, Indian, 273, Plate 261
Heart of Jesus, 89
Heart's-ease, 316
Heath
    bell, 142
    blackberried, 136
    bog, 142
    Cornish, 142
    crossleaf, 142
    Darley, 142
    moor, 142
    Scotch, 142
    spring, 142, Plate 116
    twisted, 142
    wandering, 142
    winter, 142
Heathberry, 136
Heather, Plate 53
    beach, 188, Plate 161
    common, 92
    false, 121, 188, Plate 90
    golden, 188

    ground, 188
    Monox, 136
    mountain beach, 188
    Scotch, 92
    snow, 142
    woolly beach, 188
Hebe
    Chatham, 169
    ground, 169
Hebe 'Autumn Glory', 169
Hebe 'Carl Teschner', 169
Hebe chathamica, 169
Hebe decumbens, 169
Hebe pinguifolia 'Pagei', 169, Plate 149
Hedera, 169
Hedera canariensis, 170
    'Azorica', 170
    'Gloire de Marengo', see 'Souvenir de Marengo',
    'Ravensholst', 170
    'Souvenir de Marengo', 170
    'Striata', 170
    'Variegata', see 'Souvenir de Marengo'
Hedera colchica, 170
    'Dentata', 170
    'Dentata Variegata', 170
    'Gold Leaf', 170
    'Paddy's Pride', 170
    'Sulfur Heart', 170
Hedera helix, 150, 170
    'Argenteo-Variegata', 170
    'Atropurpurea', see 'Minima'
    'Baltica', 170
    'Brocamp', 171
    'Bulgaria', 171
    'Buttercup', 171
    'Caecilia', 171
    'California Fan', 171
    'California Gold', 171
    'Duckfoot', 171
    'Flamenco', 171
    'Galaxy', 171
    'Glacier', 171
    'Goldheart', 171
    'Hahn's', 171
    'Hahn's Self-branching', see 'Hahn's'
    'Harrison', 171
    'Hibernica', 171
    'Hummingbird', 171
    'Jubilee', 171
    'Little Diamond', 171
    'Maculata', 171
    'Midget', 171
    'Miniature Green Ripples', 171
    'Minima', 171
    'Needlepoint', 171
    'Pedata', 171

'Pixie', 171
'Savannah', 171
'Schaffer Three', 171
'Silverdust', 171
'Thorndale', 171, Plate 150
'Walthamensis', 171
'Webfoot', 171
'Woerner', 171
Hedyotis caerulea, 37, 171, Plate 151
Helianthemum × hybridus, 172
Helianthemum nummularium, 172
   'Amy Baring', 172
   'Apricot', 172
   'Ben Afflick', 172
   'Ben Nevis', 172
   'Bright Spot', 172
   'Cerise Queen', 172
   'Dazzler', 172
   'Eloise', 172
   'Fireball', 172
   'Flame', 172
   'Goldilocks', 172
   'Henfield Brilliant', 172
   'Jubilee', 172
   'Mrs. C. W. Earle', see 'Fireball'
   var. *multiplex,* 172
   'Mutabile', 172
   'Orange Surprise', 172
   'Pink', 172
   'Red', 172
   'Rosa Konigin', see 'Rose Queen'
   'Rose Glory', 172
   'Rose Queen', 172
   'Watergate Rose', 172
   'Wisley Pink', 172, Plate 152
   'Wisley Primrose', 172
   'Wisley White', 172
Helictotrichon sempervirens, 48, 173,
   Plate 153
   'Saphirsprudel', 173
Heliotrope, winter, 251
Hellebore, bear's foot, 174
Helleborus atrorubens, 174
Helleborus foetidus, 174
   'Bowles Form', 174
   'Green Giant', 174
   'Italian Form', 174
   'Miss Jekyll', 174
   'Sienna', 174
   'Sierra Nevada Form', 174
   'Sopron', 174
   'Tros-os-Montes', 174
   'Wester Flisk', 174
Helleborus niger, 173
   var. *altifolius,* 174
   'Angustifolius', 174
   'Blackthorn Strain', 174
   'Eva', 174
   'Foliis Variegatus', 174
   'Harvington Hybrids', 174

'Higham's Variety', 174
'Ladham's Variety', 174
'Louis Cobbett', 174
subsp. *macranthus,* 174
'Madame Fourcade', 174
'Major', 174
'Marion', 174
'Pixie', 174
'Potter's Wheel', 174
'Praecox', 174
'St. Brigid', 174
'Sunset', 174
'Trotter's Form', 174
'White Magic', 174
Helleborus orientalis, 174, Plate 154
   'Guttatus', 174
   'Medallion', 174
Helleborus viridis, 174
   subsp. *occidentalis* 'Pailhès', 174
Helmet pod, 199
Hemerocallis, 175, Plate 155
Hemerocallis aurantiaca, 175
   'Major', 175
Hemerocallis fulva, 175
   'Cypriana', 175
   'Europa', 175
   'Flore Pleno', 175
   'Kwanso', 175
   var. *littorea,* 176
Hemerocallis × hybridus, 176
   'Alec Allen', 177
   'Always Afternoon', 177
   'Amadeus', 177
   'Antique Carrousel', 177
   'Apple Tart', 177
   'Barbara Mitchell', 177
   'Baroody', 177
   'Becky Lynn', 177
   'Bertie Ferris', 177
   'Bette Davis Eyes', 177
   'Betty Woods', 177
   'Black Eyed Stella', 177
   'Black Eyed Susan', 177
   'Blake Allen', 177
   'Brocaded Gown', 177
   'Chester Cyclone', 177
   'Chicago Knobby', 177
   'Chorus Line', 178
   'Christmas Is', 178
   'Condilla', 178
   'Dancing Shiva', 178
   'Dan Tau', 178
   'Ed Murray', 178
   'Eenie Weenie', 178
   'Ellen Christine', 178
   'Fairy Tale Pink', 178
   'Fama', 178
   'Flutterbye', 178
   'Forsyth Lemon Drop', 178
   'Frances Joiner', 178

'Fred Ham', 178
'Golden Prize', 178
'Golden Scroll', 178
'Hamlet', 178
'Happy Returns', 178
'Janet Gayle', 178
'Janice Brown', 178
'Jason Salter', 178
'Joan Senior', 178
'Kate Carpenter', 178
'Kindly Light', 178
'Lemon Lollypop', 178
'Little Business', 178
'Little Deeke', 178
'Little Grapette', 178
'Lots of Pizazz', 179
'Lullaby Baby', 179
'Magic Obsession', 179
'Malaysian Monarch', 179
'Mandala', 179
'Martha Adams', 179
'Mary Todd', 179
'Merry Witch', 179
'Ming Snow', 179
'Mini Pearl', 179
'Mini Stella', 179
'Moroccan Summer', 179
'My Belle', 179
'My Friend Nell', 179
'My Pet', 179
'Nagasaki', 179
'Neal Berry', 179
'Olive Bailey Langdon', 179
'Open Hearth', 179
'Ornate Ruffles', 179
'Paper Butterfly', 179
'Pardon Me', 179
'Picotee Princess', 179
'Pink Corduroy', 179
'Praire Blue Eyes', 179
'Prester John', 179
'Princess Ellen', 179
'Rachael My Love', 179
'Raindrop', 179
'Red Rum', 179
'Ruffled Apricot', 180
'Russian Rhapsody', 180
'Sebastian', 180
'Seductor', 180
'Seductress', 180
'Siloam Bertie Ferris', 180
'Siloam Bo Peep', 180
'Siloam Byelo', 180
'Siloam Double Classic', 180
'Siloam Jim Cooper', 180
'Siloam June Bug', 180
'Siloam Merrill Kent', 180
'Siloam Virginia Henson', 180
'Smoky Mountain Autumn', 180
'Snowy Apparition', 180

[*Hemerocallis* × *hybridus*]
    'Sombrero Way', 180
    'Stella de Oro', 180
    'Strawberry Candy', 180
    'Sugar Cookie', 180
    'Super Purple', 180
    'Sweet Shalimar', 180
    'Tuscawilla Dave Talbott', 180
    'Venetian Lace', 180
    'Vintage Bordeaux', 180
    'Vision of Beauty', 180
    'Whooperee', 180
    'Wilson Spider', 181
    'Winsome Lady', 181
    'Wynnson', 181
    'Zinfandel', 181
Hemerocallis lilioasphodelus, 181
Hemerocallis middendorffii, 181
Hemlock
    Canadian, 39, 307, Plate 301
    creeping, 300
    ground, 300
Hen and chickens, 136, 293
Herb
    blue, 132
    carpenter's, 61
    Elfin, 121
Herb Christopher, 240
Herb Gerard, 58
Herb trinity, 316
Herniaria glabra, 181, Plate 156
Herniary, 181
Heuchera americana, 37, 182, 183
    'Chocolate Veil', 182
    'Dale's Strain', 182
    'Emerald Veil', 182
    'Garnet', 182
    'Ring of Fire', 182
    'Sunset', 182
Heuchera × *brizoides,* 37, 182, 183,
        304
    'Amethyst Myst', 183
    'Bloom's Variety', 183
    'Can-Can', 183
    'Canyon Pink', 183
    'Cappuccino', 183
    'Carousel', 183
    'Cascade Dawn', 183
    'Cathedral Windows', 183
    'Chiqui', 183
    'Chocolate Ruffles', 183
    'Chocolate Veil', 183
    'Coral Cloud', 183
    'Frosty', 183
    'Lace Ruffles', 183
    'Martha's Compact', 183
    'Mayfair', 183
    'Mint Julip', 183
    'Montrose Ruby', 183
    'Oakington Jewel', 183

'Palace Passion', 183
'Palace Purple', 183
'Persian Carpet', 183
'Pewter Moon', 183
'Pewter Veil', 183'
'Pluie de Feu', 183
'Purple Petticoats', 183
'Purple Sails', 183
'Rain of Fire', see 'Pluie de Feu'
'Raspberry Regal', 183
'Regal Robe', 183
'Ruby Ruffles', 183
'Ruby Veil', 183
'Ruffles', 183
'Scintillation', 183
'Silver Shadows', 183
'Splendour', 183
'Stormy Seas', 183
'Tattletale', 183
'Velvet Night', 183
'Whirlwind', 183
'White Cloud', 183
'White Marble', 183
'White Spires', 183
Heuchera cylindrica, 183
Heuchera micrantha, 37, 183
Heuchera pilosissima, 37, 183
Heuchera sanguinea, 37, 181, 183,
        Plate 157
    'Alba', 182
    'Apple Blossom', 182
    'Bressingham Blaze', 182
    'Bressingham Hybrids', 182
    'Chartreuse', 182
    'Chatterbox', 182
    'Cherry Splash', 182
    'Coral Splash', 182
    'Fairy Cups', 182
    'Fire Sprite', 182
    'Firebird', 182
    'Freedom', 182
    'Garnet', 182
    'Green Ivory', 182
    'Jack Frost', 182
    'June Bride', 182
    'Matin Bells', 182
    'Mt. St. Helens', 182
    'Patricia Louise', 182
    'Pink Splash', 182
    'Queen of Hearts', 182
    'Rhapsody', 182
    'Rosamund', 182
    'Salt and Pepper', 182
    'Scarlet Sentinel', 182
    'Shere Variety', 182
    'Silver Veil', 182
    'Snowflakes', 182
    'Snow Storm', 182
    'Splendens', 182
    'Splish Splash', 182

'Virginalis', 182
Heuchera villosa, 37, 183
    var. *macrorhiza,* 183
    'Purpurea', 183
× *Heucherella tiarelloides,* 304
    'Bridget Bloom', 304
    'Crimson Clouds', 304
    'Pink Frost', 304
    'Rosalie', 304
    'Snow White', 304
    'White Blush', 304
Hobble, dog, 211
Holcus mollis 'Albo-variegatus', 48,
        184, Plate 158
Holly, 192
    box-leaved, 193
    Chinese, 193, Plate 165
    dwarf Chinese, 193
    ground, 104
    horned, 193
    Japanese, 193
    Oregon grape, 221
    Yaupon, 37, 193
Honey plant, 224
Honeysuckle
    Brown's hybrid, 215
    bush, 36, 132, Plate 104
    dwarf bush, 132
    dwarf emerald mound, 217
    everblooming, 216
    evergreen, 38, 216
    goldflame, 216
    Henry's, 216
    Japanese, 216
    privet, 216
    royal carpet, 216, Plate 192
    sweet, 216
    yellow-flowered, 38, 216
    yellow-net, 216
Hops, wild, 108
Horsetail
    common, 37, 140, Plate 115
    variegated, 37, 141
    woodland, 37, 141
Hosta, 184
    blue, 186
    blunt-leaved, 185
    Fortune's, 185, Plate 159
    fragrant, 185
    narrow-leaved, 185
    Siebold, 185
    wavy leaved, 185
Hosta, 184
Hosta 'Abiqua Drinking Gourd', 186
Hosta 'Antioch', 186
Hosta 'August Moon', 186
Hosta 'Big Daddy', 186
Hosta 'Blue Angel', 186
Hosta 'Blue Cadet', 186
Hosta 'Blue Diamond', 186

Hosta 'Blue Wedgewood', 186
Hosta 'Bright Glow', 186
Hosta 'Brim Cup', 186
Hosta 'Camelot', 186
Hosta 'Daybreak', 186
Hosta decorata, 185
Hosta 'Diamond Tierra', 186
Hosta 'Don Stevens', 186
Hosta 'Ellerbroek', 186
Hosta fluctuans, 185
   'Variegata', 185
Hosta fortunei, 185
   'Aoki', 185
   'Aureo-marginata', 185, Plate 159
   'Gloriosa', 185
   'Gold Standard', 185
   'Hyacinthina', 185
   'Marginato-alba', 185
Hosta 'Fragrant Blue', 186
Hosta 'Fragrant Bouquet', 186
Hosta 'Francee', 186
Hosta 'Frosted Jade', 186
Hosta 'Ginko Craig', 186
Hosta 'Gold Edger', 186
Hosta 'Golden Scepter', 186
Hosta 'Golden Tiara', 186
Hosta 'Gold Standard', 186
Hosta 'Green Fountain', 186
Hosta 'Green Gold', 186
Hosta 'Ground Master', 186
Hosta 'Hadspen Blue', 187
Hosta 'Halcyon', 187
Hosta 'Honeybells', 187
Hosta 'Inniswood', 187
Hosta 'Janet', 187
Hosta 'June', 187
Hosta kikutii', 186
Hosta 'Krossa Regal', 187
Hosta lancifolia, 185
Hosta 'Leona Fraim', 187
Hosta 'Love Pat', 187
Hosta 'Midas Touch', 187
Hosta montana, 185
   'Aureo-marginata', 185
   'Mountain Snow', 185
   'On Stage', 185
   var. *praeflorens*, 185
Hosta 'Night Before Christmas', 187
Hosta 'North Hills', 187
Hosta 'Patriot', 187
Hosta 'Paul's Glory', 187
Hosta plantaginea, 185
   'Aphrodite', 185
   'Grandiflora', 185
Hosta 'Royal Standard', 187
Hosta 'Sea Thunder', 187
Hosta 'Shade Fanfare', 187
Hosta 'Shade Master', 187
Hosta sieboldiana, 185
   'Alba', 185

'Aurora Borealis', 185
'Elegans', 185
'Francis Williams', 185
'Golden Sunburst', 185
'Great Expectations', 185
'Helen Doriot', 185
'Louisa', 185
'May T. Watts', 185
'Northern Halo', 185
'Robusta', 185
Hosta 'Snow Crust', 187
Hosta 'So Sweet', 187
Hosta 'Spritzer', 187
Hosta 'Striptease', 187
Hosta 'Sugar and Cream', 187
Hosta 'Sum and Substance', 187
Hosta 'Sun Power', 187
Hosta 'Thomas Hogg', see *H. decorata*
Hosta 'Tiny Tears', 187
Hosta undulata, 185
   'Albo-marginata', 186
   'Erromena', 186
   'Univittata', 186
   'Univittata Middle Ridge', 186
   'Variegata', 186
Hosta ventricosa, 186
   'Aureo-maculata', 186
   'Aureo-marginata', 186
Hosta 'White Christmas', 187
Hosta 'Wide Brim', 187
Hosta 'Yellow River', 187
Hosta 'Yellow Splash Rim', 187
Hosta yingeri, 186
Houseleek, 292, Plate 281
   cobweb, 293
   mountain, 293
   roof, 293
   Russian, 293
   sand loving
   spiderweb, 293
Houttuynia, 187, Plate 160
Houttuynia cordata, 187
   'Chameleon', 188
   'Plena', 188
   'Variegata', 188, Plate 160
Huckleberry, box, 37, 157, Plate 137
Hudsonia
   heatherlike, 188
   woolly, 188
Hudsonia ericoides, 37, 188
   forma *leucantha*, 188
Hudsonia montana, 37, 188
Hudsonia tomentosa, 37, 188, Plate 161
   var. *intermedia*, 188
Hundreds and thousands, 268
Huperzia lucidula, see *Lycopodium lucidulum*

Hydrangea, climbing, 189, Plate 162
Hydrangea anomala subsp. *petiolaris*, 189, Plate 162
   'Skyland's', 189
Hylotelephium populifolium, see *Sedum populifolium*
Hylotelephium spectabile, see *Sedum spectabile*
Hylotelephium telephium, 290
Hypericum, 189
Hypericum acmosepalum, see *H. beanii*
Hypericum androsaemum, 190, 191
   'Albury Purple', 191
   'Glacier', 191
Hypericum beanii, 191
Hypericum buckleyi, 37, 190
Hypericum calycinum, 190, 191
Hypericum cerastoides, 191
Hypericum coris, 190
Hypericum × *cyanthiflorum* 'Gold Cup', 191
Hypericum ellipticum, 37, 190
Hypericum forrestii, 191
Hypericum 'Hidcote', 191, Plate 164
Hypericum kouytchense 'Sungold', 191
Hypericum moseranum, 191
Hypericum olympicum, 190
   var. *citrinum*, 190
   forma *minus*, 190
   forma *minus* 'Sulphureum', 190
   forma *uniflorum* 'Sunburst', 191
Hypericum patulum, 190, 191
   var. *henryi*, see *H. beanii*
   'Hidcote', see *H.* 'Hidcote'
   'Sunburst', see *H. olympicum* forma *uniflorum* 'Sunburst'
   'Sungold', see *H. kouytchense* 'Sungold'
Hypericum polyphyllum, see *H. olympicum* forma *minus*
Hypericum pseudohenryi, see *H. beanii*
Hypericum reptans, 191
Hypericum tomentosum, 191

Iberis candolleana, 192
Iberis gibraltarica, 192
Iberis pruitii, 192
Iberis saxatilis, 192
Iberis sayana, 192
Iberis sempervirens, 191
   'Alexander's White', 192
   'Autumn Beauty', 192
   'Autumn Snow', see 'Autumn Beauty'
   'Christmas Snow', 192
   'Kingwood Compact', 192
   'Little Gem', 192

[*Iberis sempervirens*]
  'October Glory', 192
  'Purity', 192
  'Pygmaea', 1922
  'Snow Mantle', 192
  'Snowflake', 192, Plate 164
  'Weisserzwerg', see 'Little Gem'
Ice plant, 205, Plate 62
  bush, 206
  cloud-loving, 125, Plate 97
  Cooper's hardy, 125
  hairy, 133
  purple, 206
  rosy, 133, Plate 106
  showy, 206, Plate 179
  trailing, 125, 206
Ilex, 192
Ilex cornuta, 193
  'Berries Jubilee', 193
  'Burfordii Nana', 193
  'Carissa', 193
  'Rotunda', 193
Ilex crenata, 193
  'Compacta', 193
  'Convexa', 193
  'Green Island', 193
  'Helleri', 193, Plate 165
  'Hetzii', 193
  'Kingsville', 193
  'Kingsville Green Cushion', 193
Ilex vomitoria, 37, 193
  'Nana', 193
  'Shelling's Dwarf', 193
  'Stoke's Dwarf', see 'Shelling's
    Dwarf'
  'Straughans', 193
Imperata cylindrica 'Red Baron', 48,
    193, Plate 166
Inch plant, giant, 306
Indian-paint, 284
Indigo
  Kirilow, 194
  white Chinese, 194, Plate 167
Indigofera incarnata, 194, Plate 167
  var. *alba*, 194
Indigofera kirilowii, 194
Innocence, 171
Inside-out flower, 40, 310, Plate 303
Iris
  Alaskan, 37, 197
  blue flag, 37
  crested dwarf, 195
  dwarf bearded, 196
  dwarf crested, 37, 195
  Japanese, 195
  larger blue flag, 37
  poison, 197
  roof, 197
  sweet, 196
  wall, 197

  wild, 197
  yellow water, 196, Plate 169
Iris attica, 196
Iris chamaeiris, 196
Iris cristata, 37, 195
  'Abbey's Violet', 195
  'Alba', 195
  'Baby Blue', 195
  'Eco Little Bird', 195
  'Shenandoah Sky Light', 195
  'Summer Storm', 195
  'Vein Mountain', 195
Iris ensata, 195
  'Beni-Tsubaki', 196
  'Confetti Shower', 196
  'Crystal Halo', 196
  'Ebb and Flow', 196
  'Freckled Geisha', 196
  'Frilled Enchantment', 196
  'Frosted Pyramid', 196
  'Henry's White', 196
  'Joyous Troubadour', 196
  'Joy Peters', 196
  'Light At Dawn', 196
  'Lilac Peaks', 196
  'Little Snow Man', 196
  'Oriental Eyes', 196
  'Over the Waves', 196
  'Pink Pearl', 196
  'Prairie Noble', 196
  'Reign of Glory', 196
  'Rose Adagio', 196
  'Sparkling Sapphire', 196
  'Storm At Sea', 196
  'Summer Moon', 196
  'Summer Storm', 196
  'Tideline', 196
  'Variegata', 196
  'Winged Sprite', 196
Iris hexagona, 197
Iris kaempferi, 196
Iris pallida, 196
  'Albo-variegata', 196, Plate 168
  'Argentea', 196
  'Aurea-variegata', see 'Variegata'
  var. *dalmatica*, 196
  'Variegata', 196
  'Zebra', see 'Albo-variegata'
Iris pseudacorus, 196, Plate 169
  'Alba', 196
  'Bastardii', 196
  'Flore-Plena', 196
  'Golden Queen', 196
  'Nana', 196
  'Variegata', 196
Iris pumila, 196
  'Alba', 196
  'Atropurpurea', 196
  'Aurea', 197
  'Cherry Garden', 197

  'Cyanea', 197
  'Lutea', 197
  'Navy Doll', 197
  'Ritz', 197
  'Sunrise Pink', 197
  'Truely', 197
Iris setosa, 37, 197
  var. *canadensis*, 197
  'Kosho En', 197
  'Nana', 197
Iris tectorum, 197
  'Alba', 197
Iris versicolor, 37, 197
  'Alba', 197
  'Kermesina', 197
Iris virginica, 37, 197
Isotoma fluviatilis, see *Pratia
    pedunculata*
Itea virginica, 198
  'Beppu', 198
  'Henry's Garnet', 37, 198, Plate
    170
  'Sarah Eve', 198
Ivy, 169
  Algerian, 170
  American, 243
  bird's foot, 171
  Canary Island, 170
  Colchis, 170
  coliseum, 121
  English, 150, 170, Plate 150
  five-leaved, 243
  fragrant, 170
  Kenilworth, 121, Plate 91
  Madeira, 170
  Persian, 170
  spider, 105
  switch, 211
  toadflax basket, 122

Jacob's ladder, 39, 259, Plate 246
  creeping, 39, 259
Jasmine
  Chinese star, 306
  Confederate, 306
  primrose, 198
  showy, 198
  star, 306, Plate 299
  winter, 199, Plate 171
  yellow star, 306
Jasminum floridum, 198
Jasminum mesnyi, 198
Jasminum nudiflorum, 198, Plate 171
Jeffersonia diphylla, 37, 199, Plate
    172
Jeffersonia dubia, 199
Jessamine
  Carolina, 37, 158, Plate 139
  Carolina yellow, 158
  yellow, 158

yellow false, 158
Jet sedge, 95
Johnny-jumper, 316
Johnny-jump-up, 316
Jovibarba arenaria, 200
Jovibarba heuffelii, 200
   'Apache', 200
   'Beacon Hill', 200
   'Bloodstone', 200
   'Cameo', 200
   'Giuseppi Spiny', 200
   'Gold Bug', 200
   'Inferno', 200
   'Miller's Violet', 200
   'Mystique', 200, Plate 173
   'Tan', 200
   'Xanthoheuff', 200
Jovibarba hirta, 200
   'Borealis'
   'Bulgaria', 200
   'Emerald Spring', 200
   'Sierra Nevada', 200
   'Smeryouka', 200
Jovibarba sobolifera, 200
Juniper, 200
   Canadian, 201
   Chinese, 201
   common, 37, 201
   communal, 201
   creeping, 37, 202
   Davurian, 202, Plate 175
   English, 201
   horizontal, 202, Plate 174 and 278
   Japanese garden, 202
   Rocky Mountain, 37, 203
   savin, 202
   shore, 201
   singleseed, 203
   tam, 203
Juniper thrift, 75
Juniperus, 200
Juniperus chinensis, 201
   'Emerald Sea', 201
   'Fruitlandii', 201
   'Gold Coast', 201
   'Gold Lace', 201
   'Holbert', 201
   'Old Gold', 201
   'Pfitzeriana', 201
   'Pfitzeriana Aurea', 201
   'Pfitzeriana Compacta', 201
   'Pfitzeriana Sarcoxie', 201
   'San Jose', 201
   var. *sargentii,* 201
   var. *sargentii* 'Glauca', 201
   'Saybrook Gold', 201
   'Sea Spray', 201
Juniperus communis, 37, 201
   var. *depressa,* 201

   'Depressa Aurea', 201
   'Depressed Star', 201
   'Effusa', 201
   'Nana', 201
   'Saxatilis', 201
   'Siberica', 201
Juniperus conferta, 201
   'Blue Pacific', 201
   'Boulevard', 201
   'Compacta', 201
   'Emerald Sea', 202
Juniperus davurica, 202
   'Expansa', 202
   'Expansa Aureospicata', 202
   'Expansa Variegata', 202, Plate 175
   'Parsonii', see 'Expansa'
Juniperus horizontalis, 37, 202
   'Adpressa', 202
   'Aurea', 202
   'Bar Harbor', 202
   'Blue Chip', 202, Plate 174
   'Blue Horizon', 202
   'Blue Rug', see 'Wiltonii'
   'Emerald Spreader', 202
   'Hughes', 202
   'Huntington Blue', 202
   'Icee Blue', 202
   'Jade Spreader', 202
   'Mother Lode', 202
   'Pancake', 202
   'Plumosa', 202
   'Turquoise Spreader', 202
   'Variegata', 202
   'Wiltonii', 202
Juniperus procumbens, 202
   'Green Mound', 202
   'Nana', 202
   'Nana Californica', 202
   'Nana Greenmound', 202
Juniperus sabina, 202
   'Arcadia', 202
   'Arcadia Compacta', 202
   'Blue Danube', 202
   'Blue Forest', 202
   'Broadmoor', 203
   'Buffalo', 203
   'Calgary Carpet', 203
   'Moor-dense', 203
   'Sierra Spreader', 203
   'Skandia', 203
   'Tamariscifolia', 202
   'Tamariscifolia New Blue', 203
   'Variegata', 203
Juniperus scopulorum, 37, 203
   'Blue Creeper', 203
   'Monam', 203
Juniperus squamata, 203
   'Blue Carpet', 203
   'Blue Star', 203

   'Holger', 203
   'Prostrata', 203
   'Variegata', 203
Juniperus virginiana 37, 203
   'Gray Owl', 203
   'Silver Spreader', 203
Jupiter's beard, 99, Plate 61

Kalanchoe
   Christmas, 203, Plate 176
   Fedtschenkoi, 204
Kalanchoe blossfeldiana, 203, Plate 176
Kalanchoe fedtschenkoi, 204
Kalanchoe laciniata, 204
Kalanchoe marmorata, 204
Kalanchoe tomentosa, 204
Kalanchoe tubiflora, 204
King's cure, 104
Kinnikinick, 71
Kisses, 316
Kiss me, 316
Knotweed
   dwarf Japanese, 147
   pinkhead, 250
   Virginia, 38, 250
Kumazasa, 48, 286

Lace plant, 65
Lace vine, silver, 148
Ladder to heaven, 111
Ladies delight, 316
Ladies finger, 217
Lad's love, dwarf, 76
Lady's mantle, 64, Plate 15
   alpine, 64
Lagwort, 251
Lamb's ear, 297, Plate 287
Lamiastrum, 204
Lamiastrum galeobdolon, 204
   'Compacta', 204
   'Herman's Pride', 204
   'Variegata', 204, Plate 177
Lamium maculatum, 205
   'Album', 205
   'Aureum', 205
   'Beacon Silver', 205
   'Beedham's White', 205
   'Chequers', 205
   'Elizabeth De Maas', 205
   'Pink Pewter', 205
   'Shell Pink', 205
   'White Nancy', 205, Plate 178
Lampranthus, 100, 125, 133, 205
Lampranthus aurantiacus, 206
   'Glaucus', 206
   'Gold Nugget', 206
   'Sunman', 206
Lampranthus filicaulis, 206
Lampranthus productus, 206

Lampranthus spectabilis, 206, Plate
    179
Lantana
    hybrid, 206, Plate 180
    trailing, 207
    weeping, 207
Lantana camara, 206
Lantana × hybrida, 206, Plate 180
    'American Red', 206
    'Carnival', 206
    'Christine', 207
    'Confetti', 207
    'Cream Carpet', 207
    'Dwarf Pink', 207
    'Dwarf White', 207
    'Dwarf Yellow', 207
    'Golden Glow', 207
    'Gold Mound', 207
    'Gold Rush', 207
    'Irene', 207
    'Kathleen', 207
    'Miss Huff', 207
    'New Gold', 207
    'Radiation', 207
    'Spreading Sunset', 207
    'Spreading Sunshine', 207
    'Sunburst', 207
    'Tangerine', 207
    'Variegata', 207
    'Yellow Spreader', 207
Lantana montevidensis, 206, 207
    'Lavender Swirl', 207
    'Veluntina White', 207
    'White Lightnin', 207
Lathyrus latifolius, 207, Plate 181
    'Albus', 207
    'Pink Pearl', 207
    'Red Pearl', 207
    'Splendens', 207
    'White Pearl', 207
Laurel
    dwarf Australian, 258
    trailing mountain, 138
Laurentia fluviatilis, see *Pratia
        pedunculata*
Lavandula angustifolia, 208
    'Alba', 208
    'Baby White', 208
    'Bowles', 208
    'Carrol Gardens', 208
    'Compacta', 208
    'Dutch', 208
    'Dwarf Blue', 208
    'Fragrance', 208
    'Gigantea', 208
    'Graves', 208
    'Grey Lady', 208
    'Hidcote Blue', 208
    'Hidcote Giant', 208
    'Hidcote Pink', 208

'Jean Davis', 208
'Lady Lavender', 208, Plate 182
'Mitchem', 208
'Mitchem Grey', 208
'Munstead Dwarf', 208
'Nana', 208
'Nana Baby White'
'Rosea', 208
'Royal Velvet', 208
'Sachet', 208
'Silver Frost', 208
'Twickle Purple', 208
'Waltham', 208
Lavandula × intermedia, 208
    'Dutchmill', 208
    'Fred Boutin', 208
    'Grosso', 208
    'Provence', 208
    'Seal', 208
Lavandula latifolia, 208
Lavandula stoechas, 208
    'Alba', 208
    'Atlas', 208
    'Otto Quest', 208
    'Papillon', 208
    subsp. *pedunculata,* 209
Lavender
    French, 208
    spike, 208
    true, 208, Plate 182
Lavender cotton, 285
    green, 285
Leadwort
    blue, 101
    Chinese, 101
Leather flower, 107
Leatherleaf, 36, 102
    bog, 102, Plate 66
Ledum decumbens, 37, 209
Ledum groenlandicum, 37, 209, Plate
    183
    'Compactum', 209
    forma *denudatum,* 209
Leiophyllum buxifolium, 38, 209,
        Plate 184
    var. *hugeri,* 210
    'Nanum', 210
    'Procumbens', 210
    var. *prostratum,* see 'Procumbens'
Leopard plant, 212, Plate 188
Leucanthemum vulgare, 210, Plate
    185
    'May Queen', 210
Leucothoe
    coast, 210
    drooping, 211, Plate 186
Leucothoe axillaris, 38, 210
Leucothoe fontanesiana, 38, 211
    'Girard's Rainbow', 211, Plate 186
    'Nana', 211

'Rainbow', see 'Girard's Rainbow'
Leucothoe 'Scarletta', 211
Leymus arenarius 'Glaucus', 38, 48,
    211, Plate 187
Leymus mollis, 38, 48, 212
Leymus racemosus 'Glaucus', 38, 212
Leymus tritichoides, 38, 212
    'Gray Dawn', 212
    'Shoshone', 212
Life-of-man, 132, 290
Ligularia
    narrow spiked, 213
    parsley, 212
    toothed, 212
Ligularia dentata, 212
    'Dark Beauty', 213
    'Desdemona', 213
    'Orange Queen', 213
    'Othello', 213
Ligularia stenocephala, 213
    'The Rocket', 213
Ligularia tussilaginea, 212
    'Argentea', 212
    'Aurea-maculata', 212, Plate 188
    'Crispata', 212
Lily
    blue African, 60
    blue plantain, 186
    blunt-leaved plantain, 185
    Conval, 111
    flag, 197
    Fortune's plantain, 185
    fragrant plantain, 185
    Kaffir, 109, Plate 75
    liver, 197
    narrow-leaved plantain, 185
    plantain, 184
    scarlet Kaffir, 109
    Siebold plantain, 185
    snake, 197
    wavy leaved plantain, 185
Lily-of-the-field, 68
Lily-of-the-Nile, 60
Lily of the valley, 36, 111, Plate 78
    Mountain, 36, 112
Lily-turf, 213
    black, 236
    blue, 214, Plate 190
    creeping, 214
    dwarf, 236, Plate 218
    Jaburan, 236
    white, 236
Ling, 92
Lingonberry, 309
Linnaea borealis, 38, 213, Plate 189
    var. *americana,* 213
    var. *longiflora,* 213
Lion's foot, 64
Lippia
    creeping, 254, Plate 240

garden, 254
Liriope, 213
Liriope exiliflora, 214
Liriope muscari, 214
  'Big Blue', 214
  'Christmas Tree', 214
  'Densiflora', 214
  'Evergreen Giant', 214
  'Gold Band', 214
  'Green Midget', 214
  'John Burch', 214
  'Lilac Beauty', 214
  'Majestic', 214
  'Monroe's # 2', 214
  'Monroe's White', 214
  'Peedee Ingot', 214
  'Purple Bouquet', 214
  'Royal Purple', 214
  'Samantha', 214
  'Silver Midget', 214
  'Silvery Sunproof', 214
  'Variegata', 214, Plate 190
  'Webster's Wideleaf', 214
Liriope spicata, 214
  'Franklin Mint', 214
Lithodora
  acid-soil, 215
  spreading, 215, Plate 191
Lithodora diffusa, 215
  'Alba', 215
  'Grace Ward', 215, Plate 191
  'Heavenly Blue', 215
  'Lohbrunner White', 215
Little washer woman, 171
Live forever, 290
Live long, 290
London pride, 288
Lonicera americana, 216
Lonicera × brownii, 215
  'Dropmore Scarlet', 216
Lonicera caprifolium, 216
Lonicera flava, 38, 216
Lonicera × heckrottii, 216
Lonicera henryi, 216
Lonicera hirsuta, 215
Lonicera japonica, 216
  'Aureo-reticulata', 216
  'Halliana', 216
  'Purpurea', 216
  var. *repens,* 216
Lonicera pileata, 216, Plate 192
Lonicera sempervirens, 38, 215, 216
  'Cedar Lane', 217
  'Dreer's Everblooming', 217
  'Magnifica', 217
  'Red Coral', 217
  'Red Trumpet', 217
  'Rubra', 217
  'Sulphurea', 217
  'Superba', 217

Lonicera xylosteum
  'Emerald Mound', 217
  'Mini Globe', 217
  'Nana', 217
Loosestrife, 220
  dense-flowered, 221
  gooseneck, 220
  Japanese, 221
  swamp, 124
Lotus berthelotii, 217
Lotus corniculatus, 217, Plate 193
  'Pleniflorus', 217
  'Tenuifolium', 217
Lotus pinnatus, 38, 217
Love flowers, 60
Love-in-idleness, 316
Love-in-winter, 104
Lungwort, 268
  common, 268
  cowslip, 269
  long-leaved, 269
  red, 269
  soft, 269
Luzula, 218
Luzula luzuloides, 218
Luzula nivea, 218, Plate 194
Luzula sylvatica, 218
  var. *marginata,* 218
Lycopodium, 218
Lycopodium clavatum, 38, 219
Lycopodium complanatum, 38, 220, Plate 195
Lycopodium dendroideum, 38, 219
Lycopodium lucidulum, 38, 220
Lycopodium obscurum, 38, 219
  var. *dendroideum,* see *L. dendroideum*
Lycopodium tristachyum, 38, 219
Lysimachia clethroides, 220
Lysimachia congestiflora, 221
  'Eco Dark Satin', 221
Lysimachia japonica, 221
  var. *minuta,* 221
Lysimachia nummularia, 220
  'Aurea', 220, Plate 196

Madwort, 83
  rock, 83
Mahonia
  Cascades, 38, Plate 197
  creeping, 38, 221
Mahonia aquifolium, 221
  'Apollo', 221
  'Compactum', 221
  'Mayhan Strain', 221
Mahonia nervosa, 38, 221, Plate 197
Mahonia repens, 38, 221
Maiden's wreath, 153, Plate 131
Maid's ruin, dwarf, 76

Mallow, poppy, 35, 92, Plate 52
Manzanita, 71
  dune, 35, 73
  Hooker, 35, 72
  Little Sur, 35, 72
  Monterey, 72
  pinemat, 35, 72
Maple, vine, 225
Maranta leuconeura, 222, Plate 198
  var. *erythroneura,* 222
  var. *kerchoveana,* 222
  var. *massangeana,* 222
Marguerite, 86
  blue, 148, Plate 124
Marjoram
  dwarf, 238
  hop, 238
Marlberry, 74
Marram, 35, 48, 66, Plate 17
Master of the woods, 154
Matricaria recutita, 103
Matteuccia struthiopteris, 38, 46, 222, Plate 199
Mayflower, 111, 138
Mazus
  creeping, 223, Plate 200
  dwarf, 223
  white flowered Japanese, 223
Mazus japonicus 'Albiflorus', 223
Mazus pumilio, 223
Mazus reptans, 223, Plate 200
Meadowsweet, 80, 150
Mealberry, 71
Melampodium, 223
  white-flowered, 223
Melampodium cinerium, 224, Plate 201
Melampodium leucanthum, 38, 223
Melissa officinalis, 224, Plate 202
  'Aurea', 225
  'Variegata', 225
Menispermum canadense, 38, 225, Plate 203
Menispermum dauricum, 225
Mentha, 225
Mentha × gentilis, 226
  'Emerald-N-Gold', 226
Mentha × piperita, 226
  var. *citrata,* 226
  var. *vulgaris,* 226
Mentha pulegium, 226
  'Nana', 226
Mentha requienii, 227, Plate 204
Mentha spicata, 227
Mesembryanthemum, 100
Mexican gem, 36, 136, Plate 110
Microbiota decussata, 227, Plate 205
Milfoil, 56

Milkwort, ground, 260, Plate 247
Mind-your-own-business, 294
Mint, 225
    Corsican, 227, Plate 204
    creeping, 227
    garden, 227
    lemon, 226
    variegated downy, 226
    variegated ginger, 226
    variegated red, 226
    variegated scotch, 226
Miscanthus sinensis, 48, 228
    'Adagio', 228, Plate 206
    'Gracillimus Nana', 228
    'Kleine Fontaene', 228
    'Kleine Silberspinne', 228
    'Morning Light', 228
    'Nippon', 228
    'Yaku Jima', 228
Mitchella repens, 38, 228, Plate 207
    var. *leucocarpa,* 229
Mitrewort, false, 304
Mock orange, dwarf, 258
Molded wax, 36, 136
Moneywort, 220
    Japanese, 221
Monkey's face, 316
Monox, 136
Moonseed, 38, 225
    Canadian, 225, Plate 203
Moose flower, 271
Morning glory
    bush, 112, Plate 79
    ground, 113
Mosaic plant, 150
Moss
    clubfoot, 219
    flowering, 271
    Iceland 292
    Irish, 294
    Japanese, 294
    pyxie, 39, 271, Plate 258
    short leaved pyxie, 39, 271
Mother-in-law plant, 89
Mother-of-thousands, 287, 294
Mountain ash, dwarf Chinese, 295,
    Plate 284
Mountain avens, 36
Mountain lover, 243
Muehlenbeckia axillaris, 229, Plate
    208
Muehlenbeckia complexa, 229
Mugwort, western, 77
Musc de bois, 154
Myoporum, 230, Plate 209
    prostrate, 230
Myoporum debile, 229
Myoporum 'Pacifica', 230
Myoporum parvifolium, 229, Plate
    209

'Burgundy Carpet', 230
'Putah Creek', 230
Myosotis scorpioides, 230, Plate 210
    'Alba', 230
    'Count Waldersee', see 'Graf
        Waldersee'
    'Graf Waldersee', 230
    'Meernixe', 230
    'Perle von Ronneberg', 230
    'Pinkie', 230
    'Rosea', 230
    'Sapphire', 230
    'Sea Nymph', see 'Meernixe'
    'Semperflorens', 230
    'Thuringen', 230
Myrtle, 314
    Allegheny sand, 210
    barren, 71
    sand, 38, 209, Plate 184
Myrtle-flag, 57
Myrtus, 244

Nandina, 231
Nandina domestica, 231
    'Atropurpurea Nana', 231, Plate
        211
    'Compacta', see 'Nana'
    'Harbor Dwarf', 231
    'Minima', see 'Pygmaea'
    'Moon Bay', 231
    'Nana', 231
    'Purpurea Dwarf', see
        'Atropurpurea Nana'
    'Pygmaea', 231
    'Wood's Dwarf', 231
Navelwort, 234
Nepeta cataria, 231
Nepeta × faassenii, 231, 232
    'Six Hills Giant', 231
Nepeta gigantea, see *Nepeta ×
    faassenii* 'Six Hills Giant'
Nepeta mussinii, 232, Plate 212
    'Blue Dwarf', 232
    'Blue Wonder', 232
    'Snowflake', 232
    'White Wonder', 232
Nephrolepis exaltata, 46, 232, Plate
    213
    'Bostoniensis', 232
    'Compacta', 232
    'Compacta Cristata', 232
    'Dallasii', see 'Compacta'
    'Dwarf Boston', 232
    'Fluffy Ruffles', 232
    'New York', 232
    var. *rooseveltii,* 232
    'Whitmanii', 232
Nerve plant, 150
Nettle
    golden dead, 204, 205

spotted dead, 205, Plate 178
New Zealand brass buttons, 120,
    Plate 88
Nierembergia hippomanica var.
    violacea, 233, Plate 214
    'Purple Robe', 233
Nierembergia repens, 232
Nine hooks, 64
Nippon-bells, 294
None so pretty, 316
Nose-bleed, 56

Oconee bells, 39, 294
Oenothera, 233
Oenothera berlandieri, 38, 233
    'Siskiyou', 233
Oenothera biennis, 233
Oenothera drummondii, 38, 233
Oenothera fruticosa, 38, 234
    'Erica Robin', 234
    subsp. *glauca,* 234
    var. *linearis,* 234
    'Summer Solstice', 234
Oenothera missouriensis, 38, 234
Oenothera tetragona, 38, 234
    'Fireworks', 234, Plate 215
    'Fyrverkeri', see 'Fireworks'
    'Highlight', 234
    'Hoheslicht', see 'Highlight'
    'Yellow River', 234
Old man, 76, 293
Old woman, 77, 293
Oleander, wild, 124
Omphalodes verna, 234, Plate 216
    'Alba', 235
    'Grandiflora', 235
Onion, bog, 240
Onoclea sensibilis, 38, 46, 235, Plate
    217
    var. *interrupta,* 235
Ophiopogon clarkei, 236
Ophiopogon jaburan, 236
    'Aureus', 236
    'Evergreen Giant', 236
    'Variegatus', 236
    'Vittatus', see 'Variegatus'
Ophiopogon japonicus, 236, Plate
    218
    'Comet', 236
    var. *compacta,* 236
    'Gyoku Ryu', 236
    'Kigimafukiduma', 236
    'Kioto', 236
    'Nanus Variegatus', 236
    'Nippon', 236
    'Shiroshima Ryu', 236
    'Silver Mist', see
        'Kigimafukiduma'
    'Silver Showers', see 'Variegatus'
    'Super Dwarf', 236

'Variegatus', 236
Ophiopogon planiscapus 'Nigrescens',
   236
Opuntia
   big root, 38, 237
Opuntia erinacea
   var. hystricina, 237
   var. ursina, 38, 237
Opuntia humifusa, 38, 237, Plate
   219
   var. greenii, 237
Opuntia juniperina, 38, 237
Opuntia macrorhiza, 38, 237
   var. pottsii, 237
Opuntia phaeacantha, 38, 238
   var. camanchica, 238
Oregano
   creeping, 238
   dwarf, 238
   smooth-leaved, Plate 220
Origanum dictamnus, 238
Origanum laevigatum, 238
   'Herrenhausen', 238, Plate 220
Origanum vulgare, 238
   'Aureum', 238
   'Compacta Nana', 238
Orostachys aggregatum, 239
Orostachys iwarenge, 239, Plate 221
Orpine, 288, 290
   garden, 290
Osmunda cinnamomea, 38, 46, 239,
   Plate 222
Osmunda claytoniana, 38, 46, 240
Osmunda regalis, 38, 46, 240
   var. cristata, 240
   var. gracilis, 240
   var. palustris, 240
   'Purpurascens', 240
   var. spectabilis, 240
Osteospermum fruticosum, 240, Plate
   223
   'African Queen', 240
   'Burgundy Mound', 240
   'Snow White', 240
   'White Cloud', see 'Snow White'
Our Lady's Tears, 111
Oxalis
   Oregon, 38, 241, Plate 224
Oxalis 'Iron Cross', 241
Oxalis oregana, 38, 241, Plate 224
Oxalis regnelii, 241
   'Purpurea', 241
   'Triangularis', 241

Pachysandra
   Allegheny, 38, 242
   Japanese, 241
Pachysandra axillaris, 242
Pachysandra procumbens, 38, 242
   'Forest Green', 242

Pachysandra terminalis, 241, Plate
   225
   'Cabbage Leaf', 242
   'Cut Leaf', 242
   'Green Carpet', 242
   'Green Sheen', 242
   'Kingwood', 242
   'Variegata', 242
Painted lady, 36, 136
Panda plant, 204
Panicum virgatum, 38, 48, 242
   'Cloud Nine', 242
   'Haense Herms', 242
   'Heavy Metal', 242, Plate 226
   'Pathfinder', 242
   'Rehbraun', 242
   'Rotstrahlbusch', 242
   'Squaw', 242
   'Strictum', 242
   'Warrior', 242
Pansy
   European wild, 316
   field, 316
   miniature, 316
   tricolor, 316
Parilla, yellow, 225
Parrot's beak, 217
Parthenocissus henryana, 243
Parthenocissus inserta, 243
Parthenocissus quinquefolia, 38, 243,
   Plate 227
   'Engelmannii', 243
   var. engelmannii, see
      'Engelmannii'
   'Saint Paulii', 243
   var. saint paulii, see 'Saint Paulii'
Parthenocissus thomsonii, 243
Partridge berry, 38, Plate 207
Pasque flower, European, 270, Plate
   256
Pastel del risco, 59
Pauson, 284
Paxistima
   Canby, 243
   myrtle, 244
   Oregon, 38, 244
Paxistima canbyi, 38, 243, Plate 228
Paxistima myrsinites, 38, 244
Pea
   crow, 136
   ground squirrel, 199
   wild sweet, 207
   winged, 217
Peace in the home, 294
Pearl berry
   creeping, 37, 156
Pearlwort, Corsican, 281, Plate 268
Pelargonium crispum, 244
Pelargonium denticulatum, 245
Pelargonium × fragans, 245, Plate 229

Pelargonium grossularioides, 245
Pelargonium mellissinum, 245
Pelargonium nervosum, 245
Pelargonium odoratissimum, 245
Pelargonium peltatum, 244
   'Charles Monselet', 244
   'Charles Turner', 244
   'Comtesse Degrey', 244
   'Giant Lavender', 244
   'Jeanne d'Arc', 244
   'L'Elegante', 244
   'Riga', 244
   'Sugar Baby', 244
   'Tavira', 244
Pelargonium tomentosum, 245
Pelican's beak, 217
Peltiphyllum peltatum, 38, 245, Plate
   230
   var. nana, 245
Pennisetum alopecuroides, 48, 245
   'Cassian', 246
   var. caudatum, see P. caudatum
   var. compressum, 246
   'Hameln', 246
   'Herbstzauber', 246
   'Japonicum', 246
   'Little Bunny', 246
   'Moudry', 246
   'National Arboretum', 246
   'Purpurea', 246
   var. viridescens, 246
   'Weserbergland', 246
Pennisetum caudatum, 48, 246
Pennisetum incomptum, 48, 246
Pennisetum japonicum, see P.
   alopecuroides 'Japonicum'
Pennisetum orientale, 48, 246
Pennisetum setaceum, 48, 246, Plate
   231
   'Atrosanguineum', 246
   'Cupreum', 246
   'Rubrum', 246
   'Rubrum Compactum', 246
Pennyroyal, 226
   dwarf, 226
Pennywort, 121
Penstemon
   creeping red, 247
   pineleaf, 38, 247, Plate 232
   shrubby, 247
Penstemon fructicosus var. scouleri,
   247
   'Albus', 247
   'Purple Gem', 247
   'Red Cultivar', 247
   'Six Hills', 247
Penstemon pinifolius, 38, 247, Plate
   232
   'Mersea Yellow', 247
Pen-wiper, 204

370   Index of Plant Names

Peperomia
oval-leaf, 248, Plate 233
Sander's, 247
watermelon, 247
Peperomia argyreia, 247
Peperomia arifolia, 248
Peperomia obtusifolia, 248, Plate 233
'Alba', 248
'Albo-marginata', 248
'Albo-marginata Minima', 248
'Silver Edge', see 'Albo-marginata'
'Variegata', 248
Pepperbush, 'Hummingbird' sweet,
109
Pepper face, 248
Peppermint, 226
black, 226
Periwinkle
big leaved, 314
common, 314, Plate 307 and 308
dwarf, 314
greater, 314
lesser, 314
running, 314
Pernettya
Chilean, 248, Plate 234
Tasmania, 248
Pernettya mucronata, 248, Plate 234
'Alba', 248
'Cherry Ripe', 248
'Coccinea', 248
'Davis's Hybrids', 248
'Dwarf Form', 248
'Lilacina', 248
'Pink Pearl', 248
'Purpurea', 248
'Rosie'
'Sea Shell', 248
'White Pearl', 248
Pernettya tasmanica, 248
Perovskia, Caspian, 249
Perovskia abrotanoides, 249
Perovskia artemesioides, 249
Perovskia atriplicifolia, 249
'Blue Haze', 249
'Blue Mist', 249
'Blue Spire', 249
'Filigran', 249
'Longin', 249, Plate 235
Persicaria affinis, 250, Plate 236
'Border Jewel', 250
'Darjeeling Red', 250
'Donald Lowndes', 250
Persicaria bistorta, 250
'Superbum', 250
Persicaria capitatum, 250
Persicaria filiformis, 38, 249
'Painter's Palette', 250
'Variegata', 250
Persicaria vacciniifolia, 250

Petasites albus, 251
Petasites fragans, 251
Petasites hybridus, 251
Petasites japonicus, 252
'Giganteus', 252, Plate 237
Petasites palmata, 38, 252
Petasites sagittata, 38, 252
Petasites trigonophylla, 38, 252
Phalaris arundinacea, 39, 48, 252
'Dwarf Garters', 252
'Feesey's Form', 252
'Luteo-Picta', 252
'Picta' 252, Plate 238
'Tricolor', 252
Pheasant's wings, 65
Phegopteris connectilis, see *Thelypteris
connectilis*
Phegopteris hexagonoptera, see
Thelypteris hexagonoptera
Phlox
blue, 253
creeping, 39, 253
hybrid, 253
moss, 254
mountain, 254
trailing, 39, 253
wild blue, 39, 253
Phlox divaricata, 39, 253
'Dirigo Ice', 253
'Fullers White', 253
subsp. *lamphamii,* 253
subsp. *lamphamii* forma *candida,*
253
'Louisiana', 253
Phlox 'Frondosa', 253
Phlox nivalis, 39, 253
'Eco Brilliant', 253
'Eco Flirtie Eyes', 253
Phlox 'Perfection', 253
Phlox × procumbens, 253
'Millstream Variety', 253
'Variegata', 253
Phlox stolonifera, 39, 253
var. *alba,* 253
'Blue Ridge', 254
'Bruce's White', 254
'Iridescens', 254
'Light Pink', 254
'Pink Ridge', 254
'Porter's Purple', 254
'Sherwood Purple', 254
'Violet Queen', 254
Phlox subulata, 39, 253, 254, Plate
239
'Alba', 254
'Alexander's Surprise', 254
'Alexander's Wild Rose', 254
'Atropurpurea', 254
'Blue Emerald', 254
'Blue Hills', 254

'Brilliant', 254
'Chuckles', 254
'Crimson Beauty', 254
'Daniel's Cushion', 254
'Emerald Cushion', 254
'Emerald Pink', 254
'Exquisite', 254
'Laura', 254
'Millstream Daphne', 254
'Millstream Juniper', 254
'Profusion', 254
'Red Wings', 254
'Rosea', 254
'Scarlet Flame', 254
'Sneewittchen', 254
'White Delight', 254
Phlox 'Vivid', 254
Phyla nodiflora, 254, Plate 240
var. *canescens,* 254
var. *rosea,* 254
'Rosea', see var. *rosea*
Picea abies, 39, 255
'Nidiformis', 255
'Pendula', 255, Plate 241
'Procumbens', 255
'Pseudoprostrata', 255
'Repens', 255
Picea pungens, 39, 255
'Glauca Pendula', 255
'Glauca Procumbens', 255
'Glauca Prostrata', 255
Pickaback plant, 305
Piggyback plant, 39, 305, Plate 298
Pig squeak, 87
Pilea
creeping, 256
round-leaved, 256
watermelon, 255
Pilea cadierei, 255, Plate 242
'Minima', 256
Pilea depressa, 256
Pilea nummularifolia, 256
Pimpernel
blue, 67
Monell's, 67, Plate 20
Pine
Austrian, 257
dwarf mountain, 257
dwarf mugo, 257
eastern white, 39, 257
flat-branch ground, 219
gray, 256
ground, 219
jack, 39, 256
Japanese red, 257
Japanese white, 257
limber, 39, 257
mugo, 257, Plate 243
noble, 104
prince's, 104

princess, 219
Scotch, 257
running, 220
Swiss mountain, 257
white, 257
Pine barren beauty, 271
Pink, 128
    Allwood, 129
    cheddar, 129
    grass, 129
    ground, 254
    maiden, 129
    moss, 39, 254, Plate 239
    old-fashioned, 129
    sand, 129
Pinus banksiana, 39, 256
    'Uncle Foggy', 256
Pinus densiflora 'Prostrata', 257
Pinus flexilis 'Glauca Pendula', 39,
    257
Pinus mugo, 257, Plate 243
    'Gnom', 257
    var. *mugho*, see var. *mugus*
    var. *mugus*, 257
    var. *pumilio*, 257
Pinus nigra 'Hornibrookiana', 257
Pinus parviflora 'Bergman', 257
Pinus strobus, 39, 257
    'Haird's Broom', 257
    'Merrimack', 257
    'Ottawa', 257
Pinus sylvestris, 257
    'Albyn's Prostrate', 257
    'Hillside Creeper', 257
Pipsissewa, 36, 104, Plate 69
    spotted, 36, 105
    striped, 105
Pittosporum tobira
    'Creme de Mint', 258
    'Wheeler's Dwarf', 258, Plate 244
Pleioblastus, 258
Pleioblastus auricoma, 48, 259, Plate
    245
    'Nana', 259
Pleioblastus humilis, 48, 259
    var. *pumilus*, 259
Pleioblastus pygmaeus, 48, 259
    'Akebeno', 259
    'Tanake', 259
Pleioblastus variegatus, 48, 259
Pleioblastus viridi-striata, see *P.
    auricoma*
Plum
    fox, 71
    meal, 71
    natal, 96, Plate 56
Plumbago, 101
    dwarf, 101, Plate 65
Polemonium
    creeping, 259

salmon, 260
Polemonium boreale, 39, 259
Polemonium caeruleum, 39, 259,
    260, Plate 246
    var. *album*, 260
    'Breeze of Anjou', see 'Brise d'
        Anjou'
    'Brise d' Anjou', 260
    var. *himalayanum*, 260
    var. *himalayanum*, 'Album', 260
    var. *himalayanum*, 'Gracile', 260
    var. *himalayanum*, 'Variegatum',
        260
    var. *lacteum*, 260
    'Sapphire', 260
Polemonium carneum, 260
Polemonium humile, see *P. boreale*
Polemonium reptans, 39, 259
    'Alba', 259
    'Blue Pearl', 259
    'Konigsee', 259
Polyanthus, 266
Polygala chamaebuxus, 260, Plate
    247
    'Grandiflora', 260
    var. *rhodoptera*, 260
Polygala vayredae, 260
Polygonatum, 260
Polygonatum biflorum, 39, 261
Polygonatum commutatum, 39, 261
Polygonatum hybridum, 261
Polygonatum multiflorum, 262
Polygonatum odoratum, 261, Plate
    248
    var. *thunbergii*, 262
    'Variegatum', 262
Polygonum affine, see *Persicaria affinis*
Polygonum bistorta, see *Persicaria
    bistorta*
Polygonum capitatum, see *Persicaria
    capitatum*
Polygonum cuspidatum Compactum',
    see *Fallopia japonica*
    'Compacta'
Polygonum filiforme, see *Persicaria
    filiformis*
Polygonum reynoutria 'Compactum',
    see *Fallopia japonica*
    'Compacta'
Polypodium aureum, 39, 46, 262
Polypodium virginianum, 39, 46,
    262, Plate 249
Polypody
    golden, 39, 46, 262
    limestone, 167
    pale mountain, 166
    rock, 39, 46, 262, Plate 249
    tender three-branched, 166
Polystichum acrostichoides, 39, 46,
    262, Plate 250

'Crispum', 262
'Cristatum', 262
'Incisum', 262
'Multifidum', 262
Polystichum braunii, 39, 46, 263
Polystichum lonchitis, 39, 46, 263
Polystichum munitum, 39, 46, 263
    'Crested', 263
    'Crisped Form', 263
Polystichum setiferum, 46, 263
    'Capitatum', 263
    'Congestum', 263
    'Congestum Cristatum', 263
    'Cristatum', 263
    'Cristulatum', 263
    'Divisilobum Plumosum', 263
    'Imbricatum', 263
    'Percristatum', 263
    'Plumosum Bevis', 263
    'Plumosum Gracillimum', 263
    'Plumosum Grande', 263
    'Polydactylum', 263
    'Pulcherrimum', 263
    'Rotundatum', 263
Popotillo, 137
Poppy
    celandine, 39, 298, Plate 289
    yellow, 298
Pork and beans, 291
Potentilla, 263
Potentilla, strawberry, 152
Potentilla × anglica, 265
Potentilla anserina, 39, 263, Plate
    251
    forma *sericea*, 264
Potentilla atrosanguinea, 264
    'Gibson's Scarlet', 264
    var. *leucochroa*, 264
    'Red', 264
    'William Rollison', 264
    'Yellow Queen', 264
Potentilla cinerea, 264
Potentilla crantzii, 265
Potentilla fruticosa, 39, 264
    'Abbotswood', 264
    'Donard Gold', 264
    'Elizabeth', 264
    'Farreri Prostrata', 264
    'Gold Carpet', 264
    'Gold Finger', 264
    'Gold Star', 264
    'Goldteppich', 264
    'Hollandia Gold', 264
    'Klondike', 264
    'Kobold', 264
    'Longacre', 264
    'Manchu', 264
    var. *mandshurica*, see 'Manchu'
    'McKay's White', 264
    'Mount Everest', 264

[*Potentilla fruticosa*]
  'Pink Pearl', 264
  'Pretty Polly', 265
  'Red Ace', 265
  'Royal Flush', 265
  'Sunset', 265
  'Sutter's Gold', see 'Elizabeth'
  'Tangerine', 265
  'Tilford Cream', 265
  'Woodbridge Gold', 265
  'Yellow Gem', 265
  'Yellow Queen', 265
Potentilla nepalensis, 265
Potentilla tabernaemontani, 265
  'Nana', 265
  'Orange Flame', 265
Potentilla × tonguei, 265
Potentilla tridentata, 39, 265
  'Minima', 265
Potentilla verna, see *P. tabernaemontani*
Pot-of-gold, 115
Poverty grass, 188
Pratia angulata, 266, Plate 252
  'Treadwellii', see var. *treadwellii*
  var. *treadwellii*, 266
Pratia pedunculata, 265, 266
Prayer plant, 222, Plate 198
Prickly pear, 38, 237, Plate 219
Primrose
  auricula, 267
  Baja, 38, 233
  common, 267
  eared, 267
  English, 266, 267
  evening, 233
  Himalayan, 267
  Japanese, 267, Plate 253
  Mexican, 38, 233
  Missouri, 38
  polyanthus, 266
  toothed, 267
Primula auricula, 266, 267
  'Alba', 267
  'Blue Wave', 267
  'Copper King', 267
  'Dale's Red', 267
  'Gold of Ophir', 267
  'Old Red Dusty Miller', 267
  'Old Yellow Dusty Miller', 267
  'The Mikado', 267
  'Winifred', 267
Primula denticulata, 267
Primula japonica, 267, Plate 253
  'Miller's Crimson', 267
  'Postford White', 267
  var. *rosea*, 267
Primula × polyantha, 266
  Barnhaven hybrids, 266
  'Giant Bouquet', 266

  'Monarch', 266
  'Pacific Giant Hybrids', 266
Primula rubra, 267
Primula tommasinii, see *P. × variabilis*
Primula × variabilis, 267
Primula veris, 267
  'Coccinea', 267
  'Kleynii', 267
  'Lutea', 267
  subsp. *macrocalyx*, 267
Primula viscosa, 267
Primula vulgaris, 267
  'Alba', 267
  'Atropurpurea', 267
  'Lilacina', 267
  'Lutea', 267
  'Rosea', 267
  'Rubra', 267
Prunella grandiflora, 268, Plate 254
  'Alba', 268
  'Loveliness', 268
  'Rosea', 268
  'Rotkappchen', 268
  'Rubra', 268
Prunus, 146
Puccoon
  red, 284
  white, 284
Puccoon-root, 284
Pussy ears, 204
Pussytoes
  common, 35, 69
  plantainleaf, 35, 70, Plate 23
Pulmonaria angustifolia, 269
  'Alba', 269
  'April Opal', 269
  'Azurea', 269
  'Benediction', 269
  'Mawson's Variety', 269
  'Munstead Blue', 269
  'Rubra', 269
Pulmonaria 'Apple Frost', 270
Pulmonaria 'Berries and Cream', 270
Pulmonaria 'David Ward', 270
Pulmonaria 'Excalibur', 270
Pulmonaria 'Little Star', 270
Pulmonaria longifolia, 269
  'Bertram Anderson', 269
  subsp. *cevennensis*, 269
  'Little Blue', 269
Pulmonaria 'Milky Way', 270
Pulmonaria mollis, 269
  'Royal Blue', 269
Pulmonaria officinalis, 269
  'Alba', 269
  'Cambridge Blue', 269
  'White Wings', 269
Pulmonaria 'Purple Haze', 270
Pulmonaria 'Regal Ruffles', 270

Pulmonaria rubra, 269
  'Albocorollata', 269
  'Bowles' Variety', 269
  'Redstart', 269
  'Salmon Glow', 269
Pulmonaria saccharata, 268
  'Alba', 269
  'Argentea', 269
  'Baby Blue', 269
  'Boughton Blue', 269
  'British Sterling', 269
  'Coral', 269
  'Highdown', 269
  'Leopard', 269
  'Mrs. Moon', 269, Plate 255
  'Pierre's Pure Pink', 269
  'Pink Dawn', 269
  'Roy Davidson', 269
  'Sissinghurst White', 269
Pulmonaria 'Silver Dollar', 270
Pulmonaria 'Silver Streamers', 270
Pulmonaria 'Spilled Milk', 270
Pulmonaria villarsae, 269
  'Margery Fish', 269
Pulsatilla vulgaris, 270, Plate 256
  var. *alba*, 270
  var. *grandis*, 270
  var. *rubra*, 270
Pyracantha coccinea 'Lowboy', 271
Pyracantha koidzumii, 271
  'Santa Cruz', 271
  'Walderi Prostrata', 271
Pyracantha 'Red Elf', 271
Pyracantha 'Ruby Mound', 271, Plate 257
Pyrole, 104
Pyxidanthera barbulata, 39, 271, Plate 258
Pyxidanthera brevifolia, 39, 271
Pyxie, 271

Quaker bonnets, 171
Quaker ladies, 171
Quakers, 88

Rabbit tracks, 222
Ram's-claws, 272
Ranunculus repens, 39, 272, Plate 259
  'Flore-Pleno', see 'Pleniflorus'
  'Pleniflorus', 272
Raoulia, 272
Raoulia australis, 272, Plate 260
Raoulia eximia, 273
Raoulia glabra, 272
Raoulia grandiflora, 273
Raoulia haastii, 273
Raoulia mammilaris, 273
Raoulia subsericea, 272
Raoulia tenuicaulis, 272

Raphiolepis, 273
Raphiolepis 'Ballerina', 273
Raphiolepis 'Charisma', 273
Raphiolepis 'Clara', 273
Raphiolepis 'Coates Crimson', 273
Raphiolepis × *delacourii*, 273
Raphiolepis 'Indian Princess', 273
Raphiolepis indica, 273, Plate 261
Raphiolepis 'Minor', 273
Raphiolepis 'Pink Cloud', 273
Raphiolepis 'Pink Dancer', 273
Raphiolepis 'Snow White', 273
Raphiolepis 'Spring Rapture', 273
Raphiolepis umbellata, 273
Raphiolepis 'White Enchantress', 273
Rapper dandies, 71
Ratstripper, canby, 38, 243, Plate 228
Red cedar
    Colorado, 203
    eastern, 203
Red cogon, 48
Reed, sand, 48, 66
Reed-grass
    long leaved, 91
    sand, 48, 91, Plate 51
Rheumatism weed, 104
Rhododendron, Lapland, 39
Rhododendron
    Girard Hybrids, 274
    Glenn Dale Hybrids, 274
    Indicum Hybrids, 274
    Kurume Azaleas, 275
    P.J.M. cultivars, 275
    Polly Hill's North Tisbury Hybrids, 275–276
    Robin Hill Hybrids, 276
Rhododendron 'Album', 275
Rhododendron 'Alex', 275
Rhododendron 'Alexander', 275
Rhododendron 'Balsaminiflorum', 274
Rhododendron 'Barbara M. Humphreys', 276
Rhododendron 'Beth Bullard', 275
Rhododendron 'Betty Ann Voss', 276
Rhododendron 'Blue Tip', 276
Rhododendron 'Bridesmaid', 275
Rhododendron carolinianum, 275
Rhododendron 'Chanson', 276
Rhododendron 'Christie', 276
Rhododendron 'Congo', 276
Rhododendron 'Conversation Piece', 276
Rhododendron 'Coral Bells', 275
Rhododendron dauricum var. *sempervirens*, 275
Rhododendron 'Dorothy Hayden', 276
Rhododendron 'Dorothy Rees', 276

Rhododendron 'Early Bent', 276
Rhododendron 'Eunice Updike', 276
Rhododendron fastigiatum, 276
Rhododendron 'Flame Creeper', 275
Rhododendron 'Flame Dance', 276
Rhododendron 'Frosty', 276
Rhododendron 'Gabrielle Hill', 275
Rhododendron 'George Harding', 276
Rhododendron 'Gillie', 276
Rhododendron 'Girard National Beauty', 274
Rhododendron 'Girard's Scarlet', 274
Rhododendron 'Givenda', 276
Rhododendron 'Glamora', 276
Rhododendron 'Glencora', 276
Rhododendron 'Gresham', 276
Rhododendron 'Greta', 276
Rhododendron 'Guerdon', 274
Rhododendron 'Gwenda', 276
Rhododendron 'Hexe', 275
Rhododendron 'Hilda Niblett', 276
Rhododendron 'Hill's Single Red', 275
Rhododendron 'Hino-crimson', 275
Rhododendron 'Hinodegiri', 275
Rhododendron 'Hotline', 276
Rhododendron 'Jeanne Weeks', 276
Rhododendron 'Jeff Hill', 276
Rhododendron 'Joseph Hill', 276
Rhododendron kaempferi, 275
Rhododendron kiusianum, 275
    'Album', 275
    'Benichidori', 275
    'Benisuzume', 275
    'Hanekomachi', 275
    'Harunoumi', 275
    'Komo Kulshan', 275
    'Rose', 275
    'Ukon', 275
Rhododendron 'Kozan', 275
Rhododendron 'Lady Louise', 276
Rhododendron 'Lady Robin', 276
Rhododendron lapponicum, 39, 275
Rhododendron 'Laura Morland', 276
Rhododendron 'Le Belle Helene', 276
Rhododendron 'Low Red Frilled', 275
Rhododendron 'Macrantha', 275
Rhododendron 'Macrantha Double', 275
Rhododendron 'Maria Derby', 276
Rhododendron 'Marilee', 276
Rhododendron 'Michael Hill', 276
Rhododendron 'Molly Fordham', 275
Rhododendron 'Mrs. Emil Hager', 276
Rhododendron 'Mrs. Villars', 276
Rhododendron mucronatum, 274
Rhododendron nahakarai, 275
Rhododendron obtusum, 275

Rhododendron 'Octavian', 276
Rhododendron 'Olga Niblett', 276
Rhododendron 'Peg Hugger', 276
Rhododendron 'Pink Pancake', 276
Rhododendron 'Polar Sea', 274
Rhododendron pulchrum, 274
Rhododendron 'Purple Gem', 276
Rhododendron 'Purple Imp', 276
Rhododendron racemosum 'Compactum', 276
Rhododendron 'Ramapo', 276
Rhododendron 'Redmond', 276
Rhododendron 'Red Tip', 276
Rhododendron 'Robin Dale', 276
Rhododendron 'Robin Hill Gillie', 276
Rhododendron 'Roseanne', 276
Rhododendron 'Sagittarius', 274
Rhododendron 'Seafoam', 274
Rhododendron 'Sherwood Orchid', 275
Rhododendron 'Sherwood Red', 275
Rhododendron simsii, 274
Rhododendron 'Sir Robert', 276
Rhododendron 'Snow', 275
Rhododendron 'Snowclad', 274
Rhododendron 'Susannah Hill', 276
Rhododendron 'Trill', 276
Rhododendron 'Vestal', 274
Rhododendron 'Wards', 275
Rhododendron 'Watchet', 276
Rhododendron 'White Moon', 276
Rhododendron williamsianum, 276, Plate 262
Rhododendron 'Wintergreen', 276
Rhododendron 'Yaku', 276
Rhododendron yakusimanum, 276
    'Mist Maiden', 277
    'Yaku Duchess', 277
    'Yaku Princess', 277
    'Yaku Queen', 277
Rhubarb, bog, 251
Rhus aromatica, 39, 277
    'Gro-low', 277, Plate 263
Ribbon grass, variegated, 252
Ribbon plant, 105
Rockberry, 71
Root
    red, 284
    rheumatism, 199
Rosa 'Alba Meidiland', 278
Rosa blanda, 39, 278, Plate 264
    forma *alba*, 278
    forma *augustier*, 278
Rosa 'Flower Carpet', 278
Rosa 'Fuchsia Meidiland', 278
Rosa 'Hindawn', 279
Rosa 'Hinvory', 279
Rosa 'Noatraum', 278
Rosa 'Pearl Meidiland', 279

Rosa 'Pink Meidiland', 279
Rosa polyantha 'Nearly Wild', 279
Rosa 'Red Meidiland', 279
Rosa 'Scarlet Meidiland', 279
Rosa 'Scarlet Spreader', 279
Rosa 'Snow Carpet', 279
Rosa spinosissima 'Petite Pink
    Scotch', 279
Rosa 'White Meidiland', 279
Rosa wichuraiana, 279
    'Curiosity', 279
    'Hiawatha', 279
    'Poterifolia', 279
Rose
    baby sun, 70, Plate 24
    Christmas, 173
    green Mexican, 36, 136
    hybrid rock, 106
    Lenten, 174, Plate 154
    meadow, 278
    memorial, 279
    petite pink scotch, 279
    sageleaf rock, 106, Plate 72
    small, 115
    smooth, 39, 278, Plate 264
    sun, 172, Plate 152
    white Mexican, 136
    wrinkleleaf rock, 106
Rosebay, Lapland, 275
Rosemary, 279, Plate 265
    bog, 35, 68, Plate 21
    Cumberland, 36, 111, Plate 77
    marsh, 35, 68
    wild, 209
Rose-of-Sharon, 190
Roses, Meidiland, 278
Rosmarinus officinalis, 279
    'Collingwood Ingram', 280
    'Huntington Carpet', 280, Plate
        265
    'Lockwood de Forest', 280
    'Prostratus', 280
Royal osmund, 240
Rubber plant
    American, 248
    baby, 248
    creeping, 149
Rubus, Taiwanese creeping, 280,
    Plate 266
Rubus calycinoides 'Emerald Carpet',
    280, Plate 266
Rudbeckia deamii, see *R. fulgida* var.
    deamii
Rudbeckia fulgida, 281
    var. *deamii*, 281
    var. *fulgida*, 281
    'Oraile', 281
    var. *sullivantii*, 281
    var. *sullivantii* 'Goldsturm', 281,
        Plate 267

Rudbeckia speciosa var. *sullivantii*, see
    R. fulgida var. *sullivantii*
Rupturewort, 181, Plate 156
Rush
    dwarf scouring, 37, 141
    fern, 110
    greater wood, 218
    scouring, 140
    snowy wood, 218, Plate 194
    wood, 218
Rye
    beardless wild, 38, 212
    Siberian wild, 212
    Volga wild, 212

Sage
    Bethlehem, 268, Plate 255
    common, 283
    garden, 283
    meadow, 283
    Russian, 249, Plate 235
    scarlet, 283
    silver-leaved, Plate 270
    true, 283
    white, 77
Sagebrush
    fringed, 35, 77
Sagina subulata, 281, Plate 268
    'Aurea', 281
Saint John's Wort, 189
    Blue Ridge, 37, 190
    creeping, 190
    Coris, 190
    creeping, 191
    goldencup, 190, Plate 163
    Olympic, 190
    pale, 37, 190
Salal, 37, 156
Salix arenaria, see *S. repens*
    'Argentea'
Salix purpurea 'Gracilis', 282
Salix purpurea 'Nana', 282
Salix repens, 282
    var. *arenaria*, see 'Argentea'
    'Argentea', 282
    'Boyd's Pendulous'
    var. *nitida*, see 'Argentea'
Salix rosmarinifolia, 282
Salix tristis, 39, 282
Salix uva-ursi, 39, 282
Salix yezoalpina, 282, Plate 269
Saltbush
    Australian, 82
    creeping, 82, Plate 38
Salt-rheum weed, 103
Salvia argentea, 283, Plate 270
Salvia officinalis, 283
    'Albiflora', 283
    'Aurea', 283
    'Dwarf', 283

    'Purpurascens', 283
    'Purpurea', 283
    'Tricolor', 283
Salvia × *superba*, 283
    'East Friesland', 284
    'Lubeca', 284
    'May Delight', 284
    'May Night', 284
    'Ostfriesland', see 'East Friesland'
Sandberry, 71
Sandwort
    arctic, 35, 74
    larchleaf, 74
    moss, 74
    mountain, 74, Plate 30
Sanguinaria canadensis, 39, 284,
    Plate 271
    'Major', 284
    'Multiplex', 284
Sanguinary, 56
Santolina chamaecyparissus, 285,
    Plate 272
Santolina virens, 285
Saponaria ocymoides, 285, Plate 273
    'Alba', 285
    'Carnea', 285
    var. *floribunda*, 285
    'Gillian Shermon', 285
    'Rosea', 285
    'Rubra', 285
    'Splendens', 285
    'Splendissima', 285
    'Versicolor', 285
Sarcococca
    dwarf Himalayan, 286, Plate 274
    fragrant, 286
Sarcococca hookeriana
    var. *digyna*, 286
    var. *humilis*, 286, Plate 274
Sarcococca humilis, see *S. hookeriana*
    var. *humilis*
Sarsaparilla
    Texas, 225
    yellow, 225
Sasa ruscifolia, 286
    var. *chinensis*, 286
Sasa veitchii, 48, 286
    'Nana', 287, Plate 275
Satureja, smooth leaved, 39, 287
Satureja douglasii, 39, 287, Plate 276
Satureja glabella, 39, 287
Satureja glabra, 287
Savin, creeping, 202
Savory, 287
    calamint, 91, Plate 50
Saxifraga spathularis, 288
Saxifraga stolonifera, 287, Plate 277
    'Tricolor', 288
Saxifraga umbrosa, 288
Saxifraga × *urbium*, 288

'Aureopunctata', 288
'Chamber's Pink Pride', 288
'Covillei', 288
'Minor', see var. *primuloides*
var. *primuloides*, 288
var. *primuloides* 'Elliott's Variety', 288
var. *primuloides* 'Ingwersen's Variety', 288
'Variegata', 288
Saxifrage, strawberry, 287, Plate 277
Scab plant, New Zealand, 272, Plate 260
Scabish, 234
Scirpus, 141
Scrub pine, 256
Sealwort, 261
Sea-sedge, 57
Sedge
  black, 36, 95, 96
  blue, 36, 95
  'Evergold' Japanese, 95, Plate 55
  drooping, 96
  heath, 95
  Japanese, 95,
  Morrow's, 95
  palm, 36, 95
  pendulous, 96
  plantain-leaved, 36, 96
Sedum, 288
Sedum acre, 289
  'Aureum', 289
  var. *aureum*, see 'Aureum'
  'Elegans', 289
  var. *elegans*, see 'Elegans'
  'Majus', 289
  var. *majus*, see 'Majus'
  'Minus', 289
  var. *minus*, see 'Minus'
Sedum alboroseum, 289
  'Frosty Morn', 289
  'Mediovariegatum', 289
Sedum cauticola, 291, 292
Sedum ellacombianum, 289, Plate 278
Sedum 'Harvest Moon', 289
Sedum kamtschaticum, 289
  var. *floriferum*, 290
  'Takahira Dake', 290
  'Variegatum', 290
Sedum laxum subsp. *heckneri*, 290
Sedum lydium, 290
Sedum maximum 'Atropurpureum', 292
Sedum middendorfianum, 290
  var. *diffusum*, 290
Sedum 'Moonglow', 290
Sedum nevii, 39, 290
Sedum populifolium, 290
Sedum purpureum, 290

'Autumn Joy', 291
'Bittoniense', 291
'Herbstfreude', see 'Autumn Joy'
'Indian Chief', 291
'Munstead Dark Red', 291
'Rosea-variegatum', 291
Sedum reflexum, 291
Sedum rubrotinctum, 291
Sedum 'Ruby Glow', 291
Sedum 'Silver Moon', 289, 290
Sedum spathulifolium, 39, 290, 291
  'Cape Blanco', 291, Plate 279
  var. *carneum*, 289
  'Purpureum', 291
Sedum spectabile, 291
  'Album', 291
  var. *atropurpurea*, 291
  'Brilliant', 291, Plate 280
  'Carmen', 291
  'Chubby Fingers', 291
  'Coral Carpet', 291
  'Humile', 291
  'Meteor', 291
  'Nigra', 291
  'Pink Chablis', 291
  'Purpureum', 291
  'Star Dust', 291
  'Variegatum', 291
Sedum spurium, 291
  'Bronze Carpet', 292
  'Dragon's Blood', 292
  'Elizabeth', 292
  'Glowing Fire', see 'Elizabeth'
  'Purple Carpet', 292
  'Purpurteppich', 292
  'Red Carpet', 292
  'Scharbuser Blut', see 'Dragon's Blood'
  'Splendens', 292
  'Tricolor', 292
Sedum 'Sunset Cloud', 292
Sedum telephium, see *S. purpureum*
Sedum ternatum, 39, 292
  'White Waters', 292
Sedum 'Vera Jameson', 292
Self-heal, large-flowered, 268, Plate 254
Sempervivum, 292, Plate 281
Sempervivum arachnoideum, 293
  var. *tomentosum*, 293
Sempervivum calcareum, 293
  'Giuseppi', 293
  'Greenii', 293
  'Sir William Lawrence', 293
Sempervivum 'Collector Anchisi', 293
Sempervivum 'Emerald Giant', 293
Sempervivum 'Godaert', 293
Sempervivum 'Lilac Time', 293
Sempervivum 'Maria Laach', 293

Sempervivum 'Maroon Queen', 293
Sempervivum montanum, 293
  var. *braunii*, 293
Sempervivum 'Pistachio', 293
Sempervivum 'Red Devil', 293
Sempervivum 'Royanum', 293
Sempervivum ruthenicum, 293
Sempervivum tectorum, 293
  subsp. *alpinum*, 293
  subsp. *calcareum*, see *S. calcareum*
  'Robustum', 293
Sempervivum 'Wendy', 293
Shallon, 156
Shamrock
  false, 241
  false purple leaf, 241
  'Iron Cross' false, 241
Sheepburr, redspine, 54
Sheep foot, 217
Shell-flower, 103
Shepherd's crook, 220
Shinwood, 300
Shoes-and-stockings, 217
Shortia galacifolia, 39, 294
Shortia soldanelloides, 294, Plate 282
  forma *alpina*, 294
  var. *ilicifolia*, 294
  var. *magna*, 294
Shortia uniflora, 294
  'Grandiflora', 294
Shrub, lace, 297
Sicklewort, 61
Silver feather, 39, 263, Plate 251
Silver nerve plant, 150
Silver plant, 150
Silver threads, 150
Silverweed, 263
Sitfast, 272
Small lawn leaf, 131
Smilacina racemosa, 261
Snakebeard, 236
Snake bite, 284
Snakeroot, Indian, 78
Snakeweed, black, 79, 250
Sneezeweed, 56
Sneezewort, 35, 56
Snowball, Mexican, 136
Snow-in-summer, 101, Plate 64
Soapwort, rock, 285, Plate 273
Soldiers and sailors, 268
Soleirolia soleirolii, 294, Plate 283
  'Aurea', 295
Solomon's seal, 260
  fragrant, 262, Plate 211
  giant, 261
  great, 261
  hairy, 39, 261
  small, 261
  smooth, 39, 261
  true King, 261

Sorbus reducta, 295, Plate 284
Sorrel, redwood, 241
Southernwood, dwarf, 76
Spartina pectinata, 295
    'Aureo-marginata', 295, Plate 285
    'Variegata', see 'Aureo-marginata'
Spearmint, 227
Speedwell, 311
    common, 312
    creeping, 312
    drug, 312
    germander, 312
    harebell, 312
    Hungarian, 312
    woolly, 312, Plate 305
Spider flower, 163
    Australian, 164
    creeping, 165
    holly leaf, 164
    spider net
    woolly, 164
Spider plant, 105, Plate 70
Spiderwort, 306
    common, 307
    Virginia, 39, 307
    white-flowered, 306, Plate 300
Spirea, Plate 286
    daphne, 296
    false, 80
    Japanese, 296
Spiraea albiflora, 296
Spiraea × bumalda, 296
    'Anthony Waterer', 296
    'Crispa', 296
    'Dakota Goldcharm', 296
    'Dart's Red', 296
    'Flaming Mound', 296
    'Flowering Mound', 296
    'Glowing Mound', 296
    'Golden Carpet', 296
    'Gold Flame', 296
    'Gold Mound', 296, Plate 286
    'Gumball', 296
    'Lightning Mound', 296
    'Neon Flash', 296
    'Norman', 296
    'Sparkling Carpet', 296
Spiraea 'Dolchica', 296
Spiraea japonica, 296
    'Alpina', 296
    var. *alpina,* see 'Alpina'
    'Little Princess', 296
    'Magic Carpet', 296
    'Nana', see 'Alpina'
    'Nyewoods', 296
    'Shirobana', 296
Spleenwort, narrow-leaved, 35, 82
Spotted Mary, 268
Spreader, silver, 76, 77

Spruce
    bird's nest, 255
    Colorado, 39, 255
    Norway, 39, 255, Plate 241
Spurge
    cushion, 146
    cypress, 146
    Japanese, 241, Plate 125
    spruce-leaved, 146
Stachys byzantina, 297, Plate 287
    'Big Ears', see 'Helen von Stein'
    'Cotton Ball', 297
    'Helen von Stein', 297
    'Primrose Heron', 297
    'Sheila McQueen', see 'Cotton Ball'
    'Silver Carpet', 297
Stachys macrantha, 297
    'Alba', 297
    'Robusta', 297
    'Rosea', 297
    'Superba', 297
    'Violacea', 297
Staggerweed, 130
Stanchgrass, 56
Star of Bethlehem, 171
Stephanandra
    crisped, 297, Plate 288
    dwarf cutleaf, 297
Stephanandra incisa 'Crispa', 297, Plate 288
Stepmother, 316
St. John's wort, see Saint John's Wort
Stonecrop, 288
    Christmas cheer, 291
    elegant, 136
    Ellacombe's, 289, Plate 278
    evergreen, 290
    goldmoss, 289
    Kamchatka, 289
    Lydian, 290
    Middendorff, 290
    mountain, 292
    poplar-leaved, 290
    purple, 290, Plate 280
    showy, 291
    soft-leaved, 239, Plate 221
    spatula-leaved, 34, 39, 291
    spruce-leaved, 291
    three-leaved, 292
    two-row, 291
    wild, 39, 292
Strawberry
    barren, 40, 318, Plate 311
    beach, 152, 316
    Chiloe, 37, 152
    dry, 318
    European, 152, Plate 130
    Indian, 135

    mock, 135, 318, Plate 109
    sow-teat, 152
    Virginia, 152
    woodland, 152
    wild, 37, 152
    yellow, 318
Stylophorum diphyllum, 39, 298, Plate 289
Sumac
    fragrant, 39, 277, Plate 263
    lemon, 277
    sweet scented, 277
Summersweet, 'Hummingbird', 109
Suncups, 234
Sundrops, 233
    four-angled, 234, Plate 215
    common, 38, 234
Sweet box, dwarf Himalayan, 286
Sweet-cane, 57
Sweet fern, 36, 110, Plate 76
Sweet ferry, 110
Sweet-grass, 57
Sweet hay, 163
Sweet-hurts, 308
Sweet Mary, 224
Sweet-myrtle, 57
Sweet-root, 57
Sweet-rush, 57
Sweet slumber, 284
Sweetspire, 'Henry's Garnet' Virginia, 198, Plate 170
Sweet William, wild, 253
Symphoricarpos × chenaultii 'Hancock', 298
Symphoricarpos orbiculatus, 39, 298, Plate 290
    'Foliis Variegatus', see 'Variegatus'
    'Leucocarpus', 298
    'Variegatus', 298
Symphytum asperum, 299
Symphytum grandiflorum, 299, Plate 291
Symphytum officinale 'Coccineum', 299
Symphytum × rubrum, 299
Symphytum × uplandicum, 299
    'Variegatum', 299

Tanacetum parthenium, 299
    'Alba', 299
    'Aureum', 299, Plate 292
    'Crispum', 300
    'Golden Ball', 300
    'Golden Feather', 300
    'Golden Moss', 300
    'Silver Bell', 300
    'Snowball', see 'Silver Bell'
    'Tom Thumb White Stars', 300
    'Ultra Double White', 300

Tansy
  dog's, 263
  goose, 263
  white, 55, 56
  wild, 263
Tassel-white, 'Henry's Garnet', 198
Taxus baccata, 300, 301
  'Cavendishii', 300
  'Repandens', 300
  'Repens Aurea', 300, Plate 293
Taxus canadensis, 39, 300
Taxus cuspidata, 300, 301
  'Cross Spreading', 301
  'Densa', 301
Taxus × media, 301
  'Chadwickii', 301
  'Densiformis', 301
  'Everlow', 301
  'Sebian', 301
  'Ward', 301
  'Wardii', see 'Ward'
Tea
  Brigham, 137
  crystal, 209
  Labrador, 37, 209, Plate 183
  Mexican, 137
  Mormon, 137
  narrow-leaved Labrador, 209
  Nevada, 37, 137
  squaw, 137
Tears, baby's, 294, Plate 283
Ten commandments, 222
Tetterroot, 284
Teucrium chamaedrys, 301
  var. *prostratum,* 301, Plate 294
Thelypteris, 82, 301
Thelypteris connectilis, 39, 46, 301,
  302
Thelypteris hexagonoptera, 39, 46,
  302
Thelypteris noveboracensis, 39, 46,
  302, Plate 295
Thousand leaf, 56
Thousand mothers, 305
Thousand-seal, 56
Thrift
  common, 75
  maritime, 75, Plate 31
Thyme
  Azorican, 303
  caraway, 303
  common, 304
  creeping, 302
  creeping red, 302
  early, 303
  garden, 304
  golden, Plate 182
  hairy, 303
  lemon, 303, Plate 296
  mother of, 302

  wild, 302
Thymus caespitosa, 303
Thymus × citriodorus, 303, Plate 296
  'Anderson's Gold', see 'Bertram
    Anderson'
  'Argenteus, 303
  'Aureus', 303
  'Bertram Anderson', 303
  'E. B. Anderson', see 'Bertram
    Anderson'
  'Minus', 303
  'Silver Queen', 303
Thymus herba-barona, 303
Thymus praecox, 303
  subsp. *arcticus,* 303
  subsp. *arcticus* 'Alba', 303
  subsp. *arcticus* 'Minus', 303
  subsp. *lanuginosis,* see *T.
    pseudolanuginosus*
  subsp. *skorpilii,* 303
Thymus pseudolanuginosus, 303
Thymus pulegioides, 303
Thymus serpyllum, 303
  'Albus', 304
  'Argenteus', 304
  'Aureus', 304
  var. *coccineus,* 304
  'Minus', 304
  'Roseus', 304
Thymus vulgaris, 302, 304
Tiarella
  mapleleaf, 305
  Wherry's, 305, Plate 297
Tiarella 'Brandywine', 305
Tiarella cordifolia, 39, 304
  var. *collina,* 304, 305
  'Dunvegan', 304
  'Erika Leigh', 304
  'Filigree Lace', 304
  'Major', 304
  'Marmorata', 304
  'Montrose Selection', 304
  'Oakleaf', 304
  'Purpurea', 304
Tiarella 'Eco Eyed Glossy', 305
Tiarella 'Eco Rambling Silhouette',
  305
Tiarella 'Eco Red Heart', 305
Tiarella 'Eco Running Tapestry', 305
Tiarella 'Eco Splotched Velvet', 305
Tiarella 'Filigree Lace', 305
Tiarella 'Laird of Skye', 305
Tiarella 'Slick Rock', 305
Tiarella trifoliata, 304
Tiarella wherryi, 39, 305, Plate 297
Tickseed, 114
  dwarf-eared, 115
  pink, 36, 115
  whorled, 115
Timothy, white, 184

Tolmiea menziesii, 39, 305, Plate
  298
Torch plant, 65
Trachelospermum asiaticum, 306
  'Elegant', 306
  'Nana', 306
  'Nortex', see 'Nana'
Trachelospermum jasminoides, 306,
  Plate 299
  'Madison', 306
  'Variegatum', 306
Tradescantia albiflora, 306
  'Albovittata', 306, Plate 300
  'Aurea', 306
  'Laekenensis', 306
  'Variegata', 306
Tradescantia × andersoniana, 307
  'Bilberry Ice', 307
  'Blue Stone', 307
  'Blushing Bride', 307
  'Carmine Glow', 307
  'China Blue', 307
  'Concord Grape', 307
  'Hawaiian Punch', 307
  'Innocence', 307
  'Iris Prichard', 307
  'Isis', 307
  'James C. Weguelin', 307
  'Leonora', 307
  'Little Doll', 307
  'Navajo Princess', 307
  'Osprey', 307
  'Pauline', 307
  'Purewell Giant', 307
  'Purple Dome', 307
  'Purple Passion', 307
  'Purple Profusion', 307
  'Red Cloud', 307
  'Snowcap', 307
  'True Blue', 307
  'Valor', 307
  'Zwanenburg', 307
Tradescantia fluminensis, 306
  'Variegata', 307
Tradescantia subaspera, 307
Tradescantia virginiana, 39, 307
Traveler's Joy, 108
Treasure flower, 158
Trinity, 316
Trumpet flower, evening, 158
Tsuga canadensis, 39, 307
  'Bennett', 308
  'Cole', 308, Plate 301
  'Cole's Prostrate', see 'Cole'
  'Pendula', 308
  'Pendula Sargentii', 308
  'Prostrata', 308
  'Sherwood Compact', 308
Tuft, golden, 83, Plate 40
Tulip, pine, 104

Turkeyberry, 298
Turkey corn, 130
Turkey tangle, 254
Turmeric, 284
Turtle-bloom, 103
Turtle-head
    Lyon's, 104
    red, 103, Plate 68
    white, 104
Twinberry, 228
Twinflower, 38, 213, Plate 189
Twinleaf, 37, 199, Plate 172
Two-eyed Mary, 228

Umbrella plant, 38, Plate 230
Universe plant, 71, 245
Uva-ursi, 71

Vaccinium angustifolium, 39, 308
Vaccinium corymbosum, 308
Vaccinium crassifolium, 39, 309
    'Bloodstone', 309
    'Well's Delight', 309
Vaccinium deliciosum, 40, 309
Vaccinium macrocarpon, 40, 309,
        Plate 302
    'Beckwith', 309
    'Ben Lear', 309
    'Bennett', 309
    'Cropper', 309
    'Hamilton', 309
    'Langlois', 309
    'LeMunyon Honkers', 309
    'McFarlin', 309
    'Olsons', 309
Vaccinium ovatum, 309
Vaccinium vitis-idaea, 40, 309
    'Erntesegen', 309
    'Korealle', 309
    var. *majus,* 309
    var. *minus,* 309
    'Red Pearl', 309
Valerian
    Greek, 259
    red, 99
Vancouveria, golden, 40, 310
Vancouveria chrysantha, 40, 310
Vancouveria hexandra, 40, 310
Vancouveria planipetala, 40, 310,
        Plate 303
Vegetable sulfur, 219
Venus's pride, 171
Verbena
    clump, 311
    Dakota, 40, 311
    moss, 311, Plate 304
    Peruvian, 311
    rose, 40, 311
Verbena, 310
Verbena bipinnatifida, 40, 311

Verbena canadensis, 40, 311
    'Candidissima', 311
    'Compacta', 311
    'Gene Cline', 311
    'Homestead Purple', 311
    'Lavender', 311
    'Rosea', 311
    'St. Paul', 311
Verbena peruviana, 311
    'Bubble Gum', 311
    'Lipstick', 311
    'Mini Red', 311
    'Red', 311
    'Saint Paul', 311
Verbena tenuisecta, 311, Plate 304
    'Alba', 311
Veronica, 311
Veronica, common, 312
Veronica chamaedrys, 312
    'Alba', 312
Veronica 'Goodness Grows', 312
Veronica incana, 312, Plate 305
Veronica latifolia 'Prostrata', 312
Veronica officinalis, 312
Veronica prostrata, 312
    'Alba', 312
    'Heavenly Blue', 312
    'Lodden Blue', 312
    'Mrs. Holt', 312
    'Nana', 312
    'Rosea', 312
    'Spode Blue', 312
    'Trehane', 312
Veronica repens, 312
    'Alba', 312
    'Rosea', 312
Veronica 'Sunny Border Blue', 312
Vervain, 310
    creeping, 311
    Dakota, 311
    rose, 311
Vetch
    crown, 117, Plate 85
    deer, 38, 217
Vetchling, 207
Viburnum, David, 313, Plate 306
Viburnum davidii, 313, Plate 306
    'Jermyn's Globe', 313
Vinca difformis, 314
    var. *dubia,* 314
Vinca major, 313
    'Alba', 313
    'Elegantissima', see 'Variegata'
    'Gold Vein', 313
    var. *hirsuta,* see var. *pubescens*
    'Morning Glory', 313
    var. *pubescens,* 314
    'Reticulata', 314
    'Variegata', 314
Vinca minor, 314, Plate 307

    'Alba', 314
    'Alboplena', 314
    'Alpina', see 'Flore Pleno'
    'Argenteo-variegata', 314
    'Atropurpurea', 314
    'Aureo-variegata', 314
    'Blue & Gold', 314
    'Bowlesii', 314
    'Bowles' Variety', see 'Bowlesii'
    'Dart's Blue', 314
    'Emily', 314
    'Flore Pleno', 314
    'Gertrude Jekyll', 314
    'Gold Heart', 314
    'Golden', 314
    'La Grave', see 'Bowlesii'
    'Multiplex', see 'Flore Pleno'
    'Ralph Shugert', 314, Plate 308
    'Sterling Silver', 314
    'Valley Glow', 314
Vinca herbacea, 314
Vine
    chocolate, 63
    complex wire, 229
    creeping wire, 229, Plate 208
    deer, 213
    love, 108
    Monkshood, 67
    perennial pea, 207, Plate 181
    Pollyana, 294
    squaw, 228
    vase, 107
Viola alba, 316
Viola hederacea, 315
Viola labradorica, 40, 315, Plate 309
    var. *purpurea,* 315
Viola odorata, 315, 316
    'Charm', 316
    'Czar', 316
    'Double Russian', 316
    'Duchesse de Parme', 316
    'Lady Hume Campbell', 316
    'Marie Louise', 316
    'Parma', 316
    'Queen Charlotte', 316
    'Red Giant', 316
    'Rosina', 316
    'Royal Elk', 316
    'Royal Robe', 316
    'White Czar', 316
    'White Queen', 316
Viola sororia, 40, 316
    forma *albiflora,* 316
    'Freckles', 316
Viola tricolor, 316
Violet
    Australian, 315
    butterfly, 316
    common, 40, 316
    dooryard, 316

florist's, 315
    garden, 316
    ivy-leaved, 315
    Labrador, 40, 315, Plate 309
    sister, 316
    sweet, 315
    woolly blue, 316
Virgin Mary's milkdrops, 268
Virginia creeper, 38
Virgin's bower, 36, 107, 108
Vitis, 108, 317
Vitis riparia, 40, 317, Plate 310
    var. *praecox,* 317
    var. *syrticola,* 317
Vygie, 100

Waldmeister, 154
Waldsteinia fragarioides, 40, 318,
        Plate 311
Waldsteinia geoides, 318
Waldsteinia lobata, 318
Waldsteinia ternata, 318
Walking anthericum, 105
Wallflower, creeping gold, 144, Plate
        119
Wandering Jew, 306
Wand flower, 153
Wart plant, 168
Wattle, sweet, 53
Wax flower, 104
White leaf, 150
Widow's-tears, 307
Wild beet, 234
Wild betony, 133
Wild red top, 242
Willow
    bearberry, 39, 282
    creeping, 282
    dwarf arctic, 282
    dwarf basket, 282

dwarf gray, 39, 282
    dwarf purple osier, 282
    'Henry's Garnet' Virginia, 198
Willow-herb, 36, 124, Plate 96
    milk, 124
Wind flower, 68
Winecups, 92
Winterberry, 155
Wintercreeper, 145
    bitter, 104
    common, 37, 155
    fragrant, 104
    Miquel, 37, 156
    Oregon, 37, 156
    purple, 145, 150
    spotted, 105
    striped, 105
Wintergreen, common, 155, Plate
        136
Wire ling, 136
Witch's moneybags, 290
Woadwaxen
    cushion, 159
    dyer's, 159
    German, 159
    silky-leaf, 159, Plate 140
Woodbine, 108, 243
    Carolina wild, 158
    Italian, 216
Woodruff, sweet, 154, Plate 134
Woodwardia areolata, 40, 46, 319
Woodwardia virginica, 40, 46, 319,
        Plate 312
Wormwood, 35, 76
    beach, 77, Plate 33
    Caucasian, 77
    satiny, 77

Xanthorhiza simplicissima, 319, Plate
        313

Yarrow, 55
    common, 56
    fernleaf, 55
    Greek, 55
    woolly, 56
Yeddo, 273
Yellow gowan, 272
Yellow-root, 319, Plate 313
    shrub, 319
Yerba buena, 39, 287, Plate 276
Yew
    American, 300
    Anglo-Japanese, 301
    berried, 300, Plate 293
    Canadian, 39, 300
    dwarf, 300
    English, 300
    intermediate, 301
    Japanese, 300
    prostrate Japanese plum, 100,
        Plate 63
Youth-on-age, 305

Zauschneria californica, 40, 320,
        Plate 314
    subsp. *alba,* 320
    subsp. *arizonica,* 320
    subsp. *cana,* 320
    'Catalina Form', 320
    'Compact Form', 320
    'Dublin', 320
    'Etteri', 320
    subsp. *latifolia,* 320
    'Solidarity Pink', 320
    subsp. *splendens,* 320
    'U.C. Hybrid', 320
Zingiber officinale, 78
Zoysia tenuifolia, 48, 320, Plate 315